nicem
UPDATE
OF
NONBOOK
MEDIA

Volume 2
1973-74

NATIONAL INFORMATION CENTER FOR EDUCATIONAL MEDIA (NICEM)

UNIVERSITY OF SOUTHERN CALIFORNIA

UNIVERSITY PARK

LOS ANGELES, CALIFORNIA 90007

Volume 2, (October, 1973)

NICEM UPDATE OF NONBOOK MEDIA

Library of Congress Catalog Card Number: 73–85030
Volume 2, (October, 1973)

Contents

Preface

Since 1964 NICEM has provided over 12,000 institutions, individuals and agencies involved in the process of education indices, non-print book catalogs and other formatted information from its computerized data banks at the University of Southern California.

NICEM is now offering the monthly (10 volumes) *Update of Non-book Media* which supplements and updates the fourteen basic volumes listed below:

Index to 16mm Educational Films 4th edition (3 vol.)
Index to 35mm Filmstrips 4th edition (2 vol.)
Index to Educational Audio Tapes 2nd edition
Index to Educational Video Tapes 2nd edition
Index to Educational Records 2nd edition
Index to 8mm Cartridges 3rd edition
Index to Educational Overhead Transparencies 3rd edition
Index to Educational Slides 1st edition
Index to Producers and Distributors 2nd edition
Index to Black History and Studies — Multimedia 2nd edition
Index to Ecology — Multimedia 2nd edition
Index to Health and Safety Education — Multimedia 1st edition
Index to Vocational and Technical Education — Multimedia 1st edition
Index to Psychology — Multimedia 1st edition

Until other more sophisticated means of information dissemination become economically viable, NICEM will provide for its users a complete monthly update of its indexes every other year beginning with this school year 1973–1974 and providing completely new editions of the Indexes in the alternate years. For example, complete new editions of the Indexes will be available in 1975–1976 with monthly updates again available in 1976–1977.

It is the intention of the University of Southern California to continue providing an expanded non-print information service to the national and international educational and library communities as a non-profit function.

Producers and/or Distributors of films, filmstrips, transparancies, and slidesets are invited to submit new nonbook media production information on the Library of Congress — NICEM "Master Input Form." These input forms are available from the Library of Congress, processing department, Descriptive Cataloging Division, Washington, D.C., 20540. All other nonbook media information should be submitted directly to NICEM, University of Southern California, Los Angeles, California 90007.

M. THOMAS RISNER, Ph. D.
Director
National Information Center for Educational Media

Introduction

The *NICEM Update* — Multimedia is a monthly subscription service for the school year 1973-74 which updates the following NICEM Indexes:

Index to 16mm Educational Films 4th edition
Index to 35mm filmstrips 4th edition
Index to Educational Audio Tapes 2nd edition
Index to Educational Video Tapes 2nd edition
Index to Educational Records 2nd edition
Index to 8mm Cartridges 3rd edition
Index to Educational Overhead Transparencies 3rd edition
Index to Educational Slides 1st edition
Index to Producers and Distributors 2nd edition
Index to Black History and Studies — Multimedia 2nd edition
Index to Ecology — Multimedia 2nd edition
Index to Health and Safety Education — Multimedia 1st edition
Index to Vocational and Technical Education — Multimedia 1st edition
Index to Psychology — Multimedia 1st edition

These reference sources including the *NICEM Update* are generated from computerized master banks at the University of Southern California.

Contents

This volume is divided into three principal sections:

1. Subject Guide to non-book media: This section is preceded by a "Subject Heading Outline" and the "Index to Subject Headings."

2. Alphabetical Guide to non-book media

3. Directory of Producers and Distributors include separate alphabetical listings by code and by name. The Code section lists the latest addresses for most entries.

Subject Guide to Non-book Media

The *Subject Guide* is preceded by the *Subject Heading Outline,* which lists the major subject categories and subject headings to be found in the Index, and the *Index to Subject Headings* which provides a cross index to the subject headings as well as expands the number of headings for searching by subject or topic.

The *Subject Guide* is organized as follows:

    Major Heading
    Sub-Heading
followed by Titles in each media in alphabetical order.

Example:

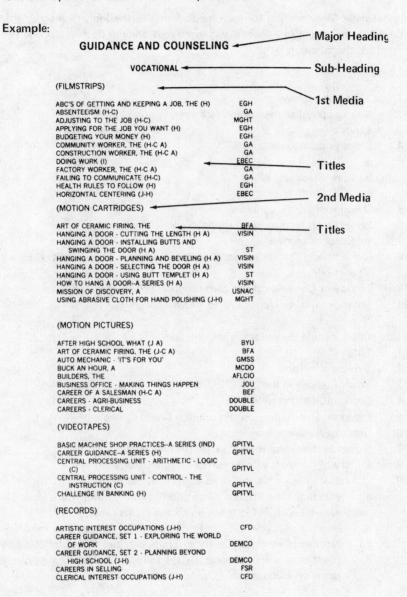

This arrangement allows the user to go directly to the media titles for which he is searching.

Alphabetical Guide to Non-book Media

Each media is allocated an *Alphabetical Guide* section by alpha order. (See Table of Contents)

The *Alphabetical Guide* section for each media contains the individual series titles listed alphabetically by title. Each title belonging to a series is also listed separately in its own alphabetical position. Individual title entries include the following data:

1. Title with subtitle
2. Size and physical description (see explanation below).
3. Length
4. Stock or color code
   a. C—Color
   b. B—Black and White
   c. X—Both
5. Description of the contents
6. Series title reference when applicable
7. Audience or grade level
8. Producer and Distributor code. (Also, some production credit codes are given.)
9. Year of release
10. Library of Congress catalog card number. (When available.)
11. Broadcast quality (applicable to Video Tapes)

Series title entries include the following information:
1. Title
2. Version or edition
3. Year of release in the U.S.
4. Description of the series content
5. Producer, Distributor, and Production Credit Codes
6. Grade or Audience level
7. Names of individual titles in series with length for each title
8. Library of Congress catalog number. (When available)
9. Individual titles within the series contain the following information:
   a. Running time (16mm films [MP], 8mm Motion Cartridges [MC], Video Tapes [MV], Audio Tapes [RT]) followed by the Media Code.
   b. Number of frames (35mm Filmstrips [FS]) followed by the Media Code.
   c. Number of overlays (Overhead Transparencies [TR]) followed by the Media Code.
   d. Number of sides (Records [RD]) followed by the Media Code. Some entries indicate the bands on each record.

Audience and/or Grade Levels

The audience levels are to be interpreted as follows:
K	Pre-school to kindergarten
P	Primary
I	Intermediate (4-6)
J	Junior High School (7-9)
H	High School (10-12)
C	Junior College, College, and University

T	Teacher Education (Designed for training teachers)
A	Adult education and general use
S	Special Education (Designed for special audiences such as physically handicapped, mentally retarded, and gifted)
R	Religious (Designed to project a religious message, moral, or philosophy)
PRO	Professional Use (Designed for such groups as medicine, dentistry, and law)
IND	Industrial Use (Designed for use in industrial training)

Physical Description

This index lists all titles alphabetically by media in the "Alphabetical Guide. The following physical descriptions apply to the different media:

1. 35mm Filmstrips
   a. Filmstrip
   b. Filmstrip with Captions
   c. Sound Filmstrip — Record
   d. Filmstrip with Script
   e. Sound Filmstrip — Audio Tape

2. 8mm Motion Catridge (Those preceded with an "S" indicate availability in Super 8)
   a. S8mm Cartridge Optical Sound
   b. S8mm Cartridge Magnetic Sound
   c. S8mm Cartridge Silent
   d. S8mm Cartridge with Audio Tape
   e. 8mm Cartridge Optical Sound
   f. 8mm Cartridge Magnetic Sound
   g. 8mm Cartridge Silent
   h. 8mm Cartridge with Audio Tape

3. 16mm Motion Picture
   a. 16mm Film Optical Sound
   b. 16mm Film Magnetic Sound
   c. 16mm Film Silent

4. Video Tapes
   a. 1 inch Video Tape
   b. 2 inch Video Tape
   c. 3/4 inch Video Tape

5. Records
   a. 33 1/3 RPM 10 inch Record
   b. 45 RPM 10 inch Record
   c. 16 2/3 RPM 10 inch Record
   d. 78 RPM 10 inch Record
   e. 33 1/3 RPM 12 inch Record
   f. 45 RPM 12 inch Record
   g. 16 2/3 RPM 12 inch Record
   h. 78 RPM 12 inch Record
   i. 33 1/3 RPM 5 inch Record
   j. 45 RPM 5 inch Record
   k. 78 RPM 5 inch Record
   l. 16 2/3 RPM 5 inch Record

m.   33 1/3 RPM 7 inch Record
n.   45 RPM 7 inch Record
o.   78 RPM 7 inch Record
p.   26 2/3 RPM 7 inch Record

6.   Audio Tapes
      a.   1 7/8 IPS Audio Tape Cassette
      b.   1 7/8 IPS 1/2 Track Audio Tape
      c.   1 7/8 IPS 1 Track Audio Tape
      d.   1 7/8 IPS 8 Track Audio Tape
      e.   1 7/8 IPS 4 Track Audio Tape
      f.   1 7/8 IPS 2 Track Audio Tape
      g.   3 3/4 IPS 1/2 Track Audio Tape
      h.   3 3/4 IPS 1 Track Audio Tape
      i.   3 3/4 IPS 2 Track Audio Tape
      j.   3 3/4 IPS 4 Track Audio Tape
      k.   3 3/4 IPS 8 Track Audio Tape
      l.   15 IPS 1/2 Track Audio Tape
      m.   15 IPS 1 Track Audio Tape
      n.   15 IPS 2 Track Audio Tape
      o.   15 IPS 4 Track Audio Tape
      p.   15 IPS 8 Track Audio Tape
      q.   7 1/2 IPS 1/2 Track Audio Tape
      r.   7 1/2 IPS 1 Track Audio Tape
      s.   7 1/2 IPS 2 Track Audio Tape
      t.   7 1/2 IPS 4 Track Audio Tape
      u.   7 1/2 IPS 8 Track Audio Tape

7.   Transparencies (When the letter [M] appears, it indicates a "Master" transparency). The basic sizes of commercially prepared transparencies are: 10" x 10"; 7" x 7"; 8" x 10"; 7" x 8"; 9" x 11"; 10" x 12"; 9" x 15".

      There are four basic types (physical descriptions) of overhead transparencies:

      a.   The "Prepared Transparency" is one which has been conceived, field tested, and manufactured by a producer and is sold to the educator or institution ready for instrucitonal use.

      b.   The "Transparency Master," is the material from which copies are made through the use of copying equipment by the user.

      c.   The "Operable Transparency" is sometimes referred to as "moving parts devices" which are three-dimensional and almost never have overlays.

      d.   The "Polarized Transparency" requires a Polaroid Spinner. It can have overlays and gives as the projected image the appearance of motion.

      Often transparency titles are available in several different types as defined above.

Computer Alphabetizing

Computer alphabetizing differs slightly from that normally used, that is, everything is filed in strict alphabetical order space by space, employing a difinite filing order. For example, abbreviations such as VD (for "Venereal Disease") file as a word spelled VD rather than as V-E-N-E-R-E-A-L D-I-S-E-A-S-E. For the same reason the articles **a, an,** or **the** are placed at the end of the title; otherwise if would file on the article; for example, the title **Art of Art Fogery, The** instead of **The Art of Art Forgery.** Nothing (spaces) comes before symbols (such as commas) so that **Automation, PT 1-Revolutionary Development** will come after all other titles beginning with the word **Automation** , such as **Automation in Today's Modern Office.** The complete filing order is as follows: nothing, symbols, letter, numbers.

Foreign language titles are entered alphabetically by article, for example: **LE PETIT MARINIER** will be located alphabetically in the **"L's".**

Directory of Producers and Distributors

The Producer (PROD) listed is the person or organization sometimes called the sponsor who originally created and/or owned the medium. The distributor (DIST) is the person or organization that handles the exclusive sale, lease, or rental of the title.

Alphabetically by Code

This listing provides the interpretation of the producer code, distributor code, and production credit code as found in the last line of each title record in the "Alphabetical Guide" and the Code found in the "Subject Guide" to the far right of the title. This listing also includes addresses and cross-references to related companies where applicable. The code following each title in the "Subject Guide" is the Distributor Code.

Alphabetically by Name

This listing enumerates the codes assigned to producers and distributors.

How to use this Index

The sections of this Index are organized to permit sequential access to information. The organization is based on the functional use of the Index with a minimum of handling. The three methods used for locating materials quickly are: (1) by title, (2) by term or topic, and (3) by subject guide.

Locating Titles by Media

The "Alphabetical Guide" lists each media titles in alpha order. (See table of contents.) The "Alphabetical Guide" is the largest section of the book and contains the most information about the title.

Individual titles and series titles are listed in alphabetical order — punctuation, spaces, and all — and as the titles appear on the media . (See section on computer alphabetizing in the "Introduction.")

Locating Titles by Subject

Three indexes precede the main section of this book. The largest of these is the "Subject Guide" which lists titles appearing in the "Alphabetical Guide" under subject headings. These are general headings with subheadings.

The **update** provides titles listed alphabetically by media under the appropriate major category and subheading. The "Subject Heading Outline" lists all of the headings used in the "Subject Guide" and should be useful in familiarizing oneself with the "Subject Guide."

The "Index to Subject Headings" has been designed to afford even greater access to the "Subject Guide". The headings listed in this index are more specific than those in the "Subject Guide" and listed below each of these are the appropriate headings where titles on this subject will be found in the "Subject Guide."

For example, the "Index to Subject Headings" lists the heading **Color.** Beneath that five headings are listed. **Fine Arts and Science-Physical** are main headings in the "Subject Guide" and Art-General, Basic Physical Science-Light and Color, and Physics-Light and Color are the respective subheadings where titles relating to these aspects of the subject will be found in the "Subject Guide."

SUBJECT HEADING OUTLINE

AGRICULTURE

AGRICULTURE - GENERAL
AGRICULTURE - CROPS
AGRICULTURE - ENGINEERING
AGRICULTURE - LIVESTOCK
AGRICULTURE - SOCIETIES
FARM WORK
GARDENING
INSECTS AND PESTS
MACHINERY AND TOOLS
PLANT DISEASES
PLANT SCIENCE
SOIL CONSERVATION
STUDY AND TEACHING

BIOGRAPHY

FAMOUS AMERICANS (OTHER THAN PRESIDENTS)
PERSONALITIES OF OTHER COUNTRIES
PRESIDENTS OF THE UNITED STATES

BUSINESS AND ECONOMICS

ADVERTISING
CAPITALISM
COMPETITION
CORPORATIONS
COST AND STANDARD OF LIVING
DEPRESSIONS
ECONOMICS - GENERAL
ECONOMIC CONDITIONS
ECONOMIC POLICY
ECONOMIC SYSTEM - U S
FINANCE
INCOME TAX
INDUSTRY
INFLATION
INVESTMENTS
LABOR AND MANAGEMENT
MANUFACTURING
MONEY AND BANKING
OFFICE PROCEDURES
SALESMANSHIP AND MARKETING
SECURITIES
SMALL BUSINESS
STOCK EXCHANGE
SUPERVISION
TAXATION
TRADE

CIVICS AND POLITICAL SYSTEMS

CITIZENSHIP - GENERAL
CITIZENSHIP - HOLIDAYS
CIVIL RIGHTS
CIVIL SERVICE
COMMUNISM
CONSTITUTION - U S
CONSTITUTIONAL HISTORY
CONSTITUTIONAL LAW
CONSTITUTIONS
DEMOCRACY
EXECUTIVE POWER
FEDERAL GOVERNMENT
FOREIGN POLICY - U S
GOVERNMENT - U S
LAW
MILITARY SCIENCE
NATIONALISM
POLITICAL ETHICS
POLITICAL PARTIES
POLITICS - U S
REPRESENTATIVE GOVERNMENT
RIGHT AND LEFT
STATE RIGHTS
SUFFRAGE
TAXATION
UNITED NATIONS
UTOPIAS

EDUCATION

ADMINISTRATION
AIMS AND OBJECTIVES
BUSINESS EDUCATION
COLLEGES AND UNIVERSITIES
COUNSELING
CURRICULA
EDUCATIONAL INNOVATION
EDUCATIONAL PSYCHOLOGY
EDUCATIONAL TECHNOLOGY
ELEMENTARY
EXPERIMENTAL METHODS
HIGHER EDUCATION
LIBRARY SCIENCE
PRESCHOOL
SECONDARY
SPECIAL
STATISTICS
STUDY AND METHODS
TEACHER AND TEACHING

TESTS AND MEASUREMENTS
VOCATIONAL EDUCATION

ENGLISH LANGUAGE

GRAMMAR
LINGUISTICS
READING AND EXPRESSION
READING INSTRUCTION
SPEECH - GENERAL
SPEECH - PHONICS
VOCABULARY - GENERAL
VOCABULARY - SPELLING
WRITING

FINE ARTS

ART - GENERAL
ART - HISTORY
ARCHITECTURE
ARTISTS AND THEIR WORKS
ART OBJECTS
ARTS AND CRAFTS
BRONZES
CERAMICS
CHILDREN'S ART ACTIVITIES
COLLAGE
CREATIVITY
DANCE
DESIGN, DECORATIVE
DRAWING
ENGRAVING AND ETCHING
JAZZ MUSIC
MOTION PICTURES
MUSIC - GENERAL
MUSIC - EDUCATION
MUSIC - INSTRUMENTAL
MUSIC - VOCAL
MUSICIANS
NEGROES IN LITERATURE AND ART
PAINTING
PHOTOGRAPHY, ARTISTIC
SCULPTURE
SOUND
THEATER

FOREIGN LANGUAGE

FRENCH
GERMAN
ITALIAN
SPANISH
FOREIGN LANGUAGE - OTHER

GEOGRAPHY - U S

GEOGRAPHY, U S - GENERAL
ALASKA
CALIFORNIA
HARBORS - U S
HAWAII
HISTORICAL GEOGRAPHY
MIDDLE ATLANTIC STATES
MIDDLE WEST AND GREAT PLAINS STATES
MOUNTAINS
NATIONAL PARKS - U S
NORTHEASTERN STATES
NORTHWESTERN STATES
ORE DEPOSITS
PHYSICAL GEOGRAPHY
RIVERS - U S
ROCKY MOUNTAIN STATES
SCENERY
SOUTHWESTERN STATES
VOYAGES AND TRAVELS
WESTERN STATES

GEOGRAPHY - WORLD

GEOGRAPHY, WORLD - GENERAL
AFGHANISTAN AND NEPAL
AFRICA
ASIA - GENERAL
AUSTRALIA
BALKANS
CARIBBEAN
CHINA
CORAL REEFS AND ISLANDS
DESERTS - WORLD
ECONOMIC GEOGRAPHY
EUROPE - EASTERN
EUROPE - WESTERN
FRANCE
GEOGRAPHY, ANCIENT
GEOGRAPHY, COMMERCIAL
GEOGRAPHY, HISTORICAL
GEOGRAPHY, MILITARY
GEOGRAPHY, PHYSICAL
GEOGRAPHY, PICTURES, ILLUSTRATIONS
GEOGRAPHY, POLITICAL
GEOGRAPHY, SOCIAL

GEYSERS
GLACIERS
GREAT BRITAIN
INDIA AND PAKISTAN
IRELAND
ITALY
JAPAN
LOW COUNTRIES
MAPS
MEXICO
MIDDLE EAST
MOUNTAINS
NATURAL RESOURCES, DISTRIBUTION
OCEANIA
PHILIPPINES
POLAR REGIONS
RIVERS AND OCEANS - WORLD
SCANDINAVIA AND FINLAND
SOUTH AMERICA
SOUTHEAST ASIA
SWITZERLAND
UNION OF SOVIET SOCIALIST REPUBLICS
TURKEY
VOLCANOES
VOYAGES AND TRAVEL

GUIDANCE AND COUNSELING

BLIND AND DEAF
DATING AND COURTSHIP
EDUCATIONAL
EMPLOYMENT
HOME AND FAMILY
INTERVIEWING
PERSONAL
PERSONNEL MANAGEMENT
PERSONNEL SERVICE, EDUCATION
PROFESSIONS
SOCIAL
VETERANS
VOCATIONAL
WELFARE

HEALTH AND SAFETY

ALCOHOL
DENTAL CARE
DENTISTRY
DIET
DRIVER EDUCATION
FIRST AID
MEDICINE
MENTAL HYGIENE
NARCOTICS
PERSONAL HYGIENE
PUBLIC HEALTH
REHABILITATION
SAFETY - GENERAL
SAFETY - FIRE
SAFETY - HOME AND COMMUNITY
SAFETY - PLAYGROUND AND SCHOOL
SEXUAL HYGIENE
SMOKING
VENEREAL DISEASE

HISTORY - U S

HISTORY, U S - GENERAL
AMERICAN COLONIES
AMERICAN HERITAGE FROM THE OLD WORLD
CONSTITUTIONAL HISTORY
DOCUMENTS
FRONTIER AND EXPANSION
IMMIGRATION
INDUSTRIAL REVOLUTION
MILITARY
NEGRO HISTORY - GENERAL
NEGRO HISTORY - AFRICA - CULTURE
NEGRO HISTORY - CIVIL RIGHTS
NEGRO HISTORY - CONSUMER
NEGRO HISTORY - ECONOMIC CONDITIONS
NEGRO HISTORY - EMPLOYMENT
NEGRO HISTORY - FAMOUS PERSONALITIES
NEGRO HISTORY - LITERATURE
NEGRO HISTORY - 1915 TO PRESENT
NEGRO HISTORY - RECREATION AND SPORTS
NEGRO HISTORY - SOCIAL PROBLEMS
NEGRO HISTORY - SONGS AND MUSIC
U S HISTORY - DISCOVERY AND EXPLORATION
U S HISTORY - COLONIAL PERIOD TO 1776
U S HISTORY - REVOLUTIONARY PERIOD TO 1783
U S HISTORY - 1783-1860
U S HISTORY - CIVIL WAR PERIOD TO 1900
U S HISTORY - 1900 TO PRESENT
WORLD WAR II - 1939-1945

HISTORY - WORLD

HISTORY, WORLD - GENERAL
AFRICA
ANCIENT WORLD
ARCHEOLOGY

ASIA
CHINA, ANCIENT
CHURCH
CULTURES AND PERIODS
DISCOVERY AND EXPLORATION
EUROPE
GEOGRAPHY
GREAT DISCOVERIES
HISTORICAL SOCIETIES
INTERNATIONAL AFFAIRS
LATIN AMERICA
MEDIEVAL TIMES
MIDDLE EAST
NORTH AMERICA
ORIENT
RENAISSANCE
REVOLUTIONARY AND NAPOLEONIC PERIOD
ROME, ANCIENT
SCIENCE AND LEARNING, MODERN HISTORY
SCIENCE AND SOCIETY, MODERN HISTORY
STUDY AND TEACHING
SYRIA-PALESTINE, ANCIENT
TWENTIETH CENTURY - GENERAL
WESTERN EUROPE, AGE OF THE CRUSADES
WESTERN EUROPE, MIDDLE AGES
WORLD FROM 1939
WORLD WAR II - 1939-1945

HOME ECONOMICS

HOME ECONOMICS - GENERAL
CHILDREN - CARE AND HYGIENE
CLOTHING AND DRESS
CONSUMER EDUCATION
FOOD AND COOKING
GROOMING
HOME MANAGEMENT
HOUSEHOLD EQUIPMENT AND SUPPLIES
HOUSEHOLD PEST
NURSING
STANDARD OF LIVING

INDUSTRIAL AND TECHNICAL EDUCATION

AUTOMATION, GENERAL
AUTOMATION, AUTOMATIC MACHINERY
AUTOMATION, COMPUTER CONTROL
AUTOMATION, SYSTEMS ENGINEERING
AUTOMOBILE, GENERAL
AUTOMOBILE, BRAKES
AUTOMOBILE, ENGINES
AUTOMOBILE, REPAIRING AND MAINTENANCE
AVIATION, GENERAL (AERONAUTICS)
AVIATION, FLIGHT EDUCATION
AVIATION, MISSILES
AVIATION, SPACE
AVIATION, STRUCTURES
CONSTRUCTION, GENERAL
CONSTRUCTION, ARCHITECTURE
CONSTRUCTION, BUILDING
CONSTRUCTION, CONCRETE
CONSTRUCTION, ENGINEERING
CONSTRUCTION, ROADS
ELECTRICAL WORK, GENERAL
ELECTRICAL WORK, WELDING AND SOLDERING
ELECTRICAL WORK, WIRING
ELECTRONICS, GENERAL
ELECTRONICS, CIRCUITS
ELECTRONICS, COMPUTERS
ELECTRONICS, RADIO AND TELEVISION
ELECTRONICS, SEMICONDUCTORS
ELECTRONICS, TELEPHONE AND TELEGRAPH
ELECTRONICS, TRANSISTORS
ENGINEERING, GENERAL
ENGINEERING, MARINE
ENGINEERING, MINING
ENGINEERING, NUCLEAR
ENGINEERING, WATER-SUPPLY
ENGINES AND POWER SYSTEMS, GENERAL
ENGINES AND POWER SYSTEMS, DIESEL
ENGINES AND POWER SYSTEMS, GAS AND OIL ENGINES
ENGINES AND POWER SYSTEMS, JET ENGINES
ENGINES AND POWER SYSTEMS, ROCKET ENGINES
ENGINES AND POWER SYSTEMS, STEAM ENGINES
MACHINE SHOP AND METALWORK, GENERAL
MACHINE SHOP AND METALWORK, IRONWORK
MACHINE SHOP AND METALWORK, STEEL
MACHINE SHOP AND METALWORK, TOOLS, EQUIPMENT AND SAFETY
MACHINE SHOP AND METALWORK, WELDING
PHOTOGRAPHY, GENERAL
PHOTOGRAPHY, ASTRONOMICAL PHOTOGRAPHY
PHOTOGRAPHY, CAMERAS
PHOTOGRAPHY, COLOR PHOTOGRAPHY
PHOTOGRAPHY, EXPERIMENTAL
PHOTOGRAPHY, MOVING PICTURE PHOTOGRAPHY
PHOTOGRAPHY, NATURE PHOTOGRAPHY
PHOTOGRAPHY, PHOTOMECHANICAL PROCESSES
PHOTOGRAPHY, SLIDES (PHOTOGRAPHY)
PHOTOGRAPHY, SLOW-MOTION
PHOTOGRAPHY, STILLS
PHOTOGRAPHY, TIME-LAPSE
PRINTING AND GRAPHIC ARTS, GENERAL

REFRIGERATION, GENERAL
REFRIGERATION, COMPRESSED AIR
WOODWORK, GENERAL
WOODWORK, FINISHING
WOODWORK, FURNITURE
WOODWORK, MACHINERY, TOOLS AND SAFETY

LITERATURE

LITERATURE - GENERAL
AUTHORS AND THEIR WORKS
CHILDREN'S STORIES
CHRISTIAN LITERATURE, EARLY
CRITICISM
DRAMA
FABLES
FAIRY TALES
FICTION
FOLKLORE
HISTORY AND CRITICISM
MEDIEVAL
NEGRO LITERATURE
NOVELS
POETRY
REALISM
ROMANTICISM
SAGAS
SATIRE
SHORT STORY
STYLE, LITERARY
WIT AND HUMOR

MATHEMATICS

MATHEMATICS - GENERAL
ALGEBRA
ARITHMETIC - GENERAL
ARITHMETIC - ADDITION
ARITHMETIC - DECIMALS
ARITHMETIC - DIVISION
ARITHMETIC - FRACTIONS
ARITHMETIC - MULTIPLICATION
ARITHMETIC - RATIO AND PROPORTION
ARITHMETIC - SUBTRACTION
COMPUTERS
EQUATIONS, THEORY OF
FORMULAS, MATHEMATICAL
FUNCTIONS, MATHEMATICAL--SEE CALCULUS
GEOMETRY
GRAPHS AND CHARTS, MATHEMATICAL
LOGIC, MATHEMATICAL
MATHEMATICS - STUDY AND TEACHING
MEASUREMENT - GENERAL
MEASUREMENT - AREA
MEASUREMENT - MEASURING INSTRUMENTS
MEASUREMENT - METRIC SYSTEM
NUMBERS AND NUMERATION SYSTEMS
OPERATIONS, MATHEMATICAL
ORDERED RELATIONS
PROBABILITIES, MATHEMATICAL
PROBLEM SOLVING, MATHEMATICAL
PROPERTIES, MATHEMATICAL
SENTENCES, MATHEMATICAL
SETS
SLIDE RULE
SYMBOLS AND VOCABULARY, MATHEMATICAL
TABLES, MATHEMATICAL
TEACHING AND METHODS
TRIGONOMETRY

PHYSICAL EDUCATION

ATHLETICS
BASEBALL
BASKETBALL
DRILL (NON MILITARY)
EXERCISE
FIELD AND TRACK
FITNESS
FOOTBALL
GAMES
GOLF
GYMNASTICS
HOCKEY
RECREATION
SOCCER
SPORTS
SPORTS, WATER
SPORTS, WINTER
TENNIS

PSYCHOLOGY

PSYCHOLOGY - GENERAL
PSYCHOLOGY, GENERAL - EDUCATION AND TRAINING
PSYCHOLOGY, GENERAL - HISTORY
PSYCHOLOGY, GENERAL - PARAPSYCHOLOGY
PSYCHOLOGY, GENERAL - PHILOSOPHY
PSYCHOLOGY, GENERAL - PROFESSIONAL DEVELOPMENTS
PSYCHOLOGY, GENERAL - THEORY AND SYSTEMS
ANIMAL - SENSORY PROCESSES
ANIMAL - SOCIAL AND SEXUAL BEHAVIOR
CLINICAL - GENERAL

CLINICAL - BEHAVIOR DISORDER
CLINICAL - COMMUNITY SERVICES
CLINICAL - COUNSELING AND GUIDANCE
CLINICAL - GERIATRICS
CLINICAL - MENTAL HEALTH AND REHABILITATION
CLINICAL - MENTAL RETARDATION
CLINICAL - MENTAL SYMPTOMS
CLINICAL - NEUROLOGICAL DISORDER
CLINICAL - NEUROSIS AND EMOTIONAL DISTURBANCE
CLINICAL - PHYSICAL HANDICAP
CLINICAL - PHYSICAL ILLNESS
CLINICAL - PSYCHOANALYTIC INTERPRETATION
CLINICAL - PSYCHOSIS
CLINICAL - PSYCHOSOMATIC DISORDER
CLINICAL - PSYCHOTHERAPY AND ANALYSIS
CLINICAL - SPEECH DISORDER
DEVELOPMENTAL, ADOLESCENCE
DEVELOPMENTAL, CHILDHOOD (CHILD GROWTH AND DEVELOPMENT)
DEVELOPMENTAL, CHILDHOOD - ABILITIES
DEVELOPMENTAL, CHILDHOOD - LEARNING
DEVELOPMENTAL, CHILDHOOD - PERCEPTION
EDUCATIONAL - GENERAL
EDUCATIONAL - ATTITUDE AND ADJUSTMENT
EDUCATIONAL - ATTITUDE AND ADJUSTMENT - HIGH SCHOOL AND COLLEGE
EDUCATIONAL - ATTITUDE AND ADJUSTMENT - NURSERY AND ELEMENTARY
EDUCATIONAL - EDUCATIONAL AND CAREER GUIDANCE
EDUCATIONAL - SCHOOL LEARNING AND ACHIEVEMENT
EDUCATIONAL - SPECIAL EDUCATION
EDUCATIONAL - SPECIAL EDUCATION - REMEDIAL EDUCATION
EDUCATIONAL - TEACHING METHOD
EXPERIMENTAL - DECISION AND CHOICE BEHAVIOR
EXPERIMENTAL - ENVIRONMENTAL EFFECTS
EXPERIMENTAL - HYPNOSIS AND SUGGESTIBILITY
EXPERIMENTAL - LEARNING
EXPERIMENTAL - MOTIVATION AND FMOTION
EXPERIMENTAL - MOTOR PERFORMANCE
EXPERIMENTAL - PERCEPTION
EXPERIMENTAL - REACTION TIME
EXPERIMENTAL - SLEEP, FATIGUE AND DREAMS
EXPERIMENTAL - THINKING
METHODOLOGY & RESEARCH TECHNOLOGY - EXPERIMENTS AND OBSERVATIONS
RESEARCH AND TESTING
PERSONALITY - GENERAL
PERSONALITY - CREATIVITY
PERSONALITY - INTELLIGENCE
PERSONALITY - PERSONALITY MEASUREMENTS
PERSONALITY - PERSONALITY TRAIT PROCESSES .
PERSONNEL AND INDUSTRIAL - ADVERTISING AND CONSUMER PSYCHOLOGY
PERSONNEL AND INDUSTRIAL - DRIVING AND SAFETY
PERSONNEL AND INDUSTRIAL - MANAGEMENT AND ORGANIZATION
PERSONNEL AND INDUSTRIAL - PERFORMANCE AND JOB SATISFACTION
PERSONNEL AND INDUSTRIAL - SELECTION AND PLACEMENT
PERSONNEL AND INDUSTRIAL - VOCATIONAL CHOICE AND GUIDANCE
PHYSIOLOGICAL - GENERAL
PHYSIOLOGICAL - BIOCHEMISTRY - DRUG EFFECTS - HUMAN
PHYSIOLOGICAL - ENVIRONMENT
PHYSIOLOGICAL - GENETICS
PHYSIOLOGICAL - NEUROLOGY
PHYSIOLOGICAL - SENSORY PHYSIOLOGY
SOCIAL - ATTITUDES AND OPINIONS
SOCIAL - COMMUNICATION
SOCIAL - COMMUNICATION - LANGUAGE
SOCIAL - CULTURE AND SOCIAL PROCESSES
SOCIAL - GROUP AND INTERPERSONAL PROCESSES
SOCIAL - SEXUAL BEHAVIOR
SOCIAL - SMOKING AND DRUG AND ALCOHOL

RELIGION AND PHILOSOPHY

CHRISTIANITY
FATE AND FATALISM
HINDUISM
HINDU PHILOSOPHY
HOLIDAYS - RELIGIOUS
HUMANISM
JUDAISM
LOGIC
MODERN PHILOSOPHY
MYTHOLOGY
PHILOSOPHY
RELIGIOUS CEREMONIES
RELIGIOUS EDUCATION
SECTS
SKEPTICISM

SCIENCE

HISTORY
LABORATORY TECHNIQUES - GENERAL
LABORATORY TECHNIQUES - BIOLOGY

LABORATORY TECHNIQUES - CHEMISTRY
LABORATORY TECHNIQUES - MEDICINE
LABORATORY TECHNIQUES - PHYSICS
SCIENCE, STUDY AND TEACHING - GENERAL
SCIENCE, STUDY AND TEACHING - BIOLOGY
SCIENTIFIC METHOD
VOCATIONS, SCIENCE - LIFE SCIENCES

SCIENCE - NATURAL

SCIENCE, NATURAL - GENERAL
BASIC LIFE SCIENCE, ANIMALS - GENERAL
BASIC LIFE SCIENCE, ANIMALS - AMPHIBIANS
BASIC LIFE SCIENCE, ANIMALS - BIRDS
BASIC LIFE SCIENCE, ANIMALS - FARM
BASIC LIFE SCIENCE, ANIMALS - FISH
BASIC LIFE SCIENCE, ANIMALS - HABITATIONS
BASIC LIFE SCIENCE, ANIMALS - HABITS AND
BEHAVIOR
BASIC LIFE SCIENCE, ANIMALS - INSECTS
BASIC LIFE SCIENCE, ANIMALS - MAMMALS
BASIC LIFE SCIENCE, ANIMALS - PETS
BASIC LIFE SCIENCE, ANIMALS - REPTILES
BASIC LIFE SCIENCE, ANIMALS - SEA ANIMALS
BASIC LIFE SCIENCE, ANIMALS - ZOO
BASIC LIFE SCIENCE, HUMAN BODY - GENERAL
BASIC LIFE SCIENCE, HUMAN BODY - BONES AND
MUSCLES
BASIC LIFE SCIENCE, HUMAN BODY - DIGESTION
BASIC LIFE SCIENCE, HUMAN BODY - EARS
BASIC LIFE SCIENCE, HUMAN BODY - EYES
BASIC LIFE SCIENCE, HUMAN BODY - GROWTH
AND DEVELOPMENT
BASIC LIFE SCIENCE, HUMAN BODY - HEART AND
CIRCULATION
BASIC LIFE SCIENCE, HUMAN BODY - NERVOUS
SYSTEM
BASIC LIFE SCIENCE, HUMAN BODY -
RESPIRATION
BASIC LIFE SCIENCE, HUMAN BODY - TEETH
BASIC LIFE SCIENCE, PLANTS - GENERAL
BASIC LIFE SCIENCE, PLANTS - FLOWERS
BASIC LIFE SCIENCE, PLANTS - GROWTH AND
DEVELOPMENT
BASIC LIFE SCIENCE, PLANTS - LEAVES, ROOTS,
STEMS
BASIC LIFE SCIENCE, PLANTS - PROCESSES
BASIC LIFE SCIENCE, PLANTS - SEEDS
BASIC LIFE SCIENCE, PLANTS - TREES
BASIC LIFE SCIENCE, SEASONS
BIOLOGY, BIOCHEMISTRY
BIOLOGY, BOTANY - GENERAL
BIOLOGY, BOTANY - FUNGI AND MOLDS
BIOLOGY, BOTANY - LEAVES, ROOTS, STEMS
BIOLOGY, BOTANY - LIFE CYCLES
BIOLOGY, BOTANY - PROCESSES
BIOLOGY, BOTANY - TYPES OF PLANTS
BIOLOGY, CELLULAR
BIOLOGY, ECOLOGY - GENERAL
BIOLOGY, ECOLOGY - ADAPTATION
BIOLOGY, ECOLOGY - AIR POLLUTION
BIOLOGY, ECOLOGY - BIRDS
BIOLOGY, ECOLOGY - DESERT
BIOLOGY, ECOLOGY - ENVIRONMENT
BIOLOGY, ECOLOGY - FOREST
BIOLOGY, ECOLOGY - MARINE
BIOLOGY, ECOLOGY - NATURAL RESOURCES
CONSERVATION
BIOLOGY, ECOLOGY - NOISE POLLUTION
BIOLOGY, ECOLOGY - PLANTS AND ANIMALS
BIOLOGY, ECOLOGY - POND AND MARSH
BIOLOGY, ECOLOGY - POPULATION
BIOLOGY, ECOLOGY - RECYCLING
BIOLOGY, ECOLOGY - SOIL CONSERVATION
BIOLOGY, ECOLOGY - URBANIZATION
ENVIRONMENT
BIOLOGY, ECOLOGY - WATER SUPPLY
BIOLOGY, EVOLUTION
BIOLOGY, GENETICS
BIOLOGY, MICROBIOLOGY
BIOLOGY, PHYSIOLOGY (HUMAN) - GENERAL
BIOLOGY, PHYSIOLOGY (HUMAN) - ANATOMY
BIOLOGY, PHYSIOLOGY (HUMAN) - BLOOD
BIOLOGY, PHYSIOLOGY (HUMAN) - DIGESTION
BIOLOGY, PHYSIOLOGY (HUMAN) - EARS
BIOLOGY, PHYSIOLOGY (HUMAN) - EYES
BIOLOGY, PHYSIOLOGY (HUMAN) - HEART AND
CIRCULATION
BIOLOGY, PHYSIOLOGY (HUMAN) - NERVOUS
SYSTEM
BIOLOGY, PHYSIOLOGY (HUMAN) - REPRODUCTION
BIOLOGY, PHYSIOLOGY (HUMAN) - RESPIRATION

BIOLOGY, ZOOLOGY - GENERAL
BIOLOGY, ZOOLOGY - AMPHIBIANS
BIOLOGY, ZOOLOGY - ANATOMY
BIOLOGY, ZOOLOGY - BIRDS
BIOLOGY, ZOOLOGY - FISH
BIOLOGY, ZOOLOGY - HABITATIONS
BIOLOGY, ZOOLOGY - HABITS AND BEHAVIOR
BIOLOGY, ZOOLOGY - INSECTS
BIOLOGY, ZOOLOGY - LIFE CYCLES
BIOLOGY, ZOOLOGY - MAMMALS
BIOLOGY, ZOOLOGY - SEA ANIMALS
BIOLOGY, ZOOLOGY - WORMS
CONSERVATION AND NATURAL RESOURCES

SCIENCE - PHYSICAL

SCIENCE, PHYSICAL - GENERAL
BASIC PHYSICAL SCIENCE - AIR
BASIC PHYSICAL SCIENCE - CHEMICAL CHANGE
BASIC PHYSICAL SCIENCE - EARTH
BASIC PHYSICAL SCIENCE - ELECTRICITY AND
MAGNETISM
BASIC PHYSICAL SCIENCE - ENERGY AND MATTER
BASIC PHYSICAL SCIENCE - FIRE
BASIC PHYSICAL SCIENCE - FORCE AND MOTION
BASIC PHYSICAL SCIENCE - HEAT AND FRICTION
BASIC PHYSICAL SCIENCE - LIGHT AND COLOR
BASIC PHYSICAL SCIENCE - LIQUIDS
BASIC PHYSICAL SCIENCE - MACHINES
BASIC PHYSICAL SCIENCE - PHYSICAL CHANGE
BASIC PHYSICAL SCIENCE - SOUND
BASIC PHYSICAL SCIENCE - SPACE AND SOLAR
SYSTEM
BASIC PHYSICAL SCIENCE - WEATHER AND
CLIMATE
CHEMISTRY - GENERAL
CHEMISTRY - ACIDS, BASES, SALTS
CHEMISTRY - ALLOYS AND METALS
CHEMISTRY - ATOMIC THEORY
CHEMISTRY - CARBONS
CHEMISTRY - ELEMENTS
CHEMISTRY - MATTER
CHEMISTRY - WATER
EARTH SCIENCE - GENERAL
EARTH SCIENCE - ARCHAEOLOGY
EARTH SCIENCE - ASTRONOMY
EARTH SCIENCE - GEOLOGY
EARTH SCIENCE - METEOROLOGY
EARTH SCIENCE - OCEANOGRAPHY
PHYSICS - ATOMIC AND NUCLEAR ENERGY
PHYSICS - ELECTRICITY AND MAGNETISM
PHYSICS - ENERGY AND MATTER
PHYSICS - FORCE AND MOTION
PHYSICS - HEAT AND FRICTION
PHYSICS - LIGHT AND COLOR
PHYSICS - LIQUIDS AND HYDRAULICS
PHYSICS - MECHANICS
PHYSICS - SOUND

SOCIAL SCIENCE

SOCIAL SCIENCE - GENERAL
BASIC NEEDS - CLOTHING, FOOD, SHELTER
CITIZENSHIP
COMMUNICATIONS
COMMUNITY CENTERS
COMMUNITY LIFE
CONSUMPTION (ECONOMICS)
COST AND STANDARD OF LIVING
FACTORY SYSTEM
FARM LIFE
FARM PRODUCE - MARKETING
FOOD ADULTERATION AND INSPECTION
HOME AND SCHOOL
INDIANS
INDIANS OF NORTH AMERICA - GENERAL
INDIANS OF NORTH AMERICA - CANADA
INDIANS OF NORTH AMERICA - GOVERNMENT
RELATIONS
INDIANS OF NORTH AMERICA - HISTORY
INDIANS OF NORTH AMERICA - ORIGIN
INDIANS OF NORTH AMERICA - RELIGION AND
MYTHOLOGY
INDIANS OF NORTH AMERICA - RESERVATIONS
INDIANS OF NORTH AMERICA - SOCIAL
CONDITIONS
INDIANS OF NORTH AMERICA - SOCIAL LIFE AND
CUSTOMS
INDIANS OF NORTH AMERICA - WARS
INDUSTRIAL MOBILIZATION
INDUSTRIALIZATION

INDUSTRY AND STATE
INTERNATIONAL ECONOMIC RELATIONS
LABOR AND LABORING CLASSES
MANNERS AND CUSTOMS
MAPS AND GLOBES
NATURAL RESOURCES
NEWSPAPER
NUTRITION
POSTAL SERVICE
RAILROADS
RELIGION, PRIMITIVE
TELECOMMUNICATION
TRANSPORTATION - GENERAL
TRANSPORTATION - AIR
TRANSPORTATION - HIGHWAY
TRANSPORTATION - LAND
TRANSPORTATION - WATER
UNDERDEVELOPED AREAS

SOCIOLOGY

ANTHROPOLOGY
AUTOMATION
BEHAVIOR
BIRTH CONTROL
BIRTH RATE
CHILD WELFARE
CITIES AND TOWNS
CIVILIZATION
CLASS DISTINCTION
COMMUNITY AGENCIES
COMMUNITY CENTERS
COST AND STANDARD OF LIVING
COUNTRY LIFE
COURTSHIP
CRIME
CRIME AND CRIMINALS
DISCRIMINATION
DIVORCE
DOMESTIC RELATIONS
EDUCATIONAL SOCIOLOGY
ETHNOLOGY
FAMILY
FARM LIFE
GERIATRICS
HEREDITY
HOUSING
HUMAN RELATIONS
IMMIGRATION AND EMIGRATION
INDIVIDUALISM
JUVENILE DELINQUENCY
LABOR AND LABORING CLASSES
LEISURE
LIQUOR PROBLEM
MAN - INFLUENCE OF ENVIRONMENT
MANNERS AND CUSTOMS
MARRIAGE AND THE FAMILY
MARRIAGE CUSTOMS AND RITES
MIGRATION, INTERNAL
MORTALITY
NARCOTICS PROBLEMS
NATIONAL CHARACTERISTICS
PARENT AND CHILD
POPULATION
PREJUDICES AND ANTIPATHIES
PRISONS
PROBLEM CHILDREN
PUBLIC HEALTH
PUBLIC WELFARE
PUNISHMENT
RACE PROBLEMS
RECREATION
SEMITIC RACE
SEXUAL ETHICS
SOCIAL CHANGE
SOCIAL CLASSES
SOCIAL CONDITIONS
SOCIAL ETHICS
SOCIAL GROUP WORK
SOCIAL PROBLEMS
SOCIAL PSYCHOLOGY
SOCIAL WORK
SOCIETY, PRIMITIVE
SOCIOLOGY, RURAL
SUICIDE
UNEMPLOYED
URBANIZATION
U S - FOREIGN POPULATION
U S - IMMIGRATION AND EMIGRATION
U S - RACE QUESTION
WELFARE WORK IN INDUSTRY

3

INDEX TO SUBJECT HEADINGS

ATMOSPHERE
SCIENCE - PHYSICAL
BASIC PHYSICAL SCIENCE - WEATHER AND CLIMATE
EARTH SCIENCE - METEOROLOGY

ATOMIC ENERGY
SCIENCE - PHYSICAL
PHYSICS - ATOMIC AND NUCLEAR ENERGY

ATOMIC THEORY
SCIENCE - PHYSICAL
CHEMISTRY - ATOMIC THEORY

AUDIO-VISUAL
EDUCATION
EDUCATIONAL TECHNOLOGY

AUSTRALIA
GEOGRAPHY - WORLD
AUSTRALIA

AUSTRIA
GEOGRAPHY - WORLD
AUSTRIA

AUTHORS AND THEIR WORKS
LITERATURE
AUTHORS AND THEIR WORKS

AUTO SHOP
INDUSTRIAL AND TECHNICAL EDUCATION
AUTOMOBILE

AUTOMATION
MATHEMATICS
COMPUTERS
SOCIOLOGY
AUTOMATION

AUTOMOBILES
HEALTH AND SAFETY
DRIVER EDUCATION
INDUSTRIAL AND TECHNICAL EDUCATION
AUTOMOBILE
SOCIAL SCIENCE
TRANSPORTATION - LAND

AUTUMN
SCIENCE - NATURAL
BASIC LIFE SCIENCE - SEASONS

AVIATION
INDUSTRIAL AND TECHNICAL EDUCATION
AVIATION
SOCIAL SCIENCE
TRANSPORTATION - AIR

BABIES
HOME ECONOMICS
CHILDREN - CARE AND HYGIENE
PSYCHOLOGY
CHILD GROWTH AND DEVELOPMENT

BACTERIA
SCIENCE - NATURAL
BIOLOGY - MICROBIOLOGY

BADMINTON
PHYSICAL EDUCATION
SPORTS

BALKANS
GEOGRAPHY - WORLD
BALKANS

BALLET
FINE ARTS
DANCE

BAND INSTRUMENTS
FINE ARTS
MUSIC - INSTRUMENTS

BANKING
BUSINESS AND ECONOMICS
MONEY AND BANKING

BASEBALL
PHYSICAL EDUCATION
BASEBALL
SPORTS

BASES
SCIENCE - PHYSICAL
CHEMISTRY - ACIDS, BASES, SALTS

BASIC NEEDS - CLOTHING, FOOD, SHELTER
SOCIAL SCIENCE
BASIC NEEDS - CLOTHING, FOOD, SHELTER

BASKETBALL
PHYSICAL EDUCATION
BASKETBALL
SPORTS

BEAR
SCIENCE - NATURAL
BASIC LIFE SCIENCE, ANIMALS - MAMMALS
BIOLOGY, ZOOLOGY - MAMMALS

BEE
SCIENCE - NATURAL
BASIC LIFE SCIENCE, ANIMALS - INSECTS
BIOLOGY, ZOOLOGY - INSECTS

BEHAVIOR, ANIMAL
SCIENCE - NATURAL
BASIC LIFE SCIENCE, ANIMAL - HABITS AND BEHAVIOR
BIOLOGY, ZOOLOGY - HABITS AND BEHAVIOR

BEHAVIOR, HUMAN
PSYCHOLOGY
PSYCHOLOGY - GENERAL

BELGIUM
GEOGRAPHY - WORLD
LOW COUNTRIES

BELGIUM - HISTORY
HISTORY - WORLD
EUROPE

BERLIN
GEOGRAPHY - WORLD
GERMANY

BICYCLE SAFETY
HEALTH AND SAFETY
SAFETY - BICYCLE

BILL OF RIGHTS
CIVICS AND POLITICAL SYSTEMS
CONSTITUTION
HISTORY - U S
DOCUMENTS

BIOCHEMISTRY
SCIENCE - NATURAL
BIOLOGY - BIOCHEMISTRY

BIOGRAPHY
BIOGRAPHY

BIOLOGY
SCIENCE - NATURAL

BIRDS
SCIENCE - NATURAL
BASIC LIFE SCIENCE, ANIMALS - BIRDS
BIOLOGY, ZOOLOGY - BIRDS

BIRTH CONTROL
SOCIOLOGY
BIRTH CONTROL
MARRIAGE AND THE FAMILY
POPULATION

BLOOD
SCIENCE - NATURAL
BASIC LIFE SCIENCE, HUMAN BODY - HEART AND CIRCULATION
BIOLOGY, PHYSIOLOGY(HUMAN) - BLOOD

BOATS
SOCIAL SCIENCE
TRANSPORTATION - WATER

BOLIVIA
GEOGRAPHY - WORLD
SOUTH AMERICA

BONES
SCIENCE - NATURAL
BASIC LIFE SCIENCE, HUMAN BODY - BONES AND MUSCLES
BIOLOGY, PHYSIOLOGY (HUMAN) - ANATOMY

BORNEO
GEOGRAPHY - WORLD
SOUTHEAST ASIA

BOTANY
SCIENCE - NATURAL
BIOLOGY, BOTANY

BRAZIL
GEOGRAPHY - WORLD
SOUTH AMERICA

BRITAIN
GEOGRAPHY - WORLD
GREAT BRITAIN

BRITAIN - HISTORY
HISTORY - WORLD
EUROPE

BRITISH COLUMBIA
GEOGRAPHY - WORLD
CANADA

BRITISH COMMONWEALTH
GEOGRAPHY - WORLD
BRITISH COMMONWEALTH

BRITISH ISLES
GEOGRAPHY - WORLD
GREAT BRITAIN
IRELAND

BROTHERHOOD
SOCIOLOGY
HUMAN RELATIONS

BRYCE CANYON NATIONAL PARK
GEOGRAPHY - U S
NATIONAL PARKS - U S

BUDDHISM
RELIGION AND PHILOSOPHY
BUDDHISM

BUDGETING
BUSINESS AND ECONOMICS
BUDGETS
HOME ECONOMICS
HOME MANAGEMENT

BUENOS AIRES
GEOGRAPHY - WORLD
SOUTH AMERICA

BUSINESS
BUSINESS AND ECONOMICS

BUTTERFLY
SCIENCE - NATURAL
BASIC LIFE SCIENCE, ANIMALS - INSECTS
BIOLOGY, ZOOLOGY - INSECTS

CALCULUS
MATHEMATICS
CALCULUS

CALIFORNIA
GEOGRAPHY - U S
CALIFORNIA

CALIFORNIA - HISTORY
HISTORY - U S
FRONTIER AND EXPANSION
U S HISTORY - GENERAL

CAMERAS
INDUSTRIAL AND TECHNICAL EDUCATION
PHOTOGRAPHY

CAMPING
PHYSICAL EDUCATION
RECREATION

CANADA
GEOGRAPHY - WORLD
CANADA

CANADA - HISTORY
HISTORY - WORLD
NORTH AMERICA

CANALS
GEOGRAPHY - WORLD
CANALS - WORLD

CAPITALISM
BUSINESS AND ECONOMICS
CAPITALISM
ECONOMIC SYSTEM - U S

CARBONS
SCIENCE - PHYSICAL
CHEMISTRY - CARBONS

CAREERS
GUIDANCE AND COUNSELING
VOCATIONAL
MATHEMATICS
VOCATIONS, MATHEMATICS
SCIENCE
VOCATIONS, SCIENCE - GENERAL
VOCATIONS, SCIENCE - CHEMISTRY
VOCATIONS, SCIENCE - LIFE SCIENCE
VOCATIONS, SCIENCE - PHYSICAL SCIENCE

CARIBBEAN
GEOGRAPHY - WORLD
CARIBBEAN

CARS
INDUSTRIAL AND TECHNICAL EDUCATION
AUTOMOBILE
SOCIAL SCIENCE
TRANSPORTATION - LAND

CELLS
SCIENCE - NATURAL
BASIC LIFE SCIENCE, HUMAN BODY - CELLS
BIOLOGY - CELLULAR

CELLULAR BIOLOGY
SCIENCE - NATURAL
BIOLOGY - CELLULAR

CENTRAL AMERICA
GEOGRAPHY - WORLD
CENTRAL AMERICA

CENTRAL AMERICA - HISTORY
HISTORY - WORLD
LATIN AMERICA

CERAMICS
FINE ARTS
CERAMICS

CHALK BOARDS
EDUCATION
EDUCATIONAL TECHNOLOGY

CHARTS
MATHEMATICS
GRAPHS AND CHARTS, MATHEMATICAL

CHEMICAL CHANGE
SCIENCE - PHYSICAL
BASIC PHYSICAL SCIENCE - CHEMICAL CHANGE

CHEMISTRY
SCIENCE - PHYSICAL
CHEMISTRY - GENERAL

CHILD CARE
HOME ECONOMICS
CHILDREN - CARE AND HYGIENE

CHILD DEVELOPMENT
EDUCATION
EDUCATIONAL PSYCHOLOGY
PSYCHOLOGY
CHILD GROWTH AND DEVELOPMENT

CHILDREN
HOME ECONOMICS
CHILDREN - CARE AND HYGIENE
PSYCHOLOGY
CHILD GROWTH AND DEVELOPMENT

CHILDREN'S STORIES
LITERATURE
CHILDREN'S STORIES

CHILE
GEOGRAPHY - WORLD
SOUTH AMERICA

CHINA
GEOGRAPHY - WORLD
CHINA

CHINA - HISTORY
HISTORY - WORLD
ORIENT

CHRISTIAN EDUCATION
RELIGION AND PHILOSOPHY
CHRISTIANITY

CHRISTIANITY
RELIGION AND PHILOSOPHY
CHRISTIANITY

CHRISTMAS
RELIGION AND PHILOSOPHY
HOLIDAYS - RELIGIOUS

CIRCLE
MATHEMATICS
GEOMETRY

CIRCULATION
SCIENCE - NATURAL
BASIC LIFE SCIENCE, HUMAN BODY - HEART
AND CIRCULATION
BIOLOGY, PHYSIOLOGY(HUMAN) - HEART AND
CIRCULATION

CIRCUS
PHYSICAL EDUCATION
RECREATION
SOCIAL SCIENCE
COMMUNITY LIFE

CITIES, U S
GEOGRAPHY - U S
(LISTED UNDER STATE OR REGION)

CITIES, WORLD
(LISTED UNDER STATE OR REGION)

CITIZENSHIP
CIVICS AND POLITICAL SYSTEMS
CITIZENSHIP

CITRUS
AGRICULTURE
AGRICULTURE - CROPS

CITY LIFE
SOCIAL SCIENCE
COMMUNITY LIFE
SOCIOLOGY
URBANIZATION

CIVICS
CIVICS AND POLITICAL SYSTEMS

CIVIL DEFENSE
HEALTH AND SAFETY
SAFETY - GENERAL

CIVIL RIGHTS
CIVICS AND POLITICAL SYSTEMS
CIVIL RIGHTS
SOCIOLOGY
HUMAN RELATIONS

CIVIL WAR
HISTORY - U S
U S HISTORY - CIVIL WAR PERIOD TO 1900

CLAY IN ART
FINE ARTS
CERAMICS

CLIMATE
SCIENCE - PHYSICAL
BASIC PHYSICAL SCIENCE - WEATHER AND
CLIMATE
EARTH SCIENCE - METEOROLOGY

CLOTHING
HOME ECONOMICS
CLOTHING AND DRESS
SOCIAL SCIENCE
BASIC NEEDS - CLOTHING, FOOD, SHELTER

CLOUDS
SCIENCE - PHYSICAL
BASIC PHYSICAL SCIENCE - WEATHER AND
CLIMATE

COLDS
HEALTH AND SAFETY
PERSONAL HYGIENE

COLLEGES
EDUCATION
AIMS AND OBJECTIVES
COLLEGES AND UNIVERSITIES
GUIDANCE AND COUNSELING
EDUCATIONAL

COLLOIDS
SCIENCE - PHYSICAL
CHEMISTRY - COLLOIDS

COLOMBIA
GEOGRAPHY - WORLD
SOUTH AMERICA

COLONIAL PERIOD
HISTORY - U S
U S HISTORY - COLONIAL PERIOD TO 1776

COLOR
FINE ARTS
ART - GENERAL
SCIENCE - PHYSICAL
BASIC PHYSICAL SCIENCE - LIGHT AND COLOR
PHYSICS - LIGHT AND COLOR

COMMON MARKET
BUSINESS AND ECONOMICS
TRADE

COMMUNICATION
SOCIAL SCIENCE
COMMUNICATION

COMMUNISM
CIVICS AND POLITICAL SYSTEMS
COMMUNISM

COMMUNITY AGENCIES
SOCIOLOGY
COMMUNITY AGENCIES

COMMUNITY LIFE
SOCIAL SCIENCE
COMMUNITY LIFE

COMMUNITY HEALTH
HEALTH AND SAFETY
PUBLIC HEALTH

COMMUNITY HELPERS
SOCIAL SCIENCE
COMMUNITY LIFE

COMPASS
SOCIAL SCIENCE
MAPS AND GLOBES

COMPETITION
BUSINESS AND ECONOMICS
COMPETITION
ECONOMIC SYSTEM - U S

COMPOSERS
FINE ARTS
ARTISTS AND THEIR WORKS

COMPOSITION
ENGLISH LANGUAGE
WRITING

COMPUTERS
MATHEMATICS
COMPUTERS
SOCIOLOGY
AUTOMATION

CONCERTS
FINE ARTS
CONCERTS
MUSIC - GENERAL

CONDUCTING A MEETING
ENGLISH LANGUAGE
SPEECH - DISCUSSION TECHNIQUES

CONGRESS
CIVICS AND POLITICAL SYSTEMS
GOVERNMENT - U S

CONSERVATION
AGRICULTURE
SOIL CONSERVATION
SCIENCE - NATURAL
CONSERVATION AND NATURAL RESOURCES

CONSTITUTION
CIVICS AND POLITICAL SYSTEMS
CONSTITUTION

CONSTITUTION - HISTORY
HISTORY - U S
DOCUMENTS

CONSTRUCTION
INDUSTRIAL AND TECHNICAL EDUCATION
CONSTRUCTION

CONSUMER EDUCATION
HOME ECONOMICS
CONSUMER EDUCATION
HOME MANAGEMENT

COOKING
HOME ECONOMICS
FOOD AND COOKING

COPPER
BUSINESS AND ECONOMICS
INDUSTRY
INDUSTRIAL AND TECHNICAL EDUCATION
MACHINE SHOP AND METALWORK

COSTA RICA
GEOGRAPHY - WORLD
CENTRAL AMERICA

COTTON
AGRICULTURE
AGRICULTURE - CROPS

COUNSELING
EDUCATION
COUNSELING

COUNTRY LIFE
SOCIAL SCIENCE
FARM LIFE

COURTESY
GUIDANCE AND COUNSELING
SOCIAL

COURTSHIP
GUIDANCE AND COUNSELING
DATING AND COURTSHIP

COWS
AGRICULTURE
LIVESTOCK
SCIENCE - NATURAL
BASIC LIFE SCIENCE, ANIMALS - FARM

CRAYON RESIST
FINE ARTS
ARTS AND CRAFTS

CREATIVITY
FINE ARTS
CREATIVITY

CREDIT
BUSINESS AND ECONOMICS
CREDIT
MONEY AND BANKING

CRIME
SOCIOLOGY
CRIME
CRIME AND CRIMINALS

CRIMINOLOGY
SOCIOLOGY
CRIME
CRIME AND CRIMINALS

CROPS
AGRICULTURE
AGRICULTURE - CROPS

CRUSADES
HISTORY - WORLD
MEDIEVAL TIMES

CUBA
GEOGRAPHY - WORLD
CARIBBEAN

CULTURES
SOCIOLOGY
ANTHROPOLOGY

CUSTOMS
SOCIOLOGY
ANTHROPOLOGY

CZECHOSLOVAKIA
GEOGRAPHY - WORLD
EUROPE - EASTERN

DAIRY
AGRICULTURE
AGRICULTURE - LIVESTOCK
SOCIAL SCIENCE
BASIC NEEDS - CLOTHING, FOOD, SHELTER

DAM CONSTRUCTION
INDUSTRIAL AND TECHNICAL EDUCATION
CONSTRUCTION

DAMS
GEOGRAPHY - U S
RIVERS - U S

DANCE
FINE ARTS
DANCE
DANCE MUSIC

DANUBE
GEOGRAPHY - WORLD
RIVERS AND OCEANS - WORLD

DATING
GUIDANCE AND COUNSELING
DATING AND COURTSHIP

DEAFNESS
EDUCATION
SPECIAL
GUIDANCE AND COUNSELING
BLIND AND DEAF

DECIMALS
MATHEMATICS
ARITHMETIC - DECIMALS

DECLARATION OF INDEPENDENCE
HISTORY - U S
DOCUMENTS

DECORATING
HOME ECONOMICS
HOME MANAGEMENT

DELINQUENCY
SOCIOLOGY
JUVENILE DELINQUENCY

DEMOCRACY
CIVICS AND POLITICAL SYSTEMS
DEMOCRACY

DENMARK
GEOGRAPHY - WORLD
SCANDINAVIA AND FINLAND

DENTAL HEALTH
HEALTH AND SAFETY
DENTAL CARE

DENTISTRY
HEALTH AND SAFETY
DENTISTRY

DESERTS
GEOGRAPHY - U S
DESERTS - U S
GEOGRAPHY - WORLD
DESERTS - WORLD
SCIENCE - NATURAL
BIOLOGY, ECOLOGY - DESERT

DESIGN
FINE ARTS
ART - GENERAL

DIET
HEALTH AND SAFETY
DIET

DIGESTION
SCIENCE - NATURAL
BASIC LIFE SCIENCE, HUMAN BODY -
DIGESTION
BIOLOGY, PHYSIOLOGY(HUMAN) - DIGESTION

DINOSAURS
SCIENCE - PHYSICAL
EARTH SCIENCE - ARCHAEOLOGY

DISADVANTAGED
EDUCATION
SPECIAL

DISCOVERY AND EXPLORATION
HISTORY - U S
DISCOVERY AND EXPLORATION
HISTORY - WORLD
DISCOVERY AND EXPLORATION

DISCUSSION TECHNIQUES
ENGLISH LANGUAGE
SPEECH - DISCUSSION TECHNIQUES

DISEASES
HEALTH AND SAFETY
MEDICINE
PUBLIC HEALTH

DISSECTION
SCIENCE
LABORATORY TECHNIQUES - GENERAL
LABORATORY TECHNIQUES - BIOLOGY
LABORATORY TECHNIQUES - MEDICINE

DIVISION
MATHEMATICS
ARITHMETIC - DIVISION

DOCTORS
HEALTH AND SAFETY
MEDICINE

DOCUMENTS
HISTORY - U S
DOCUMENTS

DRAFTING
INDUSTRIAL AND TECHNICAL EDUCATION
MECHANICAL AND ENGINEERING DRAWING

DRAMA
LITERATURE
DRAMA

DRAWING
FINE ARTS
DRAWING

DRESS
HOME ECONOMICS
CLOTHING AND DRESS

DRILLING
INDUSTRIAL AND TECHNICAL EDUCATION
MACHINE SHOP AND METALWORK

DRINKING
HEALTH AND SAFETY
ALCOHOL

DRIVER EDUCATION
HEALTH AND SAFETY
DRIVER EDUCATION

DRIVER TRAINING
HEALTH AND SAFETY
DRIVER EDUCATION

DRIVING
HEALTH AND SAFETY
DRIVER EDUCATION

DROPOUT
EDUCATION
COUNSELING

DRUGS
HEALTH AND SAFETY
NARCOTICS

DRY MOUNTING
EDUCATION
EDUCATIONAL TECHNOLOGY

DUTCH
GEOGRAPHY - WORLD
LOW COUNTRIES
FOREIGN LANGUAGE
DUTCH

EARS
SCIENCE - NATURAL
BASIC LIFE SCIENCE, HUMAN BODY - EARS

EARTH
SCIENCE - PHYSICAL
BASIC PHYSICAL SCIENCE - EARTH

EARTH SCIENCE
SCIENCE - PHYSICAL

EARTHQUAKES
SCIENCE - PHYSICAL
EARTH SCIENCE - GEOLOGY

EARTHWORM
SCIENCE - NATURAL
BIOLOGY, ZOOLOGY - WORMS

ECOLOGY
SCIENCE - NATURAL
BIOLOGY, ECOLOGY

ECONOMIC GEOGRAPHY
GEOGRAPHY - WORLD
ECONOMIC GEOGRAPHY

ECONOMICS
BUSINESS AND ECONOMICS

ECUADOR
GEOGRAPHY - WORLD
SOUTH AMERICA

EDUCATION
EDUCATION

EDUCATIONAL INNOVATION
EDUCATION
EDUCATIONAL INNOVATION

EDUCATIONAL PSYCHOLOGY
EDUCATION
EDUCATIONAL PSYCHOLOGY

EGGS
AGRICULTURE
AGRICULTURE - LIVESTOCK
SOCIAL SCIENCE
BASIC NEEDS - CLOTHING, FOOD, SHELTER

EGYPT
GEOGRAPHY - WORLD
AFRICA

EGYPT - HISTORY
HISTORY - WORLD
ANCIENT WORLD

EIRE
GEOGRAPHY - WORLD
IRELAND

EL SALVADOR
GEOGRAPHY - WORLD
CENTRAL AMERICA

ELECTIONS
CIVICS AND POLITICAL SYSTEMS
POLITICS

ELECTRICA
HEALTH AND SAFETY
SAFETY - HOME AND COMMUNITY
INDUSTRIAL AND TECHNICAL EDUCATION
ELECTRICAL WORK AND ELECTRONICS

ELECTRICAL WORK
INDUSTRIAL AND TECHNICAL EDUCATION
ELECTRICAL WORK AND ELECTRONICS

ELECTRICITY
SCIENCE - PHYSICAL
BASIC PHYSICAL SCIENCE - ELECTRICITY AND
MAGNETISM
PHYSICS - ELECTRICITY AND MAGNETISM

ELECTRONICS
INDUSTRIAL AND TECHNICAL EDUCATION
ELECTRICAL WORK AND ELECTRONICS

ELECTRONS
SCIENCE - PHYSICAL
PHYSICS - ELECTRICITY AND MAGNETISM

ELEMENTS
SCIENCE - PHYSICAL
CHEMISTRY - ELEMENTS

EMBRYO
SCIENCE - NATURAL
BIOLOGY - MICROBIOLOGY

ENERGY
SCIENCE - PHYSICAL
BASIC PHYSICAL SCIENCE - ENERGY AND
MATTER
PHYSICS - ENERGY AND MATTER

ENGINEERING
INDUSTRIAL AND TECHNICAL EDUCATION
ENGINEERING

ENGINEERING DRAWING
INDUSTRIAL AND TECHNICAL EDUCATION
MECHANICAL AND ENGINEERING DRAWING

ENGINES AND POWER SYSTEMS
INDUSTRIAL AND TECHNICAL EDUCATION
ENGINES AND POWER SYSTEMS

ENGINES, AUTO
INDUSTRIAL AND TECHNICAL EDUCATION
AUTOMOBILE

ENGINES, AVIATION
INDUSTRIAL AND TECHNICAL EDUCATION
AVIATION

ENGINES, JET
INDUSTRIAL AND TECHNICAL EDUCATION
ENGINES AND POWER SYSTEMS

ENGLAND
GEOGRAPHY - WORLD
GREAT BRITAIN

ENGLAND - HISTORY
HISTORY - WORLD
EUROPE

ENGLISH LANGUAGE
ENGLISH LANGUAGE

ENGLISH LANGUAGE - HISTORY
ENGLISH LANGUAGE
LINGUISTICS

ENGRAVING
FINE ARTS
ENGRAVING AND ETCHING

ENVIRONMENT
SCIENCE - NATURAL
BIOLOGY, ECOLOGY - ENVIRONMENT

EQUATIONS
MATHEMATICS
ALGEBRA
EQUATIONS, THEORY OF

EROSION
AGRICULTURE
SOIL CONSERVATION

ESKIMOS
GEOGRAPHY - U S
ALASKA

ETCHING
FINE ARTS
ENGRAVING AND ETCHING

ETHIOPIA
GEOGRAPHY - WORLD
AFRICA

EUROPE
HISTORY - WORLD
EUROPE

EUROPE - EASTERN
GEOGRAPHY - WORLD
EUROPE - EASTERN

EUROPE - HISTORY
HISTORY - WORLD
EUROPE

EUROPE - WESTERN
GEOGRAPHY - WORLD
EUROPE - WESTERN

EVOLUTION
SCIENCE - NATURAL
BIOLOGY - EVOLUTION

EXERCISE
HEALTH AND SAFETY
PERSONAL HYGIENE
PHYSICAL EDUCATION
EXERCISE
FITNESS

EXPLORATION
HISTORY - U S
DISCOVERY AND EXPLORATION
HISTORY - WORLD
DISCOVERY AND EXPLORATION

EYES
SCIENCE - NATURAL
BASIC LIFE SCIENCE, HUMAN BODY - EYES
BIOLOGY, PHYSIOLOGY(HUMAN) - EYES

F B I
SOCIOLOGY
CRIME

FABLES
LITERATURE
CHILDREN'S STORIES
FABLES

FABRICS
HOME ECONOMICS
CLOTHING AND DRESS

FAIRS
SOCIAL SCIENCE
FARM LIFE

FAIRY TALES
LITERATURE
CHILDREN'S STORIES

FAMILY
GUIDANCE AND COUNSELING
MARRIAGE AND THE FAMILY
SOCIOLOGY
HOME AND FAMILY

FARM ANIMALS
SCIENCE - NATURAL
BASIC LIFE SCIENCE, ANIMALS - FARM
SOCIAL SCIENCE
FARM LIFE

FARM LIFE
SOCIAL SCIENCE
FARM LIFE

FARM PRODUCTS - ANIMAL
AGRICULTURE
AGRICULTURE - LIVESTOCK

FARM PRODUCTS - PLANT
AGRICULTURE
AGRICULTURE - CROPS

FARM WORK
AGRICULTURE
FARM WORK

FARMS AND FARMING
AGRICULTURE
AGRICULTURE - GENERAL
SOCIAL SCIENCE
FARM LIFE

FASCISM
CIVICS AND POLITICAL SYSTEMS
FASCISM

FEDERAL AGENCIES
CIVICS AND POLITICAL SYSTEMS
GOVERNMENT - U S

FICTION
LITERATURE
FICTION
NOVELS

FIELD TRIPS
EDUCATION
EDUCATIONAL TECHNOLOGY

FILING
BUSINESS AND ECONOMICS
OFFICE PROCEDURES

FILMS (EDUCATIONAL)
EDUCATION
EDUCATIONAL TECHNOLOGY

FILMS (EXPERIMENTAL)
FINE ARTS
MOTION PICTURES

FILMS (FEATURE)
FINE ARTS
MOTION PICTURES

FINGER PAINTING
FINE ARTS
PAINTING

FINLAND
GEOGRAPHY - WORLD
SCANDINAVIA AND FINLAND

FIRE
SCIENCE - PHYSICAL
BASIC PHYSICAL SCIENCE - FIRE

FIRE SAFETY
HEALTH AND SAFETY
SAFETY - FIRE

FIREMEN
HEALTH AND SAFETY
SAFETY - FIRE
SOCIAL SCIENCE
COMMUNITY LIFE

FIRST AID
HEALTH AND SAFETY
FIRST AID

FISH
SCIENCE - NATURAL
BASIC LIFE SCIENCE, ANIMALS - FISH
BIOLOGY, ZOOLOGY - FISH

FISHING
PHYSICAL EDUCATION
RECREATION

FISHING INDUSTRY
BUSINESS AND ECONOMICS
INDUSTRY

FLAG, AMERICAN
CIVICS AND POLITICAL SYSTEMS
CITIZENSHIP - AMERICAN FLAG

FLAG, AMERICAN - HISTORY
HISTORY - U S
HISTORY, U S - GENERAL

FLIGHT
INDUSTRIAL AND TECHNICAL EDUCATION
AVIATION
SCIENCE - PHYSICAL
PHYSICS - AERODYNAMICS
SOCIAL SCIENCE
TRANSPORTATION - AIR

FLOWER ARRANGING
PHYSICAL EDUCATION
RECREATION

FLOWERS
SCIENCE - NATURAL
BASIC LIFE SCIENCE, PLANTS - FLOWERS
BIOLOGY, BOTANY - TYPES OF PLANTS

FOLK DANCING
FINE ARTS
DANCE

FOLK MUSIC
FINE ARTS
MUSIC - VOCAL

FOLKLORE
LITERATURE
FOLKLORE

FOOD
HOME ECONOMICS
FOOD AND COOKING
SOCIAL SCIENCE
BASIC NEEDS - CLOTHING, FOOD, SHELTER

FOOD PROBLEMS
GEOGRAPHY - WORLD
ECONOMIC GEOGRAPHY

FOOTBALL
PHYSICAL EDUCATION
FOOTBALL
SPORTS

FORCE
SCIENCE - PHYSICAL
BASIC PHYSICAL SCIENCE - FORCE AND
MOTION
PHYSICS - FORCE AND MOTION

FOREIGN LANGUAGE
FOREIGN LANGUAGE

FOREIGN POLICY - U S
CIVICS AND POLITICAL SYSTEMS
FOREIGN POLICY - U S

FOREIGN TRADE
BUSINESS AND ECONOMICS
TRADE

FORESTS
SCIENCE - NATURAL
BIOLOGY, ECOLOGY - FOREST
CONSERVATION AND NATURAL RESOURCES

FORMOSA
GEOGRAPHY - WORLD
CHINA

FORMULAS
MATHEMATICS
FORMULAS, MATHEMATICAL

FOSSILS
SCIENCE - NATURAL
BIOLOGY - EVOLUTION
SCIENCE - PHYSICAL
EARTH SCIENCE - ARCHAEOLOGY

FRACTIONS
MATHEMATICS
ARITHMETIC - FRACTIONS

FRANCE
GEOGRAPHY - WORLD
FRANCE

FRANCE - HISTORY
HISTORY - WORLD
EUROPE

FREE ENTERPRISE
BUSINESS AND ECONOMICS
ECONOMIC SYSTEM - U S

FRENCH LANGUAGE
FOREIGN LANGUAGE
FRENCH

FRICTION
SCIENCE - PHYSICAL
BASIC PHYSICAL SCIENCE - HEAT AND
FRICTION
PHYSICS - HEAT AND FRICTION

FROG
SCIENCE - NATURAL
BASIC LIFE SCIENCE, ANIMALS - AMPHIBIANS
BIOLOGY, ZOOLOGY - AMPHIBIANS

FRONTIER AND EXPANSION
HISTORY - U S
FRONTIER AND EXPANSION

FRUIT
AGRICULTURE
AGRICULTURE - CROPS

FUNCTIONS
MATHEMATICS
CALCULUS
FUNCTIONS, MATHEMATICAL

FUNGI
SCIENCE - NATURAL
BIOLOGY, BOTANY - FUNGI AND MOLDS

GANGES RIVER
GEOGRAPHY - WORLD
RIVERS AND OCEANS - WORLD

GARDENING
PHYSICAL EDUCATION
RECREATION

GENES
SCIENCE - NATURAL
BIOLOGY - GENETICS

GENETICS
SCIENCE - NATURAL
BIOLOGY - GENETICS

GEOGRAPHY
GEOGRAPHY - U S
GEOGRAPHY - WORLD

GEOLOGY
SCIENCE - PHYSICAL
EARTH SCIENCE - GEOLOGY

GEOMETRY
MATHEMATICS
GEOMETRY

GERIATRICS
SOCIOLOGY
GERIATRICS

GERMAN LANGUAGE
FOREIGN LANGUAGE
GERMAN

GERMANY
GEOGRAPHY - WORLD
GERMANY

GERMANY - HISTORY
HISTORY - WORLD
EUROPE

GHANA
GEOGRAPHY - WORLD
AFRICA

GIFTED
EDUCATION
SPECIAL

GLACIER PARK
GEOGRAPHY - U S
NATIONAL PARKS - U S

GLACIERS
GEOGRAPHY - WORLD
GLACIERS
SCIENCE - PHYSICAL
EARTH SCIENCE - GEOLOGY

GLOBES
SOCIAL SCIENCE
MAPS AND GLOBES

GOLD
BUSINESS AND ECONOMICS
INDUSTRY

GOLD RUSH
HISTORY - U S
FRONTIER AND EXPANSION

GOLF
PHYSICAL EDUCATION
GOLF
SPORTS

GOVERNMENT
CIVICS AND POLITICAL SYSTEMS

GOVERNMENT - U S
CIVICS AND POLITICAL SYSTEMS
GOVERNMENT - U S

GRAINS
AGRICULTURE
AGRICULTURE - CROPS

GRAMMAR
ENGLISH LANGUAGE
GRAMMAR

GRAND CANYON - NATIONAL
GEOGRAPHY - U S
NATIONAL PARKS - U S

GRAPHIC ARTS
INDUSTRIAL AND TECHNICAL EDUCATION
PRINTING AND GRAPHIC ARTS

GRAPHS
MATHEMATICS
MATHEMATICS - GENERAL
GRAPHS AND CHARTS, MATHEMATICAL

GRASSLANDS
SCIENCE - NATURAL
BIOLOGY, ECOLOGY - GRASSLANDS

GRAVITY
SCIENCE - PHYSICAL
BASIC PHYSICAL SCIENCE - FORCE AND
MOTION

GREAT BRITAIN
GEOGRAPHY - WORLD
GREAT BRITAIN

GREAT LAKES
GEOGRAPHY - U S
MIDDLE WEST AND GREAT PLAINS STATES

GREECE
GEOGRAPHY - WORLD
BALKANS

GREECE - ANCIENT HISTORY
HISTORY - WORLD
ANCIENT WORLD

GREENLAND
GEOGRAPHY - WORLD
POLAR REGIONS

GRINDING
INDUSTRIAL AND TECHNICAL EDUCATION
MACHINE SHOP AND METALWORK

GROOMING
HOME ECONOMICS
GROOMING

GUATEMALA
GEOGRAPHY - WORLD
CENTRAL AMERICA

GUIDANCE
GUIDANCE AND COUNSELING

GYMNASTICS
PHYSICAL EDUCATION
GYMNASTICS
SPORTS

HABITATIONS, ANIMAL
SCIENCE - NATURAL
BASIC LIFE SCIENCE, ANIMALS - HABITATIONS
BIOLOGY, ZOOLOGY - HABITATIONS

HAITI
GEOGRAPHY - WORLD
CARIBBEAN

HAND WRITING
ENGLISH LANGUAGE
WRITING

HARBORS
GEOGRAPHY - U S
HARBORS - U S

HAWAII
GEOGRAPHY - U S
HAWAII

HAWAII - HISTORY
HISTORY - U S
HISTORY, U S - GENERAL

HEALTH
HEALTH AND SAFETY

HEART
SCIENCE - NATURAL
BASIC LIFE SCIENCE, HUMAN BODY - HEART
AND CIRCULATION
BIOLOGY, PHYSIOLOGY(HUMAN) - HEART AND
CIRCULATION

HEAT
SCIENCE - PHYSICAL
BASIC PHYSICAL SCIENCE - HEAT AND
FRICTION
PHYSICS - HEAT AND FRICTION

HELICOPTERS
SOCIAL SCIENCE
TRANSPORTATION - AIR

HEREDITY
SOCIOLOGY
HEREDITY
SCIENCE - NATURAL
BIOLOGY - GENETICS

HIGHWAYS
SOCIAL SCIENCE
TRANSPORTATION - LAND

HINDUISM
RELIGION AND PHILOSOPHY
HINDUISM

HISTORY
HISTORY - U S
HISTORY - WORLD

HISTORY, U S - OVERVIEW
HISTORY - U S
HISTORY, U S - GENERAL

HISTORY, WORLD - OVERVIEW
HISTORY - WORLD
HISTORY, WORLD - GENERAL

HISTORY OF ART
FINE ARTS
ART - HISTORY

HISTORY OF MATHEMATICS
MATHEMATICS
HISTORY - MATHEMATICS

HOBBIES
PHYSICAL EDUCATION
RECREATION

HOCKEY
PHYSICAL EDUCATION
HOCKEY
SPORTS

HOLIDAYS - PATRIOTIC
CIVICS AND POLITICAL SYSTEMS
CITIZENSHIP - HOLIDAYS

HOLIDAYS - RELIGIOUS
RELIGION AND PHILOSOPHY
HOLIDAYS - RELIGIOUS

HOLLAND
GEOGRAPHY - WORLD
LOW COUNTRIES

HOME AND FAMILY
GUIDANCE AND COUNSELING
HOME AND FAMILY

HOME AND SCHOOL
SOCIAL SCIENCE
HOME AND SCHOOL

HOME ECONOMICS
HOME ECONOMICS

HOME MANAGEMENT
HOME ECONOMICS
HOME MANAGEMENT

HOME SAFETY
HEALTH AND SAFETY
SAFETY - HOME AND COMMUNITY

HOMES
SOCIAL SCIENCE
BASIC NEEDS - CLOTHING, FOOD, SHELTER
SOCIOLOGY
HOME

HONDURAS
GEOGRAPHY - WORLD
CENTRAL AMERICA

HONG KONG
GEOGRAPHY - WORLD
CHINA

HOPI INDIANS
SOCIAL SCIENCE
INDIANS OF NORTH AMERICA

HORSEMANSHIP
PHYSICAL EDUCATION
RECREATION

HOUSE CONSTRUCTION
  INDUSTRIAL AND TECHNICAL EDUCATION
  CONSTRUCTION

HOUSES
  SOCIAL SCIENCE
  BASIC NEEDS - CLOTHING, FOOD, SHELTER
  HOME AND SCHOOL

HUMAN BODY
  HEALTH AND SAFETY
  PERSONAL HYGIENE
  SCIENCE - NATURAL
  BASIC LIFE SCIENCE, HUMAN BODY
  BIOLOGY, PHYSIOLOGY(HUMAN)

HUMAN RELATIONS
  SOCIOLOGY
  HUMAN RELATIONS

HUNGARY
  GEOGRAPHY - WORLD
  EUROPE - EASTERN

HYDRAULICS
  SCIENCE - PHYSICAL
  PHYSICS - LIQUIDS AND HYDRAULICS

HYGIENE
  HEALTH AND SAFETY
  PERSONAL HYGIENE

ICELAND
  GEOGRAPHY - WORLD
  POLAR REGIONS

IMMIGRATION - HISTORY
  HISTORY - U S
  IMMIGRATION
  SOCIOLOGY
  IMMIGRATION AND EMIGRATION

IMMUNIZATION
  HEALTH AND SAFETY
  PERSONAL HYGIENE

INDIA
  GEOGRAPHY - WORLD
  INDIA AND PAKISTAN

INDIA - HISTORY
  HISTORY - WORLD
  INDIA

INDIANS - CULTURE
  SOCIOLOGY
  ANTHROPOLOGY

INDIANS - U S
  SOCIAL SCIENCE
  INDIANS OF NORTH AMERICA

INDIVIDUAL DIFFERENCES
  EDUCATION
  EDUCATIONAL PSYCHOLOGY

INDONESIA
  GEOGRAPHY - WORLD
  SOUTHEAST ASIA

INDUSTRIAL ARTS
  INDUSTRIAL AND TECHNICAL EDUCATION

INDUSTRIAL MANAGEMENT
  BUSINESS AND ECONOMICS
  LABOR AND MANAGEMENT

INDUSTRY
  BUSINESS AND ECONOMICS
  INDUSTRY

INNOVATION (EDUCATIONAL)
  EDUCATION
  EDUCATIONAL INNOVATION

INSECTS
  SCIENCE - NATURAL
  BASIC LIFE SCIENCE, ANIMALS - INSECTS
  BIOLOGY, ZOOLOGY - INSECTS

INSTRUCTIONAL MATERIALS
  EDUCATION
  EDUCATIONAL TECHNOLOGY

INSTRUCTIONAL TECHNOLOGY
  EDUCATION
  EDUCATIONAL TECHNOLOGY

INSTRUMENTS, MUSICAL
  FINE ARTS
  MUSIC - INSTRUMENTAL

INSURANCE
  BUSINESS AND ECONOMICS
  INSURANCE

INTERIOR DECORATING
  HOME ECONOMICS
  HOME MANAGEMENT

IRAN
  GEOGRAPHY - WORLD
  MIDDLE EAST

IRELAND
  GEOGRAPHY - WORLD
  IRELAND

ISLAM
  RELIGION AND PHILOSOPHY
  ISLAMISM

ISRAEL
  GEOGRAPHY - WORLD
  MIDDLE EAST

ITALY
  GEOGRAPHY - WORLD
  ITALY

JAMAICA
  GEOGRAPHY - WORLD
  CARIBBEAN

JAPAN
  GEOGRAPHY - WORLD
  JAPAN

JAPAN - HISTORY
  HISTORY - WORLD
  ORIENT

JET ENGINES
  INDUSTRIAL AND TECHNICAL EDUCATION
  ENGINES AND POWER SYSTEMS

JOBS
  GUIDANCE
  VOCATIONAL

JOURNALISM
  LITERATURE
  JOURNALISM
  SOCIAL SCIENCE
  COMMUNICATION

JUDAISM
  RELIGION AND PHILOSOPHY
  JUDAISM

JUDGES
  CIVICS AND POLITICAL SYSTEMS
  LAW

JUDICIAL PROCESS
  CIVICS AND POLITICAL SYSTEMS
  LAW

JUSTICE
  CIVICS AND POLITICAL SYSTEMS
  LAW

JUVENILE DELINQUENCY
  SOCIOLOGY
  JUVENILE DELINQUENCY

KITCHEN
  HOME ECONOMICS
  FOOD AND COOKING

LABOR AND MANAGEMENT
  BUSINESS AND ECONOMICS
  LABOR AND MANAGEMENT

LABORATORY TECHNIQUES
  SCIENCE
  LABORATORY TECHNIQUES - GENERAL
  LABORATORY TECHNIQUES - BIOLOGY
  LABORATORY TECHNIQUES - CHEMISTRY
  LABORATORY TECHNIQUES - MEDICINE
  LABORATORY TECHNIQUES - PHYSICS

LAPLAND
  GEOGRAPHY - WORLD
  SCANDINAVIA AND FINLAND

LATIN AMERICA
  GEOGRAPHY - WORLD
  SOUTH AMERICA

LATIN AMERICA - HISTORY
  HISTORY - WORLD
  LATIN AMERICA

LATIN LANGUAGE
  FOREIGN LANGUAGE
  LATIN

LATITUDE
  SOCIAL SCIENCE
  MAPS AND GLOBES

LAW
  CIVICS AND POLITICAL SYSTEMS
  LAW

LAWYERS
  CIVICS AND POLITICAL SYSTEMS
  LAW

LEARNING
  EDUCATION
  EDUCATIONAL PSYCHOLOGY

LEAVES
  SCIENCE - NATURAL
  BASIC LIFE SCIENCE, PLANTS - LEAVES, ROOTS, STEMS
  BIOLOGY, BOTANY - LEAVES, ROOTS, STEMS

LEGENDS
  LITERATURE
  FOLKLORE

LEISURE TIME
  SOCIOLOGY
  LEISURE

LENSES
  SCIENCE - PHYSICAL
  PHYSICS - LIGHT AND COLOR

LETTER WRITING
  ENGLISH LANGUAGE
  WRITING

LEVERS
  SCIENCE - PHYSICAL
  BASIC PHYSICAL SCIENCE - MACHINES

LIBRARIES
  EDUCATION
  LIBRARY SCIENCE
  SOCIAL SCIENCE
  COMMUNITY LIFE

LIBRARY SCIENCE
  EDUCATION
  LIBRARY SCIENCE

LIFE CYCLES
  SCIENCE - NATURAL
  BIOLOGY, BOTANY - LIFE CYCLES
  BIOLOGY, ZOOLOGY - LIFE CYCLES

LIGHT
  SCIENCE - PHYSICAL
  BASIC PHYSICAL SCIENCE - LIGHT AND COLOR
  PHYSICS - LIGHT AND COLOR

LINGUISTICS
ENGLISH LANGUAGE
LINGUISTICS

LIQUIDS
SCIENCE - PHYSICAL
BASIC PHYSICAL SCIENCE - LIQUIDS
PHYSICS - LIQUIDS AND HYDRAULICS

LISTENING
ENGLISH LANGUAGE
READING AND EXPRESSION

LITERATURE
LITERATURE

LITHOGRAPHY
INDUSTRIAL AND TECHNICAL EDUCATION
PRINTING AND GRAPHIC ARTS

LIVESTOCK
AGRICULTURE
AGRICULTURE - LIVESTOCK

LOCOMOTIVES
SOCIAL SCIENCE
TRANSPORTATION - LAND

LOCUS
MATHEMATICS
GEOMETRY

LOGARITHMS
MATHEMATICS
SLIDE RULE
TRIGONOMETRY

LONDON
GEOGRAPHY - WORLD
GREAT BRITAIN

LONGITUDE
SOCIAL SCIENCE
MAPS AND GLOBES

LOW COUNTRIES
GEOGRAPHY - WORLD
LOW COUNTRIES

LSD
HEALTH AND SAFETY
NARCOTICS

LUMBER
BUSINESS AND ECONOMICS
INDUSTRY

LUXEMBOURG
GEOGRAPHY - WORLD
LOW COUNTRIES

MACHINE SHOP
INDUSTRIAL AND TECHNICAL EDUCATION
MACHINE SHOP AND METALWORK

MACHINES
SCIENCE - PHYSICAL
BASIC PHYSICAL SCIENCE - MACHINES

MACHINING
INDUSTRIAL AND TECHNICAL EDUCATION
MACHINE SHOP AND METALWORK

MAGNETISM
SCIENCE - PHYSICAL
BASIC PHYSICAL SCIENCE - ELECTRICITY AND
MAGNETISM
PHYSICS - ELECTRICITY AND MAGNETISM

MAIL
SOCIAL SCIENCE
COMMUNICATIONS

MAILMEN
SOCIAL SCIENCE
COMMUNITY LIFE

MAKE-UP
FINE ARTS
THEATER

MALAYA
GEOGRAPHY - WORLD
SOUTHEAST ASIA

MAMMALS
SCIENCE - NATURAL
BASIC LIFE SCIENCE, ANIMALS - MAMMALS
BIOLOGY, ZOOLOGY - MAMMALS

MANAGEMENT AND LABOR
BUSINESS AND ECONOMICS
LABOR AND MANAGEMENT

MANAGEMENT TRAINING
BUSINESS AND ECONOMICS
LABOR AND MANAGEMENT

MANITOBA
GEOGRAPHY - WORLD
CANADA

MANNERS
GUIDANCE AND COUNSELING
PERSONAL
SOCIOLOGY
MANNERS AND CUSTOMS

MANUFACTURING
BUSINESS AND ECONOMICS
MANUFACTURING

MAPS AND GLOBES
SOCIAL SCIENCE
MAPS AND GLOBES

MARIJUANA
HEALTH AND SAFETY
NARCOTICS

MARINE LIFE
SCIENCE - NATURAL
BIOLOGY, ECOLOGY - MARINE

MARKETING
BUSINESS AND ECONOMICS
SALESMANSHIP AND MARKETING

MARRIAGE AND THE FAMILY
SOCIOLOGY
MARRIAGE AND THE FAMILY

MARSH
SCIENCE - NATURAL
BIOLOGY, ECOLOGY - POND AND MARSH

MATHEMATICS
MATHEMATICS

MATHEMATICS - HISTORY
MATHEMATICS
HISTORY - MATHEMATICS

**MATHEMATICS - TEACHING AND
METHODS**
MATHEMATICS
TEACHING AND METHODS - MATHEMATICS

MATTER
SCIENCE - PHYSICAL
BASIC PHYSICAL SCIENCE - ENERGY AND
MATTER
CHEMISTRY - MATTER
PHYSICS - ENERGY AND MATTER

MEASUREMENT(EDUCATIONAL)
EDUCATION
TESTS AND MEASUREMENT

MEASUREMENT(MATHEMATICAL)
BIOLOGY - CELLULAR

MENTAL HEALTH
PSYCHOLOGY
MENTAL HEALTH AND REHABILITATION

MENTAL SYMPTOMS - CLINIC
PSYCHOLOGY
CLINICAL - MENTAL SYMPTOMS

METAL SHOP
INDUSTRIAL AND TECHNICAL EDUCATION
MACHINE SHOP AND METALWORK

METAL WORK
FINE ARTS
ARTS AND CRAFTS
INDUSTRIAL AND TECHNICAL EDUCATION
MACHINE SHOP AND METALWORK

METALS
SCIENCE - PHYSICAL
CHEMISTRY - ALLOYS AND METALS

METAMORPHOSIS
SCIENCE - NATURAL
BASIC LIFE SCIENCE, ANIMALS - INSECTS
BIOLOGY, ZOOLOGY - INSECTS

METEOROLOGY
SCIENCE - PHYSICAL
EARTH SCIENCE - METEOROLOGY

METHODS
EDUCATION
STUDY AND METHODS

METRIC SYSTEM
MATHEMATICS
MEASUREMENT - GENERAL
MEASUREMENT - METRIC SYSTEM

MEXICO
GEOGRAPHY - WORLD
MEXICO

MEXICO - HISTORY
HISTORY - WORLD
LATIN AMERICA

MICROBES
SCIENCE - NATURAL
BIOLOGY - MICROBIOLOGY

MICROBIOLOGY
SCIENCE - NATURAL
BIOLOGY - MICROBIOLOGY

MICROORGANISMS
SCIENCE - NATURAL
BIOLOGY - MICROBIOLOGY

MICROSCOPE
SCIENCE
LABORATORY TECHNIQUES - GENERAL
LABORATORY TECHNIQUES - BIOLOGY
LABORATORY TECHNIQUES - CHEMISTRY
LABORATORY TECHNIQUES - MEDICINE
LABORATORY TECHNIQUES - PHYSICS

MIDDLE AGES
HISTORY - WORLD
MEDIEVAL TIMES

MIDDLE EAST
GEOGRAPHY - WORLD
MIDDLE EAST

MIDDLE EAST - HISTORY
HISTORY - WORLD
MIDDLE EAST

MIDDLE WESTERN U S
GEOGRAPHY - U S
MIDDLE WEST AND GREAT PLAINS STATES

MILITARY SCIENCE
CIVICS AND POLITICAL SYSTEMS
MILITARY SCIENCE

MISSION LIFE
HISTORY - U S
FRONTIER AND EXPANSION

MISSISSIPPI RIVER
GEOGRAPHY - U S
RIVERS - U S

MITOSIS
SCIENCE - NATURAL
BIOLOGY - CELLULAR

MOBILES
FINE ARTS
ARTS AND CRAFTS

MOLDING
INDUSTRIAL AND TECHNICAL EDUCATION
MACHINE SHOP AND METALWORK

MOLDS (BIOLOGY)
SCIENCE - NATURAL
BIOLOGY, BOTANY - FUNGI AND MOLDS

MONEY
BUSINESS AND ECONOMICS
MONEY AND BANKING

MONROE DOCTRINE
CIVICS AND POLITICAL SYSTEMS
FOREIGN POLICY - U S

MONTREAL
GEOGRAPHY - WORLD
CANADA

MOON
SCIENCE - PHYSICAL
BASIC PHYSICAL SCIENCE - SPACE AND SOLAR
SYSTEM
EARTH SCIENCE - ASTRONOMY

MOROCCO
GEOGRAPHY - WORLD
AFRICA

MOSAICS
FINE ARTS
ARTS AND CRAFTS

MOSSES
SCIENCE - NATURAL
BIOLOGY, BOTANY - TYPES OF PLANTS

MOTION
SCIENCE - PHYSICAL
BASIC PHYSICAL SCIENCE - FORCE AND
MOTION
PHYSICS - FORCE AND MOTION

MOTION PICTURES
FINE ARTS
MOTION PICTURES

MOTION STUDY
BUSINESS AND ECONOMICS
TIME AND MOTION STUDY

MOUNT RAINIER NATIONAL PARK
GEOGRAPHY - U S
NATIONAL PARKS - U S

MOUNTAINS
GEOGRAPHY - WORLD
(LISTED UNDER COUNTRY OR REGION)
SCIENCE - PHYSICAL
EARTH SCIENCE - GEOLOGY

MULTIPLICATION
MATHEMATICS
ARITHMETIC - MULTIPLICATION

MURALS
FINE ARTS
ARTS AND CRAFTS

MUSCLES
SCIENCE - NATURAL
BASIC LIFE SCIENCE, HUMAN BODY - BONES
AND MUSCLES
BIOLOGY, PHYSIOLOGY (HUMAN) - ANATOMY

MUSIC
FINE ARTS
MUSIC

MUSICAL COMPOSITIONS
FINE ARTS
MUSIC - GENERAL

MUSICAL INSTRUMENTS
FINE ARTS
MUSIC - INSTRUMENTAL

MYTHS
LITERATURE
FOLKLORE

NANKING
GEOGRAPHY - WORLD
CHINA

NARCOTICS
HEALTH AND SAFETY
NARCOTICS
SOCIOLOGY
NARCOTICS PROBLEMS

NATIONAL PARKS
GEOGRAPHY - U S
NATIONAL PARKS - U S

NATIONAL SHRINES
GEOGRAPHY - U S
NATIONAL PARKS - U S

NATIONALISM
CIVICS AND GOVERNMENT
NATIONALISM

NATURAL RESOURCES
SCIENCE - NATURAL
CONSERVATION AND NATURAL RESOURCES

NATURAL SELECTION
SCIENCE - NATURAL
BIOLOGY - EVOLUTION

NAVAJO INDIANS
SOCIAL SCIENCE
INDIANS OF NORTH AMERICA

NEGRO HISTORY
HISTORY - U S
NEGRO HISTORY - GENERAL
NEGRO HISTORY - AFRICA PAST
NEGRO HISTORY - 1492-1865
NEGRO HISTORY - 1866-1915
NEGRO HISTORY - CIVIL WAR PERIOD

NEIGHBORHOOD
SOCIAL SCIENCE
COMMUNITY LIFE

NEPAL
GEOGRAPHY - WORLD
AFGHANISTAN AND NEPAL

NERVOUS SYSTEM
PSYCHOLOGY
NEUROLOGY
SCIENCE - NATURAL
BASIC LIFE SCIENCE, HUMAN BODY -
NERVOUS SYSTEM

NETHERLANDS
GEOGRAPHY - WORLD
LOW COUNTRIES

NEW ENGLAND
GEOGRAPHY - U S
NORTHEASTERN STATES

NEW YORK
GEOGRAPHY - U S
MIDDLE ATLANTIC STATES

NEW ZEALAND
GEOGRAPHY - WORLD
OCEANIA

NEWFOUNDLAND
GEOGRAPHY - WORLD
CANADA

NEWSPAPERS
SOCIAL SCIENCE
COMMUNICATION

NIGERIA
GEOGRAPHY - WORLD
AFRICA

NOMADS
GEOGRAPHY - WORLD
DESERTS - WORLD

NORTH AMERICA
HISTORY - WORLD
NORTH AMERICA

NORTH POLE
GEOGRAPHY - WORLD
POLAR REGIONS

NORTHEASTERN U S
GEOGRAPHY - U S
NORTHEASTERN STATES

NORTHWESTERN U S
GEOGRAPHY - U S
NORTHWESTERN STATES

NORWAY
GEOGRAPHY - WORLD
SCANDINAVIA AND FINLAND

NOSE
SCIENCE - NATURAL
BASIC LIFE SCIENCE, HUMAN BODY - NOSE
AND THROAT
BIOLOGY, PHYSIOLOGY(HUMAN) - NOSE AND
THROAT

NOVA SCOTIA
GEOGRAPHY - WORLD
CANADA

NOVELS
LITERATURE
NOVELS

NUCLEAR ENERGY
SCIENCE - PHYSICAL
PHYSICS - ATOMIC AND NUCLEAR ENERGY

NUMBER THEORY
MATHEMATICS
NUMBERS AND NUMERATION SYSTEMS
SETS

NURSING
HOME ECONOMICS
NURSING

NUTRITION
HEALTH AND SAFETY
DIET

OASIS
GEOGRAPHY - WORLD
DESERTS - WORLD

OCCUPATIONS
GUIDANCE AND COUNSELING
VOCATIONAL

OCEANIA
GEOGRAPHY - WORLD
OCEANIA

OCEANOGRAPHY
SCIENCE - PHYSICAL
EARTH SCIENCE - OCEANOGRAPHY

OCEANS
GEOGRAPHY - WORLD
RIVERS AND OCEANS - WORLD
SCIENCE - PHYSICAL
EARTH SCIENCE - OCEANOGRAPHY

OFFICE PROCEDURES
BUSINESS AND ECONOMICS
OFFICE PROCEDURES

OIL
BUSINESS AND ECONOMICS
INDUSTRY

ONTARIO
GEOGRAPHY - WORLD
CANADA

PONY EXPRESS
HISTORY - U S
FRONTIER AND EXPANSION

POPULATION
SOCIOLOGY
POPULATION

PORTRAITS
FINE ARTS
PAINTING

PORTUGAL
GEOGRAPHY - WORLD
SPAIN AND PORTUGAL

PORTUGUESE LANGUAGE
FOREIGN LANGUAGE
PORTUGUESE

POSTAL SERVICE
SOCIAL SCIENCE
COMMUNICATION

POSTURE
HEALTH AND SAFETY
PERSONAL HYGIENE
PHYSICAL EDUCATION
POSTURE

POTTERY
FINE ARTS
CERAMICS

POULTRY
AGRICULTURE
AGRICULTURE - LIVESTOCK
SCIENCE - NATURAL
BASIC LIFE SCIENCE, ANIMALS - FARM

PREHISTORIC TIMES
HISTORY - WORLD
PREHISTORIC TIMES

PREJUDICE
SOCIOLOGY
HUMAN RELATIONS
PREJUDICES AND ANTIPATHIES

PRENATAL CARE
PSYCHOLOGY
CHILD GROWTH AND DEVELOPMENT

PRESIDENT
CIVICS AND POLITICAL SYSTEMS
GOVERNMENT - U S

PRESIDENTS, U S
BIOGRAPHY
PRESIDENTS OF THE U S

PRESS
SOCIAL SCIENCE
COMMUNICATION

PRINTING
INDUSTRIAL AND TECHNICAL EDUCATION
PRINTING AND GRAPHIC ARTS

PRINTING, PHOTOGRAPHIC
INDUSTRIAL AND TECHNICAL EDUCATION
PHOTOGRAPHY

PROBABILITIES, MATHEMATICAL
MATHEMATICS
PROBABILITIES, MATHEMATICAL

PRODUCTIVITY
BUSINESS AND ECONOMICS
ECONOMIC SYSTEM - U S

PROFESSIONS
GUIDANCE AND COUNSELING
VOCATIONAL

PROJECTORS AND PROJECTION
EDUCATION
EDUCATIONAL TECHNOLOGY

PROPERTIES, MATHEMATICAL
MATHEMATICS
PROBABILITIES, MATHEMATICAL

PROPORTION
MATHEMATICS
ARITHMETIC - RATIO AND PROPORTION

PROTOZOA
SCIENCE - NATURAL
BIOLOGY - MICROBIOLOGY

PSYCHOLOGY
PSYCHOLOGY

PUBLIC HEALTH
HEALTH AND SAFETY
PUBLIC HEALTH
SOCIOLOGY
PUBLIC HEALTH

PUEBLO INDIANS
SOCIAL SCIENCE
INDIANS OF NORTH AMERICA

PUERTO RICO
GEOGRAPHY - WORLD
CARIBBEAN

PUNCTUATION
ENGLISH LANGUAGE
GRAMMAR

PUPPETS
FINE ARTS
ARTS AND CRAFTS

QUEBEC
GEOGRAPHY - WORLD
CANADA

RACE RELATIONS
SOCIOLOGY
HUMAN RELATIONS

RADIATION
SCIENCE - PHYSICAL
PHYSICS - ATOMIC AND NUCLEAR ENERGY

RADAR
INDUSTRIAL AND TECHNICAL EDUCATION
ELECTRICAL WORK AND ELECTRONICS

RADIO
SOCIAL SCIENCE
COMMUNICATION

RADIO SERVICING
INDUSTRIAL AND TECHNICAL EDUCATION
ELECTRICAL WORK AND ELECTRONICS

RADIOACTIVITY
SCIENCE - PHYSICAL
PHYSICS - ATOMIC AND NUCLEAR ENERGY

RAILROADS
SOCIAL SCIENCE
TRANSPORTATION - LAND

RAIN
SCIENCE - PHYSICAL
BASIC PHYSICAL SCIENCE - WEATHER AND
CLIMATE

RANCH LIFE
SOCIAL SCIENCE
FARM LIFE

RATIO
MATHEMATICS
ARITHMETIC - RATIO AND PROPORTION

READING AND EXPRESSION
ENGLISH LANGUAGE
READING AND EXPRESSION

READING INSTRUCTION
ENGLISH LANGUAGE
READING INSTRUCTION

READING READINESS
ENGLISH LANGUAGE
READING AND EXPRESSION

RECONSTRUCTION
HISTORY - U S
U S HISTORY - CIVIL WAR PERIOD TO 1900

RECREATION - COMMUNITY
PHYSICAL EDUCATION
RECREATION

RECREATION - GENERAL
PHYSICAL EDUCATION
RECREATION

REFLECTION
SCIENCE - PHYSICAL
PHYSICS - LIGHT AND COLOR

REFRACTION
SCIENCE - PHYSICAL
PHYSICS - LIGHT AND COLOR

REFRIGERATION
INDUSTRIAL AND TECHNICAL EDUCATION
REFRIGERATION

REHABILITATION
HEALTH AND SAFETY
REHABILITATION

RELIGION
RELIGION AND PHILOSOPHY

RENAISSANCE
HISTORY - WORLD
RENAISSANCE

REPRODUCTION(ANIMAL)
SCIENCE - NATURAL
BASIC LIFE SCIENCE, ANIMALS - HABITS AND
BEHAVIOR
BIOLOGY, ZOOLOGY - HABITS AND BEHAVIOR
BIOLOGY, ZOOLOGY - LIFE CYCLES

REPRODUCTION(HUMAN)
SCIENCE - NATURAL
BASIC LIFE SCIENCE, HUMAN BODY - GROWTH
AND DEVELOPMENT
BIOLOGY, PHYSIOLOGY(HUMAN) -
REPRODUCTION

REPRODUCTION(PLANT)
SCIENCE - NATURAL
BASIC LIFE SCIENCE, PLANTS - GROWTH AND
DEVELOPMENT
BIOLOGY, BOTANY - LIFE CYCLES

REPTILES
SCIENCE - NATURAL
BASIC LIFE SCIENCE, ANIMALS - REPTILES
BIOLOGY, ZOOLOGY - REPTILES

RESEARCH, SCIENTIFIC
SCIENCE
LABORATORY TECHNIQUES - GENERAL
LABORATORY TECHNIQUES - BIOLOGY
LABORATORY TECHNIQUES - CHEMISTRY
LABORATORY TECHNIQUES - MEDICINE
LABORATORY TECHNIQUES - PHYSICS

RESEARCH AND TESTING
EDUCATION
TESTS AND MEASUREMENT
PSYCHOLOGY
RESEARCH AND TESTING

RESPIRATION
SCIENCE - NATURAL
BASIC LIFE SICENCE, HUMAN BODY -
RESPIRATION
BIOLOGY, PHYSIOLOGY(HUMAN) - RESPIRATION

RESPONSIBILITY
GUIDANCE AND COUNSELING
SOCIAL

RETARDED
EDUCATION
SPECIAL

RETIREMENT
SOCIOLOGY
GERIATRICS
LEISURE

REVOLUTIONARY PERIOD
HISTORY - U S
U S HISTORY - REVOLUTIONARY PERIOD TO
1783

RHINE
GEOGRAPHY - WORLD
RIVERS AND OCEANS - WORLD

RICE
AGRICULTURE
AGRICULTURE - CROPS

RIO DE JANEIRO
GEOGRAPHY - WORLD
SOUTH AMERICA

RIVERS
GEOGRAPHY - U S
RIVERS - U S
GEOGRAPHY - WORLD
RIVERS AND OCEANS - WORLD

ROCKS
SCIENCE - PHYSICAL
EARTH SCIENCE - GEOLOGY

ROMANIA
GEOGRAPHY - WORLD
BALKANS

ROME
GEOGRAPHY - WORLD
ITALY

ROME - HISTORY
HISTORY - WORLD
ANCIENT TIMES

ROOTS
SCIENCE - NATURAL
BASIC LIFE SCIENCE, PLANTS - LEAVES, ROOTS,
STEMS
BIOLOGY, BOTANY - LEAVES, ROOTS, STEMS

RUBBER
BUSINESS AND ECONOMICS
INDUSTRY

RUSSIA
GEOGRAPHY - WORLD
UNION OF SOVIET SOCIALIST REPUBLICS
HISTORY - WORLD
RUSSIA

RUSSIAN LANGUAGE
FOREIGN LANGUAGE
RUSSIAN

SAFETY
HEALTH AND SAFETY

SAFETY EDUCATION
HEALTH AND SAFETY

SAHARA
GEOGRAPHY - WORLD
DESERTS - WORLD

SALESMANSHIP
BUSINESS AND ECONOMICS
SALESMANSHIP AND MARKETING

SALTS
SCIENCE - PHYSICAL
CHEMISTRY - ACIDS, BASES, SALTS

SAMOA
GEOGRAPHY - WORLD
OCEANIA

SARDINIA
GEOGRAPHY - WORLD
ITALY

SATELLITES
SCIENCE - PHYSICAL
BASIC PHYSICAL SCIENCE - SPACE AND SOLAR
SYSTEM
EARTH SCIENCE - ASTRONOMY

SCANDINAVIA
GEOGRAPHY - WORLD
SCANDINAVIA AND FINLAND

SCHOOL SAFETY
HEALTH AND SAFETY
SAFETY - PLAYGROUND AND SCHOOL

SCHOOLS
EDUCATION
AIMS AND OBJECTIVES
GUIDANCE AND COUNSELING
EDUCATIONAL
SOCIAL SCIENCE
HOME AND SCHOOL

SCIENCE
SCIENCE
SCIENCE - NATURAL
SCIENCE - PHYSICAL

SCIENCE CAREERS
SCIENCE
VOCATIONS, SCIENCE - GENERAL
VOCATIONS, SCIENCE - CHEMISTRY
VOCATIONS, SCIENCE - LIFE SCIENCES
VOCATIONS, SCIENCE - PHYSICAL SCIENCES

SCIENCE FAIR
SCIENCE
SCIENTIFIC METHOD

SCIENCE - HISTORY
SCIENCE
HISTORY

SCIENTIFIC METHOD
SCIENCE
SCIENTIFIC METHOD

SCOTLAND
GEOGRAPHY - WORLD
GREAT BRITAIN

SCULPTURE
FINE ARTS
SCULPTURE

SEA
GEOGRAPHY - WORLD
RIVERS AND OCEANS - WORLD

SEA LIFE
SCIENCE - NATURAL
BASIC LIFE SCIENCE, ANIMALS - SEA ANIMALS
BIOLOGY, ECOLOGY - MARINE
BIOLOGY, ZOOLOGY - SEA ANIMALS

SEAPORTS
SOCIAL SCIENCE
TRANSPORTATION - WATER

SEASONS
SCIENCE - NATURAL
BASIC LIFE SCIENCE - SEASONS

SECRETARIAL SKILLS
BUSINESS AND ECONOMICS
OFFICE PROCEDURES

SECRETARIAL TRAINING
BUSINESS AND ECONOMICS
OFFICE PROCEDURES

SEEDS
SCIENCE - NATURAL
BASIC LIFE SCIENCE, PLANTS - SEEDS
BIOLOGY, BOTANY - SEEDS

SEINE
GEOGRAPHY - WORLD
RIVERS AND OCEANS - WORLD

SENTENCE STRUCTURE
ENGLISH LANGUAGE
GRAMMAR

SET THEORY
MATHEMATICS
NUMBERS AND NUMBER SYSTEMS
SETS

SETS AND NUMBERS
MATHEMATICS
NUMBERS AND NUMBER SYSTEMS
SETS

SEWING
HOME ECONOMICS
CLOTHING AND DRESS

SHAKESPEARE'S PLAYS
LITERATURE
DRAMA

SHEEP
AGRICULTURE
AGRICULTURE - LIVESTOCK
SOCIAL SCIENCE
FARM LIFE

SHELTER
SOCIAL SCIENCE
BASIC NEEDS - CLOTHING, FOOD, SHELTER

SHIPS
SOCIAL SCIENCE
TRANSPORTATION - WATER

SHORT STORY
LITERATURE
SHORT STORY

SHORTHAND
BUSINESS AND ECONOMICS
OFFICE PROCEDURES

SIAM
GEOGRAPHY - WORLD
SOUTHEAST ASIA

SICILY
GEOGRAPHY - WORLD
ITALY

SILK SCREEN PRINTING
FINE ARTS
ARTS AND CRAFTS

SINGAPORE
GEOGRAPHY - WORLD
SOUTHEAST ASIA

SKETCHING
FINE ARTS
DRAWING

SKIING
PHYSICAL EDUCATION
RECREATION
SPORTS

SKIN DIVING
PHYSICAL EDUCATION
SPORTS

SLIDE RULE
MATHEMATICS
SLIDE RULE

SMOKING
HEALTH AND SAFETY
SMOKING

SNAKES
SCIENCE - NATURAL
BASIC LIFE SCIENCE, ANIMALS - REPTILES
BIOLOGY, ZOOLOGY - REPTILES

SOCCER
PHYSICAL EDUCATION
SOCCER
SPORTS

SOCIAL DEVELOPMENT
GUIDANCE AND COUNSELING
SOCIAL

17

SOCIAL PROBLEMS
SOCIOLOGY
SOCIAL PROBLEMS

SOCIAL SCIENCE
SOCIAL SCIENCE

SOCIAL WORK
SOCIOLOGY
SOCIAL WORK

SOCIOLOGY
SOCIOLOGY

SOFTBALL
PHYSICAL EDUCATION
SPORTS

SOIL MANAGEMENT
AGRICULTURE
SOIL CONSERVATION

SOLAR SYSTEM
SCIENCE - PHYSICAL
BASIC PHYSICAL SCIENCE - SPACE AND SOLAR
SYSTEM
EARTH SCIENCE - ASTRONOMY

SOLDERING
INDUSTRIAL AND TECHNICAL EDUCATION
ELECTRICAL WORK AND ELECTRONICS

SONGS AND SINGING
FINE ARTS
MUSIC - VOCAL

SOUND
SCIENCE - PHYSICAL
BASIC PHYSICAL SCIENCE - SOUND
PHYSICS - SOUND

SOUTH AFRICA
GEOGRAPHY - WORLD
AFRICA

SOUTH AMERICA
GEOGRAPHY - WORLD
SOUTH AMERICA
HISTORY - WORLD
LATIN AMERICA

SOUTH PACIFIC
GEOGRAPHY - WORLD
OCEANIA

SOUTH VIETNAM
GEOGRAPHY - WORLD
SOUTHEAST ASIA

SOUTHEAST ASIA
GEOGRAPHY - WORLD
SOUTHEAST ASIA

SOUTHERN U S
GEOGRAPHY - U S
SOUTHERN AND SOUTHEASTERN STATES

SOUTHWESTERN U S
GEOGRAPHY - U S
SOUTHWESTERN STATES

SPACE
SCIENCE - PHYSICAL
BASIC PHYSICAL SCIENCE - SPACE AND SOLAR
SYSTEM
EARTH SCIENCE - ASTRONOMY

SPAIN
GEOGRAPHY - WORLD
SPAIN AND PORTUGAL

SPANISH LANGUAGE
FOREIGN LANGUAGE
SPANISH

SPECIAL EDUCATION
EDUCATION
SPECIAL

SPEECH
ENGLISH LANGUAGE
SPEECH

SPELLING
ENGLISH LANGUAGE
VOCABULARY - SPELLING

SPIDERS
SCIENCE - NATURAL
BASIC LIFE SCIENCE, ANIMALS - INSECTS
BIOLOGY, ZOOLOGY - INSECTS

SPORTS
PHYSICAL EDUCATION
SPORTS

SPRING
SCIENCE - NATURAL
BASIC LIFE SCIENCE - SEASONS

SQUARE DANCING
FINE ARTS
DANCE

ST LAWRENCE SEAWAY
GEOGRAPHY - WORLD
CANADA
RIVERS AND OCEANS - WORLD

STAGECRAFT
FINE ARTS
THEATER

STAR-SPANGLED BANNER
HISTORY - U S
U S HISTORY - 1783-1860

STARS
SCIENCE - PHYSICAL
BASIC PHYSICAL SCIENCE - SPACE AND SOLAR
SYSTEM
EARTH SCIENCE - ASTRONOMY

STATISTICS
MATHEMATICS
STATISTICS, MATHEMATICAL

STATUES
FINE ARTS
SCULPTURE

STEEL
BUSINESS AND ECONOMICS
INDUSTRY

STORMS
SCIENCE - PHYSICAL
EARTH SCIENCE - METEOROLOGY

STORY WRITING
ENGLISH LANGUAGE
WRITING

STREET SAFETY
HEALTH AND SAFETY
SAFETY - HOME AND COMMUNITY

STRIKES
BUSINESS AND ECONOMICS
LABOR AND MANAGEMENT

STUDY HABITS
GUIDANCE AND COUNSELING
EDUCATIONAL

SUBTRACTION
MATHEMATICS
ARITHMETIC - SUBTRACTION

SUEZ CANAL
GEOGRAPHY - WORLD
CANALS - WORLD

SUGAR
AGRICULTURE
AGRICULTURE - CROPS

SUMMER
SCIENCE - NATURAL
BASIC LIFE SCIENCE - SEASONS

SUN
SCIENCE - PHYSICAL
BASIC PHYSICAL SCIENCE - SPACE AND SOLAR
SYSTEM
EARTH SCIENCE - ASTRONOMY

SUPERVISION
BUSINESS AND ECONOMICS
SUPERVISION

SUPERVISORY TRAINING
BUSINESS AND ECONOMICS
SUPERVISION

SUPREME COURT
CIVICS AND POLITICAL SYSTEMS
GOVERNMENT - U S

SURFING
PHYSICAL EDUCATION
SPORTS

SURGERY, DENTAL
HEALTH AND SAFETY
DENTISTRY

SURGERY, MEDICAL
HEALTH AND SAFETY
MEDICINE

SWEDEN
GEOGRAPHY - WORLD
SCANDINAVIA AND FINLAND

SWIMMING
PHYSICAL EDUCATION
SPORTS

SWISS
GEOGRAPHY - WORLD
SWITZERLAND

SWITZERLAND
GEOGRAPHY - WORLD
SWITZERLAND

SYMBOLS, MATHEMATICA
MATHEMATICS
SYMBOLS AND VOCABULARY, MATHEMATICAL

TABLES, MATHEMATICAL
MATHEMATICS
TABLES, MATHEMATICAL

TAIWAN
GEOGRAPHY - WORLD
CHINA

TAPE RECORDING
EDUCATION
EDUCATIONAL TECHNOLOGY

TEACHERS AND TEACHING
EDUCATION
TEACHER AND TEACHING

TEACHING METHODS
EDUCATION
STUDY AND METHODS

TECHNOLOGY(EDUCATIONAL)
EDUCATION
EDUCATIONAL TECHNOLOGY

TEENAGERS
PSYCHOLOGY
ADOLESCENCE

TEETH
HEALTH AND SAFETY
DENTAL CARE
SCIENCE - NATURAL
BASIC LIFE SCIENCE, HUMAN BODY - TEETH

TELEPHONE
SOCIAL SCIENCE
COMMUNICATION

TELEVISION
SOCIAL SCIENCE
COMMUNICATION

TELEVISION (EDUCATIONAL)
EDUCATION
EDUCATIONAL TECHNOLOGY

TELEVISION SERVICING
INDUSTRIAL AND TECHNICAL EDUCATION
ELECTRICAL WORK AND ELECTRONICS

TENNIS
PHYSICAL EDUCATION
SPORTS
TENNIS

TESTING(EDUCATIONAL)
EDUCATION
TESTS AND MEASUREMENT

TESTING(PSYCHOLOGY)
PSYCHOLOGY
TESTING AND RESEARCH

TEXAS
GEOGRAPHY - U S
SOUTHWESTERN STATES

THAILAND
GEOGRAPHY - WORLD
SOUTHEAST ASIA

THEATER ARTS
FINE ARTS
THEATER

THERMOMETERS
SCIENCE
LABORATORY TECHNIQUES - GENERAL
LABORATORY TECHNIQUES - BIOLOGY
LABORATORY TECHNIQUES - CHEMISTRY
LABORATORY TECHNIQUES - MEDICINE
LABORATORY TECHNIQUES - PHYSICS

THROAT
SCIENCE - NATURAL
BASIC LIFE SCIENCE, HUMAN BODY - NOSE
AND THROAT
BIOLOGY, PHYSIOLOGY(HUMAN) - NOSE AND
THROAT

TIBET
GEOGRAPHY - WORLD
ASIA - GENERAL

TIDES
SCIENCE - PHYSICAL
EARTH SCIENCE - OCEANOGRAPHY

TIME
MATHEMATICS
MEASUREMENT - GENERAL

TIME AND MOTION
BUSINESS AND ECONOMICS
TIME AND MOTION STUDY

TOKYO
GEOGRAPHY - WORLD
JAPAN

TOOLS
INDUSTRIAL AND TECHNICAL EDUCATION
MACHINE SHOP AND METALWORK

TRACK AND FIELD
PHYSICAL EDUCATION
SPORTS

TRADE
BUSINESS AND ECONOMICS
TRADE

TRAINS
SOCIAL SCIENCE
TRANSPORTATION - LAND

TRANSISTORS
INDUSTRIAL AND TECHNICAL EDUCATION
ELECTRICAL WORK AND ELECTRONICS

TRANSPORTATION - AIR
SOCIAL SCIENCE
TRANSPORTATION - AIR

TRANSPORTATION - GENERAL
SOCIAL SCIENCE
TRANSPORTATION - GENERAL

TRANSPORTATION - LAND
SOCIAL SCIENCE
TRANSPORTATION - LAND

TRANSPORTATION - WATER
SOCIAL SCIENCE
TRANSPORTATION - WATER

TREES
SCIENCE - NATURAL
BASIC LIFE SCIENCE, PLANTS - TREES
BIOLOGY, BOTANY - TYPES OF PLANTS

TRIANGLES
MATHEMATICS
GEOMETRY

TRIGONOMETRY
MATHEMATICS
TRIGONOMETRY

TUBES, ELECTRICAL
INDUSTRIAL AND TECHNICAL EDUCATION
ELECTRICAL WORK AND ELECTRONICS

TUMBLING
PHYSICAL EDUCATION
SPORTS

TUNISIA
GEOGRAPHY - WORLD
MIDDLE EAST

TURKEY
GEOGRAPHY - WORLD
TURKEY

TWENTIETH CENTURY
HISTORY - U S
U S HISTORY - 1900 TO PRESENT
HISTORY - WORLD
TWENTIETH CENTURY - GENERAL

TYPE SETTING
INDUSTRIAL AND TECHNICAL EDUCATION
PRINTING AND GRAPHIC ARTS

TYPING
BUSINESS AND ECONOMICS
OFFICE PROCEDURES

U S - OVERVIEW
GEOGRAPHY - U S
GEOGRAPHY, U S - GENERAL

U S ECONOMIC SYSTEM
BUSINESS AND ECONOMICS
ECONOMIC SYSTEM - U S

**UNION OF SOVIET SOCIALIST
REPUBLICS**
GEOGRAPHY - WORLD
UNION OF SOVIET SOCIALIST REPUBLICS

UNIONS
BUSINESS AND ECONOMICS
LABOR AND MANAGEMENT

UNITED KINGDOM
GEOGRAPHY - WORLD
GREAT BRITAIN

UNITED NATIONS
CIVICS AND POLITICAL SYSTEMS
UNITED NATIONS

UNIVERSE
SCIENCE - PHYSICAL
BASIC PHYSICAL SCIENCE - SPACE AND SOLAR
SYSTEM
EARTH SCIENCE - ASTRONOMY

UNIVERSITIES
EDUCATION
AIMS AND OBJECTIVES

URBANIZATION
SOCIOLOGY
URBANIZATION

URUGUAY
GEOGRAPHY - WORLD
SOUTH AMERICA

VACATIONING
PHYSICAL EDUCATION
RECREATION

VANDALISM
SOCIOLOGY
JUVENILE DELINQUENCY

VEGETABLES
AGRICULTURE
AGRICULTURE - CROPS
SOCIAL SCIENCE
BASIC NEEDS - CLOTHING, FOOD, SHELTER

VENEZUELA
GEOGRAPHY - WORLD
SOUTH AMERICA

VENICE
GEOGRAPHY - WORLD
ITALY

VERBS
ENGLISH LANGUAGE
GRAMMAR

VETERINARY MEDICINE
AGRICULTURE
ANIMAL HUSBANDRY
HEALTH AND SAFETY
MEDICINE

VIKINGS
HISTORY - WORLD
DISCOVERY AND EXPLORATION

VISUAL HEARING
ENGLISH LANGUAGE
SPEECH - GENERAL

VOCABULARY SKILLS
ENGLISH LANGUAGE
VOCABULARY

VOCAL MUSIC
FINE ARTS
MUSIC - VOCAL

VOCATIONAL GUIDANCE
GUIDANCE AND COUNSELING
VOCATIONAL

VOLCANOS
GEOGRAPHY - WORLD
VOLCANOS
SCIENCE - PHYSICAL
EARTH SCIENCE - GEOLOGY

VOLLEYBALL
PHYSICAL EDUCATION
SPORTS

VOLUME
MATHEMATICS
MEASUREMENT - GENERAL
MEASUREMENT - VOLUME

VOTING
CIVICS AND POLITICAL SYSTEMS
POLITICS

WAR OF 1812
HISTORY - U S
U S HISTORY - 1783-1860

WASHINGTON, D C
GEOGRAPHY - U S
WASHINGTON, D C

WATER
SCIENCE - PHYSICAL
CHEMISTRY - WATER

WATER CONSERVATION
SCIENCE - NATURAL
CONSERVATION AND NATURAL RESOURCES

WATER SAFETY
HEALTH AND SAFETY
SAFETY - WATER

WATERCOLOR
FINE ARTS
PAINTING

WEATHER
SCIENCE - PHYSICAL
BASIC PHYSICAL SCIENCE - WEATHER AND
CLIMATE
EARTH SCIENCE - METEOROLOGY

WEIGHING
SCIENCE
LABORATORY TECHNIQUES

WEAVING
FINE ARTS
ARTS AND CRAFTS

WESTERN U S
GEOGRAPHY - U S
WESTERN STATES

WEST INDIES
GEOGRAPHY - WORLD
CARIBBEAN

WESTWARD EXPANSION
HISTORY - U S
FRONTIER AND EXPANSION

WHEAT
AGRICULTURE
AGRICULTURE - CROPS

WHEELS
SCIENCE - PHYSICAL
BASIC PHYSICAL SCIENCE - MACHINES

WHITE HOUSE
GEOGRAPHY - U S
WASHINGTON, D C

WILLIAMSBURG
HISTORY - U S
U S HISTORY - COLONIAL PERIOD TO 1776

WIND
SCIENCE - PHYSICAL
BASIC PHYSICAL SCIENCE - WEATHER AND
CLIMATE
EARTH SCIENCE - METEOROLOGY

WINTER
SCIENCE - NATURAL
BASIC LIFE SCIENCE - SEASONS

WOOD PRODUCTS
BUSINESS AND ECONOMICS
INDUSTRY

WOODWORK
INDUSTRIAL AND TECHNICAL EDUCATION
WOODWORK

WORD SKILLS
ENGLISH LANGUAGE
VOCABULARY

WORK
SCIENCE - PHYSICAL
PHYSICS - ENERGY AND MATTER

WORLD AFFAIRS
CIVICS AND POLITICAL SYSTEMS
FOREIGN POLICY - U S

WORLD FOOD PROBLEM
GEOGRAPHY - WORLD
ECONOMIC GEOGRAPHY
SOCIOLOGY
POPULATION

WORLD TRADE
BUSINESS AND ECONOMICS
TRADE

WORLD WAR I
HISTORY - WORLD
WORLD WAR I

WORLD WAR II
HISTORY - WORLD
WORLD WAR II

WORMS
SCIENCE - NATURAL
BIOLOGY, ZOOLOGY - WORMS

WRESTLING
PHYSICAL EDUCATION
SPORTS

WRITERS
LITERATURE
AUTHORS AND THEIR WORKS

WRITING
ENGLISH LANGUAGE
WRITING

YELLOWSTONE NATIONAL PARK
GEOGRAPHY - U S
NATIONAL PARKS - U S

YOSEMITE NATIONAL PARK
GEOGRAPHY - U S
NATIONAL PARKS - U S

YUGOSLAVIA
GEOGRAPHY - WORLD
BALKANS

ZION NATIONAL PARK
GEOGRAPHY - U S
NATIONAL PARKS - U S

ZOO ANIMALS
SCIENCE - NATURAL
BASIC LIFE SCIENCE, ANIMALS - ZOO

ZOOLOGY
SCIENCE - NATURAL
BIOLOGY, ZOOLOGY
END

SUBJECT GUIDE

AGRICULTURE

AGRICULTURE - GENERAL

(FILMSTRIPS)

AGRICULTURE AND THE ECOSYSTEM (H-C)	UILVAS
CALIFORNIA CONFLICT - MIGRANT FARM WORKERS (J-H A)	SVE
COMMUNES IN CHINA	EGH
CZECHOSLOVAKIA - AGRICULTURE AND INDUSTRY	MGHT
EASTERN EUROPE--A SERIES	MGHT
HUNGARY - AGRICULTURE TODAY	MGHT
IDENTIFICATION OF ELECTRIC WIRING ITEMS (H-C)	UILVAS
ONE HUNDRED AND THIRTY BILLION DOLLAR FOOD ASSEMBLY LINE (C A)	USDA
ONE PHASE OF THE BLACK MARKET IN MEAT	USOPA
POLAND - AGRICULTURE TODAY	MGHT
RANCH LIFE	EGH
RESOURCES, AGRICULTURE AND INDUSTRY	EGH
WORK OF THE PEOPLE OF CHINA	EGH

(MOTION PICTURES)

FLOWERS FOR DAHLIA	ALDEN
MECHANISMS OF SCATTERING SEEDS	IWANMI
MOSHAV, THE - ISRAEL'S MIDDLE WAY	ALDEN
NAHAL	ALDEN
YESTERDAY'S FARM (P-J)	BFA

AGRICULTURE - CROPS

(FILMSTRIPS)

TILLAGE ALTERNATIVES (H-C A)	USDA
TIMBER - WASHINGTON'S MOST VALUABLE CROP (J-H A)	SVE

(MOTION CARTRIDGES)

GLUTEN DEVELOPMENT	IOWA

(MOTION PICTURES)

FRESH CHILLED SUNSHINE	MTP

(TRANSPARENCIES)

CORN (K-P)	LEART

AGRICULTURE - ENGINEERING

(MOTION CARTRIDGES)

DEALER'S ROLE, THE	GEIGY

AGRICULTURE - LIVESTOCK

(FILMSTRIPS)

CLIPPING AND TRIMMING DAIRY CATTLE (H-C)	UILVAS

(MOTION PICTURES)

CHAROLAIS REPORT, THE	MTP
THOSE ANIMALS ON THE FARM (K-P)	CLBELL

AGRICULTURE - SOCIETIES

(FILMSTRIPS)

AGRICULTURE AND THE ECOSYSTEM (H-C)	UILVAS

FARM WORK

(FILMSTRIPS)

CALIFORNIA CONFLICT - MIGRANT FARM WORKERS (J-H A)	SVE
CLIPPING AND TRIMMING DAIRY CATTLE (H-C)	UILVAS
SAFE USE OF PESTICIDES ON THE FARM (H-C A)	USDA
TILLAGE ALTERNATIVES (H-C A)	USDA

(MOTION PICTURES)

SAFE OPERATION OF FARM TRACTORS (J-C A)	CUNIV

GARDENING

(FILMSTRIPS)

GREENHOUSES - USES AND DESIGN (H-C)	UILVAS
GROUND COVERS AND THEIR USES (H-C)	UILVAS
GROWING THINGS--A SERIES (P-J)	TERF

(MOTION PICTURES)

BEAUTY AND COMFORT OUTDOORS	MTP
ROOTS AND ALL	MTP

INSECTS AND PESTS

(FILMSTRIPS)

SAFE USE OF PESTICIDES ON THE FARM (H-C A)	USDA
TILLAGE ALTERNATIVES (H-C A)	USDA

(MOTION PICTURES)

BEAUTY AND COMFORT OUTDOORS	MTP
MOSQUITO	IWANMI
NEMATODE (J-C)	EBEC

MACHINERY AND TOOLS

(FILMSTRIPS)

TILLAGE ALTERNATIVES (H-C A)	USDA

(MOTION PICTURES)

SAFE OPERATION OF FARM TRACTORS (J-C A)	CUNIV

PLANT DISEASES

(MOTION PICTURES)

BEAUTY AND COMFORT OUTDOORS	MTP

PLANT SCIENCE

(FILMSTRIPS)

GREENHOUSES - USES AND DESIGN (H-C)	UILVAS
GROUND COVERS AND THEIR USES (H-C)	UILVAS

(MOTION PICTURES)

BEAUTY AND COMFORT OUTDOORS	MTP
ROOTS AND ALL	MTP

SOIL CONSERVATION

(FILMSTRIPS)

AGRICULTURE AND THE ECOSYSTEM (H-C)	UILVAS

(AUDIO TAPES)

SYLVANIA STORY, THE (H A)	USOE

STUDY AND TEACHING

(FILMSTRIPS)

IDENTIFICATION OF ELECTRIC WIRING ITEMS (H-C)	UILVAS

(MOTION CARTRIDGES)

DEALER'S ROLE, THE	GEIGY

BIOGRAPHY

FAMOUS AMERICANS (OTHER THAN PRESIDENTS)

(FILMSTRIPS)

AUTOMOBILE, THE (HENRY FORD) (P)	EDPRC
CRISPUS ATTUCKS (I-H)	CORF
FAMOUS PATRIOTS OF THE AMERICAN REVOLUTION--A SERIES (I-H)	CORF
HAYM SALOMON (I-H)	CORF
JOHN PAUL JONES (I-H)	CORF
MOLLY PITCHER (I-H)	CORF
NATHANAEL GREENE (I-H)	CORF
PATRICK HENRY (I-H)	CORF

(MOTION PICTURES)

AFFAIRS OF A MAN, THE (J-C A)	FORD
BENJAMIN FRANKLIN AND THE MID-ATLANTIC SIGNERS	RMI
BING CROSBY'S WASHINGTON STATE (I-C A)	SCREEI
FILMMAKING TECHNIQUES - ACTING (I-C A)	AIMS
IMOGEN CUNNINGHAM, PHOTOGRAPHER	AMERFI
JOHN ADAMS AND THE NEW ENGLAND SIGNERS	RMI
SATCHMO AND ALL THAT JAZZ (I-C A)	HEARST
THOMAS JEFFERSON AND THE SOUTHERN SIGNERS	RMI
TO THE SPIRIT OF '76--A SERIES (J-C)	RMI
WONDERFUL WORLD OF SPORT - BASKETBALL--A SERIES (J-C A)	AMERFI
WONDERFUL WORLD OF SPORT - FOOTBALL--A SERIES (J-C A)	AMERFI

(RECORDS)

AUTOBIOGRAPHY OF FREDERICK DOUGLASS	BOW
D-DAY PLUS 20	CAED

(TRANSPARENCIES)

A PHILIP RANDOLPH (J-H)	LEART
ADAM CLAYTON POWELL (J-H)	LEART
ALEXANDER DUMAS (J-H)	LEART
ALTHEA GIBSON (J-H)	LEART
BENJAMIN BENNEKER (J-H)	LEART
BENJAMIN L DAVIS (J-H)	LEART
BILL COSBY (J-H)	LEART
BIOGRAPHIES OF OUTSTANDING NEGRO AMERICANS--A SERIES (J-H)	LEART
BLANCHE K BRUCE (J-H)	LEART
BOB GIBSON (J-H)	LEART
BOOKER T WASHINGTON (J-H)	LEART
CARTER G WOODSON (J-H)	LEART
CHARLES DREW (J-H)	LEART
COUNTEE CULLEN (J-H)	LEART
CRISPUS ATTUCKS (J-H)	LEART
DENMARK VESEY (J-H)	LEART
DUKE ELLINGTON (J-H)	LEART
FREDERICK A DOUGLASS (J-H)	LEART
GEORGE WASHINGTON CARVER (J-H)	LEART
GRANVILLE WOODS (J-H)	LEART
GWENDOLYN BROOKS (J-H)	LEART
HARRIET TUBMAN (J-H)	LEART
HARRY BELAFONTE (J-H)	LEART
HENRY O TANNER (J-H)	LEART
JACK JOHNSON (J-H)	LEART
JACKIE ROBINSON (J-H)	LEART
JAMES BROWN (J-H)	LEART
JAMES WELDON JOHNSON (J-H)	LEART
JAN MATZELIGER (J-H)	LEART
JOE LOUIS (J-H)	LEART
LANGSTON HUGHES (J-H)	LEART
LEONTYNE PRICE (J-H)	LEART
LOUIS 'SATCHMO' ARMSTRONG (J-H)	LEART
MAHALIA JACKSON (J-H)	LEART
MALCOLM X (J-H)	LEART
MARCUS GARVEY (J-H)	LEART
MARIAN ANDERSON (J-H)	LEART
MARTIN LUTHER KING (J-H)	LEART
MARY MC LEOD BETHUNE (J-H)	LEART
MATTHEW HENSON (J-H)	LEART
NAT TURNER (J-H)	LEART
PAUL LAURENCE DUNBAR (J-H)	LEART
PHYLLIS WHEATLEY (J-H)	LEART
RALPH J BUNCHE (J-H)	LEART
RICHARD WRIGHT (J-H)	LEART
ROBERT SMALLS (J-H)	LEART
SAMMY DAVIS JR (J-H)	LEART
SIDNEY POITIER (J-H)	LEART
STOKELY CARMICHAEL (J-H)	LEART
THURGOOD MARSHALL (J-H)	LEART
W C HANDY (J-H)	LEART

WILLIAM E B DU BOIS (J-H)   LEART
WILLIE MAYS (J-H)   LEART
WILTON N CHAMBERLAIN (J-H)   LEART

PERSONALITIES OF OTHER COUNTRIES

(FILMSTRIPS)

ALBERT SCHWEITZER (2ND ED) (I-H)   CARMAN
ALEXANDER THE GREAT AND THE
   ANCIENTS (I-J)   SED
CAPTAIN COOK, ALEXANDER MAC
   KENZIE AND LEWIS AND CLARK
   (I-J)   SED
COLUMBUS, BALBOA AND MAGELLAN (I-
   J)   SED
EXPLORATION - MAN'S QUEST FOR
   KNOWLEDGE--A SERIES (I-J)   SED
EXPLORING AFRICA (I-J)   SED
GREAT MEN AND ARTISTS   EGH
GREAT MEN AND ARTISTS   EGH
SPANISH CONQUERORS AND
   COLONIZERS (I-J)   SED
VIKINGS, THE ARABS AND MARCO
   POLO, THE (I-J)   SED

(MOTION PICTURES)

KRISHNAMURTI (H-C A)   TIMLIF
POPE PAUL'S VISIT TO ISRAEL   ALDEN
PRIME MINISTER GOLDA MEIR'S
   VISIT TO THE USA IN 1969   ALDEN
ROOTS OF MADNESS   XEROX
VISION OF CHAIM WEIZMANN   ALDEN

(RECORDS)

D-DAY PLUS 20   CAED

(TRANSPARENCIES)

SHAKESPEARE--A SERIES   BETECL

PRESIDENTS OF THE UNITED STATES

(FILMSTRIPS)

GREAT DEPRESSION, THE -
   CAUSES, EFFECTS, SOLUTIONS,
   PT 2 (J-C)   EAV

(MOTION PICTURES)

BENJAMIN FRANKLIN AND THE MID-
   ATLANTIC SIGNERS   RMI
BIOGRAPHY OF A CHAIR (J-C A)   FORD
JOHN ADAMS AND THE NEW ENGLAND
   SIGNERS   RMI
THOMAS JEFFERSON AND THE
   SOUTHERN SIGNERS   RMI

(RECORDS)

D-DAY PLUS 20   CAED

BUSINESS AND ECONOMICS

ADVERTISING

(MOTION PICTURES)

ADVERTISING   BEF
ADVERTISING - INFORMATION,
   PERSUASION OR DECEPTION (I-C)   JOU
ADVERTISING AND COMPETITION   MTP

(AUDIO TAPES)

MESSAGE FROM OUR SPONSOR, A (I-J)   CORF

CAPITALISM

(FILMSTRIPS)

GREAT DEPRESSION, THE -
   CAUSES, EFFECTS, SOLUTIONS,
   PT 4 (J-C)   EAV

COMPETITION

(FILMSTRIPS)

GOOD GOODIES   BFA

(MOTION PICTURES)

ADVERTISING AND COMPETITION   MTP

CORPORATIONS

(FILMSTRIPS)

COMPANY AND THE COMMUNITY, THE,
   PT 1   CREATV
COMPANY AND THE COMMUNITY, THE,
   PT 2   CREATV
COMPANY ORGANIZATION, PT 1   CREATV
COMPANY ORGANIZATION, PT 2   CREATV

(MOTION PICTURES)

PARTNERS, THE (J-C A)   UMITV

COST AND STANDARD OF LIVING

(FILMSTRIPS)

CONSUMERISM - THE DANGERS OF
   AFFLUENCE, PT 1   ASPRSS
CONSUMERISM - THE DANGERS OF
   AFFLUENCE, PT 2   ASPRSS
DOING IT ALL ON A BUDGET   EGH
LOOKING GREAT ON A SHOESTRING--A
   SERIES   EGH

(MOTION PICTURES)

WHAT EVERY MANAGER NEEDS TO
   KNOW ABOUT MARKETING, PT 1
   - THE MERITT CASE   BNA
WHAT EVERY MANAGER NEEDS TO
   KNOW ABOUT MARKETING, PT 2
   - WHAT BUSINESS ARE YOU ...   BNA

DEPRESSIONS

(FILMSTRIPS)

DOING IT ALL ON A BUDGET   EGH
GREAT DEPRESSION, THE -
   CAUSES, EFFECTS, SOLUTIONS,
   PT 4 (J-C)   EAV
GREAT DEPRESSION, THE -
   CAUSES, EFFECTS, SOLUTIONS,
   PT 2 (J-C)   EAV
GREAT DEPRESSION, THE -
   CAUSES, EFFECTS, SOLUTIONS,
   PT 3 (J-C)   EAV
GREAT DEPRESSION, THE -
   CAUSES, EFFECTS, SOLUTIONS,
   PT 1 (J-C)   EAV

ECONOMICS - GENERAL

(FILMSTRIPS)

ECONOMIC DECISION MAKING -
   WHAT, HOW AND FOR WHOM (I-
   H)   DOUBLE
ECONOMICS--A SERIES (I-H)   DOUBLE
GREAT DEPRESSION, THE -
   CAUSES, EFFECTS, SOLUTIONS,
   PT 4 (J-C)   EAV
GREAT DEPRESSION, THE -
   CAUSES, EFFECTS, SOLUTIONS,
   PT 2 (J-C)   EAV
GREAT DEPRESSION, THE -
   CAUSES, EFFECTS, SOLUTIONS,
   PT 3 (J-C)   EAV
MEXICO - AN ECONOMY IN TRANSITION
   (I-H)   DOUBLE
MIXED ECONOMY OF THE UNITED
   STATES (I-H)   DOUBLE
RESOURCES, AGRICULTURE AND
   INDUSTRY   EGH

(MOTION PICTURES)

OCEANOGRAPHIC PREDICTION SYSTEM   USNAC

(TRANSPARENCIES)

ACCUMULATING CAPITAL FOR
   INVESTMENTS (J-H)   LEART
AFTER THE 'TAKE-OFF' - A DRIVE TO
   MATURITY (J-H)   LEART
BANKS ACCUMULATE AND DISTRIBUTE
   CAPITAL (J-H)   LEART
BASIC SOCIAL STUDIES CONCEPTS
   - ECONOMICS--A SERIES (J-H)   LEART
BASIC SOCIAL STUDIES CONCEPTS
   - POLITICS, SOCIAL-ECONOMIC
   INTERDEPENDENCE--A SERIES (J-H)   LEART
BUSINESS - WHAT COMES BEFORE
   PROFIT (J-H)   LEART
BUSINESS ORGANIZATION AND
   OWNERSHIP (J-H)   LEART
CHAPTER ACTIVITIES   COF
CONSUMPTION AND ECONOMICS (J-H)   LEART
CONTESTS AND AWARDS PROGRAM   COF
CREATIVE MARKETING PROJECT   COF
DECA CREED, THE   COF
DECA GROWTH AND WHY JOIN DECA   COF

DECA OFFICERS, TERMINOLOGY,
   EXCITEMENT   COF
DEFINITION OF ECONOMIC ROLE (J-H)   LEART
DIFFERENT MEDIUMS OF
   EXCHANGE ARE USED IN
   DIFFERENT TYPES OF MARKETS (J-H)   LEART
DISTRIBUTIVE EDUCATION CLUBS
   OF AMERICA--A SERIES   COF
DOES FOREIGN AID MEAN FOREIGN
   CONTROL (J-H)   LEART
DOMESTIC SYSTEM VS FACTORY (J-H)   LEART
ECONOMIC INTERDEPENDENCE OF
   PEOPLE (J-H)   LEART
ECONOMIC PHILOSOPHY IN
   TRADITIONAL SOCIETY (J-H)   LEART
ECONOMICS - ECONOMIC HISTORY--A
   SERIES (J-H)   LEART
ECONOMICS - ECONOMICS IN ACTION--A
   SERIES (J-H)   LEART
ECONOMICS - POLITICAL ECONOMY
   AND PHILOSOPHY --A SERIES (J-
   H)   LEART
ECONOMICS IN A DEVELOPING NATION
   (J-H)   LEART
ECONOMICS IN A TRADITIONAL SOCIETY
   (J-H)   LEART
ECONOMICS TERMS (J-H)   LEART
EDUCATION AND ECONOMICS (J-H)   LEART
FACTORS IN ECONOMIC GROWTH (J-H)   LEART
FACTORS OF PRODUCTION (J-H)   LEART
FEDERAL BUDGET - INCOME AND
   EXPENDITURES (J-H)   LEART
GUILD VS LABOR UNION   LEART
HISTORY OF RECORD KEEPING (J-H)   LEART
HOW BANKS WORK (J-H)   LEART
HOW DO CHECKS REPLACE MONEY (J-
   H)   LEART
HOW PRICE IS DETERMINED (J-H)   LEART
HOW TO EXPAND PRODUCTION (J-H)   LEART
HOW WE MEASURE ECONOMIC GROWTH
   (J-H)   LEART
INDUSTRIAL REVOLUTION IS A 'TAKE-
   OFF' (J-H)   LEART
INDUSTRIAL REVOLUTION TODAY (J-H)   LEART
INTERNATIONAL COMMERCIAL POLICY
   (J-H)   LEART
LABOR AND ECONOMICS (J-H)   LEART
MATURITY - HIGH MASS CONSUMPTION
   (J-H)   LEART
MONEY - HISTORY, TYPES AND
   PURPOSES (J-H)   LEART
NATIONAL DECA WEEK   COF
NATIONAL GOALS OF DECA   COF
NATURAL RESOURCES AND ECONOMICS
   (J-H)   LEART
OFFICIAL ITEMS   COF
ORIENTATION TO DISTRIBUTIVE
   EDUCATION--A SERIES   COF
PATTERNS OF CONSUMPTION -
   MARKETING (J-H)   LEART
PER CAPITA INCOME AND
   CONSUMPTION (J-H)   LEART
POST SECONDARY DIVISION   COF
PRODUCTION DEPENDS ON DEMAND (J-
   H)   LEART
REQUIREMENTS OF A 'TAKE-OFF' (J-H)   LEART
ROLE OF U S GOVERNMENT IN
   ECONOMICS VS ROLE OF SOVIET
   GOVERNMENT (J-H)   LEART
SAVINGS AND INVESTMENTS (J-H)   LEART
SECTORS OF A MODERN ECONOMY (J-
   H)   LEART
SOCIAL INSTITUTIONS AND ECONOMICS
   (J-H)   LEART
STAGES OF ECONOMIC GROWTH (J-H)   LEART
TAXES AND THE INDIVIDUAL (J-H)   LEART
TODAY'S ISMS (J-H)   LEART
TOWN AND ECONOMICS (J-H)   LEART
TYPES OF MARKET AND EXCHANGES (J-
   H)   LEART
TYPES OF PRODUCTION (J-H)   LEART
VALUES IN ECONOMIC DECISION (J-H)   LEART
WHAT DECA SYMBOLIZES   COF
WHAT IS CAPITAL (J-H)   LEART
WHAT IS ECONOMIC GROWTH (J-H)   LEART
WHAT IS ECONOMIC PLANNING (J-H)   LEART
WHAT IS ECONOMICS (J-H)   LEART
WHAT IS SOCIAL STUDIES - AN
   INTERDISCIPLINARY APPROACH
   (J-H)   LEART

ECONOMIC CONDITIONS

(FILMSTRIPS)

ECONOMIC DECISION MAKING -
   WHAT, HOW AND FOR WHOM (I-
   H)   DOUBLE
ECONOMICS--A SERIES (I-H)   DOUBLE
MEXICO - AN ECONOMY IN TRANSITION
   (I-H)   DOUBLE
RESOURCES, AGRICULTURE AND
   INDUSTRY   EGH
SEATTLE - A CITY FACES CRISIS (J-H A)   SVE

(MOTION PICTURES)

ADVERTISING AND COMPETITION   MTP

GROWING PAINS FOR THE COMMON
MARKET — HEARST

(TRANSPARENCIES)

BASIC SOCIAL STUDIES CONCEPTS
- ECONOMICS--A SERIES (J-H) — LEART
BASIC SOCIAL STUDIES CONCEPTS
- POLITICS, SOCIAL-ECONOMIC
INTERDEPENDENCE--A SERIES
(J-H) — LEART
BUSINESS ORGANIZATION AND
OWNERSHIP (J-H) — LEART
CONSUMPTION AND ECONOMICS (J-H) — LEART
DEFINITION OF ECONOMIC ROLE (J-H) — LEART
ECONOMIC INTERDEPENDENCE OF
PEOPLE (J-H) — LEART
ECONOMICS IN A DEVELOPING NATION
(J-H) — LEART
ECONOMICS IN A TRADITIONAL SOCIETY
(J-H) — LEART
FACTORS IN ECONOMIC GROWTH (J-H) — LEART
FACTORS OF PRODUCTION (J-H) — LEART
HOW BANKS WORK (J-H) — LEART
HOW DO CHECKS REPLACE MONEY (J-
H) — LEART
HOW PRICE IS DETERMINED (J-H) — LEART
INDUSTRIAL REVOLUTION IS A 'TAKE-
OFF' (J-H) — LEART
INTERACTION OF POLITICAL,
SOCIAL AND ECONOMIC CAUSES
AND EFFECTS (J-H) — LEART
LABOR AND ECONOMICS (J-H) — LEART
MATURITY - HIGH MASS CONSUMPTION
(J-H) — LEART
MONEY - HISTORY, TYPES AND
PURPOSES (J-H) — LEART
NATURAL RESOURCES AND ECONOMICS
(J-H) — LEART
TAXES AND THE INDIVIDUAL (J-H) — LEART
TYPES OF MARKET AND EXCHANGES (J-
H) — LEART
TYPES OF PRODUCTION (J-H) — LEART
VALUES IN ECONOMIC DECISION (J-H) — LEART
WHAT IS CAPITAL (J-H) — LEART
WHAT IS ECONOMIC GROWTH (J-H) — LEART
WHAT IS ECONOMICS (J-H) — LEART

ECONOMIC POLICY

(FILMSTRIPS)

ECONOMIC DECISION MAKING -
WHAT, HOW AND FOR WHOM (I-
H) — DOUBLE
ECONOMICS--A SERIES (I-H) — DOUBLE
MEXICO - AN ECONOMY IN TRANSITION
(I-H) — DOUBLE

(TRANSPARENCIES)

BANKS ACCUMULATE AND DISTRIBUTE
CAPITAL (J-H) — LEART
BASIC SOCIAL STUDIES CONCEPTS
- ECONOMICS--A SERIES (J-H) — LEART
BUSINESS ORGANIZATION AND
OWNERSHIP (J-H) — LEART
CONSUMPTION AND ECONOMICS (J-H) — LEART
DEFINITION OF ECONOMIC ROLE (J-H) — LEART
DIFFERENT MEDIUMS OF
EXCHANGE ARE USED IN
DIFFERENT TYPES OF MARKETS (J-H) — LEART
ECONOMIC INTERDEPENDENCE OF
PEOPLE (J-H) — LEART
ECONOMIC PHILOSOPHY IN
TRADITIONAL SOCIETY (J-H) — LEART
FACTORS OF PRODUCTION (J-H) — LEART
GROWTH OF INTERNATIONAL TRADE
AND COMMERCE (J-H) — LEART
HOW BANKS WORK (J-H) — LEART
HOW DO CHECKS REPLACE MONEY (J-
H) — LEART
HOW PRICE IS DETERMINED (J-H) — LEART
INTERNATIONAL COMMERCIAL POLICY
(J-H) — LEART
LABOR AND ECONOMICS (J-H) — LEART
MONEY - HISTORY, TYPES AND
PURPOSES (J-H) — LEART
NATURAL RESOURCES AND ECONOMICS
(J-H) — LEART
PRICES AND THE ROLE OF
GOVERNMENT (J-H) — LEART
TAXES AND THE INDIVIDUAL (J-H) — LEART
TYPES OF MARKET AND EXCHANGES (J-
H) — LEART
TYPES OF PRODUCTION (J-H) — LEART
VALUES IN ECONOMIC DECISION (J-H) — LEART
WHAT IS CAPITAL (J-H) — LEART
WHAT IS ECONOMIC GROWTH (J-H) — LEART
WHAT IS ECONOMICS (J-H) — LEART

ECONOMIC SYSTEM - U S

(FILMSTRIPS)

MIXED ECONOMY OF THE UNITED
STATES (I-H) — DOUBLE
NATION OF OWNERS--A SERIES — XEROX

(MOTION PICTURES)

ACTION FOR CHANGE (I-C A) — SCREEI

(AUDIO TAPES)

USE OF BANKS (H-C) — INSKY

(TRANSPARENCIES)

BASIC SOCIAL STUDIES CONCEPTS
- ECONOMICS--A SERIES (J-H) — LEART
BUSINESS ORGANIZATION AND
OWNERSHIP (J-H) — LEART
CONSUMPTION AND ECONOMICS (J-H) — LEART
DEFINITION OF ECONOMIC ROLE (J-H) — LEART
ECONOMIC INTERDEPENDENCE OF
PEOPLE (J-H) — LEART
FACTORS OF PRODUCTION (J-H) — LEART
FEDERAL BUDGET - INCOME AND
EXPENDITURES (J-H) — LEART
HOW BANKS WORK (J-H) — LEART
HOW DO CHECKS REPLACE MONEY (J-
H) — LEART
HOW PRICE IS DETERMINED (J-H) — LEART
LABOR AND ECONOMICS (J-H) — LEART
MONEY - HISTORY, TYPES AND
PURPOSES (J-H) — LEART
NATURAL RESOURCES AND ECONOMICS
(J-H) — LEART
ROLE OF U S GOVERNMENT IN
ECONOMICS VS ROLE OF SOVIET
GOVERNMENT (J-H) — LEART
TAXES AND THE INDIVIDUAL (J-H) — LEART
TYPES OF MARKET AND EXCHANGES (J-
H) — LEART
TYPES OF PRODUCTION (J-H) — LEART
VALUES IN ECONOMIC DECISION (J-H) — LEART
WHAT IS CAPITAL (J-H) — LEART
WHAT IS ECONOMIC GROWTH (J-H) — LEART
WHAT IS ECONOMICS (J-H) — LEART

FINANCE

(MOTION PICTURES)

MULTIPLE CHOICE (J-C A) — INDSLF
WHAT EVERY MANAGER NEEDS TO
KNOW ABOUT MARKETING, PT 1
- THE MERITT CASE — BNA
WHAT EVERY MANAGER NEEDS TO
KNOW ABOUT MARKETING, PT 2
- WHAT BUSINESS ARE YOU ... — BNA
WHAT EVERY MANAGER NEEDS TO
KNOW ABOUT LONG-RANGE
PLANNING, PT 1 - THE MERITT CASE — BNA
WHAT EVERY MANAGER NEEDS TO
KNOW ABOUT LONG-RANGE
PLANNING, PT 2 - INVENT YOUR ... — BNA

(TRANSPARENCIES)

ACCUMULATING CAPITAL FOR
INVESTMENTS (J-H) — LEART

INCOME TAX

(MOTION PICTURES)

ACTION FOR CHANGE (I-C A) — SCREEI
DEATH AND TAXES — BEF

INDUSTRY

(FILMSTRIPS)

COMPANY AND THE COMMUNITY, THE,
PT 1 — CREATV
COMPANY AND THE COMMUNITY, THE,
PT 2 — CREATV
COMPANY ORGANIZATION, PT 1 — CREATV
COMPANY ORGANIZATION, PT 2 — CREATV
CZECHOSLOVAKIA - AGRICULTURE AND
INDUSTRY — MGHT
EASTERN EUROPE--A SERIES — MGHT
HUNGARY - INDUSTRY AND PROGRESS — MGHT
LOS ANGELES - CITY OF AUTOMOBILES
(J-H A) — SVE
ONE HUNDRED AND THIRTY
BILLION DOLLAR FOOD
ASSEMBLY LINE (C A) — USDA
POLAND - INDUSTRY AND PROGRESS — MGHT
SEATTLE - A CITY FACES CRISIS (J-H A) — SVE
TIMBER - WASHINGTON'S MOST
VALUABLE CROP (J-H A) — SVE

(MOTION PICTURES)

AFFAIRS OF A MAN, THE (J-C A) — FORD
CAREERS IN LARGE INDUSTRY — VOFI
CHILDREN'S WORLD - MEXICO (K-I) — AVED
CUTTING CREW, THE (H-C A) — RARIG
ENGINEERS, THE — MTP
FUTURES IN STEEL — MTP
LANDING TEAM, THE (H-C A) — RARIG
LOGGING SAFETY--A SERIES (H-C A) — RARIG

MAKING OF FINE CHINA — MTP
NEVER UNDERESTIMATE THE POWER
OF A WOMAN (H-C) — UEUWIS
OPPORTUNITIES IN HOTELS AND
MOTELS — USNAC
OPPORTUNITIES IN LOGGING — RARIG
OPPORTUNITIES IN WELDING — USNAC
STORY OF AMERICAN WHISKEY — MTP
VERA PAINTS IBIZA IN THE SUN (J-C A) — SCHLAT
VISTAS OF ISRAEL, NO. 2 — ALDEN
VISTAS OF ISRAEL, NO. 3 — ALDEN
WROUGHT IRON - YESTERDAY, TODAY,
TOMORROW — MTP

INFLATION

(MOTION PICTURES)

MONEY, MONEY, MONEY (P-J) — TEXFLM

INVESTMENTS

(MOTION PICTURES)

HOW TO BUY STOCK — BEF

(TRANSPARENCIES)

ACCUMULATING CAPITAL FOR
INVESTMENTS (J-H) — LEART
SAVINGS AND INVESTMENTS (J-H) — LEART

LABOR AND MANAGEMENT

(FILMSTRIPS)

CALIFORNIA CONFLICT - MIGRANT FARM
WORKERS (J-H A) — SVE
TRY TO JOIN OUR UNION (I-J) — SNBRST

(MOTION PICTURES)

BRIDGE OF FRIENDSHIP — ALDEN
MANAGEMENT PRACTICE--A SERIES — BNA
VOICE OF LA RAZA — GREAVW
WHAT EVERY MANAGER NEEDS TO
KNOW ABOUT INFORMATION
SYSTEMS, PT 1 - THE MERITT CASE — BNA
WHAT EVERY MANAGER NEEDS TO
KNOW ABOUT INFORMATION
SYSTEMS, PT 2 - THE COMPUTER ... — BNA
WHAT EVERY MANAGER NEEDS TO
KNOW ABOUT MARKETING, PT 1
- THE MERITT CASE — BNA
WHAT EVERY MANAGER NEEDS TO
KNOW ABOUT MARKETING, PT 2
- WHAT BUSINESS ARE YOU ... — BNA
WHAT EVERY MANAGER NEEDS TO
KNOW ABOUT LONG-RANGE
PLANNING, PT 1 - THE MERITT CASE — BNA
WHAT EVERY MANAGER NEEDS TO
KNOW ABOUT LONG-RANGE
PLANNING, PT 2 - INVENT YOUR ... — BNA

(TRANSPARENCIES)

GUILD VS LABOR UNION — LEART

MANUFACTURING

(FILMSTRIPS)

FORMING A CAN — EGH
HOW THINGS ARE MADE--A SERIES — EGH
LOS ANGELES - CITY OF AUTOMOBILES
(J-H A) — SVE
MAKING CLOTHING — EGH
PROCESSING SOUP — EGH

(MOTION PICTURES)

MAKING OF FINE CHINA — MTP
SAFETY IN PLYWOOD OPERATIONS (J-C
A) — RARIG
WHAT IS BUSINESS (H-C A) — SAIF
WROUGHT IRON - YESTERDAY, TODAY,
TOMORROW — MTP
YANKEE CALLING — FENWCK

MONEY AND BANKING

(MOTION PICTURES)

MONEY, MONEY, MONEY (P-J) — TEXFLM
WITHIN THE CIRCLE — ALDEN

(AUDIO TAPES)

USE OF BANKS (H-C) — INSKY

(TRANSPARENCIES)

BANKS ACCUMULATE AND DISTRIBUTE
CAPITAL (J-H) — LEART

DIFFERENT MEDIUMS OF
  EXCHANGE ARE USED IN
  DIFFERENT TYPES OF MARKETS (J-H) LEART
HOW BANKS WORK (J-H) LEART
HOW DO CHECKS REPLACE MONEY (J-H) LEART
MONEY - HISTORY, TYPES AND
PURPOSES (J-H) LEART

OFFICE PROCEDURES

(MOTION PICTURES)

ADDRESSING MACHINE BEF
BEST FOR BEGINNERS BEF
CENTRAC - ONE BOLD STEP BEF
CORRECT TELEPHONE COURTESY BEF
INTEGRATED DATA PROCESSING BEF
PERSON TO PERSON - MAKING
  COMMUNICATIONS WORK FOR
  YOU (H-C A) SAIF
PRINCIPLES OF PAPERWORK
  MANAGEMENT - BETTER
  CORRESPONDENCE PRACTICE BEF
WHAT DO WE LOOK LIKE TO OTHERS
(H-C A) SAIF

(VIDEOTAPES)

ADDRESSING ENVELOPES -
  ATTENTION AND SUBJECT LINES GPITVL
BOUND MANUSCRIPTS WITH
FOOTNOTES GPITVL
INTER-OFFICE MEMORANDUM FORMS GPITVL
INVOICE AND TELEGRAM FORMS -
CARBONS GPITVL
PLAIN AND FILL-IN POSTAL CARDS GPITVL
REVIEW - LETTERS, FORMS, REPORTS GPITVL
REVISION MARKS, UNBOUND REPORTS,
HOW TO ERASE GPITVL
SELECTIVE PRACTICE - CENTERING ON
LINE GPITVL
SELECTIVE PRACTICE - CORRECTIONS GPITVL
SELECTIVE PRACTICE - INSERTIONS GPITVL
TYPEWRITING, UNIT 6 - SKILL
  DEVELOPMENT--A SERIES GPITVL
TYPEWRITING, UNIT 7 - POSTAL
  CARDS, FORMS, MANUSCRIPTS--A
  SERIES GPITVL

(TRANSPARENCIES)

ADDRESSING ENVELOPES FOR BUSINESS
LETTERS (I) BOW
ADDRESSING ENVELOPES FOR FRIENDLY
LETTERS (I) BOW
LETTER WRITING--A SERIES (I) BOW
WRITING BUSINESS LETTERS (I) BOW
WRITING FRIENDLY LETTERS (I) BOW

SALESMANSHIP AND MARKETING

(FILMSTRIPS)

GOOD GOODIES BFA
LIVING IN ASIA TODAY - AMONG
  THE MARKETS OF AFGHANISTAN
  (P-I) CORF

(MOTION PICTURES)

ADVERTISING AND COMPETITION MTP
MANAGEMENT PRACTICE--A SERIES BNA
SALES BEF
STAGE IS YOURS, THE BEF
TOUGH-MINDED SALESMANSHIP -
  ASK FOR THE ORDER AND GET
  IT (H-C) DARTNL
WHAT EVERY MANAGER NEEDS TO
  KNOW ABOUT INFORMATION
  SYSTEMS, PT 1 - THE MERITT CASE BNA
WHAT EVERY MANAGER NEEDS TO
  KNOW ABOUT INFORMATION
  SYSTEMS, PT 2 - THE COMPUTER ... BNA
WHAT EVERY MANAGER NEEDS TO
  KNOW ABOUT MARKETING, PT 1
  - THE MERITT CASE BNA
WHAT EVERY MANAGER NEEDS TO
  KNOW ABOUT MARKETING, PT 2
  - WHAT BUSINESS ARE YOU ... BNA
WHAT EVERY MANAGER NEEDS TO
  KNOW ABOUT LONG-RANGE
  PLANNING, PT 1 - THE MERITT CASE BNA
WHAT EVERY MANAGER NEEDS TO
  KNOW ABOUT LONG-RANGE
  PLANNING, PT 2 - INVENT YOUR ... BNA

(TRANSPARENCIES)

AROUSING INTEREST COF
BASIC SALESMANSHIP--A SERIES COF
BE CONVINCING COF
BEFORE YOU MEET THE CUSTOMER COF
CREATING DESIRE COF
CUSTOMER ANALYSIS COF
DO COF
DON'T COF

DON'T SAY MAY I HELP YOU COF
FIVE MAJOR STEPS IN A SALE, THE COF
FUNCTIONS OF INDIVIDUALS COF
GAINING ATTENTION COF
GETTING ACTION COF
KEEPING UP WITH THE JONESES COF
OPENING THE SALE COF
OVERCOMING OBJECTIONS COF
PATTERNS OF CONSUMPTION -
MARKETING (J-H) LEART
PRODUCT KNOWLEDGE COF
SALES DEMONSTRATION CONTEST COF
SALES FLOW, THE COF
TURN OBJECTIONS INTO SELLING
POINTS COF
WHAT IS SELLING COF
WHEN YOU'RE NOT SELLING COF

SECURITIES

(FILMSTRIPS)

INTRODUCTION TO SECURITIES
MARKETS XEROX
NATION OF OWNERS - AN
  INTRODUCTION TO THE
  SECURITIES INDUSTRY XEROX
NATION OF OWNERS--A SERIES XEROX
OPERATIONS - WHERE THE JOB GETS
DONE, PT 1 XEROX
OPERATIONS - WHERE THE JOB GETS
DONE, PT 2 XEROX
ORDERS - WHERE THE ACTION BEGINS XEROX
THOSE REMARKABLE PIECES OF
  PAPER CALLED SECURITIES XEROX

SMALL BUSINESS

(MOTION PICTURES)

WHAT IS BUSINESS (H-C A) SAIF

STOCK EXCHANGE

(FILMSTRIPS)

GREAT DEPRESSION, THE -
  CAUSES, EFFECTS, SOLUTIONS,
  PT 4 (J-C) EAV
INTRODUCTION TO SECURITIES
MARKETS XEROX
NATION OF OWNERS - AN
  INTRODUCTION TO THE
  SECURITIES INDUSTRY XEROX
NATION OF OWNERS--A SERIES XEROX
OPERATIONS - WHERE THE JOB GETS
DONE, PT 1 XEROX
OPERATIONS - WHERE THE JOB GETS
DONE, PT 2 XEROX
ORDERS - WHERE THE ACTION BEGINS XEROX
THOSE REMARKABLE PIECES OF
  PAPER CALLED SECURITIES XEROX

(MOTION PICTURES)

HOW TO BUY STOCK BEF

SUPERVISION

(MOTION PICTURES)

BARE MINIMUM BEF

TAXATION

(MOTION PICTURES)

ACTION FOR CHANGE (I-C A) SCREEI
DEATH AND TAXES BEF

(TRANSPARENCIES)

TAXES AND THE INDIVIDUAL (J-H) LEART

TRADE

(TRANSPARENCIES)

GROWTH OF INTERNATIONAL TRADE
AND COMMERCE (J-H) LEART

CIVICS AND POLITICAL SYSTEMS

CITIZENSHIP - GENERAL

(FILMSTRIPS)

ELECTION, THE EGH
NOW YOU ARE A VOTER--A SERIES EGH

REGISTRATION AND PICKING A
CANDIDATE EGH
RIGHT TO VOTE, THE EGH
WORKING IN THE POLITICAL WORLD EGH

(MOTION PICTURES)

BASIC LAW TERMS (J-C A) PFP
CIVIL WRONG, THE (J-C A) UMITV
SECURITY MAN USNAC
SENSE OF RESPONSIBILITY, A (I-C) BFA
UNAUTHORIZED DISCLOSURE USNAC

(AUDIO TAPES)

WHO NEEDS CIVIL DEFENSE (J A) NAEB

(TRANSPARENCIES)

LIBRARY SKILLS--A SERIES BOW

CITIZENSHIP - HOLIDAYS

(FILMSTRIPS)

HOLIDAY SERIES, SET 2--A SERIES (K-P) MGHT
MEMORIAL DAY (K-P) MGHT
WASHINGTON'S BIRTHDAY (K-P) MGHT

(MOTION PICTURES)

ISRAEL'S 17TH INDEPENDENCE DAY
(1965) ALDEN

(RECORDS)

HOLIDAY RHYTHMS BOW

CIVIL RIGHTS

(MOTION PICTURES)

BASIC LAW TERMS (J-C A) PFP
BILL OF RIGHTS IN ACTION - THE
  PRIVILEGE AGAINST SELF-
  INCRIMINATION (I-C A) WILETS
CIVIL WRONG, THE (J-C A) UMITV
QUEST FOR CERTAINTY--A SERIES (J-C
A) UMITV
UNAUTHORIZED DISCLOSURE USNAC

(AUDIO TAPES)

YOU HOLD THE KEY (H A) AJC

CIVIL SERVICE

(AUDIO TAPES)

STRATEGIC IMPORTANCE OF CIVIL
DEFENSE, THE (J A) NAEB
SUMMARY AND CONCLUSIONS (J A) NAEB
WHO NEEDS CIVIL DEFENSE (J A) NAEB

COMMUNISM

(AUDIO TAPES)

STRUCTURE OF THE COMMUNIST
PARTY, PT 1 (A) PHLSAC
STRUCTURE OF THE COMMUNIST
PARTY, PT 2 (A) PHLSAC
WAR OR PEACE (A) PHLSAC

CONSTITUTION - U S

(MOTION PICTURES)

BILL OF RIGHTS IN ACTION - THE
  PRIVILEGE AGAINST SELF-
  INCRIMINATION (I-C A) WILETS

(TRANSPARENCIES)

COMPROMISE RESULTING IN THE
  TWO-HOUSE LEGISLATURE (J-H) LEART
CONSTITUTION--A SERIES BETECL
HOW A BILL BECOMES A LAW (J-H) LEART
JURISDICTION OF THE SUPREME
COURT, THE (J-H) LEART
METHODS OF AMENDING THE
CONSTITUTION (J-H) LEART
POCKET VETO, THE (J-H) LEART
POWERS OF THE PRESIDENT, THE (J-H) LEART
QUALIFICATIONS FOR HOLDING
NATIONAL OFFICE, THE (J-H) LEART
RESERVED POWERS AND DELEGATED
POWERS (J-H) LEART
SPECIFIC AMENDMENTS (J-H) LEART
SYSTEM OF CHECKS AND BALANCES,
THE (J-H) LEART
UNITED STATES GOVERNMENT
  AND HOW IT WORKS--A SERIES
  (J-H) LEART

WORK OF THE CONSTITUTIONAL
CONVENTION (J-H)   LEART

CONSTITUTIONAL HISTORY

(TRANSPARENCIES)

COMPROMISE RESULTING IN THE
   TWO-HOUSE LEGISLATURE (J-H)   LEART
CONSTITUTION--A SERIES   BETECL
HOW A BILL BECOMES A LAW (J-H)   LEART
JURISDICTION OF THE SUPREME
   COURT, THE (J-H)   LEART
METHODS OF AMENDING THE
   CONSTITUTION (J-H)   LEART
POCKET VETO, THE (J-H)   LEART
POWERS OF THE PRESIDENT, THE (J-H)   LEART
QUALIFICATIONS FOR HOLDING
   NATIONAL OFFICE, THE (J-H)   LEART
RESERVED POWERS AND DELEGATED
   POWERS (J-H)   LEART
SPECIFIC AMENDMENTS (J-H)   LEART
SYSTEM OF CHECKS AND BALANCES,
   THE (J-H)   LEART
UNITED STATES GOVERNMENT
   AND HOW IT WORKS--A SERIES
   (J-H)   LEART
WORK OF THE CONSTITUTIONAL
CONVENTION (J-H)   LEART

CONSTITUTIONAL LAW

(FILMSTRIPS)

AMERICAN FOREIGN POLICY - HOW IT
WORKS (J-H)   SED

(MOTION PICTURES)

BILL OF RIGHTS IN ACTION - THE
   PRIVILEGE AGAINST SELF-
   INCRIMINATION (I-C A)   WILETS

(TRANSPARENCIES)

HOW A BILL BECOMES A LAW (J-H)   LEART
JURISDICTION OF THE SUPREME
   COURT, THE (J-H)   LEART
METHODS OF AMENDING THE
   CONSTITUTION (J-H)   LEART
QUALIFICATIONS FOR HOLDING
   NATIONAL OFFICE, THE (J-H)   LEART
RESERVED POWERS AND DELEGATED
   POWERS (J-H)   LEART
SYSTEM OF CHECKS AND BALANCES,
   THE (J-H)   LEART
UNITED STATES GOVERNMENT
   AND HOW IT WORKS--A SERIES
   (J-H)   LEART
WORK OF THE CONSTITUTIONAL
CONVENTION (J-H)   LEART

CONSTITUTIONS

(TRANSPARENCIES)

CONSTITUTION--A SERIES   BETECL

DEMOCRACY

(AUDIO TAPES)

YOU HOLD THE KEY (H A)   AJC

(TRANSPARENCIES)

COMPROMISE RESULTING IN THE
   TWO-HOUSE LEGISLATURE (J-H)   LEART
HOW A BILL BECOMES A LAW (J-H)   LEART
JURISDICTION OF THE SUPREME
   COURT, THE (J-H)   LEART
METHODS OF AMENDING THE
   CONSTITUTION (J-H)   LEART
POCKET VETO, THE (J-H)   LEART
POWERS OF THE PRESIDENT, THE (J-H)   LEART
QUALIFICATIONS FOR HOLDING
   NATIONAL OFFICE, THE (J-H)   LEART
RESERVED POWERS AND DELEGATED
   POWERS (J-H)   LEART
SPECIFIC AMENDMENTS (J-H)   LEART
SYSTEM OF CHECKS AND BALANCES,
   THE (J-H)   LEART
UNITED STATES GOVERNMENT
   AND HOW IT WORKS--A SERIES
   (J-H)   LEART
WHAT IS AN OPEN SOCIETY (J-H)   LEART
WORK OF THE CONSTITUTIONAL
CONVENTION (J-H)   LEART

EXECUTIVE POWER

(TRANSPARENCIES)

POCKET VETO, THE (J-H)   LEART

FEDERAL GOVERNMENT

(FILMSTRIPS)

AMERICAN FOREIGN POLICY - HOW IT
WORKS (J-H)   SED

(TRANSPARENCIES)

COMPROMISE RESULTING IN THE
   TWO-HOUSE LEGISLATURE (J-H)   LEART
FEDERAL BUDGET - INCOME AND
   EXPENDITURES (J-H)   LEART
HOW A BILL BECOMES A LAW (J-H)   LEART
JURISDICTION OF THE SUPREME
   COURT, THE (J-H)   LEART
METHODS OF AMENDING THE
   CONSTITUTION (J-H)   LEART
POCKET VETO, THE (J-H)   LEART
POWERS OF THE PRESIDENT, THE (J-H)   LEART
QUALIFICATIONS FOR HOLDING
   NATIONAL OFFICE, THE (J-H)   LEART
RESERVED POWERS AND DELEGATED
   POWERS (J-H)   LEART
SPECIFIC AMENDMENTS (J-H)   LEART
SYSTEM OF CHECKS AND BALANCES,
   THE (J-H)   LEART
UNITED STATES GOVERNMENT
   AND HOW IT WORKS--A SERIES
   (J-H)   LEART
WORK OF THE CONSTITUTIONAL
CONVENTION (J-H)   LEART

FOREIGN POLICY - U S

(FILMSTRIPS)

AMERICAN FOREIGN POLICY - HOW IT
WORKS (J-H)   SED

(MOTION PICTURES)

PRIME MINISTER GOLDA MEIR'S
   VISIT TO THE USA IN 1969   ALDEN

(TRANSPARENCIES)

DOES FOREIGN AID MEAN FOREIGN
CONTROL (J-H)   LEART

GOVERNMENT - U S

(MOTION PICTURES)

SECURITY MAN   USNAC
STORY OF A TRIAL   BEF

(TRANSPARENCIES)

COMPROMISE RESULTING IN THE
   TWO-HOUSE LEGISLATURE (J-H)   LEART
HOW A BILL BECOMES A LAW (J-H)   LEART
JURISDICTION OF THE SUPREME
   COURT, THE (J-H)   LEART
METHODS OF AMENDING THE
   CONSTITUTION (J-H)   LEART
POCKET VETO, THE (J-H)   LEART
POWERS OF THE PRESIDENT, THE (J-H)   LEART
QUALIFICATIONS FOR HOLDING
   NATIONAL OFFICE, THE (J-H)   LEART
RESERVED POWERS AND DELEGATED
   POWERS (J-H)   LEART
SOCIETIES FORM GOVERNMENTS (J-H)   LEART
SPECIFIC AMENDMENTS (J-H)   LEART
SYSTEM OF CHECKS AND BALANCES,
   THE (J-H)   LEART
UNITED STATES GOVERNMENT
   AND HOW IT WORKS--A SERIES
   (J-H)   LEART
WORK OF THE CONSTITUTIONAL
CONVENTION (J-H)   LEART

LAW

(FILMSTRIPS)

JAIL TERM BEFORE TRIAL (I-J)   SNBRST

(MOTION PICTURES)

BASIC LAW TERMS (J-C A)   PFP
CIVIL WRONG, THE (J-C A)   UMITV
PARTNERS, THE (J-C A)   UMITV
QUEST FOR CERTAINTY--A SERIES (J-C
A)   UMITV
STORY OF A TRIAL   BEF
UNAUTHORIZED DISCLOSURE   USNAC
UNDER THE JUGGERNAUT   AMERFI

(AUDIO TAPES)

PSYCHIATRY AND THE LAW -
   ALCOHOLISM - DRUG ABUSE   SIGINF

MILITARY SCIENCE

(FILMSTRIPS)

MY NAME IS JESUS--A SERIES (I R)   ROAS

(MOTION PICTURES)

AIRBORNE OCEANOGRAPHY -
   OCEANOGRAPHER OF THE NAVY   USNAC
CITIZEN'S ARMY   ALDEN
DAMAGE CONTROL - EFFECTS OF
   WEIGHT ON STABILITY, PT 2,
   WEIGHT CONDITION   USNAC
DAMAGE CONTROL - ELEMENTS OF
   STABILITY IN SHIP   USNAC
DAMAGE CONTROL - LOOSE WATER
   IN STABILITY, PT 1, IN INTACT
   SPACES   USNAC
DAMAGE CONTROL - THE
   METACENTER IN STABILITY, PT 2   USNAC
GLADIATORS, THE (H-C)   NLC
MEN FROM THE BOYS, THE   MTP
OCEANOGRAPHIC PREDICTION SYSTEM   USNAC
RUMOURS OF WAR (H-C A)   TIMLIF
UNAUTHORIZED DISCLOSURE   USNAC

(AUDIO TAPES)

CONSERVATIVE VS RADICAL
   BEHAVIORS - MILITARIST VS
   PACIFIST BEHAVIORS   SIGINF
MILITARY-INDUSTRIAL
   PERSONALITY - COMPASSION VS
   COMPULSION   SIGINF

NATIONALISM

(MOTION PICTURES)

SECURITY MAN   USNAC

(TRANSPARENCIES)

NATIONALIST LEADERS OF BLACK
   AFRICA (J-H)   LEART
NATIONALIST LEADERS OF NORTH
   AFRICA (J-H)   LEART
POLITICAL GEOGRAPHY AND
   NATIONALISM OF AFRICA --A
   SERIES (J-H)   LEART

POLITICAL ETHICS

(FILMSTRIPS)

POLITICS AND GOVERNMENT (J-H)   MMPRO
RIGHT TO VOTE, THE   EGH

(MOTION PICTURES)

UNDER THE JUGGERNAUT   AMERFI

(AUDIO TAPES)

VALUE-ANALYSES OF POLITICAL
IDEOLOGIES   SIGINF

(TRANSPARENCIES)

BASIC SOCIAL STUDIES CONCEPTS
   - POLITICS, SOCIAL-ECONOMIC
   INTERDEPENDENCE--A SERIES (J-H)   LEART
CULTURE VS CIVILIZATION (J-H)   LEART
ECONOMICS - POLITICAL ECONOMY
   AND PHILOSOPHY --A SERIES (J-
   H)   LEART
INTERACTION OF POLITICAL,
   SOCIAL AND ECONOMIC CAUSES
   AND EFFECTS (J-H)   LEART
SOCIETIES FORM GOVERNMENTS (J-H)   LEART
WHAT IS SOCIAL STUDIES - AN
   INTERDISCIPLINARY APPROACH
   (J-H)   LEART

POLITICAL PARTIES

(FILMSTRIPS)

POLITICS AND GOVERNMENT (J-H)   MMPRO

(MOTION PICTURES)

DIAL V FOR VOTES (C A)   DATA

(TRANSPARENCIES)

BASIC SOCIAL STUDIES CONCEPTS
   - POLITICS, SOCIAL-ECONOMIC
   INTERDEPENDENCE--A SERIES (J-H)   LEART
INTERACTION OF POLITICAL,
   SOCIAL AND ECONOMIC CAUSES
   AND EFFECTS (J-H)   LEART
SOCIETIES FORM GOVERNMENTS (J-H)   LEART

EDUCATION

POLITICS - U S

(FILMSTRIPS)

ELECTION, THE	EGH
NOW YOU ARE A VOTER--A SERIES	EGH
REGISTRATION AND PICKING A CANDIDATE	EGH
RIGHT TO VOTE, THE	EGH
WORKING IN THE POLITICAL WORLD	EGH

(MOTION PICTURES)

CAMPAIGN (H-C)	CF
DIAL V FOR VOTES (C A)	DATA

(TRANSPARENCIES)

BASIC SOCIAL STUDIES CONCEPTS - POLITICS, SOCIAL-ECONOMIC INTERDEPENDENCE--A SERIES (J-H)	LEART
INTERACTION OF POLITICAL, SOCIAL AND ECONOMIC CAUSES AND EFFECTS (J-H)	LEART
SOCIETIES FORM GOVERNMENTS (J-H)	LEART

REPRESENTATIVE GOVERNMENT

(MOTION PICTURES)

CAMPAIGN (H-C)	CF
DIAL V FOR VOTES (C A)	DATA

RIGHT AND LEFT

(AUDIO TAPES)

STRUCTURE OF THE COMMUNIST PARTY, PT 1 (A)	PHLSAC
STRUCTURE OF THE COMMUNIST PARTY, PT 2 (A)	PHLSAC
WAR OR PEACE (A)	PHLSAC

STATE RIGHTS

(MOTION PICTURES)

NAHAL	ALDEN

SUFFRAGE

(FILMSTRIPS)

ELECTION, THE	EGH
NOW YOU ARE A VOTER--A SERIES	EGH
REGISTRATION AND PICKING A CANDIDATE	EGH
RIGHT TO VOTE, THE	EGH
WORKING IN THE POLITICAL WORLD	EGH

(MOTION PICTURES)

MS - THE STRUGGLE FOR WOMEN'S RIGHTS (I-C A)	HEARST

TAXATION

(MOTION PICTURES)

ACTION FOR CHANGE (I-C A)	SCREEI

(TRANSPARENCIES)

TAXES AND THE INDIVIDUAL (J-H)	LEART

UNITED NATIONS

(FILMSTRIPS)

AMERICAN FOREIGN POLICY - HOW IT WORKS (J-H)	SED

(MOTION PICTURES)

DIAL V FOR VOTES (C A)	DATA

(AUDIO TAPES)

YOU HOLD THE KEY (H A)	AJC

(TRANSPARENCIES)

QUALIFICATIONS FOR HOLDING NATIONAL OFFICE, THE (J-H)	LEART
UNITED NATIONS ROLE IN THE INDEPENDENCE OF AFRICAN COUNTRIES (J-H)	LEART

UTOPIAS

(MOTION PICTURES)

LET'S IMAGINE - LIFE IN UTOPIA	ALDEN

EDUCATION

ADMINISTRATION

(MOTION PICTURES)

NEW ESTATE (C T)	TIMLIF

(AUDIO TAPES)

SERVICES OF UNIVERSITY AUDIO-VISUAL CENTERS (A)	KENTSU

AIMS AND OBJECTIVES

(FILMSTRIPS)

ASFEC	UNIPUB
DECIDING ON DEFENSIBLE GOALS VIA EDUCATIONAL NEEDS ASSESSMENT	VIMCET

(MOTION PICTURES)

HI, SCHOOL (J-H A)	IDEA
NEW ESTATE (C T)	TIMLIF
PLACE TO LEARN, A (A)	DUPAGE
RACE, INTELLIGENCE AND EDUCATION (H-C A)	TIMLIF
READING IS FOR US TOO (C A)	CCMFI
SUMMER JOURNAL	AMERFI
WHAT'S WRONG WITH THE SOCIAL SCIENCES (H-C A)	TIMLIF

(VIDEOTAPES)

OUR PRESENT EDUCATIONAL DILEMMA	GPITVL

(AUDIO TAPES)

THEY CAN'T WAIT (H A)	AJC

BUSINESS EDUCATION

(TRANSPARENCIES)

EDUCATION AND ECONOMICS (J-H)	LEART

COLLEGES AND UNIVERSITIES

(FILMSTRIPS)

COLLEGE - IT'S UP TO YOU, PT 1 (H)	GA
COLLEGE - IT'S UP TO YOU, PT 2 (H)	GA
COLLEGE--A SERIES (H)	GA
WHAT TO EXPECT AT COLLEGE, PT 1 (H)	GA
WHAT TO EXPECT AT COLLEGE, PT 2 (H)	GA
WHICH COLLEGE FOR YOU, PT 1 (H)	GA
WHICH COLLEGE FOR YOU, PT 2 (H)	GA

(MOTION PICTURES)

COLLEGE DAZE	AMERFI
PLACE TO LEARN, A (A)	DUPAGE

(AUDIO TAPES)

SERVICES OF UNIVERSITY AUDIO-VISUAL CENTERS (A)	KENTSU

COUNSELING

(FILMSTRIPS)

COLLEGE - IT'S UP TO YOU, PT 1 (H)	GA
COLLEGE - IT'S UP TO YOU, PT 2 (H)	GA
COLLEGE--A SERIES (H)	GA
EXPLORING CAREERS, GROUP 1--A SERIES (I-C)	SVE
HOSPITAL JOB OPPORTUNITIES--A SERIES	EGH
WHAT TO EXPECT AT COLLEGE, PT 1 (H)	GA
WHAT TO EXPECT AT COLLEGE, PT 2 (H)	GA
WHICH COLLEGE FOR YOU, PT 1 (H)	GA
WHICH COLLEGE FOR YOU, PT 2 (H)	GA

(MOTION PICTURES)

ANYTHING YOU WANT TO BE (J-C A)	EDDDW
CAREERS IN LARGE INDUSTRY	VOFI

FINDING YOURSELF AND YOUR JOB (J-C)	AMEDFL
FUTURE STREET - NEW DIRECTIONS IN CAREER EDUCATION--A SERIES (J-C)	AMEDFL
JOBS IN BAKING	USNAC
JOBS IN COSMETOLOGY	USNAC

(VIDEOTAPES)

CASE STUDIES	GPITVL
COUNSELING THE ADOLESCENT--A SERIES	GPITVL
DEMOCRATIC EVOLUTION OF SOCIETY, THE, PT 1	GPITVL
DEMOCRATIC EVOLUTION OF SOCIETY, THE, PT 2	GPITVL
EDWARD	GPITVL
GROUP DISCUSSION WITH NORMAL TEENAGERS	GPITVL
GROUP DISCUSSION WITH SCHOOL DROP-OUTS	GPITVL
JEFF	GPITVL
JUVENILE DELINQUENCY	GPITVL
MARY	GPITVL
NONI	GPITVL
ROB	GPITVL

CURRICULA

(VIDEOTAPES)

YOUR FUTURE IS NOW--A SERIES	GPITVL

(AUDIO TAPES)

VALUES OF MATHEMATICS IN SCHOOL CURRICULA (H A)	UOKLA

(TRANSPARENCIES)

BROAD GOALS OF DISTRIBUTIVE EDUCATION	COF
CHAPTER ACTIVITIES	COF
CLASSROOM-LABORATORY ACTIVITIES	COF
CLUB ACTIVITIES	COF
CONTESTS AND AWARDS PROGRAM	COF
CREATIVE MARKETING PROJECT	COF
DECA CREED, THE	COF
DECA GROWTH AND WHY JOIN DECA	COF
DECA OFFICERS, TERMINOLOGY, EXCITEMENT	COF
DEFINITION OF DISTRIBUTIVE EDUCATION	COF
DISTRIBUTIVE EDUCATION CLUBS OF AMERICA--A SERIES	COF
DISTRIBUTIVE EDUCATION IN ACTION	COF
DISTRIBUTIVE EDUCATION TRIANGLE, THE	COF
EXAMPLES OF DISTRIBUTIVE BUSINESSES	COF
EXAMPLES OF DISTRIBUTIVE OCCUPATIONS	COF
GAME - OUR MAIN STREET	COF
IN DISTRIBUTIVE EDUCATION WE WILL STUDY	COF
INTRODUCTIONS ALL AROUND	COF
MEANING OF DISTRIBUTION, THE	COF
NATIONAL DECA WEEK	COF
NATIONAL GOALS OF DECA	COF
OFFICIAL ITEMS	COF
OPPORTUNITIES THROUGH DISTRIBUTIVE EDUCATION	COF
ORIENTATION TO DISTRIBUTIVE EDUCATION--A SERIES	COF
POST SECONDARY DIVISION	COF
PURPOSES OF DECA	COF
STUDENT'S WEEKLY PRODUCTION REPORT	COF
TRAINING PLAN FOR DISTRIBUTIVE EDUCATION STUDENTS	COF
VARIOUS PROGRAMS, THE	COF
WHAT DECA SYMBOLIZES	COF

EDUCATIONAL INNOVATION

(MOTION PICTURES)

CHILDREN AS PEOPLE (H-C A)	POLYMR
CHILDREN'S CONCEPTS (C T)	TIMLIF
COPING IN SPECIAL EDUCATION - DEVELOPING OBSERVATIONAL TECHNIQUES (C)	UEUWIS
COPING IN SPECIAL EDUCATION - DEVELOPING STUDY HABITS (C)	UEUWIS
COPING IN SPECIAL EDUCATION - DISRUPTIVE BEHAVIOR (C)	UEUWIS
COPING IN SPECIAL EDUCATION - GROUPING (C)	UEUWIS
COPING IN SPECIAL EDUCATION - INDIVIDUALIZED INSTRUCTION (C)	UEUWIS
COPING IN SPECIAL EDUCATION - MOTIVATION (C)	UEUWIS
COPING IN SPECIAL EDUCATION - SOCIALIZATION (C)	UEUWIS

COPING IN SPECIAL EDUCATION--A
  SERIES (C)   UEUWIS
ENTERPRISING INFANTS (C T)   TIMLIF
EXPANDING CLASSROOM--A SERIES (C
T)   TIMLIF
PLACE TO LEARN, A (A)   DUPAGE
READING IS FOR US TOO (C A)   CCMFI
SCHOOL IS FOR CHILDREN (T)   AIMS

(VIDEOTAPES)

GROUP DISCUSSION, PT 1   GPITVL
GROUP DISCUSSION, PT 2   GPITVL
GROUP DISCUSSION, PT 3   GPITVL
OUR PRESENT EDUCATIONAL DILEMMA   GPITVL

(AUDIO TAPES)

TALKING BOOKS FOR THE BLIND (J A)   AFB
TEACHING FILM (H-C)   DAVI

EDUCATIONAL PSYCHOLOGY

(MOTION PICTURES)

CHILDREN'S CONCEPTS (C T)   TIMLIF
INFANCY (C A)   CRMP
P A T C H - POSITIVE APPROACH
  TO CHANGING HUMANS (C A)   CORF
PIAGET'S DEVELOPMENTAL THEORY
  - THE GROWTH OF INTELLIGENCE
  IN THE PRESCHOOL YEARS (A)   DAVFMS

(VIDEOTAPES)

CHANGING THE CHILD'S RELATIONSHIPS
  AND GOALS   GPITVL
CLARIFICATION OF BASIC PRINCIPLES   GPITVL
CONSEQUENCES   GPITVL
DOUGLAS   GPITVL
ENCOURAGEMENT   GPITVL
LEARNING PROBLEM, A   GPITVL
LOGICAL CONSEQUENCES AND
  PUNISHMENT   GPITVL
MOTIVATING CHILDREN TO LEARN -
  SUMMARY   GPITVL
MOTIVATING CHILDREN TO LEARN--A
  SERIES   GPITVL
OUR PRESENT EDUCATIONAL DILEMMA   GPITVL
READING DIFFICULTIES   GPITVL

EDUCATIONAL TECHNOLOGY

(FILMSTRIPS)

AUDIO-VISUAL--A SERIES   BSF
COLLEGE AUDIO-VISUAL CENTER   YAF
CREATING A MOVIE   EGH
LANGUAGE LABORATORY, THE   BSF
LIVING IN ASIA TODAY - IN A
  VILLAGE IN AMERICAN SAMOA
  (P-I)   CORF
TAPE RECORDER IN TEACHING, THE   BSF

(MOTION PICTURES)

CONSTRUCTING REALITY - A FILM ON
  FILM (P-C)   JOU
FILMMAKING FUNDAMENTALS (P-H)   AIMS
FILMMAKING TECHNIQUES - GOING ON
  LOCATION (I-C A)   AIMS
FILMMAKING TECHNIQUES--A SERIES (I-
C A)   AIMS
NATURE OF THE FILM MEDIUM, THE   PAULST
PLACE TO LEARN, A (A)   DUPAGE

(AUDIO TAPES)

SERVICES OF UNIVERSITY AUDIO-VISUAL
  CENTERS (A)   KENTSU
SLIDE AND FILM EXCHANGE (H-C)   DAVI
TEACHING FILM (H-C)   DAVI
THAT YOU MAY KNOW - AGAIN (J-C)   IU
THIRTY YEARS BEHIND A CAMERA (H-C)   DAVI
USE OF LANTERN SLIDES IN TEACHING
  (H-C)   DAVI
WHAT ARE AUDIO-VISUAL MATERIALS
  (A)   DAVI
WHAT SHALL WE LISTEN TO (J-C)   IU

ELEMENTARY

(FILMSTRIPS)

ORDER - FIRST ALWAYS COMES BEFORE
  LAST   EGH

(MOTION CARTRIDGES)

TEACHING SPANISH TO SPANISH
  SPEAKING CHILDREN (P-I)   BOUCH

(MOTION PICTURES)

CHILDREN AS PEOPLE (H-C A)   POLYMR
CHILDREN'S CONCEPTS (C T)   TIMLIF

ENTERPRISING INFANTS (C T)   TIMLIF

(RECORDS)

BASIC RHYTHMS, ALBUM 7   BOW
CHILDHOOD RHYTHMS, NO. 01   BOW
INTERPRETIVE RHYTHMS (K-I)   BOW
MACHINE RHYTHMS   BOW
RHYTHMS FROM THE LAND OF MAKE-
  BELIEVE (K-I)   BOW
RHYTHMS, DANCES AND GAMES,
  ALBUM 26   BOW
WAY OUT RECORD FOR CHILDREN, THE   BOW

EXPERIMENTAL METHODS

(MOTION PICTURES)

CHILDREN AS PEOPLE (H-C A)   POLYMR
COPING IN SPECIAL EDUCATION -
  DEVELOPING STUDY HABITS (C)   UEUWIS
EXPANDING CLASSROOM--A SERIES (C
T)   TIMLIF

HIGHER EDUCATION

(FILMSTRIPS)

COLLEGE - IT'S UP TO YOU, PT 1 (H)   GA
COLLEGE - IT'S UP TO YOU, PT 2 (H)   GA
COLLEGE--A SERIES (H)   GA
WHAT TO EXPECT AT COLLEGE, PT 1
  (H)   GA
WHAT TO EXPECT AT COLLEGE, PT 2
  (H)   GA
WHICH COLLEGE FOR YOU, PT 1 (H)   GA
WHICH COLLEGE FOR YOU, PT 2 (H)   GA

(MOTION PICTURES)

BRIDGE OF FRIENDSHIP   ALDEN
CO-OP   ALDEN
COGNITIVE DEVELOPMENT (C A)   CRMP
COLLEGE DAZE   AMERFI
PLACE TO LEARN, A (A)   DUPAGE
SEMINARS IN ISRAEL   ALDEN

(AUDIO TAPES)

WHAT SHALL WE LISTEN TO (J-C)   IU

LIBRARY SCIENCE

(MOTION PICTURES)

MULTIPLE CHOICE (J-C A)   INDSLF
PLACE TO LEARN, A (A)   DUPAGE

(AUDIO TAPES)

WHAT IS A BOOK (I-J)   INSKY

(TRANSPARENCIES)

LIBRARY SKILLS--A SERIES   BOW

PRESCHOOL

(MOTION PICTURES)

DAY CARE TODAY (C A)   POLYMR
ENTERPRISING INFANTS (C T)   TIMLIF
SCHOOL IS FOR CHILDREN (T)   AIMS

(AUDIO TAPES)

PRESCHOOL ENRICHMENT AND
  LEARNING   SIGINF
PREVENTIVE MENTAL HEALTH
  WORK WITH PRESCHOOL
  TEACHERS   SIGINF

SECONDARY

(MOTION PICTURES)

HI, SCHOOL (J-H A)   IDEA

(VIDEOTAPES)

YOUR FUTURE IS NOW--A SERIES   GPITVL

(TRANSPARENCIES)

CHAPTER ACTIVITIES   COF
CONTESTS AND AWARDS PROGRAM   COF
CREATIVE MARKETING PROJECT   COF
DECA CREED, THE   COF
DECA GROWTH AND WHY JOIN DECA   COF
DECA OFFICERS, TERMINOLOGY,
  EXCITEMENT   COF
DISTRIBUTIVE EDUCATION CLUBS
  OF AMERICA--A SERIES   COF
NATIONAL DECA WEEK   COF

NATIONAL GOALS OF DECA   COF
OFFICIAL ITEMS   COF
ORIENTATION TO DISTRIBUTIVE
  EDUCATION--A SERIES   COF
POST SECONDARY DIVISION   COF
WHAT DECA SYMBOLIZES   COF

SPECIAL

(MOTION PICTURES)

COPING IN SPECIAL EDUCATION -
  DEVELOPING OBSERVATIONAL
  TECHNIQUES (C)   UEUWIS
COPING IN SPECIAL EDUCATION -
  DEVELOPING STUDY HABITS (C)   UEUWIS
COPING IN SPECIAL EDUCATION -
  DISRUPTIVE BEHAVIOR (C)   UEUWIS
COPING IN SPECIAL EDUCATION -
  GROUPING (C)   UEUWIS
COPING IN SPECIAL EDUCATION -
  INDIVIDUALIZED INSTRUCTION
  (C)   UEUWIS
COPING IN SPECIAL EDUCATION -
  MOTIVATION (C)   UEUWIS
COPING IN SPECIAL EDUCATION -
  SOCIALIZATION (C)   UEUWIS
COPING IN SPECIAL EDUCATION--A
  SERIES (C)   UEUWIS
KIDS ARE PEOPLE, TOO (T)   CCMFI
NOBODY TOOK THE TIME (T)   AIMS
READING IS FOR US TOO (C A)   CCMFI
SCHOOL IS FOR CHILDREN (T)   AIMS

(RECORDS)

RHYTHMS, DANCES AND GAMES,
  ALBUM 26   BOW

(AUDIO TAPES)

TALKING BOOKS FOR THE BLIND (J A)   AFB
WHAT MUSIC MEANS TO THE BLIND (J
  A)   AFB

STATISTICS

(FILMSTRIPS)

DECIDING ON DEFENSIBLE GOALS
  VIA EDUCATIONAL NEEDS
  ASSESSMENT   VIMCET

STUDY AND METHODS

(FILMSTRIPS)

AUDIO-VISUAL--A SERIES   BSF
IDENTIFICATION OF ELECTRIC WIRING
  ITEMS (H-C)   UILVAS
IMPROVING YOUR STUDY SKILLS,
  SET 1 - USING THE TEXTBOOK
  PLAN--A SERIES   CREATV
IMPROVING YOUR STUDY SKILLS,
  SET 2 - INTENSIVE READING--A
  SERIES   CREATV
IMPROVING YOUR STUDY SKILLS,
  SET 3 - INTENSIVE READING
  EXERCISES--A SERIES   CREATV
TAPE RECORDER IN TEACHING, THE   BSF

(MOTION CARTRIDGES)

TEACHING SPANISH TO SPANISH
  SPEAKING CHILDREN (P-I)   BOUCH

(MOTION PICTURES)

FILMMAKING FUNDAMENTALS (P-H)   AIMS
P A T C H - POSITIVE APPROACH
  TO CHANGING HUMANS (C A)   CORF

(VIDEOTAPES)

MOTIVATING CHILDREN TO LEARN--A
  SERIES   GPITVL

(AUDIO TAPES)

WHAT ARE AUDIO-VISUAL MATERIALS
  (A)   DAVI
WHAT SHALL WE LISTEN TO (J-C)   IU

(TRANSPARENCIES)

BROAD GOALS OF DISTRIBUTIVE
  EDUCATION   COF
CHAPTER ACTIVITIES   COF
CLASSROOM-LABORATORY ACTIVITIES   COF
CLUB ACTIVITIES   COF
CONTESTS AND AWARDS PROGRAM   COF
CREATIVE MARKETING PROJECT   COF
DECA CREED, THE   COF
DECA GROWTH AND WHY JOIN DECA   COF
DECA OFFICERS, TERMINOLOGY,
  EXCITEMENT   COF

DEFINITION OF DISTRIBUTIVE
EDUCATION — COF
DISTRIBUTIVE EDUCATION CLUBS
OF AMERICA--A SERIES — COF
DISTRIBUTIVE EDUCATION IN ACTION — COF
DISTRIBUTIVE EDUCATION TRIANGLE,
THE — COF
EXAMPLES OF DISTRIBUTIVE
BUSINESSES — COF
EXAMPLES OF DISTRIBUTIVE
OCCUPATIONS — COF
GAME - OUR MAIN STREET — COF
HOW TO STUDY--A SERIES — BETECL
IN DISTRIBUTIVE EDUCATION WE WILL
STUDY — COF
INTRODUCTIONS ALL AROUND — COF
MEANING OF DISTRIBUTION, THE — COF
NATIONAL DECA WEEK — COF
NATIONAL GOALS OF DECA — COF
OFFICIAL ITEMS — COF
OPPORTUNITIES THROUGH
DISTRIBUTIVE EDUCATION — COF
ORIENTATION TO DISTRIBUTIVE
EDUCATION--A SERIES — COF
POST SECONDARY DIVISION — COF
PURPOSES OF DECA — COF
STUDENT'S WEEKLY PRODUCTION
REPORT — COF
TRAINING PLAN FOR DISTRIBUTIVE
EDUCATION STUDENTS — COF
VARIOUS PROGRAMS, THE — COF
WHAT DECA SYMBOLIZES — COF

TEACHER AND TEACHING

(FILMSTRIPS)

ORDER - FIRST ALWAYS COMES BEFORE
LAST — EGH

(MOTION CARTRIDGES)

TEACHING SPANISH TO SPANISH
SPEAKING CHILDREN (P-I) — BOUCH

(MOTION PICTURES)

COPING IN SPECIAL EDUCATION -
DEVELOPING OBSERVATIONAL
TECHNIQUES (C) — UEUWIS
COPING IN SPECIAL EDUCATION -
GROUPING (C) — UEUWIS
COPING IN SPECIAL EDUCATION -
INDIVIDUALIZED INSTRUCTION
(C) — UEUWIS
COPING IN SPECIAL EDUCATION -
MOTIVATION (C) — UEUWIS
COPING IN SPECIAL EDUCATION -
SOCIALIZATION (C) — UEUWIS
COPING IN SPECIAL EDUCATION--A
SERIES (C) — UEUWIS
EXPANDING CLASSROOM--A SERIES (C
T) — TIMLIF
KIDS ARE PEOPLE, TOO (T) — CCMFI
NEW ESTATE (C T) — TIMLIF
NOBODY TOOK THE TIME (T) — AIMS
P A T C H - POSITIVE APPROACH
TO CHANGING HUMANS (C A) — CORF
READING IS FOR US TOO (C A) — CCMFI
SUMMER JOURNAL — AMERFI

(VIDEOTAPES)

CHANGING THE CHILD'S RELATIONSHIPS
AND GOALS — GPITVL
CLARIFICATION OF BASIC PRINCIPLES — GPITVL
CONSEQUENCES — GPITVL
DOUGLAS — GPITVL
ENCOURAGEMENT — GPITVL
GROUP DISCUSSION, PT 1 — GPITVL
GROUP DISCUSSION, PT 2 — GPITVL
GROUP DISCUSSION, PT 3 — GPITVL
JEFF — GPITVL
LEARNING PROBLEM, A — GPITVL
LOGICAL CONSEQUENCES AND
PUNISHMENT — GPITVL
MOTIVATING CHILDREN TO LEARN -
SUMMARY — GPITVL
MOTIVATING CHILDREN TO LEARN--A
SERIES — GPITVL
OUR PRESENT EDUCATIONAL DILEMMA — GPITVL
READING DIFFICULTIES — GPITVL

(AUDIO TAPES)

PREVENTIVE MENTAL HEALTH
WORK WITH PRESCHOOL
TEACHERS — SIGINF
TEACHERS AS THERAPEUTIC AGENTS — SIGINF
WHAT ARE AUDIO-VISUAL MATERIALS
(A) — DAVI

(TRANSPARENCIES)

BROAD GOALS OF DISTRIBUTIVE
EDUCATION — COF
CHAPTER ACTIVITIES — COF
CLASSROOM-LABORATORY ACTIVITIES — COF

CLUB ACTIVITIES — COF
CONTESTS AND AWARDS PROGRAM — COF
CREATIVE MARKETING PROJECT — COF
DECA CREED, THE — COF
DECA GROWTH AND WHY JOIN DECA — COF
DECA OFFICERS, TERMINOLOGY,
EXCITEMENT — COF
DEFINITION OF DISTRIBUTIVE
EDUCATION — COF
DISTRIBUTIVE EDUCATION CLUBS
OF AMERICA--A SERIES — COF
DISTRIBUTIVE EDUCATION IN ACTION — COF
DISTRIBUTIVE EDUCATION TRIANGLE,
THE — COF
EXAMPLES OF DISTRIBUTIVE
BUSINESSES — COF
EXAMPLES OF DISTRIBUTIVE
OCCUPATIONS — COF
GAME - OUR MAIN STREET — COF
IN DISTRIBUTIVE EDUCATION WE WILL
STUDY — COF
INTRODUCTIONS ALL AROUND — COF
MEANING OF DISTRIBUTION, THE — COF
NATIONAL DECA WEEK — COF
NATIONAL GOALS OF DECA — COF
OFFICIAL ITEMS — COF
OPPORTUNITIES THROUGH
DISTRIBUTIVE EDUCATION — COF
ORIENTATION TO DISTRIBUTIVE
EDUCATION--A SERIES — COF
POST SECONDARY DIVISION — COF
PURPOSES OF DECA — COF
STUDENT'S WEEKLY PRODUCTION
REPORT — COF
TRAINING PLAN FOR DISTRIBUTIVE
EDUCATION STUDENTS — COF
VARIOUS PROGRAMS, THE — COF
WHAT DECA SYMBOLIZES — COF

TESTS AND MEASUREMENTS

(AUDIO TAPES)

INFORMATION FOR CANDIDATES -
THE FORMAT OF WRITTEN AND
ORAL EXAMINATIONS - HOW TO
TAKE... — SIGINF

VOCATIONAL EDUCATION

(MOTION PICTURES)

FINDING YOURSELF AND YOUR JOB (J-
C) — AMEDFL
FUTURE STREET - NEW
DIRECTIONS IN CAREER
EDUCATION--A SERIES (J-C) — AMEDFL

(TRANSPARENCIES)

JOB APPLICATION AND JOB INTERVIEW-
-A SERIES — COF

ENGLISH LANGUAGE

GRAMMAR

(FILMSTRIPS)

ACTIONS AND CONDITIONS — EGH
COMMON OBJECTS — EGH
CONQUERING COMPOSITION -
AWKWARD SHIFTS (J-H) — FSH
CONQUERING COMPOSITION -
FRAGMENTS (J-H) — FSH
CONQUERING COMPOSITION -
PRONOUNS AND ANTECEDENTS
(J-H) — FSH
CONQUERING COMPOSITION -
SENTENCE PROBLEMS-- A SERIES
(J-H) — FSH
CONQUERING COMPOSITION -
VERB-SUBJECT AGREEMENT (J-H) — FSH
DAYS, MONTHS, SEASONS, WEATHER — EGH
DESCRIBING — EGH
IN OUR DAILY LIFE — EGH
IN THE COMMUNITY — EGH
IN THE HOME — EGH
IN THE STORE — EGH
INTRODUCTION TO ENGLISH AS A
SECOND LANGUAGE --A SERIES — EGH
MORE ACTIONS AND CONDITIONS — EGH
NUMBERS AND MONEY — EGH
PRONOUNS — EGH
QUALIFYING — EGH

(MOTION PICTURES)

BRENTANO FOUNDATION BILINGUAL
FILMS--A SERIES — CAROUF

(VIDEOTAPES)

CARL AND THE CORNER MARKET (P) — GPITVL

HOW THE LAZY E RANCH GOT ITS
NAME (P) — GPITVL
INTRODUCTION TO THE VOWELS -
THE FIVE MAGIC BROTHERS (P) — GPITVL
LISTEN AND SAY - CONSONANTS
AND DIGRAPHS--A SERIES (P) — GPITVL
LISTEN AND SAY - VOWELS--A SERIES
(P) — GPITVL
LONG A - APRIL'S APRON (P) — GPITVL
LONG AND SHORT OF IT, THE (P) — GPITVL
LONG E - THE TEENY WEENY EEL (P) — GPITVL
LONG I - IDA'S ICE CREAM (P) — GPITVL
LONG O - OLE'S OLD OVERALLS (P) — GPITVL
LONG U - THE UNICORN IN THE
UNIFORM (P) — GPITVL
SHORT A - ANDY AND THE APPLE (P) — GPITVL
SHORT E - THE ELEPHANT WHO
WANTED TO GO UPSTAIRS (P) — GPITVL
SHORT I - INKY THE IMP (P) — GPITVL
SHORT O - THE OX IN THE BOX (P) — GPITVL
SHORT U - UNCLE UMBER'S UMBRELLA
(P) — GPITVL
SOMETIMES VOWEL, A (P) — GPITVL
WHEN TWO VOWELS GO WALKING (P) — GPITVL

(AUDIO TAPES)

ADJECTIVE PICTURE PUZZLES -
ADJECTIVES (P) — CORF
ADVERB ABILITY - ADVERBS (P) — CORF
LAST WORK, THE - REVIEW (P) — CORF
LITTLE NOUN RIDDLES - COMMON
NOUNS (P) — CORF
MATCHING NOUNS AND VERBS - NOUN-
VERB AGREEMENT (P) — CORF
MENDING VERB ENDINGS - IRREGULAR
VERBS (P) — CORF
MORE THAN ONE - NOUN PLURALS (P) — CORF
NAME GAMES - PROPER NOUNS (P) — CORF
NOUN MARKERS - ARTICLES (P) — CORF
SUBSTITUTE GAMES - PRONOUNS (P) — CORF
TIME TEASING VERBS - TENSE (P) — CORF
VERB MAZES - ACTION AND STATE-OF
BEING VERBS (P) — CORF
WORDS ARE FUN--A SERIES (P) — CORF

(TRANSPARENCIES)

ADJECTIVES - POSITIVE,
COMPARATIVE SUPERLATIVE (I-J) — BOW
ADVENTURES IN PHONICS--A SERIES (P-
J) — BOW
ADVERBS - POSITIVE,
COMPARATIVE SUPERLATIVE (I-J) — BOW
AVOIDING DOUBLE NEGATIVES (I-J) — BOW
BEGINNING SKILLS--A SERIES (K-P) — BOW
BLENDS AND DIGRAPHS--A SERIES — BOW
CAPITALIZATION (P-I) — BOW
COMMAS IN SERIES AND IN DIRECT
ADDRESS (P-I) — BOW
COMPARING SIMPLE AND COMPOUND
VERBS (I-J) — BOW
DISTINGUISHING PROPER AND
COMMON NOUNS (I-J) — BOW
GRAMMAR--A SERIES — BETECL
IDENTIFYING ACTION VERBS (I-J) — BOW
IDENTIFYING ADVERBIALS (I-J) — BOW
IDENTIFYING APPOSITIVES (P-I) — BOW
IDENTIFYING STATE-OF-BEING VERBS (I-
J) — BOW
INITIAL AND FINAL CONSONANTS--A
SERIES — BOW
INTRODUCING ADVERBS (I-J) — BOW
INTRODUCING QUOTATION MARKS (P-I) — BOW
LEARNING THE ALPHABET (K-P) — BOW
LET'S HAVE A NURSERY RHYME PARTY
(K-P) — BOW
ON MY WAY TO SCHOOL I SAW (K-P) — BOW
PHONIC-ANALYSIS--A SERIES — BOW
PLURAL NOUNS ENDING IN 'ES' (I-J) — BOW
PLURAL NOUNS ENDING IN 'IES' (I-J) — BOW
PLURAL NOUNS ENDING IN 'S' (I-J) — BOW
PUNCTUATING KINDS OF SENTENCES
(P-I) — BOW
PUNCTUATION - INTRODUCING KINDS
OF SENTENCES (P-I) — BOW
PUNCTUATION AND CAPITALIZATION--A
SERIES (P-I) — BOW
RECOGNIZING NOUNS (I-J) — BOW
RECOGNIZING ROOT WORDS,
PREFIXES AND SUFFIXES (I-J) — BOW
SYLLABLE AND ACCENT CLUE--A SERIES — BOW
TELL THE STORY - CHANGE THE
ENDING (K-P) — BOW
TELL THE STORY - MAKE IT RHYME (K-
P) — BOW
THREE-DIMENSIONAL LETTER SHAPES
(K-P) — BOW
THREE-DIMENSIONAL NUMERALS
AND COUNTING DISC (K-P) — BOW
THREE-DIMENSIONAL TEN FRAME (K-P) — BOW
THREE-DIMENSIONAL VISUAL
DISCRIMINATION KIT (K-P) — BOW
UNDERSTANDING ABBREVIATIONS (P-I) — BOW
UNDERSTANDING AND USING
ANTONYMS (I-J) — BOW
UNDERSTANDING AND USING
HOMONYMS (I-J) — BOW

UNDERSTANDING .AND USING
SYNONYMS (I-J) — BOW
UNDERSTANDING CONJUNCTIONS (I-J) — BOW
UNDERSTANDING CONTRACTIONS (P-I) — BOW
UNDERSTANDING PREPOSITIONS (I-J) — BOW
USING ADJECTIVES (I-J) — BOW
USING BETWEEN AND AMONG (I-J) — BOW
USING DID AND DONE (I-J) — BOW
USING I AND ME (I-J) — BOW
USING OBJECT FORM PRONOUNS (I-J) — BOW
USING POSSESSIVE NOUNS (I-J) — BOW
USING POSSESSIVE PRONOUNS (I-J) — BOW
USING PREDICATE ADJECTIVES (I-J) — BOW
USING PRONOUNS (I-J) — BOW
USING QUOTATION MARKS (P-I) — BOW
USING SAW AND SEEN (I-J) — BOW
USING THE PERIOD (P-I) — BOW
USING THE QUESTION MARK (P-I) — BOW
USING THERE, THEIR AND THEY'RE (I-J) — BOW
USING TO, TOO AND TWO (I-J) — BOW
VOWEL CHARTS--A SERIES — BOW
WORD BUILDING--A SERIES — BOW
WORD FORMS AND FUNCTIONS--A
SERIES (I-J) — BOW
WORD FUNCTION AND SENTENCE
PATTERNS--A SERIES — BOW
WORD USAGE--A SERIES (I-J) — BOW

LINGUISTICS

(FILMSTRIPS)

INTRODUCTION TO ENGLISH AS A
SECOND LANGUAGE --A SERIES — EGH

(MOTION PICTURES)

LANGUAGE DEVELOPMENT (C A) — CRMP

READING AND EXPRESSION

(MOTION PICTURES)

ELEPHANT EATS, THE, THE PENGUIN
EATS, THE - NOUN (P-I) — BFA
I WANNA BE READY (C A) — AIMS
POEM FIELD NO. 1 (J-C A) — UEVA
READING MOTIVATION--A SERIES (P-I) — BFA
RIVER OTTER (P-J) — AMEDFL
SQUIRRELS ARE UP, SQUIRRELS
ARE DOWN - ADVERBIALS OF
PLACE (P-I) — BFA
WAY FOR DIANA, A (I-J) — AIMS

(AUDIO TAPES)

CASE OF THE RED-HEADED LEAGUE (I-J) — CORF
HOW OF A TRICK, THE (I-J) — CORF
LISTENING WITH A PURPOSE--A SERIES
(I-J) — CORF
MAKING HEADLINES (I-J) — CORF
MESSAGE FROM OUR SPONSOR, A (I-J) — CORF
PEOPLE WATCHING (I-J) — CORF
PROFESSOR STRUDEL'S SECRET
FORMULA (I-J) — CORF
SECRET MISSION, THE (I-J) — CORF
TALK OF COLUMBUS, THE (I-J) — CORF
WHAT NOISES SAY (I-J) — CORF
WHAT'S IN THE NEWS (I-J) — CORF
WORD FROM THE WISE, A (I-J) — CORF
WORDS ARE FUN--A SERIES (P) — CORF
YOU BE THE JUDGE (I-J) — CORF

(TRANSPARENCIES)

ADVENTURES IN PHONICS--A SERIES (P-
J) — BOW
CLASSIFICATION-OPPOSITES-SEQUENCES-
-A SERIES — BOW
CONSONANTS WITH TWO SOUNDS--A
SERIES — COF
DIFFICULT CONSONANTS--A SERIES — COF
EASY CONSONANTS--A SERIES — COF
READING WRITING READINESS--A
SERIES — BOW

READING INSTRUCTION

(FILMSTRIPS)

ALPHABET ZOO, THE, PT 1 - A-G (K-I) — UMM
ALPHABET ZOO, THE, PT 2 - H-M (K-I) — UMM
ALPHABET ZOO, THE, PT 3 - N-T (K-I) — UMM
ALPHABET ZOO, THE, PT 4 - U-Z (K-I) — UMM
IMPROVING YOUR STUDY SKILLS,
SET 1 - USING THE TEXTBOOK
PLAN--A SERIES — CREATV
IMPROVING YOUR STUDY SKILLS,
SET 2 - INTENSIVE READING--A
SERIES — CREATV
IMPROVING YOUR STUDY SKILLS,
SET 3 - INTENSIVE READING
EXERCISES--A SERIES — CREATV

(MOTION CARTRIDGES)

SYMBOL ACCENTUATION PROGRAM--A
SERIES (P-I) — DOUBLE

(MOTION PICTURES)

READING IS FOR US TOO (C A) — CCMFI

(AUDIO TAPES)

LISTENING WITH A PURPOSE--A SERIES
(I-J) — CORF

(TRANSPARENCIES)

CONSONANTS WITH TWO SOUNDS--A
SERIES — COF
DIFFICULT CONSONANTS--A SERIES — COF
EASY CONSONANTS--A SERIES — COF

SPEECH - GENERAL

(FILMSTRIPS)

ACTIONS AND CONDITIONS — EGH
COMMON OBJECTS — EGH
DAYS, MONTHS, SEASONS, WEATHER — EGH
DESCRIBING — EGH
IN OUR DAILY LIFE — EGH
IN THE COMMUNITY — EGH
IN THE HOME — EGH
IN THE STORE — EGH
INTRODUCTION TO ENGLISH AS A
SECOND LANGUAGE --A SERIES — EGH
MORE ACTIONS AND CONDITIONS — EGH
NUMBERS AND MONEY — EGH
PRONOUNS — EGH
QUALIFYING — EGH

(MOTION PICTURES)

RIVER OTTER (P-J) — AMEDFL

SPEECH - PHONICS

(MOTION CARTRIDGES)

SYMBOL ACCENTUATION PROGRAM--A
SERIES (P-I) — DOUBLE

(VIDEOTAPES)

CARL AND THE CORNER MARKET (P) — CPITVL
HOW THE LAZY E RANCH GOT ITS
NAME (P) — GPITVL
INTRODUCTION TO THE VOWELS -
THE FIVE MAGIC BROTHERS (P) — GPITVL
LISTEN AND SAY - CONSONANTS
AND DIGRAPHS--A SERIES (P) — GPITVL
LISTEN AND SAY - VOWELS--A SERIES
(P) — GPITVL
LONG A - APRIL'S APRON (P) — GPITVL
LONG AND SHORT OF IT, THE (P) — GPITVL
LONG E - THE TEENY WEENY EEL (P) — GPITVL
LONG I - IDA'S ICE CREAM (P) — GPITVL
LONG O - OLE'S OLD OVERALLS (P) — GPITVL
LONG U - THE UNICORN IN THE
UNIFORM (P) — GPITVL
SHORT A - ANDY AND THE APPLE (P) — GPITVL
SHORT E - THE ELEPHANT WHO
WANTED TO GO UPSTAIRS (P) — GPITVL
SHORT I - INKY THE IMP (P) — GPITVL
SHORT O - THE OX IN THE BOX (P) — GPITVL
SHORT U - UNCLE UMBER'S UMBRELLA
(P) — GPITVL
SOMETIMES VOWEL, A (P) — GPITVL
WHEN TWO VOWELS GO WALKING (P) — GPITVL

(AUDIO TAPES)

WHAT NOISES SAY (I-J) — CORF

(TRANSPARENCIES)

ADVENTURES IN PHONICS--A SERIES (P-
J) — BOW
BLENDS AND DIGRAPHS--A SERIES — BOW
CONSONANTS WITH TWO SOUNDS--A
SERIES — COF
DIFFICULT CONSONANTS--A SERIES — COF
EASY CONSONANTS--A SERIES — COF
INITIAL AND FINAL CONSONANTS--A
SERIES — BOW
PHONIC-ANALYSIS--A SERIES — BOW
SPELLING GENERALIZATION--A SERIES — BOW
SYLLABLE AND ACCENT CLUE--A SERIES — BOW
VOWEL CHARTS--A SERIES — BOW
WORD BUILDING--A SERIES — BOW

VOCABULARY - GENERAL

(FILMSTRIPS)

ACTIONS AND CONDITIONS — EGH
ALPHABET ZOO, THE, PT 1 - A-G (K-I) — UMM

ALPHABET ZOO, THE, PT 2 - H-M (K-I) — UMM
ALPHABET ZOO, THE, PT 3 - N-T (K-I) — UMM
ALPHABET ZOO, THE, PT 4 - U-Z (K-I) — UMM
COMMON OBJECTS — EGH
CONQUERING COMPOSITION -
AWKWARD SHIFTS (J-H) — FSH
CONQUERING COMPOSITION -
FRAGMENTS (J-H) — FSH
CONQUERING COMPOSITION -
PRONOUNS AND ANTECEDENTS
(J-H) — FSH
CONQUERING COMPOSITION -
SENTENCE PROBLEMS-- A SERIES
(J-H) — FSH
CONQUERING COMPOSITION -
VERB-SUBJECT AGREEMENT (J-H) — FSH
DAYS, MONTHS, SEASONS, WEATHER — EGH
DESCRIBING — EGH
IN OUR DAILY LIFE — EGH
IN THE COMMUNITY — EGH
IN THE HOME — EGH
IN THE STORE — EGH
INTRODUCTION TO ENGLISH AS A
SECOND LANGUAGE --A SERIES — EGH
MORE ACTIONS AND CONDITIONS — EGH
NUMBERS AND MONEY — EGH
PRONOUNS — EGH
QUALIFYING — EGH

(MOTION PICTURES)

BRENTANO FOUNDATION BILINGUAL
FILMS--A SERIES — CAROUF
ELEPHANT EATS, THE PENGUIN
EATS, THE - NOUN (P-I) — BFA
READING MOTIVATION--A SERIES (P-I) — BFA
SQUIRRELS ARE UP, SQUIRRELS
ARE DOWN - ADVERBIALS OF
PLACE (P-I) — BFA

(RECORDS)

RHYTHMS FOR TODAY — EDLACT

(AUDIO TAPES)

ADJECTIVE PICTURE PUZZLES -
ADJECTIVES (P) — CORF
ADVERB ABILITY - ADVERBS (P) — CORF
LAST WORK, THE - REVIEW (P) — CORF
LITTLE NOUN RIDDLES - COMMON
NOUNS (P) — CORF
MATCHING NOUNS AND VERBS - NOUN-
VERB AGREEMENT (P) — CORF
MENDING VERB ENDINGS - IRREGULAR
VERBS (P) — CORF
MORE THAN ONE - NOUN PLURALS (P) — CORF
NAME GAMES - PROPER NOUNS (P) — CORF
NOUN MARKERS - ARTICLES (P) — CORF
SUBSTITUTE GAMES - PRONOUNS (P) — CORF
TIME TEASING VERBS - TENSE (P) — CORF
VERB MAZES - ACTION AND STATE-OF
BEING VERBS (P) — CORF
WORDS ARE FUN--A SERIES (P) — CORF

(TRANSPARENCIES)

ADJECTIVES - POSITIVE,
COMPARATIVE SUPERLATIVE (I-J) — BOW
ADVENTURES IN PHONICS--A SERIES (P-
J) — BOW
ADVERBS - POSITIVE,
COMPARATIVE SUPERLATIVE (I-J) — BOW
AVOIDING DOUBLE NEGATIVES (I-J) — BOW
COMPARING SIMPLE AND COMPOUND
VERBS (I-J) — BOW
DICTIONARY SKILLS--A SERIES — BOW
DISTINGUISHING PROPER AND
COMMON NOUNS (I-J) — BOW
IDENTIFYING ACTION VERBS (I-J) — BOW
IDENTIFYING ADVERBIALS (I-J) — BOW
IDENTIFYING STATE-OF-BEING VERBS (I-
J) — BOW
INTRODUCING ADVERBS (I-J) — BOW
PHONIC-ANALYSIS--A SERIES — BOW
PLURAL NOUNS ENDING IN 'ES' (I-J) — BOW
PLURAL NOUNS ENDING IN 'IES' (I-J) — BOW
PLURAL NOUNS ENDING IN 'S' (I-J) — BOW
RECOGNIZING NOUNS (I-J) — BOW
RECOGNIZING ROOT WORDS,
PREFIXES AND SUFFIXES (I-J) — BOW
SPELLING GENERALIZATION--A SERIES — BOW
UNDERSTANDING AND USING
ANTONYMS (I-J) — BOW
UNDERSTANDING AND USING
HOMONYMS (I-J) — BOW
UNDERSTANDING AND USING
SYNONYMS (I-J) — BOW
UNDERSTANDING CONJUNCTIONS (I-J) — BOW
UNDERSTANDING PREPOSITIONS (I-J) — BOW
USING ADJECTIVES (I-J) — BOW
USING BETWEEN AND AMONG (I-J) — BOW
USING DID AND DONE (I-J) — BOW
USING I AND ME (I-J) — BOW
USING OBJECT FORM PRONOUNS (I-J) — BOW
USING POSSESSIVE NOUNS (I-J) — BOW
USING POSSESSIVE PRONOUNS (I-J) — BOW
USING PREDICATE ADJECTIVES (I-J) — BOW
USING PRONOUNS (I-J) — BOW

USING SAW AND SEEN (I-J) — BOW
USING THERE, THEIR AND THEY'RE (I-J) — BOW
USING TO, TOO AND TWO (I-J) — BOW
WORD FORMS AND FUNCTIONS--A SERIES (I-J) — BOW
WORD USAGE--A SERIES (I-J) — BOW

VOCABULARY - SPELLING

(FILMSTRIPS)

ALPHABET ZOO, THE, PT 1 - A-G (K-I) — UMM
ALPHABET ZOO, THE, PT 2 - H-M (K-I) — UMM
ALPHABET ZOO, THE, PT 3 - N-T (K-I) — UMM
ALPHABET ZOO, THE, PT 4 - U-Z (K-I) — UMM

(TRANSPARENCIES)

BLENDS AND DIGRAPHS--A SERIES — BOW
DICTIONARY SKILLS--A SERIES — BOW
INITIAL AND FINAL CONSONANTS--A SERIES — BOW
PHONIC-ANALYSIS--A SERIES — BOW
SPELLING GENERALIZATION--A SERIES — BOW
SYLLABLE AND ACCENT CLUE--A SERIES — BOW
VOWEL CHARTS--A SERIES — BOW
WORD BUILDING--A SERIES — BOW

WRITING

(FILMSTRIPS)

CONQUERING COMPOSITION - AWKWARD SHIFTS (J-H) — FSH
CONQUERING COMPOSITION - FRAGMENTS (J-H) — FSH
CONQUERING COMPOSITION - PRONOUNS AND ANTECEDENTS (J-H) — FSH
CONQUERING COMPOSITION - SENTENCE PROBLEMS-- A SERIES (J-H) — FSH
CONQUERING COMPOSITION - VERB-SUBJECT AGREEMENT (J-H) — FSH
CURSIVE WRITING - CAPITAL LETTERS, PT 1 — EGH
CURSIVE WRITING - CAPITAL LETTERS, PT 2 — EGH
CURSIVE WRITING - SMALL LETTERS, PT 1 — EGH
CURSIVE WRITING - SMALL LETTERS, PT 2 — EGH
HOW WE WRITE — EGH
KINDS OF WRITING — EGH
LEARN TO WRITE WITH LETTY LETTER--A SERIES — EGH
MANUSCRIPT WRITING - SMALL LETTERS, PT 1 — EGH
MANUSCRIPT WRITING - SMALL LETTERS, PT 2 — EGH
MANUSCRIPT WRITING FOR CAPITAL LETTERS, PT 1 — EGH
MANUSCRIPT WRITING FOR CAPITAL LETTERS, PT 2 — EGH
WHY WE WRITE — EGH
WRITING READINESS — EGH

(MOTION PICTURES)

PRINCIPLES OF PAPERWORK MANAGEMENT - BETTER CORRESPONDENCE PRACTICE — BEF
THREE MAGICAL METHODS - FINDING GOOD IDEAS FOR STORIES (P-I) — ECCCW

(AUDIO TAPES)

WHAT IS A BOOK (I-J) — INSKY
YOUR HANDWRITING IS YOU--A SERIES — BASCH

(TRANSPARENCIES)

ADDRESSING ENVELOPES FOR BUSINESS LETTERS (I) — BOW
ADDRESSING ENVELOPES FOR FRIENDLY LETTERS (I) — BOW
CAPITALIZATION (P-I) — BOW
CLASSIFICATION-OPPOSITES-SEQUENCES--A SERIES — BOW
COMMAS IN SERIES AND IN DIRECT ADDRESS (P-I) — BOW
IDENTIFYING APPOSITIVES (P-I) — BOW
INTRODUCING QUOTATION MARKS (P-I) — BOW
LETTER WRITING--A SERIES (I) — BOW
PUNCTUATING KINDS OF SENTENCES (P-I) — BOW
PUNCTUATION - INTRODUCING KINDS OF SENTENCES (P-I) — BOW
PUNCTUATION AND CAPITALIZATION--A SERIES (P-I) — BOW
READING WRITING READINESS--A SERIES — BOW
UNDERSTANDING ABBREVIATIONS (P-I) — BOW
UNDERSTANDING CONTRACTIONS (P-I) — BOW
USING QUOTATION MARKS (P-I) — BOW
USING THE PERIOD (P-I) — BOW
USING THE QUESTION MARK (P-I) — BOW
WORD FUNCTION AND SENTENCE PATTERNS--A SERIES — BOW
WRITING BUSINESS LETTERS (I) — BOW
WRITING FRIENDLY LETTERS (I) — BOW

FINE ARTS

ART - GENERAL

(FILMSTRIPS)

AMERICA THE BEAUTIFUL (J-C) — SUNCOM
AMERICAN CIVILIZATION - 1783-1840--A SERIES (J-C) — SUNCOM
AMERICAN GENIUS--A SERIES (H-C) — EDDIM
AMERICAN GENIUS, 1880 - 1918 (H-C) — EDDIM
AMERICAN GENIUS, 1920 - 1940 (H-C) — EDDIM
AMERICAN GENIUS, 1940 - 1950 (H-C) — EDDIM
ARCHITECTURE AS A LANGUAGE (J-C) — SUNCOM
ARTS AND THE COMMON MAN, THE (J-C) — SUNCOM
ARTS REFLECT DAILY LIFE, THE (J-C) — SUNCOM
BRIDGES TO THE 20TH CENTURY (J-C) — SUNCOM
CHINESE ART, PT 1 (J-C A) — SCHLAT
CHINESE ART, PT 2 (J-C A) — SCHLAT
CHINESE ART, PT 3 (J-C A) — SCHLAT
COLORS EVERYWHERE - BLACK AND WHITE (K-P) — SPA
COLORS EVERYWHERE - COLORS, COLORS EVERYWHERE DO YOU KNOW THE COLORS (K-P) — SPA
COLORS EVERYWHERE - PINK AND GRAY (K-P) — SPA
COLORS EVERYWHERE - PURPLE AND BROWN (K-P) — SPA
COLORS EVERYWHERE - RED, YELLOW AND BLUE (K-P) — SPA
COLORS EVERYWHERE - RED, YELLOW, BLUE, ORANGE AND GREEN (K-P) — SPA
COLORS EVERYWHERE - WHAT IS BLUE (K-P) — SPA
COLORS EVERYWHERE - WHAT IS GREEN (K-P) — SPA
COLORS EVERYWHERE - WHAT IS ORANGE (K-P) — SPA
COLORS EVERYWHERE - WHAT IS RED (K-P) — SPA
COLORS EVERYWHERE - WHAT IS YELLOW (K-P) — SPA
COLORS EVERYWHERE--A SERIES (K-P) — SPA
DESIGN IN ART — EDPRC
HUMANITIES - A WORLD BETWEEN WARS, PT 1 (J-H) — GA
HUMANITIES - A WORLD BETWEEN WARS, PT 2 (J-H) — GA
HUMANITIES - MAN IN THE NUCLEAR AGE, PT 1 (J-H) — GA
HUMANITIES - MAN IN THE NUCLEAR AGE, PT 2 (J-H) — GA
HUMANITIES - THE DAWN OF THE TWENTIETH CENTURY, PT 1 (J-H) — GA
HUMANITIES - THE DAWN OF THE TWENTIETH CENTURY, PT 2 (J-H) — GA
PORTRAIT OF A YOUNG NATION (J-C) — SUNCOM
YOUNG AMERICA ADMIRES THE ANCIENTS (J-C) — SUNCOM

(MOTION PICTURES)

CIVILISATION, PROGRAM 03 — TIMLIF
DEVELOPING CREATIVITY (J-C A) — UEUWIS
DUNCAN GRANT AT CHARLESTON (H-C A) — MFLMC
HAND CATCHING LEAD — VISRES
WISCONSIN — VISRES

(VIDEOTAPES)

AESTHETIC STATEMENT, AN (I) — GPITVL
COLLAGE MAKING (I) — GPITVL
CREATING ART, PT 1 - LEARNING TO SEE-- A SERIES (I) — GPITVL
CREATING ART, PT 2 - LEARNING TO CREATE ART FORMS--A SERIES (I) — GPITVL
CREATING ART, PT 3 - LEARNING TO UNDERSTAND ART--A SERIES (I) — GPITVL
DRAWING (I) — GPITVL
INTENT OF ART AND ARTISTS, THE (I) — GPITVL
JUDGMENTS ABOUT ART, THE (I) — GPITVL
LEARNING TO SEE COLOR (I) — GPITVL
LEARNING TO SEE LINE AND SHAPE (I) — GPITVL
LEARNING TO SEE SPACE AND MOVEMENT (I) — GPITVL
LEARNING TO SEE TEXTURE (I) — GPITVL
LEARNING TO SEE THE SUBJECTS OF ART (I) — GPITVL
LEARNING TO SEE THE VISUAL ENVIRONMENT (I) — GPITVL
MODELING AND POTTERY MAKING (I) — GPITVL
PAINTING (I) — GPITVL
PRINTING (I) — GPITVL
SCULPTURING (I) — GPITVL
STITCHING AND WEAVING (I) — GPITVL

ART - HISTORY

(FILMSTRIPS)

AMERICA THE BEAUTIFUL (J-C) — SUNCOM
AMERICAN CIVILIZATION - 1783-1840--A SERIES (J-C) — SUNCOM
AMERICAN GENIUS--A SERIES (H-C) — EDDIM
AMERICAN GENIUS, 1880 - 1918 (H-C) — EDDIM
AMERICAN GENIUS, 1920 - 1940 (H-C) — EDDIM
AMERICAN GENIUS, 1940 - 1950 (H-C) — EDDIM
ARCHITECTURE AS A LANGUAGE (J-C) — SUNCOM
ARTS AND THE COMMON MAN, THE (J-C) — SUNCOM
ARTS REFLECT DAILY LIFE, THE (J-C) — SUNCOM
BRIDGES TO THE 20TH CENTURY (J-C) — SUNCOM
CHINESE ART, PT 1 (J-C A) — SCHLAT
CHINESE ART, PT 2 (J-C A) — SCHLAT
CHINESE ART, PT 3 (J-C A) — SCHLAT
HUMANITIES - A WORLD BETWEEN WARS, PT 1 (J-H) — GA
HUMANITIES - A WORLD BETWEEN WARS, PT 2 (J-H) — GA
HUMANITIES - THE DAWN OF THE TWENTIETH CENTURY, PT 1 (J-H) — GA
HUMANITIES - THE DAWN OF THE TWENTIETH CENTURY, PT 2 (J-H) — GA
PORTRAIT OF A YOUNG NATION (J-C) — SUNCOM
YOUNG AMERICA ADMIRES THE ANCIENTS (J-C) — SUNCOM

(MOTION PICTURES)

CIVILISATION, PROGRAM 01 — TIMLIF
CIVILISATION, PROGRAM 02 — TIMLIF
CIVILISATION, PROGRAM 03 — TIMLIF
CIVILISATION, PROGRAM 04 — TIMLIF
CIVILISATION, PROGRAM 05 — TIMLIF
CIVILISATION, PROGRAM 06 — TIMLIF
CIVILISATION, PROGRAM 07 — TIMLIF
CIVILISATION, PROGRAM 08 — TIMLIF
CIVILISATION, PROGRAM 09 — TIMLIF
CIVILISATION, PROGRAM 10 — TIMLIF
CIVILISATION, PROGRAM 11 — TIMLIF
CIVILISATION, PROGRAM 12 — TIMLIF
CIVILISATION, PROGRAM 13 — TIMLIF
CLAES OLDENBURG — VISRES
SUMMER JOURNAL — AMERFI

ARCHITECTURE

(FILMSTRIPS)

AMERICA THE BEAUTIFUL (J-C) — SUNCOM
AMERICAN CIVILIZATION - 1783-1840--A SERIES (J-C) — SUNCOM
AMERICAN CIVILIZATION - 1840-1876--A SERIES (J-C) — SUNCOM
ARCHITECTURE AS A LANGUAGE (J-C) — SUNCOM
ARTS AND THE COMMON MAN, THE (J-C) — SUNCOM
ARTS REFLECT DAILY LIFE, THE (J-C) — SUNCOM
BRIDGES TO THE 20TH CENTURY (J-C) — SUNCOM
CHINESE ART, PT 2 (J-C A) — SCHLAT
HUMANITIES - A WORLD BETWEEN WARS, PT 1 (J-H) — GA
HUMANITIES - A WORLD BETWEEN WARS, PT 2 (J-H) — GA
PORTRAIT OF A YOUNG NATION (J-C) — SUNCOM
YOUNG AMERICA ADMIRES THE ANCIENTS (J-C) — SUNCOM

(MOTION PICTURES)

CIVILISATION, PROGRAM 09 — TIMLIF
DEVELOPING CREATIVITY (J-C A) — UEUWIS
LOUIS I KAHN, ARCHITECT — VISRES
SPIRAL JETTY — VISRES

ARTISTS AND THEIR WORKS

(FILMSTRIPS)

AMERICA THE BEAUTIFUL (J-C) — SUNCOM
AMERICAN CIVILIZATION - 1783-1840--A SERIES (J-C) — SUNCOM
AMERICAN CIVILIZATION - 1840-1876--A SERIES (J-C) — SUNCOM
ARCHITECTURE AS A LANGUAGE (J-C) — SUNCOM
ARTS AND THE COMMON MAN, THE (J-C) — SUNCOM
ARTS REFLECT DAILY LIFE, THE (J-C) — SUNCOM
BRIDGES TO THE 20TH CENTURY (J-C) — SUNCOM
GREAT MEN AND ARTISTS — EGH
GREAT MEN AND ARTISTS — EGH
PORTRAIT OF A YOUNG NATION (J-C) — SUNCOM
YOUNG AMERICA ADMIRES THE ANCIENTS (J-C) — SUNCOM

(MOTION PICTURES)

ADVENTURES IN PERCEPTION (J-C A) — BFA
CIVILISATION, PROGRAM 04 — TIMLIF
CIVILISATION, PROGRAM 05 — TIMLIF

CLAES OLDENBURG — VISRES
CLAES OLDENBURG - SORT OF A COMMERCIAL FOR AN ICEBAG — VISRES
CONSTANTIN BRANCUSI — VISRES
DUNCAN GRANT AT CHARLESTON (H-C A) — MFLMC
IMOGEN CUNNINGHAM, PHOTOGRAPHER — AMERFI
LOUIS I KAHN, ARCHITECT — VISRES
LOUISE NEVELSON (C A) — CONNF
LOWELL HERRERO - THE GRAPHIC PROCESS — GRADYM
MIRROR — VISRES
NOGUCHI - A SCULPTOR'S WORLD (H-C A) — EAGLE
POTTERS OF JAPAN, PT 1 — MGHT
POTTERS OF JAPAN, PT 2 — MGHT
POTTERS OF THE USA, PT 1 — MGHT
POTTERS OF THE USA, PT 2 — MGHT
VERA PAINTS IBIZA IN THE SUN (J-C A) — SCHLAT
WALKER EVANS - HIS TIME, HIS PRESENCE, HIS SILENCE (A) — RADIM
WATERCOLOR PAINTING - ABSTRACT DESIGNS FROM NATURE WITH EDWARD BETTS — PERSPF
WATERCOLOR PAINTING - CREATIVE COLOR COLLAGE WITH EDWARD BETTS — PERSPF
WATERCOLOR PAINTING - IMAGINATIVE DESIGNS WITH ALEX ROSS — PERSPF
WATERCOLOR PAINTING - THE MARINE SCENE WITH HERB OLSEN — PERSPF
WATERCOLOR PAINTING - WORKING FROM SKETCHES WITH LOUIS J KEEP — PERSPF
WATERCOLOR PAINTING - WORKING ON LOCATION WITH EDWIN L DAHLBERG — PERSPF
WATERCOLOR PAINTING--A SERIES — PERSPF
WISCONSIN — VISRES

(VIDEOTAPES)

AESTHETIC STATEMENT, AN (I) — GPITVL
CREATING ART, PT 1 - LEARNING TO SEE-- A SERIES (I) — GPITVL
CREATING ART, PT 2 - LEARNING TO CREATE ART FORMS--A SERIES (I) — GPITVL
CREATING ART, PT 3 - LEARNING TO UNDERSTAND ART--A SERIES (I) — GPITVL
INTENT OF ART AND ARTISTS, THE (I) — GPITVL

ART OBJECTS

(FILMSTRIPS)

CHINESE ART, PT 1 (J-C A) — SCHLAT
CHINESE ART, PT 2 (J-C A) — SCHLAT

(MOTION PICTURES)

VERA PAINTS IBIZA IN THE SUN (J-C A) — SCHLAT
WATERCOLOR PAINTING - ABSTRACT DESIGNS FROM NATURE WITH EDWARD BETTS — PERSPF
WATERCOLOR PAINTING - CREATIVE COLOR COLLAGE WITH EDWARD BETTS — PERSPF
WATERCOLOR PAINTING - IMAGINATIVE DESIGNS WITH ALEX ROSS — PERSPF
WATERCOLOR PAINTING - THE MARINE SCENE WITH HERB OLSEN — PERSPF
WATERCOLOR PAINTING - WORKING FROM SKETCHES WITH LOUIS J KEEP — PERSPF
WATERCOLOR PAINTING - WORKING ON LOCATION WITH EDWIN L DAHLBERG — PERSPF

ARTS AND CRAFTS

(MOTION PICTURES)

ARTS AND CRAFTS - ARTESANIA — CAROUF
CERAMIC ART--A SERIES — MGHT
CERAMICS - WHAT, WHY, HOW — MGHT
COIL METHOD, THE — MGHT
CREATING MOSAICS AND TILES — MGHT
HANDBUILDING METHODS — MGHT
IT HAPPENED IN HUALFIN, PT 3 - ELINDA OF THE VALLEY — PIC
JAPAN'S LIVING CRAFTS (J-C A) — AMEDFL
POTTERS OF JAPAN, PT 1 — MGHT
POTTERS OF JAPAN, PT 2 — MGHT
POTTERS OF THE USA, PT 1 — MGHT
POTTERS OF THE USA, PT 2 — MGHT
UKIYO-E, A FLOATING WORLD OF JAPANESE PAINTING — VISRES
VISTAS OF ISRAEL, NO. 4 — ALDEN
YANKEE CALLING — FENWCK

(VIDEOTAPES)

MODELING AND POTTERY MAKING (I) — GPITVL

BRONZES

(FILMSTRIPS)

CHINESE ART, PT 1 (J-C A) — SCHLAT

(MOTION PICTURES)

CIVILISATION--A SERIES — TIMLIF

CERAMICS

(MOTION PICTURES)

CERAMIC ART--A SERIES — MGHT
CERAMICS - WHAT, WHY, HOW — MGHT
COIL METHOD, THE — MGHT
CREATING MOSAICS AND TILES — MGHT
HANDBUILDING METHODS — MGHT
MAKING OF FINE CHINA — MTP
POTTERS OF JAPAN, PT 1 — MGHT
POTTERS OF JAPAN, PT 2 — MGHT
POTTERS OF THE USA, PT 1 — MGHT
POTTERS OF THE USA, PT 2 — MGHT

(VIDEOTAPES)

MODELING AND POTTERY MAKING (I) — GPITVL

CHILDREN'S ART ACTIVITIES

(FILMSTRIPS)

COLORS EVERYWHERE--A SERIES (K-P) — SPA

(MOTION PICTURES)

ART FOR BEGINNERS - FUN WITH LINES (P) — CORF

(VIDEOTAPES)

AESTHETIC STATEMENT, AN (I) — GPITVL
COLLAGE MAKING (I) — GPITVL
CREATING ART, PT 1 - LEARNING TO SEE-- A SERIES (I) — GPITVL
CREATING ART, PT 2 - LEARNING TO CREATE ART FORMS--A SERIES (I) — GPITVL
CREATING ART, PT 3 - LEARNING TO UNDERSTAND ART--A SERIES (I) — GPITVL
DRAWING (I) — GPITVL
INTENT OF ART AND ARTISTS, THE (I) — GPITVL
JUDGMENTS ABOUT ART, THE (I) — GPITVL
LEARNING TO SEE COLOR (I) — GPITVL
LEARNING TO SEE LINE AND SHAPE (I) — GPITVL
LEARNING TO SEE SPACE AND MOVEMENT (I) — GPITVL
LEARNING TO SEE TEXTURE (I) — GPITVL
LEARNING TO SEE THE SUBJECTS OF ART (I) — GPITVL
LEARNING TO SEE THE VISUAL ENVIRONMENT (I) — GPITVL
MODELING AND POTTERY MAKING (I) — GPITVL
PAINTING (I) — GPITVL
PRINTING (I) — GPITVL
SCULPTURING (I) — GPITVL
STITCHING AND WEAVING (I) — GPITVL

(RECORDS)

BASIC RHYTHMS, ALBUM 7 — BOW

COLLAGE

(VIDEOTAPES)

COLLAGE MAKING (I) — GPITVL

CREATIVITY

(FILMSTRIPS)

AMERICA THE BEAUTIFUL (J-C) — SUNCOM
AMERICAN CIVILIZATION - 1783-1840--A SERIES (J-C) — SUNCOM
AMERICAN CIVILIZATION - 1840-1876--A SERIES (J-C) — SUNCOM
ARCHITECTURE AS A LANGUAGE (J-C) — SUNCOM
ARTS AND THE COMMON MAN, THE (J-C) — SUNCOM
ARTS REFLECT DAILY LIFE, THE (J-C) — SUNCOM
BRIDGES TO THE 20TH CENTURY (J-C) — SUNCOM
COLORS EVERYWHERE - BLACK AND WHITE (K-P) — SPA
COLORS EVERYWHERE - COLORS, COLORS EVERYWHERE DO YOU KNOW THE COLORS (K-P) — SPA
COLORS EVERYWHERE - PINK AND GRAY (K-P) — SPA
COLORS EVERYWHERE - PURPLE AND BROWN (K-P) — SPA
COLORS EVERYWHERE - RED, YELLOW AND BLUE (K-P) — SPA
COLORS EVERYWHERE - RED, YELLOW, BLUE, ORANGE AND GREEN (K-P) — SPA
COLORS EVERYWHERE - WHAT IS BLUE (K-P) — SPA
COLORS EVERYWHERE - WHAT IS GREEN (K-P) — SPA
COLORS EVERYWHERE - WHAT IS ORANGE (K-P) — SPA
COLORS EVERYWHERE - WHAT IS RED (K-P) — SPA
COLORS EVERYWHERE - WHAT IS YELLOW (K-P) — SPA
COLORS EVERYWHERE--A SERIES (K-P) — SPA
CREATING A MOVIE — EGH
CREATING A MOVIE — EGH
DESIGN IN ART — EDPRC
PORTRAIT OF A YOUNG NATION (J-C) — SUNCOM
YOUNG AMERICA ADMIRES THE ANCIENTS (J-C) — SUNCOM

(MOTION CARTRIDGES)

BELL — ABCMED
BULLS — ABCMED
WHY MAN CREATES (A) — PFP

(MOTION PICTURES)

ANN, A PORTRAIT — AMERFI
ART FOR BEGINNERS - FUN WITH LINES (P) — CORF
BALLET ADAGIO (J-C A) — PFP
CHANGES, CHANGES (K-P) — WWS
DEVELOPING CREATIVITY (J-C A) — UEUWIS
OUT OF HANDS (P-I) — HRAW
POEM FIELD NO. 1 (J-C A) — UEVA
SUMMER JOURNAL — AMERFI
THREE MAGICAL METHODS - FINDING GOOD IDEAS FOR STORIES (P-I) — ECCCW
WATERCOLOR PAINTING - ABSTRACT DESIGNS FROM NATURE WITH EDWARD BETTS — PERSPF
WATERCOLOR PAINTING - CREATIVE COLOR COLLAGE WITH EDWARD BETTS — PERSPF
WATERCOLOR PAINTING - IMAGINATIVE DESIGNS WITH ALEX ROSS — PERSPF
WATERCOLOR PAINTING - THE MARINE SCENE WITH HERB OLSEN — PERSPF
WATERCOLOR PAINTING - WORKING FROM SKETCHES WITH LOUIS J KEEP — PERSPF
WATERCOLOR PAINTING - WORKING ON LOCATION WITH EDWIN L DAHLBERG — PERSPF
WAY FOR DIANA, A (I-J) — AIMS

(RECORDS)

BASIC RHYTHMS, ALBUM 7 — BOW
DANCE, SING AND LISTEN AGAIN (K-I) — BOW
DANCE, SING AND LISTEN AGAIN AND AGAIN (K-I) — BOW
INTERPRETIVE RHYTHMS (K-I) — BOW
MACHINE RHYTHMS — BOW
RHYTHMS FROM THE LAND OF MAKE-BELIEVE (K-I) — BOW
WAY OUT RECORD FOR CHILDREN, THE — BOW

DANCE

(MOTION PICTURES)

ANN, A PORTRAIT — AMERFI
BALLET ADAGIO (J-C A) — PFP

(RECORDS)

DANCE, SING AND LISTEN AGAIN (K-I) — BOW
DANCE, SING AND LISTEN AGAIN AND AGAIN (K-I) — BOW
RHYTHMS, DANCES AND GAMES, ALBUM 26 — BOW

DESIGN, DECORATIVE

(FILMSTRIPS)

DESIGN IN ART — EDPRC
HISTORY OF STYLE AND VOGUE, A — EGH
SKETCHING (I) — EGH

(MOTION PICTURES)

WITHIN THE CIRCLE — ALDEN

FINE ARTS

DRAWING

(FILMSTRIPS)

SKETCHING (I) — EGH

(MOTION CARTRIDGES)

SHAPES AND SYMMETRY, UNIT 4 -
HOW TO REPRESENT THREE
DIMENSIONAL SHAPES--A SERIES — XEROX

(MOTION PICTURES)

BLACK AND WHITE (I-C) — PFP

(VIDEOTAPES)

DRAWING (I) — GPITVL

ENGRAVING AND ETCHING

(FILMSTRIPS)

SKETCHING (I) — EGH

JAZZ MUSIC

(MOTION PICTURES)

SATCHMO AND ALL THAT JAZZ (I-C A) — HEARST

MOTION PICTURES

(FILMSTRIPS)

CREATING A MOVIE — EGH
CREATING A MOVIE — EGH
LITERATURE AND THE FILM - BEAUTY
AND THE BEAST (I-C) — EDDIM
LITERATURE AND THE FILM - BLACK
ORPHEUS (I-C) — EDDIM
LITERATURE AND THE FILM - OLIVER
TWIST (I-C) — EDDIM
LITERATURE AND THE FILM - THE
IMPORTANCE OF BEING EARNEST
(I-C) — EDDIM
LITERATURE AND THE FILM--A SERIES
(I-C) — EDDIM

(MOTION PICTURES)

ART MAKEUP - GREEN, BLACK, WHITE,
PINK — VISRES
C - CALICLOTH — VISRES
CONSTRUCTING REALITY - A FILM ON
FILM (P-C) — JOU
END OF THE ART WORLD — VISRES
FILMMAKING FUNDAMENTALS (P-H) — AIMS
FILMMAKING TECHNIQUES - ACTING (I-C
A) — AIMS
FILMMAKING TECHNIQUES - GOING ON
LOCATION (I-C A) — AIMS
FILMMAKING TECHNIQUES - LIGHTING
(I-C A) — AIMS
FILMMAKING TECHNIQUES - MAKE-UP
(I-C A) — AIMS
FILMMAKING TECHNIQUES - STAGE
LIGHTING (I-C A) — AIMS
FILMMAKING TECHNIQUES - STUNTS (I-
C A) — AIMS
FILMMAKING TECHNIQUES--A SERIES (I-
C A) — AIMS
FRANK FILM (J-C A) — PFP
GOLDEN AGE OF COMEDY — CAROUF
LOVE AND FILM (H-C A) — BFA
MIRROR — VISRES
NATURE OF THE FILM MEDIUM, THE — PAULST
POSITIVE-NEGATIVE — VISRES
SIX SHORT FILMS (H-C A) — BFA
T HYBRID V-1 — VISRES
T HYBRID V-2 — VISRES

(AUDIO TAPES)

TEACHING FILM (H-C) — DAVI

MUSIC - GENERAL

(FILMSTRIPS)

MUSIC APPRECIATION--A SERIES — EAV
PETER AND THE WOLF (K-H) — EAV

(MOTION PICTURES)

CIVILISATION, PROGRAM 09 — TIMLIF
GRAVEL SPRINGS FIFE AND DRUM (H-C
A) — IU

(RECORDS)

AUF HOHER SEE — GMS
BASIC RHYTHMS, ALBUM 7 — BOW

CHILD'S INTRODUCTION TO AMERICAN
FOLK SONGS, A — SPA
CHILDHOOD RHYTHMS, NO. 01 — BOW
DANCE, SING AND LISTEN AGAIN (K-I) — BOW
DANCE, SING AND LISTEN AGAIN AND
AGAIN (K-I) — BOW
FOLK MUSIC OF FRANCE — BOW
HARK TO OUR HERITAGE — BOW
HEIMWEH NACH ST PAUL — GMS
INDIAN FOLK MUSIC — CAED
INTERPRETIVE RHYTHMS (K-I) — BOW
LINCOLN PORTRAIT AND NEW ENGLAND
TRIPTYCH — BOW
MACHINE RHYTHMS — BOW
PEARLY'S PROVERBS AND FOLK TUNES — GMS
POEMS AND SONGS FOR YOUNGER
CHILDREN — SPA
RHYTHMIC ACTIVITY — BOW
RHYTHMS FROM THE LAND OF MAKE-
BELIEVE (K-I) — BOW
RHYTHMS, DANCES AND GAMES,
ALBUM 26 — BOW
WAY OUT RECORD FOR CHILDREN, THE — BOW

(AUDIO TAPES)

WHAT MUSIC MEANS TO THE BLIND (J
A) — AFB

MUSIC - EDUCATION

(FILMSTRIPS)

BEETHOVEN'S NINTH SYMPHONY, ODE
TO JOY — EAV
CHARLES IVES - HOLIDAYS -
WASHINGTON'S BIRTHDAY AND
THE FOURTH OF JULY — EAV
FANTASIA ON GREENSLEEVES -
VAUGHAN WILLIAMS — EAV
MUSIC APPRECIATION--A SERIES — EAV

(MOTION PICTURES)

ASSOCIATES OF THE VIOLIN — IWANMI

MUSIC - INSTRUMENTAL

(FILMSTRIPS)

BEETHOVEN'S NINTH SYMPHONY, ODE
TO JOY — FAV
CHARLES IVES - HOLIDAYS -
WASHINGTON'S BIRTHDAY AND
THE FOURTH OF JULY — EAV
FANTASIA ON GREENSLEEVES -
VAUGHAN WILLIAMS — EAV
MUSIC APPRECIATION--A SERIES — EAV

(MOTION PICTURES)

ASSOCIATES OF THE VIOLIN — IWANMI
JESUS TRIP, THE (C A) — TIMLIF
PETER AND THE WOLF — DISNEY
TEMPEST, THE — VISRES
WIND INSTRUMENT, THE — IWANMI

(RECORDS)

HOLIDAY RHYTHMS — BOW
LINCOLN PORTRAIT AND NEW ENGLAND
TRIPTYCH — BOW
RHYTHM IS FUN (P-I) — BOW
RHYTHMIC ACTIVITY — BOW

(AUDIO TAPES)

SCHERZO, SYMPHONY NO. 1 (I-C A) — UILL
SUITE OF OLD AMERICAN DANCES (I-C
A) — UILL
SYMPHONY IN B FLAT (I-C A) — UILL
ZANONI (I-C A) — UILL

MUSIC - VOCAL

(MOTION PICTURES)

BIG YELLOW TAXI — PFP
BLACK AND WHITE (I-C) — PFP

(RECORDS)

CHILD'S INTRODUCTION TO AMERICAN
FOLK SONGS, A — SPA
MUSIC OF IRELAND — SPA

MUSICIANS

(MOTION PICTURES)

SATCHMO AND ALL THAT JAZZ (I-C A) — HEARST

(TRANSPARENCIES)

DUKE ELLINGTON (J-H) — LEART

HARRY BELAFONTE (J-H) — LEART
LEONTYNE PRICE (J-H) — LEART
LOUIS 'SATCHMO' ARMSTRONG (J-H) — LEART
MAHALIA JACKSON (J-H) — LEART
MARIAN ANDERSON (J-H) — LEART
SAMMY DAVIS JR (J-H) — LEART
W C HANDY (J-H) — LEART

NEGROES IN LITERATURE AND ART

(TRANSPARENCIES)

BIOGRAPHIES OF OUTSTANDING
NEGRO AMERICANS--A SERIES (J-
H) — LEART
LANGSTON HUGHES (J-H) — LEART
PAUL LAURENCE DUNBAR (J-H) — LEART

PAINTING

(FILMSTRIPS)

AMERICA THE BEAUTIFUL (J-C) — SUNCOM
AMERICAN CIVILIZATION - 1783-1840--A
SERIES (J-C) — SUNCOM
AMERICAN CIVILIZATION - 1840-1876--A
SERIES (J-C) — SUNCOM
ARCHITECTURE AS A LANGUAGE (J-C) — SUNCOM
ARTS AND THE COMMON MAN, THE (J-
C) — SUNCOM
ARTS REFLECT DAILY LIFE, THE (J-C) — SUNCOM
BRIDGES TO THE 20TH CENTURY (J-C) — SUNCOM
CHINESE ART, PT 3 (J-C A) — SCHLAT
PORTRAIT OF A YOUNG NATION (J-C) — SUNCOM
YOUNG AMERICA ADMIRES THE
ANCIENTS (J-C) — SUNCOM

(MOTION PICTURES)

ADVENTURES IN PERCEPTION (J-C A) — BFA
CIVILISATION, PROGRAM 11 — TIMLIF
UKIYO-E, A FLOATING WORLD OF
JAPANESE PAINTING — VISRES
WATERCOLOR PAINTING -
ABSTRACT DESIGNS FROM
NATURE WITH EDWARD BETTS — PERSPF
WATERCOLOR PAINTING - CREATIVE
COLOR COLLAGE WITH EDWARD
BETTS — PERSPF
WATERCOLOR PAINTING -
IMAGINATIVE DESIGNS WITH
ALEX ROSS — PERSPF
WATERCOLOR PAINTING - THE
MARINE SCENE WITH HERB
OLSEN — PERSPF
WATERCOLOR PAINTING - WORKING
FROM SKETCHES WITH LOUIS J
KEEP — PERSPF
WATERCOLOR PAINTING - WORKING
ON LOCATION WITH EDWIN L
DAHLBERG — PERSPF
WATERCOLOR PAINTING--A SERIES — PERSPF

(VIDEOTAPES)

PAINTING (I) — GPITVL

PHOTOGRAPHY, ARTISTIC

(MOTION PICTURES)

ART MAKEUP - GREEN, BLACK, WHITE,
PINK — VISRES
C - CALICLOTH — VISRES
HAND CATCHING LEAD — VISRES
IMOGEN CUNNINGHAM, PHOTOGRAPHER — AMERFI
MIRROR — VISRES
POP (H-C A) — BFA
POSITIVE-NEGATIVE — VISRES
T HYBRID V-1 — VISRES
T HYBRID V-2 — VISRES
TEMPEST, THE — VISRES
WATERSMITH (I-C A) — TIMLIF
WISCONSIN — VISRES

SCULPTURE

(FILMSTRIPS)

AMERICA THE BEAUTIFUL (J-C) — SUNCOM
AMERICAN CIVILIZATION - 1783-1840--A
SERIES (J-C) — SUNCOM
AMERICAN CIVILIZATION - 1840-1876--A
SERIES (J-C) — SUNCOM
ARCHITECTURE AS A LANGUAGE (J-C) — SUNCOM
ARTS AND THE COMMON MAN, THE (J-
C) — SUNCOM
ARTS REFLECT DAILY LIFE, THE (J-C) — SUNCOM
BRIDGES TO THE 20TH CENTURY (J-C) — SUNCOM
CHINESE ART, PT 2 (J-C A) — SCHLAT
PORTRAIT OF A YOUNG NATION (J-C) — SUNCOM
YOUNG AMERICA ADMIRES THE
ANCIENTS (J-C) — SUNCOM

(MOTION PICTURES)

CIVILISATION, PROGRAM 10	TIMLIF
CLAES OLDENBURG - SORT OF A COMMERCIAL FOR AN ICEBAG	VISRES
CONSTANTIN BRANCUSI	VISRES
LOUISE NEVELSON (C A)	CONNF
NOGUCHI - A SCULPTOR'S WORLD (H-C A)	EAGLE

(VIDEOTAPES)

SCULPTURING (I)	GPITVL

SOUND

(MOTION PICTURES)

SOUNDS OF NATURE	AVEXP

THEATER

(FILMSTRIPS)

CREATING A MOVIE	EGH

(MOTION PICTURES)

FILMMAKING TECHNIQUES - ACTING (I-C A)	AIMS
THEATER IN SHAKESPEARE'S TIME, THE (J-C A)	BFA

(RECORDS)

EUGENE IONESCO - LA CANTATRICE CHAUVE, LA LECON	GMS
GERARD PHILIPE - TNP	GMS
HOMMAGE A CHARLES DULLIN	GMS
HOMMAGE A LOUIS JOUVET	GMS
PIERRE CORNEILLE - CINNA	GMS
PIERRE CORNEILLE - CINNA, EXTRAITS	GMS
PIERRE CORNEILLE - HORACE	GMS
PIERRE CORNEILLE - POLYEUCTE (EXTRAITS)	GMS

(TRANSPARENCIES)

SHAKESPEARE--A SERIES	BETECL

FOREIGN LANGUAGE

FRENCH

(FILMSTRIPS)

CANDIDE - LE TEXTE ET LA VIE DE VOLTAIRE (H-C)	ALEP
COMICAL SITUATIONS OF EVERYDAY LIFE, PT 1 (FRENCH) (J-H)	ALEP
COMICAL SITUATIONS OF EVERYDAY LIFE, PT 2 (FRENCH) (J-H)	ALEP

(RECORDS)

AGRIPPA D'AUBIGNE - L'HIVER DE LA VIE (EXTRAIT)	GMS
AGRIPPA D'AUBIGNE - O FRANCE DESOLEE	GMS
ALBERT CAMUS - EXCERPTS	GMS
ALBERT CAMUS - L'ETRANGER	GMS
ALBERT CAMUS - SELECTIONS	GMS
ALFRED JARRY - LE BAIN DU ROI	GMS
ALPHONSE ALLAIS (1854-1905)	GMS
ALPHONSE ALLAIS, POEMES DIT PAR PIERRE BRASSEUR	GMS
ALPHONSE DAUDET - LETTRES DE MON MOULIN, LE SOUS-PREFET AUX CHAMPS	GMS
ANATOLE FRANCE - HISTOIRE CONTEMPORAINE	GMS
ANATOLE FRANCE - PIERRE NOZIERE	GMS
ANATOLE FRANCE (EXTRAITS)	GMS
ANDRE BRETON - L'UNION LIBRE	GMS
ANDRE CHENIER - LA JEUNE CAPTIVE	GMS
ANDRE CHENIER - LA JEUNE TARENTINE	GMS
ANDRE CHENIER - TOUJOURS CE SOUVENIR M'ATTENDRIT ET ME TOUCHE	GMS
ANDRE CHENIER (1762-1764)	GMS
ANDRE CHENIER, I	GMS
ANDRE CHENIER, II	GMS
ANDRE GIDE	GMS
ANDRE GIDE - ENTRETIENS AVEC JEAN AMROUCHE	GMS
ANDRE GIDE (EXTRAITS)	GMS
BABAR EN FAMILLE	GMS
BABAR ET CE COQUIN D'ARTHUR	GMS
BABAR ET LE PERE NOEL	GMS
BABAR ET LE PROFESSEUR GRIFATON	GMS
BABAR STORIES--A SERIES	GMS

BLAISE CENDRARS	GMS
BLAISE CENDRARS - HOTEL NOTRE-DAME, ILES	GMS
BLAISE CENDRARS - LE VENTRE DE MA MERE, LES PAQUES A NEW YORK	GMS
CHANSON DE ROLAND (MORT D'OLIVER ET DE ROLAND)	GMS
CHARLES BAUDELAIRE - CORRESPONDANCES	GMS
CHARLES BAUDELAIRE - LA MUSIQUE	GMS
CHARLES BAUDELAIRE - LES FLEURS DU MAL	GMS
CHARLES BAUDELAIRE - RECUEILLEMENT	GMS
CHARLES BAUDELAIRE - RECUEILLEMENT, LA CHEVELURE	GMS
CHARLES BAUDELAIRE - VISAGES DE BAUDELAIRE	GMS
CHARLES BAUDELAIRE, I	GMS
CHARLES BAUDELAIRE, II	GMS
CHARLES BAUDELAIRE, III	GMS
CHARLES BAUDELAIRE, IV	GMS
COLETTE - APRES L'ORAGE	GMS
COLETTE - CHERI, GIGI	GMS
COLETTE - DIALOGUE DES BETES	GMS
COLETTE (EXTRAITS)	GMS
COLETTE VOUS PARLE	GMS
DENIS DIDEROT - LE NEVEU DE RAMEAU, I	GMS
DENIS DIDEROT - LE NEVEU DE RAMEAU, II	GMS
DENIS DIDEROT - LE NEVEU DE RAMEAU, III	GMS
DENIS DIDEROT - PARADOXE SUR LE COMEDIEN	GMS
DENIS DIDEROT - SALON	GMS
EDMOND ET JULES GONCOURT - GERMINIE LACERTEUX	GMS
EDMOND HARAUCOURT - RONDEL DE L'ADIEU	GMS
EUGENE FROMENTIN - COCHER DE SOLEIL, LE PHARE DES BALEINES	GMS
EUGENE FROMENTIN - DOMINIQUE	GMS
EUGENE FROMENTIN - LE PHARE DES BALEINES	GMS
EUGENE IONESCO - LA CANTATRICE CHAUVE, LA LECON	GMS
FEDERICO GARCIA LORCA	GMS
FELIX ARVERS - SONNET	GMS
FRANCIS CARCO	GMS
FRANCIS JAMMES - J'AIME L'ANE	GMS
FRANCIS JAMMES - JEAN MARCHAT READS (FRENCH)	GMS
FRANCIS JAMMES - JEAN NEGRONI RECITES (FRENCH)	GMS
FRANCIS JAMMES - LA SALLE A MANGER	GMS
FRANCIS JAMMES - PRIERE POUR MONTER AU PARADIS AVEC LES ANES	GMS
FRANCOIS FENELON - LES AVENTURES DE TELEMAQUE	GMS
FRANCOIS VICOMTE DE CHATEAUBRIAND	GMS
FRANCOIS VICOMTE DE CHATEAUBRIAND - LE GENIE DU CHRISTIANISME, RENE	GMS
FRANCOIS VICOMTE DE CHATEAUBRIAND - LE GENIE DU CHRISTIANISME, LES RUINES	GMS
FRANCOIS VICOMTE DE CHATEAUBRIAND - RENE	GMS
FRANCOIS VICOMTE DE CHATEAUBRIAND - RENE, REVERIES DE RENE	GMS
FRANCOIS VICOMTE DE CHATEAUBRIAND - TEMOIN DE HISTOIRE	GMS
FRANCOIS VICOMTE DE CHATEAUBRIAND - UNE NUIT DANS LES DESERTS DU NOUVEAU MONDE	GMS
GEORGES DE BUFFON - EPOQUES DE LA NATURE VII	GMS
GERARD PHILIPE - TNP	GMS
GUILLAUME APOLLINAIRE	GMS
GUILLAUME APOLLINAIRE - HOMMAGE A APPOLLINAIRE	GMS
GUILLAUME APOLLINAIRE - LE PONT MIRABEAU	GMS
GUILLAUME APOLLINAIRE - POEMES, I	GMS
GUILLAUME APOLLINAIRE - POEMES, II	GMS
GUILLAUME APOLLINAIRE - POEMES, III	GMS
GUILLAUME APOLLINAIRE - POEMES, IV	GMS
GUILLAUME APOLLINAIRE - POEMES, V	GMS
GUSTAVE FLAUBERT - DANS LA FORET DE FONTAINEBLEAU	GMS
GUSTAVE FLAUBERT - FORET DE FONTAINEBLEAU	GMS
GUSTAVE FLAUBERT - MADAME BOVARY (EXTRAITS)	GMS
GUSTAVE FLAUBERT (1821-1880)	GMS
HOMMAGE A CHARLES DULLIN	GMS
HOMMAGE A LOUIS JOUVET	GMS
HONORE DE BALZAC - LE FAISEUR	GMS
HONORE DE BALZAC - LE PERE GORIOT	GMS
JACQUES-BENIGNE BOSSUET	GMS
JACQUES-BENIGNE BOSSUET -	

ORAISON FUNEBRE D'HENRIETTE D'ANGLETERRE	GMS
JEAN COCTEAU - HOMMAGE A JEAN COCTEAU	GMS
JEAN COCTEAU - JEAN MERCURE RECITES (FRENCH)	GMS
JEAN COCTEAU - LES MARIES DE LA TOUR EIFFEL	GMS
JEAN COCTEAU (1889-1963)	GMS
JEAN DE LA BRUYERE - LES CARACTERES DE LA SOCIETE ET DE LA CONVERSATION, GITON ET PHEDON	GMS
JEAN DE LA BRUYERE - LES CARACTERES DE LA VILLE	GMS
JEAN GIONO	GMS
JEAN GIONO - EN HAUTE PROVENCE	GMS
JEAN GIONO - LA MOISSON	GMS
JEAN GIRAUDOUX	GMS
JEAN GIRAUDOUX - PARIS, PRIERE SUR LA TOUR EIFFEL	GMS
JEAN GIRAUDOUX (EXTRAITS)	GMS
JEAN VILAR - GRANDES HEURES DU TNP	GMS
JEAN-PIERRE DE FLORIAN - LA CARPE ET LES CARPILLIONS	GMS
JOACHIM DU BELLAY	GMS
JOACHIM DU BELLAY - HEUREUX QUI, COMME ULYSSE	GMS
JOACHIM DU BELLAY - LE BEAU VOYAGE	GMS
JOACHIM DU BELLAY - LE REGRET	GMS
JOACHIM DU BELLAY - SONNET	GMS
JOSE-MARIA DE HEREDIA - EPITAPHE D'UNE SAUTERELLE	GMS
JOSE-MARIA DE HEREDIA - LES CONQUERANTS	GMS
JOSE-MARIA DE HEREDIA - MARIS STELLA	GMS
JOSEPH BEDIER - PETIT CRU	GMS
JULES LAFORGUE - COMPLAINTE DE L'OUBLI DES MORTS	GMS
JULES LAFORGUE - COMPLAINTE SUR CERTAINS ENNUIS	GMS
JULES LAFORGUE - LOCUTION DES PIERROTS, SOIR DE CARNAVAL, L'IMPOSSIBLE	GMS
JULES LAFORGUE - RENE LEFEVRE RECITES (FRENCH)	GMS
LA BATAILLE DE QADECH	GMS
LA CHANSON DE ROLAND	GMS
LA CHANSON DE ROLAND (L'EPISODE DE RONCEVAUX)	GMS
LA VOIX DE PAUL ELUARD	GMS
LAURENT GILBERT - ADIEUX A LA VIE	GMS
LEON PAUL FARGUE - NOCTURNE	GMS
LES POETES EN FRANCE	GMS
LOUIS ARAGON	GMS
LOUIS ARAGON - AMOURS	GMS
LOUIS ARAGON - LES LILAS ET LES ROSES	GMS
LOUIS LABE - POEMES	GMS
LOUIS-FERDINAND CELINE	GMS
LOUISE LABE - JE VIS, JE MEURS	GMS
LOUISE LABE - TANT QUE MES YEUX	GMS
MADAME DE LA FAYETTE - LA PRINCESSE DE CLEVES	GMS
MADAME DE LA FAYETTE - LA PRINCESSE DE CLEVES	GMS
MARCEL ACHARD - DISCOURS SOUS LA COUPOLE	GMS
MARCEL ACHARD - MARLBOROUGH S'EN VA-T-EN GUERRE	GMS
MARCEL ACHARD - VOULEZ-VOUS JOUER AVEC MOI	GMS
MARCEL AYME - LES CONTES DU CHAT PERCHE	GMS
MAURICE BARRES - LE PRINTEMPS	GMS
MAURICE FOMBEURE	GMS
MAURICE FOMBEURE - MENUISIER DU ROI	GMS
MAURICE FOMBEURE - NOSTALGIE	GMS
MAURICE GENEVOIX - LES POISSONS DE LA LOIRE	GMS
MAX JACOB - ALAIN CUNY RECITES (FRENCH)	GMS
MAX JACOB - LE KAMICHI	GMS
PAUL CLAUDEL - EXCERPTS (FRENCH)	GMS
PAUL CLAUDEL - L'ANNONCE FAITE A MARIE	GMS
PAUL CLAUDEL - L'ESPRIT ET L'EAU	GMS
PAUL CLAUDEL - LE VIERGE A MIDI	GMS
PAUL CLAUDEL, I	GMS
PAUL CLAUDEL, II	GMS
PAUL ELUARD	GMS
PAUL ELUARD - DONNER A VOIR	GMS
PAUL ELUARD - GERARD PHILIPE RECITES (FRENCH)	GMS
PAUL ELUARD - L'AMOUREUSE	GMS
PAUL ELUARD (1895-1952)	GMS
PAUL FORT - CHANSON D'UN BERGER SURPRIS PAR LA NEIGE	GMS
PAUL FORT - COMPLAINTE DU PETIT CHEVAL BLANC, LA	
PAUL FORT - LA RONDE	GMS
PAUL FORT - LE BONHEUR, LA RONDE AUTOUR DU MONDE	GMS
PAUL FORT (1872-1960)	GMS

PAUL-LOUIS COURIER DE MERE - UNE AVENTURE EN CALABRE	GMS
PEARLY'S PROVERBS AND FOLK TUNES	GMS
PIERRE CORNEILLE - CINNA	GMS
PIERRE CORNEILLE - CINNA, EXTRAITS	GMS
PIERRE CORNEILLE - HORACE	GMS
PIERRE CORNEILLE - POLYEUCTE (EXTRAITS)	GMS
PIERRE DE BEAUMARCHAIS - LE MARIAGE DE FIGARO (COMPLETE)	GMS
PIERRE DE BEAUMARCHAIS - LE MARIAGE DE FIGARO (EXTRAITS)	GMS
PIERRE DE BEAUMARCHAIS - LE MARIAGE DE FIGARO (EXTRAITS)	GMS
PIERRE DE BEAUMARCHAIS - LE MARIAGE DE FIGARO ACTE I, SCENE 1, ACTE V, SCENE 3	GMS
PIERRE-AMBROISE CHODERLOS DE LACIOS - LES LIAISONS DANGEREUSES	GMS
PRESENCE DE ALBERT CAMUS	GMS
REMY DE GOURMONT - JEANNE	GMS
RENE CHAR	GMS
RENE CHAR - L'INOFFENSIF, LA SORGUE	GMS
RENE GUY CADOU	GMS
ROGER FRISON-ROCHE - ASCENSION DU DRU (MONT BLANC)	GMS
ROLAND DORGELES - CHATEAU DES BROUILLARDS	GMS
SAMUEL BECKETT - OH LES BEAUX JOURS (EXTRAITS)	GMS
THEODORE DE BANVILLE - LE SAUT DE TREMPLIN	GMS
THEOPHILE GAUTIER - LE CAPITAINE FRACASSE	GMS
THEOPHILE GAUTIER - PAYSAGE NOCTURNE	GMS
TRISTAN CORBIERE - LA PARDON DE SAINTE-ANNE LA-PALUD (EXTRAIT)	GMS
VICTOR HUGO - CE SIECLE AVAIT DEUX ANS	GMS
VICTOR HUGO - LA CAMPAGNE DE RUSSIE	GMS
VICTOR HUGO - LA ROSE DE L'INFANTE, CHANSON D'AUTOMNE	GMS
VICTOR HUGO - LE FIN DE SATAN (EXTRAITS)	GMS
VICTOR HUGO - LES MISERABLES (COSETTE)	GMS
VICTOR HUGO - LES MISERABLES (EXTRAITS)	GMS
VICTOR HUGO - LES MISERABLES (GAVROCHE)	GMS
VICTOR HUGO - NOTRE-DAME DE PARIS	GMS
VICTOR HUGO (EXTRAITS)	GMS

GERMAN

(FILMSTRIPS)

COMICAL SITUATIONS OF EVERYDAY LIFE, PT 1 (GERMAN) (J-H)	ALEP
COMICAL SITUATIONS OF EVERYDAY LIFE, PT 2 (GERMAN) (J-H)	ALEP

(RECORDS)

AUF HOHER SEE	GMS
HEIMWEH NACH ST PAUL	GMS

ITALIAN

(FILMSTRIPS)

COMICAL SITUATIONS OF EVERYDAY LIFE, PT 1 (ITALIAN) (J-H)	ALEP
COMICAL SITUATIONS OF EVERYDAY LIFE, PT 2 (ITALIAN) (J-H)	ALEP

SPANISH

(FILMSTRIPS)

COMICAL SITUATIONS OF EVERYDAY LIFE, PT 1 (SPANISH) (J-H)	ALEP
COMICAL SITUATIONS OF EVERYDAY LIFE, PT 2 (SPANISH) (J-H)	ALEP
LA FERIA POTOSINA - UN PASEO EN ACAPULCO	STDYSC
LA JUVENTUD DE AMERICA LATINA--A SERIES	STDYSC
LA JUVENTUD DE LA CIUDAD	STDYSC
LA JUVENTUD DE LA PROVINCIA	STDYSC
LAS ESCUELAS SECONDARIAS	STDYSC
LATIN TEENAGERS JUNIOR--A SERIES	STDYSC
NUESTRO MUNDO DE VISTAS Y	

SONIDOS, GRUPO 1-- A SERIES (P)	SVE
VISTAS Y SONIDOS DE LA TIENDA DE ANIMALES CASEROS (P)	SVE
VISTAS Y SONIDOS DEL PARQUE DE DIVERSIONES	SVE

(MOTION CARTRIDGES)

TEACHING SPANISH TO SPANISH SPEAKING CHILDREN (P-I)	BOUCH

(MOTION PICTURES)

ALL ABOUT ANIMALS - TODO SOBRE LOS ANIMALES	CAROUF
ARTS AND CRAFTS - ARTESANIA	CAROUF
AT THE FIRE STATION	CAROUF
AT THE MARKET - EN EL MERCADO	CAROUF
BIG TREES, THE - LOS ARBOLES GRANDES	CAROUF
BOATS AND BRIDGES - BARCOS Y PUENTES	CAROUF
BRENTANO FOUNDATION BILINGUAL FILMS--A SERIES	CAROUF
COUNTING AND COLORS - EL CONTAR Y COLORES	CAROUF
DAY IN THE PARK, A	CAROUF
DID YOU EVER MILK A COW - JAMAS HAS EXTRAIDO LECHE DE UNA VACA	CAROUF
FIESTA	CAROUF
FIREMEN GO TO SCHOOL, TOO - LOS BOMBEROS VAN A LA ESCUELA, TAMBIEN	CAROUF
FIRST DAY, NEW FRIENDS - PRIMER DIA, NUEVOS AMIGOS	CAROUF
FROM WHEEL TO WING - DESDE LA RUEDA HASTA EL AVION	CAROUF
GET READY FOR THE RANCH - PREPARATE PARA EL RANCHO	CAROUF
GET READY FOR THE ZOO - PREPARATE PARA EL JARDIN ZOOLOGICO	CAROUF
LET'T VISIT THE FIREMEN - VAMOS A VISITAR A LA BOMBEROS	CAROUF
MEXICO	CAROUF
OUR FAMILY ALBUM - NUESTRO ALBUM DE LA FAMILIA	CAROUF
OUR FIRST PLANE RIDE - NUESTRO PRIMER VIAJE EN AVION	CAROUF
PEPE TEACHES US - PEPE NOS ENSENA	CAROUF
TOUCHDOWNS AND HORSES - GOLES Y CABALLOS	CAROUF
TRAINS AND MORE TRAINS - TRENES Y MAS TRENES	CAROUF
TRIP TO RANCHO VERDE, A	CAROUF
WE EXPLORE CHINATOWN - NOSOTROS EXPLORAMOS CHINATOWN	CAROUF
WE GO TO A DAIRY FARM	CAROUF
WE REMEMBER THE FARM - RECORDAMOS EL RANCHO	CAROUF
WE SEE THE BABY ZOO - VEMOS EL ZOOLOGICO INFANTIL	CAROUF
WE VISIT THE POST OFFICE - VISITAMOS LA CASA DE CORREOS	CAROUF
WE VISIT THE ZOO - VISITAMOS EL JARDIN ZOOLOGICO	CAROUF

FOREIGN LANGUAGE - OTHER

(FILMSTRIPS)

ACTIONS AND CONDITIONS	EGH
COMMON OBJECTS	EGH
DAYS, MONTHS, SEASONS, WEATHER	EGH
DESCRIBING	EGH
IN OUR DAILY LIFE	EGH
IN THE COMMUNITY	EGH
IN THE HOME	EGH
IN THE STORE	EGH
INTRODUCTION TO ENGLISH AS A SECOND LANGUAGE --A SERIES	EGH
LANGUAGE LABORATORY, THE	BSF
MORE ACTIONS AND CONDITIONS	EGH
NUMBERS AND MONEY	EGH
PRONOUNS	EGH
QUALIFYING	EGH
TAPE RECORDER IN TEACHING, THE	BSF

GEOGRAPHY - U S

GEOGRAPHY, U S - GENERAL

(FILMSTRIPS)

FOCUS ON AMERICA - THE PACIFIC STATES--A SERIES (J-H A)	SVE

(MOTION PICTURES)

INVITATION TO THE EAST	MTP

ALASKA

(FILMSTRIPS)

ALASKA - THE LAST AMERICAN FRONTIER (J-H)	SED

(MOTION PICTURES)

ALASKA'S BUSH PILOT HERITAGE (I-H)	DISNEY
ALASKAN GOLD RUSH, THE (I-C)	DISNEY
CHALLENGE OF THE ARCTIC	ARIC

CALIFORNIA

(FILMSTRIPS)

CALIFORNIA CONFLICT - MIGRANT FARM WORKERS (J-H A)	SVE
FOCUS ON AMERICA - THE PACIFIC STATES--A SERIES (J-H A)	SVE
LOS ANGELES - CITY OF AUTOMOBILES (J-H A)	SVE
NEW TOWN - VALENCIA, CALIFORNIA (J-H A)	SVE

(MOTION PICTURES)

FIFTH STREET (C A)	DRMINC

HARBORS - U S

(MOTION PICTURES)

BUILDING A HARBOR (I-J)	AIMS

HAWAII

(MOTION PICTURES)

HAWAII	PUI

HISTORICAL GEOGRAPHY

(MOTION PICTURES)

ALASKAN GOLD RUSH, THE (I-C)	DISNEY
NORFOLK TOUR	MTP
SPOKANE RIVER, THE (I-C A)	NWFLMP

MIDDLE ATLANTIC STATES

(MOTION PICTURES)

CAROLINAS, THE	MTP
NEW YORK - THE ANYTIME CITY	MTP
NEW YORK CITY	MTP
POPCORN LADY (I-C A)	SCHLAT
STATE OF ENCHANTMENT	MTP

MIDDLE WEST AND GREAT PLAINS STATES

(MOTION PICTURES)

TOUR OF GRANT'S FARM, A	MTP

(AUDIO TAPES)

SUN SHINES BRIGHT, THE (H A)	USOE

MOUNTAINS

(MOTION PICTURES)

SKIING ABOVE THE CLOUDS	RARIG

NATIONAL PARKS - U S

(MOTION PICTURES)

WHITE FACE OF YELLOWSTONE	MTP

NORTHEASTERN STATES

(MOTION PICTURES)

CHILDREN AS PEOPLE (H-C A)	POLYMR
VOICES FROM MAINE (J-C A)	POLYMR
WE THE ENEMY	FENWCK
YANKEE CALLING	FENWCK

NORTHWESTERN STATES

(FILMSTRIPS)

ALASKA - THE LAST AMERICAN FRONTIER (J-H)	SED

BONNEVILLE DAM - POWERHOUSE
OF THE COLUMBIA RIVER (J-H A)   SVE
FOCUS ON AMERICA - THE PACIFIC
STATES--A SERIES (J-H A)   SVE
NORTHWEST FILMSTRIPS--A SERIES   UWASHP
OLYMPIC COAST INDIANS TODAY   UWASHP
RAIN FORESTS OF THE NORTHWEST
COAST   UWASHP
SEATTLE - A CITY FACES CRISIS (J-H A)   SVE
TIMBER - WASHINGTON'S MOST
VALUABLE CROP (J-H A)   SVE

(MOTION PICTURES)

BING CROSBY'S WASHINGTON STATE (I-
C A)   SCREEI
SKIING ABOVE THE CLOUDS   RARIG
SPOKANE RIVER, THE (I-C A)   NWFLMP
STORY OF TWO CREEKS, THE   UEUWIS

ORE DEPOSITS

(MOTION PICTURES)

ALASKAN GOLD RUSH, THE (I-C)   DISNEY

PHYSICAL GEOGRAPHY

(FILMSTRIPS)

ALASKA - THE LAST AMERICAN
FRONTIER (J-H)   SED

(MOTION PICTURES)

BING CROSBY'S WASHINGTON STATE (I-
C A)   SCREEI
SPOKANE RIVER, THE (I-C A)   NWFLMP

RIVERS - U S

(MOTION PICTURES)

SPOKANE RIVER, THE (I-C A)   NWFLMP

ROCKY MOUNTAIN STATES

(MOTION PICTURES)

SPIRAL JETTY   VISRES
YOU HOO - I'M A BIRD   MTP

SCENERY

(MOTION PICTURES)

BING CROSBY'S WASHINGTON STATE (I-
C A)   SCREEI

SOUTHWESTERN STATES

(FILMSTRIPS)

DANISH FIELD, THE (J-C A)   INTXC

VOYAGES AND TRAVELS

(MOTION PICTURES)

BING CROSBY'S WASHINGTON STATE (I-
C A)   SCREEI
CAROLINAS, THE   MTP
INVITATION TO THE EAST   MTP
STATE OF ENCHANTMENT   MTP
TOUR OF GRANT'S FARM, A   MTP

WESTERN STATES

(FILMSTRIPS)

BONNEVILLE DAM - POWERHOUSE
OF THE COLUMBIA RIVER (J-H A)   SVE
FOCUS ON AMERICA - THE PACIFIC
STATES--A SERIES (J-H A)   SVE
LOS ANGELES - CITY OF AUTOMOBILES
(J-H A)   SVE

GEOGRAPHY - WORLD

GEOGRAPHY, WORLD - GENERAL

(FILMSTRIPS)

NEW FRIENDS FROM DISTANT
LANDS - THE CULTURE WE
SHARE--A SERIES (P-I)   PATED

(MOTION PICTURES)

PORT OF CALL--A SERIES   PUI

AFGHANISTAN AND NEPAL

(FILMSTRIPS)

LIVING IN ASIA TODAY - AMONG
THE MARKETS OF AFGHANISTAN
(P-I)   CORF

AFRICA

(FILMSTRIPS)

ALBERT SCHWEITZER (2ND ED) (I-H)   CARMAN
ANIMALS TO KNOW - AFRICA, PT 1 (P-I)   BFA
ANIMALS TO KNOW - AFRICA, PT 2 (P-I)   BFA
DAY IN THE CONGO, A   DOUBLE
LIVING IN AFRICA TODAY - A CITY
FAMILY OF MOROCCO (P-I)   CORF
LIVING IN AFRICA TODAY - A CITY
FAMILY OF MALI (P-I)   CORF
LIVING IN AFRICA TODAY - A
PROFESSIONAL OF GHANA (P-I)   CORF
LIVING IN AFRICA TODAY - A
SUBURBAN FAMILY OF SOUTH
AFRICA (P-I)   CORF
LIVING IN AFRICA TODAY - A
VILLAGE FAMILY OF THE UPPER
VOLTA (P-I)   CORF
LIVING IN AFRICA TODAY - A
VILLAGE FAMILY OF MALI (P-I)   CORF
LIVING IN AFRICA TODAY - A
VILLAGE FAMILY OF ZAIRE (P-I)   CORF
LIVING IN AFRICA TODAY - A
WHITE FARM FAMILY OF KENYA
(P-I)   CORF
LIVING IN AFRICA TODAY--A SERIES (P-I)   CORF
ON SAFARI IN EAST AFRICA (P-C)   DWYLIE

(MOTION CARTRIDGES)

SCAVENGERS OF AFRICA (P-I)   DOUBLE

(MOTION PICTURES)

DRY SEASON, THE   CMC
KENYA   PUI
LIVING WOOD - AFRICAN MASKS AND
MYTHS (I-H A)   GRADYM
SEARCH FOR THE NILE--A SERIES (J-C
A)   TIMLIF
UMBRELLA MAN, THE   MGHT
ZANZIBAR   PUI

(RECORDS)

FOLK AND FAIRY TALES FROM AFRICA   SPA

(TRANSPARENCIES)

COLONIES TO INDEPENDENCE (J-H)   LEART
COUNTRY OF NIGERIA, THE (J-H)   LEART
EUROPEAN PARTITION AGREEMENTS
1884-1885 (J-H)   LEART
NATIONALIST LEADERS OF BLACK
AFRICA (J-H)   LEART
NATIONALIST LEADERS OF NORTH
AFRICA (J-H)   LEART
POLITICAL DIVISIONS AS OF 1968 -
AFRICA (J-H)   LEART
POLITICAL GEOGRAPHY AND
NATIONALISM OF AFRICA --A
SERIES (J-H)   LEART
POLITICALLY SOVEREIGN STATES OF
AFRICA (J-H)   LEART
PURPOSES AND AIMS OF THE OAU (J-
H)   LEART
REGIONAL ORGANIZATIONS IN AFRICA
(J-H)   LEART
REPUBLIC OF SOUTH AFRICA (J-H)   LEART
STRUCTURE OF THE OAU (J-H)   LEART
UHURU (J-H)   LEART
UNITED NATIONS ROLE IN THE
INDEPENDENCE OF AFRICAN
COUNTRIES (J-H)   LEART

ASIA - GENERAL

(FILMSTRIPS)

ASFEC   UNIPUB
LIVING IN ASIA TODAY--A SERIES (P-I)   CORF

(MOTION PICTURES)

ROOTS OF MADNESS   XEROX

AUSTRALIA

(MOTION CARTRIDGES)

LUNGFISH AND OTHER AUSTRALIAN
ANIMALS (P-I)   DOUBLE

BALKANS

(FILMSTRIPS)

GREECE (P-I)   PATED

(MOTION PICTURES)

GREECE   PUI
STAKE IN THE FUTURE, A (J-C A)   NAGLEP

CARIBBEAN

(MOTION PICTURES)

HAITI   PUI

CHINA

(FILMSTRIPS)

CHINESE ART, PT 1 (J-C A)   SCHLAT
CHINESE ART, PT 2 (J-C A)   SCHLAT
CHINESE ART, PT 3 (J-C A)   SCHLAT
COMMUNES IN CHINA   EGH
EDUCATION AND COMMUNICATION IN
CHINA   EGH
HEALTH SERVICES IN CHINA   EGH
INSIDE THE PEOPLE'S REPUBLIC OF
CHINA--A SERIES   EGH
LIVING IN ASIA TODAY - WITH A
CITY FAMILY OF TAIWAN (P-I)   CORF
PEOPLE OF CHINA, THE   EGH
TRADE AND TRANSPORTATION IN
CHINA   EGH
WORK OF THE PEOPLE OF CHINA   EGH

(MOTION PICTURES)

CHINA - A HOLE IN THE BAMBOO
CURTAIN (I-C A)   CAROUF
GLADIATORS, THE (H-C)   , NLC

CORAL REEFS AND ISLANDS

(FILMSTRIPS)

LIVING IN ASIA TODAY - ON THE
ISLAND OF BALI IN INDONESIA
(P-I)   CORF

(MOTION PICTURES)

BIRTH OF JAPANESE ISLANDS   IWANMI
LIFE ON THE REEF   IWANMI

DESERTS - WORLD

(FILMSTRIPS)

BALANCE OF LIFE IN A DESERT   SED
DESERT LIFE--A SERIES   SED
HOW DESERT ANIMALS SURVIVE   SED

(MOTION CARTRIDGES)

DESERT, THE (I-J)   HESTER

(MOTION PICTURES)

ISRAEL'S NATIONAL WATER CARRIER   ALDEN
ISRAEL'S QUEST FOR WATER   ALDEN

ECONOMIC GEOGRAPHY

(FILMSTRIPS)

EASTERN EUROPE--A SERIES   MGHT
MEXICO - AN ECONOMY IN TRANSITION
(I-H)   DOUBLE
RESOURCES, AGRICULTURE AND
INDUSTRY   EGH
RESOURCES, AGRICULTURE AND
INDUSTRY   EGH
WHAT IS HOLLAND   EGH

(MOTION PICTURES)

LIFE FROM THE DEAD SEA   ALDEN

EUROPE - EASTERN

(FILMSTRIPS)

CZECHOSLOVAKIA - AGRICULTURE AND INDUSTRY	MGHT
EASTERN EUROPE--A SERIES	MGHT
HUNGARY - AGRICULTURE TODAY	MGHT
HUNGARY - INDUSTRY AND PROGRESS	MGHT
POLAND - AGRICULTURE TODAY	MGHT
POLAND - INDUSTRY AND PROGRESS	MGHT

(MOTION PICTURES)

GROWING PAINS FOR THE COMMON MARKET	HEARST

EUROPE - WESTERN

(MOTION PICTURES)

GROWING PAINS FOR THE COMMON MARKET	HEARST

FRANCE

(RECORDS)

FOLK AND FAIRY TALES FROM FRANCE	SPA
FOLK MUSIC OF FRANCE	BOW

GEOGRAPHY, ANCIENT

(AUDIO TAPES)

WONDERS OF THE ANCIENT WORLD (H-C)	NGART

GEOGRAPHY, COMMERCIAL

(FILMSTRIPS)

RESOURCES, AGRICULTURE AND INDUSTRY	EGH
RESOURCES, AGRICULTURE AND INDUSTRY	EGH
TRADE AND TRANSPORTATION IN CHINA	EGH
WHAT IS GREAT BRITAIN	EGH
WORK OF THE PEOPLE OF CHINA	EGH

(MOTION PICTURES)

MOSHAV, THE - ISRAEL'S MIDDLE WAY	ALDEN

GEOGRAPHY, HISTORICAL

(FILMSTRIPS)

CITIES OF ITALY	EGH
CITIES OF ROME AND FLORENCE	EGH
FLORENCE AND VENICE	EGH
WHAT IS GREAT BRITAIN	EGH
WHAT IS HOLLAND	EGH

(MOTION PICTURES)

CHILDREN'S WORLD - MEXICO (K-I)	AVED
ISRAEL - THE HOLY LAND (J-C A)	AMEDFL
YEARS OF DESTINY	ALDEN

GEOGRAPHY, MILITARY

(MOTION PICTURES)

CITIZEN'S ARMY	ALDEN
SIX DAYS IN JUNE	ALDEN

GEOGRAPHY, PHYSICAL

(FILMSTRIPS)

CITY LIFE	EGH
GREAT BRITAIN - A REGIONAL STUDY--A SERIES	EGH
HOLLAND - A REGIONAL STUDY--A SERIES	EGH
ITALY - A REGIONAL SURVEY--A SERIES	EGH
ITALY - THE LAND	EGH
ITALY - THE LAND	EGH
LAND, FEATURES AND CITIES	EGH
LAND, FEATURES AND CITIES	EGH
PEOPLE OF CHINA, THE	EGH
RANCH LIFE	EGH
TRADE AND TRANSPORTATION IN CHINA	EGH
WHAT IS GREAT BRITAIN	EGH
WHAT IS HOLLAND	EGH
WORK OF THE PEOPLE OF CHINA	EGH

(MOTION PICTURES)

CHILDREN'S WORLD - MEXICO (K-I)	AVED
DRY SEASON, THE	CMC
OFF THE BEATEN TRACK IN ISRAEL	ALDEN
SEARCH FOR THE NILE--A SERIES (J-C A)	TIMLIF
STRATA	IWANMI
VISTAS OF ISRAEL, NO. 4	ALDEN

GEOGRAPHY, PICTURES, ILLUSTRATIONS

(FILMSTRIPS)

ITALY - THE LAND	EGH
WHAT IS GREAT BRITAIN	EGH
WHAT IS HOLLAND	EGH

(MOTION PICTURES)

INVITATION TO THE EAST	MTP
VACATION FUN IN ISRAEL	ALDEN

GEOGRAPHY, POLITICAL

(FILMSTRIPS)

WHAT IS GREAT BRITAIN	EGH
WHAT IS HOLLAND	EGH

(MOTION PICTURES)

GLADIATORS, THE (H-C)	NLC
HOME AT LAST	ALDEN
PLIGHT OF SOVIET JEWELRY, THE - LET MY PEOPLE GO	ALDEN
SOVIET BUILD-UP IN THE MIDDLE EAST	ALDEN
THIRD TEMPLE, THE	ALDEN
YEARS OF DESTINY	ALDEN

(TRANSPARENCIES)

COLONIES TO INDEPENDENCE (J-H)	LEART
COUNTRY OF NIGERIA, THE (J-H)	LEART
EUROPEAN PARTITION AGREEMENTS 1884-1885 (J-H)	LEART
NATIONALIST LEADERS OF BLACK AFRICA (J-H)	LEART
NATIONALIST LEADERS OF NORTH AFRICA (J-H)	LEART
POLITICAL DIVISIONS AS OF 1968 - AFRICA (J-H)	LEART
POLITICAL GEOGRAPHY AND NATIONALISM OF AFRICA --A SERIES (J-H)	LEART
POLITICALLY SOVEREIGN STATES OF AFRICA (J-H)	LEART
PURPOSES AND AIMS OF THE OAU (J-H)	LEART
REGIONAL ORGANIZATIONS IN AFRICA (J-H)	LEART
REPUBLIC OF SOUTH AFRICA (J-H)	LEART
STRUCTURE OF THE OAU (J-H)	LEART
UHURU (J-H)	LEART
UNITED NATIONS ROLE IN THE INDEPENDENCE OF AFRICAN COUNTRIES (J-H)	LEART

GEOGRAPHY, SOCIAL

(FILMSTRIPS)

ALASKA - THE LAST AMERICAN FRONTIER (J-H)	SED
CHIHUAHUA - LIFE IN A NORTHERN MEXICAN CITY	EGH
CHILDREN	EGH
CITY LIFE	EGH
COMMUNES IN CHINA	EGH
COMMUNITY DEVELOPMENT IN MICHOACAN	EGH
FOCUS ON AMERICA - THE PACIFIC STATES--A SERIES (J-H A)	SVE
GREAT BRITAIN - A REGIONAL STUDY--A SERIES	EGH
HOLLAND - A REGIONAL STUDY--A SERIES	EGH
INSIDE THE PEOPLE'S REPUBLIC OF CHINA--A SERIES	EGH
ITALIAN CULTURE AND RECREATION	EGH
ITALIAN HOME AND FAMILY, THE	EGH
ITALIANS AT WORK	EGH
ITALY - A REGIONAL STUDY--A SERIES	EGH
ITALY - A REGIONAL SURVEY--A SERIES	EGH
LIFE IN BRITAIN	EGH
LIFE IN BRITAIN	EGH
LIFEWAYS OF THE PEOPLE - SOUTH AMERICA--A SERIES	EGH
LIVING IN AFRICA TODAY - A CITY FAMILY OF MALI (P-I)	CORF
LIVING IN AFRICA TODAY - A PROFESSIONAL OF GHANA (P-I)	CORF
LIVING IN AFRICA TODAY - A SUBURBAN FAMILY OF SOUTH AFRICA (P-I)	CORF
LIVING IN AFRICA TODAY - A VILLAGE FAMILY OF MALI (P-I)	CORF
LIVING IN AFRICA TODAY - A VILLAGE FAMILY OF ZAIRE (P-I)	CORF
LIVING IN AFRICA TODAY - A WHITE FARM FAMILY OF KENYA (P-I)	CORF
LIVING IN AFRICA TODAY--A SERIES (P-I)	CORF
LIVING IN ASIA TODAY - AMONG THE MARKETS OF AFGHANISTAN (P-I)	CORF
LIVING IN ASIA TODAY - AT A SCHOOL IN KYOTO, JAPAN (P-I)	CORF
LIVING IN ASIA TODAY - AT A VILLAGE WEDDING IN THE PUNJAB, INDIA (P-I)	CORF
LIVING IN ASIA TODAY - IN A VILLAGE IN AMERICAN SAMOA (P-I)	CORF
LIVING IN ASIA TODAY - ON HOUSEBOATS IN KASHMIR (P-I)	CORF
LIVING IN ASIA TODAY - ON THE ISLAND OF BALI IN INDONESIA (P-I)	CORF
LIVING IN ASIA TODAY - WITH A CITY FAMILY OF TAIWAN (P-I)	CORF
LIVING IN ASIA TODAY - WITH A FISH SELLER IN MALAYSIA (P-I)	CORF
LIVING IN ASIA TODAY--A SERIES (P-I)	CORF
MEXICO - A COMMUNITY STUDY--A SERIES	EGH
PEOPLE OF CHINA, THE	EGH
TOWN AND VILLAGE IN THE MOUNTAINS OF PUEBLA	EGH
VILLAGE LIFE	EGH
VILLAGE OF ZIHUATANEJO AND ITS TURTLE INDUSTRY	EGH
WHAT IS GREAT BRITAIN	EGH
WHAT IS HOLLAND	EGH

(MOTION PICTURES)

KIBBUTZ, A	ALDEN
LET'S IMAGINE - LIFE IN UTOPIA	ALDEN
OFF THE BEATEN TRACK IN ISRAEL	ALDEN
VACATION FUN IN ISRAEL	ALDEN
YEARS OF DESTINY	ALDEN

GEYSERS

(MOTION PICTURES)

VOLCANOES AND HOT SPRINGS	IWANMI

GLACIERS

(MOTION PICTURES)

STORY OF TWO CREEKS, THE	UEUWIS

GREAT BRITAIN

(FILMSTRIPS)

ENGLAND (P-I)	PATED
GREAT BRITAIN - A REGIONAL STUDY--A SERIES	EGH
LAND, FEATURES AND CITIES	EGH
LIFE IN BRITAIN	EGH
RESOURCES, AGRICULTURE AND INDUSTRY	EGH
WHAT IS GREAT BRITAIN	EGH

(RECORDS)

FOLK AND FAIRY TALES FROM ENGLAND	SPA

(TRANSPARENCIES)

SHAKESPEARE--A SERIES	BETECL

INDIA AND PAKISTAN

(FILMSTRIPS)

LIVING IN ASIA TODAY - AT A VILLAGE WEDDING IN THE PUNJAB, INDIA (P-I)	CORF
LIVING IN ASIA TODAY - ON HOUSEBOATS IN KASHMIR (P-I)	CORF
WILDLIFE SANCTUARIES OF INDIA	AVEXP

(MOTION PICTURES)

INDIA	PUI
PAKISTAN	PUI
WORK OF GOMIS, THE (J-C A)	WASHBF

(RECORDS)

INDIAN FOLK MUSIC	CAED

IRELAND

(RECORDS)

MUSIC OF IRELAND   SPA

ITALY

(FILMSTRIPS)

CITIES OF ITALY   EGH
CITIES OF ITALY   EGH
CITIES OF ROME AND FLORENCE   EGH
CITIES OF ROME AND FLORENCE   EGH
FLORENCE AND VENICE   EGH
FLORENCE AND VENICE   EGH
GREAT MEN AND ARTISTS   EGH
GREAT MEN AND ARTISTS   EGH
ITALIAN CULTURE AND RECREATION   EGH
ITALIAN CULTURE AND RECREATION   EGH
ITALIAN HOME AND FAMILY, THE   EGH
ITALIANS AT WORK   EGH
ITALY (P-I)   PATED
ITALY - A REGIONAL STUDY--A SERIES   EGH
ITALY - A REGIONAL SURVEY--A SERIES   EGH
ITALY - THE LAND   EGH
ITALY - THE LAND   EGH

(RECORDS)

FOLK AND FAIRY TALES FROM ITALY   SPA

JAPAN

(FILMSTRIPS)

JAPAN   TF
LIVING IN ASIA TODAY - AT A
  SCHOOL IN KYOTO, JAPAN (P-I)   CORF

(MOTION PICTURES)

BIRTH OF JAPANESE ISLANDS   IWANMI
BIRTH OF MOUNT FUJI   IWANMI
FORM OF VOLCANOES, THE   IWANMI
JAPAN   PUI
JAPAN'S LIVING CRAFTS (J-C A)   AMEDFL
JAPANESE CHILDREN   IWANMI
POTTERS OF JAPAN, PT 1   MGHT
POTTERS OF JAPAN, PT 2   MGHT
SAND HILLS   IWANMI
STALACTITE GROTTO   IWANMI
STRATA   IWANMI
TOKYO - THE FIFTY-FIRST VOLCANO (H-C
A)   TIMLIF
UKIYO-E, A FLOATING WORLD OF
JAPANESE PAINTING   VISRES

(RECORDS)

FOLK AND FAIRY TALES FROM JAPAN   SPA

LOW COUNTRIES

(FILMSTRIPS)

DANISH FIELD, THE (J-C A)   INTXC
HOLLAND - A REGIONAL STUDY--A
SERIES   EGH
LAND, FEATURES AND CITIES   EGH
LIFE IN HOLLAND   EGH
RESOURCES, AGRICULTURE AND
INDUSTRY   EGH
WHAT IS HOLLAND   EGH

MAPS

(MOTION CARTRIDGES)

CONTOUR MAPPING (P)   HUBDSC
MAP READING--A SERIES (P)   HUBDSC

MEXICO

(FILMSTRIPS)

CHIHUAHUA - LIFE IN A NORTHERN
MEXICAN CITY   EGH
COMMUNITY DEVELOPMENT IN
MICHOACAN   EGH
COMPARATIVE PATHOGENIC
BACTERIOLOGY, PT 1   SAUNDW
MEXICO - A COMMUNITY STUDY--A
SERIES   EGH
MEXICO - AN ECONOMY IN TRANSITION
(I-H)   DOUBLE
TOWN AND VILLAGE IN THE
MOUNTAINS OF PUEBLA   EGH
VILLAGE OF ZIHUATANEJO AND ITS
TURTLE INDUSTRY   EGH

(MOTION- PICTURES)

CHILDREN'S WORLD - MEXICO (K-I)   AVED
MEXICO   CAROUF
YO SOY CHICANO (ENGLISH) (H-C A)   IU

(RECORDS)

FOLK AND FAIRY TALES FROM MEXICO   SPA

MIDDLE EAST

(FILMSTRIPS)

LEBANON (P-I)   PATED

(MOTION PICTURES)

BRIDGE OF FRIENDSHIP   ALDEN
CHILDREN OF THE KIBBUTZ (I-C A)   ACI
CHILDREN, THE   AMERFI
CITIZEN'S ARMY   ALDEN
CO-OP   ALDEN
DOCTOR IN THE DESERT   ALDEN
EGYPT   PUI
FLOWERS FOR DAHLIA   ALDEN
HANUKKAH   ALDEN
HOME AT LAST   ALDEN
IN SEARCH OF HISTORY   ALDEN
ISRAEL   PUI
ISRAEL IN THE FAMILY OF NATIONS   ALDEN
ISRAEL'S NATIONAL WATER CARRIER   ALDEN
ISRAEL'S QUEST FOR WATER   ALDEN
ISRAEL'S 17TH INDEPENDENCE DAY
(1965)   ALDEN
IT WAS THE CUSTOM   ALDEN
JERUSALEM - HERE WE COME   ALDEN
KIBBUTZ, A   ALDEN
LAND OF HOPE AND PRAYER   ALDEN
LAND SPEAKS OUT, THE   ALDEN
LET MY PEOPLE GO   ALDEN
LET'S IMAGINE - LIFE IN UTOPIA   ALDEN
LIFE FROM THE DEAD SEA   ALDEN
LOVING YOUNG COMPANY   ALDEN
MOSHAV, THE - ISRAEL'S MIDDLE WAY   ALDEN
NAHAL   ALDEN
OFF THE BEATEN TRACK IN ISRAEL   ALDEN
PASSOVER   ALDEN
PLIGHT OF SOVIET JEWELRY, THE -
  LET MY PEOPLE GO   ALDEN
POPE PAUL'S VISIT TO ISRAEL   ALDEN
PRIME MINISTER GOLDA MEIR'S
  VISIT TO THE USA IN 1969   ALDEN
PURIM   ALDEN
RHYTHM OF TOMMORW   ALDEN
SCENES OF NATURAL RESERVE   ALDEN
SEMINARS IN ISRAEL   ALDEN
SHAVUOTH   ALDEN
SIX DAYS IN JUNE   ALDEN
SOVIET BUILD-UP IN THE MIDDLE EAST   ALDEN
STORY OF STAMPS, THE   ALDEN
SUCCOTH   ALDEN
SYRIA   PUI
THIRD TEMPLE, THE   ALDEN
THIS IS OUR FARM   ALDEN
TIBERIAS - LAND OF THE EMPERORS   ALDEN
TURKEY   PUI
VACATION FUN IN ISRAEL   ALDEN
VISTAS OF ISRAEL, NO. 1   ALDEN
VISTAS OF ISRAEL, NO. 2   ALDEN
VISTAS OF ISRAEL, NO. 3   ALDEN
VISTAS OF ISRAEL, NO. 4   ALDEN
WITHIN THE CIRCLE   ALDEN
YEARS OF DESTINY   ALDEN

MOUNTAINS

(FILMSTRIPS)

FOLD MOUNTAINS (I-H)   VISPUB
VOLCANOES, PT 1 (I-H)   VISPUB
VOLCANOES, PT 2 (I-H)   VISPUB

(MOTION PICTURES)

BIRTH OF MOUNT FUJI   IWANMI

NATURAL RESOURCES, DISTRIBUTION

(FILMSTRIPS)

BONNEVILLE DAM - POWERHOUSE
  OF THE COLUMBIA RIVER (J-H A)   SVE
RESOURCES, AGRICULTURE AND
INDUSTRY   EGH
ROCKS AND MINERALS (I-H)   VISPUB
TIMBER - WASHINGTON'S MOST
VALUABLE CROP (J-H A)   SVE

(MOTION PICTURES)

LIFE FROM THE DEAD SEA   ALDEN
STAKE IN THE FUTURE, A (J-C A)   NAGLEP
VISTAS OF ISRAEL, NO. 2   ALDEN
VISTAS OF ISRAEL, NO. 3   ALDEN

OCEANIA

(FILMSTRIPS)

LIVING IN ASIA TODAY - IN A
  VILLAGE IN AMERICAN SAMOA
  (P-I)   CORF

PHILIPPINES

(MOTION PICTURES)

ALCOHOLISM - A MODEL OF DRUG
DEPENDENCY (C A)   CRMP

POLAR REGIONS

(MOTION PICTURES)

CHALLENGE OF THE ARCTIC   ARIC

RIVERS AND OCEANS - WORLD

(FILMSTRIPS)

BONNEVILLE DAM - POWERHOUSE
  OF THE COLUMBIA RIVER (J-H A)   SVE
RIVERS, PT 1 (I-H)   VISPUB
RIVERS, PT 2 (I-H)   VISPUB
RIVERS, PT 3 (I-H)   VISPUB
SEA, THE - DEPOSITION (I-H)   VISPUB
SEA, THE - EROSION (I-H)   VISPUB
TRADE AND TRANSPORTATION IN
CHINA   EGH

(MOTION PICTURES)

LIFE FROM THE DEAD SEA   ALDEN
RIVERS   IWANMI
SEARCH FOR THE NILE--A SERIES (J-C
A)   TIMLIF

(AUDIO TAPES)

WHY AN OCEAN - THE OCEAN'S
HISTORY (J-H)   VOA

SCANDINAVIA AND FINLAND

(RECORDS)

FOLK AND FAIRY TALES FROM
DENMARK   SPA

SOUTH AMERICA

(FILMSTRIPS)

CHILDREN   EGH
CITY LIFE   EGH
INDUSTRIAL WORKER   EGH
LIFE OF THE LEISURE CLASS   EGH
LIFEWAYS OF THE PEOPLE - SOUTH
  AMERICA--A SERIES   EGH
POLITICS AND GOVERNMENT (J-H)   MMPRO
RANCH LIFE   EGH
VILLAGE LIFE   EGH

SOUTHEAST ASIA

(FILMSTRIPS)

LIVING IN ASIA TODAY - ON THE
  ISLAND OF BALI IN INDONESIA
  (P-I)   CORF
LIVING IN ASIA TODAY - WITH A
  FISH SELLER IN MALAYSIA (P-I)   CORF

(MOTION PICTURES)

BALI   PUI
CEYLON   PUI
HONG KONG   PUI
SINGAPORE   PUI
THREE FAMILIES OF MALAYSIA (I)   CORF

SWITZERLAND

(FILMSTRIPS)

CHRISTMAS IN A NOISY VILLAGE (K-P)   VIP

UNION OF SOVIET SOCIALIST REPUBLICS

(FILMSTRIPS)

FISH IN THE FOREST - A RUSSIAN
FOLKTALE (I)   GA

(MOTION PICTURES)

PLIGHT OF SOVIET JEWELRY, THE · LET MY PEOPLE GO	ALDEN
SOVIET BUILD-UP IN THE MIDDLE EAST	ALDEN

(RECORDS)

FOLK AND FAIRY TALES FROM RUSSIA	SPA

TURKEY

(FILMSTRIPS)

TURKEY (P-I)	PATED

(MOTION PICTURES)

TURKEY	PUI

VOLCANOES

(FILMSTRIPS)

VOLCANOES, PT 1 (I-H)	VISPUB
VOLCANOES, PT 2 (I-H)	VISPUB

(MOTION PICTURES)

BIRTH OF MOUNT FUJI	IWANMI
FORM OF VOLCANOES, THE	IWANMI
PROPERTIES OF CLAY	IWANMI
VOLCANOES AND HOT SPRINGS	IWANMI

(VIDEOTAPES)

HOW IS THE EARTH'S SURFACE CHANGED BY INTERNAL FORCES (I)	GPITVL

VOYAGES AND TRAVEL

(MOTION PICTURES)

LAND SPEAKS OUT, THE	ALDEN
LOVING YOUNG COMPANY	ALDEN
OFF THE BEATEN TRACK IN ISRAEL	ALDEN
PORT OF CALL--A SERIES	PUI
TIBERIAS · LAND OF THE EMPERORS	ALDEN
VACATION FUN IN ISRAEL	ALDEN

GUIDANCE AND COUNSELING

BLIND AND DEAF

(AUDIO TAPES)

TALKING BOOKS FOR THE BLIND (J A)	AFB
WHAT MUSIC MEANS TO THE BLIND (J A)	AFB

DATING AND COURTSHIP

(FILMSTRIPS)

DATING DATA (J-C A)	RMI
HOT TIPS ON BASIC BEAUTY, FASHION, GROOMING AND DATING--A SERIES (J-C A)	RMI
PERSONALITY PLUS (J-C A)	RMI

(MOTION PICTURES)

ADOLESCENCE AND SEXUAL IDENTITY (H-C A)	CHM
COPING IN SPECIAL EDUCATION · SOCIALIZATION (C)	UEUWIS
PICTURE, THE	AMERFI

(AUDIO TAPES)

TOO YOUNG TO MARRY	BASCH

(TRANSPARENCIES)

BASIS OF ROMANTIC IDEAL (J)	LEART
BEING YOURSELF (J)	LEART
BREAKING OFF (J)	LEART
CARS AND DATES (J)	LEART
CASUAL-STEADY DATING (J)	LEART
CATEGORIES OF DATING BEHAVIOR (J)	LEART
COMMUNICATION CONFUSION (J)	LEART
COMPLEXITY OF LOVE (J)	LEART
DATING AND PARTYING	LEART
DATING BEHAVIOR (J)	LEART
DATING BEHAVIORS AND EXPECTATIONS (J)	LEART
DATING RELATIONS · DATING CATEGORIES--A SERIES (J)	LEART
DATING RELATIONS · DATING PROBLEMS--A SERIES (J)	LEART
DATING RELATIONS · DIMENSIONS OF DATING--A SERIES (J)	LEART
DATING RELATIONS · EVALUATING DATING BEHAVIOR --A SERIES (J)	LEART
DATING RELATIONS · MATURE LOVE--A SERIES (J)	LEART
DATING RELATIONS · MIXED DATING--A SERIES (J)	LEART
DATING RELATIONS · POPULARITY--A SERIES (J)	LEART
DATING RELATIONS · ROMANCE AND PEOPLE--A SERIES (J)	LEART
DATING RELATIONS · THE FIRST DATE--A SERIES (J)	LEART
DIMENSIONS OF SEXUAL ATTRACTION · FEMALE (J)	LEART
DIMENSIONS OF SEXUAL ATTRACTION · MALE (J)	LEART
DOING THINGS (J)	LEART
DRINKING AND DATING (J)	LEART
FIRST DATE, THE · COSTS (J)	LEART
FIRST DATE, THE · GROUP ACTIVITIES (J)	LEART
FIRST DATE, THE · HOW (J)	LEART
FIRST DATE, THE · WHAT TO DO (J)	LEART
FIRST DATE, THE · WHO (J)	LEART
FRIENDLINESS (J)	LEART
IDEAL AND YOUR PARENTS (J)	LEART
IDEAL FEMALE (J)	LEART
IDEAL MALE (J)	LEART
IDEALIZATION AND FANTASY (J)	LEART
INDIVIDUAL DIFFERENCES IN CAPACITY (J)	LEART
INFATUATION (J)	LEART
INTERACTION WITH PEOPLE (J)	LEART
INTRODUCTION OF ROMANCE (J)	LEART
INTRODUCTION TO LOVE (J)	LEART
LASTING LOVE (J)	LEART
LEARNING HOW TO SAY NO (J)	LEART
LEARNING HOW TO VARY THE TEMPO (J)	LEART
LOVE IS BOTH STURDY AND PERISHABLE (J)	LEART
MIXED DATING AMONG RACES (J)	LEART
MIXED DATING AMONG RELIGIONS (J)	LEART
NORMAL ATTRACTION OF THE SEXES, PT 1	LEART
NORMAL ATTRACTION OF THE SEXES, PT 2	LEART
PLAYING THE FIELD (J)	LEART
PSYCHOLOGICAL DIMENSIONS AND DATING BEHAVIOR (J)	LEART
SELF IMAGE (J)	LEART
SERIOUS-STEADY DATING (J)	LEART
SETTING STANDARDS ON DATES (J)	LEART
SEX AND DATING · CONSEQUENCES (J)	LEART
SEX AND DATING · GUILT AND SHAME (J)	LEART
SEX AND DATING · REPUTATION (J)	LEART
STEADY DATES (J)	LEART
SUMMARY OF DATING CATEGORIES (J)	LEART
SUMMARY OF DATING PROBLEMS (J)	LEART
SUMMARY OF ROMANTIC LOVE (J)	LEART
SURFACE APPEAL (J)	LEART
TRAITS OF POPULARITY (J)	LEART
WHAT IS ROMANTIC LOVE (J)	LEART

EDUCATIONAL

(FILMSTRIPS)

COLLEGE · IT'S UP TO YOU, PT 1 (H)	GA
COLLEGE · IT'S UP TO YOU, PT 2 (H)	GA
COLLEGE--A SERIES (H)	GA
IMPROVING YOUR STUDY SKILLS, SET 1 · USING THE TEXTBOOK PLAN--A SERIES	CREATV
IMPROVING YOUR STUDY SKILLS, SET 2 · INTENSIVE READING--A SERIES	CREATV
IMPROVING YOUR STUDY SKILLS, SET 3 · INTENSIVE READING EXERCISES--A SERIES	CREATV
TAKING CARE OF THINGS AROUND ME BOOKS	BFA
WHAT TO EXPECT AT COLLEGE, PT 1 (H)	GA
WHAT TO EXPECT AT COLLEGE, PT 2 (H)	GA
WHICH COLLEGE FOR YOU, PT 1 (H)	GA
WHICH COLLEGE FOR YOU, PT 2 (H)	GA

(MOTION PICTURES)

COLLEGE DAZE	AMERFI
MEN FROM THE BOYS, THE	MTP
WAY FOR DIANA, A (I-J)	AIMS

(VIDEOTAPES)

YOUR FUTURE IS NOW--A SERIES	GPITVL

(AUDIO TAPES)

COLLEGE OR JOB	BASCH
MOVING · NEW SCHOOL, NEW PLAYMATES	BASCH
SCHOOL DROP OUT	BASCH

WHAT IS A BOOK (I-J)	INSKY
WHAT SHALL WE LISTEN TO (J-C)	IU

(TRANSPARENCIES)

DICTIONARY SKILLS--A SERIES	BOW
HOW TO STUDY--A SERIES	BETECL
LIBRARY SKILLS--A SERIES	BOW

EMPLOYMENT

(MOTION PICTURES)

ANYTHING YOU WANT TO BE (J-C A)	EDDDW
CAREERS IN LARGE INDUSTRY	VOFI
I WANT TO WORK FOR YOUR COMPANY (H-C A)	SAIF
OPPORTUNITIES FOR THE DISADVANTAGED (J-H)	AMEDFL
OPPORTUNITIES IN HOTELS AND MOTELS	USNAC
OPPORTUNITIES IN WELDING	USNAC
THAT JOB INTERVIEW	USNAC
YOUR NEW JOB (H-C A)	SAIF

(TRANSPARENCIES)

APPLICATION LETTER	COF
CARD OF INTRODUCTION (SAMPLE)	COF
COMPARE VIEWPOINTS	COF
DATA SHEET	COF
DURING THE INTERVIEW	COF
EMPLOYEE'S WITHHOLDING EXEMPTION CERTIFICATE	COF
GET ACQUAINTED WITH YOURSELF	COF
INTERVIEW RATING SHEET	COF
JOB APPLICATION AND JOB INTERVIEW--A SERIES	COF
JOB APPLICATION FORM	COF
OVERVIEW OF JOB APPLICATION AND JOB INTERVIEW	COF
PREPARATION	COF
RELATED ITEMS FOR CLASSROOM DISCUSSION	COF
SOCIAL SECURITY AND TAX ACCOUNT NUMBER	COF
TIPS FOR THE INTERVIEW	COF

HOME AND FAMILY

(FILMSTRIPS)

LIVING IN AFRICA TODAY · A CITY FAMILY OF MOROCCO (P-I)	CORF
LIVING IN AFRICA TODAY · A CITY FAMILY OF MALI (P-I)	CORF
LIVING IN AFRICA TODAY · A SUBURBAN FAMILY OF SOUTH AFRICA (P-I)	CORF
LIVING IN AFRICA TODAY · A VILLAGE FAMILY OF THE UPPER VOLTA (P-I)	CORF
LIVING IN AFRICA TODAY · A VILLAGE FAMILY OF MALI (P-I)	CORF
LIVING IN AFRICA TODAY · A VILLAGE FAMILY OF ZAIRE (P-I)	CORF
LIVING IN AFRICA TODAY · A WHITE FARM FAMILY OF KENYA (P-I)	CORF
LIVING IN ASIA TODAY · ON THE ISLAND OF BALI IN INDONESIA (P-I)	CORF

(MOTION PICTURES)

BIRTH (H-C A)	VERITE
BIRTH (H-C A)	VERITE
CRIME IN THE HOME (J-C A)	AIMS
CRIME ON THE STREETS (J-C A)	AIMS
DECIDING (P-I)	CENTEF
EDUCATION FOR FAMILY LIFE (H-C A)	CHM
EXECUTIVE'S WIFE, THE (A)	UEUWIS
FAIR CHANCE (H-C A)	DATA
FIRE SAFETY · HALL OF FLAME (P-I)	SAGENA
GRANDMOTHER, THE	AMERFI
SHOW ME THE WAY TO GO HOME	MTP
THREE FAMILIES OF MALAYSIA (I)	CORF
WHEN EVERY MINUTE COUNTS	MTP

(VIDEOTAPES)

CHANGING THE CHILD'S RELATIONSHIPS AND GOALS	GPITVL
CLARIFICATION OF BASIC PRINCIPLES	GPITVL
CONSEQUENCES	GPITVL
DOUGLAS	GPITVL
EDWARD	GPITVL
ENCOURAGEMENT	GPITVL
LOGICAL CONSEQUENCES AND PUNISHMENT	GPITVL
MOTIVATING CHILDREN TO LEARN · SUMMARY	GPITVL

(AUDIO TAPES)

FAMILY SURVIVORS OF SUICIDE	SIGINF
IT TAKES A WOMAN--A SERIES	BASCH

MOVING - NEW HOME, NEW NEIGHBORHOOD — BASCH
RIGHT TO FREEDOM, THE (H A) — WNAD

(TRANSPARENCIES)

ADOLESCENT CHANGE (H) — BOW
FAMILY OF CHILDREN (K-P) — LEART
GENERAL TOPICS--A SERIES (H) — BOW
HEREDITY (BASIC) (H) — BOW
MOM AND ME (K-P) — LEART
OVUM AND SPERM PHOTO (H) — BOW
SINGLE FULL-TERM FETUS (X-RAY) (H) — BOW
TWIN X-RAY (H) — BOW
TWINS (H) — BOW
TYPES OF FAMILIES (J-H) — LEART

INTERVIEWING

(MOTION PICTURES)

I WANT TO WORK FOR YOUR COMPANY (H-C A) — SAIF
THAT JOB INTERVIEW — USNAC

(TRANSPARENCIES)

APPLICATION LETTER — COF
CARD OF INTRODUCTION (SAMPLE) — COF
COMPARE VIEWPOINTS — COF
DATA SHEET — COF
DURING THE INTERVIEW — COF
EMPLOYEE'S WITHHOLDING EXEMPTION CERTIFICATE — COF
GET ACQUAINTED WITH YOURSELF — COF
INTERVIEW RATING SHEET — COF
JOB APPLICATION AND JOB INTERVIEW--A SERIES — COF
JOB APPLICATION FORM — COF
OVERVIEW OF JOB APPLICATION AND JOB INTERVIEW — COF
PREPARATION — COF
RELATED ITEMS FOR CLASSROOM DISCUSSION — COF
SOCIAL SECURITY AND TAX ACCOUNT NUMBER — COF
TIPS FOR THE INTERVIEW — COF

PERSONAL

(FILMSTRIPS)

APPETITE OF A BIRD — FI
ARE SEX AND LOVE THE SAME THING — EGH
ATTITUDES ABOUT HUMAN SEXUALITY — EGH
COLLEGE - IT'S UP TO YOU, PT 1 (H) — GA
COLLEGE - IT'S UP TO YOU, PT 2 (H) — GA
COLLEGE--A SERIES (H) — GA
DATING DATA (J-C A) — RMI
DOCTOR'S VIEWPOINT — EGH
DRUGS AND YOUR FUTURE — EGH
ECOLOGY OF OUR BODIES — EGH
EXPLORING CAREERS, GROUP 1--A SERIES (I-C) — SVE
FACE FACTS — EGH
FACE FACTS (J-C A) — RMI
FASHION FORMULAS (J-C A) — RMI
FEMALE OF THE SPECIES, THE — EGH
FIGURE FACTS — EGH
FINDING WHAT'S RIGHT FOR YOU — EGH
GOING TO THE DOCTOR, DENTIST AND HOSPITAL--A SERIES — EGH
GOOD GROOMING (J-C A) — RMI
HISTORY OF STYLE AND VOGUE, A — EGH
HOT TIPS ON BASIC BEAUTY, FASHION, GROOMING AND DATING--A SERIES (J-C A) — RMI
HUMAN SEXUALITY--A SERIES — EGH
LET'S LOOK AT DRUGS--A SERIES — EGH
LEWIS-LIES-A-LOT — EGH
LOOKING GREAT ON A SHOESTRING--A SERIES — EGH
MARIJUANA, STIMULANTS AND DEPRESSANTS — EGH
MARRIAGE AND FAMILIES — EGH
MILES MUGWUMP AND FRANNIE FRANTIC — EGH
MODELING MANNERS (J-C A) — RMI
NOW YOU ARE A VOTER--A SERIES — EGH
OOPSIES, THE — PHOTO
OUR INSTINCTS AND WHY WE HAVE THEM — EGH
PERSONALITY PLUS (J-C A) — RMI
PUTTING IT TOGETHER SO IT WORKS — EGH
TAKING CARE OF THINGS AROUND ME - BOOKS — BFA
TRY, TRY AGAIN — EGH
WHAT TO EXPECT AT COLLEGE, PT 1 (H) — GA
WHAT TO EXPECT AT COLLEGE, PT 2 (H) — GA
WHICH COLLEGE FOR YOU, PT 1 (H) — GA
WHICH COLLEGE FOR YOU, PT 2 (H) — GA

(MOTION PICTURES)

A TO B — AMERFI

ADOLESCENCE AND SEXUAL IDENTITY (H-C A) — CHM
ALADDIN — PUI
ALCOHOL - HOW MUCH IS TOO MUCH (I) — AIMS
ALCOHOL - OUR NUMBER ONE DRUG (I-H) — OF
ALCOHOL PROBLEM, THE - WHAT DO YOU THINK (I-C) — EBEC
ALI BABA — PUI
ANN, A PORTRAIT — AMERFI
AUTUMN FIRE — MGHT
BEACH PARTY, THE — PAULST
BERKELEY CHRISTMAS, A — AMERFI
BILL OF RIGHTS IN ACTION - THE PRIVILEGE AGAINST SELF-INCRIMINATION (I-C A) — WILETS
CAUGHT (J-C) — NRMA
CHANGES, CHANGES (K-P) — WWS
CHECK IT OUT (J-H A) — NEWD
COLLEGE DAZE — AMERFI
CRIME ON THE STREETS (J-C A) — AIMS
DECIDING (P-I) — CENTEF
DEPENDENCE - A NEW DEFINITION (C A) — CRMP
DRUG PROBLEM, THE - WHAT DO YOU THINK (J-H) — EBEC
DRUMMER BOY, THE — PUI
EDUCATION FOR FAMILY LIFE (H-C A) — CHM
ENJOYING YOUR CONTACT LENSES (PRO) — DATA
FAIRY TALE TIME--A SERIES — PUI
FINDING YOURSELF AND YOUR JOB (J-C) — AMEDFL
FLYING TRUNK, THE — PUI
FRANKENSTEIN IN A FISHBOWL — AMERFI
GOLDEN BIRD, THE — PUI
GOLDEN GOOSE, THE — PUI
GOLDEN TOUCH, THE — PUI
GRANDMOTHER, THE — AMERFI
HANSEL AND GRETEL — PUI
HOW TO MAKE A WOMAN (C A) — POLYMR
I WANNA BE READY (C A) — AIMS
IMPLOSION — AMERFI
LEFT, RIGHT MOVIE, THE (K-P S) — GRADYM
LEO THE LION-HEARTED — PUI
LOVE'S BEGINNINGS (P) — CAHILL
PICKLES (H-C A) — BFA
PICTURE, THE — AMERFI
RAPUNZEL — PUI
RUMPELSTILTSKIN — PUI
SEARCH FOR ALTERNATE LIFE-STYLES AND PHILOSOPHIES, THE (J-C A) — FLMFR
SENSE OF RESPONSIBILITY, A (I-C) — BFA
SINBAD — PUI
SOLDIER AND THE DRAGON, THE — PUI
TAILOR'S ADVENTURE, THE — PUI
TIN SOLDIER, THE — PUI
WAY FOR DIANA, A (I-J) — AIMS
WELL OF WISDOM, THE — PUI
WHAT FIXED ME — AMERFI
WHAT WOULD YOU DO (P-I) — ATLAP
WHATEVER IS FUN (P-J) — CCMFI
WHERE'S THE TROUBLE (K-P) — GRADYM
WORLD'S GREATEST FREAK SHOW, THE (P-I) — XEROX
YOU (P-I) — CENTEF

(VIDEOTAPES)

BECAUSE IT'S FUN — NITC
HOW DO YOU SHOW — NITC

(AUDIO TAPES)

ADOLESCENCE — BASCH
ALCOHOLISM — BASCH
BECOMING A PARENT — BASCH
CAREER WIFE — BASCH
COLLEGE OR JOB — BASCH
DISCONTENTED HOUSEWIFE — BASCH
INFIDELITY — BASCH
INSECURITY — BASCH
IT TAKES A WOMAN--A SERIES — BASCH
MOVIES — BASCH
MOVING - NEW HOME, NEW NEIGHBORHOOD — BASCH
MOVING - NEW SCHOOL, NEW PLAYMATES — BASCH
ON BECOMING IN-LAWS — BASCH
ON BEING WIDOWED — BASCH
OUR EMOTIONS — BASCH
SCHOOL DROP OUT — BASCH
SOUND OF THE WAY YOU LOOK, THE (I-J) — MINNOE
TOO YOUNG TO MARRY — BASCH
WHAT MAKES A HAPPY MARRIAGE — BASCH
WHAT'S YOUR PROBLEM--A SERIES — BASCH

(TRANSPARENCIES)

APPAREL AND POSTURE AFFECT YOUR ATTITUDE — COF
ATTITUDES (H) — LEART
BABY AND ME (K-P) — LEART
BABY FOR A YEAR (K-P) — LEART
BASIS OF ROMANTIC IDEAL (J) — LEART
BEING YOURSELF (J) — LEART

BREAKING OFF (J) — LEART
CARS AND DATES (J) — LEART
CLEANLINESS INFLUENCES HEALTH — LEART
COMPLEXITY OF LOVE (J) — LEART
DAD AND ME (K-P) — LEART
DAILY SCHEDULE FOR GOOD GROOMING, A — COF
DATING AND PARTYING — LEART
DATING RELATIONS - DATING CATEGORIES--A SERIES (J) — LEART
DATING RELATIONS - DATING PROBLEMS--A SERIES (J) — LEART
DATING RELATIONS - DIMENSIONS OF DATING--A SERIES (J) — LEART
DATING RELATIONS - EVALUATING DATING BEHAVIOR --A SERIES (J) — LEART
DATING RELATIONS - MATURE LOVE--A SERIES (J) — LEART
DATING RELATIONS - POPULARITY--A SERIES (J) — LEART
DATING RELATIONS - ROMANCE AND PEOPLE--A SERIES (J) — LEART
DATING RELATIONS - THE FIRST DATE--A SERIES (J) — LEART
DIMENSIONS OF SEXUAL ATTRACTION - FEMALE (J) — LEART
DIMENSIONS OF SEXUAL ATTRACTION - MALE (J) — LEART
DIVERGENCE OF ATTITUDES OF ADULTS LIVING ON YOUR BLOCK (H) — LEART
DOES GOOD GROOMING PAY OFF — COF
DOING THINGS (J) — LEART
DRESS FOR THE WEATHER — LEART
DRINKING AND DATING (J) — LEART
EMOTION AND BODY FUNCTIONS — LEART
EMOTIONS AND SOCIAL ATTITUDES - ATTITUDES, VALUES--A SERIES (H) — LEART
EXERCISE AND ACTIVITIES — LEART
FAVORITE THINGS (K-P) — LEART
FOOD AFFECTS GROWTH — LEART
FOOD, FUN, REST (K-P) — LEART
FRIENDLINESS (J) — LEART
GOOD GROOMING GAME A — COF
GOOD GROOMING GAME B — COF
GOOD GROOMING RULES — COF
GOOD GROOMING--A SERIES — COF
HOW DO YOU MEASURE UP, NO. 1 — COF
HOW DO YOU MEASURE UP, NO. 2 — COF
HOW EMOTIONS ARE EXPRESSED — LEART
IDEAL AND YOUR PARENTS (J) — LEART
IDEAL FEMALE (J) — LEART
IDEAL MALE (J) — LEART
IDEALIZATION AND FANTASY (J) — LEART
IMPORTANCE OF A PLEASANT FACE AND VOICE — , COF
INDIVIDUAL DIFFERENCES IN CAPACITY (J) — LEART
INFATUATION (J) — LEART
INTERACTION WITH PEOPLE (J) — LEART
INTRODUCTION OF ROMANCE (J) — LEART
INTRODUCTION TO LOVE (J) — LEART
ITEMS FOR THE WORKING GIRL'S HANDBAG — COF
ITEMS TO BE CARRIED BY THE WORKING MAN — COF
JOB REQUIREMENTS IN DRESS — COF
LASTING LOVE (J) — LEART
LEARNING HOW TO SAY NO (J) — LEART
LEARNING HOW TO VARY THE TEMPO (J) — LEART
LIFE SCIENCE - GROWING UP--A SERIES (K-P) — LEART
LOVE IS BOTH STURDY AND PERISHABLE (J) — LEART
MOM AND ME (K-P) — LEART
NARROW VS BROAD EXPERIMENTATION IN ATTITUDES (H) — LEART
NORMAL ATTRACTION OF THE SEXES, PT 1 — LEART
NORMAL ATTRACTION OF THE SEXES, PT 2 — LEART
PROPER SLEEP IS IMPORTANT TO HEALTH — LEART
PSYCHOLOGICAL DIMENSIONS AND DATING BEHAVIOR (J) — LEART
SELECTING A HAIR STYLE — COF
SELECTING CLOTHING FOR YOUR BUDGET — COF
SELF IMAGE (J) — LEART
SETTING STANDARDS ON DATES (J) — LEART
SEX AND DATING - CONSEQUENCES (J) — LEART
SEX AND DATING - GUILT AND SHAME (J) — LEART
SEX AND DATING - REPUTATION (J) — LEART
SEX EDUCATION - DEVELOPMENT OF CONCEPTS AND ATTITUDES--A SERIES — LEART
SEX EDUCATION - PHYSICAL CARE AND SELF RESPECT--A SERIES — LEART
SOURCE OF ATTITUDES OF THE HIGH SCHOOL PERSON (H) — LEART
STEADY DATES (J) — LEART
SUMMARY OF DATING PROBLEMS (J) — LEART
SUMMARY OF GOOD GROOMING FACTORS, PT 1 — COF
SUMMARY OF GOOD GROOMING FACTORS, PT 2 — COF

SUMMARY OF ROMANTIC LOVE (J)	LEART
SURFACE APPEAL (J)	LEART
TASTES (H)	LEART
TRAITS OF POPULARITY (J)	LEART
UNDERSTANDING MALENESS AND FEMALENESS	LEART
UNDERSTANDING SEXUALITY	LEART
VALUES IN THE ADULT (H)	LEART
WEEKLY SCHEDULE FOR GOOD GROOMING, A	COF
WELL-DRESSED YOUNG WORKING MAN, THE	COF
WELL-DRESSED YOUNG WORKING WOMAN, THE	COF
WHAT IS ROMANTIC LOVE (J)	LEART
WHAT MAKES PERSONALITIES DIFFERENT	LEART
YOUR ATTITUDE IN FIVE YEARS (H)	LEART

PERSONNEL MANAGEMENT

(FILMSTRIPS)

HOSPITAL ADMINISTRATION	EGH

(MOTION PICTURES)

MULTIPLE CHOICE (J-C A)	INDSLF
OPPORTUNITIES IN HOTELS AND MOTELS	USNAC
OPPORTUNITIES IN WELDING	USNAC

PERSONNEL SERVICE, EDUCATION

(TRANSPARENCIES)

JOB APPLICATION AND JOB INTERVIEW--A SERIES	COF

PROFESSIONS

(FILMSTRIPS)

HOSPITAL ADMINISTRATION	EGH
LIVING IN AFRICA TODAY - A PROFESSIONAL OF GHANA (P-I)	CORF

(MOTION PICTURES)

ANYTHING YOU WANT TO BE (J-C A)	EDDDW
NEVER UNDERESTIMATE THE POWER OF A WOMAN (H-C)	UEUWIS
UNIVERSE AND OTHER THINGS, THE	MTP

(TRANSPARENCIES)

JOB APPLICATION AND JOB INTERVIEW--A SERIES	COF

SOCIAL

(FILMSTRIPS)

AMERICAN GENIUS, 1960 - 1970 (H-C)	EDDIM
APPETITE OF A BIRD	FI
ARE SEX AND LOVE THE SAME THING	EGH
ATTITUDES ABOUT HUMAN SEXUALITY	EGH
COMICAL SITUATIONS OF EVERYDAY LIFE, PT 1 (J-H)	ALEP
COMICAL SITUATIONS OF EVERYDAY LIFE, PT 2 (J-H)	ALEP
CONCRETE CHARLEY DUMPLING	COMICO
FACES OF MAN (H-C A)	ARGSC
FEMALE OF THE SPECIES, THE	EGH
GUIDES FOR GROWING--A SERIES	EGH
HUMAN SEXUALITY--A SERIES	EGH
LET'S LOOK AT DRUGS--A SERIES	EGH
MAGICAL COQUI (P)	UMM
MARRIAGE AND FAMILIES	EGH
ONCE UPON A COMPULSION	KELLRP
OUR INSTINCTS AND WHY WE HAVE THEM	EGH
PRINCESS ECOL VISITS THE PLANET THRAE	EGH

(MOTION PICTURES)

A TO B	AMERFI
ALCOHOL - OUR NUMBER ONE DRUG (I-H)	OF
ALFRED	AMERFI
AUTUMN FIRE	MGHT
BASIC LAW TERMS (J-C A)	PFP
BEACH PARTY, THE	PAULST
BERKELEY CHRISTMAS, A	AMERFI
BROWN RICE	AMERFI
BY THE PEOPLE (J-C A)	FILIM
CAMPAIGN (H-C)	CF
COLLEGE DAZE	AMERFI
COPING IN SPECIAL EDUCATION - SOCIALIZATION (C)	UEUWIS
CORRECT TELEPHONE COURTESY	BEF
DIAL V FOR VOTES (C A)	DATA
DRUG PROBLEM, THE - WHAT DO YOU THINK (J-H)	EBEC

EVOLUTION	LCOA
FACES (K-P)	SCHLAT
FAIR CHANCE (H-C A)	DATA
FAIRY TALE TIME--A SERIES	PUI
FRANKENSTEIN IN A FISHBOWL	AMERFI
IMPLOSION	AMERFI
INTERVIEW WITH GARRETT HARDIN (J-C A)	HRAW
IT HAPPENED IN HUALFIN, PT 1 - WHEN THE WIND IS SILENT	PIC
JUNIOR FIREMEN	LACFD
KEEP COOL (J-C)	BFA
LOVE AND FILM (H-C A)	BFA
LOVE'S BEGINNINGS (P)	CAHILL
MISTER MAGROOTER'S MARVELOUS MACHINE (I-C A)	BOSUST
OUT OF HANDS (P-I)	HRAW
PARK ON OUR BLOCK, A (J-C A)	WASHBF
PERSON TO PERSON - MAKING COMMUNICATIONS WORK FOR YOU (H-C A)	SAIF
PICTURE, THE	AMERFI
PORCH GLIDER	AMERFI
SEVENTH MANDARIN, THE (I)	XEROX
STILL	AMERFI
STRAWBERRIES - WITH CREAM	MTP
SURVIVAL OF SPACESHIP EARTH	WB
THEORIST ROOM	AMERFI
TO BE A FRIEND (J-H)	BBF
TUB FILM (J-C A)	BFA
TUP TUP (J-C A)	BFA
WHAT DO WE LOOK LIKE TO OTHERS (H-C A)	SAIF
WHAT FIXED ME	AMERFI
WHAT WOULD YOU DO (P-I)	ATLAP
WHATEVER IS FUN (P-J)	CCMFI
YOUR NEW JOB (H-C A)	SAIF

(AUDIO TAPES)

COMPASSION - TOWARD A SCIENCE OF VALUE--A SERIES	SIGINF
ON BECOMING IN-LAWS	BASCH
SUN SHINES BRIGHT, THE (H A)	USOE
WHAT'S YOUR PROBLEM--A SERIES	BASCH
YANKEE DOODLEBUG AND THE AW-THAT'S NOTHIN' (P-I)	UTEX

(TRANSPARENCIES)

ATTITUDES (H)	LEART
BASIC SOCIAL STUDIES CONCEPTS - SOCIETY--A SERIES (J-H)	LEART
BEING YOURSELF (J)	LEART
DATING RELATIONS - DATING CATEGORIES--A SERIES (J)	LEART
DATING RELATIONS - DATING PROBLEMS--A SERIES (J)	LEART
DATING RELATIONS - DIMENSIONS OF DATING--A SERIES (J)	LEART
DATING RELATIONS - EVALUATING DATING BEHAVIOR --A SERIES (J)	LEART
DATING RELATIONS - MATURE LOVE--A SERIES (J)	LEART
DATING RELATIONS - MIXED DATING--A SERIES (J)	LEART
DATING RELATIONS - POPULARITY--A SERIES (J)	LEART
DATING RELATIONS - ROMANCE AND PEOPLE--A SERIES (J)	LEART
DATING RELATIONS - THE FIRST DATE--A SERIES (J)	LEART
DIVERGENCE OF ATTITUDES OF ADULTS LIVING ON YOUR BLOCK (H)	LEART
DOING THINGS (J)	LEART
EMOTIONS AND SOCIAL ATTITUDES - ATTITUDES, VALUES--A SERIES (H)	LEART
FRIENDLINESS (H)	LEART
HOW DOES SOCIETY TEACH ITS VALUES (J-H)	LEART
INTERACTION WITH PEOPLE (J)	LEART
NARROW VS BROAD EXPERIMENTATION IN ATTITUDES (H)	LEART
PSYCHOLOGICAL DIMENSIONS AND DATING BEHAVIOR (J)	LEART
RELIGION AND SOCIETY (J-H)	LEART
SEX EDUCATION - DEVELOPMENT OF CONCEPTS AND ATTITUDES--A SERIES	LEART
SOURCE OF ATTITUDES OF THE HIGH SCHOOL PERSON (H)	LEART
SURFACE APPEAL (J)	LEART
TASTES (H)	LEART
TRAITS OF POPULARITY (J)	LEART
VALUES IN THE ADULT (H)	LEART
WHAT ARE SOCIAL VALUES AND NORMS (J-H)	LEART
WHAT IS A SOCIAL INSTITUTION (J-H)	LEART
WHAT IS A SOCIETY (J-H)	LEART
WHAT IS AN OPEN SOCIETY (J-H)	LEART
YOUR ATTITUDE IN FIVE YEARS (H)	LEART

VETERANS

(MOTION PICTURES)

THAT JOB INTERVIEW	USNAC

VOCATIONAL

(FILMSTRIPS)

AIRLINE CABIN ATTENDANT, THE (I-C)	SVE
AUTOMOTIVE MECHANIC, THE (I-C)	SVE
BROADCAST TECHNICIAN, THE (I-C)	SVE
DIET CLERK AND FRY COOK	EGH
EXPLORING CAREERS, GROUP 1--A SERIES (I-C)	SVE
FOOD SERVICE WORKER	EGH
HOSPITAL ADMINISTRATION	EGH
HOSPITAL JOB OPPORTUNITIES--A SERIES	EGH
INHALATION THERAPY TECHNICIAN	EGH
LONG HAUL TRUCK DRIVER, THE (I-C)	SVE
MAINTENANCE MECHANIC, ELECTRICIAN AND CUSTODIAN	EGH
MEDICAL ASSISTANT	EGH
NEWSPAPER REPORTER, THE (I-C)	SVE
NUCLEAR TECHNICIAN	EGH
NURSE	EGH
NURSE'S AIDE	EGH
TELEPHONE INSTALLER, THE (I-C)	SVE
X-RAY TECHNICIAN	EGH

(MOTION PICTURES)

ANYTHING YOU WANT TO BE (J-C A)	EDDDW
CAREERS IN LARGE INDUSTRY	VOFI
FINDING YOURSELF AND YOUR JOB (J-C)	AMEDFL
FUTURE STREET - NEW DIRECTIONS IN CAREER EDUCATION A SERIES (J-C)	AMEDFL
FUTURES IN STEEL	MTP
I WANT TO WORK FOR YOUR COMPANY (H-C A)	SAIF
INTERN - A LONG YEAR (J-C)	EBEC
JOBS IN BAKING	USNAC
JOBS IN COSMETOLOGY	USNAC
MEN FROM THE BOYS, THE	MTP
NEVER UNDERESTIMATE THE POWER OF A WOMAN (H-C)	UEUWIS
OPPORTUNITIES FOR THE DISADVANTAGED (J-H)	AMEDFL
OPPORTUNITIES IN HOTELS AND MOTELS	USNAC
OPPORTUNITIES IN LOGGING	RARIG
OPPORTUNITIES IN WELDING	USNAC
OUT OF HANDS (P-I)	HRAW
THAT JOB INTERVIEW	USNAC
UNIVERSE AND OTHER THINGS, THE	MTP
WHAT IS BUSINESS (H-C A)	SAIF
WHAT'S IT ALL ABOUT, HARRY (IND)	DATA
YOUR NEW JOB (H-C A)	SAIF

(VIDEOTAPES)

ADDRESSING ENVELOPES - ATTENTION AND SUBJECT LINES	GPITVL
BOUND MANUSCRIPTS WITH FOOTNOTES	GPITVL
DATA PROCESSING, UNIT 4 - APPLICATIONS AND CAREER OPPORTUNITIES--A SERIES	GPITVL
INTER-OFFICE MEMORANDUM FORMS	GPITVL
INVOICE AND TELEGRAM FORMS - CARBONS	GPITVL
PLAIN AND FILL-IN POSTAL CARDS	GPITVL
REVIEW - LETTERS, FORMS, REPORTS	GPITVL
REVISION MARKS, UNBOUND REPORTS, HOW TO ERASE	GPITVL
SELECTIVE PRACTICE - CENTERING ON LINE	GPITVL
SELECTIVE PRACTICE - CORRECTIONS	GPITVL
SELECTIVE PRACTICE - INSERTIONS	GPITVL
TYPEWRITING, UNIT 6 - SKILL DEVELOPMENT--A SERIES	GPITVL
TYPEWRITING, UNIT 7 - POSTAL CARDS, FORMS, MANUSCRIPTS--A SERIES	GPITVL

(AUDIO TAPES)

CAREER WIFE	BASCH
COLLEGE OR JOB	BASCH

(TRANSPARENCIES)

APPLICATION LETTER	COF
CARD OF INTRODUCTION (SAMPLE)	COF
COMPARE VIEWPOINTS	COF
DATA SHEET	COF
DURING THE INTERVIEW	COF
EMPLOYEE'S WITHHOLDING EXEMPTION CERTIFICATE	COF
GET ACQUAINTED WITH YOURSELF	COF
INTERVIEW RATING SHEET	COF
JOB APPLICATION AND JOB INTERVIEW--A SERIES	COF

JOB APPLICATION FORM COF
OVERVIEW OF JOB APPLICATION AND
JOB INTERVIEW COF
PREPARATION COF
RELATED ITEMS FOR CLASSROOM
DISCUSSION COF
SOCIAL SECURITY AND TAX ACCOUNT
NUMBER COF
TIPS FOR THE INTERVIEW COF

WELFARE

(MOTION PICTURES)

ALFRED AMERFI
SRO (SINGLE ROOM OCCUPANCY) (H-C
A) CAROUF

HEALTH AND SAFETY

ALCOHOL

(FILMSTRIPS)

ALCOHOL - PARENTS AND THEIR
POTIONS (P-I) EBEC
ALCOHOL AND TOBACCO EGH
DECISION IS YOURS, THE NAVA

(MOTION PICTURES)

ALCOHOL - HOW MUCH IS TOO MUCH
(I) AIMS
ALCOHOL - OUR NUMBER ONE DRUG (I-
H) OF
ALCOHOL PROBLEM, THE - WHAT DO
YOU THINK (I-C) EBEC
ALCOHOLISM - A MODEL OF DRUG
DEPENDENCY (C A) CRMP
ROLE OF YEAST IWANMI

(AUDIO TAPES)

ALCOHOLISM BASCH
DEFINITION OF ALCOHOLISM, THE SIGINF
PSYCHIATRY AND THE LAW -
ALCOHOLISM - DRUG ABUSE SIGINF

(TRANSPARENCIES)

DRINKING AND DATING (J) LEART

DENTAL CARE

(FILMSTRIPS)

BRUSHING AWAY TOOTH DECAY (P-I) DISNEY
CASE OF THE CROOKED TEETH, THE (P-
I) DISNEY
GOING TO THE DENTIST EGH
MAGIC POTION, THE (P-I) DISNEY
MEET YOUR TEETH (P-I) DISNEY
PRACTICING GOOD HEALTH, SET 2
- YOUR MOUTH SPEAKING--A
SERIES (P-I) DISNEY
SAFETY OF THE MOUTH (P-I) DISNEY
TALE OF TWO TEETH, A (P-I) DISNEY
WHY VISIT THE DENTIST (P-I) DISNEY

(MOTION PICTURES)

D IS FOR DENTIST (K-P) AMDA
DENTAL CARE UNDER GENERAL
ANAESTHESIA FOR THE
CEREBRAL PALSIED PATIENT (C A) RARIG

(VIDEOTAPES)

DENTAL HEALTH--A SERIES (P-I) GPITVL
KEEP IT CLEAN (P-I) GPITVL
KID, YOU'VE GOT A DIRTY MOUTH (P-I) GPITVL
SALLY HAD A SWEET TOOTH, NOW IT'S
GONE (P-I) GPITVL
WINNING TEAM, THE (P-I) GPITVL

DENTISTRY

(FILMSTRIPS)

GOING TO THE DENTIST EGH

(MOTION PICTURES)

ANIMAL TEETH IWANMI
D IS FOR DENTIST (K-P) AMDA
DENTAL CARE UNDER GENERAL
ANAESTHESIA FOR THE
CEREBRAL PALSIED PATIENT (C A) RARIG

(VIDEOTAPES)

DENTAL HEALTH--A SERIES (P-I) GPITVL
KEEP IT CLEAN (P-I) GPITVL

KID, YOU'VE GOT A DIRTY MOUTH (P-I) GPITVL
SALLY HAD A SWEET TOOTH, NOW IT'S
GONE (P-I) GPITVL
WINNING TEAM, THE (P-I) GPITVL

DIET

(FILMSTRIPS)

DIET CLERK AND FRY COOK EGH
FOOD SERVICE WORKER EGH
OOPSIES, THE PHOTO

(MOTION PICTURES)

EARTHBREAD - A NATURAL FOOD (I-C) FPRD

(VIDEOTAPES)

DENTAL HEALTH--A SERIES (P-I) GPITVL
KEEP IT CLEAN (P-I) GPITVL
KID, YOU'VE GOT A DIRTY MOUTH (P-I) GPITVL
SALLY HAD A SWEET TOOTH, NOW IT'S
GONE (P-I) GPITVL
WINNING TEAM, THE (P-I) GPITVL

DRIVER EDUCATION

(FILMSTRIPS)

DECISION IS YOURS, THE NAVA

(MOTION PICTURES)

CRITICAL DRIVING PATTERNS FMCMP
DRIVER EDUCATION--A SERIES FMCMP
DRIVING IN TRAFFIC FMCMP
RURAL DRIVING FMCMP

FIRST AID

(FILMSTRIPS)

HAVING STITCHES AND GETTING A
CAST EGH
MEDICAL ASSISTANT EGH
NUCLEAR TECHNICIAN EGH
X-RAY TECHNICIAN EGH

MEDICINE

(FILMSTRIPS)

CANCER, SERIES 3 - TREATMENT
MODALITIES WITH IMPLICATIONS
FOR NURSING CARE--A SERIES CONMED
CHEMOTHERAPY CONMED
COLOSTOMY CONMED
DIET CLERK AND FRY COOK EGH
FOOD SERVICE WORKER EGH
GOING INTO THE HOSPITAL EGH
GOING TO THE DOCTOR EGH
GUIDE TO WHEELCHAIR TRANSFER
TECHNIQUES, A KRI
HAVING AN OPERATION EGH
HAVING STITCHES AND GETTING A
CAST EGH
HEAD AND NECK SURGERY CONMED
HEALTH SERVICES IN CHINA EGH
HOSPITAL ADMINISTRATION EGH
HOSPITAL SAFETY--A SERIES (PRO) TRNAID
HYSTERECTOMY FOR UTERINE CANCER CONMED
INHALATION THERAPY TECHNICIAN EGH
INTRODUCTION TO CANCER SURGERY -
MASTECTOMY CONMED
MAINTENANCE MECHANIC, ELECTRICIAN
AND CUSTODIAN EGH
MEDICAL ASSISTANT EGH
MEDICINE - PEOPLE AND PILLS (P-I) EBEC
NEUROSCIENCES DAUNDW
NUCLEAR TECHNICIAN EGH
NURSE EGH
NURSE'S AIDE EGH
RADIOTHERAPY I CONMED
RADIOTHERAPY II CONMED
WHAT YOU WILL FIND IN A HOSPITAL EGH
X-RAY TECHNICIAN EGH

(MOTION PICTURES)

BIOENGINEERS, THE USNAC
CAPRI PROGRAM, THE (C A) SAFECO
CLINICAL EVALUATION OF THE
JUGULAR VENOUS PULSE (PRO) AMEDA
DOCTOR IN THE DESERT ALDEN
FRANKENSTEIN IN A FISHBOWL AMERFI
HEART, THE - ATTACK CRMP
INTERN - A LONG YEAR (J-C) EBEC
MIMI (J-C A) BBF
MOSQUITO IWANMI
QUICK BILLY AMERFI
WORK OF GOMIS, THE (J-C A) WASHBF

(AUDIO TAPES)

BIBLIOGRAPHY - HOW TO STUDY
FOR BOARDS - SAMPLE
EXAMINATIONS SIGINF
CLINICAL ASPECTS OF THE
PSYCHIATRIC MANAGEMENT OF
BURNED AND DISFIGURED CHILDREN SIGINF
HOSPITAL MANAGEMENT OF
DISTURBED ADOLESCENTS, THE,
PT 1 SIGINF
HOSPITAL MANAGEMENT OF
DISTURBED ADOLESCENTS, THE,
PT 2 SIGINF
INFORMATION FOR CANDIDATES -
THE FORMAT OF WRITTEN AND
ORAL EXAMINATIONS - HOW TO
TAKE... SIGINF
PREPARATION FOR CERTIFICATION
BY THE AMERICAN BOARD OF
PSYCHIATRY AND NEUROLOGY--A
SERIES SIGINF
SAMPLE EXAMINATIONS - THE
CONCEPT OF SCHIZOPHRENIA SIGINF
SCHIZOPHRENIA - THE CONCEPT
OF NEUROSIS AND PSYCHOSIS -
SPECIFIC NEUROSES SIGINF
SPECIFIC NEUROSES - SPECIFIC
PSYCHOSES - THE CONCEPT OF
DEPRESSION SIGINF
SUICIDE - HOMICIDE - THE
CONCEPT OF
PSYCHOPHYSIOLOGIC DISORDERS SIGINF
TO DIE THAT OTHERS MAY LIVE (I) MINSA

MENTAL HYGIENE

(MOTION PICTURES)

FRAGILE EGOS (H-C A) WGBH
INTRODUCTION TO PSYCHOTHERAPY,
AN (PRO) VIDEOG

NARCOTICS

(FILMSTRIPS)

DOCTOR'S VIEWPOINT EGH
DRUGS - A TRICK, A TRAP--A SERIES EBEC
DRUGS AND CHILDREN, PT 1 (I) EDLACT
DRUGS AND CHILDREN, PT 2 (I) EDLACT
DRUGS AND YOUR FUTURE EGH
ECOLOGY OF OUR BODIES EGH
HARD DRUGS, THE - THE BOTTOM OF
THE TRAP (P-I) EBEC
LET'S LOOK AT DRUGS--A SERIES EGH
MARIJUANA AND GLUE - KIDS, TRICKS
AND TRAPS (P-I) EBEC
MARIJUANA, STIMULANTS AND
DEPRESSANTS EGH
MARY JANE AND BUTTERFLY EGH
MEDICINE - PEOPLE AND PILLS (P-I) EBEC

(MOTION PICTURES)

DRUG PROBLEM, THE - WHAT DO YOU
THINK (J-H) EBEC
TAKING CARE OF BUSINESS AMERFI
WE HAVE AN ADDICT IN THE HOUSE
(J-C A) DOUBLE

(AUDIO TAPES)

DRUG ABUSE - SOMATIC
THERAPIES - PSYCHIATRIC
DISORDERS OF CHILDHOOD SIGINF
MANAGEMENT OF DRUG ABUSE IN
THE OUTPATIENT
PSYCHOTHERAPY OF ADOLESCENTS,
THE SIGINF
PATTERNS OF DRUG ABUSE
AMONG MIDDLE-CLASS
ADOLESCENTS SIGINF
PSYCHIATRY AND THE LAW -
ALCOHOLISM - DRUG ABUSE SIGINF
SOCIOLOGIC PERSPECTIVES OF THE
MARIJUANA CONTROVERSY SIGINF

(TRANSPARENCIES)

DEPRESSANTS (H) BOW
DRUG ABUSE--A SERIES (H) BOW
DRUGS AND THE LAW (H) BOW
GLUE SNIFFING (H) BOW
HALLUCINOGENIC DRUGS (H) BOW
MARIJUANA (H) BOW
NARCOTICS (H) BOW
STIMULANTS (H) BOW
USES AND ABUSES (H) BOW

PERSONAL HYGIENE

(FILMSTRIPS)

BRUSHING AWAY TOOTH DECAY (P-I) DISNEY

CASE OF THE CROOKED TEETH, THE (P-I) — DISNEY
DOCTOR'S VIEWPOINT — EGH
ECOLOGY OF OUR BODIES — EGH
GOING INTO THE HOSPITAL — EGH
GOING TO THE DENTIST — EGH
GOING TO THE DOCTOR — EGH
GOING TO THE DOCTOR, DENTIST AND HOSPITAL--A SERIES — EGH
HAVING AN OPERATION — EGH
HAVING STITCHES AND GETTING A CAST — EGH
MAGIC POTION, THE (P-I) — DISNEY
MARIJUANA, STIMULANTS AND DEPRESSANTS — EGH
MEET YOUR TEETH (P-I) — DISNEY
PRACTICING GOOD HEALTH, SET 2 - YOUR MOUTH SPEAKING--A SERIES (P-I) — DISNEY
SAFETY OF THE MOUTH (P-I) — DISNEY
TALE OF TWO TEETH, A (P-I) — DISNEY
WHAT YOU WILL FIND IN A HOSPITAL — EGH.
WHY VISIT THE DENTIST (P-I) — DISNEY

(MOTION PICTURES)

ALCOHOL - HOW MUCH IS TOO MUCH (I) — AIMS
ALCOHOL - OUR NUMBER ONE DRUG (I-H) — OF
ALCOHOLISM - A MODEL OF DRUG DEPENDENCY (C A) — CRMP
ENJOYING YOUR CONTACT LENSES (PRO) — DATA
LIFE AND HEALTH FILM--A SERIES — CRMP
NUTRITION - THE INNER ENVIRONMENT (P-J) — AMEDFL

(AUDIO TAPES)

SOUND OF THE WAY YOU LOOK, THE (I-J) — MINNOE

(TRANSPARENCIES)

CLEANLINESS INFLUENCES HEALTH — LEART
DRESS FOR THE WEATHER — LEART
EMOTION AND BODY FUNCTIONS — LEART
EXERCISE AND ACTIVITIES — LEART
FOOD AFFECTS GROWTH — LEART
FOOD, FUN, REST (K-P) — LEART
PROPER SLEEP IS IMPORTANT TO HEALTH — LEART
SEX EDUCATION - PHYSICAL CARE AND SELF RESPECT--A SERIES — LEART

PUBLIC HEALTH

(FILMSTRIPS)

CANCER, SERIES 3 - TREATMENT MODALITIES WITH IMPLICATIONS FOR NURSING CARE--A SERIES — CONMED
CHEMOTHERAPY — CONMED
COLOSTOMY — CONMED
DIET CLERK AND FRY COOK — EGH
FOOD SERVICE WORKER — EGH
GOING INTO THE HOSPITAL — EGH
GOING TO THE DOCTOR — EGH
HAVING AN OPERATION — EGH
HAVING STITCHES AND GETTING A CAST — EGH
HEAD AND NECK SURGERY — CONMED
HEALTH SERVICES IN CHINA — EGH
HOSPITAL ADMINISTRATION — EGH
HOSPITAL SAFETY--A SERIES (PRO) — TRNAID
HYSTERECTOMY FOR UTERINE CANCER — CONMED
INHALATION THERAPY TECHNICIAN — EGH
INTRODUCTION TO CANCER SURGERY - MASTECTOMY — CONMED
MAINTENANCE MECHANIC, ELECTRICIAN AND CUSTODIAN — EGH
MEDICAL ASSISTANT — EGH
NUCLEAR TECHNICIAN — EGH
NURSE — EGH
NURSE'S AIDE — EGH
RADIOTHERAPY I — CONMED
RADIOTHERAPY II — CONMED
WHAT YOU WILL FIND IN A HOSPITAL — EGH
X-RAY TECHNICIAN — EGH

(MOTION PICTURES)

CAPRI PROGRAM, THE (C A) — SAFECO
CHECK IT OUT (J-H A) — NEWD
DOCTOR IN THE DESERT — ALDEN
LOOK WHAT'S GOING AROUND (H-C A) — CF
MIMI (J-C A) — BBF
MOSQUITO — IWANMI
VD - ATTACK PLAN (J-H) — DISNEY
WORK OF GOMIS, THE (J-C A) — WASHBF

(VIDEOTAPES)

DENTAL HEALTH--A SERIES (P-I) — GPITVL
KEEP IT CLEAN (P-I) — GPITVL
KID, YOU'VE GOT A DIRTY MOUTH (P-I) — GPITVL

SALLY HAD A SWEET TOOTH, NOW IT'S GONE (P-I) — GPITVL
WINNING TEAM, THE (P-I) — GPITVL

(AUDIO TAPES)

TO DIE THAT OTHERS MAY LIVE (I) — MINSA

REHABILITATION

(FILMSTRIPS)

GOING TO THE DOCTOR — EGH
GUIDE TO WHEELCHAIR TRANSFER TECHNIQUES, A — KRI

(MOTION PICTURES)

ALCOHOLISM - A MODEL OF DRUG DEPENDENCY (C A) — CRMP
CAPRI PROGRAM, THE (C A) — SAFECO
CENTER OF LIFE (J-C A) — GRANDY
NUTRITION - THE INNER ENVIRONMENT (P-J) — AMEDFL
QUICK BILLY — AMERFI
TAKING CARE OF BUSINESS — AMERFI
UMBRELLA MAN, THE — MGHT

(AUDIO TAPES)

HOSPITAL MANAGEMENT OF DISTURBED ADOLESCENTS, THE, PT 1 — SIGINF
HOSPITAL MANAGEMENT OF DISTURBED ADOLESCENTS, THE, PT 2 — SIGINF

SAFETY - GENERAL

(FILMSTRIPS)

DECISION IS YOURS, THE — NAVA
DEPUTY MARV — LYCEUM
HOSPITAL SAFETY--A SERIES (PRO) — TRNAID

(MOTION CARTRIDGES)

HOW TO USE HAMMERS — VISIN
HOW TO USE SAWS — VISIN

(MOTION PICTURES)

BARE MINIMUM — BEF
CUTTING CREW, THE (H-C A) — RARIG
LANDING TEAM, THE (H-C A) — RARIG
LOGGING SAFETY--A SERIES (H-C A) — RARIG
PRIMARY SAFETY - ON THE WAY TO SCHOOL — CORF
SAFETY IN PLYWOOD OPERATIONS (J-C A) — RARIG
SENSE OF RESPONSIBILITY, A (I-C) — BFA

(AUDIO TAPES)

STRATEGIC IMPORTANCE OF CIVIL DEFENSE, THE (J A) — NAEB
SUMMARY AND CONCLUSIONS (J A) — NAEB
WHO NEEDS CIVIL DEFENSE (J A) — NAEB

SAFETY - FIRE

(FILMSTRIPS)

HOSPITAL SAFETY--A SERIES (PRO) — TRNAID

(MOTION PICTURES)

ENEMY IS FIRE, THE (J-C A) — RARIG
FIRE SAFETY - HALL OF FLAME (P-I) — SAGENA
FIRE WEATHER (J-C A) — RARIG
FOREST FIRE PROTECTION--A SERIES (J-C A) — RARIG
GLOVE BOX FIRES — USNAC
JUNIOR FIREMEN — LACFD
SAFETY IN PLYWOOD OPERATIONS (J-C A) — RARIG

SAFETY - HOME AND COMMUNITY

(FILMSTRIPS)

DECISION IS YOURS, THE — NAVA
DEPUTY MARV — LYCEUM

(MOTION PICTURES)

CRIME IN THE HOME (J-C A) — AIMS
CRIME ON THE STREETS (J-C A) — AIMS
JUNIOR FIREMEN — LACFD
WHEN EVERY MINUTE COUNTS — MTP

SAFETY - PLAYGROUND AND SCHOOL

(MOTION PICTURES)

PRIMARY SAFETY - ON THE WAY TO SCHOOL — CORF

SEXUAL HYGIENE

(MOTION PICTURES)

HUMAN REPRODUCTION (H-C A) — CHM
VENEREAL DISEASE (H-C A) — CHM

(TRANSPARENCIES)

ADOLESCENT CHANGE (H) — BOW
BABY AT ONE MONTH — LEART
BIRTH OF THE BABY — LEART
BREAST DEVELOPMENT AND PURPOSE — LEART
CARE OF MALE REPRODUCTIVE ORGANS — LEART
CARE OF THE BODY DURING MENSTRUATION — LEART
CLEANLINESS INFLUENCES HEALTH — LEART
COMPARATIVE SIZES - BOYS AND GIRLS 11 YEARS — LEART
COMPARATIVE SIZES - BOYS AND GIRLS 12 YEARS — LEART
COMPARATIVE SIZES - BOYS AND GIRLS 13 YEARS — LEART
COMPARATIVE SIZES - BOYS AND GIRLS 14 YEARS — LEART
CROSS-SECTION OF PENIS — LEART
DATING AND PARTYING — LEART
DESCENT OF THE TESTICLES — LEART
DRESS FOR THE WEATHER — LEART
EFFECTS OF GONORRHEA — LEART
EFFECTS OF SYPHILIS — LEART
EMBRYO TO BABY — LEART
EMOTION AND BODY FUNCTIONS — LEART
ENDOCRINE GLANDS — LEART
EXERCISE AND ACTIVITIES — LEART
FEMALE ORGANS OF EXCRETION AND REPRODUCTION — LEART
FEMALE REPRODUCTIVE ORGANS - FRONT VIEW — LEART
FERTILIZATION — LEART
FOOD AFFECTS GROWTH — LEART
GENERAL TOPICS--A SERIES (H) — BOW
GONORRHEA — LEART
GROWTH OF BODY HAIR — LEART
GROWTH OF THE BABY, PT 1 — LEART
GROWTH OF THE BABY, PT 2 — LEART
HEREDITY (BASIC) (H) — BOW
HORMONES AND EMOTIONAL EFFECTS, PT 1 — LEART
HORMONES AND EMOTIONAL EFFECTS, PT 2 — LEART
HOW EMOTIONS ARE EXPRESSED — LEART
IMPLANTATION — LEART
INGUINAL AND SPERMATIC CORD — LEART
MALE ORGANS OF EXCRETION AND REPRODUCTION — LEART
MENSTRUATION — LEART
MULTIPLE OVULATION AND FERTILIZATION — LEART
NORMAL ATTRACTION OF THE SEXES, PT 1 — LEART
NORMAL ATTRACTION OF THE SEXES, PT 2 — LEART
OVULATION — LEART
OVUM AND SPERM PHOTO (H) — BOW
PASSAGE OF PLACENTA — LEART
PHYSICAL CHANGES - BOYS — LEART
PHYSICAL CHANGES - GIRLS — LEART
PITUITARY GLAND — LEART
PROPER SLEEP IS IMPORTANT TO HEALTH — LEART
PUBESCENCE - THE AGE OF PUBERTY — LEART
REASONS FOR ERECTION — LEART
REPRODUCTIVE CELL DIVISION - GROWTH — LEART
SEMINAL EMISSIONS — LEART
SEPARATION OF MOTHER AND BABY — LEART
SEX EDUCATION - DEVELOPMENT OF CONCEPTS AND ATTITUDES--A SERIES — LEART
SEX EDUCATION - DEVELOPMENTAL PATTERNS OF PUBESCENT BOYS--A SERIES — LEART
SEX EDUCATION - GROWTH AND THE ENDOCRINE GLANDS--A SERIES — LEART
SEX EDUCATION - PHYSICAL CARE AND SELF RESPECT--A SERIES — LEART
SEX EDUCATION - THE BABY - ITS CONCEPTION, GROWTH AND BIRTH--A SERIES — LEART
SEX EDUCATION - UNDERSTANDING VENEREAL DISEASE--A SERIES — LEART
SINGLE FULL-TERM FETUS (X-RAY) (H) — BOW
SPERM — LEART
SYPHILIS — LEART
TWIN X-RAY (H) — BOW
TWINNING — LEART
TWINS (H) — BOW

TYPES OF PROTECTION   LEART
UNDERSTANDING MALENESS AND
FEMALENESS   LEART
UNDERSTANDING SEXUALITY   LEART
VENEREAL DISEASE   LEART
WAYS OF CONTROL   LEART
WHAT MAKES PERSONALITIES
DIFFERENT   LEART

SMOKING

(FILMSTRIPS)

ALCOHOL AND TOBACCO   EGH
MARIJUANA AND GLUE - KIDS, TRICKS
AND TRAPS (P-I)   EBEC
TOBACCO - A PUFF OF POISON (P-I)   EBEC

VENEREAL DISEASE

(MOTION PICTURES)

CHECK IT OUT (J-H A)   NEWD
LOOK WHAT'S GOING AROUND (H-C A)   CF
VD - ATTACK PLAN (J-H)   DISNEY
VENEREAL DISEASE (H-C A)   CHM

(TRANSPARENCIES)

EFFECTS OF GONORRHEA   LEART
EFFECTS OF SYPHILIS   LEART
GONORRHEA   LEART
SEX EDUCATION -
UNDERSTANDING VENEREAL
DISEASE--A SERIES   LEART
SYPHILIS   LEART
VENEREAL DISEASE   LEART

HISTORY - U S

HISTORY, U S - GENERAL

(FILMSTRIPS)

AMERICAN GENIUS--A SERIES (H-C)   EDDIM
AMERICAN GENIUS, 1880 - 1918 (H-C)   EDDIM
AMERICAN GENIUS, 1920 - 1940 (H-C)   EDDIM
AMERICAN GENIUS, 1940 - 1950 (H-C)   EDDIM
CIVIL WAR AS IT HAPPENED--A SERIES   TECVIS
CONCEPT-CENTERED LESSONS IN
AMERICAN HISTORY, UNIT 1--A
SERIES   FPC
CRISPUS ATTUCKS (I-H)   CORF
DANISH FIELD, THE (J-C A)   INTXC
FAMOUS PATRIOTS OF THE
AMERICAN REVOLUTION--A
SERIES (I-H)   CORF
HAYM SALOMON (I-H)   CORF
JOHN PAUL JONES (I-H)   CORF
MAKING OF THE AMERICAN
NATION, PT 1 - THE
COLONIZATION OF AMERICA   FPC
MAKING OF THE AMERICAN
NATION, PT 2 - THE AMERICAN
REVOLUTION   FPC
MOLLY PITCHER (I-H)   CORF
NATHANAEL GREENE (I-H)   CORF
PATRICK HENRY (I-H)   CORF

(MOTION PICTURES)

NORFOLK TOUR   MTP
TO THE SPIRIT OF '76--A SERIES (J-C)   RMI

(RECORDS)

HARK TO OUR HERITAGE   BOW

(TRANSPARENCIES)

CONSTITUTION--A SERIES   BETECL

AMERICAN COLONIES

(FILMSTRIPS)

MAKING OF THE AMERICAN
NATION, PT 1 - THE
COLONIZATION OF AMERICA   FPC

(MOTION PICTURES)

ANGRY COLONIES - 1763 - 1774   RMI
FLAMES OF REVOLUTION -
SEPTEMBER 1774 - JUNE, 1776   RMI
SEEDS OF REBELLION - VIKINGS TO
1763   RMI

(RECORDS)

HARK TO OUR HERITAGE   BOW

AMERICAN HERITAGE FROM THE OLD WORLD

(FILMSTRIPS)

CONCEPT-CENTERED LESSONS IN
AMERICAN HISTORY, UNIT 1--A
SERIES   FPC
DANISH FIELD, THE (J-C A)   INTXC
MAKING OF THE AMERICAN
NATION, PT 1 - THE
COLONIZATION OF AMERICA   FPC
MAKING OF THE AMERICAN
NATION, PT 2 - THE AMERICAN
REVOLUTION   FPC

(MOTION PICTURES)

IMMIGRANT EXPERIENCE, THE -
THE LONG, LONG JOURNEY   LCOA
SEEDS OF REBELLION - VIKINGS TO
1763   RMI
TO THE SPIRIT OF '76--A SERIES (J-C)   RMI

CONSTITUTIONAL HISTORY

(MOTION PICTURES)

BENJAMIN FRANKLIN AND THE MID-
ATLANTIC SIGNERS   RMI
DECLARATION OF INDEPENDENCE,
JUNE 1776 - JANUARY, 1777   RMI
JOHN ADAMS AND THE NEW ENGLAND
SIGNERS   RMI
THOMAS JEFFERSON AND THE
SOUTHERN SIGNERS   RMI
TO THE SPIRIT OF '76--A SERIES (J-C)   RMI

(TRANSPARENCIES)

CONSTITUTION--A SERIES   BETECL

DOCUMENTS

(MOTION PICTURES)

BENJAMIN FRANKLIN AND THE MID-
ATLANTIC SIGNERS   RMI
DECLARATION OF INDEPENDENCE,
JUNE 1776 - JANUARY, 1777   RMI
JOHN ADAMS AND THE NEW ENGLAND
SIGNERS   RMI
THOMAS JEFFERSON AND THE
SOUTHERN SIGNERS   RMI

FRONTIER AND EXPANSION

(FILMSTRIPS)

ALASKA - THE LAST AMERICAN
FRONTIER (J-H)   SED
AMERICAN WEST IN LITERATURE, THE,
PT 1 (J)   GA
AMERICAN WEST IN LITERATURE, THE,
PT 2 (J)   GA
DANISH FIELD, THE (J-C A)   INTXC

(MOTION PICTURES)

ALASKAN GOLD RUSH, THE (I-C)   DISNEY
YESTERDAY'S FARM (P-J)   BFA

(RECORDS)

HARK TO OUR HERITAGE   BOW

IMMIGRATION

(FILMSTRIPS)

AMERICAN ADVENTURE--A SERIES (I-J)   FIELEP
BLACK AMERICANS (I-J)   FIELEP
DANISH FIELD, THE (J-C A)   INTXC
GERMAN AMERICANS (I-J)   FIELEP
HAYM SALOMON (I-H)   CORF
ITALIAN AMERICANS (I-J)   FIELEP
JOHN PAUL JONES (I-H)   CORF
MEXICAN AMERICANS (I-J)   FIELEP
NEW AMERICANS (I-J)   FIELEP

(MOTION PICTURES)

IMMIGRANT EXPERIENCE, THE -
THE LONG, LONG JOURNEY   LCOA

INDUSTRIAL REVOLUTION

(MOTION PICTURES)

CIVILISATION, PROGRAM 13   TIMLIF

MILITARY

(MOTION PICTURES)

RUMOURS OF WAR (H-C A)   TIMLIF

NEGRO HISTORY - GENERAL

(FILMSTRIPS)

BLACK AMERICANS (I-J)   FIELEP

NEGRO HISTORY - AFRICA - CULTURE

(MOTION PICTURES)

GRAVEL SPRINGS FIFE AND DRUM (H-C
A)   IU

NEGRO HISTORY - CIVIL RIGHTS

(RECORDS)

AUTOBIOGRAPHY OF FREDERICK
DOUGLASS   BOW

NEGRO HISTORY - CONSUMER

(TRANSPARENCIES)

POLITICAL GEOGRAPHY AND
NATIONALISM OF AFRICA --A
SERIES (J-H)   LEART

NEGRO HISTORY - ECONOMIC CONDITIONS

(MOTION PICTURES)

INNER CITY DWELLER - WORK (H-C A)   IU

NEGRO HISTORY - EMPLOYMENT

(MOTION PICTURES)

INNER CITY DWELLER - WORK (H-C A)   IU

NEGRO HISTORY - FAMOUS PERSONALITIES

(TRANSPARENCIES)

A PHILIP RANDOLPH (J-H)   LEART
ADAM CLAYTON POWELL (J-H)   LEART
ALEXANDER DUMAS (J-H)   LEART
ALTHEA GIBSON (J-H)   LEART
BENJAMIN BENNEKER (J-H)   LEART
BENJAMIN L DAVIS (J-H)   LEART
BILL COSBY (J-H)   LEART
BIOGRAPHIES OF OUTSTANDING
NEGRO AMERICANS--A SERIES (J-
H)   LEART
BLANCHE K BRUCE (J-H)   LEART
BOB GIBSON (J-H)   LEART
BOOKER T WASHINGTON (J-H)   LEART
CARTER G WOODSON (J-H)   LEART
CHARLES DREW (J-H)   LEART
COUNTEE CULLEN (J-H)   LEART
CRISPUS ATTUCKS (J-H)   LEART
DENMARK VESEY (J-H)   LEART
DUKE ELLINGTON (J-H)   LEART
FREDERICK A DOUGLASS (J-H)   LEART
GEORGE WASHINGTON CARVER (J-H)   LEART
GRANVILLE WOODS (J-H)   LEART
GWENDOLYN BROOKS (J-H)   LEART
HARRIET TUBMAN (J-H)   LEART
HARRY BELAFONTE (J-H)   LEART
HENRY O TANNER (J-H)   LEART
JACK JOHNSON (J-H)   LEART
JACKIE ROBINSON (J-H)   LEART
JAMES BROWN (J-H)   LEART
JAMES WELDON JOHNSON (J-H)   LEART
JAN MATZELIGER (J-H)   LEART
JOE LOUIS (J-H)   LEART
LANGSTON HUGHES (J-H)   LEART
LEONTYNE PRICE (J-H)   LEART
LOUIS 'SATCHMO' ARMSTRONG (J-H)   LEART
MAHALIA JACKSON (J-H)   LEART
MALCOLM X (J-H)   LEART
MARCUS GARVEY (J-H)   LEART
MARIAN ANDERSON (J-H)   LEART
MARTIN LUTHER KING (J-H)   LEART
MARY MC LEOD BETHUNE (J-H)   LEART
MATTHEW HENSON (J-H)   LEART
NAT TURNER (J-H)   LEART
PAUL LAURENCE DUNBAR (J-H)   LEART
PHYLLIS WHEATLEY (J-H)   LEART
RALPH J BUNCHE (J-H)   LEART
RICHARD WRIGHT (J-H)   LEART
ROBERT SMALLS (J-H)   LEART
SAMMY DAVIS JR (J-H)   LEART
SIDNEY POITIER (J-H)   LEART
STOKELY CARMICHAEL (J-H)   LEART

THURGOOD MARSHALL (J-H)   LEART
W C HANDY (J-H)   LEART
WILLIAM E B DU BOIS (J-H)   LEART
WILLIE MAYS (J-H)   LEART
WILTON N CHAMBERLAIN (J-H)   LEART

NEGRO HISTORY - LITERATURE

(MOTION PICTURES)

RIGHT ON (J-C A)   NLC

NEGRO HISTORY - 1915 TO PRESENT

(TRANSPARENCIES)

POLITICAL GEOGRAPHY AND
   NATIONALISM OF AFRICA --A
   SERIES (J-H)   LEART

NEGRO HISTORY - RECREATION AND SPORTS

(TRANSPARENCIES)

ALTHEA GIBSON (J-H)   LEART
BOB GIBSON (J-H)   LEART
JACKIE ROBINSON (J-H)   LEART
WILLIE MAYS (J-H)   LEART
WILTON N CHAMBERLAIN (J-H)   LEART

NEGRO HISTORY - SOCIAL PROBLEMS

(AUDIO TAPES)

DEVELOPMENTAL CRISES IN BLACK
   ADOLESCENTS   SIGINF
NORMAL AND ABNORMAL
   BEHAVIOR OF ADOLESCENCE-- A
   SERIES   SIGINF

NEGRO HISTORY - SONGS AND MUSIC

(MOTION PICTURES)

GRAVEL SPRINGS FIFE AND DRUM (H-C
A)   IU

(TRANSPARENCIES)

DUKE ELLINGTON (J-H)   LEART
HARRY BELAFONTE (J-H)   LEART
LEONTYNE PRICE (J-H)   LEART
LOUIS 'SATCHMO' ARMSTRONG (J-H)   LEART
MAHALIA JACKSON (J-H)   LEART
MARIAN ANDERSON (J-H)   LEART
SAMMY DAVIS JR (J-H)   LEART
W C HANDY (J-H)   LEART

U S HISTORY - DISCOVERY AND EXPLORATION

(MOTION PICTURES)

SEEDS OF REBELLION - VIKINGS TO
1763   RMI

U S HISTORY - COLONIAL PERIOD TO 1776

(MOTION PICTURES)

ANGRY COLONIES - 1763 - 1774   RMI
DECLARATION OF INDEPENDENCE,
   JUNE 1776 - JANUARY, 1777   RMI
FLAMES OF REVOLUTION -
   SEPTEMBER 1774 - JUNE, 1776   RMI

U S HISTORY - REVOLUTIONARY PERIOD TO 1783

(FILMSTRIPS)

CRISPUS ATTUCKS (I-H)   CORF
FAMOUS PATRIOTS OF THE
   AMERICAN REVOLUTION--A
   SERIES (I-H)   CORF
HAYM SALOMON (I-H)   CORF
JOHN PAUL JONES (I-H)   CORF
MAKING OF THE AMERICAN
   NATION, PT 2 - THE AMERICAN
   REVOLUTION   FPC
MOLLY PITCHER (I-H)   CORF
NATHANAEL GREENE (I-H)   CORF
PATRICK HENRY (I-H)   CORF

(MOTION PICTURES)

DECLARATION OF INDEPENDENCE,
   JUNE 1776 - JANUARY, 1777   RMI
FLAMES OF REVOLUTION -
   SEPTEMBER 1774 - JUNE, 1776   RMI

U S HISTORY - 1783-1860

(FILMSTRIPS)

AMERICA THE BEAUTIFUL (J-C)   SUNCOM
AMERICAN CIVILIZATION - 1783-1840--A
   SERIES (J-C)   SUNCOM
AMERICAN CIVILIZATION - 1840-1876--A
   SERIES (J-C)   SUNCOM
ARCHITECTURE AS A LANGUAGE (J-C)   SUNCOM
ARTS AND THE COMMON MAN, THE (J-
   C)   SUNCOM
ARTS REFLECT DAILY LIFE, THE (J-C)   SUNCOM
BRIDGES TO THE 20TH CENTURY (J-C)   SUNCOM
PORTRAIT OF A YOUNG NATION (J-C)   SUNCOM
YOUNG AMERICA ADMIRES THE
   ANCIENTS (J-C)   SUNCOM

(MOTION PICTURES)

BENJAMIN FRANKLIN AND THE MID-
   ATLANTIC SIGNERS   RMI
JOHN ADAMS AND THE NEW ENGLAND
   SIGNERS   RMI
THOMAS JEFFERSON AND THE
   SOUTHERN SIGNERS   RMI

U S HISTORY - CIVIL WAR PERIOD TO 1900

(FILMSTRIPS)

AMERICA THE BEAUTIFUL (J-C)   SUNCOM
AMERICAN CIVILIZATION - 1840-1876--A
   SERIES (J-C)   SUNCOM
AMERICAN GENIUS--A SERIES (H-C)   EDDIM
AMERICAN GENIUS, 1880 - 1918 (H-C)   EDDIM
AMERICAN GENIUS, 1920 - 1940 (H-C)   EDDIM
AMERICAN GENIUS, 1940 - 1950 (H-C)   EDDIM
ARCHITECTURE AS A LANGUAGE (J-C)   SUNCOM
ARTILLERY IN THE CIVIL WAR   TECVIS
ARTS REFLECT DAILY LIFE, THE (J-C)   SUNCOM
BRIDGES TO THE 20TH CENTURY (J-C)   SUNCOM
CIVIL WAR AS IT HAPPENED--A SERIES   TECVIS
DANISH FIELD, THE (J-C A)   INTXC
FOOT SOLDIER, THE   TECVIS
HOW WE KNOW ABOUT THE CIVIL WAR   TECVIS
SUPPORTING SERVICES   TECVIS
TOLL OF THE CIVIL WAR, THE   TECVIS
WAR ON THE WATER, THE   TECVIS

(MOTION PICTURES)

BIOGRAPHY OF A CHAIR (J-C A)   FORD

(TRANSPARENCIES)

BEGINNING OF THE CIVIL WAR - 1860-
   1861 (I-H)   BOW
CIVIL WAR IN 1862 (I-H)   BOW
CIVIL WAR IN 1863 (I-H)   BOW
CIVIL WAR IN 1864 (I-H)   BOW
CIVIL WAR IN 1865 (I-H)   BOW
CIVIL WAR--A SERIES (I-H)   BOW

U S HISTORY - 1900 TO PRESENT

(FILMSTRIPS)

AMERICAN GENIUS--A SERIES (H-C)   EDDIM
AMERICAN GENIUS, 1880 - 1918 (H-C)   EDDIM
AMERICAN GENIUS, 1920 - 1940 (H-C)   EDDIM
AMERICAN GENIUS, 1940 - 1950 (H-C)   EDDIM
GREAT DEPRESSION, THE -
   CAUSES, EFFECTS, SOLUTIONS,
   PT 4 (J-C)   EAV
GREAT DEPRESSION, THE -
   CAUSES, EFFECTS, SOLUTIONS,
   PT 2 (J-C)   EAV
GREAT DEPRESSION, THE -
   CAUSES, EFFECTS, SOLUTIONS,
   PT 3 (J-C)   EAV
GREAT DEPRESSION, THE -
   CAUSES, EFFECTS, SOLUTIONS,
   PT 1 (J-C)   EAV

(MOTION PICTURES)

CHILDREN, THE   AMERFI
INNER CITY DWELLER - WORK (H-C A)   IU
LANTON MILLS   AMERFI
VIETNAM EPILOGUE   HEARST

WORLD WAR II - 1939-1945

(RECORDS)

D-DAY PLUS 20   CAED

HISTORY, WORLD - GENERAL

(FILMSTRIPS)

CITY IN HISTORY, THE, PT 1 (J-C A)   EDDIM
CITY IN HISTORY, THE, PT 2 (J-C A)   EDDIM

(MOTION PICTURES)

CIVILISATION--A SERIES   TIMLIF
MONEY, MONEY, MONEY (P-J)   TEXFLM

(AUDIO TAPES)

HISTORY AND HUMAN EVOLUTION   SIGINF

(TRANSPARENCIES)

MAN'S COMMUNITY EXPANDS
   THROUGH THE AGES (J-H)   LEART
WHY A SOCIETY NEEDS TO STUDY IT'S
   PAST (J-H)   LEART

AFRICA

(FILMSTRIPS)

ALBERT SCHWEITZER (2ND ED) (I-H)   CARMAN
EXPLORING AFRICA (I-J)   SED

(TRANSPARENCIES)

COLONIES TO INDEPENDENCE (J-H)   LEART
COUNTRY OF NIGERIA, THE (J H)   LEART
EUROPEAN PARTITION AGREEMENTS
   1884-1885 (J-H)   LEART
NATIONALIST LEADERS OF BLACK
   AFRICA (J-H)   LEART
NATIONALIST LEADERS OF NORTH
   AFRICA (J-H)   LEART
POLITICAL DIVISIONS AS OF 1968 -
   AFRICA (J-H)   LEART
POLITICAL GEOGRAPHY AND
   NATIONALISM OF AFRICA --A
   SERIES (J-H)   LEART
POLITICALLY SOVEREIGN STATES OF
   AFRICA (J-H)   LEART
PURPOSES AND AIMS OF THE OAU (J-
   H)   LEART
REGIONAL ORGANIZATIONS IN AFRICA
   (J-H)   LEART
REPUBLIC OF SOUTH AFRICA (J-H)   LEART
STRUCTURE OF THE OAU (J-H)   LEART
UHURU (J-H)   LEART
UNITED NATIONS ROLE IN THE
   INDEPENDENCE OF AFRICAN
   COUNTRIES (J-H)   LEART

ANCIENT WORLD

(FILMSTRIPS)

ANCIENT CIVILIZATIONS OF THE
   AMERICAS--A SERIES (I-J)   EBEC
AZTECS, THE (I-J)   EBEC
GREECE (P-I)   PATED
INCAS, THE (I-J)   EBEC
MAYAS, THE (I-J)   EBEC

(AUDIO TAPES)

WONDERS OF THE ANCIENT WORLD (H-
   C)   NGART

ARCHEOLOGY

(MOTION PICTURES)

IN SEARCH OF HISTORY   ALDEN
RETURN TO MASADA   ALDEN

ASIA

(MOTION PICTURES)

ROOTS OF MADNESS   XEROX
VIETNAM EPILOGUE   HEARST

CHINA, ANCIENT

(MOTION PICTURES)

ROOTS OF MADNESS   XEROX

CHURCH

(MOTION PICTURES)

CIVILISATION, PROGRAM 06	TIMLIF
CIVILISATION, PROGRAM 07	TIMLIF
REFORMATION - AGE OF REVOLT (J-H)	EBEC

CULTURES AND PERIODS

(FILMSTRIPS)

ALEXANDER THE GREAT AND THE ANCIENTS (I-J)	SED
AMERICAN GENIUS--A SERIES (H-C)	EDDIM
AMERICAN GENIUS, 1880 - 1918 (H-C)	EDDIM
AMERICAN GENIUS, 1920 - 1940 (H-C)	EDDIM
AMERICAN GENIUS, 1940 - 1950 (H-C)	EDDIM
AMERICAN GENIUS, 1960 - 1970 (H-C)	EDDIM
AZTECS	UMM
BEGINNINGS	UMM
CAPTAIN COOK, ALEXANDER MAC KENZIE AND LEWIS AND CLARK (I-J)	SED
CITIES OF ITALY	EGH
CITIES OF ROME AND FLORENCE	EGH
CLASSIC MAYA	UMM
CLASSIC MEXICANS	UMM
COLUMBUS, BALBOA AND MAGELLAN (I-J)	SED
CONCEPT-CENTERED LESSONS IN AMERICAN HISTORY, UNIT 1--A SERIES	FPC
EXPLORATION - MAN'S QUEST FOR KNOWLEDGE--A SERIES (I-J)	SED
EXPLORING AFRICA (I-J)	SED
FLORENCE AND VENICE	EGH
GREAT MEN AND ARTISTS	EGH
HUMANITIES - A WORLD BETWEEN WARS, PT 1 (J-H)	GA
HUMANITIES - A WORLD BETWEEN WARS, PT 2 (J-H)	GA
HUMANITIES - THE DAWN OF THE TWENTIETH CENTURY, PT 1 (J-H)	GA
HUMANITIES - THE DAWN OF THE TWENTIETH CENTURY, PT 2 (J-H)	GA
ITALIAN CULTURE AND RECREATION	EGH
ITALY - A REGIONAL STUDY--A SERIES	EGH
JAPAN	TF
MAKING OF THE AMERICAN NATION, PT 1 - THE COLONIZATION OF AMERICA	FPC
MAKING OF THE AMERICAN NATION, PT 2 - THE AMERICAN REVOLUTION	FPC
MEXICAN EPIC - BEFORE THE CONQUEST--A SERIES	UMM
SPANISH CONQUERORS AND COLONIZERS (I-J)	SED
TOLTECS	UMM
TURKEY (P-I)	PATED
VIKINGS, THE ARABS AND MARCO POLO, THE (I-J)	SED

(MOTION PICTURES)

CIVILISATION--A SERIES	TIMLIF
CIVILISATION, PROGRAM 01	TIMLIF
CIVILISATION, PROGRAM 02	TIMLIF
CIVILISATION, PROGRAM 03	TIMLIF
CIVILISATION, PROGRAM 04	TIMLIF
CIVILISATION, PROGRAM 05	TIMLIF
CIVILISATION, PROGRAM 06	TIMLIF
CIVILISATION, PROGRAM 07	TIMLIF
CIVILISATION, PROGRAM 08	TIMLIF
CIVILISATION, PROGRAM 09	TIMLIF
CIVILISATION, PROGRAM 10	TIMLIF
CIVILISATION, PROGRAM 11	TIMLIF
CIVILISATION, PROGRAM 12	TIMLIF
CIVILISATION, PROGRAM 13	TIMLIF
REFORMATION - AGE OF REVOLT (J-H)	EBEC
THEATER IN SHAKESPEARE'S TIME, THE (J-C A)	BFA

(TRANSPARENCIES)

SHAKESPEARE--A SERIES	BETECL

DISCOVERY AND EXPLORATION

(FILMSTRIPS)

ALEXANDER THE GREAT AND THE ANCIENTS (I-J)	SED
CAPTAIN COOK, ALEXANDER MAC KENZIE AND LEWIS AND CLARK (I-J)	SED
COLUMBUS, BALBOA AND MAGELLAN (I-J)	SED
EXPLORATION - MAN'S QUEST FOR KNOWLEDGE--A SERIES (I-J)	SED
EXPLORING AFRICA (I-J)	SED
SPANISH CONQUERORS AND COLONIZERS (I-J)	SED
VIKINGS, THE ARABS AND MARCO POLO, THE (I-J)	SED

EUROPE

(MOTION PICTURES)

REFORMATION - AGE OF REVOLT (J-H)	EBEC

GEOGRAPHY

(MOTION PICTURES)

RETURN TO MASADA	ALDEN

GREAT DISCOVERIES

(FILMSTRIPS)

ALEXANDER THE GREAT AND THE ANCIENTS (I-J)	SED
AUTOMOBILE, THE (HENRY FORD) (P)	EDPRC
CAPTAIN COOK, ALEXANDER MAC KENZIE AND LEWIS AND CLARK (I-J)	SED
COLUMBUS, BALBOA AND MAGELLAN (I-J)	SED
EXPLORATION - MAN'S QUEST FOR KNOWLEDGE--A SERIES (I-J)	SED
EXPLORING AFRICA (I-J)	SED
SPANISH CONQUERORS AND COLONIZERS (I-J)	SED
VIKINGS, THE ARABS AND MARCO POLO, THE (I-J)	SED

(MOTION PICTURES)

SEARCH FOR THE NILE--A SERIES (J-C A)	TIMLIF

(AUDIO TAPES)

TO DIE THAT OTHERS MAY LIVE (I)	MINSA

HISTORICAL SOCIETIES

(FILMSTRIPS)

ANCIENT CIVILIZATIONS OF THE AMERICAS--A SERIES (I-J)	EBEC
MEXICAN EPIC - BEFORE THE CONQUEST--A SERIES	UMM
TURKEY (P-I)	PATED

INTERNATIONAL AFFAIRS

(MOTION PICTURES)

ISRAEL IN THE FAMILY OF NATIONS	ALDEN
SOVIET BUILD-UP IN THE MIDDLE EAST	ALDEN

LATIN AMERICA

(FILMSTRIPS)

AZTECS	UMM
BEGINNINGS	UMM
CLASSIC MAYA	UMM
CLASSIC MEXICANS	UMM
MEXICAN EPIC - BEFORE THE CONQUEST--A SERIES	UMM
TOLTECS	UMM

(MOTION PICTURES)

YO SOY CHICANO (ENGLISH) (H-C A)	IU

MEDIEVAL TIMES

(MOTION PICTURES)

CIVILISATION, PROGRAM 01	TIMLIF
CIVILISATION, PROGRAM 02	TIMLIF
CIVILISATION, PROGRAM 03	TIMLIF

(AUDIO TAPES)

SWORD AND SICKLE (I-J)	INSKY

MIDDLE EAST

(MOTION PICTURES)

CITIZEN'S ARMY	ALDEN
HOME AT LAST	ALDEN
IN SEARCH OF HISTORY	ALDEN
ISRAEL - THE HOLY LAND (J-C A)	AMEDFL
ISRAEL IN THE FAMILY OF NATIONS	ALDEN
LET MY PEOPLE GO	ALDEN
RETURN TO MASADA	ALDEN
SIX DAYS IN JUNE	ALDEN
STORY OF STAMPS, THE	ALDEN
THIRD TEMPLE, THE	ALDEN
TIBERIAS - LAND OF THE EMPERORS	ALDEN

VISION OF CHAIM WEIZMANN	ALDEN
YEARS OF DESTINY	ALDEN

NORTH AMERICA

(FILMSTRIPS)

ANCIENT CIVILIZATIONS OF THE AMERICAS--A SERIES (I-J)	EBEC
AZTECS, THE (I-J)	EBEC
INCAS, THE (I-J)	EBEC
MAYAS, THE (I-J)	EBEC

ORIENT

(FILMSTRIPS)

CHINESE ART, PT 1 (J-C A)	SCHLAT
CHINESE ART, PT 2 (J-C A)	SCHLAT
CHINESE ART, PT 3 (J-C A)	SCHLAT

(MOTION PICTURES)

ROOTS OF MADNESS	XEROX

RENAISSANCE

(FILMSTRIPS)

ITALY (P-I)	PATED

(MOTION PICTURES)

CIVILISATION, PROGRAM 04	TIMLIF
CIVILISATION, PROGRAM 05	TIMLIF
CIVILISATION, PROGRAM 06	TIMLIF
CIVILISATION, PROGRAM 08	TIMLIF

REVOLUTIONARY AND NAPOLEONIC PERIOD

(MOTION PICTURES)

CIVILISATION, PROGRAM 10	TIMLIF
CIVILISATION, PROGRAM 12	TIMLIF

ROME, ANCIENT

(FILMSTRIPS)

CITIES OF ROME AND FLORENCE	EGH

(MOTION PICTURES)

CIVILISATION, PROGRAM 01	TIMLIF
RETURN TO MASADA	ALDEN
TIBERIAS - LAND OF THE EMPERORS	ALDEN

SCIENCE AND LEARNING, MODERN HISTORY

(AUDIO TAPES)

HISTORY AND HUMAN EVOLUTION	SIGINF
HUMANISTIC AND POSITIVIST PHILOSOPHIES OF SCIENCE	SIGINF
NEW APPROACH TO HUMAN EVOLUTION - INTRODUCTION	SIGINF
THERAPEUTIC ALLIANCE AND THE EARLY STAGES OF TREATMENT, THE	SIGINF

SCIENCE AND SOCIETY, MODERN HISTORY

(MOTION PICTURES)

CIVILISATION, PROGRAM 08	TIMLIF

STUDY AND TEACHING

(AUDIO TAPES)

HISTORY AND HUMAN EVOLUTION	SIGINF

(TRANSPARENCIES)

WHY A SOCIETY NEEDS TO STUDY IT'S PAST (J-H)	LEART

SYRIA-PALESTINE, ANCIENT

(MOTION PICTURES)

ISRAEL - THE HOLY LAND (J-C A)	AMEDFL

TWENTIETH CENTURY - GENERAL

(FILMSTRIPS)

HUMANITIES - A WORLD BETWEEN WARS, PT 1 (J-H)	GA

HUMANITIES - A WORLD BETWEEN WARS, PT 2 (J-H)   GA
HUMANITIES - THE DAWN OF THE TWENTIETH CENTURY, PT 1 (J-H)   GA
HUMANITIES - THE DAWN OF THE TWENTIETH CENTURY, PT 2 (J-H)   GA

(MOTION PICTURES)

CIVILISATION, PROGRAM 13   TIMLIF
SIX DAYS IN JUNE   ALDEN
VIETNAM EPILOGUE   HEARST

WESTERN EUROPE, AGE OF THE CRUSADES

(MOTION PICTURES)

CIVILISATION, PROGRAM 02   TIMLIF

WESTERN EUROPE, MIDDLE AGES

(MOTION PICTURES)

CIVILISATION, PROGRAM 01   TIMLIF
CIVILISATION, PROGRAM 02   TIMLIF

WORLD FROM 1939

(FILMSTRIPS)

JAPAN   TF

WORLD WAR II - 1939-1945

(FILMSTRIPS)

JAPAN   TF

(MOTION PICTURES)

LET MY PEOPLE GO   ALDEN

(RECORDS)

D-DAY PLUS 20   CAED

HOME ECONOMICS

HOME ECONOMICS - GENERAL

(MOTION PICTURES)

EXECUTIVE'S WIFE, THE (A)   UEUWIS

CHILDREN - CARE AND HYGIENE

(MOTION PICTURES)

CHILDBIRTH (J-C A)   POLYMR
NOT ME ALONE (H-C A)   POLYMR
TALKING ABOUT BREASTFEEDING (H-C A)   POLYMR

CLOTHING AND DRESS

(FILMSTRIPS)

FASHION FORMULAS (J-C A)   RMI
FINDING WHAT'S RIGHT FOR YOU   EGH
HISTORY OF STYLE AND VOGUE, A   EGH
HOT TIPS ON BASIC BEAUTY, FASHION, GROOMING AND DATING--A SERIES (J-C A)   RMI
MAKING CLOTHING   EGH
MODELING MANNERS (J-C A)   RMI
PUTTING IT TOGETHER SO IT WORKS   EGH

(MOTION CARTRIDGES)

MAKING IT IN FASHION - THE BASICS OF CLOTHING CONSTRUCTION, PT 1--A SERIES   DOUBLE
MAKING IT IN FASHION - THE BASICS OF CLOTHING CONSTRUCTION, PT 2--A SERIES   DOUBLE

(MOTION PICTURES)

BARE MINIMUM   BEF
SCIENCE OF FOOTWEAR, THE   IWANMI
VERA PAINTS IBIZA IN THE SUN (J-C A)   SCHLAT

CONSUMER EDUCATION

(FILMSTRIPS)

CONSUMERISM - THE DANGERS OF AFFLUENCE, PT 1   ASPRSS

CONSUMERISM - THE DANGERS OF AFFLUENCE, PT 2   ASPRSS
DOING IT ALL ON A BUDGET   EGH
LOOKING GREAT ON A SHOESTRING--A SERIES   EGH
ONE HUNDRED AND THIRTY BILLION DOLLAR FOOD ASSEMBLY LINE (C A)   USDA
ONE PHASE OF THE BLACK MARKET IN MEAT   USOPA
RECIPES USING NON-INSTANT, NONFAT DRY MILK AND OTHER DONATED FOODS (A)   USDA

(MOTION PICTURES)

ADVERTISING - INFORMATION, PERSUASION OR DECEPTION (I-C)   JOU
DEATH AND TAXES   BEF
DECIDING (P-I)   CENTEF

FOOD AND COOKING

(FILMSTRIPS)

DIET CLERK AND FRY COOK   EGH
FOOD SERVICE WORKER   EGH
ONE HUNDRED AND THIRTY BILLION DOLLAR FOOD ASSEMBLY LINE (C A)   USDA
PROCESSING SOUP   EGH
RECIPES USING NON-INSTANT, NONFAT DRY MILK AND OTHER DONATED FOODS (A)   USDA

(MOTION PICTURES)

CHICKEN SOUP (J-C A)   CAROUF
EARTHBREAD - A NATURAL FOOD (I-C)   FPRD
FOOD PREPARATION TERMS, PT 1 (J-C A)   EPRI
FOOD PREPARATION TERMS, PT 2 (J-C A)   EPRI
FOOD PREPARATION--A SERIES (J-C A)   EPRI
FRESH CHILLED SUNSHINE   MTP
JOBS IN BAKING   USNAC
STORY OF LAVER   IWANMI
TUNA FROM CATCH TO THE CAN   MTP
YEAST   IWANMI

GROOMING

(FILMSTRIPS)

BRUSHING AWAY TOOTH DECAY (P-I)   DISNEY
CASE OF THE CROOKED TEETH, THE (P-I)   DISNEY
FACE FACTS   EGH
FACE FACTS (J-C A)   RMI
FIGURE FACTS   EGH
FINDING WHAT'S RIGHT FOR YOU   EGH
GOOD GROOMING (J-C A)   RMI
HISTORY OF STYLE AND VOGUE, A   EGH
HOT TIPS ON BASIC BEAUTY, FASHION, GROOMING AND DATING--A SERIES (J-C A)   RMI
MAGIC POTION, THE (P-I)   DISNEY
MEET YOUR TEETH (P-I)   DISNEY
PRACTICING GOOD HEALTH, SET 2 - YOUR MOUTH SPEAKING--A SERIES (P-I)   DISNEY
PUTTING IT TOGETHER SO IT WORKS   EGH
SAFETY OF THE MOUTH (P-I)   DISNEY
WHY VISIT THE DENTIST (P-I)   DISNEY

(MOTION PICTURES)

JOBS IN COSMETOLOGY   USNAC
WHAT DO WE LOOK LIKE TO OTHERS (H-C A)   SAIF

(AUDIO TAPES)

SOUND OF THE WAY YOU LOOK, THE (I-J)   MINNOE

(TRANSPARENCIES)

APPAREL AND POSTURE AFFECT YOUR ATTITUDE   COF
CLEANLINESS INFLUENCES HEALTH   LEART
DAILY SCHEDULE FOR GOOD GROOMING, A   COF
DOES GOOD GROOMING PAY OFF   COF
DRESS FOR THE WEATHER   LEART
EMOTION AND BODY FUNCTIONS   LEART
EXERCISE AND ACTIVITIES   LEART
FOOD AFFECTS GROWTH   LEART
GOOD GROOMING GAME A   COF
GOOD GROOMING GAME B   COF
GOOD GROOMING RULES   COF
GOOD GROOMING--A SERIES   COF
HOW DO YOU MEASURE UP, NO. 1   COF
HOW DO YOU MEASURE UP, NO. 2   COF
IMPORTANCE OF A PLEASANT FACE AND VOICE   COF

ITEMS FOR THE WORKING GIRL'S HANDBAG   COF
ITEMS TO BE CARRIED BY THE WORKING MAN   COF
JOB REQUIREMENTS IN DRESS   COF
PROPER SLEEP IS IMPORTANT TO HEALTH   LEART
SELECTING A HAIR STYLE   COF
SELECTING CLOTHING FOR YOUR BUDGET   COF
SEX EDUCATION - PHYSICAL CARE AND SELF RESPECT--A SERIES   LEART
SUMMARY OF GOOD GROOMING FACTORS, PT 1   COF
SUMMARY OF GOOD GROOMING FACTORS, PT 2   COF
WEEKLY SCHEDULE FOR GOOD GROOMING, A   COF
WELL-DRESSED YOUNG WORKING MAN, THE   COF
WELL-DRESSED YOUNG WORKING WOMAN, THE   COF

HOME MANAGEMENT

(FILMSTRIPS)

DOING IT ALL ON A BUDGET   EGH
EXTERIOR BUILDING MATERIALS FOR YOUR HOME (J-C A)   USDA
HOUSE PESTS AND PARASITES (I-H)   COMG
HOUSING--A SERIES (J-C A)   USDA
PLANNING THE BEDROOM (J-C A)   USDA

(MOTION PICTURES)

BEAUTY AND COMFORT OUTDOORS   MTP
EXECUTIVE'S WIFE, THE (A)   UEUWIS

HOUSEHOLD EQUIPMENT AND SUPPLIES

(FILMSTRIPS)

CRAFTING A CHAIR   EGH

(MOTION PICTURES)

FOOD PREPARATION TERMS, PT 1 (J-C A)   EPRI
FOOD PREPARATION TERMS, PT 2 (J-C A)   EPRI

HOUSEHOLD PEST

(FILMSTRIPS)

HOUSE PESTS AND PARASITES (I-H)   COMG

NURSING

(FILMSTRIPS)

CANCER, SERIES 3 - TREATMENT MODALITIES WITH IMPLICATIONS FOR NURSING CARE--A SERIES   CONMED
GUIDE TO WHEELCHAIR TRANSFER TECHNIQUES, A   KRI
HOSPITAL SAFETY--A SERIES (PRO)   TRNAID
NURSE   EGH
NURSE'S AIDE   EGH

(MOTION PICTURES)

BEDBATH, THE - EMOTIONAL SUPPORT (IND)   COPI
BEDBATH, THE - PROCEDURE (IND)   COPI
GIVING A BEDPAN OR URINAL (IND)   COPI
NURSE'S AIDE, ORDERLY AND ATTENDANT--A SERIES (IND)   COPI
OBSERVATION OF FECES AND URINE (IND)   COPI
PREVENTION AND CARE OF DECUBITI (IND)   COPI
SKIN, THE - FUNCTION AND CARE (IND)   COPI

(AUDIO TAPES)

BORDERLINE PATIENT, THE   SIGINF
HOSPITAL MANAGEMENT OF DISTURBED ADOLESCENTS, THE, PT 1   SIGINF
HOSPITAL MANAGEMENT OF DISTURBED ADOLESCENTS, THE, PT 2   SIGINF
PATIENTS WHO BEHAVE BADLY   SIGINF

STANDARD OF LIVING

(FILMSTRIPS)

CONSUMERISM - THE DANGERS OF AFFLUENCE, PT 1   ASPRSS

CONSUMERISM - THE DANGERS OF AFFLUENCE, PT 2	ASPRSS
DOING IT ALL ON A BUDGET	EGH
LOOKING GREAT ON A SHOESTRING--A SERIES	EGH

INDUSTRIAL AND TECHNICAL EDUCATION

AUTOMATION, GENERAL

(MOTION PICTURES)

CARGO ON THE GO	BEF
STORY OF THE U S MAIL	BEF

AUTOMATION, AUTOMATIC MACHINERY

(MOTION PICTURES)

TOY DEVICES	IWANMI

(VIDEOTAPES)

CENTRAL PROCESSING UNIT - LOGIC AND CONTROL	GPITVL
CENTRAL PROCESSING UNIT - THE COMPUTER'S ARITHMETIC	GPITVL
COMPUTER APPLICATIONS - CAREER OPPORTUNITIES	GPITVL
COMPUTER MEMORY AND DATA REPRESENTATION	GPITVL
DATA PROCESSING - REVIEW	GPITVL
DATA PROCESSING, UNIT 1 - INTRODUCTION TO DATA PROCESSING--A SERIES	GPITVL
DATA PROCESSING, UNIT 2 - THE COMPUTER AND HOW IT WORKS--A SERIES	GPITVL
DATA PROCESSING, UNIT 3 - INSTRUCTING THE COMPUTER--A SERIES	GPITVL
DATA PROCESSING, UNIT 4 - APPLICATIONS AND CAREER OPPORTUNITIES--A SERIES	GPITVL
DECISION TABLES AND INTRODUCTION TO COMPUTER PROGRAMMING	GPITVL
FLOWCHARTING	GPITVL
FLOWCHARTING AND INTRODUCTION TO DECISION TABLES	GPITVL
HISTORY OF ADP AND INTRODUCTION TO UNIT RECORD DATA PROCESSING	GPITVL
HOW COMPUTERS WORK	GPITVL
INPUT-OUTPUT AND SECONDARY MEMORY	GPITVL
INPUT-OUTPUT DEVICES, PT 1	GPITVL
INPUT-OUTPUT DEVICES, PT 2	GPITVL
INSTRUCTING THE COMPUTER	GPITVL
INSTRUCTING THE COMPUTER AND THE OPERATING SYSTEM	GPITVL
INTRODUCTION TO ELECTRONIC DATA PROCESSING - THE COMPUTER	GPITVL
INTRODUCTION TO FLOWCHARTING	GPITVL
MACHINE LANGUAGE PROGRAMMING, PT 1	GPITVL
MACHINE LANGUAGE PROGRAMMING, PT 2	GPITVL
MACHINE LANGUAGE PROGRAMMING, PT 3	GPITVL
PROBLEM ORIENTED LANGUAGES - COBOL	GPITVL
PROBLEM ORIENTED LANGUAGES - FORTRAN	GPITVL
PROBLEM ORIENTED LANGUAGES - REPORT PROGRAM GENERATOR RPG	GPITVL
RECORD LAYOUT AND PRINT CHART	GPITVL
RECORDING MACHINES, THE	GPITVL
SYMBOLIC PROGRAMMING - ASSEMBLER LANGUAGE	GPITVL
TELEPROCESSING AND TIME SHARING SYSTEMS	GPITVL
UNIT RECORD APPLICATIONS	GPITVL
WHY'S OF DATA PROCESSING, THE	GPITVL

AUTOMATION, COMPUTER CONTROL

(FILMSTRIPS)

COMPUTER SYSTEM, THE (H)	EBEC
HISTORY OF THE COMPUTER, THE (H)	EBEC
HOW COMPUTERS WORK--A SERIES (H)	EBEC
INPUT-OUTPUT - HOW COMPUTERS READ AND WRITE (H)	EBEC
NUMBER SYSTEMS - THE COMPUTER'S VOCABULARY (H)	EBEC
SOFTWARE AND HARDWARE AT WORK (H)	EBEC

(VIDEOTAPES)

CENTRAL PROCESSING UNIT - LOGIC AND CONTROL	GPITVL
CENTRAL PROCESSING UNIT - THE COMPUTER'S ARITHMETIC	GPITVL
COMPUTER APPLICATIONS - CAREER OPPORTUNITIES	GPITVL
COMPUTER MEMORY AND DATA REPRESENTATION	GPITVL
DATA PROCESSING - REVIEW	GPITVL
DATA PROCESSING, UNIT 1 - INTRODUCTION TO DATA PROCESSING--A SERIES	GPITVL
DATA PROCESSING, UNIT 2 - THE COMPUTER AND HOW IT WORKS--A SERIES	GPITVL
DATA PROCESSING, UNIT 3 - INSTRUCTING THE COMPUTER--A SERIES	GPITVL
DATA PROCESSING, UNIT 4 - APPLICATIONS AND CAREER OPPORTUNITIES--A SERIES	GPITVL
DECISION TABLES AND INTRODUCTION TO COMPUTER PROGRAMMING	GPITVL
FLOWCHARTING	GPITVL
FLOWCHARTING AND INTRODUCTION TO DECISION TABLES	GPITVL
HISTORY OF ADP AND INTRODUCTION TO UNIT RECORD DATA PROCESSING	GPITVL
HOW COMPUTERS WORK	GPITVL
INPUT-OUTPUT AND SECONDARY MEMORY	GPITVL
INPUT-OUTPUT DEVICES, PT 1	GPITVL
INPUT-OUTPUT DEVICES, PT 2	GPITVL
INSTRUCTING THE COMPUTER	GPITVL
INSTRUCTING THE COMPUTER AND THE OPERATING SYSTEM	GPITVL
INTRODUCTION TO ELECTRONIC DATA PROCESSING - THE COMPUTER	GPITVL
INTRODUCTION TO FLOWCHARTING	GPITVL
MACHINE LANGUAGE PROGRAMMING, PT 1	GPITVL
MACHINE LANGUAGE PROGRAMMING, PT 2	GPITVL
MACHINE LANGUAGE PROGRAMMING, PT 3	GPITVL
PROBLEM ORIENTED LANGUAGES - COBOL	GPITVL
PROBLEM ORIENTED LANGUAGES - FORTRAN	GPITVL
PROBLEM ORIENTED LANGUAGES - REPORT PROGRAM GENERATOR RPG	GPITVL
RECORD LAYOUT AND PRINT CHART	GPITVL
RECORDING MACHINES, THE	GPITVL
SYMBOLIC PROGRAMMING - ASSEMBLER LANGUAGE	GPITVL
TELEPROCESSING AND TIME SHARING SYSTEMS	GPITVL
UNIT RECORD APPLICATIONS	GPITVL
WHY'S OF DATA PROCESSING, THE	GPITVL

AUTOMATION, SYSTEMS ENGINEERING

(FILMSTRIPS)

AUTOMOTIVE MECHANIC, THE (I-C)	SVE

AUTOMOBILE, GENERAL

(FILMSTRIPS)

AUTO BODY - PAINTING	MTSJC
HOW A CAR IS ASSEMBLED	EGH

(MOTION PICTURES)

AFFAIRS OF A MAN, THE (J-C A)	FORD
WONDERFUL WORLD OF SPORT - CARS, AUTO RACING --A SERIES (J-C A)	AMERFI

AUTOMOBILE, BRAKES

(FILMSTRIPS)

BASIC PARTS AND PRINCIPLES (J-C A)	BERGL
HOW TO RELINE DISK-TYPE BRAKES (J-C A)	BERGL
HOW TO RELINE DRUM-TYPE BRAKES (J-C A)	BERGL
HYDRAULIC BRAKE SYSTEM EXPLAINED--A SERIES (J-C A)	BERGL
PROBLEMS - CAUSES AND CORRECTIONS (J-C A)	BERGL
SERVICING THE HYDRAULIC SYSTEM - DISK-TYPE (J-C A)	BERGL
SERVICING THE HYDRAULIC SYSTEM - DRUM-TYPE (J-C A)	BERGL

AUTOMOBILE, ENGINES

(FILMSTRIPS)

BASIC PARTS AND OPERATION (J-C A)	BERGL
CARBURETION, IGNITION AND COOLING (J-C A)	BERGL
HOW TO DO A VALVE JOB (J-C A)	BERGL
INTERNAL COMBUSTION ENGINE EXPLAINED--A SERIES (J-C A)	BERGL
LUBRICATION AND VALVE OPERATION (J-C A)	BERGL
VALVE PROBLEMS - CAUSES AND CORRECTIONS (J-C A)	BERGL

AUTOMOBILE, REPAIRING AND MAINTENANCE

(FILMSTRIPS)

AUTO BODY - PAINTING	MTSJC
BASIC PARTS AND PRINCIPLES (J-C A)	BERGL
HOW TO DO A VALVE JOB (J-C A)	BERGL
HOW TO RELINE DISK-TYPE BRAKES (J-C A)	BERGL
HOW TO RELINE DRUM-TYPE BRAKES (J-C A)	BERGL
HYDRAULIC BRAKE SYSTEM EXPLAINED--A SERIES (J-C A)	BERGL
PROBLEMS - CAUSES AND CORRECTIONS (J-C A)	BERGL
SERVICING THE HYDRAULIC SYSTEM - DISK-TYPE (J-C A)	BERGL
SERVICING THE HYDRAULIC SYSTEM - DRUM-TYPE (J-C A)	BERGL
VALVE PROBLEMS - CAUSES AND CORRECTIONS (J-C A)	BERGL

(MOTION PICTURES)

PERMANENT PROTECTION	MTP

AVIATION, GENERAL (AERONAUTICS)

(MOTION PICTURES)

WONDERFUL WORLD OF SPORT - FLYING--A SERIES (J-C A)	AMERFI

(TRANSPARENCIES)

AIRPLANE (H)	BOW

AVIATION, FLIGHT EDUCATION

(FILMSTRIPS)

AIRLINE CABIN ATTENDANT, THE (I-C)	SVE

(TRANSPARENCIES)

FLIGHT PRINCIPLES (H)	BOW

AVIATION, MISSILES

(MOTION PICTURES)

STEPPING STONES IN SPACE (I-C A)	HEARST

AVIATION, SPACE

(FILMSTRIPS)

DIVIDENDS FROM SPACE (I-J)	DOUBLE
EAGLE HAS LANDED, THE - MAN ON THE MOON (I-J)	DOUBLE
HISTORY OF ASTRONAUTICS, THE, PT 1 (I-J)	DOUBLE
HISTORY OF ASTRONAUTICS, THE, PT 2 (I-J)	DOUBLE
MAN ON THE MOON--A SERIES (I-J)	DOUBLE
STATIONS IN SPACE (I-J)	DOUBLE

(MOTION PICTURES)

APOLLO 17 - ON THE SHOULDERS OF GIANTS (J-C A)	NASA
ERTS - EARTH RESOURCES TECHNOLOGY SATELLITE (J-C A)	NASA
NEW VIEW OF SPACE, A (J-C A)	NASA
STEPPING STONES IN SPACE (I-C A)	HEARST

AVIATION, STRUCTURES

(MOTION PICTURES)

STEPPING STONES IN SPACE (I-C A)	HEARST

CONSTRUCTION, GENERAL

(FILMSTRIPS)

HOW WE BUILD BRIDGES	EGH
HOW WE BUILD CITIES	EGH
HOW WE BUILD HOUSES	EGH
HOW WE BUILD ROADS	EGH
HOW WE BUILD SHIPS	EGH
HOW WE BUILD SKYSCRAPERS	EGH
HOW WE BUILD THINGS--A SERIES	EGH

(MOTION CARTRIDGES)

HOW TO USE HAMMERS	VISIN

(MOTION PICTURES)

SPIRAL JETTY	VISRES

CONSTRUCTION, ARCHITECTURE

(FILMSTRIPS)

HOW WE BUILD BRIDGES	EGH
HOW WE BUILD CITIES	EGH
HOW WE BUILD HOUSES	EGH
HOW WE BUILD SKYSCRAPERS	EGH

CONSTRUCTION, BUILDING

(FILMSTRIPS)

EXTERIOR BUILDING MATERIALS FOR YOUR HOME (J-C A)	USDA
HOUSING--A SERIES (J-C A)	USDA
HOW WE BUILD BRIDGES	EGH
HOW WE BUILD SHIPS	EGH
HOW WE BUILD SKYSCRAPERS	EGH
PLANNING THE BEDROOM (J-C A)	USDA

CONSTRUCTION, CONCRETE

(FILMSTRIPS)

HOW WE BUILD SKYSCRAPERS	EGH

(MOTION PICTURES)

DAMS	IWANMI

CONSTRUCTION, ENGINEERING

(FILMSTRIPS)

HOW WE BUILD BRIDGES	EGH
HOW WE BUILD CITIES	EGH
HOW WE BUILD HOUSES	EGH
HOW WE BUILD ROADS	EGH
HOW WE BUILD SHIPS	EGH
HOW WE BUILD SKYSCRAPERS	EGH

(MOTION PICTURES)

BRIDGE CONSTRUCTION	IWANMI
DAMS	IWANMI
VISTAS OF ISRAEL, NO. 2	ALDEN

CONSTRUCTION, ROADS

(FILMSTRIPS)

HOW WE BUILD ROADS	EGH

(MOTION PICTURES)

VISTAS OF ISRAEL, NO. 1	ALDEN

ELECTRICAL WORK, GENERAL

(FILMSTRIPS)

MAINTENANCE MECHANIC, ELECTRICIAN AND CUSTODIAN	EGH

(MOTION PICTURES)

ELECTRIC BULB SCIENCE	IWANMI

(TRANSPARENCIES)

ELECTRICAL SWITCHES (H)	BOW

ELECTRICAL WORK, WELDING AND SOLDERING

(MOTION PICTURES)

OPPORTUNITIES IN WELDING	USNAC

ELECTRICAL WORK, WIRING

(FILMSTRIPS)

IDENTIFICATION OF ELECTRIC WIRING ITEMS (H-C)	UILVAS

ELECTRONICS, GENERAL

(FILMSTRIPS)

HISTORY OF THE COMPUTER, THE (H)	EBEC
HOW COMPUTERS WORK--A SERIES (H)	EBEC

(MOTION PICTURES)

PHOTO TUBES	IWANMI
WHEN EVERY MINUTE COUNTS	MTP

(VIDEOTAPES)

UNDERSTANDING SEMICONDUCTORS COURSE OUTLINE --A SERIES (IND)	TXINLC

(TRANSPARENCIES)

BATTERIES (H)	BOW
CIRCUITS (H)	BOW
COMPASS (H)	BOW
EARTH'S MAGNETIC FIELD (H)	BOW
ELECTRIC BELL (H)	BOW
ELECTRIC MOTOR (H)	BOW
ELECTROSCOPE (H)	BOW
GENERATING STATION (H)	BOW
LAWS OF MAGNETISM (H)	BOW
MAGNETISM AND ELECTRICITY--A SERIES (H)	BOW
TELEGRAPH (H)	BOW
TELEPHONE (H)	BOW
TELEVISION (H)	BOW

ELECTRONICS, CIRCUITS

(VIDEOTAPES)

UNDERSTANDING SEMICONDUCTORS COURSE OUTLINE --A SERIES (IND)	TXINLC

ELECTRONICS, COMPUTERS

(FILMSTRIPS)

COMPUTER SCIENCE--A SERIES	AVDEV
COMPUTER SYSTEM, THE (H)	EBEC
HARDWARE AND FUNDAMENTAL CONCEPTS	AVDEV
HISTORY OF THE COMPUTER, THE (H)	EBEC
HOW COMPUTERS WORK--A SERIES (H)	EBEC
INPUT-OUTPUT - HOW COMPUTERS READ AND WRITE (H)	EBEC
NUMBER SYSTEMS - THE COMPUTER'S VOCABULARY (H)	EBEC
PRINCIPLES OF FLOWCHARTS	AVDEV
PROGRAMMING - HOW TO ORDER A COMPUTER AROUND (H)	EBEC
PROGRAMMING IN FORTRAN, PT 1	AVDEV
PROGRAMMING IN FORTRAN, PT 2	AVDEV
SOFTWARE AND HARDWARE AT WORK (H)	EBEC

(MOTION PICTURES)

ADDRESSING MACHINE	BEF
INTEGRATED DATA PROCESSING	BEF

ELECTRONICS, RADIO AND TELEVISION

(FILMSTRIPS)

BROADCAST TECHNICIAN, THE (I-C)	SVE

(AUDIO TAPES)

SPOTS BEFORE YOUR EYES (J-C)	IU
TELEVISION	BASCH

ELECTRONICS, SEMICONDUCTORS

(VIDEOTAPES)

UNDERSTANDING SEMICONDUCTORS COURSE OUTLINE --A SERIES (IND)	TXINLC

ELECTRONICS, TELEPHONE AND TELEGRAPH

(FILMSTRIPS)

TELEPHONE INSTALLER, THE (I-C)	SVE

(MOTION PICTURES)

WHAT'S IT ALL ABOUT, HARRY (IND)	DATA

ELECTRONICS, TRANSISTORS

(VIDEOTAPES)

UNDERSTANDING SEMICONDUCTORS COURSE OUTLINE --A SERIES (IND)	TXINLC

ENGINEERING, GENERAL

(MOTION PICTURES)

CHALLENGE OF THE ARCTIC	ARIC
ENGINEERS, THE	MTP
FUTURES IN STEEL	MTP
UNIVERSE AND OTHER THINGS, THE	MTP

ENGINEERING, MARINE

(MOTION PICTURES)

BUILDING A HARBOR (I-J)	AIMS

ENGINEERING, MINING

(MOTION PICTURES)

LIFE FROM THE DEAD SEA	ALDEN

ENGINEERING, NUCLEAR

(FILMSTRIPS)

NUCLEAR TECHNICIAN	EGH

(MOTION PICTURES)

PEACEFUL USE OF NUCLEAR EXPLOSIVES (H-C A)	TIMLIF
TO BOTTLE THE SUN	USAEC

(VIDEOTAPES)

BOMBARDING THINGS (I-J)	GPITVL
DISCOVERING THE ATOM (I-J)	GPITVL
LIVING IN A NUCLEAR AGE--A SERIES (I-J)	GPITVL
NUCLEAR ENERGY AND LIVING THINGS (I-J)	GPITVL
POWER FROM THE ATOM (I-J)	GPITVL
RADIOISOTOPES (I-J)	GPITVL
SOCIETY AND THINGS NUCLEAR (I-J)	GPITVL

ENGINEERING, WATER-SUPPLY

(MOTION PICTURES)

DAMS	IWANMI

ENGINES AND POWER SYSTEMS, GENERAL

(FILMSTRIPS)

BASIC PARTS AND OPERATION (J-C A)	BERGL
CARBURETION, IGNITION AND COOLING (J-C A)	BERGL
HOW TO DO A VALVE JOB (J-C A)	BERGL
INTERNAL COMBUSTION ENGINE EXPLAINED--A SERIES (J-C A)	BERGL
LUBRICATION AND VALVE OPERATION (J-C A)	BERGL
VALVE PROBLEMS - CAUSES AND CORRECTIONS (J-C A)	BERGL

(MOTION PICTURES)

SHIPBOARD VIBRATIONS, PT 3 - VIBRATION, EXCITATION AND RESPONSE	USNAC

(TRANSPARENCIES)

DIESEL ENGINE (H)	BOW
ENGINES--A SERIES (H)	BOW
FOUR-CYCLE ENGINE (H)	BOW
INTERNAL COMBUSTION ENGINE (H)	BOW
JET ENGINE (H)	BOW
ROCKET ENGINE (H)	BOW
STEAM ENGINE (H)	BOW

ENGINES AND POWER SYSTEMS, DIESEL

(TRANSPARENCIES)

DIESEL ENGINE (H)	BOW
ENGINES--A SERIES (H)	BOW

ENGINES AND POWER SYSTEMS, GAS AND OIL ENGINES

(FILMSTRIPS)

BASIC PARTS AND OPERATION (J-C A)	BERGL
CARBURETION, IGNITION AND COOLING (J-C A)	BERGL
HOW TO DO A VALVE JOB (J-C A)	BERGL
INTERNAL COMBUSTION ENGINE EXPLAINED--A SERIES (J-C A)	BERGL
LIVING WITH NATURAL GAS	LILC
LUBRICATION AND VALVE OPERATION (J-C A)	BERGL
VALVE PROBLEMS - CAUSES AND CORRECTIONS (J-C A)	BERGL

(TRANSPARENCIES)

ENGINES--A SERIES (H)	BOW

ENGINES AND POWER SYSTEMS, JET ENGINES

(TRANSPARENCIES)

ENGINES--A SERIES (H)	BOW
JET ENGINE (H)	BOW

ENGINES AND POWER SYSTEMS, ROCKET ENGINES

(TRANSPARENCIES)

ENGINES--A SERIES (H)	BOW
ROCKET ENGINE (H)	BOW

ENGINES AND POWER SYSTEMS, STEAM ENGINES

(TRANSPARENCIES)

ENGINES--A SERIES (H)	BOW
STEAM ENGINE (H)	BOW

MACHINE SHOP AND METALWORK, GENERAL

(FILMSTRIPS)

INTRODUCTION TO OXYACETYLENE WELDING	LIBFSC

MACHINE SHOP AND METALWORK, IRONWORK

(MOTION PICTURES)

WROUGHT IRON - YESTERDAY, TODAY, TOMORROW	MTP

MACHINE SHOP AND METALWORK, STEEL

(MOTION PICTURES)

FUTURES IN STEEL	MTP
SHAPERS OF STAINLESS STEEL, THE	MTP

MACHINE SHOP AND METALWORK, TOOLS, EQUIPMENT AND SAFETY

(FILMSTRIPS)

INTRODUCTION TO OXYACETYLENE WELDING	LIBFSC

(MOTION CARTRIDGES)

HOW TO USE SAWS	VISIN

MACHINE SHOP AND METALWORK, WELDING

(FILMSTRIPS)

INTRODUCTION TO OXYACETYLENE WELDING	LIBFSC

(MOTION PICTURES)

OPPORTUNITIES IN WELDING	USNAC

PHOTOGRAPHY, GENERAL

(FILMSTRIPS)

CAMERA SYSTEMS (J-C A)	ARIZSU
CAMERA, THE (J-C A)	ARIZSU
COMPOSITION (J-C A)	ARIZSU
CREATIVE PHOTOGRAPHY - CAMERA--A SERIES (J-C A)	ARIZSU
EXPOSURE (J-C A)	ARIZSU
LIGHTING, PT 1 (J-C A)	ARIZSU
LIGHTING, PT 2 (J-C A)	ARIZSU

X-RAY TECHNICIAN	EGH

(MOTION PICTURES)

CONSTRUCTING REALITY - A FILM ON FILM (P-C)	JOU
IMOGEN CUNNINGHAM, PHOTOGRAPHER	AMERFI
PHOTO TUBES	IWANMI
WALKER EVANS - HIS TIME, HIS PRESENCE, HIS SILENCE (A)	RADIM

(AUDIO TAPES)

THIRTY YEARS BEHIND A CAMERA (H-C)	DAVI

(TRANSPARENCIES)

PHOTOGRAPHY (H)	BOW

PHOTOGRAPHY, ASTRONOMICAL PHOTOGRAPHY

(MOTION PICTURES)

NEW VIEW OF SPACE, A (J-C A)	NASA

PHOTOGRAPHY, CAMERAS

(FILMSTRIPS)

CAMERA SYSTEMS (J-C A)	ARIZSU
CAMERA, THE (J-C A)	ARIZSU
COMPOSITION (J-C A)	ARIZSU
CREATIVE PHOTOGRAPHY - CAMERA--A SERIES (J-C A)	ARIZSU
EXPOSURE (J-C A)	ARIZSU
LIGHTING, PT 1 (J-C A)	ARIZSU
LIGHTING, PT 2 (J-C A)	ARIZSU

(MOTION PICTURES)

NATURE OF THE FILM MEDIUM, THE	PAULST

(AUDIO TAPES)

THIRTY YEARS BEHIND A CAMERA (H-C)	DAVI

PHOTOGRAPHY, COLOR PHOTOGRAPHY

(FILMSTRIPS)

COMPOSITION (J-C A)	ARIZSU
CREATIVE PHOTOGRAPHY - CAMERA--A SERIES (J-C A)	ARIZSU
EXPOSURE (J-C A)	ARIZSU
LIGHTING, PT 1 (J-C A)	ARIZSU
LIGHTING, PT 2 (J-C A)	ARIZSU

PHOTOGRAPHY, EXPERIMENTAL

(FILMSTRIPS)

COMPOSITION (J-C A)	ARIZSU
CREATIVE PHOTOGRAPHY - CAMERA--A SERIES (J-C A)	ARIZSU
EXPOSURE (J-C A)	ARIZSU
LIGHTING, PT 1 (J-C A)	ARIZSU
LIGHTING, PT 2 (J-C A)	ARIZSU

(MOTION PICTURES)

ART MAKEUP - GREEN, BLACK, WHITE, PINK	VISRES
BLACK MASS	AMERFI
C - CALICLOTH	VISRES
END OF THE ART WORLD	VISRES
FRANK FILM (J-C A)	PFP
HAND CATCHING LEAD	VISRES
MIRROR	VISRES
POSITIVE-NEGATIVE	VISRES
QUICK BILLY	AMERFI
RAZOR BLADES	AMERFI
SIX SHORT FILMS (H-C A)	BFA
SLICE OF GOLD	AMERFI
STILL	AMERFI
T HYBRID V-1	VISRES
T HYBRID V-2	VISRES
TEMPEST, THE	VISRES
THEORIST ROOM	AMERFI
WATER SMITH	AMERFI
WISCONSIN	VISRES

PHOTOGRAPHY, MOVING PICTURE PHOTOGRAPHY

(FILMSTRIPS)

CREATING A MOVIE	EGH
CREATING A MOVIE	EGH

(MOTION PICTURES)

C - CALICLOTH	VISRES
CONSTRUCTING REALITY - A FILM ON FILM (P-C)	JOU
FILMMAKING FUNDAMENTALS (P-H)	AIMS

FILMMAKING TECHNIQUES - ACTING (I-C A)	AIMS
FILMMAKING TECHNIQUES - GOING ON LOCATION (I-C A)	AIMS
FILMMAKING TECHNIQUES - LIGHTING (I-C A)	AIMS
FILMMAKING TECHNIQUES - MAKE-UP (I-C A)	AIMS
FILMMAKING TECHNIQUES - STAGE LIGHTING (I-C A)	AIMS
FILMMAKING TECHNIQUES - STUNTS (I-C A)	AIMS
FILMMAKING TECHNIQUES--A SERIES (I-C A)	AIMS
LOVE AND FILM (H-C A)	BFA
NATURE OF THE FILM MEDIUM, THE	PAULST
POP (H-C A)	BFA
T HYBRID V-2	VISRES
TEMPEST, THE	VISRES

(AUDIO TAPES)

THIRTY YEARS BEHIND A CAMERA (H-C)	DAVI

PHOTOGRAPHY, NATURE PHOTOGRAPHY

(MOTION PICTURES)

SOUNDS OF NATURE	AVEXP

PHOTOGRAPHY, PHOTOMECHANICAL PROCESSES

(MOTION PICTURES)

NATURE OF THE FILM MEDIUM, THE	PAULST
PHOTO TUBES	IWANMI

PHOTOGRAPHY, SLIDES (PHOTOGRAPHY)

(AUDIO TAPES)

SLIDE AND FILM EXCHANGE (H-C)	DAVI
USE OF LANTERN SLIDES IN TEACHING (H-C)	DAVI

PHOTOGRAPHY, SLOW-MOTION

(MOTION PICTURES)

OBSERVATION OF ICE	IWANMI
STORY OF SLOW MOTION PHOTOGRAPHY	IWANMI

PHOTOGRAPHY, STILLS

(MOTION PICTURES)

WALKER EVANS - HIS TIME, HIS PRESENCE, HIS SILENCE (A)	RADIM

PHOTOGRAPHY, TIME-LAPSE

(MOTION PICTURES)

STORY OF LAPSE PHOTOGRAPHY	IWANMI

PRINTING AND GRAPHIC ARTS, GENERAL

(MOTION PICTURES)

BLACK AND WHITE (I-C)	PFP
CIVILISATION, PROGRAM 06	TIMLIF
LOWELL HERRERO - THE GRAPHIC PROCESS	GRADYM

(VIDEOTAPES)

PRINTING (I)	GPITVL

REFRIGERATION, GENERAL

(MOTION PICTURES)

REFRIGERATION - COMPRESSOR CONTROLS	USNAC
REFRIGERATION - CONDENSER CONTROLS	USNAC
STORY OF THE REFRIGERATOR	IWANMI

(TRANSPARENCIES)

REFRIGERATION (H)	BOW

REFRIGERATION, COMPRESSED AIR

(MOTION PICTURES)

REFRIGERATION - COMPRESSOR CONTROLS	USNAC

REFRIGERATION - CONDENSER
CONTROLS USNAC

WOODWORK, GENERAL

(FILMSTRIPS)

CRAFTING A CHAIR EGH

WOODWORK, FINISHING

(FILMSTRIPS)

CRAFTING A CHAIR EGH

WOODWORK, FURNITURE

(FILMSTRIPS)

CRAFTING A CHAIR EGH

WOODWORK, MACHINERY, TOOLS AND SAFETY

(MOTION PICTURES)

SAFETY IN PLYWOOD OPERATIONS (J-C
A) RARIG

LITERATURE

LITERATURE - GENERAL

(FILMSTRIPS)

AMERICAN GENIUS--A SERIES (H-C) EDDIM
AMERICAN GENIUS, 1880 - 1918 (H-C) EDDIM
AMERICAN GENIUS, 1920 - 1940 (H-C) EDDIM
AMERICAN GENIUS, 1940 - 1950 (H-C) EDDIM
AMERICAN ROMANTICISM (J-C) EAV
AMERICAN WEST IN LITERATURE, THE,
PT 1 (J) GA
AMERICAN WEST IN LITERATURE, THE,
PT 2 (J) GA
BEGINNINGS OF REALISM, THE (J-C) EAV
BETWEEN THE WARS (J-C) EAV
CANDIDE - LE TEXTE ET LA VIE DE
VOLTAIRE (H-C) ALEP
DEVELOPMENT OF THE AMERICAN
SHORT STORY--A SERIES (J-C) EAV
FABLES AND FACTS--A SERIES (P-I) TERF
HUMANITIES - A WORLD BETWEEN
WARS, PT 1 (J-H) GA
HUMANITIES - A WORLD BETWEEN
WARS, PT 2 (J-H) GA
HUMANITIES - MAN IN THE NUCLEAR
AGE, PT 1 (J-H) GA
HUMANITIES - MAN IN THE NUCLEAR
AGE, PT 2 (J-H) GA
LITERATURE AND THE FILM--A SERIES
(I-C) EDDIM
SHORT STORY TODAY, THE (J-C) EAV
STORY OF ROBIN HOOD, PT 1 DISNEY
STORY OF ROBIN HOOD, PT 2 DISNEY

(MOTION PICTURES)

CIVILISATION, PROGRAM 03 TIMLIF
CIVILISATION, PROGRAM 06 TIMLIF
THEATER IN SHAKESPEARE'S TIME, THE
(J-C A) BFA

(VIDEOTAPES)

DRAMA - THE PLAY READ (J-H) GPITVL
DRAMA - THE PLAY SEEN (J-H) GPITVL
EDWIN ARLINGTON ROBINSON - A
SAMPLING (J-H) GPITVL
EMILY DICKINSON - ESSENTIAL OILS (J-
H) GPITVL
EMILY DICKINSON - PERSPECTIVES (J-H) GPITVL
ERNEST HEMINGWAY - FOCUS ON
DEATH (J-H) GPITVL
EUGENE O'NEILL - THE EMPEROR
JONES (J-H) GPITVL
EUGENE O'NEILL - THE HAIRY APE (J-H) GPITVL
FROM FRANKLIN TO FROST - PROSPECT
(J-H) GPITVL
FROM FRANKLIN TO FROST -
RETROSPECT (J-H) GPITVL
FROM FRANKLIN TO FROST--A SERIES
(J-H) GPITVL
NARRATIVE FICTION - REPETITION AND
CONTRAST (J-H) GPITVL
RALPH WALDO EMERSON -
EMERSON'S CRITICAL THEORY (J-
H) GPITVL
RALPH WALDO EMERSON -
INTRODUCTION (J-H) GPITVL
RALPH WALDO EMERSON - METER-
MAKING ARGUMENTS (J-H) GPITVL

RALPH WALDO EMERSON - SELF-
RELIANCE, EMERSON'S
PHILOSOPHY (J-H) GPITVL

(RECORDS)

ALFRED JARRY - LE BAIN DU ROI GMS
ALPHONSE DAUDET - LETTRES DE
MON MOULIN, LE SOUS-PREFET
AUX CHAMPS GMS
ANATOLE FRANCE - HISTOIRE
CONTEMPORAINE GMS
ANATOLE FRANCE - PIERRE NOZIERE GMS
ANATOLE FRANCE (EXTRAITS) GMS
ANDRE BRETON - L'UNION LIBRE GMS
ANDRE CHENIER - LA JEUNE CAPTIVE GMS
ANDRE CHENIER - LA JEUNE
TARENTINE GMS
ANDRE CHENIER - TOUJOURS CE
SOUVENIR M'ATTENDRIT ET ME
TOUCHE GMS
ANDRE CHENIER, I GMS
ANDRE CHENIER, II GMS
ANDRE GIDE GMS
ANDRE GIDE - ENTRETIENS AVEC JEAN
AMROUCHE GMS
ANDRE GIDE (EXTRAITS) GMS
BLAISE CENDRARS GMS
BLAISE CENDRARS - HOTEL NOTRE-
DAME, ILES GMS
BLAISE CENDRARS - LE VENTRE DE
MA MERE, LES PAQUES A NEW
YORK GMS
CHARLES BAUDELAIRE - LA MUSIQUE GMS
CHARLES BAUDELAIRE -
RECUEILLEMENT GMS
CHARLES BAUDELAIRE -
RECUEILLEMENT, LA CHEVELURE GMS
COLETTE - APRES L'ORAGE GMS
COLETTE - CHERI, GIGI GMS
COLETTE - DIALOGUE DES BETES GMS
COLETTE (EXTRAITS) GMS
COLETTE VOUS PARLE GMS
DENIS DIDEROT - LE NEVEU DE
RAMEAU, I GMS
DENIS DIDEROT - LE NEVEU DE
RAMEAU, II GMS
DENIS DIDEROT - LE NEVEU DE
RAMEAU, III GMS
DENIS DIDEROT - PARADOXE SUR LE
COMEDIEN GMS
DENIS DIDEROT - SALON GMS
E E CUMMINGS, LECTURING AND
READING SIX NONLECTURES--A
SERIES (H-C) CAED
EDMOND ET JULES GONCOURT -
GERMINIE LACERTEUX GMS
EDMOND HARAUCOURT - RONDEL DE
L'ADIEU GMS
EUGENE FROMENTIN - COCHER DE
SOLEIL, LE PHARE DES BALEINES GMS
EUGENE FROMENTIN - DOMINIQUE GMS
EUGENE FROMENTIN - LE PHARE DES
BALEINES GMS
EUGENE IONESCO - LA CANTATRICE
CHAUVE, LA LECON GMS
FEDERICO GARCIA LORCA GMS
FRANCIS JAMMES - J'AIME L'ANE GMS
FRANCIS JAMMES - JEAN MARCHAT
READS (FRENCH) GMS
FRANCIS JAMMES - JEAN NEGRONI
RECITES (FRENCH) GMS
FRANCIS JAMMES - LA SALLE A
MANGER GMS
FRANCIS JAMMES - PRIERE POUR
MONTER AU PARADIS AVEC LES
ANES GMS
FRANCOIS FENELON - LES AVENTURES
DE TELEMAQUE GMS
FRANCOIS VICOMTE DE
CHATEAUBRIAND GMS
FRANCOIS VICOMTE DE
CHATEAUBRIAND - LE GENIE DU
CHRISTIANISME, RENE GMS
FRANCOIS VICOMTE DE
CHATEAUBRIAND - LE GENIE DU
CHRISTIANISME, LES RUINES GMS
FRANCOIS VICOMTE DE
CHATEAUBRIAND - RENE GMS
FRANCOIS VICOMTE DE
CHATEAUBRIAND - RENE,
REVERIES DE RENE GMS
FRANCOIS VICOMTE DE
CHATEAUBRIAND - TEMOIN DE
HISTOIRE GMS
FRANCOIS VICOMTE DE
CHATEAUBRIAND - UNE NUIT
DANS LES DESERTS DU NOUVEAU
MONDE GMS
GEORGES DE BUFFON - EPOQUES DE LA
NATURE VII GMS
GUSTAVE FLAUBERT - DANS LA
FORET DE FONTAINEBLEAU GMS
GUSTAVE FLAUBERT - FORET DE
FONTAINEBLEAU GMS
GUSTAVE FLAUBERT - MADAME BOVARY
(EXTRAITS) GMS
GUSTAVE FLAUBERT (1821-1880) GMS
HOMMAGE A CHARLES DULLIN GMS

HOMMAGE A LOUIS JOUVET GMS
JACQUES-BENIGNE BOSSUET GMS
JACQUES-BENIGNE BOSSUET -
ORAISON FUNEBRE D'HENRIETTE
D'ANGLETERRE GMS
JEAN COCTEAU - HOMMAGE A JEAN
COCTEAU GMS
JEAN COCTEAU - JEAN MERCURE
RECITES (FRENCH) GMS
JEAN COCTEAU - LES MARIES DE LA
TOUR EIFFEL GMS
JEAN DE LA BRUYERE - LES
CARACTERES DE LA SOCIETE ET
DE LA CONVERSATION, GITON ET
PHEDON GMS
JEAN DE LA BRUYERE - LES
CARACTERES DE LA VILLE GMS
JEAN GIONO GMS
JEAN GIONO - EN HAUTE PROVENCE GMS
JEAN GIONO - LA MOISSON GMS
JEAN GIRAUDOUX GMS
JEAN GIRAUDOUX - PARIS, PRIERE
SUR LA TOUR EIFFEL GMS
JEAN GIRAUDOUX (EXTRAITS) GMS
JEAN-PIERRE DE FLORIAN - LA
CARPE ET LES CARPILLIONS GMS
JOACHIM DU BELLAY GMS
JOACHIM DU BELLAY - HEUREUX QUI,
COMME ULYSSE GMS
JOACHIM DU BELLAY - LE BEAU
VOYAGE GMS
JOACHIM DU BELLAY - LE REGRET GMS
JOACHIM DU BELLAY - SONNET GMS
JOSE-MARIA DE HEREDIA -
EPITAPHE D'UNE SAUTERELLE GMS
JOSE-MARIA DE HEREDIA - LES
CONQUERANTS GMS
JOSE-MARIA DE HEREDIA - MARIS
STELLA GMS
JOSEPH BEDIER - PETIT CRU GMS
JULES LAFORGUE - COMPLAINTE
DE L'OUBLI DES MORTS GMS
JULES LAFORGUE - COMPLAINTE
SUR CERTAINS ENNUIS GMS
JULES LAFORGUE - LOCUTION DES
PIERROTS, SOIR DE CARNAVAL,
L'IMPOSSIBLE GMS
JULES LAFORGUE - RENE LEFEVRE
RECITES (FRENCH) GMS
LAURENT GILBERT - ADIEU A LA VIE GMS
LEON PAUL FARGUE - NOCTURNE GMS
LOUIS LABE - POEMES GMS
LOUIS-FERDINAND CELINE GMS
LOUISE LABE - JE VIS, JE MEURS GMS
LOUISE LABE - TANT QUE MES YEUX GMS
MADAME DE LA FAYETTE - LA
PRINCESSE DE CLEVES GMS
MADAME DE LA FAYETTE - LA
PRINCESSE DE CLEVES GMS
MAURICE FOMBEURE GMS
MAURICE FOMBEURE - MENUISIER DU
ROI GMS
MAURICE FOMBEURE - NOSTALGIE GMS
MAURICE GENEVOIX - LES POISSONS DE
LA LOIRE GMS
MAX JACOB - ALAIN CUNY RECITES
(FRENCH) GMS
MAX JACOB - LE KAMICHI GMS
NONLECTURE FIVE - I AND NOW AND
HIM (H-C) CAED
NONLECTURE FOUR - I AND YOU AND
IS (H-C) CAED
NONLECTURE ONE - I AND MY
PARENTS (H-C) CAED
NONLECTURE SIX - I AND AM AND
SANTA CLAUS (H-C) CAED
NONLECTURE THREE - I AND
SELFDISCOVERY (H-C) CAED
NONLECTURE TWO - I AND THEIR SON
(H-C) CAED
PAUL CLAUDEL - EXCERPTS (FRENCH) GMS
PAUL CLAUDEL - L'ANNONCE FAITE A
MARIE GMS
PAUL CLAUDEL - L'ESPRIT ET L'EAU GMS
PAUL CLAUDEL - LE VIERGE A MIDI GMS
PAUL CLAUDEL, I GMS
PAUL CLAUDEL, II GMS
PAUL ELUARD (1895-1952) GMS
PAUL FORT - CHANSON D'UN
BERGER SURPRIS PAR LA NEIGE GMS
PAUL FORT - COMPLAINTE DU
PETIT CHEVAL BLANC, LA
GRENOUILLE BLEUE GMS
PAUL FORT - LA RONDE GMS
PAUL FORT - LE BONHEUR, LA
RONDE AUTOUR DU MONDE GMS
PAUL FORT (1872-1960) GMS
PAUL-LOUIS COURIER DE MERE -
UNE AVENTURE EN CALABRE GMS
PIERRE DE BEAUMARCHAIS - LE
MARIAGE DE FIGARO (COMPLETE) GMS
PIERRE DE BEAUMARCHAIS - LE
MARIAGE DE FIGARO (EXTRAITS) GMS
PIERRE DE BEAUMARCHAIS - LE
MARIAGE DE FIGARO (EXTRAITS) GMS
PIERRE DE BEAUMARCHAIS - LE
MARIAGE DE FIGARO ACTE I,
SCENE 1, ACTE V, SCENE 3 GMS
PIERRE-AMBROISE CHODERLOS DE

LACIOS · LES LIAISONS DANGEREUSES   GMS
REMY DE GOURMONT · JEANNE   GMS
RENE CHAR   GMS
RENE CHAR · L'INOFFENSIF, LA SORGUE   GMS
RENE GUY CADOU   GMS
ROGER FRISON-ROCHE · ASCENSION DU DRU (MONT BLANC)   GMS
ROLAND DORGELES · CHATEAU DES BROUILLARDS   GMS
SAMUEL BECKETT · OH LES BEAUX JOURS (EXTRAITS)   GMS
SHORT STORIES OF SAKI, THE, VOL 1   CAED
SHORT STORIES OF SAKI, THE, VOL 2   CAED
THEOPHILE GAUTIER · LE CAPITAINE FRACASSE   GMS
THEOPHILE GAUTIER · PAYSAGE NOCTURNE   GMS
TRISTAN CORBIERE · LA PARDON DE SAINTE-ANNE LA-PALUD (EXTRAIT)   GMS
VICTOR HUGO · CE SIECLE AVAIT DEUX ANS   GMS
VICTOR HUGO · LA CAMPAGNE DE RUSSIE   GMS
VICTOR HUGO · LA ROSE DE L'INFANTE, CHANSON D'AUTOMNE   GMS
VICTOR HUGO · LE FIN DE SATAN (EXTRAITS)   GMS
VICTOR HUGO · LES MISERABLES (COSETTE)   GMS
VICTOR HUGO · LES MISERABLES (EXTRAITS)   GMS
VICTOR HUGO · LES MISERABLES (GAVROCHE)   GMS
VICTOR HUGO · NOTRE-DAME DE PARIS   GMS
VICTOR HUGO (EXTRAITS)   GMS

(AUDIO TAPES)

WHO IS THE CENSOR WHAT (A)   UTS

AUTHORS AND THEIR WORKS

(FILMSTRIPS)

HUMANITIES · THE DAWN OF THE TWENTIETH CENTURY, PT 1 (J-H)   GA
HUMANITIES · THE DAWN OF THE TWENTIETH CENTURY, PT 2 (J-H)   GA

(MOTION PICTURES)

POETRY OF BRIAN PATTEN, THE (J-C A)   LONWTV
RIGHT ON (J-C A)   NLC
TRIALS OF FRANZ KAFKA, THE (H-C A)   FOTH

(VIDEOTAPES)

ARTHUR MILLER · DEATH OF A SALESMAN, PT 1 (J-H)   GPITVL
ARTHUR MILLER · DEATH OF A SALESMAN, PT 2 (J-H)   GPITVL
BENJAMIN FRANKLIN · MORALS AND THE MAN (J-H)   GPITVL
BENJAMIN FRANKLIN · POOR RICHARD AND THE MAXIM, THE STYLE OF WIT (J-H)   GPITVL
BENJAMIN FRANKLIN · THE FORMING OF A STYLE (J-H)   GPITVL
BENJAMIN FRANKLIN · THE LENGTHENED MAXIM, FORMAL SATIRE (J-H)   GPITVL
EDGAR ALLAN POE · POE'S POETIC THEORY AND PRACTICE (J-H)   GPITVL
EDGAR ALLAN POE · THE FALL OF THE HOUSE OF USHER (J-H)   GPITVL
EDGAR ALLAN POE · THE PURLOINED LETTER (J-H)   GPITVL
EDGAR ALLEN POE · ASSESSMENT (J-H)   GPITVL
EDWIN ARLINGTON ROBINSON · A SAMPLING (J-H)   GPITVL
EDWIN ARLINGTON ROBINSON · ASSESSMENT (J-H)   GPITVL
EDWIN ARLINGTON ROBINSON · CHARACTERISTIC (J-H)   GPITVL
EDWIN ARLINGTON ROBINSON · EROS TURANNOS, MR FLOOD'S PARTY (J-H)   GPITVL
EMILY DICKINSON · A SAMPLING (J-H)   GPITVL
EMILY DICKINSON · ESSENTIAL OILS (J-H)   GPITVL
EMILY DICKINSON · PERSPECTIVES (J-H)   GPITVL
EMILY DICKINSON · STYLE (J-H)   GPITVL
ERNEST HEMINGWAY · BIG TWO HEARTED RIVER (J-H)   GPITVL
ERNEST HEMINGWAY · FOCUS ON DEATH (J-H)   GPITVL
ERNEST HEMINGWAY · THE OLD MAN AND THE SEA, PT 1 (J-H)   GPITVL
ERNEST HEMINGWAY · THE OLD MAN AND THE SEA, PT 2 (J-H)   GPITVL
FROM FRANKLIN TO FROST · PROSPECT (J-H)   GPITVL
FROM FRANKLIN TO FROST--A SERIES (J-H)   GPITVL

MARK TWAIN · CRITICAL THEORY (J-H)   GPITVL
MARK TWAIN · FROGS, JAYS AND HUMOR (J-H)   GPITVL
MARK TWAIN · HUCK FINN · CHARACTER AND GROWTH (J-H)   GPITVL
MARK TWAIN · THE ADVENTURES OF HUCKLEBERRY FINN (J-H)   GPITVL
NARRATIVE FICTION · DIVIDE AND CONQUER, THE MEANING OF ANALYSIS (J-H)   GPITVL
NATHANIEL HAWTHORNE · THE AMBITIOUS GUEST (J-H)   GPITVL
NATHANIEL HAWTHORNE · THE MINISTER'S BLACK VEIL (J-H)   GPITVL
NATHANIEL HAWTHORNE · THE SCARLET LETTER AND THE FORTUNATE FALL (J-H)   GPITVL
NATHANIEL HAWTHORNE · THE WORLD OF THE SCARLET LETTER AND ITS STRUCTURE (J-H)   GPITVL
RALPH WALDO EMERSON · EMERSON'S CRITICAL THEORY (J-H)   GPITVL
RALPH WALDO EMERSON · EMERSON'S DISCIPLE, THOREAU (J-H)   GPITVL
RALPH WALDO EMERSON · INTRODUCTION (J-H)   GPITVL
RALPH WALDO EMERSON · METER-MAKING ARGUMENTS (J-H)   GPITVL
RALPH WALDO EMERSON · SELF-RELIANCE, EMERSON'S PHILOSOPHY (J-H)   GPITVL
ROBERT FROST · A SAMPLING (J-H)   GPITVL
ROBERT FROST · FACT, FORM, PROCESS AND MEANING (J-H)   GPITVL
ROBERT FROST · PERSPECTIVES (J-H)   GPITVL
ROBERT FROST · SIMPLICITY AND COMPLEXITY (J-H)   GPITVL
STEPHEN CRANE · THE BLUE HOTEL (J-H)   GPITVL
STEPHEN CRANE · THE BRIDE COMES TO YELLOW SKY (J-H)   GPITVL
STEPHEN CRANE · THE RED BADGE OF COURAGE, PT 1 (J-H)   GPITVL
STEPHEN CRANE · THE RED BADGE OF COURAGE, PT 2 (J-H)   GPITVL
WALT WHITMAN · DRUM TAPS (J-H)   GPITVL
WALT WHITMAN · SONG OF MYSELF, PT 1 (J-H)   GPITVL
WALT WHITMAN · SONG OF MYSELF, PT 2 (J-H)   GPITVL
WALT WHITMAN · WHEN LILACS IN THE DOORYARD BLOOM'D (J-H)   GPITVL

(RECORDS)

ALBERT CAMUS · EXCERPTS   GMS
ALBERT CAMUS · L'ETRANGER   GMS
ALBERT CAMUS · SELECTIONS   GMS
BAT POET, THE   CAED
E E CUMMINGS READING HIS POETRY (H-C)   CAED
E E CUMMINGS, LECTURING AND READING SIX NONLECTURES--A SERIES (H-C)   CAED
GUILLAUME APOLLINAIRE · LE PONT MIRABEAU   GMS
HILDA CONKLING READING HER POETRY   CAED
JEAN COCTEAU (1889-1963)   GMS
LA VOIX DE PAUL ELUARD   GMS
LOUIS ARAGON · AMOURS   GMS
LOUIS-FERDINAND CELINE   GMS
MARCEL ACHARD · DISCOURS SOUS LA COUPOLE   GMS
MARCEL ACHARD · MARLBOROUGH S'EN VA-T-EN GUERRE   GMS
MARCEL ACHARD · VOULEZ-VOUS JOUER AVEC MOI   GMS
NONLECTURE FIVE · I AND NOW AND HIM (H-C)   CAED
NONLECTURE FOUR · I AND YOU AND IS (H-C)   CAED
NONLECTURE ONE · I AND MY PARENTS (H-C)   CAED
NONLECTURE SIX · I AND AM AND SANTA CLAUS (H-C)   CAED
NONLECTURE THREE · I AND SELFDISCOVERY (H-C)   CAED
NONLECTURE TWO · I AND THEIR SON (H-C)   CAED
PAUL ELUARD   GMS
PAUL ELUARD · DONNER A VOIR   GMS
PAUL ELUARD · GERARD PHILIPE RECITES (FRENCH)   GMS
PAUL ELUARD · L'AMOUREUSE   GMS
PRESENCE DE ALBERT CAMUS   GMS
RANDALL JARRELL READS AND DISCUSSES HIS POEMS AGAINST WAR   CAED
THEODORE ROETHKE READS HIS POETRY (H-C)   CAED

(AUDIO TAPES)

WHAT IS A BOOK (I-J)   INSKY

(TRANSPARENCIES)

LANGSTON HUGHES (J-H)   LEART
PAUL LAURENCE DUNBAR (J-H)   LEART
SHAKESPEARE--A SERIES   BETECL

CHILDREN'S STORIES

(FILMSTRIPS)

AIR (P-I)   TERF
ALADDIN (K-P)   STNHM
ALL THE ANIMALS WERE ANGRY (P-I)   BFA
BRODERICK (P-I)   BFA
CHILDREN'S STORIES--A SERIES (K-P)   STNHM
CINDERELLA (K-P)   STNHM
DON QUIXOTE (K-P)   STNHM
DR DOOLITTLE (K-P)   STNHM
DRAGON STEW (P-I)   BFA
FABLES AND FACTS--A SERIES (P-I)   TERF
FIRE (P-I)   TERF
FIVE NAUGHTY MARBLES (K-P)   STNHM
GOLDEN FISH, THE (K-P)   STNHM
HEAVENS (P-I)   TERF
LAZY CAT, THE (K-P)   STNHM
LIFE COMES TO THE WORLD (P-I)   TERF
LITTLE RED RIDING HOOD (K-P)   STNHM
MAGICAL COQUI (P)   UMM
PETER AND THE WOLF (K-P)   STNHM
PETER AND THE WOLF (K-H)   EAV
PINOCCHIO (K-P)   STNHM
PUSS IN BOOTS (K-P)   STNHM
SNOW WHITE (K-P)   STNHM
SORCERER'S APPRENTICE, THE (K-P)   STNHM
STORY SERIES 6--A SERIES (P-I)   BFA
SUN (P-I)   TERF
THREE BEARS, THE (K-P)   STNHM
THUMBELINA (K-P)   STNHM
THUNDER AND LIGHTNING (P-I)   TERF
TIGER IN THE TEAPOT, THE (P-I)   BFA
TOM THUMB (K-P)   STNHM
TWINKLE NOSE, THE FIREFLY   EGH
TWO DERVISHES, THE (K-P)   STNHM
UGLY DUCKLING, THE (K-P)   STNHM
WATER (P-I)   TERF
WORLD IS BORN, THE (P-I)   TERF

(MOTION PICTURES)

BOY NAMED CHARLIE BROWN, A   SWANK
CARNIVAL, THE · THE STORY OF A GIRL AND A GOLDFISH (P)   XEROX
PETER AND THE WOLF   DISNEY
SEVENTH MANDARIN, THE (I)   XEROX
SHOW ME THE WAY TO GO HOME   MTP
TUB FILM (J-C A)   BFA
WHATEVER IS FUN (P-J)   CCMFI
WHITE MANE   CCMFI
WORLD'S GREATEST FREAK SHOW, THE (P-I)   XEROX
ZEBRAS (K-I)   TEXFLM

(RECORDS)

BABAR EN FAMILLE   GMS
BABAR ET CE COQUIN D'ARTHUR   GMS
BABAR ET LE PERE NOEL   GMS
BABAR ET LE PROFESSEUR GRIFATON   GMS
BABAR STORIES--A SERIES   GMS
BRER RABBIT AND MORE BRER RABBIT   SPA
GOLDILOCKS AND THE THREE BEARS, HEREAFTER THIS, DICK WITTINGTON AND HIS CAT   SPA
GULLIVER'S TRAVELS   CAED
HILAIRE BELLOC · CAUTIONARY TALES (K-H)   CAED
IRISH FAIRY TALES   SPA
WIND IN THE WILLOWS, THE   SPA

(AUDIO TAPES)

RAPUNZEL AND THE GOLDEN BIRD (I)   UTEX

CHRISTIAN LITERATURE, EARLY

(MOTION PICTURES)

WALLS OF TIME, THE (J-C A)   PFP

(RECORDS)

TWO CANTERBURY TALES IN MIDDLE ENGLISH · THE PARDONER'S PROLOGUE AND TALE AND THE NUNS (C)..   CAED
TWO CANTERBURY TALES IN MODERN ENGLISH · THE PARDONER'S TALE AND THE MILLER'S TALE (C)   CAED

CRITICISM

(FILMSTRIPS)

MODERN NOVEL, THE · CATCHER IN THE RYE (I-C)   EDDIM

DRAMA

(FILMSTRIPS)

LITERATURE AND THE FILM - THE IMPORTANCE OF BEING EARNEST (I-C)	EDDIM

(MOTION PICTURES)

DIARY OF A MAD HOUSEWIFE (C A)	SWANK
DON JUAN TENORIO - 1970 (H-C)	UWISC

(VIDEOTAPES)

ARTHUR MILLER - DEATH OF A SALESMAN, PT 1 (J-H)	GPITVL
ARTHUR MILLER - DEATH OF A SALESMAN, PT 2 (J-H)	GPITVL
DRAMA - THE PLAY READ (J-H)	GPITVL
DRAMA - THE PLAY SEEN (J-H)	GPITVL
EUGENE O'NEILL - THE EMPEROR JONES (J-H)	GPITVL
EUGENE O'NEILL - THE HAIRY APE (J-H)	GPITVL

(RECORDS)

GERARD PHILIPE - TNP	GMS
PIERRE CORNEILLE - CINNA	GMS
PIERRE CORNEILLE - CINNA, EXTRAITS	GMS
PIERRE CORNEILLE - HORACE	GMS
PIERRE CORNEILLE - POLYEUCTE (EXTRAITS)	GMS

FABLES

(FILMSTRIPS)

AIR (P-I)	TERF
ALL THE ANIMALS WERE ANGRY (P-I)	RFA
BRODERICK (P-I)	BFA
DRAGON STEW (P-I)	BFA
FABLES AND FACTS--A SERIES (P-I)	TERF
FIRE (P-I)	TERF
HEAVENS (P-I)	TERF
LIFE COMES TO THE WORLD (P-I)	TERF
PETER AND THE WOLF (K-H)	EAV
STORY SERIES 6--A SERIES (P-I)	BFA
SUN (P-I)	TERF
THUNDER AND LIGHTNING (P-I)	TERF
TIGER IN THE TEAPOT, THE (P-I)	BFA
WATER (P-I)	TERF
WORLD IS BORN, THE (P-I)	TERF

(MOTION PICTURES)

PETER AND THE WOLF	DISNEY

FAIRY TALES

(FILMSTRIPS)

ALADDIN (K-P)	STNHM
CHILDREN'S STORIES--A SERIES (K-P)	STNHM
CINDERELLA (K-P)	STNHM
DON QUIXOTE (K-P)	STNHM
DR DOOLITTLE (K-P)	STNHM
FIVE NAUGHTY MARBLES (K-P)	STNHM
GOLDEN FISH, THE (K-P)	STNHM
LAZY CAT, THE (K-P)	STNHM
LITERATURE AND THE FILM - BEAUTY AND THE BEAST (I-C)	EDDIM
LITTLE RED RIDING HOOD (K-P)	STNHM
PETER AND THE WOLF (K-P)	STNHM
PINOCCHIO (K-P)	STNHM
PUSS IN BOOTS (K-P)	STNHM
SNOW WHITE (K-P)	STNHM
SORCERER'S APPRENTICE, THE (K-P)	STNHM
THREE BEARS, THE (K-P)	STNHM
THUMBELINA (K-P)	STNHM
TOM THUMB (K-P)	STNHM
TWINKLE NOSE, THE FIREFLY	EGH
TWO DERVISHES, THE (K-P)	STNHM
UGLY DUCKLING, THE (K-P)	STNHM

(MOTION PICTURES)

ALADDIN	PUI
ALI BABA	PUI
DRUMMER BOY, THE	PUI
FAIRY TALE TIME--A SERIES	PUI
FLYING TRUNK, THE	PUI
GOLDEN BIRD, THE	PUI
GOLDEN GOOSE, THE	PUI
GOLDEN TOUCH, THE	PUI
HANSEL AND GRETEL	PUI
LEO THE LION-HEARTED	PUI
RAPUNZEL	PUI
RUMPELSTILTSKIN	PUI
SINBAD	PUI
SOLDIER AND THE DRAGON, THE	PUI
TAILOR'S ADVENTURE, THE	PUI
TIN SOLDIER, THE	PUI
WELL OF WISDOM, THE	PUI

(RECORDS)

BRER RABBIT AND MORE BRER RABBIT	SPA
FOLK AND FAIRY TALES FROM AFRICA	SPA
FOLK AND FAIRY TALES FROM DENMARK	SPA
FOLK AND FAIRY TALES FROM ENGLAND	SPA
FOLK AND FAIRY TALES FROM FRANCE	SPA
FOLK AND FAIRY TALES FROM GERMANY	SPA
FOLK AND FAIRY TALES FROM ITALY	SPA
FOLK AND FAIRY TALES FROM JAPAN	SPA
FOLK AND FAIRY TALES FROM MEXICO	SPA
FOLK AND FAIRY TALES FROM RUSSIA	SPA
GOLDILOCKS AND THE THREE BEARS, HEREAFTER THIS, DICK WITTINGTON AND HIS CAT	SPA
IRISH FAIRY TALES	SPA

(AUDIO TAPES)

RAPUNZEL AND THE GOLDEN BIRD (I)	UTEX

FICTION

(FILMSTRIPS)

AIR (P-I)	TERF
AMERICAN WEST IN LITERATURE, THE, PT 1 (J)	GA
AMERICAN WEST IN LITERATURE, THE, PT 2 (J)	GA
CHILDREN'S STORIES--A SERIES (K-P)	STNHM
FABLES AND FACTS--A SERIES (P-I)	TERF
FIRE (P-I)	TERF
FISH IN THE FOREST - A RUSSIAN FOLKTALE (I)	GA
HEAVENS (P-I)	TERF
LIFE COMES TO THE WORLD (P-I)	TERF
MODERN NOVEL, THE - CATCHER IN THE RYE (I-C)	EDDIM
STORY OF ROBIN HOOD, PT 1	DISNEY
STORY OF ROBIN HOOD, PT 1	DISNEY
STORY OF ROBIN HOOD, PT 2	DISNEY
STORY OF ROBIN HOOD, PT 2	DISNEY
SUN (P-I)	TERF
THUNDER AND LIGHTNING (P-I)	TERF
WATER (P-I)	TERF
WORLD IS BORN, THE (P-I)	TERF

(MOTION PICTURES)

TELL-TALE HEART, THE	AMERFI

(VIDEOTAPES)

NARRATIVE FICTION - DIVIDE AND CONQUER, THE MEANING OF ANALYSIS (J-H)	GPITVL
NARRATIVE FICTION - REPETITION AND CONTRAST (J-H)	GPITVL
NARRATIVE FICTION - THE STORY AS ART, THE THING MADE (J-H)	GPITVL

(RECORDS)

CANTERVILLE GHOST, THE (J-C)	CAED
HILAIRE BELLOC - CAUTIONARY TALES (K-H)	CAED
MONKEY'S PAW AND THE INTERUPTION, THE (H-C)	CAED

(AUDIO TAPES)

RAPUNZEL AND THE GOLDEN BIRD (I)	UTEX

FOLKLORE

(FILMSTRIPS)

ALADDIN (K-P)	STNHM
CHILDREN'S STORIES--A SERIES (K-P)	STNHM
CINDERELLA (K-P)	STNHM
DON QUIXOTE (K-P)	STNHM
DR DOOLITTLE (K-P)	STNHM
FISH IN THE FOREST - A RUSSIAN FOLKTALE (I)	GA
FIVE NAUGHTY MARBLES (K-P)	STNHM
GOLDEN FISH, THE (K-P)	STNHM
LAZY CAT, THE (K-P)	STNHM
LITERATURE AND THE FILM - BLACK ORPHEUS (I-C)	EDDIM
LITTLE RED RIDING HOOD (K-P)	STNHM
PETER AND THE WOLF (K-P)	STNHM
PINOCCHIO (K-P)	STNHM
PUSS IN BOOTS (K-P)	STNHM
SNOW WHITE (K-P)	STNHM
SORCERER'S APPRENTICE, THE (K-P)	STNHM
STORY OF ROBIN HOOD, PT 1	DISNEY
STORY OF ROBIN HOOD, PT 1	DISNEY
STORY OF ROBIN HOOD, PT 2	DISNEY
STORY OF ROBIN HOOD, PT 2	DISNEY
THREE BEARS, THE (K-P)	STNHM
THUMBELINA (K-P)	STNHM
TOM THUMB (K-P)	STNHM
TWO DERVISHES, THE (K-P)	STNHM

UGLY DUCKLING, THE (K-P)	STNHM

(RECORDS)

FOLK AND FAIRY TALES FROM AFRICA	SPA
FOLK AND FAIRY TALES FROM DENMARK	SPA
FOLK AND FAIRY TALES FROM ENGLAND	SPA
FOLK AND FAIRY TALES FROM FRANCE	SPA
FOLK AND FAIRY TALES FROM GERMANY	SPA
FOLK AND FAIRY TALES FROM ITALY	SPA
FOLK AND FAIRY TALES FROM JAPAN	SPA
FOLK AND FAIRY TALES FROM MEXICO	SPA
FOLK AND FAIRY TALES FROM RUSSIA	SPA

HISTORY AND CRITICISM

(FILMSTRIPS)

LITERATURE AND THE FILM - BEAUTY AND THE BEAST (I-C)	EDDIM
LITERATURE AND THE FILM - BLACK ORPHEUS (I-C)	EDDIM
LITERATURE AND THE FILM - OLIVER TWIST (I-C)	EDDIM
LITERATURE AND THE FILM - THE IMPORTANCE OF BEING EARNEST (I-C)	EDDIM
LITERATURE AND THE FILM--A SERIES (I-C)	EDDIM
MODERN NOVEL, THE - CATCHER IN THE RYE (I-C)	EDDIM

(AUDIO TAPES)

WESTMINISTER BRIDGE (C A)	IU
WHAT DOES A POEM MEAN (C A)	WEUD

(TRANSPARENCIES)

SHAKESPEARE--A SERIES	BETECL

MEDIEVAL

(RECORDS)

LE MORTE D'ARTHUR	CAED
TWO CANTERBURY TALES IN MIDDLE ENGLISH - THE PARDONER'S PROLOGUE AND TALE AND THE NUNS (C)..	CAED
TWO CANTERBURY TALES IN MODERN ENGLISH - THE PARDONER'S TALE AND THE MILLER'S TALE (C)	CAED

NEGRO LITERATURE

(MOTION PICTURES)

RIGHT ON (J-C A)	NLC

(TRANSPARENCIES)

LANGSTON HUGHES (J-H)	LEART
PAUL LAURENCE DUNBAR (J-H)	LEART

NOVELS

(FILMSTRIPS)

AMERICAN GENIUS, 1940 - 1950 (H-C)	EDDIM
MODERN NOVEL, THE - CATCHER IN THE RYE (I-C)	EDDIM

(MOTION PICTURES)

TRIALS OF FRANZ KAFKA, THE (H-C A)	FOTH

(VIDEOTAPES)

ERNEST HEMINGWAY - THE OLD MAN AND THE SEA, PT 1 (J-H)	GPITVL
ERNEST HEMINGWAY - THE OLD MAN AND THE SEA, PT 2 (J-H)	GPITVL
FROM FRANKLIN TO FROST--A SERIES (J-H)	GPITVL
NATHANIEL HAWTHORNE - THE SCARLET LETTER AND THE FORTUNATE FALL (J-H)	GPITVL
NATHANIEL HAWTHORNE - THE WORLD OF THE SCARLET LETTER AND ITS STRUCTURE (J-H)	GPITVL
STEPHEN CRANE - THE RED BADGE OF COURAGE, PT 1 (J-H)	GPITVL
STEPHEN CRANE - THE RED BADGE OF COURAGE, PT 2 (J-H)	GPITVL

(RECORDS)

ALBERT CAMUS - EXCERPTS	GMS
ALBERT CAMUS - L'ETRANGER	GMS
ALBERT CAMUS - SELECTIONS	GMS

GULLIVER'S TRAVELS	CAED	MODERN ENGLISH · THE PARDONER'S TALE AND THE MILLER'S		NATHANIEL HAWTHORNE · THE MINISTER'S BLACK VEIL (J-H)	GPITVL
LE MORTE D'ARTHUR	CAED	TALE (C)	CAED	SAMPLING, A (J-H)	GPITVL
		VICTORIAN POETRY (J-C)	CAED	SELECTION, ORDER, EMPHASIS (J-H)	GPITVL
POETRY		WHEN WE WERE VERY YOUNG (P-I)	CAED	STEPHEN CRANE · THE BLUE HOTEL (J-H)	GPITVL
				STEPHEN CRANE · THE BRIDE COMES	
(FILMSTRIPS)		**(AUDIO TAPES)**		TO YELLOW SKY (J-H)	GPITVL

POETRY

(FILMSTRIPS)

AMERICAN WEST IN LITERATURE, THE, PT 1 (J)	GA
AMERICAN WEST IN LITERATURE, THE, PT 2 (J)	GA

(MOTION PICTURES)

POEM FIELD NO. 1 (J-C A)	UEVA
POETRY OF BRIAN PATTEN, THE (J-C A)	LONWTV
RIGHT ON (J-C A)	NLC

(VIDEOTAPES)

EDGAR ALLAN POE · POE'S POETIC THEORY AND PRACTICE (J-H)	GPITVL
EDGAR ALLEN POE · ASSESSMENT (J-H)	GPITVL
EDWIN ARLINGTON ROBINSON · ASSESSMENT (J-H)	GPITVL
EDWIN ARLINGTON ROBINSON · CHARACTERISTIC (J-H)	GPITVL
EDWIN ARLINGTON ROBINSON · EROS TURANNOS, MR FLOOD'S PARTY (J-H)	GPITVL
EMILY DICKINSON · A SAMPLING (J-H)	GPITVL
EMILY DICKINSON · STYLE (J-H)	GPITVL
FROM FRANKLIN TO FROST · PROSPECT (J-H)	GPITVL
FROM FRANKLIN TO FROST · RETROSPECT (J-H)	GPITVL
FROM FRANKLIN TO FROST--A SERIES (J-H)	GPITVL
POETRY · DICTION (J-H)	GPITVL
POETRY · IMAGERY (J-H)	GPITVL
POETRY · RHYME (J-H)	GPITVL
POETRY · RHYTHM (J-H)	GPITVL
ROBERT FROST · A SAMPLING (J-H)	GPITVL
ROBERT FROST · FACT, FORM, PROCESS AND MEANING (J-H)	GPITVL
ROBERT FROST · PERSPECTIVES (J-H)	GPITVL
ROBERT FROST · SIMPLICITY AND COMPLEXITY (J-H)	GPITVL
WALT WHITMAN · DRUM TAPS (J-H)	GPITVL
WALT WHITMAN · SONG OF MYSELF, PT 1 (J-H)	GPITVL
WALT WHITMAN · SONG OF MYSELF, PT 2 (J-H)	GPITVL
WALT WHITMAN · WHEN LILACS IN THE DOORYARD BLOOM'D (J-H)	GPITVL

(RECORDS)

ANDRE CHENIER · LA JEUNE CAPTIVE	GMS
ANDRE CHENIER · LA JEUNE TARENTINE	GMS
ANDRE CHENIER · TOUJOURS CE SOUVENIR M'ATTENDRIT ET ME TOUCHE	GMS
ANDRE CHENIER (1762-1764)	GMS
ANDRE CHENIER, I	GMS
ANDRE CHENIER, II	GMS
BAT POET, THE	CAED
BLAISE CENDRARS	GMS
CLASSICS OF ENGLISH POETRY FOR THE ELEMENTARY CURRICULUM (K-P)	CAED
DYLAN THOMAS READS THE POETRY OF W B YEATS AND OTHERS (H-C)	CAED
E E CUMMINGS READING HIS POETRY (H-C)	CAED
FRANCIS CARCO	GMS
GUILLAUME APOLLINAIRE · POEMES, I	GMS
GUILLAUME APOLLINAIRE · POEMES, II	GMS
GUILLAUME APOLLINAIRE · POEMES, III	GMS
GUILLAUME APOLLINAIRE · POEMES, IV	GMS
GUILLAUME APOLLINAIRE · POEMES, V	GMS
HILDA CONKLING READING HER POETRY	CAED
JEAN COCTEAU (1889-1963)	GMS
LA VOIX DE PAUL ELUARD	GMS
LOUIS ARAGON · AMOURS	GMS
PAUL ELUARD	GMS
PAUL ELUARD · DONNER A VOIR	GMS
PAUL ELUARD · GERARD PHILIPE RECITES (FRENCH)	GMS
PAUL ELUARD · L'AMOUREUSE	GMS
POEMS AND SONGS FOR YOUNGER CHILDREN	SPA
POETRY OF GEORGE GORDON BYRON	CAED
POETRY OF PERCY BYSSHE SHELLEY (H-C)	CAED
RANDALL JARRELL READS AND DISCUSSES HIS POEMS AGAINST WAR	CAED
THEODORE ROETHKE READS HIS POETRY (H-C)	CAED
TWO CANTERBURY TALES IN MIDDLE ENGLISH · THE PARDONER'S PROLOGUE AND TALE AND THE NUNS (C)..	CAED
TWO CANTERBURY TALES IN	

(AUDIO TAPES)

WESTMINISTER BRIDGE (C A)	IU
WHAT DOES A POEM MEAN (C A)	WEUD

(TRANSPARENCIES)

LANGSTON HUGHES (J-H)	LEART
PAUL LAURENCE DUNBAR (J-H)	LEART

REALISM

(FILMSTRIPS)

BEGINNINGS OF REALISM, THE (J-C)	EAV

ROMANTICISM

(FILMSTRIPS)

AMERICAN ROMANTICISM (J-C)	EAV

SAGAS

(RECORDS)

CHANSON DE ROLAND (MORT D'OLIVER ET DE ROLAND)	GMS
LA BATAILLE DE QADECH	GMS
LA CHANSON DE ROLAND	GMS
LA CHANSON DE ROLAND (L'EPISODE DE RONCEVAUX)	GMS

SATIRE

(FILMSTRIPS)

ONCE UPON A COMPULSION	KELLRP

(MOTION PICTURES)

BLAZE GLORY (J-C A)	PFP
LANTON MILLS	AMERFI
PICKLES (H-C A)	BFA

(VIDEOTAPES)

BENJAMIN FRANKLIN · THE LENGTHENED MAXIM, FORMAL SATIRE (J-H)	GPITVL
HUMOR · SATIRE (J-H)	GPITVL

(RECORDS)

MODEST PROPOSAL, A	CAED

SHORT STORY

(FILMSTRIPS)

AMERICAN ROMANTICISM (J-C)	EAV
BEGINNINGS OF REALISM, THE (J-C)	EAV
BETWEEN THE WARS (J-C)	EAV
DEVELOPMENT OF THE AMERICAN SHORT STORY--A SERIES (J-C)	EAV
SHORT STORY TODAY, THE (J-C)	EAV

(MOTION PICTURES)

TELL-TALE HEART, THE	AMERFI
TRIALS OF FRANZ KAFKA, THE (H-C A)	FOTH

(VIDEOTAPES)

BENJAMIN FRANKLIN · MORALS AND THE MAN (J-H)	GPITVL
BENJAMIN FRANKLIN · POOR RICHARD AND THE MAXIM, THE STYLE OF WIT (J-H)	GPITVL
BENJAMIN FRANKLIN · THE FORMING OF A STYLE (J-H)	GPITVL
EDGAR ALLAN POE · POE'S POETIC THEORY AND PRACTICE (J-H)	GPITVL
EDGAR ALLAN POE · THE FALL OF THE HOUSE OF USHER (J-H)	GPITVL
EDGAR ALLAN POE · THE PURLOINED LETTER (J-H)	GPITVL
ERNEST HEMINGWAY · BIG TWO HEARTED RIVER (J-H)	GPITVL
FROM FRANKLIN TO FROST--A SERIES (J-H)	GPITVL
NARRATIVE FICTION · DIVIDE AND CONQUER, THE MEANING OF ANALYSIS (J-H)	GPITVL
NARRATIVE FICTION · THE STORY AS ART, THE THING MADE (J-H)	GPITVL
NATHANIEL HAWTHORNE · THE AMBITIOUS GUEST (J-H)	GPITVL

(RECORDS)

CANTERVILLE GHOST, THE (J-C)	CAED
MONKEY'S PAW AND THE INTERUPTION, THE (H-C)	CAED
SHORT STORIES OF SAKI, THE, VOL 1	CAED
SHORT STORIES OF SAKI, THE, VOL 2	CAED

STYLE, LITERARY

(VIDEOTAPES)

BENJAMIN FRANKLIN · THE FORMING OF A STYLE (J-H)	GPITVL
EDWIN ARLINGTON ROBINSON · CHARACTERISTIC (J-H)	GPITVL
EMILY DICKINSON · STYLE (J-H)	GPITVL
FROM FRANKLIN TO FROST--A SERIES (J-H)	GPITVL
MARK TWAIN · CRITICAL THEORY (J-H)	GPITVL
MARK TWAIN · HUCK FINN · CHARACTER AND GROWTH (J-H)	GPITVL
NARRATIVE FICTION · REPETITION AND CONTRAST (J-H)	GPITVL
ROBERT FROST · FACT, FORM, PROCESS AND MEANING (J-H)	GPITVL
ROBERT FROST · SIMPLICITY AND COMPLEXITY (J-H)	GPITVL

(AUDIO TAPES)

WHAT DOES A POEM MEAN (C A)	WEUD

WIT AND HUMOR

(FILMSTRIPS)

COMICAL SITUATIONS OF EVERYDAY LIFE, PT 1 (J-H)	ALEP
COMICAL SITUATIONS OF EVERYDAY LIFE, PT 2 (J-H)	ALEP

(MOTION PICTURES)

BOY NAMED CHARLIE BROWN, A	SWANK
CHICKEN SOUP (J-C A)	CAROUF
GOLDEN AGE OF COMEDY	CAROUF
LOVE AND FILM (H-C A)	BFA
MISTER MAGROOTER'S MARVELOUS MACHINE (I-C A)	BOSUST
ZEBRAS (K-I)	TEXFLM

(VIDEOTAPES)

BENJAMIN FRANKLIN · POOR RICHARD AND THE MAXIM, THE STYLE OF WIT (J-H)	GPITVL
HUMOR · HUMOR (J-H)	GPITVL
MARK TWAIN · CRITICAL THEORY (J-H)	GPITVL
MARK TWAIN · FROGS, JAYS AND HUMOR (J-H)	GPITVL
MARK TWAIN · HUCK FINN · CHARACTER AND GROWTH (J-H)	GPITVL
MARK TWAIN · THE ADVENTURES OF HUCKLEBERRY FINN (J-H)	GPITVL

MATHEMATICS

MATHEMATICS · GENERAL

(FILMSTRIPS)

BASIC ARITHMETIC SKILLS--A SERIES	CREATV
BASIC COMPUTATIONAL SKILLS--A SERIES	CREATV
COMPUTER SCIENCE--A SERIES	AVDEV
DECIMAL FRACTIONS--A SERIES	CREATV
DEVELOPMENT OF OUR NUMBER SYSTEM (J-H)	VIEWLX
HARDWARE AND FUNDAMENTAL CONCEPTS	AVDEV
MATH · DECIMAL NUMERATION--A SERIES (J-H)	VIEWLX
MATHEMATICS · FUNDAMENTAL OPERATIONS--A SERIES (J-H)	VIEWLX
MATHEMATICS · GRAPHING--A SERIES (I-H)	VIEWLX
MEASUREMENT--A SERIES	CREATV
PRINCIPLES OF FLOWCHARTS	AVDEV
PROGRAMMING IN FORTRAN, PT 1	AVDEV
PROGRAMMING IN FORTRAN, PT 2	AVDEV
USING NUMBER PAIRS (P)	EDPRC

MATHEMATICS

(MOTION PICTURES)

INFINITY (J-C A)	AIMS

(VIDEOTAPES)

ANGLES AND OTHER FIGURES (I)	GPITVL
CIRCLES (I)	GPITVL
CURVES (I)	GPITVL
DEVICES IN THEIR HANDS - MATH IN THEIR MINDS --A SERIES	GPITVL
FUN WITH THE MINI-COMPUTER	GPITVL
GREAT GAME CONTEST, THE (I)	GPITVL
INTRODUCING SETS (I)	GPITVL
JOINING SETS, ADDITION (I)	GPITVL
MATH FACTORY, MODULE 1 - SETS--A SERIES (I)	GPITVL
MATH FACTORY, MODULE 2 - GEOMETRY--A SERIES (I)	GPITVL
NONEQUIVALENT SETS, INEQUALITIES (I)	GPITVL
POINTS AND LINE SEGMENTS (I)	GPITVL
SEPARATING SETS (I)	GPITVL
SET NUMERATION (I)	GPITVL
SLIDING IN FRACTIONS	GPITVL
TAKE A CHANCE - LEARN PROBABILITY	GPITVL
TILES TEACH MATHEMATICS	GPITVL

(AUDIO TAPES)

STAMP COLLECTING AND MATHEMATICIANS (H A)	UOKLA
VALUES OF MATHEMATICS IN SCHOOL CURRICULA (H A)	UOKLA

(TRANSPARENCIES)

ADDITION OF FRACTIONS (P-I)	LEART
ADDITION TABLE (P-I)	LEART
ASSOCIATIVE LAW - GROUPING (P-I)	LEART
BAR GRAPH (P-I)	LEART
BASE FOUR (P-I)	LEART
BASE FOUR - ADDING AND SUBTRACTING (P-I)	LEART
BASE FOUR ADDITION TABLE (P-I)	LEART
BASE FOUR MULTIPLICATION TABLE (P-I)	LEART
BASIC PRINCIPLES (P-I)	LEART
BEGINNING SKILLS--A SERIES (K-P)	BOW
CALENDAR (P-I)	LEART
CIRCLE (P-I)	LEART
CLOCK (P-I)	LEART
COMMUTATIVE LAW (P-I)	LEART
CONVERSION CHART (P-I)	LEART
DECIMAL NUMBER LINE - ADDITION AND SUBTRACTION (P-I)	LEART
DECIMAL NUMBER LINE - MULTIPLICATION AND DIVISION (P-I)	LEART
DEGREE MEASUREMENT - CIRCLE (P-I)	LEART
ELEMENTARY-JUNIOR HIGH MATHEMATICS--A SERIES (P-I)	LEART
EMPTY SET (P-I)	LEART
EQUIVALENT SETS (P-I)	LEART
EQUIVALENT SETS (MULTIPLICATION SERIES) (P-I)	LEART
FRACTIONAL NUMBER LINE (P-I)	LEART
FREQUENCY DISTRIBUTION TABLE AND LINE GRAPH (P-I)	LEART
GRAPHING (P-I)	LEART
LEARNING THE ALPHABET (K-P)	BOW
LET'S HAVE A NURSERY RHYME PARTY (K-P)	BOW
LIQUID MEASURE (P-I)	LEART
MAP PROBLEMS (P-I)	LEART
MATHEMATICAL SYMBOLS (P-I)	LEART
MEASUREMENT--A SERIES	BETECL
METRIC SYSTEM (P-I)	LEART
MODERN BASE TEN ABACUS (P-I)	LEART
MULTIPLICATION OF FRACTIONS (P-I)	LEART
MULTIPLICATION PRINCIPLES (P-I)	LEART
MULTIPLICATION TABLE (P-I)	LEART
NAMES FOR NUMBERS (P-I)	LEART
NATURAL ORDER OF NUMBERS, NO. 1 (P-I)	LEART
NATURAL ORDER OF NUMBERS, NO. 2 (P-I)	LEART
NON-EQUIVALENT SETS (P-I)	LEART
NUMBER FACTS, PT 1 (P-I)	LEART
NUMBER FACTS, PT 2 (P-I)	LEART
NUMBER FACTS, PT 3 (P-I)	LEART
NUMBER FACTS, PT 4 (P-I)	LEART
NUMBER FACTS, PT 5 (P-I)	LEART
NUMBER FACTS, PT 6 (P-I)	LEART
NUMBER FACTS, PT 7 (P-I)	LEART
NUMBER FACTS, PT 8 (P-I)	LEART
NUMBER FACTS, PT 9 (P-I)	LEART
NUMBER LINE (P-I)	LEART
NUMBER LINE - SIGNED NUMBERS (P-I)	LEART
NUMBER LINE (MULT SERIES) (P-I)	LEART
NUMERATION SYSTEMS--A SERIES	BETECL
ON MY WAY TO SCHOOL I SAW (K-P)	BOW
PASCAL'S TRIANGLE (P-I)	LEART
PATTERN FORMATIONS (P-I)	LEART
PLANE FIGURES (P-I)	LEART
PROPERTIES OF SETS (P-I)	LEART
PYTHAGOREAN THEOREM (P-I)	LEART
REGULAR SOLIDS (P-I)	LEART
SET, A (P-I)	LEART
SETS AND SUBSETS (P-I)	LEART
SIEVE OF ERATOSTHENES (P-I)	LEART
SIMPLE GEOMETRIC FIGURES (P-I)	LEART
SKIP COUNTING (P-I)	LEART
SOLID FIGURES (P-I)	LEART
SQUARE (P-I)	LEART
SUBTRACTION - TAKE AWAY (P-I)	LEART
SUBTRACTION OF FRACTIONS (P-I)	LEART
SYSTEMS OF WRITING NUMERALS (P-I)	LEART
TABLE OF MEASURE (P-I)	LEART
TELL THE STORY - CHANGE THE ENDING (K-P)	BOW
TELL THE STORY - MAKE IT RHYME (K-P)	BOW
TEMPERATURE (P-I)	LEART
THREE-DIMENSIONAL LETTER SHAPES (K-P)	BOW
THREE-DIMENSIONAL NUMERALS AND COUNTING DISC (K-P)	BOW
THREE-DIMENSIONAL TEN FRAME (K-P)	BOW
THREE-DIMENSIONAL VISUAL DISCRIMINATION KIT (K-P)	BOW
TIME ZONES (P-I)	LEART
UNDERSTANDING MATH CONCEPTS--A SERIES (I-J)	BOW
UNION OF SETS (P-I)	LEART
UNITS OF TIME - YEAR, MONTH, DAY (P-I)	LEART
VENN DIAGRAMS - INTERSECTION OF SETS (P-I)	LEART
VENN DIAGRAMS - SETS AND SUBSETS, IDENTICAL SETS, INTERSECTING SETS, DISJOINT SETS (P-I)	LEART
VISUALIZING CROSS SECTIONS - INTERSECTION OF PLANE AND CUBE (P-I)	LEART
VISUALIZING CROSS SECTIONS - INTERSECTION OF PLANE AND SPHERE (P-I)	LEART
VISUALIZING CROSS SECTIONS - INTERSECTION OF PLANE AND CYLINDER (P-I)	LEART
VISUALIZING CROSS SECTIONS - INTERSECTION OF PLANE AND CONE (P-I)	LEART
VOCABULARY (P-I)	LEART

ALGEBRA

(FILMSTRIPS)

FACTORING NUMBERS (J-H)	VIEWLX
FOUR QUADRANTS (I-H)	VIEWLX
GRAPHING AN EQUATION (I-H)	VIEWLX
MATHEMATICS - GRAPHING--A SERIES (I-H)	VIEWLX
MULTIPLYING FACTORS (J-H)	VIEWLX
POINT COORDINATES - QUADRANT ONE (I-H)	VIEWLX

(TRANSPARENCIES)

ADDITION AND MULTIPLICATION OF RADICALS	LEART
ADDITION OF COMPLEX NUMBERS	LEART
ALGEBRA, FIRST YEAR - FUNCTIONS--A SERIES	LEART
ALGEBRA, FIRST YEAR - QUADRATIC SENTENCES--A SERIES	LEART
ALGEBRA, FIRST YEAR - REAL NUMBERS--A SERIES	LEART
ALGEBRA, FIRST YEAR - SYSTEM OF LINEAR EQUATIONS--A SERIES	LEART
ALGEBRA, FIRST YEAR - WORD PROBLEMS--A SERIES	LEART
ALGEBRA, SECOND YEAR - ALGEBRAIC EXPRESSIONS --A SERIES	LEART
ALGEBRA, SECOND YEAR - COMPLEX NUMBERS--A SERIES	LEART
ALGEBRA, SECOND YEAR - CONICS--A SERIES	LEART
ALGEBRA, SECOND YEAR - DETERMINANTS--A SERIES	LEART
ALGEBRA, SECOND YEAR - FACTORING--A SERIES	LEART
ALGEBRA, SECOND YEAR - LINES AND PLANES--A SERIES	LEART
ALGEBRA, SECOND YEAR - LOGARITHMS--A SERIES	LEART
ALGEBRA, SECOND YEAR - RADICALS--A SERIES	LEART
ALGEBRA, SECOND YEAR - SOLUTION PROBLEMS	LEART
ALGEBRA, SECOND YEAR - STRUCTURE OF ALGEBRA-- A SERIES	LEART
ALGEBRA, SECOND YEAR - WORK PROBLEMS	LEART
ALGEBRA, SECOND YEAR - WORK PROBLEMS--A SERIES	LEART
ALGEBRAIC SOLUTION OF SYSTEM OF THREE EQUATIONS	LEART
ALGEBRAIC SOLUTION OF SYSTEM WITH ONE QUADRATIC AND ONE LINEAR	LEART
ALGEBRAIC SOLUTION OF SYSTEM WITH TWO QUADRATIC EQUATIONS	LEART
ANTILOGARITHMS	LEART
BASE TEN DIGIT PROBLEMS	LEART
CALCULATING WITH LOGARITHMS	LEART
CHANGING BASES IN LOGARITHMS	LEART
COMBINING ALGEBRAIC FRACTIONS	LEART
COMBINING RADICAL EXPRESSIONS	LEART
COMMON LOGARITHM - TABLES	LEART
COMPLEX FRACTIONS	LEART
COMPLEX NUMBERS	LEART
CONJUGATE COMPLEX NUMBERS	LEART
CRAMER'S RULE	LEART
DEFINITION OF LOGARITHM	LEART
DETERMINANT PROPERTIES FIVE AND SIX	LEART
DETERMINANT PROPERTIES ONE AND TWO	LEART
DETERMINANT PROPERTIES THREE AND FOUR	LEART
DETERMINANT PROPERTY SEVEN	LEART
DETERMINANTS - DEFINITION AND MINORS	LEART
DIFFERENCE OF TWO SQUARES	LEART
DIRECT VARIATION	LEART
DISCRIMINANT	LEART
ELLIPSE - DEFINITION	LEART
EQUATION AND GRAPHING OF ELLIPSE	LEART
EQUATIONS WITH LOGARITHMS AND EXPONENTS	LEART
EQUATIONS WITH RATIONAL ALGEBRAIC EXPRESSIONS	LEART
EVALUATING DETERMINANTS	LEART
EXPANDING A DETERMINANT	LEART
EXTENDING THE NUMBER LINE TO INCLUDE IRRATIONAL NUMBERS	LEART
FACTORING BY GROUPING	LEART
FACTORING BY USING EQUIVALENT EXPRESSIONS	LEART
GRAPH OF SYSTEM WITH ONE QUADRATIC AND ONE LINEAR EQUATION	LEART
GRAPH OF SYSTEM WITH TWO QUADRATIC EQUATIONS	LEART
GRAPH OF Y EQUALS B TO THE X POWER	LEART
GRAPHICAL SOLUTION OF INEQUALITIES IN TWO VARIABLES	LEART
GRAPHING A FIRST-DEGREE EQUATION IN THREE VARIABLES	LEART
GRAPHING SOLUTION OF A SYSTEM OF THREE EQUATIONS	LEART
HYPERBOLA - DEFINITION	LEART
HYPERBOLA - GRAPHING AND EQUATION	LEART
HYPERBOLA OF FORM XY EQUALS K	LEART
INTERPOLATING FOR ANTILOGARITHMS	LEART
INTERPOLATION IN TABLES	LEART
INVERSE OF SUM AND OF PRODUCT	LEART
INVERSES OF EQUALS	LEART
LINEAR INTERPOLATION	LEART
LOGARITHM OF A PRODUCT	LEART
LOGARITHM OF A QUOTIENT AND A POWER	LEART
MENSURATION PROBLEMS	LEART
MIXTURE PROBLEMS	LEART
MIXTURE, INVESTMENT AND RATIO PROBLEMS	LEART
MOTION PROBLEMS	LEART
MULTIPLICATION OF COMPLEX NUMBERS	LEART
MULTIPLICATION PROPERTY OF ZERO	LEART
MULTIPLYING AND DIVIDING RATIONAL ALGEBRAIC FRACTIONS	LEART
NATURE OF ROOTS OF QUADRATIC EQUATIONS	LEART
PARABOLA - DEFINITION AND EQUATION	LEART
PARABOLA - SKETCHING	LEART
PARALLEL LINES	LEART
PERPENDICULAR LINES	LEART
POSSIBLE RELATIONS OF THREE PLANES IN SPACE	LEART
POSTULATES FOR A FIELD	LEART
PRODUCTS OF ROOTS	LEART
PROPERTIES OF ROOTS OF QUADRATIC EQUATIONS	LEART
QUADRATIC FORMULA	LEART
QUOTIENTS OF COMPLEX NUMBERS	LEART
RADICAL EQUATIONS	LEART
RATIONAL EXPONENTS	LEART
RATIONAL NUMBERS	LEART
RIGHT DISTRIBUTIVE PROPERTY	LEART
ROOTS OF NUMBERS	LEART
SIMPLIFYING RADICALS	LEART
SLOPE OF A STRAIGHT LINE	LEART
SOLVING OF QUADRATIC INEQUALITIES	LEART
SOLVING QUADRATIC EQUATIONS BY FACTORING	LEART
SUBTRACTION AND DIVISION	LEART
SUM AND PRODUCT OF ROOTS	LEART
SUM OR DIFFERENCE OF TWO CUBES	LEART
THEOREMS ON INVERSES, PT 1	LEART
THEOREMS ON INVERSES, PT 2	LEART
THREE-DIMENSIONAL COORDINATE SYSTEM	LEART
TWO VELOCITY MOTION PROBLEMS	LEART
TWO-POINT AND POINT-SLOPE	LEART

UNION OF SETS (P-I) — LEART
USING DETERMINANTS — LEART
WORK PROBLEMS — LEART
WRITING EQUATIONS — LEART
WRITING EQUATIONS - EXAMPLES — LEART
ZERO PRODUCTS — LEART

ARITHMETIC - GENERAL

(FILMSTRIPS)

BASIC ARITHMETIC SKILLS--A SERIES — CREATV
BASIC COMPUTATIONAL SKILLS--A SERIES — CREATV

(RECORDS)

SQUARE THAT NUMBER — SPA

(TRANSPARENCIES)

FUNCTIONS — LEART
INVERSE VARIATION — LEART
NUMERATION SYSTEMS--A SERIES — BETECL

ARITHMETIC - ADDITION

(FILMSTRIPS)

BASIC ARITHMETIC SKILLS--A SERIES — CREATV

(VIDEOTAPES)

FUN WITH THE MINI-COMPUTER — GPITVL
JOINING SETS, ADDITION (I) — GPITVL
SLIDING IN FRACTIONS — GPITVL

(TRANSPARENCIES)

ADDITION OF FRACTIONS (P-I) — LEART
ADDITION TABLE (P-I) — LEART
BASE FOUR ADDITION TABLE (P-I) — LEART
INVERSE OF SUM AND OF PRODUCT — LEART

ARITHMETIC - DECIMALS

(FILMSTRIPS)

DECIMAL FRACTIONS (J-H) — VIEWLX
DECIMAL FRACTIONS--A SERIES — CREATV
DECIMAL SYSTEM (J-H) — VIEWLX
MATH - DECIMAL NUMERATION--A SERIES — VIEWLX

(TRANSPARENCIES)

DECIMAL NUMBER LINE - ADDITION AND SUBTRACTION (P-I) — LEART
DECIMAL NUMBER LINE - MULTIPLICATION AND DIVISION (P-I) — LEART
REPEATING DECIMALS — LEART

ARITHMETIC - DIVISION

(FILMSTRIPS)

BASIC ARITHMETIC SKILLS--A SERIES — CREATV
DIVISION - COMPUTATION I (P) — EDPRC
DIVISION - COMPUTATION II (P) — EDPRC
DIVISION PROGRAM, THE — CREATV

(TRANSPARENCIES)

DECIMAL NUMBER LINE - MULTIPLICATION AND DIVISION (P-I) — LEART
SUBTRACTION AND DIVISION — LEART

ARITHMETIC - FRACTIONS

(FILMSTRIPS)

DECIMAL FRACTIONS (J-H) — VIEWLX
DECIMAL FRACTIONS--A SERIES — CREATV
FRACTIONS (P) — EDPRC

(VIDEOTAPES)

SLIDING IN FRACTIONS — GPITVL
TAKE A CHANCE - LEARN PROBABILITY — GPITVL

(TRANSPARENCIES)

ADDITION OF FRACTIONS (P-I) — LEART
ALGEBRA, SECOND YEAR - ALGEBRAIC EXPRESSIONS --A SERIES — LEART
ALGEBRA, SECOND YEAR - FACTORING -A SERIES — LEART
COMBINING ALGEBRAIC FRACTIONS — LEART
COMPLEX FRACTIONS — LEART
DECIMAL NUMBER LINE - ADDITION AND SUBTRACTION (P-I) — LEART

DECIMAL NUMBER LINE - MULTIPLICATION AND DIVISION (P-I) — LEART
ELEMENTARY-JUNIOR HIGH MATHEMATICS--A SERIES (P-I) — LEART
FRACTIONAL NUMBER LINE (P-I) — LEART
LIQUID MEASURE (P-I) — LEART
MODERN BASE TEN ABACUS (P-I) — LEART
MULTIPLICATION OF FRACTIONS (P-I) — LEART
MULTIPLYING AND DIVIDING RATIONAL ALGEBRAIC FRACTIONS — LEART
NUMBER FACTS, PT 4 (P-I) — LEART
RATIONALIZING THE DENOMINATOR — LEART
SUBTRACTION OF FRACTIONS (P-I) — LEART

ARITHMETIC - MULTIPLICATION

(FILMSTRIPS)

BASIC ARITHMETIC SKILLS--A SERIES — CREATV
DIVISION - COMPUTATION II (P) — EDPRC
FACTORING NUMBERS (J-H) — VIEWLX
MULTIPLICATION PROGRAM, THE — CREATV
MULTIPLYING FACTORS (J-H) — VIEWLX

(TRANSPARENCIES)

BASE FOUR MULTIPLICATION TABLE (P-I) — LEART
DECIMAL NUMBER LINE - MULTIPLICATION AND DIVISION (P-I) — LEART
INVERSE OF SUM AND OF PRODUCT — LEART
MULTIPLICATION OF FRACTIONS (P-I) — LEART
MULTIPLICATION PRINCIPLES (P-I) — LEART
MULTIPLICATION PROPERTY OF ZERO — LEART
MULTIPLICATION TABLE (P-I) — LEART
PRODUCTS OF ADDITIVE INVERSES — LEART
SOLVING QUADRATIC EQUATIONS BY FACTORING — LEART

ARITHMETIC - RATIO AND PROPORTION

(VIDEOTAPES)

TAKE A CHANCE - LEARN PROBABILITY — GPITVL

(TRANSPARENCIES)

ALGEBRA, FIRST YEAR - FUNCTIONS--A SERIES — LEART
RATIO AND PROPORTION — LEART

ARITHMETIC - SUBTRACTION

(FILMSTRIPS)

SUBTRACTION PROGRAM — CREATV

(VIDEOTAPES)

FUN WITH THE MINI-COMPUTER — GPITVL
SEPARATING SETS (I) — GPITVL
SLIDING IN FRACTIONS — GPITVL

(TRANSPARENCIES)

NUMERATION SYSTEMS--A SERIES — BETECL
SUBTRACTION - TAKE AWAY (P-I) — LEART
SUBTRACTION AND DIVISION — LEART
SUBTRACTION OF FRACTIONS (P-I) — LEART

COMPUTERS

(FILMSTRIPS)

COMPUTER SCIENCE--A SERIES — AVDEV
COMPUTER SYSTEM, THE (H) — EBEC
HARDWARE AND FUNDAMENTAL CONCEPTS — AVDEV
HISTORY OF THE COMPUTER, THE (H) — EBEC
HOW COMPUTERS WORK--A SERIES (H) — EBEC
INPUT-OUTPUT - HOW COMPUTERS READ AND WRITE (H) — EBEC
NUMBER SYSTEMS - THE COMPUTER'S VOCABULARY (H) — EBEC
PRINCIPLES OF FLOWCHARTS — AVDEV
PROGRAMMING - HOW TO ORDER A COMPUTER AROUND (H) — EBEC
PROGRAMMING IN FORTRAN, PT 1 — AVDEV
PROGRAMMING IN FORTRAN, PT 2 — AVDEV
SOFTWARE AND HARDWARE AT WORK (H) — EBEC

EQUATIONS, THEORY OF

(FILMSTRIPS)

GRAPHING AN EQUATION (I-H) — VIEWLX

(TRANSPARENCIES)

ALGEBRA, FIRST YEAR -

QUADRATIC SENTENCES--A SERIES — LEART
ALGEBRA, FIRST YEAR - SYSTEM OF LINEAR EQUATIONS--A SERIES — LEART
ALGEBRA, SECOND YEAR - ALGEBRAIC EXPRESSIONS --A SERIES — LEART
ALGEBRA, SECOND YEAR - DETERMINANTS--A SERIES — LEART
ALGEBRAIC SOLUTION OF SYSTEM OF THREE EQUATIONS — LEART
ALGEBRAIC SOLUTION OF SYSTEMS OF LINEAR EQUATIONS — LEART
EQUATION AND GRAPHING OF ELLIPSE — LEART
EQUATIONS WITH RATIONAL ALGEBRAIC EXPRESSIONS — LEART
GRAPH OF SYSTEM WITH ONE QUADRATIC AND ONE LINEAR EQUATION — LEART
GRAPH OF SYSTEM WITH TWO QUADRATIC EQUATIONS — LEART
GRAPHING A FIRST-DEGREE EQUATION IN THREE VARIABLES — LEART
GRAPHING SOLUTION OF A SYSTEM OF THREE EQUATIONS — LEART
HYPERBOLA - GRAPHING AND EQUATION — LEART
INVERSES OF EQUALS — LEART
NATURE OF ROOTS OF QUADRATIC EQUATIONS — LEART
PARABOLA - DEFINITION AND EQUATION — LEART
PROPERTIES OF EQUATIONS — LEART
PROPERTIES OF ROOTS OF QUADRATIC EQUATIONS — LEART
RADICAL EQUATIONS — LEART
SLOPE OF THE GRAPH OF AN EQUATION — LEART
SOLVING OF QUADRATIC INEQUALITIES — LEART
SOLVING QUADRATIC EQUATIONS BY FACTORING — LEART
WRITING EQUATIONS — LEART
WRITING EQUATIONS - EXAMPLES — LEART

FORMULAS, MATHEMATICAL

(TRANSPARENCIES)

QUADRATIC FORMULA — LEART

FUNCTIONS, MATHEMATICAL--SEE CALCULUS

(TRANSPARENCIES)

ALGEBRA, FIRST YEAR - FUNCTIONS--A SERIES — LEART
DIRECT VARIATION — LEART
FUNCTIONS — LEART

GEOMETRY

(FILMSTRIPS)

GEOMETRY (P) — EDPRC

(MOTION CARTRIDGES)

SHAPES AND SYMMETRY, UNIT 1 - RECOGNIZING TWO-DIMENSIONAL SHAPES--A SERIES — XEROX
SHAPES AND SYMMETRY, UNIT 2 - RECOGNIZING THREE-DIMENSIONAL SHAPES--A SERIES — XEROX
SHAPES AND SYMMETRY, UNIT 3 - SYMMETRY--A SERIES — XEROX
SHAPES AND SYMMETRY, UNIT 4 - HOW TO REPRESENT THREE DIMENSIONAL SHAPES--A SERIES — XEROX
SHAPES AND SYMMETRY, UNIT 5 - PLANES THROUGH SOLIDS--A SERIES — XEROX

(VIDEOTAPES)

ANGLES AND OTHER FIGURES (I) — GPITVL
CIRCLES (I) — GPITVL
CURVES (I) — GPITVL
GREAT GAME CONTEST, THE (I) — GPITVL
MATH FACTORY, MODULE 1 - SETS--A SERIES (I) — GPITVL
MATH FACTORY, MODULE 2 - GEOMETRY--A SERIES (I) — GPITVL
POINTS AND LINE SEGMENTS (I) — GPITVL
STRETCH A RUBBER BAND AND LEARN GEOMETRY — GPITVL

(TRANSPARENCIES)

AREAS AS COVERING (P-I) — LEART
CIRCLE (P-I) — LEART
CIRCULAR REGION (P-I) — LEART
DEGREE MEASUREMENT - CIRCLE (P-I) — LEART
ELEMENTARY GEOMETRY - AREA AS A MEASURE OF COVERING--A SERIES (P-I) — LEART
PARALLELOGRAM REGION (P-I) — LEART

PASCAL'S TRIANGLE (P-I)   LEART
PLANE FIGURES (P-I)   LEART
PYTHAGOREAN THEOREM (P-I)   LEART
RECTANGULAR COORDINATE SYSTEM   LEART
RECTANGULAR REGION (P-I)   LEART
SIMPLE GEOMETRIC FIGURES (P-I)   LEART
SQUARE (P-I)   LEART
TRIANGULAR REGION (P-I)   LEART
VISUALIZING CROSS SECTIONS -
   INTERSECTION OF PLANE AND
   CUBE (P-I)   LEART
VISUALIZING CROSS SECTIONS -
   INTERSECTION OF PLANE AND
   SPHERE (P-I)   LEART
VISUALIZING CROSS SECTIONS -
   INTERSECTION OF PLANE AND
   CYLINDER (P-I)   LEART
VISUALIZING CROSS SECTIONS -
   INTERSECTION OF PLANE AND
   CONE (P-I)   LEART

GRAPHS AND CHARTS, MATHEMATICAL

(FILMSTRIPS)

COMPUTER SCIENCE--A SERIES   AVDEV
FOUR QUADRANTS (I-H)   VIEWLX
GRAPHING AN EQUATION (I-H)   VIEWLX
HARDWARE AND FUNDAMENTAL
CONCEPTS   AVDEV
MATHEMATICS - GRAPHING--A SERIES (I-
H)   VIEWLX
POINT COORDINATES - QUADRANT ONE
(I-H)   VIEWLX
PRINCIPLES OF FLOWCHARTS   AVDEV
PROGRAMMING IN FORTRAN, PT 1   AVDEV
PROGRAMMING IN FORTRAN, PT 2   AVDEV

(VIDEOTAPES)

WHAT DO YOU DO WITH NUMBERS (I)   GPITVL

(TRANSPARENCIES)

ALGEBRA, FIRST YEAR - SYSTEM OF
   LINEAR EQUATIONS--A SERIES   LEART
ALGEBRA, SECOND YEAR - CONICS--A
SERIES   LEART
ALGEBRA, SECOND YEAR - LINES
   AND PLANES--A SERIES   LEART
BAR GRAPH (P-I)   LEART
EQUATION AND GRAPHING OF ELLIPSE   LEART
FREQUENCY DISTRIBUTION TABLE AND
LINE GRAPH (P-I)   LEART
GRAPH OF A LINEAR EQUATION IN TWO
VARIABLES   LEART
GRAPH OF SYSTEM WITH ONE
   QUADRATIC AND ONE LINEAR
   EQUATION   LEART
GRAPH OF SYSTEM WITH TWO
QUADRATIC EQUATIONS   LEART
GRAPH OF Y EQUALS B TO THE X
POWER   LEART
GRAPHING (P-I)   LEART
GRAPHS OF OPEN SENTENCES IN TWO
VARIABLES   LEART
HYPERBOLA - GRAPHING AND
EQUATION   LEART
PARABOLA - SKETCHING   LEART
SLOPE INTERCEPT FORM   LEART
SLOPE OF THE GRAPH OF AN
EQUATION   LEART
UNITS OF TIME - YEAR, MONTH, DAY
(P-I)   LEART
VENN DIAGRAMS - INTERSECTION OF
SETS (P-I)   LEART

LOGIC, MATHEMATICAL

(FILMSTRIPS)

ORDER - FIRST ALWAYS COMES BEFORE
LAST   EGH

MATHEMATICS - STUDY AND TEACHING

(MOTION PICTURES)

ENTERPRISING INFANTS (C T)   TIMLIF

(VIDEOTAPES)

DEVICES IN THEIR HANDS - MATH
   IN THEIR MINDS --A SERIES   GPITVL
FUN WITH THE MINI-COMPUTER   GPITVL
SLIDING IN FRACTIONS   GPITVL
STRETCH A RUBBER BAND AND LEARN
GEOMETRY   GPITVL
TAKE A CHANCE - LEARN PROBABILITY   GPITVL
TILES TEACH MATHEMATICS   GPITVL

(AUDIO TAPES)

VALUES OF MATHEMATICS IN SCHOOL
CURRICULA (H A)   UOKLA

(TRANSPARENCIES)

UNDERSTANDING MATH CONCEPTS--A
SERIES (I-J)   BOW

MEASUREMENT - GENERAL

(FILMSTRIPS)

MEASUREMENT--A SERIES   CREATV

(MOTION PICTURES)

MEANING OF TIME IN SCIENCE, THE (H-
C)   EBEC
MEASURING INSTRUMENTS   IWANMI
ONCE UPON A TIME (P-J)   TEXFLM

(VIDEOTAPES)

CIRCLES (I)   GPITVL
GREAT GAME CONTEST, THE (I)   GPITVL
MATH FACTORY, MODULE 2 -
GEOMETRY--A SERIES (I)   GPITVL
WHAT DO YOU DO WITH NUMBERS (I)   GPITVL

(TRANSPARENCIES)

BAR GRAPH (P-I)   LEART
BASE FOUR (P-I)   LEART
BASE FOUR - ADDING AND
SUBTRACTING (P-I)   LEART
BASE FOUR ADDITION TABLE (P-I)   LEART
BASE FOUR MULTIPLICATION TABLE (P-
I)   LEART
BASIC PRINCIPLES (P-I)   LEART
CALENDAR (P-I)   LEART
CIRCLE (P-I)   LEART
CLOCK (P-I)   LEART
COMMUTATIVE LAW (P-I)   LEART
CONVERSION CHART (P-I)   LEART
DECIMAL NUMBER LINE - ADDITION
AND SUBTRACTION (P-I)   LEART
DECIMAL NUMBER LINE -
   MULTIPLICATION AND DIVISION
   (P-I)   LEART
DEGREE MEASUREMENT - CIRCLE (P-I)   LEART
ELEMENTARY-JUNIOR HIGH
MATHEMATICS--A SERIES (P-I)   LEART
EMPTY SET (P-I)   LEART
EQUIVALENT SETS (P-I)   LEART
EQUIVALENT SETS (MULTIPLICATION
SERIES) (P-I)   LEART
FRACTIONAL NUMBER LINE (P-I)   LEART
FREQUENCY DISTRIBUTION TABLE AND
LINE GRAPH (P-I)   LEART
GRAPHING (P-I)   LEART
LIQUID MEASURE (P-I)   LEART
MAP PROBLEMS (P-I)   LEART
MATHEMATICAL SYMBOLS (P-I)   LEART
MEASUREMENT IN ASTRONOMY--A
SERIES (I-J)   BOW
MEASURING INDIRECTLY (I-J)   BOW
MEASURING THE EARTH (I-J)   BOW
MEASURING THE MOON (I-J)   BOW
MEASURING THE SPEED OF LIGHT (I-J)   BOW
MEASURING TO MARS (I-J)   BOW
MEASURING TO THE STARS (I-J)   BOW
MEASURING TO THE SUN (I-J)   BOW
METRIC SYSTEM (P-I)   LEART
MODELS OF SOLAR SYSTEM (I-J)   BOW
MODERN BASE TEN ABACUS (P-I)   LEART
MULTIPLICATION TABLE (P-I)   LEART
NATURAL ORDER OF NUMBERS, NO. 2
(P-I)   LEART
NUMBER FACTS, PT 4 (P-I)   LEART
NUMBER FACTS, PT 6 (P-I)   LEART
NUMBER FACTS, PT 7 (P-I)   LEART
NUMBER FACTS, PT 8 (P-I)   LEART
NUMBER FACTS, PT 9 (P-I)   LEART
NUMBER LINE (P-I)   LEART
NUMBER LINE - SIGNED NUMBERS (P-I)   LEART
NUMBER LINE (MULT SERIES) (P-I)   LEART
PASCAL'S TRIANGLE (P-I)   LEART
PATTERN FORMATIONS (P-I)   LEART
PLANE FIGURES (P-I)   LEART
PROPERTIES OF SETS (P-I)   LEART
PYTHAGOREAN THEOREM (P-I)   LEART
RECTANGULAR COORDINATE SYSTEM   LEART
REGULAR SOLIDS (P-I)   LEART
SET, A (P-I)   LEART
SETS AND SUBSETS (P-I)   LEART
SIEVE OF ERATOSTHENES (P-I)   LEART
SIMPLE GEOMETRIC FIGURES (P-I)   LEART
SKIP COUNTING (P-I)   LEART
SOLID FIGURES (P-I)   LEART
SQUARE (P-I)   LEART
SUBTRACTION - TAKE AWAY (P-I)   LEART
TABLE OF MEASURE (P-I)   LEART
TEMPERATURE (P-I)   LEART
TIME ZONES (P-I)   LEART
UNION OF SETS (P-I)   LEART
UNITS OF TIME - YEAR, MONTH, DAY
(P-I)   LEART
VENN DIAGRAMS - INTERSECTION OF
SETS (P-I)   LEART
VENN DIAGRAMS - SETS AND
   SUBSETS, IDENTICAL SETS,

INTERSECTING SETS, DISJOINT SETS
(P-I)   LEART
VISUALIZING CROSS SECTIONS -
   INTERSECTION OF PLANE AND
   CUBE (P-I)   LEART
VISUALIZING CROSS SECTIONS -
   INTERSECTION OF PLANE AND
   SPHERE (P-I)   LEART
VISUALIZING CROSS SECTIONS -
   INTERSECTION OF PLANE AND
   CYLINDER (P-I)   LEART
VISUALIZING CROSS SECTIONS -
   INTERSECTION OF PLANE AND
   CONE (P-I)   LEART

MEASUREMENT - AREA

(TRANSPARENCIES)

AREAS AS COVERING (P-I)   LEART
CIRCULAR REGION (P-I)   LEART
ELEMENTARY GEOMETRY - AREA
   AS A MEASURE OF COVERING--A
   SERIES (P-I)   LEART
PARALLELOGRAM REGION (P-I)   LEART
RECTANGULAR REGION (P-I)   LEART
TRIANGULAR REGION (P-I)   LEART

MEASUREMENT - MEASURING INSTRUMENTS

(MOTION PICTURES)

MEASURING INSTRUMENTS   IWANMI

(TRANSPARENCIES)

BALANCE BEAM SCALE (H)   BOW
INSTRUMENTS AND TECHNIQUES OF
SCIENCE--A SERIES (H)   BOW
MEASUREMENT--A SERIES   BETECL
PREPARING SLIDES (H)   BOW
PSYCHROMETER (H)   BOW
TELESCOPE (H)   BOW
TESTING FOR MINERALS (H)   BOW
THERMOMETER (H)   BOW

MEASUREMENT - METRIC SYSTEM

(MOTION CARTRIDGES)

METRIC SYSTEM, THE, PT 1   VISIN

(VIDEOTAPES)

STRETCH A RUBBER BAND AND LEARN
GEOMETRY   GPITVL

(TRANSPARENCIES)

MEASUREMENT--A SERIES   BETECL
METRIC SYSTEM (P-I)   LEART

NUMBERS AND NUMERATION SYSTEMS

(FILMSTRIPS)

DEVELOPMENT OF OUR NUMBER
SYSTEM (J-H)   VIEWLX

(MOTION CARTRIDGES)

METRIC SYSTEM, THE, PT 1   VISIN

(MOTION PICTURES)

COUNTING AND COLORS - EL CONTAR Y
COLORES   CAROUF
INFINITY (J-C A)   AIMS

(VIDEOTAPES)

INTRODUCING SETS (I)   GPITVL
SET NUMERATION (I)   GPITVL

(TRANSPARENCIES)

ADDITION AND MULTIPLICATION OF
RADICALS   LEART
ADDITION OF COMPLEX NUMBERS   LEART
ALGEBRA, FIRST YEAR - REAL
NUMBERS--A SERIES   LEART
ALGEBRA, SECOND YEAR -
   COMPLEX NUMBERS--A SERIES   LEART
ALGEBRA, SECOND YEAR - RADICALS--A
SERIES   LEART
ALGEBRAIC SOLUTION OF SYSTEMS
   OF LINEAR EQUATIONS   LEART
BASE FOUR (P-I)   LEART
BASE FOUR - ADDING AND
SUBTRACTING (P-I)   LEART
BASE FOUR ADDITION TABLE (P-I)   LEART
COMPLEX NUMBERS   LEART
CONJUGATE COMPLEX NUMBERS   LEART
DECIMAL NUMBER LINE - ADDITION
AND SUBTRACTION (P-I)   LEART

DISCRIMINANT	LEART
EXTENDING THE NUMBER LINE TO INCLUDE IRRATIONAL NUMBERS	LEART
FRACTIONAL NUMBER LINE (P-I)	LEART
GRAPH OF A LINEAR EQUATION IN TWO VARIABLES	LEART
GRAPHICAL SOLUTION OF INEQUALITIES IN TWO VARIABLES	LEART
INVERSE VARIATION	LEART
INVERSES OF EQUALS	LEART
IRRATIONAL NUMBERS	LEART
MODERN BASE TEN ABACUS (P-I)	LEART
MULTIPLICATION OF COMPLEX NUMBERS	LEART
MULTIPLICATION PROPERTY OF ZERO	LEART
NAMES FOR NUMBERS (P-I)	LEART
NATURAL ORDER OF NUMBERS, NO. 1 (P-I)	LEART
NATURAL ORDER OF NUMBERS, NO. 2 (P-I)	LEART
NTH ROOTS	LEART
NUMBER FACTS, PT 1 (P-I)	LEART
NUMBER FACTS, PT 2 (P-I)	LEART
NUMBER FACTS, PT 3 (P-I)	LEART
NUMBER FACTS, PT 4 (P-I)	LEART
NUMBER FACTS, PT 5 (P-I)	LEART
NUMBER FACTS, PT 6 (P-I)	LEART
NUMBER FACTS, PT 7 (P-I)	LEART
NUMBER FACTS, PT 8 (P-I)	LEART
NUMBER FACTS, PT 9 (P-I)	LEART
NUMBER LINE - SIGNED NUMBERS (P-I)	LEART
NUMBER LINE (MULT SERIES) (P-I)	LEART
NUMERATION SYSTEMS--A SERIES	BETECL
PROPERTIES OF EQUALITY	LEART
PROPERTIES OF EQUATIONS	LEART
PROPERTIES OF SQUARE ROOTS	LEART
QUOTIENTS OF COMPLEX NUMBERS	LEART
RATIONAL NUMBERS	LEART
RATIONALIZING THE DENOMINATOR	LEART
REAL NUMBERS	LEART
RECTANGULAR COORDINATE SYSTEM	LEART
RELATIONS	LEART
REPEATING DECIMALS	LEART
SIMPLIFYING RADICALS	LEART
SKIP COUNTING (P-I)	LEART
SLOPE INTERCEPT FORM	LEART
SQUARE ROOTS	LEART
SYSTEMS OF WRITING NUMERALS (P-I)	LEART
ZERO PRODUCTS	LEART

OPERATIONS, MATHEMATICAL

(FILMSTRIPS)

BASES AND EXPONENTS (J-H)	VIEWLX
MATHEMATICS - FUNDAMENTAL OPERATIONS--A SERIES (J-H)	VIEWLX

(TRANSPARENCIES)

ALGEBRA, SECOND YEAR - COMPLEX NUMBERS--A SERIES	LEART
ALGEBRA, SECOND YEAR - FACTORING- -A SERIES	LEART
ALGEBRA, SECOND YEAR - STRUCTURE OF ALGEBRA-- A SERIES	LEART
ALGEBRAIC SOLUTION OF SYSTEM OF THREE EQUATIONS	LEART
COMBINING ALGEBRAIC FRACTIONS	LEART
COMBINING RADICAL EXPRESSIONS	LEART
FACTORING BY GROUPING	LEART
FACTORING BY USING EQUIVALENT EXPRESSIONS	LEART
NATURE OF ROOTS OF QUADRATIC EQUATIONS	LEART
PRODUCTS OF ADDITIVE INVERSES	LEART
PROPERTIES OF ROOTS OF QUADRATIC EQUATIONS	LEART
SOLVING OF QUADRATIC INEQUALITIES	LEART
SUM OR DIFFERENCE OF TWO CUBES	LEART

ORDERED RELATIONS

(FILMSTRIPS)

USING NUMBER PAIRS (P)	EDPRC

(TRANSPARENCIES)

GRAPH OF A LINEAR EQUATION IN TWO VARIABLES	LEART
IRRATIONAL NUMBERS	LEART
NATURAL ORDER OF NUMBERS, NO. 1 (P-I)	LEART
NATURAL ORDER OF NUMBERS, NO. 2 (P-I)	LEART
RELATIONS	LEART

PROBABILITIES, MATHEMATICAL

(VIDEOTAPES)

TAKE A CHANCE - LEARN PROBABILITY	GPITVL

PROBLEM SOLVING, MATHEMATICAL

(FILMSTRIPS)

FACTORING NUMBERS (J-H)	VIEWLX

(TRANSPARENCIES)

ALGEBRA, FIRST YEAR - WORD PROBLEMS--A SERIES	LEART
ALGEBRA, SECOND YEAR - SOLUTION PROBLEMS	LEART
ALGEBRA, SECOND YEAR - WORK PROBLEMS	LEART
ALGEBRA, SECOND YEAR - WORK PROBLEMS--A SERIES	LEART
ALGEBRAIC SOLUTION OF SYSTEMS OF LINEAR EQUATIONS	LEART
BASE TEN DIGIT PROBLEMS	LEART
GRAPHICAL SOLUTION OF INEQUALITIES IN TWO VARIABLES	LEART
MAP PROBLEMS (P-I)	LEART
MENSURATION PROBLEMS	LEART
MIXTURE PROBLEMS	LEART
MIXTURE, INVESTMENT AND RATIO PROBLEMS	LEART
MOTION PROBLEMS	LEART
RATIO AND PROPORTION	LEART
RATIONALIZING THE DENOMINATOR	LEART
REAL NUMBERS	LEART
RELATIONS	LEART
SIMPLIFYING RADICALS	LEART
SOLUTION SET OF AN OPEN SENTENCE IN TWO VARIABLES	LEART
SQUARE ROOTS	LEART
TWO VELOCITY MOTION PROBLEMS	LEART
WORK PROBLEMS	LEART

PROPERTIES, MATHEMATICAL

(MOTION CARTRIDGES)

SHAPES AND SYMMETRY, UNIT 1 - RECOGNIZING TWO-DIMENSIONAL SHAPES--A SERIES	XEROX
SHAPES AND SYMMETRY, UNIT 2 - RECOGNIZING THREE- DIMENSIONAL SHAPES--A SERIES	XEROX
SHAPES AND SYMMETRY, UNIT 3 - SYMMETRY--A SERIES	XEROX
SHAPES AND SYMMETRY, UNIT 4 - HOW TO REPRESENT THREE DIMENSIONAL SHAPES--A SERIES	XEROX
SHAPES AND SYMMETRY, UNIT 5 - PLANES THROUGH SOLIDS--A SERIES	XEROX

(TRANSPARENCIES)

ALGEBRA, SECOND YEAR - DETERMINANTS--A SERIES	LEART
ALGEBRA, SECOND YEAR - STRUCTURE OF ALGEBRA-- A SERIES	LEART
ASSOCIATIVE LAW - GROUPING (P-I)	LEART
COMMUTATIVE LAW (P-I)	LEART
CRAMER'S RULE	LEART
PROPERTIES OF EQUALITY	LEART
PROPERTIES OF EQUATIONS	LEART
PROPERTIES OF SETS (P-I)	LEART
PROPERTIES OF SQUARE ROOTS	LEART
RIGHT DISTRIBUTIVE PROPERTY	LEART
THEOREMS ON INVERSES, PT 1	LEART
THEOREMS ON INVERSES, PT 2	LEART

SENTENCES, MATHEMATICAL

(TRANSPARENCIES)

GRAPHS OF OPEN SENTENCES IN TWO VARIABLES	LEART
SOLUTION SET OF AN OPEN SENTENCE IN TWO VARIABLES	LEART

SETS

(MOTION PICTURES)

INFINITY (J-C A)	AIMS

(VIDEOTAPES)

INTRODUCING SETS (I)	GPITVL
JOINING SETS, ADDITION (I)	GPITVL
MATH FACTORY, MODULE 1 - SETS--A SERIES (I)	GPITVL
NONEQUIVALENT SETS, INEQUALITIES (I)	GPITVL
SEPARATING SETS (I)	GPITVL

(TRANSPARENCIES)

ADDITION TABLE (P-I)	LEART
ASSOCIATIVE LAW - GROUPING (P-I)	LEART
BAR GRAPH (P-I)	LEART

BASE FOUR (P-I)	LEART
BASE FOUR - ADDING AND SUBTRACTING (P-I)	LEART
BASE FOUR ADDITION TABLE (P-I)	LEART
BASE FOUR MULTIPLICATION TABLE (P-I)	LEART
DECIMAL NUMBER LINE - MULTIPLICATION AND DIVISION (P-I)	LEART
ELEMENTARY-JUNIOR HIGH MATHEMATICS--A SERIES (P-I)	LEART
EMPTY SET (P-I)	LEART
EQUIVALENT SETS (P-I)	LEART
EQUIVALENT SETS (MULTIPLICATION SERIES) (P-I)	LEART
FRACTIONAL NUMBER LINE (P-I)	LEART
NON-EQUIVALENT SETS (P-I)	LEART
NUMBER FACTS, PT 1 (P-I)	LEART
PROPERTIES OF SETS (P-I)	LEART
SET, A (P-I)	LEART
SETS AND SUBSETS (P-I)	LEART
SOLUTION SET OF AN OPEN SENTENCE IN TWO VARIABLES	LEART
UNION OF SETS (P-I)	LEART
VENN DIAGRAMS - SETS AND SUBSETS, IDENTICAL SETS, INTERSECTING SETS, DISJOINT SETS (P-I)	LEART

SLIDE RULE

(TRANSPARENCIES)

ANTILOGARITHMS	LEART
CALCULATING WITH LOGARITHMS	LEART
CHANGING BASES IN LOGARITHMS	LEART
COMMON LOGARITHM - TABLES	LEART
DEFINITION OF LOGARITHM	LEART
EQUATIONS WITH LOGARITHMS AND EXPONENTS	LEART
INTERPOLATING FOR ANTILOGARITHMS	LEART
LOGARITHM OF A PRODUCT	LEART
LOGARITHM OF A QUOTIENT AND A POWER	LEART

SYMBOLS AND VOCABULARY, MATHEMATICAL

(FILMSTRIPS)

BASES AND EXPONENTS (J-H)	VIEWLX
DEVELOPMENT OF OUR NUMBER SYSTEM (J-H)	VIEWLX

(MOTION PICTURES)

INFINITY (J-C A)	AIMS

(VIDEOTAPES)

NONEQUIVALENT SETS, INEQUALITIES (I)	GPITVL

(TRANSPARENCIES)

ADDITION AND MULTIPLICATION OF RADICALS	LEART
ALGEBRA, FIRST YEAR - REAL NUMBERS--A SERIES	LEART
ALGEBRA, SECOND YEAR - RADICALS--A SERIES	LEART
DEFINITION OF LOGARITHM	LEART
DETERMINANTS - DEFINITION AND MINORS	LEART
ELLIPSE - DEFINITION	LEART
EQUATIONS WITH LOGARITHMS AND EXPONENTS	LEART
EXTENDING THE NUMBER LINE TO INCLUDE IRRATIONAL NUMBERS	LEART
GRAPH OF A LINEAR EQUATION IN TWO VARIABLES	LEART
GRAPHS OF OPEN SENTENCES IN TWO VARIABLES	LEART
HYPERBOLA - DEFINITION	LEART
INVERSE OF SUM AND OF PRODUCT	LEART
INVERSE VARIATION	LEART
INVERSES OF EQUALS	LEART
IRRATIONAL NUMBERS	LEART
MATHEMATICAL SYMBOLS (P-I)	LEART
NAMES FOR NUMBERS (P-I)	LEART
NTH ROOTS	LEART
PARABOLA - DEFINITION AND EQUATION	LEART
PRODUCTS OF ADDITIVE INVERSES	LEART
PROPERTIES OF EQUALITY	LEART
RATIO AND PROPORTION	LEART
REPEATING DECIMALS	LEART
SLOPE INTERCEPT FORM	LEART
SLOPE OF THE GRAPH OF AN EQUATION	LEART
SQUARE ROOTS	LEART
UNITS OF TIME - YEAR, MONTH, DAY (P-I)	LEART
VENN DIAGRAMS - INTERSECTION OF SETS (P-I)	LEART
VISUALIZING CROSS SECTIONS - INTERSECTION OF PLANE AND CYLINDER (P-I)	LEART

VOCABULARY (P-I)   LEART

TABLES, MATHEMATICAL

(TRANSPARENCIES)

ALGEBRA, SECOND YEAR - LOGARITHMS-
-A SERIES   LEART
COMMON LOGARITHM - TABLES   LEART
DEFINITION OF LOGARITHM   LEART
EQUATIONS WITH LOGARITHMS AND
EXPONENTS   LEART
INTERPOLATION IN TABLES   LEART

TEACHING AND METHODS

(VIDEOTAPES)

DEVICES IN THEIR HANDS - MATH
IN THEIR MINDS --A SERIES   GPITVL
FUN WITH THE MINI-COMPUTER   GPITVL
GREAT GAME CONTEST, THE (I)   GPITVL
MATH FACTORY, MODULE 2 -
GEOMETRY--A SERIES (I)   GPITVL
SLIDING IN FRACTIONS   GPITVL
STRETCH A RUBBER BAND AND LEARN
GEOMETRY   GPITVL
TAKE A CHANCE - LEARN PROBABILITY   GPITVL
TILES TEACH MATHEMATICS   GPITVL

(RECORDS)

SQUARE THAT NUMBER   SPA

TRIGONOMETRY

(TRANSPARENCIES)

NATURE OF ROOTS OF QUADRATIC
EQUATIONS   LEART
PROPERTIES OF ROOTS OF QUADRATIC
EQUATIONS   LEART
SOLVING OF QUADRATIC INEQUALITIES   LEART

PHYSICAL EDUCATION

ATHLETICS

(MOTION PICTURES)

ADOLPH RUPP (J-C A)   AMERFI
AFL - WIVES (J-C A)   AMERFI
ARMY-NAVY HIGHLIGHTS (J-C A)   AMERFI
BEACH VOLLEY BALL (J-C A)   AMERFI
CALVIN MURPHY (J-C A)   AMERFI
CHARLIE POLITE (J-C A)   AMERFI
COACHES STORY (J-C A)   AMERFI
COLLEGE CHEERLEADERS, NO. 1 (J-C A)   AMERFI
COLLEGE CHEERLEADERS, NO. 2 (J-C A)   AMERFI
COLLEGE FOOTBALL, HANRATTY,
SEYMOUR (J-C A)   AMERFI
CONSERVATION - TURTLE RESEARCH (J-
C A)   AMERFI
CURLING - SCORING (J-C A)   AMERFI
CURLING - STRATEGY (J-C A)   AMERFI
DAVE BING (J-C A)   AMERFI
DEFENSE (J-C A)   AMERFI
DEFENSIVE BACKS (J-C A)   AMERFI
DYNAMICS OF JUDO   IWANMI
FATHER AND SON (J-C A)   AMERFI
FIGURE SKATING - FREE SKATING (J-C
A)   AMERFI
FIREBIRDS (J-C A)   AMERFI
FRAN TARKENTON (J-C A)   AMERFI
GYPSY JOE HARRIS (J-C A)   AMERFI
HOMER JONES (J-C A)   AMERFI
HOWARD PORTER (J-C A)   AMERFI
ICE CANOE RACING (J-C A)   AMERFI
JIM NANCE (J-C A)   AMERFI
JOE FRAZIER - CHAMPION IN TRAINING
(J-C A)   AMERFI
JOE NAMATH (J-C A)   AMERFI
K C EXERCISE (J-C A)   AMERFI
KENTUCKY STYLE (J-C A)   AMERFI
KICKER STORY (J-C A)   AMERFI
LADY BOXER (J-C A)   AMERFI
LITTLE MAN - MIKE GARRETT (J-C A)   AMERFI
MIKE REED (J-C A)   AMERFI
NEIL WALK (J-C A)   AMERFI
OSCAR ROBERTSON (J-C A)   AMERFI
OVER THE LINE - BEACH SPORTS (J-C
A)   AMERFI
PETE MARAVICH (J-C A)   AMERFI
PRO FOOTBALL - DUMP THE
QUARTERBACK (J-C A)   AMERFI
PRO FOOTBALL - RUNNERS (J-C A)   AMERFI
QUEBEC WINTER CARNIVAL (J-C A)   AMERFI
RADIO-OPERATED RACERS - MODELISTS
(J-C A)   AMERFI
RECEIVERS (J-C A)   AMERFI
REFEREE STORY (J-C A)   AMERFI
RESEARCH (J-C A)   AMERFI

SCOTTISH GAMES - CROSS-SECTION (J-C
A)   AMERFI
SCOTTISH GAMES - TOSSING CABOR (J-C
A)   AMERFI
SKATING - PEGGY FLEMING (J-C A)   AMERFI
SKEET SHOOTING (J-C A)   AMERFI
SOCCER - PELE (J-C A)   AMERFI
SPENCER HAYWARD (J-C A)   AMERFI
STEVE VAN BUREN (J-C A)   AMERFI
SWARTHMORE - HUDDLE (J-C A)   AMERFI
SWARTHMORE - SMALL COLLEGE
FOOTBALL (J-C A)   AMERFI
TIGERS TRAINING (J-C A)   AMERFI
TOM PAINE (J-C A)   AMERFI
TRAP SHOOTING (J-C A)   AMERFI
TWO-PLATOON (J-C A)   AMERFI
VARIOUS SPORTS - THIRTY POINTS TO
FITNESS (J-C A)   AMERFI
WONDERFUL WORLD OF SPORT -
AEROBICS--A SERIES (J-C A)   AMERFI
WONDERFUL WORLD OF SPORT -
BASKETBALL--A SERIES (J-C A)   AMERFI
WONDERFUL WORLD OF SPORT -
BOXING--A SERIES (J-C A)   AMERFI
WONDERFUL WORLD OF SPORT -
FOOTBALL--A SERIES (J-C A)   AMERFI
WONDERFUL WORLD OF SPORT -
OTHER--A SERIES (J-C A)   AMERFI

BASEBALL

(MOTION PICTURES)

ASTROTURF (J-C A)   AMERFI
BASE RUNNING (J-C A)   AMERFI
BASEBALL   IWANMI
BASEBALL CLINIC (J-C A)   AMERFI
BASEBALL'S UFO, THE SPITBALL (J-C A)   AMERFI
BAT BOY (J-C A)   AMERFI
BILLY MUFFET (J-C A)   AMERFI
BROADCASTER STORY (J-C A)   AMERFI
BROOKS ROBINSON (J-C A)   AMERFI
CARL YASTRZEMSKI (J-C A)   AMERFI
DUCKY MEDWICK (J-C A)   AMERFI
FRANK ROBINSON (J-C A)   AMERFI
HANK AARON - CONSISTENT HITTER (J-
C A)   AMERFI
HANK AARON - HITTING (J-C A)   AMERFI
HOW TO SET UP BATTERS (J-C A)   AMERFI
JOE TORRE (J-C A)   AMERFI
KNUCKLEBALL, THE - HOYT WHILHELM
(J-C A)   AMERFI
LOWELL HERRERO - THE GRAPHIC
PROCESS   GRADYM
MAX PATKIN (J-C A)   AMERFI
RED SCHOENDIST (J-C A)   AMERFI
RELIEF PITCHER STORY (J-C A)   AMERFI
ROY CAMPANELLA - WHAT HAPPENED
TO (J-C A)   AMERFI
SCOREKEEPER (J-C A)   AMERFI
SLIP PITCH (J-C A)   AMERFI
SONNY JACKSON - BUNTING (J-C A)   AMERFI
SPITBALL STORY (J-C A)   AMERFI
SWITCH HITTING STORY (J-C A)   AMERFI
TIME MC CARVER (J-C A)   AMERFI
TRAINER (J-C A)   AMERFI
UMPIRE SCHOOL (J-C A)   AMERFI
UMPIRE'S TOUCH PLAYS (J-C A)   AMERFI
WONDERFUL WORLD OF SPORT -
BASEBALL--A SERIES (J-C A)   AMERFI

(TRANSPARENCIES)

BOB GIBSON (J-H)   LEART
JACKIE ROBINSON (J-H)   LEART

BASKETBALL

(MOTION PICTURES)

ADOLPH RUPP (J-C A)   AMERFI
CALVIN MURPHY (J-C A)   AMERFI
COACHES STORY (J-C A)   AMERFI
DAVE BING (J-C A)   AMERFI
DEFENSE (J-C A)   AMERFI
DICK VAN ARSDALE - DEFENSIVE PLAY,
PT 1 (J-C)   SCHLAT
DICK VAN ARSDALE - DEFENSIVE PLAY,
PT 2 (J-C)   SCHLAT
FATHER AND SON (J-C A)   AMERFI
HOWARD PORTER (J-C A)   AMERFI
JACK MARIN - FORWARD PLAY, PT 1 (J-
C)   SCHLAT
JACK MARIN - FORWARD PLAY, PT 2 (J-
C)   SCHLAT
JO JO WHITE - OFFENSIVE GUARD, PT 1
(J-C)   SCHLAT
JO JO WHITE - OFFENSIVE GUARD, PT 2
(J-C)   SCHLAT
KENTUCKY STYLE (J-C A)   AMERFI
NEIL WALK (J-C A)   AMERFI
OSCAR ROBERTSON (J-C A)   AMERFI
PETE MARAVICH (J-C A)   AMERFI
REFEREE STORY (J-C A)   AMERFI
SPENCER HAYWARD (J-C A)   AMERFI
TIGERS TRAINING (J-C A)   AMERFI
TOM PAINE (J-C A)   AMERFI

WILLIS REED - CENTER PLAY, PT 1 (J-C)   SCHLAT
WILLIS REED - CENTER PLAY, PT 2 (J-C)   SCHLAT
WILLIS REED BASKETBALL--A SERIES (J-
C)   SCHLAT
WONDERFUL WORLD OF SPORT -
BASKETBALL--A SERIES (J-C A)   AMERFI

(TRANSPARENCIES)

WILLIE MAYS (J-H)   LEART
WILTON N CHAMBERLAIN (J-H)   LEART

DRILL (NON MILITARY)

(MOTION PICTURES)

BULLSEYE   MTP

EXERCISE

(FILMSTRIPS)

FIGURE FACTS   EGH

(MOTION PICTURES)

BOB BEDNARSKI (J-C A)   AMERFI
ROMAN MIELEC (J-C A)   AMERFI
WEIGHTLIFTING - TRAINING (J-C A)   AMERFI
WEIGHTLIFTING - WHAT IS IT (J-C A)   AMERFI
WONDERFUL WORLD OF SPORT -
WEIGHTLIFTING--A SERIES (J-C A)   AMERFI

FIELD AND TRACK

(MOTION PICTURES)

BATON PASS (J-C A)   AMERFI
MILE RELAY (J-C A)   AMERFI
PENN RELAYS (J-C A)   AMERFI
TARTAN TRACK (J-C A)   AMERFI
WONDERFUL WORLD OF SPORT -
TRACK AND FIELD--A SERIES (J-C
A)   AMERFI

FITNESS

(MOTION PICTURES)

BOB BEDNARSKI (J-C A)   AMERFI
RESEARCH (J-C A)   AMERFI
ROMAN MIELEC (J-C A)   AMERFI
VARIOUS SPORTS - THIRTY POINTS TO
FITNESS (J-C A)   AMERFI
WEIGHTLIFTING - TRAINING (J-C A)   AMERFI
WEIGHTLIFTING - WHAT IS IT (J-C A)   AMERFI
WONDERFUL WORLD OF SPORT -
AEROBICS--A SERIES (J-C A)   AMERFI
WONDERFUL WORLD OF SPORT -
WEIGHTLIFTING--A SERIES (J-C A)   AMERFI

FOOTBALL

(MOTION PICTURES)

AFL - WIVES (J-C A)   AMERFI
ARMY-NAVY HIGHLIGHTS (J-C A)   AMERFI
COLLEGE CHEERLEADERS, NO. 1 (J-C A)   AMERFI
COLLEGE CHEERLEADERS, NO. 2 (J-C A)   AMERFI
COLLEGE FOOTBALL, HANRATTY,
SEYMOUR (J-C A)   AMERFI
DEFENSIVE BACKS (J-C A)   AMERFI
FIREBIRDS (J-C A)   AMERFI
FRAN TARKENTON (J-C A)   AMERFI
HOMER JONES (J-C A)   AMERFI
JIM NANCE (J-C A)   AMERFI
JOE NAMATH (J-C A)   AMERFI
K C EXERCISE (J-C A)   AMERFI
KICKER STORY (J-C A)   AMERFI
LITTLE MAN - MIKE GARRETT (J-C A)   AMERFI
MIKE REED (J-C A)   AMERFI
PRO FOOTBALL - DUMP THE
QUARTERBACK (J-C A)   AMERFI
PRO FOOTBALL - RUNNERS (J-C A)   AMERFI
RECEIVERS (J-C A)   AMERFI
STEVE VAN BUREN (J-C A)   AMERFI
SWARTHMORE - HUDDLE (J-C A)   AMERFI
SWARTHMORE - SMALL COLLEGE
FOOTBALL (J-C A)   AMERFI
TWO-PLATOON (J-C A)   AMERFI
WONDERFUL WORLD OF SPORT -
FOOTBALL--A SERIES (J-C A)   AMERFI

GAMES

(MOTION PICTURES)

BEACH VOLLEY BALL (J-C A)   AMERFI
CONSERVATION - TURTLE RESEARCH (J-
C A)   AMERFI
CURLING - SCORING (J-C A)   AMERFI
CURLING - STRATEGY (J-C A)   AMERFI

OVER THE LINE - BEACH SPORTS (J-C A) AMERFI
RADIO-OPERATED RACERS - MODELISTS (J-C A) AMERFI
SCOTTISH GAMES - CROSS-SECTION (J-C A) AMERFI
SCOTTISH GAMES - TOSSING CABOR (J-C A) AMERFI
SKEET SHOOTING (J-C A) AMERFI
TRAP SHOOTING (J-C A) AMERFI
WONDERFUL WORLD OF SPORT - OTHER--A SERIES (J-C A) AMERFI

(VIDEOTAPES)

BECAUSE IT'S FUN NITC

(RECORDS)

RHYTHMS FOR TODAY EDLACT

GOLF

(MOTION PICTURES)

BALTUSROL - THE FOURTH HOLE (J-C A) AMERFI
JOE DEY - PIN PLACEMENT (J-C A) AMERFI
LADIES GOLF - CATHY WENTWORTH (J-C A) AMERFI
MERION - THE ELEVENTH (J-C A) AMERFI
MERION - THE FIRST (J-C A) AMERFI
MIKE BONALLACK (J-C A) AMERFI
SCROTA - THE SECOND (J-C A) AMERFI
WONDERFUL WORLD OF SPORT - GOLF--A SERIES (J-C A) AMERFI

GYMNASTICS

(MOTION PICTURES)

BALANCE BEAM (J-C A) AMERFI
BEGINNING GYMNASTICS (J-C A) AMERFI
FLOOR EXERCISE (J-C A) AMERFI
PARALLEL BARS (J-C A) AMERFI
STILL RINGS (J-C A) AMERFI
TRAMPOLINE - GARY ERWIN (J-C A) AMERFI
TRAMPOLINE COMPETITION (J-C A) SPORTI
UNEVEN PARALLEL BARS (J-C A) AMERFI
WONDERFUL WORLD OF SPORT - GYMNASTICS--A SERIES (J-C A) AMERFI

HOCKEY

(MOTION PICTURES)

GOALIE (J-C A) AMERFI
GOALIE EQUIPMENT STORY (J-C A) AMERFI
HOCKEY STICK STORY (J-C A) AMERFI
PENALTY STORY (J-C A) AMERFI
POWER PLAY (J-C A) AMERFI
WONDERFUL WORLD OF SPORT - HOCKEY--A SERIES (J-C A) AMERFI

RECREATION

(FILMSTRIPS)

GOOD HORSEMANSHIP (H-C) UILVAS
ON SAFARI IN EAST AFRICA (P-C) DWYLIE

(MOTION PICTURES)

AMATEUR POLO (J-C A) AMERFI
AQUA SUMMER (I-C A) NWFCMP
AUCTION STORY (J-C A) AMERFI
BASS FISHING (J-C A) AMERFI
BREAKING A YEARLING (J-C A) AMERFI
CARDIGAN BAY - HARNESS WINNER (J-C A) AMERFI
CAST NETTING (J-C A) AMERFI
CHILDREN'S WORLD - MEXICO (K-I) AVED
DANCER FARM - BERT HANOVER (J-C A) AMERFI
DEVON HORSE SHOW (J-C A) AMERFI
DR FAGER (J-C A) AMERFI
FLORIDA BREEDING (J-C A) AMERFI
FLY CASTING (J-C A) AMERFI
GALLOP, TROT, PACE (J-C A) AMERFI
GUNNING THE FLYWAYS MTP
HARNESS - HAMBLETONIAN (J-C A) AMERFI
HARNESS - SU MAC LAD (J-C A) AMERFI
HARNESS - YEARLING STORY (J-C A) AMERFI
HORSE RACE - CHART CALLER (J-C A) AMERFI
HORSE RACE - FILM PATROL (J-C A) AMERFI
HORSE RACE - THE CLOCKER (J-C A) AMERFI
HORSE RACE - THE STARTING GATE (J-C A) AMERFI
ICE FISHING (J-C A) AMERFI
NEVELE PRIDE - TROTTER (J-C A) AMERFI
OVER THE LINE - BEACH SPORTS (J-C A) AMERFI
REEL CASTING (J-C A) AMERFI
RODEO SCHOOL - BAREBACK RIDING (J-C A) AMERFI
RODEO SCHOOL - BULL RIDING (J-C A) AMERFI
RODEO SCHOOL - GRADUATE (J-C A) AMERFI

RODEO SCHOOL - LARRY MAHAN (J-C A) AMERFI
RODEO SCHOOL - SADDLE BRONC RIDE (J-C A) AMERFI
SKEET SHOOTING (J-C A) AMERFI
SKIING ABOVE THE CLOUDS RARIG
SNATCH - HOOK FISHING (J-C A) AMERFI
THIS IS CAMPING (I-C A) IU
THOROUGHBRED - THE NEW BOY (J-C A) AMERFI
THOROUGHBRED - THE STARTING GATE (J-C A) AMERFI
TIPS ON TRAP MTP
TRICK CASTING (J-C A) AMERFI
VACATION FUN IN ISRAEL ALDEN
WAY TO GO, THE (A) SFI
WONDERFUL WORLD OF SPORT - CARS, AUTO RACING --A SERIES (J-C A) AMERFI
WONDERFUL WORLD OF SPORT - FISHING--A SERIES (J-C A) AMERFI
WONDERFUL WORLD OF SPORT - HORSES, RACING, POLO, RODEO- -A SERIES (J-C A) AMERFI
WONDERFUL WORLD OF SPORT - SKIING--A SERIES (J-C A) AMERFI
WONDERFUL WORLD OF SPORT - SNOWMOBILES--A SERIES (J-C A) AMERFI

SOCCER

(MOTION PICTURES)

HOW DOES A YACHT SAIL IWANMI
SOCCER - PELE (J-C A) AMERFI

SPORTS

(FILMSTRIPS)

GOOD HORSEMANSHIP (H-C) UILVAS

(MOTION PICTURES)

ADOLPH RUPP (J-C A) AMERFI
AEROBATICS - AERIAL ACROBATICS (J-C A) AMERFI
AFL - WIVES (J-C A) AMERFI
AMATEUR POLO (J-C A) AMERFI
AMERICA'S CUP (J-C A) AMERFI
ANTIQUE CARS - DUSENBERG, MERCEDES, BUGATTI (J-C A) AMERFI
ANTIQUE CARS - PIERCE ARROW (J-C A) AMERFI
ANTIQUE PLANES - F3F AND SPITFIRE (J-C A) AMERFI
ARMY-NAVY HIGHLIGHTS (J-C A) AMERFI
ASTROTURF (J-C A) AMERFI
AUCTION STORY (J-C A) AMERFI
BALANCE BEAM (J-C A) AMERFI
BALTUSROL - THE FOURTH HOLE (J-C A) AMERFI
BASE RUNNING (J-C A) AMERFI
BASEBALL CLINIC (J-C A) AMERFI
BASEBALL'S UFO, THE SPITBALL (J-C A) AMERFI
BASS FISHING (J-C A) AMERFI
BAT BOY (J-C A) AMERFI
BATON PASS (J-C A) AMERFI
BEACH VOLLEY BALL (J-C A) AMERFI
BEGINNERS (J-C A) AMERFI
BEGINNING GYMNASTICS (J-C A) AMERFI
BILLY MUFFET (J-C A) AMERFI
BLUE ANGELS - BEHIND THE ACT - MECHANICS (J-C A) AMERFI
BLUE ANGELS - NAVY'S FORMATION FLYERS (J-C A) AMERFI
BREAKING A YEARLING (J-C A) AMERFI
BREEZY AIRPLANE (J-C A) AMERFI
BROADCASTER STORY (J-C A) AMERFI
BROOKS ROBINSON (J-C A) AMERFI
BULLSEYE MTP
CALVIN MURPHY (J-C A) AMERFI
CARDIGAN BAY - HARNESS WINNER (J-C A) AMERFI
CARL YASTRZEMSKI (J-C A) AMERFI
CAST NETTING (J-C A) AMERFI
CATAMARANS (J-C A) AMERFI
CHARLIE POLITE (J-C A) AMERFI
CLASSIC CARS, THE 1930 BENTLEY (J-C A) AMERFI
CLAUDE FRANTZ (J-C A) AMERFI
COACHES STORY (J-C A) AMERFI
COLLEGE CHEERLEADERS, NO. 1 (J-C A) AMERFI
COLLEGE CHEERLEADERS, NO. 2 (J-C A) AMERFI
COLLEGE FOOTBALL, HANRATTY, SEYMOUR (J-C A) AMERFI
CONSERVATION - TURTLE RESEARCH (J-C A) AMERFI
CONSTRUCTING REALITY - A FILM ON FILM (P-C) JOU
COUNTERS FOR TAKEDOWNS FROM A STANDING POSITION (J-C A) EDCOM
COXSWAIN STORY (J-C A) AMERFI
CURLING - SCORING (J-C A) AMERFI
CURLING - STRATEGY (J-C A) AMERFI
DANCER FARM - BERT HANOVER (J-C A) AMERFI
DAVE BING (J-C A) AMERFI
DEFENSE (J-C A) AMERFI
DEFENSIVE BACKS (J-C A) AMERFI
DEVON HORSE SHOW (J-C A) AMERFI

DICK VAN ARSDALE - DEFENSIVE PLAY, PT 1 (J-C) SCHLAT
DICK VAN ARSDALE - DEFENSIVE PLAY, PT 2 (J-C) SCHLAT
DIVING - BASICS (J-C A) AMERFI
DIVING - LESLEY BUSH (J-C A) AMERFI
DR FAGER (J-C A) AMERFI
DRAG BOATS (J-C A) AMERFI
DRAG RACING - CHRISTMAS TREE (J-C A) AMERFI
DRAG RACING - DON GARLITS (J-C A) AMERFI
DRAG RACING - FUNNY CARS (J-C A) AMERFI
DRAG RACING - SIGHTS AND SOUNDS (J-C A) AMERFI
DRAG RACING - SLINGSHOT DRAGSTERS (J-C A) AMERFI
DRIVING SCHOOL - TRAINING RACERS (J-C A) AMERFI
DUCKY MEDWICK (J-C A) AMERFI
DUNE BUGGIES - FUN CARS (J-C A) AMERFI
DUNE BUGGIES - IN FLEET (J-C A) AMERFI
DUNE BUGGIES - OFF-THE-ROAD RACING (J-C A) AMERFI
DYNAMICS OF JUDO IWANMI
EPEE, THE (J-C A) AMERFI
FATHER AND SON (J-C A) AMERFI
FIGURE SKATING - FREE SKATING (J-C A) AMERFI
FIREBIRDS (J-C A) AMERFI
FLOAT PARTY - DOWN THE RIVER (J-C A) AMERFI
FLOOR EXERCISE (J-C A) AMERFI
FLORIDA BREEDING (J-C A) AMERFI
FLY CASTING (J-C A) AMERFI
FLYING - STUNTING (J-C A) AMERFI
FOIL (J-C A) AMERFI
FRAN TARKENTON (J-C A) AMERFI
FRANK ROBINSON (J-C A) AMERFI
GALLOP, TROT, PACE (J-C A) AMERFI
GOALIE (J-C A) AMERFI
GOALIE EQUIPMENT STORY (J-C A) AMERFI
GOING FOR THE PIN (J-C A) AMERFI
GYPSY JOE HARRIS (J-C A) AMERFI
GYROCOPTERS (J-C A) AMERFI
HANK AARON - CONSISTENT HITTER (J-C A) AMERFI
HANK AARON - HITTING (J-C A) AMERFI
HARNESS - HAMBLETONIAN (J-C A) AMERFI
HARNESS - SU MAC LAD (J-C A) AMERFI
HARNESS - YEARLING STORY (J-C A) AMERFI
HOCKEY STICK STORY (J-C A) AMERFI
HOMEBUILTS (J-C A) AMERFI
HOMER JONES (J-C A) AMERFI
HORSE RACE - CHART CALLER (J-C A) AMERFI
HORSE RACE - FILM PATROL (J-C A) AMERFI
HORSE RACE - THE CLOCKER (J-C A) AMERFI
HORSE RACE - THE STARTING GATE (J-C A) AMERFI
HOW DOES A YACHT SAIL IWANMI
HOW TO RIDE THEM (J-C A) AMERFI
HOW TO SET UP BATTERS (J-C A) AMERFI
HOWARD PORTER (J-C A) AMERFI
ICE BOATS (J-C A) AMERFI
ICE CANOE RACING (J-C A) AMERFI
ICE FISHING (J-C A) AMERFI
INTERMEDIATE (COMPANION DOGS) (J-C A) AMERFI
JACK MARIN - FORWARD PLAY, PT 1 (J-C) SCHLAT
JACK MARIN - FORWARD PLAY, PT 2 (J-C) SCHLAT
JIM NANCE (J-C A) AMERFI
JO JO WHITE - OFFENSIVE GUARD, PT 1 (J-C) SCHLAT
JO JO WHITE - OFFENSIVE GUARD, PT 2 (J-C) SCHLAT
JOE DEY - PIN PLACEMENT (J-C A) AMERFI
JOE FRAZIER - CHAMPION IN TRAINING (J-C A) AMERFI
JOE NAMATH (J-C A) AMERFI
JOE TORRE (J-C A) AMERFI
K C EXERCISE (J-C A) AMERFI
KARATE (J-C A) PFP
KENTUCKY STYLE (J-C A) AMERFI
KICKER STORY (J-C A) AMERFI
KNUCKLEBALL, THE - HOYT WHILHELM (J-C A) AMERFI
LABRADORS IN TRAINING (J-C A) AMERFI
LABRADORS, LAND RETRIEVING (J-C A) AMERFI
LABRADORS, WATER RETRIEVING (J-C A) AMERFI
LADIES GOLF - CATHY WENTWORTH (J-C A) AMERFI
LADY BOXER (J-C A) AMERFI
LE CYCLISTE (J-C A) ALBM
LITTLE MAN - MIKE GARRETT (J-C A) AMERFI
MAESTRO, THE (J-C A) AMERFI
MAX PATKIN (J-C A) AMERFI
MERION - THE ELEVENTH (J-C A) AMERFI
MERION - THE FIRST (J-C A) AMERFI
MIKE BONALLACK (J-C A) AMERFI
MIKE REED (J-C A) AMERFI
MILE RELAY (J-C A) AMERFI
NEIL WALK (J-C A) AMERFI
NEVELE PRIDE - TROTTER (J-C A) AMERFI
NOVICE COMPANION (J-C A) AMERFI
OLD PLANE - BEARCAT (J-C A) AMERFI
OSCAR ROBERTSON (J-C A) AMERFI
OVER THE LINE - BEACH SPORTS (J-C A) AMERFI

PARALLEL BARS (J-C A)	AMERFI
PENALTY STORY (J-C A)	AMERFI
PENN RELAYS (J-C A)	AMERFI
PETE MARAVICH (J-C A)	AMERFI
POWER PLAY (J-C A)	AMERFI
PRO FOOTBALL - DUMP THE QUARTERBACK (J-C A)	AMERFI
PRO FOOTBALL - RUNNERS (J-C A)	AMERFI
QUEBEC WINTER CARNIVAL (J-C A)	AMERFI
RACING (FACTORY) TEAM (J-C A)	AMERFI
RACING (LACONIA N H) (J-C A)	AMERFI
RADIO-OPERATED RACERS - MODELISTS (J-C A)	AMERFI
RECEIVERS (J-C A)	AMERFI
RED SCHOENDIST (J-C A)	AMERFI
REEL CASTING (J-C A)	AMERFI
REFEREE STORY (J-C A)	AMERFI
RELIEF PITCHER STORY (J-C A)	AMERFI
RESEARCH (J-C A)	AMERFI
RESTORATION (J-C A)	AMERFI
RODEO SCHOOL - BAREBACK RIDING (J-C A)	AMERFI
RODEO SCHOOL - BULL RIDING (J-C A)	AMERFI
RODEO SCHOOL - GRADUATE (J-C A)	AMERFI
RODEO SCHOOL - LARRY MAHAN (J-C A)	AMERFI
RODEO SCHOOL - SADDLE BRONC RIDE (J-C A)	AMERFI
ROY CAMPANELLA - WHAT HAPPENED TO (J-C A)	AMERFI
SABER (J-C A)	AMERFI
SAILING - 'E' SLOOPS (J-C A)	AMERFI
SAILING - SUNFISH REGATTA (J-C A)	AMERFI
SCOREKEEPER (J-C A)	AMERFI
SCOTTISH GAMES - CROSS-SECTION (J-C A)	AMERFI
SCOTTISH GAMES - TOSSING CABOR (J-C A)	AMERFI
SCROTA - THE SECOND (J-C A)	AMERFI
SCUBA - FLORIDA'S UNDERWATER STATE PARK (J-C A)	AMERFI
SCUBA - SLURP GUN (J-C A)	AMERFI
SCUBA - SPANISH WRECK (J-C A)	AMERFI
SHELL STORY (J-C A)	AMERFI
SKATING	IWANMI
SKATING - PEGGY FLEMING (J-C A)	AMERFI
SKEET SHOOTING (J-C A)	AMERFI
SKI INSTRUCTORS (J-C A)	AMERFI
SKI PATROL - GENERAL (J-C A)	AMERFI
SKI PATROL - RESCUE (J-C A)	AMERFI
SKIING - BASICS (J-C A)	AMERFI
SKY DIVING - BARBARA ROQUEMORE (J-C A)	AMERFI
SKY DIVING - U S TEAM (J-C A)	AMERFI
SKY DIVING - WHAT IS IT (J-C A)	AMERFI
SLED DOGS - ALASKAN HUSKY (J-C A)	AMERFI
SLED DOGS - BIG-TIME TEAM (J-C A)	AMERFI
SLED DOGS - RACING (J-C A)	AMERFI
SLIP PITCH (J-C A)	AMERFI
SNATCH - HOOK FISHING (J-C A)	AMERFI
SNOW SAFARI (J-C A)	AMERFI
SOARING - MOOD STORY (J-C A)	AMERFI
SOARING - TEST PILOT (J-C A)	AMERFI
SOCCER - PELE (J-C A)	AMERFI
SONNY JACKSON - BUNTING (J-C A)	AMERFI
SPENCER HAYWARD (J-C A)	AMERFI
SPITBALL STORY (J-C A)	AMERFI
STEVE VAN BUREN (J-C A)	AMERFI
STILL RINGS (J-C A)	AMERFI
SURFING - CORKY CARROLL (J-C A)	AMERFI
SURFING - JOYCE HOFFMAN (J-C A)	AMERFI
SWARTHMORE - HUDDLE (J-C A)	AMERFI
SWARTHMORE - SMALL COLLEGE FOOTBALL (J-C A)	AMERFI
SWIMMING - BASIC STROKES (J-C A)	AMERFI
SWIMMING AND DIVING - HOW CHAMPIONSHIPS ARE WON (J-C A)	AMERFI
SWIMMING AND DIVING - TRAINING (J-C A)	AMERFI
SWITCH HITTING STORY (J-C A)	AMERFI
TAKEDOWNS FROM A STANDING POSITION (J-C A)	EDCOM
TARTAN TRACK (J-C A)	AMERFI
THOROUGHBRED - THE NEW BOY (J-C A)	AMERFI
THOROUGHBRED - THE STARTING GATE (J-C A)	AMERFI
TIGERS TRAINING (J-C A)	AMERFI
TIME MC CARVER (J-C A)	AMERFI
TIPS ON TRAP	MTP
TOM PAINE (J-C A)	AMERFI
TRAINER (J-C A)	AMERFI
TRAMPOLINE - GARY ERWIN (J-C A)	AMERFI
TRAMPOLINE COMPETITION (J-C A)	SPORTI
TRAP SHOOTING (J-C A)	AMERFI
TRICK CASTING (J-C A)	AMERFI
TWO-PLATOON (J-C A)	AMERFI
UMPIRE SCHOOL (J-C A)	AMERFI
UMPIRE'S TOUCH PLAYS (J-C A)	AMERFI
UNEVEN PARALLEL BARS (J-C A)	AMERFI
UTILITY DOGS (J-C A)	AMERFI
VARIOUS SPORTS - THIRTY POINTS TO FITNESS (J-C A)	AMERFI
VESPER STORY (J-C A)	AMERFI
WILLIS REED - CENTER PLAY, PT 1 (J-C)	SCHLAT
WILLIS REED - CENTER PLAY, PT 2 (J-C)	SCHLAT
WILLIS REED BASKETBALL--A SERIES (J-C)	SCHLAT
WINNING WRESTLING BY JOE BEGALA--A SERIES (J-C A)	EDCOM

WONDERFUL WORLD OF SPORT - AEROBICS--A SERIES (J-C A)	AMERFI
WONDERFUL WORLD OF SPORT - BASEBALL--A SERIES (J-C A)	AMERFI
WONDERFUL WORLD OF SPORT - BASKETBALL--A SERIES (J-C A)	AMERFI
WONDERFUL WORLD OF SPORT - BOATING--A SERIES (J-C A)	AMERFI
WONDERFUL WORLD OF SPORT - BOXING--A SERIES (J-C A)	AMERFI
WONDERFUL WORLD OF SPORT - CARS, AUTO RACING --A SERIES (J-C A)	AMERFI
WONDERFUL WORLD OF SPORT - DOGS--A SERIES (J-C A)	AMERFI
WONDERFUL WORLD OF SPORT - FENCING--A SERIES (J-C A)	AMERFI
WONDERFUL WORLD OF SPORT - FISHING--A SERIES (J-C A)	AMERFI
WONDERFUL WORLD OF SPORT - FLYING--A SERIES (J-C A)	AMERFI
WONDERFUL WORLD OF SPORT - FOOTBALL--A SERIES (J-C A)	AMERFI
WONDERFUL WORLD OF SPORT - GOLF--A SERIES (J-C A)	AMERFI
WONDERFUL WORLD OF SPORT - GYMNASTICS--A SERIES (J-C A)	AMERFI
WONDERFUL WORLD OF SPORT - HOCKEY--A SERIES (J-C A)	AMERFI
WONDERFUL WORLD OF SPORT - HORSES, RACING, POLO, RODEO--A SERIES (J-C A)	AMERFI
WONDERFUL WORLD OF SPORT - OTHER--A SERIES (J-C A)	AMERFI
WONDERFUL WORLD OF SPORT - ROWING--A SERIES (J-C A)	AMERFI
WONDERFUL WORLD OF SPORT - SKIING--A SERIES (J-C A)	AMERFI
WONDERFUL WORLD OF SPORT - SNOWMOBILES--A SERIES (J-C A)	AMERFI
WONDERFUL WORLD OF SPORT - SWIM, DIVE, SCUBA, SURF--A SERIES (J-C A)	AMERFI
WONDERFUL WORLD OF SPORT - TRACK AND FIELD--A SERIES (J-C A)	AMERFI
WONDERFUL WORLD OF SPORT - WRESTLING--A SERIES (J-C A)	AMERFI

SPORTS, WATER

(MOTION PICTURES)

AMERICA'S CUP (J-C A)	AMERFI
AQUA SUMMER (I-C A)	NWFCMP
BASS FISHING (J-C A)	AMERFI
CAST NETTING (J-C A)	AMERFI
CATAMARANS (J-C A)	AMERFI
COXSWAIN STORY (J-C A)	AMERFI
DIVING - BASICS (J-C A)	AMERFI
DIVING - LESLEY BUSH (J-C A)	AMERFI
DRAG BOATS (J-C A)	AMERFI
FLOAT PARTY - DOWN THE RIVER (J-C A)	AMERFI
FLY CASTING (J-C A)	AMERFI
HOW DOES A YACHT SAIL	IWANMI
ICE BOATS (J-C A)	AMERFI
ICE FISHING (J-C A)	AMERFI
REEL CASTING (J-C A)	AMERFI
SAILING - 'E' SLOOPS (J-C A)	AMERFI
SAILING - SUNFISH REGATTA (J-C A)	AMERFI
SCUBA - FLORIDA'S UNDERWATER STATE PARK (J-C A)	AMERFI
SCUBA - SLURP GUN (J-C A)	AMERFI
SCUBA - SPANISH WRECK (J-C A)	AMERFI
SHELL STORY (J-C A)	AMERFI
SNATCH - HOOK FISHING (J-C A)	AMERFI
SURFING - CORKY CARROLL (J-C A)	AMERFI
SURFING - JOYCE HOFFMAN (J-C A)	AMERFI
SWIMMING - BASIC STROKES (J-C A)	AMERFI
SWIMMING AND DIVING - HOW CHAMPIONSHIPS ARE WON (J-C A)	AMERFI
SWIMMING AND DIVING - TRAINING (J-C A)	AMERFI
TRICK CASTING (J-C A)	AMERFI
VESPER STORY (J-C A)	AMERFI
WATERSMITH (I-C A)	TIMLIF
WONDERFUL WORLD OF SPORT - BOATING--A SERIES (J-C A)	AMERFI
WONDERFUL WORLD OF SPORT - FISHING--A SERIES (J-C A)	AMERFI
WONDERFUL WORLD OF SPORT - ROWING--A SERIES (J-C A)	AMERFI
WONDERFUL WORLD OF SPORT - SWIM, DIVE, SCUBA, SURF--A SERIES (J-C A)	AMERFI

SPORTS, WINTER

(MOTION CARTRIDGES)

SKIING - STEM CHRISTIE	ATHI
SKIING - STEM TURN	ATHI

(MOTION PICTURES)

BEGINNERS (J-C A)	AMERFI

CURLING - SCORING (J-C A)	AMERFI
CURLING - STRATEGY (J-C A)	AMERFI
FIGURE SKATING - FREE SKATING (J-C A)	AMERFI
GUNNING THE FLYWAYS	MTP
HOW TO RIDE THEM (J-C A)	AMERFI
ICE CANOE RACING (J-C A)	AMERFI
QUEBEC WINTER CARNIVAL (J-C A)	AMERFI
RACING (FACTORY) TEAM (J-C A)	AMERFI
RACING (LACONIA N H) (J-C A)	AMERFI
SKATING - PEGGY FLEMING (J-C A)	AMERFI
SKI	IWANMI
SKI INSTRUCTORS (J-C A)	AMERFI
SKI PATROL - GENERAL (J-C A)	AMERFI
SKI PATROL - RESCUE (J-C A)	AMERFI
SKIING - BASICS (J-C A)	AMERFI
SKIING ABOVE THE CLOUDS	RARIG
SNOW SAFARI (J-C A)	AMERFI
WONDERFUL WORLD OF SPORT - OTHER--A SERIES (J-C A)	AMERFI
WONDERFUL WORLD OF SPORT - SKIING--A SERIES (J-C A)	AMERFI
WONDERFUL WORLD OF SPORT - SNOWMOBILES--A SERIES (J-C A)	AMERFI
YOU HOO - I'M A BIRD	MTP

TENNIS

(TRANSPARENCIES)

ALTHEA GIBSON (J-H)	LEART

PSYCHOLOGY

PSYCHOLOGY - GENERAL

(MOTION PICTURES)

INTRODUCTION TO PSYCHOTHERAPY, AN (PRO)	VIDEOG

PSYCHOLOGY, GENERAL - EDUCATION AND TRAINING

(AUDIO TAPES)

BIBLIOGRAPHY - HOW TO STUDY FOR BOARDS - SAMPLE EXAMINATIONS	SIGINF
INFORMATION FOR CANDIDATES - THE FORMAT OF WRITTEN AND ORAL EXAMINATIONS - HOW TO TAKE...	SIGINF
PREPARATION FOR CERTIFICATION BY THE AMERICAN BOARD OF PSYCHIATRY AND NEUROLOGY--A SERIES	SIGINF
SAMPLE EXAMINATIONS - THE CONCEPT OF SCHIZOPHRENIA	SIGINF

PSYCHOLOGY, GENERAL - HISTORY

(AUDIO TAPES)

SCHOOLS OF PSYCHODYNAMIC THEORY - THE HISTORY OF PSYCHIATRY	SIGINF

PSYCHOLOGY, GENERAL - PARAPSYCHOLOGY

(AUDIO TAPES)

FACT OR FANTASY--A SERIES	BASCH

PSYCHOLOGY, GENERAL - PHILOSOPHY

(MOTION PICTURES)

SEARCH FOR ALTERNATE LIFE-STYLES AND PHILOSOPHIES, THE (J-C A)	FLMFR

PSYCHOLOGY, GENERAL - PROFESSIONAL DEVELOPMENTS

(AUDIO TAPES)

BIBLIOGRAPHY - HOW TO STUDY FOR BOARDS - SAMPLE EXAMINATIONS	SIGINF
CLINICAL PSYCHOPATHOLOGY--A SERIES	SIGINF
EPIDEMIOLOGY - ETIOLOGY - PSYCHOLOGICAL TESTING - SCHOOLS OF PSYCHODYNAMIC THEORY	SIGINF
INFORMATION FOR CANDIDATES - THE FORMAT OF WRITTEN AND ORAL EXAMINATIONS - HOW TO TAKE...	SIGINF

NEW APPROACH TO HUMAN EVOLUTION
- INTRODUCTION   SIGINF
NEW APPROACH TO HUMAN
  EVOLUTION - SUMMATION AND
  CONCLUSIONS   SIGINF
NEW APPROACH TO HUMAN
EVOLUTION--A SERIES   SIGINF
PREPARATION FOR CERTIFICATION
  BY THE AMERICAN BOARD OF
  PSYCHIATRY AND NEUROLOGY--A
  SERIES   SIGINF
RECENT ATTITUDES TOWARD HUMAN
EVOLUTION   SIGINF
SPECIAL CLINICAL PROBLEMS IN
  INTENSIVE PSYCHOTHERAPY--A
  SERIES   SIGINF

PSYCHOLOGY, GENERAL - THEORY AND SYSTEMS

(MOTION PICTURES)

COGNITIVE DEVELOPMENT (C A)   CRMP
DEVELOPMENTAL PSYCHOLOGY FILM--A
SERIES (C A)   CRMP
EMOTIONAL DEVELOPMENT (C A)   CRMP
MORAL DEVELOPMENT (C A)   CRMP

(AUDIO TAPES)

BEHAVIOR DISORDERS OF CHILDREN--A
SERIES   SIGINF
BEHAVIOR MODIFICATION
  STRATEGIES FOR CHILD
  PSYCHOTHERAPISTS--A SERIES   SIGINF
BEHAVIORISM AND
  PSYCHOANALYSIS - COGNITIVE
  STYLES, CONTENTS AND ORIGINS   SIGINF
CLINICAL PSYCHOPATHOLOGY--A SERIES   SIGINF
EPIDEMIOLOGY - ETIOLOGY -
  PSYCHOLOGICAL TESTING -
  SCHOOLS OF PSYCHODYNAMIC
  THEORY   SIGINF
FACTS, PRACTICES, THEORIES AND
  VALUES - A VALUE THEORY OF
  TRUTH   SIGINF
LIMITATIONS OF PSYCHOTHERAPY, THE   SIGINF
NEW APPROACH TO HUMAN EVOLUTION
- INTRODUCTION   SIGINF
NEW APPROACH TO HUMAN
  EVOLUTION - SUMMATION AND
  CONCLUSIONS   SIGINF
NEW APPROACH TO HUMAN
EVOLUTION--A SERIES   SIGINF
NORMAL AND ABNORMAL
  BEHAVIOR OF ADOLESCENCE-- A
  SERIES   SIGINF
PREPARATION FOR CERTIFICATION
  BY THE AMERICAN BOARD OF
  PSYCHIATRY AND NEUROLOGY--A
  SERIES   SIGINF
RECENT ATTITUDES TOWARD HUMAN
EVOLUTION   SIGINF
SCHOOLS OF PSYCHODYNAMIC
  THEORY - THE HISTORY OF
  PSYCHIATRY   SIGINF

ANIMAL - SENSORY PROCESSES

(MOTION PICTURES)

CONDITIONED REFLEX   IWANMI

ANIMAL - SOCIAL AND SEXUAL BEHAVIOR

(MOTION PICTURES)

LIFE OF A MONKEY, THE   IWANMI

CLINICAL - GENERAL

(AUDIO TAPES)

CLINICAL PSYCHOPATHOLOGY--A SERIES   SIGINF
TOPICS IN CLINICAL PSYCHIATRY--A
SERIES   SIGINF

CLINICAL - BEHAVIOR DISORDER

(AUDIO TAPES)

ACCELERATION TECHNIQUES   SIGINF
ACUTE SCHIZOPHRENIA, PT 1   SIGINF
ACUTE SCHIZOPHRENIA, PT 2   SIGINF
ADOLESCENT PATIENT AND THE
FAMILY, THE   SIGINF
ADOLESCENT WITH A COMMUNICATION
DISORDER, THE   SIGINF
ANGER INHIBITION PROBLEMS, PT 1   SIGINF
ANGER INHIBITION PROBLEMS, PT 2   SIGINF
ASSESSING FOR BEHAVIOR CHANGE   SIGINF
ASSESSMENT OF CHANGE IN
CHILDREN'S BEHAVIOR   SIGINF
BASIC STRATEGIES FOR MODIFYING
  CHILDREN'S BEHAVIOR   SIGINF

BEHAVIOR DISORDERS OF CHILDHOOD   SIGINF
BEHAVIOR DISORDERS OF CHILDREN--A
SERIES   SIGINF
BEHAVIOR MODIFICATION
  STRATEGIES FOR CHILD
  PSYCHOTHERAPISTS--A SERIES   SIGINF
BORDERLINE PATIENT, THE   SIGINF
CEREBRAL DYSFUNCTION   SIGINF
CEREBRAL DYSFUNCTION - SEIZURE
DISORDERS   SIGINF
CEREBRAL DYSFUNCTION - 14 AND
  SIX CYCLES POSITIVE EEG
  SPIKING   SIGINF
CHILD PEERS AS THERAPEUTIC AGENTS   SIGINF
COGNITIVE PERFORMANCE - PROGRESS
VS PRODUCT   SIGINF
CONTINGENCY MANAGEMENT   SIGINF
CURRENT ISSUES AND PROBLEMS
IN SUICIDE PREVENTION   SIGINF
DECELERATION TECHNIQUES   SIGINF
DELINQUENT AND PROMISCUOUS
HOMOSEXUAL BEHAVIOR   SIGINF
DEPRESSION - CLINICAL PICTURES AND
TREATMENT   SIGINF
DEPRESSION - DIFFERENTIAL
  DIAGNOSIS AND RECENT
  BIOCHEMISTRY   SIGINF
DEPRESSION - REACTION OR DISEASE   SIGINF
DEPRESSION AND SUICIDE   SIGINF
DEVELOPMENT OF AGGRESSION
  AND AGGRESSION ANXIETY   SIGINF
DEVELOPMENTAL CRISES IN BLACK
ADOLESCENTS   SIGINF
DIAGNOSIS AND TREATMENT OF
  PSEUDONEUROTIC
  SCHIZOPHRENIA, THE   SIGINF
DIAGNOSTIC PROCESS AND THE
  PLANNING OF TREATMENT, THE   SIGINF
DRUG ABUSE - SOMATIC
  THERAPIES - PSYCHIATRIC
  DISORDERS OF CHILDHOOD   SIGINF
EMERGENCY PSYCHIATRIC TREATMENT   SIGINF
EXAMPLES AND DISCUSSION OF
SUICIDE CALLS, PT 1   SIGINF
EXAMPLES AND DISCUSSION OF
SUICIDE CALLS, PT 2   SIGINF
EXTRAVERSION AND NEUROTICISM
  - ORIGINS OF PERSONALITY
  TRAITS AND SOCIAL ATTITUDES   SIGINF
FAMILY TREATMENT OF SCHOOL
PHOBIAS   SIGINF
GENERAL SYSTEMS - DIAGNOSTIC
CONCEPTS   SIGINF
GOALS FOR BEHAVIOR THERAPY WITH
CHILDREN, THE   SIGINF
INITIAL EVALUATION, THE   SIGINF
INPATIENT MANAGEMENT OF
  BORDERLINE PATIENTS, THE   SIGINF
LIMITATIONS OF PSYCHOTHERAPY, THE   SIGINF
MANAGEMENT OF THE DEPENDENT
ADOLESCENT   SIGINF
MENTAL AND PHYSICAL, THE   SIGINF
MISCELLANEOUS TECHNIQUES   SIGINF
NEUROSIS, CHARACTER AND BIOLOGY   SIGINF
OBSERVATIONAL LEARNING   SIGINF
OBSESSING AND LEARNING   SIGINF
OBSESSIONS AND PHOBIAS   SIGINF
PARENTS AS THERAPEUTIC AGENTS   SIGINF
PATIENTS WHO BEHAVE BADLY   SIGINF
PHOBIC AND ANXIETY STATES   SIGINF
PREVENTIVE MENTAL HEALTH
  WORK WITH PRESCHOOL
  TEACHERS   SIGINF
PSYCHIATRIC DISORDERS OF
  CHILDHOOD - CHILD
  PSYCHOTHERAPY - MARITAL
  MALADJUSTMENT AND...   SIGINF
PSYCHOLOGICAL FUNCTIONS OF THE
COUNTER CULTURE   SIGINF
PSYCHOTHERAPEUTIC INTERACTION,
THE   SIGINF
PSYCHOTHERAPIST, THE   SIGINF
RE-GRIEF WORK FOR THE
PATHOLOGICAL MOURNER   SIGINF
RECENT CONTRIBUTIONS TOWARD
A THEORY OF PAIN BEHAVIOR   SIGINF
REGRESSION AND ITS PREVENTION   SIGINF
REGRESSION AND SEMANTIC
  SPEECH IN HYSTERIA AND
  SCHIZOPHRENIA   SIGINF
SCHIZOPHRENIC PATIENT, THE   SIGINF
SELF-ADMINISTERED BEHAVIOR
THERAPY FOR CHILDREN   SIGINF
SEVERELY NEUROTIC AND THE
PSYCHOTIC ADOLESCENT, THE   SIGINF
SISSIES AND TOMBOYS - CROSS
GENDER BEHAVIOR IN CHILDREN   SIGINF
SPECIAL CLINICAL PROBLEMS IN
  INTENSIVE PSYCHOTHERAPY--A
  SERIES   SIGINF
SUICIDE AND DEPRESSION   SIGINF
SUICIDE AND VIOLENCE   SIGINF
TEACHERS AS THERAPEUTIC AGENTS   SIGINF
THERAPEUTIC ALLIANCE AND THE
  EARLY STAGES OF TREATMENT,
  THE   SIGINF
THERAPEUTIC COMMUNITY, THE   SIGINF
THERAPY OF COMMON CHILDHOOD
DISORDERS--A SERIES   SIGINF

TOPICS IN CLINICAL PSYCHIATRY--A
SERIES   SIGINF
TRANSFERENCE AND
COUNTERTRANSFERENCE   SIGINF
TRANSFERENCE MANIFESTATIONS
  AND THEIR MANAGEMENT   SIGINF
USE OF SOMATIC TREATMENTS IN
SCHIZOPHRENIA   SIGINF
VIOLENCE IN CLINICAL STATES -
SYNDROMES   SIGINF
VIOLENCE IN CLINICAL STATES -
TREATMENT   SIGINF

CLINICAL - COMMUNITY SERVICES

(AUDIO TAPES)

ACUTE SCHIZOPHRENIA, PT 1   SIGINF
ACUTE SCHIZOPHRENIA, PT 2   SIGINF
DEPRESSION - CLINICAL PICTURES AND
TREATMENT   SIGINF
DEPRESSION - DIFFERENTIAL
  DIAGNOSIS AND RECENT
  BIOCHEMISTRY   SIGINF
FAMILY THERAPY - GROUP
  THERAPY - COMMUNITY
  PSYCHIATRY   SIGINF
GENERAL SYSTEMS - DIAGNOSTIC
CONCEPTS   SIGINF
INNOVATIVE SERVICES FOR YOUTH   SIGINF
THERAPEUTIC COMMUNITY, THE   SIGINF
TOPICS IN CLINICAL PSYCHIATRY--A
SERIES   SIGINF
VIOLENCE IN CLINICAL STATES -
SYNDROMES   SIGINF
VIOLENCE IN CLINICAL STATES -
TREATMENT   SIGINF

CLINICAL - COUNSELING AND GUIDANCE

(VIDEOTAPES)

CASE STUDIES   GPITVL
COUNSELING THE ADOLESCENT--A
SERIES   GPITVL
DEMOCRATIC EVOLUTION OF SOCIETY,
THE, PT 1   GPITVL
DEMOCRATIC EVOLUTION OF SOCIETY,
THE, PT 2   GPITVL
EDWARD   GPITVL
GROUP DISCUSSION WITH NORMAL
TEENAGERS   GPITVL
GROUP DISCUSSION WITH SCHOOL
DROP-OUTS   GPITVL
JEFF   GPITVL
JUVENILE DELINQUENCY   GPITVL
MARY   GPITVL
NONI   GPITVL
ROB   GPITVL

(AUDIO TAPES)

ACUTE SCHIZOPHRENIA, PT 1   SIGINF
ACUTE SCHIZOPHRENIA, PT 2   SIGINF
ASSESSMENT OF SUICIDAL RISK   SIGINF
DEPRESSION - CLINICAL PICTURES AND
TREATMENT   SIGINF
DEPRESSION - DIFFERENTIAL
  DIAGNOSIS AND RECENT
  BIOCHEMISTRY   SIGINF
FAMILY SURVIVORS OF SUICIDE   SIGINF
GENERAL SYSTEMS - DIAGNOSTIC
CONCEPTS   SIGINF
HOW TO ESTABLISH A SUICIDE
PREVENTION PROGRAM   SIGINF
INNOVATIVE SERVICES FOR YOUTH   SIGINF
MANAGEMENT OF THE SUICIDAL
PERSON   SIGINF
SUICIDE - AN OVERVIEW   SIGINF
SUICIDE AND SUICIDE PREVENTION--A
SERIES   SIGINF
SUICIDE AND THE TERMINALLY ILL   SIGINF
SUICIDE IN PRISON   SIGINF
SUICIDE, SUICIDE ATTEMPTS AND SELF-
MUTILATION   SIGINF
THERAPEUTIC COMMUNITY, THE   SIGINF
TOPICS IN CLINICAL PSYCHIATRY--A
SERIES   SIGINF
VIOLENCE IN CLINICAL STATES -
SYNDROMES   SIGINF
VIOLENCE IN CLINICAL STATES -
TREATMENT   SIGINF

CLINICAL - GERIATRICS

(AUDIO TAPES)

GERIATRIC PSYCHIATRY   SIGINF

CLINICAL - MENTAL HEALTH AND REHABILITATION

(FILMSTRIPS)

GOD'S CHILDREN   UWLA

PSYCHOLOGY

(MOTION PICTURES)

FRAGILE EGOS (H-C A)   WGBH

(AUDIO TAPES)

ACUTE SCHIZOPHRENIA, PT 1   SIGINF
ACUTE SCHIZOPHRENIA, PT 2   SIGINF
ASSESSMENT OF CHANGE IN
  CHILDREN'S BEHAVIOR   SIGINF
ASSESSMENT OF SUICIDAL RISK   SIGINF
CLINICAL ASPECTS OF THE
  PSYCHIATRIC MANAGEMENT OF
  BURNED AND DISFIGURED CHILDREN   SIGINF
CLINICAL PSYCHOPATHOLOGY--A SERIES   SIGINF
CURRENT ISSUES AND PROBLEMS
  IN SUICIDE PREVENTION
DEPRESSION - CLINICAL PICTURES AND
  TREATMENT   SIGINF
DEPRESSION - DIFFERENTIAL
  DIAGNOSIS AND RECENT
  BIOCHEMISTRY   SIGINF
DEPRESSION AND SUICIDE   SIGINF
DIAGNOSIS AND TREATMENT OF
  PSEUDONEUROTIC
  SCHIZOPHRENIA, THE   SIGINF
FAMILY SURVIVORS OF SUICIDE   SIGINF
GENERAL SYSTEMS - DIAGNOSTIC
  CONCEPTS   SIGINF
HOW TO ESTABLISH A SUICIDE
  PREVENTION PROGRAM   SIGINF
INPATIENT MANAGEMENT OF
  BORDERLINE PATIENTS, THE   SIGINF
MANAGEMENT OF THE SUICIDAL
  PERSON   SIGINF
OBSESSIONS AND PHOBIAS   SIGINF
PSYCHOLOGICAL FUNCTIONS OF THE
  COUNTER CULTURE   SIGINF
RE-GRIEF WORK FOR THE
  PATHOLOGICAL MOURNER   SIGINF
RECENT CONTRIBUTIONS TOWARD
  A THEORY OF PAIN BEHAVIOR   SIGINF
REGRESSION AND SEMANTIC
  SPEECH IN HYSTERIA AND
  SCHIZOPHRENIA   SIGINF
SEVERELY NEUROTIC AND THE
  PSYCHOTIC ADOLESCENT, THE   SIGINF
SUICIDE - AN OVERVIEW   SIGINF
SUICIDE AND SUICIDE PREVENTION--A
  SERIES   SIGINF
SUICIDE AND THE TERMINALLY ILL   SIGINF
SUICIDE AND VIOLENCE   SIGINF
SUICIDE IN PRISON   SIGINF
SUICIDE, SUICIDE ATTEMPTS AND SELF-
  MUTILATION   SIGINF
THERAPEUTIC COMMUNITY, THE   SIGINF
TOPICS IN CLINICAL PSYCHIATRY--A
  SERIES   SIGINF
USE OF SOMATIC TREATMENTS IN
  SCHIZOPHRENIA   SIGINF
VIOLENCE IN CLINICAL STATES -
  SYNDROMES   SIGINF
VIOLENCE IN CLINICAL STATES -
  TREATMENT   SIGINF

CLINICAL - MENTAL RETARDATION

(MOTION PICTURES)

NOBODY TOOK THE TIME (T)   AIMS

CLINICAL - MENTAL SYMPTOMS

(AUDIO TAPES)

ACCELERATION TECHNIQUES   SIGINF
ANGER INHIBITION PROBLEMS, PT 1   SIGINF
ANGER INHIBITION PROBLEMS, PT 2   SIGINF
ASSESSING FOR BEHAVIOR CHANGE   SIGINF
BASIC STRATEGIES FOR MODIFYING
  CHILDREN'S BEHAVIOR   SIGINF
BEHAVIOR MODIFICATION
  STRATEGIES FOR CHILD
  PSYCHOTHERAPISTS--A SERIES   SIGINF
CHILD PEERS AS THERAPEUTIC AGENTS   SIGINF
CLINICAL ASPECTS OF MINIMAL BRAIN
  DYSFUNCTION   SIGINF
CONTINGENCY MANAGEMENT   SIGINF
CURRENT ISSUES AND PROBLEMS
  IN SUICIDE PREVENTION   SIGINF
DECELERATION TECHNIQUES   SIGINF
DEPRESSION - REACTION OR DISEASE   SIGINF
DEPRESSION AND SUICIDE   SIGINF
DIAGNOSIS AND TREATMENT OF
  PSEUDONEUROTIC
  SCHIZOPHRENIA, THE   SIGINF
EXAMPLES AND DISCUSSION OF
  SUICIDE CALLS, PT 1   SIGINF
EXAMPLES AND DISCUSSION OF
  SUICIDE CALLS, PT 2   SIGINF
EXTRAVERSION AND NEUROTICISM
  - ORIGINS OF PERSONALITY
  TRAITS AND SOCIAL ATTITUDES   SIGINF
FACT OR FANTASY--A SERIES   BASCH
GENERAL SYSTEMS - DIAGNOSTIC
  CONCEPTS   SIGINF

GOALS FOR BEHAVIOR THERAPY WITH
  CHILDREN, THE   SIGINF
INPATIENT MANAGEMENT OF
  BORDERLINE PATIENTS, THE   SIGINF
MISCELLANEOUS TECHNIQUES   SIGINF
OBSERVATIONAL LEARNING   SIGINF
OBSESSIONS AND PHOBIAS   SIGINF
PARENTS AS THERAPEUTIC AGENTS   SIGINF
PSYCHOLOGICAL FUNCTIONS OF THE
  COUNTER CULTURE   SIGINF
RE-GRIEF WORK FOR THE
  PATHOLOGICAL MOURNER   SIGINF
RECENT CONTRIBUTIONS TOWARD
  A THEORY OF PAIN BEHAVIOR   SIGINF
REGRESSION AND SEMANTIC
  SPEECH IN HYSTERIA AND
  SCHIZOPHRENIA   SIGINF
SELF-ADMINISTERED BEHAVIOR
  THERAPY FOR CHILDREN   SIGINF
SEVERELY NEUROTIC AND THE
  PSYCHOTIC ADOLESCENT, THE   SIGINF
SUICIDE AND VIOLENCE   SIGINF
TEACHERS AS THERAPEUTIC AGENTS   SIGINF
THERAPEUTIC COMMUNITY, THE   SIGINF
THERAPY OF COMMON CHILDHOOD
  DISORDERS--A SERIES   SIGINF
TOPICS IN CLINICAL PSYCHIATRY--A
  SERIES   SIGINF

CLINICAL - NEUROLOGICAL DISORDER

(FILMSTRIPS)

INTRODUCTION TO THE
  NEUROSCIENCES, AN   SAUNDW

(AUDIO TAPES)

CEREBRAL DYSFUNCTION   SIGINF
CEREBRAL DYSFUNCTION - SEIZURE
  DISORDERS   SIGINF
CEREBRAL DYSFUNCTION - 14 AND
  SIX CYCLES POSITIVE EEG
  SPIKING   SIGINF
CLINICAL ASPECTS OF MINIMAL BRAIN
  DYSFUNCTION   SIGINF

**CLINICAL - NEUROSIS AND EMOTIONAL
DISTURBANCE**

(AUDIO TAPES)

ACCELERATION TECHNIQUES   SIGINF
ACUTE SCHIZOPHRENIA, PT 1   SIGINF
ACUTE SCHIZOPHRENIA, PT 2   SIGINF
ANGER INHIBITION PROBLEMS, PT 1   SIGINF
ANGER INHIBITION PROBLEMS, PT 2   SIGINF
ASSESSING FOR BEHAVIOR CHANGE   SIGINF
BASIC STRATEGIES FOR MODIFYING
  CHILDREN'S BEHAVIOR   SIGINF
BEHAVIOR MODIFICATION
  STRATEGIES FOR CHILD
  PSYCHOTHERAPISTS--A SERIES   SIGINF
CHILD PEERS AS THERAPEUTIC AGENTS   SIGINF
CLINICAL PSYCHOPATHOLOGY--A SERIES   SIGINF
CONTINGENCY MANAGEMENT   SIGINF
DECELERATION TECHNIQUES   SIGINF
DEPRESSION - REACTION OR DISEASE   SIGINF
DEPRESSION AND SUICIDE   SIGINF
DEVELOPMENT OF AGGRESSION
  AND AGGRESSION ANXIETY   SIGINF
DIAGNOSIS AND TREATMENT OF
  PSEUDONEUROTIC
  SCHIZOPHRENIA, THE   SIGINF
EXAMPLES AND DISCUSSION OF
  SUICIDE CALLS, PT 1   SIGINF
EXAMPLES AND DISCUSSION OF
  SUICIDE CALLS, PT 2   SIGINF
EXTRAVERSION AND NEUROTICISM
  - ORIGINS OF PERSONALITY
  TRAITS AND SOCIAL ATTITUDES   SIGINF
GENERAL SYSTEMS - DIAGNOSTIC
  CONCEPTS   SIGINF
GOALS FOR BEHAVIOR THERAPY WITH
  CHILDREN, THE   SIGINF
INPATIENT MANAGEMENT OF
  BORDERLINE PATIENTS, THE   SIGINF
MISCELLANEOUS TECHNIQUES   SIGINF
NEUROSIS, CHARACTER AND BIOLOGY   SIGINF
OBSERVATIONAL LEARNING   SIGINF
OBSESSIONS AND PHOBIAS   SIGINF
PSYCHOLOGICAL FUNCTIONS OF THE
  COUNTER CULTURE   SIGINF
RE-GRIEF WORK FOR THE
  PATHOLOGICAL MOURNER   SIGINF
RECENT CONTRIBUTIONS TOWARD
  A THEORY OF PAIN BEHAVIOR   SIGINF
REGRESSION AND SEMANTIC
  SPEECH IN HYSTERIA AND
  SCHIZOPHRENIA   SIGINF
SCHIZOPHRENIA - THE CONCEPT
  OF NEUROSIS AND PSYCHOSIS
  SPECIFIC NEUROSES   SIGINF
SELF-ADMINISTERED BEHAVIOR
  THERAPY FOR CHILDREN   SIGINF
SEVERELY NEUROTIC AND THE
  PSYCHOTIC ADOLESCENT, THE   SIGINF

SPECIFIC NEUROSES - SPECIFIC
  PSYCHOSES - THE CONCEPT OF
  DEPRESSION   SIGINF
SUICIDE AND VIOLENCE   SIGINF
TEACHERS AS THERAPEUTIC AGENTS   SIGINF
THERAPY OF COMMON CHILDHOOD
  DISORDERS--A SERIES   SIGINF
TOPICS IN CLINICAL PSYCHIATRY--A
  SERIES   SIGINF

CLINICAL - PHYSICAL HANDICAP

(MOTION PICTURES)

MIMI (J-C A)   BBF

CLINICAL - PHYSICAL ILLNESS

(MOTION PICTURES)

THEORIST ROOM   AMERFI

(AUDIO TAPES)

CLINICAL ASPECTS OF THE
  PSYCHIATRIC MANAGEMENT OF
  BURNED AND DISFIGURED CHILDREN   SIGINF

CLINICAL - PSYCHOANALYTIC INTERPRETATION

(AUDIO TAPES)

ACCELERATION TECHNIQUES   SIGINF
ASSESSING FOR BEHAVIOR CHANGE   SIGINF
BASIC STRATEGIES FOR MODIFYING
  CHILDREN'S BEHAVIOR   SIGINF
BEHAVIOR MODIFICATION
  STRATEGIES FOR CHILD
  PSYCHOTHERAPISTS--A SERIES   SIGINF
BEHAVIORISM AND
  PSYCHOANALYSIS - COGNITIVE
  STYLES, CONTENTS AND ORIGINS   SIGINF
CHILD PEERS AS THERAPEUTIC AGENTS   SIGINF
CONTINGENCY MANAGEMENT   SIGINF
DECELERATION TECHNIQUES   SIGINF
EMERGENCY PSYCHIATRIC TREATMENT   SIGINF
GOALS FOR BEHAVIOR THERAPY WITH
  CHILDREN, THE   SIGINF
MISCELLANEOUS TECHNIQUES   SIGINF
OBSERVATIONAL LEARNING   SIGINF
PARENTS AS THERAPEUTIC AGENTS   SIGINF
SELF-ADMINISTERED BEHAVIOR
  THERAPY FOR CHILDREN   SIGINF
SLEEP AND PSYCHOPATHOLOGY   SIGINF
STRATEGIES OF CHILD PSYCHOTHERAPY   SIGINF
TEACHERS AS THERAPEUTIC AGENTS   SIGINF
TERMINATION OF THE TREATMENT OF
  ADOLESCENTS   SIGINF

CLINICAL - PSYCHOSIS

(AUDIO TAPES)

STRATEGIES OF CHILD PSYCHOTHERAPY   SIGINF

CLINICAL - PSYCHOSOMATIC DISORDER

(AUDIO TAPES)

MENTAL AND PHYSICAL, THE   SIGINF
PSYCHOTHERAPEUTIC INTERACTION,
  THE   SIGINF
SUICIDE - HOMICIDE - THE
  CONCEPT OF
  PSYCHOPHYSIOLOGIC DISORDERS   SIGINF
USE OF SOMATIC TREATMENTS IN
  SCHIZOPHRENIA   SIGINF

CLINICAL - PSYCHOTHERAPY AND ANALYSIS

(MOTION PICTURES)

INTRODUCTION TO PSYCHOTHERAPY,
  AN (PRO)   VIDEOG

(AUDIO TAPES)

ACCELERATION TECHNIQUES   SIGINF
ADOLESCENT PATIENT AND THE
  FAMILY, THE   SIGINF
ASSESSING FOR BEHAVIOR CHANGE   SIGINF
BASIC STRATEGIES FOR MODIFYING
  CHILDREN'S BEHAVIOR   SIGINF
BEHAVIOR DISORDERS OF CHILDREN--A
  SERIES   SIGINF
BEHAVIOR MODIFICATION
  STRATEGIES FOR CHILD
  PSYCHOTHERAPISTS--A SERIES   SIGINF
BEHAVIORISM AND
  PSYCHOANALYSIS - COGNITIVE
  STYLES, CONTENTS AND ORIGINS   SIGINF
BORDERLINE PATIENT, THE   SIGINF
CONTINGENCY MANAGEMENT   SIGINF

DECELERATION TECHNIQUES | SIGINF
DIAGNOSTIC PROCESS AND THE
  PLANNING OF TREATMENT, THE | SIGINF
EMERGENCY PSYCHIATRIC TREATMENT | SIGINF
FAMILY THERAPY - GROUP
  THERAPY - COMMUNITY
  PSYCHIATRY | SIGINF
GOALS FOR BEHAVIOR THERAPY WITH
CHILDREN, THE | SIGINF
INITIAL EVALUATION, THE | SIGINF
LEARNING DISABILITIES -
  PSYCHOTHERAPY AND
  ADOLESCENT SUBCULTURES | SIGINF
LIMITATIONS OF PSYCHOTHERAPY, THE | SIGINF
MANAGEMENT OF THE DEPENDENT
ADOLESCENT | SIGINF
MENTAL AND PHYSICAL, THE | SIGINF
MISCELLANEOUS TECHNIQUES | SIGINF
NEUROSIS, CHARACTER AND BIOLOGY | SIGINF
OBSERVATIONAL LEARNING | SIGINF
OBSESSING AND LEARNING | SIGINF
PATIENTS WHO BEHAVE BADLY | SIGINF
PHOBIC AND ANXIETY STATES | SIGINF
PREPARATION FOR CERTIFICATION
  BY THE AMERICAN BOARD OF
  PSYCHIATRY AND NEUROLOGY--A
  SERIES | SIGINF
PSYCHIATRIC DISORDERS OF
  CHILDHOOD - CHILD
  PSYCHOTHERAPY - MARITAL
  MALADJUSTMENT AND... | SIGINF
PSYCHOTHERAPEUTIC INTERACTION,
THE | SIGINF
PSYCHOTHERAPIST, THE | SIGINF
PSYCHOTHERAPY OF ADOLESCENTS--A
SERIES | SIGINF
REGRESSION AND ITS PREVENTION | SIGINF
SAMPLE EXAMINATIONS - THE
  CONCEPT OF SCHIZOPHRENIA | SIGINF
SCHIZOPHRENIA - THE CONCEPT
  OF NEUROSIS AND PSYCHOSIS -
  SPECIFIC NEUROSES | SIGINF
SCHIZOPHRENIC PATIENT, THE | SIGINF
SLEEP AND PSYCHOPATHOLOGY | SIGINF
SPECIAL CLINICAL PROBLEMS IN
  INTENSIVE PSYCHOTHERAPY--A
  SERIES | SIGINF
SPECIFIC NEUROSES - SPECIFIC
  PSYCHOSES - THE CONCEPT OF
  DEPRESSION | SIGINF
STRATEGIES OF CHILD PSYCHOTHERAPY | SIGINF
SUICIDE - HOMICIDE - THE
  CONCEPT OF
  PSYCHOPHYSIOLOGIC DISORDERS | SIGINF
SUICIDE AND DEPRESSION | SIGINF
TERMINATION OF THE TREATMENT OF
ADOLESCENTS | SIGINF
THERAPEUTIC ALLIANCE AND THE
  EARLY STAGES OF TREATMENT,
  THE | SIGINF
TRANSFERENCE AND
COUNTERTRANSFERENCE | SIGINF
TRANSFERENCE MANIFESTATIONS
  AND THEIR MANAGEMENT | SIGINF

CLINICAL - SPEECH DISORDER

(AUDIO TAPES)

ADOLESCENT WITH A COMMUNICATION
DISORDER, THE | SIGINF

DEVELOPMENTAL, ADOLESCENCE

(MOTION PICTURES)

A TO B | AMERFI
ADOLESCENCE AND SEXUAL IDENTITY
(H-C A) | CHM
BEACH PARTY, THE | PAULST
BROWN RICE | AMERFI
PORCH GLIDER | AMERFI

(VIDEOTAPES)

CASE STUDIES | GPITVL
COUNSELING THE ADOLESCENT--A
SERIES | GPITVL
DEMOCRATIC EVOLUTION OF SOCIETY,
THE, PT 1 | GPITVL
DEMOCRATIC EVOLUTION OF SOCIETY,
THE, PT 2 | GPITVL
GROUP DISCUSSION WITH NORMAL
TEENAGERS | GPITVL
GROUP DISCUSSION WITH SCHOOL
DROP-OUTS | GPITVL
GROUP DISCUSSION WITH TEENAGERS | GPITVL
JEFF | GPITVL
JUVENILE DELINQUENCY | GPITVL
MARY | GPITVL
NONI | GPITVL
ROB | GPITVL

(AUDIO TAPES)

ADOLESCENCE | BASCH
ADOLESCENT AND HIS PARENTS, THE | SIGINF

ADOLESCENT PATIENT AND THE
  FAMILY, THE | SIGINF
ADOLESCENT WITH A COMMUNICATION
DISORDER, THE | SIGINF
ADOLESCENTS AND ADULTS | SIGINF
DELINQUENT AND PROMISCUOUS
HOMOSEXUAL BEHAVIOR | SIGINF
DEVELOPMENTAL CRISES IN BLACK
ADOLESCENTS | SIGINF
DIAGNOSTIC PROCESS AND THE
  PLANNING OF TREATMENT, THE | SIGINF
HOSPITAL MANAGEMENT OF
  DISTURBED ADOLESCENTS, THE,
  PT 1 | SIGINF
HOSPITAL MANAGEMENT OF
  DISTURBED ADOLESCENTS, THE,
  PT 2 | SIGINF
INITIAL EVALUATION, THE | SIGINF
INNOVATIVE SERVICES FOR YOUTH | SIGINF
LEARNING DISABILITIES -
  PSYCHOTHERAPY AND
  ADOLESCENT SUBCULTURES | SIGINF
MANAGEMENT OF DRUG ABUSE IN
  THE OUTPATIENT
  PSYCHOTHERAPY OF ADOLESCENTS,
  THE | SIGINF
MANAGEMENT OF THE DEPENDENT
ADOLESCENT | SIGINF
NORMAL AND ABNORMAL
  BEHAVIOR OF ADOLESCENCE-- A
  SERIES | SIGINF
PATTERNS OF DRUG ABUSE
  AMONG MIDDLE-CLASS
  ADOLESCENTS | SIGINF
PSYCHOLOGICAL DEVELOPMENT DURING
ADOLESCENCE | SIGINF
PSYCHOTHERAPY OF ADOLESCENTS--A
SERIES | SIGINF
REGRESSION AND ITS PREVENTION | SIGINF
SEVERELY NEUROTIC AND THE
  PSYCHOTIC ADOLESCENT, THE | SIGINF
TERMINATION OF THE TREATMENT OF
ADOLESCENTS | SIGINF
THERAPEUTIC ALLIANCE AND THE
  EARLY STAGES OF TREATMENT,
  THE | SIGINF
TRANSFERENCE AND
COUNTERTRANSFERENCE | SIGINF
TRANSFERENCE MANIFESTATIONS
  AND THEIR MANAGEMENT | SIGINF

(TRANSPARENCIES)

DATING RELATIONS - DATING
  CATEGORIES--A SERIES (J) | LEART
DATING RELATIONS - DIMENSIONS
  OF DATING--A SERIES (J) | LEART
DATING RELATIONS - EVALUATING
  DATING BEHAVIOR --A SERIES (J) | LEART
DATING RELATIONS - MIXED DATING--A
SERIES (J) | LEART
DATING RELATIONS - THE FIRST DATE-
-A SERIES (J) | LEART
SEX EDUCATION - DEVELOPMENT
  OF CONCEPTS AND ATTITUDES--A
  SERIES | LEART

**DEVELOPMENTAL, CHILDHOOD (CHILD GROWTH
AND DEVELOPMENT)**

(FILMSTRIPS)

CHILDREN | EGH
DRUGS AND CHILDREN, PT 1 (I) | EDLACT
DRUGS AND CHILDREN, PT 2 (I) | EDLACT

(MOTION PICTURES)

ADOLESCENCE AND SEXUAL IDENTITY
(H-C A) | CHM
CHILDREN OF THE KIBBUTZ (I-C A) | ACI
CHILDREN'S CONCEPTS (C T) | TIMLIF
COGNITIVE DEVELOPMENT (C A) | CRMP
DAY CARE TODAY (C A) | POLYMR
DEVELOPMENTAL PSYCHOLOGY FILM--A
SERIES (C A) | CRMP
GRANDMOTHER, THE | AMERFI
INFANCY (C A) | CRMP
LANGUAGE DEVELOPMENT (C A) | CRMP
WHAT FIXED ME | AMERFI

(VIDEOTAPES)

HOME SWEET HOME | NITC
I DARE YOU | NITC

(AUDIO TAPES)

ACCELERATION TECHNIQUES | SIGINF
ANGER INHIBITION PROBLEMS, PT 1 | SIGINF
ANGER INHIBITION PROBLEMS, PT 2 | SIGINF
ASSESSING FOR BEHAVIOR CHANGE | SIGINF
ASSESSMENT OF CHANGE IN
CHILDREN'S BEHAVIOR | SIGINF
BASIC STRATEGIES FOR MODIFYING
  CHILDREN'S BEHAVIOR | SIGINF
BEHAVIOR DISORDERS OF CHILDHOOD | SIGINF

BEHAVIOR DISORDERS OF CHILDREN--A
SERIES | SIGINF
BEHAVIOR MODIFICATION
  STRATEGIES FOR CHILD
  PSYCHOTHERAPISTS--A SERIES | SIGINF
CHILD PEERS AS THERAPEUTIC AGENTS | SIGINF
CONTINGENCY MANAGEMENT | SIGINF
DECELERATION TECHNIQUES | SIGINF
DEVELOPMENT OF AGGRESSION
  AND AGGRESSION ANXIETY | SIGINF
EGOCENTRISM IN CHILDREN AND
ADOLESCENTS | SIGINF
FAMILY TREATMENT OF SCHOOL
PHOBIAS | SIGINF
GOALS FOR BEHAVIOR THERAPY WITH
CHILDREN, THE | SIGINF
MISCELLANEOUS TECHNIQUES | SIGINF
OBSERVATIONAL LEARNING | SIGINF
PARENTS AS THERAPEUTIC AGENTS | SIGINF
PRESCHOOL ENRICHMENT AND
LEARNING | SIGINF
PROBLEMS RESULTING FROM THE
  DEPRIVATION OF PARENTAL
  AFFECTION, PT 1 | SIGINF
PROBLEMS RESULTING FROM THE
  DEPRIVATION OF PARENTAL
  AFFECTION, PT 2 | SIGINF
PSYCHIATRIC DISORDERS OF
  CHILDHOOD - CHILD
  PSYCHOTHERAPY - MARITAL
  MALADJUSTMENT AND... | SIGINF
PSYCHOGENIC LEARNING DISORDERS,
PT 1 | SIGINF
PSYCHOGENIC LEARNING DISORDERS,
PT 2 | SIGINF
PSYCHOGENIC LEARNING DISORDERS,
PT 3 | SIGINF
PSYCHOLOGICAL REACTIONS TO
DIVORCE, PT 1 | SIGINF
PSYCHOLOGICAL REACTIONS TO
DIVORCE, PT 2 | SIGINF
PSYCHOLOGICAL REACTIONS TO
DIVORCE, PT 3 | SIGINF
SELF-ADMINISTERED BEHAVIOR
  THERAPY FOR CHILDREN | SIGINF
SELF-ESTEEM PROBLEMS, PT 1 | SIGINF
SELF-ESTEEM PROBLEMS, PT 2 | SIGINF
SISSIES AND TOMBOYS - CROSS
  GENDER BEHAVIOR IN CHILDREN | SIGINF
TEACHERS AS THERAPEUTIC AGENTS | SIGINF
THERAPY OF COMMON CHILDHOOD
  DISORDERS--A SERIES | SIGINF

DEVELOPMENTAL, CHILDHOOD - ABILITIES

(MOTION PICTURES)

I WANNA BE READY (C A) | AIMS
INFANCY (C A) | CRMP

DEVELOPMENTAL, CHILDHOOD - LEARNING

(FILMSTRIPS)

LEWIS-LIES-A-LOT | EGH
TRY, TRY AGAIN | EGH

(MOTION PICTURES)

COPING IN SPECIAL EDUCATION -
  MOTIVATION (C) | UEUWIS
EMOTIONAL DEVELOPMENT (C A) | CRMP
LEFT, RIGHT MOVIE, THE (K-P S) | GRADYM
MORAL DEVELOPMENT (C A) | CRMP
PIAGET'S DEVELOPMENTAL THEORY
  - THE GROWTH OF INTELLIGENCE
  IN THE PRESCHOOL YEARS (A) | DAVFMS
WHERE'S THE TROUBLE (K-P) | GRADYM

(VIDEOTAPES)

LEARNING PROBLEM, A | GPITVL
MOTIVATING CHILDREN TO LEARN--A
SERIES | GPITVL

DEVELOPMENTAL, CHILDHOOD - PERCEPTION

(MOTION PICTURES)

CHANGES, CHANGES (K-P) | WWS
COGNITIVE DEVELOPMENT (C A) | CRMP
DEVELOPMENTAL PSYCHOLOGY FILM--A
SERIES (C A) | CRMP
FACES (K-P) | SCHLAT
LEFT, RIGHT MOVIE, THE (K-P S) | GRADYM
PIAGET'S DEVELOPMENTAL THEORY
  - THE GROWTH OF INTELLIGENCE
  IN THE PRESCHOOL YEARS (A) | DAVFMS
WAY FOR DIANA, A (I-J) | AIMS
WHERE'S THE TROUBLE (K-P) | GRADYM

(VIDEOTAPES)

CLARIFICATION OF BASIC PRINCIPLES | GPITVL
CONSEQUENCES | GPITVL
DOUGLAS | GPITVL

ENCOURAGEMENT   GPITVL
HOW BIG IS YOUR WORLD (I)   GPITVL
LOGICAL CONSEQUENCES AND
   PUNISHMENT   GPITVL

(AUDIO TAPES)

COGNITIVE PERFORMANCE · PROGRESS
VS PRODUCT   SIGINF

EDUCATIONAL · GENERAL

(MOTION PICTURES)

CHILDREN AS PEOPLE (H-C A)   POLYMR

EDUCATIONAL · ATTITUDE AND ADJUSTMENT

(MOTION PICTURES)

NEW ESTATE (C T)   TIMLIF
P A T C H · POSITIVE APPROACH
   TO CHANGING HUMANS (C A)   CORF

(VIDEOTAPES)

CLARIFICATION OF BASIC PRINCIPLES   GPITVL
CONSEQUENCES   GPITVL
EDWARD   GPITVL
ENCOURAGEMENT   GPITVL
LOGICAL CONSEQUENCES AND
   PUNISHMENT   GPITVL
MOTIVATING CHILDREN TO LEARN ·
   SUMMARY   GPITVL

(AUDIO TAPES)

BEHAVIOR DISORDERS OF CHILDHOOD   SIGINF
CLINICAL ASPECTS OF THE
   PSYCHIATRIC MANAGEMENT OF
   BURNED AND DISFIGURED CHILDREN   SIGINF
DEVELOPMENT OF AGGRESSION
   AND AGGRESSION ANXIETY   SIGINF
DEVELOPMENTAL CRISES IN BLACK
   ADOLESCENTS   SIGINF
EGOCENTRISM IN CHILDREN AND
   ADOLESCENTS   SIGINF
EXISTENCE THEORY OF
   PERSONALITY · EMPIRICAL
   STUDIES OF THE SELF CONCEPT   SIGINF
FAMILY TREATMENT OF SCHOOL
   PHOBIAS   SIGINF
INSECURITY   BASCH
KNOWLEDGE OF VALUES ·
   AUTHORITARIAN PERSONALITY   SIGINF
ON BEING WIDOWED   BASCH
PATTERNS OF DRUG ABUSE
   AMONG MIDDLE-CLASS
   ADOLESCENTS   SIGINF
PSYCHOGENIC LEARNING DISORDERS,
   PT 1   SIGINF
PSYCHOGENIC LEARNING DISORDERS,
   PT 2   SIGINF
PSYCHOGENIC LEARNING DISORDERS,
   PT 3   SIGINF
PSYCHOLOGICAL DEVELOPMENT DURING
   ADOLESCENCE   SIGINF
PSYCHOLOGICAL REACTIONS TO
   DIVORCE, PT 1   SIGINF
PSYCHOLOGICAL REACTIONS TO
   DIVORCE, PT 2   SIGINF
PSYCHOLOGICAL REACTIONS TO
   DIVORCE, PT 3   SIGINF
PSYCHOTHERAPY OF ADOLESCENTS··A
   SERIES   SIGINF
SELF-ESTEEM PROBLEMS, PT 1   SIGINF
SELF-ESTEEM PROBLEMS, PT 2   SIGINF
SISSIES AND TOMBOYS · CROSS
   GENDER BEHAVIOR IN CHILDREN   SIGINF
THERAPY OF COMMON CHILDHOOD
   DISORDERS··A SERIES   SIGINF

(TRANSPARENCIES)

EMOTIONS AND SOCIAL ATTITUDES
   · ATTITUDES, VALUES··A SERIES
   (H)   LEART

**EDUCATIONAL · ATTITUDE AND ADJUSTMENT ·
HIGH SCHOOL AND COLLEGE**

(MOTION PICTURES)

ADOLESCENCE AND SEXUAL IDENTITY
   (H-C A)   CHM
COLLEGE DAZE   AMERFI

(VIDEOTAPES)

GROUP DISCUSSION WITH TEENAGERS   GPITVL
JEFF   GPITVL
ROB   GPITVL

**EDUCATIONAL · ATTITUDE AND ADJUSTMENT ·
NURSERY AND ELEMENTARY**

(MOTION PICTURES)

CHILDREN AS PEOPLE (H-C A)   POLYMR
CHILDREN'S CONCEPTS (C T)   TIMLIF
COGNITIVE DEVELOPMENT (C A)   CRMP
DAY CARE TODAY (C A)   POLYMR
ENTERPRISING INFANTS (C T)   TIMLIF

(VIDEOTAPES)

CHANGING THE CHILD'S RELATIONSHIPS
AND GOALS   GPITVL
DOUGLAS   GPITVL
MOTIVATING CHILDREN TO LEARN--A
SERIES   GPITVL

(AUDIO TAPES)

PREVENTIVE MENTAL HEALTH
   WORK WITH PRESCHOOL
   TEACHERS   SIGINF

**EDUCATIONAL · EDUCATIONAL AND CAREER
GUIDANCE**

(FILMSTRIPS)

WORKING IN THE POLITICAL WORLD   EGH

**EDUCATIONAL · SCHOOL LEARNING AND
ACHIEVEMENT**

(FILMSTRIPS)

ORDER · FIRST ALWAYS COMES BEFORE
LAST   EGH

(MOTION PICTURES)

CHILDREN'S CONCEPTS (C T)   TIMLIF
COPING IN SPECIAL EDUCATION ·
   INDIVIDUALIZED INSTRUCTION
   (C)   UEUWIS
ENTERPRISING INFANTS (C T)   TIMLIF
INFANCY (C A)   CRMP
NEW ESTATE (C T)   TIMLIF
SCHOOL IS FOR CHILDREN (T)   AIMS

(VIDEOTAPES)

DOUGLAS   GPITVL
GROUP DISCUSSION, PT 1   GPITVL
GROUP DISCUSSION, PT 2   GPITVL
GROUP DISCUSSION, PT 3   GPITVL
LEARNING PROBLEM, A   GPITVL
MOTIVATING CHILDREN TO LEARN ·
   SUMMARY   GPITVL
MOTIVATING CHILDREN TO LEARN--A
   SERIES   GPITVL
READING DIFFICULTIES   GPITVL

(AUDIO TAPES)

LEARNING DISABILITIES ·
   PSYCHOTHERAPY AND
   ADOLESCENT SUBCULTURES   SIGINF
PSYCHOGENIC LEARNING DISORDERS,
   PT 1   SIGINF
PSYCHOGENIC LEARNING DISORDERS,
   PT 2   SIGINF
PSYCHOGENIC LEARNING DISORDERS,
   PT 3   SIGINF

(TRANSPARENCIES)

HOW TO STUDY··A SERIES   BETECL

EDUCATIONAL · SPECIAL EDUCATION

(MOTION PICTURES)

COPING IN SPECIAL EDUCATION ·
   DEVELOPING OBSERVATIONAL
   TECHNIQUES (C)   UEUWIS
COPING IN SPECIAL EDUCATION ·
   DEVELOPING STUDY HABITS (C)   UEUWIS
COPING IN SPECIAL EDUCATION ·
   DISRUPTIVE BEHAVIOR (C)   UEUWIS
COPING IN SPECIAL EDUCATION ·
   GROUPING (C)   UEUWIS
COPING IN SPECIAL EDUCATION ·
   INDIVIDUALIZED INSTRUCTION
   (C)   UEUWIS
COPING IN SPECIAL EDUCATION ·
   MOTIVATION (C)   UEUWIS
COPING IN SPECIAL EDUCATION ·
   SOCIALIZATION (C)   UEUWIS
COPING IN SPECIAL EDUCATION--A
   SERIES (C)   UEUWIS
NOBODY TOOK THE TIME (T)   AIMS
READING IS FOR US TOO (C A)   CCMFI
SCHOOL IS FOR CHILDREN (T)   AIMS

(VIDEOTAPES)

LEARNING PROBLEM, A   GPITVL

(AUDIO TAPES)

WHAT MUSIC MEANS TO THE BLIND (J
A)   AFB

**EDUCATIONAL · SPECIAL EDUCATION · REMEDIAL
EDUCATION**

(MOTION PICTURES)

KIDS ARE PEOPLE, TOO (T)   CCMFI
NOBODY TOOK THE TIME (T)   AIMS
READING IS FOR US TOO (C A)   CCMFI
SCHOOL IS FOR CHILDREN (T)   AIMS

(VIDEOTAPES)

READING DIFFICULTIES   GPITVL

EDUCATIONAL · TEACHING METHOD

(FILMSTRIPS)

DECIDING ON DEFENSIBLE GOALS
   VIA EDUCATIONAL NEEDS
   ASSESSMENT   VIMCET

(MOTION PICTURES)

COPING IN SPECIAL EDUCATION ·
   DEVELOPING OBSERVATIONAL
   TECHNIQUES (C)   UEUWIS
COPING IN SPECIAL EDUCATION ·
   DEVELOPING STUDY HABITS (C)   UEUWIS
COPING IN SPECIAL EDUCATION ·
   DISRUPTIVE BEHAVIOR (C)   UEUWIS
COPING IN SPECIAL EDUCATION ·
   GROUPING (C)   UEUWIS
COPING IN SPECIAL EDUCATION ·
   INDIVIDUALIZED INSTRUCTION
   (C)   UEUWIS
COPING IN SPECIAL EDUCATION ·
   MOTIVATION (C)   UEUWIS
COPING IN SPECIAL EDUCATION ·
   SOCIALIZATION (C)   UEUWIS
COPING IN SPECIAL EDUCATION--A
   SERIES (C)   UEUWIS

(VIDEOTAPES)

GROUP DISCUSSION, PT 1   GPITVL
GROUP DISCUSSION, PT 2   GPITVL
GROUP DISCUSSION, PT 3   GPITVL
MOTIVATING CHILDREN TO LEARN--A
   SERIES   GPITVL

**EXPERIMENTAL · DECISION AND CHOICE
BEHAVIOR**

(FILMSTRIPS)

MILES MUGWUMP AND FRANNIE
FRANTIC   EGH

(MOTION PICTURES)

ADVENTURES IN PERCEPTION (J-C A)   BFA

(AUDIO TAPES)

NORMAL AND ABNORMAL
   BEHAVIOR OF ADOLESCENCE·· A
   SERIES   SIGINF
WHAT SHALL WE LISTEN TO (J-C)   IU

EXPERIMENTAL · ENVIRONMENTAL EFFECTS

(MOTION PICTURES)

SURVIVAL OF SPACESHIP EARTH   WB

(VIDEOTAPES)

OUR PRESENT EDUCATIONAL DILEMMA   GPITVL

EXPERIMENTAL · HYPNOSIS AND SUGGESTIBILITY

(AUDIO TAPES)

WHO CAN BE HYPNOTIZED   SIGINF

EXPERIMENTAL · LEARNING

(AUDIO TAPES)

BIOLOGICAL EVOLUTION OF
   INTELLIGENCE, THE   SIGINF
GENES AND INTELLIGENCE   SIGINF
PRESCHOOL ENRICHMENT AND
   LEARNING   SIGINF
PREVENTIVE MENTAL HEALTH
   WORK WITH PRESCHOOL
   TEACHERS   SIGINF

PSYCHOGENIC LEARNING DISORDERS,
PT 1 — SIGINF
PSYCHOGENIC LEARNING DISORDERS,
PT 2 — SIGINF
PSYCHOGENIC LEARNING DISORDERS,
PT 3 — SIGINF

EXPERIMENTAL - MOTIVATION AND EMOTION

(VIDEOTAPES)

CHANGING THE CHILD'S RELATIONSHIPS
AND GOALS — GPITVL
CLARIFICATION OF BASIC PRINCIPLES — GPITVL

(AUDIO TAPES)

COMPASSION - TOWARD A SCIENCE
OF VALUE--A SERIES — SIGINF
DISCONTENTED HOUSEWIFE — BASCH
INTRODUCTION - COMPASSION IN
GREAT PHILOSOPHIES AND
RELIGIONS — SIGINF
IT TAKES A WOMAN--A SERIES — BASCH
OUR EMOTIONS — BASCH
WHAT MAKES A HAPPY MARRIAGE — BASCH
WHAT'S YOUR PROBLEM--A SERIES — BASCH

EXPERIMENTAL - MOTOR PERFORMANCE

(MOTION PICTURES)

LEFT, RIGHT MOVIE, THE (K-P S) — GRADYM
SCHOOL IS FOR CHILDREN (T) — AIMS

EXPERIMENTAL - PERCEPTION

(MOTION PICTURES)

MORAL DEVELOPMENT (C A) — CRMP
SIX SHORT FILMS (H-C A) — BFA
SLICE OF GOLD — AMERFI

(VIDEOTAPES)

GROUP DISCUSSION WITH TEENAGERS — GPITVL

(AUDIO TAPES)

EXISTENCE THEORY OF
PERSONALITY - EMPIRICAL
STUDIES OF THE SELF CONCEPT — SIGINF

EXPERIMENTAL - REACTION TIME

(MOTION PICTURES)

COPING IN SPECIAL EDUCATION -
DISRUPTIVE BEHAVIOR (C) — UEUWIS
THEORIST ROOM — AMERFI

EXPERIMENTAL - SLEEP, FATIGUE AND DREAMS

(AUDIO TAPES)

SLEEP AND PSYCHOPATHOLOGY — SIGINF

EXPERIMENTAL - THINKING

(MOTION PICTURES)

CHILDREN'S CONCEPTS (C T) — TIMLIF

(AUDIO TAPES)

BIOLOGICAL EVOLUTION OF
INTELLIGENCE, THE — SIGINF
COGNITIVE CONSISTENCY -
PSYCHOSOCIAL ISOMORPHISM — SIGINF
COGNITIVE PERFORMANCE - PROGRESS
VS PRODUCT — SIGINF
GENES AND INTELLIGENCE — SIGINF

METHODOLOGY & RESEARCH TECHNOLOGY - EXPERIMENTS AND OBSERVATIONS

(AUDIO TAPES)

FACT OR FANTASY--A SERIES — BASCH

RESEARCH AND TESTING

(AUDIO TAPES)

CLINICAL PSYCHOPATHOLOGY--A SERIES — SIGINF
INFORMATION FOR CANDIDATES -
THE FORMAT OF WRITTEN AND
ORAL EXAMINATIONS - HOW TO
TAKE... — SIGINF
NORMAL AND ABNORMAL

BEHAVIOR OF ADOLESCENCE-- A
SERIES — SIGINF

PERSONALITY - GENERAL

(MOTION PICTURES)

ADOLESCENCE AND SEXUAL IDENTITY
(H-C A) — CHM
DEPENDENCE - A NEW DEFINITION (C
A) — CRMP
EMOTIONAL DEVELOPMENT (C A) — CRMP
TUP TUP (J-C A) — BFA

(AUDIO TAPES)

EXISTENCE THEORY OF
PERSONALITY - EMPIRICAL
STUDIES OF THE SELF CONCEPT — SIGINF

PERSONALITY - CREATIVITY

(MOTION CARTRIDGES)

WHY MAN CREATES (A) — PFP

(MOTION PICTURES)

CHANGES, CHANGES (K-P) — WWS
DEVELOPING CREATIVITY (J-C A) — UEUWIS
SUMMER JOURNAL — AMERFI
THREE MAGICAL METHODS -
FINDING GOOD IDEAS FOR
STORIES (P-I) — ECCCW

PERSONALITY - INTELLIGENCE

(MOTION PICTURES)

PIAGET'S DEVELOPMENTAL THEORY
- THE GROWTH OF INTELLIGENCE
IN THE PRESCHOOL YEARS (A) — DAVFMS
RACE, INTELLIGENCE AND EDUCATION
(H-C A) — TIMLIF

(AUDIO TAPES)

BIOLOGICAL EVOLUTION OF
INTELLIGENCE, THE — SIGINF
COGNITIVE CONSISTENCY -
PSYCHOSOCIAL ISOMORPHISM — SIGINF

PERSONALITY - PERSONALITY MEASUREMENTS

(MOTION PICTURES)

PIAGET'S DEVELOPMENTAL THEORY
- THE GROWTH OF INTELLIGENCE
IN THE PRESCHOOL YEARS (A) — DAVFMS

PERSONALITY - PERSONALITY TRAIT PROCESSES

(VIDEOTAPES)

CHANGING THE CHILD'S RELATIONSHIPS
AND GOALS — GPITVL
CLARIFICATION OF BASIC PRINCIPLES — GPITVL
ENCOURAGEMENT — GPITVL
MOTIVATING CHILDREN TO LEARN -
SUMMARY — GPITVL

(AUDIO TAPES)

ASSESSMENT OF CHANGE IN
CHILDREN'S BEHAVIOR — SIGINF
EXISTENCE THEORY OF
PERSONALITY - EMPIRICAL
STUDIES OF THE SELF CONCEPT — SIGINF

PERSONNEL AND INDUSTRIAL - ADVERTISING AND CONSUMER PSYCHOLOGY

(FILMSTRIPS)

DOING IT ALL ON A BUDGET — EGH

(MOTION PICTURES)

ADVERTISING — BEF
ADVERTISING - INFORMATION,
PERSUASION OR DECEPTION (I-C) — JOU
ADVERTISING AND COMPETITION — MTP
DECIDING (P-I) — CENTEF
STAGE IS YOURS, THE — BEF
TOUGH-MINDED SALESMANSHIP -
ASK FOR THE ORDER AND GET
IT (H-C) — DARTNL

(AUDIO TAPES)

MESSAGE FROM OUR SPONSOR, A (I-J) — CORF

(TRANSPARENCIES)

BASIC SALESMANSHIP--A SERIES — COF
JOB APPLICATION AND JOB INTERVIEW-
-A SERIES — COF

PERSONNEL AND INDUSTRIAL - DRIVING AND SAFETY

(MOTION PICTURES)

CRITICAL DRIVING PATTERNS — FMCMP
DRIVER EDUCATION--A SERIES — FMCMP
DRIVING IN TRAFFIC — FMCMP
RURAL DRIVING — FMCMP

PERSONNEL AND INDUSTRIAL - MANAGEMENT AND ORGANIZATION

(FILMSTRIPS)

COMPANY AND THE COMMUNITY, THE,
PT 1 — CREATV
COMPANY AND THE COMMUNITY, THE,
PT 2 — CREATV
COMPANY ORGANIZATION, PT 1 — CREATV
COMPANY ORGANIZATION, PT 2 — CREATV
NATION OF OWNERS - AN
INTRODUCTION TO THE
SECURITIES INDUSTRY — XEROX
NATION OF OWNERS--A SERIES — XEROX

(MOTION PICTURES)

BRIDGE OF FRIENDSHIP — ALDEN
MANAGEMENT PRACTICE--A SERIES — BNA
WHAT EVERY MANAGER NEEDS TO
KNOW ABOUT INFORMATION
SYSTEMS, PT 1 - THE MERITT CASE — BNA
WHAT EVERY MANAGER NEEDS TO
KNOW ABOUT INFORMATION
SYSTEMS, PT 2 - THE COMPUTER ... — BNA
WHAT IS BUSINESS (H-C A) — SAIF

PERSONNEL AND INDUSTRIAL - PERFORMANCE AND JOB SATISFACTION

(FILMSTRIPS)

COMPANY AND THE COMMUNITY, THE,
PT 1 — CREATV
COMPANY AND THE COMMUNITY, THE,
PT 2 — CREATV
COMPANY ORGANIZATION, PT 1 — CREATV
COMPANY ORGANIZATION, PT 2 — CREATV

(MOTION PICTURES)

FINDING YOURSELF AND YOUR JOB (J-
C) — AMEDFL
IN LIVING COLOR (H-C A) — DATA
YOUR NEW JOB (H-C A) — SAIF

PERSONNEL AND INDUSTRIAL - SELECTION AND PLACEMENT

(TRANSPARENCIES)

JOB APPLICATION AND JOB INTERVIEW-
-A SERIES — COF

PERSONNEL AND INDUSTRIAL - VOCATIONAL CHOICE AND GUIDANCE

(FILMSTRIPS)

EXPLORING CAREERS, GROUP 1--A
SERIES (I-C) — SVE

(MOTION PICTURES)

FINDING YOURSELF AND YOUR JOB (J-
C) — AMEDFL
FUTURE STREET - NEW
DIRECTIONS IN CAREER
EDUCATION--A SERIES (J-C) — AMEDFL
FUTURES IN STEEL — MTP
MULTIPLE CHOICE (J-C A) — INDSLF
OPPORTUNITIES IN HOTELS AND
MOTELS — USNAC
OPPORTUNITIES IN WELDING — USNAC

(VIDEOTAPES)

DATA PROCESSING, UNIT 4 -
APPLICATIONS AND CAREER
OPPORTUNITIES--A SERIES — GPITVL

PHYSIOLOGICAL - GENERAL

(MOTION PICTURES)

DEATHSTYLES — AMERFI

PHYSIOLOGICAL · BIOCHEMISTRY · DRUG EFFECTS · HUMAN

(FILMSTRIPS)

ALCOHOL · PARENTS AND THEIR POTIONS (P-I)	EBEC
DRUGS AND CHILDREN, PT 1 (I)	EDLACT
DRUGS AND CHILDREN, PT 2 (I)	EDLACT
MEDICINE · PEOPLE AND PILLS (P-I)	EBEC

(MOTION PICTURES)

ALCOHOL · HOW MUCH IS TOO MUCH (I)	AIMS
ALCOHOL · OUR NUMBER ONE DRUG (I-H)	OF
ALCOHOL PROBLEM, THE · WHAT DO YOU THINK (I-C)	EBEC
DRUG PROBLEM, THE · WHAT DO YOU THINK (J-H)	EBEC

PHYSIOLOGICAL · ENVIRONMENT

(MOTION PICTURES)

SLICE OF GOLD	AMERFI

PHYSIOLOGICAL · GENETICS

(MOTION PICTURES)

EMBRYOLOGICAL DEVELOPMENT (H-C A)	CHM
RACE, INTELLIGENCE AND EDUCATION (H-C A)	TIMLIF

PHYSIOLOGICAL · NEUROLOGY

(FILMSTRIPS)

INTRODUCTION TO THE NEUROSCIENCES, AN	SAUNDW
NEUROSCIENCES	DAUNDW

(MOTION PICTURES)

CONDITIONED REFLEX	IWANMI
SYSTEM AND WORKINGS OF A NERVE	IWANMI

PHYSIOLOGICAL · SENSORY PHYSIOLOGY

(VIDEOTAPES)

EXTENDING OUR SENSES (I)	GPITVL
HOW DO YOU KNOW (I)	GPITVL

SOCIAL · ATTITUDES AND OPINIONS

(FILMSTRIPS)

AMERICAN GENIUS, 1960 · 1970 (H-C)	EDDIM
ONCE UPON A COMPULSION	KELLRP

(MOTION PICTURES)

BEACH PARTY, THE	PAULST
BERKELEY CHRISTMAS, A	AMERFI
BROWN RICE	AMERFI
COLLEGE DAZE	AMERFI
DEATHSTYLES	AMERFI
EDUCATION FOR FAMILY LIFE (H-C A)	CHM
JESUS TRIP, THE (C A)	TIMLIF
KRISHNAMURTI (H-C A)	TIMLIF
RACE, INTELLIGENCE AND EDUCATION (H-C A)	TIMLIF
RUMOURS OF WAR (H-C A)	TIMLIF
TUP TUP (J-C A)	BFA
WE HAVE AN ADDICT IN THE HOUSE (J-C A)	DOUBLE
WHAT FIXED ME	AMERFI
WHAT'S WRONG WITH THE SOCIAL SCIENCES (H-C A)	TIMLIF

(VIDEOTAPES)

EDUCATION VS EDUCATION	SCCOE
GROUP DISCUSSION WITH TEENAGERS	GPITVL
OBJECTIVE · ACCULTURATION	SCCOE
OUTLOOK	SCCOE
UNCONSCIOUS CULTURAL CLASHES--A SERIES	SCCOE

(AUDIO TAPES)

COMPASSION · TOWARD A SCIENCE OF VALUE--A SERIES	SIGINF
CONSERVATIVE VS RADICAL BEHAVIORS · MILITARIST VS PACIFIST BEHAVIORS	SIGINF
INTRODUCTION · COMPASSION IN GREAT PHILOSOPHIES AND RELIGIONS	SIGINF

KNOWLEDGE OF VALUES · AUTHORITARIAN PERSONALITY	SIGINF
PSYCHOLOGICAL DEVELOPMENT DURING ADOLESCENCE	SIGINF
YANKEE DOODLEBUG AND THE AW-THAT'S NOTHIN' (P-I)	UTEX
YOU ARE THE TARGET (J-C)	INSKY

(TRANSPARENCIES)

DATING RELATIONS · DATING PROBLEMS--A SERIES (J)	LEART
DATING RELATIONS · POPULARITY--A SERIES (J)	LEART
WHAT ARE SOCIAL VALUES AND NORMS (J-H)	LEART

SOCIAL · COMMUNICATION

(MOTION PICTURES)

BY THE PEOPLE (J-C A)	FILIM
PERSON TO PERSON · MAKING COMMUNICATIONS WORK FOR YOU (H-C A)	SAIF
TO BE A FRIEND (J-H)	BBF
WHAT DO WE LOOK LIKE TO OTHERS (H-C A)	SAIF

(AUDIO TAPES)

EVOLUTION OF COMMUNICATION, THE	SIGINF

SOCIAL · COMMUNICATION · LANGUAGE

(MOTION PICTURES)

LANGUAGE DEVELOPMENT (C A)	CRMP

(VIDEOTAPES)

SOLUTIONS IN COMMUNICATIONS · INTRODUCTORY LESSON (I)	SCCOE

SOCIAL · CULTURE AND SOCIAL PROCESSES

(MOTION PICTURES)

BERKELEY CHRISTMAS, A	AMERFI
EMOTIONAL DEVELOPMENT (C A)	CRMP
FRANKENSTEIN IN A FISHBOWL	AMERFI
JESUS TRIP, THE (C A)	TIMLIF
LOVE'S BEGINNINGS (P)	CAHILL
STRAWBERRIES · WITH CREAM	MTP

(VIDEOTAPES)

BECAUSE IT'S FUN	NITC
CUSTOMS	SCCOE
GRAND ASSUMPTIONS	SCCOE
LOOK ME IN THE EYE	SCCOE
OBJECTIVE · ACCULTURATION	SCCOE
OUTLOOK	SCCOE
UNCONSCIOUS CULTURAL CLASHES--A SERIES	SCCOE

(AUDIO TAPES)

BIOLOGY, MORALITY AND SOCIAL COHESION	SIGINF
CAREER WIFE	BASCH
COMPASSION · TOWARD A SCIENCE OF VALUE--A SERIES	SIGINF
DISCONTENTED HOUSEWIFE	BASCH
EVOLUTION OF COMMUNICATION, THE	SIGINF
EVOLUTION OF WITHIN-GROUP COOPERATION, THE	SIGINF
INSTINCT PROBLEM, THE	SIGINF
INTERGROUP COMPETITION AND PRIMATE EVOLUTION	SIGINF
NEW APPROACH TO HUMAN EVOLUTION · INTRODUCTION	SIGINF
NEW APPROACH TO HUMAN EVOLUTION · SUMMATION AND CONCLUSIONS	SIGINF
NEW APPROACH TO HUMAN EVOLUTION--A SERIES	SIGINF
PSYCHOLOGICAL FUNCTIONS OF THE COUNTER CULTURE	SIGINF
RECENT ATTITUDES TOWARD HUMAN EVOLUTION	SIGINF
TOO YOUNG TO MARRY	BASCH
WHAT MAKES A HAPPY MARRIAGE	BASCH
WHAT'S YOUR PROBLEM--A SERIES	BASCH

SOCIAL · GROUP AND INTERPERSONAL PROCESSES

(FILMSTRIPS)

ALCOHOL AND TOBACCO	EGH
ALIENATION AND MASS SOCIETY, PT 1	SED
ALIENATION AND MASS SOCIETY, PT 2	SED
APPETITE OF A BIRD	FI
DOCTOR'S VIEWPOINT	EGH

DRUGS AND YOUR FUTURE	EGH
ECOLOGY OF OUR BODIES	EGH
LET'S LOOK AT DRUGS--A SERIES	EGH
MARIJUANA, STIMULANTS AND DEPRESSANTS	EGH
MARY JANE AND BUTTERFLY	EGH
ONCE UPON A COMPULSION	KELLRP
OUR INSTINCTS AND WHY WE HAVE THEM	EGH
PILLS IN A PILL CULTURE	EGH

(MOTION PICTURES)

A TO B	AMERFI
BERKELEY CHRISTMAS, A	AMERFI
CHILDREN AS PEOPLE (H-C A)	POLYMR
COPING IN SPECIAL EDUCATION · SOCIALIZATION (C)	UEUWIS
DEPENDENCE · A NEW DEFINITION (C A)	CRMP
FLOWERS FOR DAHLIA	ALDEN
FRANKENSTEIN IN A FISHBOWL	AMERFI
PERSON TO PERSON · MAKING COMMUNICATIONS WORK FOR YOU (H-C A)	SAIF
PORCH GLIDER	AMERFI
STRAWBERRIES · WITH CREAM	MTP
TO BE A FRIEND (J-H)	BBF
WHAT DO WE LOOK LIKE TO OTHERS (H-C A)	SAIF
YOU (P-I)	CENTEF

(VIDEOTAPES)

GETTING EVEN	NITC
I DARE YOU	NITC

(AUDIO TAPES)

BIOLOGY, MORALITY AND SOCIAL COHESION	SIGINF
CLINICAL ASPECTS OF THE PSYCHIATRIC MANAGEMENT OF BURNED AND DISFIGURED CHILDREN	SIGINF
COMPASSION · TOWARD A SCIENCE OF VALUE--A SERIES	SIGINF
EGOCENTRISM IN CHILDREN AND ADOLESCENTS	SIGINF
EVOLUTION OF COMMUNICATION, THE	SIGINF
EVOLUTION OF WITHIN-GROUP COOPERATION, THE	SIGINF
FAMILY THERAPY · GROUP THERAPY · COMMUNITY PSYCHIATRY	SIGINF
INSTINCT PROBLEM, THE	SIGINF
INTERGROUP COMPETITION AND PRIMATE EVOLUTION	SIGINF
KNOWLEDGE OF VALUES · AUTHORITARIAN PERSONALITY	SIGINF
NEW APPROACH TO HUMAN EVOLUTION · INTRODUCTION	SIGINF
NEW APPROACH TO HUMAN EVOLUTION · SUMMATION AND CONCLUSIONS	SIGINF
NEW APPROACH TO HUMAN EVOLUTION--A SERIES	SIGINF
RECENT ATTITUDES TOWARD HUMAN EVOLUTION	SIGINF

(TRANSPARENCIES)

DATING RELATIONS · DATING CATEGORIES--A SERIES (J)	LEART
DATING RELATIONS · DATING PROBLEMS--A SERIES (J)	LEART
DATING RELATIONS · DIMENSIONS OF DATING--A SERIES (J)	LEART
DATING RELATIONS · EVALUATING DATING BEHAVIOR --A SERIES (J)	LEART
DATING RELATIONS · MATURE LOVE--A SERIES (J)	LEART
DATING RELATIONS · POPULARITY--A SERIES (J)	LEART
DATING RELATIONS · ROMANCE AND PEOPLE--A SERIES (J)	LEART
DATING RELATIONS · THE FIRST DATE--A SERIES (J)	LEART
GROUP PRESSURES (J-H)	LEART
SEX EDUCATION · DEVELOPMENT OF CONCEPTS AND ATTITUDES--A SERIES	LEART
WHAT MAKES PERSONALITIES DIFFERENT	LEART

SOCIAL · SEXUAL BEHAVIOR

(FILMSTRIPS)

ARE SEX AND LOVE THE SAME THING	EGH
ATTITUDES ABOUT HUMAN SEXUALITY	EGH
FEMALE OF THE SPECIES, THE	EGH
HUMAN SEXUALITY--A SERIES	EGH
OUR INSTINCTS AND WHY WE HAVE THEM	EGH

(MOTION PICTURES)

ADOLESCENCE AND SEXUAL IDENTITY
(H-C A)   CHM
HOW TO MAKE A WOMAN (C A)   POLYMR
HUMAN REPRODUCTION (H-C A)   CHM
INTRODUCTION TO SEX EDUCATION (H-
C A)   CHM
LOVE AND FILM (H-C A)   BFA
SEX IN AMERICAN CULTURE--A SERIES
(H-C A)   CHM

(AUDIO TAPES)

AFFINITIES OUT OF DESPERATION -
THE 'MRS ROBINSON'
SYNDROME   SIGINF
BEHAVIOR DISORDERS OF CHILDREN--A
SERIES   SIGINF
BEYOND SEXUAL IDENTITY   SIGINF
CAN LOVE AND SEX SURVIVE THE
ELIMINATION OF SEXISM   SIGINF
DELINQUENT AND PROMISCUOUS
HOMOSEXUAL BEHAVIOR   SIGINF
EXISTENTIAL ASPECTS OF SEXUAL
JEALOUSY   SIGINF
GAY AFFINITIES AND THE HELPING
PROFESSIONS   SIGINF
IDENTITIES AND AFFINITIES - THE
PROBLEM OF JUSTICE IN
MARRIAGE AND OTHER UNIONS--A
SERIES   SIGINF
IDENTITIES AND AFFINITIES - THE
PROBLEM OF JUSTICE IN
MARRIAGE AND OTHER UNIONS - ...   SIGINF
IS MARRIAGE MORAL   SIGINF
OEDIPUS COMPLEX AND SEXISM, THE   SIGINF
STATE OF THE UNION, PRESENT AND
FUTURE, THE   SIGINF
STILL-UNACCEPTABLE AFFINITIES -
OLDER WOMEN YOUNGER MEN
LIAISONS   SIGINF
TRAUMA OF EVENTLESSNESS, THE   SIGINF
UPROOTING AND ROLE-
TRANSFERENCE - ISSUES OF
IDENTITY CRISES IN WIVES   SIGINF

(TRANSPARENCIES)

DATING RELATIONS - DATING
PROBLEMS--A SERIES (J)   LEART
DATING RELATIONS - DIMENSIONS
OF DATING--A SERIES (J)   LEART
DIMENSIONS OF SEXUAL ATTRACTION -
FEMALE (J)   LEART
DIMENSIONS OF SEXUAL ATTRACTION -
MALE (J)   LEART

SOCIAL - SMOKING AND DRUG AND ALCOHOL

(FILMSTRIPS)

ALCOHOL - PARENTS AND THEIR
POTIONS (P-I)   EBEC
DRUGS - A TRICK, A TRAP--A SERIES   EBEC
DRUGS AND CHILDREN, PT 1 (I)   EDLACT
DRUGS AND CHILDREN, PT 2 (I)   EDLACT
HARD DRUGS, THE - THE BOTTOM OF
THE TRAP (P-I)   EBEC
MARIJUANA AND GLUE - KIDS, TRICKS
AND TRAPS (P-I)   EBEC
MEDICINE - PEOPLE AND PILLS (P-I)   EBEC
TOBACCO - A PUFF OF POISON (P-I)   EBEC

(MOTION PICTURES)

ALCOHOL - HOW MUCH IS TOO MUCH
(I)   AIMS
ALCOHOL - OUR NUMBER ONE DRUG (I-
H)   OF
ALCOHOL PROBLEM, THE - WHAT DO
YOU THINK (I-C)   EBEC
ALCOHOLISM - A MODEL OF DRUG
DEPENDENCY (C A)   CRMP
CENTER OF LIFE (J-C A)   GRANDY
DRUG PROBLEM, THE - WHAT DO YOU
THINK (J-H)   EBEC
LIFE AND HEALTH FILM--A SERIES   CRMP
TAKING CARE OF BUSINESS   AMERFI
WE HAVE AN ADDICT IN THE HOUSE
(J-C A)   DOUBLE

(AUDIO TAPES)

ALCOHOLISM   BASCH
DEFINITION OF ALCOHOLISM, THE   SIGINF
DRUG ABUSE - SOMATIC
THERAPIES - PSYCHIATRIC
DISORDERS OF CHILDHOOD   SIGINF
MANAGEMENT OF DRUG ABUSE IN
THE OUTPATIENT
PSYCHOTHERAPY OF ADOLESCENTS,
THE   SIGINF
PATTERNS OF DRUG ABUSE
AMONG MIDDLE-CLASS
ADOLESCENTS   SIGINF
PSYCHIATRY AND THE LAW -
ALCOHOLISM - DRUG ABUSE   SIGINF

SOCIOLOGIC PERSPECTIVES OF THE
MARIJUANA CONTROVERSY   SIGINF

(TRANSPARENCIES)

DEPRESSANTS (H)   BOW
DRUG ABUSE--A SERIES (H)   BOW
DRUGS AND THE LAW (H)   BOW
GLUE SNIFFING (H)   BOW
HALLUCINOGENIC DRUGS (H)   BOW
MARIJUANA (H)   BOW
NARCOTICS (H)   BOW
STIMULANTS (H)   BOW
USES AND ABUSES (H)   BOW

RELIGION AND PHILOSOPHY

CHRISTIANITY

(FILMSTRIPS)

BUILDING ON THE ROCK (I R)   ROAS
DECIDING FOR MYSELF (I R)   ROAS
GROWING UP (I R)   ROAS
I AM RISEN AND WITH YOU (I R)   ROAS
MY FRIENDS AND FOLLOWERS (I R)   ROAS
MY GREATEST WORK (I R)   ROAS
MY LAND AND MY PEOPLE (I R)   ROAS
MY NAME IS JESUS--A SERIES (I R)   ROAS
SHEPHERDS AND WISEMEN (I R)   ROAS
SIGNS AND WONDERS (I R)   ROAS
TURNING TOWARD JERUSALEM (I R)   ROAS

(MOTION PICTURES)

BERKELEY CHRISTMAS, A   AMERFI
ISRAEL - THE HOLY LAND (J-C A)   AMEDFL
JESUS TRIP, THE (C A)   TIMLIF
LAND OF HOPE AND PRAYER   ALDEN
POPE PAUL'S VISIT TO ISRAEL   ALDEN
VISTAS OF ISRAEL, NO. 4   ALDEN

FATE AND FATALISM

(MOTION PICTURES)

DEATHSTYLES   AMERFI

HINDUISM

(MOTION PICTURES)

HINDU RITUAL SANDHYA, THE   CMC

HINDU PHILOSOPHY

(MOTION PICTURES)

SAMADHI (H-C A)   UWFKD
SEARCH FOR ALTERNATE LIFE-
STYLES AND PHILOSOPHIES, THE
(J-C A)   FLMFR

HOLIDAYS - RELIGIOUS

(FILMSTRIPS)

CHRISTMAS IN A NOISY VILLAGE (K-P)   VIP
EASTER (K-P)   MGHT
HOLIDAY SERIES, SET 2--A SERIES (K-P)   MGHT
PASSOVER (K-P)   MGHT

(MOTION PICTURES)

BERKELEY CHRISTMAS, A   AMERFI
HANUKKAH   ALDEN
PASSOVER   ALDEN
PURIM   ALDEN
SHAVUOTH   ALDEN
SUCCOTH   ALDEN

HUMANISM

(MOTION PICTURES)

CIVILISATION, PROGRAM 13   TIMLIF

JUDAISM

(FILMSTRIPS)

PASSOVER (K-P)   MGHT

(MOTION PICTURES)

HANUKKAH   ALDEN
JERUSALEM - HERE WE COME   ALDEN
PASSOVER   ALDEN
PURIM   ALDEN
SHAVUOTH   ALDEN

VISION OF CHAIM WEIZMANN   ALDEN

LOGIC

(FILMSTRIPS)

RATIONALISM   EGH

MODERN PHILOSOPHY

(MOTION PICTURES)

JESUS TRIP, THE (C A)   TIMLIF
KRISHNAMURTI (H-C A)   TIMLIF
SEARCH FOR ALTERNATE LIFE-
STYLES AND PHILOSOPHIES, THE
(J-C A)   FLMFR

MYTHOLOGY

(FILMSTRIPS)

AIR (P-I)   TERF
FABLES AND FACTS--A SERIES (P-I)   TERF
FIRE (P-I)   TERF
LIFE COMES TO THE WORLD (P-I)   TERF
THUNDER AND LIGHTNING (P-I)   TERF
WATER (P-I)   TERF
WORLD IS BORN, THE (P-I)   TERF

PHILOSOPHY

(VIDEOTAPES)

RALPH WALDO EMERSON -
EMERSON'S DISCIPLE, THOREAU
(J-H)   GPITVL
RALPH WALDO EMERSON - SELF-
RELIANCE, EMERSON'S
PHILOSOPHY (J-H)   GPITVL

(AUDIO TAPES)

HUMANISTIC AND POSITIVIST
PHILOSOPHIES OF SCIENCE   SIGINF
INTRODUCTION - COMPASSION IN
GREAT PHILOSOPHIES AND
RELIGIONS   SIGINF
PHILOSOPHIES OF MAN AND VALUE
- SCIENTIFIC METHODS   SIGINF

RELIGIOUS CEREMONIES

(MOTION PICTURES)

HINDU RITUAL SANDHYA, THE   CMC

RELIGIOUS EDUCATION

(FILMSTRIPS)

BUILDING ON THE ROCK (I R)   ROAS
DECIDING FOR MYSELF (I R)   ROAS
GROWING UP (I R)   ROAS
I AM RISEN AND WITH YOU (I R)   ROAS
MY FRIENDS AND FOLLOWERS (I R)   ROAS
MY GREATEST WORK (I R)   ROAS
MY LAND AND MY PEOPLE (I R)   ROAS
MY NAME IS JESUS--A SERIES (I R)   ROAS
SHEPHERDS AND WISEMEN (I R)   ROAS
SIGNS AND WONDERS (I R)   ROAS
TURNING TOWARD JERUSALEM (I R)   ROAS

(TRANSPARENCIES)

RELIGION AND SOCIETY (J-H)   LEART

SECTS

(MOTION PICTURES)

KRISHNAMURTI (H-C A)   TIMLIF

SKEPTICISM

(AUDIO TAPES)

FACT OR FANTASY--A SERIES   BASCH

SCIENCE

HISTORY

(FILMSTRIPS)

FABLES AND FACTS--A SERIES (P-I)   TERF
HISTORY OF ASTRONAUTICS, THE, PT 1
(I-J)   DOUBLE

HISTORY OF ASTRONAUTICS, THE, PT 2
(I-J) — DOUBLE
HISTORY OF THE COMPUTER, THE (H) — EBEC

(MOTION PICTURES)

STEPPING STONES IN SPACE (I-C A) — HEARST

(VIDEOTAPES)

DISCOVERING THE ATOM (I-J) — GPITVL
HUNCHES AND GUESSES (I) — GPITVL

(AUDIO TAPES)

TO DIE THAT OTHERS MAY LIVE (I) — MINSA

LABORATORY TECHNIQUES - GENERAL

(FILMSTRIPS)

COMPARATIVE PATHOGENIC
BACTERIOLOGY, PT 1 — SAUNDW
COMPARATIVE PATHOGENIC
BACTERIOLOGY, PT 2 — SAUNDW

(MOTION PICTURES)

AIRBORNE OCEANOGRAPHY -
OCEANOGRAPHER OF THE NAVY — USNAC
BATHYMETRY - DISCOVERING THE
OCEAN FLOOR - CHARTING THE
OCEAN FLOOR — AIMS
MICROSCOPE — IWANMI
NEW VIEW OF SPACE, A (J-C A) — NASA

(VIDEOTAPES)

CRYSTAL CLEAR (I) — GPITVL
DRAWING A PICTURE OF NATURE (I) — GPITVL
EXPLORING PLANTS (I) — GPITVL
HOT AND COLD (I) — GPITVL
HUNCHES AND GUESSES (I) — GPITVL
MAGNET EARTH, THE (I) — GPITVL
PUSH AND PULL (I) — GPITVL
SEESAWS, SLIDES AND SWINGS (I) — GPITVL
WHAT DO YOU DO WITH NUMBERS (I) — GPITVL
WHAT DO YOU THINK (I) — GPITVL

(TRANSPARENCIES)

BALANCE BEAM SCALE (H) — BOW
INSTRUMENTS AND TECHNIQUES OF
SCIENCE--A SERIES (H) — BOW
PREPARING SLIDES (H) — BOW
PSYCHROMETER (H) — BOW
TELESCOPE (H) — BOW
TESTING FOR MINERALS (H) — BOW
THERMOMETER (H) — BOW

LABORATORY TECHNIQUES - BIOLOGY

(FILMSTRIPS)

ANIMAL HISTOLOGY (I-H) — COMG

(MOTION PICTURES)

BIOENGINEERS, THE — USNAC
MICROSCOPE — IWANMI

LABORATORY TECHNIQUES - CHEMISTRY

(MOTION CARTRIDGES)

STRUCTURE AND
STEREOCHEMISTRY -
CONFORMATION OF
CYCLOHEXANE — HRAW
STRUCTURE AND
STEREOCHEMISTRY - DRAWING
STRUCTURES, PT 1 — HRAW
STRUCTURE AND
STEREOCHEMISTRY - DRAWING
STRUCTURES, PT 2 — HRAW

(MOTION PICTURES)

CRYSTALLIZATION — IWANMI
OBSERVATION OF BOILING — IWANMI
OBSERVATION OF ICE — IWANMI
SCIENCE OF WATER DROPS — IWANMI
STORY OF MOLECULE — IWANMI
WATER PRESSURE — IWANMI
WATER SURFACE — IWANMI

(VIDEOTAPES)

EXPLORING GASES (I) — GPITVL

LABORATORY TECHNIQUES - MEDICINE

(FILMSTRIPS)

CANCER, SERIES 3 - TREATMENT

MODALITIES WITH IMPLICATIONS
FOR NURSING CARE--A SERIES — CONMED
CHEMOTHERAPY — CONMED
COLOSTOMY — CONMED
HEAD AND NECK SURGERY — CONMED
HYSTERECTOMY FOR UTERINE CANCER — CONMED
INTRODUCTION TO CANCER SURGERY
MASTECTOMY — CONMED
RADIOTHERAPY I — CONMED
RADIOTHERAPY II — CONMED

(MOTION PICTURES)

CLINICAL EVALUATION OF THE
JUGULAR VENOUS PULSE (PRO) — AMEDA

LABORATORY TECHNIQUES - PHYSICS

(MOTION PICTURES)

ATMOSPHERIC PRESSURE — IWANMI
DISCOVERY OF THE VACUUM — IWANMI
HOW TO MEASURE TEMPERATURE — IWANMI
NATURE OF MATTER, THE - AN ATOMIC
VIEW (C A) — CRMP
SCIENCE OF FIRE — IWANMI
SURFACE TENSION — IWANMI

SCIENCE, STUDY AND TEACHING - GENERAL

(MOTION PICTURES)

MEANING OF TIME IN SCIENCE, THE (H-
C) — EBEC

(AUDIO TAPES)

HUMANISTIC AND POSITIVIST
PHILOSOPHIES OF SCIENCE — SIGINF

SCIENCE, STUDY AND TEACHING - BIOLOGY

(FILMSTRIPS)

RATIONALISM — EGH

SCIENTIFIC METHOD

(FILMSTRIPS)

FABLES AND FACTS--A SERIES (P-I) — TERF

(MOTION PICTURES)

BIOENGINEERS, THE — USNAC
CONTINENTS ADRIFT - A STUDY OF
THE SCIENTIFIC METHOD (J-C) — AMEDFL
ICE COLUMNS — IWANMI
INSECTS, OBSERVATION AND
COLLECTION — IWANMI
MEANING OF TIME IN SCIENCE, THE (H-
C) — EBEC
SCIENCE IN AN AQUARIUM — IWANMI

(VIDEOTAPES)

CRYSTAL CLEAR (I) — GPITVL
DRAWING A PICTURE OF NATURE (I) — GPITVL
EXPLORING GASES (I) — GPITVL
EXPLORING PLANTS (I) — GPITVL
EXTENDING OUR SENSES (I) — GPITVL
HOT AND COLD (I) — GPITVL
HUNCHES AND GUESSES (I) — GPITVL
MAGNET EARTH, THE (I) — GPITVL
PUSH AND PULL (I) — GPITVL
SEESAWS, SLIDES AND SWINGS (I) — GPITVL
WHAT DO YOU DO WITH NUMBERS (I) — GPITVL
WHAT DO YOU THINK (I) — GPITVL

VOCATIONS, SCIENCE - LIFE SCIENCES

(MOTION PICTURES)

BIOENGINEERS, THE — USNAC

SCIENCE - NATURAL

SCIENCE, NATURAL - GENERAL

(FILMSTRIPS)

ADAPTATIONS FOR LIFE — EGH
ANIMAL HISTOLOGY (I-H) — COMG
ENERGY AND LIFE — EGH
LIFE - A UNIQUE PHENOMENON--A
SERIES — EGH
PERPETUATING LIFE — EGH
RATIONALISM — EGH
WHAT IS LIFE — EGH

(MOTION PICTURES)

BIOLOGY TODAY FILM--A SERIES — CRMP
EVOLUTION — LCOA
LIVING CELL, THE (J-C A) — HAR
NATURE'S EVER CHANGING
COMMUNITIES (I-J) — JOU
TUNE INTO NATURE (I-C A) — NVFP

(VIDEOTAPES)

LET'S EXPLORE SCIENCE--A SERIES (I) — GPITVL
PUSH AND PULL (I) — GPITVL
SORTING THINGS (I) — GPITVL
WHAT ARE THE CHARACTERISTICS OF
LIVING THINGS (I) — GPITVL

(TRANSPARENCIES)

AT THE BEACH (K-P) — LEART
CORNER OF THE FIELD (K-P) — LEART
EDGE OF THE POND (K-P) — LEART
EDGE OF THE WOODS (K-P) — LEART
IN THE GROUND (K-P) — LEART
LIFE SCIENCE - GROWING UP--A SERIES
(K-P) — LEART
LIFE SCIENCE - LIVING SOMEWHERE--A
SERIES (K-P) — LEART
LIVING THINGS NEAR HOME (K-P) — LEART
LIVING THINGS NEAR SCHOOL (K-P) — LEART
PLACES WHERE THINGS LIVE (K-P) — LEART

BASIC LIFE SCIENCE, ANIMALS - GENERAL

(FILMSTRIPS)

ANIMAL KINGDOM--A SERIES — LIFE
ANIMALS — MSCF
ANIMALS TO KNOW - AFRICA, PT 1 (P-I) — BFA
ANIMALS TO KNOW - AFRICA, PT 2 (P-I) — BFA
ANIMALS--A SERIES — MSCF
COLLECTOR, THE — FI
EMBRYOLOGY II - FROG AND CHICK — EGH
WHAT IS IT (TEST SCRIPT) — MSCF
WILDLIFE SANCTUARIES OF INDIA — AVEXP

(MOTION CARTRIDGES)

GRAZING ANIMALS OF AFRICA (P-I) — DOUBLE
HARMFUL INSECTS (P-I) — DOUBLE
KINDS OF EYES (P) — VISED
LIONS HUNTING IMPALA (P-I) — DOUBLE
PLANT AND ANIMAL
INTERDEPENDENCE--A SERIES (P-I) — DOUBLE
SCAVENGERS OF AFRICA (P-I) — DOUBLE

(MOTION PICTURES)

ANIMAL DEVELOPMENT — IWANMI
ANIMAL TEETH — IWANMI
DOGS, CATS AND RABBITS, PT 1 (K-I) — TEXFLM
DOGS, CATS AND RABBITS, PT 2 (K-I) — TEXFLM
DOGS, CATS AND RABBITS, PT 3 (K-I) — TEXFLM
FEET OF ANIMALS — IWANMI

(VIDEOTAPES)

HOW ARE ANIMALS ADAPTED FOR
SURVIVAL (I) — GPITVL
HOW ARE ANIMALS CLASSIFIED (I) — GPITVL

(TRANSPARENCIES)

AMOEBA, THE (I-H) — BOW
ANIMAL CELL TYPES (I-H) — BOW
BABY ANIMALS (K-P) — LEART
BACTERIAL CELL TYPES (I-H) — BOW
EDGE OF THE POND (K-P) — LEART
EDGE OF THE WOODS (K-P) — LEART
EUGLENA, THE (I-H) — BOW
FOSSIL PROTOZOANS (I-H) — BOW
FRESHWATER ALGAE (I-H) — BOW
FRESHWATER PROTOZOANS (I-H) — BOW
IN THE GROUND (K-P) — LEART
LIVING THINGS NEAR HOME (K-P) — LEART
LIVING THINGS NEAR SCHOOL (K-P) — LEART
MICROSCOPIC LIFE--A SERIES (I-H) — BOW
PARAMECIUM, THE (I-H) — BOW
PLACES WHERE THINGS LIVE (K-P) — LEART
PLANT AND ANIMAL CELLS COMPARED
(I-H) — BOW
PLANT CELL TYPES (I-H) — BOW
SMALL POND LIFE (I-H) — BOW

BASIC LIFE SCIENCE, ANIMALS - AMPHIBIANS

(FILMSTRIPS)

DEVELOPMENT OF THE FROG, THE,
PT 1 - MATING OF FROGS (I-H) — CARMAN
DEVELOPMENT OF THE FROG, THE,
PT 2 - GROWTH OF THE
TADPOLE (I-H) — CARMAN

(MOTION CARTRIDGES)

TADPOLE TO TOAD (P-I) — DOUBLE

(TRANSPARENCIES)

FROG - LIFE CYCLE (K-P)   LEART

BASIC LIFE SCIENCE, ANIMALS - BIRDS

(MOTION CARTRIDGES)

AFRICAN BIRDS (P-I) DOUBLE
MEAT EATERS, PT 2--A SERIES (P-I) DOUBLE
MOUNTAIN BIRDS (P-I) DOUBLE
NESTING HABITS OF WATER BIRDS (P-I) DOUBLE
OSPREY - BIRD OF PREY (P-I) DOUBLE
PELICANS (P-I) DOUBLE
SWAMP BIRDS (P-I) DOUBLE
VERTEBRATE CONTRASTS, PT 1--A
SERIES (P-I) DOUBLE
VERTEBRATE CONTRASTS, PT 2--A
SERIES (P-I) DOUBLE
WATER BIRD STRUCTURE FOR
SURVIVAL--A SERIES (P-I) DOUBLE
WATER BIRDS GATHERING FOOD, PT 1
(P-I) DOUBLE
WATER BIRDS GATHERING FOOD, PT 2
(P-I) DOUBLE

(TRANSPARENCIES)

HEN AND CHICKS (K-P) LEART

BASIC LIFE SCIENCE, ANIMALS - FARM

(MOTION PICTURES)

THOSE ANIMALS ON THE FARM (K-P) CLBELL

BASIC LIFE SCIENCE, ANIMALS - FISH

(MOTION CARTRIDGES)

COURTSHIP RITUAL OF STICKLEBACK
FISH (P-I) DOUBLE
JAWFISH (P-I) DOUBLE

(MOTION PICTURES)

BIRTH OF KILLIFISH IWANMI
HOW DO FISH SWIM IWANMI
SCIENCE IN AN AQUARIUM IWANMI
TUNA FROM CATCH TO THE CAN MTP

BASIC LIFE SCIENCE, ANIMALS - HABITATIONS

(FILMSTRIPS)

ANIMAL KINGDOM--A SERIES LIFE
ANIMALS TO KNOW - AFRICA, PT 1 (P-I) BFA
ANIMALS TO KNOW - AFRICA, PT 2 (P-I) BFA
MONKEYS AND APES, PT 1 LIFE
MONKEYS AND APES, PT 2 LIFE

(MOTION CARTRIDGES)

AMERICAN MOUNTAIN ANIMALS (P-I) DOUBLE
BEAVER DAM AND LODGE (P-I) DOUBLE
BOTTLENOSE DOLPHIN (P-I) DOUBLE
CHEETAH HUNTING FOOD (P-I) DOUBLE
COURTSHIP RITUAL OF STICKLEBACK
FISH (P-I) DOUBLE
CRABS (P-I) DOUBLE
DIVING SPIDER (P-I) DOUBLE
LAND ANIMALS--A SERIES (P-I) DOUBLE
LUNGFISH AND OTHER AUSTRALIAN
ANIMALS (P-I) DOUBLE
MANTA AND STING RAYS (P-I) DOUBLE
MOSQUITO - EGGS TO LARVAE (P-I) DOUBLE
NESTING HABITS OF WATER BIRDS (P-I) DOUBLE
NORTH AMERICAN PECCARY (P-I) DOUBLE
OCEAN ANIMALS--A SERIES (P-I) DOUBLE
OCEAN FOOD CHAINS--A SERIES (P-I) DOUBLE
OCTOPUS (P-I) DOUBLE
PLANKTON EATERS (P-I) DOUBLE
POND COMMUNITY--A SERIES (P-I) DOUBLE
SMALL WATER ANIMALS IN PONDS--A
SERIES (P-I) DOUBLE
SPOTTED SKUNK (P-I) DOUBLE
SURVIVAL ON THE CORAL REEF (P-I) DOUBLE
SWAMP ANIMALS UNDERWATER (P-I) DOUBLE
WATER ANIMALS HUNTING FOOD, PT 1
(P-I) DOUBLE
WATER ANIMALS HUNTING FOOD, PT 2
(P-I) DOUBLE
WATER BIRDS GATHERING FOOD, PT 1
(P-I) DOUBLE

(MOTION PICTURES)

FOREST FISHERMAN - STORY OF AN
OTTER ACI
HOW DO FISH SWIM IWANMI

(VIDEOTAPES)

WHAT ANIMALS LIVE IN COMMUNITIES
(I) GPITVL

BASIC LIFE SCIENCE, ANIMALS - HABITS AND BEHAVIOR

(FILMSTRIPS)

ANIMAL KINGDOM--A SERIES LIFE
ANIMALS TO KNOW - AFRICA, PT 1 (P-I) BFA
ANIMALS TO KNOW - AFRICA, PT 2 (P-I) BFA
ANNUAL MIGRATION OF THE
CALIFORNIA GRAY WHALE SDCDE
DEVELOPMENT OF THE FROG, THE,
PT 1 - MATING OF FROGS (I-H) CARMAN
DEVELOPMENT OF THE FROG, THE,
PT 2 - GROWTH OF THE
TADPOLE (I-H) CARMAN
HOW DESERT ANIMALS SURVIVE SED
MONKEYS AND APES, PT 1 LIFE
MONKEYS AND APES, PT 2 LIFE

(MOTION CARTRIDGES)

AFRICAN BIRDS (P-I) DOUBLE
ALLIGATORS HUNTING (P-I) DOUBLE
ANTHILL PROTECTION, PT 1 (SOCIAL
INSECTS) (P-I) DOUBLE
ANTS - TUNNEL BUILDING (P-I) DOUBLE
BEAVER DAM AND LODGE (P-I) DOUBLE
BISON HERDS (P-I) DOUBLE
CARIBOU (P-I) DOUBLE
COURTSHIP RITUAL OF STICKLEBACK
FISH (P-I) DOUBLE
DINOSAURS - MEAT EATERS (P-I) DOUBLE
DINOSAURS - PLANT EATERS (P-I) DOUBLE
DIVING SPIDER (P-I) DOUBLE
DUCKBILLED PLATYPUS - MOTHER AND
BABIES (P-I) DOUBLE
ELEPHANTS FEEDING (P-I) DOUBLE
GIANT LAND TORTOISE (P-I) DOUBLE
GRAZING ANIMALS OF AFRICA (P-I) DOUBLE
INSECTS REPRODUCE--A SERIES (P-I) DOUBLE
JAWFISH (P-I) DOUBLE
KINDS OF EYES (P) VISED
LEAF-CUTTING ANTS (P-I) DOUBLE
LEMMING IN MIGRATION (P-I) DOUBLE
LIFE CYCLE OF THE BUTTERFLY (P-I) DOUBLE
LOCUST REPRODUCTION - NYMPH TO
ADULT (P-I) DOUBLE
LUNGFISH AND OTHER AUSTRALIAN
ANIMALS (P-I) DOUBLE
MARINE IGUANA OF THE GALAPAGOS
ISLANDS (P-I) DOUBLE
MOSQUITO - EGGS TO LARVAE (P-I) DOUBLE
MOSQUITO - LARVA TO ADULT (P-I) DOUBLE
NESTING HABITS OF WATER BIRDS (P-I) DOUBLE
OUT OF THE SEA, ONTO THE LAND--A
SERIES (P-I) DOUBLE
PLANT-EATING ANIMALS (P-I) DOUBLE
POND COMMUNITY--A SERIES (P-I) DOUBLE
QUEEN BEE LAYING EGGS (P-I) DOUBLE
REPTILES--A SERIES (P-I) DOUBLE
SMALL WATER ANIMALS IN PONDS--A
SERIES (P-I) DOUBLE
SOCIAL ANIMALS--A SERIES (P-I) DOUBLE
SOCIAL INSECTS--A SERIES (P-I) DOUBLE
SPIDERS - CAPTURING OF PREY (P-I) DOUBLE
SWAMP ANIMALS UNDERWATER (P-I) DOUBLE
SWAMP BIRDS (P-I) DOUBLE
TADPOLE TO TOAD (P-I) DOUBLE
TOAD SURVIVAL ADAPTATIONS (P-I) DOUBLE
UNUSUAL INSTINCTS--A SERIES (P-I) DOUBLE
VERTEBRATE CONTRASTS, PT 2--A
SERIES (P-I) DOUBLE
WATER ANIMALS HUNTING FOOD, PT 2
(P-I) DOUBLE
WATER BIRD STRUCTURE FOR
SURVIVAL--A SERIES (P-I) DOUBLE
WATER BIRDS GATHERING FOOD, PT 1
(P-I) DOUBLE
WATER BIRDS GATHERING FOOD, PT 2
(P-I) DOUBLE

(MOTION PICTURES)

BIRTH OF KILLIFISH IWANMI
DRAGONFLIES IWANMI
HOW DO FISH SWIM IWANMI
INSECTS, OBSERVATION AND
COLLECTION IWANMI
RIVER OTTER (P-J) AMEDFL
SINGING INSECTS OF AUTUMN IWANMI
STARFISH'S REALM, THE WHTCAP
STORY OF RESPIRATION IWANMI
SYMBIOSIS (J-H) BFA
WHITE MANE CCMFI

(VIDEOTAPES)

WHAT ANIMALS LIVE IN COMMUNITIES
(I) GPITVL
WHAT ARE SOME SPECIAL FORMS OF
BEHAVIOR (I) GPITVL

BASIC LIFE SCIENCE, ANIMALS - INSECTS

(FILMSTRIPS)

COLLECTOR, THE FI

(MOTION CARTRIDGES)

ANTHILL PROTECTION, PT 1
(INVERTEBRATES, PT 2) (P-I) DOUBLE
ANTHILL PROTECTION, PT 1 (SOCIAL
ANIMALS) (P-I) DOUBLE
ANTHILL PROTECTION, PT 1 (SOCIAL
INSECTS) (P-I) DOUBLE
ANTS - TUNNEL BUILDING (P-I) DOUBLE
CENTIPEDES, MILLIPEDES AND
SCORPIONS (P-I) DOUBLE
DIVING SPIDER (P-I) DOUBLE
HARMFUL INSECTS (P-I) DOUBLE
HELPFUL INSECTS (P-I) DOUBLE
HUNTER ANTS (P-I) DOUBLE
INSECTS ARE MUCH ALIKE--A SERIES (P-
I) DOUBLE
INSECTS REPRODUCE--A SERIES (P-I) DOUBLE
INVERTEBRATES, PT 1--A SERIES (P-I) DOUBLE
INVERTEBRATES, PT 2--A SERIES (P-I) DOUBLE
LEAF-CUTTING ANTS (P-I) DOUBLE
LIFE CYCLE OF THE BUTTERFLY (P-I) DOUBLE
LOCUST REPRODUCTION - NYMPH TO
ADULT (P-I) DOUBLE
LOCUST STRUCTURES - EXTERNAL (P-I) DOUBLE
MEAT EATERS, PT 2--A SERIES (P-I) DOUBLE
MOSQUITO - EGGS TO LARVAE (P-I) DOUBLE
MOSQUITO - LARVA TO ADULT (P-I) DOUBLE
MOSQUITO STRUCTURES - EXTERNAL
(P-I) DOUBLE
QUEEN BEE LAYING EGGS (P-I) DOUBLE
RAISING A QUEEN BEE (P-I) DOUBLE
SOCIAL INSECTS--A SERIES (P-I) DOUBLE
SPIDER WASP, PT 1 (P-I) DOUBLE
SPIDERS - CAPTURING OF PREY (P-I) DOUBLE

(MOTION PICTURES)

DRAGONFLIES IWANMI
EYES OF INSECTS IWANMI
INSECTS, OBSERVATION AND
COLLECTION IWANMI
SINGING INSECTS OF AUTUMN IWANMI

(TRANSPARENCIES)

INSECT LIFE CYCLE (K-P) LEART

BASIC LIFE SCIENCE, ANIMALS - MAMMALS

(FILMSTRIPS)

ANNUAL MIGRATION OF THE
CALIFORNIA GRAY WHALE SDCDE
BROWN BAT, THE MSCF
ELEPHANT SEAL, THE MSCF
ELEPHANT, THE MSCF
GIRAFFE, THE MSCF
GORILLA, THE MSCF
LION, THE MSCF
PLATYPUS, THE MSCF
POLAR BEAR, THE MSCF

(MOTION CARTRIDGES)

AMERICAN MOUNTAIN ANIMALS (P-I) DOUBLE
ARCTIC MUSK OX (P-I) DOUBLE
BEAVER DAM AND LODGE (P-I) DOUBLE
BISON HERDS (P-I) DOUBLE
BOTTLENOSE DOLPHIN (P-I) DOUBLE
CARIBOU (P-I) DOUBLE
CHEETAH HUNTING FOOD (P-I) DOUBLE
DUCKBILLED PLATYPUS - MOTHER AND
BABIES (P-I) DOUBLE
ELEPHANTS FEEDING (P-I) DOUBLE
LAND ANIMALS--A SERIES (P-I) DOUBLE
LEMMING IN MIGRATION (P-I) DOUBLE
LEOPARD HUNTING FOOD (P-I) DOUBLE
LIONS HUNTING IMPALA (P-I) DOUBLE
MEAT EATERS, PT 1--A SERIES (P-I) DOUBLE
MEAT EATERS, PT 2--A SERIES (P-I) DOUBLE
NORTH AMERICAN PECCARY (P-I) DOUBLE
PRIDE OF LIONS (P-I) DOUBLE
SPOTTED SKUNK (P-I) DOUBLE
VERTEBRATE CONTRASTS, PT 1--A
SERIES (P-I) DOUBLE
VERTEBRATE CONTRASTS, PT 2--A
SERIES (P-I) DOUBLE
WOLVES HUNTING (P-I) DOUBLE

(MOTION PICTURES)

ABOUT CATS (P-J) METROM
FOREST FISHERMAN - STORY OF AN
OTTER ACI

BASIC LIFE SCIENCE, ANIMALS - PETS

(MOTION PICTURES)

ABOUT CATS (P-J) METROM
CARNIVAL, THE - THE STORY OF A
GIRL AND A GOLDFISH (P) XEROX
DOGS, CATS AND RABBITS, PT 1 (K-I) TEXFLM
DOGS, CATS AND RABBITS, PT 2 (K-I) TEXFLM
DOGS, CATS AND RABBITS, PT 3 (K-I) TEXFLM

INTERMEDIATE (COMPANION DOGS) (J-C A)   AMERFI
LABRADORS IN TRAINING (J-C A)   AMERFI
LABRADORS, LAND RETRIEVING (J-C A)   AMERFI
LABRADORS, WATER RETRIEVING (J-C A)   AMERFI
NOVICE COMPANION (J-C A)   AMERFI
SLED DOGS - ALASKAN HUSKY (J-C A)   AMERFI
SLED DOGS - BIG-TIME TEAM (J-C A)   AMERFI
SLED DOGS - RACING (J-C A)   AMERFI
TUB FILM (J-C A)   BFA
UTILITY DOGS (J-C A)   AMERFI
WONDERFUL WORLD OF SPORT - DOGS- -A SERIES (J-C A)   AMERFI

BASIC LIFE SCIENCE, ANIMALS - REPTILES

(MOTION CARTRIDGES)

ALLIGATORS HUNTING (P-I)   DOUBLE
DINOSAURS - MEAT EATERS (P-I)   DOUBLE
DINOSAURS - PLANT EATERS (P-I)   DOUBLE
GIANT LAND TORTOISE (P-I)   DOUBLE
MARINE IGUANA OF THE GALAPAGOS ISLANDS (P-I)   DOUBLE
MEAT EATERS, PT 1--A SERIES (P-I)   DOUBLE
REPTILES--A SERIES (P-I)   DOUBLE
SNAKES OF THE AMAZON (P-I)   DOUBLE
TOAD SURVIVAL ADAPTATIONS (P-I)   DOUBLE
VERTEBRATE CONTRASTS, PT 1--A SERIES (P-I)   DOUBLE
VERTEBRATE CONTRASTS, PT 2--A SERIES (P-I)   DOUBLE

(MOTION PICTURES)

STORY OF RESPIRATION   IWANMI

BASIC LIFE SCIENCE, ANIMALS - SEA ANIMALS

(MOTION CARTRIDGES)

ANIMAL LIFE IN A DROP OF WATER (INVERTEBRATES (P-I)   DOUBLE
BOTTLENOSE DOLPHIN (P-I)   DOUBLE
CRABS (P-I)   DOUBLE
ECHINODERMS AND SEA SQUIRTS (P-I)   DOUBLE
HERMIT CRABS (P-I)   DOUBLE
INVERTEBRATES, PT 1--A SERIES (P-I)   DOUBLE
INVERTEBRATES, PT 2--A SERIES (P-I)   DOUBLE
MANTA AND STING RAYS (P-I)   DOUBLE
MARINE IGUANA OF THE GALAPAGOS ISLANDS (P-I)   DOUBLE
MEAT EATERS, PT 2--A SERIES (P-I)   DOUBLE
OCEAN ANIMALS--A SERIES (P-I)   DOUBLE
OCEAN FOOD CHAINS--A SERIES (P-I)   DOUBLE
OCTOPUS (P-I)   DOUBLE
PLANKTON EATERS (P-I)   DOUBLE
SALT WATER INVERTEBRATES--A SERIES (P-I)   DOUBLE
SEA ANIMALS OF THE SHALLOWS--A SERIES (P-I)   DOUBLE
SEA SLUGS (P-I)   DOUBLE
SURVIVAL ON THE CORAL REEF (P-I)   DOUBLE
TIDEPOOL LIFE, PT 1 (P-I)   DOUBLE

(MOTION PICTURES)

LIFE ON THE REEF   IWANMI
STARFISH'S REALM, THE   WHTCAP

BASIC LIFE SCIENCE, ANIMALS - ZOO

(FILMSTRIPS)

ANIMAL KINGDOM--A SERIES   LIFE
ANIMALS TO KNOW - AFRICA, PT 1 (P-I)   BFA
ANIMALS TO KNOW - AFRICA, PT 2 (P-I)   BFA
ELEPHANT, THE   MSCF
GIRAFFE, THE   MSCF
GORILLA, THE   MSCF
LION, THE   MSCF
MONKEYS AND APES, PT 1   LIFE
MONKEYS AND APES, PT 2   LIFE
PLATYPUS, THE   MSCF
POLAR BEAR, THE   MSCF

BASIC LIFE SCIENCE, HUMAN BODY - GENERAL

(MOTION PICTURES)

FACES (K-P)   SCHLAT
MUSCLE - A STUDY OF INTEGRATION   CRMP

(TRANSPARENCIES)

SKIN (H)   BOW
TEETH COME AND GO (K-P)   LEART

BASIC LIFE SCIENCE, HUMAN BODY - BONES AND MUSCLES

(FILMSTRIPS)

MUSCLE - PHYSIOLOGICAL CHARACTERISTICS (H-C A)   HRAW

(MOTION PICTURES)

BIOLOGY TODAY FILM--A SERIES   CRMP
LIVING BONE, THE   IWANMI
MUSCLE - A STUDY OF INTEGRATION   CRMP
SCIENCE OF FOOTWEAR, THE   IWANMI

(TRANSPARENCIES)

BONE JOINTS (H)   BOW
SKELETAL SYSTEM (H)   BOW
TEETH COME AND GO (K-P)   LEART

BASIC LIFE SCIENCE, HUMAN BODY - DIGESTION

(TRANSPARENCIES)

DIGESTIVE SYSTEM (H)   BOW

BASIC LIFE SCIENCE, HUMAN BODY - EARS

(TRANSPARENCIES)

EAR (H)   BOW

BASIC LIFE SCIENCE, HUMAN BODY - EYES

(TRANSPARENCIES)

EYE (H)   BOW
VISION DEFECTS (H)   BOW

BASIC LIFE SCIENCE, HUMAN BODY - GROWTH AND DEVELOPMENT

(TRANSPARENCIES)

BABY AND ME (K-P)   LEART
BABY FOR A YEAR (K-P)   LEART
DAD AND ME (K-P)   LEART
FAMILY OF CHILDREN (K-P)   LEART
FAVORITE THINGS (K-P)   LEART
FOOD, FUN, REST (K-P)   LEART
HOW HEAVY (K-P)   LEART
HOW TALL (K-P)   LEART
MANY COLORS (K-P)   LEART
MANY FEET (K-P)   LEART
MANY HANDS (K-P)   LEART
MOM AND ME (K-P)   LEART

BASIC LIFE SCIENCE, HUMAN BODY - HEART AND CIRCULATION

(MOTION PICTURES)

HEART, THE - ATTACK   CRMP

(TRANSPARENCIES)

CIRCULATORY SYSTEM (H)   BOW
HEART (H)   BOW

BASIC LIFE SCIENCE, HUMAN BODY - NERVOUS SYSTEM

(FILMSTRIPS)

INTRODUCTION TO THE NEUROSCIENCES, AN   SAUNDW

(VIDEOTAPES)

EXTENDING OUR SENSES (I)   GPITVL
HOW DO YOU KNOW (I)   GPITVL

(TRANSPARENCIES)

NERVOUS SYSTEM (H)   BOW

BASIC LIFE SCIENCE, HUMAN BODY - RESPIRATION

(TRANSPARENCIES)

RESPIRATORY SYSTEM (H)   BOW

BASIC LIFE SCIENCE, HUMAN BODY - TEETH

(FILMSTRIPS)

MEET YOUR TEETH (P-I)   DISNEY
PRACTICING GOOD HEALTH, SET 2 - YOUR MOUTH SPEAKING--A SERIES (P-I)   DISNEY
TALE OF TWO TEETH, A (P-I)   DISNEY

(TRANSPARENCIES)

MOM AND ME (K-P)   LEART
TEETH COME AND GO (K-P)   LEART
TOOTH STRUCTURE (H)   BOW

BASIC LIFE SCIENCE, PLANTS - GENERAL

(MOTION CARTRIDGES)

GLUTEN DEVELOPMENT   IOWA
HARMFUL INSECTS (P-I)   DOUBLE
LIONS HUNTING IMPALA (P-I)   DOUBLE
PLANT AND ANIMAL INTERDEPENDENCE--A SERIES (P-I)   DOUBLE
SCAVENGERS OF AFRICA (P-I)   DOUBLE

(MOTION PICTURES)

GROWTH OF PLANTS   IWANMI
STORY OF MUSHROOMS   IWANMI
STORY OF POLLEN   IWANMI
SUNFLOWER, THE   IWANMI
VEGETABLE CELLS   IWANMI
WONDERS OF THE CACTUS   IWANMI

(VIDEOTAPES)

EXPLORING PLANTS (I)   GPITVL
HOW ARE GREEN PLANTS ALIKE (I)   GPITVL
HOW ARE NON-GREEN PLANTS ALIKE (I)   GPITVL
HOW ARE PLANTS CLASSIFIED (I)   GPITVL

(TRANSPARENCIES)

CHARACTERISTIC OF DECIDUOUS TREES (H)   BOW
CLASSIFICATION (H)   BOW
CORN (K-P)   LEART
EVERGREEN IDENTIFICATION (H)   BOW
FERTILIZATION (H)   BOW
GERMINATION (H)   BOW
GRAFTING (H)   BOW
HEREDITY (H)   BOW
LEAF IDENTIFICATION (H)   BOW
LEAF STRUCTURE (H)   BOW
MOLD (H)   BOW
MUSHROOM (H)   BOW
PHOTOSYNTHESIS (H)   BOW
PLANT CELL (H)   BOW
PLANT TRANSPIRATION (H)   BOW
PLANTING BULBS AND TUBERS (H)   BOW
PLANTS--A SERIES (H)   BOW
TERRARIUM CONSTRUCTION (H)   BOW
TREE BUDS (H)   BOW
TREE TRUNK STRUCTURE (H)   BOW

BASIC LIFE SCIENCE, PLANTS - FLOWERS

(MOTION CARTRIDGES)

DESERT FLOWERS (P-I)   DOUBLE
FLOWERS OPENING (P-I)   DOUBLE

(MOTION PICTURES)

STORY OF POLLEN   IWANMI
SUNFLOWER, THE   IWANMI

BASIC LIFE SCIENCE, PLANTS - GROWTH AND DEVELOPMENT

(FILMSTRIPS)

FAMILY OF TREES, THE (P-J)   TERF
GROWING THINGS--A SERIES (P-J)   TERF
HOW PLANTS GROW (P-J)   TERF
JUNGLE AND DESERT PLANTS (P-J)   TERF
PLANT LIFE IN THE WATERS (P-J)   TERF
PRAIRIE AND MOUNTAIN PLANTS (P-J)   TERF
RARE AND EXOTIC PLANTS (P-J)   TERF

(MOTION CARTRIDGES)

AMAZON JUNGLE (P-I)   DOUBLE
CARNIVOROUS PLANTS (P-I)   DOUBLE
DESERT FLOWERS (P-I)   DOUBLE
DESERT PLANTS (P-I)   DOUBLE
FLOWERS OPENING (P-I)   DOUBLE
FRESH WATER ALGAE (P-I)   DOUBLE
FRUIT RIPENING (P-I)   DOUBLE
MOUNTAINS (P-I)   DOUBLE
PLANTS GROW IN MANY PLACES--A SERIES (P-I)   DOUBLE
PLANTS GROWING--A SERIES (P-I)   DOUBLE

(MOTION PICTURES)

GROWTH OF PLANTS   IWANMI
PERFORMANCE OF ROOTS, STEMS AND LEAVES   IWANMI
STORY OF MUSHROOMS   IWANMI
VEGETABLE CELLS   IWANMI
WHAT DO SEEDS NEED TO SPROUT (P)   CORF

(TRANSPARENCIES)

BEANS - BLOOM AND SEED (K-P)   LEART
BLOOM TO FRUIT (K-P)   LEART

BASIC LIFE SCIENCE, PLANTS - LEAVES, ROOTS, STEMS

(MOTION PICTURES)

CACTUS, THE - ADAPTATIONS FOR
SURVIVAL (I-J)   EBEC
PERFORMANCE OF ROOTS, STEMS AND
LEAVES   IWANMI

(TRANSPARENCIES)

BEANS - BLOOM AND SEED (K-P)   LEART
LEAF IDENTIFICATION (H)   BOW
LEAF STRUCTURE (H)   BOW

BASIC LIFE SCIENCE, PLANTS - PROCESSES

(FILMSTRIPS)

FAMILY OF TREES, THE (P-J)   TERF
GROWING THINGS--A SERIES (P-J)   TERF
HOW PLANTS GROW (P-J)   TERF
JUNGLE AND DESERT PLANTS (P-J)   TERF
PLANT LIFE IN THE WATERS (P-J)   TERF
PRAIRIE AND MOUNTAIN PLANTS (P-J)   TERF
RARE AND EXOTIC PLANTS (P-J)   TERF

(MOTION CARTRIDGES)

PLANTS REPRODUCE--A SERIES (P-I)   DOUBLE
SEED DISPERSAL (P-I)   DOUBLE
SEEDS SPROUTING (P-I)   DOUBLE
SELF-PLANTING SEEDS (P-I)   DOUBLE

(MOTION PICTURES)

CACTUS, THE - ADAPTATIONS FOR
SURVIVAL (I-J)   EBEC
SYMBIOSIS (J-H)   BFA
WHAT DO SEEDS NEED TO SPROUT (P)   CORF
WONDERS OF THE CACTUS   IWANMI

(VIDEOTAPES)

WHAT GREEN PLANTS REPRODUCE BY
OTHER MEANS (I)   GPITVL
WHAT GREEN PLANTS REPRODUCE BY
SEEDS (I)   GPITVL

(TRANSPARENCIES)

FERTILIZATION (H)   BOW
GERMINATION (H)   BOW
PHOTOSYNTHESIS (H)   BOW
PLANT TRANSPIRATION (H)   BOW

BASIC LIFE SCIENCE, PLANTS - SEEDS

(MOTION CARTRIDGES)

SEED DISPERSAL (P-I)   DOUBLE
SEEDS SPROUTING (P-I)   DOUBLE
SELF-PLANTING SEEDS (P-I)   DOUBLE

(MOTION PICTURES)

MECHANISMS OF SCATTERING SEEDS   IWANMI
WHAT DO SEEDS NEED TO SPROUT (P)   CORF

(VIDEOTAPES)

WHAT GREEN PLANTS REPRODUCE BY
SEEDS (I)   GPITVL

(TRANSPARENCIES)

BEANS - BLOOM AND SEED (K-P)   LEART
LIFE SCIENCE - COMING TO LIFE--A
SERIES (K-P)   LEART
SEEDS IN FRUIT, VEGETABLES (K-P)   LEART

BASIC LIFE SCIENCE, PLANTS - TREES

(FILMSTRIPS)

FAMILY OF TREES, THE (P-J)   TERF

(MOTION PICTURES)

CELEBRATION OF LIFE - TREES (P-I)   BFA

(TRANSPARENCIES)

CHARACTERISTIC OF DECIDUOUS TREES
(H)   BOW
EVERGREEN IDENTIFICATION (H)   BOW
TREE BUDS (H)   BOW
TREE TRUNK STRUCTURE (H)   BOW

BASIC LIFE SCIENCE, SEASONS

(MOTION PICTURES)

AQUA SUMMER (I-C A)   NWFCMP
CELEBRATION OF LIFE - TREES (P-I)   BFA
TUNE INTO NATURE (I-C A)   NVFP

BIOLOGY, BIOCHEMISTRY

(FILMSTRIPS)

A-V LECTURES IN BIOLOGY   SAUNDW
ADAPTATIONS FOR LIFE   EGH
ENERGY AND LIFE   EGH
LIFE - A UNIQUE PHENOMENON--A
SERIES   EGH
PERPETUATING LIFE   EGH
WHAT IS LIFE   EGH

(MOTION PICTURES)

BIOENGINEERS, THE   USNAC

BIOLOGY, BOTANY - GENERAL

(FILMSTRIPS)

ALGAE AND FUNGI   EGH
GROUND COVERS AND THEIR USES (H-
C)   UILVAS
MOSSES AND FERNS   EGH
ROOTS, STEMS AND LEAVES - DICOTS   EGH
ROOTS, STEMS AND LEAVES -
MONOCOTS   EGH

(MOTION PICTURES)

WATER IN THE WILDERNESS (I-C A)   CLBELL

(TRANSPARENCIES)

CHARACTERISTIC OF DECIDUOUS TREES
(H)   BOW
CLASSIFICATION (H)   BOW
EVERGREEN IDENTIFICATION (H)   BOW
FERTILIZATION (H)   BOW
GERMINATION (H)   BOW
GRAFTING (H)   BOW
HEREDITY (H)   BOW
LEAF IDENTIFICATION (H)   BOW
LEAF STRUCTURE (H)   BOW
MOLD (H)   BOW
MUSHROOM (H)   BOW
PHOTOSYNTHESIS (H)   BOW
PLANT CELL (H)   BOW
PLANT CELL TYPES (I-H)   BOW
PLANT TRANSPIRATION (H)   BOW
PLANTING BULBS AND TUBERS (H)   BOW
PLANTS--A SERIES (H)   BOW
TERRARIUM CONSTRUCTION (H)   BOW
TREE BUDS (H)   BOW
TREE TRUNK STRUCTURE (H)   BOW

BIOLOGY, BOTANY - FUNGI AND MOLDS

(FILMSTRIPS)

ALGAE AND FUNGI   EGH

(MOTION PICTURES)

ROLE OF YEAST   IWANMI
STORY OF MUSHROOMS   IWANMI

(TRANSPARENCIES)

MOLD (H)   BOW
MUSHROOM (H)   BOW

BIOLOGY, BOTANY - LEAVES, ROOTS, STEMS

(FILMSTRIPS)

ROOTS, STEMS AND LEAVES -
MONOCOTS   EGH

(MOTION PICTURES)

PERFORMANCE OF ROOTS, STEMS AND
LEAVES   IWANMI

BIOLOGY, BOTANY - LIFE CYCLES

(MOTION PICTURES)

STORY OF POLLEN   IWANMI
VEGETABLE CELLS   IWANMI

(TRANSPARENCIES)

LIFE SCIENCE - COMING TO LIFE--A
SERIES (K-P)   LEART

BIOLOGY, BOTANY - PROCESSES

(MOTION PICTURES)

CACTUS, THE - ADAPTATIONS FOR
SURVIVAL (I-J)   EBEC
SUNFLOWER, THE   IWANMI
SYMBIOSIS (J-H)   BFA

BIOLOGY, BOTANY - TYPES OF PLANTS

(FILMSTRIPS)

MOSSES AND FERNS   EGH
ROOTS, STEMS AND LEAVES - DICOTS   EGH
ROOTS, STEMS AND LEAVES -
MONOCOTS   EGH

(MOTION PICTURES)

CACTUS, THE - ADAPTATIONS FOR
SURVIVAL (I-J)   EBEC
WONDERS OF THE CACTUS   IWANMI

BIOLOGY, CELLULAR

(FILMSTRIPS)

HUMAN HISTOLOGY - SYSTEMS   EGH
HUMAN HISTOLOGY - TISSUE   EGH
METHOD, ASSESSMENT AND
EVALUATION   EGH
PROTOZOA   EGH

(MOTION CARTRIDGES)

ANIMAL LIFE IN A DROP OF
   WATER (LIFE IN SINGLE CELLS)
   (P-I)   DOUBLE
FRESH WATER MICROORGANISMS (P-I)   DOUBLE
LIFE IN SINGLE CELLS--A SERIES (P-I) DOUBLE
MICROSCOPIC ANIMALS - PROTOZOA (P-
I)   DOUBLE
MICROSCOPIC WATER ANIMALS (P-I)   DOUBLE

(MOTION PICTURES)

BIOLOGY TODAY FILM--A SERIES   CRMP
LIVING CELL, THE (J-C A)   HAR
VEGETABLE CELLS   IWANMI

BIOLOGY, ECOLOGY - GENERAL

(FILMSTRIPS)

AGRICULTURE AND THE ECOSYSTEM (H-
C)   UILVAS
AIR POLLUTION, PT 1 - LOCAL
   CONTINENTAL AND NATURAL   CARMAN
PRINCESS ECOL VISITS THE PLANET
THRAE   EGH

(MOTION PICTURES)

INTERVIEW WITH GARRETT HARDIN (J-C
A)   HRAW
NATURE'S EVER CHANGING
COMMUNITIES (I-J)   JOU
RECYCLED REFLECTIONS (I-C A)   FLMFR

(VIDEOTAPES)

HOW ARE ANIMALS ADAPTED FOR
SURVIVAL (I)   GPITVL
SCIENCE IS DISCOVERY--A SERIES (I)   GPITVL

(TRANSPARENCIES)

CONSERVATION--A SERIES (H)   BOW

BIOLOGY, ECOLOGY - ADAPTATION

(FILMSTRIPS)

ADAPTATIONS FOR LIFE   EGH
EQUATORIAL FORESTS   CARMAN

(MOTION CARTRIDGES)

TOAD SURVIVAL ADAPTATIONS (P-I)   DOUBLE

(MOTION PICTURES)

CACTUS, THE - ADAPTATIONS FOR
SURVIVAL (I-J)   EBEC

(VIDEOTAPES)

WHAT ARE SOME SPECIAL FORMS OF
BEHAVIOR (I)   GPITVL

SCIENCE - NATURAL

BIOLOGY, ECOLOGY - AIR POLLUTION

(FILMSTRIPS)

AIR POLLUTION, PT 1 - LOCAL CONTINENTAL AND NATURAL	CARMAN
LOS ANGELES - CITY OF AUTOMOBILES (J-H A)	SVE

BIOLOGY, ECOLOGY - BIRDS

(MOTION PICTURES)

SCENES OF NATURAL RESERVE	ALDEN

BIOLOGY, ECOLOGY - DESERT

(FILMSTRIPS)

BALANCE OF LIFE IN A DESERT	SED
DESERT LIFE--A SERIES	SED
HOW DESERT ANIMALS SURVIVE	SED

(MOTION CARTRIDGES)

DESERT PLANTS (P-I)	DOUBLE
DESERT, THE (I-J)	HESTER

BIOLOGY, ECOLOGY - ENVIRONMENT

(FILMSTRIPS)

ADAPTATIONS FOR LIFE	EGH
AGRICULTURE AND THE ECOSYSTEM (H-C)	UILVAS
AIR POLLUTION, PT 1 - LOCAL CONTINENTAL AND NATURAL	CARMAN
BALANCE OF LIFE IN A DESERT	SED
BONNEVILLE DAM - POWERHOUSE OF THE COLUMBIA RIVER (J-H A)	SVE
CONCRETE CHARLEY DUMPLING	COMICO
DESERT LIFE--A SERIES	SED
ENERGY CRISIS, THE - REPORT FROM PLANET 32 (I)	TERF
HOW DESERT ANIMALS SURVIVE	SED
PRINCESS ECOL VISITS THE PLANET THRAE	EGH

(MOTION PICTURES)

DEPENDENCE - A NEW DEFINITION (C A)	CRMP
ERTS - EARTH RESOURCES TECHNOLOGY SATELLITE (J-C A)	NASA
NATURE'S EVER CHANGING COMMUNITIES (I-J)	JOU
PARK ON OUR BLOCK, A (J-C A)	WASHBF
STARFISH'S REALM, THE	WHTCAP
SURVIVAL OF SPACESHIP EARTH	WB
THIS IS CAMPING (I-C A)	IU
VOICES FROM MAINE (J-C A)	POLYMR
WE THE ENEMY	FENWCK

(VIDEOTAPES)

HOW IS BALANCE IN AN ENVIRONMENT MAINTAINED (I)	GPITVL
WHAT HAPPENS WHEN ENVIRONMENTAL CONDITIONS ARE ALTERED (I)	GPITVL
WHERE ARE LIVING THINGS FOUND (I)	GPITVL

(TRANSPARENCIES)

AT THE BEACH (K-P)	LEART
CORNER OF THE FIELD (K-P)	LEART
EDGE OF THE POND (K-P)	LEART
EDGE OF THE WOODS (K-P)	LEART
IN THE GROUND (K-P)	LEART
LIFE SCIENCE - LIVING SOMEWHERE--A SERIES (K-P)	LEART
LIVING THINGS NEAR HOME (K-P)	LEART
LIVING THINGS NEAR SCHOOL (K-P)	LEART
PLACES WHERE THINGS LIVE (K-P)	LEART

BIOLOGY, ECOLOGY - FOREST

(FILMSTRIPS)

EQUATORIAL FORESTS	CARMAN
RAIN FORESTS OF THE NORTHWEST COAST	UWASHP
TIMBER - WASHINGTON'S MOST VALUABLE CROP (J-H A)	SVE

(MOTION PICTURES)

ENEMY IS FIRE, THE (J-C A)	RARIG
FIRE WEATHER (J-C A)	RARIG
FOREST FIRE PROTECTION--A SERIES (J-C A)	RARIG
FOREST FISHERMAN - STORY OF AN OTTER	ACI

BIOLOGY, ECOLOGY - MARINE

(FILMSTRIPS)

SEA, THE - DEPOSITION (I-H)	VISPUB
SEA, THE - EROSION (I-H)	VISPUB

(MOTION CARTRIDGES)

OCEAN FOOD CHAINS--A SERIES (P-I)	DOUBLE

(MOTION PICTURES)

BATHYMETRY - DISCOVERING THE OCEAN FLOOR - CHARTING THE OCEAN FLOOR	AIMS
BEACH INTELLIGENCE - WAVES, BREAKERS AND SURF	AIMS
LIFE AND HEALTH FILM--A SERIES	CRMP
LIFE ON THE SAND BEACH	IWANMI
OCEAN PHENOMENON - THE DEEP SCATTERING LAYER	USNAC
SCIENCE IN AN AQUARIUM	IWANMI
STARFISH'S REALM, THE	WHTCAP

(TRANSPARENCIES)

ANIMALS OF THE DEEP (I-H)	BOW
ANIMALS OF THE OPEN OCEAN (I-H)	BOW
DIVISIONS OF THE OCEAN (I-H)	BOW
FOOD WEB (I-H)	BOW
ISLAND AND CORAL REEF FORMATION (I-H)	BOW
MAN IN THE OCEAN (I-H)	BOW
OCEAN CURRENTS (I-H)	BOW
OCEANOGRAPHY--A SERIES (I-H)	BOW
PLANKTON (I-H)	BOW
SEASHORE LIFE - COLD ROCKY SHORES (I-H)	BOW
SEASHORE LIFE - TEMPERATE MARSHY SHORES (I-H)	BOW
SEASHORE LIFE - WARM SANDY SHORES (I-H)	BOW
SUBMARINE GEOLOGY (I-H)	BOW
TOOLS OF THE OCEANOGRAPHER (I-H)	BOW

BIOLOGY, ECOLOGY - NATURAL RESOURCES CONSERVATION

(MOTION PICTURES)

ERTS - EARTH RESOURCES TECHNOLOGY SATELLITE (J-C A)	NASA
INTERVIEW WITH GARRETT HARDIN (J-C A)	HRAW
WATER IN THE WILDERNESS (I-C A)	CLBELL

(TRANSPARENCIES)

CONSERVATION--A SERIES (H)	BOW
EROSION (H)	BOW
FLOODING (H)	BOW
FOREST FIRE (H)	BOW
NATURAL RESOURCES (H)	BOW
POLLUTION (H)	BOW
SOIL DEPLETION (H)	BOW

BIOLOGY, ECOLOGY - NOISE POLLUTION

(MOTION PICTURES)

NOISE AND ITS EFFECTS ON HEALTH (J-C A)	FLMFR
QUIET, PLEASE	WILCOX

BIOLOGY, ECOLOGY - PLANTS AND ANIMALS

(MOTION CARTRIDGES)

HARMFUL INSECTS (P-I)	DOUBLE
LIONS HUNTING IMPALA (P-I)	DOUBLE
PLANT AND ANIMAL INTERDEPENDENCE--A SERIES (P-I)	DOUBLE
SCAVENGERS OF AFRICA (P-I)	DOUBLE

(MOTION PICTURES)

LIVING CELL, THE (J-C A)	HAR
SCENES OF NATURAL RESERVE	ALDEN
SYMBIOSIS (J-H)	BFA

(VIDEOTAPES)

HOW IS BALANCE IN AN ENVIRONMENT MAINTAINED (I)	GPITVL
WHAT HAPPENS WHEN ENVIRONMENTAL CONDITIONS ARE ALTERED (I)	GPITVL

(TRANSPARENCIES)

PLANT AND ANIMAL CELLS COMPARED (I-H)	BOW

BIOLOGY, ECOLOGY - POND AND MARSH

(MOTION CARTRIDGES)

BEAVER DAM AND LODGE (P-I)	DOUBLE
COURTSHIP RITUAL OF STICKLEBACK FISH (P-I)	DOUBLE
DIVING SPIDER (P-I)	DOUBLE
MOSQUITO - EGGS TO LARVAE (P-I)	DOUBLE
NESTING HABITS OF WATER BIRDS (P-I)	DOUBLE
POND COMMUNITY--A SERIES (P-I)	DOUBLE
SMALL WATER ANIMALS IN PONDS--A SERIES (P-I)	DOUBLE
SWAMP ANIMALS UNDERWATER (P-I)	DOUBLE
WATER ANIMALS HUNTING FOOD, PT 2 (P-I)	DOUBLE
WATER BIRDS GATHERING FOOD, PT 1 (P-I)	DOUBLE

(MOTION PICTURES)

OZE SWAMP	IWANMI
STORY OF THE PLANKTON	IWANMI

(VIDEOTAPES)

WHAT IS IN A POND (I)	GPITVL

(TRANSPARENCIES)

SMALL POND LIFE (I-H)	BOW

BIOLOGY, ECOLOGY - POPULATION

(MOTION PICTURES)

POPULATION EXPANSION AND BIRTH CONTROL (H-C A)	CHM

BIOLOGY, ECOLOGY - RECYCLING

(MOTION PICTURES)

RECYCLED REFLECTIONS (I-C A)	FLMFR

BIOLOGY, ECOLOGY - SOIL CONSERVATION

(AUDIO TAPES)

SYLVANIA STORY, THE (H A)	USOE

(TRANSPARENCIES)

CONSERVATION--A SERIES (H)	BOW
EROSION (H)	BOW
FLOODING (H)	BOW
FOREST FIRE (H)	BOW
NATURAL RESOURCES (H)	BOW
POLLUTION (H)	BOW
SOIL DEPLETION (H)	BOW

BIOLOGY, ECOLOGY - URBANIZATION ENVIRONMENT

(MOTION PICTURES)

ABANDONMENT OF THE CITIES, THE (J-C A)	NBCTV
FROM CAVE TO CITY (I-C)	FLMFR

BIOLOGY, ECOLOGY - WATER SUPPLY

(FILMSTRIPS)

HOW DESERT ANIMALS SURVIVE	SED

(MOTION PICTURES)

ISRAEL'S NATIONAL WATER CARRIER	ALDEN
ISRAEL'S QUEST FOR WATER	ALDEN
WATER IN THE WILDERNESS (I-C A)	CLBELL
WATER SMITH	AMERFI

(VIDEOTAPES)

WHAT IS THE WATER CYCLE (I)	GPITVL

BIOLOGY, EVOLUTION

(FILMSTRIPS)

ADAPTATIONS FOR LIFE	EGH
ENERGY AND LIFE	EGH
LIFE - A UNIQUE PHENOMENON--A SERIES	EGH
PERPETUATING LIFE	EGH
WHAT IS LIFE	EGH

(MOTION CARTRIDGES)

DINOSAURS - MEAT EATERS (P-I)	DOUBLE

LUNGFISH AND OTHER AUSTRALIAN
ANIMALS (P-I)   DOUBLE
MARINE IGUANA OF THE GALAPAGOS
ISLANDS (P-I)   DOUBLE
OUT OF THE SEA, ONTO THE LAND--A
SERIES (P-I)   DOUBLE
TADPOLE TO TOAD (P-I)   DOUBLE

(MOTION PICTURES)

ANIMAL TEETH   IWANMI
EVOLUTION   LCOA
EYES OF INSECTS   IWANMI
FEET OF ANIMALS   IWANMI
FOSSILS   IWANMI

(AUDIO TAPES)

BIOLOGICAL EVOLUTION OF
INTELLIGENCE, THE   SIGINF
BIOLOGY, MORALITY AND SOCIAL
COHESION   SIGINF
EVOLUTION OF COMMUNICATION, THE   SIGINF
EVOLUTION OF WITHIN-GROUP
COOPERATION, THE   SIGINF
GENES AND HUMAN EVOLUTION   SIGINF
GENES AND INTELLIGENCE   SIGINF
HISTORY AND HUMAN EVOLUTION   SIGINF
INSTINCT PROBLEM, THE   SIGINF
INTERGROUP COMPETITION AND
PRIMATE EVOLUTION   SIGINF
NEW APPROACH TO HUMAN EVOLUTION
- INTRODUCTION   SIGINF
NEW APPROACH TO HUMAN
EVOLUTION - SUMMATION AND
CONCLUSIONS   SIGINF
NEW APPROACH TO HUMAN
EVOLUTION--A SERIES   SIGINF
RECENT ATTITUDES TOWARD HUMAN
EVOLUTION   SIGINF

BIOLOGY, GENETICS

(FILMSTRIPS)

A-V LECTURES IN BIOLOGY   SAUNDW
MITOSIS AND MEIOSIS   EGH

(MOTION PICTURES)

RACE, INTELLIGENCE AND EDUCATION
(H-C A)   TIMLIF

(AUDIO TAPES)

BIOLOGICAL EVOLUTION OF
INTELLIGENCE, THE   SIGINF
GENES AND HUMAN EVOLUTION   SIGINF
GENES AND INTELLIGENCE   SIGINF
NEW APPROACH TO HUMAN
EVOLUTION--A SERIES   SIGINF

BIOLOGY, MICROBIOLOGY

(FILMSTRIPS)

ALGAE AND FUNGI   EGH
ANIMAL HISTOLOGY (I-H)   COMG
BASIC ASPECTS OF MOLECULAR
BIOLOGY   MTSJC
COMPARATIVE PATHOGENIC
BACTERIOLOGY, PT 1   SAUNDW
COMPARATIVE PATHOGENIC
BACTERIOLOGY, PT 2   SAUNDW
EARTHWORM - TYPICAL INVERTEBRATE   EGH
EMBRYOLOGY I - HYDRA AND STARFISH   EGH
EMBRYOLOGY II - FROG AND CHICK   EGH
HUMAN HISTOLOGY - SYSTEMS   EGH
HUMAN HISTOLOGY - TISSUE   EGH
METHOD, ASSESSMENT AND
EVALUATION   EGH
MICROSCOPIC SPECIMENS - A
  RESOURCE UNIT--A SERIES   EGH
MITOSIS AND MEIOSIS   EGH
MOSSES AND FERNS   EGH
PROTOZOA   EGH
ROOTS, STEMS AND LEAVES - DICOTS   EGH
ROOTS, STEMS AND LEAVES -
MONOCOTS   EGH

(MOTION CARTRIDGES)

ANIMAL LIFE IN A DROP OF
  WATER (LIFE IN SINGLE CELLS)
  (P-I)   DOUBLE
FRESH WATER MICROORGANISMS (P-I)   DOUBLE
LIFE IN SINGLE CELLS--A SERIES (P-I)   DOUBLE
MICROSCOPIC ANIMALS - PROTOZOA (P-
I)   DOUBLE
MICROSCOPIC WATER ANIMALS (P-I)   DOUBLE

(MOTION PICTURES)

SYMBIOSIS (J-H)   BFA

(TRANSPARENCIES)

AMOEBA, THE (I-H)   BOW
ANIMAL CELL TYPES (I-H)   BOW
BACTERIAL CELL TYPES (I-H)   BOW
EUGLENA, THE (I-H)   BOW
FOSSIL PROTOZOANS (I-H)   BOW
FRESHWATER ALGAE (I-H)   BOW
FRESHWATER PROTOZOANS (I-H)   BOW
MICROSCOPIC LIFE--A SERIES (I-H)   BOW
PARAMECIUM, THE (I-H)   BOW
PLANT AND ANIMAL CELLS COMPARED
(I-H)   BOW
PLANT CELL TYPES (I-H)   BOW
SMALL POND LIFE (I-H)   BOW

BIOLOGY, PHYSIOLOGY (HUMAN) - GENERAL

(FILMSTRIPS)

ADAPTATIONS FOR LIFE   EGH
ENERGY AND LIFE   EGH
FUNCTION OF THE KIDNEY (H-C A)   HRAW
HUMAN ANATOMY AND PHYSIOLOGY--A
SERIES (H-C A)   HRAW
LIFE - A UNIQUE PHENOMENON--A
SERIES   EGH
MOVEMENTS OF THE HUMAN BODY (H-
C A)   HRAW
MUSCLE - PHYSIOLOGICAL
CHARACTERISTICS (H-C A)   HRAW
PERPETUATING LIFE   EGH
WHAT IS LIFE   EGH

(MOTION PICTURES)

BIRTH OF A BABY (H-C A)   CHM
EMBRYOLOGICAL DEVELOPMENT (H-C A)   CHM
HOW TO MAKE A WOMAN (C A)   POLYMR
MUSCLE - A STUDY OF INTEGRATION   CRMP

(TRANSPARENCIES)

HUMAN BODY--A SERIES (H)   BOW

BIOLOGY, PHYSIOLOGY (HUMAN) - ANATOMY

(FILMSTRIPS)

FUNCTION OF THE KIDNEY (H-C A)   HRAW
HUMAN ANATOMY AND PHYSIOLOGY--A
SERIES (H-C A)   HRAW
HUMAN HISTOLOGY - SYSTEMS   EGH
HUMAN HISTOLOGY - TISSUE   EGH
INTRODUCTION TO THE
NEUROSCIENCES, AN   SAUNDW
MOVEMENTS OF THE HUMAN BODY (H-
C A)   HRAW
MUSCLE - PHYSIOLOGICAL
CHARACTERISTICS (H-C A)   HRAW
NERVOUS SYSTEM - REFLEX ARC (H-C
A)   HRAW
NERVOUS SYSTEM - THE AUTONOMIC
NERVOUS SYSTEM (H-C A)   HRAW
NERVOUS SYSTEM - TRANSMISSION (H-
C A)   HRAW

(MOTION PICTURES)

EAR, THE   IWANMI
LIVING BONE, THE   IWANMI

(TRANSPARENCIES)

BREAST DEVELOPMENT AND PURPOSE   LEART
CARE OF MALE REPRODUCTIVE ORGANS   LEART
CARE OF THE BODY DURING
MENSTRUATION   LEART
CROSS-SECTION OF PENIS   LEART
DESCENT OF THE TESTICLES   LEART
FEMALE ORGANS OF EXCRETION AND
REPRODUCTION   LEART
FEMALE REPRODUCTIVE ORGANS -
FRONT VIEW   LEART
GROWTH OF BODY HAIR   LEART
INGUINAL AND SPERMATIC CORD   LEART
MALE ORGANS OF EXCRETION AND
REPRODUCTION   LEART
MENSTRUATION   LEART
OVULATION   LEART
PHYSICAL CHANGES - BOYS   LEART
PHYSICAL CHANGES - GIRLS   LEART
REASONS FOR ERECTION   LEART
SEMINAL EMISSIONS   LEART
SEX EDUCATION - DEVELOPMENTAL
PATTERNS OF PUBESCENT BOYS-
-A SERIES   LEART
SPERM   LEART
TYPES OF PROTECTION   LEART
WAYS OF CONTROL   LEART

BIOLOGY, PHYSIOLOGY (HUMAN) - BLOOD

(FILMSTRIPS)

CIRCULATION - BLOOD CIRCULATION (H-
C A)   HRAW
CIRCULATION - BLOOD PRESSURE (H-C
A)   HRAW

(MOTION PICTURES)

BLOOD   IWANMI
CLINICAL EVALUATION OF THE
JUGULAR VENOUS PULSE (PRO)   AMEDA

BIOLOGY, PHYSIOLOGY (HUMAN) - DIGESTION

(FILMSTRIPS)

DIGESTION - CONCEPTS OF DIGESTION
(H-C A)   HRAW
DIGESTION OF FOODS (H-C A)   HRAW

BIOLOGY, PHYSIOLOGY (HUMAN) - EARS

(FILMSTRIPS)

FUNCTION OF THE EAR (H-C A)   HRAW

(MOTION PICTURES)

EAR, THE   IWANMI
NOISE AND ITS EFFECTS ON HEALTH
(J-C A)   FLMFR

BIOLOGY, PHYSIOLOGY (HUMAN) - EYES

(FILMSTRIPS)

FUNCTION OF THE EYE (H-C A)   HRAW
OPTICAL PRINCIPLES (H-C A)   HRAW

(MOTION PICTURES)

MICROSCOPE   IWANMI

BIOLOGY, PHYSIOLOGY (HUMAN) - HEART AND
CIRCULATION

(FILMSTRIPS)

CIRCULATION - BLOOD CIRCULATION (H-
C A)   HRAW
CIRCULATION - BLOOD PRESSURE (H-C
A)   HRAW
CIRCULATION - FUNCTION OF THE
HEART (H-C A)   HRAW

(MOTION PICTURES)

CLINICAL EVALUATION OF THE
JUGULAR VENOUS PULSE (PRO)   AMEDA

BIOLOGY, PHYSIOLOGY (HUMAN) - NERVOUS
SYSTEM

(FILMSTRIPS)

INTRODUCTION TO THE
NEUROSCIENCES, AN   SAUNDW
NERVOUS SYSTEM - REFLEX ARC (H-C
A)   HRAW
NERVOUS SYSTEM - THE AUTONOMIC
NERVOUS SYSTEM (H-C A)   HRAW
NERVOUS SYSTEM - TRANSMISSION (H-
C A)   HRAW
NEUROSCIENCES   DAUNDW

(MOTION PICTURES)

CONDITIONED REFLEX   IWANMI
SYSTEM AND WORKINGS OF A NERVE   IWANMI

(AUDIO TAPES)

CEREBRAL DYSFUNCTION   SIGINF
CEREBRAL DYSFUNCTION - SEIZURE
DISORDERS   SIGINF
CEREBRAL DYSFUNCTION - 14 AND
SIX CYCLES POSITIVE EEG
SPIKING   SIGINF
CLINICAL ASPECTS OF MINIMAL BRAIN
DYSFUNCTION   SIGINF

BIOLOGY, PHYSIOLOGY (HUMAN) - REPRODUCTION

(FILMSTRIPS)

MITOSIS AND MEIOSIS   EGH

(MOTION PICTURES)

BIRTH (H-C A)	VERITE
BIRTH (H-C A)	VERITE
BIRTH OF A BABY (H-C A)	CHM
CHILDBIRTH (J-C A)	POLYMR
EMBRYOLOGICAL DEVELOPMENT (H-C A)	CHM
HUMAN REPRODUCTION (H-C A)	CHM
NOT ME ALONE (H-C A)	POLYMR

(TRANSPARENCIES)

ADOLESCENT CHANGE (H)	BOW
BABY AT ONE MONTH	LEART
BIRTH OF THE BABY	LEART
BREAST DEVELOPMENT AND PURPOSE	LEART
CARE OF MALE REPRODUCTIVE ORGANS	LEART
CARE OF THE BODY DURING MENSTRUATION	LEART
CLEANLINESS INFLUENCES HEALTH	LEART
COMPARATIVE SIZES - BOYS AND GIRLS 11 YEARS	LEART
COMPARATIVE SIZES - BOYS AND GIRLS 12 YEARS	LEART
COMPARATIVE SIZES - BOYS AND GIRLS 13 YEARS	LEART
COMPARATIVE SIZES - BOYS AND GIRLS 14 YEARS	LEART
CROSS-SECTION OF PENIS	LEART
DESCENT OF THE TESTICLES	LEART
DRESS FOR THE WEATHER	LEART
EFFECTS OF GONORRHEA	LEART
EFFECTS OF SYPHILIS	LEART
EMBRYO TO BABY	LEART
EMOTION AND BODY FUNCTIONS	LEART
ENDOCRINE GLANDS	LEART
EXERCISE AND ACTIVITIES	LEART
FEMALE ORGANS OF EXCRETION AND REPRODUCTION	LEART
FEMALE REPRODUCTIVE ORGANS - FRONT VIEW	LEART
FERTILIZATION	LEART
FOOD AFFECTS GROWTH	LEART
GENERAL TOPICS--A SERIES (H)	BOW
GONORRHEA	LEART
GROWTH OF BODY HAIR	LEART
GROWTH OF THE BABY, PT 1	LEART
GROWTH OF THE BABY, PT 2	LEART
HEREDITY (BASIC) (H)	BOW
HORMONES AND EMOTIONAL EFFECTS, PT 1	LEART
HORMONES AND EMOTIONAL EFFECTS, PT 2	LEART
IMPLANTATION	LEART
INGUINAL AND SPERMATIC CORD	LEART
MALE ORGANS OF EXCRETION AND REPRODUCTION	LEART
MENSTRUATION	LEART
MULTIPLE OVULATION AND FERTILIZATION	LEART
OVULATION	LEART
OVUM AND SPERM PHOTO (H)	BOW
PASSAGE OF PLACENTA	LEART
PHYSICAL CHANGES - BOYS	LEART
PHYSICAL CHANGES - GIRLS	LEART
PITUITARY GLAND	LEART
PROPER SLEEP IS IMPORTANT TO HEALTH	LEART
PUBESCENCE - THE AGE OF PUBERTY	LEART
REASONS FOR ERECTION	LEART
REPRODUCTIVE CELL DIVISION - GROWTH	LEART
SELF DISCIPLINE	LEART
SEMINAL EMISSIONS	LEART
SEPARATION OF MOTHER AND BABY	LEART
SEX EDUCATION - DEVELOPMENT OF CONCEPTS AND ATTITUDES--A SERIES	LEART
SEX EDUCATION - DEVELOPMENTAL PATTERNS OF PUBESCENT BOYS- -A SERIES	LEART
SEX EDUCATION - GROWTH AND THE ENDOCRINE GLANDS--A SERIES	LEART
SEX EDUCATION - PHYSICAL CARE AND SELF RESPECT--A SERIES	LEART
SEX EDUCATION - THE BABY - ITS CONCEPTION, GROWTH AND BIRTH--A SERIES	LEART
SEX EDUCATION - UNDERSTANDING VENEREAL DISEASE--A SERIES	LEART
SINGLE FULL-TERM FETUS (X-RAY) (H)	BOW
SPERM	LEART
SYPHILIS	LEART
TWIN X-RAY (H)	BOW
TWINNING	LEART
TWINS (H)	BOW
TYPES OF PROTECTION	LEART
VENEREAL DISEASE	LEART
WAYS OF CONTROL	LEART

BIOLOGY, PHYSIOLOGY (HUMAN) - RESPIRATION

(FILMSTRIPS)

RESPIRATION - GAS EXCHANGE (H-C A)	HRAW

RESPIRATION - MECHANICS OF VENTILATION (H-C A)	HRAW

(MOTION PICTURES)

STORY OF RESPIRATION	IWANMI

BIOLOGY, ZOOLOGY - GENERAL

(FILMSTRIPS)

ADAPTATIONS FOR LIFE	EGH
ANIMAL HISTOLOGY (I-H)	COMG
ANIMALS	MSCF
ANIMALS--A SERIES	MSCF
BASIC ASPECTS OF MOLECULAR BIOLOGY	MTSJC
COMPARATIVE PATHOGENIC BACTERIOLOGY, PT 1	SAUNDW
COMPARATIVE PATHOGENIC BACTERIOLOGY, PT 2	SAUNDW
ENERGY AND LIFE	EGH
LIFE - A UNIQUE PHENOMENON--A SERIES	EGH
MICROTUBULES IN ECHINOSPHAERIUM NUCLEOFILUM	HRAW
PERPETUATING LIFE	EGH
WHAT IS IT (TEST SCRIPT)	MSCF
WHAT IS LIFE	EGH

(MOTION PICTURES)

MUSCLE - A STUDY OF INTEGRATION	CRMP

(TRANSPARENCIES)

AMOEBA, THE (I-H)	BOW
ANIMAL CELL TYPES (I-H)	BOW
BACTERIAL CELL TYPES (I-H)	BOW
BIRD ADAPTATION (H)	BOW
BIRD EMBRYOLOGY (H)	BOW
BIRD IDENTIFICATION (H)	BOW
BIRD MIGRATION (H)	BOW
BIRD NESTS (H)	BOW
BIRD STRUCTURE (H)	BOW
EUGLENA, THE (I-H)	BOW
EVOLUTION OF THE HORSE (H)	BOW
FEEDER CONSTRUCTION (H)	BOW
FOSSIL PROTOZOANS (I-H)	BOW
FRESHWATER ALGAE (I-H)	BOW
FRESHWATER PROTOZOANS (I-H)	BOW
MAMMALS' HOMES (H)	BOW
MICROSCOPIC LIFE--A SERIES (I-H)	BOW
PARAMECIUM, THE (I-H)	BOW
PLANT AND ANIMAL CELLS COMPARED (I-H)	BOW
PLANT CELL TYPES (I-H)	BOW
SMALL POND LIFE (I-H)	BOW
STRUCTURE OF MAMMALS (H)	BOW
UNUSUAL MAMMALS (H)	BOW
VERTEBRATE ANIMALS (H)	BOW
WARM-BLOODED VERTEBRATES--A SERIES (H)	BOW

BIOLOGY, ZOOLOGY - AMPHIBIANS

(FILMSTRIPS)

DEVELOPMENT OF THE FROG, THE, PT 1 - MATING OF FROGS (I-H)	CARMAN
DEVELOPMENT OF THE FROG, THE, PT 2 - GROWTH OF THE TADPOLE (I-H)	CARMAN

(MOTION PICTURES)

BIRTH OF A FROG	IWANMI

BIOLOGY, ZOOLOGY - ANATOMY

(MOTION PICTURES)

ANIMAL TEETH	IWANMI
FEET OF ANIMALS	IWANMI

BIOLOGY, ZOOLOGY - BIRDS

(TRANSPARENCIES)

BIRD ADAPTATION (H)	BOW
BIRD EMBRYOLOGY (H)	BOW
BIRD IDENTIFICATION (H)	BOW
BIRD MIGRATION (H)	BOW
BIRD NESTS (H)	BOW
BIRD STRUCTURE (H)	BOW
EVOLUTION OF THE HORSE (H)	BOW
FEEDER CONSTRUCTION (H)	BOW
MAMMALS' HOMES (H)	BOW
STRUCTURE OF MAMMALS (H)	BOW
UNUSUAL MAMMALS (H)	BOW
VERTEBRATE ANIMALS (H)	BOW
WARM-BLOODED VERTEBRATES--A SERIES (H)	BOW

BIOLOGY, ZOOLOGY - FISH

(MOTION PICTURES)

BIRTH OF KILLIFISH	IWANMI
HOW DO FISH SWIM	IWANMI

BIOLOGY, ZOOLOGY - HABITATIONS

(MOTION PICTURES)

NEMATODE (J-C)	EBEC

BIOLOGY, ZOOLOGY - HABITS AND BEHAVIOR

(FILMSTRIPS)

ADAPTATIONS FOR LIFE	EGH
DEVELOPMENT OF THE FROG, THE, PT 1 - MATING OF FROGS (I-H)	CARMAN
MICROTUBULES IN ECHINOSPHAERIUM NUCLEOFILUM	HRAW

(MOTION PICTURES)

ANIMAL DEVELOPMENT	IWANMI
BIRTH OF KILLIFISH	IWANMI
OFFSPRINGS HATCHING FROM EGGS	IWANMI
STORY OF RESPIRATION	IWANMI

BIOLOGY, ZOOLOGY - INSECTS

(MOTION PICTURES)

DRAGONFLIES	IWANMI
EYES OF INSECTS	IWANMI
INSECTS, OBSERVATION AND COLLECTION	IWANMI
LIFE CYCLE OF A DRAGONFLY	IWANMI
MOSQUITO	IWANMI
SINGING INSECTS OF AUTUMN	IWANMI

BIOLOGY, ZOOLOGY - LIFE CYCLES

(FILMSTRIPS)

DEVELOPMENT OF THE FROG, THE, PT 1 - MATING OF FROGS (I-H)	CARMAN
DEVELOPMENT OF THE FROG, THE, PT 2 - GROWTH OF THE TADPOLE (I-H)	CARMAN
EMBRYOLOGY I - HYDRA AND STARFISH	EGH
EMBRYOLOGY II - FROG AND CHICK	EGH
MITOSIS AND MEIOSIS	EGH

(MOTION PICTURES)

BIRTH OF A FROG	IWANMI
LIFE CYCLE OF A DRAGONFLY	IWANMI
LIFE OF A MONKEY, THE	IWANMI
MOSQUITO	IWANMI
OFFSPRINGS HATCHING FROM EGGS	IWANMI

(TRANSPARENCIES)

LIFE SCIENCE - COMING TO LIFE--A SERIES (K-P)	LEART

BIOLOGY, ZOOLOGY - MAMMALS

(MOTION PICTURES)

LIFE OF A MONKEY, THE	IWANMI

(TRANSPARENCIES)

BIRD ADAPTATION (H)	BOW
BIRD EMBRYOLOGY (H)	BOW
BIRD IDENTIFICATION (H)	BOW
BIRD MIGRATION (H)	BOW
BIRD NESTS (H)	BOW
BIRD STRUCTURE (H)	BOW
FEEDER CONSTRUCTION (H)	BOW
MAMMALS' HOMES (H)	BOW
STRUCTURE OF MAMMALS (H)	BOW
UNUSUAL MAMMALS (H)	BOW
VERTEBRATE ANIMALS (H)	BOW
WARM-BLOODED VERTEBRATES--A SERIES (H)	BOW

BIOLOGY, ZOOLOGY - SEA ANIMALS

(FILMSTRIPS)

EMBRYOLOGY I - HYDRA AND STARFISH	EGH

(MOTION PICTURES)

LIFE ON THE REEF	IWANMI
STARFISH'S REALM, THE	WHTCAP
STORY OF RESPIRATION	IWANMI

(TRANSPARENCIES)

ANIMALS OF THE DEEP (I-H)	BOW
ANIMALS OF THE OPEN OCEAN (I-H)	BOW
DIVISIONS OF THE OCEAN (I-H)	BOW
FOOD WEB (I-H)	BOW
ISLAND AND CORAL REEF FORMATION (I-H)	BOW
MAN IN THE OCEAN (I-H)	BOW
OCEAN CURRENTS (I-H)	BOW
OCEANOGRAPHY--A SERIES (I-H)	BOW
PLANKTON (I-H)	BOW
SEASHORE LIFE - COLD ROCKY SHORES (I-H)	BOW
SEASHORE LIFE - TEMPERATE MARSHY SHORES (I-H)	BOW
SEASHORE LIFE - WARM SANDY SHORES (I-H)	BOW
SUBMARINE GEOLOGY (I-H)	BOW
TOOLS OF THE OCEANOGRAPHER (I-H)	BOW

BIOLOGY, ZOOLOGY - WORMS

(FILMSTRIPS)

EARTHWORM - TYPICAL INVERTEBRATE	EGH

(MOTION PICTURES)

NEMATODE (J-C)	EBEC

CONSERVATION AND NATURAL RESOURCES

(FILMSTRIPS)

ENERGY CRISIS, THE - AN HISTORICAL REVIEW (I)	TERF
ENERGY CRISIS, THE - REPORT FROM PLANET 32 (I)	TERF
ON SAFARI IN EAST AFRICA (P-C)	DWYLIE
SCHOOL TIMES KIT - APRIL--A SERIES (I)	TERF

(MOTION PICTURES)

CHALLENGE OF THE ARCTIC	ARIC
ENEMY IS FIRE, THE (J-C A)	RARIG
ERTS - EARTH RESOURCES TECHNOLOGY SATELLITE (J-C A)	NASA
FIRE WEATHER (J-C A)	RARIG
FOREST FIRE PROTECTION--A SERIES (J-C A)	RARIG
SCENES OF NATURAL RESERVE	ALDEN
THIS IS CAMPING (I-C A)	IU
TO BOTTLE THE SUN	USAEC

(TRANSPARENCIES)

CONSERVATION--A SERIES (H)	BOW
EROSION (H)	BOW
FLOODING (H)	BOW
FOREST FIRE (H)	BOW
NATURAL RESOURCES (H)	BOW
POLLUTION (H)	BOW
SOIL DEPLETION (H)	BOW

SCIENCE - PHYSICAL

SCIENCE, PHYSICAL - GENERAL

(FILMSTRIPS)

FABLES AND FACTS--A SERIES (P-I)	TERF

(MOTION PICTURES)

MEASURING INSTRUMENTS	IWANMI
ONCE UPON A TIME (P-J)	TEXFLM
SCIENCE OF VACUUM	IWANMI
SCIENCE TODAY FILM--A SERIES	CRMP
SCIENCE TODAY--A SERIES (C A)	CRMP

(VIDEOTAPES)

HOW BIG IS YOUR WORLD (I)	GPITVL
LET'S EXPLORE SCIENCE--A SERIES (I)	GPITVL
PUSH AND PULL (I)	GPITVL
SCIENCE IS DISCOVERY--A SERIES (I)	GPITVL
SORTING THINGS (I)	GPITVL

(TRANSPARENCIES)

AIRPLANE (H)	BOW
APPLIED SCIENCE--A SERIES (H)	BOW
BALANCE BEAM SCALE (H)	BOW
BUOYANCY (H)	BOW
COMPUTER (H)	BOW
ELECTRICAL SWITCHES (H)	BOW
FLIGHT PRINCIPLES (H)	BOW
HEATING A HOME (H)	BOW
INSTRUMENTS AND TECHNIQUES OF SCIENCE--A SERIES (H)	BOW
LIFT PUMP (H)	BOW
OIL WELL (H)	BOW
PHOTOGRAPHY (H)	BOW

PREPARING SLIDES (H)	BOW
PSYCHROMETER (H)	BOW
REFRIGERATION (H)	BOW
SYNTHETIC FIBERS (H)	BOW
TELESCOPE (H)	BOW
TESTING FOR MINERALS (H)	BOW
THERMOMETER (H)	BOW
WATER FILTRATION PLANT (H)	BOW

BASIC PHYSICAL SCIENCE - AIR

(MOTION PICTURES)

ATMOSPHERIC PRESSURE	IWANMI
DISCOVERY OF THE VACUUM	IWANMI
HOW DOES A YACHT SAIL	IWANMI
SCIENCE OF VACUUM	IWANMI

(VIDEOTAPES)

SCIENCE IS DISCOVERY--A SERIES (I)	GPITVL
WHAT MAKES AIR MOVE (I)	GPITVL

BASIC PHYSICAL SCIENCE - CHEMICAL CHANGE

(FILMSTRIPS)

HOT AND COLD - EARLY SCIENCE CONCEPTS (K-I)	TROLA

(MOTION CARTRIDGES)

SEPARATING THE ELEMENTS OF WATER	DOUBLE

(MOTION PICTURES)

ACID AND ALKALI	IWANMI

BASIC PHYSICAL SCIENCE - EARTH

(FILMSTRIPS)

ENERGY CRISIS, THE - REPORT FROM PLANET 32 (I)	TERF
ORIGINS OF THE EARTH--A SERIES (I-H)	VISPUB
SCHOOL TIMES KIT - APRIL--A SERIES (I)	TERF

(VIDEOTAPES)

HOW IS THE EARTH'S SURFACE CHANGED BY INTERNAL FORCES (I)	GPITVL
HOW IS THE EARTH'S SURFACE CHANGED BY WATER (I)	GPITVL
HOW IS THE EARTH'S SURFACE CHANGED BY WIND (I)	GPITVL
SCIENCE IS DISCOVERY--A SERIES (I)	GPITVL
WHAT IS THE EARTH'S SURFACE LIKE (I)	GPITVL

BASIC PHYSICAL SCIENCE - ELECTRICITY AND MAGNETISM

(MOTION PICTURES)

ELECTRIC BULB SCIENCE	IWANMI
MAGNET, THE	IWANMI

(VIDEOTAPES)

HOW CAN ELECTRICAL ENERGY MAKE THINGS MOVE (I)	GPITVL
SCIENCE IS DISCOVERY--A SERIES (I)	GPITVL
WHAT MAKES ELECTRIC CURRENT FLOW (I)	GPITVL

(TRANSPARENCIES)

BATTERIES (H)	BOW
CIRCUITS (H)	BOW
COMPASS (H)	BOW
EARTH'S MAGNETIC FIELD (H)	BOW
ELECTRIC BELL (H)	BOW
ELECTRIC MOTOR (H)	BOW
ELECTROSCOPE (H)	BOW
GENERATING STATION (H)	BOW
LAWS OF MAGNETISM (H)	BOW
MAGNETISM AND ELECTRICITY--A SERIES (H)	BOW
TELEGRAPH (H)	BOW
TELEPHONE (H)	BOW
TELEVISION (H)	BOW

BASIC PHYSICAL SCIENCE - ENERGY AND MATTER

(FILMSTRIPS)

ENERGY CRISIS, THE - AN HISTORICAL REVIEW (I)	TERF
GAS/LIQUID/SOLID, PT 1	RAYM
SCHOOL TIMES KIT - APRIL--A SERIES (I)	TERF

(MOTION PICTURES)

FOAM	IWANMI

(VIDEOTAPES)

HOW DOES TEMPERATURE AFFECT MATTER (I)	GPITVL
SCIENCE IS DISCOVERY--A SERIES (I)	GPITVL
WHAT ARE THE PROPERTIES OF MATTER (I)	GPITVL
WHAT IS MATTER (I)	GPITVL

BASIC PHYSICAL SCIENCE - FIRE

(MOTION PICTURES)

SCIENCE OF FIRE	IWANMI

BASIC PHYSICAL SCIENCE - FORCE AND MOTION

(MOTION PICTURES)

CENTRIFUGAL FORCE	IWANMI
INERTIA	IWANMI
MOVEMENT OF THE PENDULUM	IWANMI
MOVEMENT OF THE TOP	IWANMI
SURFACE TENSION	IWANMI
VISUALIZATION OF FORCE	IWANMI

BASIC PHYSICAL SCIENCE - HEAT AND FRICTION

(FILMSTRIPS)

HOT AND COLD - EARLY SCIENCE CONCEPTS (K-I)	TROLA

(MOTION PICTURES)

HOW TO MEASURE TEMPERATURE	IWANMI
STORY OF THE REFRIGERATOR	IWANMI
UTILIZATION OF SOLAR HEAT	IWANMI

(VIDEOTAPES)

WHAT MAKES WATER MOVE (I)	GPITVL

(TRANSPARENCIES)

HOW TEMPERATURE AFFECTS US (K-P)	BOW
HOW TO USE THE THERMOMETER (K-P)	BOW
LEARNING TO READ THE THERMOMETER (K-P)	BOW
TEMPERATURE--A SERIES (K-P)	BOW

BASIC PHYSICAL SCIENCE - LIGHT AND COLOR

(FILMSTRIPS)

COLORS EVERYWHERE--A SERIES (K-P)	SPA

(MOTION CARTRIDGES)

WHAT IS A SHADOW	VISED

(MOTION PICTURES)

LIGHT OF DAY, THE	GRADYM
REFRACTION AND SHADOW OF LIGHT	IWANMI
REFRACTION OF LIGHT	IWANMI
WHAT IS LIGHT, PT 1	IWANMI
WHAT IS LIGHT, PT 2	IWANMI

(VIDEOTAPES)

LEARNING TO SEE COLOR (I)	GPITVL

BASIC PHYSICAL SCIENCE - LIQUIDS

(MOTION CARTRIDGES)

SEPARATING THE ELEMENTS OF WATER	DOUBLE

(VIDEOTAPES)

WHAT IS THE WATER CYCLE (I)	GPITVL

BASIC PHYSICAL SCIENCE - MACHINES

(TRANSPARENCIES)

FIRST CLASS LEVER (H)	BOW
GEARS (H)	BOW
INCLINED PLANE (H)	BOW
MACHINES--A SERIES (H)	BOW
PULLEY (H)	BOW
SECOND CLASS LEVER (H)	BOW
THIRD CLASS LEVER (H)	BOW

BASIC PHYSICAL SCIENCE - PHYSICAL CHANGE

(FILMSTRIPS)

FOLD MOUNTAINS (I-H)	VISPUB
HOT AND COLD - EARLY SCIENCE CONCEPTS (K-I)	TROLA
ICE, PT 1 (I-H)	VISPUB
ICE, PT 2 (I-H)	VISPUB
ICE, PT 3 (I-H)	VISPUB
ORIGINS OF THE EARTH--A SERIES (I-H)	VISPUB
RATIONALISM	EGH
RIVERS, PT 1 (I-H)	VISPUB
RIVERS, PT 2 (I-H)	VISPUB
RIVERS, PT 3 (I-H)	VISPUB
ROCKS AND MINERALS (I-H)	VISPUB
SEA, THE - DEPOSITION (I-H)	VISPUB
SEA, THE - EROSION (I-H)	VISPUB
VOLCANOES, PT 1 (I-H)	VISPUB
VOLCANOES, PT 2 (I-H)	VISPUB

(MOTION PICTURES)

ICE COLUMNS	IWANMI
OBSERVATION OF BOILING	IWANMI
STATES OF MATTER, THE	CRMP

BASIC PHYSICAL SCIENCE - SOUND

(MOTION PICTURES)

ASSOCIATES OF THE VIOLIN	IWANMI
QUIET, PLEASE	WILCOX
SOUNDS OF NATURE	AVEXP
WIND INSTRUMENT, THE	IWANMI

(AUDIO TAPES)

SOUND OF A CITY, THE (I)	IU

BASIC PHYSICAL SCIENCE - SPACE AND SOLAR SYSTEM

(FILMSTRIPS)

DIVIDENDS FROM SPACE (I-J)	DOUBLE
EAGLE HAS LANDED, THE - MAN ON THE MOON (I-J)	DOUBLE
HISTORY OF ASTRONAUTICS, THE, PT 1 (I-J)	DOUBLE
HISTORY OF ASTRONAUTICS, THE, PT 2 (I-J)	DOUBLE
MAN ON THE MOON--A SERIES (I-J)	DOUBLE
STATIONS IN SPACE (I-J)	DOUBLE

(MOTION PICTURES)

APOLLO 17 - ON THE SHOULDERS OF GIANTS (J-C A)	NASA
STEPPING STONES IN SPACE (I-C A)	HEARST

(VIDEOTAPES)

ARE ALL STARS ALIKE (I)	GPITVL
HOW BIG IS THE UNIVERSE (I)	GPITVL
SCIENCE IS DISCOVERY--A SERIES (I)	GPITVL
WHAT ARE PLANETS (I)	GPITVL
WHY DO ECLIPSES OCCUR (I)	GPITVL
WHY DO TEMPERATURES OF PLANETS VARY (I)	GPITVL
WHY DOES THE SUN'S POSITION SEEM TO CHANGE (I)	GPITVL

(AUDIO TAPES)

SMALL OBSERVATORIES (H A)	UOKLA

BASIC PHYSICAL SCIENCE - WEATHER AND CLIMATE

(MOTION CARTRIDGES)

ARCTIC THAW, PT 1 (P-I)	DOUBLE
CLOUDS (P-I)	DOUBLE
FLASH FLOOD (P-I)	DOUBLE
MOUNTAIN STORM (P-I)	DOUBLE
WEATHER--A SERIES (P-I)	DOUBLE

(MOTION PICTURES)

ATMOSPHERIC PRESSURE	IWANMI
DRY SEASON, THE	CMC
FIRE WEATHER (J-C A)	RARIG
ICE COLUMNS	IWANMI
KNOW YOUR CLOUDS	USNAC
PARTICLES OF SNOW	IWANMI
TYPHOON, PT 1	IWANMI
TYPHOON, PT 2	IWANMI
WHAT TRIGGERS SNOWSLIDES	IWANMI
WINDOW FROST	IWANMI
WINTERLUDE	MTP

(TRANSPARENCIES)

ASTRONOMY--A SERIES (H)	BOW

ATMOSPHERE (H)	BOW
CLIMATE (H)	BOW
CLOUDS (H)	BOW
DAY AND NIGHT (H)	BOW
ECLIPSES (H)	BOW
HOW TEMPERATURE AFFECTS US (K-P)	BOW
HOW TO USE THE THERMOMETER (K-P)	BOW
LEARNING TO READ THE THERMOMETER (K-P)	BOW
MOON (H)	BOW
SEASONS (H)	BOW
SOLAR SYSTEMS (H)	BOW
STAR CHART (H)	BOW
TEMPERATURE--A SERIES (K-P)	BOW
WARM AND COLD FRONTS (H)	BOW
WATER CYCLE (H)	BOW
WEATHER--A SERIES (H)	BOW
WIND CIRCULATION (H)	BOW

CHEMISTRY - GENERAL

(MOTION CARTRIDGES)

STRUCTURE AND STEREOCHEMISTRY - CONFORMATION OF CYCLOHEXANE	HRAW
STRUCTURE AND STEREOCHEMISTRY - DRAWING STRUCTURES, PT 1	HRAW
STRUCTURE AND STEREOCHEMISTRY - DRAWING STRUCTURES, PT 2	HRAW

(MOTION PICTURES)

CRYSTALLIZATION	IWANMI
OBSERVATION OF ICE	IWANMI

CHEMISTRY - ACIDS, BASES, SALTS

(MOTION PICTURES)

ACID AND ALKALI	IWANMI

CHEMISTRY - ALLOYS AND METALS

(MOTION PICTURES)

PERMANENT PROTECTION	MTP
WROUGHT IRON - YESTERDAY, TODAY, TOMORROW	MTP

CHEMISTRY - ATOMIC THEORY

(MOTION PICTURES)

STORY OF MOLECULE	IWANMI

(VIDEOTAPES)

HOW ARE ATOMS COMBINED (I)	GPITVL
HOW MANY KINDS OF ATOMS EXIST (I)	GPITVL

CHEMISTRY - CARBONS

(FILMSTRIPS)

BASIC ASPECTS OF MOLECULAR BIOLOGY	MTSJC

CHEMISTRY - ELEMENTS

(MOTION PICTURES)

ORIGIN OF THE ELEMENTS, THE (C A)	CRMP
ORIGIN OF THE ELEMENTS, THE	CRMP
STATES OF MATTER, THE	CRMP

(VIDEOTAPES)

HOW ARE ATOMS COMBINED (I)	GPITVL

CHEMISTRY - MATTER

(MOTION PICTURES)

NATURE OF MATTER, THE - AN ATOMIC VIEW	CRMP
STATES OF MATTER, THE (C A)	CRMP

CHEMISTRY - WATER

(FILMSTRIPS)

ICE, PT 1 (I-H)	VISPUB
ICE, PT 2 (I-H)	VISPUB
ICE, PT 3 (I-H)	VISPUB

(MOTION PICTURES)

OBSERVATION OF BOILING	IWANMI
PARTICLES OF SNOW	IWANMI
SCIENCE OF WATER DROPS	IWANMI
WATER PRESSURE	IWANMI
WATER SURFACE	IWANMI
WINDOW FROST	IWANMI

(VIDEOTAPES)

WHAT IS THE WATER CYCLE (I)	GPITVL

EARTH SCIENCE - GENERAL

(FILMSTRIPS)

FOLD MOUNTAINS (I-H)	VISPUB
ICE, PT 1 (I-H)	VISPUB
ICE, PT 2 (I-H)	VISPUB
ICE, PT 3 (I-H)	VISPUB
ORIGINS OF THE EARTH--A SERIES (I-H)	VISPUB
RATIONALISM	EGH
RIVERS, PT 1 (I-H)	VISPUB
RIVERS, PT 2 (I-H)	VISPUB
RIVERS, PT 3 (I-H)	VISPUB
ROCKS AND MINERALS (I-H)	VISPUB
SEA, THE - DEPOSITION (I-H)	VISPUB
SEA, THE - EROSION (I-H)	VISPUB
VOLCANOES, PT 1 (I-H)	VISPUB
VOLCANOES, PT 2 (I-H)	VISPUB

(MOTION PICTURES)

BIRTH OF JAPANESE ISLANDS	IWANMI
CONTINENTS ADRIFT - A STUDY OF THE SCIENTIFIC METHOD (J-C)	AMEDFL
DEPENDENCE - A NEW DEFINITION (C A)	CRMP
HOW ARE LAKES MADE	IWANMI
PROPERTIES OF CLAY	IWANMI
STALACTITE GROTTO	IWANMI
STRATA	IWANMI
STRATA	IWANMI
WHAT TRIGGERS SNOWSLIDES	IWANMI

(AUDIO TAPES)

WHY AN OCEAN - THE OCEAN'S HISTORY (J-H)	VOA

(TRANSPARENCIES)

EARTH AND SKY--A SERIES (K-P)	BOW
FAULT MOUNTAINS (H)	BOW
FOLDED MOUNTAINS (H)	BOW
GEOLOGIC TIME (H)	BOW
GEOLOGY--A SERIES (H)	BOW
GLACIATION (H)	BOW
HOW THE EARTH REVOLVES (K-P)	BOW
HOW THE EARTH ROTATES (K-P)	BOW
HOW THE MOON SENDS LIGHT (K-P)	BOW
LEARNING ABOUT LIGHT AND SHADOWS (K-P)	BOW
ROCK CYCLE (H)	BOW
VOLCANO (H)	BOW
WHAT IS DAY, WHAT IS NIGHT (K-P)	BOW

EARTH SCIENCE - ARCHAEOLOGY

(MOTION PICTURES)

FOSSILS	IWANMI
SAND HILLS	IWANMI
SHELL-HEAP AND EARTHENWARE, A	IWANMI

EARTH SCIENCE - ASTRONOMY

(FILMSTRIPS)

DIVIDENDS FROM SPACE (I-J)	DOUBLE
EAGLE HAS LANDED, THE - MAN ON THE MOON (I-J)	DOUBLE
HISTORY OF ASTRONAUTICS, THE, PT 1 (I-J)	DOUBLE
HISTORY OF ASTRONAUTICS, THE, PT 2 (I-J)	DOUBLE
MAN ON THE MOON--A SERIES (I-J)	DOUBLE
STATIONS IN SPACE (I-J)	DOUBLE

(MOTION PICTURES)

ORIGIN OF THE ELEMENTS, THE (C A)	CRMP

(VIDEOTAPES)

ARE ALL STARS ALIKE (I)	GPITVL
HOW BIG IS THE UNIVERSE (I)	GPITVL
WHAT ARE PLANETS (I)	GPITVL
WHY DO ECLIPSES OCCUR (I)	GPITVL
WHY DO TEMPERATURES OF PLANETS VARY (I)	GPITVL
WHY DOES THE SUN'S POSITION SEEM TO CHANGE (I)	GPITVL

(AUDIO TAPES)

SMALL OBSERVATORIES (H A)   UOKLA

(TRANSPARENCIES)

ASTRONOMY--A SERIES (H)   BOW
DAY AND NIGHT (H)   BOW
EARTH AND SKY--A SERIES (H)   BOW
ECLIPSES (H)   BOW
HOW THE EARTH REVOLVES (K-P)   BOW
HOW THE EARTH ROTATES (K-P)   BOW
HOW THE MOON SENDS LIGHT (K-P)   BOW
LEARNING ABOUT LIGHT AND SHADOWS (K-P)   BOW
MEASUREMENT IN ASTRONOMY--A SERIES (I-J)   BOW
MEASURING INDIRECTLY (I-J)   BOW
MEASURING THE EARTH (I-J)   BOW
MEASURING THE MOON (I-J)   BOW
MEASURING THE SPEED OF LIGHT (I-J)   BOW
MEASURING TO MARS (I-J)   BOW
MEASURING TO THE STARS (I-J)   BOW
MEASURING TO THE SUN (I-J)   BOW
MODELS OF SOLAR SYSTEM (I-J)   BOW
MOON (H)   BOW
SEASONS (H)   BOW
SOLAR SYSTEMS (H)   BOW
STAR CHART (H)   BOW
WHAT IS DAY, WHAT IS NIGHT (K-P)   BOW

EARTH SCIENCE - GEOLOGY

(FILMSTRIPS)

FOLD MOUNTAINS (I-H)   VISPUB
ICE, PT 1 (I-H)   VISPUB
ICE, PT 2 (I-H)   VISPUB
ICE, PT 3 (I-H)   VISPUB
ORIGINS OF THE EARTH--A SERIES (I-H)   VISPUB
RIVERS, PT 1 (I-H)   VISPUB
RIVERS, PT 2 (I-H)   VISPUB
RIVERS, PT 3 (I-H)   VISPUB
ROCKS AND MINERALS (I-H)   VISPUB
SEA, THE - DEPOSITION (I-H)   VISPUB
SEA, THE - EROSION (I-H)   VISPUB
VOLCANOES, PT 1 (I-H)   VISPUB
VOLCANOES, PT 2 (I-H)   VISPUB

(MOTION PICTURES)

BIRTH OF JAPANESE ISLANDS   IWANMI
CONTINENTS ADRIFT - A STUDY OF THE SCIENTIFIC METHOD (J-C)   AMEDFL
HOW ARE LAKES MADE   IWANMI
PROPERTIES OF CLAY   IWANMI
RIVERS   IWANMI
SAND HILLS   IWANMI
STALACTITE GROTTO   IWANMI
STORY OF TWO CREEKS, THE   UEUWIS
STRATA   IWANMI
STRATA   IWANMI

(VIDEOTAPES)

HOW IS THE EARTH'S SURFACE CHANGED BY INTERNAL FORCES (I)   GPITVL
HOW IS THE EARTH'S SURFACE CHANGED BY WATER (I)   GPITVL
HOW IS THE EARTH'S SURFACE CHANGED BY WIND (I)   GPITVL
WHAT IS THE EARTH'S SURFACE LIKE (I)   GPITVL
WHAT MAKES WATER MOVE (I)   GPITVL

(TRANSPARENCIES)

FAULT MOUNTAINS (H)   BOW
FOLDED MOUNTAINS (H)   BOW
GEOLOGIC TIME (H)   BOW
GEOLOGY--A SERIES (H)   BOW
GLACIATION (H)   BOW
ROCK CYCLE (H)   BOW
VOLCANO (H)   BOW

EARTH SCIENCE - METEOROLOGY

(MOTION CARTRIDGES)

ARCTIC THAW, PT 1 (P-I)   DOUBLE
CLOUDS (P-I)   DOUBLE
FLASH FLOOD (P-I)   DOUBLE
MOUNTAIN STORM (P-I)   DOUBLE
WEATHER--A SERIES (P-I)   DOUBLE

(MOTION PICTURES)

DRY SEASON, THE   CMC
TYPHOON, PT 1   IWANMI
TYPHOON, PT 2   IWANMI
WINTERLUDE   MTP

(VIDEOTAPES)

WHAT MAKES AIR MOVE (I)   GPITVL

(TRANSPARENCIES)

ATMOSPHERE (H)   BOW
CLIMATE (H)   BOW
CLOUDS (H)   BOW
WARM AND COLD FRONTS (H)   BOW
WATER CYCLE (H)   BOW
WEATHER--A SERIES (H)   BOW
WIND CIRCULATION (H)   BOW

EARTH SCIENCE - OCEANOGRAPHY

(FILMSTRIPS)

SEA, THE - DEPOSITION (I-H)   VISPUB
SEA, THE - EROSION (I-H)   VISPUB

(MOTION PICTURES)

AIRBORNE OCEANOGRAPHY - OCEANOGRAPHER OF THE NAVY   USNAC
BATHYMETRY - DISCOVERING THE OCEAN FLOOR - CHARTING THE OCEAN FLOOR   AIMS
BEACH INTELLIGENCE - WAVES, BREAKERS AND SURF   AIMS
CONTINENTS ADRIFT - A STUDY OF THE SCIENTIFIC METHOD (J-C)   AMEDFL
OCEAN PHENOMENON - THE DEEP SCATTERING LAYER   USNAC
OCEANOGRAPHIC PREDICTION SYSTEM   USNAC
WAVES ON THE SEASHORE   IWANMI

(AUDIO TAPES)

WHY AN OCEAN - THE OCEAN'S HISTORY (J-H)   VOA

(TRANSPARENCIES)

ANIMALS OF THE DEEP (I-H)   BOW
ANIMALS OF THE OPEN OCEAN (I-H)   BOW
DIVISIONS OF THE OCEAN (I-H)   BOW
FOOD WEB (I-H)   BOW
ISLAND AND CORAL REEF FORMATION (I-H)   BOW
MAN IN THE OCEAN (I-H)   BOW
OCEAN CURRENTS (I-H)   BOW
OCEANOGRAPHY--A SERIES (I-H)   BOW
PLANKTON (I-H)   BOW
SEASHORE LIFE - COLD ROCKY SHORES (I-H)   BOW
SEASHORE LIFE - TEMPERATE MARSHY SHORES (I-H)   BOW
SEASHORE LIFE - WARM SANDY SHORES (I-H)   BOW
SUBMARINE GEOLOGY (I-H)   BOW
TOOLS OF THE OCEANOGRAPHER (I-H)   BOW

PHYSICS - ATOMIC AND NUCLEAR ENERGY

(MOTION PICTURES)

ENERGY - A CONVERSATION   CRMP
GLOVE BOX FIRES   USNAC
NATURE OF MATTER, THE - AN ATOMIC VIEW   CRMP
ORIGIN OF THE ELEMENTS, THE   CRMP
PEACEFUL USE OF NUCLEAR EXPLOSIVES (H-C A)   TIMLIF
RUMOURS OF WAR (H-C A)   TIMLIF
STORY OF MOLECULE   IWANMI
WORLD OF X-RAYS, THE   IWANMI

(VIDEOTAPES)

BOMBARDING THINGS (I-J)   GPITVL
DISCOVERING THE ATOM (I-J)   GPITVL
LIVING IN A NUCLEAR AGE--A SERIES (I-J)   GPITVL
NUCLEAR ENERGY AND LIVING THINGS (I-J)   GPITVL
POWER FROM THE ATOM (I-J)   GPITVL
RADIOISOTOPES (I-J)   GPITVL
SOCIETY AND THINGS NUCLEAR (I-J)   GPITVL

(TRANSPARENCIES)

ATOMIC ENERGY--A SERIES (H)   BOW
ATOMIC FISSION (H)   BOW
ATOMIC FUSION (H)   BOW
ATOMIC STRUCTURE (H)   BOW
CHEMICAL CHANGE (H)   BOW
ENGINES (H)   BOW
NUCLEAR REACTOR (H)   BOW
PERIODIC CHART (H)   BOW

PHYSICS - ELECTRICITY AND MAGNETISM

(MOTION PICTURES)

MAGNET, THE   IWANMI

(TRANSPARENCIES)

BATTERIES (H)   BOW

CIRCUITS (H)   BOW
COMPASS (H)   BOW
EARTH'S MAGNETIC FIELD (H)   BOW
ELECTRIC BELL (H)   BOW
ELECTRIC MOTOR (H)   BOW
ELECTROSCOPE (H)   BOW
GENERATING STATION (H)   BOW
LAWS OF MAGNETISM (H)   BOW
MAGNETISM AND ELECTRICITY--A SERIES (H)   BOW
TELEGRAPH (H)   BOW
TELEPHONE (H)   BOW
TELEVISION (H)   BOW

PHYSICS - ENERGY AND MATTER

(MOTION PICTURES)

ENERGY - A CONVERSATION   CRMP
ENERGY - A CONVERSATION (C A)   CRMP
FOAM   IWANMI
NATURE OF MATTER, THE - AN ATOMIC VIEW (C A)   CRMP
STATES OF MATTER, THE (C A)   CRMP
STATES OF MATTER, THE   CRMP
TO BOTTLE THE SUN   USAEC

PHYSICS - FORCE AND MOTION

(MOTION PICTURES)

BASEBALL   IWANMI
BEACH INTELLIGENCE - WAVES, BREAKERS AND SURF   AIMS
CENTRIFUGAL FORCE   IWANMI
DAMAGE CONTROL - EFFECTS OF WEIGHT ON STABILITY, PT 2, WEIGHT CONDITION   USNAC
DAMAGE CONTROL - ELEMENTS OF STABILITY IN SHIP   USNAC
DAMAGE CONTROL - LOOSE WATER IN STABILITY, PT 1, IN INTACT SPACES   USNAC
DAMAGE CONTROL - THE METACENTER IN STABILITY, PT 2   USNAC
INERTIA   IWANMI
MEANING OF TIME IN SCIENCE, THE (H-C)   EBEC
MOVEMENT OF THE TOP   IWANMI
SHIPBOARD VIBRATIONS, PT 3 - VIBRATION, EXCITATION AND RESPONSE   USNAC
SKATING   IWANMI
SKI   IWANMI
SURFACE TENSION   IWANMI
TOY DEVICES   IWANMI
VISUALIZATION OF FORCE   IWANMI
WAVES ON THE SEASHORE   IWANMI
WHAT TRIGGERS SNOWSLIDES   IWANMI

PHYSICS - HEAT AND FRICTION

(MOTION PICTURES)

HOW TO MEASURE TEMPERATURE   IWANMI
SKATING   IWANMI
SKI   IWANMI
STORY OF THE REFRIGERATOR   IWANMI
UTILIZATION OF SOLAR HEAT   IWANMI

(TRANSPARENCIES)

HEATING A HOME (H)   BOW

PHYSICS - LIGHT AND COLOR

(MOTION PICTURES)

NATURE OF MATTER, THE - AN ATOMIC VIEW (C A)   CRMP
REFRACTION AND SHADOW OF LIGHT   IWANMI
REFRACTION OF LIGHT   IWANMI
WHAT IS LIGHT, PT 1   IWANMI
WHAT IS LIGHT, PT 2   IWANMI

(TRANSPARENCIES)

COLOR WHEEL (I-H)   BOW
COMBINING COLORS (I-H)   BOW
EXPERIMENTING WITH LIGHT AND OBJECTS (I-H)   BOW
EXPERIMENTS WITH COLORED LIGHT (I-H)   BOW
EXPERIMENTS WITH COLORED OBJECTS (I-H)   BOW
HOW COLOR PICTURES ARE MADE (I-H)   BOW
HOW LENSES WORK (I-H)   BOW
LAW OF REFLECTION (I-H)   BOW
LIGHT AND COLOR--A SERIES (I-H)   BOW
LIGHT AND DARKNESS (I-H)   BOW
LIGHT--A SERIES (I-C)   BOW
MATERIALS AND LIGHT (I-C)   BOW
MICROSCOPE (I-C)   BOW
PRIMARY COLORS OF LIGHT (I-C)   BOW
PRISM AND SPECTRUM (I-H)   BOW

REFLECTION OF LIGHT (I-C) BOW
REFRACTION AND LENSES (I-C) BOW
REFRACTION OF LIGHT (I-H) BOW
SPECTRUM (I-C) BOW
TWO WAYS TO PRODUCE COLOR (I-H) BOW

PHYSICS - LIQUIDS AND HYDRAULICS

(FILMSTRIPS)

GAS/LIQUID/SOLID, PT 1 RAYM

PHYSICS - MECHANICS

(MOTION PICTURES)

GEAR IWANMI

PHYSICS - SOUND

(MOTION PICTURES)

NOISE AND ITS EFFECTS ON HEALTH
(J-C A) FLMFR
QUIET, PLEASE WILCOX

(TRANSPARENCIES)

REFLECTION OF SOUND (I-C) BOW
SONAR (I-C) BOW
SOUND REPRODUCTION (I-C) BOW
SOUND WAVES (I-C) BOW
SOUND--A SERIES (I-C) BOW
SPEECH (I-C) BOW
VIBRATION AND TRAVEL (I-C) BOW

SOCIAL SCIENCE

SOCIAL SCIENCE - GENERAL

(FILMSTRIPS)

DAY IN THE CONGO, A DOUBLE

(MOTION PICTURES)

FROM CAVE TO CITY (I-C) FLMFR
WHAT'S WRONG WITH THE SOCIAL
SCIENCES (H-C A) TIMLIF

(TRANSPARENCIES)

BASIC SOCIAL STUDIES CONCEPTS
- ECONOMICS--A SERIES (J-H) LEART
BASIC SOCIAL STUDIES CONCEPTS
- POLITICS, SOCIAL-ECONOMIC
INTERDEPENDENCE--A SERIES (J-H) LEART
BASIC SOCIAL STUDIES CONCEPTS
- SOCIETY--A SERIES (J-H) LEART
HOW DOES SOCIETY TEACH ITS VALUES
(J-H) LEART
WHAT IS A SOCIAL INSTITUTION (J-H) LEART
WHAT IS A SOCIETY (J-H) LEART
WHAT IS AN OPEN SOCIETY (J-H) LEART
WHAT IS SOCIAL STUDIES - AN
INTERDISCIPLINARY APPROACH
(J-H) LEART
WHY A SOCIETY NEEDS TO STUDY IT'S
PAST (J-H) LEART

BASIC NEEDS - CLOTHING, FOOD, SHELTER

(FILMSTRIPS)

CONSUMERISM - THE DANGERS OF
AFFLUENCE, PT 1 ASPRSS
CONSUMERISM - THE DANGERS OF
AFFLUENCE, PT 2 ASPRSS
HOW THINGS ARE MADE--A SERIES EGH
HOW WE BUILD THINGS--A SERIES EGH
LIVING IN ASIA TODAY - AMONG
THE MARKETS OF AFGHANISTAN
(P-I) CORF
LIVING IN ASIA TODAY - WITH A
FISH SELLER IN MALAYSIA (P-I) CORF
LIVING WITH NATURAL GAS LILC
ONE HUNDRED AND THIRTY
BILLION DOLLAR FOOD
ASSEMBLY LINE (C A) USDA
TAKING CARE OF THINGS AROUND ME -
BOOKS BFA

(MOTION PICTURES)

BREAD (I-C A) HRAW
FRESH CHILLED SUNSHINE MTP
NUTRITION - THE INNER ENVIRONMENT
(P-J) AMEDFL
OUT OF HANDS (P-I) HRAW
TUNA FROM CATCH TO THE CAN MTP

CITIZENSHIP

(FILMSTRIPS)

ELECTION, THE EGH
NOW YOU ARE A VOTER--A SERIES EGH
REGISTRATION AND PICKING A
CANDIDATE EGH
RIGHT TO VOTE, THE EGH
WORKING IN THE POLITICAL WORLD EGH

(TRANSPARENCIES)

LIBRARY SKILLS--A SERIES BOW

COMMUNICATIONS

(FILMSTRIPS)

HUMANITIES - A WORLD BETWEEN
WARS, PT 1 (J-H) GA
HUMANITIES - A WORLD BETWEEN
WARS, PT 2 (J-H) GA

(MOTION PICTURES)

STORY OF THE U S MAIL BEF

(VIDEOTAPES)

SOLUTIONS IN COMMUNICATIONS -
INTRODUCTORY LESSON (T) SCCOE

(AUDIO TAPES)

MESSAGE FROM OUR SPONSOR, A (I-J) CORF
MOVIES BASCH
SEVENTEENTH CENTURY BEGINNING (J-
C) IU
SPOTS BEFORE YOUR EYES (J-C) IU
TELEVISION BASCH
THAT YOU MAY KNOW - AGAIN (J-C) IU
WHAT'S NEWS (J-C) INSKY
WHO PAYS FOR THE NEWS (J-C) IU
YOU ARE THE TARGET (J-C) INSKY

(TRANSPARENCIES)

ADDRESSING ENVELOPES FOR BUSINESS
LETTERS (I) BOW
ADDRESSING ENVELOPES FOR FRIENDLY
LETTERS (I) BOW
LETTER WRITING--A SERIES (I) BOW
WRITING BUSINESS LETTERS (I) BOW
WRITING FRIENDLY LETTERS (I) BOW

COMMUNITY CENTERS

(MOTION PICTURES)

CENTER OF LIFE (J-C A) GRANDY
MULTIPLE CHOICE (J-C A) INDSLF

COMMUNITY LIFE

(FILMSTRIPS)

CITIES OF ITALY EGH
CITIES OF ROME AND FLORENCE EGH
CITY - HOW AMERICA LIVES--A SERIES AVNA
CITY IN HISTORY, THE, PT 1 (J-C A) EDDIM
CITY IN HISTORY, THE, PT 2 (J-C A) EDDIM
CITY LIFE EGH
HOW WE BUILD CITIES EGH
HOW WE BUILD SKYSCRAPERS EGH
LIVING IN AFRICA TODAY - A CITY
FAMILY OF MOROCCO (P-I) CORF
LIVING IN AFRICA TODAY - A CITY
FAMILY OF MALI (P-I) CORF
LIVING IN AFRICA TODAY - A
PROFESSIONAL OF GHANA (P-I) CORF
LIVING IN AFRICA TODAY - A
SUBURBAN FAMILY OF SOUTH
AFRICA (P-I) CORF
LIVING IN AFRICA TODAY - A
VILLAGE FAMILY OF THE UPPER
VOLTA (P-I) CORF
LIVING IN AFRICA TODAY - A
VILLAGE FAMILY OF MALI (P-I) CORF
LIVING IN AFRICA TODAY - A
VILLAGE FAMILY OF ZAIRE (P-I) CORF
LIVING IN AFRICA TODAY--A SERIES (P-I) CORF
LIVING IN ASIA TODAY - AT A
SCHOOL IN KYOTO, JAPAN (P-I) CORF
LIVING IN ASIA TODAY - IN A
VILLAGE IN AMERICAN SAMOA
(P-I) CORF
LIVING IN ASIA TODAY - WITH A
CITY FAMILY OF TAIWAN (P-I) CORF
LOS ANGELES - CITY OF AUTOMOBILES
(J-H A) SVE
NEW TOWN - VALENCIA, CALIFORNIA (J-
H A) SVE
SEATTLE - A CITY FACES CRISIS (J-H A) SVE
VILLAGE LIFE EGH

(MOTION CARTRIDGES)

CITIES--A SERIES (I-C) BFA
CITIES, THE - A CITY IS TO LIVE IN, PT
1 (I-C) BFA
CITIES, THE - A CITY IS TO LIVE IN, PT
2 (I-C) BFA

(MOTION PICTURES)

BREAD (I-C A) HRAW
BUILDING A HARBOR (I-J) AIMS
CHILDREN OF THE KIBBUTZ (I-C A) ACI
FLOWERS FOR DAHLIA ALDEN
FROM CAVE TO CITY (I-C) FLMFR
JUNIOR FIREMEN LACFD
KIBBUTZ, A ALDEN
LET'S IMAGINE - LIFE IN UTOPIA ALDEN
LIGHT OF DAY, THE GRADYM
NEW YORK - THE ANYTIME CITY MTP
NEW YORK CITY MTP
PARK ON OUR BLOCK, A (J-C A) WASHBF

(AUDIO TAPES)

SOUND OF A CITY, THE (I) IU
WOMEN DID IT, THE (H A) USOE
YANKEE DOODLEBUG AND THE AW-
THAT'S NOTHIN' (P-I) UTEX

(TRANSPARENCIES)

MAN'S COMMUNITY EXPANDS
THROUGH THE AGES (J-H) LEART

CONSUMPTION (ECONOMICS)

(FILMSTRIPS)

CONSUMERISM - THE DANGERS OF
AFFLUENCE, PT 1 ASPRSS
CONSUMERISM - THE DANGERS OF
AFFLUENCE, PT 2 ASPRSS
ECONOMIC DECISION MAKING -
WHAT, HOW AND FOR WHOM (I-
H) DOUBLE
ECONOMICS--A SERIES (I-H) DOUBLE
GOOD GOODIES BFA
LOOKING GREAT ON A SHOESTRING--A
SERIES EGH
MIXED ECONOMY OF THE UNITED
STATES (I-H) DOUBLE
NATION OF OWNERS--A SERIES XEROX

(MOTION PICTURES)

DECIDING (P-I) CENTEF
MONEY, MONEY, MONEY (P-J) TEXFLM
WHAT IS BUSINESS (H-C A) SAIF

(AUDIO TAPES)

USE OF BANKS (H-C) INSKY

(TRANSPARENCIES)

ACCUMULATING CAPITAL FOR
INVESTMENTS (J-H) LEART
AFTER THE 'TAKE-OFF' - A DRIVE TO
MATURITY (J-H) LEART
BANKS ACCUMULATE AND DISTRIBUTE
CAPITAL (J-H) LEART
BASIC SOCIAL STUDIES CONCEPTS
- ECONOMICS--A SERIES (J-H) LEART
BASIC SOCIAL STUDIES CONCEPTS
- POLITICS, SOCIAL-ECONOMIC
INTERDEPENDENCE--A SERIES (J-H) LEART
BUSINESS - WHAT COMES BEFORE
PROFIT (J-H) LEART
BUSINESS ORGANIZATION AND
OWNERSHIP (J-H) LEART
CONSUMPTION AND ECONOMICS (J-H) LEART
DEFINITION OF ECONOMIC ROLE (J-H) LEART
DIFFERENT MEDIUMS OF
EXCHANGE ARE USED IN
DIFFERENT TYPES OF MARKETS (J-H) LEART
DOES FOREIGN AID MEAN FOREIGN
CONTROL (J-H) LEART
DOMESTIC SYSTEM VS FACTORY (J-H) LEART
ECONOMIC INTERDEPENDENCE OF
PEOPLE (J-H) LEART
ECONOMIC PHILOSOPHY IN
TRADITIONAL SOCIETY (J-H) LEART
ECONOMICS - ECONOMIC HISTORY--A
SERIES (J-H) LEART
ECONOMICS - ECONOMICS IN ACTION--A
SERIES (J-H) LEART
ECONOMICS - POLITICAL ECONOMY
AND PHILOSOPHY --A SERIES (J-
H) LEART
ECONOMICS IN A DEVELOPING NATION
(J-H) LEART
ECONOMICS IN A TRADITIONAL SOCIETY
(J-H) LEART
ECONOMICS TERMS (J-H) LEART
EDUCATION AND ECONOMICS (J-H) LEART
FACTORS IN ECONOMIC GROWTH (J-H) LEART
FACTORS OF PRODUCTION (J-H) LEART

FEDERAL BUDGET - INCOME AND
EXPENDITURES (J-H)   LEART
GROWTH OF INTERNATIONAL TRADE
AND COMMERCE (J-H)   LEART
GUILD VS LABOR UNION   LEART
HISTORY OF RECORD KEEPING (J-H)   LEART
HOW BANKS WORK (J-H)   LEART
HOW DO CHECKS REPLACE MONEY (J-
H)   LEART
HOW PRICE IS DETERMINED (J-H)   LEART
HOW TO EXPAND PRODUCTION (J-H)   LEART
HOW WE MEASURE ECONOMIC GROWTH
(J-H)   LEART
INDUSTRIAL REVOLUTION IS A 'TAKE-
OFF' (J-H)   LEART
INDUSTRIAL REVOLUTION TODAY (J-H)   LEART
INTERNATIONAL COMMERCIAL POLICY
(J-H)   LEART
INTERNATIONAL TRADE AND FINANCE
(J-H)   LEART
LABOR AND ECONOMICS (J-H)   LEART
MATURITY - HIGH MASS CONSUMPTION
(J-H)   LEART
MONEY - HISTORY, TYPES AND
PURPOSES (J-H)   LEART
NATURAL RESOURCES AND ECONOMICS
(J-H)   LEART
PATTERNS OF CONSUMPTION -
MARKETING (J-H)   LEART
PER CAPITA INCOME AND
CONSUMPTION (J-H)   LEART
PRICES AND THE ROLE OF
GOVERNMENT (J-H)   LEART
PRODUCTION DEPENDS ON DEMAND (J-
H)   LEART
REQUIREMENTS OF A 'TAKE-OFF' (J-H)   LEART
ROLE OF U S GOVERNMENT IN
ECONOMICS VS ROLE OF SOVIET
GOVERNMENT (J-H)   LEART
SAVINGS AND INVESTMENTS (J-H)   LEART
SECTORS OF A MODERN ECONOMY (J-
H)   LEART
STAGES OF ECONOMIC GROWTH (J-H)   LEART
TAXES AND THE INDIVIDUAL (J-H)   LEART
TODAY'S ISMS (J-H)   LEART
TOWN AND ECONOMICS (J-H)   LEART
TYPES OF MARKET AND EXCHANGES (J-
H)   LEART
TYPES OF PRODUCTION (J-H)   LEART
VALUES IN ECONOMIC DECISION (J-H)   LEART
WHAT IS CAPITAL (J-H)   LEART
WHAT IS ECONOMIC GROWTH (J-H)   LEART
WHAT IS ECONOMIC PLANNING (J-H)   LEART
WHAT IS ECONOMICS (J-H)   LEART

COST AND STANDARD OF LIVING

(FILMSTRIPS)

TAKING CARE OF THINGS AROUND ME -
BOOKS   BFA

(TRANSPARENCIES)

ACCUMULATING CAPITAL FOR
INVESTMENTS (J-H)   LEART
AFTER THE 'TAKE-OFF' - A DRIVE TO
MATURITY (J-H)   LEART
BANKS ACCUMULATE AND DISTRIBUTE
CAPITAL (J-H)   LEART
BUSINESS - WHAT COMES BEFORE
PROFIT (J-H)   LEART
DIFFERENT MEDIUMS OF
EXCHANGE ARE USED IN
DIFFERENT TYPES OF MARKETS (J-H)   LEART
DOMESTIC SYSTEM VS FACTORY (J-H)   LEART
ECONOMICS - ECONOMIC HISTORY--A
SERIES (J-H)   LEART
ECONOMICS - ECONOMICS IN ACTION--A
SERIES (J-H)   LEART
ECONOMICS IN A DEVELOPING NATION
(J-H)   LEART
ECONOMICS IN A TRADITIONAL SOCIETY
(J-H)   LEART
ECONOMICS TERMS (J-H)   LEART
FACTORS IN ECONOMIC GROWTH (J-H)   LEART
GROWTH OF INTERNATIONAL TRADE
AND COMMERCE (J-H)   LEART
HISTORY OF RECORD KEEPING (J-H)   LEART
HOW TO EXPAND PRODUCTION (J-H)   LEART
HOW WE MEASURE ECONOMIC GROWTH
(J-H)   LEART
INDUSTRIAL REVOLUTION IS A 'TAKE-
OFF' (J-H)   LEART
INDUSTRIAL REVOLUTION TODAY (J-H)   LEART
INTERNATIONAL COMMERCIAL POLICY
(J-H)   LEART
INTERNATIONAL TRADE AND FINANCE
(J-H)   LEART
MATURITY - HIGH MASS CONSUMPTION
(J-H)   LEART
PATTERNS OF CONSUMPTION -
MARKETING (J-H)   LEART
PER CAPITA INCOME AND
CONSUMPTION (J-H)   LEART
PRICES AND THE ROLE OF
GOVERNMENT (J-H)   LEART

PRODUCTION DEPENDS ON DEMAND (J-
H)   LEART
REQUIREMENTS OF A 'TAKE-OFF' (J-H)   LEART
SAVINGS AND INVESTMENTS (J-H)   LEART
SECTORS OF A MODERN ECONOMY (J-
H)   LEART
STAGES OF ECONOMIC GROWTH (J-H)   LEART
TOWN AND ECONOMICS (J-H)   LEART
WHAT IS ECONOMIC PLANNING (J-H)   LEART

FACTORY SYSTEM

(FILMSTRIPS)

FORMING A CAN   EGH
MAKING CLOTHING   EGH

(TRANSPARENCIES)

BANKS ACCUMULATE AND DISTRIBUTE
CAPITAL (J-H)   LEART
BUSINESS - WHAT COMES BEFORE
PROFIT (J-H)   LEART
DOMESTIC SYSTEM VS FACTORY (J-H)   LEART
ECONOMICS - ECONOMIC HISTORY--A
SERIES (J-H)   LEART
ECONOMICS - ECONOMICS IN ACTION--A
SERIES (J-H)   LEART
ECONOMICS IN A DEVELOPING NATION
(J-H)   LEART
FACTORS IN ECONOMIC GROWTH (J-H)   LEART
GROWTH OF INTERNATIONAL TRADE
AND COMMERCE (J-H)   LEART
HOW TO EXPAND PRODUCTION (J-H)   LEART
HOW WE MEASURE ECONOMIC GROWTH
(J-H)   LEART
INDUSTRIAL REVOLUTION IS A 'TAKE-
OFF' (J-H)   LEART
INDUSTRIAL REVOLUTION TODAY (J-H)   LEART
INTERNATIONAL COMMERCIAL POLICY
(J-H)   LEART
INTERNATIONAL TRADE AND FINANCE
(J-H)   LEART
MATURITY - HIGH MASS CONSUMPTION
(J-H)   LEART
PATTERNS OF CONSUMPTION -
MARKETING (J-H)   LEART
PER CAPITA INCOME AND
CONSUMPTION (J-H)   LEART
PRICES AND THE ROLE OF
GOVERNMENT (J-H)   LEART
PRODUCTION DEPENDS ON DEMAND (J-
H)   LEART
REQUIREMENTS OF A 'TAKE-OFF' (J-H)   LEART
SAVINGS AND INVESTMENTS (J-H)   LEART
SECTORS OF A MODERN ECONOMY (J-
H)   LEART
STAGES OF ECONOMIC GROWTH (J-H)   LEART
TOWN AND ECONOMICS (J-H)   LEART
WHAT IS ECONOMIC PLANNING (J-H)   LEART

FARM LIFE

(FILMSTRIPS)

LIVING IN AFRICA TODAY - A
VILLAGE FAMILY OF THE UPPER
VOLTA (P-I)   CORF
LIVING IN AFRICA TODAY - A
VILLAGE FAMILY OF MALI (P-I)   CORF
LIVING IN AFRICA TODAY - A
WHITE FARM FAMILY OF KENYA
(P-I)   CORF

(MOTION PICTURES)

CHILDREN OF THE KIBBUTZ (I-C A)   ACI
FLOWERS FOR DAHLIA   ALDEN
KIBBUTZ, A   ALDEN
LIGHT OF DAY, THE   GRADYM
THIS IS OUR FARM   ALDEN
THOSE ANIMALS ON THE FARM (K-P)   CLBELL
YESTERDAY'S FARM (P-J)   BFA

(AUDIO TAPES)

SYLVANIA STORY, THE (H A)   USOE

FARM PRODUCE - MARKETING

(FILMSTRIPS)

LIVING IN ASIA TODAY - AMONG
THE MARKETS OF AFGHANISTAN
(P-I)   CORF

(MOTION CARTRIDGES)

GLUTEN DEVELOPMENT   IOWA

(MOTION PICTURES)

CHAROLAIS REPORT, THE   MTP

FOOD ADULTERATION AND INSPECTION

(FILMSTRIPS)

ONE HUNDRED AND THIRTY
BILLION DOLLAR FOOD
ASSEMBLY LINE (C A)   USDA

HOME AND SCHOOL

(FILMSTRIPS)

HOW WE BUILD HOUSES   EGH
LIVING IN ASIA TODAY - AT A
SCHOOL IN KYOTO, JAPAN (P-I)   CORF
TAKING CARE OF THINGS AROUND ME -
BOOKS   BFA

(AUDIO TAPES)

MOVING - NEW HOME, NEW
NEIGHBORHOOD   BASCH
MOVING - NEW SCHOOL, NEW
PLAYMATES   BASCH
THEY CAN'T WAIT (H A)   AJC

INDIANS

(FILMSTRIPS)

AFTER THE SETTLERS CAME   EGH
ANCIENT CIVILIZATIONS OF THE
AMERICAS--A SERIES (I-J)   EBEC
AZTECS, THE (I-J)   EBEC
EARLY AMERICAN INDIAN   EGH
INCAS, THE (I-J)   EBEC
INDIANS OF AMERICA--A SERIES   EGH
MAYAS, THE (I-J)   EBEC
NORTHWEST FILMSTRIPS--A SERIES   UWASHP
OLYMPIC COAST INDIANS TODAY   UWASHP
PLAINS INDIANS, THE   EGH
RAIN FORESTS OF THE NORTHWEST
COAST   UWASHP

INDIANS OF NORTH AMERICA - GENERAL

(FILMSTRIPS)

AFTER THE SETTLERS CAME   EGH
EARLY AMERICAN INDIAN   EGH
INDIANS OF AMERICA--A SERIES   EGH
PLAINS INDIANS, THE   EGH

(MOTION PICTURES)

NATION WITHIN A NATION, A (I-C A)   HEARST

INDIANS OF NORTH AMERICA - CANADA

(MOTION PICTURES)

INDIAN MEMENTO (J-C A)   NFBC

**INDIANS OF NORTH AMERICA - GOVERNMENT
RELATIONS**

(FILMSTRIPS)

AFTER THE SETTLERS CAME   EGH

INDIANS OF NORTH AMERICA - HISTORY

(FILMSTRIPS)

AFTER THE SETTLERS CAME   EGH
EARLY AMERICAN INDIAN   EGH
INDIANS OF AMERICA--A SERIES   EGH
PLAINS INDIANS, THE   EGH

(MOTION PICTURES)

INDIAN MEMENTO (J-C A)   NFBC

INDIANS OF NORTH AMERICA - ORIGIN

(FILMSTRIPS)

EARLY AMERICAN INDIAN   EGH

**INDIANS OF NORTH AMERICA - RELIGION AND
MYTHOLOGY**

(FILMSTRIPS)

AFTER THE SETTLERS CAME   EGH

INDIANS OF NORTH AMERICA - RESERVATIONS

(FILMSTRIPS)

PLAINS INDIANS, THE — EGH

(MOTION PICTURES)

NATION WITHIN A NATION, A (I-C A) — HEARST

INDIANS OF NORTH AMERICA - SOCIAL CONDITIONS

(FILMSTRIPS)

AFTER THE SETTLERS CAME — EGH
OLYMPIC COAST INDIANS TODAY — UWASHP
RAIN FORESTS OF THE NORTHWEST COAST — UWASHP

(MOTION PICTURES)

NATION WITHIN A NATION, A (I-C A) — HEARST

INDIANS OF NORTH AMERICA - SOCIAL LIFE AND CUSTOMS

(FILMSTRIPS)

EARLY AMERICAN INDIAN — EGH
OLYMPIC COAST INDIANS TODAY — UWASHP
PLAINS INDIANS, THE — EGH

(MOTION PICTURES)

NATION WITHIN A NATION, A (I-C A) — HEARST

INDIANS OF NORTH AMERICA - WARS

(FILMSTRIPS)

AFTER THE SETTLERS CAME — EGH

INDUSTRIAL MOBILIZATION

(FILMSTRIPS)

INDUSTRIAL WORKER — EGH

(MOTION PICTURES)

RHYTHM OF TOMMORW — ALDEN

INDUSTRIALIZATION

(FILMSTRIPS)

AMERICAN GENIUS, 1880 - 1918 (H-C) — EDDIM
FORMING A CAN — EGH
INDUSTRIAL WORKER — EGH
MAKING CLOTHING — EGH

(MOTION PICTURES)

BIG YELLOW TAXI — PFP
BRIDGE OF FRIENDSHIP — ALDEN

(TRANSPARENCIES)

BANKS ACCUMULATE AND DISTRIBUTE CAPITAL (J-H) — LEART
BUSINESS - WHAT COMES BEFORE PROFIT (J-H) — LEART
DOMESTIC SYSTEM VS FACTORY (J-H) — LEART
ECONOMICS - ECONOMIC HISTORY--A SERIES (J-H) — LEART
ECONOMICS - ECONOMICS IN ACTION--A SERIES (J-H) — LEART
ECONOMICS IN A DEVELOPING NATION (J-H) — LEART
FACTORS IN ECONOMIC GROWTH (J-H) — LEART
GROWTH OF INTERNATIONAL TRADE AND COMMERCE (J-H) — LEART
HOW TO EXPAND PRODUCTION (J-H) — LEART
HOW WE MEASURE ECONOMIC GROWTH (J-H) — LEART
INDUSTRIAL REVOLUTION IS A 'TAKE-OFF' (J-H) — LEART
INDUSTRIAL REVOLUTION TODAY (J-H) — LEART
INTERNATIONAL COMMERCIAL POLICY (J-H) — LEART
INTERNATIONAL TRADE AND FINANCE (J-H) — LEART
MATURITY - HIGH MASS CONSUMPTION (J-H) — LEART
PATTERNS OF CONSUMPTION - MARKETING (J-H) — LEART
PER CAPITA INCOME AND CONSUMPTION (J-H) — LEART
PRICES AND THE ROLE OF GOVERNMENT (J-H) — LEART
PRODUCTION DEPENDS ON DEMAND (J-H) — LEART

REQUIREMENTS OF A 'TAKE-OFF' (J-H) — LEART
SAVINGS AND INVESTMENTS (J-H) — LEART
SECTORS OF A MODERN ECONOMY (J-H) — LEART
STAGES OF ECONOMIC GROWTH (J-H) — LEART
TOWN AND ECONOMICS (J-H) — LEART
WHAT IS ECONOMIC PLANNING (J-H) — LEART

INDUSTRY AND STATE

(TRANSPARENCIES)

DOES FOREIGN AID MEAN FOREIGN CONTROL (J-H) — LEART
ECONOMIC PHILOSOPHY IN TRADITIONAL SOCIETY (J-H) — LEART
ECONOMICS - POLITICAL ECONOMY AND PHILOSOPHY --A SERIES (J-H) — LEART
EDUCATION AND ECONOMICS (J-H) — LEART
FEDERAL BUDGET - INCOME AND EXPENDITURES (J-H) — LEART
GUILD VS LABOR UNION — LEART
ROLE OF U S GOVERNMENT IN ECONOMICS VS ROLE OF SOVIET GOVERNMENT (J-H) — LEART
TODAY'S ISMS (J-H) — LEART

INTERNATIONAL ECONOMIC RELATIONS

(MOTION PICTURES)

GROWING PAINS FOR THE COMMON MARKET — HEARST

(TRANSPARENCIES)

DIFFERENT MEDIUMS OF EXCHANGE ARE USED IN DIFFERENT TYPES OF MARKETS (J-H) — LEART
DOES FOREIGN AID MEAN FOREIGN CONTROL (J-H) — LEART
ECONOMIC PHILOSOPHY IN TRADITIONAL SOCIETY (J-H) — LEART
ECONOMICS - ECONOMICS IN ACTION--A SERIES (J-H) — LEART
ECONOMICS - POLITICAL ECONOMY AND PHILOSOPHY --A SERIES (J-H) — LEART
ECONOMICS IN A DEVELOPING NATION (J-H) — LEART
EDUCATION AND ECONOMICS (J-H) — LEART
FEDERAL BUDGET - INCOME AND EXPENDITURES (J-H) — LEART
GUILD VS LABOR UNION — LEART
HOW TO EXPAND PRODUCTION (J-H) — LEART
HOW WE MEASURE ECONOMIC GROWTH (J-H) — LEART
INTERNATIONAL COMMERCIAL POLICY (J-H) — LEART
INTERNATIONAL TRADE AND FINANCE (J-H) — LEART
PATTERNS OF CONSUMPTION - MARKETING (J-H) — LEART
PER CAPITA INCOME AND CONSUMPTION (J-H) — LEART
PRICES AND THE ROLE OF GOVERNMENT (J-H) — LEART
PRODUCTION DEPENDS ON DEMAND (J-H) — LEART
ROLE OF U S GOVERNMENT IN ECONOMICS VS ROLE OF SOVIET GOVERNMENT (J-H) — LEART
SAVINGS AND INVESTMENTS (J-H) — LEART
SECTORS OF A MODERN ECONOMY (J-H) — LEART
TODAY'S ISMS (J-H) — LEART
WHAT IS ECONOMIC PLANNING (J-H) — LEART

LABOR AND LABORING CLASSES

(TRANSPARENCIES)

DOES FOREIGN AID MEAN FOREIGN CONTROL (J-H) — LEART
ECONOMIC PHILOSOPHY IN TRADITIONAL SOCIETY (J-H) — LEART
ECONOMICS - POLITICAL ECONOMY AND PHILOSOPHY --A SERIES (J-H) — LEART
EDUCATION AND ECONOMICS (J-H) — LEART
FEDERAL BUDGET - INCOME AND EXPENDITURES (J-H) — LEART
GUILD VS LABOR UNION — LEART
ROLE OF U S GOVERNMENT IN ECONOMICS VS ROLE OF SOVIET GOVERNMENT (J-H) — LEART
TODAY'S ISMS (J-H) — LEART

MANNERS AND CUSTOMS

(FILMSTRIPS)

ANCIENT CIVILIZATIONS OF THE AMERICAS--A SERIES (I-J) — EBEC

AZTECS, THE (I-J) — EBEC
CHILDREN — EGH
CHRISTMAS IN A NOISY VILLAGE (K-P) — VIP
CITIES OF ITALY — EGH
CITIES OF ROME AND FLORENCE — EGH
COMMUNES IN CHINA — EGH
DAY IN THE CONGO, A — DOUBLE
ENGLAND (P-I) — PATED
FLORENCE AND VENICE — EGH
GREAT MEN AND ARTISTS — EGH
GREECE (P-I) — PATED
INCAS, THE (I-J) — EBEC
ITALIAN CULTURE AND RECREATION — EGH
ITALIAN CULTURE AND RECREATION — EGH
ITALIAN HOME AND FAMILY, THE — EGH
ITALY (P-I) — PATED
ITALY - A REGIONAL STUDY--A SERIES — EGH
ITALY - THE LAND — EGH
JAPAN — TF
LEBANON (P-I) — PATED
LIFE IN BRITAIN — EGH
LIFE IN HOLLAND — EGH
LIFE OF THE LEISURE CLASS — EGH
LIFEWAYS OF THE PEOPLE - SOUTH AMERICA--A SERIES — EGH
LIVING IN AFRICA TODAY - A CITY FAMILY OF MOROCCO (P-I) — CORF
LIVING IN AFRICA TODAY - A CITY FAMILY OF MALI (P-I) — CORF
LIVING IN AFRICA TODAY - A PROFESSIONAL OF GHANA (P-I) — CORF
LIVING IN AFRICA TODAY - A SUBURBAN FAMILY OF SOUTH AFRICA (P-I) — CORF
LIVING IN AFRICA TODAY - A VILLAGE FAMILY OF THE UPPER VOLTA (P-I) — CORF
LIVING IN AFRICA TODAY - A VILLAGE FAMILY OF MALI (P-I) — CORF
LIVING IN AFRICA TODAY - A VILLAGE FAMILY OF ZAIRE (P-I) — CORF
LIVING IN AFRICA TODAY - A WHITE FARM FAMILY OF KENYA (P-I) — CORF
LIVING IN AFRICA TODAY--A SERIES (P-I) — CORF
LIVING IN ASIA TODAY - AT A SCHOOL IN KYOTO, JAPAN (P-I) — CORF
LIVING IN ASIA TODAY - AT A VILLAGE WEDDING IN THE PUNJAB, INDIA (P-I) — CORF
LIVING IN ASIA TODAY - IN A VILLAGE IN AMERICAN SAMOA (P-I) — CORF
LIVING IN ASIA TODAY - ON HOUSEBOATS IN KASHMIR (P-I) — CORF
LIVING IN ASIA TODAY - ON THE ISLAND OF BALI IN INDONESIA (P-I) — CORF
LIVING IN ASIA TODAY - WITH A CITY FAMILY OF TAIWAN (P-I) — CORF
LIVING IN ASIA TODAY - WITH A FISH SELLER IN MALAYSIA (P-I) — CORF
LIVING IN ASIA TODAY--A SERIES (P-I) — CORF
MAYAS, THE (I-J) — EBEC
NEW FRIENDS FROM DISTANT LANDS - THE CULTURE WE SHARE--A SERIES (P-I) — PATED
PEOPLE OF CHINA, THE — EGH
RANCH LIFE — EGH
TURKEY (P-I) — PATED
VILLAGE LIFE — EGH
WHAT IS GREAT BRITAIN — EGH
WHAT IS HOLLAND — EGH
WILDLIFE SANCTUARIES OF INDIA — AVEXP

(MOTION PICTURES)

BALI — PUI
CEYLON — PUI
CHILDREN OF THE KIBBUTZ (I-C A) — ACI
CHILDREN'S WORLD - MEXICO (K-I) — AVED
DRY SEASON, THE — CMC
EGYPT — PUI
GREECE — PUI
HAITI — PUI
HANUKKAH — ALDEN
HAWAII — PUI
HONG KONG — PUI
INDIA — PUI
ISRAEL — PUI
IT WAS THE CUSTOM — ALDEN
JAPAN — PUI
JAPANESE CHILDREN — IWANMI
JERUSALEM - HERE WE COME — ALDEN
KENYA — PUI
LIVING WOOD - AFRICAN MASKS AND MYTHS (I-H A) — GRADYM
PAKISTAN — PUI
PASSOVER — ALDEN
PLIGHT OF SOVIET JEWELRY, THE - LET MY PEOPLE GO — ALDEN
PORT OF CALL--A SERIES — PUI
PURIM — ALDEN
SHAVUOTH — ALDEN
SINGAPORE — PUI
SUCCOTH — ALDEN
SYRIA — PUI
THREE FAMILIES OF MALAYSIA (I) — CORF
TURKEY — PUI

ZANZIBAR	PUI

MAPS AND GLOBES

(MOTION CARTRIDGES)

CONTOUR MAPPING (P)	HUBDSC
MAP READING--A SERIES (P)	HUBDSC

NATURAL RESOURCES

(FILMSTRIPS)

BONNEVILLE DAM - POWERHOUSE OF THE COLUMBIA RIVER (J-H A)	SVE
ENERGY CRISIS, THE - AN HISTORICAL REVIEW (I)	TERF
ENERGY CRISIS, THE - REPORT FROM PLANET 32 (I)	TERF
LIVING WITH NATURAL GAS	LILC
SCHOOL TIMES KIT - APRIL--A SERIES (I)	TERF
TIMBER - WASHINGTON'S MOST VALUABLE CROP (J-H A)	SVE

(MOTION PICTURES)

CHALLENGE OF THE ARCTIC	ARIC
ERTS - EARTH RESOURCES TECHNOLOGY SATELLITE (J-C A)	NASA
INTERVIEW WITH GARRETT HARDIN (J-C A)	HRAW
STAKE IN THE FUTURE, A (J-C A)	NAGLEP
TO BOTTLE THE SUN	USAEC
VISTAS OF ISRAEL, NO. 3	ALDEN

(TRANSPARENCIES)

NATURAL RESOURCES AND ECONOMICS (J-H)	LEART

NEWSPAPER

(FILMSTRIPS)

NEWSPAPER REPORTER, THE (I-C)	SVE

(AUDIO TAPES)

SEVENTEENTH CENTURY BEGINNING (J-C)	IU
WHAT'S NEWS (J-C)	INSKY
WHO PAYS FOR THE NEWS (J-C)	IU

NUTRITION

(FILMSTRIPS)

DIET CLERK AND FRY COOK	EGH
FOOD SERVICE WORKER	EGH
OOPSIES, THE	PHOTO
PROCESSING SOUP	EGH
TALE OF TWO TEETH, A (P-I)	DISNEY

(MOTION PICTURES)

EARTHBREAD - A NATURAL FOOD (I-C)	FPRD
NUTRITION - THE INNER ENVIRONMENT (P-J)	AMEDFL

POSTAL SERVICE

(MOTION PICTURES)

STORY OF STAMPS, THE	ALDEN
STORY OF THE U S MAIL	BEF

(AUDIO TAPES)

STAMP COLLECTING AND MATHEMATICIANS (H A)	UOKLA

RAILROADS

(MOTION PICTURES)

POP (H-C A)	BFA

RELIGION, PRIMITIVE

(MOTION PICTURES)

LIVING WOOD - AFRICAN MASKS AND MYTHS (I-H A)	GRADYM

TELECOMMUNICATION

(MOTION PICTURES)

WHAT'S IT ALL ABOUT, HARRY (IND)	DATA

(AUDIO TAPES)

SPOTS BEFORE YOUR EYES (J-C)	IU

TRANSPORTATION - GENERAL

(FILMSTRIPS)

TRADE AND TRANSPORTATION IN CHINA	EGH

(MOTION PICTURES)

CARGO ON THE GO	BEF

TRANSPORTATION - AIR

(MOTION PICTURES)

ALASKA'S BUSH PILOT HERITAGE (I-H)	DISNEY
CARGO ON THE GO	BEF

TRANSPORTATION - HIGHWAY

(FILMSTRIPS)

DECISION IS YOURS, THE	NAVA
HOW WE BUILD ROADS	EGH
LONG HAUL TRUCK DRIVER, THE (I-C)	SVE

TRANSPORTATION - LAND

(FILMSTRIPS)

AUTOMOBILE, THE (HENRY FORD) (P)	EDPRC

TRANSPORTATION - WATER

(FILMSTRIPS)

HOW WE BUILD SHIPS	EGH

(MOTION PICTURES)

BUILDING A HARBOR (I-J)	AIMS
DAMAGE CONTROL - EFFECTS OF WEIGHT ON STABILITY, PT 2, WEIGHT CONDITION	USNAC
DAMAGE CONTROL - ELEMENTS OF STABILITY IN SHIP	USNAC
DAMAGE CONTROL - LOOSE WATER IN STABILITY, PT 1, IN INTACT SPACES	USNAC
DAMAGE CONTROL - THE METACENTER IN STABILITY, PT 2	USNAC
SHIPBOARD VIBRATIONS, PT 3 - VIBRATION, EXCITATION AND RESPONSE	USNAC

UNDERDEVELOPED AREAS

(MOTION PICTURES)

ISRAEL'S NATIONAL WATER CARRIER	ALDEN
ISRAEL'S QUEST FOR WATER	ALDEN
RHYTHM OF TOMMORW	ALDEN

SOCIOLOGY

ANTHROPOLOGY

(TRANSPARENCIES)

CULTURE VS CIVILIZATION (J-H)	LEART
HOW CUSTOMS CHANGE (J-H)	LEART
HOW DOES SOCIETY TEACH ITS VALUES (J-H)	LEART
MAN'S COMMUNITY EXPANDS THROUGH THE AGES (J-H)	LEART
WHAT IS A SOCIETY (J-H)	LEART
WHY A SOCIETY NEEDS TO STUDY IT'S PAST (J-H)	LEART

AUTOMATION

(MOTION PICTURES)

AFFAIRS OF A MAN, THE (J-C A)	FORD
RHYTHM OF TOMMORW	ALDEN

BEHAVIOR

(FILMSTRIPS)

ALIENATION AND MASS SOCIETY, PT 1	SED
ALIENATION AND MASS SOCIETY, PT 2	SED
ARE SEX AND LOVE THE SAME THING	EGH
ATTITUDES ABOUT HUMAN SEXUALITY	EGH

FEMALE OF THE SPECIES, THE	EGH
HUMAN SEXUALITY--A SERIES	EGH
MILES MUGWUMP AND FRANNIE FRANTIC	EGH
OUR INSTINCTS AND WHY WE HAVE THEM	EGH

(MOTION PICTURES)

A TO B	AMERFI
BERKELEY CHRISTMAS, A	AMERFI
COGNITIVE DEVELOPMENT (C A)	CRMP
DEPENDENCE - A NEW DEFINITION (C A)	CRMP
DEVELOPMENTAL PSYCHOLOGY FILM--A SERIES (C A)	CRMP
EMOTIONAL DEVELOPMENT (C A)	CRMP
FRANKENSTEIN IN A FISHBOWL	AMERFI
MORAL DEVELOPMENT (C A)	CRMP
WHAT'S WRONG WITH THE SOCIAL SCIENCES (H-C A)	TIMLIF

(VIDEOTAPES)

MARY	GPITVL
ROB	GPITVL

(AUDIO TAPES)

BEHAVIOR DISORDERS OF CHILDREN--A SERIES	SIGINF
BEHAVIOR MODIFICATION STRATEGIES FOR CHILD PSYCHOTHERAPISTS--A SERIES	SIGINF
CONSERVATIVE VS RADICAL BEHAVIORS - MILITARIST VS PACIFIST BEHAVIORS	SIGINF
SPECIAL CLINICAL PROBLEMS IN INTENSIVE PSYCHOTHERAPY--A SERIES	SIGINF
SUICIDE AND SUICIDE PREVENTION--A SERIES	SIGINF
SUICIDE AND VIOLENCE	SIGINF

(TRANSPARENCIES)

EMOTIONS AND SOCIAL ATTITUDES - ATTITUDES, VALUES--A SERIES (H)	LEART

BIRTH CONTROL

(MOTION PICTURES)

FAIR CHANCE (H-C A)	DATA
POPULATION EXPANSION AND BIRTH CONTROL (H-C A)	CHM

BIRTH RATE

(MOTION PICTURES)

POPULATION EXPANSION AND BIRTH CONTROL (H-C A)	CHM

CHILD WELFARE

(VIDEOTAPES)

HOME SWEET HOME	NITC

CITIES AND TOWNS

(FILMSTRIPS)

CITIES OF ITALY	EGH
CITIES OF ITALY	EGH
CITIES OF ROME AND FLORENCE	EGH
CITIES OF ROME AND FLORENCE	EGH
CITY - HOW AMERICA LIVES--A SERIES	AVNA
CITY IN HISTORY, THE, PT 1 (J-C A)	EDDIM
CITY IN HISTORY, THE, PT 2 (J-C A)	EDDIM
CITY LIFE	EGH
DYNAMISM OR DECAY	AVNA
FLORENCE AND VENICE	EGH
FLORENCE AND VENICE	EGH
GREAT MEN AND ARTISTS	EGH
HERITAGE OF GREATNESS	AVNA
HOW WE BUILD CITIES	EGH
HOW WE BUILD HOUSES	EGH
ITALIAN CULTURE AND RECREATION	EGH
ITALY - A REGIONAL STUDY--A SERIES	EGH
ITALY - THE LAND	EGH
LOS ANGELES - CITY OF AUTOMOBILES (J-H A)	SVE
NEW TOWN - VALENCIA, CALIFORNIA (J-H A)	SVE
SEATTLE - A CITY FACES CRISIS (J-H A)	SVE

(MOTION CARTRIDGES)

CITIES--A SERIES (I-C)	BFA
CITIES, THE - A CITY IS TO LIVE IN, PT 1 (I-C)	BFA

CITIES, THE - A CITY IS TO LIVE IN, PT 2 (I-C)   BFA
CITIES, THE - DILEMMA IN BLACK AND WHITE, PT 1 (I-C)   BFA
CITIES, THE - DILEMMA IN BLACK AND WHITE, PT 2 (I-C)   BFA
CITIES, THE - TO BUILD A FUTURE, PT 1 (I-C)   BFA
CITIES, THE - TO BUILD A FUTURE, PT 2 (I-C)   BFA

(MOTION PICTURES)

ABANDONMENT OF THE CITIES, THE (J-C A)   NBCTV
FIFTH STREET (C A)   DRMINC
NEW YORK - THE ANYTIME CITY   MTP
NEW YORK CITY   MTP
POPCORN LADY (I-C A)   SCHLAT
TOKYO - THE FIFTY-FIRST VOLCANO (H-C A)   TIMLIF
VISTAS OF ISRAEL, NO. 1   ALDEN

(AUDIO TAPES)

SOUND OF A CITY, THE (I)   IU

CIVILIZATION

(FILMSTRIPS)

AMERICAN CIVILIZATION - 1783-1840--A SERIES (J-C)   SUNCOM
ANCIENT CIVILIZATIONS OF THE AMERICAS--A SERIES (I-J) EBEC
ARTS AND THE COMMON MAN, THE (J-C)   SUNCOM
PORTRAIT OF A YOUNG NATION (J-C)   SUNCOM
YOUNG AMERICA ADMIRES THE ANCIENTS (J-C)   SUNCOM

(MOTION PICTURES)

CIVILISATION--A SERIES   TIMLIF
CIVILISATION, PROGRAM 01   TIMLIF
CIVILISATION, PROGRAM 02   TIMLIF
CIVILISATION, PROGRAM 03   TIMLIF
CIVILISATION, PROGRAM 04   TIMLIF
CIVILISATION, PROGRAM 05   TIMLIF
CIVILISATION, PROGRAM 06   TIMLIF
CIVILISATION, PROGRAM 07   TIMLIF
CIVILISATION, PROGRAM 08   TIMLIF
CIVILISATION, PROGRAM 09   TIMLIF
CIVILISATION, PROGRAM 10   TIMLIF
CIVILISATION, PROGRAM 11   TIMLIF
CIVILISATION, PROGRAM 12   TIMLIF
CIVILISATION, PROGRAM 13   TIMLIF

(TRANSPARENCIES)

CULTURE VS CIVILIZATION (J-H)   LEART

CLASS DISTINCTION

(AUDIO TAPES)

NORMAL AND ABNORMAL BEHAVIOR OF ADOLESCENCE-- A SERIES   SIGINF
PATTERNS OF DRUG ABUSE AMONG MIDDLE-CLASS ADOLESCENTS   SIGINF

COMMUNITY AGENCIES

(MOTION PICTURES)

AGED, THE (H-C A)   CAROUF
OPPORTUNITIES FOR THE DISADVANTAGED (J-H)   AMEDFL
PARK ON OUR BLOCK, A (J-C A)   WASHBF
STRAWBERRIES - WITH CREAM   MTP

(AUDIO TAPES)

INNOVATIVE SERVICES FOR YOUTH   SIGINF
WOMEN DID IT, THE (H A)   USOE

COMMUNITY CENTERS

(FILMSTRIPS)

COMPANY AND THE COMMUNITY, THE, PT 1   CREATV
COMPANY AND THE COMMUNITY, THE, PT 2   CREATV
GOD'S CHILDREN   UWLA

(MOTION PICTURES)

DAY CARE TODAY (C A)   POLYMR
INTERN - A LONG YEAR (J-C)   EBEC
STRAWBERRIES - WITH CREAM   MTP

COST AND STANDARD OF LIVING

(FILMSTRIPS)

CONSUMERISM - THE DANGERS OF AFFLUENCE, PT 1   ASPRSS
CONSUMERISM - THE DANGERS OF AFFLUENCE, PT 2   ASPRSS

COUNTRY LIFE

(FILMSTRIPS)

RANCH LIFE   EGH

COURTSHIP

(TRANSPARENCIES)

LOVE IS BOTH STURDY AND PERISHABLE (J)   LEART

CRIME

(FILMSTRIPS)

ONE PHASE OF THE BLACK MARKET IN MEAT   USOPA

(MOTION PICTURES)

BASIC LAW TERMS (J-C A)   PFP
CAUGHT (J-C)   NRMA
CRIME IN THE HOME (J-C A)   AIMS
CRIME ON THE STREETS (J-C A)   AIMS
LANTON MILLS   AMERFI
TAKING CARE OF BUSINESS   AMERFI
UNDER THE JUGGERNAUT   AMERFI
WHEN EVERY MINUTE COUNTS   MTP

(AUDIO TAPES)

SUICIDE AND VIOLENCE   SIGINF

CRIME AND CRIMINALS

(FILMSTRIPS)

HANGMAN'S KNOT VERSUS THE PAROLE BOARD (I-J)   SNBRST
JAIL TERM BEFORE TRIAL (I-J)   SNBRST
MIND BLOWERS--A SERIES (I-J)   SNBRST

(MOTION PICTURES)

BASIC LAW TERMS (J-C A)   PFP
CAUGHT (J-C)   NRMA
CRIME ON THE STREETS (J-C A)   AIMS
LANTON MILLS   AMERFI
TAKING CARE OF BUSINESS   AMERFI
UNDER THE JUGGERNAUT   AMERFI

(AUDIO TAPES)

SUICIDE - HOMICIDE - THE CONCEPT OF PSYCHOPHYSIOLOGIC DISORDERS   SIGINF
SUICIDE IN PRISON   SIGINF

DISCRIMINATION

(FILMSTRIPS)

HANGMAN'S KNOT VERSUS THE PAROLE BOARD (I-J)   SNBRST
HOW TO CLOSE OPEN HOUSING (I-J)   SNBRST
JAIL TERM BEFORE TRIAL (I-J)   SNBRST
MIND BLOWERS--A SERIES (I-J)   SNBRST
TRY TO JOIN OUR UNION (I-J)   SNBRST

(MOTION PICTURES)

VOICE OF LA RAZA   GREAVW

(AUDIO TAPES)

TERMITES IN THE HOUSE (H A)   AJC

(TRANSPARENCIES)

DATING RELATIONS - MIXED DATING--A SERIES (J) LEART
MIXED DATING AMONG RELIGIONS (J)   LEART

DIVORCE

(AUDIO TAPES)

PSYCHOLOGICAL REACTIONS TO DIVORCE, PT 1   SIGINF
PSYCHOLOGICAL REACTIONS TO DIVORCE, PT 2   SIGINF

DOMESTIC RELATIONS

(MOTION PICTURES)

AIN'T GONNA EAT MY MIND (J-C A)   CAROUF

(AUDIO TAPES)

RIGHT TO FREEDOM, THE (H A)   WNAD

EDUCATIONAL SOCIOLOGY

(FILMSTRIPS)

EDUCATION AND COMMUNICATION IN CHINA   EGH

(MOTION PICTURES)

COLLEGE DAZE   AMERFI
HI, SCHOOL (J-H A)   IDEA
NEW ESTATE (C T)   TIMLIF
PLACE TO LEARN, A (A)   DUPAGE

(VIDEOTAPES)

EDUCATION VS EDUCATION   SCCOE

(AUDIO TAPES)

SUN SHINES BRIGHT, THE (H A)   USOE
THEY CAN'T WAIT (H A)   AJC

ETHNOLOGY

(FILMSTRIPS)

AMERICAN ADVENTURE--A SERIES (I-J)   FIELEP
BLACK AMERICANS (I-J)   FIELEP
BLUE GOOTCHES, THE   EGH
FAT BLACK MACK   EGH
GERMAN AMERICANS (I-J)   FIELEP
ITALIAN AMERICANS (I-J)   FIELEP
MEXICAN AMERICANS (I-J)   FIELEP

(MOTION PICTURES)

THREE FAMILIES OF MALAYSIA (I)   CORF

FAMILY

(FILMSTRIPS)

CITY - HOW AMERICA LIVES--A SERIES   AVNA
DYNAMISM OR DECAY   AVNA
HERITAGE OF GREATNESS   AVNA
MARRIAGE AND FAMILIES   EGH

(MOTION PICTURES)

EDUCATION FOR FAMILY LIFE (H-C A)   CHM
EXECUTIVE'S WIFE, THE (A)   UEUWIS
FAIR CHANCE (H-C A)   DATA
INTRODUCTION TO SEX EDUCATION (H-C A)   CHM
POPULATION EXPANSION AND BIRTH CONTROL (H-C A) CHM
WE HAVE AN ADDICT IN THE HOUSE (J-C A)   DOUBLE

(AUDIO TAPES)

ADOLESCENT AND HIS PARENTS, THE   SIGINF
ADOLESCENT PATIENT AND THE FAMILY, THE   SIGINF
ADOLESCENTS AND ADULTS   SIGINF
BECOMING A PARENT   BASCH
BEHAVIOR DISORDERS OF CHILDREN--A SERIES   SIGINF
IT TAKES A WOMAN--A SERIES   BASCH
ON BECOMING IN-LAWS   BASCH
ON BEING WIDOWED   BASCH
PARENTS AS THERAPEUTIC AGENTS   SIGINF
PROBLEMS RESULTING FROM THE DEPRIVATION OF PARENTAL AFFECTION, PT 1   SIGINF
PROBLEMS RESULTING FROM THE DEPRIVATION OF PARENTAL AFFECTION, PT 2   SIGINF
PSYCHOLOGICAL REACTIONS TO DIVORCE, PT 1   SIGINF
PSYCHOLOGICAL REACTIONS TO DIVORCE, PT 2   SIGINF
PSYCHOLOGICAL REACTIONS TO DIVORCE, PT 3   SIGINF
RIGHT TO FREEDOM, THE (H A)   WNAD

(TRANSPARENCIES)

TYPES OF FAMILIES (J-H)   LEART

FARM LIFE

(FILMSTRIPS)

RANCH LIFE   EGH

(MOTION PICTURES)

FLOWERS FOR DAHLIA   ALDEN
KIBBUTZ, A   ALDEN
THIS IS OUR FARM   ALDEN
YESTERDAY'S FARM (P-J)   BFA

(AUDIO TAPES)

SYLVANIA STORY, THE (H A)   USOE

GERIATRICS

(MOTION PICTURES)

AGED, THE (H-C A)   CAROUF
IT HAPPENED IN HUALFIN, PT 1 -
   WHEN THE WIND IS SILENT   PIC
NEW DEAL (H-C A)   CAROUF

HEREDITY

(MOTION PICTURES)

RACE, INTELLIGENCE AND EDUCATION
(H-C A)   TIMLIF

HOUSING

(FILMSTRIPS)

EXTERIOR BUILDING MATERIALS FOR
YOUR HOME (J-C A)   USDA
HOUSING--A SERIES (J-C A)   USDA
HOW TO CLOSE OPEN HOUSING (I-J)   SNBRST
MIND BLOWERS--A SERIES (I-J)   SNBRST
PLANNING THE BEDROOM (J-C A)   USDA

(MOTION PICTURES)

ALFRED   AMERFI

(AUDIO TAPES)

TERMITES IN THE HOUSE (H A)   AJC

HUMAN RELATIONS

(FILMSTRIPS)

APPETITE OF A BIRD   FI
BLUE GOOTCHES, THE   EGH
COMICAL SITUATIONS OF EVERYDAY
LIFE, PT 1 (J-H)   ALEP
COMICAL SITUATIONS OF EVERYDAY
LIFE, PT 2 (J-H)   ALEP
DATING DATA (J-C A)   RMI
FACES OF MAN (H-C A)   ARGSC
FAT BLACK MACK   EGH
GUIDES FOR GROWING--A SERIES   EGH
MAGICAL COQUI (P)   UMM
PERSONALITY PLUS (J-C A)   RMI

(MOTION PICTURES)

AIN'T GONNA EAT MY MIND (J-C A)   CAROUF
AUTUMN FIRE   MGHT
BRIDGE OF FRIENDSHIP   ALDEN
CHILDREN AS PEOPLE (H-C A)   POLYMR
CO-OP   ALDEN
DIARY OF A MAD HOUSEWIFE (C A)   SWANK
GLADIATORS, THE (H-C)   NLC
GRANDMOTHER, THE   AMERFI
KEEP COOL (J-C)   BFA
KIDS ARE PEOPLE, TOO (T)   CCMFI
LOVE AND FILM (H-C A)   BFA
LOVE'S BEGINNINGS (P)   CAHILL
MIMI (J-C A)   BBF
PICKLES (H-C A)   BFA
PICTURE, THE   AMERFI
PORCH GLIDER   AMERFI
SEMINARS IN ISRAEL   ALDEN
THIS IS CAMPING (I-C A)   IU
TO BE A FRIEND (J-H)   BBF
WHAT WOULD YOU DO (P-I)   ATLAP
YOU (P-I)   CENTEF

(VIDEOTAPES)

BECAUSE IT'S FUN   NITC
BUT NAMES WILL NEVER HURT   NITC
CUSTOMS   SCCOE
EDUCATION VS EDUCATION   SCCOE
GETTING EVEN   NITC
GRAND ASSUMPTIONS   SCCOE
I DARE YOU   NITC
LOOK ME IN THE EYE   SCCOE
OBJECTIVE - ACCULTURATION   SCCOE

OUTLOOK   SCCOE
UNCONSCIOUS CULTURAL CLASHES--A
SERIES   SCCOE

(AUDIO TAPES)

ADOLESCENTS AND ADULTS   SIGINF
AFFINITIES OUT OF DESPERATION -
   THE 'MRS ROBINSON'
   SYNDROME   SIGINF
COMPASSION - TOWARD A SCIENCE
   OF VALUE--A SERIES   SIGINF
CONSERVATIVE VS RADICAL
   BEHAVIORS - MILITARIST VS
   PACIFIST BEHAVIORS   SIGINF
FACTS, PRACTICES, THEORIES AND
   VALUES - A VALUE THEORY OF
   TRUTH   SIGINF
HUMANISTIC AND POSITIVIST
   PHILOSOPHIES OF SCIENCE   SIGINF
IDENTITIES AND AFFINITIES - THE
   PROBLEM OF JUSTICE IN
   MARRIAGE AND OTHER UNIONS--A
   SERIES   SIGINF
IDENTITIES AND AFFINITIES - THE
   PROBLEM OF JUSTICE IN
   MARRIAGE AND OTHER UNIONS - ...   SIGINF
INTRODUCTION - COMPASSION IN
   GREAT PHILOSOPHIES AND
   RELIGIONS   SIGINF
IS MARRIAGE MORAL   SIGINF
IT TAKES A WOMAN--A SERIES   BASCH
MILITARY-INDUSTRIAL
   PERSONALITY - COMPASSION VS
   COMPULSION   SIGINF
MOVING - NEW SCHOOL, NEW
   PLAYMATES   BASCH
PHILOSOPHIES OF MAN AND VALUE
   - SCIENTIFIC METHODS   SIGINF
PROBLEMS RESULTING FROM THE
   DEPRIVATION OF PARENTAL
   AFFECTION, PT 1   SIGINF
PROBLEMS RESULTING FROM THE
   DEPRIVATION OF PARENTAL
   AFFECTION, PT 2   SIGINF
PSYCHOLOGICAL REACTIONS TO
   DIVORCE, PT 1   SIGINF
PSYCHOLOGICAL REACTIONS TO
   DIVORCE, PT 2   SIGINF
PSYCHOLOGICAL REACTIONS TO
   DIVORCE, PT 3   SIGINF
RIGHT TO FREEDOM, THE (H A)   WNAD
STILL-UNACCEPTABLE AFFINITIES -
   OLDER WOMEN YOUNGER MEN
   LIAISONS   SIGINF
VALUE-ANALYSES OF POLITICAL
   IDEOLOGIES   SIGINF
YANKEE DOODLEBUG AND THE AW-
   THAT'S NOTHIN' (P-I)   UTEX

(TRANSPARENCIES)

BASIC SOCIAL STUDIES CONCEPTS
   - SOCIETY--A SERIES (J-H)   LEART
DATING RELATIONS - MIXED DATING--A
   SERIES (J)   LEART
GROUP PRESSURES (J-H)   LEART
HOW CUSTOMS CHANGE (J-H)   LEART
HOW DOES SOCIETY TEACH ITS VALUES
(J-H)   LEART
MIXED DATING AMONG CLASSES (J)   LEART
MIXED DATING AMONG RACES (J)   LEART
MIXED DATING AMONG RELIGIONS (J)   LEART
RELIGION AND SOCIETY (J-H)   LEART
SOCIAL INSTITUTIONS MATCH THE LIFE
   CYCLE (J-H)   LEART
TYPES OF FAMILIES (J-H)   LEART
WHAT ARE SOCIAL VALUES AND NORMS
(J-H)   LEART
WHAT IS A SOCIAL INSTITUTION (J-H)   LEART
WHAT IS A SOCIETY (J-H)   LEART
WHAT IS AN OPEN SOCIETY (J-H)   LEART
WHY A SOCIETY NEEDS TO STUDY IT'S
PAST (J-H)   LEART

IMMIGRATION AND EMIGRATION

(FILMSTRIPS)

DANISH FIELD, THE (J-C A)   INTXC

(MOTION PICTURES)

IMMIGRANT EXPERIENCE, THE -
   THE LONG, LONG JOURNEY   LCOA
ROSE ARGOFF (H-C A)   CAROUF

INDIVIDUALISM

(MOTION PICTURES)

A TO B   AMERFI
ANN, A PORTRAIT   AMERFI
CIVILISATION, PROGRAM 04   TIMLIF
KRISHNAMURTI (H-C A)   TIMLIF

SEARCH FOR ALTERNATE LIFE-
   STYLES AND PHILOSOPHIES, THE
   (J-C A)   FLMFR

JUVENILE DELINQUENCY

(VIDEOTAPES)

JUVENILE DELINQUENCY   GPITVL

(AUDIO TAPES)

NORMAL AND ABNORMAL
   BEHAVIOR OF ADOLESCENCE-- A
   SERIES   SIGINF

LABOR AND LABORING CLASSES

(FILMSTRIPS)

ALIENATION AND MASS SOCIETY, PT 1   SED
CALIFORNIA CONFLICT - MIGRANT FARM
   WORKERS (J-H A)   SVE
EDUCATION AND COMMUNICATION IN
   CHINA   EGH
SEATTLE - A CITY FACES CRISIS (J-H A)   SVE
TRY TO JOIN OUR UNION (I-J)   SNBRST

(MOTION PICTURES)

INNER CITY DWELLER - WORK (H-C A)   IU

LEISURE

(FILMSTRIPS)

COLLECTOR, THE   FI

(MOTION PICTURES)

AQUA SUMMER (I-C A)   NWFCMP
VACATION FUN IN ISRAEL   ALDEN
WAY TO GO, THE (A)   SFI

LIQUOR PROBLEM

(MOTION PICTURES)

ALCOHOL - HOW MUCH IS TOO MUCH
(I)   AIMS
ALCOHOL - OUR NUMBER ONE DRUG (I-
H)   OF
ALCOHOL PROBLEM, THE - WHAT DO
   YOU THINK (I-C)   EBEC
ALCOHOLISM - A MODEL OF DRUG
   DEPENDENCY (C A)   CRMP
CENTER OF LIFE (J-C A)   GRANDY
FIFTH STREET (C A)   DRMINC
STORY OF AMERICAN WHISKEY   MTP

(AUDIO TAPES)

ALCOHOLISM   BASCH
DEFINITION OF ALCOHOLISM, THE   SIGINF
PSYCHIATRY AND THE LAW -
   ALCOHOLISM - DRUG ABUSE   SIGINF

MAN - INFLUENCE OF ENVIRONMENT

(FILMSTRIPS)

ALIENATION AND MASS SOCIETY, PT 2   SED
ASFEC   UNIPUB
CHIHUAHUA - LIFE IN A NORTHERN
   MEXICAN CITY   EGH
COMMUNITY DEVELOPMENT IN
   MICHOACAN   EGH
CONCRETE CHARLEY DUMPLING   COMICO
ENERGY CRISIS, THE - REPORT FROM
   PLANET 32 (I)   TERF
EQUATORIAL FORESTS   CARMAN
EXPLORATION - MAN'S QUEST FOR
   KNOWLEDGE--A SERIES (I-J)   SED
FACES OF MAN (H-C A)   ARGSC
HOW WE BUILD CITIES   EGH
HOW WE BUILD HOUSES   EGH
HUMANITIES - MAN IN THE NUCLEAR
   AGE, PT 1 (J-H)   GA
HUMANITIES - MAN IN THE NUCLEAR
   AGE, PT 2 (J-H)   GA
HUMANITIES - THE DAWN OF THE
   TWENTIETH CENTURY, PT 1 (J-H)   GA
HUMANITIES - THE DAWN OF THE
   TWENTIETH CENTURY, PT 2 (J-H)   GA
INDUSTRIAL WORKER   EGH
MEXICO - A COMMUNITY STUDY--A
   SERIES   EGH
PRINCESS ECOL VISITS THE PLANET
   THRAE   EGH
TOWN AND VILLAGE IN THE
   MOUNTAINS OF PUEBLA   EGH
VILLAGE OF ZIHUATANEJO AND ITS
   TURTLE INDUSTRY   EGH

(MOTION PICTURES)

BY THE PEOPLE (J-C A)	FILIM
DEVELOPING CREATIVITY (J-C A)	UEUWIS
EMOTIONAL DEVELOPMENT (C A)	CRMP
FROM CAVE TO CITY (I-C)	FLMFR
JAPANESE CHILDREN	IWANMI
LIVING OFF THE LAND	AMERFI
NOISE AND ITS EFFECTS ON HEALTH (J-C A)	FLMFR
PEACEFUL USE OF NUCLEAR EXPLOSIVES (H-C A)	TIMLIF
RUMOURS OF WAR (H-C A)	TIMLIF
SLICE OF GOLD	AMERFI
SURVIVAL OF SPACESHIP EARTH	WB
TOKYO - THE FIFTY-FIRST VOLCANO (H-C A)	TIMLIF
TRIALS OF FRANZ KAFKA, THE (H-C A)	FOTH
VOICES FROM MAINE (J-C A)	POLYMR

(TRANSPARENCIES)

SEX EDUCATION - DEVELOPMENT OF CONCEPTS AND ATTITUDES--A SERIES	LEART

MANNERS AND CUSTOMS

(FILMSTRIPS)

ALIENATION AND MASS SOCIETY, PT 1	SED
ALIENATION AND MASS SOCIETY, PT 2	SED
ANCIENT CIVILIZATIONS OF THE AMERICAS--A SERIES (I-J)	EBEC
ASFEC	UNIPUB
CHIHUAHUA - LIFE IN A NORTHERN MEXICAN CITY	EGH
CITIES OF ITALY	EGH
CITIES OF ROME AND FLORENCE	EGH
CITY - HOW AMERICA LIVES--A SERIES	AVNA
COMMUNES IN CHINA	EGH
COMMUNITY DEVELOPMENT IN MICHOACAN	EGH
DRUGS - A TRICK, A TRAP--A SERIES	EBEC
FLORENCE AND VENICE	EGH
GREAT MEN AND ARTISTS	EGH
ITALIAN CULTURE AND RECREATION	EGH
ITALIAN CULTURE AND RECREATION	EGH
ITALIAN HOME AND FAMILY, THE	EGH
ITALIANS AT WORK	EGH
ITALY - A REGIONAL STUDY--A SERIES	EGH
ITALY - THE LAND	EGH
LEBANON (P-I)	PATED
LIVING IN AFRICA TODAY - A CITY FAMILY OF MOROCCO (P-I)	CORF
LIVING IN AFRICA TODAY--A SERIES (P-I)	CORF
LIVING IN ASIA TODAY - AMONG THE MARKETS OF AFGHANISTAN (P-I)	CORF
LIVING IN ASIA TODAY - AT A SCHOOL IN KYOTO, JAPAN (P-I)	CORF
LIVING IN ASIA TODAY - AT A VILLAGE WEDDING IN THE PUNJAB, INDIA (P-I)	CORF
LIVING IN ASIA TODAY - IN A VILLAGE IN AMERICAN SAMOA (P-I)	CORF
LIVING IN ASIA TODAY - ON HOUSEBOATS IN KASHMIR (P-I)	CORF
LIVING IN ASIA TODAY - ON THE ISLAND OF BALI IN INDONESIA (P-I)	CORF
LIVING IN ASIA TODAY - WITH A CITY FAMILY OF TAIWAN (P-I)	CORF
LIVING IN ASIA TODAY - WITH A FISH SELLER IN MALAYSIA (P-I)	CORF
LIVING IN ASIA TODAY--A SERIES (P-I)	CORF
MEXICO - A COMMUNITY STUDY--A SERIES	EGH
NEW FRIENDS FROM DISTANT LANDS - THE CULTURE WE SHARE--A SERIES (P-I)	PATED
PEOPLE OF CHINA, THE	EGH
PILLS IN A PILL CULTURE	EGH
POLITICS AND GOVERNMENT (J-H)	MMPRO
TOWN AND VILLAGE IN THE MOUNTAINS OF PUEBLA	EGH
VILLAGE OF ZIHUATANEJO AND ITS TURTLE INDUSTRY	EGH

(MOTION PICTURES)

BALI	PUI
CEYLON	PUI
CHILDREN OF THE KIBBUTZ (I-C A)	ACI
CHINA - A HOLE IN THE BAMBOO CURTAIN (I-C A)	CAROUF
CO-OP	ALDEN
DRY SEASON, THE	CMC
EGYPT	PUI
FLOWERS FOR DAHLIA	ALDEN
GREECE	PUI
HAITI	PUI
HAWAII	PUI
HINDU RITUAL SANDHYA, THE	CMC
HONG KONG	PUI
INDIA	PUI
ISRAEL	PUI

IT HAPPENED IN HUALFIN, PT 1 - WHEN THE WIND IS SILENT	PIC
IT HAPPENED IN HUALFIN, PT 2 - THE CLAY	PIC
IT HAPPENED IN HUALFIN, PT 3 - ELINDA OF THE VALLEY	PIC
JAPAN	PUI
JAPANESE CHILDREN	IWANMI
KENYA	PUI
KIBBUTZ, A	ALDEN
LANGUAGE DEVELOPMENT (C A)	CRMP
LET'S IMAGINE - LIFE IN UTOPIA	ALDEN
LIVING WOOD - AFRICAN MASKS AND MYTHS (I-H A)	GRADYM
OFF THE BEATEN TRACK IN ISRAEL	ALDEN
PAKISTAN	PUI
PORT OF CALL--A SERIES	PUI
SINGAPORE	PUI
SYRIA	PUI
TURKEY	PUI
YO SOY CHICANO (ENGLISH) (H-C A)	IU
ZANZIBAR	PUI

(VIDEOTAPES)

CUSTOMS	SCCOE

(AUDIO TAPES)

COMPASSION - TOWARD A SCIENCE OF VALUE--A SERIES	SIGINF
INTRODUCTION - COMPASSION IN GREAT PHILOSOPHIES AND RELIGIONS	SIGINF
PHILOSOPHIES OF MAN AND VALUE - SCIENTIFIC METHODS	SIGINF

(TRANSPARENCIES)

HOW CUSTOMS CHANGE (J-H)	LEART

MARRIAGE AND THE FAMILY

(FILMSTRIPS)

DRUGS AND CHILDREN, PT 1 (I)	EDLACT
DRUGS AND CHILDREN, PT 2 (I)	EDLACT
MARRIAGE AND FAMILIES	EGH

(MOTION PICTURES)

ADOLESCENCE AND SEXUAL IDENTITY (H-C A)	CHM
AUTUMN FIRE	MGHT
BIRTH (H-C A)	VERITE
BIRTH (H-C A)	VERITE
BIRTH OF A BABY (H-C A)	CHM
CHILDBIRTH (J-C A)	POLYMR
CRIME IN THE HOME (J-C A)	AIMS
DIARY OF A MAD HOUSEWIFE (C A)	SWANK
EXECUTIVE'S WIFE, THE (A)	UEUWIS
IMPLOSION	AMERFI
INTRODUCTION TO SEX EDUCATION (H-C A)	CHM
NOT ME ALONE (H-C A)	POLYMR
TALKING ABOUT BREASTFEEDING (H-C A)	POLYMR

(AUDIO TAPES)

BECOMING A PARENT	BASCH
CAREER WIFE	BASCH
DISCONTENTED HOUSEWIFE	BASCH
IDENTITIES AND AFFINITIES - THE PROBLEM OF JUSTICE IN MARRIAGE AND OTHER UNIONS--A SERIES	SIGINF
IDENTITIES AND AFFINITIES - THE PROBLEM OF JUSTICE IN MARRIAGE AND OTHER UNIONS - ...	SIGINF
INFIDELITY	BASCH
IS MARRIAGE MORAL	SIGINF
ON BECOMING IN-LAWS	BASCH
PSYCHIATRIC DISORDERS OF CHILDHOOD - CHILD PSYCHOTHERAPY - MARITAL MALADJUSTMENT AND...	SIGINF
TOO YOUNG TO MARRY	BASCH
UPROOTING AND ROLE-TRANSFERENCE - ISSUES OF IDENTITY CRISES IN WIVES	SIGINF
WHAT MAKES A HAPPY MARRIAGE	BASCH
WHAT'S YOUR PROBLEM--A SERIES	BASCH

MARRIAGE CUSTOMS AND RITES

(FILMSTRIPS)

LIVING IN ASIA TODAY - AT A VILLAGE WEDDING IN THE PUNJAB, INDIA (P-I)	CORF

(MOTION PICTURES)

IT WAS THE CUSTOM	ALDEN

MIGRATION, INTERNAL

(MOTION PICTURES)

IMMIGRANT FROM AMERICA (J-C A)	REPRO

MORTALITY

(MOTION PICTURES)

DEATHSTYLES	AMERFI

NARCOTICS PROBLEMS

(FILMSTRIPS)

ALCOHOL - PARENTS AND THEIR POTIONS (P-I)	EBEC
ALCOHOL AND TOBACCO	EGH
DOCTOR'S VIEWPOINT	EGH
DRUGS - A TRICK, A TRAP--A SERIES	EBEC
DRUGS AND YOUR FUTURE	EGH
ECOLOGY OF OUR BODIES	EGH
HARD DRUGS, THE - THE BOTTOM OF THE TRAP (P-I)	EBEC
LET'S LOOK AT DRUGS--A SERIES	EGH
MARIJUANA AND GLUE - KIDS, TRICKS AND TRAPS (P-I)	EBEC
MARIJUANA, STIMULANTS AND DEPRESSANTS	EGH
MARY JANE AND BUTTERFLY	EGH
MEDICINE - PEOPLE AND PILLS (P-I)	EBEC
PILLS IN A PILL CULTURE	EGH

(MOTION PICTURES)

DRUG PROBLEM, THE - WHAT DO YOU THINK (J-H)	EBEC
TAKING CARE OF BUSINESS	AMERFI
WE HAVE AN ADDICT IN THE HOUSE (J-C A)	DOUBLE

(AUDIO TAPES)

DRUG ABUSE - SOMATIC THERAPIES - PSYCHIATRIC DISORDERS OF CHILDHOOD	SIGINF
MANAGEMENT OF DRUG ABUSE IN THE OUTPATIENT PSYCHOTHERAPY OF ADOLESCENTS, THE	SIGINF
NORMAL AND ABNORMAL BEHAVIOR OF ADOLESCENCE-- A SERIES	SIGINF
PSYCHIATRY AND THE LAW - ALCOHOLISM - DRUG ABUSE	SIGINF
SOCIOLOGIC PERSPECTIVES OF THE MARIJUANA CONTROVERSY	SIGINF

(TRANSPARENCIES)

DEPRESSANTS (H)	BOW
DRUG ABUSE--A SERIES (H)	BOW
DRUGS AND THE LAW (H)	BOW
GLUE SNIFFING (H)	BOW
HALLUCINOGENIC DRUGS (H)	BOW
MARIJUANA (H)	BOW
NARCOTICS (H)	BOW
STIMULANTS (H)	BOW
USES AND ABUSES (H)	BOW

NATIONAL CHARACTERISTICS

(FILMSTRIPS)

ASFEC	UNIPUB

(MOTION PICTURES)

LOVE AND FILM (H-C A)	BFA

PARENT AND CHILD

(FILMSTRIPS)

GOD'S CHILDREN	UWLA
MARRIAGE AND FAMILIES	EGH

(MOTION PICTURES)

EDUCATION FOR FAMILY LIFE (H-C A)	CHM
LOVE'S BEGINNINGS (P)	CAHILL

(VIDEOTAPES)

DOUGLAS	GPITVL
EDWARD	GPITVL
HOME SWEET HOME	NITC
MARY	GPITVL
NONI	GPITVL

(AUDIO TAPES)

ADOLESCENT AND HIS PARENTS, THE	SIGINF

ADOLESCENTS AND ADULTS	SIGINF
BECOMING A PARENT	BASCH
PARENTS AS THERAPEUTIC AGENTS	SIGINF
PROBLEMS RESULTING FROM THE DEPRIVATION OF PARENTAL AFFECTION, PT 1	SIGINF
PROBLEMS RESULTING FROM THE DEPRIVATION OF PARENTAL AFFECTION, PT 2	SIGINF
PSYCHOLOGICAL REACTIONS TO DIVORCE, PT 1	SIGINF
PSYCHOLOGICAL REACTIONS TO DIVORCE, PT 2	SIGINF
PSYCHOLOGICAL REACTIONS TO DIVORCE, PT 3	SIGINF
RIGHT TO FREEDOM, THE (H A)	WNAD

POPULATION

(MOTION PICTURES)

BREAD (I-C A)	HRAW
POPULATION EXPANSION AND BIRTH CONTROL (H-C A)	CHM

(AUDIO TAPES)

SUICIDE IN PRISON	SIGINF

PREJUDICES AND ANTIPATHIES

(FILMSTRIPS)

HOW TO CLOSE OPEN HOUSING (I-J)	SNBRST
TRY TO JOIN OUR UNION (I-J)	SNBRST

(MOTION PICTURES)

IN LIVING COLOR (H-C A)	DATA
VOICE OF LA RAZA	GREAVW
WHAT WOULD YOU DO (P-I)	ATLAP

(VIDEOTAPES)

BUT NAMES WILL NEVER HURT	NITC

PRISONS

(FILMSTRIPS)

HANGMAN'S KNOT VERSUS THE PAROLE BOARD (I-J)	SNBRST
HOW TO CLOSE OPEN HOUSING (I-J)	SNBRST
JAIL TERM BEFORE TRIAL (I-J)	SNBRST
MIND BLOWERS--A SERIES (I-J)	SNBRST
TRY TO JOIN OUR UNION (I-J)	SNBRST

PROBLEM CHILDREN

(AUDIO TAPES)

SCHOOL DROP OUT	BASCH

PUBLIC HEALTH

(FILMSTRIPS)

ALCOHOL - PARENTS AND THEIR POTIONS (P-I)	EBEC
DRUGS - A TRICK, A TRAP--A SERIES	EBEC
HARD DRUGS, THE - THE BOTTOM OF THE TRAP (P-I)	EBEC
MARIJUANA AND GLUE - KIDS, TRICKS AND TRAPS (P-I)	EBEC
MEDICINE - PEOPLE AND PILLS (P-I)	EBEC
TOBACCO - A PUFF OF POISON (P-I)	EBEC

(MOTION PICTURES)

BIOENGINEERS, THE	USNAC
CAPRI PROGRAM, THE (C A)	SAFECO
CENTER OF LIFE (J-C A)	GRANDY
CHECK IT OUT (J-H A)	NEWD
HEART, THE - ATTACK	CRMP
LIFE AND HEALTH FILM--A SERIES	CRMP
NOISE AND ITS EFFECTS ON HEALTH (J-C A)	FLMFR
VD - ATTACK PLAN (J-H)	DISNEY
VENEREAL DISEASE (H-C A)	CHM
WORK OF GOMIS, THE (J-C A)	WASHBF

PUBLIC WELFARE

(FILMSTRIPS)

ALCOHOL - PARENTS AND THEIR POTIONS (P-I)	EBEC
CHEMOTHERAPY	CONMED
COLOSTOMY	CONMED
DRUGS - A TRICK, A TRAP--A SERIES	EBEC
HARD DRUGS, THE - THE BOTTOM OF THE TRAP (P-I)	EBEC
HEAD AND NECK SURGERY	CONMED

HYSTERECTOMY FOR UTERINE CANCER	CONMED
INTRODUCTION TO CANCER SURGERY - MASTECTOMY	CONMED
MARIJUANA AND GLUE - KIDS, TRICKS AND TRAPS (P-I)	EBEC
MEDICINE - PEOPLE AND PILLS (P-I)	EBEC
RADIOTHERAPY I	CONMED
RADIOTHERAPY II	CONMED
TOBACCO - A PUFF OF POISON (P-I)	EBEC

(MOTION PICTURES)

AGED, THE (H-C A)	CAROUF
ALFRED	AMERFI
NEW DEAL (H-C A)	CAROUF
ROSE ARGOFF (H-C A)	CAROUF
SRO (SINGLE ROOM OCCUPANCY) (H-C A)	CAROUF
UMBRELLA MAN, THE	MGHT
WAY IT IS, THE (C A)	SYNCRO

PUNISHMENT

(FILMSTRIPS)

HANGMAN'S KNOT VERSUS THE PAROLE BOARD (I-J)	SNBRST
JAIL TERM BEFORE TRIAL (I-J)	SNBRST
MIND BLOWERS--A SERIES (I-J)	SNBRST

(MOTION PICTURES)

CAUGHT (J-C)	NRMA
TAKING CARE OF BUSINESS	AMERFI

RACE PROBLEMS

(FILMSTRIPS)

BLACK AMERICANS (I-J)	FIELEP
BLUE GOOTCHES, THE	EGH
FAT BLACK MACK	EGH
GERMAN AMERICANS (I-J)	FIELEP
ITALIAN AMERICANS (I-J)	FIELEP
MEXICAN AMERICANS (I-J)	FIELEP

(MOTION CARTRIDGES)

CITIES, THE - DILEMMA IN BLACK AND WHITE, PT 1 (I-C)	BFA
CITIES, THE - DILEMMA IN BLACK AND WHITE, PT 2 (I-C)	BFA

(AUDIO TAPES)

DEVELOPMENTAL CRISES IN BLACK ADOLESCENTS	SIGINF

RECREATION

(MOTION PICTURES)

THIS IS CAMPING (I-C A)	IU
VISTAS OF ISRAEL, NO. 2	ALDEN
VISTAS OF ISRAEL, NO. 3	ALDEN
WAY TO GO, THE (A)	SFI

SEMITIC RACE

(MOTION PICTURES)

HOME AT LAST	ALDEN
IT WAS THE CUSTOM	ALDEN
JERUSALEM - HERE WE COME	ALDEN
LET MY PEOPLE GO	ALDEN
PLIGHT OF SOVIET JEWELRY, THE - LET MY PEOPLE GO	ALDEN
THIRD TEMPLE, THE	ALDEN

SEXUAL ETHICS

(FILMSTRIPS)

ARE SEX AND LOVE THE SAME THING	EGH
ATTITUDES ABOUT HUMAN SEXUALITY	EGH
FEMALE OF THE SPECIES, THE	EGH
HUMAN SEXUALITY--A SERIES	EGH
OUR INSTINCTS AND WHY WE HAVE THEM	EGH

(MOTION PICTURES)

BEACH PARTY, THE	PAULST
INTRODUCTION TO SEX EDUCATION (H-C A)	CHM
LOOK WHAT'S GOING AROUND (H-C A)	CF
SEX IN AMERICAN CULTURE--A SERIES (H-C A)	CHM

(AUDIO TAPES)

AFFINITIES OUT OF DESPERATION - THE 'MRS ROBINSON' SYNDROME	SIGINF

BEYOND SEXUAL IDENTITY	SIGINF
CAN LOVE AND SEX SURVIVE THE ELIMINATION OF SEXISM	SIGINF
DELINQUENT AND PROMISCUOUS HOMOSEXUAL BEHAVIOR	SIGINF
EXISTENTIAL ASPECTS OF SEXUAL JEALOUSY	SIGINF
GAY AFFINITIES AND THE HELPING PROFESSIONS	SIGINF
IDENTITIES AND AFFINITIES - THE PROBLEM OF JUSTICE IN MARRIAGE AND OTHER UNIONS--A SERIES	SIGINF
IDENTITIES AND AFFINITIES - THE PROBLEM OF JUSTICE IN MARRIAGE AND OTHER UNIONS - ...	SIGINF
INFIDELITY	BASCH
IS MARRIAGE MORAL	SIGINF
OEDIPUS COMPLEX AND SEXISM, THE	SIGINF
STATE OF THE UNION, PRESENT AND FUTURE, THE	SIGINF
STILL-UNACCEPTABLE AFFINITIES - OLDER WOMEN YOUNGER MEN LIAISONS	SIGINF
TRAUMA OF EVENTLESSNESS, THE	SIGINF
UPROOTING AND ROLE-TRANSFERENCE - ISSUES OF IDENTITY CRISES IN WIVES	SIGINF
WHO IS THE CENSOR WHAT (A)	UTS

(TRANSPARENCIES)

DATING AND PARTYING	LEART
DATING RELATIONS - DATING PROBLEMS--A SERIES (J)	LEART
DATING RELATIONS - DIMENSIONS OF DATING--A SERIES (J)	LEART
DIMENSIONS OF SEXUAL ATTRACTION - FEMALE (J)	LEART
DIMENSIONS OF SEXUAL ATTRACTION - MALE (J)	LEART
HOW EMOTIONS ARE EXPRESSED	LEART
LEARNING HOW TO SAY NO (J)	LEART
LEARNING HOW TO VARY THE TEMPO (J)	LEART
NORMAL ATTRACTION OF THE SEXES, PT 1	LEART
NORMAL ATTRACTION OF THE SEXES, PT 2	LEART
SETTING STANDARDS ON DATES (J)	LEART
SEX AND DATING - CONSEQUENCES (J)	LEART
SEX AND DATING - GUILT AND SHAME (J)	LEART
SEX AND DATING - REPUTATION (J)	LEART
UNDERSTANDING MALENESS AND FEMALENESS	LEART
UNDERSTANDING SEXUALITY	LEART
WHAT MAKES PERSONALITIES DIFFERENT	LEART

SOCIAL CHANGE

(FILMSTRIPS)

AMERICAN GENIUS--A SERIES (H-C)	EDDIM
HUMANITIES - A WORLD BETWEEN WARS, PT 1 (J-H)	GA
HUMANITIES - A WORLD BETWEEN WARS, PT 2 (J-H)	GA
HUMANITIES - MAN IN THE NUCLEAR AGE, PT 1 (J-H)	GA
HUMANITIES - MAN IN THE NUCLEAR AGE, PT 2 (J-H)	GA
HUMANITIES - THE DAWN OF THE TWENTIETH CENTURY, PT 1 (J-H)	GA
HUMANITIES - THE DAWN OF THE TWENTIETH CENTURY, PT 2 (J-H)	GA

(MOTION PICTURES)

BY THE PEOPLE (J-C A)	FILIM
FROM CAVE TO CITY (I-C)	FLMFR
NATION WITHIN A NATION, A (I-C A)	HEARST
POPCORN LADY (I-C A)	SCHLAT

(TRANSPARENCIES)

HOW CUSTOMS CHANGE (J-H)	LEART
MAN'S COMMUNITY EXPANDS THROUGH THE AGES (J-H)	LEART

SOCIAL CLASSES

(FILMSTRIPS)

ALIENATION AND MASS SOCIETY, PT 1	SED
ALIENATION AND MASS SOCIETY, PT 2	SED
CHILDREN	EGH
LIFE OF THE LEISURE CLASS	EGH

(MOTION PICTURES)

IT HAPPENED IN HUALFIN, PT 1 - WHEN THE WIND IS SILENT	PIC
IT HAPPENED IN HUALFIN, PT 2 - THE CLAY	PIC

IT HAPPENED IN HUALFIN, PT 3 -
 ELINDA OF THE VALLEY   PIC

(TRANSPARENCIES)

BASIC SOCIAL STUDIES CONCEPTS
 - SOCIETY--A SERIES (J-H)   LEART
GROUP PRESSURES (J-H)   LEART
HOW CUSTOMS CHANGE (J-H)   LEART
HOW DOES SOCIETY TEACH ITS VALUES
 (J-H)   LEART
RELIGION AND SOCIETY (J-H)   LEART
TYPES OF FAMILIES (J-H)   LEART
WHAT ARE SOCIAL CLASSES (J-H)   LEART
WHAT ARE SOCIAL VALUES AND NORMS
 (J-H)   LEART
WHAT IS A SOCIAL INSTITUTION (J-H)   LEART
WHAT IS A SOCIETY (J-H)   LEART
WHAT IS AN OPEN SOCIETY (J-H)   LEART
WHY A SOCIETY NEEDS TO STUDY IT'S
 PAST (J-H)   LEART

SOCIAL CONDITIONS

(FILMSTRIPS)

ALIENATION AND MASS SOCIETY, PT 1   SED
ALIENATION AND MASS SOCIETY, PT 2   SED
AMERICAN GENIUS, 1960 - 1970 (H-C)   EDDIM
APPETITE OF A BIRD   FI
DRUGS - A TRICK, A TRAP--A SERIES   EBEC
FISH IN THE FOREST - A RUSSIAN
 FOLKTALE (I)   GA
HANGMAN'S KNOT VERSUS THE PAROLE
 BOARD (I-J)   SNBRST
HOW TO CLOSE OPEN HOUSING (I-J)   SNBRST
HUMANITIES - MAN IN THE NUCLEAR
 AGE, PT 1 (J-H)   GA
HUMANITIES - MAN IN THE NUCLEAR
 AGE, PT 2 (J-H)   GA
JAIL TERM BEFORE TRIAL (I-J)   SNBRST
MARY JANE AND BUTTERFLY   EGH
MIND BLOWERS--A SERIES (I-J)   SNBRST
ONCE UPON A COMPULSION   KELLRP
SEATTLE - A CITY FACES CRISIS (J-H A)   SVE
TRY TO JOIN OUR UNION (I-J)   SNBRST

(MOTION PICTURES)

ABANDONMENT OF THE CITIES, THE (J-
 C A)   NBCTV
AIN'T GONNA EAT MY MIND (J-C A)   CAROUF
BIG YELLOW TAXI   PFP
BREAD (I-C A)   HRAW
BY THE PEOPLE (J-C A)   FILIM
CHILDREN, THE   AMERFI
FAIR CHANCE (H-C A)   DATA
FIFTH STREET (C A)   DRMINC
FRANKENSTEIN IN A FISHBOWL   AMERFI
GLADIATORS, THE (H-C)   NLC
IT HAPPENED IN HUALFIN, PT 2 - THE
 CLAY   PIC
IT HAPPENED IN HUALFIN, PT 3 -
 ELINDA OF THE VALLEY   PIC
JAPANESE CHILDREN   IWANMI
JESUS TRIP, THE (C A)   TIMLIF
LIVING OFF THE LAND   AMERFI
PORCH GLIDER   AMERFI
RIGHT ON (J-C A)   NLC
RUMOURS OF WAR (H-C A)   TIMLIF
SEVENTH MANDARIN, THE (I)   XEROX
THEORIST ROOM   AMERFI
TOKYO - THE FIFTY-FIRST VOLCANO (H-C
 A)   TIMLIF
UNDER THE JUGGERNAUT   AMERFI
VOICES FROM MAINE (J-C A)   POLYMR
WAY IT IS, THE (C A)   SYNCRO
YO SOY CHICANO (ENGLISH) (H-C A)   IU

(AUDIO TAPES)

PSYCHOLOGICAL FUNCTIONS OF THE
 COUNTER CULTURE   SIGINF
SUN SHINES BRIGHT, THE (H A)   USOE
WOMEN DID IT, THE (H A)   USOE

(TRANSPARENCIES)

BASIC SOCIAL STUDIES CONCEPTS
 - POLITICS, SOCIAL-ECONOMIC
 INTERDEPENDENCE--A SERIES (J-H)   LEART
BASIC SOCIAL STUDIES CONCEPTS
 - SOCIETY--A SERIES (J-H)   LEART
GROUP PRESSURES (J-H)   LEART
HOW CUSTOMS CHANGE (J-H)   LEART
INTERACTION OF POLITICAL,
 SOCIAL AND ECONOMIC CAUSES
 AND EFFECTS (J-H)   LEART
SOCIAL INSTITUTIONS AND ECONOMICS
 (J-H)   LEART
SOCIAL INSTITUTIONS MATCH THE LIFE
 CYCLE (J-H)   LEART
WHAT ARE SOCIAL CLASSES (J-H)   LEART
WHAT IS A SOCIETY (J-H)   LEART
WHAT IS AN OPEN SOCIETY (J-H)   LEART
WHY A SOCIETY NEEDS TO STUDY IT'S
 PAST (J-H)   LEART

SOCIAL ETHICS

(FILMSTRIPS)

LEWIS-LIES-A-LOT   EGH

(MOTION PICTURES)

LOVE AND FILM (H-C A)   BFA
MORAL DEVELOPMENT (C A)   CRMP

(AUDIO TAPES)

AFFINITIES OUT OF DESPERATION -
 THE 'MRS ROBINSON'
 SYNDROME   SIGINF
BEYOND SEXUAL IDENTITY   SIGINF
BIOLOGY, MORALITY AND SOCIAL
 COHESION   SIGINF
CAN LOVE AND SEX SURVIVE THE
 ELIMINATION OF SEXISM   SIGINF
COMPASSION - TOWARD A SCIENCE
 OF VALUE--A SERIES   SIGINF
CONSERVATIVE VS RADICAL
 BEHAVIORS - MILITARIST VS
 PACIFIST BEHAVIORS   SIGINF
DELINQUENT AND PROMISCUOUS
 HOMOSEXUAL BEHAVIOR   SIGINF
EXISTENTIAL ASPECTS OF SEXUAL
 JEALOUSY   SIGINF
FACTS, PRACTICES, THEORIES AND
 VALUES - A VALUE THEORY OF
 TRUTH   SIGINF
GAY AFFINITIES AND THE HELPING
 PROFESSIONS   SIGINF
HUMANISTIC AND POSITIVIST
 PHILOSOPHIES OF SCIENCE   SIGINF
IDENTITIES AND AFFINITIES - THE
 PROBLEM OF JUSTICE IN
 MARRIAGE AND OTHER UNIONS--A
 SERIES   SIGINF
IDENTITIES AND AFFINITIES - THE
 PROBLEM OF JUSTICE IN
 MARRIAGE AND OTHER UNIONS - ...   SIGINF
INTRODUCTION - COMPASSION IN
 GREAT PHILOSOPHIES AND
 RELIGIONS   SIGINF
IS MARRIAGE MORAL   SIGINF
KNOWLEDGE OF VALUES -
 AUTHORITARIAN PERSONALITY   SIGINF
MILITARY-INDUSTRIAL
 PERSONALITY - COMPASSION VS
 COMPULSION   SIGINF
OEDIPUS COMPLEX AND SEXISM, THE   SIGINF
PHILOSOPHIES OF MAN AND VALUE
 - SCIENTIFIC METHODS   SIGINF
STATE OF THE UNION, PRESENT AND
 FUTURE, THE   SIGINF
STILL-UNACCEPTABLE AFFINITIES -
 OLDER WOMEN YOUNGER MEN
 LIAISONS   SIGINF
TRAUMA OF EVENTLESSNESS, THE   SIGINF
UPROOTING AND ROLE-
 TRANSFERENCE - ISSUES OF
 IDENTITY CRISES IN WIVES   SIGINF
VALUE-ANALYSES OF POLITICAL
 IDEOLOGIES   SIGINF

(TRANSPARENCIES)

BASIC SOCIAL STUDIES CONCEPTS
 - SOCIETY--A SERIES (J-H)   LEART
DATING RELATIONS - DATING
 CATEGORIES--A SERIES (J)   LEART
DATING RELATIONS - DIMENSIONS
 OF DATING--A SERIES (J)   LEART
DATING RELATIONS - EVALUATING
 DATING BEHAVIOR --A SERIES (J)   LEART
DATING RELATIONS - MIXED DATING--A
 SERIES (J)   LEART
DATING RELATIONS - THE FIRST DATE-
 -A SERIES (J)   LEART
GROUP PRESSURES (J-H)   LEART
HOW DOES SOCIETY TEACH ITS VALUES
 (J-H)   LEART
RELIGION AND SOCIETY (J-H)   LEART
SOCIAL INSTITUTIONS MATCH THE LIFE
 CYCLE (J-H)   LEART
TYPES OF FAMILIES (J-H)   LEART
WHAT ARE SOCIAL CLASSES (J-H)   LEART
WHAT ARE SOCIAL VALUES AND NORMS
 (J-H)   LEART
WHAT IS A SOCIAL INSTITUTION (J-H)   LEART
WHAT IS A SOCIETY (J-H)   LEART
WHAT IS AN OPEN SOCIETY (J-H)   LEART
WHY A SOCIETY NEEDS TO STUDY IT'S
 PAST (J-H)   LEART

SOCIAL GROUP WORK

(MOTION PICTURES)

PARK ON OUR BLOCK, A (J-C A)   WASHBF
STRAWBERRIES - WITH CREAM   MTP

(AUDIO TAPES)

WOMEN DID IT, THE (H A)   USOE

SOCIAL PROBLEMS

(FILMSTRIPS)

ALCOHOL - PARENTS AND THEIR
 POTIONS (P-I)   EBEC
ALCOHOL AND TOBACCO   EGH
ALIENATION AND MASS SOCIETY, PT 1   SED
ALIENATION AND MASS SOCIETY, PT 2   SED
AMERICAN GENIUS, 1960 - 1970 (H-C)   EDDIM
CITY - HOW AMERICA LIVES--A SERIES   AVNA
DOCTOR'S VIEWPOINT   EGH
DRUGS - A TRICK, A TRAP--A SERIES   EBEC
DRUGS AND YOUR FUTURE   EGH
DYNAMISM OR DECAY   AVNA
ECOLOGY OF OUR BODIES   EGH
HANGMAN'S KNOT VERSUS THE PAROLE
 BOARD (I-J)   SNBRST
HARD DRUGS, THE - THE BOTTOM OF
 THE TRAP (P-I)   EBEC
HERITAGE OF GREATNESS   AVNA
HOW TO CLOSE OPEN HOUSING (I-J)   SNBRST
JAIL TERM BEFORE TRIAL (I-J)   SNBRST
LET'S LOOK AT DRUGS--A SERIES   EGH
MARIJUANA AND GLUE - KIDS, TRICKS
 AND TRAPS (P-I)   EBEC
MARIJUANA, STIMULANTS AND
 DEPRESSANTS   EGH
MARY JANE AND BUTTERFLY   EGH
MEDICINE - PEOPLE AND PILLS (P-I)   EBEC
MIND BLOWERS--A SERIES (I-J)   SNBRST
PILLS IN A PILL CULTURE   EGH
TOBACCO - A PUFF OF POISON (P-I)   EBEC
TRY TO JOIN OUR UNION (I-J)   SNBRST

(MOTION PICTURES)

AGED, THE (H C A)   CAROUF
AIN'T GONNA EAT MY MIND (J-C A)   CAROUF
ALFRED   AMERFI
ANYTHING YOU WANT TO BE (J-C A)   EDDDW
CENTER OF LIFE (J-C A)   GRANDY
CHILDREN, THE   AMERFI
FAIR CHANCE (H-C A)   DATA
FIFTH STREET (C A)   DRMINC
INNER CITY DWELLER - WORK (H-C A)   IU
IT HAPPENED IN HUALFIN, PT 1 -
 WHEN THE WIND IS SILENT   PIC
IT HAPPENED IN HUALFIN, PT 2 - THE
 CLAY   PIC
IT HAPPENED IN HUALFIN, PT 3 -
 ELINDA OF THE VALLEY   PIC
JAPANESE CHILDREN   IWANMI
LIVING OFF THE LAND   AMERFI
MS - THE STRUGGLE FOR WOMEN'S
 RIGHTS (I-C A)   HEARST
NEW DEAL (H-C A)   CAROUF
NOBODY TOOK THE TIME (T)   AIMS
NOISE AND ITS EFFECTS ON HEALTH
 (J-C A)   FLMFR
OPPORTUNITIES FOR THE
 DISADVANTAGED (J-H)   AMEDFL
RIGHT ON (J-C A)   NLC
ROSE ARGOFF (H-C A)   CAROUF
SEVENTH MANDARIN, THE (I)   XEROX
SRO (SINGLE ROOM OCCUPANCY) (H-C
 A)   CAROUF
UNDER THE JUGGERNAUT   AMERFI
WE HAVE AN ADDICT IN THE HOUSE
 (J-C A)   DOUBLE
WHAT'S WRONG WITH THE SOCIAL
 SCIENCES (H-C A)   TIMLIF

(AUDIO TAPES)

ASSESSMENT OF SUICIDAL RISK   SIGINF
BIOLOGY, MORALITY AND SOCIAL
 COHESION   SIGINF
FAMILY SURVIVORS OF SUICIDE   SIGINF
INFIDELITY   BASCH
MANAGEMENT OF THE SUICIDAL
 PERSON   SIGINF
SCHOOL DROP OUT   BASCH
SUICIDE - AN OVERVIEW   SIGINF
SUICIDE AND DEPRESSION   SIGINF
SUICIDE AND SUICIDE PREVENTION--A
 SERIES   SIGINF
SUICIDE AND THE TERMINALLY ILL   SIGINF
SUICIDE IN PRISON   SIGINF
SUICIDE, SUICIDE ATTEMPTS AND SELF-
 MUTILATION   SIGINF
SUN SHINES BRIGHT, THE (H A)   USOE
WHO IS THE CENSOR WHAT (A)   UTS
WOMEN DID IT, THE (H A)   USOE

(TRANSPARENCIES)

BASIC SOCIAL STUDIES CONCEPTS
 - SOCIETY--A SERIES (J-H)   LEART
GROUP PRESSURES (J-H)   LEART
WHAT IS A SOCIETY (J-H)   LEART
WHAT IS AN OPEN SOCIETY (J-H)   LEART

SOCIAL PSYCHOLOGY

(MOTION PICTURES)

DEATHSTYLES	AMERFI
DEPENDENCE - A NEW DEFINITION (C A)	CRMP
FRANKENSTEIN IN A FISHBOWL	AMERFI
IN LIVING COLOR (H-C A)	DATA

(AUDIO TAPES)

YOU ARE THE TARGET (J-C)	INSKY

(TRANSPARENCIES)

BASIC SALESMANSHIP--A SERIES	COF
LOVE IS BOTH STURDY AND PERISHABLE (J)	LEART

SOCIAL WORK

(MOTION PICTURES)

WAY IT IS, THE (C A)	SYNCRO

SOCIETY, PRIMITIVE

(MOTION PICTURES)

LIVING WOOD - AFRICAN MASKS AND MYTHS (I-H A)	GRADYM

SOCIOLOGY, RURAL

(FILMSTRIPS)

CALIFORNIA CONFLICT - MIGRANT FARM WORKERS (J-H A)	SVE

(MOTION PICTURES)

YESTERDAY'S FARM (P-J)	BFA

SUICIDE

(AUDIO TAPES)

ASSESSMENT OF SUICIDAL RISK	SIGINF
CURRENT ISSUES AND PROBLEMS IN SUICIDE PREVENTION	SIGINF
DEPRESSION AND SUICIDE	SIGINF
EXAMPLES AND DISCUSSION OF SUICIDE CALLS, PT 1	SIGINF
EXAMPLES AND DISCUSSION OF SUICIDE CALLS, PT 2	SIGINF
FAMILY SURVIVORS OF SUICIDE	SIGINF
HOW TO ESTABLISH A SUICIDE PREVENTION PROGRAM	SIGINF
MANAGEMENT OF THE SUICIDAL PERSON	SIGINF
SUICIDE - AN OVERVIEW	SIGINF
SUICIDE - HOMICIDE - THE CONCEPT OF PSYCHOPHYSIOLOGIC DISORDERS	SIGINF

SUICIDE AND DEPRESSION	SIGINF
SUICIDE AND SUICIDE PREVENTION--A SERIES	SIGINF
SUICIDE AND THE TERMINALLY ILL	SIGINF
SUICIDE AND VIOLENCE	SIGINF
SUICIDE IN PRISON	SIGINF
SUICIDE, SUICIDE ATTEMPTS AND SELF-MUTILATION	SIGINF

UNEMPLOYED

(MOTION PICTURES)

INNER CITY DWELLER - WORK (H-C A)	IU
OPPORTUNITIES FOR THE DISADVANTAGED (J-H)	AMEDFL

URBANIZATION

(FILMSTRIPS)

ALIENATION AND MASS SOCIETY, PT 1	SED
ALIENATION AND MASS SOCIETY, PT 2	SED
AMERICAN GENIUS, 1880 - 1918 (H-C)	EDDIM
CITY - HOW AMERICA LIVES--A SERIES	AVNA
CITY IN HISTORY, THE, PT 1 (J-C A)	EDDIM
CITY IN HISTORY, THE, PT 2 (J-C A)	EDDIM
CITY LIFE	EGH
DYNAMISM OR DECAY	AVNA
HERITAGE OF GREATNESS	AVNA
HOW WE BUILD CITIES	EGH
HOW WE BUILD HOUSES	EGH

(MOTION CARTRIDGES)

CITIES, THE - A CITY IS TO LIVE IN, PT 1 (I-C)	BFA
CITIES, THE - A CITY IS TO LIVE IN, PT 2 (I-C)	BFA
CITIES, THE - TO BUILD A FUTURE, PT 1 (I-C)	BFA
CITIES, THE -- TO BUILD A FUTURE, PT 2 (I-C)	BFA

(MOTION PICTURES)

ABANDONMENT OF THE CITIES, THE (J-C A)	NBCTV
BIG YELLOW TAXI	PFP
FIFTH STREET (C A)	DRMINC
FROM CAVE TO CITY (I-C)	FLMFR
SLICE OF GOLD	AMERFI
TOKYO - THE FIFTY-FIRST VOLCANO (H-C A)	TIMLIF

U S - FOREIGN POPULATION

(FILMSTRIPS)

AMERICAN ADVENTURE--A SERIES (I-J)	FIELEP
BLACK AMERICANS (I-J)	FIELEP
GERMAN AMERICANS (I-J)	FIELEP
ITALIAN AMERICANS (I-J)	FIELEP
MEXICAN AMERICANS (I-J)	FIELEP
NEW AMERICANS (I-J)	FIELEP

(MOTION PICTURES)

IMMIGRANT EXPERIENCE, THE - THE LONG, LONG JOURNEY	LCOA
ROSE ARGOFF (H-C A)	CAROUF

U S - IMMIGRATION AND EMIGRATION

(FILMSTRIPS)

AMERICAN ADVENTURE--A SERIES (I-J)	FIELEP
BLACK AMERICANS (I-J)	FIELEP
DANISH FIELD, THE (J-C A)	INTXC
GERMAN AMERICANS (I-J)	FIELEP
ITALIAN AMERICANS (I-J)	FIELEP
MEXICAN AMERICANS (I-J)	FIELEP
NEW AMERICANS (I-J)	FIELEP

(MOTION PICTURES)

IMMIGRANT FROM AMERICA (J-C A)	REPRO

U S - RACE QUESTION

(FILMSTRIPS)

AMERICAN ADVENTURE--A SERIES (I-J)	FIELEP
BLACK AMERICANS (I-J)	FIELEP
BLUE GOOTCHES, THE	EGH
FAT BLACK MACK	EGH
GERMAN AMERICANS (I-J)	FIELEP
ITALIAN AMERICANS (I-J)	FIELEP
MEXICAN AMERICANS (I-J)	FIELEP

(MOTION PICTURES)

AIN'T GONNA EAT MY MIND (J-C A)	CAROUF
BLACK AND WHITE (I-C)	PFP
INNER CITY DWELLER - WORK (H-C A)	IU
ROSE ARGOFF (H-C A)	CAROUF
VOICE OF LA RAZA	GREAVW
WAY IT IS, THE (C A)	SYNCRO
YO SOY CHICANO (ENGLISH) (H-C A)	IU

(AUDIO TAPES)

NORMAL AND ABNORMAL BEHAVIOR OF ADOLESCENCE-- A SERIES	SIGINF

(TRANSPARENCIES)

DATING RELATIONS - MIXED DATING--A SERIES (J)	LEART

WELFARE WORK IN INDUSTRY

(FILMSTRIPS)

COMPANY AND THE COMMUNITY, THE, PT 1	CREATV
COMPANY AND THE COMMUNITY, THE, PT 2	CREATV

(MOTION PICTURES)

UMBRELLA MAN, THE	MGHT

ALPHABETICAL GUIDE TO 35mm FILMSTRIPS

A

A-V LECTURES IN BIOLOGY   C 50 FRS
SOUND FILMSTRIP - AUDIO TAPE
PRESENTS VIEWS ON THE SUBJECTS OF BIOENER-
GETICS AND POPULAR GENETICS.
LC NO. 72-734130
PROD-SAUNDW   DIST-SAUNDW   1972

ACTIONS AND CONDITIONS   C 84 FRS
SOUND FILMSTRIP - AUDIO TAPE
DESCRIBES COMMON TERMS CONNECTED WITH
ACTIONS AND CONDITIONS. FROM THE INTRO-
DUCTION TO ENGLISH AS A SECOND LANGUAGE
SERIES.
PROD-EGH   DIST-EGH   1972

ADAPTATIONS FOR LIFE   C 42 FRS
SOUND FILMSTRIP - AUDIO TAPE
DESCRIBES THE ADAPTATIONS THAT HAVE AL-
LOWED VARIOUS KINDS OF ORGANISMS TO SUR-
VIVE. FROM THE LIFE - A UNIQUE PHENOMENON
SERIES.
PROD-EGH   DIST-EGH   1972

ADAPTATIONS FOR LIFE   C 45 FRS
SOUND FILMSTRIP - AUDIO TAPE
DESCRIBES THE ADAPTATIONS THAT HAVE AL-
LOWED VARIOUS KINDS OF ORGANISMS TO SUR-
VIVE. FROM THE LIFE - A UNIQUE PHENOMENON
SERIES.
LC NO. 72-736547
PROD-EGH   DIST-EGH

AFTER THE SETTLERS CAME   C 29 FRS
SOUND FILMSTRIP - AUDIO TAPE
SHOWS THE DIFFERENCES AND THE FEUDS THAT
EXISTED BETWEEN THE INDIANS AND THE SET-
TLERS. FROM THE INDIANS OF AMERICA SERIES.
PROD-EGH   DIST-EGH   1972

**AGRICULTURE AND THE
ECOSYSTEM**   C 47 FRS
FILMSTRIP WITH SCRIPT   H-C
DISCUSSES ECOLOGY, ECOSYSTEM, ENERGY AND
NUTRIENT FLOW, FOOD CHAINS, LIFE CYCLES AND
VARIOUS WAYS OF IMPROVING OUR ENVIRON-
MENT.
LC NO. 73-733311
PROD-UILVAS   DIST-UILVAS   1972

AIR   C 40 FRS
SOUND FILMSTRIP - AUDIO TAPE   P-I
SEE SERIES TITLE FOR DESCRIPTIVE STATEMENT.
FROM THE FABLES AND FACTS SERIES.
PROD-TERF   DIST-TERF   1973

**AIR POLLUTION, PT 1 - LOCAL
CONTINENTAL AND NATURAL**   C 41 FRS
FILMSTRIP
SHOWS EXAMPLES OF PRESENT AIR POLLUTION
PROBLEMS AND THE PLACES IN WHICH IT COMES
FROM.
LC NO. 72-737217
PROD-DWYLIE   DIST-CARMAN   PRODN-SCORER   1971

**AIRLINE CABIN ATTENDANT,
THE**   C 85 FRS
SOUND FILMSTRIP - RECORD   I-C
TELLS ABOUT THE TRAINING, FUNCTION AND
LIFE-STYLE OF STEWARDESSES WHILE POINTING
OUT THE MANY NEW OPPORTUNITIES NOW FOR
MALE EMPLOYEES. FROM THE EXPLORING CA-
REERS, GROUP 1 SERIES.
LC NO. 73-733179
PROD-SVE   DIST-SVE   1973

ALADDIN   C 31 FRS
SOUND FILMSTRIP - AUDIO TAPE   K-P
DESCRIBES HOW A MAGIC LAMP IS THE SOURCE
OF CHANGE IN THE LIVES OF ALADDIN AND ALL
THOSE WHO ARE CLOSE TO HIM. FROM THE CHIL-
DREN'S STORIES SERIES.
LC NO. 72-737489
PROD-STNHM   DIST-STNHM   1972

**ALASKA - THE LAST AMERICAN
FRONTIER**   C 212 FRS
SOUND FILMSTRIP - RECORD   J-H
GIVES A PICTORIAL OVERVIEW OF THE 'GREAT
ALONE,' ITS LAND AND ITS PEOPLE. SURVEYS THE
HISTORY OF ALASKA FROM THE TIMES OF THE

18TH CENTURY RUSSIAN FUR TRADERS THROUGH
THE FIGHT FOR STATEHOOD FOLLOWING WORLD
WAR II. DISCUSSES THE SITUATION OF ALASKA'S
NATIVES AND THEIR NEED FOR PRODUCTIVE
LAND THAT WILL AFFORD THEM ECONOMIC INDE-
PENDENCE FROM THE FEDERAL GOVERNMENT.
LC NO. 73-732525
PROD-SED   DIST-SED   1973

ALBERT SCHWEITZER (2ND ED)   B 40 FRS
FILMSTRIP WITH SCRIPT   I-H
SHOWS SCHWEITZER'S WORK IN AFRICA AS A
DOCTOR, AS A MISSIONARY WORKER AND AS AN
ARCHITECT AND BUILDER.
LC NO. 72-737240
PROD-COMB   DIST-CARMAN   1959

**ALCOHOL - PARENTS AND
THEIR POTIONS**   B 74 FRS
SOUND FILMSTRIP - AUDIO TAPE   P-I
PRESENTS THE EFFECTS OF ALCOHOL ON THE HU-
MAN BODY. DISCUSSES THE REASONS PEOPLE
DRINK. EXPLORES THE IMPLICATIONS OF WIDE-
SPREAD USE OF ALCOHOL, INCLUDING CAUSE OF
TRAFFIC ACCIDENTS AND DEPENDENCY. STUDIES
THE QUESTIONS AND PROBLEMS RAISED BY THE
MINIMUM AGE LIMIT OF DRINKING. FROM THE
DRUGS - A TRICK, A TRAP SERIES.
LC NO. 72-737372
PROD-EBEC   DIST-EBEC   1972

ALCOHOL AND TOBACCO   C 52 FRS
SOUND FILMSTRIP - AUDIO TAPE
DESCRIBES THE EFFECTS OF THE UNWISE USE OF
ALCOHOL AND TOBACCO. FROM THE LET'S LOOK
AT DRUGS SERIES.
PROD-EGH   DIST-EGH   1972

**ALEXANDER THE GREAT AND
THE ANCIENTS**   C 58 FRS
SOUND FILMSTRIP - AUDIO TAPE   I-J
EXAMINES THE EARLY MEDITERRANEAN PEO-
PLES, MINOANS AND PHOENICIANS, AS EXAMPLES
OF COMMERCIAL EMPIRE BUILDERS WHOSE
ECONOMIES DEPENDED ON SEAFARING. DEALS
WITH THE EXPLOITS OF ALEXANDER THE GREAT,
INCLUDING AN ACCOUNT OF HIS TRAVELS AND
THE DIFFERENT VARIABLES THAT MOTIVATED
HIM. FROM THE EXPLORATION - MAN'S QUEST
FOR KNOWLEDGE SERIES.
LC NO. 73-732518
PROD-SED   DIST-SED   1972

ALGAE AND FUNGI   C 46 FRS
FILMSTRIP
PRESENTS MICROSCOPIC PICTURES OF A SE-
LECTED GROUP OF ALGAE AND FUNGI. FROM THE
MICROSCOPIC SPECIMENS - A RESOURCE UNIT SE-
RIES.
PROD-EGH   DIST-EGH   1972

**ALIENATION AND MASS
SOCIETY, PT 1**   C 95 FRS
SOUND FILMSTRIP - AUDIO TAPE
DEFINES ALIENATION, FIRST AS ASSOCIATED
WITH PEOPLE AND SITUATIONS IN URBAN SET-
TINGS AND THEN AS EXPERIENCED BY THE POOR,
THE MIDDLE CLASS, THE WEALTHY AND THE
YOUNG.
LC NO. 72-734805
PROD-ASPRSS   DIST-SED   1972

**ALIENATION AND MASS
SOCIETY, PT 2**   C 94 FRS
SOUND FILMSTRIP - AUDIO TAPE
DEFINES ALIENATION, FIRST AS ASSOCIATED
WITH PEOPLE AND SITUATIONS IN URBAN SET-
TINGS AND THEN AS EXPERIENCED BY THE POOR,
THE MIDDLE CLASS, THE WEALTHY AND THE
YOUNG.
LC NO. 72-734805
PROD-ASPRSS   DIST-SED   1972

ALL THE ANIMALS WERE ANGRY   C 51 FRS
SOUND FILMSTRIP - AUDIO TAPE   P-I
PRESENTS A STORY WHICH PROVIDES AN OPPOR-
TUNITY TO EXPLORE ALTERNATIVE WAYS TO DEAL
WITH TRYING SITUATIONS. FROM THE STORY SE-
RIES 6 SERIES.
LC NO. 72-737104
PROD-BFA   DIST-BFA   1972

**ALPHABET ZOO, THE, PT 1 -
A-G**   C 30 FRS
FILMSTRIP WITH CAPTIONS   K-I
PRESENTS A PICTURE DICTIONARY SHOWING ANI-
MALS IN ALPHABETICAL ORDER.
LC NO. 72-737214
PROD-UMM   DIST-UMM   1973

**ALPHABET ZOO, THE, PT 2 -
H-M**   C 30 FRS
FILMSTRIP WITH CAPTIONS   K-I
PRESENTS A PICTURE DICTIONARY SHOWING ANI-
MALS IN ALPHABETICAL ORDER.
LC NO. 72-737214
PROD-UMM   DIST-UMM   1973

**ALPHABET ZOO, THE, PT 3 -
N-T**   C 30 FRS
FILMSTRIP WITH CAPTIONS   K-I
PRESENTS A PICTURE DICTIONARY SHOWING ANI-
MALS IN ALPHABETICAL ORDER.
LC NO. 72-737214
PROD-UMM   DIST-UMM   1973

**ALPHABET ZOO, THE, PT 4 -
U-Z**   C 30 FRS
FILMSTRIP WITH CAPTIONS   K-I
PRESENTS A PICTURE DICTIONARY SHOWING ANI-
MALS IN ALPHABETICAL ORDER.
LC NO. 72-737214
PROD-UMM   DIST-UMM   1973

AMERICA THE BEAUTIFUL   C 74 FRS
SOUND FILMSTRIP - RECORD   J-C
SEE SERIES TITLE FOR DESCRIPTIVE STATEMENT.
FROM THE AMERICAN CIVILIZATION - 1840-1876
SERIES.
PROD-SUNCOM   DIST-SUNCOM   1973

**AMERICAN ADVENTURE--A
SERIES**   I-J
POINTS OUT THE ETHNIC DIVERSITY OF THE
AMERICAN POPULATION AND TRACES ITS HIS-
TORY, MAINLY THROUGH IMMIGRATION. DEALS
WITH INDIVIDUAL GROUPS WHICH DIFFER
WIDELY IN HISTORY, ASSIMILATION AND CUR-
RENT IDENTIFICATION.
PROD-FIELEP   DIST-FIELEP   1972

BLACK AMERICANS   120 FRS
GERMAN AMERICANS   85 FRS
ITALIAN AMERICANS   93 FRS
MEXICAN AMERICANS   121 FRS
NEW AMERICANS   111 FRS

**AMERICAN CIVILIZATION - 1783-
1840--A SERIES**   J-C
EXAMINES THE HISTORY AND IDEALS OF OUR NA-
TION'S EARLY YEARS THROUGH THE SUBJECTS
AND STYLES OF ITS GREAT NATIVE ARTISTS. COR-
RELATES HISTORY, PAINTING, ARCHITECTURE
AND SCULPTURE AND SHOWS EARLY AMERICA'S
SENSE OF PURPOSE AND FUNDAMENTAL RE-
SPECT FOR THE COMMON MAN.
LC NO. 73-733276
PROD-SUNCOM   DIST-SUNCOM   1973

ARTS AND THE COMMON MAN, THE   71 FRS
PORTRAIT OF A YOUNG NATION   80 FRS
YOUNG AMERICA ADMIRES THE
ANCIENTS   80 FRS

**AMERICAN CIVILIZATION - 1840-
1876--A SERIES**   J-C
EXAMINES THE MOOD AND TONE OF AMERICAN
SOCIETY IMMEDIATELY PRECEDING, DURING AND
AFTER THE CIVIL WAR. INTEGRATES HISTORY,
PAINTING, ARCHITECTURE AND SCULPTURE AND
OUTLINES THE RAPID CHANGES AND INSTABILITY
OF THE YEARS 1840-1876.
LC NO. 73-733275
PROD-SUNCOM   DIST-SUNCOM   1973

AMERICA THE BEAUTIFUL   74 FRS
ARCHITECTURE AS A LANGUAGE   80 FRS
ARTS REFLECT DAILY LIFE, THE   80 FRS
BRIDGES TO THE 20TH CENTURY   80 FRS

**AMERICAN FOREIGN POLICY -
HOW IT WORKS**   C 179 FRS
SOUND FILMSTRIP - RECORD   J-H
POINTS OUT THAT FOREIGN POLICY DECISIONS
EMERGE FROM A COMPLEX SYSTEM OF BUREAUS
AND AGENCIES, SOME CREATED BY THE CONSTI-
TUTION, OTHERS BY CONGRESS OR THE PRESI-
DENT. EXPLAINS HOW THE SYSTEM DEVELOPED,

B

HOW IT ALL WORKS AND HOW THE FEDERAL SYSTEM OF CHECKS AND BALANCES OPERATES TO CONTROL IT.
LC NO. 73-732529
PROD-SED   DIST-SED   1972

AMERICAN GENIUS--A SERIES
                                             H-C
ILLUSTRATES THE CHANGES IN U S CULTURE AND SOCIETY BETWEEN 1880 AND 1970.
PROD-EDDIM   DIST-EDDIM   1972

AMERICAN GENIUS, 1880 - 1918
AMERICAN GENIUS, 1920 - 1940
AMERICAN GENIUS, 1940 - 1950
AMERICAN GENIUS, 1960 - 1970

AMERICAN GENIUS, 1880 - 1918
                SOUND FILMSTRIP - AUDIO TAPE   C   H-C
DESCRIBES THE EFFECTS OF GROWING INDUSTRIALIZATION AND URBANIZATION DURING THE GILDED AGE, USING THE WRITINGS OF MARK TWAIN, HENRY JAMES AND WILLIAM HOWELLS AND THE PAINTINGS OF CASSATT, EAKINS, HOMER, DUCHAMP AND OTHERS TO ILLUSTRATE THE SOCIOCULTURAL CONCERNS OF THE TIME. FROM THE AMERICAN GENIUS SERIES.
LC NO. 72-737517
PROD-EDDIM   DIST-EDDIM   1972

AMERICAN GENIUS, 1920 - 1940
                SOUND FILMSTRIP - AUDIO TAPE   C   H-C
CONTRASTS THE WILD, BOOTLEGGING TWENTIES WITH THE BITTERLY SOBER THIRTIES, INCORPORATING AS ARTISTIC COMMENT ON FITZGERALD, POUND, ELIOT AND FAULKNER, THE PAINTINGS OF BEN SHAHN, THOMAS HART BENTON AND GEORGIA O'KEEFE. FROM THE AMERICAN GENIUS SERIES.
LC NO. 72-737520
PROD EDDIM   DIST EDDIM   1972

AMERICAN GENIUS, 1940 - 1950
                SOUND FILMSTRIP - AUDIO TAPE   C   H-C
USES THE NOVELS OF MAILER, MC CULLERS, JAMES JOYCE AND TRUMAN CAPOTE AND THE NOVELS OF ARTHUR MILLER AND TENNESSEE WILLIAMS TO EXPRESS THE DISINTEGRATION OF THE CONFORMIST VALUES IN THE 1950'S, FURTHER ILLUSTRATED BY THE FRAGMENTED AND ABSTRACT PAINTINGS OF DEKOONING AND POLLACK. FROM THE AMERICAN GENIUS SERIES.
LC NO. 72-737518
PROD-EDDIM   DIST-EDDIM   1972

AMERICAN GENIUS, 1960 - 1970
                SOUND FILMSTRIP - AUDIO TAPE   C   H-C
SHOWS HOW THE EMERGING SOCIAL CONSCIOUSNESS OF THE 1960'S ERUPTED IN PHYSICAL VIOLENCE AND FOUND EXPRESSION IN ANTI-HERO MOVIES, PAP AND POP ART, THE LIVING THEATER AND ROCK MUSIC. FROM THE AMERICAN GENIUS SERIES.
LC NO. 72-737519
PROD-EDDIM   DIST-EDDIM   1972

AMERICAN ROMANTICISM   C 63 FRS
                SOUND FILMSTRIP - RECORD   J-C
SEE SERIES TITLE FOR DESCRIPTIVE STATEMENT. FROM THE DEVELOPMENT OF THE AMERICAN SHORT STORY SERIES. PT 1
LC NO. 77-734751
PROD-EAV   DIST-EAV   1969

AMERICAN WEST IN LITERATURE, THE, PT 1   C 73 FRS
                SOUND FILMSTRIP - AUDIO TAPE   J
HELPS STUDENTS LEARN TO DISTINGUISH SUBSTANCE FROM MYTH IN LITERATURE ABOUT THE AMERICAN WEST.
LC NO. 73-733112
PROD-GA   DIST-GA   1973

AMERICAN WEST IN LITERATURE, THE, PT 2   C 68 FRS
                SOUND FILMSTRIP - AUDIO TAPE   J
HELPS STUDENTS LEARN TO DISTINGUISH SUBSTANCE FROM MYTH IN LITERATURE ABOUT THE AMERICAN WEST.
LC NO. 73-733112
PROD-GA   DIST-GA   1973

ANCIENT CIVILIZATIONS OF THE AMERICAS--A SERIES
                                             I-J
TRACES THE HISTORIES OF THE GREAT ANCIENT INDIAN CIVILIZATIONS OF AMERICA. ILLUSTRATES IMPORTANT ASPECTS OF THEIR CULTURE AND EVALUATES THEIR ACHIEVEMENTS.
PROD-EBEC   DIST-EBEC   1972

AZTECS, THE   53 FRS
INCAS, THE   47 FRS
MAYAS, THE   60 FRS

ANIMAL HISTOLOGY   C 25 FRS
                FILMSTRIP WITH SCRIPT   I-H
INTRODUCES PUPILS TO THE APPEARANCE AND INTERPRETATION OF MICROSCOPICAL PREPARATIONS. HELPS THE PUPILS TO UNDERSTAND THE SECTIONS THEY WILL BE LOOKING AT WHEN DOING DIRECT MICROSCOPE WORK.
LC NO. 72-737262
PROD-COMG   DIST-COMG   1961

ANIMAL KINGDOM--A SERIES
PROD-LIFE   DIST-LIFE   1970

MONKEYS AND APES, PT 1   67 FRS
MONKEYS AND APES, PT 2   70 FRS

ANIMALS   C
                FILMSTRIP WITH CAPTIONS
FROM THE ANIMALS SERIES.
LC NO. 72-734417
PROD-LIEB   DIST-MSCF   1970

ANIMALS TO KNOW - AFRICA, PT 1   C 68 FRS
                SOUND FILMSTRIP - AUDIO TAPE   P-I
PRESENTS ANIMALS IN LIVING SITUATIONS. INTRODUCES A NUMBER OF ZOO ANIMALS AND EXPLAINS SOMETHING ABOUT THEIR BACKGROUND, THEIR ADAPTABILITY TO ZOO LIFE AND THE SPECIAL CARE GIVEN THEM BY THE ZOO ATTENDANTS.
LC NO. 72-737087
PROD-BFA   DIST-BFA   1972

ANIMALS TO KNOW - AFRICA, PT 2   C 60 FRS
                SOUND FILMSTRIP - AUDIO TAPE   P-I
PRESENTS ANIMALS IN LIVING SITUATIONS. INTRODUCES A NUMBER OF ZOO ANIMALS AND EXPLAINS SOMETHING ABOUT THEIR BACKGROUND, THEIR ADAPTABILITY TO ZOO LIFE AND THE SPECIAL CARE GIVEN THEM BY THE ZOO ATTENDANTS.
LC NO. 72-737088
PROD-BFA   DIST-BFA   1972

ANIMALS--A SERIES
LC NO. 72-734417
PROD-LIEB   DIST-MSCF   1970

ANIMALS
BROWN BAT, THE
ELEPHANT SEAL, THE
ELEPHANT, THE
GIRAFFE, THE
GORILLA, THE
LION, THE
PLATYPUS, THE
POLAR BEAR, THE
WHAT IS IT (TEST SCRIPT)

ANNUAL MIGRATION OF THE CALIFORNIA GRAY WHALE   C 35 FRS
                SOUND FILMSTRIP - RECORD
PRESENTS AN EXAMINATION OF THE MIGRATORY AND BREEDING BEHAVIOR OF THE CALIFORNIA GRAY WHALE.
LC NO. 72-735350
PROD-SDCDE   DIST-SDCDE   PRODN-CER   1971

APPETITE OF A BIRD   C
                FILMSTRIP
USES ANIMATION AND LIVE ACTION TO PORTRAY THE PROBLEMS OF THE RELATIONSHIP BETWEEN MAN AND WOMAN.
LC NO. 72-702781
PROD-LESAM   DIST-FI   1972

ARCHITECTURE AS A LANGUAGE   C 80 FRS
                SOUND FILMSTRIP - RECORD   J-C
SEE SERIES TITLE FOR DESCRIPTIVE STATEMENT. FROM THE AMERICAN CIVILIZATION - 1840-1876 SERIES.
PROD-SUNCOM   DIST-SUNCOM   1973

ARE SEX AND LOVE THE SAME THING   C 64 FRS
                SOUND FILMSTRIP - AUDIO TAPE
DISCUSSES SEX WITHOUT RELATIONSHIP VERSUS LOVE AS THE TOTAL MUTUAL CLOSENESS AND RESPONSE, BOTH PHYSICAL AND PSYCHOLOGICAL, OF TWO CARING PERSONS. FROM THE HUMAN SEXUALITY SERIES.
PROD-EGH   DIST-EGH   1972

ARTILLERY IN THE CIVIL WAR   C 45 FRS
                SOUND FILMSTRIP - RECORD
EXPLAINS THE USE OF ARTILLERY IN THE CIVIL WAR. FROM THE CIVIL WAR AS IT HAPPENED SERIES.
LC NO. 72-735143
PROD-EDREC   DIST-TECVIS   1970

ARTS AND THE COMMON MAN, THE   C 71 FRS
                SOUND FILMSTRIP - RECORD   J-C
SEE SERIES TITLE FOR DESCRIPTIVE STATEMENT. FROM THE AMERICAN CIVILIZATION - 1783-1840 SERIES.
PROD-SUNCOM   DIST-SUNCOM   1973

ARTS REFLECT DAILY LIFE, THE   C 80 FRS
                SOUND FILMSTRIP - RECORD   J-C
SEE SERIES TITLE FOR DESCRIPTIVE STATEMENT. FROM THE AMERICAN CIVILIZATION - 1840-1876 SERIES.
PROD-SUNCOM   DIST-SUNCOM   1973

ASFEC   B 67 FRS
                FILMSTRIP
SHOWS THE WORK DONE BY THE ARAB STATES FUNDAMENTAL EDUCATION CENTER.
LC NO. 72-740205
PROD-ASFEC   DIST-UNIPUB   1955

ATTITUDES ABOUT HUMAN SEXUALITY   C 53 FRS
                SOUND FILMSTRIP - AUDIO TAPE
EXPLORES ATTITUDES TOWARDS SEXUALITY TO HELP PEOPLE UNDERSTAND THEMSELVES AND BASE RELATIONSHIPS WITH OTHERS ON HONESTY, RESPONSIBILITY, PERSONAL GROWTH AND MATURITY, OPENNESS AND COMMITMENT. FROM THE HUMAN SEXUALITY SERIES.
PROD-EGH   DIST-EGH   1972

AUDIO-VISUAL--A SERIES
PROD-BSF   DIST-BSF   1966

LANGUAGE LABORATORY, THE   55 FRS
TAPE RECORDER IN TEACHING, THE   59 FRS

AUTO BODY - PAINTING   C 35 FRS
                SOUND FILMSTRIP - AUDIO TAPE
DEMONSTRATES THE USE OF THE PAINT GUN, PATTERN SETTINGS AND SPRAYING TECHNIQUES.
LC NO. 72-735114
PROD-MTSJC   DIST-MTSJC   1971

AUTOMOBILE, THE (HENRY FORD)   C 56 FRS
                FILMSTRIP WITH CAPTIONS   P
USES CAPTIONED DRAWINGS TO PRESENT THE STORY OF HENRY FORD AND THE CAR HE BUILT. SHOWS THAT THE MODEL T WAS THE MEANS FOR PROVIDING ALMOST EVERYONE WITH AUTOMOBILE TRANSPORTATION. FROM THE IMPORTANT INVENTORS, LEVEL 3 SERIES.
LC NO. 72-737074
PROD-EDPRC   DIST-EDPRC

AUTOMOTIVE MECHANIC, THE   C 91 FRS
                SOUND FILMSTRIP - RECORD   I-C
HIGHLIGHTS THE PROBLEM-SOLVING APTITUDES GENERALLY FOUND IN GOOD AUTOMOTIVE MECHANICS. FROM THE EXPLORING CAREERS, GROUP 1 SERIES.
LC NO. 73-733178
PROD-SVE   DIST-SVE   1973

AZTECS   C 57 FRS
                FILMSTRIP WITH SCRIPT
FROM THE MEXICAN EPIC - BEFORE THE CONQUEST SERIES.
LC NO. 75-732593
PROD-UMM   DIST-UMM

AZTECS, THE   C 53 FRS
                SOUND FILMSTRIP - AUDIO TAPE   I-J
INTRODUCES THE CULTURE, GOVERNMENT, RELIGION AND ACHIEVEMENTS OF THE AZTECS AND THEIR GREAT EMPIRE. STUDIES THE CAPITAL CITY, THEIR INTRICATE RELIGIOUS SYSTEM AND THEIR ART AND ARCHITECTURE. FROM THE ANCIENT CIVILIZATIONS OF THE AMERICAS SERIES.
LC NO. 72-737365

PROD-EBEC   DIST-EBEC   1972

B

BALANCE OF LIFE IN A DESERT   C 56 FRS
FILMSTRIP WITH SCRIPT
STRESSES THE INTERDEPENDENCE OF ALL LIVING
THINGS. FROM THE DESERT LIFE SERIES. NO. 4
LC NO. 72-735809
PROD-SED   DIST-SED   1972

BASES AND EXPONENTS   C 29 FRS
SOUND FILMSTRIP - RECORD   J-H
INTRODUCES EXPONENTIAL NOTATION AS A DE-
VICE TO EXPRESS REPEATED FACTORS COM-
PACTLY WITH EMPHASIS ON THE MEANING OF
BASE AND EXPONENT. FROM THE MATHEMATICS -
FUNDAMENTAL OPERATIONS SERIES.
LC NO. 73-732673
PROD-UNISYS   DIST-VIEWLX   1972

**BASIC ARITHMETIC SKILLS--A
SERIES**
PRESENTS LESSONS ON ADDITION, MULTIPLICA-
TION AND DIVISION.
LC NO. 72-735675
PROD-CREATV   DIST-CREATV

**BASIC ASPECTS OF MOLECULAR
BIOLOGY**   C .42 FRS
SOUND FILMSTRIP - AUDIO TAPE
PROVIDES A BASIC INTRODUCTION TO MOLECU-
LAR BIOLOGY, WITH INSTRUCTIONS FOR USING
THE HGS MODEL KIT TO BUILD MODELS OF OR-
GANIC MOLECULES.
LC NO. 72-735001
PROD-MTSJC   DIST-MTSJC   1971

**BASIC COMPUTATIONAL SKILLS-
-A SERIES**

PROD-CREATV   DIST-CREATV

DIVISION PROGRAM, THE   90 FRS
MULTIPLICATION PROGRAM, THE   90 FRS
SUBTRACTION PROGRAM, THE   90 FRS

BASIC PARTS AND OPERATION   C
SOUND FILMSTRIP - RECORD   J-C A
SEE SERIES TITLE FOR DESCRIPTIVE STATEMENT.
FROM THE INTERNAL COMBUSTION ENGINE EX-
PLAINED SERIES.
PROD-BERGL   DIST-BERGL   1972

BASIC PARTS AND PRINCIPLES   C
SOUND FILMSTRIP - RECORD   J-C A
SEE SERIES TITLE FOR DESCRIPTIVE STATEMENT.
FROM THE HYDRAULIC BRAKE SYSTEM EX-
PLAINED SERIES.
PROD-BERGL   DIST-BERGL   1972

**BEETHOVEN'S NINTH
SYMPHONY, ODE TO JOY**   B 122 FRS
SOUND FILMSTRIP - RECORD
USES PHOTOGRAPHS OF PEOPLE FROM ALL PARTS
OF THE WORLD TO ILLUSTRATE THE BROTHER-
HOOD OF MAN THEME OF THE FOURTH MOVE-
MENT OF BEETHOVEN'S 'NINTH SYMPHONY.'
FROM THE MUSIC APPRECIATION SERIES.
LC NO. 72-736268
PROD-EAV   DIST-EAV

BEGINNINGS   C 57 FRS
FILMSTRIP WITH SCRIPT
FROM THE MEXICAN EPIC - BEFORE THE
CONQUEST SERIES.
LC NO. 75-732593
PROD-UMM   DIST-UMM

BEGINNINGS OF REALISM, THE   C 59 FRS
SOUND FILMSTRIP - RECORD   J-C
SEE SERIES TITLE FOR DESCRIPTIVE STATEMENT.
FROM THE DEVELOPMENT OF THE AMERICAN
SHORT STORY SERIES. PT 2
LC NO. 77-734751
PROD-EAV   DIST-EAV   1969

BETWEEN THE WARS   C 50 FRS
SOUND FILMSTRIP - RECORD   J-C
SEE SERIES TITLE FOR DESCRIPTIVE STATEMENT.
FROM THE DEVELOPMENT OF THE AMERICAN
SHORT STORY SERIES. PT 3
LC NO. 77-734751
PROD-EAV   DIST-EAV   1969

BLACK AMERICANS   C 120 FRS
SOUND FILMSTRIP - RECORD   I-J
SEE SERIES TITLE FOR DESCRIPTIVE STATEMENT.
FROM THE AMERICAN ADVENTURE SERIES.
LC NO. 72-737419
PROD-FIELEP   DIST-FIELEP   1972

BLUE GOOTCHES, THE   C 55 FRS
SOUND FILMSTRIP - AUDIO TAPE
PRESENTS A MODERN PARABLE CONCERNING
RACE RELATIONS. FROM THE GUIDES FOR GROW-
ING SERIES.
LC NO. 72-736524
PROD-EGH   DIST-EGH   1972

**BONNEVILLE DAM -
POWERHOUSE OF THE
COLUMBIA RIVER**   C 93 FRS
SOUND FILMSTRIP - AUDIO TAPE   J-H A
EXPLAINS THAT DEVELOPMENT OF THE COLUM-
BIA RIVER AS A SOURCE OF HYDROELECTRIC
POWER- FOR THE PACIFIC NORTHWEST HAS BEEN
BENEFICIAL, BUT SOME PEOPLE THINK DEVELOP-
MENT THREATENS THE WILDERNESS AREA SO
LOVED BY THOSE WHO LIVE THERE. PROFILES THE
FAMILIES OF THE MEN WHO WORK AT BONNE-
VILLE DAM - AND LIVE BESIDE THE MAGNIFICENT
COLUMBIA RIVER. FROM THE FOCUS ON AMERICA
- THE PACIFIC STATES SERIES.
LC NO. 73-733160
PROD-SVE   DIST-SVE   1972

**BRIDGES TO THE 20TH
CENTURY**   C 80 FRS
SOUND FILMSTRIP - RECORD   J-C
SEE SERIES TITLE FOR DESCRIPTIVE STATEMENT.
FROM THE AMERICAN CIVILIZATION - 1840-1876
SERIES.
PROD-SUNCOM   DIST-SUNCOM   1973

BROADCAST TECHNICIAN, THE   C 89 FRS
SOUND FILMSTRIP - RECORD   I-C
SHOWS A VARIETY OF TECHNICIANS IN RADIO
AND TV AND ZEROS IN ON A SOUND ENGINEER.
FROM THE EXPLORING CAREERS, GROUP 1 SE-
RIES.
LC NO. 73-733175
PROD-SVE   DIST-SVE   1973

BRODERICK   C 55 FRS
SOUND FILMSTRIP - AUDIO TAPE   P-I
PRESENTS A STORY WHICH ENCOURAGES STU-
DENTS TO READ AS ONE WAY OF EXPLORING THE
WORLD AROUND THEM AND TO TRY NEW ACTIVI-
TIES. FROM THE STORY SERIES 6 SERIES.
LC NO. 72-737107
PROD-BFA   DIST-BFA   1972

BROWN BAT, THE   C
FILMSTRIP WITH CAPTIONS
FROM THE ANIMALS SERIES.
LC NO. 72-734417
PROD-LIEB   DIST-MSCF   1970

BRUSHING AWAY TOOTH DECAY
C 40 FRS
SOUND FILMSTRIP - AUDIO TAPE   P-I
SHOWS HOW OUR FRIEND THE TOOTHBRUSH,
WHEN USED PROPERLY AFTER MEALS AND
SNACKS, CAN PREVENT THE TOOTH DECAY VIL-
LAIN FROM BORING THROUGH THE ENAMEL AND
DENTINE AND ATTACKING THE PULP AT THE
HEART OF THE TOOTH. FROM THE PRACTICING
GOOD HEALTH, SET 2 - YOUR MOUTH SPEAKING
SERIES.
LC NO. 73-733194
PROD-DISNEY   DIST-DISNEY   1973

BUILDING ON THE ROCK   C 37 FRS
SOUND FILMSTRIP - RECORD   I R
GIVES A FIRST-PERSON PRESENTATION OF THE
LIFE OF JESUS. POINTS OUT THAT FAITH IN JESUS
IS THE CORNERSTONE OF THE CHRISTIAN COM-
MUNITY. PRESENTS GOSPEL NARRATIVES SHOW-
ING HOW JESUS WAS REJECTED BY THE PEOPLE
IN HIS HOMETOWN BECAUSE HE REFUSED TO DO
MIRACLES FOR THEM, HOW THE MIRACLE OF
LOAVES AND FISHES PROMPTED MEN TO SHARE
AND HOW THE TRANSFIGURATION CHANGED THE
DISCIPLES. FROM THE MY NAME IS JESUS SERIES.
LC NO. 72-737434

PROD-ROAS   DIST-ROAS   1972

C

**CALIFORNIA CONFLICT -
MIGRANT FARM WORKERS**   C 94 FRS
SOUND FILMSTRIP - AUDIO TAPE   J-H A
EXAMINES CALIFORNIA'S AGRICULTURALLY RICH
CENTRAL VALLEY AND REVIEWS THE HISTORY OF
THE VALLEY'S CONFLICT BETWEEN FARM LABOR-
ERS AND OWNERS. FOCUSES ON RECENT EF-
FORTS TO UNIONIZE THE FARM LABORERS OF THE
REGION. FROM THE FOCUS ON AMERICA - THE PA-
CIFIC STATES SERIES.
LC NO. 73-733158
PROD-SVE   DIST-SVE   1972

CAMERA SYSTEMS   B 77 FRS
SOUND FILMSTRIP - AUDIO TAPE   J-C A
ILLUSTRATES THE ACCESSORIES WHICH MAKE UP
A CAMERA SYSTEM, INCLUDING LENSES, VIEW-
FINDER SYSTEMS, MOTOR DRIVES, FILTERS,
FLASH SYSTEMS AND PANORAMA HEADS. DIS-
CUSSES METHODS AND PROCEDURES FOR AC-
TION, CLOSE-UP AND SEQUENCE PHOTOGRAPHY.
FROM THE CREATIVE PHOTOGRAPHY - CAMERA
SERIES.
LC NO. 73-732513
PROD-ARIZSU   DIST-ARIZSU   1973

CAMERA, THE   B 70 FRS
SOUND FILMSTRIP - AUDIO TAPE   J-C A
ILLUSTRATES CAMERAS OF VARIOUS TYPES
WHICH USE POPULAR FILM SIZES. DISCUSSES
THEIR ADVANTAGES AND DISADVANTAGES AND
SHOWS VIEWFINDERS, SHUTTERS AND EXPOSURE
CONTROL SYSTEMS. FROM THE CREATIVE PHO-
TOGRAPHY - CAMERA SERIES.
LC NO. 73-732511
PROD-ARIZSU   DIST-ARIZSU   1973

**CANCER, SERIES 3 -
TREATMENT MODALITIES WITH
IMPLICATIONS FOR NURSING
CARE--A SERIES**

PROD-CONMED   DIST-CONMED   1972

CHEMOTHERAPY   106 FRS
COLOSTOMY   115 FRS
HEAD AND NECK SURGERY   119 FRS
HYSTERECTOMY FOR UTERINE CANCER   80 FRS
INTRODUCTION TO CANCER SURGERY -
MASTECTOMY   109 FRS
RADIOTHERAPY I   102 FRS
RADIOTHERAPY II   106 FRS

**CANDIDE - LE TEXTE ET LA VIE
DE VOLTAIRE**   C 120 FRS
SOUND FILMSTRIP - AUDIO TAPE   H-C
A FRENCH LANGUAGE FILMSTRIP. ILLUSTRATES
THE ENTIRE BOOK, 'CANDIDE,' FROM THE OPEN-
ING SCENE OF THE CHATEAU IN WESTPHALIA UN-
TIL THE LAST SCENE, 'ONE MUST CULTIVATE
ONE'S GARDEN.'
LC NO. 73-733000
PROD-ALEP   DIST-ALEP   1973

**CAPTAIN COOK, ALEXANDER
MAC KENZIE AND LEWIS AND
CLARK**   C 58 FRS
SOUND FILMSTRIP - AUDIO TAPE   I-J
RELATES THE ORGANIZED, SCIENTIFIC EXPEDI-
TIONS OF CAPTAIN COOK ALONG WITH A REVIEW
OF THE LONG SEARCH FOR A NORTHWEST PAS-
SAGE THROUGH THE U S. MENTIONS JACQUES
CARTIER, SAMUEL DE CHAMPLAIN, HENRY HUD-
SON AND GEORGE VANCOUVER. FROM THE EXPLO-
RATION - MAN'S QUEST FOR KNOWLEDGE SERIES.
LC NO. 73-732523
PROD-SED   DIST-SED   1972

**CARBURETION, IGNITION AND
COOLING**   C
SOUND FILMSTRIP - RECORD   J-C A
SEE SERIES TITLE FOR DESCRIPTIVE STATEMENT.
FROM THE INTERNAL COMBUSTION ENGINE EX-
PLAINED SERIES.
PROD-BERGL   DIST-BERGL   1972

**CASE OF THE CROOKED TEETH,
THE**   C 42 FRS
SOUND FILMSTRIP - AUDIO TAPE   P-I
TELLS THE MYSTERY STORY OF HOW AN IRREGU-
LAR TOOTH GOT THAT WAY. OUTLINES GOOD
MANNERS FOR THE BRACE WEARER AND HIS
PEERS. FROM THE PRACTICING GOOD HEALTH,
SET 2 - YOUR MOUTH SPEAKING SERIES.
LC NO. 73-733200
PROD-DISNEY   DIST-DISNEY   1973

**CHARLES IVES - HOLIDAYS -
WASHINGTON'S BIRTHDAY AND
THE FOURTH OF JULY**   C 100 FRS
        SOUND FILMSTRIP - RECORD
PRESENTS HISTORICAL SCENES OF THE SEASONS
AND SCENES OF FESTIVITIES ASSOCIATED WITH
WASHINGTON'S BIRTHDAY AND FOURTH OF JULY,
ACCOMPANIED BY THE MUSIC OF CHARLES IVES.
FROM THE MUSIC APPRECIATION SERIES.
    LC NO. 72-736382
PROD-EAV   DIST-EAV

CHEMOTHERAPY   C 106 FRS
        SOUND FILMSTRIP - RECORD
DISCUSSES THE ACTION AND USE OF FOUR TYPES
OF ANTINEOPLASTIC DRUGS. FROM THE CANCER,
SERIES 3 - TREATMENT MODALITIES WITH IMPLI-
CATIONS FOR NURSING CARE SERIES. NO. 7
    LC NO. 72-733179
PROD-CONMED   DIST-CONMED   1972

**CHIHUAHUA - LIFE IN A
NORTHERN MEXICAN CITY**   C 37 FRS
        SOUND FILMSTRIP - AUDIO TAPE
DESCRIBES THE VARIOUS FACTORS IN THE LIFE
PATTERN OF CHIHUAHUA. FROM THE MEXICO - A
COMMUNITY STUDY SERIES.
PROD-EGH   DIST-EGH   1972

CHILDREN   C 50 FRS
        SOUND FILMSTRIP - AUDIO TAPE
DESCRIBES THE LIFE OF THE CHILDREN AND
SHOWS THE CONTRAST BETWEEN THE POOR AND
THE PROSPEROUS. FROM THE LIFEWAYS OF THE
PEOPLE - SOUTH AMERICA SERIES.
PROD-EGH   DIST-EGH   1972

CHILDREN'S STORIES--A SERIES
                            K-P
PROD-STNHM   DIST-STNHM   1972

ALADDIN	31 FRS
CINDERELLA	30 FRS
DON QUIXOTE	31 FRS
DR DOOLITTLE	36 FRS
FIVE NAUGHTY MARBLES	33 FRS
GOLDEN FISH, THE	30 FRS
LAZY CAT, THE	24 FRS
LITTLE RED RIDING HOOD	28 FRS
PETER AND THE WOLF	45 FRS
PINOCCHIO	34 FRS
PUSS IN BOOTS	29 FRS
SNOW WHITE	32 FRS
SORCERER'S APPRENTICE, THE	32 FRS
THREE BEARS, THE	30 FRS
THUMBELINA	31 FRS
TOM THUMB	35 FRS
TWO DERVISHES, THE	30 FRS
UGLY DUCKLING, THE	30 FRS

CHINESE ART, PT 1   C 68 FRS
        SOUND FILMSTRIP - AUDIO TAPE   J-C A
PRESENTS THE DISCOVERY AND DESCRIPTION OF
ANCIENT CHINESE POTTERY AND BRONZES FROM
NEOLITHIC TIMES TO THE T'ANG DYNASTY.
    LC NO. 73-733067
PROD-SCHLAT   DIST-SCHLAT   1973

CHINESE ART, PT 2   C 97 FRS
        SOUND FILMSTRIP - AUDIO TAPE   J-C A
DISCUSSES CHINESE ARCHITECTURE, SCULPTURE,
POTTERY AND MINOR ART FORMS TO THE PRE-
SENT DAY.
    LC NO. 73-733067
PROD-SCHLAT   DIST-SCHLAT   1973

CHINESE ART, PT 3   C 96 FRS
        SOUND FILMSTRIP - AUDIO TAPE   J-C A
INTRODUCES CHINESE PAINTING FORMS FROM
EARLIEST TIMES IN THE FIRST MILLENIUM BC TO
THE PRESENT.
    LC NO. 73-733067
PROD-SCHLAT   DIST-SCHLAT   1973

**CHRISTMAS IN A NOISY
VILLAGE**   C 32 FRS
        SOUND FILMSTRIP - AUDIO TAPE   K-P
DESCRIBES THE PREPARATION FOR AND CELE-
BRATION OF CHRISTMAS IN A SMALL SWEDISH
VILLAGE, AS SEEN THROUGH THE ACTIVITIES OF
THE CHILDREN WHO LIVE THERE.
    LC NO. 73-732654
PROD-VIP   DIST-VIP   1973

CINDERELLA   C 30 FRS
        SOUND FILMSTRIP - AUDIO TAPE   K-P
PRESENTS THE CLASSIC TALE OF CINDERELLA
WHO WORKS HARD AND OBEDIENTLY SERVES
HER STEPMOTHER AND STEPSISTERS. FROM THE
CHILDREN'S STORIES SERIES.
    LC NO. 73-732806
PROD-STNHM   DIST-STNHM   1972

**CIRCULATION - BLOOD
CIRCULATION**   C
        FILMSTRIP WITH SCRIPT   H-C A
FROM THE HUMAN ANATOMY AND PHYSIOLOGY
SERIES.
PROD-HRAW   DIST-HRAW   1973

**CIRCULATION - BLOOD
PRESSURE**   C
        FILMSTRIP WITH SCRIPT   H-C A
FROM THE HUMAN ANATOMY AND PHYSIOLOGY
SERIES.
PROD-HRAW   DIST-HRAW   1973

**CIRCULATION - FUNCTION OF
THE HEART**   C
        FILMSTRIP WITH SCRIPT   H-C A
FROM THE HUMAN ANATOMY AND PHYSIOLOGY
SERIES.
PROD-HRAW   DIST-HRAW   1973

CITIES OF ITALY   C 49 FRS
        SOUND FILMSTRIP - AUDIO TAPE
DESCRIBES THE HISTORIC PAST AND THE PRE-
SENT IN SEVERAL ITALIAN CITIES. FROM THE IT-
ALY - A REGIONAL SURVEY SERIES.
    LC NO. 72-736588
PROD-EGH   DIST-EGH   1972

CITIES OF ITALY   C 57 FRS
        SOUND FILMSTRIP - AUDIO TAPE
PRESENTS THE HISTORY AND DESCRIPTION OF
SEVERAL ITALIAN CITIES. FROM THE ITALY - A RE-
GIONAL STUDY SERIES.
    LC NO. 72-736588
PROD-EGH   DIST-EGH   1972

**CITIES OF ROME AND
FLORENCE**   C 47 FRS
        SOUND FILMSTRIP - AUDIO TAPE
DESCRIBES THE MANY HISTORIC AND MODERN
AREAS OF ROME AND FLORENCE. FROM THE ITALY
- A REGIONAL SURVEY SERIES.
    LC NO. 72-736589
PROD-EGH   DIST-EGH   1972

**CITIES OF ROME AND
FLORENCE**   C 55 FRS
        SOUND FILMSTRIP - AUDIO TAPE
DESCRIBES THE MANY HISTORIC AND MODERN
AREAS OF ROME AND FLORENCE. FROM THE ITALY
- A REGIONAL STUDY SERIES.
    LC NO. 72-736589
PROD-EGH   DIST-EGH   1972

**CITY - HOW AMERICA LIVES--A
SERIES**
EXAMINES HOW AND WHY AMERICA BECAME AN
URBAN NATION. SHOWS HOW A TYPICAL FAMILY
LIVES IN AN URBAN ENVIRONMENT AND DIS-
CUSSES THE MULTIPLE PROBLEMS OF THE CITIES
TODAY.
    LC NO. 72-736412
PROD-AVNA   DIST-AVNA   1972

DYNAMISM OR DECAY	67 FRS
HERITAGE OF GREATNESS	72 FRS

CITY IN HISTORY, THE, PT 1   C 78 FRS
        SOUND FILMSTRIP - RECORD   J-C A
COVERS THE ECONOMIC, SOCIAL AND POLITICAL
EVOLUTION OF THE CITY. TRACES THE CITY FROM
ITS ANCIENT ORIGINS THROUGH THE GRECO-RO-
MAN CIVILIZATION TO THE WALLED CITY OF THE
MIDDLE AGES AND THE BURGEONING CITIES OF
THE RENAISSANCE.
    LC NO. 72-737515
PROD-EDDIM   DIST-EDDIM   1973

CITY IN HISTORY, THE, PT 2   C 92 FRS
        SOUND FILMSTRIP - RECORD   J-C A
COVERS THE ECONOMIC, SOCIAL AND POLITICAL
EVOLUTION OF THE CITY. EXPLORES THE AMERI-
CAN CITY FROM THE FIRST COLONIAL SETTLE-
MENTS TO THE CONTEMPORARY MEGALOPOLIS,
NOTING THE SIGNIFICANCE OF SOCIAL MOBILITY,
THE INDUSTRIAL REVOLUTION, THE FRONTIER
AND THE MATERIAL AND SOCIAL DECAY OF MOD-
ERN, SPRAWLING URBAN CENTERS.
    LC NO. 72-737515
PROD-EDDIM   DIST-EDDIM   1973

CITY LIFE   C 52 FRS
        SOUND FILMSTRIP - AUDIO TAPE
DESCRIBES THE FEATURES OF MODERN CITY LIFE
IN SOUTH AMERICA AND DISCUSSES THE URBAN
TENDENCIES OF THE REGION. FROM THE
LIFEWAYS OF THE PEOPLE - SOUTH AMERICA SE-
RIES.
PROD-EGH   DIST-EGH   1972

**CIVIL WAR AS IT HAPPENED--A
SERIES**
PROD-EDREC   DIST-TECVIS   1970

ARTILLERY IN THE CIVIL WAR	45 FRS
FOOT SOLDIER, THE	60 FRS
HOW WE KNOW ABOUT THE CIVIL WAR	34 FRS
SUPPORTING SERVICES	48 FRS
TOLL OF THE CIVIL WAR, THE	49 FRS
WAR ON THE WATER, THE	44 FRS

CLASSIC MAYA   C 58 FRS
        FILMSTRIP WITH SCRIPT
FROM THE MEXICAN EPIC - BEFORE THE
CONQUEST SERIES.
    LC NO. 75-732593
PROD-UMM   DIST-UMM

CLASSIC MEXICANS   C 56 FRS
        FILMSTRIP WITH SCRIPT
FROM THE MEXICAN EPIC - BEFORE THE
CONQUEST SERIES.
    LC NO. 75-732593
PROD-UMM   DIST-UMM

**CLIPPING AND TRIMMING
DAIRY CATTLE**   C 34 FRS
        FILMSTRIP WITH CAPTIONS   H-C
ILLUSTRATES THE STEP-BY-STEP PREPARATION OF
CLIPPING DAIRY CATTLE.
    LC NO. 73-733317
PROD-UILVAS   DIST-UILVAS   1972

COLLECTOR, THE   C
                      FILMSTRIP
TELLS ABOUT A MAN WHO COLLECTS BUTTER-
FLIES AND LACKS ONE SPECIMEN.
    LC NO. 72-702797
PROD-ZAGREB   DIST-FI   1972

**COLLEGE - IT'S UP TO YOU, PT
1**   C 68 FRS
        SOUND FILMSTRIP - AUDIO TAPE   H
PRESENTS FRANK INTERVIEWS WITH COLLEGE
AND HIGH SCHOOL STUDENTS, HELPING YOUNG
PEOPLE FIND VALID PERSONAL CRITERIA FOR
MAKING THEIR OWN COLLEGE DECISIONS. SUG-
GESTS BASIC POINTS OF REFERENCE. FROM THE
COLLEGE SERIES.
    LC NO. 72-737465
PROD-GA   DIST-GA   1972

**COLLEGE - IT'S UP TO YOU, PT
2**   C 68 FRS
        SOUND FILMSTRIP - AUDIO TAPE   H
PRESENTS FRANK INTERVIEWS WITH COLLEGE
AND HIGH SCHOOL STUDENTS, HELPING YOUNG
PEOPLE FIND VALID PERSONAL CRITERIA FOR
MAKING THEIR OWN COLLEGE DECISIONS. SUG-
GESTS BASIC POINTS OF REFERENCE. FROM THE
COLLEGE SERIES.
    LC NO. 72-737465
PROD-GA   DIST-GA   1972

COLLEGE AUDIO-VISUAL CENTER
                            B 37 FRS
        FILMSTRIP WITH SCRIPT
SHOWS HOW THE AUDIOVISUAL AIDS CENTER OF
A COLLEGE IS SET UP TO SERVE ITS CAMPUS,
SCHOOLS AND PEOPLE OF ITS AREA. FROM THE
AUDIO-VISUAL SERIES.
    LC NO. FIA52-2447
PROD-YAF   DIST-YAF   1948

COLLEGE--A SERIES
                            H
PROD-GA   DIST-GA   1972

COLLEGE - IT'S UP TO YOU, PT 1	68 FRS
COLLEGE - IT'S UP TO YOU, PT 2	68 FRS
WHAT TO EXPECT AT COLLEGE, PT 1	69 FRS
WHAT TO EXPECT AT COLLEGE, PT 2	72 FRS
WHICH COLLEGE FOR YOU, PT 1	74 FRS
WHICH COLLEGE FOR YOU, PT 2	62 FRS

**COLORS EVERYWHERE - BLACK
AND WHITE**   C 46 FRS
        SOUND FILMSTRIP - AUDIO TAPE   K-P
SEE SERIES TITLE FOR DESCRIPTIVE STATEMENT.
FROM THE COLORS EVERYWHERE SERIES.
PROD-SPA   DIST-SPA   1972

**COLORS EVERYWHERE -
COLORS, COLORS EVERYWHERE
DO YOU KNOW THE COLORS**   C 32 FRS
        SOUND FILMSTRIP - AUDIO TAPE   K-P
SEE SERIES TITLE FOR DESCRIPTIVE STATEMENT.
FROM THE COLORS EVERYWHERE SERIES.
PROD-SPA   DIST-SPA   1972

COLORS EVERYWHERE - PINK AND GRAY C 38 FRS
SOUND FILMSTRIP - AUDIO TAPE K-P
SEE SERIES TITLE FOR DESCRIPTIVE STATEMENT.
FROM THE COLORS EVERYWHERE SERIES.
PROD-SPA DIST-SPA 1972

COLORS EVERYWHERE - PURPLE AND BROWN C 37 FRS
SOUND FILMSTRIP - AUDIO TAPE K-P
SEE SERIES TITLE FOR DESCRIPTIVE STATEMENT.
FROM THE COLORS EVERYWHERE SERIES.
PROD-SPA DIST-SPA 1972

COLORS EVERYWHERE - RED, YELLOW AND BLUE C 27 FRS
SOUND FILMSTRIP - AUDIO TAPE K-P
SEE SERIES TITLE FOR DESCRIPTIVE STATEMENT.
FROM THE COLORS EVERYWHERE SERIES.
PROD-SPA DIST-SPA 1972

COLORS EVERYWHERE - RED, YELLOW, BLUE, ORANGE AND GREEN C 35 FRS
SOUND FILMSTRIP - AUDIO TAPE K-P
SEE SERIES TITLE FOR DESCRIPTIVE STATEMENT.
FROM THE COLORS EVERYWHERE SERIES.
PROD-SPA DIST-SPA 1972

COLORS EVERYWHERE - WHAT IS BLUE C 27 FRS
SOUND FILMSTRIP - AUDIO TAPE K-P
SEE SERIES TITLE FOR DESCRIPTIVE STATEMENT.
FROM THE COLORS EVERYWHERE SERIES.
PROD-SPA DIST-SPA 1972

COLORS EVERYWHERE - WHAT IS GREEN C 25 FRS
SOUND FILMSTRIP - AUDIO TAPE K-P
SEE SERIES TITLE FOR DESCRIPTIVE STATEMENT.
FROM THE COLORS EVERYWHERE SERIES.
PROD-SPA DIST-SPA 1972

COLORS EVERYWHERE - WHAT IS ORANGE C 25 FRS
SOUND FILMSTRIP - AUDIO TAPE K-P
SEE SERIES TITLE FOR DESCRIPTIVE STATEMENT.
FROM THE COLORS EVERYWHERE SERIES.
PROD-SPA DIST-SPA 1972

COLORS EVERYWHERE - WHAT IS RED C 33 FRS
SOUND FILMSTRIP - AUDIO TAPE K-P
SEE SERIES TITLE FOR DESCRIPTIVE STATEMENT.
FROM THE COLORS EVERYWHERE SERIES.
PROD-SPA DIST-SPA 1972

COLORS EVERYWHERE - WHAT IS YELLOW C 25 FRS
SOUND FILMSTRIP - AUDIO TAPE K-P
SEE SERIES TITLE FOR DESCRIPTIVE STATEMENT.
FROM THE COLORS EVERYWHERE SERIES.
PROD-SPA DIST-SPA 1972

COLORS EVERYWHERE--A SERIES
K-P
INTRODUCES COLORS THROUGH PERSONIFICATION OF THE COLOR AND IDENTIFICATION OF EACH COLOR BY PARTICULAR SHAPES OR OBJECTS AND AN APPROPRIATE MUSICAL ACCOMPANIMENT.
LC NO. 70-739153
PROD-SPA DIST-SPA 1972

COLORS EVERYWHERE - BLACK AND WHITE 46 FRS
COLORS EVERYWHERE - COLORS,
COLORS EVERYWHERE-- 32 FRS
COLORS EVERYWHERE - PINK AND GRAY 38 FRS
COLORS EVERYWHERE - PURPLE AND BROWN 37 FRS
COLORS EVERYWHERE - RED, YELLOW AND BLUE 27 FRS
COLORS EVERYWHERE - RED, YELLOW, BLUE, ORANGE-- 35 FRS
COLORS EVERYWHERE - WHAT IS BLUE 27 FRS
COLORS EVERYWHERE - WHAT IS GREEN 25 FRS
COLORS EVERYWHERE - WHAT IS ORANGE 25 FRS
COLORS EVERYWHERE - WHAT IS RED 33 FRS
COLORS EVERYWHERE - WHAT IS YELLOW 25 FRS

COLOSTOMY C 115 FRS
SOUND FILMSTRIP - RECORD
DESCRIBES VARIOUS SURGICAL PROCEDURES EMPLOYED IN TREATMENT OF CANCER OF THE COLON AND RECTUM, WITH EMPHASIS ON ABDOMINOPERINEAL RESECTION FOR CANCER OF THE

RECTUM. FROM THE CANCER, SERIES 3 - TREATMENT MODALITIES WITH IMPLICATIONS FOR NURSING CARE SERIES. NO. 3
LC NO. 72-733175
PROD-CONMED DIST-CONMED 1972

COLUMBUS, BALBOA AND MAGELLAN C 58 FRS
SOUND FILMSTRIP - AUDIO TAPE I-J
COMPARES COLUMBUS' EXPEDITIONS TO HIS 'INDIES' AND THEIR CONTRIBUTION TO THE REDRAWING OF THE MAP OF THE WORLD TO THE MORE IMMEDIATELY PRODUCTIVE VENTURES OF VASCO DE GAMA. DISCUSSES BALBOA'S DISCOVERY OF THE GREAT SOUTH SEA, AS WELL AS THE SAGA OF MAGELLAN AND THE FIRST CIRCUMNAVIGATION OF THE GLOBE. FROM THE EXPLORATION - MAN'S QUEST FOR KNOWLEDGE SERIES.
LC NO. 73-732521
PROD-SED DIST-SED 1972

COMICAL SITUATIONS OF EVERYDAY LIFE, PT 1 B 37 FRS
SOUND FILMSTRIP - AUDIO TAPE J-H
PRESENTS A SERIES OF VERY FUNNY COMICAL DRAWINGS DESCRIBING LIFE SITUATIONS.
LC NO. 72-737554
PROD-ALEP DIST-ALEP 1972

COMICAL SITUATIONS OF EVERYDAY LIFE, PT 1 (FRENCH) B 37 FRS
SOUND FILMSTRIP - AUDIO TAPE J-H
PRESENTS A SERIES OF VERY FUNNY COMICAL DRAWINGS DESCRIBING LIFE SITUATIONS.
LC NO. 72-737554
PROD-ALEP DIST-ALEP 1972

COMICAL SITUATIONS OF EVERYDAY LIFE, PT 1 (GERMAN) B 37 FRS
SOUND FILMSTRIP - AUDIO TAPE J-H
PRESENTS A SERIES OF VERY FUNNY COMICAL DRAWINGS DESCRIBING LIFE SITUATIONS.
LC NO. 72-737554
PROD-ALEP DIST-ALEP 1972

COMICAL SITUATIONS OF EVERYDAY LIFE, PT 1 (SPANISH) B 37 FRS
SOUND FILMSTRIP - AUDIO TAPE J-H
PRESENTS A SERIES OF VERY FUNNY COMICAL DRAWINGS DESCRIBING LIFE SITUATIONS.
LC NO. 72-737554
PROD-ALEP DIST-ALEP 1972

COMICAL SITUATIONS OF EVERYDAY LIFE, PT 1 (ITALIAN) B 37 FRS
SOUND FILMSTRIP - AUDIO TAPE J-H
PRESENTS A SERIES OF VERY FUNNY COMICAL DRAWINGS DESCRIBING LIFE SITUATIONS.
LC NO. 72-737554
PROD-ALEP DIST-ALEP 1972

COMICAL SITUATIONS OF EVERYDAY LIFE, PT 2 B 37 FRS
SOUND FILMSTRIP - AUDIO TAPE J-H
PRESENTS A SERIES OF VERY FUNNY COMICAL DRAWINGS DESCRIBING LIFE SITUATIONS.
LC NO. 72-737554
PROD-ALEP DIST-ALEP 1972

COMICAL SITUATIONS OF EVERYDAY LIFE, PT 2 (FRENCH) B 37 FRS
SOUND FILMSTRIP - AUDIO TAPE J-H
PRESENTS A SERIES OF VERY FUNNY COMICAL DRAWINGS DESCRIBING LIFE SITUATIONS.
LC NO. 72-737554
PROD-ALEP DIST-ALEP 1972

COMICAL SITUATIONS OF EVERYDAY LIFE, PT 2 (GERMAN) B 37 FRS
SOUND FILMSTRIP - AUDIO TAPE J-H
PRESENTS A SERIES OF VERY FUNNY COMICAL DRAWINGS DESCRIBING LIFE SITUATIONS.
LC NO. 72-737554
PROD-ALEP DIST-ALEP 1972

COMICAL SITUATIONS OF EVERYDAY LIFE, PT 2 (SPANISH) B 37 FRS
SOUND FILMSTRIP - AUDIO TAPE J-H
PRESENTS A SERIES OF VERY FUNNY COMICAL DRAWINGS DESCRIBING LIFE SITUATIONS.
LC NO. 72-737554
PROD-ALEP DIST-ALEP 1972

COMICAL SITUATIONS OF EVERYDAY LIFE, PT 2 (ITALIAN) B 37 FRS
SOUND FILMSTRIP - AUDIO TAPE J-H
PRESENTS A SERIES OF VERY FUNNY COMICAL DRAWINGS DESCRIBING LIFE SITUATIONS.
LC NO. 72-737554
PROD-ALEP DIST-ALEP 1972

COMMON OBJECTS C 84 FRS
SOUND FILMSTRIP - AUDIO TAPE
DESCRIBES TERMS RELATED TO COMMON OBJECTS. FROM THE INTRODUCTION TO ENGLISH AS A SECOND LANGUAGE SERIES.
PROD-EGH DIST-EGH 1972

COMMUNES IN CHINA C 50 FRS
SOUND FILMSTRIP - AUDIO TAPE
TELLS WHAT THE CHINESE COMMUNE IS, HOW IT IS ORGANIZED AND HOW EFFECTIVE IT IS. FROM THE INSIDE THE PEOPLE'S REPUBLIC OF CHINA SERIES.
PROD-EGH DIST-EGH 1972

COMMUNITY DEVELOPMENT IN MICHOACAN C 36 FRS
SOUND FILMSTRIP - AUDIO TAPE
ILLUSTRATES THE PROBLEMS AND THE ATTEMPTS TO SOLVE THEM IN THE COMMUNITY OF TACAMBARO. FROM THE MEXICO - A COMMUNITY STUDY SERIES.
PROD-EGH DIST-EGH 1972

COMPANY AND THE COMMUNITY, THE, PT 1 C
SOUND FILMSTRIP - AUDIO TAPE
EXAMINES THE RELATIONSHIP BETWEEN THE COMPANY AND THE COMMUNITY. SHOWS HOW TO DEVELOP POSITIVE JOB ATTITUDES THROUGH AN UNDERSTANDING OF COMPANY OPERATIONS. FROM THE JOB ATTITUDES, SET 1 SERIES.
LC NO. 72-736053
PROD-CREATV DIST-CREATV

COMPANY AND THE COMMUNITY, THE, PT 2 C
SOUND FILMSTRIP - AUDIO TAPE
EXAMINES THE RELATIONSHIP BETWEEN THE COMPANY AND THE COMMUNITY. SHOWS HOW TO DEVELOP POSITIVE JOB ATTITUDES THROUGH AN UNDERSTANDING OF COMPANY OPERATIONS. FROM THE JOB ATTITUDES, SET 1 SERIES.
LC NO. 72-736053
PROD-CREATV DIST-CREATV

COMPANY ORGANIZATION, PT 1
C
SOUND FILMSTRIP - AUDIO TAPE
SHOWS HOW TO DEVELOP POSITIVE JOB ATTITUDES THROUGH AN UNDERSTANDING OF HOW A COMPANY IS ORGANIZED. FROM THE JOB ATTITUDES, SET 3 SERIES.
LC NO. 72-736056
PROD-CREATV DIST-CREATV

COMPANY ORGANIZATION, PT 2
C
SOUND FILMSTRIP - AUDIO TAPE
SHOWS HOW TO DEVELOP POSITIVE JOB ATTITUDES THROUGH AN UNDERSTANDING OF HOW A COMPANY IS ORGANIZED. FROM THE JOB ATTITUDES, SET 3 SERIES.
LC NO. 72-736056
PROD-CREATV DIST-CREATV

COMPARATIVE PATHOGENIC BACTERIOLOGY, PT 1 C 60 FRS
FILMSTRIP WITH CAPTIONS
PRESENTS ILLUSTRATIONS DESIGNED TO ACHIEVE EASE OF RECOGNITION AND DIAGNOSIS OF GRAM NEGATIVE BACTERIA, GRAM POSITIVE AEROBIC AND ANAEROBIC BACTERIA, RODS AND COCCI AND MISCELLANEOUS OTHER BACTERIA.
LC NO. 72-736826
PROD-SAUNDW DIST-SAUNDW 1972

COMPARATIVE PATHOGENIC BACTERIOLOGY, PT 2 C 51 FRS
FILMSTRIP WITH CAPTIONS
PRESENTS ILLUSTRATIONS DESIGNED TO ACHIEVE EASE OF RECOGNITION AND DIAGNOSIS OF GRAM NEGATIVE BACTERIA, GRAM POSITIVE AEROBIC AND ANAEROBIC BACTERIA, RODS AND COCCI AND MISCELLANEOUS OTHER BACTERIA.
LC NO. 72-736826
PROD-SAUNDW DIST-SAUNDW 1972

COMPOSITION B 81 FRS
SOUND FILMSTRIP - AUDIO TAPE J-C A
ILLUSTRATES GUIDELINES FOR GOOD COMPOSITION, INCLUDING THE PRINCIPLES OF SUBJECT PLACEMENT, BALANCE, BACKGROUND AND FOREGROUND, OPTICAL PERSPECTIVE, CAMERA ANGLE

AND OPTICAL PERSPECTIVE. FROM THE CREATIVE PHOTOGRAPHY - CAMERA SERIES.
LC NO. 73-735514
PROD-ARIZSU   DIST-ARIZSU   1973

COMPUTER SCIENCE--A SERIES
LC NO. 73-732500
PROD-AVDEV   DIST-AVDEV   1972

HARDWARE AND FUNDAMENTAL
CONCEPTS   60 FRS
PRINCIPLES OF FLOWCHARTS   60 FRS
PROGRAMMING IN FORTRAN, PT 1   60 FRS
PROGRAMMING IN FORTRAN, PT 2   60 FRS

COMPUTER SYSTEM, THE   B 82 FRS
SOUND FILMSTRIP - RECORD   H
LISTS VARIOUS USES OF THE COMPUTER AND IN-
TRODUCES THE TWO ESSENTIAL ELEMENTS OF A
COMPUTER SYSTEM, HARDWARE AND SOFTWARE.
PRESENTS THE INPUT, PROCESSING, STORAGE
AND OUTPUT OF THE HARDWARE. FROM THE
HOW COMPUTERS WORK SERIES.
LC NO. 73-732745
PROD-EBEC   DIST-EBEC   1972

**CONCEPT-CENTERED LESSONS
IN AMERICAN HISTORY, UNIT
1--A SERIES**
PROD-VISTAP   DIST-FPC

MAKING OF THE AMERICAN NATION, PT
1 - THE --   23 FRS
MAKING OF THE AMERICAN NATION, PT
2 - THE --   23 FRS

CONCRETE CHARLEY DUMPLING   C
FILMSTRIP
EXPLAINS HOW MAN'S DESIRE FOR ORDER
THREATENS HIS ENVIRONMENT.
LC NO. 72-702886
PROD-COMICO   DIST-COMICO   1970

**CONQUERING COMPOSITION -
AWKWARD SHIFTS**   C 50 FRS
SOUND FILMSTRIP - RECORD   J-H
SEE SERIES TITLE FOR DESCRIPTIVE STATEMENT.
FROM THE CONQUERING COMPOSITION - SEN-
TENCE PROBLEMS SERIES.
LC NO. 73-732813
PROD-FSH   DIST-FSH   1972

**CONQUERING COMPOSITION -
FRAGMENTS**   C 46 FRS
SOUND FILMSTRIP - RECORD   J-H
SEE SERIES TITLE FOR DESCRIPTIVE STATEMENT.
FROM THE CONQUERING COMPOSITION - SEN-
TENCE PROBLEMS SERIES.
LC NO. 73-732810
PROD-FSH   DIST-FSH   1972

**CONQUERING COMPOSITION -
PRONOUNS AND ANTECEDENTS**   C 45 FRS
SOUND FILMSTRIP - RECORD   J-H
SEE SERIES TITLE FOR DESCRIPTIVE STATEMENT.
FROM THE CONQUERING COMPOSITION - SEN-
TENCE PROBLEMS SERIES.
LC NO. 73-732812
PROD-FSH   DIST-FSH   1972

**CONQUERING COMPOSITION -
SENTENCE PROBLEMS-- A
SERIES**   J-H
ILLUSTRATES COMMON MISTAKES IN COMPOSI-
TION AND THE WAYS IN WHICH THEY CAN BE
CORRECTED. FOCUSES ON SUCH PROBLEMS AS
INCOMPLETE SENTENCE FRAGMENTS, AGREE-
MENT OF SUBJECT AND VERB, AMBIGUOUS PRO-
NOUN REFERENCES AND AWKWARD SENTENCE
CONSTRUCTION.
PROD-FSH   DIST-FSH   1972

CONQUERING COMPOSITION -
AWKWARD SHIFTS   50 FRS
CONQUERING COMPOSITION -
FRAGMENTS   46 FRS
CONQUERING COMPOSITION -
PRONOUNS AND --   45 FRS
CONQUERING COMPOSITION - VERB-
SUBJECT --   53 FRS

**CONQUERING COMPOSITION -
VERB-SUBJECT AGREEMENT**   C 53 FRS
SOUND FILMSTRIP - RECORD   J-H
SEE SERIES TITLE FOR DESCRIPTIVE STATEMENT.
FROM THE CONQUERING COMPOSITION - SEN-
TENCE PROBLEMS SERIES.
LC NO. 73-732811
PROD-FSH   DIST-FSH   1972

**CONSUMERISM - THE DANGERS
OF AFFLUENCE, PT 1**   C 109 FRS
SOUND FILMSTRIP - RECORD
SHOWS HOW THE CONSUMER IS AFFECTED BY
THE CONDITIONS OF THE MARKETPLACE, THE
FEDERAL AGENCIES AND CREDIT RATING INSTI-
TUTIONS.
LC NO. 72-735089
PROD-ASPRSS   DIST-ASPRSS   1972

**CONSUMERISM - THE DANGERS
OF AFFLUENCE, PT 2**   C 87 FRS
SOUND FILMSTRIP - RECORD
SHOWS HOW THE CONSUMER IS AFFECTED BY
THE CONDITIONS OF THE MARKETPLACE, THE
FEDERAL AGENCIES AND CREDIT RATING INSTI-
TUTIONS.
LC NO. 72-735089
PROD-ASPRSS   DIST-ASPRSS   1972

CRAFTING A CHAIR   C 49 FRS
SOUND FILMSTRIP - AUDIO TAPE
SHOWS THE STEPS INVOLVED IN MAKING FURNI-
TURE. FROM THE HOW THINGS ARE MADE SERIES.
LC NO. 72-736553
PROD-EGH   DIST-EGH   1972

CREATING A MOVIE   C 47 FRS
SOUND FILMSTRIP - AUDIO TAPE
SHOWS THE STEPS INVOLVED IN CREATING AND
PRODUCING A MOVIE. FROM THE HOW THINGS
ARE MADE SERIES.
LC NO. 72-736548
PROD-EGH   DIST-EGH   1972

CREATING A MOVIE   C 50 FRS
SOUND FILMSTRIP - AUDIO TAPE
SHOWS THE STEPS INVOLVED IN CREATING AND
PRODUCING A MOVIE. FROM THE HOW THINGS
ARE MADE SERIES.
LC NO. 72-736548
PROD-EGH   DIST-EGH

**CREATIVE PHOTOGRAPHY -
CAMERA--A SERIES**   J-C A
PROD-ARIZSU   DIST-ARIZSU   1973

CAMERA SYSTEMS   77 FRS
CAMERA, THE   70 FRS
COMPOSITION   81 FRS
EXPOSURE   80 FRS
LIGHTING, PT 1   67 FRS
LIGHTING, PT 2   85 FRS

CRISPUS ATTUCKS   C 44 FRS
SOUND FILMSTRIP - AUDIO TAPE   I-H
DESCRIBES THE LIFE OF THE FIRST BLACK MAN
TO DIE DURING THE AMERICAN REVOLUTION AT
THE BOSTON MASSACRE. FROM THE FAMOUS PA-
TRIOTS OF THE AMERICAN REVOLUTION SERIES.
LC NO. 73-732979
PROD-CORF   DIST-CORF   1973

**CURSIVE WRITING - CAPITAL
LETTERS, PT 1**   C 64 FRS
SOUND FILMSTRIP - AUDIO TAPE
TEACHES CURSIVE WRITING THROUGH THE USE
OF VERSE AND PROSE. FROM THE LEARN TO
WRITE WITH LETTY LETTER SERIES.
PROD-EGH   DIST-EGH   1972

**CURSIVE WRITING - CAPITAL
LETTERS, PT 2**   C 74 FRS
SOUND FILMSTRIP - AUDIO TAPE
TEACHES CURSIVE WRITING THROUGH THE USE
OF VERSE AND PROSE. FROM THE LEARN TO
WRITE WITH LETTY LETTER SERIES.
PROD-EGH   DIST-EGH   1972

**CURSIVE WRITING - SMALL
LETTERS, PT 1**   C 59 FRS
SOUND FILMSTRIP - AUDIO TAPE
TEACHES CURSIVE WRITING THROUGH THE USE
OF VERSE AND PROSE. FROM THE LEARN TO
WRITE WITH LETTY LETTER SERIES.
PROD-EGH   DIST-EGH   1972

**CURSIVE WRITING - SMALL
LETTERS, PT 2**   C 75 FRS
SOUND FILMSTRIP - AUDIO TAPE
TEACHES CURSIVE WRITING THROUGH THE USE
OF VERSE AND PROSE. FROM THE LEARN TO
WRITE WITH LETTY LETTER SERIES.
PROD-EGH   DIST-EGH   1972

**CZECHOSLOVAKIA -
AGRICULTURE AND INDUSTRY**   C 41 FRS
FILMSTRIP
SEE SERIES TITLE FOR DESCRIPTIVE STATEMENT.
FROM THE EASTERN EUROPE SERIES.
LC NO. 72-734721
PROD-MGHT   DIST-MGHT   1972

D

DANISH FIELD, THE   C 71 FRS
SOUND FILMSTRIP - AUDIO TAPE   J-C A
DEPICTS THE HISTORY OF THE LARGEST DANISH
SETTLEMENT IN TEXAS AND MENTIONS THE
OTHER DANES WHO HAVE CONTRIBUTED TO THE
HISTORY OF TEXAS. DESCRIBES SOME OF THE
DANISH HERITAGE AS WELL AS THE CHANGE THAT
COMES TO A GROUP OF IMMIGRANTS IN A NEW
LAND.
LC NO. 72-737570
PROD-INTXC   DIST-INTXC   1972

DATING DATA   C 100 FRS
SOUND FILMSTRIP - RECORD   J-C A
HELPS GIRLS ESTABLISH A NORMAL AND HEALTHY
RELATIONSHIP WITH BOYS BY DEVELOPING THEIR
OWN PERSONALITIES AND INDIVIDUALISM.
SHOWS THEM HOW TO BE ATTRACTIVE TO BOYS,
HOW TO GAIN IN POPULARITY AND WHAT TO
AVOID. FROM THE HOT TIPS ON BASIC BEAUTY,
FASHION, GROOMING AND DATING SERIES.
LC NO. 72-737341
PROD-RMI   DIST-RMI   1972

DAY IN THE CONGO, A   C 47 FRS
SOUND FILMSTRIP - RECORD
SHOWS THE EFFECTS OF WESTERNIZATION AND
THE PRESERVATION OF TRADITION IN THE CONGO
AS EXEMPLIFIED BY THE PERSONAL LIVES OF TWO
CONGOLESE BOYS.
LC NO. 72-735272
PROD-DOUBLE   DIST-DOUBLE   1971

**DAYS, MONTHS, SEASONS,
WEATHER**   C 82 FRS
SOUND FILMSTRIP - AUDIO TAPE
DESCRIBES THE SIMPLE TERMINOLOGY OF THE
SUBJECT AND DISCUSSES RELATED VERBS. FROM
THE INTRODUCTION TO ENGLISH AS A SECOND
LANGUAGE SERIES.
PROD-EGH   DIST-EGH   1972

DECIDING FOR MYSELF   C 36 FRS
SOUND FILMSTRIP - RECORD   I R
GIVES A FIRST-PERSON PRESENTATION OF THE
LIFE OF JESUS. INTRODUCES THE ADULT JESUS
IN HIS MOMENT OF DECISION AT THE BEGINNING
OF HIS MINISTRY. INCLUDES JOHN THE BAPTIST,
BAPTISM OF JESUS, THE TEMPTATIONS, MO-
MENTS OF DECISION, THE VALUES OF JESUS AND
HIS MISSION OF LIFE AND SERVICE. FROM THE MY
NAME IS JESUS SERIES.
LC NO. 72-737431
PROD-ROAS   DIST-ROAS   1972

**DECIDING ON DEFENSIBLE
GOALS VIA EDUCATIONAL
NEEDS ASSESSMENT**   C 29 FRS
SOUND FILMSTRIP - AUDIO TAPE
PROPOSES A STRATEGY FOR SURVEYING THE
PREFERENCES OF VARIOUS REPRESENTATIVE
GROUPS IN ORDER TO ESTABLISH EDUCATIONAL
GOALS.
LC NO. 72-736814
PROD-POPHAM   DIST-VIMCET   PRODN-CONSFI

DECIMAL FRACTIONS   C 65 FRS
SOUND FILMSTRIP - RECORD   J-H
SHOWS THE PLACE VALUES FOR POSITIVE INTE-
GERS TO EXTEND IN AN EVER INCREASING SERIES
OF POWERS OF TEN. FROM THE MATH - DECIMAL
NUMERATION SERIES.
LC NO. 73-733100
PROD-UNISYS   DIST-VIEWLX   1973

DECIMAL FRACTIONS--A SERIES
PRESENTS LESSONS ON DECIMAL FRACTIONS.
LC NO. 72-735678
PROD-CREATV   DIST-CREATV

DECIMAL SYSTEM   C 28 FRS
SOUND FILMSTRIP - RECORD   J-H
EXAMINES THE PLACE VALUE STRUCTURE OF THE
DECIMAL SYSTEM. FROM THE MATH - DECIMAL
NUMERATION SERIES.
LC NO. 73-733099
PROD-UNISYS   DIST-VIEWLX   1973

DECISION IS YOURS, THE　　　　C　93 FRS
　　　　SOUND FILMSTRIP - AUDIO TAPE
PRESENTS A PROGRAM DESIGNED TO ALERT THE
STUDENT TO THE PROBLEMS OF ALCOHOL AND
DRIVING.
　　LC NO. 72-736207
PROD-NHTSA　　DIST-NAVA　　PRODN-ADTSEA　　1972

DEPUTY MARV　　　　　　　　C　65 FRS
　　　　SOUND FILMSTRIP - RECORD
TEACHES BASIC SAFETY RULES TO CHILDREN.
　　LC NO. 72-734178
PROD-LYCEUM　　　　DIST-LYCEUM　　　　1972

DESCRIBING　　　　　　　　　C　82 FRS
　　　　SOUND FILMSTRIP - AUDIO TAPE
TEACHES THE STUDENT SOME OF THE MORE
COMMON DESCRIPTIVE WORDS. FROM THE IN-
TRODUCTION TO ENGLISH AS A SECOND LAN-
GUAGE SERIES.
PROD-EGH　　　　　DIST-EGH　　　　　1972

DESERT LIFE--A SERIES

PROD-SED　　　　　DIST-SED　　　　　1972

BALANCE OF LIFE IN A DESERT　　　56 FRS
HOW DESERT ANIMALS SURVIVE　　　59 FRS

DESIGN IN ART　　　　　　　　C　38 FRS
　　　　FILMSTRIP WITH CAPTIONS
DEFINES AND ILLUSTRATES THE USE OF DESIGN
IN ART.
　　LC NO. 72-734793
PROD-EDPRC　　　　DIST-EDPRC　　　　1971

DEVELOPMENT OF OUR
NUMBER SYSTEM　　　　　　　C　26 FRS
　　　　SOUND FILMSTRIP - RECORD　J-H
EXAMINES SEVERAL PRIMITIVE METHODS OF TAL-
LYING TO SHOW THEIR LIMITATIONS IN REPRE-
SENTING LARGE NUMBERS. FROM THE MATH -
DECIMAL NUMERATION SERIES.
　　LC NO. 73-733097
PROD-UNISYS　　　　DIST-VIEWLX　　　1973

DEVELOPMENT OF THE
AMERICAN SHORT STORY--A
SERIES
　　　　　　　　　　　　　　　J-C
TRACES THE DEVELOPMENT OF THE SHORT
STORY.
　　LC NO. 77-734751
PROD-EAV　　　　　DIST-EAV　　　　　1969

AMERICAN ROMANTICISM　　　　　63 FRS
BEGINNINGS OF REALISM, THE　　　59 FRS
BETWEEN THE WARS　　　　　　　50 FRS
SHORT STORY TODAY, THE　　　　59 FRS

DEVELOPMENT OF THE FROG,
THE, PT 1 - MATING OF FROGS
　　　　　　　　　　　　　B　23 FRS
　　　　FILMSTRIP WITH SCRIPT　I-H
SHOWS THE MATING OF FROGS, THE FERTILIZA-
TION OF THE EGGS AND THE STAGES OF DEVELOP-
MENT TO A FULL-GROWN FROG.
　　LC NO. 72-737239
PROD-COMG　　　　DIST-CARMAN　　　1946

DEVELOPMENT OF THE FROG,
THE, PT 2 - GROWTH OF THE
TADPOLE　　　　　　　　　　B　29 FRS
　　　　FILMSTRIP WITH SCRIPT　I-H
CONCENTRATES ON THE GROWTH AND META-
MORPHOSIS OF THE TADPOLE. SHOWS DIFFERENT
EXPERIMENTS INVOLVING THE OVA OF THE FROG.
　　LC NO. 72-737238
PROD-COMG　　　　DIST-CARMAN　　　1946

DIET CLERK AND FRY COOK　　C　50 FRS
　　　　SOUND FILMSTRIP - AUDIO TAPE
DESCRIBES THE FUNCTION OF THE DIET AND FRY
COOK. FROM THE HOSPITAL JOB OPPORTUNITIES
SERIES.
PROD-EGH　　　　　DIST-EGH　　　　　1972

DIGESTION - CONCEPTS OF
DIGESTION　　　　　　　　　　C
　　　　FILMSTRIP WITH SCRIPT　H-C A
FROM THE HUMAN ANATOMY AND PHYSIOLOGY
SERIES.
PROD-HRAW　　　　DIST-HRAW　　　　1973

DIGESTION OF FOODS　　　　　C
　　　　FILMSTRIP WITH SCRIPT　H-C A
FROM THE HUMAN ANATOMY AND PHYSIOLOGY
SERIES.
PROD-HRAW　　　　DIST-HRAW　　　　1973

DIVIDENDS FROM SPACE　　　C 114 FRS
　　　　FILMSTRIP WITH SCRIPT　I-J
SEE SERIES TITLE FOR DESCRIPTIVE STATEMENT.
FROM THE MAN ON THE MOON SERIES.
PROD-DOUBLE　　　　DIST-DOUBLE　　　1971

DIVISION - COMPUTATION I　　C　38 FRS
　　　　FILMSTRIP WITH SCRIPT　P
ILLUSTRATES THE DIVISION ALGORITHM USED IN
PROBLEMS WITH QUOTIENTS GREATER THAN ONE
HUNDRED, AND EXPLAINS HOW TO WORK PROB-
LEMS IN WHICH THE DIVISOR IS BETWEEN TEN
AND ONE HUNDRED. FROM THE MODERN MATHE-
MATICS PROGRAM, LEVEL 4, 744 SERIES.
　　LC NO. 72-733839
PROD-EDPRC　　　　DIST-EDPRC

DIVISION - COMPUTATION II　　C　41 FRS
　　　　FILMSTRIP WITH SCRIPT　P
INTRODUCES THE BASIC ALGORITHM, AND RE-
VIEWS THE RELATIONSHIP BETWEEN MULTIPLICA-
TION AND DIVISION. FROM THE MODERN MATHE-
MATICS PROGRAM, LEVEL 4, 743 SERIES.
　　LC NO. 72-733840
PROD-EDPRC　　　　DIST-EDPRC

DIVISION PROGRAM, THE　　　C　90 FRS
　　　　SOUND FILMSTRIP - AUDIO TAPE
PRESENTS A SEQUENTIAL PRESENTATION OF THE
DIVISION PROGRAM. FROM THE BASIC COMPUTA-
TIONAL SKILLS SERIES.
　　LC NO. 72-735464
PROD-CREATV　　　　DIST-CREATV

DOCTOR'S VIEWPOINT　　　　C　56 FRS
　　　　SOUND FILMSTRIP - AUDIO TAPE
DESCRIBES THE DOCTOR'S REACTIONS TO SMOK-
ING, DRINKING AND DRUG ABUSE. FROM THE
LET'S LOOK AT DRUGS SERIES.
PROD-EGH　　　　　DIST-EGH　　　　　1972

DOING IT ALL ON A BUDGET　　C　48 FRS
　　　　SOUND FILMSTRIP - AUDIO TAPE
DESCRIBES HOW TO SHOP TO GET THE MOST FOR
YOUR MONEY. FROM THE LOOKING GREAT ON A
SHOESTRING SERIES.
PROD-EGH　　　　　DIST-EGH　　　　　1972

DON QUIXOTE　　　　　　　　C　31 FRS
　　　　SOUND FILMSTRIP - AUDIO TAPE　K-P
EXPLAINS HOW SIR DON QUIXOTE, HAVING READ
MANY BOOKS OF KNIGHT-ERRANTRY, SETS OUT
TO REDRESS THE WRONGS OF THE WORLD. FROM
THE CHILDREN'S STORIES SERIES.
　　LC NO. 73-732777
PROD-STNHM　　　　DIST-STNHM　　　1972

DR DOOLITTLE　　　　　　　　C　36 FRS
　　　　SOUND FILMSTRIP - AUDIO TAPE　K-P
EXPLAINS THAT DR DOOLITTLE, WHO LIKES ANI-
MALS BETTER THAN PEOPLE, KEEPS THEM IN HIS
HOUSE AND HEALS AND CARES FOR THEM. FROM
THE CHILDREN'S STORIES SERIES.
　　LC NO. 73-732805
PROD-STNHM　　　　DIST-STNHM　　　1972

DRAGON STEW　　　　　　　C　77 FRS
　　　　SOUND FILMSTRIP - AUDIO TAPE　P-I
PRESENTS A STORY INVOLVING A KING, HIS
ROYAL CHEF AND A DRAGON. ENCOURAGES THE
VIEWER TO EXAMINE THE RELATIONSHIP BE-
TWEEN A PERSON'S BEHAVIOR TOWARDS OTHERS
AND HIS TREATMENT OF THAT PERSON. FROM
THE STORY SERIES 6 SERIES.
　　LC NO. 72-737008
PROD-BFA　　　　　DIST-BFA　　　　　1972

DRUGS - A TRICK, A TRAP--A
SERIES
PRESENTS THE USES OF DRUGS IN OUR CULTURE
TODAY. DISCUSSES THE REASONS PEOPLE USE
THEM, THE TYPES THEY USE AND THE DANGERS
OF DRUG OVERUSE AND ABUSE.
PROD-EBEC　　　　　DIST-EBEC　　　　1972

ALCOHOL - PARENTS AND THEIR
POTIONS　　　　　　　　　　　74 FRS
HARD DRUGS, THE - THE BOTTOM OF
THE TRAP　　　　　　　　　　82 FRS
MARIJUANA AND GLUE - KIDS, TRICKS
AND TRAPS　　　　　　　　　72 FRS
MEDICINE - PEOPLE AND PILLS　　58 FRS
TOBACCO - A PUFF OF POISON　　63 FRS

DRUGS AND CHILDREN, PT 1　　C　36 FRS
　　　　SOUND FILMSTRIP - AUDIO TAPE　I
PRESENTS THE STORY OF TODAY'S DRUGS, IN-
CLUDING THEIR EFFECT ON CHILDREN AND THEIR
DANGERS AND BENEFITS.
PROD-EDLACT　　　　DIST-EDLACT　　　1971

DRUGS AND CHILDREN, PT 2　　C　36 FRS
　　　　SOUND FILMSTRIP - AUDIO TAPE　I
PRESENTS THE STORY OF TODAY'S DRUGS, IN-
CLUDING THEIR EFFECT ON CHILDREN AND THEIR
DANGERS AND BENEFITS.
PROD-EDLACT　　　　DIST-EDLACT　　　1971

DRUGS AND YOUR FUTURE　　C　52 FRS
　　　　SOUND FILMSTRIP - AUDIO TAPE
DESCRIBES THE DANGERS AND THE EFFECTS OF
DRUGS ON ONE'S FUTURE. FROM THE LET'S LOOK
AT DRUGS SERIES.
PROD-EGH　　　　　DIST-EGH　　　　　1972

DYNAMISM OR DECAY　　　　C　67 FRS
　　　　SOUND FILMSTRIP - RECORD
SEE SERIES TITLE FOR DESCRIPTIVE STATEMENT.
FROM THE CITY - HOW AMERICA LIVES SERIES. PT
2
　　LC NO. 72-736412
PROD-AVNA　　　　　DIST-AVNA　　　　1972

EAGLE HAS LANDED, THE - MAN
ON THE MOON　　　　　　　　C　85 FRS
　　　　FILMSTRIP WITH SCRIPT　I-J
SEE SERIES TITLE FOR DESCRIPTIVE STATEMENT.
FROM THE MAN ON THE MOON SERIES.
PROD-DOUBLE　　　　DIST-DOUBLE　　　1971

EARLY AMERICAN INDIAN　　　C　31 FRS
　　　　SOUND FILMSTRIP - AUDIO TAPE
DESCRIBES THE ORIGINS OF THE AMERICAN INDI-
ANS AND SOME FEATURES OF THEIR LIFE DURING
THE EARLY PERIOD. FROM THE INDIANS OF AMER-
ICA SERIES.
PROD-EGH　　　　　DIST-EGH　　　　　1972

EARTHWORM - TYPICAL
INVERTEBRATE　　　　　　　C　34 FRS
　　　　FILMSTRIP
PRESENTS A MICROSCOPIC PICTURE OF THE
STRUCTURE OF EARTHWORMS. FROM THE MICRO-
SCOPIC SPECIMENS - A RESOURCE UNIT SERIES.
PROD-EGH　　　　　DIST-EGH　　　　　1972

EASTER　　　　　　　　　　　C　35 FRS
　　　　SOUND FILMSTRIP - RECORD　K-P
GIVES THE BACKGROUND OF PASSOVER AND EX-
PLAINS HOW IT IS CELEBRATED TODAY. FROM
THE HOLIDAY SERIES, SET 2 SERIES.
　　LC NO. 72-737288
PROD-MGHT　　　　　DIST-MGHT　　　　1972

EASTERN EUROPE--A SERIES
EXPLORES THE AGRICULTURE AND INDUSTRY OF
A COUNTRY IN EASTERN EUROPE.
PROD-MGHT　　　　　DIST-MGHT　　　　1972

CZECHOSLOVAKIA - AGRICULTURE AND
INDUSTRY　　　　　　　　　　41 FRS
HUNGARY - AGRICULTURE TODAY　　35 FRS
HUNGARY - INDUSTRY AND PROGRESS　37 FRS
POLAND - AGRICULTURE TODAY　　35 FRS
POLAND - INDUSTRY AND PROGRESS　37 FRS

ECOLOGY OF OUR BODIES　　　C　53 FRS
　　　　SOUND FILMSTRIP - AUDIO TAPE
DESCRIBES THE MECHANISM OF THE BODY AND
THE EFFECTS OF DRUGS UPON IT. FROM THE
LET'S LOOK AT DRUGS SERIES.
PROD-EGH　　　　　DIST-EGH　　　　　1972

ECONOMIC DECISION MAKING -
WHAT, HOW AND FOR WHOM　　C　60 FRS
　　　　FILMSTRIP WITH SCRIPT　I-H
SEE SERIES TITLE FOR DESCRIPTIVE STATEMENT.
FROM THE ECONOMICS SERIES.
PROD-DOUBLE　　　　DIST-DOUBLE　　　1972

ECONOMICS--A SERIES
　　　　　　　　　　　　　　　I-H
EXPLAINS THE BASICS OF ECONOMICS CLEARLY
AND CONCISELY. PRESENTS EXAMPLES FROM EV-
ERYDAY LIFE TO HELP RELATED ECONOMIC PRIN-
CIPLES.
　　LC NO. 72-737156
PROD-DOUBLE　　　　DIST-DOUBLE　　　1972

ECONOMIC DECISION MAKING - WHAT,
HOW AND --　　　　　　　　　60 FRS
MEXICO - AN ECONOMY IN TRANSITION　55 FRS
MIXED ECONOMY OF THE UNITED
STATES　　　　　　　　　　　55 FRS

EDUCATION AND COMMUNICATION IN CHINA   C 57 FRS
SOUND FILMSTRIP - AUDIO TAPE
SHOWS HOW EDUCATION REFLECTS THE GOALS AND VALUES OF PRESENT DAY CHINA. FROM THE INSIDE THE PEOPLE'S REPUBLIC OF CHINA SERIES.
PROD-EGH   DIST-EGH   1972

ELECTION, THE   C 38 FRS
SOUND FILMSTRIP - AUDIO TAPE
DESCRIBES THE USE OF THE VOTING MACHINE IN ELECTIONS. FROM THE NOW YOU ARE A VOTER SERIES.
LC NO. 72-736556
PROD-EGH   DIST-EGH

ELEPHANT SEAL, THE   C
FILMSTRIP WITH CAPTIONS
FROM THE ANIMALS SERIES.
LC NO. 72-734417
PROD-LIEB   DIST-MSCF   1970

ELEPHANT, THE   C
FILMSTRIP WITH CAPTIONS
FROM THE ANIMALS SERIES.
LC NO. 72-734417
PROD-LIEB   DIST-MSCF   1970

EMBRYOLOGY I - HYDRA AND STARFISH   C 42 FRS
FILMSTRIP
USES MICROSCOPIC PICTURES TO SHOW THE STRUCTURE AND THE REPRODUCTION OF THE HYDRA AND THE STARFISH. FROM THE MICROSCOPIC SPECIMENS - A RESOURCE UNIT SERIES.
PROD-EGH   DIST-EGH   1972

EMBRYOLOGY II - FROG AND CHICK   C 40 FRS
FILMSTRIP
SHOWS HOW FROG AND CHICK EMBRYOS ARE PRODUCED AND SHOWS HOW THE EMBRYOS GROW. FROM THE MICROSCOPIC SPECIMENS - A RESOURCE UNIT SERIES.
PROD-EGH   DIST-EGH   1972

ENERGY AND LIFE   C 36 FRS
SOUND FILMSTRIP - AUDIO TAPE
INTRODUCES THE STUDENT TO THE BASIC REQUIREMENTS OF ALL LIFE, ENERGY. FROM THE LIFE - A UNIQUE PHENOMENON SERIES.
PROD-EGH   DIST-EGH   1972

ENERGY CRISIS, THE - AN HISTORICAL REVIEW   C 45 FRS
SOUND FILMSTRIP - RECORD   I
PRESENTS A PICTURE OF THE FORCES WITH WHICH MAN NEEDS TO DO WORK AND WHAT FORMS OF ENERGY LIE AHEAD FOR US. FROM THE SCHOOL TIMES KIT - APRIL SERIES.
LC NO. 72-700784
PROD-TERF   DIST-TERF   1972

ENERGY CRISIS, THE - REPORT FROM PLANET 32   C 50 FRS
SOUND FILMSTRIP - RECORD   I
PRESENTS A DRAMATIC FANTASY ACCOUNT OF WHAT, IN FACT, CAN HAPPEN TO THE PLANET EARTH IF MAN IS NOT MORE CONSCIOUS OF HIS ENVIRONMENT AND ENERGY SOURCES. FROM THE SCHOOL TIMES KIT - APRIL SERIES.
LC NO. 72-700785
PROD-TERF   DIST-TERF   1972

ENGLAND   C
SOUND FILMSTRIP - AUDIO TAPE   P-I
POINTS OUT THE MANY ASPECTS OF THE CLOSELY SHARED HERITAGE OF ENGLAND AND THE UNITED STATES - POLITICAL IDEAS AND IDEALS, FORM OF GOVERNMENT AND BASIC LAW, LITERATURE AND LEGENDS, THE INDUSTRIAL REVOLUTION AND ITS EFFECTS IN ENGLAND AND IN THE UNITED STATES. FROM THE NEW FRIENDS FROM DISTANT LANDS - THE CULTURE WE SHARE SERIES.
PROD-PATED   DIST-PATED   1973

EQUATORIAL FORESTS   C 34 FRS
FILMSTRIP WITH SCRIPT
SHOWS THE VEGETATION, FAUNA, AGRICULTURE AND TRADE OF THE EQUATORIAL FORESTS AND POINTS OUT HOW MAN HAS ADAPTED TO THIS CLIMATIC REGION. FROM THE CLIMATIC REGIONS OF THE WORLD SERIES.
LC NO. 72-736985
PROD-COMG   DIST-CARMAN   PRODN-PUGH   1972

EXPLORATION - MAN'S QUEST FOR KNOWLEDGE--A SERIES   I-J
PROD-SED   DIST-SED   1972

ALEXANDER THE GREAT AND THE ANCIENTS   58 FRS
CAPTAIN COOK, ALEXANDER MACKENZIE AND LEWIS --   58 FRS
COLUMBUS, BALBOA AND MAGELLAN   58 FRS
EXPLORING AFRICA   58 FRS
SPANISH CONQUERORS AND COLONIZERS   58 FRS
VIKINGS, THE ARABS AND MARCO POLO, THE   58 FRS

EXPLORING AFRICA   C 58 FRS
SOUND FILMSTRIP - AUDIO TAPE   I-J
REVIEWS THE STRUGGLES OF SEVERAL MEN TO GAIN ACCESS TO THE NIGER AND CONTROL OF WEST AFRICA. FROM THE EXPLORATION - MAN'S QUEST FOR KNOWLEDGE SERIES.
LC NO. 73-732524
PROD-SED   DIST-SED   1972

EXPLORING CAREERS, GROUP 1--A SERIES   I-C
DETAILS THE JOB FUNCTION, EDUCATION, SKILL, TRAINING AND PRIOR EXPERIENCE REQUIRED FOR OBTAINING THE JOB, JOB AVAILABILITIES AND OCCUPATIONAL OUTLOOK FOR EMPLOYMENT OPPORTUNITY AND FINANCIAL AND PSYCHOLOGICAL REWARDS.
PROD-SVE   DIST-SVE   1973

AIRLINE CABIN ATTENDANT, THE   85 FRS
AUTOMOTIVE MECHANIC, THE   91 FRS
BROADCAST TECHNICIAN, THE   89 FRS
LONG HAUL TRUCK DRIVER, THE   91 FRS
NEWSPAPER REPORTER, THE   91 FRS
TELEPHONE INSTALLER, THE   96 FRS

EXPOSURE   B 80 FRS
SOUND FILMSTRIP - AUDIO TAPE   J-C A
EXPLAINS THE FOUR VARIABLE INTERRELATED FACTORS OF EXPOSURE - FILM SPEED, SHUTTER SPEED, APERTURE AND LIGHTING. ILLUSTRATES CORRECT USAGE OF EACH OF THESE FACTORS INCLUDING SUCH CONCEPTS AS ASA, DEPTH OF FIELD, HYPERFOCAL DISTANCE AND LIGHT METERING. FROM THE CREATIVE PHOTOGRAPHY - CAMERA SERIES.
LC NO. 73-732515
PROD-ARIZSU   DIST-ARIZSU   1973

EXTERIOR BUILDING MATERIALS FOR YOUR HOME   C 43 FRS
FILMSTRIP WITH SCRIPT   J-C A
SHOWS HOW THE PROPER SIDING CAN GIVE YOUR HOME PROTECTION, CHARM AND A LOT OF OTHER QUALITIES. HELPS THE VIEWER CHOOSE THE RIGHT SIDING FOR HIS HOME. FROM THE HOUSING SERIES.
LC NO. 73-733247
PROD-USDA   DIST-USDA   1968

FABLES AND FACTS--A SERIES   P-I
ILLUSTRATES TRADITIONAL TALES FROM THE GREEK, AMERICAN INDIAN, AUSTRALIAN, FAR EASTERN, ORIENTAL AND OTHER MYTHOLOGIES. OFFERS SCIENTIFIC EXPLANATIONS OF THE PHENOMENA.
LC NO. 72-737521
PROD-TERF   DIST-TERF   1973

AIR   40 FRS
FIRE   40 FRS
HEAVENS   40 FRS
LIFE COMES TO THE WORLD   40 FRS
SUN   40 FRS
THUNDER AND LIGHTNING   40 FRS
WATER   40 FRS
WORLD IS BORN, THE   40 FRS

FACE FACTS   C 52 FRS
SOUND FILMSTRIP - AUDIO TAPE
DESCRIBES THE PROPER DIET FOR HEALTHY SKIN AND OFFERS HINTS FOR SKIN CARE. FROM THE LOOKING GREAT ON A SHOESTRING SERIES.
PROD-EGH   DIST-EGH   1972

FACE FACTS   C 100 FRS
SOUND FILMSTRIP - RECORD   J-C A
BRINGS OUT EXPLICIT PROCEDURES FOR THE PROPER CARE OF THE SKIN AND THE HAIR AND HOW TO ACCENTUATE GOOD FEATURES THROUGH THE USE OF MAKE-UP AND HAIR ARRANGEMENT.

FROM THE HOT TIPS ON BASIC BEAUTY, FASHION, GROOMING AND DATING SERIES.
LC NO. 72-737338
PROD-RMI   DIST-RMI   1972

FACES OF MAN   C 89 FRS
SOUND FILMSTRIP - RECORD   H-C A
EXPLORES THE DIVERSITY OF MAN AS IT IS REFLECTED IN A WIDE RANGE OF COUNTENANCES AND EXPRESSIONS.
LC NO. 72-737553
PROD-ARGSC   DIST-ARGSC   1971

FACTORING NUMBERS   C 29 FRS
SOUND FILMSTRIP - RECORD   J-H
DEFINES PRIME FACTORS AND PRESENTS THE PRINCIPLES OF THE UNIQUE FACTORIZATION OF A NUMBER INTO PRIMES. FROM THE MATHEMATICS - FUNDAMENTAL OPERATIONS SERIES.
LC NO. 73-732675
PROD-UNISYS   DIST-VIEWLX   1972

FAMILY OF TREES, THE   C 40 FRS
SOUND FILMSTRIP - RECORD   P-J
SEE SERIES TITLE FOR DESCRIPTIVE STATEMENT. FROM THE GROWING THINGS SERIES.
PROD-TERF   DIST-TERF   1973

FAMOUS PATRIOTS OF THE AMERICAN REVOLUTION--A SERIES   I-H
PROD-CORF   DIST-CORF   1973

CRISPUS ATTUCKS   44 FRS
HAYM SALOMON   45 FRS
JOHN PAUL JONES   46 FRS
MOLLY PITCHER   43 FRS
NATHANAEL GREENE   47 FRS
PATRICK HENRY   44 FRS

FANTASIA ON GREENSLEEVES - VAUGHAN WILLIAMS   C 61 FRS
SOUND FILMSTRIP - RECORD
PRESENTS RALPH VAUGHAN WILLIAMS' 'FANTASIA ON GREENSLEEVES,' AGAINST A BACKGROUND OF ORIGINAL PHOTOGRAPHS OF THE ENGLISH COUNTRYSIDE AND PERFORMANCES OF TWO ENGLISH FOLKSONGS ON WHICH VAUGHAN WILLIAMS BASED HIS WORK. FROM THE MUSIC APPRECIATION SERIES.
LC NO. 72-736175
PROD-EAV   DIST-EAV

FASHION FORMULAS   C 89 FRS
SOUND FILMSTRIP - RECORD   J-C A
SHOWS HOW TO ACHIEVE FASHION THROUGH WARDROBE PLANNING AT MINIMUM EXPENSE, HOW TO SELECT THE COLORS, STYLES AND MATERIALS MOST APPROPRIATE TO THE INDIVIDUAL AND HOW TO AVOID EXTREME FADS. FROM THE HOT TIPS ON BASIC BEAUTY, FASHION, GROOMING AND DATING SERIES.
LC NO. 72-737339
PROD-RMI   DIST-RMI   1972

FAT BLACK MACK   C 46 FRS
SOUND FILMSTRIP - AUDIO TAPE
PRESENTS A MODERN PARABLE INVOLVING THE COLOR OF ONE'S SKIN. FROM THE GUIDES FOR GROWING SERIES.
LC NO. 72-736523
PROD-EGH   DIST-EGH   1972

FEMALE OF THE SPECIES, THE   C 53 FRS
SOUND FILMSTRIP - AUDIO TAPE
DESCRIBES THE GRADUALLY CHANGING IMAGE OF WOMAN FROM A PASSIVE SEX OBJECT TO A PERSON IN HER OWN RIGHT. FROM THE HUMAN SEXUALITY SERIES.
PROD-EGH   DIST-EGH   1972

FIGURE FACTS   C 41 FRS
SOUND FILMSTRIP - AUDIO TAPE
DESCRIBES THE PROPER DIET AND EXERCISE FOR A TRIM FIGURE. FROM THE LOOKING GREAT ON A SHOESTRING SERIES.
PROD-EGH   DIST-EGH   1972

FINDING WHAT'S RIGHT FOR YOU   C 46 FRS
SOUND FILMSTRIP - AUDIO TAPE
NOTES THAT THE STUDENT IS THE ONLY PERSON WHO SHOULD DECIDE WHAT KIND OF CLOTHES TO BUY. FROM THE LOOKING GREAT ON A SHOESTRING SERIES.
PROD-EGH   DIST-EGH   1972

FIRE   C 40 FRS
SOUND FILMSTRIP - AUDIO TAPE   P-I
SEE SERIES TITLE FOR DESCRIPTIVE STATEMENT.
FROM THE FABLES AND FACTS SERIES.
PROD-TERF   DIST-TERF   1973

**FISH IN THE FOREST - A
RUSSIAN FOLKTALE**   C 76 FRS
SOUND FILMSTRIP - AUDIO TAPE   I
PRESENTS A RUSSIAN FOLKTALE OF A SHREWD
PEASANT IN CONFLICT WITH AN OPPRESSIVE SO-
CIETY.
LC NO. 73-732665
PROD-GA   DIST-GA   1972

FIVE NAUGHTY MARBLES   C 33 FRS
SOUND FILMSTRIP - AUDIO TAPE   K-P
PRESENTS THE ADVENTURES OF A YOUNG BOY
AND FIVE MAGIC MARBLES WHICH HAVE THE
UNIQUE POWER OF DISAPPEARING AND REAP-
PEARING. FROM THE CHILDREN'S STORIES SE-
RIES.
LC NO. 72-737212
PROD-STNHM   DIST-STNHM   1972

FLORENCE AND VENICE   C 28 FRS
SOUND FILMSTRIP - AUDIO TAPE
DESCRIBES THE MANY HISTORIC LOCATIONS IN
BOTH FLORENCE AND VENICE. FROM THE ITALY -
A REGIONAL SURVEY SERIES.
LC NO. 72-736590
PROD-EGH   DIST-EGH   1972

FLORENCE AND VENICE   C 36 FRS
SOUND FILMSTRIP - AUDIO TAPE
DESCRIBES THE MANY HISTORIC LOCATIONS IN
BOTH FLORENCE AND VENICE. FROM THE ITALY -
A REGIONAL STUDY SERIES.
LC NO. 72-736590
PROD-EGH   DIST-EGH

**FOCUS ON AMERICA - THE
PACIFIC STATES--A SERIES**
    J-H A
PROD-SVE   DIST-SVE   1972

BONNEVILLE DAM - POWERHOUSE OF
THE COLUMBIA --   93 FRS
CALIFORNIA CONFLICT - MIGRANT FARM
WORKERS   94 FRS
LOS ANGELES - CITY OF AUTOMOBILES   83 FRS
NEW TOWN - VALENCIA, CALIFORNIA   88 FRS
SEATTLE - A CITY FACES CRISIS   79 FRS
TIMBER - WASHINGTON'S MOST
VALUABLE CROP   81 FRS

FOLD MOUNTAINS   C 38 FRS
FILMSTRIP WITH SCRIPT   I-H
SHOWS THE DIFFERENT PROCESSES BY WHICH
FOLD MOUNTAINS ARE FORMED, THE GEOGRAPHI-
CAL DISTRIBUTION OF PRESENTDAY MOUNTAINS
AND A SURVEY OF THE DIFFERENT TYPES OF
FOLDS WITH CAREFULLY SELECTED EXAMPLES OF
FOLDING. FROM THE ORIGINS OF THE EARTH SE-
RIES.
LC NO. 72-737133
PROD-VISPUB   DIST-VISPUB   1970

FOOD SERVICE WORKER   C 55 FRS
SOUND FILMSTRIP - AUDIO TAPE
DESCRIBES THE DUTIES OF THE FOOD SERVICE
WORKER WHOSE JOB IS COMPLICATED BY THE
SPECIAL DIET REQUIREMENTS OF THE MODERN
HOSPITAL. FROM THE HOSPITAL JOB OPPORTUNI-
TIES SERIES.
PROD-EGH   DIST-EGH   1972

FOOT SOLDIER, THE   C 60 FRS
SOUND FILMSTRIP - RECORD
DISCUSSES THE COMPOSITION OF THE UNION
ARMY. FROM THE CIVIL WAR AS IT HAPPENED SE-
RIES.
LC NO. 72-735142
PROD-EDREC   DIST-TECVIS   1970

FORMING A CAN   C 38 FRS
SOUND FILMSTRIP - AUDIO TAPE
GIVES THE VIEWER AN AWARENESS OF BASIC
MANUFACTURING PROCESSES. FROM THE HOW
THINGS ARE MADE SERIES.
LC NO. 72-736550
PROD-EGH   DIST-EGH   1972

FOUR QUADRANTS   C 26 FRS
SOUND FILMSTRIP - RECORD   I-H
ESTABLISHES THE NEED FOR A NEGATIVE SCALE
ON THE X AXIS AND GIVES ITS RELATION TO THE
NUMBER LINE. FROM THE MATHEMATICS -
GRAPHING SERIES.
LC NO. 72-737594
PROD-UNISYS   DIST-VIEWLX   1972

FRACTIONS   C 37 FRS
FILMSTRIP WITH SCRIPT   P
INTRODUCES THE CONCEPT OF FRACTIONS, AND
FRACTIONS IN WHICH THE NUMERATOR IS
GREATER THAN THE DENOMINATOR. FROM THE
MODERN MATHEMATICS PROGRAM, LEVEL 4, 747
SERIES.
LC NO. 72-733835
PROD-EDPRC   DIST-EDPRC

FUNCTION OF THE EAR   C
FILMSTRIP WITH SCRIPT   H-C A
FROM THE HUMAN ANATOMY AND PHYSIOLOGY
SERIES.
PROD-HRAW   DIST-HRAW   1973

FUNCTION OF THE EYE   C
FILMSTRIP WITH SCRIPT   H-C A
FROM THE HUMAN ANATOMY AND PHYSIOLOGY
SERIES.
PROD-HRAW   DIST-HRAW   1973

FUNCTION OF THE KIDNEY   C
FILMSTRIP WITH SCRIPT   H-C A
FROM THE HUMAN ANATOMY AND PHYSIOLOGY
SERIES.
PROD-HRAW   DIST-HRAW   1973

G

GAS/LIQUID/SOLID, PT 1   C 27 FRS
FILMSTRIP WITH SCRIPT
DISCUSSES THE PROPERTIES OF GASES, LIQUIDS
AND SOLIDS. FROM THE ATOMIC DIAGRAMS, NO. 7
SERIES.
LC NO. FIA68-3520
PROD-RAYM   DIST-RAYM   1967

GEOMETRY   C 28 FRS
FILMSTRIP WITH SCRIPT   P
USES PAPER FOLDING AND REFLECTION OF FIG-
URES IN A MIRROR TO ILLUSTRATE THE CONCEPT
OF SYMMETRY WITH RESPECT TO A LINE. FROM
THE MODERN MATHEMATICS PROGRAM, LEVEL 4,
739 SERIES.
LC NO. 72-733832
PROD-EDPRC   DIST-EDPRC

GERMAN AMERICANS   C 85 FRS
SOUND FILMSTRIP - RECORD   I-J
SEE SERIES TITLE FOR DESCRIPTIVE STATEMENT.
FROM THE AMERICAN ADVENTURE SERIES.
LC NO. 72-737418
PROD-FIELEP   DIST-FIELEP   1972

GIRAFFE, THE   C
FILMSTRIP WITH CAPTIONS
FROM THE ANIMALS SERIES.
LC NO. 72-734417
PROD-LIEB   DIST-MSCF   1970

GOD'S CHILDREN   C 8 FRS
FILMSTRIP
JOHNNY CASH SINGS A BALLAD WHICH TELLS THE
STORY OF A RETARDED CHILD AND HIS PARENTS,
AND HOW THEIR MUTUAL PROBLEMS ARE EASED
BY HELP THROUGH THE UNITED WAY.
LC NO. 72-702217
PROD-UWLA   DIST-UWLA   PRODN-NOWAKA

GOING INTO THE HOSPITAL   C 40 FRS
SOUND FILMSTRIP - AUDIO TAPE
TELLS THE STORY OF A LITTLE GIRL WHO HAD TO
HAVE HER TONSILS REMOVED. FROM THE GOING
TO THE DOCTOR, DENTIST AND HOSPITAL SERIES.
PROD-EGH   DIST-EGH   1972

GOING TO THE DENTIST   C 54 FRS
SOUND FILMSTRIP - AUDIO TAPE
FAMILIARIZES THE VIEWER WITH WHAT A DEN-
TIST REALLY DOES. FROM THE GOING TO THE
DOCTOR, DENTIST AND HOSPITAL SERIES.
PROD-EGH   DIST-EGH   1972

GOING TO THE DOCTOR   C 28 FRS
SOUND FILMSTRIP - AUDIO TAPE
MAKES THE THOUGHT OF GOING TO THE DOCTOR
A PLEASANT ONE. EASES THE FEAR THAT A CHILD
MAY HAVE. FROM THE GOING TO THE DOCTOR,
DENTIST AND HOSPITAL SERIES.
PROD-EGH   DIST-EGH   1972

**GOING TO THE DOCTOR,
DENTIST AND HOSPITAL--A
SERIES**
PROD-EGH   DIST-EGH   1972

GOING INTO THE HOSPITAL   40 FRS
GOING TO THE DENTIST   54 FRS
GOING TO THE DOCTOR   28 FRS
HAVING AN OPERATION   43 FRS
HAVING STITCHES AND GETTING A
CAST   47 FRS
WHAT YOU WILL FIND IN A HOSPITAL   50 FRS

GOLDEN FISH, THE   C 30 FRS
SOUND FILMSTRIP - AUDIO TAPE   K-P
EXPLAINS HOW THE LIVES OF AN OLD FISHERMAN
AND HIS WIFE ARE CHANGED WHEN HE CATCHES
A GOLDEN FISH IN HIS NET AND THE FISH OFFERS
TO GRANT ALL OF THE FISHERMAN'S WISHES IN
RETURN FOR HIS FREEDOM. FROM THE CHIL-
DREN'S STORIES SERIES.
LC NO. 72-737210
PROD-STNHM   DIST-STNHM   1972

GOOD GOODIES   C
FILMSTRIP
USES ANIMATION TO TELL THE STORY OF TWO
TRUCKS SELLING REFRESHMENTS WHO COMPETE
WITH ONE ANOTHER, EACH CLAIMING THAT ITS
OWN FOOD IS BETTER BY PUTTING UP SIGNS.
LC NO. 74-714222
PROD-BOSUST   DIST-BFA   1971

GOOD GROOMING   C 100 FRS
SOUND FILMSTRIP - RECORD   J-C A
EXPLAINS THE IMPORTANCE OF GOOD GROOMING
AND HOW TO ACHIEVE IT TO ACQUIRE SELF-RE-
SPECT, MENTAL AND PHYSICAL HEALTH AND
PROPER RELATIONSHIPS WITH OTHERS. FROM
THE HOT TIPS ON BASIC BEAUTY, FASHION,
GROOMING AND DATING SERIES.
LC NO. 72-737337
PROD-RMI   DIST-RMI   1972

GOOD HORSEMANSHIP   C 43 FRS
FILMSTRIP WITH CAPTIONS   H-C
ILLUSTRATES VARIOUS THINGS TO CHECK BEFORE
MOUNTING, HOW TO MOUNT PROPERLY, BEST PO-
SITIONS FOR THE HANDS AND FEET AND THE
PROPER POSITION IN THE SADDLE AT VARIOUS
GAITS.
LC NO. 73-733321
PROD-UILVAS   DIST-UILVAS   1972

GORILLA, THE   C
FILMSTRIP WITH CAPTIONS
FROM THE ANIMALS SERIES.
LC NO. 72-734417
PROD-LIEB   DIST-MSCF   1970

GRAPHING AN EQUATION   C 29 FRS
SOUND FILMSTRIP - RECORD   I-H
EMPHASIZES THE ONE-TO-ONE CORRESPON-
DENCE BETWEEN THE POINTS OF THE GRAPH,
THE VALUES IN THE TABLE AND THE SOLUTION
SET OF THE EQUATION. FROM THE MATHEMATICS
- GRAPHING SERIES.
LC NO. 72-737593
PROD-UNISYS   DIST-VIEWLX   1972

**GREAT BRITAIN - A REGIONAL
STUDY--A SERIES**
PROD-EGH   DIST-EGH   1972

LAND, FEATURES AND CITIES   49 FRS
LIFE IN BRITAIN   47 FRS
RESOURCES, AGRICULTURE AND
INDUSTRY   40 FRS
WHAT IS GREAT BRITAIN   49 FRS

**GREAT DEPRESSION, THE -
CAUSES, EFFECTS, SOLUTIONS,
PT 4**   C 68 FRS
SOUND FILMSTRIP - RECORD   J-C
EXPLAINS IN SIMPLE ECONOMIC TERMS THE NA-
TURE OF A CAPITALIST ECONOMY, WHY THE
STOCK MARKET ROSE AND THEN BOOMED DUR-
ING THE LATE 1920'S, WHY IT CRASHED AND WHY
A DEPRESSION FOLLOWED.
LC NO. 73-733225
PROD-EAV   DIST-EAV   1970

**GREAT DEPRESSION, THE -
CAUSES, EFFECTS, SOLUTIONS,
PT 2**   C 79 FRS
SOUND FILMSTRIP - RECORD   J-C
DEALS WITH THE MAGNITUDE OF THE CRISIS FAC-
ING FDR UPON HIS INAUGURATION, THE ATTI-
TUDES OF HIS ADMINISTRATION AND ITS VARI-
OUS PROGRAMS AIMED AT RELIEF, RECOVERY
AND REFORM.
LC NO. 73-733225

PROD-EAV   DIST-EAV   1970

**GREAT DEPRESSION, THE -
CAUSES, EFFECTS, SOLUTIONS,
PT 3**   C 81 FRS
              SOUND FILMSTRIP - RECORD   J-C
EVOKES THROUGH SONGS, VISUALS AND NARRA-
TIVE, THE FLAVOR OF LIFE IN THE 1930'S.
    LC NO. 73-733225
PROD-EAV   DIST-EAV   1970

**GREAT DEPRESSION, THE -
CAUSES, EFFECTS, SOLUTIONS,
PT 1**   C 95 FRS
              SOUND FILMSTRIP - RECORD   J-C
EXAMINES THE 1920'S AND THE BACKGROUND OF
THE DEPRESSION.
    LC NO. 73-733225
PROD-EAV   DIST-EAV   1970

GREAT MEN AND ARTISTS   C 18 FRS
              SOUND FILMSTRIP - AUDIO TAPE
DESCRIBES SEVERAL OF ITALY'S FAMOUS MEN
AND IMPORTANT ARTISTS. FROM THE ITALY - A
REGIONAL SURVEY SERIES.
    LC NO. 72-736582
PROD-EGH   DIST-EGH   1972

GREAT MEN AND ARTISTS   C 24 FRS
              SOUND FILMSTRIP - AUDIO TAPE
PRESENTS BIOGRAPHICAL MATERIAL ABOUT SEV-
ERAL OF ITALY'S FAMOUS MEN AND IMPORTANT
ARTISTS. FROM THE ITALY - A REGIONAL STUDY
SERIES.
    LC NO. 72-736582
PROD-EGH   DIST-EGH

GREECE   C
              SOUND FILMSTRIP - AUDIO TAPE   P-I
DESCRIBES THE MANY GREAT GIFTS OF ANCIENT
GREECE, IN SCULPTURE, ARCHITECTURE, DRAMA,
LITERATURE AND PHILOSOPHY AS WELL AS ITS
EARLY CONTRIBUTIONS TO MATHEMATICS, SCI-
ENCE AND THE CONCEPT OF DEMOCRACY. FROM
THE NEW FRIENDS FROM DISTANT LANDS - THE
CULTURE WE SHARE SERIES.
PROD-PATED   DIST-PATED   1973

**GREENHOUSES - USES AND
DESIGN**   C 44 FRS
              FILMSTRIP WITH CAPTIONS   H-C
DISCUSSES THINGS TO CONSIDER BEFORE BUILD-
ING A GREENHOUSE.
    LC NO. 73-733322
PROD-UILVAS   DIST-UILVAS   1971

**GROUND COVERS AND THEIR
USES**   C 60 FRS
              FILMSTRIP WITH SCRIPT   H-C
DISCUSSES 51 DIFFERENT GROUND COVERS, GIV-
ING PLANTING SUGGESTIONS, DISTANCE APART
AND FOLIAGE COLOR.
    LC NO. 73-733323
PROD-UILVAS   DIST-UILVAS   1972

GROWING THINGS--A SERIES
                                          P-J
PRESENTS A SURVEY OF THE RANGE OF PLANT
LIFE FROM HOW PLANTS GROW, INCLUDING PHO-
TOSYNTHESIS, ANATOMY AND REPRODUCTION,
TO WHY, WHEN AND WHERE THEY GROW. EX-
PLORES THE RELATIONSHIP OF PLANTS TO LIVING
THINGS AND THEIR VERSATILITY FROM BEAUTY
TO DRUGS.
    LC NO. 73-733038
PROD-TERF   DIST-TERF   1973

FAMILY OF TREES, THE   40 FRS
HOW PLANTS GROW   40 FRS
JUNGLE AND DESERT PLANTS   40 FRS
PLANT LIFE IN THE WATERS   40 FRS
PRAIRIE AND MOUNTAIN PLANTS   40 FRS
RARE AND EXOTIC PLANTS   40 FRS

GROWING UP   C 38 FRS
              SOUND FILMSTRIP - RECORD   I R
GIVES A FIRST-PERSON PRESENTATION OF THE
LIFE OF JESUS. TELLS OF HIS EXPERIENCES AS A
BOY GROWING UP IN A GALILEAN VILLAGE. FROM
THE MY NAME IS JESUS SERIES.
    LC NO. 72-737430
PROD-ROAS   DIST-ROAS   1972

**GUIDE TO WHEELCHAIR
TRANSFER TECHNIQUES, A**   C
              SOUND FILMSTRIP - RECORD
ILLUSTRATES HOW TO EXECUTE SITTING AND
STANDING TRANSFERS FROM WHEELCHAIR TO
BED, BED TO WHEELCHAIR, WHEELCHAIR TO
CHAIR AND WHEELCHAIR TO CAR.
    LC NO. 72-736286
PROD-KRI   DIST-KRI

**GUIDES FOR GROWING--A
SERIES**
PROD-EGH   DIST-EGH   1972

BLUE GOOTCHES, THE   55 FRS
FAT BLACK MACK   46 FRS
LEWIS-LIES-A-LOT   53 FRS
MARY JANE AND BUTTERFLY   16 FRS
MILES MUGWUMP AND FRANNIE
FRANTIC   52 FRS
PRINCESS ECOL VISITS THE PLANET
THRAE   44 FRS

**HANGMAN'S KNOT VERSUS THE
PAROLE BOARD**   C 61 FRS
              SOUND FILMSTRIP - AUDIO TAPE   I-J
SEE SERIES TITLE FOR DESCRIPTIVE STATEMENT.
FROM THE MIND BLOWERS SERIES.
    LC NO. 73-733278
PROD-SNBRST   DIST-SNBRST   1973

**HARD DRUGS, THE - THE
BOTTOM OF THE TRAP**   B 82 FRS
              SOUND FILMSTRIP - AUDIO TAPE   P-I
INVESTIGATES THE EFFECTS OF FOUR TYPES OF
STRONG DRUGS AND SOME REASONS FOR THEIR
USE. TRACES THE CAUSES OF DRUG EXPERIMEN-
TATION. SUGGESTS SOME ALTERNATIVES TO
DRUGS. FROM THE DRUGS - A TRICK, A TRAP SE-
RIES.
    LC NO. 72-737376
PROD-EBEC   DIST-EBEC   1972

**HARDWARE AND FUNDAMENTAL
CONCEPTS**   C 60 FRS
              SOUND FILMSTRIP - RECORD
FROM THE COMPUTER SCIENCE SERIES.
    LC NO. 73-732500
PROD-AVDEV   DIST-AVDEV   1972

HAVING AN OPERATION   C 43 FRS
              SOUND FILMSTRIP - AUDIO TAPE
COMPLETES THE STORY OF THE LITTLE GIRL'S
TONSIL OPERATION. FROM THE GOING TO THE
DOCTOR, DENTIST AND HOSPITAL SERIES.
PROD-EGH   DIST-EGH   1972

**HAVING STITCHES AND
GETTING A CAST**   C 47 FRS
              SOUND FILMSTRIP - AUDIO TAPE
TELLS OF A LITTLE BOY WHO HAD TO HAVE
STITCHES AND A LITTLE GIRL WHO HAD TO GET A
CAST PUT ON HER ARM. FROM THE GOING TO THE
DOCTOR, DENTIST AND HOSPITAL SERIES.
PROD-EGH   DIST-EGH   1972

HAYM SALOMON   C 45 FRS
              SOUND FILMSTRIP - AUDIO TAPE   I-H
PRESENTS THE LIFE OF HAYM SALOMON, A JEW-
ISH IMMIGRANT, WHO WAS INFLUENTIAL IN FI-
NANCING THE AMERICAN REVOLUTION. FROM
THE FAMOUS PATRIOTS OF THE AMERICAN REVO-
LUTION SERIES.
    LC NO. 73-732982
PROD-CORF   DIST-CORF   1973

HEAD AND NECK SURGERY   C 119 FRS
              SOUND FILMSTRIP - RECORD
DESCRIBES PROCEDURES, POSTOPERATIVE NURS-
ING MEASURES AND RESPONSIBILITIES, BOTH
PHYSICAL AND PSYCHOLOGICAL, ASSOCIATED
WITH TREATMENT OF HEAD AND NECK CANCER.
FROM THE CANCER, SERIES 3 - TREATMENT MO-
DALITIES WITH IMPLICATIONS FOR NURSING
CARE SERIES. NO. 4
    LC NO. 72-733176
PROD-CONMED   DIST-CONMED   1972

HEALTH SERVICES IN CHINA   C 43 FRS
              SOUND FILMSTRIP - AUDIO TAPE
DESCRIBES THE VARIOUS TYPES OF HEALTH SERV-
ICES AND THE PHILOSOPHY BEHIND THEM. FROM
THE INSIDE THE PEOPLE'S REPUBLIC OF CHINA
SERIES.
PROD-EGH   DIST-EGH   1972

HEAVENS   C 40 FRS
              SOUND FILMSTRIP - AUDIO TAPE   P-I
SEE SERIES TITLE FOR DESCRIPTIVE STATEMENT.
FROM THE FABLES AND FACTS SERIES.
PROD-TERF   DIST-TERF   1973

HERITAGE OF GREATNESS   C 72 FRS
              SOUND FILMSTRIP - RECORD
SEE SERIES TITLE FOR DESCRIPTIVE STATEMENT.
FROM THE CITY - HOW AMERICA LIVES SERIES. PT
1
    LC NO. 72-736412
PROD-AVNA   DIST-AVNA   1972

**HISTORY OF ASTRONAUTICS,
THE, PT 1**   C 70 FRS
              FILMSTRIP WITH SCRIPT   I-J
SEE SERIES TITLE FOR DESCRIPTIVE STATEMENT.
FROM THE MAN ON THE MOON SERIES.
PROD-DOUBLE   DIST-DOUBLE   1971

**HISTORY OF ASTRONAUTICS,
THE, PT 2**   C 86 FRS
              FILMSTRIP WITH SCRIPT   I-J
SEE SERIES TITLE FOR DESCRIPTIVE STATEMENT.
FROM THE MAN ON THE MOON SERIES.
PROD-DOUBLE   DIST-DOUBLE   1971

**HISTORY OF STYLE AND VOGUE,
A**   C 45 FRS
              SOUND FILMSTRIP - AUDIO TAPE
PRESENTS BACKGROUND INFORMATION ABOUT
STYLES OF THE PAST AND DISTINGUISHES BE-
TWEEN THE VOGUE OF THE MOMENT AND STYLES
THAT WILL LAST. FROM THE LOOKING GREAT ON A
SHOESTRING SERIES.
PROD-EGH   DIST-EGH   1972

**HISTORY OF THE COMPUTER,
THE**   B 54 FRS
              SOUND FILMSTRIP - RECORD   H
FOLLOWS SIGNIFICANT DEVELOPMENTS IN THE
EVOLUTION OF THE COMPUTER IN THE 17TH CEN-
TURY TO THE DEVELOPMENT OF THE DIGITAL
COMPUTER IN THE 1940'S. FROM THE HOW COM-
PUTERS WORK SERIES.
    LC NO. 73-732751
PROD-EBEC   DIST-EBEC   1972

**HOLIDAY SERIES, SET 2--A
SERIES**
                                          K-P
TELLS ABOUT WASHINGTON'S BIRTHDAY, PASS-
OVER, EASTER AND MEMORIAL DAY. GIVES THE
BACKGROUND OF EACH OF THESE HOLIDAYS AND
TELLS HOW THEY ARE CELEBRATED TODAY.
PROD-MGHT   DIST-MGHT   1972

EASTER   35 FRS
MEMORIAL DAY   39 FRS,
PASSOVER   41 FRS
WASHINGTON'S BIRTHDAY   51 FRS

**HOLLAND - A REGIONAL STUDY-
-A SERIES**
PROD-EGH   DIST-EGH   1972

LAND, FEATURES AND CITIES   55 FRS
LIFE IN HOLLAND   45 FRS
RESOURCES, AGRICULTURE AND
INDUSTRY   43 FRS
WHAT IS HOLLAND   54 FRS

HOSPITAL ADMINISTRATION   C 52 FRS
              SOUND FILMSTRIP - AUDIO TAPE
DESCRIBES THE BUSINESS OF RUNNING A HOSPI-
TAL. FROM THE HOSPITAL JOB OPPORTUNITIES
SERIES.
PROD-EGH   DIST-EGH   1972

**HOSPITAL JOB OPPORTUNITIES-
-A SERIES**
PROD-EGH   DIST-EGH   1972

DIET CLERK AND FRY COOK   50 FRS
FOOD SERVICE WORKER   55 FRS
HOSPITAL ADMINISTRATION   52 FRS
INHALATION THERAPY TECHNICIAN   52 FRS
MAINTENANCE MECHANIC, ELECTRICIAN
AND CUSTODIAN   63 FRS
MEDICAL ASSISTANT   56 FRS
NUCLEAR TECHNICIAN   54 FRS
NURSE   56 FRS
NURSE'S AIDE   56 FRS
X-RAY TECHNICIAN   53 FRS

HOSPITAL SAFETY--A SERIES
                                          PRO
PROVIDES A PLANNED LEARNING EXPERIENCE
ENABLING THE PARTICIPANT TO BE ALERT TO THE
PREVENTION AND CAUSES OF ACCIDENTS IN THE
HOSPITAL SETTING AND TO IDENTIFY HIS PER-
SONAL RESPONSIBILITY, ALL RESULTING IN SAFER
PATIENT CARE.
PROD-TRNAID   DIST-TRNAID   1972

ELECTRICAL HAZARDS   106 FRS
HOSPITAL FIRES - THEIR CAUSE AND
PREVENTION   135 FRS

HOSPITAL FIRES AND THE EVACUATION
OF PATIENTS   119 FRS
INCIDENTS AND ACCIDENTS   101 FRS

HOT AND COLD - EARLY
SCIENCE CONCEPTS   C 44 FRS
FILMSTRIP WITH CAPTIONS   K-I
PRESENTS SIMPLE, COLORFUL EXPLANATIONS OF
WHAT HAPPENS WHEN FIRE BURNS AND WATER
BOILS, WHEN WATER FREEZES AND ICE MELTS
AND HOW HOT AND COLD AFFECT CERTAIN
CHANGES.
LC NO. 70-735111
PROD-TROLA   DIST-TROLA   1969

HOT TIPS ON BASIC BEAUTY,
FASHION, GROOMING AND
DATING--A SERIES
     J-C A
HELPS GIRLS ESTABLISH HABITS AND GUIDELINES
WHICH WILL BRING OUT THEIR BEST INDIVIDUAL
DEVELOPMENT.
PROD-RMI   DIST-RMI   1972

DATING DATA   100 FRS
FACE FACTS   100 FRS
FASHION FORMULAS   89 FRS
GOOD GROOMING   100 FRS
MODELING MANNERS   93 FRS
PERSONALITY PLUS   91 FRS

HOUSE PESTS AND PARASITES   C 25 FRS
FILMSTRIP WITH SCRIPT   I-H
STUDIES VARIOUS HOUSE PESTS AND PARASITES
INCLUDING THE HOUSEFLY, MOSQUITO, COCK-
ROACH, MUCOR, DIPHTHERIA ORGANISM, BED-
BUG, FLEA, LOUSE AND OTHERS.
LC NO. 72-737234
PROD-COMG   DIST-COMG   1961

HOUSING--A SERIES
     J-C A
PROD-USDA   DIST-USDA   1968

EXTERIOR BUILDING MATERIALS FOR
YOUR HOME   43 FRS
PLANNING THE BEDROOM   32 FRS

HOW A CAR IS ASSEMBLED   C 43 FRS
SOUND FILMSTRIP - AUDIO TAPE
SHOWS STUDENTS HOW AN ASSEMBLY LINE
WORKS. FROM THE HOW THINGS ARE MADE SE-
RIES.
LC NO. 72-736552
PROD-EGH   DIST-EGH   1972

HOW COMPUTERS WORK--A
SERIES
     H
INTRODUCES THE ELEMENTS, HISTORY AND FU-
TURE OF COMPUTERS AS WELL AS THEIR OPERA-
TIONS.
PROD-EBEC   DIST-EBEC   1972

COMPUTER SYSTEM, THE   82 FRS
HISTORY OF THE COMPUTER, THE   54 FRS
INPUT-OUTPUT - HOW COMPUTERS
READ AND WRITE   58 FRS
NUMBER SYSTEMS - THE COMPUTER'S
VOCABULARY   53 FRS
PROGRAMMING - HOW TO ORDER A
COMPUTER AROUND   61 FRS
SOFTWARE AND HARDWARE AT WORK   64 FRS

HOW DESERT ANIMALS
SURVIVE   C 59 FRS
FILMSTRIP WITH SCRIPT
EXAMINES VARIOUS DESERT ANIMALS, POINTING
OUT THEIR ABILITY TO LIVE WHERE WATER IS
SCARCE. FROM THE DESERT LIFE SERIES. NO. 3
LC NO. 72-734808
PROD-SED   DIST-SED   1972

HOW PLANTS GROW   C 40 FRS
SOUND FILMSTRIP - RECORD   P-J
SEE SERIES TITLE FOR DESCRIPTIVE STATEMENT.
FROM THE GROWING THINGS SERIES.
PROD-TERF   DIST-TERF   1973

HOW THINGS ARE MADE--A
SERIES
PROD-EGH   DIST-EGH   1972

CRAFTING A CHAIR   49 FRS
CREATING A MOVIE   47 FRS
FORMING A CAN   38 FRS
HOW A CAR IS ASSEMBLED   43 FRS
MAKING CLOTHING   40 FRS
PROCESSING SOUP   39 FRS

HOW TO CLOSE OPEN HOUSING   C 77 FRS
SOUND FILMSTRIP - AUDIO TAPE   I-J
SEE SERIES TITLE FOR DESCRIPTIVE STATEMENT.
FROM THE MIND BLOWERS SERIES.
LC NO. 73-733279
PROD-SNBRST   DIST-SNBRST   1973

HOW TO DO A VALVE JOB   C
SOUND FILMSTRIP - RECORD   J-C A
SEE SERIES TITLE FOR DESCRIPTIVE STATEMENT.
FROM THE INTERNAL COMBUSTION ENGINE EX-
PLAINED SERIES.
PROD-BERGL   DIST-BERGL   1972

HOW TO RELINE DISK-TYPE
BRAKES   C
SOUND FILMSTRIP - RECORD   J-C A
SEE SERIES TITLE FOR DESCRIPTIVE STATEMENT.
FROM THE HYDRAULIC BRAKE SYSTEM EX-
PLAINED SERIES.
PROD-BERGL   DIST-BERGL   1972

HOW TO RELINE DRUM-TYPE
BRAKES   C
SOUND FILMSTRIP - RECORD   J-C A
SEE SERIES TITLE FOR DESCRIPTIVE STATEMENT.
FROM THE HYDRAULIC BRAKE SYSTEM EX-
PLAINED SERIES.
PROD-BERGL   DIST-BERGL   1972

HOW WE BUILD BRIDGES   C 51 FRS
SOUND FILMSTRIP - AUDIO TAPE
DESCRIBES THE PROBLEMS INVOLVED IN THE
CONSTRUCTION OF VARIOUS TYPES OF BRIDGES.
FROM THE HOW WE BUILD THINGS SERIES.
PROD-EGH   DIST-EGH   1972

HOW WE BUILD CITIES   C 48 FRS
SOUND FILMSTRIP - AUDIO TAPE
DESCRIBES THE VARIOUS CONSTRUCTION METH-
ODS IN CITY CONSTRUCTION AND THE RELATION-
SHIP OF THE CITY AND THE SURROUNDING ENVI-
RONMENT. FROM THE HOW WE BUILD THINGS SE-
RIES.
PROD-EGH   DIST-EGH   1972

HOW WE BUILD HOUSES   C 42 FRS
SOUND FILMSTRIP - AUDIO TAPE
SHOWS THE BASIC CONCEPTS OF HOUSE CON-
STRUCTION. FROM THE HOW WE BUILD THINGS
SERIES.
PROD-EGH   DIST-EGH   1972

HOW WE BUILD ROADS   C 45 FRS
SOUND FILMSTRIP - AUDIO TAPE
DESCRIBES THE PROBLEMS INVOLVED IN ROAD-
BUILDING. FROM THE HOW WE BUILD THINGS SE-
RIES.
PROD-EGH   DIST-EGH   1972

HOW WE BUILD SHIPS   C 55 FRS
SOUND FILMSTRIP - AUDIO TAPE
DESCRIBES THE MAJOR METHODS BY WHICH
MAN BUILDS SHIPS. FROM THE HOW WE BUILD
THINGS SERIES.
PROD-EGH   DIST-EGH   1972

HOW WE BUILD SKYSCRAPERS   C 42 FRS
SOUND FILMSTRIP - AUDIO TAPE
DESCRIBES THE BASIC CONSTRUCTION METHODS
USED IN BUILDING A SKYSCRAPER AND COM-
PARES THE CONSTRUCTION TO THAT OF A HOUSE.
FROM THE HOW WE BUILD THINGS SERIES.
PROD-EGH   DIST-EGH   1972

HOW WE BUILD THINGS--A
SERIES
PROD-EGH   DIST-EGH   1972

HOW WE BUILD BRIDGES   51 FRS
HOW WE BUILD CITIES   48 FRS
HOW WE BUILD HOUSES   42 FRS
HOW WE BUILD ROADS   45 FRS
HOW WE BUILD SHIPS   55 FRS
HOW WE BUILD SKYSCRAPERS   42 FRS

HOW WE KNOW ABOUT THE
CIVIL WAR   C 34 FRS
SOUND FILMSTRIP - RECORD
PRESENTS AN INTRODUCTION TO HISTORIOGRA-
PHY AS EXEMPLIFIED IN THE STUDY OF THE CIVIL
WAR. FROM THE CIVIL WAR AS IT HAPPENED SE-
RIES.
LC NO. 72-735141
PROD-EDREC   DIST-TECVIS   1970

HOW WE WRITE   C 38 FRS
SOUND FILMSTRIP - AUDIO TAPE
DESCRIBES THE PROPER CONDITIONS AND THE
PROPER MANNER OF WRITING. FROM THE LEARN
TO WRITE WITH LETTY LETTER SERIES.
PROD-EGH   DIST-EGH   1972

HUMAN ANATOMY AND
PHYSIOLOGY--A SERIES
     H-C A
LC NO. 72-736386
PROD-HRAW   DIST-HRAW   1973

CIRCULATION - BLOOD CIRCULATION
CIRCULATION - BLOOD PRESSURE
CIRCULATION - FUNCTION OF THE
HEART
DIGESTION - CONCEPTS OF DIGESTION
DIGESTION OF FOODS
FUNCTION OF THE EAR
FUNCTION OF THE EYE
FUNCTION OF THE KIDNEY
MOVEMENTS OF THE HUMAN BODY
MUSCLE - PHYSIOLOGICAL
CHARACTERISTICS
NERVOUS SYSTEM - REFLEX ARC
NERVOUS SYSTEM - THE AUTONOMIC
NERVOUS SYSTEM
NERVOUS SYSTEM - TRANSMISSION
OPTICAL PRINCIPLES
RESPIRATION - GAS EXCHANGE
RESPIRATION - MECHANICS OF
VENTILATION

HUMAN HISTOLOGY - SYSTEMS   C 37 FRS
FILMSTRIP
SHOWS MICROSCOPIC PICTURES OF VARIOUS SYS-
TEMS OF THE HUMAN BODY. FROM THE MICRO-
SCOPIC SPECIMENS - A RESOURCE UNIT SERIES.
PROD-EGH   DIST-EGH   1972

HUMAN HISTOLOGY - TISSUE   C 38 FRS
FILMSTRIP
SHOWS MICROSCOPIC PICTURES OF VARIOUS
SPECIMENS OF HUMAN TISSUE. FROM THE MI-
CROSCOPIC SPECIMENS - A RESOURCE UNIT SE-
RIES.
PROD-EGH   DIST-EGH   1972

HUMAN SEXUALITY--A SERIES
PROD-EGH   DIST-EGH   1972

ARE SEX AND LOVE THE SAME THING   64 FRS
ATTITUDES ABOUT HUMAN SEXUALITY   53 FRS
FEMALE OF THE SPECIES, THE   53 FRS
MARRIAGE AND FAMILIES   59 FRS
OUR INSTINCTS AND WHY WE HAVE
THEM   52 FRS

HUMANITIES - A WORLD
BETWEEN WARS, PT 1   C 84 FRS
SOUND FILMSTRIP - RECORD   J-H
EMPHASIZES VAST CULTURAL AND SOCIAL REOR-
GANIZATION THROUGHOUT WESTERN CIVILIZA-
TION. FOCUSES ON NEW KINDS OF LITERATURE,
ART, ARCHITECTURE, BROADCAST AND FILM.
LC NO. 73-733114
PROD-GA   DIST-GA   1972

HUMANITIES - A WORLD
BETWEEN WARS, PT 2   C 99 FRS
SOUND FILMSTRIP - RECORD   J-H
EMPHASIZES VAST CULTURAL AND SOCIAL REOR-
GANIZATION THROUGHOUT WESTERN CIVILIZA-
TION. FOCUSES ON NEW KINDS OF LITERATURE,
ART, ARCHITECTURE, BROADCAST AND FILM.
LC NO. 73-733114
PROD-GA   DIST-GA   1972

HUMANITIES - MAN IN THE
NUCLEAR AGE, PT 1   C 77 FRS
SOUND FILMSTRIP - RECORD   J-H
TRACES THE INCREASING INTERNATIONALIZA-
TION AND POPULARIZATION OF ART AND LITERA-
TURE IN A TECHNOLOGICALLY TRANSFORMED
WORLD. CONSIDERS THE NEW IMPORTANCE OF
FILM AND POPULAR MUSIC.
LC NO. 73-733113
PROD-GA   DIST-GA   1972

HUMANITIES - MAN IN THE
NUCLEAR AGE, PT 2   C 121 FRS
SOUND FILMSTRIP - RECORD   J-H
TRACES THE INCREASING INTERNATIONALIZA-
TION AND POPULARIZATION OF ART AND LITERA-
TURE IN A TECHNOLOGICALLY TRANSFORMED
WORLD. CONSIDERS THE NEW IMPORTANCE OF
FILM AND POPULAR MUSIC.
LC NO. 73-733113
PROD-GA   DIST-GA   1972

HUMANITIES - THE DAWN OF THE TWENTIETH CENTURY, PT 1
C 105 FRS
SOUND FILMSTRIP - RECORD J-H
RELATES WORKS OF G B SHAW, PROUST AND THE AMERICAN MUCKRAKERS TO EMERGING TECHNOLOGY, REVOLUTIONARY SCIENTIFIC THEORY AND MAJOR DEVELOPMENTS IN ART AND FILM.
LC NO. 73-732666
PROD-GA   DIST-GA   1972

HUMANITIES - THE DAWN OF THE TWENTIETH CENTURY, PT 2
C 97 FRS
SOUND FILMSTRIP - RECORD J-H
RELATES WORKS OF G B SHAW, PROUST AND THE AMERICAN MUCKRAKERS TO EMERGING TECHNOLOGY, REVOLUTIONARY SCIENTIFIC THEORY AND MAJOR DEVELOPMENTS IN ART AND FILM.
LC NO. 73-732666
PROD-GA   DIST-GA   1972

HUNGARY - AGRICULTURE TODAY
C 35 FRS
FILMSTRIP
SEE SERIES TITLE FOR DESCRIPTIVE STATEMENT. FROM THE EASTERN EUROPE SERIES.
LC NO. 72-734726
PROD-MGHT   DIST-MGHT   1972

HUNGARY - INDUSTRY AND PROGRESS
C 37 FRS
FILMSTRIP
SEE SERIES TITLE FOR DESCRIPTIVE STATEMENT. FROM THE EASTERN EUROPE SERIES.
LC NO. 72-734725
PROD-MGHT   DIST-MGHT   1972

HYDRAULIC BRAKE SYSTEM EXPLAINED--A SERIES
J-C A
PRESENTS A COMPLETE INTRODUCTION TO THE HYDRAULIC BRAKE SYSTEM. SHOWS THE PARTS AND THEIR OPERATIONS IN SEQUENTIAL PROCEDURE.
LC NO. 73-732672
PROD-BERGL   DIST-BERGL   1972

BASIC PARTS AND PRINCIPLES
HOW TO RELINE DISK-TYPE BRAKES
HOW TO RELINE DRUM-TYPE BRAKES
PROBLEMS - CAUSES AND CORRECTIONS
SERVICING THE HYDRAULIC SYSTEM - DISK-TYPE
SERVICING THE HYDRAULIC SYSTEM - DRUM-TYPE

HYSTERECTOMY FOR UTERINE CANCER
C 80 FRS
SOUND FILMSTRIP - RECORD
DESCRIBES PROCEDURES EMPLOYED IN TREATING CANCER OF THE CERVIX AND ENDOMETRIUM THROUGH SURGERY AND RADIOTHERAPY. FROM THE CANCER, SERIES 3 - TREATMENT MODALITIES WITH IMPLICATIONS FOR NURSING CARE SERIES. NO. 1
LC NO. 72-733173
PROD-CONMED   DIST-CONMED   1972

I AM RISEN AND WITH YOU
C 35 FRS
SOUND FILMSTRIP - RECORD I R
GIVES A FIRST-PERSON PRESENTATION OF THE LIFE OF JESUS. INCLUDES SELECTIONS FROM SEVERAL OF THE GOSPEL NARRATIVES OF THE RESURRECTION PRESENTING JESUS MANIFESTING HIMSELF TO HIS DISCIPLES IN THE ORDINARY EXPERIENCES OF THEIR DAILY LIVES, ON A JOURNEY, AT A MEAL AND FISHING ON THE LAKE OF GALILEE. FROM THE MY NAME IS JESUS SERIES.
LC NO. 72-737438
PROD-ROAS   DIST-ROAS   1972

ICE, PT 1
C 38 FRS
FILMSTRIP WITH SCRIPT I-H
ILLUSTRATES THE EFFECTS OF GLACIATION IN LOWLAND AREAS, NOW OCCUPIED BY SOME OF THE RICH NATIONS OF THE WORLD. FROM THE ORIGINS OF THE EARTH SERIES.
LC NO. 73-733001
PROD-VISPUB   DIST-VISPUB   1970

ICE, PT 2
C 39 FRS
FILMSTRIP WITH SCRIPT I-H
ILLUSTRATES THE EFFECTS OF EROSION. FROM THE ORIGINS OF THE EARTH SERIES.
LC NO. 73-733002
PROD-VISPUB   DIST-VISPUB   1970

ICE, PT 3
C 39 FRS
FILMSTRIP WITH SCRIPT I-H
SHOWS THE RESULTS OF GLACIATION IN THE MAIN VALLEYS OF HIGHLAND AREAS. FROM THE ORIGINS OF THE EARTH SERIES.
LC NO. 73-733003
PROD-VISPUB   DIST-VISPUB   1970

IDENTIFICATION OF ELECTRIC WIRING ITEMS
C 66 FRS
FILMSTRIP WITH CAPTIONS H-C
TEACHES IDENTIFICATION OF COMMONLY USED ELECTRICAL ITEMS, PRIMARILY FOR USE BY TEACHERS WHEN UNPACKING AND CHECKING ITEMS CONTAINED IN THE VOCATIONAL AGRICULTURE SERVICE WIRING LOAN BOX.
LC NO. 73-733324
PROD-UILVAS   DIST-UILVAS   1973

IMPROVING YOUR STUDY SKILLS, SET 1 - USING THE TEXTBOOK PLAN--A SERIES
EXAMINES THE ORGANIZATIONAL STRUCTURE OF THE TYPICAL TEXTBOOK.
LC NO. 72-736098
PROD-CREATV   DIST-CREATV

IMPROVING YOUR STUDY SKILLS, SET 2 - INTENSIVE READING--A SERIES
PRESENTS A DEFINITION OF INTENSIVE READING AND THE OBJECTIVES OF INTENSIVE READING AS THEY APPLY TO TEXT MATERIAL.
LC NO. 72-736099
PROD-CREATV   DIST-CREATV

IMPROVING YOUR STUDY SKILLS, SET 3 - INTENSIVE READING EXERCISES--A SERIES
PRESENTS EXERCISES IN INTENSIVE READING OF TEXT READING MATERIAL.
LC NO. 72-736100
PROD-CREATV   DIST-CREATV

IN OUR DAILY LIFE
C 78 FRS
SOUND FILMSTRIP - AUDIO TAPE
DESCRIBES COMMON TERMS USED IN OUR DAILY LIVES. FROM THE INTRODUCTION TO ENGLISH AS A SECOND LANGUAGE SERIES.
PROD-EGH   DIST-EGH   1972

IN THE COMMUNITY
C 82 FRS
SOUND FILMSTRIP - AUDIO TAPE
DESCRIBES COMMON TERMS USED IN THE COMMUNITY AND THEIR ASSOCIATED VERBS. FROM THE INTRODUCTION TO ENGLISH AS A SECOND LANGUAGE SERIES.
PROD-EGH   DIST-EGH   1972

IN THE HOME
C 84 FRS
SOUND FILMSTRIP - AUDIO TAPE
DESCRIBES COMMON HOUSEHOLD OBJECTS AND THEIR ASSOCIATED VERBS. FROM THE INTRODUCTION TO ENGLISH AS A SECOND LANGUAGE SERIES.
PROD-EGH   DIST-EGH   1972

IN THE STORE
C 84 FRS
SOUND FILMSTRIP - AUDIO TAPE
DESCRIBES COMMON TERMS ASSOCIATED WITH STORES ALONG WITH ASSOCIATED VERBS. FROM THE INTRODUCTION TO ENGLISH AS A SECOND LANGUAGE SERIES.
PROD-EGH   DIST-EGH   1972

INCAS, THE
C 47 FRS
SOUND FILMSTRIP - AUDIO TAPE I-J
PRESENTS THE CULTURE, GOVERNMENT, RELIGION AND ACHIEVEMENTS OF THE INCAS AND THEIR GREAT EMPIRE, WHICH ONCE COVERED ONE-FOURTH OF THE SOUTH AMERICAN CONTINENT. FROM THE ANCIENT CIVILIZATIONS OF THE AMERICAS SERIES.
LC NO. 72-737363
PROD-EBEC   DIST-EBEC   1972

INDIANS OF AMERICA--A SERIES
PROD-EGH   DIST-EGH   1972

AFTER THE SETTLERS CAME   29 FRS
EARLY AMERICAN INDIAN   31 FRS
PLAINS INDIANS, THE   35 FRS

INDUSTRIAL WORKER
C 54 FRS
SOUND FILMSTRIP - AUDIO TAPE
DESCRIBES THE GROWING INDUSTRIALIZATION AND ITS EFFECTS ON INDIVIDUALS AND COUNTRIES. FROM THE LIFEWAYS OF THE PEOPLE - SOUTH AMERICA SERIES.

PROD-EGH   DIST-EGH   1972

INHALATION THERAPY TECHNICIAN
C 52 FRS
SOUND FILMSTRIP - AUDIO TAPE
SHOWS THE VARIOUS ASPECTS OF THE JOB OF THE INHALATION THERAPIST. FROM THE HOSPITAL JOB OPPORTUNITIES SERIES.
PROD-EGH   DIST-EGH   1972

INPUT-OUTPUT - HOW COMPUTERS READ AND WRITE
B 58 FRS
SOUND FILMSTRIP H
DEMONSTRATES INPUT-OUTPUT METHODS AND EQUIPMENT AND EXPLAINS THE FUNCTION OF PERIPHERAL UNITS USED FOR INPUT-OUTPUT PURPOSES. DETAILS THE FUNCTIONS AND METHODS OF COMPUTER ACCESS. FROM THE HOW COMPUTERS WORK SERIES.
LC NO. 73-732750
PROD-EBEC   DIST-EBEC   1972

INSIDE THE PEOPLE'S REPUBLIC OF CHINA--A SERIES
PROD-EGH   DIST-EGH   1972

COMMUNES IN CHINA   50 FRS
EDUCATION AND COMMUNICATION IN CHINA   57 FRS
HEALTH SERVICES IN CHINA   43 FRS
PEOPLE OF CHINA, THE   53 FRS
TRADE AND TRANSPORTATION IN CHINA   75 FRS
WORK OF THE PEOPLE OF CHINA   63 FRS

INTERNAL COMBUSTION ENGINE EXPLAINED--A SERIES
J-C A
PRESENTS A COMPLETE INTRODUCTION TO THE INTERNAL COMBUSTION ENGINE, SHOWING THE PARTS AND THEIR OPERATIONS IN SEQUENTIAL PROCEDURE.
LC NO. 73-732671
PROD-BERGL   DIST-BERGL   1972

BASIC PARTS AND OPERATION
CARBURETION, IGNITION AND COOLING
HOW TO DO A VALVE JOB
LUBRICATION AND VALVE OPERATION
VALVE PROBLEMS - CAUSES AND CORRECTIONS

INTRODUCTION TO CANCER SURGERY - MASTECTOMY
C 109 FRS
SOUND FILMSTRIP - RECORD
PRESENTS THE USE OF SURGERY, RADIOTHERAPY AND CHEMOTHERAPY IN CANCER TREATMENT. FROM THE CANCER, SERIES 3 - TREATMENT MODALITIES WITH IMPLICATIONS FOR NURSING CARE SERIES. NO. 2
LC NO. 72-733172
PROD-CONMED   DIST-CONMED   1972

INTRODUCTION TO ENGLISH AS A SECOND LANGUAGE --A SERIES
PROD-EGH   DIST-EGH   1972

ACTIONS AND CONDITIONS   84 FRS
COMMON OBJECTS   84 FRS
DAYS, MONTHS, SEASONS, WEATHER   82 FRS
DESCRIBING   82 FRS
IN OUR DAILY LIFE   78 FRS
IN THE COMMUNITY   82 FRS
IN THE HOME   84 FRS
IN THE STORE   84 FRS
MORE ACTIONS AND CONDITIONS   84 FRS
NUMBERS AND MONEY   80 FRS
PRONOUNS   46 FRS
QUALIFYING   79 FRS

INTRODUCTION TO OXYACETYLENE WELDING
C 50 FRS
SOUND FILMSTRIP - AUDIO TAPE
ILLUSTRATES AND EXPLAINS THE OXYACETYLENE METHOD OF WELDING.
LC NO. 73-740693
PROD-LIBFSC   DIST-LIBFSC

INTRODUCTION TO SECURITIES MARKETS
C
SOUND FILMSTRIP - AUDIO TAPE
SEE SERIES TITLE FOR DESCRIPTIVE STATEMENT. FROM THE NATION OF OWNERS SERIES.
LC NO. 72-736600
PROD-EMP   DIST-XEROX

INTRODUCTION TO THE NEUROSCIENCES, AN
C 63 FRS
FILMSTRIP WITH SCRIPT
INCLUDES ILLUSTRATIONS RELATING TO THE BRAIN'S STRUCTURE, NEUROBRYOLOGY, NEUROCYTOLOGY AND OTHER RELATED AREAS.

LC NO. 72-736825
PROD-SAUNDW   DIST-SAUNDW

ITALIAN AMERICANS   C 93 FRS
SOUND FILMSTRIP - RECORD   I-J
SEE SERIES TITLE FOR DESCRIPTIVE STATEMENT.
FROM THE AMERICAN ADVENTURE SERIES.
LC NO. 72-737417
PROD-FIELEP   DIST-FIELEP   1972

ITALIAN CULTURE AND
RECREATION   C 24 FRS
SOUND FILMSTRIP - AUDIO TAPE
DESCRIBES SEVERAL OF THE MAJOR ELEMENTS
OF ITALIAN CIVILIZATION. FROM THE ITALY - A RE-
GIONAL SURVEY SERIES.
LC NO. 72-736587
PROD-EGH   DIST-EGH   1972

ITALIAN CULTURE AND
RECREATION   C 31 FRS
SOUND FILMSTRIP - AUDIO TAPE
DESCRIBES SEVERAL OF THE MAJOR ELEMENTS
OF ITALIAN CIVILIZATION. FROM THE ITALY - A RE-
GIONAL STUDY SERIES.
LC NO. 72-736587
PROD-EGH   DIST-EGH

ITALIAN HOME AND FAMILY,
THE   C 34 FRS
SOUND FILMSTRIP - AUDIO TAPE
DESCRIBES SOME OF THE MAJOR ELEMENTS OF
ITALIAN LIFE, AT HOME, SCHOOL AND AT THE
MARKET. FROM THE ITALY - A REGIONAL SURVEY
SERIES.
LC NO. 72-736583
PROD-EGH   DIST-EGH   1972

ITALIANS AT WORK   C 30 FRS
SOUND FILMSTRIP - AUDIO TAPE
DESCRIBES THE VARIOUS INDUSTRIES AND OCCU-
PATIONS OF THE ITALIANS. FROM THE ITALY - A
REGIONAL SURVEY SERIES.
LC NO. 72-736584
PROD-EGH   DIST-EGH   1972

ITALY   C
SOUND FILMSTRIP - AUDIO TAPE   P-I
DESCRIBES OUR INHERITANCE FROM ANCIENT,
PAGAN ROME IN ARCHITECTURE, BUILDING
METHODS, ARTS, LAW, LITERATURE AND LAN-
GUAGE. DISCUSSES THE GREAT REVIVAL IN ART,
EDUCATION AND SCIENCE WHICH BEGAN DURING
THE ITALIAN RENAISSANCE AND SPREAD
THROUGHOUT EUROPE. FROM THE NEW FRIENDS
FROM DISTANT LANDS - THE CULTURE WE SHARE
SERIES.
PROD-PATED   DIST-PATED   1973

ITALY - A REGIONAL STUDY--A
SERIES

PROD-EGH   DIST-EGH

CITIES OF ITALY   57 FRS
CITIES OF ROME AND FLORENCE   55 FRS
FLORENCE AND VENICE   36 FRS
GREAT MEN AND ARTISTS   24 FRS
ITALIAN CULTURE AND RECREATION   31 FRS
ITALY - THE LAND   38 FRS

ITALY - A REGIONAL SURVEY--A
SERIES

PROD-EGH   DIST-EGH   1972

CITIES OF ITALY   49 FRS
CITIES OF ROME AND FLORENCE   47 FRS
FLORENCE AND VENICE   28 FRS
GREAT MEN AND ARTISTS   18 FRS
ITALIAN CULTURE AND RECREATION   24 FRS
ITALIAN HOME AND FAMILY, THE   34 FRS
ITALIANS AT WORK   30 FRS
ITALY - THE LAND   32 FRS

ITALY - THE LAND   C 32 FRS
SOUND FILMSTRIP - AUDIO TAPE
DESCRIBES THE MAJOR REGIONS AND GEOGRAPH-
ICAL FEATURES OF ITALY. FROM THE ITALY - A RE-
GIONAL SURVEY SERIES.
LC NO. 72-736585
PROD-EGH   DIST-EGH   1972

ITALY - THE LAND   C 38 FRS
SOUND FILMSTRIP - AUDIO TAPE
DESCRIBES THE MAJOR REGIONS AND GEOGRAPH-
ICAL FEATURES OF ITALY. FROM THE ITALY - A RE-
GIONAL STUDY SERIES.
LC NO. 72-736585

PROD-EGH   DIST-EGH   *

J

JAIL TERM BEFORE TRIAL   C 59 FRS
SOUND FILMSTRIP - AUDIO TAPE   I-J
SEE SERIES TITLE FOR DESCRIPTIVE STATEMENT.
FROM THE MIND BLOWERS SERIES.
LC NO. 73-733281
PROD-SNBRST   DIST-SNBRST   1973

JAPAN   B 84 FRS
FILMSTRIP WITH CAPTIONS
SURVEYS LIFE IN JAPAN FROM THE PERIOD BE-
FORE WORLD WAR II TO THE PRESENT DAY.
LC NO. FI53-1244
PROD-TF   DIST-TF

JOHN PAUL JONES   C 46 FRS
SOUND FILMSTRIP - AUDIO TAPE   I-H
DEPICTS JOHN PAUL JONES, A SCOTTISH IMMI-
GRANT, WHO WAS TO BECOME THE DRIVING
FORCE BEHIND THE DEVELOPMENT OF THE AMER-
ICAN NAVY. FROM THE FAMOUS PATRIOTS OF THE
AMERICAN REVOLUTION SERIES.
LC NO. 73-732984
PROD-CORF   DIST-CORF   1973

JUNGLE AND DESERT PLANTS   C 40 FRS
SOUND FILMSTRIP - RECORD   P-J
SEE SERIES TITLE FOR DESCRIPTIVE STATEMENT.
FROM THE GROWING THINGS SERIES.
PROD-TERF   DIST-TERF   1973

K

KINDS OF WRITING   C 32 FRS
SOUND FILMSTRIP - AUDIO TAPE
DESCRIBES VARIOUS TYPES OF WRITING, BOTH
ANCIENT AND MODERN. FROM THE LEARN TO
WRITE WITH LETTY LETTER SERIES.
PROD-EGH   DIST-EGH   1972

L

LA FERIA POTOSINA - UN
PASEO EN ACAPULCO   C 44 FRS
SOUND FILMSTRIP - AUDIO TAPE
FROM THE LA JUVENTUD DE AMERICA LATINA
SERIES.
LC NO. FIA65-2707
PROD-STDYSC   DIST-STDYSC

LA JUVENTUD DE AMERICA
LATINA--A SERIES

PROD-STDYSC   DIST-STDYSC

LA FERIA POTOSINA - UN PASEO EN
ACAPULCO   44 FRS
LA JUVENTUD DE LA CIUDAD   38 FRS
LA JUVENTUD DE LA PROVINCIA   38 FRS
LAS ESCUELAS SECONDARIAS   38 FRS

LA JUVENTUD DE LA CIUDAD   C 38 FRS
SOUND FILMSTRIP - AUDIO TAPE
FROM THE LA JUVENTUD DE AMERICA LATINA
SERIES.
LC NO. FIA65-2707
PROD-STDYSC   DIST-STDYSC

LA JUVENTUD DE LA PROVINCIA   C 38 FRS
SOUND FILMSTRIP - AUDIO TAPE
FROM THE LA JUVENTUD DE AMERICA LATINA
SERIES.
LC NO. FIA65-2707
PROD-STDYSC   DIST-STDYSC

LAND, FEATURES AND CITIES   C 49 FRS
SOUND FILMSTRIP - AUDIO TAPE
OUTLINES THE MORE IMPORTANT GEOGRAPHIC
FEATURES AND SOME OF THE IMPORTANT CITIES.
FROM THE GREAT BRITAIN - A REGIONAL STUDY
SERIES.
LC NO. 72-736526
PROD-EGH   DIST-EGH   1972

LAND, FEATURES AND CITIES   C 55 FRS
SOUND FILMSTRIP - AUDIO TAPE
GIVES INFORMATION ABOUT THE GEOGRAPHY,
CLIMATE AND CITIES OF HOLLAND. FROM THE
HOLLAND - A REGIONAL STUDY SERIES.
PROD-EGH   DIST-EGH   1972

LANGUAGE LABORATORY, THE   C 55 FRS
FILMSTRIP
DESCRIBES THE AUDIO-LINGUAL APPROACH TO
TEACHING FOREIGN LANGUAGES IN THE LAN-
GUAGE LABORATORY. FROM THE AUDIO-VISUAL
SERIES.
LC NO. FIA66-3567
PROD-BSF   DIST-BSF   1966

LAS ESCUELAS SECONDARIAS   C 38 FRS
SOUND FILMSTRIP - AUDIO TAPE
FROM THE LA JUVENTUD DE AMERICA LATINA
SERIES.
LC NO. FIA65-2707
PROD-STDYSC   DIST-STDYSC

LATIN TEENAGERS JUNIOR--A
SERIES

PROD-STDYSC   DIST-STDYSC

LA FERIA POTOSINA - UN PASEO EN
ACAPULCO   44 FRS
LA JUVENTUD DE LA CIUDAD   38 FRS
LA JUVENTUD DE LA PROVINCIA   38 FRS
LAS ESCUELAS SECONDARIAS   38 FRS

LAZY CAT, THE   C 24 FRS
SOUND FILMSTRIP - AUDIO TAPE   K-P
EXPLAINS HOW A LAZY AND SELF-CENTERED CAT
IS PERSUADED TO CHANGE HIS BEHAVIOR IN A
VILLAGE WHERE ONLY ANIMALS LIVE AND WHERE
SUPPLYING THE NECESSITIES OF LIVING IS THE
RESPONSIBILITY OF EVERY ANIMAL. FROM THE
CHILDREN'S STORIES SERIES.
LC NO. 72-737494
PROD-STNHM   DIST-STNHM   1972

LEARN TO WRITE WITH LETTY
LETTER--A SERIES

PROD-EGH   DIST-EGH   1972

CURSIVE WRITING - CAPITAL LETTERS,
PT 1   64 FRS
CURSIVE WRITING - CAPITAL LETTERS,
PT 2   74 FRS
CURSIVE WRITING - SMALL LETTERS, PT
1   59 FRS
CURSIVE WRITING - SMALL LETTERS, PT
2   75 FRS
HOW WE WRITE   38 FRS
KINDS OF WRITING   32 FRS
MANUSCRIPT WRITING - SMALL
LETTERS, PT 1   64 FRS
MANUSCRIPT WRITING - SMALL
LETTERS, PT 2   45 FRS
MANUSCRIPT WRITING FOR CAPITAL
LETTERS, PT 1   64 FRS
MANUSCRIPT WRITING FOR CAPITAL
LETTERS, PT 2   56 FRS
WHY WE WRITE   30 FRS
WRITING READINESS   41 FRS

LEBANON   C
SOUND FILMSTRIP - AUDIO TAPE   P-I
TELLS OF THE SPREAD OF PHOENICIAN CULTURE,
ITS MANY ADVANCES IN MANUFACTURING AND
PRODUCTION METHODS AND ITS MAJOR CONTRI-
BUTION, THE ALPHABET. VISITS SEVERAL AN-
CIENT CITIES AS WELL AS MODERN BEIRUT AND A
CHILDREN'S SCHOOL. FROM THE NEW FRIENDS
FROM DISTANT LANDS - THE CULTURE WE SHARE
SERIES.
PROD-PATED   DIST-PATED   1973

LET'S LOOK AT DRUGS--A
SERIES

PROD-EGH   DIST-EGH   1972

ALCOHOL AND TOBACCO   52 FRS
DOCTOR'S VIEWPOINT   56 FRS
DRUGS AND YOUR FUTURE   52 FRS
ECOLOGY OF OUR BODIES   53 FRS
MARIJUANA, STIMULANTS AND
DEPRESSANTS   50 FRS
PILLS IN A PILL CULTURE   55 FRS

LEWIS-LIES-A-LOT   C 53 FRS
SOUND FILMSTRIP - AUDIO TAPE
PRESENTS THE DISTINCTION BETWEEN TRUTH
AND FALSEHOOD. FROM THE GUIDES FOR GROW-
ING SERIES.
LC NO. 72-736522
PROD-EGH   DIST-EGH   1972

**LIFE - A UNIQUE PHENOMENON-
-A SERIES**

PROD-EGH	DIST-EGH	1972

ADAPTATIONS FOR LIFE	42 FRS
ENERGY AND LIFE	36 FRS
PERPETUATING LIFE	39 FRS
WHAT IS LIFE	41 FRS

LIFE COMES TO THE WORLD   C 40 FRS
            SOUND FILMSTRIP - AUDIO TAPE   P-I
SEE SERIES TITLE FOR DESCRIPTIVE STATEMENT.
FROM THE FABLES AND FACTS SERIES.
PROD-TERF   DIST-TERF   1973

LIFE IN BRITAIN   C 47 FRS
            SOUND FILMSTRIP - AUDIO TAPE
EXAMINES SOME OF THE LIFE-STYLES OF THE
BRITISH PEOPLE. FROM THE GREAT BRITAIN - A
REGIONAL STUDY SERIES.
    LC NO. 72-736529
PROD-EGH   DIST-EGH   1972

LIFE IN HOLLAND   C 45 FRS
            SOUND FILMSTRIP - AUDIO TAPE
EXAMINES SOME OF THE LIFESTYLES OF THE
DUTCH. FROM THE HOLLAND - A REGIONAL STUDY
SERIES.
PROD-EGH   DIST-EGH   1972

LIFE OF THE LEISURE CLASS   C 51 FRS
            SOUND FILMSTRIP - AUDIO TAPE
DESCRIBES THE LIFEWAYS OF THE SOUTH AMER-
ICA LEISURE CLASSES. FROM THE LIFEWAYS OF
THE PEOPLE - SOUTH AMERICA SERIES.
PROD-EGH   DIST-EGH   1972

**LIFEWAYS OF THE PEOPLE -
SOUTH AMERICA--A SERIES**

PROD-EGH	DIST-EGH	1972

CHILDREN	50 FRS
CITY LIFE	52 FRS
INDUSTRIAL WORKER	54 FRS
LIFE OF THE LEISURE CLASS	51 FRS
RANCH LIFE	51 FRS
VILLAGE LIFE	52 FRS

LIGHTING, PT 1   B 67 FRS
            SOUND FILMSTRIP - AUDIO TAPE   J-C A
DISCUSSES TECHNICAL FACTORS OF LIGHT AND
ITS USES. FROM THE CREATIVE PHOTOGRAPHY -
CAMERA SERIES.
    LC NO. 73-732516
PROD-ARIZSU   DIST-ARIZSU   1973

LIGHTING, PT 2   B 85 FRS
            SOUND FILMSTRIP - AUDIO TAPE   J-C A
DEMONSTRATES THE POSITIONING OF LIGHTS
AND SUBJECT TO CAPTURE A MOOD TO EMPHA-
SIZE TEXTURE OR TO PRODUCE A MORE PLEASING
PICTURE. FROM THE CREATIVE PHOTOGRAPHY -
CAMERA SERIES.
    LC NO. 73-732517
PROD-ARIZSU   DIST-ARIZSU   1973

LION, THE   C
            FILMSTRIP WITH CAPTIONS
FROM THE ANIMALS SERIES.
    LC NO. 72-734417
PROD-LIEB   DIST-MSCF   1970

**LITERATURE AND THE FILM -
BEAUTY AND THE BEAST**   B 87 FRS
            SOUND FILMSTRIP - RECORD   I-C
PRESENTS MADAME LE PRINCE DE BEAUMONT'S
FAIRY TALE, 'BEAUTY AND THE BEAST' AS IT IS
TREATED BY THE AUTHOR AS WELL AS BY THE DI-
RECTOR, JEAN COCTEAU, IN THE MOVIE OF THE
SAME NAME. FROM THE LITERATURE AND THE
FILM SERIES.
    LC NO. 72-737526
PROD-EDDIM   DIST-EDDIM   1972

**LITERATURE AND THE FILM -
BLACK ORPHEUS**   C 82 FRS
            SOUND FILMSTRIP - RECORD   I-C
PRESENTS THE GREEK LEGEND OF ORPHEUS AND
EURYDICE AS IT IS TREATED BY MARCEL CAMUS
IN THE MOVIE OF THE SAME NAME. FROM THE
LITERATURE AND THE FILM SERIES.
    LC NO. 72-737527
PROD-EDDIM   DIST-EDDIM   1972

**LITERATURE AND THE FILM -
OLIVER TWIST**   C 85 FRS
            SOUND FILMSTRIP - RECORD   I-C
PRESENTS THE CHARLES DICKEN'S NOVEL, 'OLI-
VER TWIST,' AS IT IS TREATED BY DICKENS AS
WELL AS THE WAY DAVID LEAN DIRECTED THE
MOVIE OF THE SAME NAME. FROM THE LITERA-
TURE AND THE FILM SERIES.
    LC NO. 72-737529
PROD-EDDIM   DIST-EDDIM   1972

**LITERATURE AND THE FILM -
THE IMPORTANCE OF BEING
EARNEST**   C 80 FRS
            SOUND FILMSTRIP - RECORD   I-C
EXPLAINS OSCAR WILDE'S PLAY, 'THE IMPOR-
TANCE OF BEING EARNEST,' AS IT IS TREATED BY
WILDE AS WELL AS THE WAY DIRECTOR ANTHONY
ASQUITH DIRECTED THE MOVIE OF THE SAME
NAME. FROM THE LITERATURE AND THE FILM SE-
RIES.
    LC NO. 72-737528
PROD-EDDIM   DIST-EDDIM   1972

**LITERATURE AND THE FILM--A
SERIES**
                                           I-C
PRESENTS MAJOR LITERARY MASTERWORKS AS
SEEN THROUGH THE EYES OF THE WORLD'S DI-
RECTORS.
    LC NO. 72-737574
PROD-EDDIM   DIST-EDDIM   1972

LITERATURE AND THE FILM - BEAUTY AND THE BEAST	87 FRS
LITERATURE AND THE FILM - BLACK ORPHEUS	82 FRS
LITERATURE AND THE FILM - OLIVER TWIST	85 FRS
LITERATURE AND THE FILM - THE IMPORTANCE OF --	80 FRS

LITTLE RED RIDING HOOD   C 28 FRS
            SOUND FILMSTRIP - AUDIO TAPE   K-P
FOLLOWS THE EXPERIENCE OF A LITTLE GIRL WHO
MEETS WITH MISFORTUNE AND CAUSES ANXIETY
FOR OTHERS BECAUSE SHE DID NOT OBEY THE
ADVICE GIVEN TO HER BY HER MOTHER. FROM
THE CHILDREN'S STORIES SERIES.
    LC NO. 72-737497
PROD-STNHM   DIST-STNHM   1972

**LIVING IN AFRICA TODAY - A
CITY FAMILY OF MOROCCO**   C 54 FRS
            SOUND FILMSTRIP - RECORD   P-I
PRESENTS THE HOUCIN FAMILY WHO LIVES IN
AGADIR. POINTS OUT THAT THEY LIVE IN A MOS-
LEM WORLD WITH THE MODERN COVENIENCES
THAT MOST OF US ARE FAMILIAR WITH. FROM
THE LIVING IN AFRICA TODAY SERIES.
    LC NO. 73-732604
PROD-CORF   DIST-CORF   1972

**LIVING IN AFRICA TODAY - A
CITY FAMILY OF MALI**   C 48 FRS
            SOUND FILMSTRIP - RECORD   P-I
PRESENTS MR SANGARE WHO WORKS IN BA-
MAKO, THE CAPITAL OF MALI. POINTS OUT THAT
HE DRIVES TO WORK IN A CAR AND HIS FAMILY
ENJOYS A MIDDLE CLASS INCOME. FROM THE LIV-
ING IN AFRICA TODAY SERIES.
    LC NO. 73-732606
PROD-CORF   DIST-CORF   1972

**LIVING IN AFRICA TODAY - A
PROFESSIONAL OF GHANA**   C 50 FRS
            SOUND FILMSTRIP - RECORD   P-I
PRESENTS THE LAAST FAMILY WHO LIVES IN THE
CAPITAL OF GHANA. POINTS OUT THAT MR LAAST
HAS A HIGH GOVERNMENT POSITION, SO HIS FAM-
ILY LIVES COMFORTABLY. FROM THE LIVING IN AF-
RICA TODAY SERIES.
    LC NO. 73-732608
PROD-CORF   DIST-CORF   1972

**LIVING IN AFRICA TODAY - A
SUBURBAN FAMILY OF SOUTH
AFRICA**   C 50 FRS
            SOUND FILMSTRIP - RECORD   P-I
PRESENTS THE MILLS FAMILY, ENGLISH-SPEAKING
WHITE PEOPLE LIVING IN SOUTH AFRICA. POINTS
OUT THAT THEY ARE PART OF THE RULING CLASS
OF THAT COUNTRY. FROM THE LIVING IN AFRICA
TODAY SERIES.
    LC NO. 73-732610
PROD-CORF   DIST-CORF   1972

**LIVING IN AFRICA TODAY - A
VILLAGE FAMILY OF THE UPPER
VOLTA**   C 51 FRS
            SOUND FILMSTRIP - RECORD   P-I
PRESENTS THE KEPANNA FAMILY OF MARGBA.
POINTS OUT THAT THEIR LIFE IS CENTERED
AROUND FARMING AND RAISING LIVESTOCK.
FROM THE LIVING IN AFRICA TODAY SERIES.
    LC NO. 73-732605
PROD-CORF   DIST-CORF   1972

**LIVING IN AFRICA TODAY - A
VILLAGE FAMILY OF MALI**   C 49 FRS
            SOUND FILMSTRIP - RECORD   P-I
POINTS OUT THAT ONLY 30 MILES FROM BAMAKO,
THE ZOUMANA FAMILY RAISES CATTLE THAT ARE
SOLD IN THE CITY. SHOWS THAT THEIR LIFE IS
VERY DIFFERENT FROM THE SANGARES, WHO LIVE
IN MALI. FROM THE LIVING IN AFRICA TODAY SE-
RIES.
    LC NO. 73-732607
PROD-CORF   DIST-CORF   1972

**LIVING IN AFRICA TODAY - A
VILLAGE FAMILY OF ZAIRE**   C 51 FRS
            SOUND FILMSTRIP - RECORD   P-I
SHOWS THAT THE JOSEPH FAMILY LIVES BY GATH-
ERING THE THINGS THAT THE RAINFOREST PRO-
VIDES. POINTS OUT THAT THEIR LIVES ARE
CHANGING. FROM THE LIVING IN AFRICA TODAY
SERIES.
    LC NO. 73-732609
PROD-CORF   DIST-CORF   1972

**LIVING IN AFRICA TODAY - A
WHITE FARM FAMILY OF KENYA**
                                   C 51 FRS
            SOUND FILMSTRIP - RECORD   P-I
POINTS OUT THAT THE FOSTER FAMILY WILL NOT
REMAIN IN KENYA MUCH LONGER, SINCE THE
GOVERNMENT IS BREAKING UP WHITE OWNED
FARMS, CAUSING A CHANGE IN THE FOSTER'S
WAY OF LIFE. FROM THE LIVING IN AFRICA TODAY
SERIES.
    LC NO. 73-732611
PROD-CORF   DIST-CORF   1972

**LIVING IN AFRICA TODAY--A
SERIES**
                                           P-I
PRESENTS FAMILY LIFE IN A 'TYPICAL' DAY OF A
WIDE VARIETY OF AFRICAN FAMILIES, EMPHASIZ-
ING THE DIVERSITY OF CULTURES, RACES, GEO-
GRAPHIC REGIONS, CITY VERSUS VILLAGE LIFE,
OCCUPATIONS, RELIGIONS, CHILDREN AND EDU-
CATION.
PROD-CORF   DIST-CORF   1972

LIVING IN AFRICA TODAY - A CITY FAMILY OF --	54 FRS
LIVING IN AFRICA TODAY - A CITY FAMILY OF MALI	48 FRS
LIVING IN AFRICA TODAY - A PROFESSIONAL OF --	50 FRS
LIVING IN AFRICA TODAY - A SUBURBAN FAMILY OF--	50 FRS
LIVING IN AFRICA TODAY - A VILLAGE FAMILY OF --	51 FRS
LIVING IN AFRICA TODAY - A VILLAGE FAMILY OF 1-	49 FRS
LIVING IN AFRICA TODAY - A VILLAGE FAMILY OF 2-	51 FRS
LIVING IN AFRICA TODAY - A WHITE FARM FAMILY --	51 FRS

**LIVING IN ASIA TODAY -
AMONG THE MARKETS OF
AFGHANISTAN**   C 52 FRS
            SOUND FILMSTRIP - RECORD   P-I
EXAMINES THE ITEMS PEOPLE BRING TO MARKET
IN AFGHANISTAN TO SELL AND WHAT THEY FIND
TO BUY THERE TO PROVIDE AN INSIGHT INTO
HOW THEY LIVE. FROM THE LIVING IN ASIA TODAY
SERIES.
    LC NO. 73-732620
PROD-CORF   DIST-CORF   1972

**LIVING IN ASIA TODAY - AT A
SCHOOL IN KYOTO, JAPAN**   C 48 FRS
            SOUND FILMSTRIP - RECORD   P-I
PORTRAYS STUDENT LIFE IN JAPAN THROUGH
THE EYES OF KIMIE, A JAPANESE GIRL. FROM THE
LIVING IN ASIA TODAY SERIES.
    LC NO. 73-732612
PROD-CORF   DIST-CORF   1972

**LIVING IN ASIA TODAY - AT A
VILLAGE WEDDING IN THE
PUNJAB, INDIA**   C 48 FRS
            SOUND FILMSTRIP - RECORD   P-I
GIVES AN INTIMATE LOOK AT CUSTOMS AND TRA-
DITION IN THE PUNJAB THROUGH A VILLAGE
WEDDING CEREMONY. FROM THE LIVING IN ASIA
TODAY SERIES.
    LC NO. 73-732617
PROD-CORF   DIST-CORF   1972

**LIVING IN ASIA TODAY - IN A
VILLAGE IN AMERICAN SAMOA**   C 51 FRS
            SOUND FILMSTRIP - RECORD   P-I
PRESENTS A PART OF THE UNITED STATES IN THE
SOUTH PACIFIC AS THE SETTING FOR THE LELAFU
FAMILY AND EDUCATIONAL TELEVISION. FROM
THE LIVING IN ASIA TODAY SERIES.
    LC NO. 73-732614
PROD-CORF   DIST-CORF   1972

LIVING IN ASIA TODAY - ON HOUSEBOATS IN KASHMIR C 53 FRS
SOUND FILMSTRIP - RECORD P-I
DEPICTS LIFE ON THE CANALS AND LAKES OF STINAGAR IN KASHMIR. SHOWS HOW WATER REPLACES LAND AS A BASE BUT SIMILARITIES PERSIST. FROM THE LIVING IN ASIA TODAY SERIES.
LC NO. 73-732619
PROD-CORF   DIST-CORF   1972

LIVING IN ASIA TODAY - ON THE ISLAND OF BALI IN INDONESIA C 53 FRS
SOUND FILMSTRIP - RECORD P-I
EXAMINES FAMILY LIFE CENTERED AROUND RELIGIOUS ACTIVITIES ON THE ISLAND OF BALI IN INDONESIA. FROM THE LIVING IN ASIA TODAY SERIES.
LC NO. 73-732615
PROD-CORF   DIST-CORF   1972

LIVING IN ASIA TODAY - WITH A CITY FAMILY OF TAIWAN C 53 FRS
SOUND FILMSTRIP - RECORD P-I
PRESENTS A CLOSE LOOK AT DAILY ACTIVITIES OF A MAIL CLERK ON THE ISLAND OF TAIWAN. INCLUDES A VISIT TO THE CAPITAL. FROM THE LIVING IN ASIA TODAY SERIES.
LC NO. 73-732613
PROD-CORF   DIST-CORF   1972

LIVING IN ASIA TODAY - WITH A FISH SELLER IN MALAYSIA C 49 FRS
SOUND FILMSTRIP - RECORD P-I
POINTS OUT THAT THE CHOO FAMILY IS CHINESE, BUT THEY LIVE IN A MALAYSIAN VILLAGE. REVEALS WHAT THEIR LIFE IS LIKE THROUGH THEIR DAILY ACTIVITIES IN THE MARKET AND IN THE HOME. FROM THE LIVING IN ASIA TODAY SERIES.
LC NO. 73-732616
PROD-CORF   DIST-CORF   1972

LIVING IN ASIA TODAY--A SERIES P-I
SHOWS THE WAY PEOPLE IN ASIA LIVE TODAY, FROM A SCHOOL IN JAPAN TO THE MARKETS OF AFGHANISTAN.
PROD-CORF   DIST-CORF   1972

LIVING IN ASIA TODAY - AMONG THE MARKETS OF -- 52 FRS
LIVING IN ASIA TODAY - AT A SCHOOL IN KYOTO, -- 48 FRS
LIVING IN ASIA TODAY - AT A VILLAGE WEDDING -- 48 FRS
LIVING IN ASIA TODAY - IN A VILLAGE IN -- 51 FRS
LIVING IN ASIA TODAY - ON HOUSEBOATS IN -- 53 FRS
LIVING IN ASIA TODAY - ON THE ISLAND OF BALI -- 53 FRS
LIVING IN ASIA TODAY - WITH A CITY FAMILY OF -- 53 FRS
LIVING IN ASIA TODAY - WITH A FISH SELLER IN -- 49 FRS

LIVING WITH NATURAL GAS C 89 FRS
SOUND FILMSTRIP - RECORD
DEMONSTRATES THE IMPORTANCE OF NATURAL GAS AS AN ENERGY SOURCE FOR THE UNITED STATES.
LC NO. 72-735277
PROD-AMP   DIST-LILC

LONG HAUL TRUCK DRIVER, THE C 91 FRS
SOUND FILMSTRIP - RECORD I-C
PICTURES THE PHYSICAL ENDURANCE, SENSE OF RESPONSIBILITY AND DRIVING SKILLS REQUIRED OF A SUCESSFUL LONG HAUL TRUCK DRIVER. FROM THE EXPLORING CAREERS, GROUP 1 SERIES.
LC NO. 73-733180
PROD-SVE   DIST-SVE   1973

LOOKING GREAT ON A SHOESTRING--A SERIES
PROD-EGH   DIST-EGH   1972

DOING IT ALL ON A BUDGET 48 FRS
FACE FACTS 52 FRS
FIGURE FACTS 41 FRS
FINDING WHAT'S RIGHT FOR YOU 46 FRS
HISTORY OF STYLE AND VOGUE, A 45 FRS
PUTTING IT TOGETHER SO IT WORKS 48 FRS

LOS ANGELES - CITY OF AUTOMOBILES C 83 FRS
SOUND FILMSTRIP - AUDIO TAPE J-H A
EXAMINES THE INFLUENCE OF THE AUTO ON THE CITY OF LOS ANGELES, PARTICULARLY AT THE AUTO'S EFFECT ON THE RATE AND DIRECTION OF THE CITY'S GROWTH AND ITS EFFECT ON THE

POLLUTION OF THE AIR IN AND AROUND LOS ANGELES. FROM THE FOCUS ON AMERICA - THE PACIFIC STATES SERIES.
LC NO. 73-733157
PROD-SVE   DIST-SVE   1972

LUBRICATION AND VALVE OPERATION C
SOUND FILMSTRIP - RECORD J-C A
SEE SERIES TITLE FOR DESCRIPTIVE STATEMENT. FROM THE INTERNAL COMBUSTION ENGINE EXPLAINED SERIES.
PROD-BERGL   DIST-BERGL   1972

M

MAGIC POTION, THE C 30 FRS
SOUND FILMSTRIP - AUDIO TAPE P-I
PRESENTS FLUORIDE - THE MIRACLE CHEMICAL THAT CUTS DOWN ON TOOTH DECAY. EXPLAINS THAT IT ALREADY EXISTS IN THE WATER IN SOME CITIES, BUT THAT IF WE CAN'T GET IT OUT OF OUR FAUCETS, WE CAN BUY IT OR USE A TOOTHPASTE WITH FLUORIDE. FROM THE PRACTICING GOOD HEALTH, SET 2 - YOUR MOUTH SPEAKING SERIES.
LC NO. 73-733202
PROD-DISNEY   DIST-DISNEY   1973

MAGICAL COQUI C 35 FRS
SOUND FILMSTRIP - RECORD P
ILLUSTRATES A STORY FOR CHILDREN ABOUT A CHILD FROM A MINORITY GROUP.
LC NO. 72-733770
PROD-UMM   DIST-UMM

MAINTENANCE MECHANIC, ELECTRICIAN AND CUSTODIAN C 63 FRS
SOUND FILMSTRIP - AUDIO TAPE
DESCRIBES THE IMPORTANT FUNCTIONS OF THE MAINTENANCE MECHANIC, ELECTRICIAN AND CUSTODIAN. FROM THE HOSPITAL JOB OPPORTUNITIES SERIES.
PROD-EGH   DIST-EGH   1972

MAKING CLOTHING C 40 FRS
SOUND FILMSTRIP - AUDIO TAPE
SHOWS STEPS INVOLVED IN THE MASS PRODUCTION OF CLOTHING. FROM THE HOW THINGS ARE MADE SERIES.
LC NO. 72-736554
PROD-EGH   DIST-EGH   1972

MAKING OF THE AMERICAN NATION, PT 1 - THE COLONIZATION OF AMERICA C 23 FRS
FILMSTRIP WITH SCRIPT
EXAMINES THE DIFFERING ECONOMIC, RELIGIOUS AND SOCIAL REASONS OF THE ENGLISH, FRENCH AND SPANISH FOR COLONIZING THE NEW WORLD. FROM THE CONCEPT-CENTERED LESSONS IN AMERICAN HISTORY, UNIT 1 SERIES.
LC NO. 72-735150
PROD-VISTAP   DIST-FPC

MAKING OF THE AMERICAN NATION, PT 2 - THE AMERICAN REVOLUTION C 23 FRS
FILMSTRIP WITH SCRIPT
FROM THE CONCEPT-CENTERED LESSONS IN AMERICAN HISTORY, UNIT 1 SERIES.
LC NO. 72-735151
PROD-VISTAP   DIST-FPC

MAN ON THE MOON--A SERIES I-J
EXAMINES MANY ASPECTS OF THE FIELD OF ASTRONAUTICS. SHOWS HOW THE TOOLS AND METHODS DEVELOPED FOR THE SPACE AGE CAN BE APPLIED TO THE PROBLEMS OF THE '70'S. COVERS THE HISTORY OF ASTRONAUTICS, ROCKETRY AND SPACE FLIGHT.
PROD-DOUBLE   DIST-DOUBLE   1971

DIVIDENDS FROM SPACE 114 FRS
EAGLE HAS LANDED, THE - MAN ON THE MOON 85 FRS
HISTORY OF ASTRONAUTICS, THE, PT 1 70 FRS
HISTORY OF ASTRONAUTICS, THE, PT 2 86 FRS
STATIONS IN SPACE 86 FRS

MANUSCRIPT WRITING - SMALL LETTERS, PT 1 C 64 FRS
SOUND FILMSTRIP - AUDIO TAPE
TEACHES MANUSCRIPT WRITING THROUGH THE USE OF VERSE AND PROSE. FROM THE LEARN TO WRITE WITH LETTY LETTER SERIES.
PROD-EGH   DIST-EGH   1972

MANUSCRIPT WRITING - SMALL LETTERS, PT 2 C 45 FRS
SOUND FILMSTRIP - AUDIO TAPE
TEACHES MANUSCRIPT WRITING THROUGH THE USE OF VERSE AND PROSE. FROM THE LEARN TO WRITE WITH LETTY LETTER SERIES.
PROD-EGH   DIST-EGH   1972

MANUSCRIPT WRITING FOR CAPITAL LETTERS, PT 1 C 64 FRS
SOUND FILMSTRIP - AUDIO TAPE
TEACHES MANUSCRIPT WRITING THROUGH THE USE OF VERSE AND PROSE. FROM THE LEARN TO WRITE WITH LETTY LETTER SERIES.
PROD-EGH   DIST-EGH   1972

MANUSCRIPT WRITING FOR CAPITAL LETTERS, PT 2 C 56 FRS
SOUND FILMSTRIP - AUDIO TAPE
TEACHES MANUSCRIPT WRITING THROUGH THE USE OF VERSE AND PROSE. FROM THE LEARN TO WRITE WITH LETTY LETTER SERIES.
PROD-EGH   DIST-EGH   1972

MARIJUANA AND GLUE - KIDS, TRICKS AND TRAPS B 72 FRS
SOUND FILMSTRIP - AUDIO TAPE P-I
EXPLORES THE CAUSES AND EFFECTS OF SMOKING MARIJUANA AND SNIFFING GLUE. FROM THE DRUGS - A TRICK, A TRAP SERIES.
LC NO. 72-737375
PROD-EBEC   DIST-EBEC   1972

MARIJUANA, STIMULANTS AND DEPRESSANTS C 50 FRS
SOUND FILMSTRIP - AUDIO TAPE
DESCRIBES THE EFFECTS OF MARIJUANA, STIMULANTS AND DEPRESSANTS. DISCUSSES THEIR HARMFUL SUBSTANCES. FROM THE LET'S LOOK AT DRUGS SERIES.
PROD-EGH   DIST-EGH   1972

MARRIAGE AND FAMILIES C 59 FRS
SOUND FILMSTRIP - AUDIO TAPE
DISCUSSES THE CONTRIBUTION OF SENSITIVITY, AWARENESS, UNDERSTANDING AND ACCEPTANCE. FROM THE HUMAN SEXUALITY SERIES.
PROD-EGH   DIST-EGH   1972

MARY JANE AND BUTTERFLY C 16 FRS
SOUND FILMSTRIP - AUDIO TAPE
TELLS THE DANGERS OF DRUG ADDICTION. FROM THE GUIDES FOR GROWING SERIES.
LC NO. 72-736521
PROD-EGH   DIST-EGH   1972

MATH - DECIMAL NUMERATION--A SERIES J-H
PROD-UNISYS   DIST-VIEWLX   1973

DECIMAL FRACTIONS 65 FRS
DECIMAL SYSTEM 28 FRS
DEVELOPMENT OF OUR NUMBER SYSTEM 26 FRS

MATHEMATICS - FUNDAMENTAL OPERATIONS--A SERIES J-H
PROD-UNISYS   DIST-VIEWLX   1972

BASES AND EXPONENTS 29 FRS
FACTORING NUMBERS 29 FRS
MULTIPLYING FACTORS 29 FRS

MATHEMATICS - GRAPHING--A SERIES I-H
PROD-UNISYS   DIST-VIEWLX   1972

FOUR QUADRANTS 26 FRS
GRAPHING AN EQUATION 29 FRS
POINT COORDINATES - QUADRANT ONE 28 FRS

MAYAS, THE C 60 FRS
SOUND FILMSTRIP - AUDIO TAPE I-J
INTRODUCES THE CULTURE, GOVERNMENT, RELIGION AND ACHIEVEMENTS OF THE MAYAS AND THEIR GREAT EMPIRE, WHICH INCLUDED MEXICO AND CENTRAL AMERICA OF TODAY. FROM THE ANCIENT CIVILIZATIONS OF THE AMERICAS SERIES.
LC NO. 72-737364
PROD-EBEC   DIST-EBEC   1972

MEASUREMENT--A SERIES
PRESENTS ARITHMETIC LESSONS ON MEASUREMENT.
LC NO. 72-735680
PROD-CREATV   DIST-CREATV

MEDICAL ASSISTANT   C 56 FRS
SOUND FILMSTRIP - AUDIO TAPE
DESCRIBES THE MANY ASPECTS OF THE JOB OF
THE MEDICAL ASSISTANT. FROM THE HOSPITAL
JOB OPPORTUNITIES SERIES.
PROD-EGH   DIST-EGH   1972

MEDICINE - PEOPLE AND PILLS   B 58 FRS
SOUND FILMSTRIP - AUDIO TAPE P-I
DISCUSSES SOME COMMONLY USED MEDICAL
DRUGS AND THEIR EFFECTS - PENICILLIN, AMPHE-
TAMINES, TRANQUILIZERS AND ASPIRIN. PRE-
SENTS BOTH BENEFICIAL AND HARMFUL USES OF
THESE DRUGS. DESCRIBES DEPENDENCE ON
DRUGS AS PART OF OTHER ASPECTS OF MODERN
SOCIETY. FROM THE DRUGS - A TRICK, A TRAP SE-
RIES.
LC NO. 72-737371
PROD-EBEC   DIST-EBEC   1972

MEET YOUR TEETH   C 48 FRS
SOUND FILMSTRIP - AUDIO TAPE P-I
USES CARTOON CHARACTERS TO INTRODUCE THE
VARIOUS TYPES OF TEETH AND TO EXPLAIN THEIR
FUNCTIONS. FROM THE PRACTICING GOOD
HEALTH, SET 2 - YOUR MOUTH SPEAKING SERIES.
LC NO. 73-733192
PROD-DISNEY   DIST-DISNEY   1973

MEMORIAL DAY   C 39 FRS
SOUND FILMSTRIP - RECORD K-P
GIVES THE BACKGROUND OF MEMORIAL DAY AND
EXPLAINS HOW IT IS CELEBRATED TODAY. FROM
THE HOLIDAY SERIES, SET 2 SERIES.
LC NO. 72-737289
PROD-MGHT   DIST-MGHT   1972

**METHOD, ASSESSMENT AND
EVALUATION**   C 61 FRS
FILMSTRIP
PRESENTS A FILMSTRIP SUMMARY OF THE EN-
TIRE SERIES CONSISTING OF NOTES. FROM THE
MICROSCOPIC SPECIMENS - A RESOURCE UNIT SE-
RIES.
PROD-EGH   DIST-EGH   1972

MEXICAN AMERICANS   C 121 FRS
SOUND FILMSTRIP - RECORD I-J
SEE SERIES TITLE FOR DESCRIPTIVE STATEMENT.
FROM THE AMERICAN ADVENTURE SERIES.
LC NO. 72-737416
PROD-FIELEP   DIST-FIELEP   1972

**MEXICAN EPIC - BEFORE THE
CONQUEST--A SERIES**

PROD-UMM   DIST-UMM

AZTECS   57 FRS
BEGINNINGS   57 FRS
CLASSIC MAYA   58 FRS
CLASSIC MEXICANS   56 FRS
TOLTECS   59 FRS

**MEXICO - A COMMUNITY
STUDY--A SERIES**

PROD-EGH   DIST-EGH   1972

CHIHUAHUA - LIFE IN A NORTHERN
MEXICAN CITY   37 FRS
COMMUNITY DEVELOPMENT IN
MICHOACAN   36 FRS
TOWN AND VILLAGE IN THE
MOUNTAINS OF PUEBLA   41 FRS
VILLAGE OF ZIHUATANEJO AND ITS
TURTLE INDUSTRY   35 FRS

**MEXICO - AN ECONOMY IN
TRANSITION**   C 55 FRS
FILMSTRIP WITH SCRIPT I-H
SEE SERIES TITLE FOR DESCRIPTIVE STATEMENT.
FROM THE ECONOMICS SERIES.
PROD-DOUBLE   DIST-DOUBLE   1972

**MICROSCOPIC SPECIMENS - A
RESOURCE UNIT--A SERIES**

PROD-EGH   DIST-EGH   1972

ALGAE AND FUNGI   46 FRS
EARTHWORM - TYPICAL INVERTEBRATE   34 FRS
EMBRYOLOGY I - HYDRA AND STARFISH   42 FRS
EMBRYOLOGY II - FROG AND CHICK   40 FRS
HUMAN HISTOLOGY - SYSTEMS   37 FRS
HUMAN HISTOLOGY - TISSUE   38 FRS
METHOD, ASSESSMENT AND
EVALUATION   61 FRS
MITOSIS AND MEIOSIS   48 FRS
MOSSES AND FERNS   42 FRS
PROTOZOA   34 FRS
ROOTS, STEMS AND LEAVES - DICOTS   37 FRS
ROOTS, STEMS AND LEAVES -
MONOCOTS   42 FRS

**MICROTUBULES IN
ECHINOSPHAERIUM
NUCLEOFILUM**   C
FILMSTRIP WITH SCRIPT
ILLUSTRATES THAT MICROTUBULES ARE THE SUB-
STRUCTURAL ELEMENTS THAT GIVE THE AXOPO-
DIA OF ECHINOSPHAERIUM NUCLEOFILUM THEIR
RIGIDITY AND PLAY A PART IN FEEDING. FROM
THE DEVELOPMENT BIOLOGY FILM PROGRAM SE-
RIES.
LC NO. 72-702828
PROD-NSF   DIST-HRAW   PRODN-EDC   1971

**MILES MUGWUMP AND
FRANNIE FRANTIC**   C 52 FRS
SOUND FILMSTRIP - AUDIO TAPE
PRESENTS THE IMPORTANCE OF DECISION MAK-
ING RATHER THAN PROCRASTINATION, ILLUS-
TRATED THROUGH THE FABLE FORM. FROM THE
GUIDES FOR GROWING SERIES.
LC NO. 72-736520
PROD-EGH   DIST-EGH   1972

MIND BLOWERS--A SERIES
     I-J
FOCUSES ON DIFFICULT PROBLEMS IN TODAY'S
SOCIETY LONG JAIL TERMS BEFORE TRIAL, PUN-
ISHMENT AS A DETERRENT TO CRIME, DISCRIMI-
NATORY HOUSING DESPITE OPEN HOUSING LAWS
AND TRADE UNIONS FOR WHITES ONLY.
PROD-SNBRST   DIST-SNBRST   1973

HANGMAN'S KNOT VERSUS THE PAROLE
BOARD   61 FRS
HOW TO CLOSE OPEN HOUSING   77 FRS
JAIL TERM BEFORE TRIAL   59 FRS
TRY TO JOIN OUR UNION   64 FRS

MITOSIS AND MEIOSIS   C 48 FRS
FILMSTRIP
PICTURES THE BASIC PROCESSES INVOLVED IN
THE EVENTUAL DUPLICATION OF A CELL. FROM
THE MICROSCOPIC SPECIMENS - A RESOURCE
UNIT SERIES.
PROD-EGH   DIST-EGH   1972

**MIXED ECONOMY OF THE
UNITED STATES**   C 55 FRS
FILMSTRIP WITH SCRIPT I-H
SEE SERIES TITLE FOR DESCRIPTIVE STATEMENT.
FROM THE ECONOMICS SERIES.
PROD-DOUBLE   DIST-DOUBLE   1972

MODELING MANNERS   C 93 FRS
SOUND FILMSTRIP - RECORD J-C A
SHOWS THE DEVELOPMENT OF GOOD TASTE IN
CLOTHES AND THE ABILITY TO WEAR THEM WITH
POISE AND CHARM IN A FASHION SHOW, ORGA-
NIZED BY THE CLASS, WITH JOB ASSIGNMENTS
FOR EVERY GIRL AND WITH PARENTS INVITED.
FROM THE HOT TIPS ON BASIC BEAUTY, FASHION,
GROOMING AND DATING SERIES.
LC NO. 72-737340
PROD-RMI   DIST-RMI   1972

**MODERN NOVEL, THE -
CATCHER IN THE RYE**   C 85 FRS
SOUND FILMSTRIP - RECORD I-C
GIVES A CRITICAL PRESENTATION OF THE
'CATCHER IN THE RYE' BY J D SALINGER. PRE-
SENTS A CONCENTRATED PLOT FOR GREATER IM-
PACT.
LC NO. 72-737579
PROD-EDDIM   DIST-EDDIM   1972

MOLLY PITCHER   C 43 FRS
SOUND FILMSTRIP - AUDIO TAPE I-H
RECOUNTS THE ROLE OF WOMEN DURING THE
REVOLUTION AND THE ROLE OF MOLLY PITCHER.
FROM THE FAMOUS PATRIOTS OF THE AMERICAN
REVOLUTION SERIES.
LC NO. 73-732983
PROD-CORF   DIST-CORF   1973

MONKEYS AND APES, PT 1   C 67 FRS
FILMSTRIP WITH CAPTIONS
PRESENTS PHOTOGRAPHIC AND BEHAVIORAL
PROFILES OF VARIOUS MONKEYS AND APES IN
THEIR NATURAL HABITATS. FROM THE ANIMAL
KINGDOM SERIES.
LC NO. 72-736499
PROD-LIFE   DIST-LIFE   1970

MONKEYS AND APES, PT 2   C 70 FRS
FILMSTRIP WITH CAPTIONS
PRESENTS PHOTOGRAPHIC AND BEHAVIORAL
PROFILES OF VARIOUS MONKEYS AND APES IN
THEIR NATURAL HABITAT. FROM THE ANIMAL
KINGDOM SERIES.
LC NO. 72-736500
PROD-LIFE   DIST-LIFE   1970

**MORE ACTIONS AND
CONDITIONS**   C 84 FRS
SOUND FILMSTRIP - AUDIO TAPE
DESCRIBES OTHER TERMS INVOLVED WITH AC-
TIONS AND CONDITIONS. FROM THE INTRODUC-
TION TO ENGLISH AS A SECOND LANGUAGE SE-
RIES.
PROD-EGH   DIST-EGH   1972

MOSSES AND FERNS   C 42 FRS
FILMSTRIP
PRESENTS MICROSCOPIC PICTURES OF A SE-
LECTED GROUP OF MOSSES AND FERNS. FROM
THE MICROSCOPIC SPECIMENS - A RESOURCE
UNIT SERIES.
PROD-EGH   DIST-EGH   1972

**MOVEMENTS OF THE HUMAN
BODY**   C
FILMSTRIP WITH SCRIPT H-C A
FROM THE HUMAN ANATOMY AND PHYSIOLOGY
SERIES.
PROD-HRAW   DIST-HRAW   1973

**MULTIPLICATION PROGRAM,
THE**   C 90 FRS
SOUND FILMSTRIP - AUDIO TAPE
PRESENTS A SEQUENTIAL PRESENTATION OF THE
MULTIPLICATION PROGRAM. FROM THE BASIC
COMPUTATIONAL SKILLS SERIES.
LC NO. 72-735463
PROD-CREATV   DIST-CREATV

MULTIPLYING FACTORS   C 29 FRS
SOUND FILMSTRIP - RECORD J-H
ANALYZES THE RELATION OF THE MULTIPLICA-
TION OF NUMBERS AS A STEP BEYOND THE
PROCESS OF REPEATED ADDITION THROUGH THE
SEGMENTING OF A RECTANGULAR SHAPE. FROM
THE MATHEMATICS - FUNDAMENTAL OPERATIONS
SERIES.
LC NO. 73-732674
PROD-UNISYS   DIST-VIEWLX   1972

**MUSCLE - PHYSIOLOGICAL
CHARACTERISTICS**   C
FILMSTRIP WITH SCRIPT H-C A
FROM THE HUMAN ANATOMY AND PHYSIOLOGY
SERIES.
PROD-HRAW   DIST-HRAW   1973

MUSIC APPRECIATION--A SERIES

PROD-EAV   DIST-EAV

BEETHOVEN'S NINTH SYMPHONY, ODE
TO JOY   122 FRS
CHARLES IVES - HOLIDAYS -
WASHINGTON'S --   100 FRS
FANTASIA ON GREENSLEEVES -
VAUGHAN WILLIAMS   61 FRS

MY FRIENDS AND FOLLOWERS   C 36 FRS
SOUND FILMSTRIP - RECORD I R
GIVES A FIRST-PERSON PRESENTATION OF THE
LIFE OF JESUS. INTRODUCES THE FIRST DISCI-
PLES OF JESUS. ILLUSTRATES THE IMPRESSION
JESUS MAKES UPON PEOPLE. PRESENTS THE
WEDDING AT CANA AS A SIGN OF THE NEW JOY
AND FRUITFULNESS WHICH THE PRESENCE OF JE-
SUS BRINGS TO PEOPLE EVERYWHERE. FROM THE
MY NAME IS JESUS SERIES.
LC NO. 72-737432
PROD-ROAS   DIST-ROAS   1972

MY GREATEST WORK   C 35 FRS
SOUND FILMSTRIP - RECORD I R
GIVES A FIRST-PERSON PRESENTATION OF THE
LIFE OF JESUS. SHOWS THE FREEDOM AND FAITH-
FUL LOVE AND FORGIVENESS OF JESUS AS HE IS
BETRAYED BY HIS FRIENDS AND OPPOSED BY HIS
FELLOW MEN. FROM THE MY NAME IS JESUS SE-
RIES.
LC NO. 72-737436
PROD-ROAS   DIST-ROAS   1972

MY LAND AND MY PEOPLE   C 35 FRS
SOUND FILMSTRIP - RECORD I R
PRESENTS A FIRST-PERSON PRESENTATION OF
THE LIFE OF JESUS. DESCRIBES HISTORICAL, GEO-
GRAPHICAL AND CULTURAL BACKGROUNDS OF
HIS LIFE AS WELL AS POLITICAL, SOCIAL AND RELI-
GIOUS CONDITIONS. FROM THE MY NAME IS JE-
SUS SERIES.
LC NO. 72-737427
PROD-ROAS   DIST-ROAS   1972

MY NAME IS JESUS--A SERIES
     I R
PROD-ROAS   DIST-ROAS   1972

BUILDING ON THE ROCK   37 FRS
DECIDING FOR MYSELF   36 FRS
GROWING UP   38 FRS
I AM RISEN AND WITH YOU   35 FRS
MY FRIENDS AND FOLLOWERS   36 FRS
MY GREATEST WORK   35 FRS
MY LAND AND MY PEOPLE   35 FRS
SHEPHERDS AND WISEMEN   35 FRS
SIGNS AND WONDERS   36 FRS
TURNING TOWARD JERUSALEM   36 FRS

N

NATHANAEL GREENE   C 47 FRS
SOUND FILMSTRIP - AUDIO TAPE   I-H
TRACES THE BACKGROUND OF NATHANAEL
GREENE, A YOUNG QUAKER, THROUGH HIS CA-
REER AS ONE OF THE PRINCIPAL MILITARY LEAD-
ERS OF THE REVOLUTION. FROM THE FAMOUS PA-
TRIOTS OF THE AMERICAN REVOLUTION SERIES.
LC NO. 73-732979
PROD-CORF   DIST-CORF   1973

NATION OF OWNERS - AN
INTRODUCTION TO THE
SECURITIES INDUSTRY   C
SOUND FILMSTRIP - AUDIO TAPE
SEE SERIES TITLE FOR DESCRIPTIVE STATEMENT.
FROM THE NATION OF OWNERS SERIES.
LC NO. 72-736600
PROD-EMP   DIST-XEROX

NATION OF OWNERS--A SERIES
DESCRIBES THE SECURITIES INDUSTRY AND HOW
IT WORKS.
PROD-EMP   DIST-XEROX

INTRODUCTION TO SECURITIES
MARKETS
NATION OF OWNERS - AN
INTRODUCTION TO THE --
OPERATIONS - WHERE THE JOB GETS
DONE, PT 1
OPERATIONS - WHERE THE JOB GETS
DONE, PT 2
ORDERS - WHERE THE ACTION BEGINS
THOSE REMARKABLE PIECES OF PAPER
CALLED --

NERVOUS SYSTEM - REFLEX
ARC   C
FILMSTRIP WITH SCRIPT   H-C A
FROM THE HUMAN ANATOMY AND PHYSIOLOGY
SERIES.
PROD-HRAW   DIST-HRAW   1973

NERVOUS SYSTEM - THE
AUTONOMIC NERVOUS SYSTEM   C
FILMSTRIP WITH SCRIPT   H-C A
FROM THE HUMAN ANATOMY AND PHYSIOLOGY
SERIES.
PROD-HRAW   DIST-HRAW   1973

NERVOUS SYSTEM -
TRANSMISSION   C
FILMSTRIP WITH SCRIPT   H-C A
FROM THE HUMAN ANATOMY AND PHYSIOLOGY
SERIES.
PROD-HRAW   DIST-HRAW   1973

NEUROSCIENCES   C 60 FRS
FILMSTRIP WITH SCRIPT
PRESENTS AN OUTLINE OF THE NEUROSCIENCES
FOR USE IN MEDICAL EDUCATION.
LC NO. 72-734143
PROD-SAUNDW   DIST-DAUNDW

NEW AMERICANS   C 111 FRS
SOUND FILMSTRIP - RECORD   I-J
SEE SERIES TITLE FOR DESCRIPTIVE STATEMENT.
FROM THE AMERICAN ADVENTURE SERIES.
LC NO. 72-737415
PROD-FIELEP   DIST-FIELEP   1972

NEW FRIENDS FROM DISTANT
LANDS - THE CULTURE WE
SHARE--A SERIES   P-I
SHOWS THE CONTRIBUTIONS OF THESE COUN-
TRIES TO THE WORLD IN ART, ARCHITECTURE
AND OTHER FIELDS.
PROD-PATED   DIST-PATED   1973

ENGLAND
GREECE
ITALY
LEBANON
TURKEY

NEW TOWN - VALENCIA,
CALIFORNIA   C 88 FRS
SOUND FILMSTRIP - AUDIO TAPE   J-H A
EXAMINES A NEW CONCEPT IN AMERICAN COM-
MUNITIES - THE NEW TOWN. EXPLAINS A NEW
TOWN AS A TOTALLY PREPLANNED AND DI-
RECTED COMMUNITY. FROM THE FOCUS ON
AMERICA - THE PACIFIC STATES SERIES.
LC NO. 73-733159
PROD-SVE   DIST-SVE   1972

NEWSPAPER REPORTER, THE   C 91 FRS
SOUND FILMSTRIP - RECORD   I-C
FOCUSES ON A POLITICAL REPORTER AS HE GATH-
ERS THE NEWS, WRITES AND EDITS HIS STORY
AND PARTICIPATES IN THE NEWSPAPER MAKE-UP
IN THE PRESS ROOM. FROM THE EXPLORING CA-
REERS, GROUP 1 SERIES.
LC NO. 73-733176
PROD-SVE   DIST-SVE   1973

NORTHWEST FILMSTRIPS--A
SERIES

PROD-CLOPSD   DIST-UWASHP

OLYMPIC COAST INDIANS TODAY   67 FRS
RAIN FORESTS OF THE NORTHWEST
COAST   72 FRS

NOW YOU ARE A VOTER--A
SERIES

PROD-EGH   DIST-EGH

ELECTION, THE   38 FRS
REGISTRATION AND PICKING A
CANDIDATE   38 FRS
RIGHT TO VOTE, THE   45 FRS
WORKING IN THE POLITICAL WORLD   40 FRS

NUCLEAR TECHNICIAN   C 54 FRS
SOUND FILMSTRIP - AUDIO TAPE
DESCRIBES THE NUMEROUS TYPES OF EQUIP-
MENT THAT THE NUCLEAR TECHNICIAN COMES
INTO CONTACT WITH IN THE MODERN HOSPITAL.
FROM THE HOSPITAL JOB OPPORTUNITIES SE-
RIES.
PROD-EGH   DIST-EGH   1972

NUESTRO MUNDO DE VISTAS Y
SONIDOS, GRUPO 1-- A SERIES

P

PROD-SVE   DIST-SVE

VISTAS Y SONIDOS DE LA TIENDA DE
ANIMALES --   33 FRS
VISTAS Y SONIDOS DEL PARQUE DE
DIVERSIONES   41 FRS

NUMBER SYSTEMS - THE
COMPUTER'S VOCABULARY   B 53 FRS
SOUND FILMSTRIP - RECORD   H
POINTS OUT THE FOUR NUMBER SYSTEMS USED
IN DIGITAL DECIMAL AND DECIMAL SYSTEMS.
SHOWS HOW THE COMPUTER ADDS BY FOLLOW-
ING THE BASIC RULES OF BINARY ADDITION.
FROM THE HOW COMPUTERS WORK SERIES.
LC NO. 73-732747
PROD-EBEC   DIST-EBEC   1972

NUMBERS AND MONEY   C 80 FRS
SOUND FILMSTRIP - AUDIO TAPE
DESCRIBES COMMON TERMS ASSOCIATED WITH
NUMBERS AND MONEY ALONG WITH ASSOCIATED
VERBS. FROM THE INTRODUCTION TO ENGLISH AS
A SECOND LANGUAGE SERIES.
PROD-EGH   DIST-EGH   1972

NURSE   C 56 FRS
SOUND FILMSTRIP - AUDIO TAPE
DESCRIBES THE NURSE'S JOB. FROM THE HOSPI-
TAL JOB OPPORTUNITIES SERIES.
PROD-EGH   DIST-EGH   1972

NURSE'S AIDE   C 56 FRS
SOUND FILMSTRIP - AUDIO TAPE
DESCRIBES THE MAJOR FEATURES OF THE
NURSE'S AIDE. FROM THE HOSPITAL JOB OPPOR-
TUNITIES SERIES.

PROD-EGH   DIST-EGH   1972

O

OLYMPIC COAST INDIANS
TODAY   C 67 FRS
FILMSTRIP WITH SCRIPT
DISCUSSES THE NORTHWEST COAST INDIANS
AND THEIR SURVIVING TRADITIONS. FROM THE
NORTHWEST FILMSTRIPS SERIES.
LC NO. 70-734792
PROD-CLOPSD   DIST-UWASHP

ON SAFARI IN EAST AFRICA   C 42 FRS
FILMSTRIP WITH SCRIPT   P-C
SHOWS THE VARIED PLANT AND ANIMAL LIFE
THROUGHOUT EAST AFRICA. SHOWS THE NEED
FOR CONSERVATION.
LC NO. 72-737221
PROD-DWYLIE   DIST-DWYLIE   1971

ONCE UPON A COMPULSION   C 42 FRS
SOUND FILMSTRIP - RECORD
PRESENTS A HUMOROUS LOOK AT CONFORMITY.
ASKS ABOUT THE LEADER, HOW HE GOT THERE
AND WHAT REALLY GOES ON IN THE GROUP.
LC NO. 72-737334
PROD-KELLRP   DIST-KELLRP   1969

ONE HUNDRED AND THIRTY
BILLION DOLLAR FOOD
ASSEMBLY LINE   C 47 FRS
FILMSTRIP WITH SCRIPT   C A
DEPICTS THE PEOPLE AND FIRMS THAT PRODUCE
AND SUPPLY FOOD IN ANY SEASON. GIVES A
QUICK TOUR OF OTHER THINGS THAT HAPPEN
ALONG THE NATION'S FOOD ASSEMBLY LINE,
SUCH AS HOW MUCH LAND IS USED FOR FARM-
ING, HOW MUCH FOOD WE EACH GET A YEAR AND
HOW MANY CATTLE AND OTHER ANIMALS ARE
GROWN FOR FOOD.
LC NO. 73-733253
PROD-USDA   DIST-USDA   1972

ONE PHASE OF THE BLACK
MARKET IN MEAT   B 50 FRS
SOUND FILMSTRIP - AUDIO TAPE
EXPLAINS HOW BLACK MARKET MEAT IS SOLD
AND TELLS HOW THE OFFICE OF PRICE ADMINIS-
TRATION TRIES TO PREVENT ILLEGAL DISTRIBU-
TION OF MEAT.
LC NO. FI66-1875
PROD-USOPA   DIST-USOPA

OOPSIES, THE   C 22 FRS
FILMSTRIP WITH SCRIPT
PORTRAYS FICTIONAL CHARACTERS MARK AND
DAISY OOPSIE WHO HELP SHOW HOW PEOPLE BE-
COME OVERWEIGHT, AND HOW THEY CAN SLIM
DOWN THROUGH EXERCISE, DIETING AND
PROPER NUTRITION.
LC NO. 72-735280
PROD-USDA   DIST-PHOTO

OPERATIONS - WHERE THE JOB
GETS DONE, PT 1   C
SOUND FILMSTRIP - AUDIO TAPE
SEE SERIES TITLE FOR DESCRIPTIVE STATEMENT.
FROM THE NATION OF OWNERS SERIES.
LC NO. 72-736600
PROD-EMP   DIST-XEROX

OPERATIONS - WHERE THE JOB
GETS DONE, PT 2   C
SOUND FILMSTRIP - AUDIO TAPE
SEE SERIES TITLE FOR DESCRIPTIVE STATEMENT.
FROM THE NATION OF OWNERS SERIES.
LC NO. 72-736600
PROD-EMP   DIST-XEROX

OPTICAL PRINCIPLES   C
FILMSTRIP WITH SCRIPT   H-C A
FROM THE HUMAN ANATOMY AND PHYSIOLOGY
SERIES.
PROD-HRAW   DIST-HRAW   1973

ORDER - FIRST ALWAYS COMES
BEFORE LAST   C 38 FRS
SOUND FILMSTRIP - RECORD
TEACHES THE CONCEPT OF ORDER. FROM THE DE-
VELOPING ELEMENTARY CONCEPTS SERIES.
LC NO. 72-736534
PROD-EGH   DIST-EGH   1972

PROD-EGH   DIST-EGH   1972

ORDERS - WHERE THE ACTION BEGINS C
SOUND FILMSTRIP - AUDIO TAPE
SEE SERIES TITLE FOR DESCRIPTIVE STATEMENT.
FROM THE NATION OF OWNERS SERIES.
LC NO. 72-736600
PROD-EMP   DIST-XEROX

ORIGINS OF THE EARTH--A SERIES I-H

PROD-VISPUB   DIST-VISPUB   1970

FOLD MOUNTAINS   38 FRS
ICE, PT 1   38 FRS
ICE, PT 2   39 FRS
ICE, PT 3   39 FRS
RIVERS, PT 1   35 FRS
RIVERS, PT 2   37 FRS
RIVERS, PT 3   39 FRS
ROCKS AND MINERALS   41 FRS
SEA, THE - DEPOSITION   39 FRS
SEA, THE - EROSION   37 FRS
VOLCANOES, PT 1   37 FRS
VOLCANOES, PT 2   40 FRS

OUR INSTINCTS AND WHY WE HAVE THEM C 52 FRS
SOUND FILMSTRIP - AUDIO TAPE
DISCUSSES HOW A MATURE INSTINCT FOR UNION
WITH ANOTHER EXISTS NOT JUST ON A PHYSICAL
LEVEL, BUT AS A TOTAL PSYCHOLOGICAL AND
PERSONAL RELATIONSHIP OF MUTUALITY AND
SHARING. FROM THE HUMAN SEXUALITY SERIES.
PROD-EGH   DIST-EGH   1972

PASSOVER C 41 FRS
SOUND FILMSTRIP - RECORD K-P
GIVES THE BACKGROUND OF PASSOVER AND EX-
PLAINS HOW IT IS CELEBRATED TODAY. FROM
THE HOLIDAY SERIES, SET 2 SERIES.
LC NO. 72-737286
PROD-MGHT   DIST-MGHT   1972

PATRICK HENRY C 44 FRS
SOUND FILMSTRIP - AUDIO TAPE I-H
FOLLOWS PATRICK HENRY AS HE DEVELOPS FROM
A BACKCOUNTRY LAWYER TO ONE OF THE LEAD-
ING SPOKESMEN FOR THE CAUSE OF LIBERTY.
FROM THE FAMOUS PATRIOTS OF THE AMERICAN
REVOLUTION SERIES.
LC NO. 73-732978
PROD-CORF   DIST-CORF   1973

PEOPLE OF CHINA, THE C 53 FRS
SOUND FILMSTRIP - AUDIO TAPE
DESCRIBES THE PEOPLE, THEIR LAND AND THEIR
ACTIVITIES. FROM THE INSIDE THE PEOPLE'S RE-
PUBLIC OF CHINA SERIES.
PROD-EGH   DIST-EGH   1972

PERPETUATING LIFE C 39 FRS
SOUND FILMSTRIP - AUDIO TAPE
DESCRIBES THE STRATEGIES USED BY VARIOUS
SPECIES TO INSURE SURVIVAL. FROM THE LIFE - A
UNIQUE PHENOMENON SERIES.
PROD-EGH   DIST-EGH   1972

PERSONALITY PLUS C 91 FRS
SOUND FILMSTRIP - RECORD J-C A
SHOWS GIRLS HOW TO CULTIVATE THEIR HEALTH
HABITS, PERSONAL APPEARANCE, ACTIVITIES,
CONSIDERATION OF OTHERS AND THE GENUINE
INTEREST IN PEOPLE TO BRING ABOUT THEIR
HIGHEST PHYSICAL, MENTAL, MORAL AND SPIRI-
TUAL DEVELOPMENT. FROM THE HOT TIPS ON BA-
SIC BEAUTY, FASHION, GROOMING AND DATING
SERIES.
LC NO. 72-737342
PROD-RMI   DIST-RMI   1972

PETER AND THE WOLF C 45 FRS
SOUND FILMSTRIP - AUDIO TAPE K-P
PICTURES THE MEMORABLE MELODIC TALE OF PE-
TER AND THE WOLF BY SERGIO PROKOFIEV. FROM
THE CHILDREN'S STORIES SERIES.
LC NO. 73-733103
PROD-STNHM   DIST-STNHM   1972

PETER AND THE WOLF C 94 FRS
SOUND FILMSTRIP - RECORD K-H
USES ORIGINAL ILLUSTRATIONS TO PRESENT THE
STORY OF PETER AND THE WOLF, PROKOFIEV'S
COMPOSITION. FROM THE MUSIC APPRECIATION
SERIES.
LC NO. 72-737573

PROD-EAV   DIST-EAV   1972

PILLS IN A PILL CULTURE C 55 FRS
SOUND FILMSTRIP - AUDIO TAPE
DESCRIBES THE EFFECTS OF PILLS AND THE POSI-
TION PILLS HOLD IN AMERICAN CULTURE. FROM
THE LET'S LOOK AT DRUGS SERIES.
PROD-EGH   DIST-EGH   1972

PINOCCHIO C 34 FRS
SOUND FILMSTRIP - AUDIO TAPE K-P
PRESENTS THE CLASSIC TALE OF A WOODEN BOY
WHOSE UNUSUAL ADVENTURES INFLUENCE HIS
BEING CHANGED INTO A REAL BOY TO THE GREAT
JOY OF HIS PUPPET-MAKER FATHER. FROM THE
CHILDREN'S STORIES SERIES.
LC NO. 72-737492
PROD-STNHM   DIST-STNHM   1972

PLAINS INDIANS, THE C 35 FRS
SOUND FILMSTRIP - AUDIO TAPE
INTRODUCES THE LIFE AND CUSTOMS OF THE
VARIOUS TRIBES OF THE PLAINS AREA. FROM THE
INDIANS OF AMERICA SERIES.
PROD-EGH   DIST-EGH   1972

PLANNING THE BEDROOM C 32 FRS
FILMSTRIP WITH SCRIPT J-C A
TELLS THE VIEWER HOW MANY BEDROOMS HE
NEEDS, WHERE THEY SHOULD BE LOCATED, HOW
A BEDROOM MIGHT CHANGE AS ITS OCCUPANT
MATURES AND SPACE AND FURNITURE REQUIRE-
MENTS NEEDED IN A BEDROOM. FROM THE
HOUSING SERIES.
LC NO. 73-733255
PROD-USDA   DIST-USDA   1968

PLANT LIFE IN THE WATERS C 40 FRS
SOUND FILMSTRIP - RECORD P-J
SEE SERIES TITLE FOR DESCRIPTIVE STATEMENT.
FROM THE GROWING THINGS SERIES.
PROD-TERF   DIST-TERF   1973

PLATYPUS, THE C
FILMSTRIP WITH CAPTIONS
FROM THE ANIMALS SERIES.
LC NO. 72-734417
PROD-LIEB   DIST-MSCF   1970

POINT COORDINATES - QUADRANT ONE C 28 FRS
SOUND FILMSTRIP - RECORD I-H
FOLLOWS THE STEP-BY-STEP CONSTRUCTION OF
THE ELEMENTS OF THE CARTESIAN COORDINATE
SYSTEM IN QUADRANT ONE. ILLUSTRATES THE
TECHNIQUE FOR FINDING THE COORDINATES OF
A POINT ON THE PLANE AND FOR PLOTTING
POINTS WHEN THE COORDINATES ARE GIVEN.
FROM THE MATHEMATICS - GRAPHING SERIES.
LC NO. 72-737595
PROD-UNISYS   DIST-VIEWLX   1972

POLAND - AGRICULTURE TODAY C 35 FRS
FILMSTRIP
SEE SERIES TITLE FOR DESCRIPTIVE STATEMENT.
FROM THE EASTERN EUROPE SERIES.
LC NO. 72-734724
PROD-MGHT   DIST-MGHT   1972

POLAND - INDUSTRY AND PROGRESS C 37 FRS
FILMSTRIP
SEE SERIES TITLE FOR DESCRIPTIVE STATEMENT.
FROM THE EASTERN EUROPE SERIES.
LC NO. 72-734722
PROD-MGHT   DIST-MGHT   1972

POLAR BEAR, THE C
FILMSTRIP WITH CAPTIONS
FROM THE ANIMALS SERIES.
LC NO. 72-734417
PROD-LIEB   DIST-MSCF   1970

POLITICS AND GOVERNMENT C 72 FRS
SOUND FILMSTRIP - RECORD J-H
PRESENTS AN EXAMINATION OF POLITICS AND
GOVERNMENT IN LATIN AMERICA TODAY. FROM
THE LATIN AMERICA TODAY SERIES.
LC NO. 73-733220
PROD-MMPRO   DIST-MMPRO   1970

PORTRAIT OF A YOUNG NATION C 80 FRS
SOUND FILMSTRIP - RECORD J-C
SEE SERIES TITLE FOR DESCRIPTIVE STATEMENT.
FROM THE AMERICAN CIVILIZATION - 1783-1840
SERIES.
PROD-SUNCOM   DIST-SUNCOM   1973

PRACTICING GOOD HEALTH, SET 2 - YOUR MOUTH SPEAKING--A SERIES P-I

LC NO. 73-733189
PROD-DISNEY   DIST-DISNEY   1973

BRUSHING AWAY TOOTH DECAY   40 FRS
CASE OF THE CROOKED TOOTH, THE   42 FRS
MAGIC POTION, THE   30 FRS
MEET YOUR TEETH   48 FRS
SAFETY OF THE MOUTH   40 FRS
TALE OF TWO TEETH, A   42 FRS
WHY VISIT THE DENTIST   36 FRS

PRAIRIE AND MOUNTAIN PLANTS C 40 FRS
SOUND FILMSTRIP - RECORD P-J
SEE SERIES TITLE FOR DESCRIPTIVE STATEMENT.
FROM THE GROWING THINGS SERIES.
PROD-TERF   DIST-TERF   1973

PRINCESS ECOL VISITS THE PLANET THRAE C 44 FRS
SOUND FILMSTRIP - AUDIO TAPE
SHOWS THE EFFECTS OF POLLUTION. FROM THE
GUIDES FOR GROWING SERIES.
LC NO. 72-736518
PROD-EGH   DIST-EGH   1972

PRINCIPLES OF FLOWCHARTS C 60 FRS
SOUND FILMSTRIP - RECORD
FROM THE COMPUTER SCIENCE SERIES.
LC NO. 73-732500
PROD-AVDEV   DIST-AVDEV   1972

PROBLEMS - CAUSES AND CORRECTIONS C
SOUND FILMSTRIP - RECORD J-C A
SEE SERIES TITLE FOR DESCRIPTIVE STATEMENT.
FROM THE HYDRAULIC BRAKE SYSTEM EX-
PLAINED SERIES.
PROD-BERGL   DIST-BERGL   1972

PROCESSING SOUP C 39 FRS
SOUND FILMSTRIP - AUDIO TAPE
SHOWS HOW FOODS ARE PROCESSED. FROM THE
HOW THINGS ARE MADE SERIES.
LC NO. 72-736549
PROD-EGH   DIST-EGH   1972

PROGRAMMING - HOW TO ORDER A COMPUTER AROUND B 61 FRS
SOUND FILMSTRIP - RECORD H
DEMONSTRATES THE FORM IN WHICH THE PRO-
GRAM IS ORGANIZED AND WRITTEN AND SHOWS
HOW THE PROGRAM IS FED INTO THE COMPUTER
AND CONVEYED INTO A FORM IT CAN USE IN ITS
OPERATIONS. DEFINES TERMS SUCH AS FLOW
CHART, COMPILING AND DEBUGGING. FROM THE
HOW COMPUTERS WORK SERIES.
LC NO. 73-732749
PROD-EBEC   DIST-EBEC   1972

PROGRAMMING IN FORTRAN, PT 1 C 60 FRS
SOUND FILMSTRIP - RECORD
FROM THE COMPUTER SCIENCE SERIES.
LC NO. 73-732500
PROD-AVDEV   DIST-AVDEV   1972

PROGRAMMING IN FORTRAN, PT 2 C 60 FRS
SOUND FILMSTRIP - RECORD
FROM THE COMPUTER SCIENCE SERIES.
LC NO. 73-732500
PROD-AVDEV   DIST-AVDEV   1972

PRONOUNS C 46 FRS
SOUND FILMSTRIP - AUDIO TAPE
DESCRIBES THE DIFFERENCES IN PRONOUN US-
AGE IN SPANISH AND ENGLISH. FROM THE INTRO-
DUCTION TO ENGLISH AS A SECOND LANGUAGE
SERIES.
PROD-EGH   DIST-EGH   1972

PROTOZOA C 34 FRS
FILMSTRIP
PRESENTS MICROSCOPIC PICTURES OF MANY OF
THE MAJOR TYPES OF PROTOZOA. FROM THE MI-
CROSCOPIC SPECIMENS - A RESOURCE UNIT SE-
RIES.
PROD-EGH   DIST-EGH   1972

PUSS IN BOOTS C 29 FRS
SOUND FILMSTRIP - AUDIO TAPE K-P
DESCRIBES THE ACTIVITIES OF A TALKING CAT
WHO LEADS HIMSELF AND HIS MASTER FROM
RAGS TO RICHES. FROM THE CHILDREN'S STORIES
SERIES.

LC NO. 72-737211
PROD-STNHM   DIST-STNHM   1972

**PUTTING IT TOGETHER SO IT
WORKS**   C 48 FRS
          SOUND FILMSTRIP - AUDIO TAPE
DESCRIBES THE CONTENTS OF A BASIC WARD-
ROBE AND SHOWS HOW THE SEPARATE ELE-
MENTS CAN BE MIXED. FROM THE LOOKING
GREAT ON A SHOESTRING SERIES.
PROD-EGH   DIST-EGH   1972

Q

QUALIFYING   C 79 FRS
          SOUND FILMSTRIP - AUDIO TAPE
DEALS WITH QUALIFIERS SUCH AS COLOR, SIZE
AND POSITION. FROM THE INTRODUCTION TO EN-
GLISH AS A SECOND LANGUAGE SERIES.
PROD-EGH   DIST-EGH   1972

R

RADIOTHERAPY I   C 102 FRS
          SOUND FILMSTRIP - RECORD
DESCRIBES THE USE OF RADIOTHERAPY IN THE
CURE AND PALLIATION OF CANCER. FROM THE
CANCER, SERIES 3 - TREATMENT MODALITIES
WITH IMPLICATIONS FOR NURSING CARE SERIES.
NO. 5
   LC NO. 72-733177
PROD-CONMED   DIST-CONMED   1972

RADIOTHERAPY II   C 106 FRS
          SOUND FILMSTRIP - RECORD
CONSIDERS THE NATURE OF RADIOISOTOPES AND
THE THREE TYPES OF RADIATION IN RESPECT TO
NURSING CARE. FROM THE CANCER, SERIES 3 -
TREATMENT MODALITIES WITH IMPLICATIONS
FOR NURSING CARE SERIES. NO. 6
   LC NO. 72-733178
PROD-CONMED   DIST-CONMED   1972

**RAIN FORESTS OF THE
NORTHWEST COAST**   C 72 FRS
          FILMSTRIP WITH SCRIPT
DISCUSSES THE UNIQUE CONDITIONS WHICH
MAKE POSSIBLE THE GROWTH OF THE ONLY CO-
NIFEROUS RAIN FOREST IN THE WORLD AND THE
VARIETY OF PLANTS AND ANIMALS TO BE FOUND
THERE. EMPHASIZES THE ECOLOGY OF THE FOR-
EST. FROM THE NORTHWEST FILMSTRIPS SERIES.
   LC NO. 77-734794
PROD-CLOPSD   DIST-UWASHP

RANCH LIFE   C 51 FRS
          SOUND FILMSTRIP - AUDIO TAPE
DESCRIBES THE MAJOR FEATURES OF LIFE ON A
RANCH LOCATED IN THE PAMPAS. FROM THE
LIFEWAYS OF THE PEOPLE - SOUTH AMERICA SE-
RIES.
PROD-EGH   DIST-EGH   1972

RARE AND EXOTIC PLANTS   C 40 FRS
          SOUND FILMSTRIP - RECORD   P-J
SEE SERIES TITLE FOR DESCRIPTIVE STATEMENT.
FROM THE GROWING THINGS SERIES.
PROD-TERF   DIST-TERF   1973

RATIONALISM   C 26 FRS
          SOUND FILMSTRIP - AUDIO TAPE
SHOWS THAT NATURE IS UNDERSTANDABLE AND
THAT THERE ARE REASONABLE EXPLANATIONS
FOR EVENTS AND PHENOMENA. FROM THE GREAT
IDEAS IN BIOLOGY SERIES.
PROD-EGH   DIST-EGH   1970

**RECIPES USING NON-INSTANT,
NONFAT DRY MILK AND OTHER
DONATED FOODS**   C 49 FRS
          FILMSTRIP WITH SCRIPT   A
TELLS HOW TO MIX NON-INSTANT, NONFAT DRY
MILK AND HOW TO MAKE SEVEN DISHES AND A
FOOD DRINK WITH IT.
   LC NO. 73-733258
PROD-USDA   DIST-USDA   1970

**REGISTRATION AND PICKING A
CANDIDATE**   C 38 FRS
          SOUND FILMSTRIP - AUDIO TAPE
DESCRIBES THE VARIOUS PROBLEMS THAT MIGHT
BE ENCOUNTERED IN REGISTRATION FOR VOTING

AND GIVES SOME GENERAL GUIDELINES AS TO IM-
PORTANT FACTORS IN VOTING. FROM THE NOW
YOU ARE A VOTER SERIES.
   LC NO. 72-736557
PROD-EGH   DIST-EGH

**RESOURCES, AGRICULTURE AND
INDUSTRY**   C 40 FRS
          SOUND FILMSTRIP - AUDIO TAPE
GIVES AN UNDERSTANDING OF THE BASIC FAC-
TORS IN THE BRITISH ECONOMY. FROM THE
GREAT BRITAIN - A REGIONAL STUDY SERIES.
   LC NO. 72-736528
PROD-EGH   DIST-EGH   1972

**RESOURCES, AGRICULTURE AND
INDUSTRY**   C 43 FRS
          SOUND FILMSTRIP - AUDIO TAPE
GIVES AN UNDERSTANDING OF THE BASIC FAC-
TORS IN THE DUTCH ECONOMY. FROM THE HOL-
LAND - A REGIONAL STUDY SERIES.
PROD-EGH   DIST-EGH   1972

RESPIRATION - GAS EXCHANGE   C
          FILMSTRIP WITH SCRIPT   H-C A
FROM THE HUMAN ANATOMY AND PHYSIOLOGY
SERIES.
PROD-HRAW   DIST-HRAW   1973

**RESPIRATION - MECHANICS OF
VENTILATION**   C
          FILMSTRIP WITH SCRIPT   H-C A
FROM THE HUMAN ANATOMY AND PHYSIOLOGY
SERIES.
PROD-HRAW   DIST-HRAW   1973

RIGHT TO VOTE, THE   C 45 FRS
          SOUND FILMSTRIP - AUDIO TAPE
DISCUSSES THE IMPORTANCE OF THE RIGHT TO
VOTE AND THE IMPORTANCE OF VOTING. FROM
THE NOW YOU ARE A VOTER SERIES.
   LC NO. 72-736558
PROD-EGH   DIST-EGH

RIVERS, PT 1   C 35 FRS
          FILMSTRIP WITH SCRIPT   I-H
ILLUSTRATES THE CHARACTERISTIC FEATURES OF
A RIVER, TAKING AS A TYPICAL EXAMPLE THE
RIVER TEIFI AND FOLLOWING ITS COURSE. HIGH-
LIGHTS MAJOR FEATURES, INCLUDING SOURCE,
WATERFALLS, EROSION, TRANSPORT, DEPOSI-
TION, MEANDERS AND BRAIDING. FROM THE ORI-
GINS OF THE EARTH SERIES.
   LC NO. 72-737139
PROD-VISPUB   DIST-VISPUB   1972

RIVERS, PT 2   C 37 FRS
          FILMSTRIP WITH SCRIPT   I-H
EXPLAINS THE IMPORTANT ASPECTS OF RIVER AC-
TION. SHOWS THE EFFECTS OF HEADWARD ERO-
SION, VERTICAL EROSION AND FORMATIONS OF
V-SHAPED VALLEYS. FROM THE ORIGINS OF THE
EARTH SERIES.
   LC NO. 72-737140
PROD-VISPUB   DIST-VISPUB   1972

RIVERS, PT 3   C 39 FRS
          FILMSTRIP WITH SCRIPT   I-H
EXAMINES THE DIFFERENT STAGES OF RIVERS -
THE ACTIVITIES OF A RIVER IN ITS LOWER OR
PLAIN STAGE AND THE COURSE OF THE RIVER TO
THE SEA IN ESTUARIES OR ACROSS DELTAS. FROM
THE ORIGINS OF THE EARTH SERIES.
   LC NO. 72-737141
PROD-VISPUB   DIST-VISPUB   1972

ROCKS AND MINERALS   C 41 FRS
          FILMSTRIP WITH SCRIPT   I-H
ILLUSTRATES THE FORMATIONS OF THE DIFFER-
ENT KINDS OF ROCKS AND EXPLAINS THE IDEA
OF ROCK CYCLES. DESCRIBES ROCKS OF NON-OR-
GANIC AND ORGANIC ORIGIN AND THE PROCESS
OF METAMORPHOSIS. FROM THE ORIGINS OF THE
EARTH SERIES.
   LC NO. 72-737138
PROD-VISPUB   DIST-VISPUB   1972

**ROOTS, STEMS AND LEAVES -
DICOTS**   C 37 FRS
          FILMSTRIP
PRESENTS A MICROSCOPIC PICTURE OF THE
STRUCTURE OF PLANTS IN THE CLASS, DICOTYLE-
DON. FROM THE MICROSCOPIC SPECIMENS - A RE-
SOURCE UNIT SERIES.
PROD-EGH   DIST-EGH   1972

**ROOTS, STEMS AND LEAVES -
MONOCOTS**   C 42 FRS
          FILMSTRIP
PRESENTS A MICROSCOPIC PICTURE OF THE
STRUCTURE OF PLANTS IN THE SUBCLASS, MONO-
COTYLEDON. FROM THE MICROSCOPIC SPECI-
MENS - A RESOURCE UNIT SERIES.
PROD-EGH   DIST-EGH   1972

S

**SAFE USE OF PESTICIDES ON
THE FARM**   C 48 FRS
          FILMSTRIP WITH SCRIPT   H-C A
GIVES SAFETY INFORMATION ON THE USE OF PES-
TICIDES ON A LARGE SCALE.
   LC NO. 73-733260
PROD-USDA   DIST-USDA   1973

SAFETY OF THE MOUTH   C 40 FRS
          SOUND FILMSTRIP - AUDIO TAPE   P-I
SHOWS THE EFFECTS ON TOTAL DENTAL HEALTH
WHEN A TOOTH IS INJURED OR KNOCKED OUT BY
AN ACCIDENT AND OUTLINES THE CORRECT DEN-
TAL SAFETY MEASURE WHICH EVERYONE SHOULD
PRACTICE. DESCRIBES WHAT THE DENTIST CAN
DO TO REPAIR AND REPLACE TEETH THAT HAVE
BEEN CHIPPED OR OTHERWISE DAMAGED. FROM
THE PRACTICING GOOD HEALTH, SET 2 - YOUR
MOUTH SPEAKING SERIES.
   LC NO. 73-733196
PROD-DISNEY   DIST-DISNEY   1973

**SCHOOL TIMES KIT - APRIL--A
SERIES**
                                                 I
PROD-TERF   DIST-TERF   1972

ENERGY CRISIS, THE - AN HISTORICAL
REVIEW   45 FRS
ENERGY CRISIS, THE - REPORT FROM
PLANET 32   50 FRS

SEA, THE - DEPOSITION   C 39 FRS
          FILMSTRIP WITH SCRIPT   I-H
ILLUSTRATES AND EXPLAINS HOW THE SEA RE-
MOVES MATERIALS FROM THE LAND AND TRANS-
PORTS IT TO BUILD UP NEW LAND FORMATIONS.
SHOWS TYPICAL BEACH FORMATIONS AND ILLUS-
TRATES THE SEQUENCES LEADING TO THEIR FOR-
MATION. FROM THE ORIGINS OF THE EARTH SE-
RIES.
   LC NO. 72-737137
PROD-VISPUB   DIST-VISPUB   1970

SEA, THE - EROSION   C 37 FRS
          FILMSTRIP WITH SCRIPT   I-H
ILLUSTRATES THE EROSIVE POWERS OF THE SEA
AND THE RESULTS OF WAVE-ACTION, LEADING TO
THE FORMATION OF VARIOUS FEATURES SUCH AS
CLIFFS AND PLATFORMS. FROM THE ORIGINS OF
THE EARTH SERIES.
   LC NO. 72-737136
PROD-VISPUB   DIST-VISPUB   1970

SEATTLE - A CITY FACES CRISIS   C 79 FRS
          SOUND FILMSTRIP - AUDIO TAPE   J-H A
RELATES THE RECENT ECONOMIC CRISIS CAUSED
BY LAYOFFS IN SEATTLE'S AEROSPACE INDUSTRY.
SHOWS THE GENERAL EFFECT OF A DEPRESSED
ECONOMY ON THE CITY AND RELATES THE EXPE-
RIENCES OF THREE AEROSPACE WORKERS, ONE
WHO KEPT HIS JOB AND TWO WHO LOST THEIRS.
FROM THE FOCUS ON AMERICA - THE PACIFIC
STATES SERIES.
   LC NO. 73-733162
PROD-SVE   DIST-SVE   1972

**SERVICING THE HYDRAULIC
SYSTEM - DISK-TYPE**   C
          SOUND FILMSTRIP - RECORD   J-C A
SEE SERIES TITLE FOR DESCRIPTIVE STATEMENT.
FROM THE HYDRAULIC BRAKE SYSTEM EX-
PLAINED SERIES.
PROD-BERGL   DIST-BERGL   1972

**SERVICING THE HYDRAULIC
SYSTEM - DRUM-TYPE**   C
          SOUND FILMSTRIP - RECORD   J-C A
SEE SERIES TITLE FOR DESCRIPTIVE STATEMENT.
FROM THE HYDRAULIC BRAKE SYSTEM EX-
PLAINED SERIES.
PROD-BERGL   DIST-BERGL   1972

T

SHEPHERDS AND WISEMEN C 35 FRS
SOUND FILMSTRIP - RECORD I R
GIVES A FIRST-PERSON PRESENTATION OF THE
LIFE OF JESUS. DESCRIBES THE INFANCY NARRA-
TIVES FROM MATTHEW AND LUKE. TELLS OF THE
SIGNIFICANCE OF HIS BIRTH FOR ALL LEVELS OF
SOCIETY. FROM THE MY NAME IS JESUS SERIES.
LC NO. 72-737428
PROD-ROAS   DIST-ROAS   1972

SHORT STORY TODAY, THE C 59 FRS
SOUND FILMSTRIP - RECORD J-C
SEE SERIES TITLE FOR DESCRIPTIVE STATEMENT.
FROM THE DEVELOPMENT OF THE AMERICAN
SHORT STORY SERIES. PT 4
LC NO. 77-734751
PROD-EAV   DIST-EAV   1969

SIGNS AND WONDERS C 36 FRS
SOUND FILMSTRIP - RECORD I R
GIVES A FIRST-PERSON PRESENTATION OF THE
LIFE OF JESUS. INCLUDES THE GOSPEL NARRA-
TIVES OF THE MIRACLES OF JESUS, JESUS' DESIRE
TO HEAL HEARTS CRIPPLED BY SIN, THE GREAT
SIGNS THAT REVEAL WHO JESUS IS AND JESUS'
COMPASSION AS A REFLECTION OF GOD'S POWER-
FUL LOVE. FROM THE MY NAME IS JESUS SERIES.
LC NO. 72-737433
PROD-ROAS   DIST-ROAS   1972

SKETCHING C 33 FRS
SOUND FILMSTRIP - AUDIO TAPE I
PRESENTS BASIC RULES OF A FINISHED SKETCH,
THEN REPEATS FOR GREATER COMPREHENSION.
FROM THE HOW A PICTURE IS MADE SERIES.
PROD-EGH   DIST-EGH

SNOW WHITE C 32 FRS
SOUND FILMSTRIP - AUDIO TAPE K-P
DESCRIBES SNOW WHITE'S ADVENTURES WITH
THE SEVEN DWARFS, WHEN SHE'S IN HIDING
FROM HER STEPMOTHER WHO WISHES TO HAVE
HER KILLED. FROM THE CHILDREN'S STORIES SE-
RIES.
LC NO. 72-737495
PROD-STNHM   DIST-STNHM   1972

**SOFTWARE AND HARDWARE AT
WORK** B 64 FRS
SOUND FILMSTRIP - RECORD H
EXAMINES THE COMPUTER PROGRAM AND RE-
VEALS THE WAY IN WHICH THE PROGRAMMER
COMMUNICATES WITH THE MACHINE. FROM THE
HOW COMPUTERS WORK SERIES.
LC NO. 73-732746
PROD-EBEC   DIST-EBEC   1972

SORCERER'S APPRENTICE, THE C 32 FRS
SOUND FILMSTRIP - AUDIO TAPE K-P
DESCRIBES WHAT HAPPENS TO AN OVER-CONFI-
DENT SORCERER'S APPRENTICE WHO DECIDES TO
TRY HIS NEWLY LEARNED SKILL OF MANY MAGIC
TRICKS. FROM THE CHILDREN'S STORIES SERIES.
LC NO. 72-737490
PROD-STNHM   DIST-STNHM   1972

**SPANISH CONQUERORS AND
COLONIZERS** C 58 FRS
SOUND FILMSTRIP - AUDIO TAPE I-J
EXPLAINS CORTES' CONQUEST OF THE AZTEC EM-
PIRE IN RELATION TO THE AZTEC LEGEND OF A
'LIGHT GOD.' RECOUNTS PIZARRO'S EXPLOITS AS
PART OF THE CONTINUING PURSUIT OF EL DO-
RADO. FROM THE EXPLORATION - MAN'S QUEST
FOR KNOWLEDGE SERIES.
LC NO. 73-732522
PROD-SED   DIST-SED   1972

STATIONS IN SPACE C 86 FRS
FILMSTRIP WITH SCRIPT I-J
SEE SERIES TITLE FOR DESCRIPTIVE STATEMENT.
FROM THE MAN ON THE MOON SERIES.
PROD-DOUBLE   DIST-DOUBLE   1971

STORY OF ROBIN HOOD, PT 1 C 73 FRS
FILMSTRIP WITH SCRIPT
AN ADAPTATION OF THE LEGEND OF ROBIN HOOD
AND HIS BAND OF MEN. FROM THE LITERARY
CLASSICS, SET 1 SERIES.
LC NO. 72-732624
PROD-DISNEY   DIST-DISNEY

STORY OF ROBIN HOOD, PT 1 C 116 FRS
SOUND FILMSTRIP - RECORD
AN ADAPTATION OF THE LEGEND OF ROBIN HOOD
AND HIS BAND OF MEN. FROM THE LITERARY
CLASSICS, SET 1 SERIES.
LC NO. 72-732624
PROD-DISNEY   DIST-DISNEY

STORY OF ROBIN HOOD, PT 2 C 69 FRS
FILMSTRIP WITH SCRIPT
AN ADAPTATION OF THE LEGEND OF ROBIN HOOD
AND HIS BAND OF MEN. FROM THE LITERARY
CLASSICS, SET 1 SERIES.
LC NO. 72-732624
PROD-DISNEY   DIST-DISNEY

STORY OF ROBIN HOOD, PT 2 C 116 FRS
SOUND FILMSTRIP - RECORD
AN ADAPTATION OF THE LEGEND OF ROBIN HOOD
AND HIS BAND OF MEN. FROM THE LITERARY
CLASSICS, SET 1 SERIES.
LC NO. 72-732624
PROD-DISNEY   DIST-DISNEY

STORY SERIES 6--A SERIES
P-I
PROD-BFA   DIST-BFA   1972

ALL THE ANIMALS WERE ANGRY   51 FRS
BRODERICK   55 FRS
DRAGON STEW   77 FRS
TIGER IN THE TEAPOT, THE   41 FRS

SUBTRACTION PROGRAM C 90 FRS
SOUND FILMSTRIP - AUDIO TAPE
PRESENTS A SEQUENTIAL PRESENTATION OF THE
SUBTRACTION PROGRAM. FROM THE BASIC COM-
PUTATIONAL SKILLS SERIES.
LC NO. 72-735462
PROD-CREATV   DIST-CREATV

SUN C 40 FRS
SOUND FILMSTRIP - AUDIO TAPE P-I
SEE SERIES TITLE FOR DESCRIPTIVE STATEMENT.
FROM THE FABLES AND FACTS SERIES.
PROD-TERF   DIST-TERF   1973

SUPPORTING SERVICES C 48 FRS
SOUND FILMSTRIP - RECORD
SHOWS EXAMPLES OF LABOR BATTALIONS AND
ARMY ENGINEERS BUILDING, DESTROYING AND
REBUILDING INSTALLATIONS, FORTIFICATIONS,
RAILROAD BRIDGES, PONTOON BRIDGES AND
PERMANENT BRIDGES. FROM THE CIVIL WAR AS
IT HAPPENED SERIES.
LC NO. 72-735145
PROD-EDREC   DIST-TECVIS   1970

T

**TAKING CARE OF THINGS
AROUND ME - BOOKS** C 31 FRS
FILMSTRIP WITH CAPTIONS
USES CAPTIONED PICTURES TO DEMONSTRATE
TO THE CHILDREN THE IMPORTANCE OF TAKING
CARE OF THINGS AROUND THEM. FROM THE AU-
DIOVISUAL INVOLVEMENT SERIES.
LC NO. 72-734038
PROD-WERMOR   DIST-BFA   1972

TALE OF TWO TEETH, A C 42 FRS
SOUND FILMSTRIP - AUDIO TAPE P-I
TELLS THE EFFECT OF NUTRITION ON TEETH AND
GENERAL HEALTH. EXPLAINS THAT SOME FOODS
GIVE ENERGY, SOME BUILD THE BODY AND SOME
MAKE US FEEL GOOD. FROM THE PRACTICING
GOOD HEALTH, SET 2 - YOUR MOUTH SPEAKING
SERIES.
LC NO. 73-733204
PROD-DISNEY   DIST-DISNEY   1973

**TAPE RECORDER IN TEACHING,
THE** C 59 FRS
FILMSTRIP
DISCUSSES THE USE OF THE TAPE RECORDER FOR
CLASSROOM TEACHING AT ALL LEVELS. FROM THE
AUDIO-VISUAL SERIES.
LC NO. FIA66-3570
PROD-BSF   DIST-BSF   1966

TELEPHONE INSTALLER, THE C 96 FRS
SOUND FILMSTRIP - RECORD I-C
EMPHASIZES REQUIREMENTS FOR MECHANICAL
AND MANUAL DEXTERITY, ABILITY TO MEET CUS-
TOMERS, SAFE DRIVING AND OTHER SKILLS OF
TELEPHONE INSTALLERS. FROM THE EXPLORING
CAREERS, GROUP 1 SERIES.
LC NO. 73-733174
PROD-SVE   DIST-SVE   1973

**THOSE REMARKABLE PIECES OF
PAPER CALLED SECURITIES** C
SOUND FILMSTRIP - AUDIO TAPE
SEE SERIES TITLE FOR DESCRIPTIVE STATEMENT.
FROM THE NATION OF OWNERS SERIES.

LC NO. 72-736600
PROD-EMP   DIST-XEROX

THREE BEARS, THE C 30 FRS
SOUND FILMSTRIP - AUDIO TAPE K-P
EXPLAINS WHAT HAPPENS TO GOLDILOCKS ONE
DAY WHEN, OUT OF CURIOSITY, SHE WANDERS
INTO THE HOME OF THE THREE BEARS. FROM THE
CHILDREN'S STORIES SERIES.
LC NO. 72-732804
PROD-STNHM   DIST-STNHM   1973

THUMBELINA C 31 FRS
SOUND FILMSTRIP - AUDIO TAPE K-P
DESCRIBES THE ADVENTURES OF A TINY GIRL, NO
BIGGER THAN A THUMB, AS SHE IS CARRIED
AWAY BY A FROG. FROM THE CHILDREN'S STO-
RIES SERIES.
LC NO. 72-737209
PROD-STNHM   DIST-STNHM   1973

THUNDER AND LIGHTNING C 40 FRS
SOUND FILMSTRIP - AUDIO TAPE P-I
SEE SERIES TITLE FOR DESCRIPTIVE STATEMENT.
FROM THE FABLES AND FACTS SERIES.
PROD-TERF   DIST-TERF   1973

TIGER IN THE TEAPOT, THE C 41 FRS
SOUND FILMSTRIP - AUDIO TAPE P-I
PRESENTS A STORY WHICH SUGGESTS THAT
KINDNESS AND TACTFULNESS ARE USEFUL QUAL-
ITIES. FROM THE STORY SERIES 6 SERIES.
LC NO. 72-737105
PROD-BFA   DIST-BFA   1972

TILLAGE ALTERNATIVES C 48 FRS
FILMSTRIP WITH SCRIPT H-C A
SHOWS NEW DESIGNS IN FARM MACHINERY AND
IMPROVEMENT OF HERBICIDES TO CONTROL
WEEDS WHICH ARE NOW GIVING CROP PRODUC-
ERS MORE ALTERNATIVES IN TILLAGE. DISCUSSES
THESE ALTERNATIVES AND THE RESULTS OF A 28-
STATE SURVEY.
LC NO. 73-733262
PROD-USDA   DIST-USDA   1972

**TIMBER - WASHINGTON'S MOST
VALUABLE CROP** C 81 FRS
SOUND FILMSTRIP - AUDIO TAPE J-H A
DISCUSSES THE GREAT FOREST OF THE PACIFIC
NORTHWEST. RELATES THE HISTORY OF LOGGING
IN THE U S AND THE EARLY WASTING OF THE VAL-
UABLE TIMBER. FROM THE FOCUS ON AMERICA -
THE PACIFIC STATES SERIES.
LC NO. 73-733161
PROD-SVE   DIST-SVE   1972

TOBACCO - A PUFF OF POISON B 63 FRS
SOUND FILMSTRIP - AUDIO TAPE P-I
INVESTIGATES THE POISONS CONTAINED IN TO-
BACCO SMOKE. DISCUSSES THE REASONS THAT
PEOPLE START SMOKING DESPITE THE DANGERS
AND THE DIFFICULTY OF BREAKING THE SMOKING
HABIT. FROM THE DRUGS - A TRICK, A TRAP SE-
RIES.
LC NO. 72-737373
PROD-EBEC   DIST-EBEC   1972

TOLL OF THE CIVIL WAR, THE C 49 FRS
SOUND FILMSTRIP - RECORD
DEPICTS WAR'S RAVAGES, FOCUSING ON THE DE-
STRUCTION OF WAR MATERIAL AND THE MONE-
TARY COST OF THE WAR. FROM THE CIVIL WAR AS
IT HAPPENED SERIES.
LC NO. 72-735147
PROD-EDREC   DIST-TECVIS   1970

TOLTECS C 59 FRS
FILMSTRIP WITH SCRIPT
FROM THE MEXICAN EPIC - BEFORE THE
CONQUEST SERIES.
LC NO. 75-732593
PROD-UMM   DIST-UMM

TOM THUMB C 35 FRS
SOUND FILMSTRIP - AUDIO TAPE K-P
DESCRIBES THE ADVENTURES OF TOM THUMB,
THE TINY SON OF A FARMER. FROM THE CHIL-
DREN'S STORIES SERIES.
LC NO. 72-737493
PROD-STNHM   DIST-STNHM   1973

**TOWN AND VILLAGE IN THE
MOUNTAINS OF PUEBLA** C 41 FRS
SOUND FILMSTRIP - AUDIO TAPE
DESCRIBES THE SOCIAL SITUATION IN TWO
MOUNTAIN COMMUNITIES OF THE STATE OF
PUEBLA. FROM THE MEXICO - A COMMUNITY
STUDY SERIES.
PROD-EGH   DIST-EGH   1972

108

W

TRADE AND TRANSPORTATION IN CHINA C 75 FRS
SOUND FILMSTRIP · AUDIO TAPE
DESCRIBES THE POSITION OF RIVER AND OTHER TRANSPORT IN CHINA AND THE INFLUENCE OF GEOGRAPHY ON HER TRADE. FROM THE INSIDE THE PEOPLE'S REPUBLIC OF CHINA SERIES.
PROD-EGH   DIST-EGH   1972

TRY TO JOIN OUR UNION C 64 FRS
SOUND FILMSTRIP · AUDIO TAPE I-J
SEE SERIES TITLE FOR DESCRIPTIVE STATEMENT. FROM THE MIND BLOWERS SERIES.
LC NO. 73-733277
PROD-SNBRST   DIST-SNBRST   1973

TRY, TRY AGAIN C 33 FRS
SOUND FILMSTRIP · AUDIO TAPE
EXPLAINS THAT RONNIE LEARNS THAT ONE SHOULD NOT GIVE UP BECAUSE A TASK IS HARD BUT SHOULD TRY HARDER. FROM THE LITTLE THINGS THAT COUNT SERIES.
PROD-EGH   DIST-EGH   1966

TURKEY C
SOUND FILMSTRIP · AUDIO TAPE P-I
DESCRIBES THE GIFTS GIVEN TO THE WORLD BY THE MANY CIVILIZATIONS WHICH EXISTED IN THE ANCIENT LAND OF TURKEY · SMELTED IRON FROM THE HITTITE EMPIRE, COINAGE FROM LYDIA AND THE CONTRIBUTIONS OF THE GREEK COLONISTS, ROMAN CONQUERORS AND THE BYZANTINES. FROM THE NEW FRIENDS FROM DISTANT LANDS · THE CULTURE WE SHARE SERIES.
PROD-PATED   DIST-PATED   1973

TURNING TOWARD JERUSALEM C 36 FRS
SOUND FILMSTRIP · RECORD I R
GIVES A FIRST-PERSON PRESENTATION OF THE LIFE OF JESUS. PROVIDES A FURTHER UNFOLDING OF THE MEANING OF THE KINGDOM OF GOD, AS JESUS OUTLINES HIS KINGDOM TO THE PEOPLE OF ISRAEL, THE PROMISED KINGDOM WHICH IS IN ACCORD WITH THE SCRIPTURES. DESCRIBES THE MOTHER OF JAMES AND JOHN AS A SYMBOL OF SERVICE, THE RAISING OF LAZARUS AS A SYMBOL OF FAITH AND PALM SUNDAY AND THE PASSOVER MEAL AS SYMBOLS OF HUMILITY AND LOVE. FROM THE MY NAME IS JESUS SERIES.
LC NO. 72-737435
PROD-ROAS   DIST-ROAS   1972

TWINKLE NOSE, THE FIREFLY C 40 FRS
SOUND FILMSTRIP · RECORD
PRESENTS THE STORY OF TWINKLE NOSE, WHO MANAGED TO BRING CHILDREN TOGETHER TO PLAY. FROM THE CHRISTMASTORIES SERIES.
LC NO. 72-736542
PROD-EGH   DIST-EGH   1972

TWO DERVISHES, THE C 30 FRS
SOUND FILMSTRIP · AUDIO TAPE K-P
DEMONSTRATES THE GULLIBILITY OF MAN IN A TALE OF TWO DERVISHES WHO FOOLED THE PUBLIC. FROM THE CHILDREN'S STORIES SERIES.
LC NO. 72-737491
PROD-STNHM   DIST-STNHM   1973

U

UGLY DUCKLING, THE C 30 FRS
SOUND FILMSTRIP · AUDIO TAPE K-P
DESCRIBES THE ADVENTURES OF THE UGLY DUCKLING, THE LAST AND BIGGEST OF EIGHT DUCK EGGS TO HATCH. FROM THE CHILDREN'S STORIES SERIES.
LC NO. 72-737208
PROD-STNHM   DIST-STNHM   1973

USING NUMBER PAIRS C 43 FRS
FILMSTRIP WITH SCRIPT P
INTRODUCES THE CONCEPTS OF RATE PAIR AND ORDERED PAIR, AND SHOWS HOW ORDERED PAIRS OF NUMBERS CAN BE USED TO RECORD DATA. FROM THE MODERN MATHEMATICS PROGRAM, LEVEL 4, 746 SERIES.
LC NO. 72-733808

PROD-EDPRC   DIST-EDPRC

V

VALVE PROBLEMS · CAUSES AND CORRECTIONS C
SOUND FILMSTRIP · RECORD J-C A
SEE SERIES TITLE FOR DESCRIPTIVE STATEMENT. FROM THE INTERNAL COMBUSTION ENGINE EXPLAINED SERIES.
PROD-BERGL   DIST-BERGL   1972

VIKINGS, THE ARABS AND MARCO POLO, THE C 58 FRS
SOUND FILMSTRIP · AUDIO TAPE I-J
SETS THE EXPLORATIONS OF THE VIKINGS, THE ARABS AND MARCO POLO AGAINST THE BACKGROUND OF THE MIDDLE AGES. FROM THE EXPLORATION · MAN'S QUEST FOR KNOWLEDGE SERIES.
LC NO. 73-732519
PROD-SED   DIST-SED   1972

VILLAGE LIFE C 52 FRS
SOUND FILMSTRIP · AUDIO TAPE
USES BOLIVIA AS AN EXAMPLE OF VILLAGE LIFE ON THE ALTIPLANO. FROM THE LIFEWAYS OF THE PEOPLE · SOUTH AMERICA SERIES.
PROD-EGH   DIST-EGH   1972

VILLAGE OF ZIHUATANEJO AND ITS TURTLE INDUSTRY C 35 FRS
SOUND FILMSTRIP · AUDIO TAPE
DESCRIBES THE VILLAGE LIFE AND THE INFLUENCE OF THE SEA UPON IT. FROM THE MEXICO · A COMMUNITY STUDY SERIES.
PROD-EGH   DIST-EGH   1972

VISTAS Y SONIDOS DE LA TIENDA DE ANIMALES CASEROS C 33 FRS
SOUND FILMSTRIP · AUDIO TAPE P
A SPANISH LANGUAGE FILMSTRIP. FOLLOWS A FAMILY ON A VISIT TO A NEIGHBORHOOD PET SHOP. FROM THE NUESTRO MUNDO DE VISTAS Y SONIDOS, GRUPO 1 SERIES.
LC NO. 72-732899
PROD-SVE   DIST-SVE

VISTAS Y SONIDOS DEL PARQUE DE DIVERSIONES C 41 FRS
SOUND FILMSTRIP · AUDIO TAPE
A SPANISH LANGUAGE FILMSTRIP. PORTRAYS THE EXCITEMENT AND ACTIVITIES OF TWO BOYS AND THEIR PARENTS ON THE RIDES IN A CHILDREN'S AMUSEMENT PARK. FROM THE NUESTRO MUNDO DE VISTAS Y SONIDOS, GRUPO 1 SERIES.
LC NO. 72-732900
PROD-SVE   DIST-SVE

VOLCANOES, PT 1 C 37 FRS
FILMSTRIP WITH SCRIPT I-H
DESCRIBES THE MECHANISMS OF VOLCANIC ACTIVITY, EMPHASIZING THE RESULTS OF SUCH ACTIVITY. EXPLAINS THE CAUSES, FORMATION AND EFFECTS OF VOLCANOES AND SHOWS EXAMPLES OF WELL-KNOWN OR UNUSUAL VOLCANOES. FROM THE ORIGINS OF THE EARTH SERIES.
LC NO. 72-737134
PROD-VISPUB   DIST-VISPUB   1971

VOLCANOES, PT 2 C 40 FRS
FILMSTRIP WITH SCRIPT I-H
EMPHASIZES VOLCANOES ASSOCIATED WITH LANDFORMS OTHER THAN FOLD MOUNTAINS. ILLUSTRATES THE PROCESS OF RIFTING. FROM THE ORIGINS OF THE EARTH SERIES.
LC NO. 72-737135
PROD-VISPUB   DIST-VISPUB   1971

W

WAR ON THE WATER, THE C 44 FRS
SOUND FILMSTRIP · RECORD
DESCRIBES THE MAJOR ROLE OF THE NAVIES OF BOTH THE UNION AND CONFEDERATE FORCES IN THE WAR. FROM THE CIVIL WAR AS IT HAPPENED SERIES.
LC NO. 72-735146
PROD-EDREC   DIST-TECVIS   1970

WASHINGTON'S BIRTHDAY C 51 FRS
SOUND FILMSTRIP · RECORD K-P
GIVES THE BACKGROUND OF WASHINGTON'S BIRTHDAY AND EXPLAINS HOW IT IS CELEBRATED TODAY. FROM THE HOLIDAY SERIES, SET 2 SERIES.
LC NO. 72-737285
PROD-MGHT   DIST-MGHT   1972

WATER C 40 FRS
SOUND FILMSTRIP · AUDIO TAPE P-I
SEE SERIES TITLE FOR DESCRIPTIVE STATEMENT. FROM THE FABLES AND FACTS SERIES.
PROD-TERF   DIST-TERF   1973

WHAT IS GREAT BRITAIN C 49 FRS
SOUND FILMSTRIP · AUDIO TAPE
GIVES THE VIEWER A GENERAL OUTLINE OF WHAT GREAT BRITAIN IS LIKE. FROM THE GREAT BRITAIN · A REGIONAL STUDY SERIES.
LC NO. 72-736525
PROD-EGH   DIST-EGH   1972

WHAT IS HOLLAND C 54 FRS
SOUND FILMSTRIP · AUDIO TAPE
GIVES A GENERAL OUTLINE OF WHAT HOLLAND IS LIKE. FROM THE HOLLAND · A REGIONAL STUDY SERIES.
PROD-EGH   DIST-EGH   1972

WHAT IS IT (TEST SCRIPT) C
FILMSTRIP WITH CAPTIONS
FROM THE ANIMALS SERIES.
LC NO. 72-734417
PROD-LIEB   DIST-MSCF   1970

WHAT IS LIFE C 41 FRS
SOUND FILMSTRIP · AUDIO TAPE
INTRODUCES LIFE AS A SERIES OF ACTIVITIES THAT AN ORGANISM MUST CARRY ON TO BE 'ALIVE.' FROM THE LIFE · A UNIQUE PHENOMENON SERIES.
PROD-EGH   DIST-EGH   1972

WHAT TO EXPECT AT COLLEGE, PT 1 C 69 FRS
SOUND FILMSTRIP · AUDIO TAPE H
PRESENTS STUDENTS WHO DESCRIBE THEIR OWN COLLEGE EXPECTATIONS, MISCONCEPTIONS AND ADJUSTMENTS. HELPS BREAK THE GROUND FOR REALISTIC GROUP DISCUSSION AMONG COLLEGE-BOUND STUDENTS. FROM THE COLLEGE SERIES.
LC NO. 72-737467
PROD-GA   DIST-GA   1972

WHAT TO EXPECT AT COLLEGE, PT 2 C 72 FRS
SOUND FILMSTRIP · AUDIO TAPE H
PRESENTS STUDENTS WHO DESCRIBE THEIR OWN COLLEGE EXPECTATIONS, MISCONCEPTIONS AND ADJUSTMENTS. HELPS BREAK THE GROUND FOR REALISTIC GROUP DISCUSSION AMONG COLLEGE-BOUND STUDENTS. FROM THE COLLEGE SERIES.
LC NO. 72-737467
PROD-GA   DIST-GA   1972

WHAT YOU WILL FIND IN A HOSPITAL C 50 FRS
SOUND FILMSTRIP · AUDIO TAPE
CONDUCTS A GROUP OF CHILDREN AROUND A HOSPITAL, ANSWERING THEIR QUESTIONS AS THEY GO. FROM THE GOING TO THE DOCTOR, DENTIST AND HOSPITAL SERIES.
PROD-EGH   DIST-EGH   1972

WHICH COLLEGE FOR YOU, PT 1 C 74 FRS
SOUND FILMSTRIP · AUDIO TAPE H
ESTABLISHES BASIC CRITERIA FOR INTELLIGENT COLLEGE SELECTION. DISCUSSES SOCIAL, GEOGRAPHIC, ACADEMIC AND FINANCIAL CONSIDERATIONS. STIMULATES SELF-EVALUATION AND EXCHANGE OF IDEAS. FROM THE COLLEGE SERIES.
LC NO. 72-737466
PROD-GA   DIST-GA   1972

WHICH COLLEGE FOR YOU, PT 2 C 62 FRS
SOUND FILMSTRIP · AUDIO TAPE H
ESTABLISHES BASIC CRITERIA FOR INTELLIGENT COLLEGE SELECTION. DISCUSSES SOCIAL, GEOGRAPHIC, ACADEMIC AND FINANCIAL CONSIDERATIONS. STIMULATES SELF-EVALUATION AND EXCHANGE OF IDEAS. FROM THE COLLEGE SERIES.
LC NO. 72-737466
PROD-GA   DIST-GA   1972

WHY VISIT THE DENTIST   C 36 FRS
     SOUND FILMSTRIP - AUDIO TAPE   P-I
EXPLAINS THAT WE MUST VISIT DENTISTS BE-
CAUSE THEY ARE CONCERNED WITH KEEPING US
HEALTHY BY X-RAYING OUR TEETH, CLEANING
THEM, REMOVING PLAQUE, FILLING CAVITIES TO
PREVENT FURTHER DECAY, STRAIGHTENING
CROOKED TEETH WITH BRACES AND MAKING AR-
TIFICIAL TEETH TO REPLACE ANY WE MAY LOSE.
FROM THE PRACTICING GOOD HEALTH, SET 2 -
YOUR MOUTH SPEAKING SERIES.
     LC NO. 73-733198
PROD-DISNEY   DIST-DISNEY   1973

WHY WE WRITE   C 30 FRS
     SOUND FILMSTRIP - AUDIO TAPE
DESCRIBES THE VARIOUS USES OF WRITING.
FROM THE LEARN TO WRITE WITH LETTY LETTER
SERIES.
PROD-EGH   DIST-EGH   1972

**WILDLIFE SANCTUARIES OF
INDIA**   C
     FILMSTRIP
TOURS FOUR INDIAN WILDLIFE SANCTUARIES
WHICH INCLUDE SOME OF THE EARTH'S RAREST
ANIMALS, WITH A SIDE TRIP TO SEVERAL INDIAN
VILLAGES TO VIEW THEIR CRAFTS AND FOLK CUS-
TOMS. FROM THE AUDUBON WILDLIFE THEATRE
SERIES.
     LC NO. 72-701984

PROD-KEGPL   DIST-AVEXP   1971

**WORK OF THE PEOPLE OF
CHINA**   C 63 FRS
     SOUND FILMSTRIP - AUDIO TAPE
DESCRIBES THE VARIOUS TYPES OF WORK OF THE
PEOPLE IN AGRICULTURE AND IN INDUSTRY.
FROM THE INSIDE THE PEOPLE'S REPUBLIC OF
CHINA SERIES.
PROD-EGH   DIST-EGH   1972

**WORKING IN THE POLITICAL
WORLD**   C 40 FRS
     SOUND FILMSTRIP - AUDIO TAPE
DESCRIBES THE OPPORTUNITIES FOR WORK IN
POLITICS. FROM THE NOW YOU ARE A VOTER SE-
RIES.
     LC NO. 72-736555
PROD-EGH   DIST-EGH

WORLD IS BORN, THE   C 40 FRS
     SOUND FILMSTRIP - AUDIO TAPE   P-I
SEE SERIES TITLE FOR DESCRIPTIVE STATEMENT.
FROM THE FABLES AND FACTS SERIES.
PROD-TERF   DIST-TERF   1973

WRITING READINESS   C 41 FRS
     SOUND FILMSTRIP - AUDIO TAPE
DESCRIBES THE VARIOUS 'STROKES' NEEDED IN
WRITING. FROM THE LEARN TO WRITE WITH
LETTY LETTER SERIES.

PROD-EGH   DIST-EGH   1972

X

X-RAY TECHNICIAN   C 53 FRS
     SOUND FILMSTRIP - AUDIO TAPE
DISCUSSES THE MANY PHASES OF THE JOB OF
THE X-RAY TECHNICIAN, FROM TAKING THE PIC-
TURE TO DEVELOPING IT. FROM THE HOSPITAL
JOB OPPORTUNITIES SERIES.
PROD-EGH   DIST-EGH   1972

Y

**YOUNG AMERICA ADMIRES THE
ANCIENTS**   C 80 FRS
     SOUND FILMSTRIP - RECORD   J-C
SEE SERIES TITLE FOR DESCRIPTIVE STATEMENT.
FROM THE AMERICAN CIVILIZATION - 1783-1840
SERIES.
PROD-SUNCOM   DIST-SUNCOM   1973

ALPHABETICAL GUIDE TO 8mm MOTION CARTRIDGES

A

AFRICAN BIRDS   C   4 MIN
       S8MM CARTRIDGE SILENT   P-I
FROM THE VERTEBRATE CONTRASTS, PT 2
SERIES.
   LC NO. 72-703293
PROD-DOUBLE   DIST-DOUBLE   1972

ALLIGATORS HUNTING   C   4 MIN
       S8MM CARTRIDGE SILENT   P-I
FROM THE REPTILES SERIES.
   LC NO. 72-703283
PROD-DOUBLE   DIST-DOUBLE   1972

AMAZON JUNGLE   C   4 MIN
       S8MM CARTRIDGE SILENT   P-I
FROM THE PLANTS GROW IN MANY PLACES
SERIES.
   LC NO. 72-703279
PROD-DOUBLE   DIST-DOUBLE   1972

AMERICAN MOUNTAIN ANIMALS
           C   4 MIN
       S8MM CARTRIDGE SILENT   P-I
FROM THE LAND ANIMALS SERIES.
   LC NO. 72-703261
PROD-DOUBLE   DIST-DOUBLE   1972

**ANIMAL LIFE IN A DROP OF
WATER (INVERTEBRATES**   C   4 MIN
       S8MM CARTRIDGE SILENT   P-I
FROM THE INVERTEBRATES, PT 1 SERIES.
   LC NO. 72-703259
PROD-DOUBLE   DIST-DOUBLE   1972

**ANIMAL LIFE IN A DROP OF
WATER (LIFE IN SINGLE CELLS)**   C   4 MIN
       S8MM CARTRIDGE SILENT   P-I
FROM THE LIFE IN SINGLE CELLS SERIES.
   LC NO. 72-703262
PROD-DOUBLE   DIST-DOUBLE   1972

**ANTHILL PROTECTION, PT 1
(INVERTEBRATES, PT 2)**   C   4 MIN
       S8MM CARTRIDGE SILENT   P-I
FROM THE INVERTEBRATES, PT 2 SERIES.
   LC NO. 72-703260
PROD-DOUBLE   DIST-DOUBLE   1972

**ANTHILL PROTECTION, PT 1
(SOCIAL ANIMALS)**   C   4 MIN
       S8MM CARTRIDGE SILENT   P-I
FROM THE SOCIAL ANIMALS SERIES.
   LC NO. 72-703288
PROD-DOUBLE   DIST-DOUBLE   1972

**ANTHILL PROTECTION, PT 1
(SOCIAL INSECTS)**   C   4 MIN
       S8MM CARTRIDGE SILENT   P-I
FROM THE SOCIAL INSECTS SERIES.
   LC NO. 72-703289
PROD-DOUBLE   DIST-DOUBLE   1972

ANTS - TUNNEL BUILDING   C   4 MIN
       S8MM CARTRIDGE SILENT   P-I
FROM THE SOCIAL INSECTS SERIES.
   LC NO. 72-703289
PROD-DOUBLE   DIST-DOUBLE   1972

ARCTIC MUSK OX   C   4 MIN
       S8MM CARTRIDGE SILENT   P-I
FROM THE VERTEBRATE CONTRASTS, PT 1
SERIES.
   LC NO. 72-703291
PROD-DOUBLE   DIST-DOUBLE   1972

ARCTIC THAW, PT 1   C   4 MIN
       S8MM CARTRIDGE SILENT   P-I
FROM THE WEATHER SERIES.
   LC NO. 72-703295
PROD-DOUBLE   DIST-DOUBLE   1972

B

BEAVER DAM AND LODGE   C   4 MIN
       S8MM CARTRIDGE SILENT   P-I
FROM THE POND COMMUNITY SERIES.
   LC NO. 72-703282
PROD-DOUBLE   DIST-DOUBLE   1972

BELL   C   12 MIN
       S8MM CARTRIDGE SILENT
USES ANIMATION, GRAPHICS, FILM CLIPS AND
SONGS TO ILLUSTRATE VARIOUS USAGES OF THE
WORD BELL. EXAMPLES INCLUDE DUMBBELL,
BELLHOP, DOORBELL, BELLE OF THE BALL AND
THE DIVING BELL PROJECT NEMO. FROM THE
MAKE A WISH SERIES.
   LC NO. 72-701268
PROD-ABCNEW   DIST-ABCMED   1972

BISON HERDS   C   4 MIN
       S8MM CARTRIDGE SILENT   P-I
FROM THE VERTEBRATE CONTRASTS, PT 2
SERIES.
   LC NO. 72-703293
PROD-DOUBLE   DIST-DOUBLE   1972

BOTTLENOSE DOLPHIN   C   4 MIN
       S8MM CARTRIDGE SILENT   P-I
FROM THE OCEAN ANIMALS SERIES.
   LC NO. 72-703273
PROD-DOUBLE   DIST-DOUBLE   1972

BULLS   C   12 MIN
       S8MM CARTRIDGE SILENT
USES ANIMATION, GRAPHICS, FILM CLIPS AND
SONGS TO ILLUSTRATE VARIOUS MEANINGS OF
THE WORD BULL. EXAMPLES INCLUDE A NA-
TIONAL SYMBOL, A SLANG EXPRESSION, A FA-
MOUS INDIAN AND AN ANIMAL. FROM THE MAKE
A WISH SERIES.
   LC NO. 72-701267
PROD-ABCNEW   DIST-ABCMED   1972

C

CARIBOU   C   4 MIN
       S8MM CARTRIDGE SILENT   P-I
FROM THE PLANT-EATING ANIMALS SERIES.
   LC NO. 72-703278
PROD-DOUBLE   DIST-DOUBLE   1972

CARNIVOROUS PLANTS   C   4 MIN
       S8MM CARTRIDGE SILENT   P-I
FROM THE PLANTS GROWING SERIES.
   LC NO. 72-703280
PROD-DOUBLE   DIST-DOUBLE   1972

**CENTIPEDES, MILLIPEDES AND
SCORPIONS**   C   4 MIN
       S8MM CARTRIDGE SILENT   P-I
FROM THE INVERTEBRATES, PT 2 SERIES.
   LC NO. 72-703260
PROD-DOUBLE   DIST-DOUBLE   1972

CHEETAH HUNTING FOOD   C   4 MIN
       S8MM CARTRIDGE SILENT   P-I
FROM THE LAND ANIMALS SERIES.
   LC NO. 72-703261
PROD-DOUBLE   DIST-DOUBLE   1972

CITIES--A SERIES

                 I-C
PROD-CBSTV   DIST-BFA   1968

CITIES, THE - A CITY IS TO LIVE IN, PT
1   29 MIN
CITIES, THE - A CITY IS TO LIVE IN, PT
2   29 MIN
CITIES, THE - DILEMMA IN BLACK AND
WHITE, PT 1   29 MIN
CITIES, THE - DILEMMA IN BLACK AND
WHITE, PT 2   29 MIN
CITIES, THE - TO BUILD A FUTURE, PT
1   29 MIN
CITIES, THE - TO BUILD A FUTURE, PT
2   29 MIN

**CITIES, THE - A CITY IS TO
LIVE IN, PT 1**   X   29 MIN
       8MM CARTRIDGE OPTICAL SOUND   I-C
EXAMINES THE RESULTS OF 25 YEARS OF IGNO-
RANCE AND NEGLIGENCE THAT HAS LED MANY OF
THE NATION'S CITIES TO A POINT OF MAJOR CRI-
SIS. ILLUSTRATES SUCH SPREADING PROBLEMS
AS WATER AND AIR POLLUTION, DECAYING
SLUMS AND INCREASING DEPERSONALIZATION.
FROM THE CITIES SERIES.
PROD-CBSTV   DIST-BFA   1968

**CITIES, THE - A CITY IS TO
LIVE IN, PT 2**   X   29 MIN
       8MM CARTRIDGE OPTICAL SOUND   I-C
EXAMINES THE RESULTS OF 25 YEARS OF IGNO-
RANCE AND NEGLIGENCE THAT HAS LED MANY OF
THE NATION'S CITIES TO A POINT OF MAJOR CRI-
SIS. ILLUSTRATES SUCH SPREADING PROBLEMS
AS WATER AND AIR POLLUTION, DECAYING
SLUMS AND INCREASING DEPERSONALIZATION.
FROM THE CITIES SERIES.
PROD-CBSTV   DIST-BFA   1968

**CITIES, THE - DILEMMA IN
BLACK AND WHITE, PT 1**   X   29 MIN
       8MM CARTRIDGE OPTICAL SOUND   I-C
FOCUSES ATTENTION ON THE RAPIDLY GROWING
NEGRO POPULATION TRAPPED BY POVERTY AND
PREJUDICE AROUND THE INNER CORE OF THE
CITY. FROM THE CITIES SERIES.
PROD-CBSTV   DIST-BFA   1968

**CITIES, THE - DILEMMA IN
BLACK AND WHITE, PT 2**   X   29 MIN
       8MM CARTRIDGE OPTICAL SOUND   I-C
FOCUSES ATTENTION ON THE RAPIDLY GROWING
NEGRO POPULATION TRAPPED BY POVERTY AND
PREJUDICE AROUND THE INNER CORE OF THE
CITY. FROM THE CITIES SERIES.
PROD-CBSTV   DIST-BFA   1968

**CITIES, THE - TO BUILD A
FUTURE, PT 1**   X   29 MIN
       8MM CARTRIDGE OPTICAL SOUND   I-C
REVEALS VARIOUS APPROACHES TO CITY IM-
PROVEMENT AND IDENTIFIES MEANS BY WHICH
OLD CITIES MAY BE RESHAPED AND NEW ONES
BUILT. FROM THE CITIES SERIES.
PROD-CBSTV   DIST-BFA   1968

**CITIES, THE - TO BUILD A
FUTURE, PT 2**   X   29 MIN
       8MM CARTRIDGE OPTICAL SOUND   I-C
REVEALS VARIOUS APPROACHES TO CITY IM-
PROVEMENT AND IDENTIFIES MEANS BY WHICH
OLD CITIES MAY BE RESHAPED AND NEW ONES
BUILT. FROM THE CITIES SERIES.
PROD-CBSTV   DIST-BFA   1968

CLOUDS   C   4 MIN
       S8MM CARTRIDGE SILENT   P-I
FROM THE WEATHER SERIES.
   LC NO. 72-703295
PROD-DOUBLE   DIST-DOUBLE   1972

CONTOUR MAPPING   C   4 MIN
       S8MM CARTRIDGE SILENT   P
FROM THE MAP READING SERIES.
PROD-HUBDSC   DIST-HUBDSC   1971

**COURTSHIP RITUAL OF
STICKLEBACK FISH**   C   4 MIN
       S8MM CARTRIDGE SILENT   P-I
FROM THE SMALL WATER ANIMALS IN PONDS
SERIES.
   LC NO. 72-703287
PROD-DOUBLE   DIST-DOUBLE   1972

CRABS C 4 MIN
S8MM CARTRIDGE· SILENT P-I
FROM THE OCEAN FOOD CHAINS SERIES.
LC NO. 72-703274
PROD-DOUBLE DIST-DOUBLE 1972

D

DEALER'S ROLE, THE C 18 MIN
S8MM CARTRIDGE SILENT
SHOWS HOW AGRICULTURAL CHEMICAL DEALERS
AND FARMERS WORK TOGETHER TO IMPROVE
FARM PRODUCTION.
LC NO. 72-702609
PROD-GEIGY DIST-GEIGY 1972

DESERT FLOWERS C 4 MIN
S8MM CARTRIDGE SILENT P-I
FROM THE PLANTS GROWING SERIES.
LC NO. 72-703280
PROD-DOUBLE DIST-DOUBLE 1972

DESERT PLANTS C 4 MIN
S8MM CARTRIDGE SILENT P-I
FROM THE PLANTS GROW IN MANY PLACES
SERIES.
LC NO. 72-703279
PROD-DOUBLE DIST-DOUBLE 1972

DESERT, THE C 4 MIN
S8MM CARTRIDGE SILENT I-J
PRESENTS A VIEW OF THE FORMS AND COLORS
CHARACTERISTIC OF THE DESERT. FROM THE
AWARENESS SERIES.
LC NO. FIA68-2029
PROD-IIESTER DIST-IIESTER 1967

DINOSAURS - MEAT EATERS C 4 MIN
S8MM CARTRIDGE SILENT P-I
FROM THE OUT OF THE SEA, ONTO THE LAND
SERIES.
LC NO. 72-703275
PROD-DOUBLE DIST-DOUBLE 1972

DINOSAURS - PLANT EATERS C 4 MIN
S8MM CARTRIDGE SILENT P-I
FROM THE REPTILES SERIES.
LC NO. 72-703283
PROD-DOUBLE DIST-DOUBLE 1972

DIVING SPIDER C 4 MIN
S8MM CARTRIDGE SILENT P-I
FROM THE SMALL WATER ANIMALS IN PONDS
SERIES.
LC NO. 72-703287
PROD-DOUBLE DIST-DOUBLE 1972

**DUCKBILLED PLATYPUS -
MOTHER AND BABIES** C 4 MIN
S8MM CARTRIDGE SILENT P-I
FROM THE UNUSUAL INSTINCTS SERIES.
LC NO. 72-703290
PROD-DOUBLE DIST-DOUBLE 1972

E

**ECHINODERMS AND SEA
SQUIRTS** C 4 MIN
S8MM CARTRIDGE SILENT P-I
FROM THE SALT WATER INVERTEBRATES
SERIES.
LC NO. 72-703285
PROD-DOUBLE DIST-DOUBLE 1972

ELEPHANTS FEEDING C 4 MIN
S8MM CARTRIDGE SILENT P-I
FROM THE PLANT-EATING ANIMALS SERIES.
LC NO. 72-703278
PROD-DOUBLE DIST-DOUBLE 1972

F

FLASH FLOOD C 4 MIN
S8MM CARTRIDGE SILENT P-I
FROM THE WEATHER SERIES.
LC NO. 72-703295
PROD-DOUBLE DIST-DOUBLE 1972

FLOWERS OPENING C 4 MIN
S8MM CARTRIDGE SILENT P-I
FROM THE PLANTS GROWING SERIES.
LC NO. 72-703280
PROD-DOUBLE DIST-DOUBLE 1972

FRESH WATER ALGAE C 4 MIN
S8MM CARTRIDGE SILENT P-I
FROM THE PLANTS GROW IN MANY PLACES
SERIES.
LC NO. 72-703279
PROD-DOUBLE DIST-DOUBLE 1972

**FRESH WATER
MICROORGANISMS** C 4 MIN
S8MM CARTRIDGE SILENT P-I
FROM THE LIFE IN SINGLE CELLS SERIES.
LC NO. 72-703262
PROD-DOUBLE DIST-DOUBLE 1972

FRUIT RIPENING C 4 MIN
S8MM CARTRIDGE SILENT P-I
FROM THE PLANTS GROWING SERIES.
LC NO. 72-703280
PROD-DOUBLE DIST-DOUBLE 1972

G

GIANT LAND TORTOISE C 4 MIN
S8MM CARTRIDGE SILENT P-I
FROM THE VERTEBRATE CONTRASTS, PT 2
SERIES.
LC NO. 72-703293
PROD-DOUBLE DIST-DOUBLE 1972

GLUTEN DEVELOPMENT C 3 MIN
S8MM CARTRIDGE SILENT
SHOWS THE EXTRACTION OF GLUTEN FROM
WHEAT FLOUR. ILLUSTRATES ITS EXTERNAL AND
INTERNAL APPEARANCE AFTER BAKING AND
COMPARES GLUTEN IN FIVE DIFFERENT WHEAT
FLOURS. FROM THE FOOD AND NUTRITION SE-
RIES.
LC NO. 72-702651
PROD-IOWA DIST-IOWA 1972

GRAZING ANIMALS OF AFRICA C 4 MIN
S8MM CARTRIDGE SILENT P-I
FROM THE PLANT-EATING ANIMALS SERIES.
LC NO. 72-703278
PROD-DOUBLE DIST-DOUBLE 1972

H

HARMFUL INSECTS C 4 MIN
S8MM CARTRIDGE SILENT P-I
FROM THE PLANT AND ANIMAL
INTERDEPENDENCE SERIES.
LC NO. 72-703277
PROD-DOUBLE DIST-DOUBLE 1972

HELPFUL INSECTS C 4 MIN
S8MM CARTRIDGE SILENT P-I
FROM THE INVERTEBRATES, PT 1 SERIES.
LC NO. 72-703259
PROD-DOUBLE DIST-DOUBLE 1972

HERMIT CRABS C 4 MIN
S8MM CARTRIDGE SILENT P-I
FROM THE INVERTEBRATES, PT 1 SERIES.
LC NO. 72-703259
PROD-DOUBLE DIST-DOUBLE 1972

HOW TO USE HAMMERS C 13 MIN
S8MM CARTRIDGE SILENT
SHOWS VARIOUS TYPES OF HAMMERS AND HOW
TO USE THEM PROPERLY. DEMONSTRATES THE
USE OF THE NAIL SET, HOW TO DRIVE AND RE-
MOVE A NAIL AND SAFETY PROCEDURES. FROM
THE HOW TO USE HAMMERS SERIES.
LC NO. 72-703413
PROD-VISIN DIST-VISIN 1970

HOW TO USE SAWS C 13 MIN
S8MM CARTRIDGE SILENT
SHOWS VARIOUS TYPES OF SAWS AND DEMON-
STRATES HOW TO USE THEM PROPERLY. IN-
CLUDES SHARPENING AND SAFETY PROCEDURES.
FROM THE HOW TO USE SAWS SERIES.
LC NO. 72-703392
PROD-VISIN DIST-VISIN 1970

HUNTER ANTS C 4 MIN
S8MM CARTRIDGE SILENT P-I
FROM THE INSECTS ARE MUCH ALIKE SERIES.
LC NO. 72-703257
PROD-DOUBLE DIST-DOUBLE 1972

I

**INSECTS ARE MUCH ALIKE--A
SERIES**
P-I
LC NO. 72-703257
PROD-DOUBLE DIST-DOUBLE 1972

HUNTER ANTS 4 MIN
LOCUST STRUCTURES - EXTERNAL 4 MIN
MOSQUITO STRUCTURES - EXTERNAL 4 MIN
SPIDER WASP, PT 1 4 MIN

INSECTS REPRODUCE--A SERIES
P-I
LC NO. 72-703258
PROD-DOUBLE DIST-DOUBLE 1972

LIFE CYCLE OF THE BUTTERFLY 4 MIN
LOCUST REPRODUCTION - NYMPH TO
ADULT 4 MIN
MOSQUITO - EGGS TO LARVAE 4 MIN
MOSQUITO - LARVA TO ADULT 4 MIN

INVERTEBRATES, PT 1--A SERIES
P-I
LC NO. 72-703259
PROD-DOUBLE DIST-DOUBLE 1972

ANIMAL LIFE IN A DROP OF WATER
(INVERTEBRATES-- 4 MIN
HELPFUL INSECTS 4 MIN
HERMIT CRABS 4 MIN
LIFE CYCLE OF THE BUTTERFLY 4 MIN

INVERTEBRATES, PT 2--A SERIES
P-I
LC NO. 72-703260
PROD-DOUBLE DIST-DOUBLE 1972

ANTHILL PROTECTION, PT 1
(INVERTEBRATES, PT 2) 4 MIN
CENTIPEDES, MILLIPEDES AND
SCORPIONS 4 MIN
CRABS 4 MIN
ECHINODERMS AND SEA SQUIRTS 4 MIN

J

JAWFISH C 4 MIN
S8MM CARTRIDGE SILENT P-I
FROM THE UNUSUAL INSTINCTS SERIES.
LC NO. 72-703290
PROD-DOUBLE DIST-DOUBLE 1972

K

KINDS OF EYES C 4 MIN
S8MM CARTRIDGE SILENT P
SHOWS ANIMALS WITH VARIOUS TYPES OF EYES.
INCLUDES THE COMPOUND EYES OF INSECTS
AND THE EYES OF SPIDERS, AMPHIBIANS, BIRDS
AND MAMMALS.
LC NO. 73-700140
PROD-VISED DIST-VISED 1972

L

LAND ANIMALS--A SERIES
P-I
LC NO. 72-703261
PROD-DOUBLE DIST-DOUBLE 1972

AMERICAN MOUNTAIN ANIMALS 4 MIN
CHEETAH HUNTING FOOD 4 MIN
NORTH AMERICAN PECCARY 4 MIN
SPOTTED SKUNK 4 MIN

LEAF-CUTTING ANTS C 4 MIN
S8MM CARTRIDGE SILENT P-I
FROM THE PLANT-EATING ANIMALS SERIES.
LC NO. 72-703278
PROD-DOUBLE DIST-DOUBLE 1972

LEMMING IN MIGRATION C 4 MIN
S8MM CARTRIDGE SILENT P-I
FROM THE UNUSUAL INSTINCTS SERIES.
LC NO. 72-703290
PROD-DOUBLE DIST-DOUBLE 1972

LEOPARD HUNTING FOOD C 4 MIN
S8MM CARTRIDGE SILENT P-I
FROM THE MEAT EATERS, PT 1 SERIES.
LC NO. 72-703267
PROD-DOUBLE DIST-DOUBLE 1972

LIFE CYCLE OF THE BUTTERFLY C 4 MIN
S8MM CARTRIDGE SILENT P-I
FROM THE INSECTS REPRODUCE SERIES.
LC NO. 72-703258
PROD-DOUBLE DIST-DOUBLE 1972

LIFE IN SINGLE CELLS--A SERIES

P-I

LC NO. 72-703262
PROD-DOUBLE DIST-DOUBLE 1972

ANIMAL LIFE IN A DROP OF WATER
(LIFE IN -- 4 MIN
FRESH WATER MICROORGANISMS 4 MIN
MICROSCOPIC ANIMALS - PROTOZOA 4 MIN
MICROSCOPIC WATER ANIMALS 4 MIN

LIONS HUNTING IMPALA C 4 MIN
S8MM CARTRIDGE SILENT P-I
FROM THE PLANT AND ANIMAL
INTERDEPENDENCE SERIES.
LC NO. 72-703277
PROD-DOUBLE DIST-DOUBLE 1972

**LOCUST REPRODUCTION -
NYMPH TO ADULT** C 4 MIN
S8MM CARTRIDGE SILENT P-I
FROM THE INSECTS REPRODUCE SERIES.
LC NO. 72-703258
PROD-DOUBLE DIST-DOUBLE 1972

**LOCUST STRUCTURES -
EXTERNAL** C 4 MIN
S8MM CARTRIDGE SILENT P-I
FROM THE INSECTS ARE MUCH ALIKE SERIES.
LC NO. 72-703257
PROD-DOUBLE DIST-DOUBLE 1972

**LUNGFISH AND OTHER
AUSTRALIAN ANIMALS** C 4 MIN
S8MM CARTRIDGE SILENT P-I
FROM THE OUT OF THE SEA, ONTO THE LAND
- SERIES.
LC NO. 72-703275
PROD-DOUBLE DIST-DOUBLE 1972

M

**MAKING IT IN FASHION - THE
BASICS OF CLOTHING
CONSTRUCTION, PT 1--A SERIES**

LC NO. 73-701003
PROD-DOUBLE DIST-DOUBLE 1970

BUTTONHOLES 7 MIN
BUTTONS 6 MIN
CONSTRUCTING BUSTLINE AND
WAISTLINE DARTS 5 MIN
CUTTING SPECIAL FABRICS 4 MIN
PATTERN LAYOUT 5 MIN
PRESSING 6 MIN
SELECTION OF FABRICS FOR
INTERFACING, LINING,-- 7 MIN
SEWING EQUIPMENT FOR
PROFESSIONAL RESULTS 4 MIN
STAY AND DIRECTIONAL STITCHING 4 MIN

**MAKING IT IN FASHION - THE
BASICS OF CLOTHING
CONSTRUCTION, PT 2--A SERIES**

LC NO. 73-701004
PROD-DOUBLE DIST-DOUBLE 1970

APPLYING A UNIQUE ZIPPER 4 MIN
CONSTRUCTING THE COVERED BELT
AND BUCKLE 5 MIN
CONSTRUCTING THE TOP STITCHED
BELT 3 MIN
HEM PRINCIPLES 4 MIN
REINFORCING SLEEVE SEAMS 4 MIN
SEAM FINISHES 7 MIN
SETTING IN SLEEVES 4 MIN
TECHNIQUES OF HEMMING 8 MIN
WAISTLINE STAYS 3 MIN

MANTA AND STING RAYS C 4 MIN
S8MM CARTRIDGE SILENT P-I
FROM THE OCEAN ANIMALS SERIES.
LC NO. 72-703273
PROD-DOUBLE DIST-DOUBLE 1972

MAP READING--A SERIES

P

PROD-HUBDSC DIST-HUBDSC 1971

CONTOUR MAPPING 4 MIN

**MARINE IGUANA OF THE
GALAPAGOS ISLANDS** C 4 MIN
S8MM CARTRIDGE SILENT P-I
FROM THE OUT OF THE SEA, ONTO THE LAND
SERIES.
LC NO. 72-703275
PROD-DOUBLE DIST-DOUBLE 1972

MEAT EATERS, PT 1--A SERIES

P-I

LC NO. 72-703267
PROD-DOUBLE DIST-DOUBLE 1972

ALLIGATORS HUNTING 4 MIN
DINOSAURS - MEAT EATERS 4 MIN
LEOPARD HUNTING FOOD 4 MIN
WOLVES HUNTING 4 MIN

MEAT EATERS, PT 2--A SERIES

P-I

LC NO. 72-703269
PROD-DOUBLE DIST-DOUBLE 1972

LIONS HUNTING IMPALA 4 MIN
OCTOPUS 4 MIN
OSPREY - BIRD OF PREY 4 MIN
SPIDERS - CAPTURING OF PREY 4 MIN

METRIC SYSTEM, THE, PT 1 C 13 MIN
S8MM CARTRIDGE SILENT
DISCUSSES THE HISTORY AND ADVANTAGES OF
THE METRIC SYSTEM. SHOWS DECIMAL CALCULA-
TIONS AND COMPARES THE ENGLISH SYSTEM
WITH THE METRIC SYSTEM. FROM THE METRIC
SYSTEM SERIES.
LC NO. 73-700089
PROD-VISIN DIST-VISIN 1972

**MICROSCOPIC ANIMALS -
PROTOZOA** C 4 MIN
S8MM CARTRIDGE SILENT P-I
FROM THE LIFE IN SINGLE CELLS SERIES.
LC NO. 72-703262
PROD-DOUBLE DIST-DOUBLE 1972

MICROSCOPIC WATER ANIMALS C 4 MIN
S8MM CARTRIDGE SILENT P-I
FROM THE LIFE IN SINGLE CELLS SERIES.
LC NO. 72-703262
PROD-DOUBLE DIST-DOUBLE 1972

MOSQUITO - EGGS TO LARVAE C 4 MIN
S8MM CARTRIDGE SILENT P-I
FROM THE SMALL WATER ANIMALS IN PONDS
SERIES.
LC NO. 72-703287
PROD-DOUBLE DIST-DOUBLE 1972

MOSQUITO - LARVA TO ADULT C 4 MIN
S8MM CARTRIDGE SILENT P-I
FROM THE INSECTS REPRODUCE SERIES.
LC NO. 72-703258
PROD-DOUBLE DIST-DOUBLE 1972

**MOSQUITO STRUCTURES -
EXTERNAL** C 4 MIN
S8MM CARTRIDGE SILENT P-I
FROM THE INSECTS ARE MUCH ALIKE SERIES.
LC NO. 72-703257
PROD-DOUBLE DIST-DOUBLE 1972

MOUNTAIN BIRDS C 4 MIN
S8MM CARTRIDGE SILENT P-I
FROM THE VERTEBRATE CONTRASTS, PT 1
SERIES.
LC NO. 72-703291

PROD-DOUBLE DIST-DOUBLE 1972

MOUNTAIN STORM C 4 MIN
S8MM CARTRIDGE SILENT P-I
FROM THE WEATHER SERIES.
LC NO. 72-703295
PROD-DOUBLE DIST-DOUBLE 1972

MOUNTAINS C 4 MIN
S8MM CARTRIDGE SILENT P-I
FROM THE PLANTS GROW IN MANY PLACES
SERIES.
LC NO. 72-703279
PROD-DOUBLE DIST-DOUBLE 1972

N

**NESTING HABITS OF WATER
BIRDS** C 4 MIN
S8MM CARTRIDGE SILENT P-I
FROM THE POND COMMUNITY SERIES.
LC NO. 72-703282
PROD-DOUBLE DIST-DOUBLE 1972

NORTH AMERICAN PECCARY C 4 MIN
S8MM CARTRIDGE SILENT P-I
FROM THE LAND ANIMALS SERIES.
LC NO. 72-703261
PROD-DOUBLE DIST-DOUBLE 1972

O

OCEAN ANIMALS--A SERIES

P-I

LC NO. 72-703273
PROD-DOUBLE DIST-DOUBLE 1972

BOTTLENOSE DOLPHIN 4 MIN
MANTA AND STING RAYS 4 MIN
PLANKTON EATERS 4 MIN
SURVIVAL ON THE CORAL REEF 4 MIN

OCEAN FOOD CHAINS--A SERIES

P-I

LC NO. 72-703274
PROD-DOUBLE DIST-DOUBLE 1972

CRABS 4 MIN
OCTOPUS 4 MIN
PLANKTON EATERS 4 MIN
WATER ANIMALS HUNTING FOOD, PT 1 4 MIN

OCTOPUS C 4 MIN
S8MM CARTRIDGE SILENT P-I
FROM THE OCEAN FOOD CHAINS SERIES.
LC NO. 72-703274
PROD-DOUBLE DIST-DOUBLE 1972

OSPREY - BIRD OF PREY C 4 MIN
S8MM CARTRIDGE SILENT P-I
FROM THE WATER BIRD STRUCTURE FOR
SURVIVAL SERIES.
LC NO. 72-703294
PROD-DOUBLE DIST-DOUBLE 1972

**OUT OF THE SEA, ONTO THE
LAND--A SERIES**

P-I

LC NO. 72-703275
PROD-DOUBLE DIST-DOUBLE 1972

DINOSAURS - MEAT EATERS 4 MIN
LUNGFISH AND OTHER AUSTRALIAN
ANIMALS 4 MIN
MARINE IGUANA OF THE GALAPAGOS
ISLANDS 4 MIN
TADPOLE TO TOAD 4 MIN

P

PELICANS C 4 MIN
S8MM CARTRIDGE SILENT P-I
FROM THE WATER BIRD STRUCTURE FOR
SURVIVAL SERIES.
LC NO. 72-703294
PROD-DOUBLE DIST-DOUBLE 1972

PLANKTON EATERS C 4 MIN
S8MM CARTRIDGE SILENT P-I
FROM THE OCEAN ANIMALS SERIES.
LC NO. 72-703273
PROD-DOUBLE   DIST-DOUBLE   1972

**PLANT AND ANIMAL
INTERDEPENDENCE--A SERIES**
P-I

LC NO. 72-703277
PROD-DOUBLE   DIST-DOUBLE   1972

GRAZING ANIMALS OF AFRICA   4 MIN
HARMFUL INSECTS   4 MIN
LIONS HUNTING IMPALA   4 MIN
SCAVENGERS OF AFRICA   4 MIN

PLANT-EATING ANIMALS
P-I

LC NO. 72-703278
PROD-DOUBLE   DIST-DOUBLE   1972

CARIBOU   4 MIN
ELEPHANTS FEEDING   4 MIN
GRAZING ANIMALS OF AFRICA   4 MIN
LEAF-CUTTING ANTS   4 MIN

**PLANTS GROW IN MANY
PLACES--A SERIES**
P-I

LC NO. 72-703279
PROD-DOUBLE   DIST-DOUBLE   1972

AMAZON JUNGLE   4 MIN
DESERT PLANTS   4 MIN
FRESH WATER ALGAE   4 MIN
MOUNTAINS   4 MIN

PLANTS GROWING--A SERIES
P-I

LC NO. 72-703280
PROD-DOUBLE   DIST-DOUBLE   1972

CARNIVOROUS PLANTS   4 MIN
DESERT FLOWERS   4 MIN
FLOWERS OPENING   4 MIN
FRUIT RIPENING   4 MIN

PLANTS REPRODUCE--A SERIES
P-I

LC NO. 72-703281
PROD-DOUBLE   DIST-DOUBLE   1972

FRUIT RIPENING   4 MIN
SEED DISPERSAL   4 MIN
SEEDS SPROUTING   4 MIN
SELF-PLANTING SEEDS   4 MIN

POND COMMUNITY--A SERIES
P-I

LC NO. 72-703282
PROD-DOUBLE   DIST-DOUBLE   1972

BEAVER DAM AND LODGE   4 MIN
NESTING HABITS OF WATER BIRDS   4 MIN
SWAMP ANIMALS UNDERWATER   4 MIN
WATER BIRDS GATHERING FOOD, PT 1   4 MIN

PRIDE OF LIONS C 4 MIN
S8MM CARTRIDGE SILENT P-I
FROM THE SOCIAL ANIMALS SERIES.
LC NO. 72-703288
PROD-DOUBLE   DIST-DOUBLE   1972

Q

QUEEN BEE LAYING EGGS C 4 MIN
S8MM CARTRIDGE SILENT P-I
FROM THE SOCIAL INSECTS SERIES.
LC NO. 72-703289
PROD-DOUBLE   DIST-DOUBLE   1972

R

RAISING A QUEEN BEE C 4 MIN
S8MM CARTRIDGE SILENT P-I
FROM THE SOCIAL ANIMALS SERIES.
LC NO. 72-703288
PROD-DOUBLE   DIST-DOUBLE   1972

REPTILES--A SERIES
P-I

LC NO. 72-703283
PROD-DOUBLE   DIST-DOUBLE   1972

ALLIGATORS HUNTING   4 MIN
DINOSAURS - MEAT EATERS   4 MIN
DINOSAURS - PLANT EATERS   4 MIN
MARINE IGUANA OF THE GALAPAGOS
ISLANDS   4 MIN

S

**SALT WATER INVERTEBRATES--A
SERIES**
P-I

LC NO. 72-703285
PROD-DOUBLE   DIST-DOUBLE   1972

ECHINODERMS AND SEA SQUIRTS   4 MIN
OCTOPUS   4 MIN
SEA SLUGS   4 MIN
TIDEPOOL LIFE, PT 1   4 MIN

SCAVENGERS OF AFRICA C 4 MIN
S8MM CARTRIDGE SILENT P-I
FROM THE PLANT AND ANIMAL
INTERDEPENDENCE SERIES.
LC NO. 72-703277
PROD-DOUBLE   DIST-DOUBLE   1972

**SEA ANIMALS OF THE
SHALLOWS--A SERIES**
P-I

LC NO. 72-703286
PROD-DOUBLE   DIST-DOUBLE   1972

CRABS   4 MIN
OCTOPUS   4 MIN
PLANKTON EATERS   4 MIN
SURVIVAL ON THE CORAL REEF   4 MIN

SEA SLUGS C 4 MIN
S8MM CARTRIDGE SILENT P-I
FROM THE SALT WATER INVERTEBRATES
SERIES.
LC NO. 72-703285
PROD-DOUBLE   DIST-DOUBLE   1972

SEED DISPERSAL C 4 MIN
S8MM CARTRIDGE SILENT P-I
FROM THE PLANTS REPRODUCE SERIES.
LC NO. 72-703281
PROD-DOUBLE   DIST-DOUBLE   1972

SEEDS SPROUTING C 4 MIN
S8MM CARTRIDGE SILENT P-I
FROM THE PLANTS REPRODUCE SERIES.
LC NO. 72-703281
PROD-DOUBLE   DIST-DOUBLE   1972

SELF-PLANTING SEEDS C 4 MIN
S8MM CARTRIDGE SILENT P-I
FROM THE PLANTS REPRODUCE SERIES.
LC NO. 72-703281
PROD-DOUBLE   DIST-DOUBLE   1972

**SEPARATING THE ELEMENTS OF
WATER** C 3 MIN
S8MM CARTRIDGE SILENT
SHOWS THE SEPARATION OF WATER INTO ITS
COMPONENT ELEMENTS OF HYDROGEN AND OXY-
GEN BY ELECTROLYTIC DECOMPOSITION. COM-
PARES AND COMBINES VOLUMES OF HYDROGEN
AND OXYGEN GASES TO SHOW THAT THEY WILL
FORM WATER. FROM THE WATER SERIES.
LC NO. 73-700653
PROD-DOUBLE   DIST-DOUBLE   1972

**SHAPES AND SYMMETRY, UNIT
1 - RECOGNIZING TWO-
DIMENSIONAL SHAPES--A
SERIES**
ESTABLISHES THE CHARACTERISTICS OF REGULAR
PLANE SHAPES AND TAKES A TOUR OBSERVING
TWO-DIMENSIONAL SHAPES IN THE ENVIRON-
MENT. COVERS SQUARES, CIRCLES, RECTANGLES,
TRIANGLES AND ELLIPSES.
LC NO. 72-702726
PROD-XEROX   DIST-XEROX   1971

**SHAPES AND SYMMETRY, UNIT
2 - RECOGNIZING THREE-
DIMENSIONAL SHAPES--A
SERIES**
GIVES THE CHARACTERISTICS AND NAMES OF
COMMON THREEDIMENSIONAL SHAPES. COVERS

SPHERES, CYLINDERS, CONES, ELLIPSOIDS, REC-
TANGULAR SOLIDS, CUBES AND PYRAMIDS.
LC NO. 72-702724
PROD-XEROX   DIST-XEROX   1971

**SHAPES AND SYMMETRY, UNIT
3 - SYMMETRY--A SERIES** C 3 MIN
S8MM CARTRIDGE SILENT
DEMONSTRATES LINES AND PLANE SYMMETRY IN
TWO-DIMENSIONAL AND THREE-DIMENSIONAL
SHAPES AND PROVIDES EXPERIENCE IN LOOKING
FOR SYMMETRY IN FAMILIAR OBJECTS.
LC NO. 72-702729
PROD-XEROX   DIST-XEROX   1971

**SHAPES AND SYMMETRY, UNIT
4 - HOW TO REPRESENT THREE
DIMENSIONAL SHAPES--A
SERIES**
DEMONSTRATES SIMPLE METHODS OF DEVELOP-
ING TWO-DIMENSIONAL REPRESENTATIONS OF
COMMON SOLIDS AND PROVIDES ACTIVITIES
HELPFUL IN LEARNING TO DRAW CUBES, RECTAN-
GULAR SOLIDS, CONES, PYRAMIDS, SPHERES AND
CYLINDERS.
LC NO. 72-702705
PROD-XEROX   DIST-XEROX   1971

**SHAPES AND SYMMETRY, UNIT
5 - PLANES THROUGH SOLIDS--A
SERIES**
EXPLORES MANY ASPECTS OF TWO-DIMENSIONAL
PLANE SHAPES AS COMPONENTS OF THREE-DI-
MENSIONAL SOLIDS. HELPS DEVELOP THE ABILITY
TO VISUALIZE THE SHAPE OF CROSS SECTIONS
CUT THROUGH SOLID OBJECTS.
LC NO. 72-702721
PROD-XEROX   DIST-XEROX   1971

SKIING - STEM CHRISTIE C 4 MIN
S8MM CARTRIDGE SILENT
PRESENTS EXPERT SKIERS WHO DEMONSTRATE
THE STEM CHRISTIE TURN.
LC NO. 72-703319
PROD-ATHI   DIST-ATHI   1969

SKIING - STEM TURN C 4 MIN
S8MM CARTRIDGE SILENT
PRESENTS EXPERT SKIERS DEMONSTRATING THE
STEM TURN.
LC NO. 72-703317
PROD-ATHI   DIST-ATHI   1969

**SMALL WATER ANIMALS IN
PONDS--A SERIES**
P-I

LC NO. 72-703287
PROD-DOUBLE   DIST-DOUBLE   1972

COURTSHIP RITUAL OF STICKLEBACK
FISH   4 MIN
DIVING SPIDER   4 MIN
MOSQUITO - EGGS TO LARVAE   4 MIN
WATER ANIMALS HUNTING FOOD, PT 2   4 MIN

SNAKES OF THE AMAZON C 4 MIN
S8MM CARTRIDGE SILENT P-I
FROM THE VERTEBRATE CONTRASTS, PT 1
SERIES.
LC NO. 72-703291
PROD-DOUBLE   DIST-DOUBLE   1972

SOCIAL ANIMALS--A SERIES
P-I

LC NO. 72-703288
PROD-DOUBLE   DIST-DOUBLE   1972

ANTHILL PROTECTION, PT 1 (SOCIAL
ANIMALS)   4 MIN
BEAVER DAM AND LODGE   4 MIN
PRIDE OF LIONS   4 MIN
RAISING A QUEEN BEE   4 MIN

SOCIAL INSECTS--A SERIES
P-I

LC NO. 72-703289
PROD-DOUBLE   DIST-DOUBLE   1972

ANTHILL PROTECTION, PT 1 (SOCIAL
INSECTS)   4 MIN
ANTS - TUNNEL BUILDING   4 MIN
QUEEN BEE LAYING EGGS   4 MIN
RAISING A QUEEN BEE   4 MIN

SPIDER WASP, PT 1 C 4 MIN
S8MM CARTRIDGE SILENT P-I
FROM THE INSECTS ARE MUCH ALIKE SERIES.
LC NO. 72-703257
PROD-DOUBLE   DIST-DOUBLE   1972

W

SPIDERS - CAPTURING OF PREY
C 4 MIN
S8MM CARTRIDGE SILENT P-I
FROM THE UNUSUAL INSTINCTS SERIES.
LC NO. 72-703290
PROD-DOUBLE   DIST-DOUBLE   1972

SPOTTED SKUNK
C 4 MIN
S8MM CARTRIDGE SILENT P-I
FROM THE LAND ANIMALS SERIES.
LC NO. 72-703261
PROD-DOUBLE   DIST-DOUBLE   1972

STRUCTURE AND STEREOCHEMISTRY - CONFORMATION OF CYCLOHEXANE
C 4 MIN
S8MM CARTRIDGE SILENT
RATIONALIZES THE CHAIN CONFORMATION OF CY-CLOHEXANE, BEGINNING WITH A HYPOTHETICAL PLANAR MODEL. IDENTIFIES AXIAL AND EQUATO-RIAL HYDROGENS AND ILLUSTRATES INTERNU-CLEAR DISTANCES FOR CHAIN, BOAT AND TWO-BOAT CONFORMATIONS.
LC NO. 72-701871
PROD-HRAW   DIST-HRAW   1972

STRUCTURE AND STEREOCHEMISTRY - DRAWING STRUCTURES, PT 1
C 4 MIN
S8MM CARTRIDGE SILENT
SHOWS SEVERAL TYPES OF MOLECULAR MODELS REPRESENTING METHYL CHLORIDE. COMPARES EACH OF THE THREE-DIMENSIONAL MODELS TO ITS TWO-DIMENSIONAL REPRESENTATION. ILLUS-TRATES THE RELATIONSHIP BETWEEN VARIOUS ORIENTATIONS AND THE HAND-DRAWN STRUC-TURES DERIVED FROM THEM.
LC NO. 72-701867
PROD-HRAW   DIST-HRAW   1972

STRUCTURE AND STEREOCHEMISTRY - DRAWING STRUCTURES, PT 2
C 4 MIN
S8MM CARTRIDGE SILENT
DEPICTS THE PROBLEMS INVOLVED WHEN COM-PLEX MOLECULES ARE REPRESENTED BY TWO-DI-MENSIONAL DRAWINGS AS COMPARED WITH THE REPRESENTATION WHICH IS ACHIEVED IN THREE-DIMENSIONAL MOLECULAR MODELS. ILLUS-TRATES THE VALUE OF CONDENSED STRUCTURAL FORMULA.
LC NO. 72-701868
PROD-HRAW   DIST-HRAW   1972

SURVIVAL ON THE CORAL REEF
C 4 MIN
S8MM CARTRIDGE SILENT P-I
FROM THE OCEAN ANIMALS SERIES.
LC NO. 72-703273
PROD-DOUBLE   DIST-DOUBLE   1972

SWAMP ANIMALS UNDERWATER
C 4 MIN
S8MM CARTRIDGE SILENT P-I
FROM THE POND COMMUNITY SERIES.
LC NO. 72-703282
PROD-DOUBLE   DIST-DOUBLE   1972

SWAMP BIRDS
C 4 MIN
S8MM CARTRIDGE SILENT P-I
FROM THE WATER BIRD STRUCTURE FOR SURVIVAL SERIES.
LC NO. 72-703294
PROD-DOUBLE   DIST-DOUBLE   1972

SYMBOL ACCENTUATION PROGRAM--A SERIES
P-I
TEACHES SIGHT AND PHONETIC READING BY US-ING ANIMATED PICTURES AND TRANSFORMING THESE OBJECTS INTO ASSOCIATED PRINTED WORDS.
LC NO. 73-700656

PROD-DOUBLE   DIST-DOUBLE   1969

T

TADPOLE TO TOAD
C 4 MIN
S8MM CARTRIDGE SILENT P-I
FROM THE OUT OF THE SEA, ONTO THE LAND SERIES.
LC NO. 72-703275
PROD-DOUBLE   DIST-DOUBLE   1972

TEACHING SPANISH TO SPANISH SPEAKING CHILDREN
C 10 MIN
S8MM CARTRIDGE MAGNETIC SOUND P-I
TEACHES THE SPEAKING, READING AND WRITING OF SPANISH USING BLACKBOARD AND CHART AIDES.
PROD-BOUCH   DIST-BOUCH   1969

TIDEPOOL LIFE, PT 1
C 4 MIN
S8MM CARTRIDGE SILENT P-I
FROM THE SALT WATER INVERTEBRATES SERIES.
LC NO. 72-703285
PROD-DOUBLE   DIST-DOUBLE   1972

TOAD SURVIVAL ADAPTATIONS
C 4 MIN
S8MM CARTRIDGE SILENT P-I
FROM THE VERTEBRATE CONTRASTS, PT 2 SERIES.
LC NO. 72-703293
PROD-DOUBLE   DIST-DOUBLE   1972

U

UNUSUAL INSTINCTS--A SERIES
P-I
LC NO. 72-703290
PROD-DOUBLE   DIST-DOUBLE   1972

DUCKBILLED PLATYPUS - MOTHER AND BABIES   4 MIN
JAWFISH   4 MIN
LEMMING IN MIGRATION   4 MIN
SPIDERS - CAPTURING OF PREY   4 MIN

V

VERTEBRATE CONTRASTS, PT 1--A SERIES
P-I
LC NO. 72-703291
PROD-DOUBLE   DIST-DOUBLE   1972

ARCTIC MUSK OX   4 MIN
MARINE IGUANA OF THE GALAPAGOS ISLANDS   4 MIN
MOUNTAIN BIRDS   4 MIN
SNAKES OF THE AMAZON   4 MIN

VERTEBRATE CONTRASTS, PT 2--A SERIES
P-I
LC NO. 72-703293
PROD-DOUBLE   DIST-DOUBLE   1972

AFRICAN BIRDS   4 MIN
BISON HERDS   4 MIN
GIANT LAND TORTOISE   4 MIN

TOAD SURVIVAL ADAPTATIONS   4 MIN

W

WATER ANIMALS HUNTING FOOD, PT 1
C 4 MIN
S8MM CARTRIDGE SILENT P-I
FROM THE OCEAN FOOD CHAINS SERIES.
LC NO. 72-703274
PROD-DOUBLE   DIST-DOUBLE   1972

WATER ANIMALS HUNTING FOOD, PT 2
C 4 MIN
S8MM CARTRIDGE SILENT P-I
FROM THE SMALL WATER ANIMALS IN PONDS SERIES.
LC NO. 72-703287
PROD-DOUBLE   DIST-DOUBLE   1972

WATER BIRD STRUCTURE FOR SURVIVAL--A SERIES
P-I
LC NO. 72-703294
PROD-DOUBLE   DIST-DOUBLE   1972

OSPREY - BIRD OF PREY   4 MIN
PELICANS   4 MIN
SWAMP BIRDS   4 MIN
WATER BIRDS GATHERING FOOD, PT 2   4 MIN

WATER BIRDS GATHERING FOOD, PT 1
C 4 MIN
S8MM CARTRIDGE SILENT P-I
FROM THE POND COMMUNITY SERIES.
LC NO. 72-703282
PROD-DOUBLE   DIST-DOUBLE   1972

WATER BIRDS GATHERING FOOD, PT 2
C 4 MIN
S8MM CARTRIDGE SILENT P-I
FROM THE WATER BIRD STRUCTURE FOR SURVIVAL SERIES.
LC NO. 72-703294
PROD-DOUBLE   DIST-DOUBLE   1972

WEATHER--A SERIES
P-I
LC NO. 72-703295
PROD-DOUBLE   DIST-DOUBLE   1972

ARCTIC THAW, PT 1   4 MIN
CLOUDS   4 MIN
FLASH FLOOD   4 MIN
MOUNTAIN STORM   4 MIN

WHAT IS A SHADOW
C 4 MIN
S8MM CARTRIDGE SILENT
SHOWS THAT SHADOWS ARE FORMED WHEN SOMETHING IS PUT BETWEEN THE LIGHT SOURCE AND WHERE THE SHADOW APPEARS AND THAT SHADOW SHAPES ARE CHANGED BY CHANGING THE SHAPES OF THE OBJECTS OF THE ANGLE OF THE LIGHT.
LC NO. 73-700168
PROD-VISED   DIST-VISED   1972

WHY MAN CREATES
C 25 MIN
S8MM CARTRIDGE OPTICAL SOUND A
PRESENTS A SERIES OF EXPLORATIONS, EPISODES AND COMMENTS ON CREATIVITY.
LC NO. FIA68-872
PROD-BASSS   DIST-PFP   1969

WOLVES HUNTING
C 4 MIN
S8MM CARTRIDGE SILENT P-I
FROM THE MEAT EATERS, PT 1 SERIES.
LC NO. 72-703267
PROD-DOUBLE   DIST-DOUBLE   1972

115

ALPHABETICAL GUIDE TO 16mm FILMS

A

A TO B   C 35 MIN
16MM FILM OPTICAL SOUND
TELLS THE STORY OF A SIXTEEN YEAR OLD GIRL'S
SELF-DISCOVERY AND IDENTITY CRISIS. FOLLOWS
THE HEROINE'S PAINFUL EMERGENCE FROM THE
COCOON OF CONVENTION INTO A HIPPIE WORLD
AND A RELATIONSHIP WITH A BOHEMIAN BOY-
FRIEND.
PROD-AMERFI   DIST-AMERFI

ABANDONMENT OF THE CITIES,
THE   C 11 MIN
16MM FILM OPTICAL SOUND   J-C A
EXPLAINS THAT CLEVELAND, ST LOUIS AND NEW
YORK STAND AS SAD EXAMPLES OF A GROWING
PHENOMENON, THE ABANDONMENT OF CITIES.
SHOWS HOW LARGE AREAS OF MOST URBAN CEN-
TERS ARE BECOMING DESOLATE WASTELANDS OF
EMPTY STORES AND BUILDINGS WHICH ARE HOS-
TILE TO LIFE. FROM THE FIRST TUESDAY SERIES.
LC NO. 73-714191
PROD-NBCTV   DIST-NBCTV   1971

ABOUT CATS   C 11 MIN
16MM FILM OPTICAL SOUND   P-J
PRESENTS DIFFERENT TYPES OF CATS.
PROD-METROM   DIST-METROM   1972

ACID AND ALKALI   C 10 MIN
16MM FILM OPTICAL SOUND
EXPLAINS THE NEUTRALIZATION OF ACIDITY AND
ALKALINITY. SHOWS THE SEPARATION OF THE
VARIOUS LIQUIDS INTO ACIDS, ALKALIS AND NEU-
TRALS DISTINGUISHING THEM BY USING LITMUS
SOLUTION.
PROD-IWANMI   DIST-IWANMI

ACTION FOR CHANGE   C 28 MIN
16MM FILM OPTICAL SOUND   I-C A
EXPLAINS WHERE THE TAXPAYERS' MONEY GOES.
LC NO. 73-701352
PROD-SCREEI   DIST-SCREEI   1973

ADDRESSING MACHINE   C 16 MIN
16MM FILM OPTICAL SOUND
DEMONSTRATES NEW METHODS OF ADDRESSING
BY THE USE OF AN OPTICAL HIGH SPEED AD-
DRESSER. SHOWS ITS USAGE IN COMBINATION
WITH A COMPUTERIZED CARD, THEREBY ENABL-
ING IT TO GIVE VALUABLE INFORMATION IN VARI-
OUS PROJECTS.
PROD-BEF   DIST-BEF

ADOLESCENCE AND SEXUAL
IDENTITY   B 28 MIN
16MM FILM OPTICAL SOUND   H-C A
ILLUSTRATES THE EMERGENCE OF PERSONALITY
FROM CHILDHOOD THROUGH ADOLESCENCE. DIS-
CUSSES THE PROBLEM OF SEXUAL IDENTITY AT
PUBERTY AND THE FAILURE OF EARLY MAR-
RIAGES AS REFLECTIONS OF IMMATURITY. FROM
THE SEX IN AMERICA CULTURE SERIES.
LC NO. 73-701211
PROD-CHM   DIST-CHM   1967

ADOLPH RUPP   C 5 MIN
16MM FILM OPTICAL SOUND   J-C A
SEE SERIES TITLE FOR DESCRIPTIVE STATEMENT.
FROM THE WONDERFUL WORLD OF SPORT - BAS-
KETBALL SERIES.
PROD-SPORTI   DIST-AMERFI

ADVENTURES IN PERCEPTION   C 21 MIN
16MM FILM OPTICAL SOUND   J-C A
PRESENTS M C ESCHER WHO IMAGINES THE
WORLD AROUND HIM IN WAYS THAT CAN ONLY
BE DESCRIBED VISUALLY. SHOWS HIS PAINTINGS
WHICH HAVE UNUSUAL PERSPECTIVES AND DI-
MENSIONS.
LC NO. 73-701283
PROD-BFA   DIST-BFA   1973

ADVERTISING   B 27 MIN
16MM FILM OPTICAL SOUND
EXPLAINS THE ROLE OF ADVERTISING IN OUR
ECONOMY, OUR PROSPERITY AND OUR DAILY
LIVES. SHOWS METHODS USED TO STIMULATE
PRODUCTION, CREATE JOBS AND CREATE DE-
MAND FOR NEW PRODUCTS.
PROD-BEF   DIST-BEF

ADVERTISING - INFORMATION,
PERSUASION OR DECEPTION   C 13 MIN
16MM FILM OPTICAL SOUND   I-C
EXPLAINS THAT EVERY PURCHASE REPRESENTS
AN ATTEMPT TO SATISFY NEEDS AND DESIRES ON
MANY DIFFERENT LEVELS, FROM THE MOST PRAC-
TICAL TO THE MOST IRRATIONAL. SHOWS HOW
ADVERTISERS TRY TO REACH CONSUMERS ON
THESE LEVELS.
LC NO. 73-701348
PROD-ALTSUL   DIST-JOU   1973

ADVERTISING AND
COMPETITION   C 29 MIN
16MM FILM OPTICAL SOUND
PRESENTS AN OVERVIEW OF ADVERTISING'S RE-
LATION TO, AND INTERRELATIONSHIP WITH, MAR-
KETING AND GENERAL ECONOMIC CONDITIONS.
FEATURES LEADERS IN THE FIELDS OF EDUCA-
TION AND COMMUNICATIONS.
PROD-MTP   DIST-MTP

AEROBATICS - AERIAL
ACROBATICS   C 5 MIN
16MM FILM OPTICAL SOUND   J-C A
SEE SERIES TITLE FOR DESCRIPTIVE STATEMENT.
FROM THE WONDERFUL WORLD OF SPORT - FLY-
ING SERIES.
PROD-SPORTI   DIST-AMERFI

AFFAIRS OF A MAN, THE   B 30 MIN
16MM FILM OPTICAL SOUND   J-C A
TRACES THE LIFE OF HENRY FORD FROM HIS
BIRTH IN 1863 TO HIS DEATH IN 1947. TELLS THE
STORY OF FORD THE INDUSTRIALIST AND SHOWS
HIM AS A HISTORIAN AND PRESERVER OF AMERI-
CAN HERITAGE.
PROD-FORD   DIST-FORD

AFL - WIVES   C 5 MIN
16MM FILM OPTICAL SOUND   J-C A
SEE SERIES TITLE FOR DESCRIPTIVE STATEMENT.
FROM THE WONDERFUL WORLD OF SPORT - FOOT-
BALL SERIES.
PROD-SPORTI   DIST-AMERFI

AGED, THE   C 17 MIN
16MM FILM OPTICAL SOUND   H-C A
SHOWS THE PROBLEM OF THE AGED FROM THE
VIEWPOINT OF A YOUNG VIETNAM VETERAN WHO
RETURNS TO FIND THAT HIS PARENTS ARE NO
LONGER CAPABLE OF TAKING CARE OF THEM-
SELVES AND TELLS OF THE WEARY, ENDLESS VIS-
ITS TO SOCIAL AGENCIES FOR HELP.
PROD-CAROUF   DIST-CAROUF

AIN'T GONNA EAT MY MIND   C 34 MIN
16MM FILM OPTICAL SOUND   J-C A
DEPICTS CURRENT GANG WARS AND STREET LIFE
IN U S GHETTOS.
PROD-CAROUF   DIST-CAROUF

AIRBORNE OCEANOGRAPHY -
OCEANOGRAPHER OF THE NAVY
C 23 MIN
16MM FILM OPTICAL SOUND
SHOWS MAJOR AREAS OF AIRBORNE RESEARCH
CONDUCTED BY THE OCEANOGRAPHIC OFFICE. IN-
CLUDES SCENES OF LONGRANGE ICE FORECAST-
ING, MAGNETIC SURVEYING OF THE EARTH'S SUR-
FACE AND SURVEYING THE GULF STREAM.
LC NO. 73-701402
PROD-USN   DIST-USNAC   1969

ALADDIN   C
16MM FILM OPTICAL SOUND
SEE SERIES TITLE FOR DESCRIPTIVE STATEMENT.
FROM THE FAIRY TALE TIME SERIES.
PROD-PUI   DIST-PUI

ALASKA'S BUSH PILOT
HERITAGE   C 10 MIN
16MM FILM OPTICAL SOUND   I-H
EXPLAINS THE LONG RECOGNIZED IMPORTANCE
OF AIR TRAVEL IN THE NATION'S LARGEST STATE.
PRESENTS THE STORY OF THE AVIATION PRO-
GRESS PARALLELING AND CONTRIBUTING TO
ALASKA'S GROWTH.
LC NO. 73-700964
PROD-DISNEY   DIST-DISNEY   1973

ALASKAN GOLD RUSH, THE   C 6 MIN
16MM FILM OPTICAL SOUND   I-C
REVEALS WHAT LIFE WAS LIKE FOR THOSE WHO
SCRAMBLED FOR FAME AND FORTUNE IN THE
ALASKAN GOLD RUSH OF 1897.
LC NO. 73-700963
PROD-DISNEY   DIST-DISNEY   1973

ALCOHOL - HOW MUCH IS TOO
MUCH   C 11 MIN
16MM FILM OPTICAL SOUND   I
STRESSES MATURE DECISIONS REGARDING
DRINKING. INCLUDES SOME PHYSIOLOGICAL EF-
FECTS OF ALCOHOL.
LC NO. 73-715523
PROD-FILMSW   DIST-AIMS   1972

ALCOHOL - OUR NUMBER ONE
DRUG   C 11 MIN
16MM FILM OPTICAL SOUND   I-H
SHOWS THE PERSONAL, SOCIAL AND PHYSIOLOGI-
CAL EFFECTS OF DRINKING TOO MUCH.
LC NO. 73-700818
PROD-AVIS   DIST-OF   1973

ALCOHOL PROBLEM, THE -
WHAT DO YOU THINK   C 18 MIN
16MM FILM OPTICAL SOUND   I-C
EXAMINES ALCOHOL FROM THREE PERSPECTIVES
- SOCIAL ASPECTS, CHEMISTRY AND PHYSIOLOGI-
CAL EFFECTS. PRESENTS EXPERIMENTS WITH
MICE.
LC NO. 73-701360
PROD-EBEC   DIST-EBEC   1973

ALCOHOLISM - A MODEL OF
DRUG DEPENDENCY   C 20 MIN
16MM FILM OPTICAL SOUND   C A
DEALS WITH ALCOHOLISM, THE RESULT OF INDI-
VIDUAL DEPENDENCY DIFFICULTIES. SHOWS HOW
SOME PEOPLE HAVE MANAGED TO CONQUER AL-
COHOL IN THE SHORT-TERM BY SUBSTITUTING
OTHER ADDICTIONS AND HOW OTHER METHODS
THAT HELP THE ALCOHOLIC TO REALIGN HIS DE-
PENDENCY STRUCTURE IN THE LONG-TERM MAY
PROVIDE A PERMANENT CURE. FROM THE LIFE
AND HEALTH FILM SERIES.
LC NO. 73-701091
PROD-CRMP   DIST-CRMP   1972

ALFRED   B 30 MIN
16MM FILM OPTICAL SOUND
PORTRAYS A 64-YEAR-OLD MAN LIVING ON WEL-
FARE IN A SQUALID, ROACH-INFESTED ROOM IN
ONE OF NEW YORK'S UPPER WEST SIDE 'WELFARE
HOTELS.' PICTURES HIS SPIRIT WHICH HAS SOME-
HOW SURVIVED YEARS OF POVERTY, DISCOUR-
AGEMENT AND NEGLECT.
PROD-AMERFI   DIST-AMERFI

ALI BABA   C
16MM FILM OPTICAL SOUND
SEE SERIES TITLE FOR DESCRIPTIVE STATEMENT.
FROM THE FAIRY TALE TIME SERIES.
PROD-PUI   DIST-PUI

ALL ABOUT ANIMALS - TODO
SOBRE LOS ANIMALES   C 7 MIN
16MM FILM OPTICAL SOUND
DISCUSSES ANIMAL ORIGINS, NAMES AND LOCA-
TIONS OF CONTINENTS. FROM THE BRENTANO
FOUNDATION BILINGUAL FILMS SERIES.
PROD-CAROUF   DIST-CAROUF

AMATEUR POLO   C 5 MIN
16MM FILM OPTICAL SOUND   J-C A
SEE SERIES TITLE FOR DESCRIPTIVE STATEMENT.
FROM THE WONDERFUL WORLD OF SPORT -
HORSES, RACING, POLO, RODEO SERIES.
PROD-SPORTI   DIST-AMERFI

AMERICA'S CUP   C 5 MIN
16MM FILM OPTICAL SOUND   J-C A
SEE SERIES TITLE FOR DESCRIPTIVE STATEMENT.
FROM THE WONDERFUL WORLD OF SPORT - BOAT-
ING SERIES.
PROD-SPORTI   DIST-AMERFI

ANGRY COLONIES - 1763 - 1774
C 80 MIN
16MM FILM OPTICAL SOUND
EXPLAINS THAT BY 1763, THE AMERICAN COLO-
NISTS WERE DEMANDING POLITICAL SEPARATION
FROM ENGLAND AND REPEAL OF UNFAIR EXPORT

B

AND IMPORT LAWS, THE CURRENCY ACT, THE QUARTERING ACT AND THE STAMP ACT. DEPICTS THE BOSTON MASSACRE AND BOSTON TEA PARTY. FROM THE TO THE SPIRIT OF '76 SERIES.
LC NO. 73-733677
PROD-RMI   DIST-RMI

ANIMAL DEVELOPMENT   C 14 MIN
16MM FILM OPTICAL SOUND
OBSERVES A CELL UNTIL IT IS FULLY GROWN. IL-LUSTRATES THE BIRTH OF A BABY TURTLE, THE DEVELOPMENT OF A FROG, THE DEVELOPMENT OF THE GLOBEFISH AND THE HATCHING OF CHICKS.
PROD-IWANMI   DIST-IWANMI

ANIMAL TEETH   C 14 MIN
16MM FILM OPTICAL SOUND
SHOWS THE FUNCTION OF ANIMAL TEETH, IN-CLUDING DECAY PREVENTION. SHOWS THE CHANGE IN FORMS OF TEETH FROM AN EVOLU-TIONARY STANDPOINT.
PROD-IWANMI   DIST-IWANMI

ANN, A PORTRAIT   C 24 MIN
16MM FILM OPTICAL SOUND
INTRODUCES ANN HALPRIN, A UNIQUE MODERN DANCER. CAPTURES THE FORCES THAT INSPIRE HER BY JUXTAPOSING HER STRONG FAMILY TIES TO STUNNING SCENES OF HER INDIVIDUALISTIC CONTEMPORARY DANCING.
PROD-AMERFI   DIST-AMERFI

ANTIQUE CARS - DUSENBERG,
MERCEDES, BUGATTI   C 5 MIN
16MM FILM OPTICAL SOUND   J-C A
SEE SERIES TITLE FOR DESCRIPTIVE STATEMENT. FROM THE WONDERFUL WORLD OF SPORT - CARS, AUTO RACING SERIES.
PROD-SPORTI   DIST-AMERFI

ANTIQUE CARS - PIERCE
ARROW   C 5 MIN
16MM FILM OPTICAL SOUND   J-C A
SEE SERIES TITLE FOR DESCRIPTIVE STATEMENT. FROM THE WONDERFUL WORLD OF SPORT - CARS, AUTO RACING SERIES.
PROD-SPORTI   DIST-AMERFI

ANTIQUE PLANES - F3F AND
SPITFIRE   C 5 MIN
16MM FILM OPTICAL SOUND   J-C A
SEE SERIES TITLE FOR DESCRIPTIVE STATEMENT. FROM THE WONDERFUL WORLD OF SPORT - FLY-ING SERIES.
PROD-SPORTI   DIST-AMERFI

ANYTHING YOU WANT TO BE   C 88 MIN
16MM FILM OPTICAL SOUND   J-C A
PARALLELS FEMININE ROLES TO CAREER OPPOR-TUNITIES.
LC NO. 72-700975
PROD-BRNDNL   DIST-EDDDW   1973

APOLLO 17 - ON THE
SHOULDERS OF GIANTS   C 28 MIN
16MM FILM OPTICAL SOUND   J-C A
PRESENTS A HIGHLY VISUAL DOCUMENTARY OF THE APOLLO 17 JOURNEY TO TAURUW-LITTROW, THE FINAL LUNAR LANDING MISSION. DESCRIBES PREPARATION FOR A SPACE JOURNEY.
LC NO. 73-701241
PROD-NASA   DIST-NASA   1973

AQUA SUMMER   C 14 MIN
16MM FILM OPTICAL SOUND   I-C A
COMBINES THE FUN AND EXCITEMENT OF SUM-MER AT A BEAUTIFUL NORTHERN LAKE WITH WA-TER SKIING, BOATING AND SWIMMING.
LC NO. 73-701097
PROD-NWFCMP   DIST-NWFCMP   1973

ARMY-NAVY HIGHLIGHTS   C 5 MIN
16MM FILM OPTICAL SOUND   J-C A
SEE SERIES TITLE FOR DESCRIPTIVE STATEMENT. FROM THE WONDERFUL WORLD OF SPORT - FOOT-BALL SERIES.
PROD-SPORTI   DIST-AMERFI

ART FOR BEGINNERS - FUN
WITH LINES   C 11 MIN
16MM FILM OPTICAL SOUND   P
ILLUSTRATES LINES THAT CHILDREN MAKE, LINES IN MAN-MADE STRUCTURES AND LINES IN NA-TURE. INTRODUCES LINES YOU CAN MAKE ON PA-PER, ON OTHER MATERIALS AND WITH DIFFER-ENT TOOLS.
LC NO. 73-701237
PROD-CORD   DIST-CORF   1973

ART MAKEUP - GREEN, BLACK,
WHITE, PINK   C 44 MIN
16MM FILM OPTICAL SOUND
PRESENTS AN EXPERIMENTAL FILM USING ART MAKEUP.
PROD-VISRES   DIST-VISRES   1971

ARTS AND CRAFTS - ARTESANIA   C 9 MIN
16MM FILM OPTICAL SOUND
PRESENTS 'HOW-TO' CLASSROOM PROJECTS FOR MAKING GIFTS. FROM THE BRENTANO FOUNDA-TION BILINGUAL FILMS SERIES.
PROD-CAROUF   DIST-CAROUF

ASSOCIATES OF THE VIOLIN   C 14 MIN
16MM FILM OPTICAL SOUND
DEFINES THE SOUND OF THE VIOLIN AND EX-PLAINS VARIOUS RELATED STRINGED INSTRU-MENTS. USES AN EXPERIMENT TO SHOW DIFFER-ENCES IN SOUND ACCORDING TO THE LENGTH, TIGHTNESS AND THICKNESS OF STRING.
PROD-IWANMI   DIST-IWANMI

ASTROTURF   C 5 MIN
16MM FILM OPTICAL SOUND   J-C A
SEE SERIES TITLE FOR DESCRIPTIVE STATEMENT. FROM THE WONDERFUL WORLD OF SPORT - BASE-BALL SERIES.
PROD-SPORTI   DIST-AMERFI

AT THE FIRE STATION   C 8 MIN
16MM FILM OPTICAL SOUND
SHOWS CHILDREN MEETING THE FIREMEN, WATCHING CLIMBING AND JUMPING DEMON-STRATIONS, SEEING HOW HOSES AND LADDERS ARE USED AND SEEING A FIRE ENGINE CLOSE UP. FROM THE BRENTANO FOUNDATION BILINGUAL FILMS SERIES.
PROD-CAROUF   DIST-CAROUF

AT THE MARKET - EN EL
MERCADO   C 10 MIN
16MM FILM OPTICAL SOUND
SHOWS CHILDREN HOW TO BUY VEGETABLES AND COUNT CHANGE. FROM THE BRENTANO FOUNDA-TION BILINGUAL FILMS SERIES.
PROD-CAROUF   DIST-CAROUF

ATMOSPHERIC PRESSURE   C 14 MIN
16MM FILM OPTICAL SOUND
EXPLAINS THE TREMENDOUS POWER OF ATMO-SPHERIC PRESSURE WITH A SIMPLE EXPERIMENT INVOLVING A CRUSHED METAL HOT WATER CON-TAINER.
PROD-IWANMI   DIST-IWANMI

AUCTION STORY   C 5 MIN
16MM FILM OPTICAL SOUND   J-C A
SEE SERIES TITLE FOR DESCRIPTIVE STATEMENT. FROM THE WONDERFUL WORLD OF SPORT - HORSES, RACING, POLO, RODEO SERIES.
PROD-SPORTI   DIST-AMERFI

AUTUMN FIRE   B 23 MIN
16MM FILM OPTICAL SOUND
PRESENTS A SILENT LYRICAL NARRATIVE WHICH RELIES ON THE TECHNIQUES OF MONTAGE TO CONVEY MOODS AND RELATE THE STORY ABOUT A COUPLE, SEPARATED BY DISAGREEMENTS, WHO ARE REUNITED BY THEIR OWN EFFORTS AND WILL.
PROD-MGHT   DIST-MGHT

B

BALANCE BEAM   C 5 MIN
16MM FILM OPTICAL SOUND   J-C A
SEE SERIES TITLE FOR DESCRIPTIVE STATEMENT. FROM THE WONDERFUL WORLD OF SPORT - GYM-NASTICS SERIES.
PROD-SPORTI   DIST-AMERFI

BALI   C
16MM FILM OPTICAL SOUND
SEE SERIES TITLE FOR DESCRIPTIVE STATEMENT. FROM THE PORT OF CALL SERIES.
PROD-PUI   DIST-PUI

BALLET ADAGIO   C 10 MIN
16MM FILM OPTICAL SOUND   J-C A
PRESENTS AN ARTICULATION OF THE BALLET 'SPRING WATER,' DANCED BY DAVID AND ANNA MARIE HOLMES.
PROD-PFP   DIST-PFP

BALTUSROL - THE FOURTH
HOLE   C 5 MIN
16MM FILM OPTICAL SOUND   J-C A
SEE SERIES TITLE FOR DESCRIPTIVE STATEMENT. FROM THE WONDERFUL WORLD OF SPORT - GOLF SERIES.
PROD-SPORTI   DIST-AMERFI

BARE MINIMUM   B 10 MIN
16MM FILM OPTICAL SOUND
DISCUSSES PROTECTIVE CLOTHING AND EQUIP-MENT NECESSARY FROM THE VIEWPOINT OF THE FOREMAN AND THE SAFETY DIRECTOR AND REC-OMMENDS THE CARE AND USE OF SAFETY GEAR.
PROD-BEF   DIST-BEF

BASE RUNNING   C 5 MIN
16MM FILM OPTICAL SOUND   J-C A
SEE SERIES TITLE FOR DESCRIPTIVE STATEMENT. FROM THE WONDERFUL WORLD OF SPORT - BASE-BALL SERIES.
PROD-SPORTI   DIST-AMERFI

BASEBALL   C 14 MIN
16MM FILM OPTICAL SOUND
EXPLAINS THE SCIENTIFIC RELATIONS BETWEEN BASEBALL BAT AND BALL.
PROD-IWANMI   DIST-IWANMI

BASEBALL CLINIC   C 5 MIN
16MM FILM OPTICAL SOUND   J-C A
SEE SERIES TITLE FOR DESCRIPTIVE STATEMENT. FROM THE WONDERFUL WORLD OF SPORT - BASE-BALL SERIES.
PROD-SPORTI   DIST-AMERFI

BASEBALL'S UFO, THE SPITBALL   C 5 MIN
16MM FILM OPTICAL SOUND   J-C A
SEE SERIES TITLE FOR DESCRIPTIVE STATEMENT. FROM THE WONDERFUL WORLD OF SPORT - BASE-BALL SERIES.
PROD-SPORTI   DIST-AMERFI

BASIC LAW TERMS   C 20 MIN
16MM FILM OPTICAL SOUND   J-C A
SHOWS HOW YOUNG PEOPLE CAN MAKE THE LAW WORK FOR THEM, RATHER THAN AGAINST THEM. MAKES CLEAR THE DISTINCTION BETWEEN CRIMI-NAL AND CIVIL LAWS AND HELPS DEFINE OUR RIGHTS AND OUR OBLIGATIONS.
PROD-PFP   DIST-PFP

BASS FISHING   C 5 MIN
16MM FILM OPTICAL SOUND   J-C A
SEE SERIES TITLE FOR DESCRIPTIVE STATEMENT. FROM THE WONDERFUL WORLD OF SPORT - FISH-ING SERIES.
PROD-SPORTI   DIST-AMERFI

BAT BOY   C 5 MIN
16MM FILM OPTICAL SOUND   J-C A
SEE SERIES TITLE FOR DESCRIPTIVE STATEMENT. FROM THE WONDERFUL WORLD OF SPORT - BASE-BALL SERIES.
PROD-SPORTI   DIST-AMERFI

BATHYMETRY - DISCOVERING
THE OCEAN FLOOR - CHARTING
THE OCEAN FLOOR   C 16 MIN
16MM FILM OPTICAL SOUND
SHOWS THE PROCEDURES FOR TAKING AND SUB-MITTING BATHYMETRIC REPORTS AND REASONS FOR INCREASING THE QUALITY OF THESE RE-PORTS.
LC NO. 73-701403
PROD-CAHILL   DIST-AIMS   1970

BATON PASS   C 5 MIN
16MM FILM OPTICAL SOUND   J-C A
SEE SERIES TITLE FOR DESCRIPTIVE STATEMENT. FROM THE WONDERFUL WORLD OF SPORT - TRACK AND FIELD SERIES.
PROD-SPORTI   DIST-AMERFI

BEACH INTELLIGENCE - WAVES,
BREAKERS AND SURF   C 20 MIN
16MM FILM OPTICAL SOUND
EXPLAINS WAVE FORMS, EQUATIONS INVOLVED, PERIOD, VELOCITY AND WAVE LENGTHS. SHOWS HOW WAVES ARE FORMED IN THE FETCH AREA, HOW THEY TRAVEL THROUGH DECAY AND HOW REFRACTIONS TAKE PLACE IN SHOAL WATERS AND BREAKERS ON THE BEACH.
LC NO. 73-701251
PROD-CAHILL   DIST-AIMS

118

BEACH PARTY, THE C 27 MIN
16MM FILM OPTICAL·SOUND
INTRODUCES SIX HIGH SCHOOL SENIORS WHO TAKE A BEACH HOUSE FOR THE WEEKEND. SHOWS THE IMMATURITY OF A GIRL AND HER BOYFRIEND.
PROD-PAULST   DIST-PAULST

BEACH VOLLEY BALL C 5 MIN
16MM FILM OPTICAL SOUND   J-C A
SEE SERIES TITLE FOR DESCRIPTIVE STATEMENT. FROM THE WONDERFUL WORLD OF SPORT - OTHER SERIES.
PROD-SPORTI   DIST-AMERFI

BEAUTY AND COMFORT OUTDOORS C 14 MIN
16MM FILM OPTICAL SOUND
SHOWS HOW TO ELIMINATE UNDESIRABLE INSECTS, WEEDS AND PLANT DISEASES BY SPRAYING, FOGGING AND DUSTING.
PROD-MTP   DIST-MTP

BEDBATH, THE - EMOTIONAL SUPPORT C 13 MIN
16MM FILM OPTICAL SOUND   IND
SHOWS HOW TO PREPARE THE PATIENT AND SUPPLIES AND EQUIPMENT FOR GIVING A BEDBATH. EMPHASIZES OBSERVING THE CORRECT HEALTH, SAFETY AND ETHICAL MEASURES. FROM THE NURSE'S AIDE, ORDERLY AND ATTENDANT SERIES.
LC NO. 73-701044
PROD-COPI   DIST-COPI   1971

BEDBATH, THE - PROCEDURE C 15 MIN
16MM FILM OPTICAL SOUND   IND
ILLUSTRATES UTILIZATION OF THE CORRECT SEQUENCE FOR THE COMPLETE BEDBATH PROCEDURE WITH ITS ACCOMPANYING OBLIGATIONS OF PRIVACY, SAFETY AND PROVIDING EMOTIONAL SUPPORT. DESCRIBES OBSERVATION OF PATIENT'S CONDITION AND CHANGES WHICH MAY OCCUR. FROM THE NURSE'S AIDE, ORDERLY AND ATTENDANT SERIES.
LC NO. 73-701045
PROD-COPI   DIST-COPI   1971

BEGINNERS C 5 MIN
16MM FILM OPTICAL SOUND   J-C A
SEE SERIES TITLE FOR DESCRIPTIVE STATEMENT. FROM THE WONDERFUL WORLD OF SPORT - SKIING SERIES.
PROD-SPORTI   DIST-AMERFI

BEGINNING GYMNASTICS C 5 MIN
16MM FILM OPTICAL SOUND   J-C A
SEE SERIES TITLE FOR DESCRIPTIVE STATEMENT. FROM THE WONDERFUL WORLD OF SPORT - GYMNASTICS SERIES.
PROD-SPORTI   DIST-AMERFI

BENJAMIN FRANKLIN AND THE MID-ATLANTIC SIGNERS C 80 MIN
16MM FILM OPTICAL SOUND
GIVES THE BACKGROUND OF THE 21 SIGNERS OF THE CONSTITUTION FROM THE MID-ATLANTIC STATES. TELLS OF THEIR LIVES, ACHIEVEMENTS AND FATES. FROM THE THE TO THE SPIRIT OF '76 SERIES.
LC NO. 73-733681
PROD-RMI   DIST-RMI

BERKELEY CHRISTMAS, A C 47 MIN
16MM FILM OPTICAL SOUND
PORTRAYS A LOVE STORY BETWEEN TWO PEOPLE OF ENTIRELY OPPOSITE VALUES. PRESENTS A TOW-HEADED SUPER-STRAIGHT BERKELEY STUDENT FROM NEW ENGLAND, WHO WHILE DRIVING UP THE COAST ON CHRISTMAS EVE LOOKING FOR A PICK-UP, GIVES A LIFT TO A PRETTY YOUNG CALIFORNIAN, WHO TURNS OUT TO BE NINE MONTHS PREGNANT.
PROD-AMERFI   DIST-AMERFI

BEST FOR BEGINNERS C 10 MIN
16MM FILM OPTICAL SOUND
DEMONSTRATES THAT THE ELECTRIC TYPEWRITER SIMPLIFIES THE LEARNING PROCESS FOR BEGINNING TYPING STUDENTS. SHOWS THAT THE KEYBOARD IS ALSO USED IN DATA PROCESSING EQUIPMENT.
PROD-BEF   DIST-BEF

BIG TREES, THE - LOS ARBOLES GRANDES C 7 MIN
16MM FILM OPTICAL SOUND
PRESENTS A FIELD TRIP TO MUIR WOODS WITH A DISCUSSION OF BASIC BOTANY AND THE STORY OF THE REDWOODS. FROM THE BRENTANO FOUNDATION BILINGUAL FILMS SERIES.
PROD-CAROUF   DIST-CAROUF

BIG YELLOW TAXI C 4 MIN
16MM FILM OPTICAL SOUND
USES ANIMATION TO SHOW ADAM AND EVE'S LUSH PARADISE PAVED OVER BY THE ALL-POWERFUL BULLDOZERS THAT COVER THE EARTH WITH CEMENT AS JONI MITCHELL SINGS 'BIG YELLOW TAXI.'
PROD-PFP   DIST-PFP

BILL OF RIGHTS IN ACTION - THE PRIVILEGE AGAINST SELF-INCRIMINATION C 23 MIN
16MM FILM OPTICAL SOUND   I-C A
EXPLAINS THAT THE FIFTH AMENDMENT PROTECTS THE ACCUSED AGAINST COERCED CONFESSIONS.
LC NO. 73-701284
PROD-BFA   DIST-WILETS   1972

BILLY MUFFET C 5 MIN
16MM FILM OPTICAL SOUND   J-C A
SEE SERIES TITLE FOR DESCRIPTIVE STATEMENT. FROM THE WONDERFUL WORLD OF SPORT - BASEBALL SERIES.
PROD-SPORTI   DIST-AMERFI

BING CROSBY'S WASHINGTON STATE C 28 MIN
16MM FILM OPTICAL SOUND   I-C A
INTERVIEWS BING CROSBY IN HIS NATIVE STATE, WASHINGTON. EXPLAINS THAT WASHINGTON IS THE EVERGREEN STATE RANGING FROM ANACORTES TO OMAK, FROM FERRY TO FOREST AND FROM MOUNTAIN CLIMBING TO MANUFACTURING.
LC NO. 73-701354
PROD-SCREEI   DIST-SCREEI   1968

BIOENGINEERS, THE C 14 MIN
16MM FILM OPTICAL SOUND
EXPLORES THE EXCITING NEW COMBINATION OF BIOLOGY AND ENGINEERING AT OAK RIDGE NATIONAL LABORATORY WITH SPECIAL EMPHASIS ON THE INVESTIGATION OF HUMAN CELLS. STUDIES MOLECULAR BIOLOGY AND CONTROL OF DISEASE.
LC NO. 73-701363
PROD-USAECO   DIST-USNAC   1973

BIOGRAPHY OF A CHAIR B 14 MIN
16MM FILM OPTICAL SOUND   J-C A
TELLS THE STORY OF ONE OF GREENFIELD VILLAGE'S MOST IMPORTANT ARTIFACTS, THE CHAIR IN WHICH ABRAHAM LINCOLN WAS SEATED WHEN HE WAS ASSASSINATED BY JOHN WILKES BOOTH ON APRIL 14, 1865.
PROD-FORD   DIST-FORD

BIOLOGY TODAY FILM--A SERIES

PROD-CRMP   DIST-CRMP

CELL, THE - A FUNCTIONING
STRUCTURE, PT 1   29 MIN
CELL, THE - A FUNCTIONING
STRUCTURE, PT 2   32 MIN
EVOLUTION AND THE ORIGIN OF LIFE   33 MIN
MUSCLE - A STUDY OF INTEGRATION   30 MIN

BIRTH C 47 MIN
16MM FILM OPTICAL SOUND   H-C A
PRESENTS A PORTRAIT OF A MARRIAGE AND MEMORABLE RECORDING OF THE BIRTH PROCESS. FOLLOWS A COUPLE DURING THE LAST THREE MONTHS OF PREGNANCY. REVEALS HOPE AND EXPECTATIONS ABOUT LIFE.
LC NO. 73-701062
PROD-VERITE   DIST-VERITE   1968

BIRTH C 76 MIN
16MM FILM OPTICAL SOUND   H-C A
PRESENTS A PORTRAIT OF A MARRIAGE AND A MEMORABLE RECORDING OF THE BIRTH PROCESS. FOLLOWS A COUPLE DURING THE LAST THREE MONTHS OF PREGNANCY. REVEALS HOPE AND EXPECTATIONS ABOUT LIFE.
LC NO. 73-701072
PROD-VERITE   DIST-VERITE   1968

BIRTH OF A BABY B 28 MIN
16MM FILM OPTICAL SOUND   H-C A
ILLUSTRATES THE BIRTH PROCESS SHOWING HOW THE BABY PASSES THROUGH THE BIRTH CANAL. INCLUDES ILLUSTRATIONS OF BREECH BIRTHS AND TWINS, PREMATURE BIRTH, MISCARRIAGE AND ABORTION. FROM THE SEX IN AMERICA CULTURE SERIES.
LC NO. 73-701212
PROD-CHM   DIST-CHM   1967

BIRTH OF A FROG B 11 MIN
16MM FILM OPTICAL SOUND
COVERS THE ENTIRE LIFE CYCLE OF A FROG BY LAPSE PHOTOGRAPHY.
PROD-IWANMI   DIST-IWANMI

BIRTH OF JAPANESE ISLANDS C 21 MIN
16MM FILM OPTICAL SOUND
USES A MODEL TO RELATE THE HISTORY OF THE BIRTH OF THE JAPANESE ISLANDS. DISCUSSES THE ORIGIN OF ANIMALS AND PLANTS ON THE MAINLAND AT THE TIME.
PROD-IWANMI   DIST-IWANMI

BIRTH OF KILLIFISH C 14 MIN
16MM FILM OPTICAL SOUND
OBSERVES THE TINY KILLIFISH AND EXPERIMENTS ON ITS HABITS. ILLUSTRATES THE INSTINCT OF PRESERVATION OF THE SPECIES, EGG LAYING AND FERTILIZATION AND DEVELOPMENT.
PROD-IWANMI   DIST-IWANMI

BIRTH OF MOUNT FUJI C 14 MIN
16MM FILM OPTICAL SOUND
STUDIES THE STAGES OF THE COMPLEX FORMATION OF MOUNT FUJI, A BEAUTIFUL CONOID TYPE VOLCANO. DESCRIBES THE MANY PARASITE VOLCANOES AROUND MOUNT FUJI AND THE FAULT OF SHIRAITO FALLS.
PROD-IWANMI   DIST-IWANMI

BLACK AND WHITE C 4 MIN
16MM FILM OPTICAL SOUND   I-C
PRESENTS THE ANIMATED JOHN WILSON'S DRAWINGS AND GRAPHICS AS CHER SINGS ROBINSON AND ARKIN'S SONG 'THE WORLD IS BLACK, THE WORLD IS WHITE, IT TURNS BY DAY AND THEN BY NIGHT.'
PROD-PFP   DIST-PFP

BLACK MASS B 16 MIN
16MM FILM OPTICAL SOUND
PRESENTS AN EXPERIMENTAL FILM DEPICTING A CAVERNOUS, WOMB-LIKE REALM RULED BY AN ALL-PERVASIVE EVIL, WHERE MALEVOLENT FORCES CAPRICIOUSLY SELECT VICTIMS AT RANDOM.
PROD-AMERFI   DIST-AMERFI

BLAZE GLORY C 10 MIN
16MM FILM OPTICAL SOUND   J-C A
PRESENTS A SPOOF ON COWBOY MOVIES.
PROD-PFP   DIST-PFP

BLOOD C 14 MIN
16MM FILM OPTICAL SOUND
EXPLAINS THE COMPOSITION OF BLOOD AND ITS FUNCTIONS. DISCUSSES BLOOD PLASMA, RED CORPUSCLES, THE WORKINGS OF HEMOGLOBIN, BLOOD CIRCULATION, WHITE CORPUSCLES AND THEIR FUNCTION AND BLOOD TRANSFUSIONS.
PROD-IWANMI   DIST-IWANMI

BLUE ANGELS - BEHIND THE ACT - MECHANICS C 5 MIN
16MM FILM OPTICAL SOUND   J-C A
SEE SERIES TITLE FOR DESCRIPTIVE STATEMENT. FROM THE WONDERFUL WORLD OF SPORT - FLYING SERIES.
PROD-SPORTI   DIST-AMERFI

BLUE ANGELS - NAVY'S FORMATION FLYERS C 5 MIN
16MM FILM OPTICAL SOUND   J-C A
SEE SERIES TITLE FOR DESCRIPTIVE STATEMENT. FROM THE WONDERFUL WORLD OF SPORT - FLYING SERIES.
PROD-SPORTI   DIST-AMERFI

BOATS AND BRIDGES - BARCOS Y PUENTES C 13 MIN
16MM FILM OPTICAL SOUND
PRESENTS A FERRY BOAT RIDE WHERE CHILDREN SEE OCEAN LINERS, FREIGHTERS AND BARGES AND LEARN THEIR USES. FROM THE BRENTANO FOUNDATION BILINGUAL FILMS SERIES.
PROD-CAROUF   DIST-CAROUF

BOB BEDNARSKI C 5 MIN
16MM FILM OPTICAL SOUND   J-C A
SEE SERIES TITLE FOR DESCRIPTIVE STATEMENT. FROM THE WONDERFUL WORLD OF SPORT - WEIGHTLIFTING SERIES.
PROD-SPORTI   DIST-AMERFI

BOY NAMED CHARLIE BROWN, A C 85 MIN
16MM FILM OPTICAL SOUND
FEATURES THE 'PEANUTS GANG' IN THEIR FIRST MOVIE.

119

PROD-SWANK   DIST-SWANK

BREAD   C   9 MIN
          16MM FILM OPTICAL SOUND   I-C A
PRESENTS AN ANALOGY BETWEEN THE MASS
PRODUCTION OF BREAD AND THE GIANT ME-
TROPOLISES FED BY BAKERIES.
LC NO. 73-701189
PROD-KINGSP   DIST-HRAW   1972

BREAKING A YEARLING   C   5 MIN
          16MM FILM OPTICAL SOUND   J-C A
SEE SERIES TITLE FOR DESCRIPTIVE STATEMENT.
FROM THE WONDERFUL WORLD OF SPORT -
HORSES, RACING, POLO, RODEO SERIES.
PROD-SPORTI   DIST-AMERFI

BREEZY AIRPLANE   C   5 MIN
          16MM FILM OPTICAL SOUND   J-C A
SEE SERIES TITLE FOR DESCRIPTIVE STATEMENT.
FROM THE WONDERFUL WORLD OF SPORT - FLY-
ING SERIES.
PROD-SPORTI   DIST-AMERFI

**BRENTANO FOUNDATION
BILINGUAL FILMS--A SERIES**
PRESENTS A BILINGUAL FILM SERIES DIRECTED
AT THE SPANISH-SPEAKING MINORITY CHILDREN,
TO HELP THEM GROW INTO CAPABLE, INFORMED
CITIZENS AND WORK FOR A POSITIVE AND CRE-
ATIVE CHANGE IN THE SOCIAL CLIMATE.
PROD-CAROUF   DIST-CAROUF

ALL ABOUT ANIMALS - TODO SOBRE
LOS ANIMALES   7 MIN
ARTS AND CRAFTS - ARTESANIA   9 MIN
AT THE FIRE STATION   8 MIN
AT THE MARKET - EN EL MERCADO   10 MIN
BIG TREES, THE - LOS ARBOLES
GRANDES   7 MIN
BOATS AND BRIDGES - BARCOS Y
PUENTES   13 MIN
COUNTING AND COLORS - EL CONTAR Y
COLORES   9 MIN
DAY IN THE PARK, A   8 MIN
DID YOU EVER MILK A COW - JAMAS
HAS EXTRAIDO --   6 MIN
FIESTA   9 MIN
FIREMEN GO TO SCHOOL, TOO - LOS
BOMBEROS VAN --   7 MIN
FIRST DAY, NEW FRIENDS - PRIMER
DIA, NUEVOS --   7 MIN
FROM WHEEL TO WING - DESDE LA
RUEDA HASTA EL --   7 MIN
GET READY FOR THE RANCH -
PREPARATE PARA EL --   7 MIN
GET READY FOR THE ZOO - PREPARATE
PARA EL --   6 MIN
LET'S VISIT THE FIREMEN - VAMOS A
VISITAR A --   7 MIN
MEXICO   12 MIN
OUR FAMILY ALBUM - NUESTRO ALBUM
DE LA FAMILIA   7 MIN
OUR FIRST PLANE RIDE - NUESTRO
PRIMER VIAJE --   10 MIN
PEPE TEACHES US - PEPE NOS ENSENA   7 MIN
TOUCHDOWNS AND HORSES - GOLES Y
CABALLOS   6 MIN
TRAINS AND MORE TRAINS - TRENES Y
MAS TRENES   11 MIN
TRIP TO RANCHO VERDE, A   9 MIN
WE EXPLORE CHINATOWN - NOSOTROS
EXPLORAMOS --   7 MIN
WE GO TO A DAIRY FARM   8 MIN
WE REMEMBER THE FARM -
RECORDAMOS EL RANCHO   6 MIN
WE SEE THE BABY ZOO - VEMOS EL
ZOOLOGICO --   8 MIN
WE VISIT THE POST OFFICE -
VISITAMOS LA CASA --   8 MIN
WE VISIT THE ZOO - VISITAMOS EL
JARDIN --   11 MIN

BRIDGE CONSTRUCTION   C 14 MIN
          16MM FILM OPTICAL SOUND
EXAMINES VARIOUS TYPES OF BRIDGE CON-
STRUCTIONS AND THEIR RELATIVE STURDINESS.
PROD-IWANMI   DIST-IWANMI

BRIDGE OF FRIENDSHIP   B 14 MIN
          16MM FILM OPTICAL SOUND
SHOWS STUDENTS FROM MANY COUNTRIES OF
AFRICA AND ASIA ON ISRAELI STUDY GRANTS
LEARNING LABOR AND MANAGEMENT TECH-
NIQUES AND TOURING THE CHIEF INDUSTRIAL
SITES.
PROD-ALDEN   DIST-ALDEN

BROADCASTER STORY   C   5 MIN
          16MM FILM OPTICAL SOUND   J-C A
SEE SERIES TITLE FOR DESCRIPTIVE STATEMENT.
FROM THE WONDERFUL WORLD OF SPORT - BASE-
BALL SERIES.
PROD-SPORTI   DIST-AMERFI

BROOKS ROBINSON   C   5 MIN
          16MM FILM OPTICAL SOUND   J-C A
SEE SERIES TITLE FOR DESCRIPTIVE STATEMENT.
FROM THE WONDERFUL WORLD OF SPORT - BASE-
BALL SERIES.
PROD-SPORTI   DIST-AMERFI

BROWN RICE   C 28 MIN
          16MM FILM OPTICAL SOUND
TAKES A LIGHT-HEARTED VIEW OF TODAY'S TEE-
NAGERS AND SHOWS HOW THEIR ATTITUDES
HAVE CHANGED. OBSERVES EXPERIENCES IN-
VOLVING A VEGETARIAN MEAL, A FLAT TIRE, A
PARKING TICKET AND AN ASSIGNMENT TO READ
'THE ART OF LOVING.'
PROD-AMERFI   DIST-AMERFI

BUILDING A HARBOR   C 13 MIN
          16MM FILM OPTICAL SOUND   I-J
SHOWS PRELIMINARY SURVEYS, MAPPING, ECO-
LOGICAL STUDIES AND MODEL EXPERIMENTA-
TIONS BY U S ARMY CORPS OF ENGINEERS. DE-
SCRIBES GRAPHICALLY THE MEN, MACHINES AND
MATERIALS NEEDED TO CONSTRUCT BREAKWA-
TERS AND COMPLETION OF THE HARBOR FACILI-
TIES NEEDED TO SERVE THE PUBLIC.
LC NO. 73-701067
PROD-CAHILL   DIST-AIMS   1972

BULLSEYE   C 28 MIN
          16MM FILM OPTICAL SOUND
TELLS THE STORY OF AMRLIN'S EXHIBITION
SHOOTER AND WORLD CHAMPION WITH THE RI-
FLE, COL LARSON. CONTAINS HELPFUL TIPS FOR
HUNTERS AND TARGET SHOOTERS.
PROD-MTP   DIST-MTP

BY THE PEOPLE   B 81 MIN
          16MM FILM OPTICAL SOUND   J-C A
SUGGESTS ATTEMPTING CHANGE WHILE WORK-
ING QUIETLY WITHIN THE SYSTEM.
PROD-FILIM   DIST-FILIM   1973

C

C - CALICLOTH   C   4 MIN
          16MM FILM OPTICAL SOUND
USES SEMI-ABSTRACT ANIMATION TO SHOW OUT-
STANDING USE OF GRAPHIC DESIGN AND COLOR
IN FILM.
PROD-CFS   DIST-VISRES

**CACTUS, THE - ADAPTATIONS
FOR SURVIVAL**   C 14 MIN
          16MM FILM OPTICAL SOUND   I-J
EXPLAINS THAT THE CACTUS HAS BEEN ABLE TO
ADAPT SUCCESSFULLY TO HARSH ENVIRONMENTS
THROUGH ITS UNIQUE PHYSICAL CHARACTERIS-
TICS AND LIFE CYCLES. DEMONSTRATES ITS WA-
TER-CONSERVING CHARACTERISTICS.
LC NO. 73-701229
PROD-EBEC   DIST-EBEC   1973

CALVIN MURPHY   C   5 MIN
          16MM FILM OPTICAL SOUND   J-C A
SEE SERIES TITLE FOR DESCRIPTIVE STATEMENT.
FROM THE WONDERFUL WORLD OF SPORT - BAS-
KETBALL SERIES.
PROD-SPORTI   DIST-AMERFI

CAMPAIGN   C
          16MM FILM OPTICAL SOUND   H-C
PRESENTS AN ACCOUNT OF A GRASS ROOTS CAM-
PAIGN OF A WOMAN RUNNING FOR STATE SENA-
TOR. INDICATES THAT THE ENTHUSIASM OF THE
GROUP EFFORT MAKES AN ELOQUENT PLEA FOR
INVOLVEMENT IN THE ELECTORAL PROCESS.
LC NO. 73-701442
PROD-CF   DIST-CF   1973

CAPRI PROGRAM, THE   C 27 MIN
          16MM FILM OPTICAL SOUND   C A
SHOWS A MEDICALLY SUPERVISED EXERCISE PRO-
GRAM FOR HEART PATIENTS. POINTS OUT THE
COMMUNITY'S STAKE IN RAPID REHABILITATION
OF HEART ATTACK SURVIVORS. STRESSES THE
POSSIBILITY OF REBUILDING A HIGH DEGREE OF
PHYSICAL WELL-BEING.
LC NO. 73-701355
PROD-SAFECO   DIST-SAFECO   1972

**CARDIGAN BAY - HARNESS
WINNER**   C   5 MIN
          16MM FILM OPTICAL SOUND   J-C A
SEE SERIES TITLE FOR DESCRIPTIVE STATEMENT.
FROM THE WONDERFUL WORLD OF SPORT -
HORSES, RACING, POLO, RODEO SERIES.
PROD-SPORTI   DIST-AMERFI

CAREERS IN LARGE INDUSTRY   C 12 MIN
          16MM FILM OPTICAL SOUND
SHOWS MANY OF THE CAREER OPPORTUNITIES
THAT LARGE INDUSTRY HAS TO OFFER THOSE
WHO QUALIFY. USES THE NATURAL GAS INDUS-
TRY AS AN EXAMPLE.
LC NO. 73-701220
PROD-VOFI   DIST-VOFI   1973

CARGO ON THE GO   C 12 MIN
          16MM FILM OPTICAL SOUND
TAKES THE VIEWER ON A TOUR OF THE WORLD'S
LARGEST AIR CARGO CENTER AT KENNEDY INTER-
NATIONAL AIRPORT IN NEW YORK. CAPTURES
THE PACE OF JET-AGE MARKETING, AUTOMATED
GROUND HANDLING, WORLD-WIDE FLIGHT CON-
NECTION AND ROUND-THE-CLOCK SHIPPING
SERVICES.
PROD-BEF   DIST-BEF

CARL YASTRZEMSKI   C   5 MIN
          16MM FILM OPTICAL SOUND   J-C A
SEE SERIES TITLE FOR DESCRIPTIVE STATEMENT.
FROM THE WONDERFUL WORLD OF SPORT - BASE-
BALL SERIES.
PROD-SPORTI   DIST-AMERFI

**CARNIVAL, THE - THE STORY
OF A GIRL AND A GOLDFISH**   X   8 MIN
          16MM FILM OPTICAL SOUND   P
PRESENTS A YOUNG GIRL WHO WINS A GOLDFISH
AT A CARNIVAL.
LC NO. 72-702690
PROD-SOCTYS   DIST-XEROX   1972

CAROLINAS, THE   C 29 MIN
          16MM FILM OPTICAL SOUND
PRESENTS THE ENCHANTMENT OF THE CAROLI-
NAS IN A KALEIDOSCOPIC JOURNEY THROUGH FA-
MOUS HISTORICAL SITES, SCENIC MARVELS AND
PRESENT-DAY ENTERPRISES AND ACCOMPLISH-
MENTS.
PROD-MTP   DIST-MTP

CAST NETTING   C   5 MIN
          16MM FILM OPTICAL SOUND   J-C A
SEE SERIES TITLE FOR DESCRIPTIVE STATEMENT.
FROM THE WONDERFUL WORLD OF SPORT - FISH-
ING SERIES.
PROD-SPORTI   DIST-AMERFI

CATAMARANS   C   5 MIN
          16MM FILM OPTICAL SOUND   J-C A
SEE SERIES TITLE FOR DESCRIPTIVE STATEMENT.
FROM THE WONDERFUL WORLD OF SPORT - BOAT-
ING SERIES.
PROD-SPORTI   DIST-AMERFI

CAUGHT   C
          16MM FILM OPTICAL SOUND   J-C
PRESENTS TO TEENAGERS THE SERIOUS CONSE-
QUENCES OF SHOPLIFTING.
LC NO. 73-701448
PROD-CINCON   DIST-NRMA   1971

CELEBRATION OF LIFE - TREES   C 12 MIN
          16MM FILM OPTICAL SOUND   P-I
INDICATES THAT THE BEAUTY AND WONDER OF
OUR NATURAL ENVIRONMENT GIVES CAUSE FOR
CELEBRATION. JOINS A GROUP OF YOUNGSTERS
DISCOVERING AND ENJOYING EVERYTHING
ABOUT TREES AND WOODS, INCLUDING COLORS,
SHAPES, SEASONS CHANGING, FOREST ANIMALS
AND SOUNDS.
LC NO. 73-701426
PROD-BFA   DIST-BFA   1973

CENTER OF LIFE   C 20 MIN
          16MM FILM OPTICAL SOUND   J-C A
DESCRIBES TECHNIQUES AND FACILITIES USED
BY MEN'S SOCIAL SERVICE CENTERS IN FULL-TIME
REHABILITATION PROGRAMS FOR VICTIMS OF
COMPULSIVE ALCOHOLISM AND OTHER EMO-
TIONAL DISTRESSES. EMPHASIZES THE ADJUST-
MENT EX-CONVICTS AND OTHERS MUST MAKE IN
THE MODERN WORLD.
LC NO. 73-701279
PROD-SALVA   DIST-GRANDY   1973

CENTRAC - ONE BOLD STEP   C 15 MIN
          16MM FILM OPTICAL SOUND
TELLS THE STORY OF A MODERN OFFICE AND IT'S
METHOD OF RECORD KEEPING. CONTRASTS THE
OLD AND NEW WAYS OF FILING. SHOWS HOW RO-
TARY FILES AND AUTOMATIC CONVEYORS IN-
CREASE EFFICIENCY AND OFFICE PRODUCTION.
PROD-BEF   DIST-BEF

CENTRIFUGAL FORCE   C 14 MIN
        16MM FILM OPTICAL SOUND
GIVES BASIC EXPLANATIONS OF CENTRIFUGAL
FORCE IN ACTION THROUGH EXPERIMENTS OF
FORWARD AND CIRCULAR MOVEMENTS OF A BALL
ON A FLAT SURFACE.
PROD-IWANMI   DIST-IWANMI

CERAMIC ART--A SERIES
PROVIDES AN UNDERSTANDING OF THE METH-
ODS, MATERIALS AND EQUIPMENT BASIC TO THE
ART OF CERAMICS.
PROD-MGHT   DIST-MGHT

CERAMICS - WHAT, WHY, HOW   16 MIN
COIL METHOD, THE   21 MIN
CREATING MOSAICS AND TILES   15 MIN
HANDBUILDING METHODS   17 MIN
POTTERS OF JAPAN, PT 1   16 MIN
POTTERS OF JAPAN, PT 2   15 MIN
POTTERS OF THE USA, PT 1   16 MIN
POTTERS OF THE USA, PT 2   17 MIN

CERAMICS - WHAT, WHY, HOW   C 16 MIN
        16MM FILM OPTICAL SOUND
PRESENTS AN OVERALL PICTURE OF MATERIALS
AND PROCESSES USED IN THE PRODUCTION OF
CERAMICS. FROM THE CERAMIC ART SERIES.
PROD-MGHT   DIST-MGHT

CEYLON   C
        16MM FILM OPTICAL SOUND
SEE SERIES TITLE FOR DESCRIPTIVE STATEMENT.
FROM THE PORT OF CALL SERIES.
PROD-PUI   DIST-PUI

CHALLENGE OF THE ARCTIC   C 28 MIN
        16MM FILM OPTICAL SOUND
PRESENTS A COLLAGE OF LIFE IN NORTHERN
ALASKA. DEALS WITH THE RECENT DISCOVERY OF
VAST NEW PETROLEUM RESOURCES ON THE
NORTH SLOPE. DOCUMENTS THE EFFORTS BEING
MADE TO TAP URGENTLY NEEDED FUTURE
POWER SOURCES TO BENEFIT THE NATIVE POPU-
LATION AND TO CONSERVE THE REGION'S PRE-
CIOUS WILDLIFE.
PROD-ARIC   DIST-ARIC

CHANGES, CHANGES   C 6 MIN
        16MM FILM OPTICAL SOUND   K-P
SHOWS HOW BLOCKS BECOME WHATEVER A
CHILD AT PLAY IMAGINES.
LC NO. 73-701127
PROD-SCHNDL   DIST-WWS   1972

CHARLIE POLITE   C 5 MIN
        16MM FILM OPTICAL SOUND   J-C A
SEE SERIES TITLE FOR DESCRIPTIVE STATEMENT.
FROM THE WONDERFUL WORLD OF SPORT - BOX-
ING SERIES.
PROD-SPORTI   DIST-AMERFI

CHAROLAIS REPORT, THE   C 27 MIN
        16MM FILM OPTICAL SOUND
TELLS THE STORY OF THE GREAT WHITE FRENCH
BREED OF BEEF CATTLE FROM PRODUCER TO
CONSUMER.
PROD-MTP   DIST-MTP

CHECK IT OUT   C 27 MIN
        16MM FILM OPTICAL SOUND   J-H A
DISCUSSES THE IMPACT OF VD ON TWO YOUNG
PEOPLE AND THEIR FAMILIES. SUGGESTS METH-
ODS OF PREVENTION, HOW TO GET HELP WHEN
NEEDED AND DISCLOSURE OF CONTACTS AS A
WAY TO STOP FURTHER SPREADING.
LC NO. 73-700639
PROD-NEWD   DIST-NEWD   1972

CHICKEN SOUP   B 14 MIN
        16MM FILM OPTICAL SOUND   J-C A
DEMONSTRATES IN A HUMOROUS WAY HOW TO
MAKE CHICKEN SOUP.
LC NO. 73-701255
PROD-CAROUF   DIST-CAROUF   1973

CHILDBIRTH   C 17 MIN
        16MM FILM OPTICAL SOUND   J-C A
PRESENTS A SHORTENED VERSION OF 'NOT ME
ALONE,' EMPHASIZING THE INTERPERSONAL RE-
LATIONSHIPS AND THE SHARED JOY OF CHILD-
BIRTH.
PROD-POLYMR   DIST-POLYMR

CHILDREN AS PEOPLE   B 28 MIN
        16MM FILM OPTICAL SOUND   H-C A
DEPICTS THE FAYERWEATHER STREET SCHOOL OF
CAMBRIDGE, MASSACHUSETTS, WHICH ALLOWS
CHILDREN TO BE RESPONSIBLE FOR THEIR SOCIAL
AND ACADEMIC BEHAVIOR, TREATING CHILDREN
AS PEOPLE. SHOWS HOW THE CHILDREN DECIDE

WHAT THEY ARE GOING TO DO AND HOW AND
WHEN THEY ARE GOING TO DO IT.
PROD-POLYMR   DIST-POLYMR

CHILDREN OF THE KIBBUTZ   C 15 MIN
        16MM FILM OPTICAL SOUND   I-C A
PORTRAYS THE DAILY ROUTINE OF CHILDREN IN
A KIBBUTZ. NOTES HOW THE CHILDREN LIVE TO-
GETHER, LEARN AND PLAY AS A GROUP AND
GROW UP IN A FREE AND SECURE ATMOSPHERE.
LC NO. 73-701419
PROD-YANIV   DIST-ACI   1972

CHILDREN, THE   C 7 MIN
        16MM FILM OPTICAL SOUND
CONTRASTS THE WELL-FED, WELL-CLOTHED
AMERICAN CHILDREN PLAYING IN NEW YORK'S
CENTRAL PARK, INTERSPERSED WITH MARCHES
AND SUPERIMPOSED OVER POOR, UNDERNOUR-
ISHED YOUNG VIETNAMESE TO PROVIDE AN UN-
SPOKEN CRITICISM.
PROD-AMERFI   DIST-AMERFI

CHILDREN'S CONCEPTS   B 30 MIN
        16MM FILM OPTICAL SOUND   C T
PRESENTS A RECONSTRUCTION OF SOME OF PIAG-
ET'S EXPERIMENTS, DEMONSTRATING SOME OF
THE LIMITATIONS OF CHILDREN'S CONCEPTUAL
THINKING. FROM THE EXPANDING CLASSROOM
SERIES.
PROD-BBCTV   DIST-TIMLIF

CHILDREN'S WORLD - MEXICO   C
        16MM FILM OPTICAL SOUND   K-I
INTRODUCES MEXICO, INCLUDING GEOGRAPHY,
HISTORY, CULTURE, CUSTOMS, HOME INDUS-
TRIES, RECREATION AND CITIES OF MEXICO.
FROM THE CHILDREN'S WORLD SERIES.
LC NO. 73-701410
PROD-TEDFDI   DIST-AVED   1973

**CHINA - A HOLE IN THE
BAMBOO CURTAIN**   C 28 MIN
        16MM FILM OPTICAL SOUND   I-C A
PRESENTS A CHINESE ODYSSEY WHICH RANGES
FROM SHENYANG TO PEKING, SHANGHAI AND FI-
NALLY CANTON IN THE SOUTH. FOCUSES ON THE
PEOPLE, THEIR LIFESTYLES, THEIR CHILDREN IN
THE SCHOOL AND THEIR THOUGHTS OF THE PRE-
SENT AND FUTURE.
PROD-CAROUF   DIST-CAROUF

CITIZEN'S ARMY   C 15 MIN
        16MM FILM OPTICAL SOUND
SHOWS THE UNIQUE PURPOSE AND FUNCTION-
ING OF THE ISRAELI DEFENSE FORCES. DEPICTS
THE TRAINING AND CULTURAL ACTIVITIES IN
BOTH THE MEN'S AND WOMEN'S UNITS AS WELL
AS THE MANNING OF BORDER SETTLEMENTS BY
RESERVE MILITIA.
PROD-ALDEN   DIST-ALDEN

CIVIL WRONG, THE   B 29 MIN
        16MM FILM OPTICAL SOUND   J-C A
PORTRAYS THE LEGAL LIABILITIES WHICH DAILY
FACE EACH INDIVIDUAL CITIZEN IN A DAY IN THE
LIFE OF AN AVERAGE AMERICAN. DISCUSSES THE
CIVIL WRONGS AND THE WAYS IN WHICH LAWS
PROTECT THE CITIZEN FROM THESE WRONGS.
FROM THE QUEST FOR CERTAINTY SERIES.
LC NO. 73-701037
PROD-UMITV   DIST-UMITV   1962

CIVILISATION--A SERIES

PROD-BBCTV   DIST-TIMLIF

CIVILISATION, PROGRAM 01   52 MIN
CIVILISATION, PROGRAM 02   52 MIN
CIVILISATION, PROGRAM 03   52 MIN
CIVILISATION, PROGRAM 04   52 MIN
CIVILISATION, PROGRAM 05   52 MIN
CIVILISATION, PROGRAM 06   52 MIN
CIVILISATION, PROGRAM 07   52 MIN
CIVILISATION, PROGRAM 08   52 MIN
CIVILISATION, PROGRAM 09   52 MIN
CIVILISATION, PROGRAM 10   52 MIN
CIVILISATION, PROGRAM 11   52 MIN
CIVILISATION, PROGRAM 12   52 MIN
CIVILISATION, PROGRAM 13   52 MIN

CIVILISATION, PROGRAM 01   C 52 MIN
        16MM FILM OPTICAL SOUND
DISCUSSES THE SURVIVAL OF WESTERN CIVILIZA-
TION AFTER THE FALL OF ROME, WHICH MARKED
THE END OF IDEAS AND IDEALS INHERITED FROM
FIFTH CENTURY GREECE. INCLUDES A VIEW OF
THE EARLY CHRISTIANS AS CRAFTSMEN AND THE
IMPACT OF CHARLEMAGNE. FROM THE CIVILISA-
TION SERIES.
PROD-BBCTV   DIST-TIMLIF

CIVILISATION, PROGRAM 02   C 52 MIN
        16MM FILM OPTICAL SOUND
DISCUSSES THE FIRST GREAT FLOWERING OF CIVI-
LIZATION IN THE 12TH CENTURY. PORTRAYS THE
ERA OF ABBEYS AND CATHEDRALS BUILD TO
HONOR GOD, INCLUDING CLUNY, CANTERBURY,
AUTUN AND CHARTRES. FROM THE CIVILISATION
SERIES.
PROD-BBCTV   DIST-TIMLIF

CIVILISATION, PROGRAM 03   C 52 MIN
        16MM FILM OPTICAL SOUND
DISCUSSES THE GOTHIC WORLD AND THE
ACHIEVEMENTS IN ART AND LITERATURE OF THE
LATE MIDDLE AGES, INCLUDING DANTE, GIOTTO
AND THE ANJOU TAPESTRIES. PORTRAYS THE
EMERGENCE OF WOMAN AS AN IDEAL. FROM THE
CIVILISATION SERIES.
PROD-BBCTV   DIST-TIMLIF

CIVILISATION, PROGRAM 04   C 52 MIN
        16MM FILM OPTICAL SOUND
DISCUSSES THE BIRTH OF INDIVIDUALISM IN THE
EARLY RENAISSANCE. FEATURES THE GREAT
PAINTERS BOTTICELLI, MASACCIO, BELLINI, GIOR-
GIONE AND VAN EYCK. FROM THE CIVILISATION
SERIES.
PROD-BBCTV   DIST-TIMLIF

CIVILISATION, PROGRAM 05   C 52 MIN
        16MM FILM OPTICAL SOUND
DISCUSSES THE SPLENDOR OF ROME AND THE
AGE OF GENIUS, SHOWING THE WORK OF DA
VINCI, MICHELANGELO AND RAPHAEL. FROM THE
CIVILISATION SERIES.
PROD-BBCTV   DIST-TIMLIF

CIVILISATION, PROGRAM 06   C 52 MIN
        16MM FILM OPTICAL SOUND
DISCUSSES THE CLOSE OF THE 15TH CENTURY
AND GUTENBERG'S PRINTING PRESS AND THE
SPREADING OF KNOWLEDGE. INCLUDES THE
WORK OF LUTHER, ERASMUS, THOMAS MORE AND
SHAKESPEARE. FROM THE CIVILISATION SERIES.
PROD-BBCTV   DIST-TIMLIF

CIVILISATION, PROGRAM 07   C 52 MIN
        16MM FILM OPTICAL SOUND
DISCUSSES THE COUNTER-REFORMATION AND
THE REBUILDING OF ROME AS A GREAT SPIRITUAL
CENTER. POINTS OUT THAT A NEW UNITY OF
DOGMA AND PURSUIT OF PLEASURE IS REACHED.
FROM THE CIVILISATION SERIES.
PROD-BBCTV   DIST-TIMLIF

CIVILISATION, PROGRAM 08   C 52 MIN
        16MM FILM OPTICAL SOUND
DISCUSSES THE 17TH CENTURY AS REPRESENTED
BY FRANZ HALS, VERMEER AND REMBRANDT IN
THE NORTH AND MEN OF SCIENCE IN ENGLAND,
INCLUDING NEWTON AND CHRISTOPHER WREN.
FROM THE CIVILISATION SERIES.
PROD-BBCTV   DIST-TIMLIF

CIVILISATION, PROGRAM 09   C 52 MIN
        16MM FILM OPTICAL SOUND
DISCUSSES THE PURSUIT OF HAPPINESS, ROCOCO
ARCHITECTURE IN GERMANY AND MUSIC BY
BACH, HANDEL AND MOZART. FROM THE CIVILISA-
TION SERIES.
PROD-BBCTV   DIST-TIMLIF

CIVILISATION, PROGRAM 10   C 52 MIN
        16MM FILM OPTICAL SOUND
DISCUSSES THE ART AND SCULPTURE OF THE
18TH CENTURY, FOLLOWED BY THE ENLIGHTEN-
MENT IN FRANCE, ENGLAND AND THOMAS JEF-
FERSON'S AMERICA. FROM THE CIVILISATION SE-
RIES.
PROD-BBCTV   DIST-TIMLIF

CIVILISATION, PROGRAM 11   C 52 MIN
        16MM FILM OPTICAL SOUND
DISCUSSES THE WORSHIP OF NATURE AS EXEM-
PLIFIED IN SWITZERLAND, HOME OF ROUSSEAU,
AND IN ENGLAND THROUGH PAINTERS CONSTA-
BLE, MONET AND TURNER. FROM THE CIVILISA-
TION SERIES.
PROD-BBCTV   DIST-TIMLIF

CIVILISATION, PROGRAM 12   C 52 MIN
        16MM FILM OPTICAL SOUND
POINTS OUT THAT MAN'S BELIEF IN HIS NATURAL
GOODNESS IS SHATTERED IN THE 19TH CENTURY.
DISCUSSES THE FRENCH REVOLUTION, NAPO-
LEON, LORD BYRON, BEETHOVEN, BLAKE, DELA-
CROIX AND OTHERS. FROM THE CIVILISATION SE-
RIES.
PROD-BBCTV   DIST-TIMLIF

CIVILISATION, PROGRAM 13   C 52 MIN
16MM FILM OPTICAL SOUND
TAKES THE VIEWER FROM THE INDUSTRIAL REVO-
LUTION TO THE PRESENT STATE OF WESTERN
CIVILIZATION. EXAMINES THE ROOTS OF HUMANI-
TARIANISM AND THE STATE OF 20TH CENTURY
MAN'S CONSCIENCE. FROM THE CIVILISATION SE-
RIES.
PROD-BBCTV   DIST-TIMLIF

CLAES OLDENBURG   B 30 MIN
16MM FILM OPTICAL SOUND
ILLUMINATES THE CONCERNS OF CLAES OLDEN-
BURG, A MAJOR FIGURE OF THE POP ART MOVE-
MENT AND ORIGINATOR OF HAPPENINGS. SHOWS
MANY OF OLDENBURG'S WORKS OF ART.
PROD-NET   DIST-VISRES

**CLAES OLDENBURG - SORT OF
A COMMERCIAL FOR AN ICEBAG**
C 16 MIN
16MM FILM OPTICAL SOUND
REFLECTS CLAES OLDENBURG'S HIGH ESTEEM
FOR THE ICEBAG, WHICH, AFTER A LONG SEARCH,
HE SELECTED FOR HIS GIANT KINETIC SCULP-
TURE.
PROD-NET   DIST-VISRES

**CLASSIC CARS, THE 1930
BENTLEY**   C 5 MIN
16MM FILM OPTICAL SOUND   J-C A
SEE SERIES TITLE FOR DESCRIPTIVE STATEMENT.
FROM THE WONDERFUL WORLD OF SPORT - CARS,
AUTO RACING SERIES.
PROD-SPORTI   DIST-AMERFI

CLAUDE FRANTZ   C 5 MIN
16MM FILM OPTICAL SOUND   J-C A
SEE SERIES TITLE FOR DESCRIPTIVE STATEMENT.
FROM THE WONDERFUL WORLD OF SPORT -
WRESTLING SERIES.
PROD-SPORTI   DIST-AMERFI

**CLINICAL EVALUATION OF THE
JUGULAR VENOUS PULSE**   C
16MM FILM OPTICAL SOUND   PRO
SHOWS THE TECHNIQUE OF EXAMINING JUGULAR
VENOUS PULSATION AS AN AID TO DIAGNOSIS
WHEN EKG IS NOT AVAILABLE.
LC NO. 72-700016
PROD-SKF   DIST-AMEDA   1971

CO-OP   B 15 MIN
16MM FILM OPTICAL SOUND
SHOWS HOW STUDENTS FROM FRENCH-SPEAKING
AFRICAN COUNTRIES TAKE PART IN EVERYDAY
LIFE IN ISRAEL, THROUGH WORK AND STUDY.
PROD-ALDEN   DIST-ALDEN

COACHES STORY   C 5 MIN
16MM FILM OPTICAL SOUND   J-C A
SEE SERIES TITLE FOR DESCRIPTIVE STATEMENT.
FROM THE WONDERFUL WORLD OF SPORT - BAS-
KETBALL SERIES.
PROD-SPORTI   DIST-AMERFI

COGNITIVE DEVELOPMENT   C 18 MIN
16MM FILM OPTICAL SOUND   C A
SHOWS HOW A CHILD'S SENSE OF REALITY
ADAPTS AS HIS COGNITIVE CAPACITIES MATURE.
CONTRASTS THE THEORIES OF THE SWISS PSY-
CHOLOGIST, JEAN PIAGET, AS USED AT THE PA-
CIFIC OAKS COLLEGE PRESCHOOL WITH PROFES-
SOR SIEGFRIED ENGLEMANN'S BEHAVIORIST VIEW
WHICH IS BEING PRACTICED AT THE UNIVERSITY
OF OREGON. FROM THE DEVELOPMENTAL PSY-
CHOLOGY FILM SERIES.
LC NO. 73-700572
PROD-CRMP   DIST-CRMP   1973

COIL METHOD, THE   C 21 MIN
16MM FILM OPTICAL SOUND
DEMONSTRATES THE BASIC METHODS IN CE-
RAMIC ART WITH AN EXPLANATION OF EACH
PHASE OF THE WORK. FROM THE CERAMIC ART
SERIES.
PROD-MGHT   DIST-MGHT

COLLEGE CHEERLEADERS, NO. 1
C 5 MIN
16MM FILM OPTICAL SOUND   J-C A
SEE SERIES TITLE FOR DESCRIPTIVE STATEMENT.
FROM THE WONDERFUL WORLD OF SPORT - FOOT-
BALL SERIES.
PROD-SPORTI   DIST-AMERFI

COLLEGE CHEERLEADERS, NO. 2
C 5 MIN
16MM FILM OPTICAL SOUND   J-C A
SEE SERIES TITLE FOR DESCRIPTIVE STATEMENT.
FROM THE WONDERFUL WORLD OF SPORT - FOOT-
BALL SERIES.
PROD-SPORTI   DIST-AMERFI

COLLEGE DAZE   B 29 MIN
16MM FILM OPTICAL SOUND
SATIRIZES EARLY COLLEGE LIFE. INTRODUCES MI-
CHAEL PAUL, THE GANGLING HERO WHO PLUNGES
INTO THE MAELSTROM OF REGISTRATION WHERE
HE IS NUMBERED, CLASSIFIED, IBM-IFIED AND
PHOTOGRAPHED.
PROD-AMERFI   DIST-AMERFI

**COLLEGE FOOTBALL, HANRATTY,
SEYMOUR**   C 5 MIN
16MM FILM OPTICAL SOUND   J-C A
SEE SERIES TITLE FOR DESCRIPTIVE STATEMENT.
FROM THE WONDERFUL WORLD OF SPORT - FOOT-
BALL SERIES.
PROD-SPORTI   DIST-AMERFI

CONDITIONED REFLEX   C 14 MIN
16MM FILM OPTICAL SOUND
PROBES INTO CONDITIONED REFLEXES, WHICH
HAVE VERY CLOSE CONNECTIONS WITH THE
MOVEMENT OF ANIMALS. DESCRIBES THE DIFFER-
ENCE BETWEEN CONDITIONED AND NATURAL RE-
FLEXES AND GIVES EXAMPLES OF EACH.
PROD-IWANMI   DIST-IWANMI

**CONSERVATION - TURTLE
RESEARCH**   C 5 MIN
16MM FILM OPTICAL SOUND   J-C A
SEE SERIES TITLE FOR DESCRIPTIVE STATEMENT.
FROM THE WONDERFUL WORLD OF SPORT -
OTHER SERIES.
PROD-SPORTI   DIST-AMERFI

CONSTANTIN BRANCUSI   C 22 MIN
16MM FILM OPTICAL SOUND
GIVES THE VIEWER A UNIQUE OPPORTUNITY TO
OBSERVE THE BEAUTY AND THE ENORMOUS VA-
RIETY OF SCULPTURE BY CONSTANTIN BRANCUSI
WHILE BEING GUIDED BY THE AUTHORITATIVE
NARRATION OF SIDNEY GEIST.
PROD-VISRES   DIST-VISRES

**CONSTRUCTING REALITY - A
FILM ON FILM**   C 18 MIN
16MM FILM OPTICAL SOUND   P-C
DISCUSSES THE FIVE KEY ELEMENTS OF FILM
CONSTRUCTION, INCLUDING FILM TIME, FILM
SPACE, PERSPECTIVE, RHYTHM AND SOUND AS A
FILM ABOUT SPORT CAR RACING IS CONTRUCTED.
LC NO. 73-701347
PROD-ALTSUL   DIST-JOU   1973

**CONTINENTS ADRIFT - A STUDY
OF THE SCIENTIFIC METHOD**   C 15 MIN
16MM FILM OPTICAL SOUND   J-C
SHOWS HOW A SCIENTIFIC HYPOTHESIS BECOMES
ESTABLISHED IN A STUDY OF ALFRED WEGENER'S
HYPOTHESIS THAT AT ONE TIME ALL THE CONTI-
NENTS WERE ONE. DISCUSSES PALEOMAGNET-
ISM, SEA FLOOR SPREADING, MAGNETISM IN
ROCK AND THE DRIFTING MAGNETIC POLES.
LC NO. 75-712961
PROD-AMEDFL   DIST-AMEDFL   1971

**COPING IN SPECIAL EDUCATION
- DEVELOPING OBSERVATIONAL
TECHNIQUES**   C
16MM FILM OPTICAL SOUND   C
DEMONSTRATES INSTRUCTIONAL, CONTROL AND
ORGANIZATIONAL TECHNIQUES AND STRATEGIES
FOR PREVENTING OR COPING WITH CHILDREN'S
INAPPROPRIATE BEHAVIOR AND THE CUES BY
WHICH SUCH BEHAVIORS ARE OBSERVED. FROM
THE COPING IN SPECIAL EDUCATION SERIES.
LC NO. 73-701172
PROD-UEUWIS   DIST-UEUWIS   1972

**COPING IN SPECIAL EDUCATION
- DEVELOPING STUDY HABITS**   C
16MM FILM OPTICAL SOUND   C
STUDIES HABITS IN AN EXPERIMENTAL CLASS-
ROOM THROUGH INDIVIDUAL AND GROUP LEARN-
ING ACTIVITIES, INCLUDING SELECTION OF INDI-
VIDUAL LEARNING TASKS, CONSISTENT PRAISE,
INDIVIDUAL PROGRESS CHARTS AND A REWARD
SYSTEM GRANTING FREE TIME OR TOYS FOR AC-
CURATE WORK. FROM THE COPING IN SPECIAL
EDUCATION SERIES.
LC NO. 73-701167
PROD-UEUWIS   DIST-UEUWIS   1972

**COPING IN SPECIAL EDUCATION
- DISRUPTIVE BEHAVIOR**   C
16MM FILM OPTICAL SOUND   C
PRESENTS ONE TEACHER'S PHILOSOPHY FOR ED-
UCATING CHILDREN EXHIBITING DISRUPTIVE BE-
HAVIORS, HYPERACTIVITY, IMMATURITY AND PER-
SONALITY PROBLEMS. FROM THE COPING IN SPE-
CIAL EDUCATION SERIES.
LC NO. 73-701169
PROD-UEUWIS   DIST-UEUWIS   1972

**COPING IN SPECIAL EDUCATION
- GROUPING**   C
16MM FILM OPTICAL SOUND   C
EMPHASIZES THE PHILOSOPHIES OF GROUPING
AND THE USES OF TEACHER-AIDES AUTOMATED
INSTRUCTIONAL DEVICES AND INDEPENDENT
STUDY. FROM THE COPING IN SPECIAL EDUCA-
TION SERIES.
LC NO. 73-701168
PROD-UEUWIS   DIST-UEUWIS   1972

**COPING IN SPECIAL EDUCATION
- INDIVIDUALIZED INSTRUCTION**   C
16MM FILM OPTICAL SOUND   C
FEATURES A TEACHER IN A LEARNING DISABILI-
TIES CLASS DESCRIBING HER TEACHING PHILOSO-
PHY, OBJECTIVES AND METHODS. EXPLAINS THE
TYPES AND FREQUENCY OF REINFORCEMENT, IN-
DIVIDUALIZATION OF CURRICULUM, DIFFERENCES
IN DEGREES OF ABSTRACTION IN LESSON PRE-
SENTATION AND BEHAVIORAL CONTROL TECH-
NIQUES. FROM THE COPING IN SPECIAL EDUCA-
TION SERIES.
LC NO. 73-701171
PROD-UEUWIS   DIST-UEUWIS   1972

**COPING IN SPECIAL EDUCATION
- MOTIVATION**   C
16MM FILM OPTICAL SOUND   C
ILLUSTRATES DIFFERENT MOTIVATION REINFORC-
ERS TO INCREASE ATTENDING BEHAVIORS, ACA-
DEMIC ACTIVITY AND PROSOCIAL BEHAVIORS.
SHOWS HOW TO COLLECT DATA ON PUPIL BEHAV-
IORS AND SPEECH-TRAIN YOUNG DEAF CHIL-
DREN. FROM THE COPING IN SPECIAL EDUCATION
SERIES.
LC NO. 73-701170
PROD-UEUWIS   DIST-UEUWIS   1972

**COPING IN SPECIAL EDUCATION
- SOCIALIZATION**   C
16MM FILM OPTICAL SOUND   C
PRESENTS LESSONS IN VARIOUS SUBJECTS TO
PROVIDE EXAMPLES OF HOW SOCIAL LEARNING IS
INCORPORATED INTO REGULAR LESSONS IN SPE-
CIAL EDUCATION CLASSES. DISCUSSES DATING,
PEER ACCEPTANCE AND JOB TRAINING PROB-
LEMS. DESCRIBES TEACHER-PUPIL, PUPIL-
TEACHER AND PUPIL-PUPIL INTERACTIONS. FROM
THE COPING IN SPECIAL EDUCATION SERIES.
LC NO. 73-701173
PROD-UEUWIS   DIST-UEUWIS   1972

**COPING IN SPECIAL
EDUCATION--A SERIES**
C
PROD-UEUWIS   DIST-UEUWIS   1972

COPING IN SPECIAL EDUCATION -
DEVELOPING --
COPING IN SPECIAL EDUCATION -
DEVELOPING 1-
COPING IN SPECIAL EDUCATION -
DISRUPTIVE --
COPING IN SPECIAL EDUCATION -
GROUPING
COPING IN SPECIAL EDUCATION -
INDIVIDUALIZED --
COPING IN SPECIAL EDUCATION -
MOTIVATION
COPING IN SPECIAL EDUCATION -
SOCIALIZATION

**CORRECT TELEPHONE
COURTESY**   B 22 MIN
16MM FILM OPTICAL SOUND
POINTS OUT THAT HOW ONE ANSWERS A PHONE
REFLECTS AN IMAGE OF YOU AND YOUR COM-
PANY. DEMONSTRATES GOOD TELEPHONE COUR-
TESY.
PROD-BEF   DIST-BEF

**COUNTERS FOR TAKEDOWNS
FROM A STANDING POSITION**   C 16 MIN
16MM FILM OPTICAL SOUND   J-C A
DEMONSTRATES 32 COUNTERS TO TURN DEFEN-
SIVE SITUATIONS INTO OFFENSIVE ADVANTAGES
IN WRESTLING. ANALYZES EACH HOLD IN SLOW
MOTION, NORMAL SPEED AND EXTREME CLOSE-
UP PHOTOGRAPHY. FROM THE WINNING WRES-
TLING BY JOE BEGALA SERIES.
LC NO. 73-700691

PROD-EDCOM   DIST-EDCOM   1971

COUNTING AND COLORS - EL
CONTAR Y COLORES   C 9 MIN
       16MM FILM OPTICAL SOUND
DISCUSSES SENTENCE STRUCTURE USING NUM-
BERS AND COLORS. FROM THE BRENTANO FOUN-
DATION BILINGUAL FILMS SERIES.
PROD-CAROUF   DIST-CAROUF

COXSWAIN STORY   C 5 MIN
       16MM FILM OPTICAL SOUND   J-C A
SEE SERIES TITLE FOR DESCRIPTIVE STATEMENT.
FROM THE WONDERFUL WORLD OF SPORT - ROW-
ING SERIES.
PROD-SPORTI   DIST-AMERFI

CREATING MOSAICS AND TILES   C 15 MIN
       16MM FILM OPTICAL SOUND
ILLUSTRATES THE IMMENSE VARIETY AND VERSA-
TILITY OF CERAMIC TILES AND MOSAICS. DEMON-
STRATES HAND METHODS OF MAKING CLAY TILES
AND SHOWS PROCEDURES FOR STACKING, GLAZ-
ING, CEMENTING IN PLACE AND GROUTING. FROM
THE CERAMIC ART SERIES.
PROD-MGHT   DIST-MGHT

CRIME IN THE HOME   C 22 MIN
       16MM FILM OPTICAL SOUND   J-C A
PRESENTS DRAMATIC VIGNETTES TO DEMON-
STRATE EFFECTIVE WAYS TO PROTECT YOURSELF
AND YOUR PROPERTY.
   LC NO. 73-701159
PROD-AIMS   DIST-AIMS   1973

CRIME ON THE STREETS   C 18 MIN
       16MM FILM OPTICAL SOUND   J-C A
DESCRIBES HOW STREET CRIMES HAVE REACHED
ALARMING PROPORTIONS. SUGGESTS THAT BY
OUR OWN BEHAVIOR WE OFTEN ENCOURAGE
CRIMINALS AND SET UP OURSELVES AS THE VIC-
TIMS. PROPOSES WAYS FOR INDIVIDUALS TO PRO-
TECT THEMSELVES AND THEIR PROPERTY.
   LC NO. 73-701070
PROD-CAHILL   DIST-AIMS   1972

CRITICAL DRIVING PATTERNS   C 10 MIN
       16MM FILM OPTICAL SOUND
DISCUSSES MAINTAINING VEHICLE CONTROL
DURING LOSS OF VISION, LOSS OF STEERING CON-
TROL OR LOSS OF BRAKING. FROM THE DRIVER
EDUCATION SERIES.
PROD-FMCMP   DIST-FMCMP

CRYSTALLIZATION   C 14 MIN
       16MM FILM OPTICAL SOUND
OBSERVES DIFFERENT TYPES OF CRYSTALLIZA-
TION AND THEIR USES. DISCUSSES THE ORDERLY
ARRANGEMENT IN CRYSTALLIZATION, THE DIREC-
TIONAL PROPERTIES OF CRYSTAL AND THE UTILI-
ZATION OF DIRECTIONAL PROPERTIES IN CRYS-
TAL.
PROD-IWANMI   DIST-IWANMI

CURLING - SCORING   C 5 MIN
       16MM FILM OPTICAL SOUND   J-C A
SEE SERIES TITLE FOR DESCRIPTIVE STATEMENT.
FROM THE WONDERFUL WORLD OF SPORT -
OTHER SERIES.
PROD-SPORTI   DIST-AMERFI

CURLING - STRATEGY   C 5 MIN
       16MM FILM OPTICAL SOUND   J-C A
SEE SERIES TITLE FOR DESCRIPTIVE STATEMENT.
FROM THE WONDERFUL WORLD OF SPORT -
OTHER SERIES.
PROD-SPORTI   DIST-AMERFI

CUTTING CREW, THE   C 11 MIN
       16MM FILM OPTICAL SOUND   H-C A
PRESENTS A TRAINING TOOL AND SAFETY UNIT
FOR HELPING LOGGERS IN THEIR WORK OF FALL-
ING AND BUCKING TIMBER. ILLUSTRATES TYPICAL
SITUATIONS AND GIVES TIPS ON PLANNING AND
TEAMWORK. FROM THE LOGGING SAFETY SERIES.
PROD-RARIG   DIST-RARIG   1966

D

D IS FOR DENTIST   C 5 MIN
       16MM FILM OPTICAL SOUND   K-P
PREPARES CHILDREN FOR THEIR FIRST VISIT TO
THE DENTIST.
   LC NO. 73-701405
PROD-AMDA   DIST-AMDA   1970

DAMAGE CONTROL - EFFECTS
OF WEIGHT ON STABILITY, PT
2, WEIGHT CONDITION   B 23 MIN
       16MM FILM OPTICAL SOUND
SHOWS THE EFFECTS OF WEIGHT CHANGES ON
THE STABILITY OF A CRUISER IN SITUATIONS,
SUCH AS NORMAL CONDITIONS OF FULL LOAD
AND AFTER FUEL WAS USED FROM TANKS BELOW
'G' WEIGHT TAKEN ON THE TOPSIDE. DESCRIBES
WHAT HAPPENS WHEN TOPSIDE WEIGHT SHIFTS
CAUSING THE KEEL TO RISE ABOVE THE CENTER
OF GRAVITY.
   LC NO. 73-701243
PROD-USN   DIST-USNAC

DAMAGE CONTROL - ELEMENTS
OF STABILITY IN SHIP   B 37 MIN
       16MM FILM OPTICAL SOUND
DESCRIBES PRINCIPLES OF BUOYANCY AND GRAV-
ITY. SHOWS THE EFFECTS OF LOADING ON STABIL-
ITY AND PERIOD OF ROLL ON SHIPS.
   LC NO. 73-701246
PROD-USN   DIST-USNAC

DAMAGE CONTROL - LOOSE
WATER IN STABILITY, PT 1, IN
INTACT SPACES   B 13 MIN
       16MM FILM OPTICAL SOUND
DESCRIBES PRINCIPLES INVOLVING FREE SUR-
FACE. SHOWS THAT LOSS OF 'GM' VARIES DI-
RECTLY WITH THE LENGTH OF THE COMPART-
MENT AND THE CUBE OF THE WIDTH OF THE
COMPARTMENT.
   LC NO. 73-701244
PROD-USN   DIST-USNAC

DAMAGE CONTROL - THE
METACENTER IN STABILITY, PT
2   B 22 MIN
       16MM FILM OPTICAL SOUND
DESCRIBES IN TERMS OF DIPLACEMENT THE EF-
FECT ON THE METACENTER DUE TO CHANGES IN
VALUE OF 'G' RELATIONSHIP OF METACENTER
HEIGHT WITH RANGE OF STABILITY AND INITIAL
STABILITY. GIVES EXAMPLES OF A WARSHIP ON A
CRUISE AND CHANGES OF STABILITY DUE TO
CHANGES OF WEIGHT THROUGH DEPLETION OF
STORES, FUEL AND AMMUNITION.
   LC NO. 73-701245
PROD-USN   DIST-USNAC

DAMS   C 14 MIN
       16MM FILM OPTICAL SOUND
STUDIES THE MECHANICAL STRUCTURE OF DAMS.
DESCRIBES THE RELATIONSHIP BETWEEN DAM
STRENGTH AND WATER LEVEL AND SHOWS A DAM
STABILIZED BY THE WEIGHT OF THE WATER IT-
SELF.
PROD-IWANMI   DIST-IWANMI

DANCER FARM - BERT
HANOVER   C 5 MIN
       16MM FILM OPTICAL SOUND   J-C A
SEE SERIES TITLE FOR DESCRIPTIVE STATEMENT.
FROM THE WONDERFUL WORLD OF SPORT -
HORSES, RACING, POLO, RODEO SERIES.
PROD-SPORTI   DIST-AMERFI

DAVE BING   C 5 MIN
       16MM FILM OPTICAL SOUND   J-C A
SEE SERIES TITLE FOR DESCRIPTIVE STATEMENT.
FROM THE WONDERFUL WORLD OF SPORT - BAS-
KETBALL SERIES.
PROD-SPORTI   DIST-AMERFI

DAY CARE TODAY   C 30 MIN
       16MM FILM OPTICAL SOUND   C A
PROVIDES A VIEW OF THREE FUNCTIONING DAY
CARE CENTERS - A COMMUNITY-ORIENTED CEN-
TER, A FACTORY-RELATED DAY CARE CENTER FOR
CHILDREN OF EMPLOYEES AND A UNIVERSITY-RE-
LATED TEACHER TRAINING CENTER. ILLUSTRATES
THE DIVERSE POSSIBILITIES OF DAY CARE AND
THE POTENTIAL FOR MEETING THE NEEDS OF
PRESCHOOL CHILDREN.
PROD-POLYMR   DIST-POLYMR

DAY IN THE PARK, A   C 8 MIN
       16MM FILM OPTICAL SOUND
PRESENTS A FIELD TRIP TO THE PARK IN WHICH
CHILDREN MEET MOUNTED POLICEMEN AND
RIDE HORSES, PLAY FOOTBALL, HAVE A PICNIC
AND LEARN TO PICK UP PICNIC DEBRIS. FROM
THE BRENTANO FOUNDATION BILINGUAL FILMS
SERIES.
PROD-CAROUF   DIST-CAROUF

DEATH AND TAXES   C 18 MIN
       16MM FILM OPTICAL SOUND
TRACES THE HISTORY OF AMERICAN TAXATION
FROM THE TEA TAX TO PRESENT DAY FEDERAL
INCOME TAXES. GIVES TIPS ON TAX PREPARATION

AND SHOWS THE COMPUTERIZED PROCESSING OF
TAX FORMS BY THE INTERNAL REVENUE SERVICE.
PROD-BEF   DIST-BEF

DEATHSTYLES   C 50 MIN
       16MM FILM OPTICAL SOUND
SYNTHESIZES DISPARATE ELEMENTS RELATING
TO DEATH.
PROD-AMERFI   DIST-AMERFI

DECIDING   C 14 MIN
       16MM FILM OPTICAL SOUND   P-I
DOCUMENTS A SHOPPING EXCURSION BY A
BROTHER AND SISTER TO BUY A GIFT FOR THEIR
FATHER. ILLUSTRATES MANY IMPORTANT CON-
CEPTS IN PURCHASING.
   LC NO. 73-701203
PROD-CENTEF   DIST-CENTEF   1973

DECLARATION OF
INDEPENDENCE, JUNE 1776 -
JANUARY, 1777   C 80 MIN
       16MM FILM OPTICAL SOUND
FOCUSES ON THE SECOND CONTINENTAL CON-
GRESS, THE LONG DEBATE AND CONSIDERATION
GIVEN TO POLITICAL SEPARATION FROM BRITAIN,
THE DRAMATIC STORY OF THE FIVE MEN CHOSEN
TO DRAFT THE DECLARATION, THEIR PHILOSO-
PHIES AND PROBLEMS AND THE FINAL STAGES OF
THE WAR AND THE SURRENDER AT YORKTOWN.
FROM THE TO THE SPIRIT OF '76 SERIES.
   LC NO. 73-733679
PROD-RMI   DIST-RMI

DEFENSE   C 5 MIN
       16MM FILM OPTICAL SOUND   J-C A
SEE SERIES TITLE FOR DESCRIPTIVE STATEMENT.
FROM THE WONDERFUL WORLD OF SPORT - BAS-
KETBALL SERIES.
PROD-SPORTI   DIST-AMERFI

DEFENSIVE BACKS   C 5 MIN
       16MM FILM OPTICAL SOUND   J-C A
SEE SERIES TITLE FOR DESCRIPTIVE STATEMENT.
FROM THE WONDERFUL WORLD OF SPORT - FOOT-
BALL SERIES.
PROD-SPORTI   DIST-AMERFI

DENTAL CARE UNDER GENERAL
ANAESTHESIA FOR THE
CEREBRAL PALSIED PATIENT   C 16 MIN
       16MM FILM OPTICAL SOUND   C A
SHOWS THE SPECIAL CARE AND DENTAL TECH-
NIQUES THAT ARE REQUIRED TO SUCCESSFULLY
HANDLE THE CEREBRAL PALSIED PATIENT.
PROD-RARIG   DIST-RARIG

DEPENDENCE - A NEW
DEFINITION   C 25 MIN
       16MM FILM OPTICAL SOUND   C A
DEMONSTRATES HOW EVERY LIVING THING IS DE-
PENDENT ON THE RHYTHMS OF NATURE, THE IN-
FLUENCES OF TIDES AND THE PHASES OF THE
MOON ALONG WITH THE INFLUENCES OF THE
EARTH'S ELECTROSTATIC AND MAGNETIC FIELDS.
PRESENTS A PSYCHOANALYTIC MODEL OF THE
VARIOUS STAGES OF DEPENDENCY IN THE DEVEL-
OPMENT OF THE INDIVIDUAL. FROM THE LIFE
AND HEALTH FILM SERIES.
   LC NO. 73-701090
PROD-CRMP   DIST-CRMP   1972

DEVELOPING CREATIVITY   C 11 MIN
       16MM FILM OPTICAL SOUND   J-C A
DISPLAYS THE NEED FOR ARTISTIC CREATIVITY IN
SOLVING PROBLEMS OF MODERN CIVILIZATION
THROUGH ART EDUCATION. EXAMINES THE AP-
PLICATION OF ART IN SOLVING PROBLEMS OF AR-
CHITECTURE AND ENVIRONMENT.
   LC NO. 73-701178
PROD-UEUWIS   DIST-UEUWIS   1971

DEVELOPMENTAL PSYCHOLOGY
FILM--A SERIES
                            C A

PROD-CRMP   DIST-CRMP   1973

COGNITIVE DEVELOPMENT   18 MIN
EMOTIONAL DEVELOPMENT   19 MIN
LANGUAGE DEVELOPMENT   29 MIN
MORAL DEVELOPMENT   28 MIN

DEVON HORSE SHOW   C 5 MIN
       16MM FILM OPTICAL SOUND   J-C A
SEE SERIES TITLE FOR DESCRIPTIVE STATEMENT.
FROM THE WONDERFUL WORLD OF SPORT -
HORSES, RACING, POLO, RODEO SERIES.
PROD-SPORTI   DIST-AMERFI

DIAL V FOR VOTES C 30 MIN
16MM FILM OPTICAL SOUND C A
TEACHES MORE PRODUCTIVE USE OF A POLITICAL CAMPAIGN BY UTILIZING VOLUNTEER WORKERS' TELEPHONE BANKS. DEMONSTRATES THE MAJOR POLITICAL TELEPHONE ACTIVITIES INVOLVED IN GETTING OUT THE VOTE.
LC NO. 73-700525
PROD-PTELC   DIST-DATA   1970

DIARY OF A MAD HOUSEWIFE C 94 MIN
16MM FILM OPTICAL SOUND C A
EXPLORES THE DISINTEGRATION OF MARRIAGE AND ITS EFFECT ON THE INDIVIDUAL, ESPECIALLY THE WOMAN. STARS CARRIE SNODGRASS.
PROD-SWANK   DIST-SWANK

**DICK VAN ARSDALE -
DEFENSIVE PLAY, PT 1** C 12 MIN
16MM FILM OPTICAL SOUND J-C
FEATURES DICK VAN ARSDALE OF THE PHOENIX SUNS WHO EXPLAINS THE FUNDAMENTALS OF TEAM DEFENSE, THE POSITIONING OF THE FEET, PLACEMENT OF THE HANDS, FIGHTING OVER THE OFFENSIVE 'PICK' AND SWITCHING ON THE OFFENSIVE 'PICK.' FROM THE WILLIS REED BASKETBALL SERIES.
LC NO. 73-700577
PROD-SCHLAT   DIST-SCHLAT   1972

**DICK VAN ARSDALE -
DEFENSIVE PLAY, PT 2** C 11 MIN
16MM FILM OPTICAL SOUND J-C
FEATURES DICK VAN ARSDALE OF THE PHOENIX SUNS WHO EXPLAINS TEAM DEFENSE, INDIVIDUAL DEFENSE, DEFENSE AGAINST 'BACK DOORING,' BOXING OUT DEFENSE AND DEFENSIVE REBOUNDING. FROM THE WILLIS REED BASKETBALL SERIES.
LC NO. 73-700577
PROD-SCHLAT   DIST-SCHLAT   1972

**DID YOU EVER MILK A COW -
JAMAS HAS EXTRAIDO LECHE
DE UNA VACA** C 6 MIN
16MM FILM OPTICAL SOUND
PRESENTS CLASSROOM PREPARATION FOR A FIELD TRIP TO A DAIRY FARM. FROM THE BRENTANO FOUNDATION BILINGUAL FILMS SERIES.
PROD-CAROUF   DIST-CAROUF

DISCOVERY OF THE VACUUM C 14 MIN
16MM FILM OPTICAL SOUND
SHOWS THAT AIR IS NOT WEIGHTLESS AND THAT NATURE DISLIKES A VACUUM BY RE-CREATING ARISTOLES' EXPERIMENT WITH THE USE OF A COW BLADDER. DESCRIBES THE EVENTS LEADING TO THE DISCOVERY OF VACUUM WITH THE USE OF MERCURY.
PROD-IWANMI   DIST-IWANMI

DIVING - BASICS C 5 MIN
16MM FILM OPTICAL SOUND J-C A
SEE SERIES TITLE FOR DESCRIPTIVE STATEMENT. FROM THE WONDERFUL WORLD OF SPORT - SWIM, DIVE, SCUBA, SURF SERIES.
PROD-SPORTI   DIST-AMERFI

DIVING - LESLEY BUSH C 5 MIN
16MM FILM OPTICAL SOUND J-C A
SEE SERIES TITLE FOR DESCRIPTIVE STATEMENT. FROM THE WONDERFUL WORLD OF SPORT - SWIM, DIVE, SCUBA, SURF SERIES.
PROD-SPORTI   DIST-AMERFI

DOCTOR IN THE DESERT B 10 MIN
16MM FILM OPTICAL SOUND
SHOWS ISRAELI PHYSICIANS BRINGING MODERN MEDICINE TO THE DESERT BEDOUIN.
PROD-ALDEN   DIST-ALDEN

**DOGS, CATS AND RABBITS, PT
1** C 7 MIN
16MM FILM OPTICAL SOUND K-I
INCLUDES DIFFERENT TYPES OF ANIMATED BARKS AND PRESENTATIONS OF DOGS, CATS AND RABBITS.
LC NO. 73-701200
PROD-TEXFLM   DIST-TEXFLM   1973

**DOGS, CATS AND RABBITS, PT
2** C 7 MIN
16MM FILM OPTICAL SOUND K-I
INCLUDES DIFFERENT TYPES OF ANIMATED BARKS AND PRESENTATIONS OF DOGS, CATS AND RABBITS.
LC NO. 73-701200
PROD-TEXFLM   DIST-TEXFLM   1973

**DOGS, CATS AND RABBITS, PT
3** C 7 MIN
16MM FILM OPTICAL SOUND K-I
INCLUDES DIFFERENT TYPES OF ANIMATED BARKS AND PRESENTATIONS OF DOGS, CATS AND RABBITS.
LC NO. 73-701200
PROD-TEXFLM   DIST-TEXFLM   1973

DON JUAN TENORIO - 1970 C 30 MIN
16MM FILM OPTICAL SOUND H-C
PRESENTS SCENES FROM ZORRILLA'S 19TH CENTURY TRAGEDY, 'DON JUAN TENORIO.'
LC NO. 73-701175
PROD-UWISC   DIST-UWISC   1971

DR FAGER C 5 MIN
16MM FILM OPTICAL SOUND J-C A
SEE SERIES TITLE FOR DESCRIPTIVE STATEMENT. FROM THE WONDERFUL WORLD OF SPORT - HORSES, RACING, POLO, RODEO SERIES.
PROD-SPORTI   DIST-AMERFI

DRAG BOATS C 5 MIN
16MM FILM OPTICAL SOUND J-C A
SEE SERIES TITLE FOR DESCRIPTIVE STATEMENT. FROM THE WONDERFUL WORLD OF SPORT - BOATING SERIES.
PROD-SPORTI   DIST-AMERFI

**DRAG RACING - CHRISTMAS
TREE** C 5 MIN
16MM FILM OPTICAL SOUND J-C A
SEE SERIES TITLE FOR DESCRIPTIVE STATEMENT. FROM THE WONDERFUL WORLD OF SPORT - CARS, AUTO RACING SERIES.
PROD-SPORTI   DIST-AMERFI

DRAG RACING - DON GARLITS C 5 MIN
16MM FILM OPTICAL SOUND J-C A
SEE SERIES TITLE FOR DESCRIPTIVE STATEMENT. FROM THE WONDERFUL WORLD OF SPORT - CARS, AUTO RACING SERIES.
PROD-SPORTI   DIST-AMERFI

DRAG RACING - FUNNY CARS C 5 MIN
16MM FILM OPTICAL SOUND J-C A
SEE SERIES TITLE FOR DESCRIPTIVE STATEMENT. FROM THE WONDERFUL WORLD OF SPORT - CARS, AUTO RACING SERIES.
PROD-SPORTI   DIST-AMERFI

**DRAG RACING - SIGHTS AND
SOUNDS** C 5 MIN
16MM FILM OPTICAL SOUND J-C A
SEE SERIES TITLE FOR DESCRIPTIVE STATEMENT. FROM THE WONDERFUL WORLD OF SPORT - CARS, AUTO RACING SERIES.
PROD-SPORTI   DIST-AMERFI

**DRAG RACING - SLINGSHOT
DRAGSTERS** C 5 MIN
16MM FILM OPTICAL SOUND J-C A
SEE SERIES TITLE FOR DESCRIPTIVE STATEMENT. FROM THE WONDERFUL WORLD OF SPORT - CARS, AUTO RACING SERIES.
PROD-SPORTI   DIST-AMERFI

DRAGONFLIES C 14 MIN
16MM FILM OPTICAL SOUND
DESCRIBES VARIOUS SPECIES OF DRAGONFLIES AND THEIR LIFE CYCLE. INCLUDES THE JAPANESE DRAGONFLY, GINYANMA, DURUMA DRAGONFLY, ITO DRAGONFLY AND RED DRAGONFLY.
PROD-IWANMI   DIST-IWANMI

DRIVER EDUCATION--A SERIES
TEACHES THE IMPORTANCE OF SOUND PERCEPTUAL HABITS THAT WILL HELP IN MAKING ACCURATE BEHIND-THE-WHEEL DECISIONS.
PROD-FMCMP   DIST-FMCMP

CRITICAL DRIVING PATTERNS   10 MIN
DRIVING IN TRAFFIC   10 MIN
RURAL DRIVING   10 MIN

DRIVING IN TRAFFIC C 10 MIN
16MM FILM OPTICAL SOUND
DISCUSSES PROPER POSITIONING FOR MANEUVERING IN TRAFFIC. FROM THE DRIVER EDUCATION SERIES.
PROD-FMCMP   DIST-FMCMP

**DRIVING SCHOOL - TRAINING
RACERS** C 5 MIN
16MM FILM OPTICAL SOUND J-C A
SEE SERIES TITLE FOR DESCRIPTIVE STATEMENT. FROM THE WONDERFUL WORLD OF SPORT - CARS, AUTO RACING SERIES.
PROD-SPORTI   DIST-AMERFI

**DRUG PROBLEM, THE - WHAT
DO YOU THINK** C 17 MIN
16MM FILM OPTICAL SOUND J-H
STUDIES DEFINITIONS OF DRUGS AND DRUG ABUSE AS A SOCIAL AND INDIVIDUAL PROBLEM. DISCUSSES THE DANGER OF DRUG USE.
LC NO. 73-703163
PROD-EBEC   DIST-EBEC   1973

DRUMMER BOY, THE C
16MM FILM OPTICAL SOUND
SEE SERIES TITLE FOR DESCRIPTIVE STATEMENT. FROM THE FAIRY TALE TIME SERIES.
PROD-PUI   DIST-PUI

DRY SEASON, THE C 20 MIN
16MM FILM OPTICAL SOUND
PORTRAYS LIFE DURING THE DRY SEASON, WHICH COMES TO THE ABRON PEOPLE OF EAST CENTRAL AFRICA EVERY YEAR IN NOVEMBER, WHEN SCORCHING WINDS FROM THE SAHARA OVERCOME THOSE FROM THE ATLANTIC AND DESICCATE THE LAND.
PROD-CMC   DIST-CMC

DUCKY MEDWICK C 5 MIN
16MM FILM OPTICAL SOUND J-C A
SEE SERIES TITLE FOR DESCRIPTIVE STATEMENT. FROM THE WONDERFUL WORLD OF SPORT - BASEBALL SERIES.
PROD-SPORTI   DIST-AMERFI

**DUNCAN GRANT AT
CHARLESTON** X 33 MIN
16MM FILM OPTICAL SOUND H-C A
PRESENTS THE ARTIST DUNCAN GRANT IN HIS HOME IN CHARLESTON. REVIEWS GRANT'S LIFE AS AN ARTIST.
LC NO. 73-701421
PROD-MFLMC   DIST-MFLMC

DUNE BUGGIES - FUN CARS C 5 MIN
16MM FILM OPTICAL SOUND J-C A
SEE SERIES TITLE FOR DESCRIPTIVE STATEMENT. FROM THE WONDERFUL WORLD OF SPORT - CARS, AUTO RACING SERIES.
PROD-SPORTI   DIST-AMERFI

DUNE BUGGIES - IN FLEET C 5 MIN
16MM FILM OPTICAL SOUND J-C A
SEE SERIES TITLE FOR DESCRIPTIVE STATEMENT. FROM THE WONDERFUL WORLD OF SPORT - CARS, AUTO RACING SERIES.
PROD-SPORTI   DIST-AMERFI

**DUNE BUGGIES - OFF-THE-ROAD
RACING** C 5 MIN
16MM FILM OPTICAL SOUND J-C A
SEE SERIES TITLE FOR DESCRIPTIVE STATEMENT. FROM THE WONDERFUL WORLD OF SPORT - CARS, AUTO RACING SERIES.
PROD-SPORTI   DIST-AMERFI

DYNAMICS OF JUDO C 14 MIN
16MM FILM OPTICAL SOUND
PRESENTS A COMMENTARY ON THE DYNAMICS OF JUDO, A TRADITIONAL JAPANESE SPORT. DISCUSSES WHAT CAUSES THE FALL AND WHAT MAINTAINS EQUILIBRIUM.
PROD-IWANMI   DIST-IWANMI

E

EAR, THE C 14 MIN
16MM FILM OPTICAL SOUND
EXPLAINS THE STRUCTURE AND FUNCTIONS OF THE EAR AND DESCRIBES HOW THE VITAL SEMICIRCULAR CANALS GIVE BALANCE TO THE HUMAN BODY.
PROD-IWANMI   DIST-IWANMI

**EARTHBREAD - A NATURAL
FOOD** C 20 MIN
16MM FILM OPTICAL SOUND I-C
FEATURES STEP-BY-STEP INSTRUCTIONS SHOWING HOW TO MAKE A LOAF OF WHOLE GRAIN BREAD, INCLUDING SOME SPECIAL TIPS THAT PROMISE SUCCESSFUL BAKING WITH NATURAL INGREDIENTS. FROM THE NATURAL FOODS SERIES.
LC NO. 73-701407
PROD-FPRD   DIST-FPRD   1973

EDUCATION FOR FAMILY LIFE   B 28 MIN
          16MM FILM OPTICAL SOUND   H-C A
EXAMINES PARENTAL MODELS AND RESPONSIBIL-
ITIES FOR THE DEVELOPMENT OF ATTITUDES AND
VALUES WITHIN THE FAMILY. FROM THE SEX IN
AMERICA CULTURE SERIES.
          LC NO. 73-701213
PROD-CHM   DIST-CHM   1967

EGYPT   C
          16MM FILM OPTICAL SOUND
SEE SERIES TITLE FOR DESCRIPTIVE STATEMENT.
FROM THE PORT OF CALL SERIES.
PROD-PUI   DIST-PUI

ELECTRIC BULB SCIENCE   B 11 MIN
          16MM FILM OPTICAL SOUND
EXPLAINS THE PRINCIPLES AND STRUCTURE OF
THE ELECTRIC BULB.
PROD-IWANMI   DIST-IWANMI

**ELEPHANT EATS, THE PENGUIN
EATS, THE - NOUN**   C 10 MIN
          16MM FILM OPTICAL SOUND   P-I
PRESENTS BOTH ORALLY AND VISUALLY WORDS
SELECTED FROM COMMONLY USED VOCABULARY
LISTS FOR PRIMARY READERS. ENGAGES RHYME
AND MUSIC TO CREATE PATTERNS THAT AID IN
RETENTION OF THE WORDS. FROM THE READING
MOTIVATION SERIES.
          LC NO. 73-701281
PROD-BFA   DIST-BFA   1972

EMBRYOLOGICAL DEVELOPMENT
          B 28 MIN
          16MM FILM OPTICAL SOUND   H-C A
FOLLOWS THE DEVELOPMENT OF A FERTILIZED
EGG FROM ONE CELL THROUGH THE STAGES OF
THE EMBRYO TO COMPLETION OF THE FETUS. RE-
LATES THE IMPORTANCE OF GENETICS AND THE
ROLE OF DNA IN THE DETERMINATION OF SEX
AND THE OCCURRENCE OF MULTIPLE BIRTHS
AND MUTATIONS. FROM THE SEX IN AMERICA
CULTURE SERIES.
          LC NO. 73-701214
PROD-CHM   DIST-CHM   1967

EMOTIONAL DEVELOPMENT   C 19 MIN
          16MM FILM OPTICAL SOUND   C A
PRESENTS A STUDY BASED ON THE PREMISE
THAT, ALTHOUGH HUMANS MAY HAVE AN INNATE
POTENTIAL FOR AGGRESSIVE BEHAVIOR, THE
MANIFESTATION OF AGGRESSION IS LEARNED
FROM SOCIETY. FROM THE DEVELOPMENTAL PSY-
CHOLOGY FILM SERIES.
          LC NO. 73-700579
PROD-CRMP   DIST-CRMP   1973

END OF THE ART WORLD   C 40 MIN
          16MM FILM OPTICAL SOUND
USES FILM TECHNIQUES TO DEMONSTRATE COR-
RESPONDENCES OF VISUAL ARTS WITH AND
WITHOUT MOVEMENT.
PROD-VISRES   DIST-VISRES

ENEMY IS FIRE, THE   C 26 MIN
          16MM FILM OPTICAL SOUND   J-C A
EXAMINES THE EFFECTS OF TEMPERATURE AND
HUMIDITY ON FOREST FIRE POSSIBILITIES. ILLUS-
TRATES MEASURES TAKEN BY A LOGGING OPERA-
TION TO ORGANIZE FOR THE PREVENTION AND
SUPPRESSION OF FOREST FIRES. FROM THE FOR-
EST FIRE PROTECTION SERIES.
PROD-RARIG   DIST-RARIG   1952

ENERGY - A CONVERSATION   C 20 MIN
          16MM FILM OPTICAL SOUND
PRESENTS THREE VERY EMINENT SCIENTISTS, DR
LINUS PAULING OF STANFORD, DR GEORGE WALD
OF HARVARD AND DR PHILIP MORRISON OF MIT,
IN A DISCUSSION OF THE CONCEPT OF ENERGY.
FROM THE BIOLOGY TODAY FILM SERIES.
PROD-CRMP   DIST-CRMP

ENERGY - A CONVERSATION   C 27 MIN
          16MM FILM OPTICAL SOUND   C A
PRESENTS A CONVERSATION ON THE NATURE OF
ENERGY BETWEEN DR LINUS PAULING, DR
GEORGE WALD AND DR PHILIP MORRISON. DIS-
CUSSES THE DEFINITION OF ENERGY, DIFFERENT
FORMS OF ENERGY AND SOURCES OF ENERGY.
FROM THE SCIENCE TODAY SERIES.
          LC NO. 73-701093
PROD-CRMP   DIST-CRMP   1972

ENGINEERS, THE   C 26 MIN
          16MM FILM OPTICAL SOUND
SHOWS ENGINEERS IN MODERN INDUSTRY
WORKING ON WORLDWIDE PROJECTS ON THE
EARTH, IN THE WATER AND IN THE AIR.
PROD-MTP   DIST-MTP

**ENJOYING YOUR CONTACT
LENSES**   C 5 MIN
          16MM FILM OPTICAL SOUND   PRO
ILLUSTRATES A SIMPLE WAY TO REMOVE CON-
TACT LENSES, HOW TO RE-ENTER A LENS WHICH
HAS SLIPPED OUT OF POSITION, EFFECTIVE
CLEANING ROUTINES AND HOW TO KEEP LEFT
AND RIGHT LENSES SEPARATED.
          LC NO. 73-700526
PROD-PART   DIST-DATA   1969

ENTERPRISING INFANTS   B 30 MIN
          16MM FILM OPTICAL SOUND   C T
DISCUSSES EARLY INTRODUCTIONS TO READING,
WRITING AND MATHEMATICS AT A PRIMARY
SCHOOL. EXPLAINS THAT DISPLAYS OF PATTERN
AND COLOR, AND SHAPE AND TEXTURE STIMU-
LATE THE CHILDREN TO COMMUNICATE BY
PAINTING, MODELING AND WRITING. SHOWS
THAT SORTING AND COUNTING LEAD ON TO
EARLY MATHEMATICS. FROM THE EXPANDING
CLASSROOM SERIES.
PROD-BBCTV   DIST-TIMLIF

EPEE, THE   C 5 MIN
          16MM FILM OPTICAL SOUND   J-C A
SEE SERIES TITLE FOR DESCRIPTIVE STATEMENT.
FROM THE WONDERFUL WORLD OF SPORT - FENC-
ING SERIES.
PROD-SPORTI   DIST-AMERFI

**ERTS - EARTH RESOURCES
TECHNOLOGY SATELLITE**   C
          16MM FILM OPTICAL SOUND   J-C A
SHOWS WHY WE NEED TO SURVEY OUR EARTH
RESOURCES ON A WORLDWIDE SCALE AND HOW
IT IS BEING DONE USING THE EARTH RESOURCES
TECHNOLOGY SATELLITE.
          LC NO. 73-701242
PROD-NASA   DIST-NASA   1973

EVOLUTION   C 11 MIN
          16MM FILM OPTICAL SOUND
USES ANIMATION TO TELL HOW LIFE BEGAN ON
EARTH FROM ONE-CELLED AMOEBAE TO HOMO
SAPIENS.
          LC NO. 72-700226
PROD-LCOA   DIST-LCOA   1972

EXECUTIVE'S WIFE, THE   C 20 MIN
          16MM FILM OPTICAL SOUND   A
HIGHLIGHTS PROBLEMS ENCOUNTERED BY THE
EXECUTIVE'S WIFE THROUGH A SEMINAR. ILLUS-
TRATES THE FLEXIBILITY A WIFE NEEDS IN ORDER
TO MANAGE THE MANY DUTIES TO HER HUS-
BAND, HER FAMILY AND HERSELF.
          LC NO. 73-701176
PROD-UEUWIS   DIST-UEUWIS   1971

**EXPANDING CLASSROOM--A
SERIES**
          C T
SHOWS INTERESTING INNOVATIONS IN TEACHING
METHODS. COVERS A WIDE RANGE OF SITUA-
TIONS AND PROBLEMS AND APPROACHES TO
THEM.
PROD-BBCTV   DIST-TIMLIF

BUCKLEBURY FARM   30 MIN
CHILDREN'S CONCEPTS   30 MIN
DECIMALIZATION AND METRICATION   30 MIN
ELIZABETHAN VILLAGE   30 MIN
ENTERPRISING INFANTS   30 MIN
EVELINE LOWE   30 MIN
EYNSHAM   30 MIN
NEW ESTATE   30 MIN

EYES OF INSECTS   C 14 MIN
          16MM FILM OPTICAL SOUND
COMPARES THE COMPOUND EYE AND STEMMA OF
THE INSECT AND STUDIES THE EVOLUTION AND
GENETICS OF INSECTS. ILLUSTRATES THE COM-
POUND EYES OF THE DRAGONFLY, HONEYBEE
AND WATER-SPIDER AND DISCUSSES THE DEVEL-
OPMENT OF THE EYES.
PROD-IWANMI   DIST-IWANMI

F

FACES   C 5 MIN
          16MM FILM OPTICAL SOUND   K-P
POINTS OUT THAT EVERYONE HAS TWO EYES,
TWO EARS, A NOSE AND A MOUTH BUT THAT ALL
FACES ARE DIFFERENT. CREATES AN AWARENESS
OF SEEING, HEARING, SMELLING, TASTING AND
COMMUNICATING.
          LC NO. 73-700582
PROD-SCHLAT   DIST-SCHLAT   1972

FAIR CHANCE   C 15 MIN
          16MM FILM OPTICAL SOUND   H-C A
TELLS THE STORY OF A MAN STANDING OUTSIDE
A MATERNITY WARD WHO RECALLS HIS OWN
CHILDHOOD AND THE DISADVANTAGES WHICH HE
ENCOUNTERED BECAUSE OF A FAMILY WHICH
GREW TOO LARGE TOO FAST.
          LC NO. FIA60-1876
PROD-PPFA   DIST-DATA   1959

FAIRY TALE TIME--A SERIES
USES ANIMATION TO RETELL CLASSIC FAIRY TA-
LES WHICH TEACH IMPORTANT LESSONS IN GOOD
MANNERS, ETHICS AND COMMON SENSE.
PROD-PUI   DIST-PUI

ALADDIN
ALI BABA
DRUMMER BOY, THE
FLYING TRUNK, THE
GOLDEN BIRD, THE
GOLDEN GOOSE, THE
GOLDEN TOUCH, THE
HANSEL AND GRETEL
LEO THE LION-HEARTED
RAPUNZEL
RUMPELSTILTSKIN
SINBAD
SOLDIER AND THE DRAGON, THE
TAILOR'S ADVENTURE, THE
TIN SOLDIER, THE
WELL OF WISDOM, THE

FATHER AND SON   C 5 MIN
          16MM FILM OPTICAL SOUND   J-C A
SEE SERIES TITLE FOR DESCRIPTIVE STATEMENT.
FROM THE WONDERFUL WORLD OF SPORT - BAS-
KETBALL SERIES.
PROD-SPORTI   DIST-AMERFI

FEET OF ANIMALS   C 14 MIN
          16MM FILM OPTICAL SOUND
DISCUSSES THE EVOLUTION AND CHANGING
FUNCTIONS OF FEET OF ANIMALS. DESCRIBES
THE EVOLUTION OF QUADRUPEDS AND THEIR
PERFORMANCE.
PROD-IWANMI   DIST-IWANMI

FIESTA   C 9 MIN
          16MM FILM OPTICAL SOUND
PRESENTS A FIELD TRIP TO SEE MEXICAN DANC-
ING, HEAR MUSIC AND EAT NATIONAL DISHES.
FROM THE BRENTANO FOUNDATION BILINGUAL
FILMS SERIES.
PROD-CAROUF   DIST-CAROUF

FIFTH STREET   C 32 MIN
          16MM FILM OPTICAL SOUND   C A
DEPICTS THE TRAGEDY OF SKID ROW IN A SERIES
OF SHORT VIGNETTES OF LIFE ON FIFTH STREET
IN LOS ANGELES. EXPLORES THE FILTH, POVERTY
AND ALCOHOLISM OF SOCIETY'S MOST DEGENER-
ATE ENVIRONMENT.
          LC NO. 73-701087
PROD-MCANDB   DIST-DRMINC   1970

**FIGURE SKATING - FREE
SKATING**   C 5 MIN
          16MM FILM OPTICAL SOUND   J-C A
SEE SERIES TITLE FOR DESCRIPTIVE STATEMENT.
FROM THE WONDERFUL WORLD OF SPORT -
OTHER SERIES.
PROD-SPORTI   DIST-AMERFI

FILMMAKING FUNDAMENTALS   C 20 MIN
          16MM FILM OPTICAL SOUND   P-H
DESCRIBES THE BASIC FUNDAMENTALS OF MAK-
ING EIGHT MILLIMETER FILMS AS AN INDIVIDUAL
OR IN CLASS.
          LC NO. 72-700019
PROD-AIMS   DIST-AIMS   1972

**FILMMAKING TECHNIQUES -
ACTING**   C 32 MIN
          16MM FILM OPTICAL SOUND   I-C A
FOLLOWS THE TRANSITION OF A STAGE-EXPERI-
ENCED ACTOR TO A MOTION PICTURE ACTOR.
FEATURES HELEN HAYES, VINCENT PRICE, JIM
BACKUS, HENRY FONDA AND JEAN STAPLETON
DISCUSSING PROBLEM AREAS OF FILM ACTING.
FROM THE FILMMAKING TECHNIQUES SERIES.
          LC NO. 73-701050
PROD-AIMS   DIST-AIMS   1973

**FILMMAKING TECHNIQUES -
GOING ON LOCATION**   C 17 MIN
          16MM FILM OPTICAL SOUND   I-C A
POINTS OUT THAT TRUE ECONOMY THROUGH
FILMING ON LOCATION IS ONLY REALIZED BY
GOOD PRE-PRODUCTION PLANNING, ATTENTION
TO DETAIL AND LOGISTICS. COVERS MAKEUP, RE-
FLECTORS, TALENT RELEASES AND METHODS OF

MAKING ROLLING SHOTS. FROM THE FILMMAKING
TECHNIQUES SERIES.
LC NO. 73-701151
PROD-AIMS   DIST-AIMS   1973

**FILMMAKING TECHNIQUES -
LIGHTING**   C 13 MIN
          16MM FILM OPTICAL SOUND   I-C A
COVERS SOURCES OF POWER, HOOK-UP, USE OF
FILTERS FOR LIGHTS AND CAMERAS, POLAROID
FILTERS, WINDOW DIFFUSION AND REFLECTORS.
FROM THE FILMMAKING TECHNIQUES SERIES.
LC NO. 73-701153
PROD-AIMS   DIST-AIMS   1973

**FILMMAKING TECHNIQUES -
MAKE-UP**   C 17 MIN
          16MM FILM OPTICAL SOUND   I-C A
DEMONSTRATES BASIC MAKE-UP TECHNIQUES
THAT EASILY FALL WITHIN EVERYONE'S BUDGET.
ILLUSTRATES THE AGING PROCESS, APPLICATION
OF BEARDS AND MOUSTACHES, BLACK EYES, SKIN
TONES AND BUILT-UP NOSES. FROM THE FILM-
MAKING TECHNIQUES SERIES.
LC NO. 73-701154
PROD-AIMS   DIST-AIMS   1973

**FILMMAKING TECHNIQUES -
STAGE LIGHTING**   C 15 MIN
          16MM FILM OPTICAL SOUND   I-C A
DEMONSTRATES KEY LIGHT, FILL LIGHT, BACK
LIGHT AND THE KICKER AS WELL AS SPECIAL EF-
FECTS LIGHTING FOR FILMMAKING. FROM THE
FILMMAKING TECHNIQUES SERIES.
LC NO. 73-701155
PROD-AIMS   DIST-AIMS   1973

**FILMMAKING TECHNIQUES -
STUNTS**   C 13 MIN
          16MM FILM OPTICAL SOUND   I-C A
STRESSES PROPER WARM-UP EXERCISES AND
BODY CONTROL IN STUNT WORK. SHOWS TRICKS
FOR SAFEGUARDING INJURIES. FROM THE FILM-
MAKING TECHNIQUES SERIES.
LC NO. 73-701156
PROD-AIMS   DIST-AIMS   1973

**FILMMAKING TECHNIQUES--A
SERIES**
                                     I-C A
LC NO. 73-701366
PROD-AIMS   DIST-AIMS   1973

FILMMAKING TECHNIQUES - ACTING   32 MIN
FILMMAKING TECHNIQUES - GOING ON
LOCATION   17 MIN
FILMMAKING TECHNIQUES - LIGHTING   13 MIN
FILMMAKING TECHNIQUES - MAKE-UP   17 MIN
FILMMAKING TECHNIQUES - STAGE
LIGHTING   15 MIN
FILMMAKING TECHNIQUES - STUNTS   13 MIN

**FINDING YOURSELF AND YOUR
JOB**   C 17 MIN
          16MM FILM OPTICAL SOUND   J-C
SHOWS HOW TO MAKE REALISTIC CAREER DECI-
SIONS BY STARTING WITH ONE'S OWN INTER-
ESTS, ATTITUDES, EXPECTATIONS AND APTI-
TUDES. PROVIDES TESTED METHODS TO ADAPT
ONE'S SELF TO THE NEW JOB REQUIREMENTS
AND THE REVOLUTION IN TODAY'S EMPLOYMENT
MARKET. FROM THE FUTURE STREET - NEW DI-
RECTIONS IN CAREER EDUCATION SERIES.
PROD-AMEDFL   DIST-AMEDFL

FIRE SAFETY - HALL OF FLAME   C 15 MIN
          16MM FILM OPTICAL SOUND   P-I
POINTS OUT FIRE SAFETY PREVENTIVE MEASURES
INCLUDING PLAYING WITH MATCHES, CAMP FIRE
SAFETY AND DO'S AND DON'TS WHEN A HOME
FIRE BREAKS OUT.
LC NO. 73-701365
PROD-SAGENA   DIST-SAGENA   1973

FIRE WEATHER   C 22 MIN
          16MM FILM OPTICAL SOUND   J-C A
SHOWS HOW ANYONE IN THE WOODS CAN COOP-
ERATE TO PREVENT FOREST FIRES. POINTS OUT
THAT HUNTERS, FISHERMEN, CAMPERS, HIKERS
AND PICKNICKERS CAN ALSO GET VALUABLE IN-
FORMATION ON HOW THE WEATHER AFFECTS
FIRE CONDITIONS. FROM THE FOREST FIRE PRO-
TECTION SERIES.
PROD-RARIG   DIST-RARIG   1956

FIREBIRDS   C 5 MIN
          16MM FILM OPTICAL SOUND   J-C A
SEE SERIES TITLE FOR DESCRIPTIVE STATEMENT.
FROM THE WONDERFUL WORLD OF SPORT - FOOT-
BALL SERIES.
PROD-SPORTI   DIST-AMERFI

**FIREMEN GO TO SCHOOL, TOO -
LOS BOMBEROS VAN A LA
ESCUELA, TAMBIEN**   C 7 MIN
          16MM FILM OPTICAL SOUND
PRESENTS CLASSROOM FOLLOW-UP FOR THE
FIELD TRIP TO THE FIRE STATION. FROM THE
BRENTANO FOUNDATION BILINGUAL FILMS SE-
RIES.
PROD-CAROUF   DIST-CAROUF

**FIRST DAY, NEW FRIENDS -
PRIMER DIA, NUEVOS AMIGOS**   C 7 MIN
          16MM FILM OPTICAL SOUND
DISCUSSES INTRODUCTION AND NATIONAL ORI-
GINS. FROM THE BRENTANO FOUNDATION BILIN-
GUAL FILMS SERIES.
PROD-CAROUF   DIST-CAROUF

**FLAMES OF REVOLUTION -
SEPTEMBER 1774 - JUNE, 1776**   C 80 MIN
          16MM FILM OPTICAL SOUND
VISUALIZES THE AMERICAN REVOLUTION OF JUNE
'76, WHEN THE FIRST PROVINCIAL CONGRESS EM-
POWERED CALLED OUT THE FAMOUS MINUTEMEN
AND OTHER MILITIA. INCLUDES SUCH HISTORIC
SITES AS BUNKER HILL, OLD NORTH CHURCH,
LEXINGTON AND CONCORD. FROM THE TO THE
SPIRIT OF '76 SERIES.
LC NO. 73-733678
PROD-RMI   DIST-RMI

**FLOAT PARTY - DOWN THE
RIVER**   C 5 MIN
          16MM FILM OPTICAL SOUND   J-C A
SEE SERIES TITLE FOR DESCRIPTIVE STATEMENT.
FROM THE WONDERFUL WORLD OF SPORT - BOAT-
ING SERIES.
PROD-SPORTI   DIST-AMERFI

FLOOR EXERCISE   C 5 MIN
          16MM FILM OPTICAL SOUND   J-C A
SEE SERIES TITLE FOR DESCRIPTIVE STATEMENT.
FROM THE WONDERFUL WORLD OF SPORT - GYM-
NASTICS SERIES.
PROD-SPORTI   DIST-AMERFI

FLORIDA BREEDING   C 5 MIN
          16MM FILM OPTICAL SOUND   J-C A
SEE SERIES TITLE FOR DESCRIPTIVE STATEMENT.
FROM THE WONDERFUL WORLD OF SPORT -
HORSES, RACING, POLO, RODEO SERIES.
PROD-SPORTI   DIST-AMERFI

FLOWERS FOR DAHLIA   C 28 MIN
          16MM FILM OPTICAL SOUND
PORTRAYS ONE DAY IN THE LIFE OF DAHLIA, WHO
LIVES AND WORKS ON A KIBBUTZ.
PROD-ALDEN   DIST-ALDEN

FLY CASTING   C 5 MIN
          16MM FILM OPTICAL SOUND   J-C A
SEE SERIES TITLE FOR DESCRIPTIVE STATEMENT.
FROM THE WONDERFUL WORLD OF SPORT - FISH-
ING SERIES.
PROD-SPORTI   DIST-AMERFI

FLYING - STUNTING   C 5 MIN
          16MM FILM OPTICAL SOUND   J-C A
SEE SERIES TITLE FOR DESCRIPTIVE STATEMENT.
FROM THE WONDERFUL WORLD OF SPORT - FLY-
ING SERIES.
PROD-SPORTI   DIST-AMERFI

FLYING TRUNK, THE   C
          16MM FILM OPTICAL SOUND
SEE SERIES TITLE FOR DESCRIPTIVE STATEMENT.
FROM THE FAIRY TALE TIME SERIES.
PROD-PUI   DIST-PUI

FOAM   C 14 MIN
          16MM FILM OPTICAL SOUND
OBSERVES THE ACTION OF FOAM, COMPARES
SOAPSUDS AND WATER AND DISCUSSES THE
PRINCIPLE OF THE FLOATING BUBBLE.
PROD-IWANMI   DIST-IWANMI

FOIL   C 5 MIN
          16MM FILM OPTICAL SOUND   J-C A
SEE SERIES TITLE FOR DESCRIPTIVE STATEMENT.
FROM THE WONDERFUL WORLD OF SPORT - FENC-
ING SERIES.
PROD-SPORTI   DIST-AMERFI

**FOOD PREPARATION TERMS, PT
1**   C 8 MIN
          16MM FILM OPTICAL SOUND   J-C A
PRESENTS BASIC TECHNIQUES AND UTENSILS
USED IN THE PREPARATION OF FRUITS AND VEG-
ETABLES. FROM THE FOOD PREPARATION SERIES.
LC NO. 73-701148

PROD-EPRI   DIST-EPRI   1972

**FOOD PREPARATION TERMS, PT
2**   C 10 MIN
          16MM FILM OPTICAL SOUND   J-C A
ILLUSTRATES BASIC TECHNIQUES AND UTENSILS
USED IN BAKING, BOILING OR ROASTING. FROM
THE FOOD PREPARATION SERIES.
LC NO. 73-701149
PROD-EPRI   DIST-EPRI   1972

FOOD PREPARATION--A SERIES
                                     J-C A
PROD-EPRI   DIST-EPRI   1972

FOOD PREPARATION TERMS, PT 1   8 MIN
FOOD PREPARATION TERMS, PT 2   10 MIN

**FOREST FIRE PROTECTION--A
SERIES**
                                     J-C A
PROD-RARIG   DIST-RARIG

ENEMY IS FIRE, THE   26 MIN
FIRE WEATHER   22 MIN
SAFETY IN PLYWOOD OPERATIONS   10 MIN

**FOREST FISHERMAN - STORY
OF AN OTTER**   C 16 MIN
          16MM FILM OPTICAL SOUND
TELLS THE STORY OF A FOREST RANGER WHO
ADOPTS AN ORPHANED LAND OTTER, RAISES IT
TO MATURITY IN HIS HOME AND ENABLES THE
OTTER TO RETURN TO ITS NATURAL ENVIRON-
MENT.
LC NO. 73-701422
PROD-HUNGFM   DIST-ACI   1972

FORM OF VOLCANOES, THE   C 14 MIN
          16MM FILM OPTICAL SOUND
USES A MODEL TO DEMONSTRATE THE RELATION-
SHIP BETWEEN THE SHAPE OF THE VOLCANO AND
ITS FORM OF ERUPTION. POINTS OUT THE VOL-
CANIC BELTS OF THE WORLD AND THE DIFFER-
ENT TYPES OF VOLCANOES IN JAPAN.
PROD-IWANMI   DIST-IWANMI

FOSSILS   C 14 MIN
          16MM FILM OPTICAL SOUND
PRESENTS AN HISTORICAL INTRODUCTION OF
THE CHANGING VIEWS REGARDING FOSSILS. OUT-
LINES THE CORRECT VIEW REGARDING THE FOS-
SILS AND THE EVOLUTION OF LIVING CREATURES.
SHOWS REPRESENTATIVE FOSSILS IN ORDER OF
ANTIQUITY.
PROD-IWANMI   DIST-IWANMI

FRAGILE EGOS   C 35 MIN
          16MM FILM OPTICAL SOUND   H-C A
PRESENTS A TEACHING FILM FOR ALL PROFES-
SIONAL AND LAY PERSONS CONCERNED WITH
THE PROBLEM OF REHABILITATING THE MEN-
TALLY ILL.
LC NO. 72-700011
PROD-WGBH   DIST-WGBH   1968

FRAN TARKENTON   C 5 MIN
          16MM FILM OPTICAL SOUND   J-C A
SEE SERIES TITLE FOR DESCRIPTIVE STATEMENT.
FROM THE WONDERFUL WORLD OF SPORT - FOOT-
BALL SERIES.
PROD-SPORTI   DIST-AMERFI

FRANK FILM   C 9 MIN
          16MM FILM OPTICAL SOUND   J-C A
PRESENTS 11,592 SEPARATE SHOTS OF COMMON
OBJECTS THAT APPEAR EITHER ALONE OR IN REP-
ETITION, PRIMARILY FORMING COMPLEX, RAPIDLY
MOVING PATTERNS ACCOMPANIED BY TWO CON-
TINUOUS NARRATIVE SOUND TRACKS PLAYED
SIMULTANEOUSLY.
LC NO. 73-701423
PROD-PFP   DIST-PFP   1973

FRANK ROBINSON   C 5 MIN
          16MM FILM OPTICAL SOUND   J-C A
SEE SERIES TITLE FOR DESCRIPTIVE STATEMENT.
FROM THE WONDERFUL WORLD OF SPORT - BASE-
BALL SERIES.
PROD-SPORTI   DIST-AMERFI

FRANKENSTEIN IN A FISHBOWL
                                     C 43 MIN
          16MM FILM OPTICAL SOUND
PRESENTS A DOCUMENTARY ABOUT PLASTIC
SURGERY. FOLLOWS TWO 44-YEAR-OLD WOMEN,
ONE A PRETTY SOPHISTICATE STRUGGLING WITH
THE DREAMS OF THE JET SET, THE OTHER, AN
UNATTRACTIVE HOUSEWIFE SWEPT UP IN THE
MIDDLE-CLASS SOCIAL CLIMB.
PROD-AMERFI   DIST-AMERFI

FRESH CHILLED SUNSHINE   C 15 MIN
16MM FILM OPTICAL SOUND
PRESENTS A PICTORIAL VISIT TO THE ORANGE
GROVES AS WE FOLLOW THE MORNING ORANGE
JUICE FROM TREE TO TABLE.
PROD-MTP   DIST-MTP

FROM CAVE TO CITY   C 10 MIN
16MM FILM OPTICAL SOUND   I-C
USES THE ART OF PAPER SCULPTURE TO FOLLOW
THE LOGICAL STEPS THAT OCCURRED IN MAN'S
EVOLVEMENT FROM EARLY WANDERING FOOD
GATHERERS TO THE MODERN-DAY CROWDED
DWELLER IN HUGE TECHNOLOGICALLY COMPLEX
AND POLLUTED CITIES.
LC NO. 73-701221
PROD-FLMFR   DIST-FLMFR   1973

**FROM WHEEL TO WING - DESDE
LA RUEDA HASTA EL AVION**   C 7 MIN
16MM FILM OPTICAL SOUND
DISCUSSES THE HISTORY OF TRANSPORTATION
FROM EARLY TIMES TO SPACE TRAVEL. FROM THE
BRENTANO FOUNDATION BILINGUAL FILMS SE-
RIES.
PROD-CAROUF   DIST-CAROUF

**FUTURE STREET - NEW
DIRECTIONS IN CAREER
EDUCATION--A SERIES**
                                      J-C
PROD-AMEDFL   DIST-AMEDFL

DROPPING OUT   17 MIN
FINDING YOURSELF AND YOUR JOB   17 MIN
NEW CAREERS FOR WOMEN   17 MIN
NEW SCHOOLS, THE   17 MIN
OPPORTUNITIES FOR THE
DISADVANTAGED   17 MIN

FUTURES IN STEEL   C 28 MIN
16MM FILM OPTICAL SOUND
STUDIES THE BASIC STEEL INDUSTRY FROM THE
EARLY IRON WORKS AT SAUGUS, MASSACHU-
SETTS TO THE PRESENT. OUTLINES CAREER OP-
PORTUNITIES FOR COLLEGE-EDUCATED ENGI-
NEERS AND YOUNG MEN IN OTHER PROFES-
SIONS.
PROD-MTP   DIST-MTP

G

GALLOP, TROT, PACE   C 5 MIN
16MM FILM OPTICAL SOUND   J-C A
SEE SERIES TITLE FOR DESCRIPTIVE STATEMENT.
FROM THE WONDERFUL WORLD OF SPORT -
HORSES, RACING, POLO, RODEO SERIES.
PROD-SPORTI   DIST-AMERFI

GEAR   B 11 MIN
16MM FILM OPTICAL SOUND
DESCRIBES THE PROPERTIES OF THE GEAR WHICH
PLAYS AN IMPORTANT ROLE IN A MACHINE. DIS-
CUSSES THE ACTUAL PRINCIPLE OF POWER
TRANSMISSION AND ITS APPLICATION, THE FLAT
GEAR AND LEVEL GEAR AND THE MANUFACTUR-
ING OF GEAR.
PROD-IWANMI   DIST-IWANMI

**GET READY FOR THE RANCH -
PREPARATE PARA EL RANCHO**   C 7 MIN
16MM FILM OPTICAL SOUND
PRESENTS CLASSROOM PREPARATION FOR A
FIELD TRIP TO THE VEGETABLE RANCH. FROM THE
BRENTANO FOUNDATION BILINGUAL FILMS SE-
RIES.
PROD-CAROUF   DIST-CAROUF

**GET READY FOR THE ZOO -
PREPARATE PARA EL JARDIN
ZOOLOGICO**   C 6 MIN
16MM FILM OPTICAL SOUND
PRESENTS CLASSROOM PREPARATION FOR A
FIELD TRIP TO THE ZOO. FROM THE BRENTANO
FOUNDATION BILINGUAL FILMS SERIES.
PROD-CAROUF   DIST-CAROUF

GIVING A BEDPAN OR URINAL   C 18 MIN
16MM FILM OPTICAL SOUND
SHOWS HOW TO PROVIDE FOR THE PATIENT'S
PRIVACY WHILE USING THE CORRECT PROCEDURE
FOR GIVING AND REMOVING THE BEDPAN OR URI-
NAL. FROM THE NURSE'S AIDE, ORDERLY AND AT-
TENDANT SERIES.
LC NO. 73-701053
PROD-COPI   DIST-COPI   1971

GLADIATORS, THE   C 88 MIN
16MM FILM OPTICAL SOUND   H-C
TELLS THE STORY OF A COMPUTERIZED WAR
GAME BETWEEN CHINA AND THE WEST, WHICH
TAKES PLACE IN SWEDEN UNDER THE SUPERVI-
SION OF THE SWEDISH ARMY AND ITS GIANT
COMPUTER AND IS TELEVISED TO THE ENTIRE
WORLD BY AN ITALIAN SPAGHETTI COMPANY
SPONSOR.
PROD-NLC   DIST-NLC

GLOVE BOX FIRES   C 24 MIN
16MM FILM OPTICAL SOUND
SHOWS IMPROVEMENTS RELATING TO FIRE
SAFETY MADE FOR THE PLUTONIUM PROCESSING
FACILITIES OF THE ROCKY FLATS PLANT AFTER
AND AS A RESULT OF A MAJOR FIRE. ILLUSTRATES
THE FIRE PROPERTIES OF GLOVE BOX CONSTRUC-
TION MATERIALS.
LC NO. 73-701362
PROD-USAEC   DIST-USNAC   1973

GOALIE   C 5 MIN
16MM FILM OPTICAL SOUND   J-C A
SEE SERIES TITLE FOR DESCRIPTIVE STATEMENT.
FROM THE WONDERFUL WORLD OF SPORT -
HOCKEY SERIES.
PROD-SPORTI   DIST-AMERFI

GOALIE EQUIPMENT STORY   C 5 MIN
16MM FILM OPTICAL SOUND   J-C A
SEE SERIES TITLE FOR DESCRIPTIVE STATEMENT.
FROM THE WONDERFUL WORLD OF SPORT -
HOCKEY SERIES.
PROD-SPORTI   DIST-AMERFI

GOING FOR THE PIN   C 5 MIN
16MM FILM OPTICAL SOUND   J-C A
SEE SERIES TITLE FOR DESCRIPTIVE STATEMENT.
FROM THE WONDERFUL WORLD OF SPORT -
WRESTLING SERIES.
PROD-SPORTI   DIST-AMERFI

GOLDEN AGE OF COMEDY   B 86 MIN
16MM FILM OPTICAL SOUND
TAKES THE VIEWER BACK INTO THE HISTORY OF
HOLLYWOOD COMEDY FROM THE EARLY 1900'S TO
THE PRESENT. FEATURES SUCH CINEMA GREATS
AS JEAN HARLOW, CAROLE LOMBARD, WILL
ROGERS AND LAUREL AND HARDY.
PROD-CAROUF   DIST-CAROUF

GOLDEN BIRD, THE   C
16MM FILM OPTICAL SOUND
SEE SERIES TITLE FOR DESCRIPTIVE STATEMENT.
FROM THE FAIRY TALE TIME SERIES.
PROD-PUI   DIST-PUI

GOLDEN GOOSE, THE   C
16MM FILM OPTICAL SOUND
SEE SERIES TITLE FOR DESCRIPTIVE STATEMENT.
FROM THE FAIRY TALE TIME SERIES.
PROD-PUI   DIST-PUI

GOLDEN TOUCH, THE   C
16MM FILM OPTICAL SOUND
SEE SERIES TITLE FOR DESCRIPTIVE STATEMENT.
FROM THE FAIRY TALE TIME SERIES.
PROD-PUI   DIST-PUI

GRANDMOTHER, THE   C 34 MIN
16MM FILM OPTICAL SOUND
TAKES THE IDEA OF A LITTLE BOY TERRORIZED BY
HIS PARENTS AND CREATES FROM IT A VISION OF
SUBJECTIVE CHILDHOOD FEELINGS.
PROD-AMERFI   DIST-AMERFI

**GRAVEL SPRINGS FIFE AND
DRUM**   C 10 MIN
16MM FILM OPTICAL SOUND   H-C A
PRESENTS A DOCUMENTARY ON BLACK FOLKLORE
IN THE GRAVEL SPRINGS COMMUNITY OF NORTH-
ERN MISSISSIPPI WHERE AN UNUSUAL KIND OF
FIFE AND DRUM MUSIC CLOSELY RESEMBLING
WEST AFRICAN TRIBAL MUSIC, HAS SURVIVED.
LC NO. 73-700878
PROD-IU   DIST-IU   1971

GREECE   C
16MM FILM OPTICAL SOUND
SEE SERIES TITLE FOR DESCRIPTIVE STATEMENT.
FROM THE PORT OF CALL SERIES.
PROD-PUI   DIST-PUI

**GROWING PAINS FOR THE
COMMON MARKET**   B 13 MIN
16MM FILM OPTICAL SOUND
EXPLORES THE SUCCESSES AND SETBACKS IN
THE CENTURIESOLD DREAM OF A UNITED STATES

OF EUROPE. FROM THE SCREEN NEWS DIGEST SE-
RIES.
LC NO. 73-701270
PROD-HEARST   DIST-HEARST   1972

GROWTH OF PLANTS   C 14 MIN
16MM FILM OPTICAL SOUND
ILLUSTRATES THE GROWTH OF PLANTS THROUGH
OBSERVATION AND EXPERIMENTATION WITH THE
FRENCH BEAN, FROM SEED TO FULL GROWTH.
PROD-IWANMI   DIST-IWANMI

GUNNING THE FLYWAYS   C 33 MIN
16MM FILM OPTICAL SOUND
TAKES THE VIEWER ON A TOUR OF CHOICE SPOTS
WHERE DUCK HUNTING IS A PRIME ATTRACTION
IN BOTH THE UNITED STATES AND CANADA,
STARTING IN A DUCK HUNTER'S BLIND ON JAMES
BAY IN NORTHERN CANADA.
PROD-MTP   DIST-MTP

GYPSY JOE HARRIS   C 5 MIN
16MM FILM OPTICAL SOUND   J-C A
SEE SERIES TITLE FOR DESCRIPTIVE STATEMENT.
FROM THE WONDERFUL WORLD OF SPORT - BOX-
ING SERIES.
PROD-SPORTI   DIST-AMERFI

GYROCOPTERS   C 5 MIN
16MM FILM OPTICAL SOUND   J-C A
SEE SERIES TITLE FOR DESCRIPTIVE STATEMENT.
FROM THE WONDERFUL WORLD OF SPORT - FLY-
ING SERIES.
PROD-SPORTI   DIST-AMERFI

H

HAITI   C
16MM FILM OPTICAL SOUND
SEE SERIES TITLE FOR DESCRIPTIVE STATEMENT.
FROM THE PORT OF CALL SERIES.
PROD-PUI   DIST-PUI

HAND CATCHING LEAD   B 4 MIN
16MM FILM OPTICAL SOUND
SHOWS A HAND AND ARM STRETCHED OUT PAR-
ALLEL TO THE UNSEEN GROUND, AGAINST A
BACKGROUND OF PAINTED BRICK WALL, AS DULL
SHEEN, SOFT LEAD PLAQUES PLUMMET DOWN
PAST THE HAND FROM AN UNSEEN HEIGHT OUT-
SIDE THE FRAME OF THE CAMERA.
PROD-VISRES   DIST-VISRES

HANDBUILDING METHODS   C 17 MIN
16MM FILM OPTICAL SOUND
DEMONSTRATES HANDBUILDING METHODS WITH-
OUT A POTTER'S WHEEL AND WITH VERY LIMITED
EQUIPMENT. FROM THE CERAMIC ART SERIES.
PROD-MGHT   DIST-MGHT

**HANK AARON - CONSISTENT
HITTER**   C 5 MIN
16MM FILM OPTICAL SOUND   J-C A
SEE SERIES TITLE FOR DESCRIPTIVE STATEMENT.
FROM THE WONDERFUL WORLD OF SPORT - BASE-
BALL SERIES.
PROD-SPORTI   DIST-AMERFI

HANK AARON - HITTING   C 5 MIN
16MM FILM OPTICAL SOUND   J-C A
SEE SERIES TITLE FOR DESCRIPTIVE STATEMENT.
FROM THE WONDERFUL WORLD OF SPORT - BASE-
BALL SERIES.
PROD-SPORTI   DIST-AMERFI

HANSEL AND GRETEL   C
16MM FILM OPTICAL SOUND
SEE SERIES TITLE FOR DESCRIPTIVE STATEMENT.
FROM THE FAIRY TALE TIME SERIES.
PROD-PUI   DIST-PUI

HANUKKAH   C 15 MIN
16MM FILM OPTICAL SOUND
SHOWS HOW HANUKKAH, THE FESTIVAL OF
LIGHTS, IS CELEBRATED IN ISRAEL.
PROD-ALDEN   DIST-ALDEN

HARNESS - HAMBLETONIAN   C 5 MIN
16MM FILM OPTICAL SOUND   J-C A
SEE SERIES TITLE FOR DESCRIPTIVE STATEMENT.
FROM THE WONDERFUL WORLD OF SPORT -
HORSES, RACING, POLO, RODEO SERIES.
PROD-SPORTI   DIST-AMERFI

HARNESS - SU MAC LAD   C 5 MIN
        16MM FILM OPTICAL SOUND   J-C A
SEE SERIES TITLE FOR DESCRIPTIVE STATEMENT.
FROM THE WONDERFUL WORLD OF SPORT -
HORSES, RACING, POLO, RODEO SERIES.
PROD-SPORTI   DIST-AMERFI

HARNESS - YEARLING STORY   C 5 MIN
        16MM FILM OPTICAL SOUND   J-C A
SEE SERIES TITLE FOR DESCRIPTIVE STATEMENT.
FROM THE WONDERFUL WORLD OF SPORT -
HORSES, RACING, POLO, RODEO SERIES.
PROD-SPORTI   DIST-AMERFI

HAWAII   C
        16MM FILM OPTICAL SOUND
SEE SERIES TITLE FOR DESCRIPTIVE STATEMENT.
FROM THE PORT OF CALL SERIES.
PROD-PUI   DIST-PUI

HEART, THE - ATTACK   C 25 MIN
        16MM FILM OPTICAL SOUND
EXAMINES THE HEART ATTACK FROM BOTH A BIO-
LOGICAL AND SOCIAL VIEWPOINT. DESCRIBES THE
CARE OF THE HUMAN HEART AND THE CONSE-
QUENCES OF MISTREATING IT. FROM THE LIFE
AND HEALTH FILM SERIES.
PROD-CRMP   DIST-CRMP

HI, SCHOOL   C 28 MIN
        16MM FILM OPTICAL SOUND   J-H A
CONTRASTS THE NEGATIVE REPORTS THAT HAVE
PORTRAYED THE TYPICAL AMERICAN HIGH
SCHOOL AS A RATHER BLAND, QUASIPRISON EN-
VIRONMENT COMPLETELY CUT OFF FROM THE
REAL WORLD.
    LC NO. 73-701071
PROD-IDEA   DIST-IDEA   1970

HINDU RITUAL SANDHYA, THE   C 19 MIN
        16MM FILM OPTICAL SOUND
EXPLAINS THE CURRENT RITUAL PRACTICE OF
SANDHYA AND RELATES THE CEREMONY TO ITS
ANCIENT CULTURAL HERITAGE. POINTS OUT THAT
SANDHYA IS ONE OF THE FEW HINDU RITUALS
CURRENTLY PERFORMED IN INDIA WHICH HAS
ITS ROOTS IN THE MOST ANCIENT PHASE OF
HINDUISM.
PROD-CMC   DIST-CMC

HOCKEY STICK STORY   C 5 MIN
        16MM FILM OPTICAL SOUND   J-C A
SEE SERIES TITLE FOR DESCRIPTIVE STATEMENT.
FROM THE WONDERFUL WORLD OF SPORT -
HOCKEY SERIES.
PROD-SPORTI   DIST-AMERFI

HOME AT LAST   C 14 MIN
        16MM FILM OPTICAL SOUND
TELLS THE STORY OF THE REBIRTH AND REHABIL-
ITATION OF JEWS IN ISRAEL. SHOWS THE BEGIN-
NING OF A NEW LIFE FOR HALF A MILLION JEWISH
REFUGEES FROM ARAB COUNTRIES.
PROD-ALDEN   DIST-ALDEN

HOMEBUILTS   C 5 MIN
        16MM FILM OPTICAL SOUND   J-C A
SEE SERIES TITLE FOR DESCRIPTIVE STATEMENT.
FROM THE WONDERFUL WORLD OF SPORT - FLY-
ING SERIES.
PROD-SPORTI   DIST-AMERFI

HOMER JONES   C 5 MIN
        16MM FILM OPTICAL SOUND   J-C A
SEE SERIES TITLE FOR DESCRIPTIVE STATEMENT.
FROM THE WONDERFUL WORLD OF SPORT - FOOT-
BALL SERIES.
PROD-SPORTI   DIST-AMERFI

HONG KONG   C
        16MM FILM OPTICAL SOUND
SEE SERIES TITLE FOR DESCRIPTIVE STATEMENT.
FROM THE PORT OF CALL SERIES.
PROD-PUI   DIST-PUI

HORSE RACE - CHART CALLER   C 5 MIN
        16MM FILM OPTICAL SOUND   J-C A
SEE SERIES TITLE FOR DESCRIPTIVE STATEMENT.
FROM THE WONDERFUL WORLD OF SPORT -
HORSES, RACING, POLO, RODEO SERIES.
PROD-SPORTI   DIST-AMERFI

HORSE RACE - FILM PATROL   C 5 MIN
        16MM FILM OPTICAL SOUND   J-C A
SEE SERIES TITLE FOR DESCRIPTIVE STATEMENT.
FROM THE WONDERFUL WORLD OF SPORT -
HORSES, RACING, POLO, RODEO SERIES.
PROD-SPORTI   DIST-AMERFI

HORSE RACE - THE CLOCKER   C 5 MIN
        16MM FILM OPTICAL SOUND   J-C A
SEE SERIES TITLE FOR DESCRIPTIVE STATEMENT.
FROM THE WONDERFUL WORLD OF SPORT -
HORSES, RACING, POLO, RODEO SERIES.
PROD-SPORTI   DIST-AMERFI

**HORSE RACE - THE STARTING
GATE**   C 5 MIN
        16MM FILM OPTICAL SOUND   J-C A
SEE SERIES TITLE FOR DESCRIPTIVE STATEMENT.
FROM THE WONDERFUL WORLD OF SPORT -
HORSES, RACING, POLO, RODEO SERIES.
PROD-SPORTI   DIST-AMERFI

HOW ARE LAKES MADE   C 14 MIN
        16MM FILM OPTICAL SOUND
DISCUSSES THE DIFFERENT WAYS IN WHICH
LAKES ARE FORMED. ILLUSTRATES A DISLOCA-
TION LAKE, AN INLAND SEA-LAKE AND A VOL-
CANIC LAKE.
PROD-IWANMI   DIST-IWANMI

HOW DO FISH SWIM   C 14 MIN
        16MM FILM OPTICAL SOUND
DESCRIBES THE DIFFERENT HABITATS OF FISH
AND HOW THEY PROPEL THEMSELVES IN WATER.
INCLUDES THE SEA BREAM, BASS, HORSE MACK-
EREL, MORAY EEL, RAYS, SEAHORSE AND HALI-
BUT.
PROD-IWANMI   DIST-IWANMI

HOW DOES A YACHT SAIL   C 14 MIN
        16MM FILM OPTICAL SOUND
POINTS OUT THAT SKILLFUL HANDLING OF THE
SAILS ENABLES A YACHT TO MOVE FORWARD. DIS-
CUSSES THE RELATION BETWEEN SPEED AND
PRESSURE MEASURED WITH A MODEL INSIDE A
WIND TUNNEL.
PROD-IWANMI   DIST-IWANMI

HOW TO BUY STOCK   B 6 MIN
        16MM FILM OPTICAL SOUND
DISCUSSES THE PURPOSE OF INVESTMENTS AND
THE PROPER METHODS OF EVALUATING STOCKS
BEFORE PURCHASE.
PROD-BEF   DIST-BEF

HOW TO MAKE A WOMAN   C 58 MIN
        16MM FILM OPTICAL SOUND   C A
PRESENTS AN EXTRAORDINARY ILLUMINATION
OF THE MECHANISMS OF PERSONAL AND SEXUAL
RELATIONSHIPS THAT MAKE UP A WOMAN, DRAM-
ATIZED BY A SERIES OF IMPROVISATIONS BY THE
CARAVAN THEATRE IN CAMBRIDGE, MASSACHU-
SETTS.
PROD-POLYMR   DIST-POLYMR

**HOW TO MEASURE
TEMPERATURE**   C 14 MIN
        16MM FILM OPTICAL SOUND
TELLS HOW TO MEASURE HEAT RANGING FROM
SUPER LOW TEMPERATURE TO SUPER HIGH TEM-
PERATURE. DESCRIBES THE EXPANSION OF GAS
HEAT AND INCLUDES EXPERIMENTS WITH A
FLASK AND BALLOON, GAS THERMOMETER AND
MERCURY THERMOMETER.
PROD-IWANMI   DIST-IWANMI

HOW TO RIDE THEM   C 5 MIN
        16MM FILM OPTICAL SOUND   J-C A
SEE SERIES TITLE FOR DESCRIPTIVE STATEMENT.
FROM THE WONDERFUL WORLD OF SPORT -
SNOWMOBILES SERIES.
PROD-SPORTI   DIST-AMERFI

HOW TO SET UP BATTERS   C 5 MIN
        16MM FILM OPTICAL SOUND   J-C A
SEE SERIES TITLE FOR DESCRIPTIVE STATEMENT.
FROM THE WONDERFUL WORLD OF SPORT - BASE-
BALL SERIES.
PROD-SPORTI   DIST-AMERFI

HOWARD PORTER   C 5 MIN
        16MM FILM OPTICAL SOUND   J-C A
SEE SERIES TITLE FOR DESCRIPTIVE STATEMENT.
FROM THE WONDERFUL WORLD OF SPORT - BAS-
KETBALL SERIES.
PROD-SPORTI   DIST-AMERFI

HUMAN REPRODUCTION   B 28 MIN
        16MM FILM OPTICAL SOUND   H-C A
PRESENTS AN EXPLANATION OF HUMAN GROWTH
AND DEVELOPMENT INCLUDING SEX HORMONES
AND THEIR ROLE IN MENSTRUATION, OVULATION
AND MENOPAUSE. DISCUSSES THE PARALLEL DE-
VELOPMENT OF THE SPERM AND THE PROCESS OF
FERTILIZATION. FROM THE SEX IN AMERICAN
CULTURE SERIES.
    LC NO. 73-701216

PROD-CHM   DIST-CHM   1967

I WANNA BE READY   C 9 MIN
        16MM FILM OPTICAL SOUND   C A
USES EVERYDAY TASKS SUCH AS TABLE SETTING
AND HAND WASHING TO INTRODUCE THE YOUNG
CHILD TO CONCEPTS OF INDEPENDENCE AND
SELF-AWARENESS.
    LC NO. 72-700018
PROD-AIMS   DIST-AIMS   1966

**I WANT TO WORK FOR YOUR
COMPANY**   C 10 MIN
        16MM FILM OPTICAL SOUND   H-C A
DISPELS THE DILEMMA AND FRUSTRATION OF
THE FIRST JOB INTERVIEW BY PRESENTING TIPS
FOR APPROACHING THE FIRST INTERVIEW. POR-
TRAYS THE INTERACTION BETWEEN INTER-
VIEWER AND APPLICANT.
PROD-SAIF   DIST-SAIF

ICE BOATS   C 5 MIN
        16MM FILM OPTICAL SOUND   J-C A
SEE SERIES TITLE FOR DESCRIPTIVE STATEMENT.
FROM THE WONDERFUL WORLD OF SPORT - BOAT-
ING SERIES.
PROD-SPORTI   DIST-AMERFI

ICE CANOE RACING   C 5 MIN
        16MM FILM OPTICAL SOUND   J-C A
SEE SERIES TITLE FOR DESCRIPTIVE STATEMENT.
FROM THE WONDERFUL WORLD OF SPORT -
OTHER SERIES.
PROD-SPORTI   DIST-AMERFI

ICE COLUMNS   C 14 MIN
        16MM FILM OPTICAL SOUND
PRESENTS A HIGH SCHOOL GIRL'S RESEARCH
INTO THE SUBJECT OF WHERE AND HOW ICE COL-
UMNS ARE FORMED.
PROD-IWANMI   DIST-IWANMI

ICE FISHING   C 5 MIN
        16MM FILM OPTICAL SOUND   J-C A
SEE SERIES TITLE FOR DESCRIPTIVE STATEMENT.
FROM THE WONDERFUL WORLD OF SPORT - FISH-
ING SERIES.
PROD-SPORTI   DIST-AMERFI

**IMMIGRANT EXPERIENCE, THE -
THE LONG, LONG JOURNEY**   C 31 MIN
        16MM FILM OPTICAL SOUND
TELLS THE STORY OF THE AMERICAN DREAM AND
OF THE AMERICAN REALITY, AS IT WAS LIVED BY
ONE FAMILY WHO CAME TO THE UNITED STATES
FROM POLAND IN 1907.
    LC NO. 73-700232
PROD-LCOA   DIST-LCOA   1973

IMMIGRANT FROM AMERICA   C 20 MIN
        16MM FILM OPTICAL SOUND   J-C A
PRESENTS A STUDY OF THE SIMILARITIES AND
DISSIMILARITIES IN THE IMMIGRANT EXPERIENCE
AS EXPERIENCED BY THE BLACK MIGRANT FROM
THE RURAL SOUTH AND THE EUROPEAN IMMI-
GRANT TO AMERICA.
    LC NO. 70-710621
PROD-REPRO   DIST-REPRO   1971

**IMOGEN CUNNINGHAM,
PHOTOGRAPHER**   C 20 MIN
        16MM FILM OPTICAL SOUND
PORTRAYS IMOGEN CUNNINGHAM, THE PIONEER
PHOTOGRAPHER NOW IN HER 80'S. INTRODUCES
THE VIEWER TO A SENSE OF HER ACHIEVEMENT
AND A FEELING FOR HER VITALITY AND UNIQUE
RADIANCE, THROUGH INTERVIEWS, CANDID
FOOTAGE AND A LOOK AT HER OWN WORK.
PROD-AMERFI   DIST-AMERFI

IMPLOSION   B 20 MIN
        16MM FILM OPTICAL SOUND
DEALS WITH THE DISINTEGRATION OF A MAR-
RIAGE AND ITS PARTNERS. INTRODUCES A
YOUNG COUPLE WHO BEGIN THEIR LIFE TO-
GETHER IN THE MOST IDYLLIC WAY, BUT WHEN
THEIR INFANT SON DROWNS IN THE BATHTUB,
SHE DROWNS IN RELENTLESS GRIEF AND HE
DROWNS IN ALCOHOL.
PROD-AMERFI   DIST-AMERFI

IN LIVING COLOR C 12 MIN
16MM FILM OPTICAL SOUND H-C A
PRESENTS A STUDY OF THE INNER FEELINGS OF
TWO MINORITY INDIVIDUALS TO AWAKEN SUPER-
VISORS TO THE REAL ATTITUDES AND FEELINGS
BEHIND THE COOL FRONTS OF THEIR BLACK AND
SPANISH-SURNAME EMPLOYEES.
LC NO. 73-700527
PROD-PART DIST-DATA 1971

IN SEARCH OF HISTORY C 25 MIN
16MM FILM OPTICAL SOUND
DEPICTS THE ARCHAEOLOGICAL EXPEDITION OF
PROFESSOR YIGAEL YADIN IN THE JUDEAN HILL
CAVES, SEARCHING FOR THE TRACES OF THE JEW-
ISH REBELLION UNDER BAR KOKHBA AGAINST
THE ROMANS 2,000 YEARS AGO.
PROD-ALDEN DIST-ALDEN

INDIA C
16MM FILM OPTICAL SOUND
SEE SERIES TITLE FOR DESCRIPTIVE STATEMENT.
FROM THE PORT OF CALL SERIES.
PROD-PUI DIST-PUI

INDIAN MEMENTO C
16MM FILM OPTICAL SOUND J-C A
VISITS THE INDIANS OF CANADA PAVILLION AT
EXPO 67, MONTREAL. TELLS THE STORY OF THE
INDIAN IN NORTH AMERICA, RECALLING WHAT
CONTACT WITH EUROPEAN SETTLERS COST IN
FREEDOM OF MOVEMENT, LOSS OF LAND AND
LOSS OF HEALTH OF BODY AND SPIRIT.
LC NO. 73-701401
PROD-NFBC DIST-NFBC 1968

INERTIA C 14 MIN
16MM FILM OPTICAL SOUND
SHOWS THAT ALL MOVEMENTS ARE INFLUENCED
BY INERTIA AND FORCE, THROUGH THE RELATION
OF A BOY ON EXPERIMENTAL PLATFORM AND THE
MOVEMENT OF THE PLATFORM BY HIGHSPEED
PHOTOGRAPHY.
PROD-IWANMI DIST-IWANMI

INFANCY C 19 MIN
16MM FILM OPTICAL SOUND C A
PRESENTS A SURVEY OF PHYSICAL, PERCEPTUAL,
EMOTIONAL, SOCIAL LANGUAGE AND COGNITIVE
DEVELOPMENT OF HUMAN INFANTS FROM BIRTH
TO 18 MONTHS. DEMONSTRATES NEW THEORIES
ON THE ABILITIES AND CAPABILITIES OF INFANTS.
FROM THE DEVELOPMENTAL PSYCHOLOGY FILM
SERIES.
LC NO. 73-701095
PROD-CRMP DIST-CRMP 1972

INFINITY C 17 MIN
16MM FILM OPTICAL SOUND J-C A
INTRODUCES THE ANIMATED CHARACTER
GEORGE CANTOR WHO GUIDES THE WAY
THROUGH THE INVESTIGATIONS OF INFINITY.
PRESENTS EXAMPLES OF INFINITE SETS AND
PROVES THAT THERE ARE NO MORE RATIONAL
NUMBERS THAN INTEGERS.
LC NO. 73-701063
PROD-NULSEN DIST-AIMS 1972

INNER CITY DWELLER - WORK C 19 MIN
16MM FILM OPTICAL SOUND H-C A
TELLS THE STORY OF A YOUNG, UNEMPLOYED
BLACK MAN WHO MUST PROVIDE FOR HIS WIFE
AND CHILDREN. EXPLAINS THAT HE ENTERS A
JOB-TRAINING PROGRAM, ACQUIRES A DECENT
PAYING JOB AND IS SOON LAID-OFF, PLACING HIM
BACK INTO THE SAME POSITION FROM WHICH HE
STARTED.
LC NO. 73-700956
PROD-IU DIST-IU 1972

**INSECTS, OBSERVATION AND
COLLECTION** C 14 MIN
16MM FILM OPTICAL SOUND
DESCRIBES THE COLLECTION OF INSECTS, THE
VARIOUS TYPES AND THEIR CHARACTERISTICS.
SHOWS THE EQUIPMENT FOR COLLECTING IN-
SECTS AND HOW TO LOOK FOR THE HOMES OF IN-
SECTS.
PROD-IWANMI DIST-IWANMI

INTEGRATED DATA PROCESSING
C 35 MIN
16MM FILM OPTICAL SOUND
PORTRAYS THE MANY COMPONENTS OF 'INTE-
GRATED DATA PROCESSING' AND THE VARIOUS
WAYS IT MAY BE INCORPORATED INTO AN EFFI-
CIENT MODERN DATA PROCESSING SYSTEM.
PROD-BEF DIST-BEF

**INTERMEDIATE (COMPANION
DOGS)** C 5 MIN
16MM FILM OPTICAL SOUND J-C A
SEE SERIES TITLE FOR DESCRIPTIVE STATEMENT.
FROM THE WONDERFUL WORLD OF SPORT - DOGS
SERIES.
PROD-SPORTI DIST-AMERFI

INTERN - A LONG YEAR C 20 MIN
16MM FILM OPTICAL SOUND J-C
LOOKS AT THE VARIOUS DUTIES OF AN INTERN
THROUGH THE WORK OF ONE INTERN, DR KARIN
MACK. SHOWS HOW SHE DEALS WITH MEDICAL
PROBLEMS AS WELL AS THE EMOTIONAL AND HU-
MAN PROBLEMS IN A LARGE, POOR CITY HOSPI-
TAL. FROM THE WORLD OF WORK SERIES.
LC NO. 73-701164
PROD-EBEC DIST-EBEC 1972

**INTERVIEW WITH GARRETT
HARDIN** C 10 MIN
16MM FILM OPTICAL SOUND J-C A
PRESENTS GARRETT HARDIN'S VIEWS ON THE
SIGNIFICANT ECOLOGICAL PROBLEMS OF MODERN
SOCIETY. DISCUSSES THE FAILURE OF PEOPLE TO
ASSUME RESPONSIBILITY FOR THE NATURAL RE-
SOURCES FROM WHICH THEY DERIVE BENEFITS.
LC NO. 73-701369
PROD-KINGSP DIST-HRAW 1972

**INTRODUCTION TO
PSYCHOTHERAPY, AN** B 18 MIN
16MM FILM OPTICAL SOUND PRO
IDENTIFIES 16 OF THE MOST FREQUENTLY OC-
CURRING FEARS, MISCONCEPTIONS AND UNCER-
TAINTIES WHICH UNSOPHISTICATED PATIENTS
HAVE ABOUT PSYCHOTHERAPY.
LC NO. 73-700533
PROD-VIDEOG DIST-VIDEOG 1970

**INTRODUCTION TO SEX
EDUCATION** B 28 MIN
16MM FILM OPTICAL SOUND H-C A
PRESENTS A REVIEW OF TRADITIONAL AND
CHANGING ATTITUDES AND VALUES OF SEX AND
MORALITY FOR THE PHILOSOPHICAL APPROACH
TO EDUCATION FOR FAMILY LIVING. DESCRIBES
THE INFLUENCE OF FAMILY LIFE ON SEX ATTI-
TUDES AND BEHAVIORS. FROM THE SEX IN AMER-
ICAN CULTURE SERIES.
LC NO. 73-701217
PROD-CHM DIST-CHM 1967

INVITATION TO THE EAST C 28 MIN
16MM FILM OPTICAL SOUND
FEATURES A TOUR OF AMERICA BY HELICOPTER.
PROD-MTP DIST-MTP

ISRAEL C
16MM FILM OPTICAL SOUND
SEE SERIES TITLE FOR DESCRIPTIVE STATEMENT.
FROM THE PORT OF CALL SERIES.
PROD-PUI DIST-PUI

ISRAEL - THE HOLY LAND C 25 MIN
16MM FILM OPTICAL SOUND J-C A
FOLLOWS THE WAY OF JESUS, SHOWING THE
HOLY PLACES OF ISRAEL, INCLUDING GALILEE,
THE HOLY SEPULCHRE, JERUSALEM AND BETHLE-
HEM.
LC NO. 79-713509
PROD-AMEDFL DIST-AMEDFL 1970

**ISRAEL IN THE FAMILY OF
NATIONS** B 17 MIN
16MM FILM OPTICAL SOUND
HIGHLIGHTS DRAMATIC MOMENTS IN ISRAEL'S
EXPANDING INTERNATIONAL RELATIONS.
PROD-ALDEN DIST-ALDEN

**ISRAEL'S NATIONAL WATER
CARRIER** C 18 MIN
16MM FILM OPTICAL SOUND
TELLS THE STORY OF THE CONSTRUCTION OF IS-
RAEL'S BIGGEST WATER CARRIER WHICH PUMPS
SWEET WATER FROM THE LAKE OF GALILEE IN
THE NORTH ALONG 100 MILES OF TUNNELS, CA-
NALS AND PIPES TO THE NEGEV DESERT IN THE
SOUTH.
PROD-ALDEN DIST-ALDEN

ISRAEL'S QUEST FOR WATER B 22 MIN
16MM FILM OPTICAL SOUND
SHOWS HOW WATER FROM THE JORDAN RIVER
REJUVENATES ISRAEL'S PARCHED LAND.
PROD-ALDEN DIST-ALDEN

**ISRAEL'S 17TH INDEPENDENCE
DAY (1965)** C
16MM FILM OPTICAL SOUND
DEPICTS THE CELEBRATIONS ON ISRAEL'S 17TH
INDEPENDENCE DAY.
PROD-ALDEN DIST-ALDEN

**IT HAPPENED IN HUALFIN, PT 1
- WHEN THE WIND IS SILENT** B 15 MIN
16MM FILM OPTICAL SOUND
PRESENTS 84-YEAR-OLD TEMISTOCLES FIGUEROA
WHO RECOUNTS HIS LIFE IN THE CANEFIELDS
WITH THE MATTER-OF-FACTNESS OF AN OLD MAN
NO LONGER USEFUL.
PROD-PIC DIST-PIC

**IT HAPPENED IN HUALFIN, PT 2
- THE CLAY** B 15 MIN
16MM FILM OPTICAL SOUND
PRESENTS JUSTINA FIGUEROA'S NARRATIVE ON
POVERTY AND POTTERY, MINGLED WITH QUES-
TIONS AND POLITICS.
PROD-PIC DIST-PIC

**IT HAPPENED IN HUALFIN, PT 3
- ELINDA OF THE VALLEY** B 20 MIN
16MM FILM OPTICAL SOUND
TELLS THE STORY OF ANTONIA WHO LIVES IN HU-
ALFIN WITH HER DAUGHTER ELINDA AND TOILS
DAY AND NIGHT WEAVING BLANKETS FOR SALE
OR BARTER AT THE GENERAL STORE. EXPLAINS
THAT ELINDA IS HER MOTHER'S HOPE - SHE CAN
BECOME A SCHOOL TEACHER AND BREAK OUT OF
THE CYCLE OF POVERTY.
PROD-PIC DIST-PIC

IT WAS THE CUSTOM B 15 MIN
16MM FILM OPTICAL SOUND
SHOWS SOME OF THE TRADITIONS, MARRIAGE
CEREMONIES AND THE SABBATH AS PRACTICED
AND OBSERVED BY THE VARIOUS JEWISH COM-
MUNITIES LIVING IN ISRAEL.
PROD-ALDEN DIST-ALDEN

J

**JACK MARIN - FORWARD PLAY,
PT 1** C 12 MIN
16MM FILM OPTICAL SOUND J-C
FEATURES JACK MARIN OF THE NBA TEACHING
AND DEMONSTRATING THE FUNDAMENTALS OF
GOOD FORWARD PLAY. COVERS THE ART OF THE
JUMP SHOT, SQUARING UP THE BODY, RELEASING
THE BALL, VARIOUS DRIVING MOVES AND 'GOING
TO THE BASKET.' FROM THE WILLIS REED BASKET-
BALL SERIES.
LC NO. 73-701356
PROD-SCHLAT DIST-SCHLAT 1972

**JACK MARIN - FORWARD PLAY,
PT 2** C 11 MIN
16MM FILM OPTICAL SOUND J-C
FEATURES JACK MARIN OF THE NBA TEACHING
AND DEMONSTRATING THE FUNDAMENTALS OF
GOOD FORWARD PLAY. COVERS THE ART OF FOUL
SHOOTING, HOW TO DEVELOP ONE FLUID MO-
TION, DEFENSIVE REBOUNDING AND OFFENSIVE
REBOUNDING. FROM THE WILLIS REED BASKET-
BALL SERIES.
LC NO. 73-701366
PROD-SCHLAT DIST-SCHLAT 1972

JAPAN C
16MM FILM OPTICAL SOUND
SEE SERIES TITLE FOR DESCRIPTIVE STATEMENT.
FROM THE PORT OF CALL SERIES.
PROD-PUI DIST-PUI

JAPAN'S LIVING CRAFTS C 21 MIN
16MM FILM OPTICAL SOUND J-C A
EXAMINES THE WORK AND FEELINGS OF THE
CRAFTSMEN WHO PRODUCE JAPANESE CERAM-
ICS, LAQUER WARE, DYEING AND WEAVING AND
METALWORK. POINTS OUT THAT THE PEOPLE
WHO HAVE INHERITED THESE SKILLS ARE TODAY
PROTECTED BY THE JAPANESE GOVERNMENT.
LC NO. 79-708657
PROD-AMEDFL DIST-AMEDFL 1971

JAPANESE CHILDREN B 18 MIN
16MM FILM OPTICAL SOUND
DEPICTS CHILDREN IN VARIOUS PARTS OF JAPAN
AND DESCRIBES PROBLEMS RELATED TO THEIR
LIVING ENVIRONMENT. FROM THE LAND AND IN-
DUSTRY OF JAPAN SERIES.
PROD-IWANMI DIST-IWANMI

L

JERUSALEM - HERE WE COME   C 16 MIN
16MM FILM OPTICAL SOUND
SHOWS THE ANCIENT TRADITION OF A PILGRIM-
AGE TO JERUSALEM BEING REVIVED YEARLY BY
THOUSANDS OF ISRAELIS, YOUNG AND OLD, MILI-
TARY UNITS AND GROUPS FROM ABROAD, IN A
FOUR-DAY MARCH TO THE CAPITAL.
PROD-ALDEN   DIST-ALDEN

JESUS TRIP, THE   C 50 MIN
16MM FILM OPTICAL SOUND   C A
PENETRATES THE JESUS FREAKS' COMMUNES TO
ACCURATELY RECORD THE SIGNIFICANCE AND
SCOPE OF THE JESUS MOVEMENT. EXPLAINS
THAT THE LIFE STYLE OF THE JESUS MOVEMENT
IS BUILT AROUND ACID ROCK RELIGIOUS MUSIC.
PROD-BBCTV   DIST-TIMLIF

JIM NANCE   C 5 MIN
16MM FILM OPTICAL SOUND   J-C A
SEE SERIES TITLE FOR DESCRIPTIVE STATEMENT.
FROM THE WONDERFUL WORLD OF SPORT - FOOT-
BALL SERIES.
PROD-SPORTI   DIST-AMERFI

**JO JO WHITE - OFFENSIVE
GUARD, PT 1**   C 10 MIN
16MM FILM OPTICAL SOUND   J-C
FEATURES JO JO WHITE, STAR OF THE BOSTON
CELTICS, WHO ILLUSTRATES THE VARIOUS TECH-
NIQUES IN GUARD PLAY. COVERS THE JUMP
SHOT, SHOOTING BEHIND A 'PICK,' SHOOTING BE-
HIND A SCREEN, SHOOTING A LAYUP AND FREE
THROW SHOOTING. FROM THE WILLIS REED BAS-
KETBALL SERIES.
LC NO. 73-701357
PROD-SCHLAT   DIST-SCHLAT   1972

**JO JO WHITE - OFFENSIVE
GUARD, PT 2**   C 12 MIN
16MM FILM OPTICAL SOUND   J-C
FEATURES JO JO WHITE, STAR OF THE BOSTON
CELTICS, WHO ILLUSTRATES THE VARIOUS TECH-
NIQUES IN GUARD PLAY. COVERS THE CHEST
PASS, THE BOUND PASS, THE HOOK PANS, THE
BASEBALL PASS, DRIBBLING TECHNIQUES AND
MOVING WITHOUT THE BALL. FROM THE WILLIS
REED BASKETBALL SERIES.
LC NO. 73-701367
PROD-SCHLAT   DIST-SCHLAT   1972

JOBS IN BAKING   C 7 MIN
16MM FILM OPTICAL SOUND
DEPICTS A DRIVER-SALESMAN INTRODUCING A
SALES TRAINEE TO CUSTOMERS ON HIS ROUTE
AND DEMONSTRATING HIS SELLING SKILLS.
POINTS OUT THAT BACKING UP THE SALES FORCE
ARE BAKERS AND THEIR SKILLED HELPERS,
WHOSE PRODUCTS RUN FROM SIMPLE BREADS
TO WEDDING CAKES.
LC NO. 73-701058
PROD-USDL   DIST-USNAC   1968

JOBS IN COSMETOLOGY   C 10 MIN
16MM FILM OPTICAL SOUND
COVERS BEAUTY SALON OPERATORS, HAIR STYL-
ISTS, BEAUTICIANS AND THEIR SPECIALIZED AS-
SISTANTS. POINTS OUT THAT TRAINING IN THE
FIELD OF COSMETOLOGY IS OPEN TO PEOPLE
WITH NO HIGH SCHOOL DIPLOMA.
LC NO. 73-701056
PROD-USDL   DIST-USNAC   1970

JOE DEY - PIN PLACEMENT   C 5 MIN
16MM FILM OPTICAL SOUND   J-C A
SEE SERIES TITLE FOR DESCRIPTIVE STATEMENT.
FROM THE WONDERFUL WORLD OF SPORT - GOLF
SERIES.
PROD-SPORTI   DIST-AMERFI

**JOE FRAZIER - CHAMPION IN
TRAINING**   C 5 MIN
16MM FILM OPTICAL SOUND   J-C A
SEE SERIES TITLE FOR DESCRIPTIVE STATEMENT.
FROM THE WONDERFUL WORLD OF SPORT - BOX-
ING SERIES.
PROD-SPORTI   DIST-AMERFI

JOE NAMATH   C 5 MIN
16MM FILM OPTICAL SOUND   J-C A
SEE SERIES TITLE FOR DESCRIPTIVE STATEMENT.
FROM THE WONDERFUL WORLD OF SPORT - FOOT-
BALL SERIES.
PROD-SPORTI   DIST-AMERFI

JOE TORRE   C 5 MIN
16MM FILM OPTICAL SOUND   J-C A
SEE SERIES TITLE FOR DESCRIPTIVE STATEMENT.
FROM THE WONDERFUL WORLD OF SPORT - BASE-
BALL SERIES.
PROD-SPORTI   DIST-AMERFI

**JOHN ADAMS AND THE NEW
ENGLAND SIGNERS**   C 80 MIN
16MM FILM OPTICAL SOUND
GIVES THE BACKGROUND OF THE 18 NEW EN-
GLAND SIGNERS OF THE CONSTITUTION, THEIR
LIVES, ACHIEVEMENTS AND FATES. FROM THE TO
THE SPIRIT OF '76 SERIES.
LC NO. 73-733680
PROD-RMI   DIST-RMI

JUNIOR FIREMEN   C 14 MIN
16MM FILM OPTICAL SOUND
DOCUMENTS A PROGRAM ESTABLISHED BY THE
LOS ANGELES CITY FIRE DEPARTMENT TO ENLIST
THE AID OF THE CHILDREN OF THE CITY SCHOOLS
IN A COMPREHENSIVE FIRE PREVENTION DRIVE.
PROD-LACFD   DIST-LACFD

K

K C EXERCISE   C 5 MIN
16MM FILM OPTICAL SOUND   J-C A
SEE SERIES TITLE FOR DESCRIPTIVE STATEMENT.
FROM THE WONDERFUL WORLD OF SPORT - FOOT-
BALL SERIES.
PROD-SPORTI   DIST-AMERFI

KARATE   C 10 MIN
16MM FILM OPTICAL SOUND   J-C A
GIVES A BRIEF HISTORY OF KARATE, OBSERVING
SOME OF ITS BASIC PROCEDURE DEMONSTRATED
BY A GROUP OF EXPERTS FROM THE AGE OF FIVE
ON UP.
LC NO. 73-700558
PROD-PFP   DIST-PFP

KEEP COOL   C 4 MIN
16MM FILM OPTICAL SOUND   J-C
PRESENTS AN IRONIC AND HUMOROUS ESSAY ON
HOW ONE BLACK MAN TRIES TO MAKE IT BY A
NEW GOLDEN RULE - 'KEEP COOL.'
LC NO. 73-701286
PROD-BFA   DIST-BFA   1973

KENTUCKY STYLE   C 5 MIN
16MM FILM OPTICAL SOUND   J-C A
SEE SERIES TITLE FOR DESCRIPTIVE STATEMENT.
FROM THE WONDERFUL WORLD OF SPORT - BAS-
KETBALL SERIES.
PROD-SPORTI   DIST-AMERFI

KENYA   C
16MM FILM OPTICAL SOUND
SEE SERIES TITLE FOR DESCRIPTIVE STATEMENT.
FROM THE PORT OF CALL SERIES.
PROD-PUI   DIST-PUI

KIBBUTZ, A   B 40 MIN
16MM FILM OPTICAL SOUND
PRESENTS A VISIT TO A KIBBUTZ, AN ISRAELI COL-
LECTIVE VILLAGE, AND LOOKS AT ITS WAY OF LIFE.
PROD-ALDEN   DIST-ALDEN

KICKER STORY   C 5 MIN
16MM FILM OPTICAL SOUND   J-C A
SEE SERIES TITLE FOR DESCRIPTIVE STATEMENT.
FROM THE WONDERFUL WORLD OF SPORT - FOOT-
BALL SERIES.
PROD-SPORTI   DIST-AMERFI

KIDS ARE PEOPLE, TOO   C 42 MIN
16MM FILM OPTICAL SOUND   T
PRESENTS A DOCUMENTARY OF ONE TEACHER'S
ATTEMPT TO REACH DISRUPTIVE CHILDREN BY
PROVIDING A SPECIAL CLASSROOM SITUATION
WHERE THE STUDENTS CAN LEARN TO TRUST AN
ADULT AND EACH OTHER.
LC NO. 73-701190
PROD-CEURED   DIST-CCMFI   1972

KNOW YOUR CLOUDS   C 16 MIN
16MM FILM OPTICAL SOUND
DESCRIBES THE DEVELOPMENT OF THE TEN BA-
SIC KINDS OF CLOUDS, THEIR PRINCIPLE CHARAC-
TERISTICS, THEIR RELATIVE POSITIONS AND AV-
ERAGE ATTITUDES AND THEIR FLIGHT HAZARDS.
LC NO. 73-701250
PROD-USA   DIST-USNAC   1967

**KNUCKLEBALL, THE - HOYT
WHILHELM**   C 5 MIN
16MM FILM OPTICAL SOUND   J-C A
SEE SERIES TITLE FOR DESCRIPTIVE STATEMENT.
FROM THE WONDERFUL WORLD OF SPORT - BASE-
BALL SERIES.
PROD-SPORTI   DIST-AMERFI

KRISHNAMURTI   C 25 MIN
16MM FILM OPTICAL SOUND   H-C A
INTERVIEWS KRISHNAMURTI, ONE OF THE GREAT
SPIRITUAL THINKERS OF THIS CENTURY. EX-
PLAINS THAT ONCE HAILED AS WORLD TEACHER,
HE REJECTED HIS MESSIANIC ROLE AND ESTAB-
LISHED A CULT. TELLS OF HIS WORLD TRAVELS
ENCOURAGING LIBERATION OF THE MIND AND
HIS SEARCH FOR TOTAL UNDERSTANDING OF
SELF AND COMPLETE LOVE.
PROD-BBCTV   DIST-TIMLIF

L

LABRADORS IN TRAINING   C 5 MIN
16MM FILM OPTICAL SOUND   J-C A
SEE SERIES TITLE FOR DESCRIPTIVE STATEMENT.
FROM THE WONDERFUL WORLD OF SPORT - DOGS
SERIES.
PROD-SPORTI   DIST-AMERFI

LABRADORS, LAND RETRIEVING   C 5 MIN
16MM FILM OPTICAL SOUND   J-C A
SEE SERIES TITLE FOR DESCRIPTIVE STATEMENT.
FROM THE WONDERFUL WORLD OF SPORT - DOGS
SERIES.
PROD-SPORTI   DIST-AMERFI

**LABRADORS, WATER
RETRIEVING**   C 5 MIN
16MM FILM OPTICAL SOUND   J-C A
SEE SERIES TITLE FOR DESCRIPTIVE STATEMENT.
FROM THE WONDERFUL WORLD OF SPORT - DOGS
SERIES.
PROD-SPORTI   DIST-AMERFI

**LADIES GOLF - CATHY
WENTWORTH**   C 5 MIN
16MM FILM OPTICAL SOUND   J-C A
SEE SERIES TITLE FOR DESCRIPTIVE STATEMENT.
FROM THE WONDERFUL WORLD OF SPORT - GOLF
SERIES.
PROD-SPORTI   DIST-AMERFI

LADY BOXER   C 5 MIN
16MM FILM OPTICAL SOUND   J-C A
SEE SERIES TITLE FOR DESCRIPTIVE STATEMENT.
FROM THE WONDERFUL WORLD OF SPORT - BOX-
ING SERIES.
PROD-SPORTI   DIST-AMERFI

LAND OF HOPE AND PRAYER   C 14 MIN
16MM FILM OPTICAL SOUND
TELLS THE STORY OF A BAPTIST SETTLEMENT IN
THE HOLY LAND.
PROD-ALDEN   DIST-ALDEN

LAND SPEAKS OUT, THE   C 12 MIN
16MM FILM OPTICAL SOUND
POINTS OUT THAT ISRAEL IS A MODERN COUN-
TRY, ROOTED DEEPLY IN ITS HISTORIC PAST.
SHOWS CONVENIENT VACATION FACILITIES AT
SEA RESORTS AND CAMPING GROUNDS COM-
BINED WITH UNIQUE ARCHAEOLOGICAL SITES
AND BEAUTIFUL SCENERY OF THE COUNTRYSIDE.
PROD-ALDEN   DIST-ALDEN

LANDING TEAM, THE   C 10 MIN
16MM FILM OPTICAL SOUND   H-C A
EMPHASIZES THE SKILL, SAFE WORKING PROCE-
DURES AND PRODUCTIVE OPERATIONS OF THE
LANDING TEAM. SHOWS PROFESSIONAL LANDING
TEAMS AT WORK IN VARIOUS CONDITIONS, TER-
RAINS AND LOCATIONS. FROM THE LOGGING
SAFETY SERIES.
PROD-RARIG   DIST-RARIG   1968

LANGUAGE DEVELOPMENT   C 29 MIN
16MM FILM OPTICAL SOUND   C A
DISCUSSES CROSS-CULTURAL LANGUAGE PAT-
TERNS. FROM THE DEVELOPMENTAL PSYCHOLOGY
FILM SERIES.
LC NO. 73-700595
PROD-CRMP   DIST-CRMP   1973

LANTON MILLS   C 18 MIN
16MM FILM OPTICAL SOUND
FOLLOWS THE MISADVENTURES OF TWO GOOD-
BAD GUYS. INCORPORATES MANY OF THE CLASSIC
ELEMENTS OF WESTERN STYLE HOLD-UPS OF THE
PREVIOUS CENTURY IN THEIR ATTEMPTS TO
HOLD UP AND ROB A BANK IN BEVERLY HILLS,
PRESENT-DAY CALIFORNIA.
PROD-AMERFI   DIST-AMERFI

LE CYCLISTE · C 5 MIN
16MM FILM OPTICAL SOUND   J-C A
PRESENTS LE CYCLISTE, THE GREAT MASTER OF
ALL CYCLES, IN A MIME.
LC NO. 73-701225
PROD-ALBM   DIST-ALBM   1973

LEFT, RIGHT MOVIE, THE C 7 MIN
16MM FILM OPTICAL SOUND   K-P S
TEACHES AND REINFORCES THE CONCEPTS OF
LEFT AND RIGHT.
LC NO. 73-701041
PROD-GRADYM   DIST-GRADYM   1972

LEO THE LION-HEARTED C
16MM FILM OPTICAL SOUND
SEE SERIES TITLE FOR DESCRIPTIVE STATEMENT.
FROM THE FAIRY TALE TIME SERIES.
PROD-PUI   DIST-PUI

LET MY PEOPLE GO B 54 MIN
16MM FILM OPTICAL SOUND
TELLS THE HISTORIC ORDEAL OF THE JEW,
THROUGH THE HOLOCAUST TO STATEHOOD.
PROD-ALDEN   DIST-ALDEN

**LET'S IMAGINE - LIFE IN
UTOPIA** B 28 MIN
16MM FILM OPTICAL SOUND
FEATURES THE BRITISH BROADCASTING CORPO-
RATION TAKING A LOOK AT ISRAEL'S KIBBUTZ
SYSTEM.
PROD-ALDEN   DIST-ALDEN

**LET'T VISIT THE FIREMEN -
VAMOS A VISITAR A LA
BOMBEROS** C 7 MIN
16MM FILM OPTICAL SOUND
PRESENTS CLASSROOM PREPARATION FOR A
FIELD TRIP TO THE FIRE STATION. FROM THE
BRENTANO FOUNDATION BILINGUAL FILMS SE-
RIES.
PROD-CAROUF   DIST-CAROUF

**LIFE AND HEALTH FILM--A
SERIES**

PROD-CRMP   DIST-CRMP

ALCOHOLISM · A MODEL OF DRUG
DEPENDENCY   20 MIN
DEPENDENCE - A NEW DEFINITION   20 MIN
HEART, THE - ATTACK   25 MIN
HEART, THE - COUNTERATTACK   25 MIN

LIFE CYCLE OF A DRAGONFLY B 13 MIN
16MM FILM OPTICAL SOUND
COVERS THE ENTIRE LIFE CYCLE OF THE DRAGON-
FLY.
PROD-IWANMI   DIST-IWANMI

LIFE FROM THE DEAD SEA C 14 MIN
16MM FILM OPTICAL SOUND
SHOWS HOW THE RICH MINERAL RESOURCES
FROM THE DEAD SEA, THE LOWEST SPOT ON
EARTH, ARE EXTRACTED AND PROCESSED.
PROD-ALDEN   DIST-ALDEN

LIFE OF A MONKEY, THE C 14 MIN
16MM FILM OPTICAL SOUND
OBSERVES THE COMMUNITY LIFE OF MONKEYS AT
JAPAN'S MONKEY CENTER AND DESCRIBES THEIR
USE AS EXPERIMENTAL RESEARCH ANIMALS.
PROD-IWANMI   DIST-IWANMI

LIFE ON THE REEF C 14 MIN
16MM FILM OPTICAL SOUND
OBSERVES THE VARIOUS FORMS AND HABITS OF
LIFE FOUND ON THE REEFS. INCLUDES THE
ACORN BARNACLE, SEA ANEMONE, ASTEROIDS,
SEA URCHIN, SEA COW, SEA HARE, ABALONE, SEA
CUCUMBER AND OCTOPUS.
PROD-IWANMI   DIST-IWANMI

LIFE ON THE SAND BEACH C 14 MIN
16MM FILM OPTICAL SOUND
DESCRIBES LIFE ON THE SAND BEACH AND OB-
SERVES ITS FORMS AND HABITS. SHOWS VARIOUS
FORMS OF LIFE SEEN AT LOW TIDE, INCLUDING
LIVING FOSSILS, SAMISEN SHELLFISH, LUGWORMS,
CRABS, SMALL SNAILS AND CLAMS.
PROD-IWANMI   DIST-IWANMI

LIGHT OF DAY, THE C 9 MIN
16MM FILM OPTICAL SOUND
SHOWS HOW COLOR AND DAYLIGHT CHANGE IN
THE ENVIRONMENT FROM DAWN THROUGH EVE-
NING, IN THE CITY AND THE COUNTRY.
LC NO. 73-701040
PROD-GRADYM   DIST-GRADYM   1972

LITTLE MAN - MIKE GARRETT C 5 MIN
16MM FILM OPTICAL SOUND   J-C A
SEE SERIES TITLE FOR DESCRIPTIVE STATEMENT.
FROM THE WONDERFUL WORLD OF SPORT - FOOT-
BALL SERIES.
PROD-SPORTI   DIST-AMERFI

LIVING BONE, THE C 14 MIN
16MM FILM OPTICAL SOUND
DISCUSSES THE IMPORTANT ROLE OF BONES IN
LIVING ORGANISMS. DESCRIBES THE HUMAN
BONE STRUCTURE AND ILLUSTRATES THE DY-
NAMIC FEATURES OF BONES.
PROD-IWANMI   DIST-IWANMI

LIVING CELL, THE C 28 MIN
16MM FILM OPTICAL SOUND   J-C A
PRESENTS AN OVERVIEW OF THE STRUCTURE
AND FUNCTION OF LIVING PLANT AND ANIMAL
CELLS, SHOWING HOW DIFFERENT ASPECTS OF
CELL STRUCTURE AND FUNCTION ARE BEST
STUDIED IN SELECTED CELLS OF DIFFERENT
KINDS OF ORGANISMS.
LC NO. 72-701877
PROD-HAR   DIST-HAR   1972

LIVING OFF THE LAND C 32 MIN
16MM FILM OPTICAL SOUND
PRESENTS A DOCUMENTARY ABOUT MEN SURVIV-
ING IN A HOSTILE ENVIRONMENT. INTRODUCES A
FATHER AND SON WHO CLING GRIMLY TO EXIS-
TENCE BY SCAVENGING GARBAGE DUMPS FOR
SCRAP METAL. SHOWS THE OUTRAGE AT THE SO-
CIAL INJUSTICE OF CONDITIONS LIKE THIS IN
PRESENT DAY AMERICA.
PROD-AMERFI   DIST-AMERFI

**LIVING WOOD - AFRICAN
MASKS AND MYTHS** C 12 MIN
16MM FILM OPTICAL SOUND   I-H A
EXPLAINS THAT TO THE AFRICAN BLACK, THE
TREE IS A LIVING THING AND THE MASKS HE
CARVES FROM THE TREE HAVE A SPECIAL POWER,
A VITAL FORCE. ATTEMPTS TO REVEAL THIS VITAL
FORCE BY SHOWING THE MASKS OF AFRICA, AS A
TRIBESMAN RELATES THE TALES AND MYTHS OF
HIS PEOPLE.
LC NO. 73-701042
PROD-GRADYM   DIST-GRADYM   1973

LOGGING SAFETY--A SERIES
H-C A
PROD-RARIG   DIST-RARIG

CHOKERMAN, THE   11 MIN
CUTTING CREW, THE   11 MIN
LANDING TEAM, THE   10 MIN

LOOK WHAT'S GOING AROUND C
16MM FILM OPTICAL SOUND   H-C A
EMPHASIZES THE EASE OF TREATMENT, SYMP-
TOMS AND SPREAD OF VENERAL DISEASE. IN-
CLUDES A DISCUSSION BY A GROUP OF YOUNG
PEOPLE TO PRESENT ATTITUDES TO HELP DISPEL
THE SENSE OF SHAME.
LC NO. 73-701441
PROD-CF   DIST-CF   1973

LOUIS I KAHN, ARCHITECT C 27 MIN
16MM FILM OPTICAL SOUND
DEPICTS THE IMPOSING ARCHITECTURAL
ACHIEVEMENTS OF LOUIS I KAHN, THE GREAT
TEACHER WHO IS SHAPING THE CONCEPTS OF A
GENERATION OF YOUNG ARCHITECTS.
PROD-VISRES   DIST-VISRES

LOUISE NEVELSON C 25 MIN
16MM FILM OPTICAL SOUND   C A
FEATURES SCULPTRESS LOUISE NEVELSON COM-
MENTING ON HER ART AND TELLING OF THE DE-
VELOPMENT OF THE VARIOUS PERIODS IN HER
WORK.
LC NO. 73-701406
PROD-CONNF   DIST-CONNF   1971

LOVE AND FILM C 9 MIN
16MM FILM OPTICAL SOUND   H-C A
PRESENTS NATIONAL MYTHOLOGIES ABOUT LOVE.
EXPLAINS THAT LOVE MEANS WESTERNS AND
BULLETS IN AMERICA, WORKERS AND OUTDOOR
EPICS IN RUSSIA, SWORDS AND SAMURAI TALES
IN JAPAN, RIVAL LOVERS AND MOCK BEDROOM
COMEDY IN FRANCE.
LC NO. 73-701429
PROD-BFA   DIST-BFA   1973

LOVE'S BEGINNINGS C 10 MIN
16MM FILM OPTICAL SOUND   P
PORTRAYS CHILDREN AND ADULTS OF MANY ETH-
NIC GROUPS, EMPHASIZING THE FEELING AND
STRENGTH OF LOVE. DESCRIBES THE MANY

STRONG CHANNELS INTO WHICH LOVE CAN BE DI-
RECTED MAKING A CHILD'S AND AN ADULT'S LIFE
RICHER, STRONGER AND MORE MEANINGFUL.
LC NO. 73-700886
PROD-CAHILL   DIST-CAHILL   1972

LOVING YOUNG COMPANY C 16 MIN
16MM FILM OPTICAL SOUND
SHOWS GROUPS OF AMERICAN TEENAGERS VISIT-
ING ISRAEL IN THE SUMMER TIME. FOLLOWS
THEIR TOUR THROUGH THE COUNTRY, CREATING
NEW FRIENDSHIPS, ACQUAINTING THEMSELVES
WITH THE COUNTRY AND ITS PEOPLE AND HAV-
ING FUN.
PROD-ALDEN   DIST-ALDEN

**LOWELL HERRERO - THE
GRAPHIC PROCESS** C 28 MIN
16MM FILM OPTICAL SOUND
PRESENTS LOWELL HERRERO, THE CREATOR OF
THE CALENDARSCHEDULE OF THE SAN FRAN-
CISCO GIANTS BASEBALL TEAM FOR THE 1972
SEASON. SHOWS ALL PHASES OF THE WORK IN-
VOLVED IN GRAPHICS AND PRINTING.
LC NO. 73-701039
PROD-GRADYM   DIST-GRADYM

M

MAESTRO, THE C 5 MIN
16MM FILM OPTICAL SOUND   J-C A
SEE SERIES TITLE FOR DESCRIPTIVE STATEMENT.
FROM THE WONDERFUL WORLD OF SPORT - FENC-
ING SERIES.
PROD-SPORTI   DIST-AMERFI

MAGNET, THE C 14 MIN
16MM FILM OPTICAL SOUND
TRACES THE HISTORY OF THE MAGNET FROM ITS
DISCOVERY UP TO ITS USE IN MOTORS. DIS-
CUSSES THE COMPASS, BAR MAGNET, REPULSION
OF SAME POLES, ATTRACTION OF OPPOSITE POLES
AND THE EARTH'S MAGNETIC FIELD.
PROD-IWANMI   DIST-IWANMI

MAKING OF FINE CHINA C 20 MIN
16MM FILM OPTICAL SOUND
DESCRIBES BEAUTIFUL LENOX DINNERWARE AND
HOW IT IS MADE, INCLUDING STEPS IN DESIGN-
ING, MOLDING, FIRING, DECORATING AND BURN-
ISHING OF THE CHINA.
PROD-MTP   DIST-MTP

**MANAGEMENT PRACTICE--A
SERIES**
FEATURES VARIOUS EXPERTS WHO DISCUSS WITH
JOHN HUMBLE THE LESSONS TO BE LEARNED
FROM SEVERAL MANAGEMENT CASES. COVERS IN-
FORMATION SYSTEMS, MARKETING AND STRATE-
GIC PLANNING.
PROD-BNA   DIST-BNA

WHAT EVERY MANAGER NEEDS TO
KNOW ABOUT --
WHAT EVERY MANAGER NEEDS TO
KNOW ABOUT 1-
WHAT EVERY MANAGER NEEDS TO
KNOW ABOUT 2-
WHAT EVERY MANAGER NEEDS TO
KNOW ABOUT 3-
WHAT EVERY MANAGER NEEDS TO
KNOW ABOUT 4-
WHAT EVERY MANAGER NEEDS TO
KNOW ABOUT 5-

MAX PATKIN C 5 MIN
16MM FILM OPTICAL SOUND   J-C A
SEE SERIES TITLE FOR DESCRIPTIVE STATEMENT.
FROM THE WONDERFUL WORLD OF SPORT - BASE-
BALL SERIES.
PROD-SPORTI   DIST-AMERFI

**MEANING OF TIME IN SCIENCE,
THE** C 25 MIN
16MM FILM OPTICAL SOUND   H-C
EXAMINES THE CONCEPTS OF THE ENTROPY
PRINCIPLE, ASTRONOMICAL TIME, THE RELATION
OF SUBJECTIVE AND EXTERNAL TIME AND THE
DEFINITION OF A SECOND. DEMONSTRATES SCI-
ENTIFIC TIMEPIECES SUCH AS THE CYCLOTRON.
LC NO. 73-701230
PROD-EBEC   DIST-EBEC   1973

MEASURING INSTRUMENTS B 12 MIN
16MM FILM OPTICAL SOUND
PRESENTS VARIOUS TYPES OF MEASURING IN-
STRUMENTS, INCLUDING THE PLATFORM SCALE,
AUTOMATIC SCALE, BEAM BALANCE AND SPRING
SCALE.

PROD-IWANMI   DIST-IWANMI

MECHANISMS OF SCATTERING
SEEDS   C 14 MIN
              16MM FILM OPTICAL SOUND
STUDIES THE SCATTERING METHODS OF NUTS
AND SEEDS AND EXAMINES THE POWER OF SUR-
VIVAL OF PLANTS. SHOWS SEEDS THAT DEPEND
ON EXTERNAL FORCE AND SEEDS THAT DEPEND
ON THE HELP OF MAN OR ANIMALS.
PROD-IWANMI   DIST-IWANMI

MEN FROM THE BOYS, THE   C 51 MIN
              16MM FILM OPTICAL SOUND
FOLLOWS 48 DRAFTEES FROM DIFFERENT BACK-
GROUNDS THROUGH THE FIRST EIGHT WEEKS OF
THEIR BASIC TRAINING. SHOWS THEIR TESTING,
CONDITIONING AND TRAINING.
PROD-MTP   DIST-MTP

MERION - THE ELEVENTH   C 5 MIN
              16MM FILM OPTICAL SOUND   J-C A
SEE SERIES TITLE FOR DESCRIPTIVE STATEMENT.
FROM THE WONDERFUL WORLD OF SPORT - GOLF
SERIES.
PROD-SPORTI   DIST-AMERFI

MERION - THE FIRST   C 5 MIN
              16MM FILM OPTICAL SOUND   J-C A
SEE SERIES TITLE FOR DESCRIPTIVE STATEMENT.
FROM THE WONDERFUL WORLD OF SPORT - GOLF
SERIES.
PROD-SPORTI   DIST-AMERFI

MEXICO   C 12 MIN
              16MM FILM OPTICAL SOUND
DISCUSSES THE HISTORY OF MEXICO AND EXAM-
INES ANCIENT AND MODERN ARCHITECTURE
AND COLORFUL NATIVE COSTUMES. FROM THE
BRENTANO FOUNDATION BILINGUAL FILMS SE-
RIES.
PROD-CAROUF   DIST-CAROUF

MICROSCOPE   C 14 MIN
              16MM FILM OPTICAL SOUND
EXPLAINS THE PRINCIPLES AND STRUCTURE OF
THE MICROSCOPE. DISCUSSES THE CHARACTERIS-
TICS OF A CONVEX LENS, THE FUNCTION OF THE
LENS OF THE HUMAN EYE AND THE CONNECTION
BETWEEN THE COMBINATION AND IMAGE-FORM-
ING OF THE CONVEX LENS.
PROD-IWANMI   DIST-IWANMI

MIKE BONALLACK   C 5 MIN
              16MM FILM OPTICAL SOUND   J-C A
SEE SERIES TITLE FOR DESCRIPTIVE STATEMENT.
FROM THE WONDERFUL WORLD OF SPORT - GOLF
SERIES.
PROD-SPORTI   DIST-AMERFI

MIKE REED   C 5 MIN
              16MM FILM OPTICAL SOUND   J-C A
SEE SERIES TITLE FOR DESCRIPTIVE STATEMENT.
FROM THE WONDERFUL WORLD OF SPORT - FOOT-
BALL SERIES.
PROD-SPORTI   DIST-AMERFI

MILE RELAY   C 5 MIN
              16MM FILM OPTICAL SOUND   J-C A
SEE SERIES TITLE FOR DESCRIPTIVE STATEMENT.
FROM THE WONDERFUL WORLD OF SPORT -
TRACK AND FIELD SERIES.
PROD-SPORTI   DIST-AMERFI

MIMI   B 12 MIN
              16MM FILM OPTICAL SOUND   J-C A
PRESENTS A YOUNG WOMAN PARALYZED FROM
BIRTH, TALKING ABOUT HERSELF AND HER LIFE,
RELATING TO 'NORMAL' PEOPLE AND HOW THEY
RELATE TO HER.
   LC NO. 73-700891
PROD-BBF   DIST-BBF   1972

MIRROR   B 9 MIN
              16MM FILM SILENT
PRESENTS AN EXPERIMENTAL FILM BY ARTIST
ROBERT MORRIS IN WHICH A SNOWY, TREE-COV-
ERED LANDSCAPE IS SEEN IN REFLECTION.
PROD-VISRES   DIST-VISRES   1971

MISTER MAGROOTER'S
MARVELOUS MACHINE   C 8 MIN
              16MM FILM OPTICAL SOUND   I-C A
INTRODUCES MR MAGROOTER WHO DEVISES A
SIMPLE BUT INGENIOUS MACHINE THAT RE-
MOVES SEEDS FROM WATERMELONS. EXPLAINS
HOW VARIOUS PEOPLE STROLL BY AND CONVINCE
HIM TO ADD WHEELS AND GADGETS UNTIL HIS
NEW MACHINE DOES NOTHING SATISFACTORILY.
   LC NO. 73-701425

PROD-BOSUST   DIST-BOSUST   1972

MONEY, MONEY, MONEY   C 10 MIN
              16MM FILM OPTICAL SOUND   P-J
TAKES A CHILD FAR BEYOND THE MERE ARITHME-
TIC OF MONEY INTO THE EXCITING WORLD OF
SHILLINGS, DINARS, RUPEES, PESETAS AND BACK
TO DOLLARS AND CENTS. DEPICTS THE COIN AS A
MEDIUM OF EXCHANGE, A FORM OF SCULPTURE
AND A MONUMENT TO HISTORY.
   LC NO. 73-701201
PROD-AFI   DIST-TEXFLM   1972

MORAL DEVELOPMENT   C 28 MIN
              16MM FILM OPTICAL SOUND   C A
PRESENTS DR LAWRENCE KOHLBERG'S THEORY
ON MORAL DEVELOPMENT. STATES THAT ALL PEO-
PLE DEVELOP MORALITY IN CONSISTENT AND UN-
CHANGING WAYS AND THAT BEHAVIOR IS DETER-
MINED BY THE STATE OF MORAL DEVELOPMENT
THAT HAS BEEN REACHED. CONTRASTS KOHL-
BERG'S THEORY WITH THE SOCIAL LEARNING THE-
ORY. FROM THE DEVELOPMENTAL PSYCHOLOGY
FILM SERIES.
   LC NO. 73-700599
PROD-CRMP   DIST-CRMP   1973

MOSHAV, THE - ISRAEL'S
MIDDLE WAY   C 25 MIN
              16MM FILM OPTICAL SOUND
SHOWS ISRAEL'S SUCCESSFUL EXPERIMENT WITH
AGRICULTURAL AND REGIONAL PLANNING.
POINTS OUT THAT THE MOSHAV, A COOPERATIVE
SETTLEMENT, IS A MIDDLE WAY BETWEEN THE
CLOSELY-KNIT COMMUNAL KIBBUTZ AND THE IN-
DEPENDENT FARMER.
PROD-ALDEN   DIST-ALDEN

MOSQUITO   B 12 MIN
              16MM FILM OPTICAL SOUND
DESCRIBES THE BIRTH, GROWTH AND METHOD
OF EXTERMINATION OF MOSQUITOS, THE TRANS-
MITTERS OF SUCH COMMUNICABLE DISEASES AS
DENGUE FEVER, MALARIA AND JAPANESE EN-
CEPHALITIS.
PROD-IWANMI   DIST-IWANMI

MOVEMENT OF THE PENDULUM
                                      B 20 MIN
              16MM FILM OPTICAL SOUND
EXPLAINS THE SECRET OF THE PENDULUM
WHICH FOLLOWS REGULATED MOVEMENTS.
SHOWS THE DIFFERENCES IN SWING OF THE PEN-
DULUM ON THE SURFACES OF THE EARTH AND
MOON.
PROD-IWANMI   DIST-IWANMI

MOVEMENT OF THE TOP   C 14 MIN
              16MM FILM OPTICAL SOUND
USES EXPERIMENTS TO SHOW THAT THE TOP IS
PREVENTED FROM TOPPLING BY CENTRIFUGAL
FORCE.
PROD-IWANMI   DIST-IWANMI

MS - THE STRUGGLE FOR
WOMEN'S RIGHTS   B 14 MIN
              16MM FILM OPTICAL SOUND   I-C A
DEPICTS THE PEOPLE, PLACES AND EVENTS THAT
HAVE GIVEN IMPETUS AND LEADERSHIP TO THE
STRUGGLE FOR WOMEN'S RIGHTS. FROM THE
SCREEN NEWS DIGEST SERIES.
   LC NO. 73-701268
PROD-HEARST   DIST-HEARST   1972

MULTIPLE CHOICE   C
              16MM FILM OPTICAL SOUND   J-C A
PORTRAYS THE LIBRARY TRUSTEE AS HE CARRIES
OUT THE DUTIES AND RESPONSIBILITIES OF HIS
POSITION IN BOARD MEETINGS AND IN THE COM-
MUNITY. EMPHASIZES CERTAIN RESPONSIBILI-
TIES IN THE AREAS OF POLICY-MAKING, FINANCE
AND PUBLIC RELATIONS.
   LC NO. 73-701093
PROD-INDSLI   DIST-INDSLF   1972

MUSCLE - A STUDY OF
INTEGRATION   C 30 MIN
              16MM FILM OPTICAL SOUND
POINTS OUT THAT THE LEVELS OF ORGANIZATION
WITHIN HIGHER ORGANISMS CAN BE SUMMA-
RIZED AS BIOCHEMICAL, CELLULAR, TISSUE, OR-
GAN AND WHOLE ORGANISM. TAKES A UNIQUE
APPROACH TO THE INTEGRATION OF THESE LEV-
ELS INTO A FUNCTIONING WHOLE ORGANISM.
FROM THE BIOLOGY TODAY FILM SERIES.

PROD-CRMP   DIST-CRMP

NAHAL   C 10 MIN
              16MM FILM OPTICAL SOUND
SHOWS HOW ISRAEL'S NAHAL (PIONEER FIGHTING
YOUTH) COMBINES FARMING AND SOLDIERING.
PROD-ALDEN   DIST-ALDEN

NATION WITHIN A NATION, A   B 14 MIN
              16MM FILM OPTICAL SOUND   I-C A
EXAMINES THE WINDS OF CHANGE THAT ARE
SWEEPING ACROSS THE LIVES OF 140,000
NAVAJOS ON THE LARGEST INDIAN RESERVATION
IN THE WORLD. FROM THE SCREEN NEWS DIGEST
SERIES.
   LC NO. 73-701267
PROD-HEARST   DIST-HEARST   1972

NATURE OF MATTER, THE - AN
ATOMIC VIEW   C 20 MIN
              16MM FILM OPTICAL SOUND
PROBES THE NATURE OF MATTER AT ITS MOST
BASIC LEVEL, THAT OF ATOMIC AND SUB-ATOMIC
PARTICLES. EXPLORES MODERN TECHNIQUES OF
ATOMIC PHYSICS AND SUMMARIZES THE CUR-
RENT STATE OF KNOWLEDGE. FROM THE SCIENCE
TODAY FILM SERIES.
PROD-CRMP   DIST-CRMP

NATURE OF MATTER, THE - AN
ATOMIC VIEW   C 23 MIN
              16MM FILM OPTICAL SOUND   C A
VISITS THE DR ERWIN MEULLER LABORATORY AT
PENNSYLVANIA STATE UNIVERSITY TO DEMON-
STRATE THE FIELD-ION MICROSCOPE. DISCUSSES
WAVE-PARTICLE DUALITY AND SPECTROSCOPY.
FROM THE SCIENCE TODAY SERIES.
   LC NO. 73-700600
PROD-CRMP   DIST-CRMP   1972

NATURE OF THE FILM MEDIUM,
THE   C 27 MIN
              16MM FILM OPTICAL SOUND
DEMONSTRATES THE GREAT FLEXIBILITY OF THE
MOTION PICTURE MEDIUM. DISCUSSES SYMBOLS,
THE EFFECT OF VARIOUS CAMERA SPEEDS ON
THE EMOTIONS, THE PSYCHOLOGY OF SUBJEC-
TIVE CAMERA AND THE INFINITE POSSIBILITIES
OF FILM EDITING. INCLUDES CLIPS FROM 'CITIZEN
KANE,' 'HAND IN HAND,' 'REQUIEM FOR A HEAVY-
WEIGHT' AND OTHER FILMS.
PROD-PAULST   DIST-PAULST

NATURE'S EVER CHANGING
COMMUNITIES   C 14 MIN
              16MM FILM OPTICAL SOUND   I-J
DISCOVERS THE CONCEPTS OF RENEWAL,
CHANGE AND INTERDEPENDENCE IN THE NATU-
RAL WORLD. SHOWS HOW THE LIVING AND NON-
LIVING ELEMENTS IN AN AREA ARE REALLY AN IN-
TERDEPENDENT NATURAL COMMUNITY.
   LC NO. 73-701349
PROD-GLDWER   DIST-JOU   1973

NEIL WALK   C 5 MIN
              16MM FILM OPTICAL SOUND   J-C A
SEE SERIES TITLE FOR DESCRIPTIVE STATEMENT.
FROM THE WONDERFUL WORLD OF SPORT - BAS-
KETBALL SERIES.
PROD-SPORTI   DIST-AMERFI

NEMATODE   C 11 MIN
              16MM FILM OPTICAL SOUND   J-C
INTRODUCES THE SPECIES OF ROUNDWORMS OR
NEMATODA, COMMONLY FOUND IN PLANT
ROOTS.
   LC NO. 73-701398
PROD-EBEC   DIST-EBEC   1973

NEVELE PRIDE - TROTTER   C 5 MIN
              16MM FILM OPTICAL SOUND   J-C A
SEE SERIES TITLE FOR DESCRIPTIVE STATEMENT.
FROM THE WONDERFUL WORLD OF SPORT -
HORSES, RACING, POLO, RODEO SERIES.
PROD-SPORTI   DIST-AMERFI

NEVER UNDERESTIMATE THE
POWER OF A WOMAN   C 19 MIN
              16MM FILM OPTICAL SOUND   H-C
ESTIMATES THE GROWING NEED FOR AND EFFECT
OF WOMEN IN INDUSTRY AND IN SKILLED PRO-
FESSIONS, WHERE TRADITIONALLY THEY HAVE
BEEN FEW IN NUMBER.
   LC NO. 73-701177
PROD-UEUWIS   DIST-UEUWIS   1971

NEW DEAL   B 5 MIN
        16MM FILM OPTICAL SOUND   H-C A
PRESENTS A NON-NARRATIVE PORTRAIT STUDY
OF THE AGED, THE DISPLACED AND THE LONELY.
PROD-CAROUF   DIST-CAROUF

NEW ESTATE   B 30 MIN
        16MM FILM OPTICAL SOUND   C T
EXPLAINS THAT SCHOOLS ON LARGE HOUSING
PROJECTS HAVE SPECIAL PROBLEMS AND THAT
ENVIRONMENTAL STUDIES TEND TO BE SHORT
ON ARTISTIC AND HISTORICAL STIMULUS. FROM
THE EXPANDING CLASSROOM SERIES.
PROD-BBCTV   DIST-TIMLIF

NEW VIEW OF SPACE, A   C 28 MIN
        16MM FILM OPTICAL SOUND   J-C A
PRESENTS A LOOK AT THE SPACE PROGRAM
THROUGH THE USE OF THE PHOTOGRAPHIC ME-
DIUM. EMPHASIZES HOW THE VISUAL IMAGE OF
PHOTOGRAPHY HAS CONTRIBUTED TOWARD
MANY ACHIEVEMENTS IN RESEARCH AND ENGI-
NEERING, IN SPACE SCIENCE AND EXPLORATION
AND IN SPACE BENEFITS TO MANKIND.
    LC NO. 73-701277
PROD-NASA   DIST-NASA   1972

NEW YORK - THE ANYTIME CITY
                                                C 14 MIN
        16MM FILM OPTICAL SOUND
DEPICTS ALL THE THRILLS, WONDERS AND SPEC-
TACULAR SIGHTS OF THE DYNAMIC METROPOLIS,
NEW YORK.
PROD-MTP   DIST-MTP

NEW YORK CITY   C 14 MIN
        16MM FILM OPTICAL SOUND
FEATURES THE TRIP OF A YOUNG WOMAN TO
NEW YORK CITY.
PROD-MTP   DIST-MTP

NOBODY TOOK THE TIME   B 26 MIN
        16MM FILM OPTICAL SOUND   T
DEPICTS GHETTO CHILDREN HANDICAPPED WITH
LEARNING DISABILITIES AND MOST OFTEN LA-
BELED MENTALLY RETARDED. DEMONSTRATES
THAT BASIC TRUST IN HIMSELF AND OTHERS IS
THEIR FIRST NEED. SHOWS HOW HIGHLY STRUC-
TURED CLASSROOM AND PLAYGROUND TECH-
NIQUES RESULT IN AN UNDERSTANDING OF OR-
DER AND DEVELOPMENT OF LANGUAGE.
    LC NO. 73-701157
PROD-AIMS   DIST-AIMS   1973

**NOGUCHI - A SCULPTOR'S
WORLD**   C 28 MIN
        16MM FILM OPTICAL SOUND   H-C A
PRESENTS SCULPTOR ISAMU NOGUCHI TALKING
ABOUT HIS LIFE AND WORK AS HE IS SHOWN IN
DIFFERENT COUNTRIES WORKING ON DIFFERENT
PROJECTS. SHOWS EXAMPLES OF HIS WORK AS
EXHIBITED IN VARIOUS MUSEUMS AND PRE-
SENTS PHOTOGRAPHS OF HIS BALLET SET DE-
SIGNS AND FOUNTAINS AT THE OSAKA WORLD
EXPOSITION.
    LC NO. 73-700556
PROD-EAGLE   DIST-EAGLE   1972

**NOISE AND ITS EFFECTS ON
HEALTH**   C
        16MM FILM OPTICAL SOUND   J-C A
DESCRIBES THE DANGERS WHICH EXIST IN THE
HUMAN SYSTEM AS A RESULT OF NOISE. IN-
CLUDES SLOW AND PERMANENT HEARING LOSS
AND INCREASED INCIDENCE OF STRESS-INDUCED
PHYSICAL AND MENTAL ILLNESS.
    LC NO. 73-701222
PROD-FLMFR   DIST-FLMFR   1973

NORFOLK TOUR   C 24 MIN
        16MM FILM OPTICAL SOUND
PRESENTS A MEMORABLE TOUR THROUGH AMERI-
CAN HISTORY, RE-ENACTED IN COLONIAL HOMES,
ILLUSTRATED WITH OUR MIGHTIEST NAVAL BASE,
THE MAC ARTHUR MEMORIAL AND ENCHANTING
GARDENS-BY-THE-SEA.
PROD-MTP   DIST-MTP

NOT ME ALONE   C 31 MIN
        16MM FILM OPTICAL SOUND   H-C A
FOLLOWS A COUPLE AT NATURAL CHILDBIRTH
TRAINING CLASSES, PRACTICING BREATHING EX-
ERCISES AT HOME, SHARING LABOR AND DELIV-
ERY AND CARING FOR THE BABY IN THE HOSPI-
TAL.
PROD-POLYMR   DIST-POLYMR

NOVICE COMPANION   C 5 MIN
        16MM FILM OPTICAL SOUND   J-C A
SEE SERIES TITLE FOR DESCRIPTIVE STATEMENT.
FROM THE WONDERFUL WORLD OF SPORT - DOGS
SERIES.

PROD-SPORTI   DIST-AMERFI

**NURSE'S AIDE, ORDERLY AND
ATTENDANT--A SERIES**
                                                IND
PROD-COPI   DIST-COPI   1971

BEDBATH, THE - EMOTIONAL SUPPORT   13 MIN
BEDBATH, THE - PROCEDURE   15 MIN
GIVING A BEDPAN OR URINAL   18 MIN
OBSERVATION OF FECES AND URINE   19 MIN
PREVENTION AND CARE OF DECUBITI   17 MIN
SKIN, THE - FUNCTION AND CARE   16 MIN

**NUTRITION - THE INNER
ENVIRONMENT**   C 15 MIN
        16MM FILM OPTICAL SOUND   P-J
EXPLORES FROM THE EARLIEST TIME TO THE PRE-
SENT WHAT MEN HAVE EATEN, WHY AND WHAT
IT HAS DONE TO THEIR BODIES. SHOWS WHAT WE
MUST EAT AND HOW WE CAN IMPROVE OUR
HEALTH BY EATING PROPERLY. FROM THE AEF
HEALTH FILM LIBRARY SERIES.
    LC NO. 73-700969
PROD-AMEDFL   DIST-AMEDFL   1972

O

OBSERVATION OF BOILING   B 15 MIN
        16MM FILM OPTICAL SOUND
OBSERVES BOILING AND BOILING POINT, AS WELL
AS THE CHANGE IN BOILING POINT CAUSED BY
PRESSURE. ILLUSTRATES THE DIFFERENCE IN
BOILING POINTS ACCORDING TO MATERIALS.
PROD-IWANMI   DIST-IWANMI

**OBSERVATION OF FECES AND
URINE**   C 19 MIN
        16MM FILM OPTICAL SOUND   IND
ILLUSTRATES THE OBSERVATION OF THE CHARAC-
TERISTICS OF NORMAL AND ABNORMAL URINE
AND FECES AS AN INDICATOR OF THE PATIENT'S
CONDITION. FROM THE NURSE'S AIDE, ORDERLY
AND ATTENDANT SERIES.
    LC NO. 73-701055
PROD-COPI   DIST-COPI   1971

OBSERVATION OF ICE   C 14 MIN
        16MM FILM OPTICAL SOUND
OBSERVES ICE CRYSTALS IN AN EXPERIMENT
SHOWING ICE CRYSTALS FORMING BY SLOW MO-
TION PHOTOGRAPHY.
PROD-IWANMI   DIST-IWANMI

**OCEAN PHENOMENON - THE
DEEP SCATTERING LAYER**   C 29 MIN
        16MM FILM OPTICAL SOUND
DESCRIBES THE SEARCH FOR THE CAUSE OF
SOUND REFLECTING LAYERS OF MARINE LIFE LIV-
ING IN THE OCEANS OF THE WORLD AND HOW
NEW INFORMATION HAS HELPED IN SOLVING
THIS MYSTERY.
    LC NO. 73-701404
PROD-USN   DIST-USNAC   1970

**OCEANOGRAPHIC PREDICTION
SYSTEM**   C 33 MIN
        16MM FILM OPTICAL SOUND
DISCUSSES OCEANOGRAPHIC PREDICTION SYS-
TEMS AND PROGRAMS AND THEIR RELATIONSHIP
TO DEFENSE AND ECONOMIC NEEDS. TELLS HOW
PREDICTIONS INCREASE THE USE OF OCEANO-
GRAPHIC DATA FOR A FULLER UNDERSTANDING
AND EXPLORATION OF THE SEAS.
    LC NO. 73-701248
PROD-USN   DIST-USNAC   1966

**OFF THE BEATEN TRACK IN
ISRAEL**   C 28 MIN
        16MM FILM OPTICAL SOUND
PRESENTS A VIEW OF ISRAEL THROUGH THE EYES
OF A YOUNG BOY ACTING AS A TOURIST GUIDE TO
A VISITING AMERICAN.
PROD-ALDEN   DIST-ALDEN

**OFFSPRINGS HATCHING FROM
EGGS**   B 12 MIN
        16MM FILM OPTICAL SOUND
DESCRIBES THE ORGANIC CONNECTION BETWEEN
PARENTS, EGGS AND OFFSPRINGS.
PROD-IWANMI   DIST-IWANMI

OLD PLANE - BEARCAT   C 5 MIN
        16MM FILM OPTICAL SOUND   J-C A
SEE SERIES TITLE FOR DESCRIPTIVE STATEMENT.
FROM THE WONDERFUL WORLD OF SPORT - FLY-
ING SERIES.

PROD-SPORTI   DIST-AMERFI

ONCE UPON A TIME   C 11 MIN
        16MM FILM OPTICAL SOUND   P-J
EXPLORES TIME AS A PRACTICAL FORCE, AS AN
ABSTRACT CONCEPT AND AS A MEASURE OF LIFE.
CAPTURES THE ART AND WIZARDRY MAN HAS
USED OVER THE CENTURIES TO TELL TIME.
    LC NO. 73-701099
PROD-AFI   DIST-TEXFLM   1972

**OPPORTUNITIES FOR THE
DISADVANTAGED**   C 16 MIN
        16MM FILM OPTICAL SOUND   J-H
DISCUSSES THE DEVELOPMENT OF SPECIAL
STRATEGIES FOR THE MINORITY GROUP INDIVID-
UAL OR ECONOMICALLY DEPRIVED. DESCRIBES
AGENCIES AND PROGRAMS DESIGNED FOR THE
DISADVANTAGED ALONG WITH DRAMATIC EXAM-
PLES OF SUCCESS BY PEOPLE FROM MINORITY
BACKGROUNDS. FROM THE FUTURE STREET SE-
RIES.
    LC NO. 73-700966
PROD-AMEDFL   DIST-AMEDFL   1972

**OPPORTUNITIES IN HOTELS
AND MOTELS**   C 11 MIN
        16MM FILM OPTICAL SOUND
COVERS A VARIETY OF BEHIND-THE-SCENES JOBS
WITH FUTURES IN THE HOTEL AND MOTEL SERV-
ICE INDUSTRY. DESCRIBES YEAR-ROUND JOBS
FROM THE FRONT DESK, THROUGH THE KITCHEN
AND INTO THE BANQUET HALL AND COCKTAIL
LOUNGE.
    LC NO. 73-701061
PROD-USDL   DIST-USNAC   1968

OPPORTUNITIES IN LOGGING   C 28 MIN
        16MM FILM OPTICAL SOUND
SHOWS THE OPPORTUNITIES AVAILABLE TO
YOUNG MEN WHO LIKE THE OUTDOORS AND THE
CHALLENGE OF PHYSICAL WORK INCLUDING THE
OPERATION OF HEAVY EQUIPMENT. COVERS THE
MANY FACETS OF THE LOGGING INDUSTRY.
PROD-RARIG   DIST-RARIG   1967

OPPORTUNITIES IN WELDING   C 7 MIN
        16MM FILM OPTICAL SOUND
PRESENTS SCENES OF SPOT WELDING AND MAN-
UAL WELDING AT JOBS IN AIRCRAFT MAINTE-
NANCE, CONSTRUCTION AND SHIPYARDS AND
SHOWS WORKERS DOING AUTOMATIC TRACKROD,
FLEXCORE AND SHORT-ARC WELDING.
    LC NO. 73-701060
PROD-USDL   DIST-USNAC   1968

ORIGIN OF THE ELEMENTS, THE
                                                C 18 MIN
        16MM FILM OPTICAL SOUND   C A
EXPLORES THE FIVE MAJOR PROCESSES INSTRU-
MENTAL IN THE FORMATION OF ALL THE ELE-
MENTS IN THE UNIVERSE. EXPLAINS THE EVOLU-
TION OF THE UNIVERSE AND THE BIRTH, LIFE
AND DEATH OF STARS. FROM THE SCIENCE TO-
DAY SERIES.
    LC NO. 73-701094
PROD-CRMP   DIST-CRMP   1972

ORIGIN OF THE ELEMENTS, THE
                                                C 20 MIN
        16MM FILM OPTICAL SOUND
EXPLORES THE CONCURRENT NUCLEAR AND
STELLAR PROCESSES WHEREBY THE NATURAL EL-
EMENTS WERE CREATED AND CONTINUE TO BE
CREATED, WITHIN THE CORE OF EVOLVING STARS.
FROM THE SCIENCE TODAY FILM SERIES.
PROD-CRMP   DIST-CRMP

OSCAR ROBERTSON   C 5 MIN
        16MM FILM OPTICAL SOUND   J-C A
SEE SERIES TITLE FOR DESCRIPTIVE STATEMENT.
FROM THE WONDERFUL WORLD OF SPORT - BAS-
KETBALL SERIES.
PROD-SPORTI   DIST-AMERFI

**OUR FAMILY ALBUM - NUESTRO
ALBUM DE LA FAMILIA**   C 7 MIN
        16MM FILM OPTICAL SOUND
DISCUSSES FAMILY INTRODUCTION VIA PHOTO-
GRAPHS THE CHILDREN TAKE. FROM THE BREN-
TANO FOUNDATION BILINGUAL FILMS SERIES.
PROD-CAROUF   DIST-CAROUF

**OUR FIRST PLANE RIDE -
NUESTRO PRIMER VIAJE EN
AVION**   C 10 MIN
        16MM FILM OPTICAL SOUND
PRESENTS AN AIRPORT TOUR AND INSPECTION
OF THE BOEING 747. EXPLAINS A PLANE RIDE
AND AIRLINE CAREERS. FROM THE BRENTANO
FOUNDATION BILINGUAL FILMS SERIES.
PROD-CAROUF   DIST-CAROUF

OUT OF HANDS C 8 MIN
16MM FILM OPTICAL SOUND P-I
CONSIDERS THE MANY WAYS IN WHICH HUMANS
NEED AND USE THEIR HANDS. OBSERVES A MUSI-
CIAN, A TECHNICIAN, KINDERGARTNERS FINGER-
PAINTING, A POTTER, A GLASS CUTTER, A SILVER-
SMITH AND A DRAFTSMAN.
LC NO. 73-701256
PROD-KINGSP DIST-HRAW 1972

**OVER THE LINE - BEACH
SPORTS** C 5 MIN
16MM FILM OPTICAL SOUND J-C A
SEE SERIES TITLE FOR DESCRIPTIVE STATEMENT.
FROM THE WONDERFUL WORLD OF SPORT -
OTHER SERIES.
PROD-SPORTI DIST-AMERFI

OZE SWAMP C 14 MIN
16MM FILM OPTICAL SOUND
OBSERVES A SWAMP EXISTING ON A PLATEAU IN
ITS COMPLETE FORM, RARELY SEEN ELSEWHERE
IN THE WORLD. POINTS OUT THAT OZE SWAMP IS
LOCATED ON A 1,400 METER HIGH PLATEAU.
PROD-IWANMI DIST-IWANMI

P

**P A T C H - POSITIVE
APPROACH TO CHANGING
HUMANS** X 16 MIN
16MM FILM OPTICAL SOUND C A
ILLUSTRATES THE PROCESS TEACHERS GO
THROUGH TO ACQUIRE THE SKILLS FOR IMPROV-
ING STUDENTS' ACADEMIC SKILLS, CONTROLLING
THEIR INAPPROPRIATE BEHAVIOR AND MOTIVAT-
ING THEM IN A POSITIVE WAY.
LC NO. 73-701236
PROD-CORF DIST-CORF 1973

PAKISTAN C
16MM FILM OPTICAL SOUND
SEE SERIES TITLE FOR DESCRIPTIVE STATEMENT.
FROM THE PORT OF CALL SERIES.
PROD-PUI DIST-PUI

PARALLEL BARS C 5 MIN
16MM FILM OPTICAL SOUND J-C A
SEE SERIES TITLE FOR DESCRIPTIVE STATEMENT.
FROM THE WONDERFUL WORLD OF SPORT - GYM-
NASTICS SERIES.
PROD-SPORTI DIST-AMERFI

PARK ON OUR BLOCK, A B 23 MIN
16MM FILM OPTICAL SOUND J-C A
DESCRIBES HOW WITH INDIVIDUAL AND ORGANI-
ZATION PARTICIPATION IN A COMMUNITY PRO-
JECT, A NEIGHBORHOOD PARK WAS CREATED
OUT OF A GARBAGE DUMP.
LC NO. 73-701141
PROD-ROBINP DIST-WASHBF 1973

PARTICLES OF SNOW C 14 MIN
16MM FILM OPTICAL SOUND
OBSERVES NATURAL SNOW AND HIGH ALTITUDE
SNOW ARTIFICIALLY PRODUCED IN A LOW TEM-
PERATURE LABORATORY TO ILLUSTRATE DIFFER-
ENCES IN THE INDIVIDUAL SNOW PARTICLES. DE-
SCRIBES THE VARYING FORMS OF CRYSTALS AC-
CORDING TO DIFFERENT TEMPERATURES.
PROD-IWANMI DIST-IWANMI

PARTNERS, THE B
16MM FILM OPTICAL SOUND J-C A
CONSIDERS THE POINT AND PURPOSE OF THE
LAW AS PROTECTOR AND OPPORTUNITY MAKER
IN THE DAILY WORLD OF BUSINESS AFFAIRS. DIS-
CUSSES THE PARTNERSHIP AND CORPORATION
FORMS OF BUSINESS ORGANIZATION. FROM THE
QUEST FOR CERTAINTY SERIES.
LC NO. 73-701036
PROD-UMITV DIST-UMITV 1962

PASSOVER C 15 MIN
16MM FILM OPTICAL SOUND
SHOWS HOW THE FESTIVAL OF PASSOVER IS CELE-
BRATED IN ISRAEL.
PROD-ALDEN DIST-ALDEN

**PEACEFUL USE OF NUCLEAR
EXPLOSIVES** B 56 MIN
16MM FILM OPTICAL SOUND H-C A
INTRODUCES DR EDWARD TELLER, THE MAN
LARGELY RESPONSIBLE FOR THE DEVELOPMENT
OF THE H-BOMB, WHO WITH SIX OTHER NUCLEAR
SCIENTISTS, DEALS WITH THE POSITIVE APPLICA-
TIONS OF ATOMIC ENERGY.
PROD-BBCTV DIST-TIMLIF

PENALTY STORY C 5 MIN
16MM FILM OPTICAL SOUND J-C A
SEE SERIES TITLE FOR DESCRIPTIVE STATEMENT.
FROM THE WONDERFUL WORLD OF SPORT -
HOCKEY SERIES.
PROD-SPORTI DIST-AMERFI

PENN RELAYS C 5 MIN
16MM FILM OPTICAL SOUND J-C A
SEE SERIES TITLE FOR DESCRIPTIVE STATEMENT.
FROM THE WONDERFUL WORLD OF SPORT -
TRACK AND FIELD SERIES.
PROD-SPORTI DIST-AMERFI

**PEPE TEACHES US - PEPE NOS
ENSENA** C 7 MIN
16MM FILM OPTICAL SOUND
INTRODUCES WORDS FOR PARTS OF THE BODY.
FROM THE BRENTANO FOUNDATION BILINGUAL
FILMS SERIES.
PROD-CAROUF DIST-CAROUF

**PERFORMANCE OF ROOTS,
STEMS AND LEAVES** C 14 MIN
16MM FILM OPTICAL SOUND
TELLS HOW AND WHERE THE PLANT GETS THE
WATER AND NUTRITION REQUIRED FOR ITS
GROWTH. DESCRIBES THE ACTION OF ROOTS,
STEMS AND LEAVES.
PROD-IWANMI DIST-IWANMI

PERMANENT PROTECTION C 12 MIN
16MM FILM OPTICAL SOUND
POINTS OUT THAT RUST IS A LEADING DE-
STROYER OF THE AUTOMOBILE AND IS DANGER-
OUS AS WELL AS UNSIGHTLY. EXPLAINS WHAT
CAUSES RUST AND HOW YOU CAN PROTECT YOUR
CAR AGAINST IT.
PROD-MTP DIST-MTP

**PERSON TO PERSON - MAKING
COMMUNICATIONS WORK FOR
YOU** C 10 MIN
16MM FILM OPTICAL SOUND H-C A
EXPLORES FOUR AREAS OF OFFICE COMMUNICA-
TION, INCLUDING FACIAL EXPRESSION, BODY
LANGUAGE, EYE CONTACT AND VOCAL ENTHUSI-
ASM. PRESENTS EXAMPLES OF BOTH POSITIVE
AND NEGATIVE COMMUNICATION IN EACH AREA.
PROD-SAIF DIST-SAIF

PETE MARAVICH C 5 MIN
16MM FILM OPTICAL SOUND J-C A
SEE SERIES TITLE FOR DESCRIPTIVE STATEMENT.
FROM THE WONDERFUL WORLD OF SPORT - BAS-
KETBALL SERIES.
PROD-SPORTI DIST-AMERFI

PETER AND THE WOLF C 30 MIN
16MM FILM OPTICAL SOUND
PRESENTS SERGE PROKOFIEV'S ORCHESTRAL FA-
BLE 'PETER AND THE WOLF' TRANSLATED TO THE
SCREEN AS AN ANIMATED CARTOON.
PROD-DISNEY DIST-DISNEY

PHOTO TUBES C 14 MIN
16MM FILM OPTICAL SOUND
DISCUSSES THE PRINCIPLES OF PHOTO TUBES,
THE INTERIOR STRUCTURE OF THE PHOTO TUBE,
THE RELATIONSHIP BETWEEN LIGHT AND ELEC-
TRIC CURRENT AND THE FLOW OF ELECTRONS
WITH LINEAL DRAWINGS.
PROD-IWANMI DIST-IWANMI

**PIAGET'S DEVELOPMENTAL
THEORY - THE GROWTH OF
INTELLIGENCE IN THE
PRESCHOOL YEARS** C 32 MIN
16MM FILM OPTICAL SOUND A
FEATURES CHILDREN FROM THREE TO SIX YEARS
PERFORMING TASKS WHICH REVEAL HOW THEY
THINK AS THEY SORT OBJECTS, PUT THEM IN
ONE-TO-ONE CORRESPONDENCE AND ARRANGE
THEM IN ORDER OF SIZE. ILLUSTRATES DEVELOP-
MENTAL CHANGES AND CLARIFIES CERTAIN PIAG-
ETIAN TERMS OFTEN MYSTIFYING TO THE STU-
DENT OF PIAGET. FROM THE PIAGET'S DEVELOP-
MENTAL THEORY SERIES.
LC NO. 73-701278
PROD-DAVFMS DIST-DAVFMS 1972

PICKLES C 11 MIN
16MM FILM OPTICAL SOUND H-C A
COMMENTS ON THE MANY ABSURD PREDICA-
MENTS OF DAY TO DAY LIVING. USES IRONY, MET-
APHOR AND SATIRE TO FOCUS ON SOME NOT-SO-
SELF EVIDENT TRUTHS.
LC NO. 73-701431
PROD-BFA DIST-BFA 1973

PICTURE, THE C 16 MIN
16MM FILM OPTICAL SOUND
STARS BOB REINER AS A YOUNG LOSER WHO DES-
PERATELY TRIES TO MAKE IT WITH A PREGNANT
GIRL. DEPICTS HOW SHE PARRIES THE FUMBLING
ADVANCES OF HER UNWELCOME GUEST BY PLAY-
ING SOLITAIRE AND STAYING AWAKE UNTIL HE
WEARIES OF PURSUIT.
PROD-AMERFI DIST-AMERFI

PLACE TO LEARN, A C 19 MIN
16MM FILM OPTICAL SOUND A
DEALS WITH THE MULTIPURPOSE SERVICES OF A
VITAL, GROWING COMMUNITY COLLEGE LEARNING
RESOURCE CENTER.
LC NO. 73-700692
PROD-DUPAGE DIST-DUPAGE 1972

**PLIGHT OF SOVIET JEWELRY,
THE - LET MY PEOPLE GO** B 28 MIN
16MM FILM OPTICAL SOUND
POINTS OUT THAT THERE ARE THREE MILLION
JEWS LIVING IN SOVIET RUSSIA TODAY, BUT JEW-
ISH RELIGIOUS AND CULTURAL LIFE IS NON-EXIS-
TENT. EXPLAINS THAT SOMEHOW JEWISH IDEN-
TITY IS VERY MUCH ALIVE AND THE LONGING FOR
ISRAEL IS STRONGER THAN EVER, BUT ONLY A
FEW ARE ALLOWED TO EMIGRATE.
PROD-ALDEN DIST-ALDEN

POEM FIELD NO. 1 C 6 MIN
16MM FILM OPTICAL SOUND J-C A
PRESENTS A VISUAL EXPERIMENT WITH LAN-
GUAGE.
LC NO. 73-701191
PROD-UWF DIST-UEVA 1967

POETRY OF BRIAN PATTEN, THE C 24 MIN
16MM FILM OPTICAL SOUND J-C A
FEATURES LOVE POET BRIAN PATTEN READING
SELECTIONS FROM HIS OWN WORK, DESCRIBING
HOW HE FIRST BECAME INTERESTED IN WRITING
POETRY.
LC NO. 73-700688
PROD-LONWTV DIST-LONWTV 1972

POP B 3 MIN
16MM FILM OPTICAL SOUND H-C A
PRESENTS AN ANIMATED FILM WHICH MATCHES
THE VISUAL VARIATIONS PERCEIVED DURING A
TRAIN RIDE. DESCRIBES THE PULSATING RHYTHM
OF A TRAIN PASSING OVER THE RAILROAD
TRACKS.
LC NO. 73-701433
PROD-BFA DIST-BFA 1973

POPCORN LADY C 11 MIN
16MM FILM OPTICAL SOUND I-C A
VISITS A SMALL TOWN IN UPSTATE NEW YORK TO
WHICH CHANGE HAS COME SLOWLY. PORTRAYS
ONE OF THE TOWN'S MOST FAMOUS RESIDENTS,
THE POPCORN LADY AND SHOWS HER STEAM
POPCORN MACHINE OF 1925 VINTAGE.
LC NO. 73-701210
PROD-SCHLAT DIST-SCHLAT 1973

POPE PAUL'S VISIT TO ISRAEL B 10 MIN
16MM FILM OPTICAL SOUND
PRESENTS A PICTORIAL RECORD OF THE PON-
TIFF'S 1964 PILGRIMAGE TO A PART OF THE HOLY
LAND.
PROD-ALDEN DIST-ALDEN

**POPULATION EXPANSION AND
BIRTH CONTROL** B 28 MIN
16MM FILM OPTICAL SOUND H-C A
DISCUSSES WORLD POPULATION PROBLEMS AND
METHODS OF BIRTH CONTROL WHICH ARE USED
IN FAMILY PLANNING. FROM THE SEX IN AMERICA
CULTURE SERIES.
LC NO. 73-701218
PROD-CHM DIST-CHM 1967

PORCH GLIDER C 25 MIN
16MM FILM OPTICAL SOUND
TAKES THE PORCH GLIDER AS A FOCAL POINT
AND DEPICTS DAYTIME MOVEMENT, CHILDREN
RUNNING AND BICYCLES AND CARS GOING BY.
PRESENTS A POETIC AND DREAM-LIKE LOOK AT
ADOLESCENT LOVEMAKING IN THE NIGHTTIME
SCENE.
PROD-AMERFI DIST-AMERFI

PORT OF CALL--A SERIES
PRESENTS FASCINATING SAFARIS TO FAR-OFF, EX-
OTIC LANDS AS SEEN THROUGH A CHILD'S EYES.
HIGHLIGHTS THE STRANGE AND UNUSUAL CUS-
TOMS, ARCHITECTURE AND EVERY DAY THINGS
THAT ARE SO DIFFERENT FROM OURS.
PROD-PUI DIST-PUI

BALI
CEYLON
EGYPT
GREECE
HAITI
HAWAII
HONG KONG
INDIA
ISRAEL
JAPAN
KENYA
PAKISTAN
SINGAPORE
SYRIA
TURKEY
ZANZIBAR

POSITIVE-NEGATIVE   B
16MM FILM OPTICAL SOUND
RECORDS A YOUNG WOMAN'S HEAD WITH SHOULDER LEVEL STRAIGHT HAIR ROTATING FULL CIRCLE FROM PROFILE TO FULL VIEW. FEATURES A SPLIT SCREEN WITH THE RIGHT SIDE BEING POSITIVE AND THE LEFT NEGATIVE TO SHOW THE BACK OF WHAT IS SEEN AT THE RIGHT.
PROD-VISRES   DIST-VISRES   1970

POTTERS OF JAPAN, PT 1   C 16 MIN
16MM FILM OPTICAL SOUND
REVEALS THE INFLUENCE OF JAPANESE POTTERY ON WORLD CERAMICS. INCLUDES VISITS WITH FIVE FAMOUS JAPANESE CERAMISTS. FROM THE CERAMIC ART SERIES.
PROD-MGHT   DIST-MGHT

POTTERS OF JAPAN, PT 2   C 15 MIN
16MM FILM OPTICAL SOUND
REVEALS THE INFLUENCE OF JAPANESE POTTERY ON WORLD CERAMICS. INCLUDES VISITS WITH FIVE FAMOUS JAPANESE CERAMISTS. FROM THE CERAMIC ART SERIES.
PROD-MGHT   DIST-MGHT

POTTERS OF THE USA, PT 1   C 16 MIN
16MM FILM OPTICAL SOUND
SHOWS FOUR OUTSTANDING AMERICAN POTTERS AT WORK. DEMONSTRATES A WIDE VARIETY OF FORMING AND GLAZING METHODS. FROM THE CERAMIC ART SERIES.
PROD-MGHT   DIST-MGHT

POTTERS OF THE USA, PT 2   C 17 MIN
16MM FILM OPTICAL SOUND
SHOWS FOUR OUTSTANDING AMERICAN POTTERS AT WORK. DEMONSTRATES A WIDE VARIETY OF FORMING AND GLAZING METHODS. FROM THE CERAMIC ART SERIES.
PROD-MGHT   DIST-MGHT

POWER PLAY   C 5 MIN
16MM FILM OPTICAL SOUND   J-C A
SEE SERIES TITLE FOR DESCRIPTIVE STATEMENT. FROM THE WONDERFUL WORLD OF SPORT - HOCKEY SERIES.
PROD-SPORTI   DIST-AMERFI

**PREVENTION AND CARE OF
DECUBITI**   C 17 MIN
16MM FILM OPTICAL SOUND   IND
DESCRIBES THE APPEARANCE OF DECUBITI (BEDSORES), THE TYPES OF PATIENTS WHO ARE PRONE TO DEVELOP DECUBITI AND THE METHODS FOR PREVENTION AND CARE OF DECUBITI. FROM THE NURSE'S AIDE, ORDERLY AND ATTENDANT SERIES.
LC NO. 73-701054
PROD-COPI   DIST-COPI   1971

**PRIMARY SAFETY - ON THE
WAY TO SCHOOL**   C 11 MIN
16MM FILM OPTICAL SOUND
REVISED VERSION OF 'SAFETY ON THE WAY TO SCHOOL.' PRESENTS YOUNGSTERS WHO TELL ABOUT THE DRAWINGS THEY'VE MADE DEPICTING DANGERS ON THE WAY TO SCHOOL.
LC NO. 73-701238
PROD-CORF   DIST-CORF   1973

**PRIME MINISTER GOLDA MEIR'S
VISIT TO THE USA IN 1969**   B 13 MIN
16MM FILM OPTICAL SOUND
DOCUMENTS THE OFFICIAL VISIT OF THE PRIME MINISTER OF ISRAEL TO THE WHITE HOUSE, FOLLOWED BY A TRIUMPHANT TOUR FROM COAST TO COAST.
PROD-ALDEN   DIST-ALDEN

**PRINCIPLES OF PAPERWORK
MANAGEMENT - BETTER
CORRESPONDENCE PRACTICE**   C 11 MIN
16MM FILM OPTICAL SOUND
DISCUSSES THE EFFECTIVE HANDLING OF CORRESPONDENCE, INCLUDING THE ELIMINATION OF UNNECESSARY COPIES OF LETTERS, THE USE OF FORM LETTERS AND GUIDES, THE USE OF DICTATION MACHINES AND THE ELIMINATION OF UNNECESSARY FORMALITIES.
PROD-BEF   DIST-BEF

**PRO FOOTBALL - DUMP THE
QUARTERBACK**   C 5 MIN
16MM FILM OPTICAL SOUND   J-C A
SEE SERIES TITLE FOR DESCRIPTIVE STATEMENT. FROM THE WONDERFUL WORLD OF SPORT - FOOTBALL SERIES.
PROD-SPORTI   DIST-AMERFI

PRO FOOTBALL - RUNNERS   C 5 MIN
16MM FILM OPTICAL SOUND   J-C A
SEE SERIES TITLE FOR DESCRIPTIVE STATEMENT. FROM THE WONDERFUL WORLD OF SPORT - FOOTBALL SERIES.
PROD-SPORTI   DIST-AMERFI

PROPERTIES OF CLAY   C 14 MIN
16MM FILM OPTICAL SOUND
DISCUSSES THE PROPERTIES AND USE OF CLAY AS WELL AS NATURAL CALAMITIES CAUSED BY CLAY. SHOWS THE FORMATION OF A CLAY BED AND HOW A CLAY BED CAUSED BY VOLCANIC ERUPTION SETTLES.
PROD-IWANMI   DIST-IWANMI

PURIM   C 15 MIN
16MM FILM OPTICAL SOUND
SHOWS HOW THE FESTIVAL OF PURIM IS CELEBRATED IN ISRAEL.
PROD-ALDEN   DIST-ALDEN

Q

QUEBEC WINTER CARNIVAL   C 5 MIN
16MM FILM OPTICAL SOUND   J-C A
SEE SERIES TITLE FOR DESCRIPTIVE STATEMENT. FROM THE WONDERFUL WORLD OF SPORT - OTHER SERIES.
PROD-SPORTI   DIST-AMERFI

**QUEST FOR CERTAINTY--A
SERIES**
J-C A
PROD-UMITV   DIST-UMITV   1962
CIVIL WRONG, THE   29 MIN
PARTNERS, THE   29 MIN

QUICK BILLY   C 40 MIN
16MM FILM OPTICAL SOUND
PRESENTS AN EXPERIMENTAL FILM DEALING WITH BILLY'S RECOVERY FROM A LONG BOUT WITH HEPATITIS.
PROD-AMERFI   DIST-AMERFI

QUIET, PLEASE   C 24 MIN
16MM FILM OPTICAL SOUND
POINTS OUT THAT THE LEAST UNDERSTOOD OF ALL ENVIRONMENTAL HAZARDS IS NOISE POLLUTION OR UNWANTED SOUND. EXPLAINS WHAT NOISE IS, WHERE IT MOST COMMONLY OCCURS AND WHAT CAN BE DONE TO REDUCE OR ELIMINATE IT BY INDUSTRY AND RESEARCH LABORATORIES.
PROD-WILCOX   DIST-WILCOX

R

**RACE, INTELLIGENCE AND
EDUCATION**   B 56 MIN
16MM FILM OPTICAL SOUND   H-C A
INTRODUCES PROFESSOR H J EYSENCK, ADVOCATE OF THE THEORY THAT HEREDITY LARGELY INFLUENCES INTELLIGENCE. PRESENTS SIX OTHER SCIENTISTS WHO WITH EYSENCK DISCUSS THEIR CONTROVERSIAL IDEAS AS WELL AS THOSE OF OTHER AMERICAN PSYCHOLOGISTS AND SOCIOLOGISTS.
PROD-BBCTV   DIST-TIMLIF

RACING (FACTORY) TEAM   C 5 MIN
16MM FILM OPTICAL SOUND   J-C A
SEE SERIES TITLE FOR DESCRIPTIVE STATEMENT. FROM THE WONDERFUL WORLD OF SPORT - SNOWMOBILES SERIES.
PROD-SPORTI   DIST-AMERFI

RACING (LACONIA N H)   C 5 MIN
16MM FILM OPTICAL SOUND   J-C A
SEE SERIES TITLE FOR DESCRIPTIVE STATEMENT. FROM THE WONDERFUL WORLD OF SPORT - SNOWMOBILES SERIES.
PROD-SPORTI   DIST-AMERFI

**RADIO-OPERATED RACERS -
MODELISTS**   C 5 MIN
16MM FILM OPTICAL SOUND   J-C A
SEE SERIES TITLE FOR DESCRIPTIVE STATEMENT. FROM THE WONDERFUL WORLD OF SPORT - OTHER SERIES.
PROD-SPORTI   DIST-AMERFI

RAPUNZEL   C
16MM FILM OPTICAL SOUND
SEE SERIES TITLE FOR DESCRIPTIVE STATEMENT. FROM THE FAIRY TALE TIME SERIES.
PROD-PUI   DIST-PUI

RAZOR BLADES   C 26 MIN
16MM FILM OPTICAL SOUND
PRESENTS AN EXPERIMENTAL FILM TO BE SHOWN ON TWO PROJECTORS SIMULTANEOUSLY. PICTURES THE RECURRING THEME OF THE COSMIC, DYNAMIC UNITY OF OPPOSITES.
PROD-AMERFI   DIST-AMERFI

READING IS FOR US TOO   C 29 MIN
16MM FILM OPTICAL SOUND   C A
ILLUSTRATES PROCEDURES DEVELOPED BY DR D H SCOTT WHICH ENABLE MENTALLY RETARDED CHILDREN TO LEARN TO READ. DETAILS HOW A CHILD'S READING READINESS CAN BE IMPROVED THROUGH A PRE-READING PROGRAM DR SCOTT CALLS A 'FLYING START.'
LC NO. 73-701076
PROD-CCMFI   DIST-CCMFI   1970

READING MOTIVATION--A SERIES
P-I
PROD-BFA   DIST-BFA   1972
ELEPHANT EATS, THE, PENGUIN EATS,
THE - ..   10 MIN
SQUIRRELS ARE UP, SQUIRRELS ARE
DOWN - ..   10 MIN

RECEIVERS   C 5 MIN
16MM FILM OPTICAL SOUND   J-C A
SEE SERIES TITLE FOR DESCRIPTIVE STATEMENT. FROM THE WONDERFUL WORLD OF SPORT - FOOTBALL SERIES.
PROD-SPORTI   DIST-AMERFI

RECYCLED REFLECTIONS   C 12 MIN
16MM FILM OPTICAL SOUND   I-C A
SHOWS WHAT IS BEING DONE BY THE AUTOMOBILE INDUSTRY TO CONSERVE RESOURCES BY RECYCLING AUTOMOBILE BUMPERS.
LC NO. 73-701084
PROD-FLMFR   DIST-FLMFR   1973

RED SCHOENDIST   C 5 MIN
16MM FILM OPTICAL SOUND   J-C A
SEE SERIES TITLE FOR DESCRIPTIVE STATEMENT. FROM THE WONDERFUL WORLD OF SPORT - BASEBALL SERIES.
PROD-SPORTI   DIST-AMERFI

REEL CASTING   C 5 MIN
16MM FILM OPTICAL SOUND   J-C A
SEE SERIES TITLE FOR DESCRIPTIVE STATEMENT. FROM THE WONDERFUL WORLD OF SPORT - FISHING SERIES.
PROD-SPORTI   DIST-AMERFI

REFEREE STORY   C 5 MIN
16MM FILM OPTICAL SOUND   J-C A
SEE SERIES TITLE FOR DESCRIPTIVE STATEMENT. FROM THE WONDERFUL WORLD OF SPORT - BASKETBALL SERIES.
PROD-SPORTI   DIST-AMERFI

**REFORMATION - AGE OF
REVOLT**   C 24 MIN
16MM FILM OPTICAL SOUND   J-H
INTRODUCES THE POLITICAL, SOCIAL AND RELIGIOUS CLIMATE THAT EXISTED IN EUROPE DURING THE SIXTEENTH CENTURY. EMPHASIZES THE

RELIGIOUS REFORMS OF MARTIN LUTHER AS INDICATORS OF THE FUTURE TREND AND REFLECTION OF THEIR HISTORICAL CONTEXT.
LC NO. 73-701227
PROD-EBEC   DIST-EBEC   1973

REFRACTION AND SHADOW OF LIGHT   C 14 MIN
16MM FILM OPTICAL SOUND
EXPLAINS THE PRINCIPLE AND PHOTOGRAPHIC METHOD OF THE SCHLIEREN DEVICE TO LOOK INTO THE WORLD OF SHADOW WHICH CANNOT BE SEEN WITH THE NAKED EYE.
PROD-IWANMI   DIST-IWANMI

REFRACTION OF LIGHT   C 14 MIN
16MM FILM OPTICAL SOUND
EXPLAINS THE CONSTRUCTION OF LIGHT REFRACTION. SHOWS THE REFRACTION OF LIGHT BY WATER AND THE DEGREE RELATIONSHIP BETWEEN THE INCIDENCE ANGLE AND REFRACTION.
PROD-IWANMI   DIST-IWANMI

REFRIGERATION - COMPRESSOR CONTROLS   B 6 MIN
16MM FILM OPTICAL SOUND
DEPICTS HOW THE LOW PRESSURE SWITCH TURNS ON AND OFF THE COMPRESSOR MOTOR VIA MOTOR CONTROLLER AND HOW SAFETY CONTROLS PROTECT COMPRESSOR AND MOTOR.
LC NO. 73-701074
PROD-USN   DIST-USNAC   1957

REFRIGERATION - CONDENSER CONTROLS   B 5 MIN
16MM FILM OPTICAL SOUND
SHOWS CONTROLS FOR THE CONDENSER OF A REFRIGERATION SYSTEM. DEMONSTRATES HOW THE REFRIGERATION PRESSURE IN THE HIGH PRESSURE LINE IS USED BY THE WATER-REGULATING VALVE TO CONTROL THE FLOW OF WATER THROUGH THE CONDENSER. TELLS HOW USE OF THE WATER FAILURE SWITCH SERVES AS PROTECTION FOR THE COMPRESSOR.
LC NO. 73-701075
PROD-USN   DIST-USNAC   1957

RELIEF PITCHER STORY   C 5 MIN
16MM FILM OPTICAL SOUND   J-C A
SEE SERIES TITLE FOR DESCRIPTIVE STATEMENT. FROM THE WONDERFUL WORLD OF SPORT - BASEBALL SERIES.
PROD-SPORTI   DIST-AMERFI

RESEARCH   C 5 MIN
16MM FILM OPTICAL SOUND   J-C A
SEE SERIES TITLE FOR DESCRIPTIVE STATEMENT. FROM THE WONDERFUL WORLD OF SPORT - AEROBICS SERIES.
PROD-SPORTI   DIST-AMERFI

RESTORATION   C 5 MIN
16MM FILM OPTICAL SOUND   J-C A
SEE SERIES TITLE FOR DESCRIPTIVE STATEMENT. FROM THE WONDERFUL WORLD OF SPORT - CARS, AUTO RACING SERIES.
PROD-SPORTI   DIST-AMERFI

RETURN TO MASADA   B 25 MIN
16MM FILM OPTICAL SOUND
DEPICTS THE EXCAVATIONS OF MASADA, THE LAST JEWISH STRONGHOLD THAT RESISTED THE ROMAN LEGIONS IN THE FIRST MILLENNIUM.
PROD-ALDEN   DIST-ALDEN

RHYTHM OF TOMMORW   C 12 MIN
16MM FILM OPTICAL SOUND
SHOWS HOW TECHNOLOGY HELPS A NEW NATION'S PROGRESS.
PROD-ALDEN   DIST-ALDEN

RIGHT ON   C 80 MIN
16MM FILM OPTICAL SOUND   J-C A
PRESENTS DAVID NELSON, FELIPE LUCIANO AND GYLAU KAIR, BLACK REVOLUTIONARY AND SELF-PROFESSED ORIGINAL LAST POETS, PHOTOGRAPHED AGAINST THEIR GHETTO BACKGROUNDS, RECITING THEIR POETRY.
PROD-NLC   DIST-NLC

RIVER OTTER   C 12 MIN
16MM FILM OPTICAL SOUND   P-J
PRESENTS A LANGUAGE ORIENTED PROGRAM ABOUT AMERICAN WILDLIFE DESIGNED TO INCREASE STUDENTS' ORAL AND READING SKILLS. FROM THE FILMWAYS TO READING, SERIES A - ANIMAL FRIENDS SERIES.
LC NO. 73-700968
PROD-AMEDFL   DIST-AMEDFL   1972

RIVERS   C 14 MIN
16MM FILM OPTICAL SOUND
SHOWS HOW VARIOUS TYPES OF TOPOGRAPHY ARE FORMED BY THE DIFFERING ACTIONS OF RIVERS. INCLUDES ILLUSTRATIONS OF A V-SHAPED GORGE, A TERRACED RIVER BANK, AN ALLUVIAL CONE AND A DELTA.
PROD-IWANMI   DIST-IWANMI

RODEO SCHOOL - BAREBACK RIDING   C 5 MIN
16MM FILM OPTICAL SOUND   J-C A
SEE SERIES TITLE FOR DESCRIPTIVE STATEMENT. FROM THE WONDERFUL WORLD OF SPORT - HORSES, RACING, POLO, RODEO SERIES.
PROD-SPORTI   DIST-AMERFI

RODEO SCHOOL - BULL RIDING   C 5 MIN
16MM FILM OPTICAL SOUND   J-C A
SEE SERIES TITLE FOR DESCRIPTIVE STATEMENT. FROM THE WONDERFUL WORLD OF SPORT - HORSES, RACING, POLO, RODEO SERIES.
PROD-SPORTI   DIST-AMERFI

RODEO SCHOOL - GRADUATE   C 5 MIN
16MM FILM OPTICAL SOUND   J-C A
SEE SERIES TITLE FOR DESCRIPTIVE STATEMENT. FROM THE WONDERFUL WORLD OF SPORT - HORSES, RACING, POLO, RODEO SERIES.
PROD-SPORTI   DIST-AMERFI

RODEO SCHOOL - LARRY MAHAN   C 5 MIN
16MM FILM OPTICAL SOUND   J-C A
SEE SERIES TITLE FOR DESCRIPTIVE STATEMENT. FROM THE WONDERFUL WORLD OF SPORT - HORSES, RACING, POLO, RODEO SERIES.
PROD-SPORTI   DIST-AMERFI

RODEO SCHOOL - SADDLE BRONC RIDE   C 5 MIN
16MM FILM OPTICAL SOUND   J-C A
SEE SERIES TITLE FOR DESCRIPTIVE STATEMENT. FROM THE WONDERFUL WORLD OF SPORT - HORSES, RACING, POLO, RODEO SERIES.
PROD-SPORTI   DIST-AMERFI

ROLE OF YEAST   B 12 MIN
16MM FILM OPTICAL SOUND
DESCRIBES THE CHARACTERISTICS OF YEAST FUNGUS AND ITS USE. OBSERVES A SINGLE YEAST AND THE GERMINATION OF A PARENT CELL. SHOWS THE ACTION OF FERMENTATION IN CHANGING SUGAR TO ALCOHOL.
PROD-IWANMI   DIST-IWANMI

ROMAN MIELEC   C 5 MIN
16MM FILM OPTICAL SOUND   J-C A
SEE SERIES TITLE FOR DESCRIPTIVE STATEMENT. FROM THE WONDERFUL WORLD OF SPORT - WEIGHTLIFTING SERIES.
PROD-SPORTI   DIST-AMERFI

ROOTS AND ALL   C 15 MIN
16MM FILM OPTICAL SOUND
SHOWS HOW AMINO TRIAZOLE WEEDKILLER SOLVES THE PROBLEM OF CONTROLLING CANADA THISTLE, CATTAILS, POISON IVY AND OTHER TOUGH PERENNIAL WEEDS BY KILLING THE ENTIRE PLANT.
PROD-MTP   DIST-MTP

ROOTS OF MADNESS   B 58 MIN
16MM FILM OPTICAL SOUND
COVERS THE YEARS FROM THE END OF THE MANCHU DYNASTY TO THE ADVENT OF MAO TSE-TUNG, WITH DETAILS OF CHIANG KAI-SHEK AND HIS ACTIVITIES.
PROD-XEROX   DIST-XEROX

ROSE ARGOFF   B 6 MIN
16MM FILM OPTICAL SOUND   H-C A
DEPICTS THE LIFE OF ROSE ARGOFF, A 75-YEAR-OLD RUSSIAN EMIGRANT WHO SUBSISTS ON HER SOCIAL SECURITY AND A SMALL UNION PENSION AND WILL NOT APPLY FOR WELFARE. SHOWS HER LIFE ON THE LOWER EAST SIDE OF NEW YORK, VICTIMIZED BY ADDICTS AND WITH STREETS THAT ARE UNSAFE.
PROD-CAROUF   DIST-CAROUF

ROY CAMPANELLA - WHAT HAPPENED TO   C 5 MIN
16MM FILM OPTICAL SOUND   J-C A
SEE SERIES TITLE FOR DESCRIPTIVE STATEMENT. FROM THE WONDERFUL WORLD OF SPORT - BASEBALL SERIES.
PROD-SPORTI   DIST-AMERFI

RUMOURS OF WAR   C 60 MIN
16MM FILM OPTICAL SOUND
PRESENTS A BEHIND-THE-SCENES VIEW OF MAN'S POWER TO DESTROY ALL HUMANITY. EXAMINES THE MINUTEMEN MISSILE SILOS WHERE MINUTEMEN TRIGGER MEN WORK IN PAIRS, EACH ARMED TO KILL THE OTHER IN CASE OF A MENTAL BREAKDOWN.
PROD-BBCTV   DIST-TIMLIF

RUMPELSTILTSKIN   C
16MM FILM OPTICAL SOUND
SEE SERIES TITLE FOR DESCRIPTIVE STATEMENT. FROM THE FAIRY TALE TIME SERIES.
PROD-PUI   DIST-PUI

RURAL DRIVING   C 10 MIN
16MM FILM OPTICAL SOUND
DISCUSSES SPEED RELATIONSHIPS WITH OTHER VEHICLES AND ROADWAY ELEMENTS. FROM THE DRIVER EDUCATION SERIES.
PROD-FMCMP   DIST-FMCMP

S

SABER   C 5 MIN
16MM FILM OPTICAL SOUND   J-C A
SEE SERIES TITLE FOR DESCRIPTIVE STATEMENT. FROM THE WONDERFUL WORLD OF SPORT - FENCING SERIES.
PROD-SPORTI   DIST-AMERFI

SAFE OPERATION OF FARM TRACTORS   C 14 MIN
16MM FILM OPTICAL SOUND   J-C A
OUTLINES A DAILY SERVICE ROUTINE WHICH HELPS TO INSURE A SAFE TRACTOR. SHOWS THE USE OF PROTECTIVE EQUIPMENT, ROAD AND FIELD HAZARDS, HYDRAULICS AND NECESSARY SKILLS TO BECOME A CERTIFIED OPERATOR.
LC NO. 73-701077
PROD-CUNIV   DIST-CUNIV   1972

SAFETY IN PLYWOOD OPERATIONS   C 10 MIN
16MM FILM OPTICAL SOUND   J-C A
POINTS OUT SPECIFIC THINGS TO WATCH FOR IN PLYWOOD MANUFACTURING FOR BOTH NEW AND EXPERIENCED PLYWOOD EMPLOYEES. ILLUSTRATES PRINCIPLES OF INDIVIDUAL AND MANAGERIAL RESPONSIBILITY. FROM THE FOREST FIRE PROTECTION SERIES.
PROD-RARIG   DIST-RARIG   1970

SAILING - 'E' SLOOPS   C 5 MIN
16MM FILM OPTICAL SOUND   J-C A
SEE SERIES TITLE FOR DESCRIPTIVE STATEMENT. FROM THE WONDERFUL WORLD OF SPORT - BOATING SERIES.
PROD-SPORTI   DIST-AMERFI

SAILING - SUNFISH REGATTA   C 5 MIN
16MM FILM OPTICAL SOUND   J-C A
SEE SERIES TITLE FOR DESCRIPTIVE STATEMENT. FROM THE WONDERFUL WORLD OF SPORT - BOATING SERIES.
PROD-SPORTI   DIST-AMERFI

SALES   B 11 MIN
16MM FILM OPTICAL SOUND
EXAMINES A WIDE RANGE OF SALES CIRCUMSTANCES, INCLUDING DOOR TO DOOR, RETAIL AND WHOLESALE. POINTS OUT A VARIETY OF SALES REQUIREMENTS AND PROBLEMS IN EACH SITUATION.
PROD-BEF   DIST-BEF

SAMADHI   C 6 MIN
16MM FILM OPTICAL SOUND   H-C A
FEATURES BRILLIANTLY COLORED VAPORS WHICH FORM A VARIETY OF UNDULATING PATTERNS THAT UNIFY REPEATEDLY INTO CLEARLY DEFINED SPHERES CORRESPONDING IN YOGA THEORY TO LIGHTS REPRESENTING EARTH, AIR, FIRE AND WATER.
LC NO. 73-701192
PROD-BELSON   DIST-UWFKD   1967

SAND HILLS   C 14 MIN
16MM FILM OPTICAL SOUND
DISCUSSES THE FORMATION AND CHARACTERISTICS OF THE JAPANESE COASTAL SAND HILLS. GIVES AN EXAMPLE OF A SAND HILL FORMING NEAR THE MOUTH OF A RIVER.
PROD-IWANMI   DIST-IWANMI

SATCHMO AND ALL THAT JAZZ B 13 MIN
16MM FILM OPTICAL SOUND I-C A
RELIVES IN MUSIC AND WORDS THE LIFE AND
TIMES OF JAZZ IMMORTAL LOUIS ARMSTRONG.
FROM THE SCREEN NEWS DIGEST SERIES.
LC NO. 73-701269
PROD-HEARST   DIST-HEARST   1972

SCENES OF NATURAL RESERVE C 13 MIN
16MM FILM OPTICAL SOUND
SHOWS RARE ANIMAL AND BIRD SPECIES ROAM-
ING FREELY IN ISRAEL'S NATURAL RESERVES.
PROD-ALDEN   DIST-ALDEN

SCHOOL IS FOR CHILDREN C 17 MIN
16MM FILM OPTICAL SOUND T
SHOWS CHILDREN IN SPECIAL EDUCATION FOR
EXCEPTIONAL PRE-SCHOOL CHILDREN LEARNING
TO MASTER THEIR BODIES AND SHARE AND IN-
TERACT WITH ONE ANOTHER IN SPECIALLY DE-
SIGNED GROUP ACTIVITIES.
LC NO. 73-701158
PROD-AIMS   DIST-AIMS   1973

SCIENCE IN AN AQUARIUM C 14 MIN
16MM FILM OPTICAL SOUND
DESCRIBES THE RAISING OF VARIOUS KINDS OF
FISH IN A WATER TANK AND THE ESSENTIAL RE-
SEARCH INTO OCEAN WATER CONDITIONS.
PROD-IWANMI   DIST-IWANMI

SCIENCE OF FIRE C 14 MIN
16MM FILM OPTICAL SOUND
USES EXPERIMENTS TO RELATE OXIDATION AND
COMBUSTION TO FIRE FIGHTING.
PROD-IWANMI   DIST-IWANMI

SCIENCE OF FOOTWEAR, THE C 14 MIN
16MM FILM OPTICAL SOUND
STUDIES THE RELATIONSHIP BETWEEN LEG MUS-
CLES AND BONE STRUCTURE. DESCRIBES SIMPLE
FOOTWEAR OF THE PAST AND GOOD FOOTWEAR
AND SHOES ADAPTED FOR SPECIFIC USES.
PROD-IWANMI   DIST-IWANMI

SCIENCE OF VACUUM C 14 MIN
16MM FILM OPTICAL SOUND
SHOWS THE DIFFERENCE BETWEEN VACUUM AND
AIR, THE OPERATION OF THE VACUUM PUMP AND
APPLICATIONS OF THE VACUUM.
PROD-IWANMI   DIST-IWANMI

SCIENCE OF WATER DROPS C 14 MIN
16MM FILM OPTICAL SOUND
PRESENTS VARIOUS EXPERIMENTS TO ILLUS-
TRATE THE PROPERTIES OF WATER DROPS.
PROD-IWANMI   DIST-IWANMI

SCIENCE TODAY FILM--A SERIES

PROD-CRMP   DIST-CRMP

ENERGY - A CONVERSATION   20 MIN
NATURE OF MATTER, THE - AN ATOMIC
VIEW   20 MIN
ORIGIN OF THE ELEMENTS, THE   20 MIN
STATES OF MATTER, THE   20 MIN

SCIENCE TODAY--A SERIES
C A
PROD-CRMP   DIST-CRMP   1972

ENERGY - A CONVERSATION   27 MIN
NATURE OF MATTER, THE - AN ATOMIC
VIEW   23 MIN
ORIGIN OF THE ELEMENTS, THE   18 MIN
STATES OF MATTER, THE   18 MIN

SCOREKEEPER C 5 MIN
16MM FILM OPTICAL SOUND J-C A
SEE SERIES TITLE FOR DESCRIPTIVE STATEMENT.
FROM THE WONDERFUL WORLD OF SPORT - BASE-
BALL SERIES.
PROD-SPORTI   DIST-AMERFI

**SCOTTISH GAMES - CROSS-
SECTION** C 5 MIN
16MM FILM OPTICAL SOUND J-C A
SEE SERIES TITLE FOR DESCRIPTIVE STATEMENT.
FROM THE WONDERFUL WORLD OF SPORT -
OTHER SERIES.
PROD-SPORTI   DIST-AMERFI

**SCOTTISH GAMES - TOSSING
CABOR** C 5 MIN
16MM FILM OPTICAL SOUND J-C A
SEE SERIES TITLE FOR DESCRIPTIVE STATEMENT.
FROM THE WONDERFUL WORLD OF SPORT -
OTHER SERIES.

PROD-SPORTI   DIST-AMERFI

SCROTA - THE SECOND C 5 MIN
16MM FILM OPTICAL SOUND J-C A
SEE SERIES TITLE FOR DESCRIPTIVE STATEMENT.
FROM THE WONDERFUL WORLD OF SPORT - GOLF
SERIES.
PROD-SPORTI   DIST-AMERFI

**SCUBA - FLORIDA'S
UNDERWATER STATE PARK** C 5 MIN
16MM FILM OPTICAL SOUND J-C A
SEE SERIES TITLE FOR DESCRIPTIVE STATEMENT.
FROM THE WONDERFUL WORLD OF SPORT - SWIM,
DIVE, SCUBA, SURF SERIES.
PROD-SPORTI   DIST-AMERFI

SCUBA - SLURP GUN C 5 MIN
16MM FILM OPTICAL SOUND J-C A
SEE SERIES TITLE FOR DESCRIPTIVE STATEMENT.
FROM THE WONDERFUL WORLD OF SPORT - SWIM,
DIVE, SCUBA, SURF SERIES.
PROD-SPORTI   DIST-AMERFI

SCUBA - SPANISH WRECK C 5 MIN
16MM FILM OPTICAL SOUND J-C A
SEE SERIES TITLE FOR DESCRIPTIVE STATEMENT.
FROM THE WONDERFUL WORLD OF SPORT - SWIM,
DIVE, SCUBA, SURF SERIES.
PROD-SPORTI   DIST-AMERFI

**SEARCH FOR ALTERNATE LIFE-
STYLES AND PHILOSOPHIES,
THE** C 20 MIN
16MM FILM OPTICAL SOUND J-C A
EXPLORES SOME OF THE EFFORTS BEING MADE
TODAY TO FIND PERSONAL HARMONY AND A FUL-
FILLING LIFE-STYLE. VISITS A COOPERATIVE VIL-
LAGE IN THE SIERRAS WITH A LIFE-STYLE BASED
ON A YOGA PHILOSOPHY.
LC NO. 73-701224
PROD-FLMFR   DIST-FLMFR   1973

**SEARCH FOR THE NILE--A
SERIES**
J-C A
RECONSTRUCTS ONE OF THE MOST SPECTACULAR
QUESTS OF ALL TIME, THE SEARCH FOR THE
SOURCE OF THE NILE. PORTRAYS THE EVENTS AS
THEY ACTUALLY HAPPENED IN THE PLACES
WHERE THEY HAPPENED.
LC NO. 73-701098
PROD-TIMLIF   DIST-TIMLIF

SECURITY MAN B 17 MIN
16MM FILM OPTICAL SOUND
FOLLOWS A GOVERNMENT SECURITY MAN AS HE
VISITS AN INDUSTRIAL FACILITY AND POINTS OUT
SOME OF THE PROBLEMS ENCOUNTERED. SHOWS
HOW LOYAL AMERICANS COMPROMISE SECURITY
THROUGH IGNORANCE AND CARELESSNESS.
POINTS OUT THAT STRICT ADHERENCE TO ESTAB-
LISHED SECURITY REGULATIONS IS IMPERATIVE
FOR NATIONAL DEFENSE.
LC NO. 73-701249
PROD-USDD   DIST-USNAC   1961

**SEEDS OF REBELLION - VIKINGS
TO 1763** C 80 MIN
16MM FILM OPTICAL SOUND
PICTURES THE SEARCH FOR A NEW WORLD AND A
NEW WAY OF LIFE BEGINNING WITH THE VIKING
EXPEDITIONS. EXPLAINS THAT AFTER 1584, AT-
TENTION IS FOCUSED ON THE BRITISH COLONIES
AND EVENTS LEADING TOWARD THE DECLARA-
TION OF INDEPENDENCE. FROM THE TO THE
SPIRIT OF '76 SERIES.
LC NO. 73-733676
PROD-RMI   DIST-RMI

SEMINARS IN ISRAEL B 28 MIN
16MM FILM OPTICAL SOUND
PRESENTS A DOCUMENTARY ON AFRO-ASIAN STU-
DENTS IN ISRAEL.
PROD-ALDEN   DIST-ALDEN

SENSE OF RESPONSIBILITY, A C 4 MIN
16MM FILM OPTICAL SOUND I-C
USES ANIMATION TO RAISE QUESTIONS ABOUT
INDIVIDUAL RESPONSIBILITY. SHOWS HOW A
CARELESS MINE WORKER STARTS A CHAIN REAC-
TION OF ACCIDENTS WHICH ULTIMATELY BRINGS
ABOUT THE DESTRUCTION OF THE ENTIRE COUN-
TRY.
LC NO. 73-701288
PROD-BFA   DIST-BFA   1972

SEVENTH MANDARIN, THE C 13 MIN
16MM FILM OPTICAL SOUND I
USES ANIMATION TO TELL THE TALE OF A MANDA-
RIN WHO LOSES HIS EMPEROR'S KITE IN A STORM
AND WHILE SEARCHING FOR IT, DISCOVERS THAT
THE MEN, WOMEN AND CHILDREN LIVING OUT-
SIDE THE PALACE WALLS ARE POOR AND STARV-
ING.
LC NO. 73-701257
PROD-BOSUST   DIST-XEROX   1973

**SEX IN AMERICAN CULTURE--A
SERIES**
H-C A
PROD-CHM   DIST-CHM   1967

ADOLESCENCE AND SEXUAL IDENTITY   28 MIN
BIRTH OF A BABY   28 MIN
EDUCATION FOR FAMILY LIFE   28 MIN
EMBRYOLOGICAL DEVELOPMENT   28 MIN
HUMAN REPRODUCTION   28 MIN
INTRODUCTION TO SEX EDUCATION   28 MIN
POPULATION EXPANSION AND BIRTH
CONTROL   28 MIN
VENEREAL DISEASE   28 MIN

**SHAPERS OF STAINLESS STEEL,
THE** C 18 MIN
16MM FILM OPTICAL SOUND
FEATURES THE MANY AND VARIOUS APPLICA-
TIONS OF STAINLESS STEEL.
PROD-MTP   DIST-MTP

SHAVUOTH C 15 MIN
16MM FILM OPTICAL SOUND
SHOWS HOW THE FESTIVAL OF SHAVUOTH IS CEL-
EBRATED IN ISRAEL.
PROD-ALDEN   DIST-ALDEN

SHELL STORY C 5 MIN
16MM FILM OPTICAL SOUND J-C A
SEE SERIES TITLE FOR DESCRIPTIVE STATEMENT.
FROM THE WONDERFUL WORLD OF SPORT - ROW-
ING SERIES.
PROD-SPORTI   DIST-AMERFI

**SHELL-HEAP AND
EARTHENWARE, A** C 14 MIN
16MM FILM OPTICAL SOUND
SHOWS A GROUP OF JUNIOR HIGH SCHOOL STU-
DENTS SURVEYING AN EXCAVATED SHELL HEAP
WHERE STONEWARE AND EARTHENWARE OVER
3,000 YEARS OLD HAS BEEN FOUND.
PROD-IWANMI   DIST-IWANMI

**SHIPBOARD VIBRATIONS, PT 3 -
VIBRATION, EXCITATION AND
RESPONSE** B 15 MIN
16MM FILM OPTICAL SOUND
SHOWS VIBRATION EXCITATION IN THE PROPUL-
SION MACHINERY DUE TO IMBALANCE AND TO
PROPELLER THRUST VARIATION AND THE RE-
SPONSE OF THE SHIP'S STRUCTURE TO THIS EXCI-
TATION.
LC NO. FIA53-518
PROD-USN   DIST-USNAC   1953

**SHOW ME THE WAY TO GO
HOME** C 25 MIN
16MM FILM OPTICAL SOUND
PORTRAYS 'MOVING DAY' IN THE LIVES OF THE
RANDOM FAMILY.
PROD-MTP   DIST-MTP

SINBAD C
16MM FILM OPTICAL SOUND
SEE SERIES TITLE FOR DESCRIPTIVE STATEMENT.
FROM THE FAIRY TALE TIME SERIES.
PROD-PUI   DIST-PUI

SINGAPORE C
16MM FILM OPTICAL SOUND
SEE SERIES TITLE FOR DESCRIPTIVE STATEMENT.
FROM THE PORT OF CALL SERIES.
PROD-PUI   DIST-PUI

SINGING INSECTS OF AUTUMN C 14 MIN
16MM FILM OPTICAL SOUND
OBSERVES THE ARTICULATING MECHANISMS OF
THE INSECT. ILLUSTRATES VARYING SOUNDS
MADE BY THE VOCAL CORDS AND SHAPE AND
THICKNESS OF WINGS.
PROD-IWANMI   DIST-IWANMI

SIX DAYS IN JUNE B 14 MIN
16MM FILM OPTICAL SOUND
PRESENTS A COMPILATION OF NEWSREEL FILMS
FROM ISRAEL AND DOCUMENTARY MATERIAL
FROM EGYPT, SHOWING THE EVENTS WHICH LEAD
TO THE SIX DAY WAR IN JUNE, 1967. DEPICTS

THE FIGHTING DURING THE WAR AND JERUSALEM LIBERATED AND UNIFIED.
PROD-ALDEN   DIST-ALDEN

SIX SHORT FILMS   C 7 MIN
        16MM FILM OPTICAL SOUND   H-C A
USES ANIMATION TO PRESENT A SORT OF CONTEMPORARY AMERICAN CINEMAGRAPHIC PRIMITIVE, FULL OF VISUAL INCONGRUITIES IN WHICH THINGS ARE WHAT THEY SEEM AND THEN BECOME SOMETHING ELSE.
  LC NO. 73-701434
PROD-BFA   DIST-BFA   1973

SKATING   C 14 MIN
        16MM FILM OPTICAL SOUND
EXPLAINS THE REASONS WHY SKATES SLIDE. COMPARES SURFACES OF POLISHED STEEL PLATE AND ICE AND SHOWS EXPERIMENTS IN A LOW TEMPERATURE LABORATORY.
PROD-IWANMI   DIST-IWANMI

SKATING - PEGGY FLEMING   C 5 MIN
        16MM FILM OPTICAL SOUND   J-C A
SEE SERIES TITLE FOR DESCRIPTIVE STATEMENT. FROM THE WONDERFUL WORLD OF SPORT - OTHER SERIES.
PROD-SPORTI   DIST-AMERFI

SKEET SHOOTING   C 5 MIN
        16MM FILM OPTICAL SOUND   J-C A
SEE SERIES TITLE FOR DESCRIPTIVE STATEMENT. FROM THE WONDERFUL WORLD OF SPORT - OTHER SERIES.
PROD-SPORTI   DIST-AMERFI

SKI   C 14 MIN
        16MM FILM OPTICAL SOUND
PRESENTS A SCIENTIFIC EXPLANATION OF SKIING. DISCUSSES WHY SKIS SLIDE AT HIGH SPEEDS THROUGH EXPERIMENTS IN A LOW TEMPERATURE LABORATORY.
PROD-IWANMI   DIST-IWANMI

SKI INSTRUCTORS   C 5 MIN
        16MM FILM OPTICAL SOUND   J-C A
SEE SERIES TITLE FOR DESCRIPTIVE STATEMENT. FROM THE WONDERFUL WORLD OF SPORT - SKIING SERIES.
PROD-SPORTI   DIST-AMERFI

SKI PATROL - GENERAL   C 5 MIN
        16MM FILM OPTICAL SOUND   J-C A
SEE SERIES TITLE FOR DESCRIPTIVE STATEMENT. FROM THE WONDERFUL WORLD OF SPORT - SKIING SERIES.
PROD-SPORTI   DIST-AMERFI

SKI PATROL - RESCUE   C 5 MIN
        16MM FILM OPTICAL SOUND   J-C A
SEE SERIES TITLE FOR DESCRIPTIVE STATEMENT. FROM THE WONDERFUL WORLD OF SPORT - SKIING SERIES.
PROD-SPORTI   DIST-AMERFI

SKIING - BASICS   C 5 MIN
        16MM FILM OPTICAL SOUND   J-C A
SEE SERIES TITLE FOR DESCRIPTIVE STATEMENT. FROM THE WONDERFUL WORLD OF SPORT - SKIING SERIES.
PROD-SPORTI   DIST-AMERFI

SKIING ABOVE THE CLOUDS   C 13 MIN
        16MM FILM OPTICAL SOUND
FOLLOWS A PARTY OF EXPERIENCED OUTDOORSMEN AS THEY TRAVERSE GLACIER-CLAD MT RAINIER AT THE 10,000 FOOT LEVEL IN MID-WINTER.
PROD-RARIG   DIST-RARIG

**SKIN, THE - FUNCTION AND
CARE**   C 16 MIN
        16MM FILM OPTICAL SOUND   IND
GIVES THE STRUCTURE AND FUNCTION OF THE SKIN TO INCREASE THE AWARENESS AND ACTIVITY FOR MAINTAINING PROPER CLEANSING, LUBRICATION AND PROTECTION OF THE PATIENT'S SKIN. FROM THE NURSE'S AIDE, ORDERLY AND ATTENDANT SERIES.
  LC NO. 73-701046
PROD-COPI   DIST-COPI   1971

**SKY DIVING - BARBARA
ROQUEMORE**   C 5 MIN
        16MM FILM OPTICAL SOUND   J-C A
SEE SERIES TITLE FOR DESCRIPTIVE STATEMENT. FROM THE WONDERFUL WORLD OF SPORT - FLYING SERIES.
PROD-SPORTI   DIST-AMERFI

SKY DIVING - U S TEAM   C 5 MIN
        16MM FILM OPTICAL SOUND   J-C A
SEE SERIES TITLE FOR DESCRIPTIVE STATEMENT. FROM THE WONDERFUL WORLD OF SPORT - FLYING SERIES.
PROD-SPORTI   DIST-AMERFI

SKY DIVING - WHAT IS IT   C 5 MIN
        16MM FILM OPTICAL SOUND   J-C A
SEE SERIES TITLE FOR DESCRIPTIVE STATEMENT. FROM THE WONDERFUL WORLD OF SPORT - FLYING SERIES.
PROD-SPORTI   DIST-AMERFI

SLED DOGS - ALASKAN HUSKY   C 5 MIN
        16MM FILM OPTICAL SOUND   J-C A
SEE SERIES TITLE FOR DESCRIPTIVE STATEMENT. FROM THE WONDERFUL WORLD OF SPORT - DOGS SERIES.
PROD-SPORTI   DIST-AMERFI

SLED DOGS - BIG-TIME TEAM   C 5 MIN
        16MM FILM OPTICAL SOUND   J-C A
SEE SERIES TITLE FOR DESCRIPTIVE STATEMENT. FROM THE WONDERFUL WORLD OF SPORT - DOGS SERIES.
PROD-SPORTI   DIST-AMERFI

SLED DOGS - RACING   C 5 MIN
        16MM FILM OPTICAL SOUND   J-C A
SEE SERIES TITLE FOR DESCRIPTIVE STATEMENT. FROM THE WONDERFUL WORLD OF SPORT - DOGS SERIES.
PROD-SPORTI   DIST-AMERFI

SLICE OF GOLD   C 7 MIN
        16MM FILM OPTICAL SOUND
PRESENTS AN EXPERIMENTAL FILM SUGGESTING THE ONENESS OF TIME AND THE DUALITY OF EMOTIONAL PERCEPTIONS. LOOKS AT THE URBAN ENVIRONMENT.
PROD-AMERFI   DIST-AMERFI

SLIP PITCH   C 5 MIN
        16MM FILM OPTICAL SOUND   J-C A
SEE SERIES TITLE FOR DESCRIPTIVE STATEMENT. FROM THE WONDERFUL WORLD OF SPORT - BASEBALL SERIES.
PROD-SPORTI   DIST-AMERFI

SNATCH - HOOK FISHING   C 5 MIN
        16MM FILM OPTICAL SOUND   J-C A
SEE SERIES TITLE FOR DESCRIPTIVE STATEMENT. FROM THE WONDERFUL WORLD OF SPORT - FISHING SERIES.
PROD-SPORTI   DIST-AMERFI

SNOW SAFARI   C 5 MIN
        16MM FILM OPTICAL SOUND   J-C A
SEE SERIES TITLE FOR DESCRIPTIVE STATEMENT. FROM THE WONDERFUL WORLD OF SPORT - SNOWMOBILES SERIES.
PROD-SPORTI   DIST-AMERFI

SOARING - MOOD STORY   C 5 MIN
        16MM FILM OPTICAL SOUND   J-C A
SEE SERIES TITLE FOR DESCRIPTIVE STATEMENT. FROM THE WONDERFUL WORLD OF SPORT - FLYING SERIES.
PROD-SPORTI   DIST-AMERFI

SOARING - TEST PILOT   C 5 MIN
        16MM FILM OPTICAL SOUND   J-C A
SEE SERIES TITLE FOR DESCRIPTIVE STATEMENT. FROM THE WONDERFUL WORLD OF SPORT - FLYING SERIES.
PROD-SPORTI   DIST-AMERFI

SOCCER - PELE   C 5 MIN
        16MM FILM OPTICAL SOUND   J-C A
SEE SERIES TITLE FOR DESCRIPTIVE STATEMENT. FROM THE WONDERFUL WORLD OF SPORT - OTHER SERIES.
PROD-SPORTI   DIST-AMERFI

**SOLDIER AND THE DRAGON,
THE**   C
        16MM FILM OPTICAL SOUND
SEE SERIES TITLE FOR DESCRIPTIVE STATEMENT. FROM THE FAIRY TALE TIME SERIES.
PROD-PUI   DIST-PUI

SONNY JACKSON - BUNTING   C 5 MIN
        16MM FILM OPTICAL SOUND   J-C A
SEE SERIES TITLE FOR DESCRIPTIVE STATEMENT. FROM THE WONDERFUL WORLD OF SPORT - BASEBALL SERIES.
PROD-SPORTI   DIST-AMERFI

SOUNDS OF NATURE   C 16 MIN
        16MM FILM OPTICAL SOUND
FEATURES THE USE OF NATURAL SOUNDS IN CONJUNCTION WITH PHOTOGRAPHY. INTRODUCES DAN GIBSON, A PIONEER IN THIS AREA WHO ILLUSTRATES HOW SUCH RECORDINGS ARE MADE AND HIS TECHNIQUE OF USING BLINDS TO CAPTURE WILDLIFE ON FILM.
PROD-AVEXP   DIST-AVEXP   1971

**SOVIET BUILD-UP IN THE
MIDDLE EAST**   C 25 MIN
        16MM FILM OPTICAL SOUND
DOCUMENTS SOVIET INVOLVEMENT IN THE ARAB-ISRAEL CONFLICT.
PROD-ALDEN   DIST-ALDEN

SPENCER HAYWARD   C 5 MIN
        16MM FILM OPTICAL SOUND   J-C A
SEE SERIES TITLE FOR DESCRIPTIVE STATEMENT. FROM THE WONDERFUL WORLD OF SPORT - BASKETBALL SERIES.
PROD-SPORTI   DIST-AMERFI

SPIRAL JETTY   C 35 MIN
        16MM FILM OPTICAL SOUND
DOCUMENTS THE CONSTRUCTION OF ROBERT SMITHSON'S LARGEST EARTH WORK COMPLETED TO DATE, A SPIRAL JETTY JUTTING INTO THE SHALLOWS OFFSHORE OF THE GREAT SALT LAKE OF UTAH.
PROD-VISRES   DIST-VISRES   1970

SPITBALL STORY   C 5 MIN
        16MM FILM OPTICAL SOUND   J-C A
SEE SERIES TITLE FOR DESCRIPTIVE STATEMENT. FROM THE WONDERFUL WORLD OF SPORT - BASEBALL SERIES.
PROD-SPORTI   DIST-AMERFI

SPOKANE RIVER, THE   C 24 MIN
        16MM FILM OPTICAL SOUND   I-C A
TRACES THE SPOKANE RIVER FROM ITS SOURCE AT LAKE COEUR D'ALENE, IDAHO, TO ITS CONFLUENCE WITH THE MIGHTY COLUMBIA RIVER. POINTS OUT HISTORIC AND GEOGRAPHIC HIGHLIGHTS.
  LC NO. 73-701096
PROD-PRYOR   DIST-NWFLMP   1970

**SQUIRRELS ARE UP, SQUIRRELS
ARE DOWN - ADVERBIALS OF
PLACE**   C 10 MIN
        16MM FILM OPTICAL SOUND   P-I
PRESENTS BOTH ORALLY AND VISUALLY WORDS SELECTED FROM COMMONLY USED VOCABULARY LISTS FOR PRIMARY READERS. ENGAGES RHYME AND MUSIC TO CREATE PATTERNS THAT AID IN RETENTION OF THE WORDS. FROM THE READING MOTIVATION SERIES.
  LC NO. 73-701280
PROD-BFA   DIST-BFA   1972

**SRO (SINGLE ROOM
OCCUPANCY)**   C 13 MIN
        16MM FILM OPTICAL SOUND   H-C A
DEPICTS A WELFARE HOTEL WHERE THE PAINT IS FLAKING OFF THE WALLS, HOT WATER AND HEAT BARELY EXIST, TOILET FACILITIES ARE RUDIMENTARY AND THE TENANTS ARE VICTIMIZED BY THIEVES WHO STEAL THEIR WELFARE CHECKS AND EVEN THEIR FOOD.
PROD-CAROUF   DIST-CAROUF

STAGE IS YOURS, THE   C 15 MIN
        16MM FILM OPTICAL SOUND
COMPARES THE PROPER AND IMPROPER METHODS OF RETAIL SELLING AND SHOWS THE FOUR BASIC STEPS NECESSARY FOR SUCCESSFUL SELLING - APPROACH, DETERMINATION OF CUSTOMER NEEDS, PRESENTATION AND THE CLOSING OF THE SALE.
PROD-BEF   DIST-BEF

STAKE IN THE FUTURE, A   C 26 MIN
        16MM FILM OPTICAL SOUND   J-C A
FOLLOWS A WILDCAT OIL CREW ON A SEARCH FOR OIL ON A TINY GREEK ISLAND.
  LC NO. 73-700765
PROD-NAGLEP   DIST-NAGLEP   1973

STALACTITE GROTTO   C 14 MIN
        16MM FILM OPTICAL SOUND
PRESENTS AN EXPLORATION OF THE STALACTITE GROTTO TO THE WEST OF TOKYO. SHOWS THE INTERIOR OF THE STALACTITE GROTTO AND THE LIVING CREATURES IN THE GROTTO.
PROD-IWANMI   DIST-IWANMI

S

STARFISH'S REALM, THE   C 14 MIN
16MM FILM OPTICAL SOUND
HIGHLIGHTS THE RHYTHMIC NATURAL MOVE-
MENTS ACHIEVED BY VARIOUS SEA ANIMALS AS
THEY REACT TO DIFFERENT SPECIES OF STARFISH
IN THEIR NATURAL ENVIRONMENT. INCLUDES
THE TRUE LIFE DRAMA OF THE EVENTS THAT MAY
OCCUR WHEN A CRAB AND AN OCTOPUS MEET.
PROD-WHICAP   DIST-WHTCAP   1971

STATE OF ENCHANTMENT   C 29 MIN
16MM FILM OPTICAL SOUND
PRESENTS A VISIT TO THE MOST FAMOUS SCENIC
AND HISTORIC SPOTS IN NORTH CAROLINA.
PROD-MTP   DIST-MTP

STATES OF MATTER, THE   C 18 MIN
16MM FILM OPTICAL SOUND   C A
EXPLAINS THE FOUR DIVISIONS OF MATTER - LIQ-
UIDS, SOLIDS, GASES AND PLASMA. POINTS OUT
THAT THE DIVISION BETWEEN THESE STATES MAY
IN THE FUTURE PROVE TO BE LESS IMPORTANT
THAN THE UNITY THAT EXISTS BETWEEN THEM.
FROM THE SCIENCE TODAY SERIES.
LC NO. 73-701092
PROD-CRMP   DIST-CRMP   1972

STATES OF MATTER, THE   C 20 MIN
16MM FILM OPTICAL SOUND
EXAMINES THE CHARACTERISTICS OF THE STATES
OF MATTER AND THE ATOMIC AND MOLECULAR
MOVEMENTS WITHIN SOLIDS, LIQUIDS AND GA-
SES. FROM THE SCIENCE TODAY FILM SERIES.
PROD-CRMP   DIST-CRMP

STEPPING STONES IN SPACE   B 14 MIN
16MM FILM OPTICAL SOUND   I-C A
PRESENTS A CHRONICLE OF THE CONQUEST OF
SPACE FROM THE PIONEERING FLIGHTS OF DR
ROBERT HUTCHINGS GOODARD IN 1926 TO THE
LUNAR LANDING OF APOLLO 17 IN DECEMBER,
1972. FROM THE SCREEN NEWS DIGEST SERIES.
LC NO. 73-701271
PROD-HEARST   DIST-HEARST   1972

STEVE VAN BUREN   C 5 MIN
16MM FILM OPTICAL SOUND   J-C A
SEE SERIES TITLE FOR DESCRIPTIVE STATEMENT.
FROM THE WONDERFUL WORLD OF SPORT - FOOT-
BALL SERIES.
PROD-SPORTI   DIST-AMERFI

STILL   X 13 MIN
16MM FILM OPTICAL SOUND
PRESENTS AN EXPERIMENTAL FILM RECON-
STRUCTING CHILDLIKE SENSORY EXPERIENCES,
SUGGESTING A WORLD WAVERING BETWEEN THE
PRESENT AND THE PAST.
PROD-AMERFI   DIST-AMERFI

STILL RINGS   C 5 MIN
16MM FILM OPTICAL SOUND   J-C A
SEE SERIES TITLE FOR DESCRIPTIVE STATEMENT.
FROM THE WONDERFUL WORLD OF SPORT - GYM-
NASTICS SERIES.
PROD-SPORTI   DIST-AMERFI

STORY OF A TRIAL   B 22 MIN
16MM FILM OPTICAL SOUND
FOLLOWS TWO YOUNG MEN ACCUSED OF A MIS-
DEMEANOR OFFENSE FROM THEIR ARREST
THROUGH THEIR TRAIL. STRESSES THE IMPOR-
TANCE OF DUE PROCESS OF LAW.
PROD-BEF   DIST-BEF

STORY OF AMERICAN WHISKEY   C 28 MIN
16MM FILM OPTICAL SOUND
DESCRIBES THE AMERICAN WHISKEY INDUSTRY.
PROD-MTP   DIST-MTP

**STORY OF LAPSE
PHOTOGRAPHY**   C 14 MIN
16MM FILM OPTICAL SOUND
DESCRIBES THE PRINCIPLES OF LAPSE PHOTOG-
RAPHY AND EXAMINES THE SPAN OF A YEAR AS
SEEN THROUGH LAPSE PHOTOGRAPHY.
PROD-IWANMI   DIST-IWANMI

STORY OF LAVER   C 14 MIN
16MM FILM OPTICAL SOUND
EXPLAINS THAT LAVER, A TYPE OF SEAWEED, IS A
TRADITIONAL JAPANESE FOOD. TELLS THE SE-
CRET OF ITS GROWTH AND ITS ARTIFICIAL CULTI-
VATION.
PROD-IWANMI   DIST-IWANMI

STORY OF MOLECULE   C 14 MIN
16MM FILM OPTICAL SOUND
DESCRIBES THE STRUCTURE OF THE MOLECULE
AND ATOM WHICH COMPOSE MATTER AND GIVES
AN EXPLANATION OF THEIR CHARACTERISTICS ON
THE BASIC OF EXPERIMENTS.
PROD-IWANMI   DIST-IWANMI

STORY OF MUSHROOMS   C 14 MIN
16MM FILM OPTICAL SOUND
OBSERVES MUSHROOMS AND THEIR REPRODUC-
TION. DISCUSSES EDIBLE MUSHROOMS, POISON-
OUS MUSHROOMS, WHERE MUSHROOMS GROW
AND THE ECOLOGY OF THE MUSHROOM.
PROD-IWANMI   DIST-IWANMI

STORY OF POLLEN   C 14 MIN
16MM FILM OPTICAL SOUND
DESCRIBES VARIOUS MOVEMENTS OF THE POL-
LEN AND ILLUSTRATES WONDERS CONNECTED
WITH THE PRESERVATION OF DIFFERENT VARIE-
TIES OF FLOWERS. SHOWS THE SHAPES OF POL-
LEN AND THE SIZES OF DIFFERENT VARIETIES.
PROD-IWANMI   DIST-IWANMI

STORY OF RESPIRATION   C 14 MIN
16MM FILM OPTICAL SOUND
OBSERVES THE VARIOUS METHODS OF RESPIRA-
TION AMONG LIVING ORGANISMS. EXAMINES THE
ECOLOGY OF AMOEBA AND OSMOTIC ACTION, MA-
RINE ANIMALS THAT PERFORM BODY RESPIRA-
TION, THE BREATHING OF FISH AND THE RESPI-
RATION OF A CRAB.
PROD-IWANMI   DIST-IWANMI

**STORY OF SLOW MOTION
PHOTOGRAPHY**   C 14 MIN
16MM FILM OPTICAL SOUND
SHOWS WONDER OF THE WORLD CAPTURED WITH
HIGH-SPEED PHOTOGRAPHY. DESCRIBES THE
PRINCIPLES AND REALITY OF HIGH-SPEED PHO-
TOGRAPHY.
PROD-IWANMI   DIST-IWANMI

STORY OF STAMPS, THE   C 10 MIN
16MM FILM OPTICAL SOUND
RE-CREATES ISRAEL'S HISTORY THROUGH
STAMPS.
PROD-ALDEN   DIST-ALDEN

STORY OF THE PLANKTON   C 14 MIN
16MM FILM OPTICAL SOUND
DESCRIBES VARIOUS TYPES OF PLANKTON, METH-
ODS OF GATHERING PLANKTON AND OBSERVES
PLANKTON UNDER THE MICROSCOPE.
PROD-IWANMI   DIST-IWANMI

STORY OF THE REFRIGERATOR   C 14 MIN
16MM FILM OPTICAL SOUND
TELLS THE STORY OF THE DEVELOPMENT OF RE-
FRIGERATION FROM THE BASIC CHEMICAL RE-
FRIGERATOR TO THERMOELECTRIC REFRIGERA-
TORS. DISCUSSES ACHIEVING COOL TEMPERA-
TURE BY EVAPORATING ETHYL INSIDE A FLASK
AND THE FUNCTIONS OF THE EVAPORATOR, COM-
PRESSOR, MOTOR AND LIQUEFIER.
PROD-IWANMI   DIST-IWANMI

STORY OF THE U S MAIL   B 15 MIN
16MM FILM OPTICAL SOUND
COMPARES OLD AND NEW METHODS OF HAN-
DLING THE MAIL. SHOWS THE COMPLETE MECHA-
NIZATION OF THE POST OFFICE WITH NEW ELEC-
TRONIC EQUIPMENT, RELAYING AND SIGNALING,
CONVEYORS AND CODERS AS WELL AS EXPERI-
MENTAL EQUIPMENT.
PROD-BEF   DIST-BEF

STORY OF TWO CREEKS, THE   C
16MM FILM OPTICAL SOUND
PRESENTS A GEOLOGIC FIELD STUDY PROJECT
SPONSORED BY THE UNIVERSITY OF WISCONSIN
AND THE COMMITTEE FOR INSTITUTIONAL COOP-
ERATION, EXPLORING THE GLACIATION EFFECTS
AND GEOLOGIC HERITAGE OF THE WELL KNOWN
LAKE MICHIGAN SHORE SITE AT TWO CREEKS,
WISCONSIN.
LC NO. 73-701174
PROD-UEUWIS   DIST-UEUWIS   1969

STRATA   C 14 MIN
16MM FILM OPTICAL SOUND
DESCRIBES THE ORIGIN AND MOVEMENT OF
STRATUM AND EXPLAINS HOW THE JAPANESE IS-
LANDS WERE FORMED. DISCUSSES IGNEOUS AND
HYDROGENOUS ROCKS AND TELLS THE STORY OF
LAVA RESULTING FROM ERUPTION.
PROD-IWANMI   DIST-IWANMI

STRATA   C 15 MIN
16MM FILM OPTICAL SOUND
DESCRIBES HOW STRATUM IS FORMED AS WELL
AS CREASES AND DISLOCATIONS OF STRATA. IL-
LUSTRATES VARIOUS SHAPES THAT ARE CREATED
BY THESE CREASES AND DISLOCATIONS.
PROD-IWANMI   DIST-IWANMI

STRAWBERRIES - WITH CREAM   C 14 MIN
16MM FILM OPTICAL SOUND
TELLS THE STORY OF HOW PEOPLE IN MANY
WALKS OF LIFE, THROUGH COOPERATIVE ORGANI-
ZATIONS WORK TOGETHER TO HELP THEMSELVES
AND EACH OTHER.
PROD-MTP   DIST-MTP

SUCCOTH   C 15 MIN
16MM FILM OPTICAL SOUND
SHOWS HOW THE FESTIVAL OF SUCCOTH IS CELE-
BRATED IN ISRAEL.
PROD-ALDEN   DIST-ALDEN

SUMMER JOURNAL   C 43 MIN
16MM FILM OPTICAL SOUND
ATTEMPTS TO ANSWER QUESTIONS, SUCH AS
WHAT IS THE CREATIVE PROCESS, WHAT IS THE
STRANGE ALCHEMY BETWEEN AN ARTIST AND
HIS SUBJECT THAT RESULTS IN ART AND HOW
DOES A TEACHER OF ART IMPART HIS EXPERI-
ENCES AND KNOWLEDGE TO A YOUNG ART STU-
DENT. FOCUSES ON THE SKOWHEGAN SCHOOL OF
ART IN MAINE.
PROD-AMERFI   DIST-AMERFI

SUNFLOWER, THE   C 14 MIN
16MM FILM OPTICAL SOUND
EXPLAINS THE STRANGE MOVEMENT OF THE SUN-
FLOWER REVOLVING WITH THE SUN. STUDIES THE
MOVEMENT OF THE SUNFLOWER INSIDE A DARK
ROOM TO DETERMINE HOW ROTATION IS MADE,
THE EFFECT OF LIGHT SHINING ON A LEAF AND
THE TURNING OF THE STEM.
PROD-IWANMI   DIST-IWANMI

SURFACE TENSION   C 14 MIN
16MM FILM OPTICAL SOUND
USES SEVERAL EXPERIMENTS TO ILLUSTRATE THE
PROPERTIES OF SURFACE TENSION.
PROD-IWANMI   DIST-IWANMI

SURFING - CORKY CARROLL   C 5 MIN
16MM FILM OPTICAL SOUND   J-C A
SEE SERIES TITLE FOR DESCRIPTIVE STATEMENT.
FROM THE WONDERFUL WORLD OF SPORT - SWIM,
DIVE, SCUBA, SURF SERIES.
PROD-SPORTI   DIST-AMERFI

SURFING - JOYCE HOFFMAN   C 5 MIN
16MM FILM OPTICAL SOUND   J-C A
SEE SERIES TITLE FOR DESCRIPTIVE STATEMENT.
FROM THE WONDERFUL WORLD OF SPORT - SWIM,
DIVE, SCUBA, SURF SERIES.
PROD-SPORTI   DIST-AMERFI

SURVIVAL OF SPACESHIP EARTH   C 60 MIN
16MM FILM OPTICAL SOUND
PRESENTS A DEVASTATING ENVIRONMENTAL
STATEMENT, A SHOCKING BRUTAL LOOK AT SOME
OF THE WORLD TODAY WHICH MAY BECOME
MOST OF THE WORLD TOMORROW.
LC NO. 73-701359
PROD-WB   DIST-WB

SWARTHMORE - HUDDLE   C 5 MIN
16MM FILM OPTICAL SOUND   J-C A
SEE SERIES TITLE FOR DESCRIPTIVE STATEMENT.
FROM THE WONDERFUL WORLD OF SPORT - FOOT-
BALL SERIES.
PROD-SPORTI   DIST-AMERFI

**SWARTHMORE - SMALL
COLLEGE FOOTBALL**   C 5 MIN
16MM FILM OPTICAL SOUND   J-C A
SEE SERIES TITLE FOR DESCRIPTIVE STATEMENT.
FROM THE WONDERFUL WORLD OF SPORT - FOOT-
BALL SERIES.
PROD-SPORTI   DIST-AMERFI

SWIMMING - BASIC STROKES   C 5 MIN
16MM FILM OPTICAL SOUND   J-C A
SEE SERIES TITLE FOR DESCRIPTIVE STATEMENT.
FROM THE WONDERFUL WORLD OF SPORT - SWIM,
DIVE, SCUBA, SURF SERIES.
PROD-SPORTI   DIST-AMERFI

SWIMMING AND DIVING - HOW CHAMPIONSHIPS ARE WON C 5 MIN
16MM FILM OPTICAL SOUND J-C A
SEE SERIES TITLE FOR DESCRIPTIVE STATEMENT. FROM THE WONDERFUL WORLD OF SPORT - SWIM, DIVE, SCUBA, SURF SERIES.
PROD-SPORTI DIST-AMERFI

SWIMMING AND DIVING - TRAINING C 5 MIN
16MM FILM OPTICAL SOUND J-C A
SEE SERIES TITLE FOR DESCRIPTIVE STATEMENT. FROM THE WONDERFUL WORLD OF SPORT - SWIM, DIVE, SCUBA, SURF SERIES.
PROD-SPORTI DIST-AMERFI

SWITCH HITTING STORY C 5 MIN
16MM FILM OPTICAL SOUND J-C A
SEE SERIES TITLE FOR DESCRIPTIVE STATEMENT. FROM THE WONDERFUL WORLD OF SPORT - BASEBALL SERIES.
PROD-SPORTI DIST-AMERFI

SYMBIOSIS C 10 MIN
16MM FILM OPTICAL SOUND J-H
POINTS OUT THE MANY EXAMPLES IN NATURE OF ORGANISMS LIVING TOGETHER IN MUTUAL DEPENDENCE. GIVES INSIGHTS INTO THE RELATIONSHIP CALLED SYMBIOSIS.
LC NO. 73-701435
PROD-BFA DIST-BFA 1973

SYRIA C
16MM FILM OPTICAL SOUND
SEE SERIES TITLE FOR DESCRIPTIVE STATEMENT. FROM THE PORT OF CALL SERIES.
PROD-PUI DIST-PUI

SYSTEM AND WORKINGS OF A NERVE C 14 MIN
16MM FILM OPTICAL SOUND
EXPLAINS THE WORKINGS OF THE HIGHLY COMPLEX NERVOUS SYSTEM AS A SIMPLE FUNCTION OF PULSE COMMUNICATION. INCLUDES A DIAGRAM OF THE NERVOUS SYSTEM OF THE HUMAN BODY.
PROD-IWANMI DIST-IWANMI

T

T HYBRID V-1 C 13 MIN
16MM FILM OPTICAL SOUND
PRESENTS A CHARTREUSE FILTERED SPLIT-SCREEN VIDEO TAPE WITH NEGATIVE 'PUNCH IN' ON THE LEFT SIDE CONTRASTED WITH THE RIGHT SIDE IMAGE OF A MAN COUNTING IN SPANISH WHILE HIS IMAGE SHIFTS BACK AND FORTH FROM NEGATIVE TO POSITIVE.
PROD-VISRES DIST-VISRES 1971

T HYBRID V-2 C 11 MIN
16MM FILM OPTICAL SOUND
PRESENTS A USE OF SPLIT SCREEN EFFECTS AS SEEN THROUGH A CIRCULAR OPENING.
PROD-VISRES DIST-VISRES

TAILOR'S ADVENTURE, THE C
16MM FILM OPTICAL SOUND
SEE SERIES TITLE FOR DESCRIPTIVE STATEMENT. FROM THE FAIRY TALE TIME SERIES.
PROD-PUI DIST-PUI

TAKEDOWNS FROM A STANDING POSITION C 16 MIN
16MM FILM OPTICAL SOUND J-C A
DEMONSTRATES 32 TAKEDOWNS AND OUTLINES AN AGGRESSIVE ATTACK LEADING TO A QUICK PIN IN WRESTLING. ANALYZES EACH HOLD IN SLOW MOTION, NORMAL SPEED AND EXTREME CLOSE-UP PHOTOGRAPHY. FROM THE WINNING WRESTLING BY JOE BEGALA SERIES.
LC NO. 73-700690
PROD-EDCOM DIST-EDCOM 1971

TAKING CARE OF BUSINESS C 45 MIN
16MM FILM OPTICAL SOUND
DOCUMENTS THE LIFE OF CHARLIE MC GREGOR, AN EX-CON AND FORMER HEROIN ADDICT, WHO HAS SPENT 25 OF HIS 40 YEARS IN PRISON.
PROD-AMERFI DIST-AMERFI

TALKING ABOUT BREASTFEEDING C 25 MIN
16MM FILM OPTICAL SOUND H-C A
AFFIRMS THE VALUES OF BREASTFEEDING AS THE SIMPLEST, SAFEST AND MOST NUTRITIOUS WAY TO FEED AN INFANT AND HELPS ALLAY COMMON FEARS. FEATURES A NUMBER OF NURSING MOTHERS WHO HAVE OVERCOME MEDICAL PROBLEMS AND SOCIAL PRESSURES TO BREASTFEED SPEAKING OF THEIR EXPERIENCES.
PROD-POLYMR DIST-POLYMR

TARTAN TRACK C 5 MIN
16MM FILM OPTICAL SOUND J-C A
SEE SERIES TITLE FOR DESCRIPTIVE STATEMENT. FROM THE WONDERFUL WORLD OF SPORT - TRACK AND FIELD SERIES.
PROD-SPORTI DIST-AMERFI

TELL-TALE HEART, THE B 26 MIN
16MM FILM OPTICAL SOUND
PRESENTS AN ADAPTATION OF THE EDGAR ALLEN POE STORY, 'THE TELL-TALE HEART,' A STUDY IN PSYCHOLOGICAL SUSPENSE AND TERROR.
PROD-AMERFI DIST-AMERFI

TEMPEST, THE C 7 MIN
16MM FILM OPTICAL SOUND
PRESENTS A CINE-POEM IN WHICH THE IMAGES OF RUNNING HORSES ARE OPTICALLY MULTIPLIED AND DIVIDED, SYNCHRONIZED TO THE SOUND OF THE BEETHOVEN SONATA FOR PIANO, 'THE TEMPEST.'
PROD-CFS DIST-VISRES

THAT JOB INTERVIEW C 16 MIN
16MM FILM OPTICAL SOUND
STRESSES USEFUL TECHNIQUES FOR VETERANS TO USE IN JOB INTERVIEWS WITH PROSPECTIVE EMPLOYERS AND ILLUSTRATES FOR EMPLOYERS THE POSSIBLE APPLICATION OF MILITARY TRAINING TO CIVILIAN JOBS.
LC NO. 73-701059
PROD-USDL DIST-USNAC 1971

THEATER IN SHAKESPEARE'S TIME, THE C 14 MIN
16MM FILM OPTICAL SOUND J-C A
SHOWS THE GROWTH AND VITALITY OF THE THEATER IN SHAKESPEARE'S TIME IN A RE-CREATION OF THE PERIOD.
LC NO. 73-701436
PROD-BFA DIST-BFA 1973

THEORIST ROOM C 20 MIN
16MM FILM OPTICAL SOUND
PRESENTS AN EXPERIMENTAL FILM ABOUT A 'THEORIST,' AN AGELESS, SEXLESS FEMALE FIGURE WHO LOOKS OUT HER WINDOW AT THE WORLD AND SEES SUPERIMPOSED IMAGES WHICH OFTEN ARE IRONIC. SHOWS THAT HER SPECULATIONS END WHEN SHE IS HELPED BY A FRIEND. CONCLUDES BY REVEALING THAT SHE IS A SPASTIC.
PROD-AMERFI DIST-AMERFI

THIRD TEMPLE, THE C 17 MIN
16MM FILM OPTICAL SOUND
PORTRAYS MODERN ISRAEL MARCHING FORWARD IN THE WAKE OF THE PERSECUTED WANDERING JEW.
PROD-ALDEN DIST-ALDEN

THIS IS CAMPING C 18 MIN
16MM FILM OPTICAL SOUND I-C A
PRESENTS A LOOK AT ORGANIZED CAMPING AND THE MANY FACILITIES AND ACTIVITIES OFFERED CAMPERS. SHOWS HOW THE CAMPERS LEARN COOPERATION, CONSERVATION AND ECOLOGY THROUGH THEIR INVOLVEMENT WITH NATURE AND EACH OTHER.
LC NO. 73-700536
PROD-IU DIST-IU 1972

THIS IS OUR FARM C 11 MIN
16MM FILM OPTICAL SOUND
SHOWS A UNIQUE CHILDREN'S FARM IN ISRAEL.
PROD-ALDEN DIST-ALDEN

THOMAS JEFFERSON AND THE SOUTHERN SIGNERS C 80 MIN
16MM FILM OPTICAL SOUND
GIVES THE BACKGROUND OF THE 17 SOUTHERN SIGNERS OF THE CONSTITUTION. TELLS OF THEIR LIVES, ACHIEVEMENTS AND FATES. FROM THE TO THE SPIRIT OF '76 SERIES.
LC NO. 73-733683
PROD-RMI DIST-RMI

THOROUGHBRED - THE NEW BOY C 5 MIN
16MM FILM OPTICAL SOUND J-C A
SEE SERIES TITLE FOR DESCRIPTIVE STATEMENT. FROM THE WONDERFUL WORLD OF SPORT - HORSES, RACING, POLO, RODEO SERIES.
PROD-SPORTI DIST-AMERFI

THOROUGHBRED - THE STARTING GATE C 5 MIN
16MM FILM OPTICAL SOUND J-C A
SEE SERIES TITLE FOR DESCRIPTIVE STATEMENT. FROM THE WONDERFUL WORLD OF SPORT - HORSES, RACING, POLO, RODEO SERIES.
PROD-SPORTI DIST-AMERFI

THOSE ANIMALS ON THE FARM C
16MM FILM OPTICAL SOUND K-P
FOLLOWS PIGS, COWS, CHICKENS, HORSES AND SHEEP THROUGH THEIR DAILY ACTIVITIES OF SLEEPING, EATING AND MOVING ABOUT TO CAPTURE THE CHARACTER, INDIVIDUALITY AND HUMOR OF EACH ANIMAL.
LC NO. 73-701264
PROD-CLBELL DIST-CLBELL 1970

THREE FAMILIES OF MALAYSIA X 16 MIN
16MM FILM OPTICAL SOUND I
DEPICTS PEOPLE FROM THE THREE MAIN RACIAL GROUPS OF MALAYSIA - CHINESE, MALAY AND IBAN IN THE FAMILY GARDENS, CITY STORES AND SCHOOLS AND IN THE RUBBER TREE FOREST.
LC NO. 73-701239
PROD-CORF DIST-CORF 1973

THREE MAGICAL METHODS - FINDING GOOD IDEAS FOR STORIES C 13 MIN
16MM FILM OPTICAL SOUND P-I
PRESENTS TWO CHARACTERS, BIG MAX AND LITTLE MAX, WHO SEARCH FOR GOOD STORY IDEAS. ENCOURAGES THOSE WHO ARE RELUCTANT TO DEMONSTRATE ORIGINALITY AS WELL AS THOSE WHO ARE ALREADY SUCCESSFUL AT CREATIVE EXPRESSION.
LC NO. 73-700960
PROD-SAUER DIST-ECCCW 1971

TIBERIAS - LAND OF THE EMPERORS C 14 MIN
16MM FILM OPTICAL SOUND
POINTS OUT THAT THE ANCIENT TOWN OF TIBERIAS ON THE SEA OF GALILEE WAS BUILT BY HEROD AS A TRIBUTE TO THE ROMAN EMPEROR TIBERIUS. POINTS OUT ITS HISTORIC AND RELIGIOUS SIGNIFICANCE; THE NATURAL BEAUTY OF ITS SURROUNDINGS AND BOATING, WATER SKIING AND CULTURAL ACTIVITIES.
PROD-ALDEN DIST-ALDEN

TIGERS TRAINING C 5 MIN
16MM FILM OPTICAL SOUND J-C A
SEE SERIES TITLE FOR DESCRIPTIVE STATEMENT. FROM THE WONDERFUL WORLD OF SPORT - BASKETBALL SERIES.
PROD-SPORTI DIST-AMERFI

TIME MC CARVER C 5 MIN
16MM FILM OPTICAL SOUND J-C A
SEE SERIES TITLE FOR DESCRIPTIVE STATEMENT. FROM THE WONDERFUL WORLD OF SPORT - BASEBALL SERIES.
PROD-SPORTI DIST-AMERFI

TIN SOLDIER, THE C
16MM FILM OPTICAL SOUND
SEE SERIES TITLE FOR DESCRIPTIVE STATEMENT. FROM THE FAIRY TALE TIME SERIES.
PROD-PUI DIST-PUI

TIPS ON TRAP C 17 MIN
16MM FILM OPTICAL SOUND
FEATURES FRED MISSILDINE, NATIONAL AND WORLD CHAMPION, GIVING INSTRUCTIONS ON TRAPSHOOTING. INCLUDES PROPER GUN FIT, POINTING THE GUN, HOW TO CALL FOR THE TARGET AND PROPER STANCE AT POSITIONS.
PROD-MTP DIST-MTP

TO BE A FRIEND C 14 MIN
16MM FILM OPTICAL SOUND J-H
DESCRIBES FRIENDSHIPS EXPERIENCED BY YOUTH. FROM THE CIRCLE OF LIFE SERIES.
LC NO. 73-700928
PROD-BBF DIST-BBF 1973

TO BOTTLE THE SUN C 6 MIN
16MM FILM OPTICAL SOUND
EXPLORES THE POSSIBILITY OF FUSION POWER REACTORS AS AN ALTERNATIVE WAY OF SATISFYING OUR FUTURE EXPANDING ENERGY NEEDS WITH COAL, GAS AND OIL IN LIMITED SUPPLY.
LC NO. 73-701364
PROD-USAEC DIST-USAEC

TO THE SPIRIT OF '76--A SERIES
J-C
PRESENTS AN ACCOUNT OF EVENTS LEADING UP TO THE REVOLUTIONARY WAR, FROM THE VIKINGS THROUGH COLONIZATION AND THE DECLARATION OF INDEPENDENCE, WITH EMPHASIS ON THE SIGNERS OF THE DECLARATION AND THEIR FATE.
PROD-RMI   DIST-RMI   1973

ANGRY COLONIES - 1963 - 1774   80 MIN
BENJAMIN FRANKLIN AND THE MID-
ATLANTIC SIGNERS   80 MIN
DECLARATION OF INDEPENDENCE,
JUNE 1776 - --   80 MIN
FLAMES OF REVOLUTION - SEPTEMBER
1774 - --   80 MIN
JOHN ADAMS AND THE NEW ENGLAND
SIGNERS   80 MIN
SEEDS OF REBELLION - VIKINGS TO
1963   80 MIN
THOMAS JEFFERSON AND THE
SOUTHERN SIGNERS   80 MIN

**TOKYO - THE FIFTY-FIRST
VOLCANO**   C 51 MIN
          16MM FILM OPTICAL SOUND   H-C A
PROFILES TOKYO, THE WORLD'S LARGEST CITY, AND DESCRIBES THE QUALITY OF LIFE IN THIS CITY.
PROD-BBCTV   DIST-TIMLIF

TOM PAINE   C 5 MIN
          16MM FILM OPTICAL SOUND   J-C A
SEE SERIES TITLE FOR DESCRIPTIVE STATEMENT. FROM THE WONDERFUL WORLD OF SPORT - BASKETBALL SERIES.
PROD-SPORTI   DIST-AMERFI

**TOUCHDOWNS AND HORSES -
GOLES Y CABALLOS**   C 6 MIN
          16MM FILM OPTICAL SOUND
PRESENTS A FOLLOW-UP FOR THE PARK FIELD TRIP. FROM THE BRENTANO FOUNDATION BILINGUAL FILMS SERIES.
PROD-CAROUF   DIST-CAROUF

**TOUGH-MINDED SALESMANSHIP
- ASK FOR THE ORDER AND
GET IT -**   C 30 MIN
          16MM FILM OPTICAL SOUND   H-C
DISCUSSES FIVE TECHNIQUES FOR CLOSING A SALE AND TEACHES HOW TO TAKE THE FEAR OUT OF ASKING FOR THE ORDER. FROM THE TOUGH-MINDED SALESMANSHIP SERIES.
     LC NO. 73-701078
PROD-DARTNL   DIST-DARTNL   1972

TOUR OF GRANT'S FARM, A   C 14 MIN
          16MM FILM OPTICAL SOUND
PRESENTS A VISIT TO A POPULAR TOURIST ATTRACTION IN ST LOUIS WHICH FEATURES A 160-ACRE DEER PARK, A ZOO AND SIGHTSEEING TRAIN.
PROD-MTP   DIST-MTP

TOY DEVICES   C 14 MIN
          16MM FILM OPTICAL SOUND
INVESTIGATES WHAT MAKES TOYS MOVE. EXAMINES A BATTERY-DRIVEN LOCOMOTIVE, AUTOMOBILE RUN BY MOMENTUM, DUCK PROPELLED BY A SPRING AND A MODEL AIRPLANE FLOWN BY A RUBBER BAND.
PROD-IWANMI   DIST-IWANMI

TRAINER   C 5 MIN
          16MM FILM OPTICAL SOUND   J-C A
SEE SERIES TITLE FOR DESCRIPTIVE STATEMENT. FROM THE WONDERFUL WORLD OF SPORT - BASEBALL SERIES.
PROD-SPORTI   DIST-AMERFI

**TRAINS AND MORE TRAINS -
TRENES Y MAS TRENES**   C 11 MIN
          16MM FILM OPTICAL SOUND
PRESENTS AN INTRODUCTION TO FREIGHT AND COMMUTER TRAINS VIA DOCUMENTARY FOOTAGE. DISCUSSES THE 'TRAIN OF THE FUTURE' - AMTRAK. FROM THE BRENTANO FOUNDATION BILINGUAL FILMS SERIES.
PROD-CAROUF   DIST-CAROUF

TRAMPOLINE - GARY ERWIN   C 5 MIN
          16MM FILM OPTICAL SOUND   J-C A
SEE SERIES TITLE FOR DESCRIPTIVE STATEMENT. FROM THE WONDERFUL WORLD OF SPORT - GYMNASTICS SERIES.
PROD-SPORTI   DIST-AMERFI

TRAMPOLINE COMPETITION   C 5 MIN
          16MM FILM OPTICAL SOUND   J-C A
SEE SERIES TITLE FOR DESCRIPTIVE STATEMENT. FROM THE WONDERFUL WORLD OF SPORT - GYMNASTICS SERIES.
PROD-SPORTI   DIST-SPORTI

TRAP SHOOTING   C 5 MIN
          16MM FILM OPTICAL SOUND   J-C A
SEE SERIES TITLE FOR DESCRIPTIVE STATEMENT. FROM THE WONDERFUL WORLD OF SPORT - OTHER SERIES.
PROD-SPORTI   DIST-AMERFI

TRIALS OF FRANZ KAFKA, THE   B 15 MIN
          16MM FILM OPTICAL SOUND   H-C A
EXPLORES THE 'TRIALS' OF CHILDHOOD, YOUTH AND TRAGIC ADULTHOOD WHICH FRANZ KAFKA TRANSFORMED INTO NOVELS AND STORIES. HELPS IN THE UNDERSTANDING OF MODERN MAN'S ANXIETY AND ALIENATION. FROM THE FILMS FOR THE HUMANITIES SERIES.
     LC NO. 73-701106
PROD-MANTLH   DIST-FOTH   1969

TRICK CASTING   C 5 MIN
          16MM FILM OPTICAL SOUND   J-C A
SEE SERIES TITLE FOR DESCRIPTIVE STATEMENT. FROM THE WONDERFUL WORLD OF SPORT - FISHING SERIES.
PROD-SPORTI   DIST-AMERFI

TRIP TO RANCHO VERDE, A   C 9 MIN
          16MM FILM OPTICAL SOUND
DEPICTS CHILDREN MEETING THE FOREMAN, LEARNING ABOUT SEEDS, IRRIGATION AND DIFFERENT TYPES OF VEGETABLES. FROM THE BRENTANO FOUNDATION BILINGUAL FILMS SERIES.
PROD-CAROUF   DIST-CAROUF

TUB FILM   B 2 MIN
          16MM FILM OPTICAL SOUND
TELLS THE STORY OF A WOMAN AND HER SWEET VOICED KITTEN. SHOWS HOW BOTH ARE PLAYFUL AND CAREFREE, BUT ONE IS IN FOR A SURPRISE.
     LC NO. 73-701437
PROD-BFA   DIST-BFA   1973

**TUNA FROM CATCH TO THE
CAN**   C 27 MIN
          16MM FILM OPTICAL SOUND
TELLS THE STORY OF HOW TUNA IS OBTAINED BY MEN WHO RISK THEIR LIVES BATTLING THE ELEMENTS. INCLUDES THE PROCESSING AND SPECIAL CARE GIVEN TO PRESERVE THE TUNA FOR MARKETING.
PROD-MTP   DIST-MTP

TUNE INTO NATURE   C 11 MIN
          16MM FILM OPTICAL SOUND   I-C A
EXPLORES SOME OF THE DRAMATIC WONDERS OF NATURE PAINTED BY THE PASSING SEASONS OF THE YEAR.
     LC NO. 73-701197
PROD-NVFP   DIST-NVFP   1973

TUP TUP   C 9 MIN
          16MM FILM OPTICAL SOUND   J-C A
ASKS WHETHER ALL DESTRUCTION IS SELF-DESTRUCTION IN A STORY OF A LITTLE MAN WHO ATTEMPTS TO REMEDY AN ANNOYING 'THUMP, THUMP' THAT INTERRUPTS HIS PEACE AND QUIET.
     LC NO. 73-701438
PROD-BFA   DIST-BFA   1973

TURKEY   C
          16MM FILM OPTICAL SOUND
SEE SERIES TITLE FOR DESCRIPTIVE STATEMENT. FROM THE PORT OF CALL SERIES.
PROD-PUI   DIST-PUI

TWO-PLATOON   C 5 MIN
          16MM FILM OPTICAL SOUND   J-C A
SEE SERIES TITLE FOR DESCRIPTIVE STATEMENT. FROM THE WONDERFUL WORLD OF SPORT - FOOTBALL SERIES.
PROD-SPORTI   DIST-AMERFI

TYPHOON, PT 1   C 14 MIN
          16MM FILM OPTICAL SOUND
DISCUSSES THE ORIGIN AND STRUCTURE OF TYPHOONS THAT ANNUALLY CAUSE HEAVY LOSSES IN JAPAN.
PROD-IWANMI   DIST-IWANMI

TYPHOON, PT 2   C 14 MIN
          16MM FILM OPTICAL SOUND
STUDIES TYPHOON CHARACTERISTICS AND WIND PRESSURES TO DISCOVER APPROPRIATE MEASURES FOR COPING WITH TYPHOONS.
PROD-IWANMI   DIST-IWANMI

U

**UKIYO-E, A FLOATING WORLD
OF JAPANESE PAINTING**   C 20 MIN
          16MM FILM OPTICAL SOUND
PRESENTS A LARGE NUMBER OF RARELY DISPLAYED JAPANESE BRUSH PAINTINGS, THE GENRE FROM WHICH THE WORLD-FAMOUS JAPANESE WOODBLOCK PRINTS EVOLVED.
PROD-AMEDFL   DIST-VISRES

UMBRELLA MAN, THE   B 29 MIN
          16MM FILM OPTICAL SOUND
TELLS OF AN ENGLISH BUSINESSMAN IN ETHIOPIA WHO ESTABLISHES AN UMBRELLA FACTORY AND STAFFS IT ENTIRELY WITH CRIPPLED WORKERS.
PROD-MGHT   DIST-MGHT

UMPIRE SCHOOL   C 5 MIN
          16MM FILM OPTICAL SOUND   J-C A
SEE SERIES TITLE FOR DESCRIPTIVE STATEMENT. FROM THE WONDERFUL WORLD OF SPORT - BASEBALL SERIES.
PROD-SPORTI   DIST-AMERFI

UMPIRE'S TOUCH PLAYS   C 5 MIN
          16MM FILM OPTICAL SOUND   J-C A
SEE SERIES TITLE FOR DESCRIPTIVE STATEMENT. FROM THE WONDERFUL WORLD OF SPORT - BASEBALL SERIES.
PROD-SPORTI   DIST-AMERFI

UNAUTHORIZED DISCLOSURE   B 13 MIN
          16MM FILM OPTICAL SOUND
DEFINES 'UNAUTHORIZED DISCLOSURE' OF CLASSIFIED SECURITY INFORMATION. DESCRIBES HUMAN AND PROCEDURAL SAFEGUARDS TO AVOID COMPROMISES OF SECURITY INFORMATION.
     LC NO. 73-701247
PROD-USN   DIST-USNAC   1965

UNDER THE JUGGERNAUT   C 9 MIN
          16MM FILM OPTICAL SOUND
PRESENTS A SHOCKING COLLAGE OF SPEECH EVENTS, NEWS BROADCASTS, ANIMATED FIGURES AND ACTUAL PICTURES OF PEOPLE AND PLACES, BASED AROUND THE THEME OF POLITICAL ASSASSINATION.
PROD-AMERFI   DIST-AMERFI

UNEVEN PARALLEL BARS   C 5 MIN
          16MM FILM OPTICAL SOUND   J-C A
SEE SERIES TITLE FOR DESCRIPTIVE STATEMENT. FROM THE WONDERFUL WORLD OF SPORT - GYMNASTICS SERIES.
PROD-SPORTI   DIST-AMERFI

**UNIVERSE AND OTHER THINGS,
THE**   C 26 MIN
          16MM FILM OPTICAL SOUND
TELLS WHAT A CONSULTING ENGINEER IS, WHAT HE DOES AND HIS SIGNIFICANT CONTRIBUTIONS TO CITY, STATE, NATION AND WORLD.
PROD-MTP   DIST-MTP

UTILITY DOGS   C 5 MIN
          16MM FILM OPTICAL SOUND   J-C A
SEE SERIES TITLE FOR DESCRIPTIVE STATEMENT. FROM THE WONDERFUL WORLD OF SPORT - DOGS SERIES.
PROD-SPORTI   DIST-AMERFI

UTILIZATION OF SOLAR HEAT   C 14 MIN
          16MM FILM OPTICAL SOUND
TELLS HOW TO SCIENTIFICALLY UTILIZE SOLAR HEAT. DISCUSSES THE NATURAL UTILIZATION OF SOLAR HEAT, THE INDUCTION OF SOLAR HEAT, THE CRITICAL TEMPERATURE AND THE PREVENTION OF RADIATION.

W

PROD-IWANMI   DIST-IWANMI

V

VACATION FUN IN ISRAEL   C 11 MIN
16MM FILM OPTICAL SOUND
POINTS OUT THAT SUN, SEA, SURF AND VIVACITY
ARE PRESENT IN ISRAEL FOR ITS INHABITANTS
AND VISITORS.
PROD-ALDEN   DIST-ALDEN

**VARIOUS SPORTS - THIRTY
POINTS TO FITNESS**   C 5 MIN
16MM FILM OPTICAL SOUND   J-C A
SEE SERIES TITLE FOR DESCRIPTIVE STATEMENT.
FROM THE WONDERFUL WORLD OF SPORT - AER-
OBICS SERIES.
PROD-SPORTI   DIST-AMERFI

VD - ATTACK PLAN   C 16 MIN
16MM FILM OPTICAL SOUND   J-H
PRESENTS A VETERAN GERM IN THE CONTAGION
CORPS WHO OUTLINES HOW SYPHILIS AND GON-
ORRHEA CAN ATTACK MAN. POINTS OUT THE
STEPS WHICH MAN CAN FOLLOW TO DEFEAT THE
TWO DISEASES BUT EMPHASIZES THE MYTH THAT
KEEPS UNINFORMED HUMANS FROM SEEKING
TREATMENT.
LC NO. 73-700962
PROD-DISNEY   DIST-DISNEY   1973

VEGETABLE CELLS   C 14 MIN
16MM FILM OPTICAL SOUND
POINTS OUT THAT THE SPLITTING OF CELLS IS
THE SECRET OF PLANT GROWTH. USES LAPSE
PHOTOGRAPHY TO ILLUSTRATE THE ACTION OF
THE CELL AND PROTOPLASM CIRCULATION. DE-
SCRIBES CELL DISINTEGRATION AND ACTION OF
CHROMOSOMES.
PROD-IWANMI   DIST-IWANMI

VENEREAL DISEASE   B 28 MIN
16MM FILM OPTICAL SOUND   H-C A
PRESENTS A REVIEW OF BASIC INFORMATION ON
SYPHILIS AND GONORRHEA, EMPHASIZING THE
IMPORTANCE OF RECOGNIZING SYMPTOMS OF
THESE INFECTIONS AND SEEKING PROPER DIAG-
NOSIS AND TREATMENT. FROM THE SEX IN AMER-
ICA CULTURE SERIES.
LC NO. 73-701219
PROD-CHM   DIST-CHM   1967

**VERA PAINTS IBIZA IN THE
SUN**   C 20 MIN
16MM FILM OPTICAL SOUND
VISITS THE ISLAND OF IBIZA OFF THE COAST OF
SPAIN WITH AMERICAN TEXTILE DESIGNER, VERA
NEWMANN. SHOWS HOW HER SKETCH BECOMES
A DESIGN FOR A TEXTILE PRINT AND HOW ART-
ISTS, TECHNICIANS, CHEMISTS AND CRAFTSMEN
TRANSMIT VERA'S DESIGN ONTO FABRIC.
LC NO. 73-700627
PROD-SCHLAT   DIST-SCHLAT   1973

VESPER STORY   C 5 MIN
16MM FILM OPTICAL SOUND   J-C A
SEE SERIES TITLE FOR DESCRIPTIVE STATEMENT.
FROM THE WONDERFUL WORLD OF SPORT - ROW-
ING SERIES.
PROD-SPORTI   DIST-AMERFI

VIETNAM EPILOGUE   B
16MM FILM OPTICAL SOUND
PRESENTS A CHRONOLOGY OF THE SIGNIFICANT
MILESTONES IN THE VIETNAM WAR, THE LONG-
EST WAR IN AMERICAN HISTORY. FROM THE
SCREEN NEWS DIGEST SERIES.
PROD-HEARST   DIST-HEARST   1973

VISION OF CHAIM WEIZMANN   B 21 MIN
16MM FILM OPTICAL SOUND
PRESENTS A BIOGRAPHY OF ISRAEL'S FIRST PRES-
IDENT, INCORPORATING THE STORY OF ZIONISM
AND THE RE-ESTABLISHMENT OF THE JEWISH
PEOPLE IN THEIR LAND.
PROD-ALDEN   DIST-ALDEN

VISTAS OF ISRAEL, NO. 1   B 14 MIN
16MM FILM OPTICAL SOUND
FEATURES THE STORIES 'CITY ON WHEELS,'
SHOWING A GLIMPSE OF TEL AVIV AND SOME OF
THE PROBLEMS THAT IT PRESENTS TO THE TRAF-
FIC COP AND 'THE ROAD BUILDERS,' THE STORY
OF THE PAINSTAKING LABORS THAT WENT INTO
THE CONSTRUCTION OF A NEW ROAD THROUGH
THE NEGEV TO EILAT ON THE RED SEA.
PROD-ALDEN   DIST-ALDEN

VISTAS OF ISRAEL, NO. 2   B 14 MIN
16MM FILM OPTICAL SOUND
PRESENTS THE STORIES 'ON THE TOWN,' AN AC-
COUNT OF A GROUP OF DRUSE SOLDIERS SPEND-
ING AN ARMY FURLOUGH IN THE CITY OF TEL
AVIV, 'OLIVES OF JUDEA,' A HISTORIC AND CON-
TEMPORARY DESCRIPTION OF THE OLIVE INDUS-
TRY IN ISRAEL AND 'DOOR TO THE FUTURE,' AN
ACCOUNT OF THE BUILDING OF THE YARKON-
NEGEV PIPELINE.
PROD-ALDEN   DIST-ALDEN

VISTAS OF ISRAEL, NO. 3   B 14 MIN
16MM FILM OPTICAL SOUND
PRESENTS THE STORIES 'HELETZ NO. 1,' DOCU-
MENTING THE DISCOVERY OF OIL IN ISRAEL, 'BIB-
LICAL ZOO,' VIEWING THE ZOO THROUGH THE
EYES OF THREE YOUNG ISRAELI CHILDREN AND
'GOLD IN THE TREES,' AN ACCOUNT OF ISRAEL'S
ORANGE INDUSTRY.
PROD-ALDEN   DIST-ALDEN

VISTAS OF ISRAEL, NO. 4   B 14 MIN
16MM FILM OPTICAL SOUND
PRESENTS THE STORIES 'MACCABIAH,' DOCU-
MENTING THE ISRAELI OLYMPICS, 'PATTERNS OF
LIVING,' SHOWING THE UNIQUE CRAFTSMANSHIP
OF ISRAEL'S NEW IMMIGRANTS AND 'HOUSE OF
FAITH,' WHICH TAKES PLACE IN THE HISTORIC
TOWN OF NAZARETH AT THE CORNERSTONE LAY-
ING OF THE CHURCH OF THE ANNUNCIATION.
PROD-ALDEN   DIST-ALDEN

VISUALIZATION OF FORCE   C 14 MIN
16MM FILM OPTICAL SOUND
SHOWS THAT ACTION OF STRESS INSIDE MATERI-
ALS CANNOT BE MEASURED BY ORDINARY MATE-
RIALS TESTS. GIVES AN EXPLANATION OF THE
PHOTO-ELASTICITY TEST WHICH ENABLES THIS TO
BE SEEN AND MEASURED.
PROD-IWANMI   DIST-IWANMI

VOICE OF LA RAZA   C
16MM FILM OPTICAL SOUND
PRESENTS A DOCUMENTARY REPORT FROM EL
BARRIOS OF SPANISH SPEAKING AMERICA DEAL-
ING WITH JOB AND CULTURAL DISCRIMINATION
AGAINST SPANISH SURNAMED AMERICANS.
LC NO. 73-701126
PROD-EQEMOP   DIST-GREAVW   1970

VOICES FROM MAINE   C 28 MIN
16MM FILM OPTICAL SOUND   J-C A
PRESENTS ENVIRONMENTAL ISSUES IN TERMS OF
THE PEOPLE IN MAINE, INCLUDING A LOBSTER-
MAN, A TOWN MANAGER, A RETIRED SHOE FAC-
TORY WORKER, A GREAT GRANDMOTHER REMEM-
BERING HOW IT USED TO BE, THE YOUNG MEM-
BERS OF A WEAVING COMMUNE AND A DAIRY
FARMING FAMILY.
PROD-POLYMR   DIST-POLYMR

VOLCANOES AND HOT SPRINGS   C 14 MIN
16MM FILM OPTICAL SOUND
OBSERVES AND EXPLAINS THE RELATIONSHIP BE-
TWEEN VOLCANOES AND HOT SPRINGS.
PROD-IWANMI   DIST-IWANMI

W

**WALKER EVANS - HIS TIME, HIS
PRESENCE, HIS SILENCE**   B
16MM FILM OPTICAL SOUND   A
PRESENTS AN ACCUMULATION OF INDIVIDUAL
PHOTOGRAPHIC PRINTS TAKEN BY WALKER EV-
ANS.
LC NO. 73-701261
PROD-RADIM   DIST-RADIM   1970

WALLS OF TIME, THE   C 25 MIN
16MM FILM OPTICAL SOUND   J-C A
PRESENTS A DOCUMENTARY ON THE HISTORY OF
THE ENGLISH BIBLE.
LC NO. 72-702171
PROD-PFP   DIST-PFP   1972

WATER IN THE WILDERNESS   C
16MM FILM OPTICAL SOUND   I-C A
FOLLOWS THE JOURNEY OF THE RIVER OF WIL-
DERNESS DOWN FROM THE PEAKS AND CRAGS,
CARRYING THE GIFT OF LIFE TO ROOT AND LEAF.
LC NO. 73-701265
PROD-CLBELL   DIST-CLBELL   1972

WATER PRESSURE   B 20 MIN
16MM FILM OPTICAL SOUND
EXPLAINS PASCAL'S THEORY THAT PRESSURE AP-
PLIED TO A SECTION OF A LIQUID WOULD BE
TRANSMITTED EQUALLY TO THE ENTIRE LIQUID.
SHOWS THE USE OF A WATER COMPRESSOR AND
THE PRINCIPLES FOR OPERATING AN OIL JACK,
DUMP TRUCK, AUTO LIFT AND PRESSING MA-
CHINE.
PROD-IWANMI   DIST-IWANMI

WATER SMITH   C 32 MIN
16MM FILM OPTICAL SOUND
PRESENTS AN EXPERIMENTAL FILM ATTEMPTING
TO MERGE MAN AND WATER PHOTOGRAPHICALLY,
BOTH IN THE EYE AND THE MIND SO THAT THEY
BECOME AN INDIVISIBLE UNIT, WHERE THE WA-
TER BECOMES LIFE, THE MAN BECOMES PART OF
THE WATER AND THE WHOLE PICTURE BECOMES
A PORTRAIT OF MAN'S RELATIONSHIP WITH HIS
MOST VALUABLE INDISPENSABLE ELEMENT.
PROD-AMERFI   DIST-AMERFI

WATER SURFACE   C 14 MIN
16MM FILM OPTICAL SOUND
USES EXPERIMENTS TO OBSERVE THE STRANGE
PHENOMENON OCCURRING ON THE SURFACE OF
THE WATER.
PROD-IWANMI   DIST-IWANMI

**WATERCOLOR PAINTING -
ABSTRACT DESIGNS FROM
NATURE WITH EDWARD BETTS**   C 19 MIN
16MM FILM OPTICAL SOUND
WATCHES EDWARD BETTS AS HE MAKES SEVERAL
PENCIL DRAWINGS AT A QUARRY. SHOWS HOW HE
DEVELOPS ONE OF HIS DRAWINGS INTO AN
ACRYLIC WATERCOLOR IN HIS STUDIO. FROM THE
WATERCOLOR PAINTING SERIES.
LC NO. 73-700684
PROD-PERSPF   DIST-PERSPF   1973

**WATERCOLOR PAINTING -
CREATIVE COLOR COLLAGE
WITH EDWARD BETTS**   C 18 MIN
16MM FILM OPTICAL SOUND
FOLLOWS EDWARD BETTS AS HE SEEKS A NEW
MOTIF AMONG FAMILIAR MONOLITHS OF STONE,
THEN DEVELOPS HIS SKETCHES INTO A COHESIVE
DESIGN. FROM THE WATERCOLOR PAINTING SE-
RIES.
LC NO. 73-700685
PROD-PERSPF   DIST-PERSPF   1973

**WATERCOLOR PAINTING -
IMAGINATIVE DESIGNS WITH
ALEX ROSS**   C 20 MIN
16MM FILM OPTICAL SOUND
PRESENTS ALEX ROSS DEMONSTRATING HOW HE
CREATES ARRESTING PATTERNS OF VIVID COLOR
AND HOW HE USES ACRYLIC PAINT ON A TEX-
TURED MEDIA BOARD. FROM THE WATERCOLOR
PAINTING SERIES.
LC NO. 73-700682
PROD-PERSPF   DIST-PERSPF   1973

**WATERCOLOR PAINTING - THE
MARINE SCENE WITH HERB
OLSEN**   C 19 MIN
16MM FILM OPTICAL SOUND
PRESENTS AN ARTIST DEMONSTRATING HIS
METHOD OF CREATING IMAGES OF FOG, ILLUSION
OF SOLID FORMS IN SPACE AND THE TEXTURING
OF A PAINT SURFACE WITH A BLADE. FROM THE
WATERCOLOR PAINTING SERIES.
LC NO. 73-700680
PROD-PERSPF   DIST-PERSPF   1973

**WATERCOLOR PAINTING -
WORKING FROM SKETCHES
WITH LOUIS J KEEP**   C 20 MIN
16MM FILM OPTICAL SOUND
PRESENTS ARTIST LOUIS KEEP SHOWING A COLOR
STUDY OF A CHINESE SAMPAN PLUS SEVERAL
PENCIL DRAWINGS AND THE EVOLUTION OF THE
WATERCOLOR OF THE SAMPAN. FROM THE WA-
TERCOLOR PAINTING SERIES.
LC NO. 73-700681
PROD-PERSPF   DIST-PERSPF   1973

**WATERCOLOR PAINTING -
WORKING ON LOCATION WITH
EDWIN L DAHLBERG**   C 20 MIN
16MM FILM OPTICAL SOUND
FOLLOWS THE DEVELOPMENT OF A WATERCOLOR
FROM A FEW COMPOSITIONAL SKETCHES IN PEN-
CIL, TO LINES DRAWN ON A MOUNTED SHEET OF
PAPER TO THE FINISHED WORK. FROM THE WA-
TERCOLOR PAINTING SERIES.
LC NO. 73-700683
PROD-PERSPF   DIST-PERSPF   1973

WATERCOLOR PAINTING--A SERIES

SHOWS ARTISTS IN THEIR STUDIOS OR ON LOCATION, AS THEY EXPLAIN HOW THEY LOOK AND PLAN EACH DETAIL OF A WATERCOLOR OR AN ACRYLIC PAINTING FROM START TO FINISH.
PROD-PERSPF   DIST-PERSPF   1973

WATERCOLOR PAINTING - ABSTRACT
DESIGNS FROM --   19 MIN
WATERCOLOR PAINTING - CREATIVE
COLOR COLLAGE --   18 MIN
WATERCOLOR PAINTING - IMAGINATIVE
DESIGNS --   20 MIN
WATERCOLOR PAINTING - THE MARINE
SCENE WITH --   19 MIN
WATERCOLOR PAINTING - WORKING
FROM SKETCHES --   20 MIN
WATERCOLOR PAINTING - WORKING ON
LOCATION --   20 MIN

WATERSMITH   C 32 MIN
16MM FILM OPTICAL SOUND   I-C A
PRESENTS A DOCUMENTARY ON SWIMMING. SHOWS HOW IT EVOLVES INTO A SERIES OF BEAUTIFUL ABSTRACT PATTERNS OF LINES OF ENERGY SLICING THROUGH THE ENCLOSED, THREE-DIMENSIONAL SPACE THAT IS A SWIMMING POOL.
LC NO. 73-701391
PROD-AMERFI   DIST-TIMLIF   1972

WAVES ON THE SEASHORE   C 14 MIN
16MM FILM OPTICAL SOUND
OBSERVES THE FEATURES OF WAVES LASHING THE COAST. DISCUSSES WHY THE WAVES BREAK, WHY WAVES FORM AND WAVE INTERFERENCE.
PROD-IWANMI   DIST-IWANMI

WAY FOR DIANA, A   C 16 MIN
16MM FILM OPTICAL SOUND   I-J
TELLS THE STORY OF DIANA, A 12 YEAR OLD GIRL IN THE CITY, WHO DISCOVERS NEW WORLDS THROUGH READING IN THE LIBRARY. SHOWS HOW SHE IMAGINES HERSELF IN THE SETTINGS ABOUT WHICH SHE READS.
LC NO. 79-715511
PROD-MENKNS   DIST-AIMS   1972

WAY IT IS, THE   B 50 MIN
16MM FILM OPTICAL SOUND   C A
FOLLOWS A PUERTO RICAN GHETTO FAMILY IN ITS 'LIFESPACE.' FORCES THE VIEWER TO CRITICALLY EXAMINE THE SITUATION, TO EXPLORE THE EFFECTIVENESS AND NONEFFECTIVENESS OF THE INTERVENTIONS EMPLOYED BY THE SOCIAL WORKER AND TO WEIGH SEVERAL ALTERNATIVES TO THIS TYPE OF PUBLIC WELFARE.
LC NO. 73-700812
PROD-ADELPH   DIST-SYNCRO   1970

WAY TO GO, THE   C 28 MIN
16MM FILM OPTICAL SOUND   A
COMBINES GOOD CINEMATOGRAPHY OF SCENERY, PARKS, CAMP SITES AND FAMILIES WITH A MONTAGE OF ON-SITE COMMENTS BY PARK OFFICIALS, OWNERS OF CAMP SITES AND MORE ELABORATE RECREATIONAL FACILITIES AND INDIVIDUALS WHO ARE SOLD ON CAMPING AS A FREQUENT RECREATION OR AS A WAY OF LIFE.
LC NO. 73-700996
PROD-PILOT   DIST-SFI

**WE EXPLORE CHINATOWN -
NOSOTROS EXPLORAMOS
CHINATOWN**   C 7 MIN
16MM FILM OPTICAL SOUND
DISCUSSES ORIENTAL HERITAGE AND THE CULTURE OF MANY OF OUR CITIZENS. FROM THE BRENTANO FOUNDATION BILINGUAL FILMS SERIES.
PROD-CAROUF   DIST-CAROUF

WE GO TO A DAIRY FARM   C 8 MIN
16MM FILM OPTICAL SOUND
PRESENTS A FIELD TRIP TO A DAIRY FARM IN WHICH CHILDREN MILK A COW, CLIMB TREES, RIDE ON A HAY WAGON AND MEET ANIMALS. FROM THE BRENTANO FOUNDATION BILINGUAL FILMS SERIES.
PROD-CAROUF   DIST-CAROUF

WE HAVE AN ADDICT IN THE HOUSE   C 30 MIN
16MM FILM OPTICAL SOUND   J-C A
USES DRUG ABUSE TO PROVIDE SOME INSIGHT INTO THE PSYCHOSOCIAL CAUSES OF ALIENATION AMONG YOUNG ADULTS. PROVIDES A SITUATION WHEREIN THE PARTICIPANTS CAN EXPLORE INDIVIDUAL AND GROUP ATTITUDES ABOUT DRUGS AND ABOUT INTRA-FAMILY RELATIONSHIPS.
LC NO. 73-701394
PROD-CONFON   DIST-DOUBLE   1972

**WE REMEMBER THE FARM -
RECORDAMOS EL RANCHO**   C 6 MIN
16MM FILM OPTICAL SOUND
PRESENTS A FOLLOW-UP REVIEW OF THE FIELD TRIP TO THE DAIRY FARM. FROM THE BRENTANO FOUNDATION BILINGUAL FILMS SERIES.
PROD-CAROUF   DIST-CAROUF

**WE SEE THE BABY ZOO -
VEMOS EL ZOOLOGICO
INFANTIL**   C 8 MIN
16MM FILM OPTICAL SOUND
SHOWS CHILDREN MEETING AND LEARNING HOW TO HANDLE SMALLER ANIMALS. FROM THE BRENTANO FOUNDATION BILINGUAL FILMS SERIES.
PROD-CAROUF   DIST-CAROUF

WE THE ENEMY   C 26 MIN
16MM FILM OPTICAL SOUND
PRESENTS AN EXPOSITION ON THE ENVIRONMENTAL PROBLEMS OF CONNECTICUT.
PROD-FENWCK   DIST-FENWCK

**WE VISIT THE POST OFFICE -
VISITAMOS LA CASA DE
CORREOS**   C 8 MIN
16MM FILM OPTICAL SOUND
SHOWS CHILDREN WHAT HAPPENS TO A LETTER WHEN IT IS DROPPED IN THE MAILBOX. FROM THE BRENTANO FOUNDATION BILINGUAL FILMS SERIES.
PROD-CAROUF   DIST-CAROUF

**WE VISIT THE ZOO - VISITAMOS
EL JARDIN ZOOLOGICO**   C 11 MIN
16MM FILM OPTICAL SOUND
DISCUSSES THE HISTORY AND ZOOLOGY OF ANIMALS. FROM THE BRENTANO FOUNDATION BILINGUAL FILMS SERIES.
PROD-CAROUF   DIST-CAROUF

WEIGHTLIFTING - TRAINING   C 5 MIN
16MM FILM OPTICAL SOUND   J-C A
SEE SERIES TITLE FOR DESCRIPTIVE STATEMENT. FROM THE WONDERFUL WORLD OF SPORT - WEIGHTLIFTING SERIES.
PROD-SPORTI   DIST-AMERFI

WEIGHTLIFTING - WHAT IS IT   C 5 MIN
16MM FILM OPTICAL SOUND   J-C A
SEE SERIES TITLE FOR DESCRIPTIVE STATEMENT. FROM THE WONDERFUL WORLD OF SPORT - WEIGHTLIFTING SERIES.
PROD-SPORTI   DIST-AMERFI

WELL OF WISDOM, THE   C
16MM FILM OPTICAL SOUND
SEE SERIES TITLE FOR DESCRIPTIVE STATEMENT. FROM THE FAIRY TALE TIME SERIES.
PROD-PUI   DIST-PUI

**WHAT DO SEEDS NEED TO
SPROUT**   C 11 MIN
16MM FILM OPTICAL SOUND   P
REVEALS THE NEED FOR THREE THINGS IN ORDER FOR A SEED TO GERMINATE - THE RIGHT TEMPERATURE, WATER AND AIR.
LC NO. 73-701235
PROD-CORF   DIST-CORF   1973

**WHAT DO WE LOOK LIKE TO
OTHERS**   C 10 MIN
16MM FILM OPTICAL SOUND   H-C A
PRESENTS SEVEN DIFFERENT OFFICE SITUATIONS TO PORTRAY THE NECESSITY OF MAINTAINING GOOD PERSONAL APPEARANCE, ATTITUDES, CONDUCT AND PERSONAL HABITS.
PROD-SAIF   DIST-SAIF

**WHAT EVERY MANAGER NEEDS
TO KNOW ABOUT
INFORMATION SYSTEMS, PT 1 -
THE MERITT CASE**   C
16MM FILM OPTICAL SOUND
SEE SERIES TITLE FOR DESCRIPTIVE STATEMENT. FROM THE MANAGEMENT PRACTICE SERIES.
PROD-BNA   DIST-BNA

**WHAT EVERY MANAGER NEEDS
TO KNOW ABOUT
INFORMATION SYSTEMS, PT 2 -
THE COMPUTER ...**   C
16MM FILM OPTICAL SOUND
SEE SERIES TITLE FOR DESCRIPTIVE STATEMENT. FROM THE MANAGEMENT PRACTICE SERIES.
PROD-BNA   DIST-BNA

**WHAT EVERY MANAGER NEEDS
TO KNOW ABOUT MARKETING,
PT 1 - THE MERITT CASE**   C
16MM FILM OPTICAL SOUND
SEE SERIES TITLE FOR DESCRIPTIVE STATEMENT. FROM THE MANAGEMENT PRACTICE SERIES.
PROD-BNA   DIST-BNA

**WHAT EVERY MANAGER NEEDS
TO KNOW ABOUT MARKETING,
PT 2 - WHAT BUSINESS ARE
YOU ...**   C
16MM FILM OPTICAL SOUND
SEE SERIES TITLE FOR DESCRIPTIVE STATEMENT. FROM THE MANAGEMENT PRACTICE SERIES.
PROD-BNA   DIST-BNA

**WHAT EVERY MANAGER NEEDS
TO KNOW ABOUT LONG-RANGE
PLANNING, PT 1 - THE MERITT
CASE**   C
16MM FILM OPTICAL SOUND
SEE SERIES TITLE FOR DESCRIPTIVE STATEMENT. FROM THE MANAGEMENT PRACTICE SERIES.
PROD-BNA   DIST-BNA

**WHAT EVERY MANAGER NEEDS
TO KNOW ABOUT LONG-RANGE
PLANNING, PT 2 - INVENT
YOUR ...**   C
16MM FILM OPTICAL SOUND
SEE SERIES TITLE FOR DESCRIPTIVE STATEMENT. FROM THE MANAGEMENT PRACTICE SERIES.
PROD-BNA   DIST-BNA

WHAT FIXED ME   C 20 MIN
16MM FILM OPTICAL SOUND
CENTERS ON A BOY'S FIGHT TO FREE HIMSELF FROM HIS DOMINEERING EX-PREACHER FATHER AFTER HIS MOTHER'S SUICIDE. VIEWS THE INCIDENTS THROUGH THE BOY'S EYES. INCLUDES NATIVE KENTUCKY MUSIC AND LANDSCAPE.
PROD-AMERFI   DIST-AMERFI

WHAT IS BUSINESS   C 10 MIN
16MM FILM OPTICAL SOUND   H-C A
ACQUAINTS THE STUDENT WITH WHAT A BUSINESS IS, HOW IT OPERATES, WHO OPERATES IT AND WHO IS RESPONSIBLE FOR MAKING SHORT-TERM DECISIONS AND OVERALL POLICY. OBSERVES THE OPERATION OF A ONE MAN BOUTIQUE LEATHER SHOP IN CONTRAST WITH THE OPERATION OF A LARGE MANUFACTURING COMPANY.
PROD-SAIF   DIST-SAIF

WHAT IS LIGHT, PT 1   C 14 MIN
16MM FILM OPTICAL SOUND
SHOWS THE GRANULAR CHARACTERISTICS OF LIGHT. ILLUSTRATES DIFFUSION PHENOMENON OF LIGHT IN A DARKBOX AND THE FLOW OF TINY STEEL GRAINS AND THEIR REFLECTIONS.
PROD-IWANMI   DIST-IWANMI

WHAT IS LIGHT, PT 2   C 14 MIN
16MM FILM OPTICAL SOUND
SHOWS THE SPECIAL FEATURES OF LIGHT AS WAVES. PRESENTS AN EXPERIMENT IN A RIPPLE TANK TO SHOW THE SIMILARITIES OF WAVES AND LIGHT WAVES. DEMONSTRATES REFRACTION AND TOTAL REFLECTION OF LIGHT.
PROD-IWANMI   DIST-IWANMI

WHAT TRIGGERS SNOWSLIDES   C 14 MIN
16MM FILM OPTICAL SOUND
STUDIES THE CHARACTERISTICS OF SNOW TO FIND OUT THE CAUSES OF SNOWSLIDES. OBSERVES THE VISCOSITY OF SNOW, THE PULL BETWEEN CRYSTALS AND THE CHANGE IN SNOW-DRIFTS.
PROD-IWANMI   DIST-IWANMI

WHAT WOULD YOU DO   C 8 MIN
16MM FILM OPTICAL SOUND   P-I
DEPICTS TWO CHILDREN AT PLAY; ONE BLACK, ONE WHITE. POSES PROBLEMATICAL SITUATIONS REQUIRING ACTIVE STUDENT PARTICIPATION AND ASSESSMENT OF BASIC HUMAN VALUES.
LC NO. 73-700632
PROD-ATLAP   DIST-ATLAP   1972

WHAT'S IT ALL ABOUT, HARRY   C 29 MIN
16MM FILM OPTICAL SOUND   IND
FOLLOWS A YOUNG TELEPHONE INSTALLER AS HE TAKES HIS KID BROTHER ALONG ON HIS SATURDAY ERRANDS. SHOWS HOW THEY GIVE RATINGS TO THE KINDS OF SERVICE THEY RECEIVE AND IN TURN ARE RATED ON THE CRAFT JOBS DONE THE DAY BEFORE.
LC NO. 73-700531
PROD-ILBELL   DIST-DATA   1970

WHAT'S WRONG WITH THE SOCIAL SCIENCES   B 56 MIN
16MM FILM OPTICAL SOUND   H-C A
PRESENTS PSYCHOLOGIST B F SKINNER, WHOSE UNORTHODOX VIEWS AND REFUSAL TO FOLLOW THE USUAL METHODS OF THE BEHAVIORAL SCIENCES CONTINUE TO CREATE HEATED CONTROVERSY. SHOWS FIVE EMINENT PSYCHOLOGISTS WHO PRESENT THEIR IDEAS ABOUT THE PROBLEMS OF SOCIETY TODAY.
PROD-BBCTV   DIST-TIMLIF

WHATEVER IS FUN   C 8 MIN
16MM FILM OPTICAL SOUND   P-J
USES ANIMATION TO TELL THE STORY OF A KING WHO OFFERS UNTOLD WEALTH TO ANYONE WHO CAN TEACH HIM WHAT FUN IS.
LC NO. 73-701043
PROD-DAVFMS   DIST-CCMFI   1973

WHEN EVERY MINUTE COUNTS   C 21 MIN
16MM FILM OPTICAL SOUND
DEMONSTRATES AN ELECTRIC PROTECTION SYSTEM THAT GUARDS AGAINST FIRE AND THWARTS EVEN THE MOST INGENIOUS BURGLARS.
PROD-MTP   DIST-MTP

WHERE'S THE TROUBLE   C 9 MIN
16MM FILM OPTICAL SOUND   K-P
TEACHES THE CONCEPTS OF FRONT, BACK, TOP AND BOTTOM.
LC NO. 73-701038
PROD-GRADYM   DIST-GRADYM   1972

WHITE FACE OF YELLOWSTONE   C 30 MIN
16MM FILM OPTICAL SOUND
PRESENTS SCENES OF YELLOWSTONE NATIONAL PARK IN THE WINTER, SHOWING THE PARK'S WINTERTIME ACTIVITIES.
PROD-MTP   DIST-MTP

WHITE MANE   C 30 MIN
16MM FILM OPTICAL SOUND
TELLS THE STORY OF A WILD WHITE STALLION LIVING IN FREEDOM, OF THE MEN WHO WISH TO CAPTURE HIM AND BREAK HIS SPIRIT AND OF THE BOY WHO ULTIMATELY TAMES HIM WITH LOVE.
PROD-CCMFI   DIST-CCMFI

WILLIS REED - CENTER PLAY, PT 1   C 11 MIN
16MM FILM OPTICAL SOUND   J-C
FEATURES WILLIS REED OF THE NEW YORK KNICKS ILLUSTRATING VARIOUS TECHNIQUES IN CENTER PLAY. COVERS SHOOTING, THE PUSH SHOT, THE JUMP SHOT, THE HOOK SHOT, THE LAYUP AND THE FREE THROW. FROM THE WILLIS REED BASKETBALL SERIES.
LC NO. 73-701358
PROD-SCHLAT   DIST-SCHLAT   1972

WILLIS REED - CENTER PLAY, PT 2   C 12 MIN
16MM FILM OPTICAL SOUND   J-C
FEATURES WILLIS REED OF THE NEW YORK KNICKS ILLUSTRATING VARIOUS TECHNIQUES IN CENTER PLAY. COVERS DEFENSIVE REBOUNDING, OFFENSIVE REBOUNDING, SWITCHING ON THE 'PICK' AND PROPER TRAINING TECHNIQUES. FROM THE WILLIS REED BASKETBALL SERIES.
LC NO. 73-701368
PROD-SCHLAT   DIST-SCHLAT   1972

WILLIS REED BASKETBALL--A SERIES   J-C

PROD-SCHLAT   DIST-SCHLAT   1972

DICK VAN ARSDALE - DEFENSIVE PLAY, PT 1	12 MIN
DICK VAN ARSDALE - DEFENSIVE PLAY, PT 2	11 MIN
JACK MARIN - FORWARD PLAY, PT 1	12 MIN
JACK MARIN - FORWARD PLAY, PT 2	11 MIN
JO JO WHITE - OFFENSIVE GUARD, PT 1	10 MIN
JO JO WHITE - OFFENSIVE GUARD, PT 2	12 MIN
WILLIS REED - CENTER PLAY, PT 1	11 MIN
WILLIS REED - CENTER PLAY, PT 2	12 MIN

WIND INSTRUMENT, THE   C 14 MIN
16MM FILM OPTICAL SOUND
DESCRIBES SECRETS OF WIND INSTRUMENTS PRODUCING VARYING SOUNDS FROM A SINGLE PIPE. EXPLAINS THE RESONANCE PHENOMENON OF SOUND WAVES THROUGH EXPERIMENT AND MOVING PICTURE OF A BALL TIED TO A SPRING.
PROD-IWANMI   DIST-IWANMI

WINDOW FROST   C 14 MIN
16MM FILM OPTICAL SOUND
SHOWS FROST MADE IN A LOW TEMPERATURE LABORATORY AND OBSERVES ITS STAGES OF FORMATION BY SLOW MOTION PHOTOGRAPHY. ILLUSTRATES VARIOUS KINDS OF BEAUTIFUL FROST CRYSTALS.
PROD-IWANMI   DIST-IWANMI

WINNING WRESTLING BY JOE BEGALA--A SERIES   J-C A

PROD-EDCOM   DIST-EDCOM   1971

COUNTERS FOR TAKEDOWNS FROM A STANDING POSITION	16 MIN
TAKEDOWNS FROM A STANDING POSITION	16 MIN

WINTERLUDE   C 10 MIN
16MM FILM OPTICAL SOUND
DRAMATIZES THE SEVERE PERSONAL AND BUSINESS LOSSES THAT CAN BE CAUSED BY A HEAVY SNOWFALL.
PROD-MTP   DIST-MTP

WISCONSIN   B 15 MIN
16MM FILM SILENT
EXEMPLIFIES ROBERT MORRIS' PREOCCUPATION WITH ART AS 'THE PROCESS OF BEING AND BECOMING.' PORTRAYS A ROW OF YOUNG PEOPLE IN A SNOW LANDSCAPE MOVING ABOUT IN A VARIETY OF FORMATIONS AND ASSUMING MANY DIFFERENT POSITIONS.
PROD-VISRES   DIST-VISRES   1971

WITHIN THE CIRCLE   C 12 MIN
16MM FILM OPTICAL SOUND
DEALS WITH THE PRODUCTION OF ISRAELI COINS. SHOWS HOW EXCAVATIONS OF ANCIENT COINS INSPIRE THE USE OF ANCIENT ART MOTIFS ON THE CURRENT COINS OF ISRAEL.
PROD-ALDEN   DIST-ALDEN

WONDERFUL WORLD OF SPORT - AEROBICS--A SERIES   J-C A
COVERS THE SPORTS WORLD AND PEOPLE IN IT.
PROD-SPORTI   DIST-AMERFI

RESEARCH	5 MIN
VARIOUS SPORTS - THIRTY POINTS TO FITNESS	5 MIN

WONDERFUL WORLD OF SPORT - BASEBALL--A SERIES   J-C A
COVERS THE SPORTS WORLD AND PEOPLE IN IT.
PROD-SPORTI   DIST-AMERFI

ASTROTURF	5 MIN
BASE RUNNING	5 MIN
BASEBALL CLINIC	5 MIN
BASEBALL'S UFO, THE SPITBALL	5 MIN
BAT BOY	5 MIN
BILLY MUFFET	5 MIN
BROADCASTER STORY	5 MIN
BROOKS ROBINSON	5 MIN
CARL YASTRZEMSKI	5 MIN
DUCKY MEDWICK	5 MIN
FRANK ROBINSON	5 MIN
HANK AARON - CONSISTENT HITTER	5 MIN
HANK AARON - HITTING	5 MIN
HOW TO SET UP BATTERS	5 MIN
JOE TORRE	5 MIN
KNUCKLEBALL, THE - HOYT WHILHELM	5 MIN
MAX PATKIN	5 MIN
RED SCHOENDIST	5 MIN
RELIEF PITCHER STORY	5 MIN
ROY CAMPANELLA - WHAT HAPPENED TO	5 MIN
SCOREKEEPER	5 MIN
SLIP PITCH	5 MIN
SONNY JACKSON - BUNTING	5 MIN
SPITBALL STORY	5 MIN
SWITCH HITTING STORY	5 MIN
TIME MC CARVER	5 MIN
TRAINER	5 MIN
UMPIRE SCHOOL	5 MIN
UMPIRE'S TOUCH PLAYS	5 MIN

WONDERFUL WORLD OF SPORT - BASKETBALL--A SERIES   J-C A
COVERS THE SPORTS WORLD AND PEOPLE IN IT.
PROD-SPORTI   DIST-AMERFI

ADOLPH RUPP	5 MIN
CALVIN MURPHY	5 MIN
COACHES STORY	5 MIN
DAVE BING	5 MIN
DEFENSE	5 MIN
FATHER AND SON	5 MIN
HOWARD PORTER	5 MIN
KENTUCKY STYLE	5 MIN

NEIL WALK	5 MIN
OSCAR ROBERTSON	5 MIN
PETE MARAVICH	5 MIN
REFEREE STORY	5 MIN
SPENCER HAYWARD	5 MIN
TIGERS TRAINING	5 MIN
TOM PAINE	5 MIN

WONDERFUL WORLD OF SPORT - BOATING--A SERIES   J-C A
COVERS THE SPORTS WORLD AND PEOPLE IN IT.
PROD-SPORTI   DIST-AMERFI

AMERICA'S CUP	5 MIN
CATAMARANS	5 MIN
DRAG BOATS	5 MIN
FLOAT PARTY - DOWN THE RIVER	5 MIN
ICE BOATS	5 MIN
SAILING - 'E' SLOOPS	5 MIN
SAILING - SUNFISH REGATTA	5 MIN

WONDERFUL WORLD OF SPORT - BOXING--A SERIES   J-C A
COVERS THE SPORTS WORLD AND PEOPLE IN IT.
PROD-SPORTI   DIST-AMERFI

CHARLIE POLITE	5 MIN
GYPSY JOE HARRIS	5 MIN
JOE FRAZIER - CHAMPION IN TRAINING	5 MIN
LADY BOXER	5 MIN

WONDERFUL WORLD OF SPORT - CARS, AUTO RACING --A SERIES   J-C A
COVERS THE SPORTS WORLD AND PEOPLE IN IT.
PROD-SPORTI   DIST-AMERFI

ANTIQUE CARS - DUSENBERG, MERCEDES, BUGATTI	5 MIN
ANTIQUE CARS - PIERCE ARROW	5 MIN
CLASSIC CARS, THE 1930 BENTLEY	5 MIN
DRAG RACING - CHRISTMAS TREE	5 MIN
DRAG RACING - DON GARLITS	5 MIN
DRAG RACING - FUNNY CARS	5 MIN
DRAG RACING - SIGHTS AND SOUNDS	5 MIN
DRAG RACING - SLINGSHOT DRAGSTERS	5 MIN
DRIVING SCHOOL - TRAINING RACERS	5 MIN
DUNE BUGGIES - FUN CARS	5 MIN
DUNE BUGGIES - IN FLEET	5 MIN
DUNE BUGGIES - OFF-THE-ROAD RACING	5 MIN
RESTORATION	5 MIN

WONDERFUL WORLD OF SPORT - DOGS--A SERIES   J-C A
COVERS THE SPORTS WORLD AND SOME ANIMALS IN IT.
PROD-SPORTI   DIST-AMERFI

INTERMEDIATE (COMPANION DOGS)	5 MIN
LABRADORS IN TRAINING	5 MIN
LABRADORS, LAND RETRIEVING	5 MIN
LABRADORS, WATER RETRIEVING	5 MIN
NOVICE COMPANION	5 MIN
SLED DOGS - ALASKAN HUSKY	5 MIN
SLED DOGS - BIG-TIME TEAM	5 MIN
SLED DOGS - RACING	5 MIN
UTILITY DOGS	5 MIN

WONDERFUL WORLD OF SPORT - FENCING--A SERIES   J-C A
COVERS THE SPORTS WORLD AND PEOPLE IN IT.
PROD-SPORTI   DIST-AMERFI

EPEE, THE	5 MIN
FOIL	5 MIN
MAESTRO, THE	5 MIN
SABER	5 MIN

WONDERFUL WORLD OF SPORT - FISHING--A SERIES   J-C A
COVERS THE SPORTS WORLD AND PEOPLE IN IT.
PROD-SPORTI   DIST-AMERFI

BASS FISHING	5 MIN
CAST NETTING	5 MIN
FLY CASTING	5 MIN
ICE FISHING	5 MIN
REEL CASTING	5 MIN
SNATCH - HOOK FISHING	5 MIN
TRICK CASTING	5 MIN

WONDERFUL WORLD OF SPORT - FLYING--A SERIES   J-C A
COVERS THE SPORTS WORLD AND PEOPLE IN IT.
PROD-SPORTI   DIST-AMERFI

AEROBATICS - AERIAL ACROBATICS	5 MIN
ANTIQUE PLANES - F3F AND SPITFIRE	5 MIN
BLUE ANGELS - BEHIND THE ACT - MECHANICS	5 MIN
BLUE ANGELS - NAVY'S FORMATION FLYERS	5 MIN
BREEZY AIRPLANE	5 MIN

FLYING - STUNTING	5 MIN
GYROCOPTERS	5 MIN
HOMEBUILTS	5 MIN
OLD PLANE - BEARCAT	5 MIN
SKY DIVING - BARBARA ROQUEMORE	5 MIN
SKY DIVING - U S TEAM	5 MIN
SKY DIVING - WHAT IS IT	5 MIN
SOARING - MOOD STORY	5 MIN
SOARING - TEST PILOT	5 MIN

WONDERFUL WORLD OF SPORT - FOOTBALL--A SERIES

J-C A

COVERS THE SPORTS WORLD AND SOME PEOPLE IN IT.

PROD-SPORTI   DIST-AMERFI

AFL - WIVES	5 MIN
ARMY-NAVY HIGHLIGHTS	5 MIN
COLLEGE CHEERLEADERS, NO. 1	5 MIN
COLLEGE CHEERLEADERS, NO. 2	5 MIN
COLLEGE FOOTBALL, HANRATTY, SEYMOUR	5 MIN
DEFENSIVE BACKS	5 MIN
FIREBIRDS	5 MIN
FRAN TARKENTON	5 MIN
HOMER JONES	5 MIN
JIM NANCE	5 MIN
JOE NAMATH	5 MIN
K C EXERCISE	5 MIN
KICKER STORY	5 MIN
LITTLE MAN - MIKE GARRETT	5 MIN
MIKE REED	5 MIN
PRO FOOTBALL - DUMP THE QUARTERBACK	5 MIN
PRO FOOTBALL - RUNNERS	5 MIN
RECEIVERS	5 MIN
REFEREE STORY	5 MIN
STEVE VAN BUREN	5 MIN
SWARTHMORE - HUDDLE	5 MIN
SWARTHMORE - SMALL COLLEGE FOOTBALL	5 MIN
TWO-PLATOON	5 MIN

WONDERFUL WORLD OF SPORT - GOLF--A SERIES

J-C A

COVERS THE SPORTS WORLD AND PEOPLE IN IT.

PROD-SPORTI   DIST-AMERFI

BALTUSROL - THE FOURTH HOLE	5 MIN
JOE DEY - PIN PLACEMENT	5 MIN
LADIES GOLF - CATHY WENTWORTH	5 MIN
MERION - THE ELEVENTH	5 MIN
MERION - THE FIRST	5 MIN
MIKE BONALLACK	5 MIN
SCROTA - THE SECOND	5 MIN

WONDERFUL WORLD OF SPORT - GYMNASTICS--A SERIES

J-C A

COVERS THE SPORTS WORLD AND PEOPLE IN IT.

PROD-SPORTI   DIST-AMERFI

BALANCE BEAM	5 MIN
BEGINNING GYMNASTICS	5 MIN
FLOOR EXERCISE	5 MIN
PARALLEL BARS	5 MIN
STILL RINGS	5 MIN
TRAMPOLINE - GARY ERWIN	5 MIN
TRAMPOLINE COMPETITION	5 MIN
UNEVEN PARALLEL BARS	5 MIN

WONDERFUL WORLD OF SPORT - HOCKEY--A SERIES

J-C A

COVERS THE SPORTS WORLD AND PEOPLE IN IT.

PROD-SPORTI   DIST-AMERFI

GOALIE	5 MIN
GOALIE EQUIPMENT STORY	5 MIN
HOCKEY STICK STORY	5 MIN
PENALTY STORY	5 MIN
POWER PLAY	5 MIN

WONDERFUL WORLD OF SPORT - HORSES, RACING, POLO, RODEO--A SERIES

J-C A

COVERS THE SPORTS WORLD AND PEOPLE IN IT.

PROD-SPORTI   DIST-AMERFI

AMATEUR POLO	5 MIN
AUCTION STORY	5 MIN
BREAKING A YEARLING	5 MIN
CARDIGAN BAY - HARNESS WINNER	5 MIN
DANCER FARM - BERT HANOVER	5 MIN
DEVON HORSE SHOW	5 MIN
DR FAGER	5 MIN
FLORIDA BREEDING	5 MIN
GALLOP, TROT, PACE	5 MIN
HARNESS - HAMBLETONIAN	5 MIN
HARNESS - SU MAC LAD	5 MIN
HARNESS - YEARLING STORY	5 MIN
HORSE RACE - CHART CALLER	5 MIN
HORSE RACE - FILM PATROL	5 MIN
HORSE RACE - THE CLOCKER	5 MIN
HORSE RACE - THE STARTING GATE	5 MIN
NEVELE PRIDE - TROTTER	5 MIN

RODEO SCHOOL - BAREBACK RIDING	5 MIN
RODEO SCHOOL - BULL RIDING	5 MIN
RODEO SCHOOL - GRADUATE	5 MIN
RODEO SCHOOL - LARRY MAHAN	5 MIN
RODEO SCHOOL - SADDLE BRONC RIDE	5 MIN
THOROUGHBRED - THE NEW BOY	5 MIN
THOROUGHBRED - THE STARTING GATE	5 MIN

WONDERFUL WORLD OF SPORT - OTHER--A SERIES

J-C A

COVERS THE SPORTS WORLD AND PEOPLE IN IT.

PROD-SPORTI   DIST-AMERFI

BEACH VOLLEY BALL	5 MIN
CONSERVATION - TURTLE RESEARCH	5 MIN
CURLING - SCORING	5 MIN
CURLING - STRATEGY	5 MIN
FIGURE SKATING - FREE SKATING	5 MIN
ICE CANOE RACING	5 MIN
OVER THE LINE - BEACH SPORTS	5 MIN
QUEBEC WINTER CARNIVAL	5 MIN
RADIO-OPERATED RACERS - MODELISTS	5 MIN
SCOTTISH GAMES - CROSS-SECTION	5 MIN
SCOTTISH GAMES - TOSSING CABOR	5 MIN
SKATING - PEGGY FLEMING	5 MIN
SKEET SHOOTING	5 MIN
SOCCER - PELE	5 MIN
TRAP SHOOTING	5 MIN

WONDERFUL WORLD OF SPORT - ROWING--A SERIES

J-C A

COVERS THE SPORTS WORLD AND PEOPLE IN IT.

PROD-SPORTI   DIST-AMERFI

COXSWAIN STORY	5 MIN
SHELL STORY	5 MIN
VESPER STORY	5 MIN

WONDERFUL WORLD OF SPORT - SKIING--A SERIES

J-C A

COVERS THE SPORTS WORLD AND PEOPLE IN IT.

PROD-SPORTI   DIST-AMERFI

BEGINNERS	5 MIN
SKI INSTRUCTORS	5 MIN
SKI PATROL - GENERAL	5 MIN
SKI PATROL - RESCUE	5 MIN
SKIING - BASICS	5 MIN

WONDERFUL WORLD OF SPORT - SNOWMOBILES--A SERIES

J-C A

COVERS THE SPORTS WORLD AND PEOPLE IN IT.

PROD-SPORTI   DIST-AMERFI

HOW TO RIDE THEM	5 MIN
RACING (FACTORY) TEAM	5 MIN
RACING (LACONIA N H)	5 MIN
SNOW SAFARI	5 MIN

WONDERFUL WORLD OF SPORT - SWIM, DIVE, SCUBA, SURF--A SERIES

J-C A

COVERS THE SPORTS WORLD AND PEOPLE IN IT.

PROD-SPORTI   DIST-AMERFI

DIVING - BASICS	5 MIN
DIVING - LESLEY BUSH	5 MIN
SCUBA - FLORIDA'S UNDERWATER STATE PARK	5 MIN
SCUBA - SLURP GUN	5 MIN
SCUBA - SPANISH WRECK	5 MIN
SURFING - CORKY CARROLL	5 MIN
SURFING - JOYCE HOFFMAN	5 MIN
SWIMMING - BASIC STROKES	5 MIN
SWIMMING AND DIVING - HOW CHAMPIONSHIPS ARE WON	5 MIN
SWIMMING AND DIVING - TRAINING	5 MIN

WONDERFUL WORLD OF SPORT - TRACK AND FIELD--A SERIES

J-C A

COVERS THE SPORTS WORLD AND PEOPLE IN IT.

PROD-SPORTI   DIST-AMERFI

BATON PASS	5 MIN
MILE RELAY	5 MIN
PENN RELAYS	5 MIN
TARTAN TRACK	5 MIN

WONDERFUL WORLD OF SPORT - WEIGHTLIFTING--A SERIES

J-C A

COVERS THE SPORTS WORLD AND PEOPLE IN IT.

PROD-SPORTI   DIST-AMERFI

BOB BEDNARSKI	5 MIN
ROMAN MIELEC	5 MIN
WEIGHTLIFTING - TRAINING	5 MIN
WEIGHTLIFTING - WHAT IS IT	5 MIN

WONDERFUL WORLD OF SPORT - WRESTLING--A SERIES

J-C A

COVERS THE SPORTS WORLD AND PEOPLE IN IT.

PROD-SPORTI   DIST-AMERFI

CLAUDE FRANTZ	5 MIN
GOING FOR THE PIN	5 MIN

WONDERS OF THE CACTUS   C 14 MIN

16MM FILM OPTICAL SOUND

DESCRIBES THE DEVELOPMENT AND PHYSIOLOGY OF THE EXTRAORDINARY CACTUS PLANT. ILLUSTRATES FANTASTIC SHAPES OF CACTI AND DISCUSSES THE HOME OF THE CACTI AND THEIR UNUSUAL METABOLIC FUNCTION.

PROD-IWANMI   DIST-IWANMI

WORK OF GOMIS, THE   C 50 MIN

16MM FILM OPTICAL SOUND

PRESENTS THE DOCUMENTARY STORY OF A DOCTOR IN THE VILLAGE OF POLWATTA, CEYLON, WHO PRACTICES HEALING METHODS THOUSANDS OF YEARS OLD.

LC NO. 73-701023

PROD-WASHBF   DIST-WASHBF   1970

WORLD OF X-RAYS, THE   C 14 MIN

16MM FILM OPTICAL SOUND

PRESENTS A BASIC EXPLANATION OF THE X-RAY AND THE WORLD SEEN THROUGH THE X-RAY. SHOWS THE USE OF X-RAYS FOR ANALYSIS OF THE HUMAN BODY.

PROD-IWANMI   DIST-IWANMI

WORLD'S GREATEST FREAK SHOW, THE   C 11 MIN P-I

16MM FILM OPTICAL SOUND

USES ANIMATION TO TELL THE STORY OF ALASTAIR PFLUG, AN EXCESSIVELY VAIN MAN WHOSE ONLY AIM IN LIFE IS TO BE RICH AND FAMOUS.

LC NO. 73-700784

PROD-BOSUST   DIST-XEROX   1973

WROUGHT IRON - YESTERDAY, TODAY, TOMORROW   C 20 MIN

16MM FILM OPTICAL SOUND

DESCRIBES SOME OF THE OLDER WROUGHT IRON INSTALLATIONS IN EUROPE AND AMERICA. TELLS HOW WROUGHT IRON IS MANUFACTURED, WHY IT IS UNIQUE AMONG FERROUS METALS, WHERE AND WHY IT IS SPECIFIED AND WHY IT RESISTS CORROSION AND FATIGUE.

PROD-MTP   DIST-MTP

Y

YANKEE CALLING   C 29 MIN

16MM FILM OPTICAL SOUND

RECALLS THE HISTORY OF YANKEE CRAFTSMEN, INVENTORS AND PEDDLERS WHO MADE CONNECTICUT INTO A MANUFACTURING STATE DURING THE PERIOD FROM THE END OF THE REVOLUTION TO THE START OF THE CIVIL WAR.

PROD-FENWCK   DIST-FENWCK

YEARS OF DESTINY   B 21 MIN

16MM FILM OPTICAL SOUND

TELLS WHY AND HOW A JEWISH STATE ROSE AGAIN, INDEPENDENT, IN OUR DAY. PRESENTS THE RECORD OF THE STRUGGLE FOR THAT INDEPENDENCE AND ITS RESULTS.

PROD-ALDEN   DIST-ALDEN

YEAST   C 14 MIN

16MM FILM OPTICAL SOUND

DESCRIBES THE ECOLOGY AND USES OF YEAST. ILLUSTRATES THE ACTION OF YEAST WITH EXPERIMENTAL APPARATUS. DISCUSSES THE USES OF YEAST IN WINE, RAISING BREAD, BEER FERMENTATION, JAPANESE SAKE, SOY SAUCE AND BEAN PASTE.

PROD-IWANMI   DIST-IWANMI

YESTERDAY'S FARM   C 17 MIN P-J

16MM FILM OPTICAL SOUND

POINTS OUT THAT THE OLD FARMS THAT SPREAD ACROSS NORTH AMERICA ARE RICH SOURCES OF INFORMATION ABOUT OUR PAST, SHOWING THE RUGGEDNESS OF LIFE, THE TRIALS OF THE MOVEMENT WESTWARD, THE VALUES THAT WERE HELD BY EARLY SETTLERS AND THE HOPES AND AMBITIONS OF GENERATIONS.

LC NO. 73-701289

PROD-BFA   DIST-BFA   1972

YO SOY CHICANO (ENGLISH)   C 59 MIN

16MM FILM OPTICAL SOUND   H-C A

PORTRAYS THE CHICANO EXPERIENCE, FROM ITS ROOTS IN PRE-COLUMBIAN HISTORY TO THE PRESENT, BY ACTORS WHO RECREATE KEY EVENTS IN MEXICAN HISTORY AND THROUGH INTERVIEWS WITH CHICANO LEADERS.

LC NO. 73-700537

PROD-KCET   DIST-IU   1972

YOU   C 17 MIN
          16MM FILM OPTICAL SOUND   P-I
EXAMINES THE CONCEPTS OF EMPATHY IN HU-
MAN RELATIONS THROUGH OBSERVATION OF
YOUNG BROTHERS ENGAGED IN A TYPICAL SIB-
LING ARGUMENT. SHOWS THAT WHEN THEIR AN-
GER COOLS, THEY BEGIN TO EXPLORE EACH OTH-
ER'S FEELINGS AND VIEWPOINTS.
     LC NO. 73-701214
PROD-PHENIX   DIST-CENTEF   1973

YOU HOO - I'M A BIRD   C 28 MIN
          16MM FILM OPTICAL SOUND
SHOWS THE MARVELOUS SKIING IN COLORADO,
AS WELL AS THE ACCOMPANYING FUN OF A WIN-
TER VACATION THERE.
PROD-MTP   DIST-MTP

YOUR NEW JOB   C 10 MIN
          16MM FILM OPTICAL SOUND   H-C A
DEPICTS THE EXCITEMENT, NERVOUSNESS AND
APPREHENSION OF YOUNG MEN AND WOMEN ON
THE FIRST DAY OF THEIR EMPLOYMENT. FOLLOWS
YOUNG EMPLOYEES FROM THE FIRST MINUTE TO
THE CONCLUSION OF THEIR FIRST DAY.
PROD-SAIF   DIST-SAIF

ZANZIBAR   C
          16MM FILM OPTICAL SOUND
SEE SERIES TITLE FOR DESCRIPTIVE STATEMENT.
FROM THE PORT OF CALL SERIES.
PROD-PUI   DIST-PUI

ZEBRAS   C 10 MIN
          16MM FILM OPTICAL SOUND   K-I
USES ANIMATION TO TELL THE STORY OF TWO ZE-
BRAS WHO MISPLACE ONE OF THEIR STRIPES AND
PRANCE THROUGH VARIOUS ADVENTURES BE-
FORE THEY RECOVER IT.
     LC NO. 73-701202
PROD-CHOICE   DIST-TEXFLM   1973

ALPHABETICAL GUIDE TO VIDEOTAPES

A

**ADDRESSING ENVELOPES -
ATTENTION AND SUBJECT
LINES**   B   30 MIN
       2 INCH VIDEOTAPE
FROM THE TYPEWRITING, UNIT 7 - POSTAL
CARDS, FORMS, MANUSCRIPTS SERIES.
PROD-GPITVL   DIST-GPITVL

AESTHETIC STATEMENT, AN   C   20 MIN
       2 INCH VIDEOTAPE   I
HELPS STUDENTS DEVELOP A FEELING ABOUT AN
ARTIST, HOW HE WORKS AND HOW HE UTILIZES
THE ELEMENTS OF ART. FROM THE CREATING
ART, PT 3 - LEARNING TO UNDERSTAND ART SE-
RIES.
PROD-GPITVL   DIST-GPITVL

ANGLES AND OTHER FIGURES   C   15 MIN
       2 INCH VIDEOTAPE   I
PRESENTS THE GEOMETRIC FIGURES RAY, ANGLE,
RIGHT ANGLE, SQUARE, TRIANGLE AND RECTAN-
GLE. FROM THE MATH FACTORY, MODULE 2 - GE-
OMETRY SERIES.
PROD-GPITVL   DIST-GPITVL

ARE ALL STARS ALIKE   B   15 MIN
       2 INCH VIDEOTAPE   I
POINTS OUT THAT ALL STARS IN THE UNIVERSE
GIVE OFF ENERGY IN THE FORM OF HEAT AND
LIGHT. FROM THE SCIENCE IS DISCOVERY SERIES.
PROD-GPITVL   DIST-GPITVL

**ARTHUR MILLER - DEATH OF A
SALESMAN, PT 1**   B   30 MIN
       2 INCH VIDEOTAPE   J-H
FROM THE FRANKLIN TO FROST SERIES.
PROD-GPITVL   DIST-GPITVL

**ARTHUR MILLER - DEATH OF A
SALESMAN, PT 2**   B   30 MIN
       2 INCH VIDEOTAPE   J-H
FROM THE FRANKLIN TO FROST SERIES.
PROD-GPITVL   DIST-GPITVL

B

BECAUSE IT'S FUN   C   15 MIN
       2 INCH VIDEOTAPE
EXPLORES THE GOOD FEELINGS PRODUCED BY
SKILLFULLY ENGAGING IN A PHYSICAL ACTIVITY.
INTRODUCES BILL WHO THINKS THAT WINNING IS
THE ONLY THING THAT REALLY COUNTS AND
CAN'T UNDERSTAND WHY OTHERS ENJOY THEM-
SELVES JUST PLAYING FOR THE FUN OF IT.
PROD-NITC   DIST-NITC

**BENJAMIN FRANKLIN - MORALS
AND THE MAN**   B   30 MIN
       2 INCH VIDEOTAPE   J-H
FROM THE FRANKLIN TO FROST SERIES.
PROD-GPITVL   DIST-GPITVL

**BENJAMIN FRANKLIN - POOR
RICHARD AND THE MAXIM, THE
STYLE OF WIT**   B   30 MIN
       2 INCH VIDEOTAPE   J-H
FROM THE FRANKLIN TO FROST SERIES.
PROD-GPITVL   DIST-GPITVL

**BENJAMIN FRANKLIN - THE
FORMING OF A STYLE**   B   30 MIN
       2 INCH VIDEOTAPE   J-H
FROM THE FRANKLIN TO FROST SERIES.
PROD-GPITVL   DIST-GPITVL

**BENJAMIN FRANKLIN - THE
LENGTHENED MAXIM, FORMAL
SATIRE**   B   30 MIN
       2 INCH VIDEOTAPE   J-H
FROM THE FRANKLIN TO FROST SERIES.
PROD-GPITVL   DIST-GPITVL

BOMBARDING THINGS   C   30 MIN
       2 INCH VIDEOTAPE   I-J
COVERS EFFECTS OF RADIOACTIVE MATERIALS,
ALPHA PARTICLES, BETA PARTICLES AND GAMMA
RAYS, SAFEGUARDS AND SHIELDING REQUIRE-
MENTS FOR EACH, BENEFICIAL USES OF GAMMA
IRRADIATION AND NEUTRON ACTIVATION ANALY-
SIS. FROM THE LIVING IN A NUCLEAR AGE SERIES.
PROD-GPITVL   DIST-GPITVL

**BOUND MANUSCRIPTS WITH
FOOTNOTES**   B   30 MIN
       2 INCH VIDEOTAPE
FROM THE TYPEWRITING, UNIT 7 - POSTAL
CARDS, FORMS, MANUSCRIPTS SERIES.
PROD-GPITVL   DIST-GPITVL

BUT NAMES WILL NEVER HURT   C   15 MIN
       2 INCH VIDEOTAPE
INTRODUCES AN ENGLISH-CANADIAN BOY, WHO
IN SUDDEN ANGER CALLS A YOUNG FRENCH-CA-
NADIAN A DIRTY FRENCH FROG AND THEN
COMES TO REALIZE HOW PREJUDICE SEPARATES
ONE PERSON FROM ANOTHER AND AFFECTS THE
FEELINGS OF EVERYONE INVOLVED.
PROD-NITC   DIST-NITC

C

**CARL AND THE CORNER
MARKET**   B   15 MIN
       2 INCH VIDEOTAPE   P
SEE SERIES TITLE FOR DESCRIPTIVE STATEMENT.
FROM THE LISTEN AND SAY - VOWELS SERIES.
PROD-GPITVL   DIST-GPITVL

CASE STUDIES   B   30 MIN
       2 INCH VIDEOTAPE
PRESENTS A DISCUSSION OF CASE STUDIES DEAL-
ING WITH ADOLESCENTS. FROM THE COUNSELING
THE ADOLESCENT SERIES.
PROD-GPITVL   DIST-GPITVL

**CENTRAL PROCESSING UNIT -
LOGIC AND CONTROL**   B   45 MIN
       2 INCH VIDEOTAPE
SEE SERIES TITLE FOR DESCRIPTIVE STATEMENT.
FROM THE DATA PROCESSING, UNIT 2 - THE COM-
PUTER AND HOW IT WORKS SERIES.
PROD-GPITVL   DIST-GPITVL

**CENTRAL PROCESSING UNIT -
THE COMPUTER'S ARITHMETIC**   B   45 MIN
       2 INCH VIDEOTAPE
SEE SERIES TITLE FOR DESCRIPTIVE STATEMENT.
FROM THE DATA PROCESSING, UNIT 2 - THE COM-
PUTER AND HOW IT WORKS SERIES.
PROD-GPITVL   DIST-GPITVL

**CHANGING THE CHILD'S
RELATIONSHIPS AND GOALS**   B   30 MIN
       2 INCH VIDEOTAPE
POINTS OUT THAT THE FIRST STEP IN CHANGING
A CHILD'S MOTIVATION IS OBSERVATION TO DE-
TERMINE HIS GOALS. POINTS OUT THE CONCRETE
RECOMMENDATIONS WHICH CAN BE MADE CON-
CERNING WHAT THE PARENT OR TEACHER CAN
DO TO HELP THE CHILD. FROM THE MOTIVATING
CHILDREN TO LEARN SERIES.
PROD-GPITVL   DIST-GPITVL

CIRCLES   C   15 MIN
       2 INCH VIDEOTAPE   I
INTRODUCES THE CONCEPT OF CIRCLE, DIAME-
TER AND RADIUS. FROM THE MATH FACTORY,
MODULE 2 - GEOMETRY SERIES.
PROD-GPITVL   DIST-GPITVL

**CLARIFICATION OF BASIC
PRINCIPLES**   B   30 MIN
       2 INCH VIDEOTAPE
SHOWS THAT A CHILD'S PERSONALITY CAN BE
CHANGED THROUGH ENCOURAGEMENT AND
STRESSES THE FACT THAT EACH INDIVIDUAL IS
WORTHWHILE AS HE IS. EXPLAINS THAT BY
CHANGING A CHILD'S MOTIVATION, HE BECOMES
BETTER ABLE TO FIND HIS PLACE WITHOUT THE
FEAR OF BEING INADEQUATE. FROM THE MOTI-
VATING CHILDREN TO LEARN SERIES.
PROD-GPITVL   DIST-GPITVL

COLLAGE MAKING   C   20 MIN
       2 INCH VIDEOTAPE   I
HELPS STUDENTS FIND WAYS TO COMBINE VARI-
OUS MEDIA. FROM THE CREATING ART, PT 2 -
LEARNING TO CREATE ART FORMS SERIES.
PROD-GPITVL   DIST-GPITVL

**COMPUTER APPLICATIONS -
CAREER OPPORTUNITIES**   B   45 MIN
       2 INCH VIDEOTAPE
SEE SERIES TITLE FOR DESCRIPTIVE STATEMENT.
FROM THE DATA PROCESSING, UNIT 4 - APPLICA-
TIONS AND CAREER OPPORTUNITIES SERIES.
PROD-GPITVL   DIST-GPITVL

**COMPUTER MEMORY AND DATA
REPRESENTATION**   B   45 MIN
       2 INCH VIDEOTAPE
SEE SERIES TITLE FOR DESCRIPTIVE STATEMENT.
FROM THE DATA PROCESSING, UNIT 2 - THE COM-
PUTER AND HOW IT WORKS SERIES.
PROD-GPITVL   DIST-GPITVL

CONSEQUENCES   B   30 MIN
       2 INCH VIDEOTAPE
DISCUSSES LOGICAL CONSEQUENCES AND EX-
PLAINS THE DIFFERENCE BETWEEN NATURAL
AND LOGICAL CONSEQUENCES. FROM THE MOTI-
VATING CHILDREN TO LEARN SERIES.
PROD-GPITVL   DIST-GPITVL

**COUNSELING THE ADOLESCENT-
-A SERIES**
DEMONSTRATES THE ADLERIAN TECHNIQUES OF
COUNSELING AND PSYCHOTHERAPY IN COUNSEL-
ING THE ADOLESCENT.
PROD-GPITVL   DIST-GPITVL

CASE STUDIES	30 MIN
DEMOCRATIC EVOLUTION OF SOCIETY, THE, PT 1	30 MIN
DEMOCRATIC EVOLUTION OF SOCIETY, THE, PT 2	30 MIN
GROUP DISCUSSION WITH NORMAL TEENAGERS	30 MIN
GROUP DISCUSSION WITH SCHOOL DROP-OUTS	30 MIN
JEFF	30 MIN
JUVENILE DELINQUENCY	30 MIN
MARY	30 MIN
NONI	30 MIN
ROB	30 MIN

**CREATING ART, PT 1 -
LEARNING TO SEE-- A SERIES**   I
DEFINES THE CONTENT OF ART, THE RELATION-
SHIP OF THE INDIVIDUAL TO HIS VISUAL ENVI-
RONMENT, THE VISUAL LANGUAGE OF ART AND
THE CORRELATION BETWEEN THE CHILD'S EX-
PRESSIONS AND THE ARTIST'S EXPRESSIONS.
PROD-GPITVL   DIST-GPITVL

LEARNING TO SEE COLOR	20 MIN
LEARNING TO SEE LINE AND SHAPE	20 MIN
LEARNING TO SEE SPACE AND MOVEMENT	20 MIN
LEARNING TO SEE TEXTURE	20 MIN
LEARNING TO SEE THE SUBJECTS OF ART	20 MIN
LEARNING TO SEE THE VISUAL ENVIRONMENT	20 MIN

**CREATING ART, PT 2 -
LEARNING TO CREATE ART
FORMS--A SERIES**   I
DEFINES THE CONTENT OF ART, THE RELATION-
SHIP OF THE INDIVIDUAL TO HIS VISUAL ENVI-
RONMENT, THE VISUAL LANGUAGE OF ART AND
THE CORRELATION BETWEEN THE CHILD'S EX-
PRESSIONS AND THE ARTIST'S EXPRESSIONS.
PROD-GPITVL   DIST-GPITVL

COLLAGE MAKING	20 MIN
DRAWING	20 MIN
MODELING AND POTTERY MAKING	20 MIN
PAINTING	20 MIN
PRINTING	20 MIN
SCULPTURING	20 MIN
STITCHING AND WEAVING	20 MIN

**CREATING ART, PT 3 -
LEARNING TO UNDERSTAND
ART--A SERIES**   I
DEFINES THE CONTENT OF ART, THE RELATION-
SHIP OF THE INDIVIDUAL TO HIS VISUAL ENVI-
RONMENT, THE VISUAL LANGUAGE OF ART AND

THE CORRELATION BETWEEN THE CHILD'S EX-
PRESSIONS AND THE ARTIST'S EXPRESSIONS.
PROD-GPITVL   DIST-GPITVL

AESTHETIC STATEMENT, AN   20 MIN
INTENT OF ART AND ARTISTS, THE   20 MIN
JUDGMENTS ABOUT ART, THE   20 MIN

CRYSTAL CLEAR   B 15 MIN
      2 INCH VIDEOTAPE I
DISCUSSES THE PROCESS OF EXPERIMENTATION.
FROM THE LET'S EXPLORE SCIENCE SERIES.
PROD-GPITVL   DIST-GPITVL

CURVES   C 15 MIN
      2 INCH VIDEOTAPE I
ILLUSTRATES THE DIFFERENCE BETWEEN CLOSED
CURVES AND OPEN CURVES. FROM THE MATH
FACTORY, MODULE 2 - GEOMETRY SERIES.
PROD-GPITVL   DIST-GPITVL

CUSTOMS   C 30 MIN
      2 INCH VIDEOTAPE
SEE SERIES TITLE FOR DESCRIPTIVE STATEMENT.
FROM THE UNCONSCIOUS CULTURAL CLASHES SE-
RIES.
PROD-SCCOE   DIST-SCCOE

D

DATA PROCESSING - REVIEW   B 45 MIN
      2 INCH VIDEOTAPE
SEE SERIES TITLE FOR DESCRIPTIVE STATEMENT.
FROM THE DATA PROCESSING, UNIT 4 - APPLICA-
TIONS AND CAREER OPPORTUNITIES SERIES.
PROD GPITVL   DIST-GPITVL

DATA PROCESSING, UNIT 1 -
INTRODUCTION TO DATA
PROCESSING--A SERIES
ACQUAINTS THE STUDENT WITH THE BASIC PRIN-
CIPLES OF DATA PROCESSING, WITH THE EQUIP-
MENT ITSELF AND WHAT IT CAN DO AND WITH
THE SKILLS AND TECHNIQUES NECESSARY TO
MAKE THE MACHINES FUNCTION.
PROD-GPITVL   DIST-GPITVL

HISTORY OF ADP AND INTRODUCTION
TO UNIT --   45 MIN
RECORDING MACHINES, THE   45 MIN
UNIT RECORD APPLICATIONS   45 MIN
WHY'S OF DATA PROCESSING, THE   45 MIN

DATA PROCESSING, UNIT 2 -
THE COMPUTER AND HOW IT
WORKS--A SERIES
ACQUAINTS THE STUDENT WITH THE BASIC PRIN-
CIPLES OF DATA PROCESSING, WITH THE EQUIP-
MENT ITSELF AND WHAT IT CAN DO AND WITH
THE SKILLS AND TECHNIQUES NECESSARY TO
MAKE THE MACHINES FUNCTION.
PROD-GPITVL   DIST-GPITVL

CENTRAL PROCESSING UNIT - LOGIC
AND CONTROL   45 MIN
CENTRAL PROCESSING UNIT - THE
COMPUTER'S   45 MIN
COMPUTER MEMORY AND DATA
REPRESENTATION   45 MIN
HOW COMPUTERS WORK   45 MIN
INPUT-OUTPUT AND SECONDARY
MEMORY   45 MIN
INPUT-OUTPUT DEVICES, PT 1   45 MIN
INPUT-OUTPUT DEVICES, PT 2   45 MIN
INTRODUCTION TO ELECTRONIC DATA
PROCESSING --   45 MIN

DATA PROCESSING, UNIT 3 -
INSTRUCTING THE COMPUTER-
-A SERIES
ACQUAINTS THE STUDENT WITH THE BASIC PRIN-
CIPLES OF DATA PROCESSING, WITH THE EQUIP-
MENT ITSELF AND WHAT IT CAN DO AND WITH
THE SKILLS AND TECHNIQUES NECESSARY TO
MAKE THE MACHINES FUNCTION.
PROD-GPITVL   DIST-GPITVL

DECISION TABLES AND INTRODUCTION
TO COMPUTER --   45 MIN
FLOWCHARTING   45 MIN
FLOWCHARTING AND INTRODUCTION
TO DECISION --   45 MIN
INSTRUCTING THE COMPUTER   45 MIN
INTRODUCTION TO FLOWCHARTING   45 MIN
MACHINE LANGUAGE PROGRAMMING,
PT 1   45 MIN
MACHINE LANGUAGE PROGRAMMING,
PT 2   45 MIN
MACHINE LANGUAGE PROGRAMMING,
PT 3   45 MIN
PROBLEM ORIENTED LANGUAGES -
COBOL   45 MIN

PROBLEM ORIENTED LANGUAGES -
FORTRAN   45 MIN
PROBLEM ORIENTED LANGUAGES -
REPORT PROGRAM --   45 MIN
RECORD LAYOUT AND PRINT CHART   45 MIN
SYMBOLIC PROGRAMMING - ASSEMBLER
LANGUAGE   45 MIN

DATA PROCESSING, UNIT 4 -
APPLICATIONS AND CAREER
OPPORTUNITIES--A SERIES
DISCUSSES THE APPLICATIONS AND CAREER OP-
PORTUNITIES IN DATA PROCESSING.
PROD-GPITVL   DIST-GPITVL

COMPUTER APPLICATIONS - CAREER
OPPORTUNITIES   45 MIN
DATA PROCESSING - REVIEW   45 MIN
INSTRUCTING THE COMPUTER AND THE
OPERATING --   45 MIN
TELEPROCESSING AND TIME SHARING
SYSTEMS   45 MIN

DECISION TABLES AND
INTRODUCTION TO COMPUTER
PROGRAMMING   B 45 MIN
      2 INCH VIDEOTAPE
SEE SERIES TITLE FOR DESCRIPTIVE STATEMENT.
FROM THE DATA PROCESSING, UNIT 3 - IN-
STRUCTING THE COMPUTER SERIES.
PROD-GPITVL   DIST-GPITVL

DEMOCRATIC EVOLUTION OF
SOCIETY, THE, PT 1   B 30 MIN
      2 INCH VIDEOTAPE
PRESENTS A DISCUSSION OF THE PROBLEMS OF
ADOLESCENCE IN RELATION TO OUR GENERAL
CULTURAL UPHEAVAL AND THE NEED FOR DEMO-
CRATIC LEADERSHIP. FROM THE COUNSELING
THE ADOLESCENT SERIES.
PROD-GPITVL   DIST-GPITVL

DEMOCRATIC EVOLUTION OF
SOCIETY, THE, PT 2   B 30 MIN
      2 INCH VIDEOTAPE
PRESENTS A DISCUSSION OF THE PROBLEMS OF
ADOLESCENCE IN RELATION TO OUR GENERAL
CULTURAL UPHEAVAL AND THE NEED FOR DEMO-
CRATIC LEADERSHIP. FROM THE COUNSELING
THE ADOLESCENT SERIES.
PROD-GPITVL   DIST-GPITVL

DENTAL HEALTH--A SERIES
      P-I
PROVIDES THE NECESSARY SCIENTIFIC DENTAL
INFORMATION UPON WHICH TO BASE A TEACH-
ING PROGRAM OF DENTAL HEALTH.
PROD-GPITVL   DIST-GPITVL

KEEP IT CLEAN   15 MIN
KID, YOU'VE GOT A DIRTY MOUTH   15 MIN
SALLY HAD A SWEET TOOTH, NOW IT'S
GONE   15 MIN
WINNING TEAM, THE   15 MIN

DEVICES IN THEIR HANDS -
MATH IN THEIR MINDS --A
SERIES
HELPS IMPLEMENT THE USE OF MULTISENSORY
AIDS IN THE TEACHING OF MATHEMATICS IN ELE-
MENTARY AND JUNIOR HIGH SCHOOLS.
PROD-GPITVL   DIST-GPITVL

FUN WITH THE MINI-COMPUTER   30 MIN
SLIDING IN FRACTIONS   30 MIN
STRETCH A RUBBER BAND AND LEARN
GEOMETRY   30 MIN
TAKE A CHANCE - LEARN PROBABILITY   30 MIN
TILES TEACH MATHEMATICS   30 MIN

DISCOVERING THE ATOM   C 30 MIN
      2 INCH VIDEOTAPE I-J
DISCUSSES THE SECRETS OF ATOMIC STRUCTURE,
UNSTABLE ATOMS, FISSION AND SHIELDING. PRE-
SENTS A STUDY OF CAREER OPPORTUNITIES AND
HISTORICAL DEVELOPMENT OF ATOMIC AND NU-
CLEAR KNOWLEDGE. FROM THE LIVING IN A NU-
CLEAR AGE SERIES.
PROD-GPITVL   DIST-GPITVL

DOUGLAS   B 30 MIN
      2 INCH VIDEOTAPE
PRESENTS AN INTERVIEW WITH DOUGLAS, HIS
MOTHER AND HIS TEACHER IN AN EFFORT TO UN-
DERSTAND WHY HE HAS DIFFICULTIES AND HOW
HE CAN BE HELPED. STRESSES THE PROCESS OF
ENCOURAGEMENT AS ONE OF THE ESSENTIAL
MEANS BY WHICH A CHILD CAN BE HELPED TO
CHANGE HIS OPINION OF HIMSELF. FROM THE
MOTIVATING CHILDREN TO LEARN SERIES.
PROD-GPITVL   DIST-GPITVL

DRAMA - THE PLAY READ   B 30 MIN
      2 INCH VIDEOTAPE J-H
FROM THE FRANKLIN TO FROST SERIES.
PROD-GPITVL   DIST-GPITVL

DRAMA - THE PLAY SEEN   B 30 MIN
      2 INCH VIDEOTAPE J-H
FROM THE FRANKLIN TO FROST SERIES.
PROD-GPITVL   DIST-GPITVL

DRAWING   C 20 MIN
      2 INCH VIDEOTAPE I
HELPS STUDENTS LEARN ABOUT DRAWING AND
TO FIND WAYS TO USE LINES TO CREATE QUALITY
DRAWINGS. FROM THE CREATING ART, PT 2 -
LEARNING TO CREATE ART FORMS SERIES.
PROD-GPITVL   DIST-GPITVL

DRAWING A PICTURE OF
NATURE   B 15 MIN
      2 INCH VIDEOTAPE I
EXPLAINS HOW LEARNING MAY BE INCREASED
WHEN CONCEPTUAL MODELS ARE DRAWN UP.
FROM THE LET'S EXPLORE SCIENCE SERIES.
PROD-GPITVL   DIST-GPITVL

E

EDGAR ALLAN POE - POE'S
POETIC THEORY AND PRACTICE
      B 30 MIN
      2 INCH VIDEOTAPE J-H
FROM THE FRANKLIN TO FROST SERIES.
PROD-GPITVL   DIST-GPITVL

EDGAR ALLAN POE - THE FALL
OF THE HOUSE OF USHER   B 30 MIN
      2 INCH VIDEOTAPE J-H
FROM THE FRANKLIN TO FROST SERIES.
PROD-GPITVL   DIST-GPITVL

EDGAR ALLAN POE - THE
PURLOINED LETTER   B 30 MIN
      2 INCH VIDEOTAPE J-H
FROM THE FRANKLIN TO FROST SERIES.
PROD-GPITVL   DIST-GPITVL

EDGAR ALLEN POE -
ASSESSMENT   B 30 MIN
      2 INCH VIDEOTAPE J-H
FROM THE FRANKLIN TO FROST SERIES.
PROD-GPITVL   DIST-GPITVL

EDUCATION VS EDUCATION   C 30 MIN
      2 INCH VIDEOTAPE
SEE SERIES TITLE FOR DESCRIPTIVE STATEMENT.
FROM THE UNCONSCIOUS CULTURAL CLASHES SE-
RIES.
PROD-SCCOE   DIST-SCCOE

EDWARD   B 30 MIN
      2 INCH VIDEOTAPE
PRESENTS AN INTERVIEW WITH A MOTHER AND
HER SON, EDWARD. EMPHASIZES THE NECESSITY
FOR FAMILY COUNSELING FOR THE CHILD WHO IS
MISBEHAVING. SHOWS THAT POSITIVE RECOM-
MENDATIONS SHOULD BE GIVEN FOR HELPING
NOT ONLY THE CHILD BUT ALSO THE REST OF HIS
FAMILY. FROM THE MOTIVATING CHILDREN TO
LEARN SERIES.
PROD-GPITVL   DIST-GPITVL

EDWIN ARLINGTON ROBINSON -
A SAMPLING   B 30 MIN
      2 INCH VIDEOTAPE J-H
FROM THE FRANKLIN TO FROST SERIES.
PROD-GPITVL   DIST-GPITVL

EDWIN ARLINGTON ROBINSON -
ASSESSMENT   B 30 MIN
      2 INCH VIDEOTAPE J-H
FROM THE FRANKLIN TO FROST SERIES.
PROD-GPITVL   DIST-GPITVL

EDWIN ARLINGTON ROBINSON -
CHARACTERISTIC   B 30 MIN
      2 INCH VIDEOTAPE J-H
FROM THE FRANKLIN TO FROST SERIES.
PROD-GPITVL   DIST-GPITVL

EDWIN ARLINGTON ROBINSON -
EROS TURANNOS, MR FLOOD'S
PARTY   B 30 MIN
      2 INCH VIDEOTAPE J-H
FROM THE FRANKLIN TO FROST SERIES.
PROD-GPITVL   DIST-GPITVL

EMILY DICKINSON - A SAMPLING B 30 MIN
2 INCH VIDEOTAPE J-H
FROM THE FRANKLIN TO FROST SERIES.
PROD-GPITVL   DIST-GPITVL

EMILY DICKINSON - ESSENTIAL OILS B 30 MIN
2 INCH VIDEOTAPE J-H
FROM THE FRANKLIN TO FROST SERIES.
PROD-GPITVL   DIST-GPITVL

EMILY DICKINSON - PERSPECTIVES B 30 MIN
2 INCH VIDEOTAPE J-H
FROM THE FRANKLIN TO FROST SERIES.
PROD-GPITVL   DIST-GPITVL

EMILY DICKINSON - STYLE B 30 MIN
2 INCH VIDEOTAPE J-H
FROM THE FRANKLIN TO FROST SERIES.
PROD-GPITVL   DIST-GPITVL

ENCOURAGEMENT B 30 MIN
2 INCH VIDEOTAPE
STRESSES ENCOURAGEMENT AS A MEANS TO RE-STORE IN THE CHILD FAITH IN HIMSELF, IN HIS WORK AND IN HIS SOCIAL WORTH. FROM THE MO-TIVATING CHILDREN TO LEARN SERIES.
PROD-GPITVL   DIST-GPITVL

ERNEST HEMINGWAY - BIG TWO HEARTED RIVER B 30 MIN
2 INCH VIDEOTAPE J-H
FROM THE FRANKLIN TO FROST SERIES.
PROD-GPITVL   DIST-GPITVL

ERNEST HEMINGWAY - FOCUS ON DEATH B 30 MIN
2 INCH VIDEOTAPE J-H
FROM THE FRANKLIN TO FROST SERIES.
PROD-GPITVL   DIST-GPITVL

ERNEST HEMINGWAY - THE OLD MAN AND THE SEA, PT 1 B 30 MIN
2 INCH VIDEOTAPE J-H
FROM THE FRANKLIN TO FROST SERIES.
PROD-GPITVL   DIST-GPITVL

ERNEST HEMINGWAY - THE OLD MAN AND THE SEA, PT 2 B 30 MIN
2 INCH VIDEOTAPE J-H
FROM THE FRANKLIN TO FROST SERIES.
PROD-GPITVL   DIST-GPITVL

EUGENE O'NEILL - THE EMPEROR JONES B 30 MIN
2 INCH VIDEOTAPE J-H
FROM THE FRANKLIN TO FROST SERIES.
PROD-GPITVL   DIST-GPITVL

EUGENE O'NEILL - THE HAIRY APE B 30 MIN
2 INCH VIDEOTAPE J-H
FROM THE FRANKLIN TO FROST SERIES.
PROD-GPITVL   DIST-GPITVL

EXPLORING GASES B 15 MIN
2 INCH VIDEOTAPE I
DEMONSTRATES WAYS OF COLLECTING AND PRE-PARING GASES. FROM THE LET'S EXPLORE SCI-ENCE SERIES.
PROD-GPITVL   DIST-GPITVL

EXPLORING PLANTS B 15 MIN
2 INCH VIDEOTAPE I
POINTS OUT THE VALUE OF EXPERIMENTING WITH ONE VARIABLE, WHERE POSSIBLE. FROM THE LET'S EXPLORE SCIENCE SERIES.
PROD-GPITVL   DIST-GPITVL

EXTENDING OUR SENSES B 15 MIN
2 INCH VIDEOTAPE I
DISCUSSES THE PROBLEM OF EXTENDING THE SENSES BY USING INSTRUMENTS. FROM THE LET'S EXPLORE SCIENCE SERIES.

PROD-GPITVL   DIST-GPITVL

F

FLOWCHARTING B 45 MIN
2 INCH VIDEOTAPE
SEE SERIES TITLE FOR DESCRIPTIVE STATEMENT. FROM THE DATA PROCESSING, UNIT 3 - IN-STRUCTING THE COMPUTER SERIES.
PROD-GPITVL   DIST-GPITVL

FLOWCHARTING AND INTRODUCTION TO DECISION TABLES B 45 MIN
2 INCH VIDEOTAPE
SEE SERIES TITLE FOR DESCRIPTIVE STATEMENT. FROM THE DATA PROCESSING, UNIT 3 - IN-STRUCTING THE COMPUTER SERIES.
PROD-GPITVL   DIST-GPITVL

FROM FRANKLIN TO FROST - PROSPECT B 30 MIN
2 INCH VIDEOTAPE J-H
FROM THE FRANKLIN TO FROST SERIES.
PROD-GPITVL   DIST-GPITVL

FROM FRANKLIN TO FROST - RETROSPECT B 30 MIN
2 INCH VIDEOTAPE J-H
FROM THE FRANKLIN TO FROST SERIES.
PROD-GPITVL   DIST-GPITVL

FROM FRANKLIN TO FROST--A SERIES J-H

PROD-GPITVL   DIST-GPITVL

ARTHUR MILLER - DEATH OF A SALESMAN, PT 1 — 30 MIN
ARTHUR MILLER - DEATH OF A SALESMAN, PT 2 — 30 MIN
BENJAMIN FRANKLIN - MORALS AND THE MAN — 30 MIN
BENJAMIN FRANKLIN - POOR RICHARD AND THE -- — 30 MIN
BENJAMIN FRANKLIN - THE FORMING OF A STYLE — 30 MIN
BENJAMIN FRANKLIN - THE LENGTHENED MAXIM, -- — 30 MIN
DRAMA - THE PLAY READ — 30 MIN
DRAMA - THE PLAY SEEN — 30 MIN
EDGAR ALLAN POE - POE'S POETIC THEORY AND -- — 30 MIN
EDGAR ALLAN POE - THE FALL OF THE HOUSE OF -- — 30 MIN
EDGAR ALLAN POE - THE PURLOINED LETTER — 30 MIN
EDGAR ALLEN POE - ASSESSMENT — 30 MIN
EDWIN ARLINGTON ROBINSON - A SAMPLING — 30 MIN
EDWIN ARLINGTON ROBINSON - ASSESSMENT — 30 MIN
EDWIN ARLINGTON ROBINSON - CHARACTERISTICS — 30 MIN
EDWIN ARLINGTON ROBINSON - EROS TURANNOS, MR -- — 30 MIN
EMILY DICKINSON - A SAMPLING — 30 MIN
EMILY DICKINSON - ESSENTIAL OILS — 30 MIN
EMILY DICKINSON - PERSPECTIVES — 30 MIN
EMILY DICKINSON - STYLE — 30 MIN
ERNEST HEMINGWAY - BIG TWO HEARTED RIVER — 30 MIN
ERNEST HEMINGWAY - FOCUS ON DEATH — 30 MIN
ERNEST HEMINGWAY - THE OLD MAN AND THE SEA, -- — 30 MIN
ERNEST HEMINGWAY - THE OLD MAN AND THE SEA, 1 — 30 MIN
EUGENE O'NEILL - THE EMPEROR JONES — 30 MIN
EUGENE O'NEILL - THE HAIRY APE — 30 MIN
FROM FRANKLIN TO FROST - PROSPECT — 30 MIN
FROM FRANKLIN TO FROST - RETROSPECT — 30 MIN
HUMOR - HUMOR — 30 MIN
HUMOR - SATIRE — 30 MIN
MARK TWAIN - CRITICAL THEORY — 30 MIN
MARK TWAIN - FROGS, JAYS AND HUMOR — 30 MIN
MARK TWAIN - HUCK FINN - CHARACTER AND GROWTH — 30 MIN
MARK TWAIN - THE ADVENTURES OF HUCKLEBERRY FINN — 30 MIN
NARRATIVE FICTION - DIVIDE AND CONQUER, THE -- — 30 MIN
NARRATIVE FICTION - REPETITION AND CONTRAST — 30 MIN
NARRATIVE FICTION - THE STORY AS ART, THE — 30 MIN

NATHANIEL HAWTHORNE - THE AMBITIOUS GUEST — 30 MIN
NATHANIEL HAWTHORNE - THE MINISTER'S BLACK -- — 30 MIN
NATHANIEL HAWTHORNE - THE SCARLET LETTER AND -- — 30 MIN
NATHANIEL HAWTHORNE - THE WORLD OF THE -- — 30 MIN
POETRY - DICTION — 30 MIN
POETRY - IMAGERY — 30 MIN
POETRY - RHYME — 30 MIN
POETRY - RHYTHM — 30 MIN
RALPH WALDO EMERSON - EMERSON'S CRITICAL -- — 30 MIN
RALPH WALDO EMERSON - EMERSON'S DISCIPLE, -- — 30 MIN
RALPH WALDO EMERSON - INTRODUCTION — 30 MIN
RALPH WALDO EMERSON - METER-MAKING ARGUMENTS — 30 MIN
RALPH WALDO EMERSON - SELF-RELIANCE, -- — 30 MIN
ROBERT FROST - A SAMPLING — 30 MIN
ROBERT FROST - FACT, FORM, PROCESS AND MEANING — 30 MIN
ROBERT FROST - PERSPECTIVES — 30 MIN
ROBERT FROST - SIMPLICITY AND COMPLEXITY — 30 MIN
SAMPLING, A — 30 MIN
SELECTION, ORDER, EMPHASIS — 30 MIN
STEPHEN CRANE - THE BLUE HOTEL — 30 MIN
STEPHEN CRANE - THE BRIDE COMES TO YELLOW SKY — 30 MIN
STEPHEN CRANE - THE RED BADGE OF COURAGE, PT 1 — 30 MIN
STEPHEN CRANE - THE RED BADGE OF COURAGE, PT 2 — 30 MIN
WALT WHITMAN - DRUM TAPS — 30 MIN
WALT WHITMAN - SONG OF MYSELF, PT 1 — 30 MIN
WALT WHITMAN - SONG OF MYSELF, PT 2 — 30 MIN
WALT WHITMAN - WHEN LILACS IN THE DOORYARD -- — 30 MIN

FUN WITH THE MINI-COMPUTER C 30 MIN
2 INCH VIDEOTAPE
PRESENTS THE MINI-COMPUTER TO PROVIDE A NEW AND REFRESHING WAY TO ADD AND SUB-TRACT AND FORCES THE STUDENT TO UNDER-STAND EVERY STEP THAT MUST BE TAKEN IN THE PROCESS. FROM THE DEVICES IN THEIR HANDS - MATH IN THEIR MINDS SERIES.
PROD-GPITVL   DIST-GPITVL

G

GETTING EVEN C 15 MIN
2 INCH VIDEOTAPE
PRESENTS THREE CHILDREN WHO BUILD THEIR OWN SECRET CLUB AND CLUBHOUSE, BUT IN DO-ING SO EXCLUDE SOME OF THEIR FRIENDS. DE-PICTS WHAT HAPPENS WHEN THE FRIENDS TRY TO EVEN THE SCORE, FEELINGS HARDEN ON BOTH SIDES AND A FIGHT BREAKS OUT. POINTS OUT WHAT ACCEPTANCE AND REJECTION BY A GROUP MEANS AND WHAT CAUSES PEOPLE TO ACT VENGEFULLY.
PROD-NITC   DIST-NITC

GRAND ASSUMPTIONS C 30 MIN
2 INCH VIDEOTAPE
SEE SERIES TITLE FOR DESCRIPTIVE STATEMENT. FROM THE UNCONSCIOUS CULTURAL CLASHES SE-RIES.
PROD-SCCOE   DIST-SCCOE

GREAT GAME CONTEST, THE C 15 MIN
2 INCH VIDEOTAPE I
REVIEWS THE GEOMETRIC CONCEPTS PRESENTED IN THE FIRST FOUR LESSONS AND INTRODUCES THE GEOBOARD AS A TOOL FOR LEARNING GEOM-ETRY. FROM THE MATH FACTORY, MODULE 2 - GE-OMETRY SERIES.
PROD-GPITVL   DIST-GPITVL

GROUP DISCUSSION WITH NORMAL TEENAGERS B 30 MIN
2 INCH VIDEOTAPE
PRESENTS A GROUP DISCUSSION ABOUT SCHOOL WITH ONE TENTH GRADER AND THREE ELEVENTH GRADERS. FROM THE COUNSELING THE ADOLES-CENT SERIES.
PROD-GPITVL   DIST-GPITVL

GROUP DISCUSSION WITH
SCHOOL DROP-OUTS   B   30 MIN
                    2 INCH VIDEOTAPE
PRESENTS A GROUP DISCUSSION WITH FOUR
SCHOOL DROPOUTS, AGES 16 TO 18. FROM THE
COUNSELING THE ADOLESCENT SERIES.
PROD-GPITVL   DIST-GPITVL

GROUP DISCUSSION WITH
TEENAGERS   B   30 MIN
                    2 INCH VIDEOTAPE
PRESENTS A DISCUSSION WITH TEENAGERS CEN-
TERING AROUND VALUES AND THE GENERATION
GAP. FROM THE MOTIVATING CHILDREN TO
LEARN SERIES.
PROD-GPITVL   DIST-GPITVL

GROUP DISCUSSION, PT 1   B   30 MIN
                    2 INCH VIDEOTAPE
DISCUSSES THE EFFECTIVENESS AND THE PROCE-
DURE OF REGULARLY SCHEDULED GROUP DIS-
CUSSION IN THE CLASSROOM. FROM THE MOTI-
VATING CHILDREN TO LEARN SERIES.
PROD-GPITVL   DIST-GPITVL

GROUP DISCUSSION, PT 2   B   30 MIN
                    2 INCH VIDEOTAPE
PRESENTS A GROUP OF CHILDREN, AGES 11 AND
13, IN A DEMONSTRATION OF GROUP DISCUS-
SION. FROM THE MOTIVATING CHILDREN TO
LEARN SERIES.
PROD-GPITVL   DIST-GPITVL

GROUP DISCUSSION, PT 3   B   30 MIN
                    2 INCH VIDEOTAPE
PRESENTS A GROUP OF FIVE CHILDREN, AGES 10
AND 11, TO HELP DEMONSTRATE SOME OF THE
TECHNIQUES FOR A TEACHER TO STIMULATE AN
EFFECTIVE DISCUSSION. FROM THE MOTIVATING
CHILDREN TO LEARN SERIES.
PROD-GPITVL   DIST-GPITVL

H

HISTORY OF ADP AND
INTRODUCTION TO UNIT
RECORD DATA PROCESSING   B   45 MIN
                    2 INCH VIDEOTAPE
SEE SERIES TITLE FOR DESCRIPTIVE STATEMENT.
FROM THE DATA PROCESSING, UNIT 1 - INTRO-
DUCTION TO DATA PROCESSING SERIES.
PROD-GPITVL   DIST-GPITVL

HOME SWEET HOME   C   15 MIN
                    2 INCH VIDEOTAPE
ILLUSTRATES HOW EMOTIONAL ABUSE, WHETHER
REAL OR IMAGINED, CAN AFFECT A CHILD. INTRO-
DUCES EDDIE, WHOSE PARENTS NEGLECT AND
ABUSE HIM AND HIS FRIEND STEVE, WHOSE PAR-
ENTS ARE LOVING BUT STRICT, BOTH DECIDING
TO RUN AWAY.
PROD-NITC   DIST-NITC

HOT AND COLD   B   15 MIN
                    2 INCH VIDEOTAPE   I
DISCUSSES METHODS OF COMMUNICATING.
FROM THE LET'S EXPLORE SCIENCE SERIES.
PROD-GPITVL   DIST-GPITVL

HOW ARE ANIMALS ADAPTED
FOR SURVIVAL   B   15 MIN
                    2 INCH VIDEOTAPE   I
POINTS OUT THE SPECIAL PARTS WHICH ANIMALS
POSSESS THAT ENABLE THEM TO LIVE IN THEIR
ENVIRONMENT. FROM THE SCIENCE IS DISCOV-
ERY SERIES.
PROD-GPITVL   DIST-GPITVL

HOW ARE ANIMALS CLASSIFIED   B   15 MIN
                    2 INCH VIDEOTAPE   I
SHOWS HOW ANIMALS MAY BE SEPARATED INTO
GROUPS ACCORDING TO THEIR BODY STRUC-
TURE. FROM THE SCIENCE IS DISCOVERY SERIES.
PROD-GPITVL   DIST-GPITVL

HOW ARE ATOMS COMBINED   B   15 MIN
                    2 INCH VIDEOTAPE   I
SHOWS HOW ATOMS COMBINE TO FORM ELE-
MENTS OR COMPOUNDS. FROM THE SCIENCE IS
DISCOVERY SERIES.
PROD-GPITVL   DIST-GPITVL

HOW ARE GREEN PLANTS ALIKE
                                   B   15 MIN
                    2 INCH VIDEOTAPE   I
EXPLAINS THAT GREEN PLANTS ARE RELATED
THROUGH COMMON STRUCTURE. FROM THE SCI-
ENCE IS DISCOVERY SERIES.
PROD-GPITVL   DIST-GPITVL

HOW ARE NON-GREEN PLANTS
ALIKE   B   15 MIN
                    2 INCH VIDEOTAPE   I
EXPLAINS THAT NON-GREEN PLANTS ARE RE-
LATED THROUGH COMMON STRUCTURE. FROM
THE SCIENCE IS DISCOVERY SERIES.
PROD-GPITVL   DIST-GPITVL

HOW ARE PLANTS CLASSIFIED   B   15 MIN
                    2 INCH VIDEOTAPE   I
POINTS OUT THAT STRUCTURAL SIMILARITIES
PROVIDE A BASIS FOR PLANT CLASSIFICATION.
FROM THE SCIENCE IS DISCOVERY SERIES.
PROD-GPITVL   DIST-GPITVL

HOW BIG IS THE UNIVERSE   B   15 MIN
                    2 INCH VIDEOTAPE   I
DEFINES THE UNIVERSE AS AN AGGREGATE OF
ALL THE EXISTING THINGS KNOWN TO MAN.
FROM THE SCIENCE IS DISCOVERY SERIES.
PROD-GPITVL   DIST-GPITVL

HOW BIG IS YOUR WORLD   B   15 MIN
                    2 INCH VIDEOTAPE   I
EXPLAINS THAT AS WE GROW, OUR UNDER-
STANDING OF THE WORLD GROWS AS WELL. FROM
THE SCIENCE IS DISCOVERY SERIES.
PROD-GPITVL   DIST-GPITVL

HOW CAN ELECTRICAL ENERGY
MAKE THINGS MOVE   B   15 MIN
                    2 INCH VIDEOTAPE   I
SHOWS HOW ELECTROMAGNETIC FORCES CAN BE
USED TO DO WORK. FROM THE SCIENCE IS DIS-
COVERY SERIES.
PROD-GPITVL   DIST-GPITVL

HOW COMPUTERS WORK   B   45 MIN
                    2 INCH VIDEOTAPE
SEE SERIES TITLE FOR DESCRIPTIVE STATEMENT.
FROM THE DATA PROCESSING, UNIT 2 - THE COM-
PUTER AND HOW IT WORKS SERIES.
PROD-GPITVL   DIST-GPITVL

HOW DO YOU KNOW   B   15 MIN
                    2 INCH VIDEOTAPE   I
PRESENTS AN EXPLORATION OF THE ROLE OF THE
SENSES IN LEARNING AND IN SCIENTIFIC OBSER-
VATION. FROM THE LET'S EXPLORE SCIENCE SE-
RIES.
PROD-GPITVL   DIST-GPITVL

HOW DO YOU SHOW   C   15 MIN
                    2 INCH VIDEOTAPE
PRESENTS THREE BOYS WHO EXPRESS OR WITH-
HOLD THEIR FEELINGS ABOUT VARIOUS THINGS
THAT HAPPENED TO THEM IN THE COURSE OF AN
AFTERNOON. POINTS OUT THE MANY WAYS THAT
FEELINGS CAN BE EXPRESSED.
PROD-NITC   DIST-NITC

HOW DOES TEMPERATURE
AFFECT MATTER   B   15 MIN
                    2 INCH VIDEOTAPE   I
EXPLAINS THAT THE STATE OF MATTER IS DETER-
MINED BY ITS TEMPERATURE. FROM THE SCI-
ENCE IS DISCOVERY SERIES.
PROD-GPITVL   DIST-GPITVL

HOW IS BALANCE IN AN
ENVIRONMENT MAINTAINED   B   15 MIN
                    2 INCH VIDEOTAPE   I
EXPLAINS THAT THE NUMBER OF PLANTS AND
ANIMALS IN AN ENVIRONMENT DEPENDS PARTLY
UPON THE AMOUNT OF FOOD AVAILABLE. FROM
THE SCIENCE IS DISCOVERY SERIES.
PROD-GPITVL   DIST-GPITVL

HOW IS THE EARTH'S SURFACE
CHANGED BY INTERNAL FORCES
                                   B   15 MIN
                    2 INCH VIDEOTAPE   I
SHOWS HOW THE ACTION OF EARTHQUAKES AND
VOLCANOES CAN CAUSE MAJOR CHANGES IN THE
EARTH'S SURFACE. FROM THE SCIENCE IS DIS-
COVERY SERIES.
PROD-GPITVL   DIST-GPITVL

HOW IS THE EARTH'S SURFACE
CHANGED BY WATER   B   15 MIN
                    2 INCH VIDEOTAPE   I
SHOWS HOW MOVING WATER AND ICE CAN
CHANGE THE SURFACE OF THE EARTH. FROM THE
SCIENCE IS DISCOVERY SERIES.
PROD-GPITVL   DIST-GPITVL

HOW IS THE EARTH'S SURFACE
CHANGED BY WIND   B   15 MIN
                    2 INCH VIDEOTAPE   I
SHOWS HOW WINDS CAN CHANGE THE SURFACE
OF THE EARTH. FROM THE SCIENCE IS DISCOVERY
SERIES.
PROD-GPITVL   DIST-GPITVL

HOW MANY KINDS OF ATOMS
EXIST   B   15 MIN
                    2 INCH VIDEOTAPE   I
POINTS OUT THAT THERE ARE MORE THAN ONE
HUNDRED DIFFERENT KINDS OF ATOMS. FROM
THE SCIENCE IS DISCOVERY SERIES.
PROD-GPITVL   DIST-GPITVL

HOW THE LAZY E RANCH GOT
ITS NAME   B   15 MIN
                    2 INCH VIDEOTAPE   P
SEE SERIES TITLE FOR DESCRIPTIVE STATEMENT.
FROM THE LISTEN AND SAY - VOWELS SERIES.
PROD-GPITVL   DIST-GPITVL

HUMOR - HUMOR   B   30 MIN
                    2 INCH VIDEOTAPE   J-H
FROM THE FRANKLIN TO FROST SERIES.
PROD-GPITVL   DIST-GPITVL

HUMOR - SATIRE   B   30 MIN
                    2 INCH VIDEOTAPE   J-H
FROM THE FRANKLIN TO FROST SERIES.
PROD-GPITVL   DIST-GPITVL

HUNCHES AND GUESSES   B   15 MIN
                    2 INCH VIDEOTAPE   I
EXAMINES THE USE OF HYPOTHESES AND PRE-
DICTIONS IN SCIENTIFIC RESEARCH. FROM THE
LET'S EXPLORE SCIENCE SERIES.
PROD-GPITVL   DIST-GPITVL

I

I DARE YOU   C   15 MIN
                    2 INCH VIDEOTAPE
PRESENTS CLARISSA WHO WANTS TO BE AC-
CEPTED AS A MEMBER OF THE NEIGHBORHOOD
GANG, HAS TO DECIDE WHETHER OR NOT SHE
SHOULD TAKE A POTENTIALLY DANGEROUS DARE.
CONSIDERS CHOICES THAT INVOLVE RISK AND
SAFETY, PERSONAL BELIEF AND GROUP PRES-
SURE.
PROD-NITC   DIST-NITC

INPUT-OUTPUT AND
SECONDARY MEMORY   B   45 MIN
                    2 INCH VIDEOTAPE
SEE SERIES TITLE FOR DESCRIPTIVE STATEMENT.
FROM THE DATA PROCESSING, UNIT 2 - THE COM-
PUTER AND HOW IT WORKS SERIES.
PROD-GPITVL   DIST-GPITVL

INPUT-OUTPUT DEVICES, PT 1   B   45 MIN
                    2 INCH VIDEOTAPE
SEE SERIES TITLE FOR DESCRIPTIVE STATEMENT.
FROM THE DATA PROCESSING, UNIT 2 - THE COM-
PUTER AND HOW IT WORKS SERIES.
PROD-GPITVL   DIST-GPITVL

INPUT-OUTPUT DEVICES, PT 2   B   45 MIN
                    2 INCH VIDEOTAPE
SEE SERIES TITLE FOR DESCRIPTIVE STATEMENT.
FROM THE DATA PROCESSING, UNIT 2 - THE COM-
PUTER AND HOW IT WORKS SERIES.
PROD-GPITVL   DIST-GPITVL

INSTRUCTING THE COMPUTER   B   45 MIN
                    2 INCH VIDEOTAPE
SEE SERIES TITLE FOR DESCRIPTIVE STATEMENT.
FROM THE DATA PROCESSING, UNIT 3 - IN-
STRUCTING THE COMPUTER SERIES.
PROD-GPITVL   DIST-GPITVL

INSTRUCTING THE COMPUTER AND THE OPERATING SYSTEM   B 45 MIN
2 INCH VIDEOTAPE
SEE SERIES TITLE FOR DESCRIPTIVE STATEMENT. FROM THE DATA PROCESSING, UNIT 4 - APPLICATIONS AND CAREER OPPORTUNITIES SERIES.
PROD-GPITVL   DIST-GPITVL

INTENT OF ART AND ARTISTS, THE   C 20 MIN
2 INCH VIDEOTAPE I
HELPS STUDENTS REALIZE THE INTENT OF ARTISTS AND WHAT THEY BELIEVE ABOUT THEIR OWN EXPRESSIONS. FROM THE CREATING ART, PT 3 - LEARNING TO UNDERSTAND ART SERIES.
PROD-GPITVL   DIST-GPITVL

INTER-OFFICE MEMORANDUM FORMS   B 30 MIN
2 INCH VIDEOTAPE
FROM THE TYPEWRITING, UNIT 7 - POSTAL CARDS, FORMS, MANUSCRIPTS SERIES.
PROD-GPITVL   DIST-GPITVL

INTRODUCING SETS   C 15 MIN
2 INCH VIDEOTAPE I
PRESENTS THE BASIC IDEA OF A SET AS IT RELATES TO A NUMERATION SYSTEM. FROM THE MATH FACTORY, MODULE 1 - SETS SERIES.
PROD-GPITVL   DIST-GPITVL

INTRODUCTION TO ELECTRONIC DATA PROCESSING - THE COMPUTER   B 45 MIN
2 INCH VIDEOTAPE
SEE SERIES TITLE FOR DESCRIPTIVE STATEMENT. FROM THE DATA PROCESSING, UNIT 2 - THE COMPUTER AND HOW IT WORKS SERIES.
PROD-GPITVL   DIST-GPITVL

INTRODUCTION TO FLOWCHARTING   B 45 MIN
2 INCH VIDEOTAPE
SEE SERIES TITLE FOR DESCRIPTIVE STATEMENT. FROM THE DATA PROCESSING, UNIT 3 - INSTRUCTING THE COMPUTER SERIES.
PROD-GPITVL   DIST-GPITVL

INTRODUCTION TO THE VOWELS - THE FIVE MAGIC BROTHERS   B 15 MIN
2 INCH VIDEOTAPE P
SEE SERIES TITLE FOR DESCRIPTIVE STATEMENT. FROM THE LISTEN AND SAY - VOWELS SERIES.
PROD-GPITVL   DIST-GPITVL

INVOICE AND TELEGRAM FORMS - CARBONS   B 30 MIN
2 INCH VIDEOTAPE
FROM THE TYPEWRITING, UNIT 7 - POSTAL CARDS, FORMS, MANUSCRIPTS SERIES.
PROD-GPITVL   DIST-GPITVL

J

JEFF   B 30 MIN
2 INCH VIDEOTAPE
PRESENTS AN INTERVIEW WITH A TEACHER AND A HIGH SCHOOL STUDENT WITH WHOM SHE IS HAVING DIFFICULTY. FROM THE COUNSELING THE ADOLESCENT SERIES.
PROD-GPITVL   DIST-GPITVL

JOINING SETS, ADDITION   C 15 MIN
2 INCH VIDEOTAPE I
DEVELOPS UNDERSTANDING OF THE PHYSICAL ACTIVITY WHICH RELATES TO THE ABSTRACT IDEA OF ADDITION. FROM THE MATH FACTORY, MODULE 1 - SETS SERIES.
PROD-GPITVL   DIST-GPITVL

JUDGMENTS ABOUT ART, THE   C 20 MIN
2 INCH VIDEOTAPE I
HELPS STUDENTS DEVELOP A CRITICAL AND APPRECIATIVE ATTITUDE ABOUT A WORK OF ART. FROM THE CREATING ART, PT 3 - LEARNING TO UNDERSTAND ART SERIES.
PROD-GPITVL   DIST-GPITVL

JUVENILE DELINQUENCY   B 30 MIN
2 INCH VIDEOTAPE
DISCUSSES JUVENILE DELINQUENCY AND METHODS OF WORKING WITH RESISTANT YOUTH. FROM THE COUNSELING THE ADOLESCENT SERIES.

PROD-GPITVL   DIST-GPITVL

K

KEEP IT CLEAN   B 15 MIN
2 INCH VIDEOTAPE P-I
DISCUSSES THE IMPORTANCE OF KEEPING YOUR TEETH CLEAN THE REASONS WHY YOU SHOULD, WHAT HAPPENS WHEN YOU DON'T AND THE BEST WAY IN WHICH YOU CAN. COVERS DENTAL PLAQUE AND ITS CAUSE AND PREVENTION. FROM THE DENTAL HEALTH SERIES.
PROD-GPITVL   DIST-GPITVL

KID, YOU'VE GOT A DIRTY MOUTH   B 15 MIN
2 INCH VIDEOTAPE P-I
PRESENTS GENERAL INFORMATION ABOUT DENTAL DISEASE INCLUDING THE BACTERIA THAT CAUSE TROUBLE AND THE VARIOUS FORMS OF DISEASE. COVERS THE PREVALENCE OF DENTAL PROBLEMS IN THE UNITED STATES AND THE ROLE OF DIET AND DENTAL HYGIENE. FROM THE DENTAL HEALTH SERIES.
PROD-GPITVL   DIST-GPITVL

L

LEARNING PROBLEM, A   B 30 MIN
2 INCH VIDEOTAPE
DISCUSSES THE CASE OF CHRISTOPHER, AGE 10, WHO IS HYPERACTIVE, HAS DIFFICULTIES IN READING AND SPELLING, TENDS TO FORGET AND IS MESSY. FROM THE MOTIVATING CHILDREN TO LEARN SERIES.
PROD-GPITVL   DIST-GPITVL

LEARNING TO SEE COLOR   C 20 MIN
2 INCH VIDEOTAPE I
HELPS THE STUDENT EXPLORE THE WORLD OF COLOR AND TO GRASP MEANINGS AND SIGNIFICANCE IN THE USE OF COLOR. FROM THE CREATING ART, PT 1 - LEARNING TO SEE SERIES.
PROD-GPITVL   DIST-GPITVL

LEARNING TO SEE LINE AND SHAPE   C 20 MIN
2 INCH VIDEOTAPE I
HELPS THE STUDENT LEARN ABOUT LINE AND SHAPE AND EXPOSES HIM TO THESE ART ELEMENTS AS THEY APPEAR IN HIS VISUAL WORLD. FROM THE CREATING ART, PT 1 - LEARNING TO SEE SERIES.
PROD-GPITVL   DIST-GPITVL

LEARNING TO SEE SPACE AND MOVEMENT   C 20 MIN
2 INCH VIDEOTAPE I
HELPS THE STUDENT SENSE VARIOUS MOTIONS WHICH OCCUR AND TO SEE THE RELATIONSHIPS OF SPACE AND MOTION TO VISUAL EXPRESSION. FROM THE CREATING ART, PT 1 - LEARNING TO SEE SERIES.
PROD-GPITVL   DIST-GPITVL

LEARNING TO SEE TEXTURE   C 20 MIN
2 INCH VIDEOTAPE I
HELPS THE STUDENT SEE TEXTURE AND BECOME AWARE OF ACTUAL AS WELL AS CREATED TEXTURES. FROM THE CREATING ART, PT 1 - LEARNING TO SEE SERIES.
PROD-GPITVL   DIST-GPITVL

LEARNING TO SEE THE SUBJECTS OF ART   C 20 MIN
2 INCH VIDEOTAPE I
SHOWS THE STUDENT THE SOURCES AND INSPIRATION FOR SUBJECT MATTER FOR VISUAL EXPRESSION. FROM THE CREATING ART, PT 1 - LEARNING TO SEE SERIES.
PROD-GPITVL   DIST-GPITVL

LEARNING TO SEE THE VISUAL ENVIRONMENT   C 20 MIN
2 INCH VIDEOTAPE I
HELPS STRENGTHEN THE STUDENT'S AWARENESS TO HIS VISUAL WORLD AND TO SHARPEN SENSITIVITY TO PEOPLE, OBJECTS AND THINGS. FROM THE CREATING ART, PT 1 - LEARNING TO SEE SERIES.
PROD-GPITVL   DIST-GPITVL

LET'S EXPLORE SCIENCE--A SERIES   I
PROD-GPITVL   DIST-GPITVL

CRYSTAL CLEAR	15 MIN
DRAWING A PICTURE OF NATURE	15 MIN
EXPLORING GASES	15 MIN
EXPLORING PLANTS	15 MIN
EXTENDING OUR SENSES	15 MIN
HOT AND COLD	15 MIN
HOW DO YOU KNOW	15 MIN
HUNCHES AND GUESSES	15 MIN
MAGNET EARTH, THE	15 MIN
PUSH AND PULL	15 MIN
SEESAWS, SLIDES AND SWINGS	15 MIN
SORTING THINGS	15 MIN
WHAT DO YOU DO WITH NUMBERS	15 MIN
WHAT DO YOU THINK	15 MIN

LISTEN AND SAY - CONSONANTS AND DIGRAPHS--A SERIES   P
HELPS CHILDREN BECOME AWARE OF SOME OF THE CONSONANT SOUNDS THEY WILL MEET IN EARLY READING. TEACHES IDENTIFICATION OF THE WRITTEN LETTER WHICH REPRESENTS THE SPOKEN SOUND.
PROD-GPITVL   DIST-GPITVL

B SOUND, THE - BETTY'S BONNET	15 MIN
CH SOUND, THE - CHARLIE, THE CHUBBY CHIPMUNK	15 MIN
D SOUND, THE - DICK'S DOG	15 MIN
F SOUND, THE - FIFI IS FRIGHTENED	15 MIN
H SOUND, THE - HANNAH'S NEW HAT	15 MIN
K OR HARD C SOUND, THE - CAROLINE CAT'S COUGH	15 MIN
L SOUND, THE - THE LEANING LADDER	15 MIN
M SOUND, THE - MAYBE THE MOUSE MIGHT	15 MIN
N SOUND, THE - NOBODY'S NOSE	15 MIN
R SOUND, THE - REDDY ROOSTER'S NEW TAIL	15 MIN
S SOUND, THE - MR SAM'S LITTLE TIRE	15 MIN
SH SOUND, THE - SHERMAN'S WISH	15 MIN
T SOUND, THE - THE TINIEST TICK	15 MIN
TH SOUND, THE - THIMBLE, THIMBLE IS MY NAME	15 MIN
W SOUND, THE - WILLIE WATERMELON	15 MIN
WH SOUND, THE - WHOO-OO-OO, I WANT TO GO	15 MIN

LISTEN AND SAY - VOWELS--A SERIES   P
INTRODUCES THE CONCEPT THAT LETTERS HAVE MORE THAN ONE SOUND. TEACHES THE LETTER NAMES OF THE VOWELS AND PRESENTS THE LONG AND SHORT SOUND FOR EACH VOWEL.
PROD-GPITVL   DIST-GPITVL

CARL AND THE CORNER MARKET	15 MIN
HOW THE LAZY E RANCH GOT ITS NAME	15 MIN
INTRODUCTION TO THE VOWELS - THE FIVE MAGIC --	15 MIN
LONG A - APRIL'S APRON	15 MIN
LONG AND SHORT OF IT, THE	15 MIN
LONG E - THE TEENY WEENY EEL	15 MIN
LONG I - IDA'S ICE CREAM	15 MIN
LONG O - OLE'S OLD OVERALLS	15 MIN
LONG U - THE UNICORN IN THE UNIFORM	15 MIN
SHORT A - ANDY AND THE APPLE	15 MIN
SHORT E - THE ELEPHANT WHO WANTED TO GO --	15 MIN
SHORT I - INKY THE IMP	15 MIN
SHORT O - THE OX IN THE BOX	15 MIN
SHORT U - UNCLE UMBER'S UMBRELLA	15 MIN
SOMETIMES VOWEL, A	15 MIN
WHEN TWO VOWELS GO WALKING	15 MIN

LIVING IN A NUCLEAR AGE--A SERIES   I-J
EXAMINES THE BENEFITS, DANGERS AND SAFEGUARDS OF THE NUCLEAR AGE. PROBES THE ROLE OF NUCLEAR ENERGY IN CURRENT SOCIAL ISSUES NOW PROMINENT IN THE NEWS.
PROD-GPITVL   DIST-GPITVL

BOMBARDING THINGS	30 MIN
DISCOVERING THE ATOM	30 MIN
NUCLEAR ENERGY AND LIVING THINGS	30 MIN
POWER FROM THE ATOM	30 MIN
RADIOISOTOPES	30 MIN
SOCIETY AND THINGS NUCLEAR	30 MIN

LOGICAL CONSEQUENCES AND PUNISHMENT   B 30 MIN
2 INCH VIDEOTAPE
PRESENTS A DISCUSSION CENTERING AROUND THE BASIC PRINCIPLE OF APPLYING LOGICAL CONSEQUENCES AND HOW TO DISTINGUISH THEM FROM PUNISHMENT. FROM THE MOTIVATING CHILDREN TO LEARN SERIES.
PROD-GPITVL   DIST-GPITVL

LONG A - APRIL'S APRON   B 15 MIN
2 INCH VIDEOTAPE   P
SEE SERIES TITLE FOR DESCRIPTIVE STATEMENT.
FROM THE LISTEN AND SAY - VOWELS SERIES.
PROD-GPITVL   DIST-GPITVL

LONG AND SHORT OF IT, THE   B 15 MIN
2 INCH VIDEOTAPE   P
SEE SERIES TITLE FOR DESCRIPTIVE STATEMENT.
FROM THE LISTEN AND SAY - VOWELS SERIES.
PROD-GPITVL   DIST-GPITVL

**LONG E - THE TEENY WEENY
EEL**   B 15 MIN
2 INCH VIDEOTAPE   P
SEE SERIES TITLE FOR DESCRIPTIVE STATEMENT.
FROM THE LISTEN AND SAY - VOWELS SERIES.
PROD-GPITVL   DIST-GPITVL

LONG I - IDA'S ICE CREAM   B 15 MIN
2 INCH VIDEOTAPE   P
SEE SERIES TITLE FOR DESCRIPTIVE STATEMENT.
FROM THE LISTEN AND SAY - VOWELS SERIES.
PROD-GPITVL   DIST-GPITVL

LONG O - OLE'S OLD OVERALLS   B 15 MIN
2 INCH VIDEOTAPE   P
SEE SERIES TITLE FOR DESCRIPTIVE STATEMENT.
FROM THE LISTEN AND SAY - VOWELS SERIES.
PROD-GPITVL   DIST-GPITVL

**LONG U - THE UNICORN IN
THE UNIFORM**   B 15 MIN
2 INCH VIDEOTAPE   P
SEE SERIES TITLE FOR DESCRIPTIVE STATEMENT.
FROM THE LISTEN AND SAY - VOWELS SERIES.
PROD-GPITVL   DIST-GPITVL

LOOK ME IN THE EYE   C 30 MIN
2 INCH VIDEOTAPE
SEE SERIES TITLE FOR DESCRIPTIVE STATEMENT.
FROM THE UNCONSCIOUS CULTURAL CLASHES SE-
RIES.
PROD-SCCOE   DIST-SCCOE

M

**MACHINE LANGUAGE
PROGRAMMING, PT 1**   B 45 MIN
2 INCH VIDEOTAPE
SEE SERIES TITLE FOR DESCRIPTIVE STATEMENT.
FROM THE DATA PROCESSING, UNIT 3 - IN-
STRUCTING THE COMPUTER SERIES.
PROD-GPITVL   DIST-GPITVL

**MACHINE LANGUAGE
PROGRAMMING, PT 2**   B 45 MIN
2 INCH VIDEOTAPE
SEE SERIES TITLE FOR DESCRIPTIVE STATEMENT.
FROM THE DATA PROCESSING, UNIT 3 - IN-
STRUCTING THE COMPUTER SERIES.
PROD-GPITVL   DIST-GPITVL

**MACHINE LANGUAGE
PROGRAMMING, PT 3**   B 45 MIN
2 INCH VIDEOTAPE
SEE SERIES TITLE FOR DESCRIPTIVE STATEMENT.
FROM THE DATA PROCESSING, UNIT 3 - IN-
STRUCTING THE COMPUTER SERIES.
PROD-GPITVL   DIST-GPITVL

MAGNET EARTH, THE   B 15 MIN
2 INCH VIDEOTAPE   I
EXPLAINS THE WAYS TO INTERPRET DATA. FROM
THE LET'S EXPLORE SCIENCE SERIES.
PROD-GPITVL   DIST-GPITVL

**MARK TWAIN - CRITICAL
THEORY**   B 30 MIN
2 INCH VIDEOTAPE   J-H
FROM THE FRANKLIN TO FROST SERIES.
PROD-GPITVL   DIST-GPITVL

**MARK TWAIN - FROGS, JAYS
AND HUMOR**   B 30 MIN
2 INCH VIDEOTAPE   J-H
FROM THE FRANKLIN TO FROST SERIES.
PROD-GPITVL   DIST-GPITVL

**MARK TWAIN - HUCK FINN -
CHARACTER AND GROWTH**   B 30 MIN
2 INCH VIDEOTAPE   J-H
FROM THE FRANKLIN TO FROST SERIES.
PROD-GPITVL   DIST-GPITVL

**MARK TWAIN - THE
ADVENTURES OF HUCKLEBERRY
FINN**   B 30 MIN
2 INCH VIDEOTAPE   J-H
FROM THE FRANKLIN TO FROST SERIES.
PROD-GPITVL   DIST-GPITVL

MARY   B 30 MIN
2 INCH VIDEOTAPE
PRESENTS AN INTERVIEW WITH A 13-YEAR-OLD
GIRL AND HER MOTHER. INCLUDES PROBLEMS OF
STAYING OUT LATE AT NIGHT AND OTHER MISBE-
HAVIOR. FROM THE COUNSELING THE ADOLES-
CENT SERIES.
PROD-GPITVL   DIST-GPITVL

**MATH FACTORY, MODULE 1 -
SETS--A SERIES**
INCORPORATES COLORFUL PUPPET CHARACTERS
AND A FANCIFUL FACTORY INTO INFORMAL
MATHEMATICAL LEARNING SITUATIONS.
PROD-GPITVL   DIST-GPITVL

INTRODUCING SETS   15 MIN
JOINING SETS, ADDITION   15 MIN
NONEQUIVALENT SETS, INEQUALITIES   15 MIN
SEPARATING SETS   15 MIN
SET NUMERATION   15 MIN

**MATH FACTORY, MODULE 2 -
GEOMETRY--A SERIES**
I
INCORPORATES COLORFUL PUPPET CHARACTERS
AND A FANCIFUL FACTORY INTO INFORMAL
MATHEMATICAL LEARNING SITUATIONS.
PROD-GPITVL   DIST-GPITVL

ANGLES AND OTHER FIGURES   15 MIN
CIRCLES   15 MIN
CURVES   15 MIN
GREAT GAME CONTEST, THE   15 MIN
POINTS AND LINE SEGMENTS   15 MIN

**MODELING AND POTTERY
MAKING**   C 20 MIN
2 INCH VIDEOTAPE   I
HELPS STUDENTS EXPERIMENT WITH A PLASTIC
MATERIAL AND CONSTRUCT OBJECTS OF CLAY.
FROM THE CREATING ART, PT 2 - LEARNING TO
CREATE ART FORMS SERIES.
PROD-GPITVL   DIST-GPITVL

**MOTIVATING CHILDREN TO
LEARN - SUMMARY**   B 30 MIN
2 INCH VIDEOTAPE
SEE SERIES TITLE FOR DESCRIPTIVE STATEMENT.
FROM THE MOTIVATING CHILDREN TO LEARN SE-
RIES.
PROD-GPITVL   DIST-GPITVL

**MOTIVATING CHILDREN TO
LEARN--A SERIES**
DEMONSTRATES TECHNIQUES FOR MOTIVATING
CHILDREN. SEEKS TO HELP PARENTS AND TEACH-
ERS UNDERSTAND CHILDREN BY SHOWING METH-
ODS OF DEALING WITH CHILDREN IN ORDER TO
ASSIST THEIR POSITIVE GROWTH IN SCHOOL.
PROD-GPITVL   DIST-GPITVL

CHANGING THE CHILD'S RELATIONSHIPS
AND GOALS   30 MIN
CLARIFICATION OF BASIC PRINCIPLES   30 MIN
CONSEQUENCES   30 MIN
DOUGLAS   30 MIN
EDWARD   30 MIN
ENCOURAGEMENT   30 MIN
GROUP DISCUSSION WITH TEENAGERS   30 MIN
GROUP DISCUSSION, PT 1   30 MIN
GROUP DISCUSSION, PT 2   30 MIN
GROUP DISCUSSION, PT 3   30 MIN
LEARNING PROBLEM, A   30 MIN
LOGICAL CONSEQUENCES AND
PUNISHMENT   30 MIN
MOTIVATING CHILDREN TO LEARN -
SUMMARY   30 MIN
OUR PRESENT EDUCATIONAL DILEMMA   30 MIN
READING DIFFICULTIES   30 MIN

N

**NARRATIVE FICTION - DIVIDE
AND CONQUER, THE MEANING
OF ANALYSIS**   B 30 MIN
2 INCH VIDEOTAPE   J-H
FROM THE FRANKLIN TO FROST SERIES.
PROD-GPITVL   DIST-GPITVL

**NARRATIVE FICTION -
REPETITION AND CONTRAST**   B 30 MIN
2 INCH VIDEOTAPE   J-H
FROM THE FRANKLIN TO FROST SERIES.
PROD-GPITVL   DIST-GPITVL

**NARRATIVE FICTION - THE
STORY AS ART, THE THING
MADE**   B 30 MIN
2 INCH VIDEOTAPE   J-H
FROM THE FRANKLIN TO FROST SERIES.
PROD-GPITVL   DIST-GPITVL

**NATHANIEL HAWTHORNE - THE
AMBITIOUS GUEST**   B 30 MIN
2 INCH VIDEOTAPE   J-H
FROM THE FRANKLIN TO FROST SERIES.
PROD-GPITVL   DIST-GPITVL

**NATHANIEL HAWTHORNE - THE
MINISTER'S BLACK VEIL**   B 30 MIN
2 INCH VIDEOTAPE   J-H
FROM THE FRANKLIN TO FROST SERIES.
PROD-GPITVL   DIST-GPITVL

**NATHANIEL HAWTHORNE - THE
SCARLET LETTER AND THE
FORTUNATE FALL**   B 30 MIN
2 INCH VIDEOTAPE   J-H
FROM THE FRANKLIN TO FROST SERIES.
PROD-GPITVL   DIST-GPITVL

**NATHANIEL HAWTHORNE - THE
WORLD OF THE SCARLET
LETTER AND ITS STRUCTURE**   B 30 MIN
2 INCH VIDEOTAPE   J-H
FROM THE FRANKLIN TO FROST SERIES.
PROD-GPITVL   DIST-GPITVL

**NONEQUIVALENT SETS,
INEQUALITIES**   C 15 MIN
2 INCH VIDEOTAPE   I
DEVELOPS AN UNDERSTANDING OF INEQUALITY
AND EQUALITY OF NUMBERS AND PRESENTS
SYMBOLS FOR 'EQUAL,' 'IS GREATER THAN' AND
'IS LESS THAN.' FROM THE MATH FACTORY, MOD-
ULE 1 - SETS SERIES.
PROD-GPITVL   DIST-GPITVL

NONI   B 30 MIN
2 INCH VIDEOTAPE
PRESENTS AN INTERVIEW WITH A 16-YEAR-OLD
GIRL AND HER MOTHER WITH A FOCUS ON LIFE
STYLES. FROM THE COUNSELING THE ADOLES-
CENT SERIES.
PROD-GPITVL   DIST-GPITVL

**NUCLEAR ENERGY AND LIVING
THINGS**   C 30 MIN
2 INCH VIDEOTAPE   I-J
DISCUSSES SOURCES AND USES OF RADIATION
WITH LIVING THINGS, INDIVIDUAL RADIOISO-
TOPES, NATURAL RADIATION, USEFUL AND DAM-
AGING ASPECTS OF RADIATION, SOMATIC AND GE-
NETIC EFFECTS AND APPLICATIONS IN AGRICUL-
TURE AND MEDICINE. FROM THE LIVING IN A NU-
CLEAR AGE SERIES.
PROD-GPITVL   DIST-GPITVL

O

OBJECTIVE - ACCULTURATION   C 30 MIN
2 INCH VIDEOTAPE
SEE SERIES TITLE FOR DESCRIPTIVE STATEMENT.
FROM THE UNCONSCIOUS CULTURAL CLASHES SE-
RIES.
PROD-SCCOE   DIST-SCCOE

**OUR PRESENT EDUCATIONAL
DILEMMA**   B 30 MIN
2 INCH VIDEOTAPE
PRESENTS AN EXAMINATION OF THE EDUCA-
TIONAL ENVIRONMENT OF TODAY WHERE TRADI-
TIONAL METHODS OF RAISING CHILDREN NO
LONGER BRING RESULTS. INTRODUCES THE

TELEOANALYTIC APPROACH WHICH DEALS WITH THE PURPOSES AND HOLISTIC PERCEPTION OF THE TOTAL CHILD IN HIS TOTAL ENVIRONMENT. FROM THE MOTIVATING CHILDREN TO LEARN SERIES.
PROD-GPITVL   DIST-GPITVL

OUTLOOK   C 30 MIN
2 INCH VIDEOTAPE
SEE SERIES TITLE FOR DESCRIPTIVE STATEMENT. FROM THE UNCONSCIOUS CULTURAL CLASHES SERIES.
PROD-SCCOE   DIST-SCCOE

P

PAINTING   C 20 MIN
2 INCH VIDEOTAPE   I
HELPS STUDENTS LEARN ABOUT USING PAINT AND OTHER MEDIA FOR PAINTING. FROM THE CREATING ART, PT 2 - LEARNING TO CREATE ART FORMS SERIES.
PROD-GPITVL   DIST-GPITVL

PLAIN AND FILL-IN POSTAL CARDS   B 30 MIN
2 INCH VIDEOTAPE
FROM THE TYPEWRITING, UNIT 7 - POSTAL CARDS, FORMS, MANUSCRIPTS SERIES.
PROD-GPITVL   DIST-GPITVL

POETRY - DICTION   B 30 MIN
2 INCH VIDEOTAPE   J-H
FROM THE FRANKLIN TO FROST SERIES.
PROD-GPITVL   DIST-GPITVL

POETRY - IMAGERY   B 30 MIN
2 INCH VIDEOTAPE   J-H
FROM THE FRANKLIN TO FROST SERIES.
PROD-GPITVL   DIST-GPITVL

POETRY - RHYME   B 30 MIN
2 INCH VIDEOTAPE   J-H
FROM THE FRANKLIN TO FROST SERIES.
PROD-GPITVL   DIST-GPITVL

POETRY - RHYTHM   B 30 MIN
2 INCH VIDEOTAPE   J-H
FROM THE FRANKLIN TO FROST SERIES.
PROD-GPITVL   DIST-GPITVL

POINTS AND LINE SEGMENTS   C 15 MIN
2 INCH VIDEOTAPE
INTRODUCES THE GEOMETRIC IDEAS OF POINT, LINE AND LINE SEGMENT AND CURVE. FROM THE MATH FACTORY, MODULE 2 - GEOMETRY SERIES.
PROD-GPITVL   DIST-GPITVL

POWER FROM THE ATOM   C 30 MIN
2 INCH VIDEOTAPE   I-J
DISCUSSES ECOLOGY, THE ATOM, FUSION, USE OF NUCLEAR POWER, ELEMENTS OF A POWER PLANT, SAFEGUARDS IN A POWER PLANT, DESALINIZATION AND POSSIBILITIES OF AGRI-NUCLEAR COMPLEX. FROM THE LIVING IN A NUCLEAR AGE SERIES.
PROD-GPITVL   DIST-GPITVL

PRINTING   C 20 MIN
2 INCH VIDEOTAPE   I
HELPS STUDENTS LEARN THE TECHNIQUES OF PRINTING AND HOW THESE CAN BE UTILIZED FOR VISUAL EXPRESSIONS. FROM THE CREATING ART, PT 2 - LEARNING TO CREATE ART FORMS SERIES.
PROD-GPITVL   DIST-GPITVL

PROBLEM ORIENTED LANGUAGES - COBOL   B 45 MIN
2 INCH VIDEOTAPE
SEE SERIES TITLE FOR DESCRIPTIVE STATEMENT. FROM THE DATA PROCESSING, UNIT 3 - INSTRUCTING THE COMPUTER SERIES.
PROD-GPITVL   DIST-GPITVL

PROBLEM ORIENTED LANGUAGES - FORTRAN   B 45 MIN
2 INCH VIDEOTAPE
SEE SERIES TITLE FOR DESCRIPTIVE STATEMENT. FROM THE DATA PROCESSING, UNIT 3 - INSTRUCTING THE COMPUTER SERIES.
PROD-GPITVL   DIST-GPITVL

PROBLEM ORIENTED LANGUAGES - REPORT PROGRAM GENERATOR RPG   B 45 MIN
2 INCH VIDEOTAPE
SEE SERIES TITLE FOR DESCRIPTIVE STATEMENT. FROM THE DATA PROCESSING, UNIT 3 - INSTRUCTING THE COMPUTER SERIES.
PROD-GPITVL   DIST-GPITVL

PUSH AND PULL   B 15 MIN
2 INCH VIDEOTAPE   I
COVERS THE IMPORTANCE OF MAKING USEFUL DEFINITIONS. FROM THE LET'S EXPLORE SCIENCE SERIES.
PROD-GPITVL   DIST-GPITVL

R

RADIOISOTOPES   C 30 MIN
2 INCH VIDEOTAPE   I-J
DEFINES RADIOISOTOPES AND DESCRIBES THEIR USES, INCLUDING TRACING, DATING, HALF LIFE AND DECAY AND SYSTEMS FOR NUCLEAR AUXILIARY POWER. FROM THE LIVING IN A NUCLEAR AGE SERIES.
PROD-GPITVL   DIST-GPITVL

RALPH WALDO EMERSON - EMERSON'S CRITICAL THEORY   B 30 MIN
2 INCH VIDEOTAPE   J-H
FROM THE FRANKLIN TO FROST SERIES.
PROD-GPITVL   DIST-GPITVL

RALPH WALDO EMERSON - EMERSON'S DISCIPLE, THOREAU   B 30 MIN
2 INCH VIDEOTAPE   J-H
FROM THE FRANKLIN TO FROST SERIES.
PROD-GPITVL   DIST-GPITVL

RALPH WALDO EMERSON - INTRODUCTION   B 30 MIN
2 INCH VIDEOTAPE   J-H
FROM THE FRANKLIN TO FROST SERIES.
PROD-GPITVL   DIST-GPITVL

RALPH WALDO EMERSON - METER-MAKING ARGUMENTS   B 30 MIN
2 INCH VIDEOTAPE   J-H
FROM THE FRANKLIN TO FROST SERIES.
PROD-GPITVL   DIST-GPITVL

RALPH WALDO EMERSON - SELF-RELIANCE, EMERSON'S PHILOSOPHY   B 30 MIN
2 INCH VIDEOTAPE   J-H

PROD-GPITVL   DIST-GPITVL

READING DIFFICULTIES   B 30 MIN
2 INCH VIDEOTAPE
POINTS OUT THAT THE TEACHER WHO CONCENTRATES HER EFFORTS TOWARD THE ELIMINATION OF PREVIOUS FAILURES AND WHO BUILDS UP THE CHILD WILL FIND THAT HE WILL LEARN TO READ WITH ANY METHOD SHE MAY USE OR WITH THE ONE HE RESPONDS TO BEST. FROM THE MOTIVATING CHILDREN TO LEARN SERIES.
PROD-GPITVL   DIST-GPITVL

RECORD LAYOUT AND PRINT CHART   B 45 MIN
2 INCH VIDEOTAPE
SEE SERIES TITLE FOR DESCRIPTIVE STATEMENT. FROM THE DATA PROCESSING, UNIT 3 - INSTRUCTING THE COMPUTER SERIES.
PROD-GPITVL   DIST-GPITVL

RECORDING MACHINES, THE   B 45 MIN
2 INCH VIDEOTAPE
SEE SERIES TITLE FOR DESCRIPTIVE STATEMENT. FROM THE DATA PROCESSING, UNIT 1 - INTRODUCTION TO DATA PROCESSING SERIES.
PROD-GPITVL   DIST-GPITVL

REVIEW - LETTERS, FORMS, REPORTS   B 30 MIN
2 INCH VIDEOTAPE
FROM THE TYPEWRITING, UNIT 7 - POSTAL CARDS, FORMS, MANUSCRIPTS SERIES.
PROD-GPITVL   DIST-GPITVL

REVISION MARKS, UNBOUND REPORTS, HOW TO ERASE   B 30 MIN
2 INCH VIDEOTAPE
FROM THE TYPEWRITING, UNIT 7 - POSTAL CARDS, FORMS, MANUSCRIPTS SERIES.
PROD-GPITVL   DIST-GPITVL

ROB   B 30 MIN
2 INCH VIDEOTAPE
PRESENTS AN INTERVIEW WITH A 16-YEAR-OLD BOY WHO IS HAVING ACADEMIC AND BEHAVIORAL DIFFICULTIES IN SCHOOL. FROM THE COUNSELING THE ADOLESCENT SERIES.
PROD-GPITVL   DIST-GPITVL

ROBERT FROST - A SAMPLING   B 30 MIN
2 INCH VIDEOTAPE   J-H
FROM THE FRANKLIN TO FROST SERIES.
PROD-GPITVL   DIST-GPITVL

ROBERT FROST - FACT, FORM, PROCESS AND MEANING   B 30 MIN
2 INCH VIDEOTAPE   J-H
FROM THE FRANKLIN TO FROST SERIES.
PROD-GPITVL   DIST-GPITVL

ROBERT FROST - PERSPECTIVES   B 30 MIN
2 INCH VIDEOTAPE   J-H
FROM THE FRANKLIN TO FROST SERIES.
PROD-GPITVL   DIST-GPITVL

ROBERT FROST - SIMPLICITY AND COMPLEXITY   B 30 MIN
2 INCH VIDEOTAPE   J-H
FROM THE FRANKLIN TO FROST SERIES.
PROD-GPITVL   DIST-GPITVL

S

SALLY HAD A SWEET TOOTH, NOW IT'S GONE   B 15 MIN
2 INCH VIDEOTAPE   P-I
DISCUSSES DIET AND HOW WHAT YOU EAT AFFECTS THE HEALTH OF YOUR TEETH. CONSIDERS PROBLEMS RESULTING FROM BAD FOOD CHOICES OR FROM BEING A NERVOUS NIBBLER WHO EATS OFTEN AND BRUSHES SELDOM. FROM THE DENTAL HEALTH SERIES.
PROD-GPITVL   DIST-GPITVL

SAMPLING, A   B 30 MIN
2 INCH VIDEOTAPE   J-H
FROM THE FRANKLIN TO FROST SERIES.
PROD-GPITVL   DIST-GPITVL

SCIENCE IS DISCOVERY--A SERIES

EMPHASIZES THE AREAS OF ASTRONOMY, GEOLOGY AND ECOLOGY. EXPLORES THE NATURE OF MATTER, INCLUDING PROPERTIES AND STRUCTURE ON BOTH MOLECULAR AND SUB-MOLECULAR BASES.
PROD-GPITVL   DIST-GPITVL

ARE ALL STARS ALIKE	15 MIN
HOW ARE ANIMALS ADAPTED FOR SURVIVAL	15 MIN
HOW ARE ANIMALS CLASSIFIED	15 MIN
HOW ARE ATOMS COMBINED	15 MIN
HOW ARE GREEN PLANTS ALIKE	15 MIN
HOW ARE NON-GREEN PLANTS ALIKE	15 MIN
HOW ARE PLANTS CLASSIFIED	15 MIN
HOW BIG IS THE UNIVERSE	15 MIN
HOW BIG IS YOUR WORLD	15 MIN
HOW CAN ELECTRICAL ENERGY MAKE THINGS MOVE	15 MIN
HOW DOES TEMPERATURE AFFECT MATTER	15 MIN
HOW IS BALANCE IN AN ENVIRONMENT MAINTAINED	15 MIN
HOW IS THE EARTH'S SURFACE CHANGED BY -	15 MIN
HOW IS THE EARTH'S SURFACE CHANGED BY WATER	15 MIN
HOW IS THE EARTH'S SURFACE CHANGED BY WIND	15 MIN
HOW MANY KINDS OF ATOMS EXIST	15 MIN
WHAT ANIMALS LIVE IN COMMUNITIES	15 MIN
WHAT ARE PLANETS	15 MIN
WHAT ARE SOME SPECIAL FORMS OF BEHAVIOR	15 MIN
WHAT ARE THE CHARACTERISTICS OF LIVING THINGS	15 MIN
WHAT ARE THE PROPERTIES OF MATTER	15 MIN

WHAT GREEN PLANTS REPRODUCE BY
OTHER MEANS   15 MIN
WHAT GREEN PLANTS REPRODUCE BY
SEEDS   15 MIN
WHAT HAPPENS WHEN
ENVIRONMENTAL CONDITIONS --   15 MIN
WHAT IS IN A POND   15 MIN
WHAT IS MATTER   15 MIN
WHAT IS THE EARTH'S SURFACE LIKE   15 MIN
WHAT IS THE WATER CYCLE   15 MIN
WHAT MAKES AIR MOVE   15 MIN
WHAT MAKES ELECTRIC CURRENT FLOW   15 MIN
WHAT MAKES WATER MOVE   15 MIN
WHERE ARE LIVING THINGS FOUND   15 MIN
WHY DO ECLIPSES OCCUR   15 MIN
WHY DO TEMPERATURES OF PLANETS
VARY   15 MIN
WHY DOES THE SUN'S POSITION SEEM
TO CHANGE   15 MIN

SCULPTURING   C 20 MIN
                      2 INCH VIDEOTAPE   I
HELPS STUDENTS BUILD AND DESIGN THREE-DI-
MENSIONAL FORMS. FROM THE CREATING ART,
PT 2 - LEARNING TO CREATE ART FORMS SERIES.
PROD-GPITVL   DIST-GPITVL

SEESAWS, SLIDES AND SWINGS
                              B 15 MIN
                      2 INCH VIDEOTAPE   I
USES VARIOUS LEVERS TO POINT OUT THE IMPOR-
TANCE OF SPACE-TIME COMPARISONS. FROM THE
LET'S EXPLORE SCIENCE SERIES.
PROD-GPITVL   DIST-GPITVL

SELECTION, ORDER, EMPHASIS   B 30 MIN
                      2 INCH VIDEOTAPE J-H
FROM THE FRANKLIN TO FROST SERIES.
PROD-GPITVL   DIST-GPITVL

**SELECTIVE PRACTICE -
CENTERING ON LINE**   B 30 MIN
                      2 INCH VIDEOTAPE
FROM THE TYPEWRITING, UNIT 6 - SKILL
DEVELOPMENT SERIES.
PROD-GPITVL   DIST-GPITVL

**SELECTIVE PRACTICE -
CORRECTIONS**   B 30 MIN
                      2 INCH VIDEOTAPE
FROM THE TYPEWRITING, UNIT 6 - SKILL
DEVELOPMENT SERIES.
PROD-GPITVL   DIST-GPITVL

**SELECTIVE PRACTICE -
INSERTIONS**   B 30 MIN
                      2 INCH VIDEOTAPE
FROM THE TYPEWRITING, UNIT 6 - SKILL
DEVELOPMENT SERIES.
PROD-GPITVL   DIST-GPITVL

SEPARATING SETS   C 15 MIN
                      2 INCH VIDEOTAPE   I
RELATES THE SEPARATION OF SETS TO THE OPER-
ATION OF SUBTRACTION. FROM THE MATH FAC-
TORY, MODULE 1 - SETS SERIES.
PROD-GPITVL   DIST-GPITVL

SET NUMERATION   C 15 MIN
                      2 INCH VIDEOTAPE   I
PROVIDES A BASIC EXPERIENCE IN RELATING
NUMBER AND NUMERAL. FROM THE MATH FAC-
TORY, MODULE 1 - SETS SERIES.
PROD-GPITVL   DIST-GPITVL

**SHORT A - ANDY AND THE
APPLE**   B 15 MIN
                      2 INCH VIDEOTAPE   P
SEE SERIES TITLE FOR DESCRIPTIVE STATEMENT.
FROM THE LISTEN AND SAY - VOWELS SERIES.
PROD-GPITVL   DIST-GPITVL

**SHORT E - THE ELEPHANT WHO
WANTED TO GO UPSTAIRS**   B 15 MIN
                      2 INCH VIDEOTAPE   P
SEE SERIES TITLE FOR DESCRIPTIVE STATEMENT.
FROM THE LISTEN AND SAY - VOWELS SERIES.
PROD-GPITVL   DIST-GPITVL

SHORT I - INKY THE IMP   B 15 MIN
                      2 INCH VIDEOTAPE   P
SEE SERIES TITLE FOR DESCRIPTIVE STATEMENT.
FROM THE LISTEN AND SAY - VOWELS SERIES.
PROD-GPITVL   DIST-GPITVL

**SHORT O - THE OX IN THE
BOX**   B 15 MIN
                      2 INCH VIDEOTAPE   P
SEE SERIES TITLE FOR DESCRIPTIVE STATEMENT.
FROM THE LISTEN AND SAY - VOWELS SERIES.

PROD-GPITVL   DIST-GPITVL

**SHORT U - UNCLE UMBER'S
UMBRELLA**   B 15 MIN
                      2 INCH VIDEOTAPE   P
SEE SERIES TITLE FOR DESCRIPTIVE STATEMENT.
FROM THE LISTEN AND SAY - VOWELS SERIES.
PROD-GPITVL   DIST-GPITVL

SLIDING IN FRACTIONS   C 30 MIN
                      2 INCH VIDEOTAPE
AIDS STUDENTS WHO ARE HAVING DIFFICULTY IN
ADDING AND SUBTRACING FRACTIONAL NUM-
BERS AND IN FINDING EQUIVALENT TRACTIONS.
FROM THE DEVICES IN THEIR HANDS - MATH IN
THEIR MINDS SERIES.
PROD-GPITVL   DIST-GPITVL

SOCIETY AND THINGS NUCLEAR
                              C 30 MIN
                      2 INCH VIDEOTAPE I-J
COVERS CIVIL DEFENSE PROCEDURES, NECESSITY
FOR PLANNING AND GROUP ACTION, RESULTS OF
A NUCLEAR BLAST, EFFECTS OF DISTANCE ON RA-
DIATION, PRINCIPLES OF SHIELDING, FALLOUT
SHELTERS AND WASTE DISPOSAL PROCEDURES.
FROM THE LIVING IN A NUCLEAR AGE SERIES.
PROD-GPITVL   DIST-GPITVL

**SOLUTIONS IN
COMMUNICATIONS -
INTRODUCTORY LESSON**   C 30 MIN
                      2 INCH VIDEOTAPE   T
FROM THE SOLUTIONS IN COMMUNICATING
SERIES.
PROD-SCCOE   DIST-SCCOE

SOMETIMES VOWEL, A   B 15 MIN
                      2 INCH VIDEOTAPE   P
SEE SERIES TITLE FOR DESCRIPTIVE STATEMENT.
FROM THE LISTEN AND SAY - VOWELS SERIES.
PROD-GPITVL   DIST-GPITVL

SORTING THINGS   B 15 MIN
                      2 INCH VIDEOTAPE   I
DISCUSSES THE ORGANIZATION AND CLASSIFICA-
TION OF MATERIALS. FROM THE LET'S EXPLORE
SCIENCE SERIES.
PROD-GPITVL   DIST-GPITVL

**STEPHEN CRANE - THE BLUE
HOTEL**   B 30 MIN
                      2 INCH VIDEOTAPE J-H
FROM THE FRANKLIN TO FROST SERIES.
PROD-GPITVL   DIST-GPITVL

**STEPHEN CRANE - THE BRIDE
COMES TO YELLOW SKY**   B 30 MIN
                      2 INCH VIDEOTAPE J-H
FROM THE FRANKLIN TO FROST SERIES.
PROD-GPITVL   DIST-GPITVL

**STEPHEN CRANE - THE RED
BADGE OF COURAGE, PT 1**   B 30 MIN
                      2 INCH VIDEOTAPE J-H
FROM THE FRANKLIN TO FROST SERIES.
PROD-GPITVL   DIST-GPITVL

**STEPHEN CRANE - THE RED
BADGE OF COURAGE, PT 2**   B 30 MIN
                      2 INCH VIDEOTAPE J-H
FROM THE FRANKLIN TO FROST SERIES.
PROD-GPITVL   DIST-GPITVL

STITCHING AND WEAVING   C 20 MIN
                      2 INCH VIDEOTAPE   I
HELPS STUDENTS LEARN VARIOUS TECHNIQUES
IN COMBINING THREADS AND FABRICS. FROM
THE CREATING ART, PT 2 - LEARNING TO CREATE
ART FORMS SERIES.
PROD-GPITVL   DIST-GPITVL

**STRETCH A RUBBER BAND AND
LEARN GEOMETRY**   C 30 MIN
                      2 INCH VIDEOTAPE
INTRODUCES THE STUDENT TO SOME OF THE
METRIC AND NON-METRIC PROPERTIES OF GEOM-
ETRY THROUGH THE USE OF THE GEOBOARD.
COVERS LINE SEGMENTS, TRIANGLES, QUADRI-
LATERALS, PARALLEL LINE SEGMENTS AND PER-
PENDICULAR LINE SEGMENTS. FROM THE DE-
VICES IN THEIR HANDS - MATH IN THEIR MINDS
SERIES.
PROD-GPITVL   DIST-GPITVL

**SYMBOLIC PROGRAMMING -
ASSEMBLER LANGUAGE**   B 45 MIN
                      2 INCH VIDEOTAPE
SEE SERIES TITLE FOR DESCRIPTIVE STATEMENT.
FROM THE DATA PROCESSING, UNIT 3 - IN-
STRUCTING THE COMPUTER SERIES.
PROD-GPITVL   DIST-GPITVL

T

**TAKE A CHANCE - LEARN
PROBABILITY**   C 30 MIN
                      2 INCH VIDEOTAPE
DEMONSTRATES TO THE STUDENT A RELATIVELY
NEW BUT IMPORTANT TOPIC OF ELEMENTARY
MATHEMATICS - PROBABILITY. PRESENTS CON-
CEPTS SUCH AS RATIO AND THE MEANING OF
FRACTIONAL NUMBERS. FROM THE DEVICES IN
THEIR HANDS - MATH IN THEIR MINDS SERIES.
PROD-GPITVL   DIST-GPITVL

**TELEPROCESSING AND TIME
SHARING SYSTEMS**   B 45 MIN
                      2 INCH VIDEOTAPE
SEE SERIES TITLE FOR DESCRIPTIVE STATEMENT.
FROM THE DATA PROCESSING, UNIT 4 - APPLICA-
TIONS AND CAREER OPPORTUNITIES SERIES.
PROD-GPITVL   DIST-GPITVL

TILES TEACH MATHEMATICS   C 30 MIN
                      2 INCH VIDEOTAPE
PRESENTS A BRIEF REVIEW OF THE BASIC CON-
CEPTS OF SETS. REVIEWS THESE CONCEPTS
THROUGH THE USE OF CONCRETE OBJECTS.
FROM THE DEVICES IN THEIR HANDS - MATH IN
THEIR MINDS SERIES.
PROD-GPITVL   DIST-GPITVL

**TYPEWRITING, UNIT 6 - SKILL
DEVELOPMENT--A SERIES**

PROD-GPITVL   DIST-GPITVL

SELECTIVE PRACTICE - CENTERING ON
LINE   30 MIN
SELECTIVE PRACTICE - CORRECTIONS   30 MIN
SELECTIVE PRACTICE - INSERTIONS   30 MIN

**TYPEWRITING, UNIT 7 - POSTAL
CARDS, FORMS, MANUSCRIPTS-
-A SERIES**

PROD-GPITVL   DIST-GPITVL

ADDRESSING ENVELOPES - ATTENTION
AND SUBJECT --   30 MIN
BOUND MANUSCRIPTS WITH
FOOTNOTES   30 MIN
INTER-OFFICE MEMORANDUM FORMS   30 MIN
INVOICE AND TELEGRAM FORMS -
CARBONS   30 MIN
PLAIN AND FILL-IN POSTAL CARDS   30 MIN
REVIEW - LETTERS, FORMS, REPORTS   30 MIN
REVISION MARKS, UNBOUND REPORTS,
HOW TO ERASE   30 MIN

U

**UNCONSCIOUS CULTURAL
CLASHES--A SERIES**
PRESENTS A BACKGROUND OF CULTURAL INFOR-
MATION AND UNDERLINES AREAS WHERE MISUN-
DERSTANDINGS CAN AND DO OCCUR.
PROD-SCCOE   DIST-SCCOE

CUSTOMS   30 MIN
EDUCATION VS EDUCATION   30 MIN
GRAND ASSUMPTIONS   30 MIN
LOOK ME IN THE EYE   30 MIN
OBJECTIVE - ACCULTURATION   30 MIN
OUTLOOK   30 MIN

**UNDERSTANDING
SEMICONDUCTORS COURSE
OUTLINE --A SERIES**
                                       IND
CONCERNS FUNDAMENTAL ELECTRONICS TECH-
NOLOGY. BEGINS WITH THE END SYSTEMS AND
WORKS DOWN THROUGH CIRCUITS TO COMPO-
NENTS AND SEMICONDUCTOR THEORY.
PROD-TXINLC   DIST-TXINLC

BASIC CIRCUIT FUNCTIONS IN THE
SYSTEM   60 MIN
DIGITAL INTEGRATED CIRCUITS   60 MIN
DIODE PERFORMANCE AND
SPECIFICATIONS   60 MIN

DIODES · WHAT THEY DO AND HOW
THEY WORK 60 MIN
HOW CIRCUITS MAKE DECISIONS 60 MIN
INTRODUCTION TO INTEGRATED
CIRCUITS 60 MIN
MOS AND LINEAR INTEGRATED
CIRCUITS 60 MIN
P-N-P TRANSISTOR AND TRANSISTOR
SPECIFICATIONS 60 MIN
RELATING SEMICONDUCTORS TO
SYSTEMS 60 MIN
THYRISTORS AND OPTOELECTRONICS 60 MIN
TRANSISTORS · HOW THEY WORK, HOW
THEY ARE MADE 60 MIN
WHAT ELECTRICITY DOES IN EVERY
ELECTRIC SYSTEM 60 MIN

UNIT RECORD APPLICATIONS   B 45 MIN
2 INCH VIDEOTAPE
SEE SERIES TITLE FOR DESCRIPTIVE STATEMENT.
FROM THE DATA PROCESSING, UNIT 1 · INTRO-
DUCTION TO DATA PROCESSING SERIES.
PROD-GPITVL   DIST-GPITVL

W

WALT WHITMAN · DRUM TAPS   B 30 MIN
2 INCH VIDEOTAPE   J-H
FROM THE FRANKLIN TO FROST SERIES.
PROD-GPITVL   DIST-GPITVL

**WALT WHITMAN · SONG OF
MYSELF, PT 1**
B 30 MIN
2 INCH VIDEOTAPE   J-H
FROM THE FRANKLIN TO FROST SERIES.
PROD-GPITVL   DIST-GPITVL

**WALT WHITMAN · SONG OF
MYSELF, PT 2**
B 30 MIN
2 INCH VIDEOTAPE   J-H
FROM THE FRANKLIN TO FROST SERIES.
PROD-GPITVL   DIST-GPITVL

**WALT WHITMAN · WHEN
LILACS IN THE DOORYARD
BLOOM'D**
B 30 MIN
2 INCH VIDEOTAPE   J-H
FROM THE FRANKLIN TO FROST SERIES.
PROD-GPITVL   DIST-GPITVL

**WHAT ANIMALS LIVE IN
COMMUNITIES**
B 15 MIN
2 INCH VIDEOTAPE   I
POINTS OUT THE MANY ANIMALS WHICH LIVE TO-
GETHER IN GROUPS. FROM THE SCIENCE IS DIS-
COVERY SERIES.
PROD-GPITVL   DIST-GPITVL

WHAT ARE PLANETS   B 15 MIN
2 INCH VIDEOTAPE   I
EXPLAINS THAT PLANETS ARE SATELLITES OF THE
SUN. FROM THE SCIENCE IS DISCOVERY SERIES.
PROD-GPITVL   DIST-GPITVL

**WHAT ARE SOME SPECIAL
FORMS OF BEHAVIOR**
B 15 MIN
2 INCH VIDEOTAPE   I
POINTS OUT THAT MANY KINDS OF BEHAVIOR
ARE ADAPTATIONS WHICH HELP ANIMALS LIVE IN
THEIR ENVIRONMENTS. FROM THE SCIENCE IS
DISCOVERY SERIES.
PROD-GPITVL   DIST-GPITVL

**WHAT ARE THE
CHARACTERISTICS OF LIVING
THINGS**
B 15 MIN
2 INCH VIDEOTAPE   I
SHOWS THAT LIVING THINGS GROW, MOVE, RE-
SPOND AND REPRODUCE. FROM THE SCIENCE IS
DISCOVERY SERIES.
PROD-GPITVL   DIST-GPITVL

**WHAT ARE THE PROPERTIES OF
MATTER**
B 15 MIN
2 INCH VIDEOTAPE   I
POINTS OUT THAT EVERY KIND OF MATTER HAS
ITS OWN CHARACTERISTIC PROPERTIES. FROM
THE SCIENCE IS DISCOVERY SERIES.
PROD-GPITVL   DIST-GPITVL

**WHAT DO YOU DO WITH
NUMBERS**
B 15 MIN
2 INCH VIDEOTAPE   I
DISCUSSES THE USE OF MEASUREMENT AND
GRAPHING. FROM THE LET'S EXPLORE SCIENCE
SERIES.
PROD-GPITVL   DIST-GPITVL

WHAT DO YOU THINK   B 15 MIN
2 INCH VIDEOTAPE   I
DISCUSSES THE VALUE OF PREDICTION. FROM
THE LET'S EXPLORE SCIENCE SERIES.
PROD-GPITVL   DIST-GPITVL

**WHAT GREEN PLANTS
REPRODUCE BY OTHER MEANS**   B 15 MIN
2 INCH VIDEOTAPE   I
SHOWS SOME GROUPS OF GREEN PLANTS WHICH
REPRODUCE BY VEGETATIVE MEANS OR SPORES.
FROM THE SCIENCE IS DISCOVERY SERIES.
PROD-GPITVL   DIST-GPITVL

**WHAT GREEN PLANTS
REPRODUCE BY SEEDS**
B 15 MIN
2 INCH VIDEOTAPE   I
SHOWS SOME GROUPS OF GREEN PLANTS WHICH
REPRODUCE BY SEEDS. FROM THE SCIENCE IS
DISCOVERY SERIES.
PROD-GPITVL   DIST-GPITVL

**WHAT HAPPENS WHEN
ENVIRONMENTAL CONDITIONS
ARE ALTERED**
B 15 MIN
2 INCH VIDEOTAPE   I
SHOWS HOW SEVERE ENVIRONMENTAL CHANGES
CAN AFFECT CHANGES IN THE ANIMAL AND
PLANT POPULATION. FROM THE SCIENCE IS DIS-
COVERY SERIES.
PROD-GPITVL   DIST-GPITVL

WHAT IS IN A POND   B 15 MIN
2 INCH VIDEOTAPE   I
EXPLAINS THAT EVERY LIVING THING MUST OB-
TAIN FROM ITS OWN ENVIRONMENT ALL THAT IT
NEEDS FOR LIFE, INCLUDING THE LIFE FOUND IN
A POND. FROM THE SCIENCE IS DISCOVERY SE-
RIES.
PROD-GPITVL   DIST-GPITVL

WHAT IS MATTER   B 15 MIN
2 INCH VIDEOTAPE   I
EXPLAINS THAT MATTER IS ANYTHING THAT OC-
CUPIES SPACE AND HAS WEIGHT. FROM THE SCI-
ENCE IS DISCOVERY SERIES.
PROD-GPITVL   DIST-GPITVL

**WHAT IS THE EARTH'S
SURFACE LIKE**
B 15 MIN
2 INCH VIDEOTAPE   I
EXPLAINS THAT THE SURFACE OF THE EARTH
CONSISTS OF AN UNEVEN DISTRIBUTION OF
LAND AND WATER SURROUNDED BY AIR. FROM
THE SCIENCE IS DISCOVERY SERIES.
PROD-GPITVL   DIST-GPITVL

WHAT IS THE WATER CYCLE   B 15 MIN
2 INCH VIDEOTAPE   I
POINTS OUT THAT THERE ARE MANY CYCLES OF
CHANGE IN THE WORLD, ONE OF WHICH IS THE
WATER CYCLE. FROM THE SCIENCE IS DISCOVERY
SERIES.
PROD-GPITVL   DIST-GPITVL

WHAT MAKES AIR MOVE   B 15 MIN
2 INCH VIDEOTAPE   I
EXPLAINS THAT NEAR LARGE BODIES OF WATER,
WINDS OR BREEZES BLOW NEARLY ALL THE TIME.
FROM THE SCIENCE IS DISCOVERY SERIES.
PROD-GPITVL   DIST-GPITVL

**WHAT MAKES ELECTRIC
CURRENT FLOW**
B 15 MIN
2 INCH VIDEOTAPE   I
EXAMINES THE MANY FORCES WHICH CAN CAUSE
ELECTRICITY TO FLOW. FROM THE SCIENCE IS DIS-
COVERY SERIES.
PROD-GPITVL   DIST-GPITVL

WHAT MAKES WATER MOVE   B 15 MIN
2 INCH VIDEOTAPE   I
POINTS OUT THAT THE MOVEMENTS OF WATER
MAY BE CAUSED BY UNEVEN DISTRIBUTION OF
HEAT ENERGY. FROM THE SCIENCE IS DISCOVERY
SERIES.
PROD-GPITVL   DIST-GPITVL

**WHEN TWO VOWELS GO
WALKING**
B 15 MIN
2 INCH VIDEOTAPE   P
SEE SERIES TITLE FOR DESCRIPTIVE STATEMENT.
FROM THE LISTEN AND SAY · VOWELS SERIES.
PROD-GPITVL   DIST-GPITVL

**WHERE ARE LIVING THINGS
FOUND**
B 15 MIN
2 INCH VIDEOTAPE   I
EXPLAINS THAT PART OF THE WORLD IN WHICH
AN ORGANISM LIVES IS CALLED ITS ENVIRON-
MENT. FROM THE SCIENCE IS DISCOVERY SERIES.
PROD-GPITVL   DIST-GPITVL

WHY DO ECLIPSES OCCUR   B 15 MIN
2 INCH VIDEOTAPE   I
DISCUSSES SPECIFIC RELATIVE POSITIONS OF THE
SUN, MOON AND EARTH WHICH CAUSE ECLIPSES.
FROM THE SCIENCE IS DISCOVERY SERIES.
PROD-GPITVL   DIST-GPITVL

**WHY DO TEMPERATURES OF
PLANETS VARY**
B 15 MIN
2 INCH VIDEOTAPE   I
EXPLAINS THAT THE AMOUNT OF SOLAR RADIA-
TION WHICH A PLANET RECEIVES DEPENDS UPON
ITS DISTANCE FROM THE SUN. FROM THE SCI-
ENCE IS DISCOVERY SERIES.
PROD-GPITVL   DIST-GPITVL

**WHY DOES THE SUN'S
POSITION SEEM TO CHANGE**   B 15 MIN
2 INCH VIDEOTAPE   I
POINTS OUT THAT THE APPARENT CHANGES OF
THE SUN'S POSITION IN THE SKY CAN BE MEA-
SURED AND PREDICTED. FROM THE SCIENCE IS
DISCOVERY SERIES.
PROD-GPITVL   DIST-GPITVL

**WHY'S OF DATA PROCESSING,
THE**
B 45 MIN
2 INCH VIDEOTAPE
SEE SERIES TITLE FOR DESCRIPTIVE STATEMENT.
FROM THE DATA PROCESSING, UNIT 1 · INTRO-
DUCTION TO DATA PROCESSING SERIES.
PROD-GPITVL   DIST-GPITVL

WINNING TEAM, THE   B 15 MIN
2 INCH VIDEOTAPE   P-I
POINTS OUT THAT THE TEAM FORMED BY THE CO-
OPERATIVE PATIENT AND HIS DENTIST IS THE
WINNING ONE. PRESENTS THE HISTORY OF DEN-
TISTRY FOLLOWED BY A SURVEY OF MODERN
DENTAL EQUIPMENT. CONSIDERS MAJOR DENTAL
PROBLEMS THAT REQUIRE THE ATTENTION OF AN
ORTHODONTIST. FROM THE DENTAL HEALTH SE-
RIES.
PROD-GPITVL   DIST-GPITVL

Y

**YOUR FUTURE IS NOW--A
SERIES**
B 60 MIN
2 INCH VIDEOTAPE
COVERS THE MAJOR SUBJECT MATTER AREAS
AND SKILLS OF A HIGH SCHOOL EDUCATION.
PROD-GPITVL   DIST-GPITVL

ALPHABETICAL GUIDE TO EDUCATIONAL RECORDS

A

**AGRIPPA D'AUBIGNE - L'HIVER
DE LA VIE (EXTRAIT)**   M   2 SDS
          33 1/3 RPM 12 INCH RECORD
A FRENCH LANGUAGE RECORD.
PROD-GMS   DIST-GMS

**AGRIPPA D'AUBIGNE - O
FRANCE DESOLEE**   M   2 SDS
          33 1/3 RPM 12 INCH RECORD
A FRENCH LANGUAGE RECORD.
PROD-GMS   DIST-GMS

ALBERT CAMUS - EXCERPTS   M   2 SDS
          33 1/3 RPM 12 INCH RECORD
A FRENCH LANGUAGE RECORD. INCLUDES EX-
CERPTS FROM 'L'ETRANGER,' 'LA PESTE,' 'NOCES,'
'LE MYTHE DE SISYPHE,' 'ACTUELLES 1950,' 'AC-
TUELLES III, CHRONIQUES ALGERIENNES,' 'DIS-
COURS DE SUEDE' AND 'CALIGULA.'
PROD-GMS   DIST-GMS

ALBERT CAMUS - L'ETRANGER   M   2 SDS
          33 1/3 RPM 12 INCH RECORD
A FRENCH LANGUAGE RECORD. FEATURES AL-
BERT CAMUS READING CHAPTERS I, V AND VI OF
'L'ETRANGER.'
PROD-GMS   DIST-GMS

ALBERT CAMUS - SELECTIONS   M   2 SDS
          33 1/3 RPM 12 INCH RECORD
A FRENCH LANGUAGE RECORD. FEATURES AL-
BERT CAMUS READING SELECTIONS FROM 'LA
PESTE,' 'L'ETE,' 'LA CHUTE' AND 'L'ETRANGER.'
PROD-GMS   DIST-GMS

**ALFRED JARRY - LE BAIN DU
ROI**   M   4 SDS
          33 1/3 RPM 12 INCH RECORD
A FRENCH LANGUAGE RECORD.
PROD-GMS   DIST-GMS

ALPHONSE ALLAIS (1854-1905)   M   2 SDS
          45 RPM 7 INCH RECORD
A FRENCH LANGUAGE RECORD. FEATURES R
ROCCA WHO READS ALPHONSE ALLAIS' WORKS.
PROD-GMS   DIST-GMS

    LE BON PATRON
    LE MONSIEUR ET LE QUINCAILLIER
    LE MENDIGOT
    LA SOURDE ET MUETTE
    TON-TON, TON-TAINE ET TON-TON
    AU CAFE
    ABSINTHE LUMEN

**ALPHONSE ALLAIS, POEMES DIT
PAR PIERRE BRASSEUR**   M   2 SDS
          33 1/3 RPM 12 INCH RECORD
A FRENCH LANGUAGE RECORD.
PROD-GMS   DIST-GMS

**ALPHONSE DAUDET - LETTRES
DE MON MOULIN, LE SOUS-
PREFET AUX CHAMPS**   M   2 SDS
          33 1/3 RPM 12 INCH RECORD
A FRENCH LANGUAGE RECORD.
PROD-GMS   DIST-GMS

**ANATOLE FRANCE - HISTOIRE
CONTEMPORAINE**   M   2 SDS
          33 1/3 RPM 12 INCH RECORD
A FRENCH LANGUAGE RECORD.
PROD-GMS   DIST-GMS

**ANATOLE FRANCE - PIERRE
NOZIERE**   M   2 SDS
          33 1/3 RPM 12 INCH RECORD
A FRENCH LANGUAGE RECORD.
PROD-GMS   DIST-GMS

ANATOLE FRANCE (EXTRAITS)   M   2 SDS
          33 1/3 RPM 12 INCH RECORD
A FRENCH LANGUAGE RECORD.
PROD-GMS   DIST-GMS

    LYS ROUGE (READ BY AUTHOR)
    THAIS
    LE CRIME DE SYLVESTRE BONNARD
    CRAINQUEBILLE

**ANDRE BRETON - L'UNION
LIBRE**   M   2 SDS
          33 1/3 RPM 12 INCH RECORD
A FRENCH LANGUAGE RECORD.
PROD-GMS   DIST-GMS

**ANDRE CHENIER - LA JEUNE
CAPTIVE**   M   2 SDS
          33 1/3 RPM 12 INCH RECORD
A FRENCH LANGUAGE RECORD.
PROD-GMS   DIST-GMS

**ANDRE CHENIER - LA JEUNE
TARENTINE**   M   2 SDS
          33 1/3 RPM 12 INCH RECORD
A FRENCH LANGUAGE RECORD.
PROD-GMS   DIST-GMS

**ANDRE CHENIER - TOUJOURS
CE SOUVENIR M'ATTENDRIT ET
ME TOUCHE**   M   2 SDS
          33 1/3 RPM 12 INCH RECORD
A FRENCH LANGUAGE RECORD.
PROD-GMS   DIST-GMS

ANDRE CHENIER (1762-1764)   M   2 SDS
          33 1/3 RPM 7 INCH RECORD
A FRENCH LANGUAGE RECORD. INCLUDES 'LA
JEUNE TARENTINE,' 'CAMILLE,' 'FANNY,' 'ODE,'
'LA JEUNE CAPTIVE' AND 'COMME UN DERNIER
RAYON.'
PROD-GMS   DIST-GMS

ANDRE CHENIER, I   M   2 SDS
          33 1/3 RPM 7 INCH RECORD
A FRENCH LANGUAGE RECORD. INCLUDES 'LA
JEUNE TARENTINE,' 'L'IMITATION,' 'A SES AMIS,'
'LA JEUNE CAPTIVE' AND 'IAMBES.'
PROD-GMS   DIST-GMS

ANDRE CHENIER, II   M   2 SDS
          33 1/3 RPM 12 INCH RECORD
A FRENCH LANGUAGE RECORD. INCLUDES 'SALUT,
O BELLE NUIT,' 'LA JEUNE TARENTINE,' 'LA
JEUNE CAPTIVE' AND 'IAMBES.'
PROD-GMS   DIST-GMS

ANDRE GIDE   M   2 SDS
          33 1/3 RPM 12 INCH RECORD
A FRENCH LANGUAGE RECORD.
PROD-GMS   DIST-GMS

    LA LECON DE PIANO
    LA BILLE
    HOMMAGE A ANDRE GIDE
    LES NOURRITURES TERRESTRES
    THESEE (EXTRAIT)

**ANDRE GIDE - ENTRETIENS
AVEC JEAN AMROUCHE**   M   2 SDS
          33 1/3 RPM 12 INCH RECORD
A FRENCH LANGUAGE RECORD. FEATURES EX-
TRACTS FROM 'ENTRETIENS AVEC JEAN AM-
ROUCHE,' INCLUDING 'L'OEVRE,' 'LE SCANDALE,'
'PORTRAITS' AND 'POLITIQUE.'
PROD-GMS   DIST-GMS

ANDRE GIDE (EXTRAITS)   M   2 SDS
          33 1/3 RPM 12 INCH RECORD
A FRENCH LANGUAGE RECORD.
PROD-GMS   DIST-GMS

    LES NOURRITURES TERRESTRES
    LES CAHIERS D'ANDRE WALTER
    L'IMMORALISTE
    AMYNTAS
    LE RETOUR DE L'ENFANT PRODIGUE
    LA PORTE ETROITE
    LES CAVES DU VATICAN
    LA SYMPHONIE PASTORALE
    SI LE GRAIN NE MEURT
    LES FAUX-MONNAYEURS
    OEDIPE
    THESEE

AUF HOHER SEE   S   2 SDS
          33 1/3 RPM 12 INCH RECORD
A GERMAN LANGUAGE RECORD. PRESENTS SOME
POPULAR SONGS OF GERMANY.
PROD-GMS   DIST-GMS

    IN HAMBURG, DA BIN ICH GEWESEN
    WO DIE NORDSEEWELLEN
    NIMM MICH MIT, KAPITAIN, AUF DIE REISE
    HEUT GEHT'S AN BORD
    DE HAMBURGER VEERMASTER
    ROLLING HOME
    AUCH MATROSEN HABEN EINE HEIMAT
    WIR LAGEN VOR MADAGASKAR
    WENN DAS SCHIFFERKLAVIER

**AUTOBIOGRAPHY OF FREDERICK
DOUGLASS**   M   2 SDS
          33 1/3 RPM 12 INCH RECORD
PRESENTS AN AUTOBIOGRAPHY OF FREDERICK
DOUGLASS, THE FAMOUS ANTI-SLAVERY LEADER.
INCLUDES HIS CHILDHOOD IN SLAVERY, SELF-ED-
UCATION, ESCAPE AND FIGHT FOR FREEDOM. FEA-
TURES OSSIE DAVIS READING THE AUTOBIOGRA-
PHY.
PROD-SSR   DIST-BOW

B

BABAR EN FAMILLE   M   2 SDS
          45 RPM 7 INCH RECORD
SEE SERIES TITLE FOR DESCRIPTIVE STATEMENT.
FROM THE BABAR STORIES SERIES.
PROD-GMS   DIST-GMS

**BABAR ET CE COQUIN
D'ARTHUR**   M   2 SDS
          45 RPM 7 INCH RECORD
SEE SERIES TITLE FOR DESCRIPTIVE STATEMENT.
FROM THE BABAR STORIES SERIES.
PROD-GMS   DIST-GMS

BABAR ET LE PERE NOEL   M   2 SDS
          45 RPM 7 INCH RECORD
SEE SERIES TITLE FOR DESCRIPTIVE STATEMENT.
FROM THE BABAR STORIES SERIES.
PROD-GMS   DIST-GMS

**BABAR ET LE PROFESSEUR
GRIFATON**   M   2 SDS
          45 RPM 7 INCH RECORD
SEE SERIES TITLE FOR DESCRIPTIVE STATEMENT.
FROM THE BABAR STORIES SERIES.
PROD-GMS   DIST-GMS

BABAR STORIES--A SERIES
A FRENCH LANGUAGE RECORD SERIES. PRESENTS
BABAR STORIES BASED ON THE WORKS OF JEAN
DE BRUNHOFF.
PROD-GMS   DIST-GMS

    BABAR EN FAMILLE   2 SDS
    BABAR ET CE COQUIN D'ARTHUR   2 SDS
    BABAR ET LE PERE NOEL   2 SDS
    BABAR ET LE PROFESSEUR GRIFATON   2 SDS
    HISTOIRE DE BABAR, LE PETIT
    ELEPHANT   2 SDS
    LE ROI BABAR   2 SDS
    LE VOYAGE DE BABAR   2 SDS

BASIC RHYTHMS, ALBUM 7   M   6 SDS
          78 RPM 12 INCH RECORD
PRESENTS A PROGRAM SPECIFICALLY DESIGNED
TO TEACH RHYTHMS. BEGINS WITH MUSIC FOR
CLAPPING, LUMBERING MOVEMENTS AND SWAY-
ING. INCLUDES POPULAR CHILDREN'S SONGS.
PROD-EDLACT   DIST-BOW

    MARCH OF MARIONETTES
    TO A WILD ROSE
    THE SWAN
    SPRING, BEAUTIFUL SPRING
    PARADE OF THE WOODEN SOLDIERS
    BLUE BIRD, BLUE BIRD
    SWANEE RIVER
    LITTLE BROWN JUG
    ELEPHANT WALK
    MYSTERIOSA
    SPRINGTIME
    RUSTLE OF SPRING
    TITWILLOW
    MOCKING BIRD
    FLOWERS THAT BLOOM IN THE SPRINGTIME
    PIZZICATO POLKA
    LA GIOCONDA
    CIRCUS GALLOP
    JINGLE BELLS
    SKATERS WALTZ
    POP GOES THE WEASEL
    SKIP TO MY LOU

HIPPITY HOP TO THE CANDY SHOP

BAT POET, THE   M 2 SDS
33 1/3 RPM 12 INCH RECORD
PRESENTS RANDALL JARRELL READING HIS
STORY, 'THE BAT POET,' TO CHILDREN.
PROD-CAED   DIST-CAED

BLAISE CENDRARS   M 2 SDS
33 1/3 RPM 7 INCH RECORD
A FRENCH LANGUAGE RECORD. FEATURES JEAN
SERVAIS AND RAYMONE CENDRARS WHO RECITE
CENDRARS' WORKS.
PROD-GMS   DIST-GMS

EN CE TEMPS-LA
J'ETAIS EN MON ADOLESCENCE
OR, UN VENDREDI MATIN, CE FUT AUSSI MON
TOUR
LA CLARINETTE LE PISTON UNE FLUTE AIGRE
O PARIS, GRAND FOYER CHALEUREUX
ORION
HOTEL NOTRE-DAME

**BLAISE CENDRARS - HOTEL
NOTRE-DAME, ILES**   M 2 SDS
33 1/3 RPM 12 INCH RECORD
A FRENCH LANGUAGE RECORD.
PROD-GMS   DIST-GMS

**BLAISE CENDRARS - LE VENTRE
DE MA MERE, LES PAQUES A
NEW YORK**   M 4 SDS
33 1/3 RPM 12 INCH RECORD
A FRENCH LANGUAGE RECORD.
PROD-GMS   DIST-GMS

**BRER RABBIT AND MORE BRER
RABBIT**   M 2 SDS
33 1/3 RPM 12 INCH RECORD
PRESENTS ENNIS REES READING SEVERAL POPU-
LAR CHILDREN'S STORIES.
PROD-SPA   DIST-SPA

BRER RABBIT AND THE TAR BABY
HELLO HOUSE
WINNIANIMUS GRASS
WHIPMEWHOPME CAKE
IN THE BAG, BRER WOLF AND THE LITTLE
RABS
FISHING FOR SUCKERS
BRER FOX BAGS A LESSON
BRER RABBIT'S VISIT TO AUNT MANNY-BAMMY
A DOLLAR A MINUTE
THE WULLER-DE-WUST

C

CANTERVILLE GHOST, THE   M 2 SDS
33 1/3 RPM 12 INCH RECORD   J-C
PRESENTS ANTHONY QUAYLE READING 'THE
CANTERVILLE GHOST,' A STORY BY OSCAR WILDE.
PROD-CAED   DIST-CAED

**CHANSON DE ROLAND (MORT
D'OLIVER ET DE ROLAND)**   M 2 SDS
33 1/3 RPM 7 INCH RECORD
A FRENCH LANGUAGE RECORD.
PROD-GMS   DIST-GMS

**CHARLES BAUDELAIRE -
CORRESPONDANCES**   M 4 SDS
33 1/3 RPM 12 INCH RECORD
A FRENCH LANGUAGE RECORD.
PROD-GMS   DIST-GMS

**CHARLES BAUDELAIRE - LA
MUSIQUE**   M 2 SDS
33 1/3 RPM 12 INCH RECORD
A FRENCH LANGUAGE RECORD.
PROD-GMS   DIST-GMS

**CHARLES BAUDELAIRE - LES
FLEURS DU MAL**   M 2 SDS
33 1/3 RPM 12 INCH RECORD
A FRENCH LANGUAGE RECORD. FEATURES LOUIS
JOURDAN AND EVA LE GALLIENNE READING
FROM THE WORKS OF CHARLES BAUDELAIRE.
PROD-GMS   DIST-GMS

LA MUSE MALADE
SPLEEN
PARFUM EXOTIQUE
OBSESSION
L'AMOUR DU MENSONGE
EPIGRAPHE POUR UN LIVRE CONDAMNE

**CHARLES BAUDELAIRE -
RECUEILLEMENT**   M 2 SDS
33 1/3 RPM 12 INCH RECORD
A FRENCH LANGUAGE RECORD.
PROD-GMS   DIST-GMS

**CHARLES BAUDELAIRE -
RECUEILLEMENT, LA CHEVELURE**   M 2 SDS
33 1/3 RPM 12 INCH RECORD
A FRENCH LANGUAGE RECORD.
PROD-GMS   DIST-GMS

**CHARLES BAUDELAIRE -
VISAGES DE BAUDELAIRE**   M 2 SDS
33 1/3 RPM 12 INCH RECORD
A FRENCH LANGUAGE RECORD.
PROD-GMS   DIST-GMS

AU LECTEUR
ELEVATION
CORRESPONDANCES
L'ENNEMI
LA VIE ANTERIEURE
LE VAMPIRE
LE BALCON
REVERSIBILITE
HARMONIE DU SOIR
INVITATION AU VOYAGE
MAESTA ET ERRABUNDA
PAYSAGE
CREPUSCULE DU SOIR
LE VIN DES AMANTS
RENIEMENT DE SAINT PIERRE
LA FIN DE LA JOURNEE
RECUEILLEMENT
CONFITEOR DE L'ARTISTE
LA CHAMBRE DOUBLE
LE MAUVAIS VITRIER
ENIVREZ-VOUS
LES FENETRES
ANYWHERE OUT OF THE WORLD
ASSOMMONS LES PAUVRES

CHARLES BAUDELAIRE, I   M 2 SDS
33 1/3 RPM 12 INCH RECORD
A FRENCH LANGUAGE RECORD. INCLUDES
'ENIVREZ-VOUS,' 'LA VIE ANTERIEURE,' 'LE BAL-
CON,' 'HARMONIE DU SOIR,' 'INVITATION AU VOY-
AGE,' 'REVERSIBILITE' AND 'RECUEILLEMENT.'
PROD-GMS   DIST-GMS

CHARLES BAUDELAIRE, II   M 2 SDS
33 1/3 RPM 12 INCH RECORD
A FRENCH LANGUAGE RECORD. INCLUDES
'L'ENNEMI,' 'LA GEANTE,' 'LES BIJOUX,' 'LA
CHEVELURE,' 'L'INVITATION AU VOYAGE' AND 'LE
BEAU NAVIRE.'
PROD-GMS   DIST-GMS

CHARLES BAUDELAIRE, III   M 2 SDS
33 1/3 RPM 12 INCH RECORD
A FRENCH LANGUAGE RECORD. INCLUDES 'LE
CHAT,' 'TOUT LA-HAUT' AND 'L'ALBATROS.'
PROD-GMS   DIST-GMS

CHARLES BAUDELAIRE, IV   M 2 SDS
33 1/3 RPM 12 INCH RECORD
A FRENCH LANGUAGE RECORD. INCLUDES 'LA
CLOCHE FELEE,' 'HARMONIE DU SOIR' AND 'RECU-
EILLEMENT.'
PROD-GMS   DIST-GMS

**CHILD'S INTRODUCTION TO
AMERICAN FOLK SONGS, A**   M 2 SDS
33 1/3 RPM 12 INCH RECORD
PRESENTS AMERICAN FOLK SONGS SUNG BY ED
MC CURDY.
PROD-SPA   DIST-SPA

THE THREE RAVENS
WITH MY DISHPAN ON MY KNEE
SACRAMENTO SHORE
LITTLE OLD SOD SHANTY
THE LOVELY OHIO
THE COWBOY'S DREAM
BACK BAY HILL
A FROGGY WENT A' COURTIN'
BILLY BOY
LEATHER-WINGED BAT
HUSH LITTLE BABY
THE VERY GREEN FIELDS OF IRELAND
THE BARNYARD SONG
AUNT RHODY
THE CRAWDAD SONG
KUMBAYA
HE'S GOT THE WHOLE WORLD IN HIS HANDS

CHILDHOOD RHYTHMS, NO. 01   M 6 SDS
78 RPM 10 INCH RECORD
PRESENTS FUNDAMENTAL AND CHARACTER
RHYTHMS.
PROD-EVNSR   DIST-BOW

WALK
RUN
SKIP I
MARCH
JUMP
GALLOP
SKIP II
DUCKS
CAMELS
HORSES
ELEPHANTS
TRAINS
TOPS
SOLDIERS
AIRPLANES
SWINGS
SEE-SAWS
BICYCLES
ROWBOATS
FAIRIES
WITCHES
GIANTS
DWARFS

**CLASSICS OF ENGLISH POETRY
FOR THE ELEMENTARY
CURRICULUM**   M 2 SDS
33 1/3 RPM 12 INCH RECORD   K-P
INCLUDES THE POEMS OF E B BROWNING,
BROWNING, COLERIDGE, KIPLING, LEAR, NOYES,
SCOTT AND TENNYSON.
PROD-CAED   DIST-CAED

COLETTE - APRES L'ORAGE   M 2 SDS
33 1/3 RPM 12 INCH RECORD
A FRENCH LANGUAGE RECORD.
PROD-GMS   DIST-GMS

COLETTE - CHERI, GIGI   M 2 SDS
33 1/3 RPM 12 INCH RECORD
A FRENCH LANGUAGE RECORD. FEATURES
COLETTE READING EXTRACTS FROM 'CHERI' AND
'GIGI.'
PROD-GMS   DIST-GMS

**COLETTE - DIALOGUE DES
BETES**   M 2 SDS
33 1/3 RPM 12 INCH RECORD
A FRENCH LANGUAGE RECORD.
PROD-GMS   DIST-GMS

ADAPTATION DE MUSE DALBRAY
SENTIMENTALITE
UNE VISITE
LE DINER EST EN RETARD
ELLE EST MALADE

COLETTE (EXTRAITS)   M 2 SDS
33 1/3 RPM 12 INCH RECORD
A FRENCH LANGUAGE RECORD.
PROD-GMS   DIST-GMS

CLAUDINE A L'ECOLE
DIALOGUES DES BETES
LES VRILLES DE LA VIGNE
LE VOYAGE EGOISTE
LA MAISON DE CLAUDINE
LE BLE EN HERBE
SIDO
GIGI
LA NAISSANCE DU JOUR

COLETTE VOUS PARLE   M 2 SDS
33 1/3 RPM 12 INCH RECORD
A FRENCH LANGUAGE RECORD. FEATURES
COLETTE READING EXTRACTS FROM 'SIDO,' DAN-
IELE DELORME READING 'LES CHATS DE PARIS'
AND JEAN DESAILLY READING 'LA FEMME
CACHEE.'
PROD-GMS   DIST-GMS

D

D-DAY PLUS 20   M 2 SDS
33 1/3 RPM 12 INCH RECORD
PRESENTS AN EXCITING FACTUAL DOCUMENTARY
RECORDING OF EVENTS RELATING TO THE HIS-
TORIC INVASION OF NORMANDY BY THE ALLIED
FORCES ON JUNE 6, 1944. FEATURES AS THE NAR-
RATOR THE LATE QUENTIN REYNOLDS. INCLUDES
THE VOICES OF FRANKLIN ROOSEVELT, WINSTON
CHURCHILL, DWIGHT EISENHOWER, GENERAL
MONTGOMERY, CHARLES DE GAULLE, ADOLPH
HITLER AND OTHERS.
PROD-CAED   DIST-CAED

**DANCE, SING AND LISTEN
AGAIN**   M 2 SDS
33 1/3 RPM 12 INCH RECORD   K-I
EXPOSES THE CHILD TO CONTROLLED BODY
MOVEMENT, AND PROVIDES A STIMULUS FOR

IMAGINATION AND CREATIVITY. PRESENTS A RANGE OF THOUGHT, MUSIC AND SOUND FROM THINGS MEDIEVAL THROUGH TODAY'S ELECTRONICS.
PROD-DIMFIV   DIST-BOW

DANCE, SING AND LISTEN AGAIN -
INTRODUCTION
SILENT MOVIES
TOKEY
MACHINES
FIREWORKS
CHILDREN'S HOE DOWN
MORE MEDIEVAL MUSIC
COCO REMEMBERS
JELLY DANCER
WHAT CAN SHE BE
REHEARSAL

DANCE, SING AND LISTEN AGAIN AND AGAIN   M 2 SDS
33 1/3 RPM 12 INCH RECORD   K-I
EXPOSES THE CHILD TO CONTROLLED BODY MOVEMENT AND PROVIDES A STIMULUS FOR IMAGINATION AND CREATIVITY. PRESENTS A RANGE OF THOUGHT, MUSIC AND SOUND FROM THINGS MEDIEVAL THROUGH TODAY'S ELECTRONICS.
PROD-DIMFIV   DIST-BOW

SHADOWS
CLOCKS
LITTLE PIG
COCO BOUZOUKEE
THE HAMBURGER SONG
POTS AND PANS
MORE MACHINES
THE STUBBORN BIRD
A LITTLE CONCERT

DENIS DIDEROT - LE NEVEU DE RAMEAU, I
45 RPM 7 INCH RECORD   M 2 SDS
A FRENCH LANGUAGE RECORD.
PROD-GMS   DIST-GMS

LE CARACTERE DE DIDEROT
REGRETS SUR MA VIEILLE ROBE DE CHAMBRE
PLUS LA VIE EST REMPLIE, MOINS ON Y EST ATTACHE

DENIS DIDEROT - LE NEVEU DE RAMEAU, II   M 2 SDS
33 1/3 RPM 12 INCH RECORD
A FRENCH LANGUAGE RECORD.
PROD-GMS   DIST-GMS

PRESENTATION DU NEVEU
LES GENIES ET L'ORDRE DU MONDE
GRANDEUR ET DECADENCE D'UN PARASITE
LA MORT
LE JEUNE DIDEROT
L'ART D'ENSEIGNER CE QU'ON IGNORE
LE BONHEUR ET LA VERTU
LES ENNEMIS DES PHILOSOPHES
LE NATUREL DANS L'ART
LE BRANLE DES GUEUX
LE BONHEUR DU SAGE

DENIS DIDEROT - LE NEVEU DE RAMEAU, III   M 2 SDS
33 1/3 RPM 12 INCH RECORD
A FRENCH LANGUAGE RECORD.
PROD-GMS   DIST-GMS

DENIS DIDEROT - PARADOXE SUR LE COMEDIEN   M 2 SDS
33 1/3 RPM 12 INCH RECORD
A FRENCH LANGUAGE RECORD.
PROD-GMS   DIST-GMS

DENIS DIDEROT - SALON   M 6 SDS
33 1/3 RPM 12 INCH RECORD
A FRENCH LANGUAGE RECORD.
PROD-GMS   DIST-GMS

DYLAN THOMAS READS THE POETRY OF W B YEATS AND OTHERS   M 2 SDS
33 1/3 RPM 12 INCH RECORD   H-C
PRESENTS DYLAN THOMAS READING POEMS BY YEATS, MAC NEICE, BARKER, DAVIES, LAWRENCE, AUDEN, MARLOWE AND DE LA MARE.
PROD-CAED   DIST-CAED

E

E E CUMMINGS READING HIS POETRY   M 2 SDS
33 1/3 RPM 12 INCH RECORD   H-C
PRESENTS E E CUMMINGS READING HIS POETRY. INCLUDES 'HIM, THE ACROBAT PASSAGE,' 'EIMI,

LENIN'S TOMB,' 'WHEN SERPENTS BARGAIN FOR THE RIGHT TO SQUIRM,' 'I THANK YOU GOD FOR MOST THIS AMAZING,' 'WHAT IF A MUCH OF A WHICH OF A WIND' AND OTHERS.
PROD-CAED   DIST-CAED

E E CUMMINGS, LECTURING AND READING SIX NONLECTURES--A SERIES
    H-C
PRESENTS THE CHARLES ELIOT NORTON LECTURES DELIVERED BY E E CUMMINGS AT SANDERS THEATRE IN CAMBRIDGE, MASSACHUSETTS, IN 1952-53. DESCRIBES THE AUTOBIOGRAPHY OF THE POET.
PROD-CAED   DIST-CAED

NONLECTURE FIVE - I AND NOW AND HIM   2 SDS
NONLECTURE FOUR - I AND YOU AND IS   2 SDS
NONLECTURE ONE - I AND MY PARENTS   2 SDS
NONLECTURE SIX - I AND AM AND SANTA CLAUS   2 SDS
NONLECTURE THREE - I AND SELFDISCOVERY   2 SDS
NONLECTURE TWO - I AND THEIR SON   2 SDS

EDMOND ET JULES GONCOURT - GERMINIE LACERTEUX   M 2 SDS
33 1/3 RPM 12 INCH RECORD
A FRENCH LANGUAGE RECORD.
PROD-GMS   DIST-GMS

EDMOND HARAUCOURT - RONDEL DE L'ADIEU   M 4 SDS
33 1/3 RPM 12 INCH RECORD
A FRENCH LANGUAGE RECORD.
PROD-GMS   DIST-GMS

EUGENE FROMENTIN - COCHER DE SOLEIL, LE PHARE DES BALEINES   M 2 SDS
33 1/3 RPM 12 INCH RECORD
A FRENCH LANGUAGE RECORD.
PROD-GMS   DIST-GMS

EUGENE FROMENTIN - DOMINIQUE   M 2 SDS
33 1/3 RPM 12 INCH RECORD
A FRENCH LANGUAGE RECORD.
PROD-GMS   DIST-GMS

EUGENE FROMENTIN - LE PHARE DES BALEINES   M 2 SDS
33 1/3 RPM 12 INCH RECORD
A FRENCH LANGUAGE RECORD.
PROD-GMS   DIST-GMS

EUGENE IONESCO - LA CANTATRICE CHAUVE, LA LECON   M 4 SDS
33 1/3 RPM 12 INCH RECORD
A FRENCH LANGUAGE RECORD. INCLUDES THE COMPLETE PLAYS 'LA CANTATRICE CHAUVE' AND 'LA LECON,' RECORDED AT THE THEATRE DE LA HUCHETTE.
PROD-GMS   DIST-GMS

F

FEDERICO GARCIA LORCA   M 2 SDS
33 1/3 RPM 7 INCH RECORD
A FRENCH LANGUAGE RECORD. FEATURES MARIA CASARES.
PROD-GMS   DIST-GMS

SONNET
VERLAINE
CHANSON
THAMMAR ET AMNON
MORT D'AMOUR
VOISINES, AVEC UN COUTEAU
CHANSON DE CAVALIER
MEMENTO

FELIX ARVERS - SONNET   M 2 SDS
33 1/3 RPM 12 INCH RECORD
A FRENCH LANGUAGE RECORD.
PROD-GMS   DIST-GMS

FOLK AND FAIRY TALES FROM AFRICA   M 2 SDS
33 1/3 RPM 12 INCH RECORD
PRESENTS FOLK AND FAIRY TALES FROM AFRICA.
PROD-SPA   DIST-SPA

EKUN AND OPOLO GO LOOKING FOR WIVES
ANANSI AND THE ELEPHANTS GO HUNTING
WHY WISDOM IS FOUND EVERYWHERE
THE KING'S DRUM
THE FEAST
HOW THE LIZARD LOST AND REGAINED HIS FARM
THE FISHERMAN

FOLK AND FAIRY TALES FROM DENMARK   M 2 SDS
33 1/3 RPM 12 INCH RECORD
PRESENTS FOLK AND FAIRY TALES FROM DENMARK. INCLUDES 'THE UGLY DUCKLING,' 'THE REAL PRINCESS,' 'THE RED SHOES' AND 'THE SWINEHERD.'
PROD-SPA   DIST-SPA

FOLK AND FAIRY TALES FROM ENGLAND   M 2 SDS
33 1/3 RPM 12 INCH RECORD
PRESENTS FOLK AND FAIRY TALES FROM ENGLAND READ BY CHRISTOPHER CASSON AND DAPHNE CARROLL.
PROD-SPA   DIST-SPA

THE OLD WOMAN AND HER PIG
JACK AND THE BEANSTALK
THE THREE WISHES
TEENY-TINY
THE STORY OF THE THREE LITTLE PIGS
MR VINEGAR
THE HISTORY OF TOM THUMB
THE KING O' THE CATS

FOLK AND FAIRY TALES FROM FRANCE   M 2 SDS
33 1/3 RPM 12 INCH RECORD
PRESENTS FOLK AND FAIRY TALES FROM FRANCE. INCLUDES 'LITTLE RED RIDING HOOD,' 'CINDERELLA,' 'THE FAIRIES' AND 'BLUEBEARD.'
PROD-SPA   DIST-SPA

FOLK AND FAIRY TALES FROM GERMANY   M 2 SDS
33 1/3 RPM 12 INCH RECORD
PRESENTS FOLK AND FAIRY TALES FROM GERMANY. INCLUDES 'THE FROG PRINCE,' 'THE FISHERMAN AND HIS WIFE,' 'RUMPEL-STILTS-KIN' AND 'THE GOOSE GIRL.' FEATURES EVE WATKINSON AND CHRISTOPHER CASSON READING THE TALES.
PROD-SPA   DIST-SPA

FOLK AND FAIRY TALES FROM ITALY   M 2 SDS
33 1/3 RPM 12 INCH RECORD
PRESENTS FOLK AND FAIRY TALES FROM ITALY. INCLUDES 'CATHERINE AND HER DESTINY,' 'THE TWO BROTHERS' AND 'THE GOLDEN LION.'
PROD-SPA   DIST-SPA

FOLK AND FAIRY TALES FROM JAPAN   M 2 SDS
33 1/3 RPM 12 INCH RECORD
PRESENTS FOLK AND FAIRY TALES FROM JAPAN. INCLUDES 'THE TONGUE-CAT SPARROW,' 'THE OLD MAN WHO MAKES THE TREES BLOSSOM,' 'THE FISHERMAN AND THE TORTOISE' AND 'THE STRONG BOY.'
PROD-SPA   DIST-SPA

FOLK AND FAIRY TALES FROM MEXICO   M 2 SDS
33 1/3 RPM 12 INCH RECORD
PRESENTS FOLK AND FAIRY TALES FROM MEXICO. INCLUDES 'THE BOY WHO COULD DO ANYTHING' AND OTHER MEXICAN TALES.
PROD-SPA   DIST-SPA

FOLK AND FAIRY TALES FROM RUSSIA   M 2 SDS
33 1/3 RPM 12 INCH RECORD
PRESENTS FOLK AND FAIRY TALES FROM RUSSIA.
PROD-SPA   DIST-SPA

VASILISA THE BEAUTIFUL
TSAREVICH IVAN AND GREY WOLF
THE SILVER SAUCER AND THE ROSY-CHEEKED APPLE
THE TWO IVANS
THE WOLF
THE DOG AND THE CAT

FOLK MUSIC OF FRANCE   M 2 SDS
33 1/3 RPM 12 INCH RECORD
PRESENTS 38 SONGS FROM MANY PARTS OF FRANCE. INCLUDES THE ENGLISH TRANSLATIONS.
PROD-SSR   DIST-BOW

FRANCIS CARCO   M 2 SDS
33 1/3 RPM 7 INCH RECORD
A FRENCH LANGUAGE RECORD. INTRODUCES JEAN-PIERRE AUMONT WHO RECITES SOME OF CARCO'S WORKS.

PROD-GMS   DIST-GMS

ENFANCE
RETRAITE
MONTMARTRE
L'HEURE DU POETS
TE VOILA
NUITS D'HIVER
LES AMIES
LE DOUX CABOULOT
IL PLEUT
LES FILLES DE LA NUIT
DANSE
L'AMANT SURPRIS

**FRANCIS JAMMES - J'AIME
L'ANE**   M 2 SDS
33 1/3 RPM 12 INCH RECORD
A FRENCH LANGUAGE RECORD.
PROD-GMS   DIST-GMS

**FRANCIS JAMMES - JEAN
MARCHAT READS (FRENCH)**   M 2 SDS
33 1/3 RPM 12 INCH RECORD

PROD-GMS   DIST-GMS

PRIERE POUR ALLER AU PARADIS AVEC LES
ANES
LA SALLE A MANGER
LA PETITE VIELLE
LE POETE ET L'OISEAU
L'EGLISE HABILLEE DE FEUILLES
DEMAIN FERA UN AN
LE VILLAGE A MIDI
JE NE VEUX PAS D'AUTRE JOIE

**FRANCIS JAMMES - JEAN
NEGRONI RECITES (FRENCH)**   M 2 SDS
33 1/3 RPM 12 INCH RECORD

PROD-GMS   DIST-GMS

J'ALLAIS DANS LE VERGER
LA VALLEE
LA JEUNE FILLE
TU SERAS NUE
ELEGIE QUATORZIEME
LES MYSTERES DOULOUREUX
PRIERE POUR AVOIR UNE FEMME SIMPLE
PRIERE POUR ALLER AU PARADIS AVEC LES
ANES
QU'EST-CE QUE LE BONHEUR
FINALE

**FRANCIS JAMMES - LA SALLE A
MANGER**   M 4 SDS
33 1/3 RPM 12 INCH RECORD
A FRENCH LANGUAGE RECORD.
PROD-GMS   DIST-GMS

**FRANCIS JAMMES - PRIERE
POUR MONTER AU PARADIS
AVEC LES ANES**   M 2 SDS
33 1/3 RPM 12 INCH RECORD
A FRENCH LANGUAGE RECORD.
PROD-GMS   DIST-GMS

**FRANCOIS FENELON - LES
AVENTURES DE TELEMAQUE**   M 2 SDS
33 1/3 RPM 12 INCH RECORD
A FRENCH LANGUAGE RECORD.
PROD-GMS   DIST-GMS

**FRANCOIS VICOMTE DE
CHATEAUBRIAND**   M 2 SDS
45 RPM 7 INCH RECORD
A FRENCH LANGUAGE RECORD.
PROD-GMS   DIST-GMS

LES RIVES DE MESCHACEBE
ATHENES AU SOLEIL LEVANT
LA VIE A COMBOURG
LA VAGUE DES PASSIONS CHEZ RENE

**FRANCOIS VICOMTE DE
CHATEAUBRIAND - LE GENIE DU
CHRISTIANISME, RENE**   M 2 SDS
33 1/3 RPM 12 INCH RECORD
A FRENCH LANGUAGE RECORD.
PROD-GMS   DIST-GMS

**FRANCOIS VICOMTE DE
CHATEAUBRIAND - LE GENIE DU
CHRISTIANISME, LES RUINES** M 2 SDS
33 1/3 RPM 12 INCH RECORD
A FRENCH LANGUAGE RECORD.
PROD-GMS   DIST-GMS

**FRANCOIS VICOMTE DE
CHATEAUBRIAND - RENE**   M 2 SDS
33 1/3 RPM 12 INCH RECORD
A FRENCH LANGUAGE RECORD.
PROD-GMS   DIST-GMS

**FRANCOIS VICOMTE DE
CHATEAUBRIAND - RENE,
REVERIES DE RENE**   M 2 SDS
33 1/3 RPM 12 INCH RECORD
A FRENCH LANGUAGE RECORD.
PROD-GMS   DIST-GMS

**FRANCOIS VICOMTE DE
CHATEAUBRIAND - TEMOIN DE
HISTOIRE**   M 2 SDS
33 1/3 RPM 12 INCH RECORD
A FRENCH LANGUAGE RECORD. FEATURES READ-
INGS BY PIERRE FRESNAY.
PROD-GMS   DIST-GMS

PROLOGUE - PREFACE TESTAMENTAIRE
PRESENTATION   DU   CHEVALIER   DE
CHATEAUBRIAND AU ROI LOUIS XVI
MIRABEAU
NAPOLEON, RETOUR DE L'ILE D'ELBE
WATERLOO
JUGEMENT SUR BONAPARTE
ENTREVUE AVEC LE ROI LOUIS XVIII APRES LA
RESTAURATION
L'ASSASINAT DU DUC DE BERRY
FIN DE LA MONARCHIE
REVEIL DE L'ORIENT
EPILOGUE - EL L'AVENIR

**FRANCOIS VICOMTE DE
CHATEAUBRIAND - UNE NUIT
DANS LES DESERTS DU
NOUVEAU MONDE**   M 2 SDS
33 1/3 RPM 12 INCH RECORD
A FRENCH LANGUAGE RECORD.
PROD-GMS   DIST-GMS

G

**GEORGES DE BUFFON -
EPOQUES DE LA NATURE VII**   M 22 SDS
33 1/3 RPM 12 INCH RECORD
A FRENCH LANGUAGE RECORD.
PROD-GMS   DIST-GMS

GERARD PHILIPE - TNP   M 4 SDS
33 1/3 RPM 12 INCH RECORD
A FRENCH LANGUAGE RECORD. PRESENTS THE
LATE GREAT ACTOR, GERARD PHILIPE, IN SCENES
FROM SOME OF HIS MOST FAMOUS ROLES - 'LE
PRINCE DE HOMBOURG,' 'RUY BLAS,' 'LORENZAC-
CIO,' 'ON NE BADINE PAS AVEC L'AMOUR' AND
'LES CAPRICES DE MARIANNE.'
PROD-GMS   DIST-GMS

**GOLDILOCKS AND THE THREE
BEARS, HEREAFTER THIS, DICK
WITTINGTON AND HIS CAT** M 2 SDS
33 1/3 RPM 12 INCH RECORD
PRESENTS A DRAMATIZATION OF THREE FAVOR-
ITE STORIES FOR CHILDREN.
PROD-SPA   DIST-SPA

GUILLAUME APOLLINAIRE   M 2 SDS
33 1/3 RPM 7 INCH RECORD
A FRENCH LANGUAGE RECORD. FEATURES
JACQUES DUBY'S RECITATIONS.
PROD-GMS   DIST-GMS

LE PONT MIRABEAU
LES COLCHIQUES
L'EMIGRANT DE LANDOR ROAD
CORS DE CHASSE
LA JOLIE ROUSSE
FETE
SI JE MOURAIS LA-BAS
O MA JEUNESSE ABANDONNEE

**GUILLAUME APOLLINAIRE -
HOMMAGE A APPOLLINAIRE** M 2 SDS
33 1/3 RPM 12 INCH RECORD
A FRENCH LANGUAGE RECORD.
PROD-GMS   DIST-GMS

LA CHANSON DU MAL-AIME
A LA SANTE
CREPUSCULE
SALTIMBANQUES
EMIGRANT DE LANDOR ROAD
LA BLANCHE NEIGE
MARIE
ANNIE
MARIZIBILL
L'ADIEU
O MA JEUNESSE ABANDONNEE
LA CLEF
LA PETITE AUTO
L'ADIEU DU CAVALIER
IL Y A
C'EST LOU QU'ON LA NOMMAIT
SI JE MOURAIS LA-BAS

LES SAISONS
ZONE
ANTOMNE

**GUILLAUME APOLLINAIRE - LE
PONT MIRABEAU**   M 4 SDS
33 1/3 RPM 12 INCH RECORD
A FRENCH LANGUAGE RECORD. FEATURES THE
AUTHOR GUILLAUME APOLLINAIRE, READING HIS
OWN WORK, ACCOMPANIED BY MUSIC OF ERIK
SATIE.
PROD-GMS   DIST-GMS

**GUILLAUME APOLLINAIRE -
POEMES, I**   M 2 SDS
33 1/3 RPM 12 INCH RECORD
A FRENCH LANGUAGE RECORD. FEATURES READ-
INGS OF APOLLINAIRE'S POEMS BY MOULINOT,
FURET, ROUSSIN, PERIER, DESCHAMPS AND
JEMMA.
PROD-GMS   DIST-GMS

LE BESTIARTE OU LE CORTEGE D'ORPHEE - LE
CHAT, LA PUCE, L'ECREVISSE, LA CARPE
ALCOOLS - SALTIMBANQUES, AUTOMNE, NUIT
RHENANE, LA CHANSON DU MAL-AIME, LE PONT
MIRABEAU
CALLIGRAMMES - LA BOUCLE RETROUVEE, C'EST
LOU QU'ON LA NOMMAIT, CHANT DE L'HORIZON
EN CHAMPAGNE
VITAM IMPENDERE AMORI - DANS LE
CREPUSCULE FANE, O MA JEUNESSE
ABANDONNEE
IL Y A - DANS LE JARDIN D'ANNA, ALLONS PLUS
VITE
OMBRES DE MON AMOUR - MOURMELON - LE-
GRAND, TE SOUVIENS-TU MON LOU, LE CIEL EST
EXOILE
POEMES INEDITS - ROSE GUERRIERE
POEMES - JE DONNE A MON ESPOIR

**GUILLAUME APOLLINAIRE -
POEMES, II**   M 2 SDS
33 1/3 RPM 12 INCH RECORD
A FRENCH LANGUAGE RECORD.
PROD-GMS   DIST-GMS

LE PONT MIRABEAU
LES COLCHIQUES
L'EMIGRANT DE LANDOR ROAD
LA JOLIE ROUSSE
O MA JEUNESSE ABANDONNEE

**GUILLAUME APOLLINAIRE -
POEMES, III**   M 2 SDS
33 1/3 RPM 12 INCH RECORD
A FRENCH LANGUAGE RECORD.
PROD-GMS   DIST-GMS

SI JE MOURAIS LA-BAS
LE PONT MIRABEAU
CHANSON DU MAL-AIME (EXTRAIT)

**GUILLAUME APOLLINAIRE -
POEMES, IV**   M 2 SDS
33 1/3 RPM 12 INCH RECORD
A FRENCH LANGUAGE RECORD. INCLUDES 'LE
PONT MIRABEAU' AND 'LES COLCHIQUES.'
PROD-GMS   DIST-GMS

**GUILLAUME APOLLINAIRE -
POEMES, V**   M 2 SDS
33 1/3 RPM 12 INCH RECORD
A FRENCH LANGUAGE RECORD. INCLUDES THE
'LIENS.'
PROD-GMS   DIST-GMS

GULLIVER'S TRAVELS   M 2 SDS
33 1/3 RPM 12 INCH RECORD
PRESENTS AN ABRIDGED VERSION OF 'GULLIV-
ER'S TRAVELS' READ BY ANTHONY QUAYLE.
PROD-CAED   DIST-CAED

**GUSTAVE FLAUBERT - DANS LA
FORET DE FONTAINEBLEAU** M 2 SDS
33 1/3 RPM 12 INCH RECORD
A FRENCH LANGUAGE RECORD.
PROD-GMS   DIST-GMS

**GUSTAVE FLAUBERT - FORET DE
FONTAINEBLEAU**   M 2 SDS
33 1/3 RPM 12 INCH RECORD
A FRENCH LANGUAGE RECORD.
PROD-GMS   DIST-GMS

**GUSTAVE FLAUBERT - MADAME
BOVARY (EXTRAITS)**   M 2 SDS
33 1/3 RPM 12 INCH RECORD
A FRENCH LANGUAGE RECORD.
PROD-GMS   DIST-GMS

GUSTAVE FLAUBERT (1821-1880)
M 2 SDS
33 1/3 RPM 12 INCH RECORD
A FRENCH LANGUAGE RECORD. INCLUDES EXTRACTS FROM 'MADAME BOVARY' AND 'SALAMMBÔ.'
PROD-GMS   DIST-GMS

H

HARK TO OUR HERITAGE
M 2 SDS
33 1/3 RPM 12 INCH RECORD
PRESENTS THE INSPIRING STORY OF AMERICA REDISCOVERED THROUGH SOUNDS OF THE PAST. INCLUDES SOUNDS AND SONGS OF THE RUGGED YEARS WHEN AMERICANS ALMOST FORGOT HOW TO SING.
PROD-HERTCR   DIST-BOW

BARBARA ALLEN
OLD HUNDRED
BIRD'S COURTIN' SONG
CAN'T YOU DANCE THE POLKA
MONTH OF MAY

HEIMWEH NACH ST PAUL
S 2 SDS
33 1/3 RPM 12 INCH RECORD
A GERMAN LANGUAGE RECORD. PRESENTS SOME POPULAR SONGS OF GERMANY.
PROD-GMS   DIST-GMS

AUF DER REEPERBAHN NACHTS UM HALB EINS

IN HAMBURG AN DER WATERKANT
JUNGE, KOMM BALD WIEDER
THE LONESOME STAR
DU BIST DIE LIEBE
SCHEUN MUTT DAT SIEN
FISCHMARKT VON ST PAUL
MEIN HAMBURG
TELL, SAILOR, TELL ME A STORY
SEEMANN, O SEEMANN

HILAIRE BELLOC - CAUTIONARY TALES
M 2 SDS
33 1/3 RPM 12 INCH RECORD   K-H
PRESENTS JOYCE GRENFELL READING 'ABOUT JOHN, WHO LOST A FORTUNE BY THROWING STONES,' 'JIM, WHO RAN AWAY FROM HIS NURSE AND WAS EATEN BY A LION' AND OTHERS.
PROD-CAED   DIST-CAED

HILDA CONKLING READING HER POETRY
M 2 SDS
33 1/3 RPM 12 INCH RECORD
PRESENTS HILDA CONKLING, WHO READS EXCERPTS FROM HER POETRY.
PROD-CAED   DIST-CAED

FOR YOU MOTHER
SILVER HORN
VELVETS
THERE IS A STAR
LITTLE MOUSE IN GREY VELVET

HOLIDAY RHYTHMS
M 2 SDS
33 1/3 RPM 12 INCH RECORD
PRESENTS MUSIC FROM TWO PIANOS TO ACCOMPANY SPECIAL EVENTS THE YEAR AROUND INCLUDING HOLIDAYS.
PROD-BOW   DIST-BOW

HOMMAGE A CHARLES DULLIN
M 4 SDS
33 1/3 RPM 12 INCH RECORD
A FRENCH LANGUAGE RECORD. FEATURES EXTRACTS OF HISTORIC PERFORMANCES BY ONE OF FRANCE'S GREATEST ACTORS, CHARLES DULLIN.
PROD-GMS   DIST-GMS

LES FRERES KARAMAZOV
LA VIE EST UN SONGE
LA VOLUPTE DE L'HONNEUR
LES OISEAUX
VOLPONE
MUSSE
LA PAIX
L'AVARE
RICHARD III
L'ARCHIPEL LENOIR
LA TERRE EST RONDE

HOMMAGE A LOUIS JOUVET
M 6 SDS
33 1/3 RPM 12 INCH RECORD
A FRENCH LANGUAGE RECORD. PRESENTS EXTRACTS BY LOUIS JOUVET.
PROD-GMS   DIST-GMS

PROLOGUE DE L'IMPATIENCE
LE MEDECIN MALGRE LUI
LA JALOUSIE DU BARBOUILLE
L'ECOLE DES FEMMES
STANCES A MARQUISE DE CORNEILLE
LES ENFANTS HUMILIES
TARTUFFE
RECIT DE LA MORT DE MOLIERE
LES CINQ TENTATIONS DE LA FONTAINE
KNOCK OU LE TRIOMPHE DE LA MEDECINE
LA FOLLE JOURNEE
INTRODUCTION A GIRAUDOUX - INTERMEZZO VISITATIONS, ONDINE, LA GUERRE DE TROIE N' AURA PAS LIEU **HONORE DE BALZAC - LE FAISEUR**
M 2 SDS
33 1/3 RPM 12 INCH RECORD
A FRENCH LANGUAGE RECORD. FEATURES AN EXCERPT INCLUDED IN THE COLLECTION 'HOMMAGE A DULLIN.'
PROD-GMS   DIST-GMS

HONORE DE BALZAC - LE PERE GORIOT
M 2 SDS
33 1/3 RPM 12 INCH RECORD
PROD-GMS   DIST-GMS

I

INDIAN FOLK MUSIC
M 2 SDS
33 1/3 RPM 12 INCH RECORD
PRESENTS THE DIFFERENT TYPES OF MUSIC WITH WHICH EAST INDIAN VILLAGERS ARE LIKELY TO BE FAMILIAR. INCLUDES ARCHAIC SURVIVALS, VILLAGE TEMPLE AND ART MUSIC OF POPULAR TYPES. EXPLAINS THAT MANY OF THE SONGS WERE RECORDED IN THE BENARES, A STRONGHOLD OF TRADITIONAL HINDU SOCIETY WHERE THE ANCIENT MUSICAL FORMS RESIST MODERN CHANGE.
PROD-CAED   DIST-CAED

INTERPRETIVE RHYTHMS
M 2 SDS
33 1/3 RPM 12 INCH RECORD   K-I
PRESENTS THE BASIC BEAT OF MUSIC AND SHOWS HOW TO ASSOCIATE IT WITH EVERYDAY LIFE.
PROD-CLSMAT   DIST-BOW

IRISH FAIRY TALES
M 2 SDS
33 1/3 RPM 12 INCH RECORD
PRESENTS SOME POPULAR IRISH FAIRY TALES.
PROD-SPA   DIST-SPA

HUDDEN AND DUDDEN AND DONAL O'LEARY
HOW CORMAC MACART WENT TO FAERY
BLACK HORSE, THE
ANDREW COFFEY

J

JACQUES-BENIGNE BOSSUET
M 2 SDS
33 1/3 RPM 7 INCH RECORD
A FRENCH LANGUAGE RECORD.
PROD-GMS   DIST-GMS

SERMON SUR L'EMINENTE DIGNITE DU PAUVRE

SERMON SUR LA MORT
ORAISON FUNEBRE D'HENRIETTE-ANNE D'ANGLETERRE, DUCHESSE D'ORLEANS
PERORAISON DE L'ORAISON FUNEBRE DU PRINCE DE CONDE (EXTRAITS) **JACQUES-BENIGNE BOSSUET - ORAISON FUNEBRE D'HENRIETTE D'ANGLETERRE**
M 6 SDS
33 1/3 RPM 12 INCH RECORD
A FRENCH LANGUAGE RECORD.
PROD-GMS   DIST-GMS

JACQUES-BENIGNE BOSSUET - SERMON POUR LE JOUR DE PAQUES, 1685 (EXTRAIT)
M 2 SDS
33 1/3 RPM 12 INCH RECORD
A FRENCH LANGUAGE RECORD.
PROD-GMS   DIST-GMS

JEAN COCTEAU - HOMMAGE A JEAN COCTEAU
M 2 SDS
33 1/3 RPM 12 INCH RECORD
A FRENCH LANGUAGE RECORD. FEATURES ANDRE MAURICE WHO READS FROM 'LA CRUCIFIXION,' 'LE BUSTE,' 'LE THEATRE GREC,' 'NO MAN'S LAND' AND 'L'ANGE HEURTEBISE.'
PROD-GMS   DIST-GMS

JEAN COCTEAU - JEAN MERCURE RECITES (FRENCH)
M 2 SDS
33 1/3 RPM 7 INCH RECORD
PROD-GMS   DIST-GMS

BATTERIE
LES CHEVEUX GRIS, QUAND JEUNESSE LES PORTE
JE N'AIME PAS DORMIR
MAUVAISE COMPAGNE
LIT D'AMOUR
RIEN NE M'EFFRAYE PLUS
MUSES, QUI NE SONGES A PLAIRE
LE PAQUET ROUGE
PAR LUI-MEME
LES ALLIANCES
LES VOLEURS D'ENFANTS
CONSEIL DE TOUTE IMPORTANCE
HOMMAGE A PICASSO
MUSES PARDONNEZ-MOI
DE TOUS LES PARTIS

JEAN COCTEAU - LES MARIES DE LA TOUR EIFFEL
M 2 SDS
33 1/3 RPM 12 INCH RECORD
A FRENCH LANGUAGE RECORD.
PROD-GMS   DIST-GMS

JEAN COCTEAU (1889-1963)
M 2 SDS
33 1/3 RPM 12 INCH RECORD
A FRENCH LANGUAGE RECORD.
PROD-GMS   DIST-GMS

JEAN COCTEAU VOUS PARLE
POEMES EXTRAITS DE PLAIN-CHANT (READ BY THE AUTHOR)
LA DIFFICULTE D'ETRE (EXTRAITS)
LES PARENTS TERRIBLE (ACTE I, SCENE 4)
LA MACHINE INTERNALE (ACTE II, EXTRAIT)

JEAN DE LA BRUYERE - LES CARACTERES DE LA SOCIETE ET DE LA CONVERSATION, GITON ET PHEDON
M 2 SDS
33 1/3 RPM 12 INCH RECORD
A FRENCH LANGUAGE RECORD.
PROD-GMS   DIST-GMS

JEAN DE LA BRUYERE - LES CARACTERES DE LA VILLE
M 6 SDS
33 1/3 RPM 12 INCH RECORD
A FRENCH LANGUAGE RECORD.
PROD-GMS   DIST-GMS

JEAN GIONO
M 2 SDS
33 1/3 RPM 12 INCH RECORD
A FRENCH LANGUAGE RECORD. INCLUDES READINGS FROM 'PAGES CHOISIES-UN DE BAUMUGNES,' 'REGAIN,' 'LE GRAND TROUPEAU,' 'JEAN LE BLEU,' 'LE CHANT DU MONDE,' 'QUE MA JOIE DEMEURE' AND 'LE POIDS DU CIEL.'
PROD-GMS   DIST-GMS

JEAN GIONO - EN HAUTE PROVENCE
M 2 SDS
33 1/3 RPM 12 INCH RECORD
A FRENCH LANGUAGE RECORD.
PROD-GMS   DIST-GMS

JEAN GIONO - LA MOISSON
M 2 SDS
33 1/3 RPM 12 INCH RECORD
A FRENCH LANGUAGE RECORD.
PROD-GMS   DIST-GMS

JEAN GIRAUDOUX
M 2 SDS
33 1/3 RPM 12 INCH RECORD
A FRENCH LANGUAGE RECORD. FEATURES LOUIS JOUVET IN SCENES FROM GIRAUDOUX'S WORKS.
PROD-GMS   DIST-GMS

LA GUERRE DE TROIE N'AURA PAS LIEU
ONDINE
INTERMEZZO

JEAN GIRAUDOUX - PARIS, PRIERE SUR LA TOUR EIFFEL
M 2 SDS
33 1/3 RPM 12 INCH RECORD
A FRENCH LANGUAGE RECORD.
PROD-GMS   DIST-GMS

JEAN GIRAUDOUX (EXTRAITS)
M 2 SDS
33 1/3 RPM 12 INCH RECORD
A FRENCH LANGUAGE RECORD.
PROD-GMS   DIST-GMS

PROVINCIALES
JULIETTE AU PAYS DES HOMMES
SIMON LE PATHETIQUE
AVENTURES DE JEROME BARDINI
LA GUERRE DE TROIE N'AURA PAS LIEU
JUDITH
POUR LUCRECE

INTERMEZZO
ONDINE
SIEGFRIED
ELECTRE
SODOME ET GOMORRHE

JEAN VILAR - GRANDES HEURES
DU TNP   M   4 SDS
        33 1/3 RPM 12 INCH RECORD
   A FRENCH LANGUAGE RECORD.
PROD-GMS   DIST-GMS

MEURTRE DANS LA CATHEDRALE
LA MORT DE DANTON
DON JUAN
NUCLEA
RICHARD II
LE MALADE IMAGINAIRE
RUY BLAS
CINNA
MACBETH
HENRI IV
UBU
OEDIPE
LA RESISTIBLE ASCENSION D'ARTURO UI
L'HEUREUX STRATAGEME
ROSES ROUGES POUR MOI
L'ALCADE DE ZALAMEA
LES RUSTRES
LA GUERRE DE TROIE N'AURA PAS LIEU
THOMAS MORE

JEAN-PIERRE DE FLORIAN - LA
CARPE ET LES CARPILLIONS   M   2 SDS
        33 1/3 RPM 7 INCH RECORD
   A FRENCH LANGUAGE RECORD.
PROD-GMS   DIST-GMS

JOACHIM DU BELLAY   M   2 SDS
        33 1/3 RPM 12 INCH RECORD
   A FRENCH LANGUAGE RECORD.
PROD-GMS   DIST-GMS

D'UN VANNEUR DE BLE AUX VENTS
LOUANGES D'ANJOU (EXTRAIT)
DEJA LA NUIT
TOUT CE QU'ICI LA NATURE ENVIRONNE
COMPLAINTE DU DESESPERE (EXTRAIT)
HEUREUX QUI, COMME ULYSSE
LAS, OU EST MAINTENANT
FRANCE, MERE DES ARTS

JOACHIM DU BELLAY -
HEUREUX QUI, COMME ULYSSE   M   2 SDS
        33 1/3 RPM 12 INCH RECORD
   A FRENCH LANGUAGE RECORD.
PROD-GMS   DIST-GMS

JOACHIM DU BELLAY - LE BEAU
VOYAGE   M   2 SDS
        33 1/3 RPM 12 INCH RECORD
   A FRENCH LANGUAGE RECORD.
PROD-GMS   DIST-GMS

JOACHIM DU BELLAY - LE
REGRET   M   2 SDS
        33 1/3 RPM 12 INCH RECORD
   A FRENCH LANGUAGE RECORD.
PROD-GMS   DIST-GMS

JOACHIM DU BELLAY - SONNET   M   2 SDS
        33 1/3 RPM 12 INCH RECORD
   A FRENCH LANGUAGE RECORD.
PROD-GMS   DIST-GMS

JOSE-MARIA DE HEREDIA -
EPITAPHE D'UNE SAUTERELLE   M   4 SDS
        33 1/3 RPM 12 INCH RECORD
   A FRENCH LANGUAGE RECORD.
PROD-GMS   DIST-GMS

JOSE-MARIA DE HEREDIA - LES
CONQUERANTS   M   4 SDS
        33 1/3 RPM 12 INCH RECORD
   A FRENCH LANGUAGE RECORD.
PROD-GMS   DIST-GMS

JOSE-MARIA DE HEREDIA -
MARIS STELLA   M   2 SDS
        33 1/3 RPM 12 INCH RECORD
   A FRENCH LANGUAGE RECORD.
PROD-GMS   DIST-GMS

JOSEPH BEDIER - PETIT CRU   M   2 SDS
        33 1/3 RPM 12 INCH RECORD
   A FRENCH LANGUAGE RECORD.
PROD-GMS   DIST-GMS

JULES LAFORGUE - COMPLAINTE
DE L'OUBLI DES MORTS   M   2 SDS
        33 1/3 RPM 12 INCH RECORD
   A FRENCH LANGUAGE RECORD.
PROD-GMS   DIST-GMS

JULES LAFORGUE - COMPLAINTE
SUR CERTAINS ENNUIS   M   2 SDS
        33 1/3 RPM 12 INCH RECORD
   A FRENCH LANGUAGE RECORD.
PROD-GMS   DIST-GMS

JULES LAFORGUE - LOCUTION
DES PIERROTS, SOIR DE
CARNAVAL, L'IMPOSSIBLE   M   2 SDS
        33 1/3 RPM 12 INCH RECORD
   A FRENCH LANGUAGE RECORD.
PROD-GMS   DIST-GMS

JULES LAFORGUE - RENE
LEFEVRE RECITES (FRENCH)   M   2 SDS
        33 1/3 RPM 7 INCH RECORD
PROD-GMS   DIST-GMS

AVERTISSEMENT
COMPLAINTE DE LA LUNE EN PROVINCE
COMPLAINTE SUR CERTAINS ENNUIS
COMPLAINTE DU ROI DE THULE
COMPLAINTE DU PAUVRE JEUNE HOMME
AVANT-DERNIER MOT
LOCUTIONS DES PIERROTS (XII AND XVI)
L'HIVER QUE VIENT

L

LA BATAILLE DE QADECH   M   2 SDS
        33 1/3 RPM 12 INCH RECORD
   A FRENCH LANGUAGE RECORD. PRESENTS THE
EGYPTIAN EPIC POEM TRANSLATED BY S SAUNE-
RON AND READ BY JEAN DESCHAMPS.
PROD-GMS   DIST-GMS

LA CHANSON DE ROLAND   M   2 SDS
        33 1/3 RPM 12 INCH RECORD
   A FRENCH LANGUAGE RECORD.
PROD-GMS   DIST-GMS

LA CHANSON DE ROLAND
(L'EPISODE DE RONCEVAUX)   M   2 SDS
        33 1/3 RPM 12 INCH RECORD
   A FRENCH LANGUAGE RECORD. FEATURES THE
MOST IMPORTANT PASSAGES OF THE 'CHANSON
DE ROLAND,' WHICH ARE THOSE RELATING TO
THE DEATH OF ROLAND. PRESENTS THE ORIGINAL
VERSION PRESERVING THE RHYTHM AND MOST
OF THE WORKS, WITH ONLY A FEW TOUCHES
ADDED TO AID THE COMPREHENSION.
PROD-GMS   DIST-GMS

LA VOIX DE PAUL ELUARD   M   2 SDS
        33 1/3 RPM 12 INCH RECORD
   A FRENCH LANGUAGE RECORD. PRESENTS THE
AUTHOR PAUL ELUARD RECITING HIS OWN
POEMS.
PROD-GMS   DIST-GMS

PREMIER POEMES
CAPITALE DE LA DOULEUR
LES YEUX FERTILES
COURS NATUREL (LA VICTOIRE DE GUERNICA)
POESIE ET VERITE (LIBERTE)
LES SEPT POEMES D'AMOUR EN GUERRE
AU RENDEZ-VOUS ALLEMAND
LINGERES LEGERES
POESIE ININTERROMPUE
LE DUR DESIR DE DURER
LE LIVRE OUVERT
A L'INTERIEUR DE LA VUE
LE PHENIX
POUVOIR TOUT DIRE

LAURENT GILBERT - ADIEUX A
LA VIE   M   2 SDS
        33 1/3 RPM 12 INCH RECORD
   A FRENCH LANGUAGE RECORD.
PROD-GMS   DIST-GMS

LE MORTE D'ARTHUR   M   2 SDS
        33 1/3 RPM 12 INCH RECORD
   PRESENTS SIOBHAN MC KENNA READING THE
LANCELOT AND GUENEVER SEQUENCES.
PROD-CAED   DIST-CAED

LEON PAUL FARGUE -
NOCTURNE   M   4 SDS
        33 1/3 RPM 12 INCH RECORD
   A FRENCH LANGUAGE RECORD.
PROD-GMS   DIST-GMS

LES POETES EN FRANCE   M   4 SDS
        33 1/3 RPM 12 INCH RECORD
   A FRENCH LANGUAGE RECORD. FEATURES THE
WORKS OF 43 AUTHORS FROM RUTEBEUF TO MI-
CHAUX, RECITED BY 25 COMEDIANS, INCLUDING
JEAN DESAILLY, JEAN VILAR, GERARD PHILIPE,
DENIS MANUEL AND OTHERS. INCLUDES THE
WORKS OF RONSARD, MAROT, CORNEILLE, LA-
MARTINE, NERVAL, MUSSET, BANVILLE, VOLTAIRE,
PASCAL, LA FONTAINE, VERLAINE, ARAGON, PE-
GUY AND OTHERS.
PROD-GMS   DIST-GMS

LINCOLN PORTRAIT AND NEW
ENGLAND TRIPTYCH   M   2 SDS
        33 1/3 RPM 12 INCH RECORD
   PRESENTS ANDRE KOSTELANETZ AND THE NEW
YORK PHILHARMONIC PERFORMING COPLAND'S
AND SCHUMANN'S WORKS WITH CARL SAND-
BURG SPEAKING. INCLUDES 'BARBER'S INTER-
MEZZO' FROM ACT IV OF 'VANESSA.'
PROD-SSR   DIST-BOW

LOUIS ARAGON   M   2 SDS
        33 1/3 RPM 12 INCH RECORD
   A FRENCH LANGUAGE RECORD.
PROD-GMS   DIST-GMS

UN AIR EMBAUME
POEMES DE CAPE ET D'EPEE
LES AMANTS SEPARES
RICHARD II QUARANTE
AMOUR D'ELSA
LE CRI DU BUTOR

LOUIS ARAGON - AMOURS   M   2 SDS
        33 1/3 RPM 7 INCH RECORD
   A FRENCH LANGUAGE RECORD. FEATURES POEMS
RECITED BY THE AUTHOR, LOUIS ARAGON.
PROD-GMS   DIST-GMS

AMOUR DE MONS PAYS - LES LILAS ET LES
   ROSES
RICHARD II
QUARANTE
LA ROSE ET LE RESEDA
PARIS
AMOUR D'ELSA - LES YEUX D'ELSA
ELSA AU MIROIR
AMOUR D'ELSA

LOUIS ARAGON - LES LILAS ET
LES ROSES   M   4 SDS
        33 1/3 RPM 12 INCH RECORD
   A FRENCH LANGUAGE RECORD.
PROD-GMS   DIST-GMS

LOUIS LABE - POEMES   M   2 SDS
        33 1/3 RPM 7 INCH RECORD
   A FRENCH LANGUAGE RECORD. INCLUDES 'EPI-
TRE DEDICATOIRE,' 'ELEGIE III' AND 'SONNETS.'
PROD-GMS   DIST-GMS

LOUIS-FERDINAND CELINE   M   2 SDS
        33 1/3 RPM 7 INCH RECORD
   A FRENCH LANGUAGE RECORD. FEATURES CELINE
READING 'CELINE VOUR PARLE,' PIERRE BRAS-
SEUR READING AN EXTRACT FROM 'LE VOYAGE
AU BOUT DE LA NUIT' AND AN EXTRACT FROM
'MORT A CREDIT' READ BY ARLETTY.
PROD-GMS   DIST-GMS

LOUISE LABE - JE VIS, JE
MEURS   M   2 SDS
        33 1/3 RPM 12 INCH RECORD
   A FRENCH LANGUAGE RECORD.
PROD-GMS   DIST-GMS

LOUISE LABE - TANT QUE MES
YEUX   M   2 SDS
        33 1/3 RPM 12 INCH RECORD
   A FRENCH LANGUAGE RECORD.
PROD-GMS   DIST-GMS

M

MACHINE RHYTHMS   M   2 SDS
        33 1/3 RPM 12 INCH RECORD
   PRESENTS THE RHYTHMS OF MACHINES, CARS
AND TRUCKS TO HELP CHILDREN FEEL THE
RHYTHMS ASSOCIATED WITH EACH.
PROD-CLSMAT   DIST-BOW

MADAME DE LA FAYETTE - LA PRINCESSE DE CLEVES   M 2 SDS
33 1/3 RPM 12 INCH RECORD
A FRENCH LANGUAGE RECORD.
PROD-GMS   DIST-GMS

MADAME DE LA FAYETTE - LA PRINCESSE DE CLEVES   M 6 SDS
33 1/3 RPM 12 INCH RECORD
A FRENCH LANGUAGE RECORD.
PROD-GMS   DIST-GMS

MARCEL ACHARD - DISCOURS SOUS LA COUPOLE   M 2 SDS
33 1/3 RPM 12 INCH RECORD
A FRENCH LANGUAGE RECORD. FEATURES A RE-CEPTION AT THE ACADEMIE FRANCAISE.
PROD-GMS   DIST-GMS

MARCEL ACHARD - MARLBOROUGH S'EN VA-T-EN GUERRE   M 2 SDS
33 1/3 RPM 12 INCH RECORD
A FRENCH LANGUAGE RECORD. FEATURES THE AUTHOR MARCEL ACHARD READING HIS OWN WORK.
PROD-GMS   DIST-GMS

MARCEL ACHARD - VOULEZ-VOUS JOUER AVEC MOI   M 2 SDS
33 1/3 RPM 12 INCH RECORD
A FRENCH LANGUAGE RECORD. FEATURES THE AUTHOR MARCEL ACHARD READING HIS OWN WORK.
PROD-GMS   DIST-GMS

MARCEL AYME - LES CONTES DU CHAT PERCHE   M 2 SDS
33 1/3 RPM 12 INCH RECORD
A FRENCH LANGUAGE RECORD.
PROD-GMS   DIST-GMS

MAURICE BARRES - LE PRINTEMPTS   M 2 SDS
33 1/3 RPM 12 INCH RECORD
A FRENCH LANGUAGE RECORD.
PROD-GMS   DIST-GMS

MAURICE FOMBEURE   M 2 SDS
33 1/3 RPM 7 INCH RECORD
A FRENCH LANGUAGE RECORD. FEATURES JEAN-LOUIS JEMMA RECITING.
PROD-GMS   DIST-GMS

NAIF
ARBRES
BATELIER DE L'ALLIER
LE RETOUR DE SERGENT
PLUIE DU SOIR
PREUILLY-SUR-CLAISE
CHEVAUX DE BOIS
CHEVAUX DE MON ENFANCE
SOLITUDE
PAYSAGES URBAINS
D'UNE AUBE ETRANGE
ILS S'EN VONT AUX VEILLEES
QUEL EST CE COEUR
MARINE
JUGEMENT DERNIER

MAURICE FOMBEURE - MENUISIER DU ROI   M 2 SDS
33 1/3 RPM 7 INCH RECORD
A FRENCH LANGUAGE RECORD.
PROD-GMS   DIST-GMS

MAURICE FOMBEURE - NOSTALGIE   M 2 SDS
33 1/3 RPM 12 INCH RECORD
A FRENCH LANGUAGE RECORD.
PROD-GMS   DIST-GMS

MAURICE GENEVOIX - LES POISSONS DE LA LOIRE   M 2 SDS
33 1/3 RPM 12 INCH RECORD
A FRENCH LANGUAGE RECORD.
PROD-GMS   DIST-GMS

MAX JACOB - ALAIN CUNY RECITES (FRENCH)   M 2 SDS
33 1/3 RPM 7 INCH RECORD

PROD-GMS   DIST-GMS

POUR LES ENFANTS ET POUR LES RAFFINES
LUEURS DANS LES TENEBRES
LA GUERRE
GLOIRE, CAMBIOLAGE OU REVOLUTION
IL SE PEUT
MILLE REGRETS
VILLONELLE
LA SALTIMBANQUE EN WAGON DE TROISIEME CLASSE
LUNE COULEUR DE SANG
CONFESSION DE L'AUTEUR, SON PORTRAIT EN CRABE

MAX JACOB - LE KAMICHI   M 4 SDS
33 1/3 RPM 12 INCH RECORD
A FRENCH LANGUAGE RECORD.
PROD-GMS   DIST-GMS

MODEST PROPOSAL, A   M 2 SDS
33 1/3 RPM 12 INCH RECORD
PRESENTS PATRICK MAGGE READING 'A MODEST PROPOSAL,' OF SCATHING POLITICAL SATIRE.
PROD-CAED   DIST-CAED

MONKEY'S PAW AND THE INTERUPTION, THE   M 2 SDS
33 1/3 RPM 12 INCH RECORD   H-C
PRESENTS ANTHONY QUAYLE READING TWO MAS-TERPIECES OF PROSE BY W W JACOBS. INCLUDES 'THE MONKEY'S PAW' AND 'THE INTERRUPTION.'
PROD-CAED   DIST-CAED

MUSIC OF IRELAND   M 2 SDS
33 1/3 RPM 12 INCH RECORD
PRESENTS A COLLECTION OF 13 POPULAR IRISH MELODIES, INCLUDING 'HERE THE RIVER SHAN-NON FLOWS' AND 'GRAND OLD COUNTRY.' FEA-TURES PHILIP MC CAFFREY SINGING THESE IRISH TUNES.
PROD-SPA   DIST-SPA

N

NONLECTURE FIVE - I AND NOW AND HIM   M 2 SDS
33 1/3 RPM 12 INCH RECORD   H-C
SEE SERIES TITLE FOR DESCRIPTIVE STATEMENT. FROM THE E E CUMMINGS, LECTURING AND READING SIX NONLECTURES SERIES.
PROD-CAED   DIST-CAED

NONLECTURE FOUR - I AND YOU AND IS   M 2 SDS
33 1/3 RPM 12 INCH RECORD   H-C
SEE SERIES TITLE FOR DESCRIPTIVE STATEMENT. FROM THE E E CUMMINGS, LECTURING AND READING SIX NONLECTURES SERIES.
PROD-CAED   DIST-CAED

NONLECTURE ONE - I AND MY PARENTS   M 2 SDS
33 1/3 RPM 12 INCH RECORD   H-C
SEE SERIES TITLE FOR DESCRIPTIVE STATEMENT. FROM THE E E CUMMINGS, LECTURING AND READING SIX NONLECTURES SERIES.
PROD-CAED   DIST-CAED

NONLECTURE SIX - I AND AM AND SANTA CLAUS   M 2 SDS
33 1/3 RPM 12 INCH RECORD   H-C
SEE SERIES TITLE FOR DESCRIPTIVE STATEMENT. FROM THE E E CUMMINGS, LECTURING AND READING SIX NONLECTURES SERIES.
PROD-CAED   DIST-CAED

NONLECTURE THREE - I AND SELFDISCOVERY   M 2 SDS
33 1/3 RPM 12 INCH RECORD   H-C
SEE SERIES TITLE FOR DESCRIPTIVE STATEMENT. FROM THE E E CUMMINGS, LECTURING AND READING SIX NONLECTURES SERIES.
PROD-CAED   DIST-CAED

NONLECTURE TWO - I AND THEIR SON   M 2 SDS
33 1/3 RPM 12 INCH RECORD   H-C
SEE SERIES TITLE FOR DESCRIPTIVE STATEMENT. FROM THE E E CUMMINGS, LECTURING AND READING SIX NONLECTURES SERIES.

PROD-CAED   DIST-CAED

P

PAUL CLAUDEL - EXCERPTS (FRENCH)   M 2 SDS
33 1/3 RPM 12 INCH RECORD
PROD-GMS   DIST-GMS

VERS D'EXIL
CORONA BENIGNITATIS ANNI DEI (BALLADE, LE JOUR DES CADEAUX)
CINQ GRANDES ODES
LE CHEMIN DE LA CROIX
PARTAGE DE MIDI (ACTE I)
L'OTAGE (ACTE II)
L'ANNONCE FAITE A MARIE (ACTE III)
LE SOULIER DE SATIN (PRIERE DE PROUHEZE)

PAUL CLAUDEL - L'ANNONCE FAITE A MARIE   M 2 SDS
33 1/3 RPM 12 INCH RECORD
A FRENCH LANGUAGE RECORD. PRESENTS EX-TRACTS FROM 'L'ANNONCE FAITE A MARIE,' IN-CLUDING THE PROLOGUE, ACT I, SCENE 3, ACT II, SCENES 3 AND 4, ACT III, SCENE 3 AND ACT IV, SCENE 2.
PROD-GMS   DIST-GMS

PAUL CLAUDEL - L'ESPRIT ET L'EAU   M 2 SDS
33 1/3 RPM 12 INCH RECORD
A FRENCH LANGUAGE RECORD.
PROD-GMS   DIST-GMS

PAUL CLAUDEL - LE VIERGE A MIDI   M 2 SDS
33 1/3 RPM 12 INCH RECORD
A FRENCH LANGUAGE RECORD.
PROD-GMS   DIST-GMS

PAUL CLAUDEL, I   M 2 SDS
33 1/3 RPM 7 INCH RECORD
A FRENCH LANGUAGE RECORD. INCLUDES PER-FORMANCES BY THE COMEDIE FRANCAISE.
PROD-GMS   DIST-GMS

LA VIERGE A MIDI
VERLAINE
A LA MEMOIRE DE L'ABBE DANIEL FONTAINE
L'ENFANT JESUS DE PRAGUE
LA SAINTE FACE

PAUL CLAUDEL, II   M 2 SDS
33 1/3 RPM 7 INCH RECORD
A FRENCH LANGUAGE RECORD. INCLUDES PER-FORMANCES BY THE COMEDIE FRANCAISE.
PROD-GMS   DIST-GMS

SAINT-LOUIS
SAINT-JEAN L'EVANGELISTE
SAINTE-SCOLASTIQUE
NOTRE-DAME AUXILIATRICE
LE JOUR DES CADEAUX

PAUL ELUARD   M 2 SDS
33 1/3 RPM 12 INCH RECORD
A FRENCH LANGUAGE RECORD.
PROD-GMS   DIST-GMS

POUR VIVRE ICI
L'AMOUREUSE
NUITS PARTAGEES
DIMANCHE APRES-MIDI
LIBERTE
COUVRE-FEU
JE NE SUIS PAS SEUL
POESIE ININTERROMPUE
NOTRE VIE

PAUL ELUARD - DONNER A VOIR   M 2 SDS
33 1/3 RPM 12 INCH RECORD
A FRENCH LANGUAGE RECORD.
PROD-GMS   DIST-GMS

PAUL ELUARD - GERARD PHILIPE RECITES (FRENCH)   M 2 SDS
33 1/3 RPM 7 INCH RECORD
PROD-GMS   DIST-GMS

POUR VIVRE ICI
L'AMOURE
USE
NUITS PARTAGEES
DIMANCHE APRES-MIDI
LIBERTE
COUVRE-FEU
JE NE SUIS PAS SEUL

PROD-CAED   DIST-CAED

POESIE ININTERROMPUE
NOTRE VIE
PRINTEMPS
BONNE JUSTICE
LA POESIE DOIT AVOIR POUR BUT LA VERITE
PRACTIQUE

PAUL ELUARD - L'AMOUREUSE   M 4 SDS
      33 1/3 RPM 12 INCH RECORD
A FRENCH LANGUAGE RECORD.
PROD-GMS   DIST-GMS

PAUL ELUARD (1895-1952)   M 2 SDS
      45 RPM 7 INCH RECORD
A FRENCH LANGUAGE RECORD.
PROD-GMS   DIST-GMS

    LIBERTE
    BONNE JUSTICE
    OU ES-TU, ME VOIS-TU, M'ENTENDS-TU
    QUELQUES-UNS DES MOTS QUI
    ICI
    LA MORT, L'AMOUR, LA VIE

**PAUL FORT - CHANSON D'UN
BERGER SURPRIS PAR LA NEIGE**
      M 2 SDS
      33 1/3 RPM 7 INCH RECORD
A FRENCH LANGUAGE RECORD.
PROD-GMS   DIST-GMS

**PAUL FORT - COMPLAINTE DU
PETIT CHEVAL BLANC, LA
GRENOUILLE BLEUE**   M 2 SDS
      33 1/3 RPM 12 INCH RECORD
A FRENCH LANGUAGE RECORD.
PROD-GMS   DIST-GMS

PAUL FORT - LA RONDE   M 4 SDS
      33 1/3 RPM 12 INCH RECORD
A FRENCH LANGUAGE RECORD.
PROD-GMS   DIST-GMS

**PAUL FORT - LE BONHEUR, LA
RONDE AUTOUR DU MONDE**   M 2 SDS
      33 1/3 RPM 12 INCH RECORD
A FRENCH LANGUAGE RECORD.
PROD-GMS   DIST-GMS

PAUL FORT (1872-1960)   M 2 SDS
      45 RPM 7 INCH RECORD
A FRENCH LANGUAGE RECORD.
PROD-GMS   DIST-GMS

    LA FRANCE
    LOUIS XI, CURIEUX HOMME
    LA RONDE AUTOUR DU MONDE
    LE BONHEUR
    LE PETIT CHEVAL
    PHILOMELE
    TOUT EST SUPPOSABLE ET REVE

**PAUL-LOUIS COURIER DE MERE
- UNE AVENTURE EN CALABRE**   M 2 SDS
      33 1/3 RPM 12 INCH RECORD
A FRENCH LANGUAGE RECORD.
PROD-GMS   DIST-GMS

**PEARLY'S PROVERBS AND FOLK
TUNES**   S 2 SDS
      33 1/3 RPM 12 INCH RECORD
PRESENTS FAVORITE FRENCH FOLK SONGS AND
PROVERBS.
PROD-GMS   DIST-GMS

    AU CLAIRE DE LA LUNE
    SUR LE PONT D'AVIGNON
    IL ETAIT UNE BERGERE
    MA NORMANDIE
    ALOUETTE
    FRERE JACQUES
    LA MARSEILLAISE
    DON'T COUNT YOUR CHICKENS
    WHEN THE CAT'S AWAY
    A BIRD IN HAND
    NEVER PUT OFF TILL TOMORROW
    MARCH WINDS AND APRIL SHOWERS
    ALL IS NOT GOLD
    THE LAST STRAW BREAKS
    A ROLLING STONE
    BETTER LATE THAN NEVER
    TIME IS MONEY

PIERRE CORNEILLE - CINNA   M 2 SDS
      33 1/3 RPM 12 INCH RECORD
A FRENCH LANGUAGE RECORD.
PROD-GMS   DIST-GMS

**PIERRE CORNEILLE - CINNA,
EXTRAITS**   M 2 SDS
      33 1/3 RPM 12 INCH RECORD
A FRENCH LANGUAGE RECORD. FEATURES LES CO-
MEDIENS DE LA PLEIADE PERFORMING ACT I

SCENES 3 AND 4, ACT II, SCENE 1, ACT II, SCENES
4 AND 5, ACT IV, SCENE 2 AND ACT V, SCENES 1
AND 3 OF 'CINNA.'
PROD-GMS   DIST-GMS

PIERRE CORNEILLE - HORACE   M 2 SDS
      33 1/3 RPM 12 INCH RECORD
A FRENCH LANGUAGE RECORD. FEATURES THE
COMEDIE FRANCAISE PERFORMING 'HORACE.'
PROD-GMS   DIST-GMS

**PIERRE CORNEILLE -
POLYEUCTE (EXTRAITS)**   M 2 SDS
      33 1/3 RPM 12 INCH RECORD
A FRENCH LANGUAGE RECORD. FEATURES EX-
CERPTS OF 'POLYEUCTE.' INCLUDES ACT I,
SCENES 1, 2 AND 4, ACT II, SCENES 2 AND 6, ACT
III, SCENES 3, 4 AND 5, ACT IV, SCENES 2, 3, 4
AND 6 AND ACT V, SCENES 2, 3, 5 AND 6.
PROD-GMS   DIST-GMS

**PIERRE DE BEAUMARCHAIS - LE
MARIAGE DE FIGARO
(COMPLETE)**   M 6 SDS
      33 1/3 RPM 12 INCH RECORD
A FRENCH LANGUAGE RECORD. FEATURES LA CO-
MEDIE FRANCAISE.
PROD-GMS   DIST-GMS

**PIERRE DE BEAUMARCHAIS - LE
MARIAGE DE FIGARO
(EXTRAITS)**   M 2 SDS
      45 RPM 7 INCH RECORD
A FRENCH LANGUAGE RECORD. FEATURES JULIEN
BERTHEAU, ANTOINETTE MOYA, PHILIPPE DES-
BEUF, ANNIE DARMES AND JACQUES BUTIN IN
ACT 2, SCENE 21 AND ACT 3, SCENE 5 OF 'LE
MARIAGE DE FIGARO.'
PROD-GMS   DIST-GMS

**PIERRE DE BEAUMARCHAIS - LE
MARIAGE DE FIGARO
(EXTRAITS)**   M 2 SDS
      45 RPM 7 INCH RECORD
A FRENCH LANGUAGE RECORD. FEATURES ACT 5,
SCENE 3 OF 'LE MARIAGE DE FIGARO,' FIGARO'S
MONOLOGUE. INCLUDES ACT 5, SCENE 8.
PROD-GMS   DIST-GMS

**PIERRE DE BEAUMARCHAIS - LE
MARIAGE DE FIGARO ACTE I,
SCENE 1, ACTE V, SCENE 3**   M 2 SDS
      33 1/3 RPM 12 INCH RECORD
A FRENCH LANGUAGE RECORD.
PROD-GMS   DIST-GMS

**PIERRE-AMBROISE CHODERLOS
DE LACLOS - LES LIAISONS
DANGEREUSES**   M 2 SDS
      33 1/3 RPM 12 INCH RECORD
A FRENCH LANGUAGE RECORD. FEATURES AN EX-
TRACT FROM 'LES LIAISONS DANGEREUSES,' AND
'LETTRE DE LA MARQUISE DE MERTEUIL AU VI-
COMTE DE VALMONT.'
PROD-GMS   DIST-GMS

**POEMS AND SONGS FOR
YOUNGER CHILDREN**   M 2 SDS
      33 1/3 RPM 12 INCH RECORD
INCLUDES POEMS BY AUTHORS LEAR, CARROLL,
KEATS, WHITMAN, JOHNSON AND OTHERS.
PROD-SPA   DIST-SPA

**POETRY OF GEORGE GORDON
BYRON**   M 2 SDS
      33 1/3 RPM 12 INCH RECORD
PRESENTS TYRONE POWER READING THE POETRY
OF GEORGE GORDON BYRON. INCLUDES 'SHE
WALKS IN BEAUTY,' 'ON THIS DAY I COMPLETE MY
36TH YEAR,' 'CHILDE HAROLD'S PILGRIMAGE' AND
'DON JUAN' (CANTO 1.)
PROD-CAED   DIST-CAED

**POETRY OF PERCY BYSSHE
SHELLEY**   M 2 SDS
      33 1/3 RPM 12 INCH RECORD   H-C
PRESENTS VINCENT PRICE READING THE POETRY
OF PERCY BYSSHE SHELLEY. INCLUDES 'MUSIC,'
'WHEN SOFT VOICES DIE,' 'OZYMANDIAS,' 'ODE TO
THE WEST WIND,' 'ADONAIS' AND OTHERS.
PROD-CAED   DIST-CAED

PRESENCE DE ALBERT CAMUS   M 6 SDS
      33 1/3 RPM 12 INCH RECORD
A FRENCH LANGUAGE RECORD. FEATURES AL-
BERT CAMUS READING SELECTIONS FROM HIS
WORKS, INCLUDING 'L'ETRANGER,' 'NOCES,' 'LA
PESTE,' 'L'HOMME REVOLTE,' 'CALIGULA' AND 'LA
CHUTE'.

PROD-GMS   DIST-GMS

**RANDALL JARRELL READS AND
DISCUSSES HIS POEMS
AGAINST WAR**   M 2 SDS
      33 1/3 RPM 12 INCH RECORD
PRESENTS RANDALL JARRELL READING HIS
POEMS, INCLUDING 'A LULLABY,' 'MAIL CALL,'
'THE LINES,' 'DEATH OF THE BALL-TURRET GUN-
NER,' 'EIGHTH AIR FORCE,' 'IN MONTECITO,' 'A
STREET OF SUNSET' AND OTHERS.
PROD-CAED   DIST-CAED

REMY DE GOURMONT - JEANNE   M 4 SDS
      33 1/3 RPM 12 INCH RECORD
PROD-GMS   DIST-GMS

RENE CHAR   M 2 SDS
      33 1/3 RPM 7 INCH RECORD
A FRENCH LANGUAGE RECORD. FEATURES LAU-
RENT TERZIEFF RECITING FROM THE WORKS OF
RENE CHAR.
PROD-GMS   DIST-GMS

    LE SOL DE LA NUIT
    POETES
    COMMUNE PRESENCE
    J'AI ETRANGLE MON FRERE
    REMISE
    DECLARER SON NOM
    BIENS EGAUX
    AFFRES, DETONATION, SILENCE
    A
    L'AMOUREUSE EN SECRET
    INVITATION
    REDONNEZ-LEUR
    LA SORGUE

**RENE CHAR - L'INOFFENSIF, LA
SORGUE**   M 2 SDS
      33 1/3 RPM 12 INCH RECORD
A FRENCH LANGUAGE RECORD.
PROD-GMS   DIST-GMS

RENE GUY CADOU   M 2 SDS
      33 1/3 RPM 7 INCH RECORD
A FRENCH LANGUAGE RECORD. FEATURES DANIEL
GELIN RECITING FROM THE WORKS OF RENE GUY
CADOU.
PROD-GMS   DIST-GMS

    DEVANT CET ARBRE
    JE T'ATTENDAIS AINSI
    BERRIERE LES RIDEAUX
    SYMPHONIE DE PRINTEMPS
    L'HOMME AU KEPI DE GARDE-CHASSE
    LE CHANT DE SOLITUDE
    POURQUOI N'ALLEZ-VOUS PAS A PARIS
    SANS SAVOIR QUE LA NUIT
    LETTRE A PIERRE YVERNAULT, CURE DE
    CAMPAGNE
    LA SOIREE DE DECEMBRE

RHYTHM IS FUN   M 6 SDS
      78 RPM 10 INCH RECORD   P-I
PRESENTS AN ELEMENTARY EXPLANATION OF
SIMPLE RHYTHMS. INCLUDES THE BEAT OF THE
PIANO AND THE DRUMS AND OTHER INSTRU-
MENTS WHICH CHILDREN CAN INTERPRET.
PROD-BOW   DIST-BOW

RHYTHMIC ACTIVITY   M 2 SDS
      33 1/3 RPM 12 INCH RECORD
GIVES A SIMPLE APPROACH TO THE INTRODUC-
TION OF RHYTHMIC ACTIVITIES FOR ALL AGES.
UTILIZES THE PIANO FOR ACCOMPANIMENT.
PROD-BASCHE   DIST-BOW

RHYTHMS FOR TODAY   M 4 SDS
      33 1/3 RPM 12 INCH RECORD
PRESENTS RHYTHMS WHICH INCLUDE FAMILIAR
SOUNDS AND EXPERIENCES FOR CHILDREN. EX-
PLAINS THAT EACH RHYTHM HAS A WRITTEN
RHYME WHICH CAN BE USED TO ENRICH CHIL-
DREN'S VOCABULARY.
PROD-EDLACT   DIST-EDLACT

**RHYTHMS FROM THE LAND OF
MAKE-BELIEVE**   M 2 SDS
      33 1/3 RPM 12 INCH RECORD   K-I
PRESENTS RHYTHM BY SUGGESTING VARIOUS
IMAGINATIVE ACTIVITIES, SUCH AS BECOMING
TOY SOLDIERS MARCHING, FAIRIES DANCING,
PRINCES GALLOPING AND TORTOISES WADDLING.
PROD-CLSMAT   DIST-BOW

RHYTHMS, DANCES AND GAMES, ALBUM 26   M 8 SDS
78 RPM 12 INCH RECORD
CONTAINS BEGINNING MATERIAL IN RHYTHMS, MARCHING, MIXERS, SIMPLE SINGING AND MUSICAL GAMES. EXPLAINS HOW THESE ACTIVITIES ARE USEFUL IN CLASSES FOR EXCEPTIONAL CHILDREN.
PROD-CLSMAT   DIST-BOW

ROGER FRISON-ROCHE - ASCENSION DU DRU (MONT BLANC)   M 2 SDS
33 1/3 RPM 12 INCH RECORD
A FRENCH LANGUAGE RECORD.
PROD-GMS   DIST-GMS

ROLAND DORGELES - CHATEAU DES BROUILLARDS   M 2 SDS
33 1/3 RPM 12 INCH RECORD
A FRENCH LANGUAGE RECORD.
PROD-GMS   DIST-GMS

S

SAMUEL BECKETT - OH LES BEAUX JOURS (EXTRAITS)   M 2 SDS
33 1/3 RPM 12 INCH RECORD
A FRENCH LANGUAGE RECORD.
PROD-GMS   DIST-GMS

SHORT STORIES OF SAKI, THE, VOL 1   M 2 SDS
33 1/3 RPM 12 INCH RECORD
FEATURES KEITH BAXTER READING THE SHORT STORIES OF SAKI. INCLUDES 'THE RETICENCE OF LADY ANNE,' 'GABRIEL-ERNEST' FROM 'REGINALD IN RUSSIA' AND OTHERS.
PROD-CAED   DIST-CAED

SHORT STORIES OF SAKI, THE, VOL 2   M 2 SDS
33 1/3 RPM 12 INCH RECORD
PRESENTS KEITH BAXTER READING THE SHORT STORIES OF SAKI. INCLUDES 'SREDNI VASHTAR' AND 'TOBERMORY' FROM 'THE CHRONICLES OF CLOVIS,' 'THE SEVEN CREAM JUGS' FROM 'THE TOYS OF PEACE' AND OTHERS.
PROD-CAED   DIST-CAED

SQUARE THAT NUMBER   M 2 SDS
33 1/3 RPM 12 INCH RECORD
PRESENTS 20 SHORT ARITHMETIC GAMES BASED ON TRICK PROBLEMS. EXPLAINS THAT ALL FUNDAMENTAL ARITHMETIC OPERATIONS INVOLVE THE ABILITY TO LISTEN AND FOLLOW DIRECTIONS.
PROD-SPA   DIST-SPA

T

THEODORE DE BANVILLE - LE SAUT DE TREMPLIN   M 2 SDS
33 1/3 RPM 12 INCH RECORD
A FRENCH LANGUAGE RECORD.
PROD-GMS   DIST-GMS

THEODORE ROETHKE READS HIS POETRY   M 2 SDS
33 1/3 RPM 12 INCH RECORD   H-C
PRESENTS THEODORE ROETHKE READING SOME OF HIS POEMS.
PROD-CAED   DIST-CAED

WHERE KNOCK IS OPEN WIDE
GIVE WAY, YE GATES
MY PAPA'S WALTZ
PICKLE BELT
THE CYCLE
THE DONKEY
DINKY

THEOPHILE GAUTIER - LE CAPITAINE FRACASSE   M 2 SDS
33 1/3 RPM 12 INCH RECORD
A FRENCH LANGUAGE RECORD.
PROD-GMS   DIST-GMS

PARADE
LE CHATEAU DE LA MISERE
BRIGANDS POUR LES OISEAUX
CHEZ MONSIEUR LE MARQUIS
LE GUET-APENS
LE DUEL
L'ANNEAU D'AMETHYSTE

THEOPHILE GAUTIER - PAYSAGE NOCTURNE   M 2 SDS
33 1/3 RPM 12 INCH RECORD
A FRENCH LANGUAGE RECORD.
PROD-GMS   DIST-GMS

TRISTAN CORBIERE - LA PARDON DE SAINTE-ANNE LA-PALUD (EXTRAIT)   M 2 SDS
33 1/3 RPM 12 INCH RECORD
A FRENCH LANGUAGE RECORD.
PROD-GMS   DIST-GMS

TWO CANTERBURY TALES IN MIDDLE ENGLISH - THE PARDONER'S PROLOGUE AND TALE AND THE NUNS ...   M 2 SDS
33 1/3 RPM 12 INCH RECORD   C
PRESENTS A READING IN MIDDLE ENGLISH OF 'THE PARDONER'S PROLOGUE AND TALE' AND 'THE NUNS' PRIESTS' TALE.'
PROD-CAED   DIST-CAED

TWO CANTERBURY TALES IN MODERN ENGLISH - PARDONER'S TALE AND THE MILLER'S TALE   M 2 SDS
33 1/3 RPM 12 INCH RECORD   C
PRESENTS 'THE PARDONER'S TALE,' READ BY MICHAEL MAC LIAMMOIR AND 'THE MILLER'S TALE,' READ BY STANLEY HOLLOWAY, IN THE MODERN ENGLISH TRANSLATION BY THEODORE MORRISON.
PROD-CAED   DIST-CAED

V

VICTOR HUGO - CE SIECLE AVAIT DEUX ANS   M 2 SDS
33 1/3 RPM 12 INCH RECORD
A FRENCH LANGUAGE RECORD.
PROD-GMS   DIST-GMS

VICTOR HUGO - LA CAMPAGNE DE RUSSIE   M 2 SDS
33 1/3 RPM 12 INCH RECORD
A FRENCH LANGUAGE RECORD.
PROD-GMS   DIST-GMS

VICTOR HUGO - LA ROSE DE L'INFANTE, CHANSON D'AUTOMNE   M 2 SDS
33 1/3 RPM 12 INCH RECORD
A FRENCH LANGUAGE RECORD.
PROD-GMS   DIST-GMS

VICTOR HUGO - LE FIN DE SATAN (EXTRAITS)   M 2 SDS
33 1/3 RPM 12 INCH RECORD
A FRENCH LANGUAGE RECORD.
PROD-GMS   DIST-GMS

VICTOR HUGO - LES MISERABLES (COSETTE)   M 2 SDS
33 1/3 RPM 7 INCH RECORD
A FRENCH LANGUAGE RECORD.
PROD-GMS   DIST-GMS

CHEZ LES THENARDIER (CHAP 2, LIVRE III, 2 PARTIE)
DANS LA FORET (CHAP 3, 4, 5, LIVRE III, 2 PARTIE)
COSETTE ET LA POUPEE (CHAP 8, LIVRE III, 2 PARTIE)
COSETTE SAUVEE (CHAP 2, LIVRE IV, 2 PARTIE)

VICTOR HUGO - LES MISERABLES (EXTRAITS)   M 2 SDS
33 1/3 RPM 7 INCH RECORD
A FRENCH LANGUAGE RECORD.
PROD-GMS   DIST-GMS

VICTOR HUGO - LES MISERABLES (GAVROCHE)   M 2 SDS
33 1/3 RPM 7 INCH RECORD
A FRENCH LANGUAGE RECORD.
PROD-GMS   DIST-GMS

PORTRAIT DE GAVROCHE (CHAP 13, LIVRE I, 3 PARTIE)
GAVROCHE EN MARCHE (CHAP 1, 2, LIVRE XI, 4 PARTIE)
VERS LA BARRICADE (CHAP 1, 2 LIVRE XIV, 4 PARTIE)
LA MONT DE GAVROCHE (CHAP 4, LIVRE I, 5 PARTIE)

VICTOR HUGO - NOTRE-DAME DE PARIS   M 2 SDS
33 1/3 RPM 12 INCH RECORD
A FRENCH LANGUAGE RECORD.
PROD-GMS   DIST-GMS

VICTOR HUGO (EXTRAITS)   M 2 SDS
33 1/3 RPM 7 INCH RECORD
A FRENCH LANGUAGE RECORD.
PROD-GMS   DIST-GMS

ODES ET BALLADES - MON ENFANCE
HERNANI - ACTE V, SCENE 3
NOTRE-DAME DE PARIS - QUASIMODO
RUY BLAS - ACTE III, SCENE 2
LES RAYONS ET LES OMBRES - TRISTESSE D'OLYMPIO
CHATIMENTS - SONNEZ, SONNEZ TOUJOURS
LES ANNEES FUNESTES - LE PEUPLE ETAIT DEBOUT
LES CONTEMPLATIONS - OH, JE FUS COMME FOU
L'ANNEE TERRIBLE - PREMIER JANVIER

VICTORIAN POETRY   M 2 SDS
33 1/3 RPM 12 INCH RECORD   J-C
INCLUDES POEMS BY HENRY, E B BROWNING, FITZGERALD, TENNYSON, THACKERAY, BROWNING, LEAR, C BRONTE AND OTHERS.
PROD-CAED   DIST-CAED

W

WAY OUT RECORD FOR CHILDREN, THE   M 2 SDS
33 1/3 RPM 12 INCH RECORD
SUGGESTS CREATIVE PARTICIPATION IN EVERYTHING FROM A MOTORCYCLE RIDE AND ELECTRONIC CLOCK TO MEDIEVAL DANCING AND A CONCERT.
PROD-DIMFIV   DIST-BOW

WHEN WE WERE VERY YOUNG   M 2 SDS
33 1/3 RPM 12 INCH RECORD   P-I
PRESENTS JUDITH ANDERSON READING THE POEMS OF A A MILNE. INCLUDES POEMS FROM 'WHEN WE WERE VERY YOUNG' AND 'NOW WE ARE SIX.'
PROD-CAED   DIST-CAED

WIND IN THE WILLOWS, THE   M 2 SDS
33 1/3 RPM 12 INCH RECORD
PRESENTS THE STORY OF 'THE WIND IN THE WILLOWS' BY KENNETH GRAHAME.
PROD-SPA   DIST-SPA

ALPHABETICAL GUIDE TO EDUCATIONAL AUDIO TAPES

A

ACCELERATION TECHNIQUES M 60 MIN
3 3/4 IPS 2 TRACK AUDIO TAPE
SEE SERIES TITLE FOR DESCRIPTIVE STATEMENT.
FROM THE BEHAVIOR MODIFICATION STRATEGIES
FOR CHILD PSYCHOTHERAPISTS SERIES.
PROD-SIGINF   DIST-SIGINF

ACUTE SCHIZOPHRENIA, PT 1 M 60 MIN
3 3/4 IPS 2 TRACK AUDIO TAPE
SEE SERIES TITLE FOR DESCRIPTIVE STATEMENT.
FROM THE TOPICS IN CLINICAL PSYCHIATRY SE-
RIES.
PROD-SIGINF   DIST-SIGINF

ACUTE SCHIZOPHRENIA, PT 2 M 60 MIN
3 3/4 IPS 2 TRACK AUDIO TAPE
SEE SERIES TITLE FOR DESCRIPTIVE STATEMENT.
FROM THE TOPICS IN CLINICAL PSYCHIATRY SE-
RIES.
PROD-SIGINF   DIST-SIGINF

**ADJECTIVE PICTURE PUZZLES -
ADJECTIVES** S
1 7/8 IPS AUDIO TAPE CASSETTE   P
SEE SERIES TITLE FOR DESCRIPTIVE STATEMENT.
FROM THE WORDS ARE FUN SERIES.
PROD-CORF   DIST-CORF

ADOLESCENCE M
3 3/4 IPS 2 TRACK AUDIO TAPE
SEE SERIES TITLE FOR DESCRIPTIVE STATEMENT.
FROM THE WHAT'S YOUR PROBLEM SERIES.
PROD-BASCH   DIST-BASCH

**ADOLESCENT AND HIS
PARENTS, THE** M 60 MIN
3 3/4 IPS 2 TRACK AUDIO TAPE
SEE SERIES TITLE FOR DESCRIPTIVE STATEMENT.
FROM THE PSYCHOTHERAPY OF ADOLESCENTS SE-
RIES.
PROD-SIGINF   DIST-SIGINF

**ADOLESCENT PATIENT AND THE
FAMILY, THE** M 60 MIN
3 3/4 IPS 2 TRACK AUDIO TAPE
DISCUSSES THE PSYCHODYNAMICS OF ADOLES-
CENCE, THE FAMILY AND THE THERAPY. FROM
THE SPECIAL CLINICAL PROBLEMS IN INTENSIVE
PSYCHOTHERAPY SERIES.
PROD-SIGINF   DIST-SIGINF

**ADOLESCENT WITH A
COMMUNICATION DISORDER,
THE** M 60 MIN
3 3/4 IPS 2 TRACK AUDIO TAPE
SEE SERIES TITLE FOR DESCRIPTIVE STATEMENT.
FROM THE NORMAL AND ABNORMAL BEHAVIOR
OF ADOLESCENCE SERIES.
PROD-SIGINF   DIST-SIGINF

ADOLESCENTS AND ADULTS M 60 MIN
3 3/4 IPS 2 TRACK AUDIO TAPE
SEE SERIES TITLE FOR DESCRIPTIVE STATEMENT.
FROM THE NORMAL AND ABNORMAL BEHAVIOR
OF ADOLESCENCE SERIES.
PROD-SIGINF   DIST-SIGINF

ADVERB ABILITY - ADVERBS S
1 7/8 IPS AUDIO TAPE CASSETTE   P
SEE SERIES TITLE FOR DESCRIPTIVE STATEMENT.
FROM THE WORDS ARE FUN SERIES.
PROD-CORF   DIST-CORF

**AFFINITIES OUT OF
DESPERATION - THE 'MRS
ROBINSON' SYNDROME** M 60 MIN
3 3/4 IPS 2 TRACK AUDIO TAPE
SEE SERIES TITLE FOR DESCRIPTIVE STATEMENT.
FROM THE IDENTITIES AND AFFINITIES - THE
PROBLEM OF JUSTICE IN MARRIAGE AND OTHER
UNIONS SERIES.
PROD-SIGINF   DIST-SIGINF

ALCOHOLISM M
3 3/4 IPS 2 TRACK AUDIO TAPE
SEE SERIES TITLE FOR DESCRIPTIVE STATEMENT.
FROM THE WHAT'S YOUR PROBLEM SERIES.
PROD-BASCH   DIST-BASCH

**ANGER INHIBITION PROBLEMS,
PT 1** M 60 MIN
3 3/4 IPS 2 TRACK AUDIO TAPE
SEE SERIES TITLE FOR DESCRIPTIVE STATEMENT.
FROM THE THERAPY OF COMMON CHILDHOOD
DISORDERS SERIES.
PROD-SIGINF   DIST-SIGINF

**ANGER INHIBITION PROBLEMS,
PT 2** M 60 MIN
3 3/4 IPS 2 TRACK AUDIO TAPE
SEE SERIES TITLE FOR DESCRIPTIVE STATEMENT.
FROM THE THERAPY OF COMMON CHILDHOOD
DISORDERS SERIES.
PROD-SIGINF   DIST-SIGINF

**ASSESSING FOR BEHAVIOR
CHANGE** M 60 MIN
3 3/4 IPS 2 TRACK AUDIO TAPE
SEE SERIES TITLE FOR DESCRIPTIVE STATEMENT.
FROM THE BEHAVIOR MODIFICATION STRATEGIES
FOR CHILD PSYCHOTHERAPISTS SERIES.
PROD-SIGINF   DIST-SIGINF

**ASSESSMENT OF CHANGE IN
CHILDREN'S BEHAVIOR** M 60 MIN
3 3/4 IPS 2 TRACK AUDIO TAPE
SEE SERIES TITLE FOR DESCRIPTIVE STATEMENT.
FROM THE BEHAVIOR DISORDERS OF CHILDREN
SERIES.
PROD-SIGINF   DIST-SIGINF

ASSESSMENT OF SUICIDAL RISK
M 60 MIN
3 3/4 IPS 2 TRACK AUDIO TAPE
SEE SERIES TITLE FOR DESCRIPTIVE STATEMENT.
FROM THE SUICIDE AND SUICIDE PREVENTION
SERIES.
PROD-SIGINF   DIST-SIGINF

B

**BASIC STRATEGIES FOR
MODIFYING CHILDREN'S
BEHAVIOR** M 60 MIN
3 3/4 IPS 2 TRACK AUDIO TAPE
SEE SERIES TITLE FOR DESCRIPTIVE STATEMENT.
FROM THE BEHAVIOR MODIFICATION STRATEGIES
FOR CHILD PSYCHOTHERAPISTS SERIES.
PROD-SIGINF   DIST-SIGINF

BECOMING A PARENT M
3 3/4 IPS 2 TRACK AUDIO TAPE
SEE SERIES TITLE FOR DESCRIPTIVE STATEMENT.
FROM THE WHAT'S YOUR PROBLEM SERIES.
PROD-BASCH   DIST-BASCH

**BEHAVIOR DISORDERS OF
CHILDHOOD** M 60 MIN
3 3/4 IPS 2 TRACK AUDIO TAPE
SEE SERIES TITLE FOR DESCRIPTIVE STATEMENT.
FROM THE BEHAVIOR DISORDERS OF CHILDREN
SERIES.
PROD-SIGINF   DIST-SIGINF

**BEHAVIOR DISORDERS OF
CHILDREN--A SERIES**
EMPHASIZES INNOVATIVE THERAPEUTIC AP-
PROACHES TO THE DISTURBANCES OF CHILD-
HOOD AND PRESENTS THE CURRENT THINKING
OF MANY OUTSTANDING CHILD PSYCHIATRISTS.
INCLUDES RICHARD GREEN DISCUSSING THE
TREATMENT OF CHILDREN WITH DISORDERED
PSYCHOSEXUAL DEVELOPMENT, CARL
MALMGUIST DETAILING STRATEGIES OF PSYCHO-
THERAPY WITH CHILDREN AND FRANK PITTMAN
FOCUSING ON THE FAMILY TREATMENT OF
SCHOOL PHOBIAS.
PROD-SIGINF   DIST-SIGINF

ASSESSMENT OF CHANGE IN CHILDREN'S BEHAVIOR	60 MIN
BEHAVIOR DISORDERS OF CHILDHOOD	60 MIN
CLINICAL ASPECTS OF MINIMAL BRAIN DYSFUNCTION	60 MIN
CLINICAL ASPECTS OF THE PSYCHIATRIC	60 MIN
COGNITIVE PERFORMANCE - PROGRESS VS PRODUCT	60 MIN
DEVELOPMENT OF AGGRESSION AND AGGRESSION --	60 MIN

EGOCENTRISM IN CHILDREN AND ADOLESCENTS	60 MIN
FAMILY TREATMENT OF SCHOOL PHOBIAS	60 MIN
PRESCHOOL ENRICHMENT AND LEARNING	60 MIN
PREVENTIVE MENTAL HEALTH WORK WITH PRESCHOOL --	60 MIN
SISSIES AND TOMBOYS - CROSS GENDER BEHAVIOR --	60 MIN
STRATEGIES OF CHILD PSYCHOTHERAPY	60 MIN

**BEHAVIOR MODIFICATION
STRATEGIES FOR CHILD
PSYCHOTHERAPISTS--A SERIES**
PRESENTS A GUIDE TO THE FRUSTRATING AND
CHALLENGING PROBLEMS CONFRONTING THE
THERAPIST WHO WISHES TO APPLY THE TECH-
NIQUES OF BEHAVIOR THERAPY IN WORKING
WITH CHILDREN.
PROD-SIGINF   DIST-SIGINF

ACCELERATION TECHNIQUES	60 MIN
ASSESSING FOR BEHAVIOR CHANGE	60 MIN
BASIC STRATEGIES FOR MODIFYING CHILDREN'S --	60 MIN
CHILD PEERS AS THERAPEUTIC AGENTS	60 MIN
CONTINGENCY MANAGEMENT	60 MIN
DECELERATION TECHNIQUES	60 MIN
GOALS FOR BEHAVIOR THERAPY WITH CHILDREN, THE	60 MIN
MISCELLANEOUS TECHNIQUES	60 MIN
OBSERVATIONAL LEARNING	60 MIN
PARENTS AS THERAPEUTIC AGENTS	60 MIN
SELF-ADMINISTERED BEHAVIOR THERAPY FOR CHILDREN	60 MIN
TEACHERS AS THERAPEUTIC AGENTS	60 MIN

**BEHAVIORISM AND
PSYCHOANALYSIS - COGNITIVE
STYLES, CONTENTS AND
ORIGINS** M 60 MIN
3 3/4 IPS 2 TRACK AUDIO TAPE
SEE SERIES TITLE FOR DESCRIPTIVE STATEMENT.
FROM THE COMPASSION - TOWARD A SCIENCE OF
VALUE SERIES.
PROD-SIGINF   DIST-SIGINF

BEYOND SEXUAL IDENTITY M 60 MIN
3 3/4 IPS 2 TRACK AUDIO TAPE
SEE SERIES TITLE FOR DESCRIPTIVE STATEMENT.
FROM THE IDENTITIES AND AFFINITIES - THE
PROBLEM OF JUSTICE IN MARRIAGE AND OTHER
UNIONS SERIES.
PROD-SIGINF   DIST-SIGINF

**BIBLIOGRAPHY - HOW TO
STUDY FOR BOARDS - SAMPLE
EXAMINATIONS** M 60 MIN
3 3/4 IPS 2 TRACK AUDIO TAPE
SEE SERIES TITLE FOR DESCRIPTIVE STATEMENT.
FROM THE PREPARATION FOR CERTIFICATION BY
THE AMERICAN BOARD OF PSYCHIATRY AND NEU-
ROLOGY SERIES.
PROD-SIGINF   DIST-SIGINF

**BIOLOGICAL EVOLUTION OF
INTELLIGENCE, THE** M 60 MIN
3 3/4 IPS 2 TRACK AUDIO TAPE
SEE SERIES TITLE FOR DESCRIPTIVE STATEMENT.
FROM THE NEW APPROACH TO HUMAN EVOLU-
TION SERIES.
PROD-SIGINF   DIST-SIGINF

**BIOLOGY, MORALITY AND
SOCIAL COHESION** M 60 MIN
3 3/4 IPS 2 TRACK AUDIO TAPE
SEE SERIES TITLE FOR DESCRIPTIVE STATEMENT.
FROM THE NEW APPROACH TO HUMAN EVOLU-
TION SERIES.
PROD-SIGINF   DIST-SIGINF

BORDERLINE PATIENT, THE M 60 MIN
3 3/4 IPS 2 TRACK AUDIO TAPE
DISCUSSES THERAPEUTIC UNDERSTANDING AND
THERAPEUTIC INTERVENTION. FROM THE SPECIAL
CLINICAL PROBLEMS IN INTENSIVE PSYCHOTHER-
APY SERIES.

PROD-SIGINF   DIST-SIGINF

C

**CAN LOVE AND SEX SURVIVE
THE ELIMINATION OF SEXISM**   M 60 MIN
3 3/4 IPS 2 TRACK AUDIO TAPE
SEE SERIES TITLE FOR DESCRIPTIVE STATEMENT.
FROM THE IDENTITIES AND AFFINITIES - THE
PROBLEM OF JUSTICE IN MARRIAGE AND OTHER
UNIONS SERIES.
PROD-SIGINF   DIST-SIGINF

CAREER WIFE   M
3 3/4 IPS 2 TRACK AUDIO TAPE
SEE SERIES TITLE FOR DESCRIPTIVE STATEMENT.
FROM THE WHAT'S YOUR PROBLEM SERIES.
PROD-BASCH   DIST-BASCH

**CASE OF THE RED-HEADED
LEAGUE**   S
1 7/8 IPS AUDIO TAPE CASSETTE   I-J
ASKS THE STUDENT TO USE SOPHISTICATED LIS-
TENING AND REASONING PROCESSES TO SOLVE A
DRAMATIZATION OF A SHERLOCK HOLMES MYS-
TERY STORY. FROM THE LISTENING WITH A PUR-
POSE SERIES.
PROD-CORF   DIST-CORF

CEREBRAL DYSFUNCTION   M 60 MIN
3 3/4 IPS 2 TRACK AUDIO TAPE
SEE SERIES TITLE FOR DESCRIPTIVE STATEMENT.
FROM THE TOPICS IN CLINICAL PSYCHIATRY SE-
RIES.
PROD-SIGINF   DIST-SIGINF

**CEREBRAL DYSFUNCTION -
SEIZURE DISORDERS**   M 60 MIN
3 3/4 IPS 2 TRACK AUDIO TAPE
SEE SERIES TITLE FOR DESCRIPTIVE STATEMENT.
FROM THE TOPICS IN CLINICAL PSYCHIATRY SE-
RIES.
PROD-SIGINF   DIST-SIGINF

**CEREBRAL DYSFUNCTION - 14
AND SIX CYCLES POSITIVE EEG
SPIKING**   M 60 MIN
3 3/4 IPS 2 TRACK AUDIO TAPE
SEE SERIES TITLE FOR DESCRIPTIVE STATEMENT.
FROM THE TOPICS IN CLINICAL PSYCHIATRY SE-
RIES.
PROD-SIGINF   DIST-SIGINF

**CHILD PEERS AS THERAPEUTIC
AGENTS**   M 60 MIN
3 3/4 IPS 2 TRACK AUDIO TAPE
SEE SERIES TITLE FOR DESCRIPTIVE STATEMENT.
FROM THE BEHAVIOR MODIFICATION STRATEGIES
FOR CHILD PSYCHOTHERAPISTS SERIES.
PROD-SIGINF   DIST-SIGINF

**CLINICAL ASPECTS OF MINIMAL
BRAIN DYSFUNCTION**   M 60 MIN
3 3/4 IPS 2 TRACK AUDIO TAPE
SEE SERIES TITLE FOR DESCRIPTIVE STATEMENT.
FROM THE BEHAVIOR DISORDERS OF CHILDREN
SERIES.
PROD-SIGINF   DIST-SIGINF

**CLINICAL ASPECTS OF THE
PSYCHIATRIC MANAGEMENT OF
BURNED AND DISFIGURED
CHILDREN**   M 60 MIN
3 3/4 IPS 2 TRACK AUDIO TAPE
SEE SERIES TITLE FOR DESCRIPTIVE STATEMENT.
FROM THE BEHAVIOR DISORDERS OF CHILDREN
SERIES.
PROD-SIGINF   DIST-SIGINF

**CLINICAL PSYCHOPATHOLOGY--A
SERIES**
PRESENTS EXPERTS WHO CONTRIBUTE THEIR
SPECIAL VIEWPOINTS ON SALIENT ISSUES IN
CLINICAL PSYCHOPATHOLOGY. DISCUSSES THE
USE OF SOMATIC TREATMENTS IN SCHIZOPHRE-
NIA, OUTLINES THE DIAGNOSIS AND TREATMENT
OF PSEUDONEUROTIC SCHIZOPHRENIA, AND
COMMENTS ON THE DIAGNOSIS OF ALCOHOLISM.
INCLUDES A REPORT ON EMERGENCY PSYCHIAT-
RIC TREATMENT AND A DISCUSSION ON
ANOREXIA NERVOSA.
PROD-SIGINF   DIST-SIGINF

DEFINITION OF ALCOHOLISM, THE	60 MIN
DEPRESSION - REACTION OR DISEASE	60 MIN
DIAGNOSIS AND TREATMENT OF PSEUDONEUROTIC --	60 MIN

EMERGENCY PSYCHIATRIC TREATMENT	60 MIN
INPATIENT MANAGEMENT OF BORDERLINE PATIENTS, --	60 MIN
OBSESSIONS AND PHOBIAS	60 MIN
RE-GRIEF WORK FOR THE PATHOLOGICAL MOURNER	60 MIN
RECENT CONTRIBUTIONS TOWARD A THEORY OF PAIN --	60 MIN
REGRESSION AND SEMANTIC SPEECH IN HYSTERIA	60 MIN
SLEEP AND PSYCHOPATHOLOGY	60 MIN
USE OF SOMATIC TREATMENTS IN SCHIZOPHRENIA	60 MIN
WHO CAN BE HYPNOTIZED	60 MIN

**COGNITIVE CONSISTENCY -
PSYCHOSOCIAL ISOMORPHISM**   M 60 MIN
3 3/4 IPS 2 TRACK AUDIO TAPE
SEE SERIES TITLE FOR DESCRIPTIVE STATEMENT.
FROM THE COMPASSION - TOWARD A SCIENCE OF
VALUE SERIES.
PROD-SIGINF   DIST-SIGINF

**COGNITIVE PERFORMANCE -
PROGRESS VS PRODUCT**   M 60 MIN
3 3/4 IPS 2 TRACK AUDIO TAPE
SEE SERIES TITLE FOR DESCRIPTIVE STATEMENT.
FROM THE BEHAVIOR DISORDERS OF CHILDREN
SERIES.
PROD-SIGINF   DIST-SIGINF

COLLEGE OR JOB   M
3 3/4 IPS 2 TRACK AUDIO TAPE
SEE SERIES TITLE FOR DESCRIPTIVE STATEMENT.
FROM THE WHAT'S YOUR PROBLEM SERIES.
PROD-BASCH   DIST-BASCH

**COMPASSION - TOWARD A
SCIENCE OF VALUE--A SERIES**
SURVEYS THE ROLE OF COMPASSION IN THE
GREAT PHILOSOPHIES AND RELIGIONS AND AP-
PLIES IT TO CONTEMPORARY PROBLEMS. PROVES
THE FUNCTION OF VALUE-SYSTEMS IN DIVERSE
AREAS.
PROD-SIGINF   DIST-SIGINF

BEHAVIORISM AND PSYCHOANALYSIS - COGNITIVE --	60 MIN
COGNITIVE CONSISTENCY - PSYCHOSOCIAL --	60 MIN
CONSERVATIVE VS RADICAL BEHAVIORS - --	60 MIN
EXISTENCE THEORY OF PERSONALITY - EMPIRICAL --	60 MIN
EXTRAVERSION AND NEUROTICISM - ORIGINS OF --	60 MIN
FACTS, PRACTICES, THEORIES AND VALUES - A --	60 MIN
HUMANISTIC AND POSITIVIST PHILOSOPHIES OF --	60 MIN
INTRODUCTION - COMPASSION IN GREAT --	60 MIN
KNOWLEDGE OF VALUES - AUTHORITARIAN PERSONALITY	60 MIN
MILITARY-INDUSTRIAL PERSONALITY - COMPASSION --	60 MIN
PHILOSOPHIES OF MAN AND VALUE - SCIENTIFIC --	60 MIN
VALUE-ANALYSES OF POLITICAL IDEOLOGIES	60 MIN

**CONSERVATIVE VS RADICAL
BEHAVIORS - MILITARIST VS
PACIFIST BEHAVIORS**   M 60 MIN
3 3/4 IPS 2 TRACK AUDIO TAPE
SEE SERIES TITLE FOR DESCRIPTIVE STATEMENT.
FROM THE COMPASSION - TOWARD A SCIENCE OF
VALUE SERIES.
PROD-SIGINF   DIST-SIGINF

CONTINGENCY MANAGEMENT   M 60 MIN
3 3/4 IPS 2 TRACK AUDIO TAPE
SEE SERIES TITLE FOR DESCRIPTIVE STATEMENT.
FROM THE BEHAVIOR MODIFICATION STRATEGIES
FOR CHILD PSYCHOTHERAPISTS SERIES.
PROD-SIGINF   DIST-SIGINF

**CURRENT ISSUES AND
PROBLEMS IN SUICIDE
PREVENTION**   M 60 MIN
3 3/4 IPS 2 TRACK AUDIO TAPE
SEE SERIES TITLE FOR DESCRIPTIVE STATEMENT.
FROM THE SUICIDE AND SUICIDE PREVENTION
SERIES.

PROD-SIGINF   DIST-SIGINF

D

DECELERATION TECHNIQUES   M 60 MIN
3 3/4 IPS 2 TRACK AUDIO TAPE
SEE SERIES TITLE FOR DESCRIPTIVE STATEMENT.
FROM THE BEHAVIOR MODIFICATION STRATEGIES
FOR CHILD PSYCHOTHERAPISTS SERIES.
PROD-SIGINF   DIST-SIGINF

**DEFINITION OF ALCOHOLISM,
THE**   M 60 MIN
3 3/4 IPS 2 TRACK AUDIO TAPE
SEE SERIES TITLE FOR DESCRIPTIVE STATEMENT.
FROM THE CLINICAL PSYCHOPATHOLOGY SERIES.
PROD-SIGINF   DIST-SIGINF

**DELINQUENT AND
PROMISCUOUS HOMOSEXUAL
BEHAVIOR**   M 60 MIN
3 3/4 IPS 2 TRACK AUDIO TAPE
SEE SERIES TITLE FOR DESCRIPTIVE STATEMENT.
FROM THE PSYCHOTHERAPY OF ADOLESCENTS SE-
RIES.
PROD-SIGINF   DIST-SIGINF

**DEPRESSION - CLINICAL
PICTURES AND TREATMENT**   M 60 MIN
3 3/4 IPS 2 TRACK AUDIO TAPE
SEE SERIES TITLE FOR DESCRIPTIVE STATEMENT.
FROM THE TOPICS IN CLINICAL PSYCHIATRY SE-
RIES.
PROD-SIGINF   DIST-SIGINF

**DEPRESSION - DIFFERENTIAL
DIAGNOSIS AND RECENT
BIOCHEMISTRY**   M 60 MIN
3 3/4 IPS 2 TRACK AUDIO TAPE
SEE SERIES TITLE FOR DESCRIPTIVE STATEMENT.
FROM THE TOPICS IN CLINICAL PSYCHIATRY SE-
RIES.
PROD-SIGINF   DIST-SIGINF

**DEPRESSION - REACTION OR
DISEASE**   M 60 MIN
3 3/4 IPS 2 TRACK AUDIO TAPE
SEE SERIES TITLE FOR DESCRIPTIVE STATEMENT.
FROM THE CLINICAL PSYCHOPATHOLOGY SERIES.
PROD-SIGINF   DIST-SIGINF

DEPRESSION AND SUICIDE   M 60 MIN
3 3/4 IPS 2 TRACK AUDIO TAPE
SEE SERIES TITLE FOR DESCRIPTIVE STATEMENT.
FROM THE PSYCHOTHERAPY OF ADOLESCENTS SE-
RIES.
PROD-SIGINF   DIST-SIGINF

**DEVELOPMENT OF AGGRESSION
AND AGGRESSION ANXIETY**   M 60 MIN
3 3/4 IPS 2 TRACK AUDIO TAPE
SEE SERIES TITLE FOR DESCRIPTIVE STATEMENT.
FROM THE BEHAVIOR DISORDERS OF CHILDREN
SERIES.
PROD-SIGINF   DIST-SIGINF

**DEVELOPMENTAL CRISES IN
BLACK ADOLESCENTS**   M 60 MIN
3 3/4 IPS 2 TRACK AUDIO TAPE
SEE SERIES TITLE FOR DESCRIPTIVE STATEMENT.
FROM THE NORMAL AND ABNORMAL BEHAVIOR
OF ADOLESCENCE SERIES.
PROD-SIGINF   DIST-SIGINF

**DIAGNOSIS AND TREATMENT OF
PSEUDONEUROTIC
SCHIZOPHRENIA, THE**   M 60 MIN
3 3/4 IPS 2 TRACK AUDIO TAPE
SEE SERIES TITLE FOR DESCRIPTIVE STATEMENT.
FROM THE CLINICAL PSYCHOPATHOLOGY SERIES.
PROD-SIGINF   DIST-SIGINF

**DIAGNOSTIC PROCESS AND THE
PLANNING OF TREATMENT, THE**   M 60 MIN
3 3/4 IPS 2 TRACK AUDIO TAPE
SEE SERIES TITLE FOR DESCRIPTIVE STATEMENT.
FROM THE PSYCHOTHERAPY OF ADOLESCENTS SE-
RIES.
PROD-SIGINF   DIST-SIGINF

DISCONTENTED HOUSEWIFE   M
          3 3/4 IPS 2 TRACK AUDIO TAPE
     SEE SERIES TITLE FOR DESCRIPTIVE STATEMENT.
     FROM THE WHAT'S YOUR PROBLEM SERIES.
PROD-BASCH   DIST-BASCH

DRUG ABUSE - SOMATIC
THERAPIES - PSYCHIATRIC
DISORDERS OF CHILDHOOD   M 60 MIN
          3 3/4 IPS 2 TRACK AUDIO TAPE
     SEE SERIES TITLE FOR DESCRIPTIVE STATEMENT.
     FROM THE PREPARATION FOR CERTIFICATION BY
     THE AMERICAN BOARD OF PSYCHIATRY AND NEU-
     ROLOGY SERIES.
PROD-SIGINF   DIST-SIGINF

E

EGOCENTRISM IN CHILDREN
AND ADOLESCENTS   M 60 MIN
          3 3/4 IPS 2 TRACK AUDIO TAPE
     SEE SERIES TITLE FOR DESCRIPTIVE STATEMENT.
     FROM THE BEHAVIOR DISORDERS OF CHILDREN
     SERIES.
PROD-SIGINF   DIST-SIGINF

EMERGENCY PSYCHIATRIC
TREATMENT   M 60 MIN
          3 3/4 IPS 2 TRACK AUDIO TAPE
     SEE SERIES TITLE FOR DESCRIPTIVE STATEMENT.
     FROM THE CLINICAL PSYCOPATHOLOGY SERIES.
PROD-SIGINF   DIST-SIGINF

EPIDEMIOLOGY - ETIOLOGY -
PSYCHOLOGICAL TESTING -
SCHOOLS OF PSYCHODYNAMIC
THEORY   M 60 MIN
          3 3/4 IPS 2 TRACK AUDIO TAPE
     SEE SERIES TITLE FOR DESCRIPTIVE STATEMENT.
     FROM THE PREPARATION FOR CERTIFICATION BY
     THE AMERICAN BOARD OF PSYCHIATRY AND NEU-
     ROLOGY SERIES.
PROD-SIGINF   DIST-SIGINF

EVOLUTION OF
COMMUNICATION, THE   M 60 MIN
          3 3/4 IPS 2 TRACK AUDIO TAPE
     SEE SERIES TITLE FOR DESCRIPTIVE STATEMENT.
     FROM THE NEW APPROACH TO HUMAN EVOLU-
     TION SERIES.
PROD-SIGINF   DIST-SIGINF

EVOLUTION OF WITHIN-GROUP
COOPERATION, THE   M 60 MIN
          3 3/4 IPS 2 TRACK AUDIO TAPE
     SEE SERIES TITLE FOR DESCRIPTIVE STATEMENT.
     FROM THE NEW APPROACH TO HUMAN EVOLU-
     TION SERIES.
PROD-SIGINF   DIST-SIGINF

EXAMPLES AND DISCUSSION OF
SUICIDE CALLS, PT 1   M 60 MIN
          3 3/4 IPS 2 TRACK AUDIO TAPE
     SEE SERIES TITLE FOR DESCRIPTIVE STATEMENT.
     FROM THE SUICIDE AND SUICIDE PREVENTION
     SERIES.
PROD-SIGINF   DIST-SIGINF

EXAMPLES AND DISCUSSION OF
SUICIDE CALLS, PT 2   M 60 MIN
          3 3/4 IPS 2 TRACK AUDIO TAPE
     SEE SERIES TITLE FOR DESCRIPTIVE STATEMENT.
     FROM THE SUICIDE AND SUICIDE PREVENTION
     SERIES.
PROD-SIGINF   DIST-SIGINF

EXISTENCE THEORY OF
PERSONALITY - EMPIRICAL
STUDIES OF THE SELF CONCEPT
                                   M 60 MIN
          3 3/4 IPS 2 TRACK AUDIO TAPE
     SEE SERIES TITLE FOR DESCRIPTIVE STATEMENT.
     FROM THE COMPASSION - TOWARD A SCIENCE OF
     VALUE SERIES.
PROD-SIGINF   DIST-SIGINF

EXISTENTIAL ASPECTS OF
SEXUAL JEALOUSY   M 60 MIN
          3 3/4 IPS 2 TRACK AUDIO TAPE
     SEE SERIES TITLE FOR DESCRIPTIVE STATEMENT.
     FROM THE IDENTITIES AND AFFINITIES - THE
     PROBLEM OF JUSTICE IN MARRIAGE AND OTHER
     UNIONS SERIES.
PROD-SIGINF   DIST-SIGINF

EXTRAVERSION AND
NEUROTICISM - ORIGINS OF
PERSONALITY TRAITS AND
SOCIAL ATTITUDES   M 60 MIN
          3 3/4 IPS 2 TRACK AUDIO TAPE
     SEE SERIES TITLE FOR DESCRIPTIVE STATEMENT.
     FROM THE COMPASSION - TOWARD A SCIENCE OF
     VALUE SERIES.
PROD-SIGINF   DIST-SIGINF

F

FACT OR FANTASY--A SERIES
     PRESENTS STORIES OF MENTAL PHENOMENA
     THAT CANNOT BE EXPLAINED AWAY IN ANY SET
     FORM.
PROD-BASCH   DIST-BASCH

FACTS, PRACTICES, THEORIES
AND VALUES - A VALUE
THEORY OF TRUTH   M 60 MIN
          3 3/4 IPS 2 TRACK AUDIO TAPE
     SEE SERIES TITLE FOR DESCRIPTIVE STATEMENT.
     FROM THE COMPASSION - TOWARD A SCIENCE OF
     VALUE SERIES.
PROD-SIGINF   DIST-SIGINF

FAMILY SURVIVORS OF SUICIDE
                                   M 60 MIN
          3 3/4 IPS 2 TRACK AUDIO TAPE
     SEE SERIES TITLE FOR DESCRIPTIVE STATEMENT.
     FROM THE SUICIDE AND SUICIDE PREVENTION
     SERIES.
PROD-SIGINF   DIST-SIGINF

FAMILY THERAPY - GROUP
THERAPY - COMMUNITY
PSYCHIATRY   M 60 MIN
          3 3/4 IPS 2 TRACK AUDIO TAPE
     SEE SERIES TITLE FOR DESCRIPTIVE STATEMENT.
     FROM THE PREPARATION FOR CERTIFICATION BY
     THE AMERICAN BOARD OF PSYCHIATRY AND NEU-
     ROLOGY SERIES.
PROD-SIGINF   DIST-SIGINF

FAMILY TREATMENT OF SCHOOL
PHOBIAS   M 60 MIN
          3 3/4 IPS 2 TRACK AUDIO TAPE
     SEE SERIES TITLE FOR DESCRIPTIVE STATEMENT.
     FROM THE BEHAVIOR DISORDERS OF CHILDREN
     SERIES.
PROD-SIGINF   DIST-SIGINF

G

GAY AFFINITIES AND THE
HELPING PROFESSIONS   M 60 MIN
          3 3/4 IPS 2 TRACK AUDIO TAPE
     SEE SERIES TITLE FOR DESCRIPTIVE STATEMENT.
     FROM THE IDENTITIES AND AFFINITIES - THE
     PROBLEM OF JUSTICE IN MARRIAGE AND OTHER
     UNIONS SERIES.
PROD-SIGINF   DIST-SIGINF

GENERAL SYSTEMS -
DIAGNOSTIC CONCEPTS   M 60 MIN
          3 3/4 IPS 2 TRACK AUDIO TAPE
     SEE SERIES TITLE FOR DESCRIPTIVE STATEMENT.
     FROM THE TOPICS IN CLINICAL PSYCHIATRY SE-
     RIES.
PROD-SIGINF   DIST-SIGINF

GENES AND HUMAN EVOLUTION
                                   M 60 MIN
          3 3/4 IPS 2 TRACK AUDIO TAPE
     SEE SERIES TITLE FOR DESCRIPTIVE STATEMENT.
     FROM THE NEW APPROACH TO HUMAN EVOLU-
     TION SERIES.
PROD-SIGINF   DIST-SIGINF

GENES AND INTELLIGENCE   M 60 MIN
          3 3/4 IPS 2 TRACK AUDIO TAPE
     SEE SERIES TITLE FOR DESCRIPTIVE STATEMENT.
     FROM THE NEW APPROACH TO HUMAN EVOLU-
     TION SERIES.
PROD-SIGINF   DIST-SIGINF

GERIATRIC PSYCHIATRY   M 60 MIN
          3 3/4 IPS 2 TRACK AUDIO TAPE
     SEE SERIES TITLE FOR DESCRIPTIVE STATEMENT.
     FROM THE TOPICS IN CLINICAL PSYCHIATRY SE-
     RIES.
PROD-SIGINF   DIST-SIGINF

GOALS FOR BEHAVIOR THERAPY
WITH CHILDREN, THE   M 60 MIN
          3 3/4 IPS 2 TRACK AUDIO TAPE
     SEE SERIES TITLE FOR DESCRIPTIVE STATEMENT.
     FROM THE BEHAVIOR MODIFICATION STRATEGIES
     FOR CHILD PSYCHOTHERAPISTS SERIES.
PROD-SIGINF   DIST-SIGINF

H

HISTORY AND HUMAN
EVOLUTION   M 60 MIN
          3 3/4 IPS 2 TRACK AUDIO TAPE
     SEE SERIES TITLE FOR DESCRIPTIVE STATEMENT.
     FROM THE NEW APPROACH TO HUMAN EVOLU-
     TION SERIES.
PROD-SIGINF   DIST-SIGINF

HOSPITAL MANAGEMENT OF
DISTURBED ADOLESCENTS, THE,
PT 1   M 60 MIN
          3 3/4 IPS 2 TRACK AUDIO TAPE
     SEE SERIES TITLE FOR DESCRIPTIVE STATEMENT.
     FROM THE NORMAL AND ABNORMAL BEHAVIOR
     OF ADOLESCENCE SERIES.
PROD-SIGINF   DIST-SIGINF

HOSPITAL MANAGEMENT OF
DISTURBED ADOLESCENTS, THE,
PT 2   M 60 MIN
          3 3/4 IPS 2 TRACK AUDIO TAPE
     SEE SERIES TITLE FOR DESCRIPTIVE STATEMENT.
     FROM THE NORMAL AND ABNORMAL BEHAVIOR
     OF ADOLESCENCE SERIES.
PROD-SIGINF   DIST-SIGINF

HOW OF A TRICK, THE   S
     1 7/8 IPS AUDIO TAPE CASSETTE   I-J
     EMPHASIZES LISTENING FOR HIDDEN PURPOSES.
     FROM THE LISTENING WITH A PURPOSE SERIES.
PROD-CORF   DIST-CORF

HOW TO ESTABLISH A SUICIDE
PREVENTION PROGRAM   M 60 MIN
          3 3/4 IPS 2 TRACK AUDIO TAPE
     SEE SERIES TITLE FOR DESCRIPTIVE STATEMENT.
     FROM THE SUICIDE AND SUICIDE PREVENTION
     SERIES.
PROD-SIGINF   DIST-SIGINF

HUMANISTIC AND POSITIVIST
PHILOSOPHIES OF SCIENCE   M 60 MIN
          3 3/4 IPS 2 TRACK AUDIO TAPE
     SEE SERIES TITLE FOR DESCRIPTIVE STATEMENT.
     FROM THE COMPASSION - TOWARD A SCIENCE OF
     VALUE SERIES.
PROD-SIGINF   DIST-SIGINF

I

IDENTITIES AND AFFINITIES -
THE PROBLEM OF JUSTICE IN
MARRIAGE AND OTHER UNIONS-
-A SERIES
     PROVIDES A NEW PERSPECTIVE ON THE DISCON-
     CERTING SHIFTS OF SEXUAL MORES AND MORALI-
     TIES IN CURRENT AMERICAN SOCIETY.
PROD-SIGINF   DIST-SIGINF

AFFINITIES OUT OF DESPERATION - THE
'MRS --   60 MIN
BEYOND SEXUAL IDENTITY   60 MIN
CAN LOVE AND SEX SURVIVE THE
ELIMINATION OF --   60 MIN
EXISTENTIAL ASPECTS OF SEXUAL
JEALOUSY   60 MIN
GAY AFFINITIES AND THE HELPING
PROFESSIONS   60 MIN
IDENTITIES AND AFFINITIES - THE
PROBLEM OF --   60 MIN
IS MARRIAGE MORAL   60 MIN
OEDIPUS COMPLEX AND SEXISM, THE   60 MIN
STATE OF THE UNION, PRESENT AND
FUTURE, THE   60 MIN
STILL-UNACCEPTABLE AFFINITIES -
OLDER WOMEN --   60 MIN
TRAUMA OF EVENTLESSNESS, THE   60 MIN
UPROOTING AND ROLE-TRANSFERENCE -
ISSUES OF --   60 MIN

IDENTITIES AND AFFINITIES -
THE PROBLEM OF JUSTICE IN
MARRIAGE AND OTHER UNIONS
                                   M 60 MIN
          3 3/4 IPS 2 TRACK AUDIO TAPE

SEE SERIES TITLE FOR DESCRIPTIVE STATEMENT. FROM THE IDENTITIES AND AFFINITIES - THE PROBLEM OF JUSTICE IN MARRIAGE AND OTHER UNIONS SERIES.
PROD-SIGINF   DIST-SIGINF

INFIDELITY   M
     3 3/4 IPS 2 TRACK AUDIO TAPE
SEE SERIES TITLE FOR DESCRIPTIVE STATEMENT. FROM THE WHAT'S YOUR PROBLEM SERIES.
PROD-BASCH   DIST-BASCH

INFORMATION FOR CANDIDATES - THE FORMAT OF WRITTEN AND ORAL EXAMINATIONS - HOW TO TAKE...   M 60 MIN
     3 3/4 IPS 2 TRACK AUDIO TAPE
SEE SERIES TITLE FOR DESCRIPTIVE STATEMENT. FROM THE PREPARATION FOR CERTIFICATION BY THE AMERICAN BOARD OF PSYCHIATRY AND NEUROLOGY SERIES.
PROD-SIGINF   DIST-SIGINF

INITIAL EVALUATION, THE   M 60 MIN
     3 3/4 IPS 2 TRACK AUDIO TAPE
SEE SERIES TITLE FOR DESCRIPTIVE STATEMENT. FROM THE PSYCHOTHERAPY OF ADOLESCENTS SERIES.
PROD-SIGINF   DIST-SIGINF

INNOVATIVE SERVICES FOR YOUTH   M 60 MIN
     3 3/4 IPS 2 TRACK AUDIO TAPE
SEE SERIES TITLE FOR DESCRIPTIVE STATEMENT. FROM THE NORMAL AND ABNORMAL BEHAVIOR OF ADOLESCENCE SERIES.
PROD-SIGINF   DIST-SIGINF

INPATIENT MANAGEMENT OF BORDERLINE PATIENTS, THE   M 60 MIN
     3 3/4 IPS 2 TRACK AUDIO TAPE
SEE SERIES TITLE FOR DESCRIPTIVE STATEMENT. FROM THE CLINICAL PSYCHOPATHOLOGY SERIES.
PROD-SIGINF   DIST-SIGINF

INSECURITY   M
     3 3/4 IPS 2 TRACK AUDIO TAPE
SEE SERIES TITLE FOR DESCRIPTIVE STATEMENT. FROM THE WHAT'S YOUR PROBLEM SERIES.
PROD-BASCH   DIST-BASCH

INSTINCT PROBLEM, THE   M 60 MIN
     3 3/4 IPS 2 TRACK AUDIO TAPE
SEE SERIES TITLE FOR DESCRIPTIVE STATEMENT. FROM THE NEW APPROACH TO HUMAN EVOLUTION SERIES.
PROD-SIGINF   DIST-SIGINF

INTERGROUP COMPETITION AND PRIMATE EVOLUTION   M 60 MIN
     3 3/4 IPS 2 TRACK AUDIO TAPE
SEE SERIES TITLE FOR DESCRIPTIVE STATEMENT. FROM THE NEW APPROACH TO HUMAN EVOLUTION SERIES.
PROD-SIGINF   DIST-SIGINF

INTRODUCTION - COMPASSION IN GREAT PHILOSOPHIES AND RELIGIONS   M 60 MIN
     3 3/4 IPS 2 TRACK AUDIO TAPE
SEE SERIES TITLE FOR DESCRIPTIVE STATEMENT. FROM THE COMPASSION - TOWARD A SCIENCE OF VALUE SERIES.
PROD-SIGINF   DIST-SIGINF

IS MARRIAGE MORAL   M 60 MIN
     3 3/4 IPS 2 TRACK AUDIO TAPE
SEE SERIES TITLE FOR DESCRIPTIVE STATEMENT. FROM THE IDENTITIES AND AFFINITIES - THE PROBLEM OF JUSTICE IN MARRIAGE AND OTHER UNIONS SERIES.
PROD-SIGINF   DIST-SIGINF

IT TAKES A WOMAN--A SERIES
TELLS THE STORY OF HOW WOMEN HAVE TAKEN THEIR FAMILIES IN HAND, AT MOMENTS WHEN DESPAIR MIGHT HAVE BEFALLEN THEM.
PROD-BASCH   DIST-BASCH

K

KNOWLEDGE OF VALUES - AUTHORITARIAN PERSONALITY   M 60 MIN
     3 3/4 IPS 2 TRACK AUDIO TAPE
SEE SERIES TITLE FOR DESCRIPTIVE STATEMENT. FROM THE COMPASSION - TOWARD A SCIENCE OF VALUE SERIES.
PROD-SIGINF   DIST-SIGINF

L

LAST WORK, THE - REVIEW   S
     1 7/8 IPS AUDIO TAPE CASSETTE   P
SEE SERIES TITLE FOR DESCRIPTIVE STATEMENT. FROM THE WORDS ARE FUN SERIES.
PROD-CORF   DIST-CORF

LEARNING DISABILITIES - PSYCHOTHERAPY AND ADOLESCENT SUBCULTURES   M 60 MIN
     3 3/4 IPS 2 TRACK AUDIO TAPE
SEE SERIES TITLE FOR DESCRIPTIVE STATEMENT. FROM THE PSYCHOTHERAPY OF ADOLESCENTS SERIES.
PROD-SIGINF   DIST-SIGINF

LIMITATIONS OF PSYCHOTHERAPY, THE   M 60 MIN
     3 3/4 IPS 2 TRACK AUDIO TAPE
DISCUSSES STAGES OF LIFE'S WAY AND THE ICHOMSKYAN REVOLUTION AND BEYOND. FROM THE SPECIAL CLINICAL PROBLEMS IN INTENSIVE PSYCHOTHERAPY SERIES.
PROD-SIGINF   DIST-SIGINF

LISTENING WITH A PURPOSE--A SERIES   I-J
COMBINES EXCITING LISTENING WITH ACTIVE PARTICIPATION AS THE STUDENT BECOMES DIRECTLY INVOLVED IN EACH DRAMATIC SITUATION.
PROD-CORF   DIST-CORF

CASE OF THE RED-HEADED LEAGUE
HOW OF A TRICK, THE
MAKING HEADLINES
MESSAGE FROM OUR SPONSOR, A
PEOPLE WATCHING
PROFESSOR STRUDEL'S SECRET FORMULA
SECRET MISSION, THE
TALK OF COLUMBUS, THE
WHAT NOISES SAY
WHAT'S IN THE NEWS
WORD FROM THE WISE, A
YOU BE THE JUDGE

LITTLE NOUN RIDDLES - COMMON NOUNS   S
     1 7/8 IPS AUDIO TAPE CASSETTE   P
SEE SERIES TITLE FOR DESCRIPTIVE STATEMENT. FROM THE WORDS ARE FUN SERIES.
PROD-CORF   DIST-CORF

M

MAKING HEADLINES   S
     1 7/8 IPS AUDIO TAPE CASSETTE   I-J
EMPHASIZES LISTENING FOR MAIN IDEAS. FROM THE LISTENING WITH A PURPOSE SERIES.
PROD-CORF   DIST-CORF

MANAGEMENT OF DRUG ABUSE IN THE OUTPATIENT PSYCHOTHERAPY OF ADOLESCENTS, THE   M 60 MIN
     3 3/4 IPS 2 TRACK AUDIO TAPE
SEE SERIES TITLE FOR DESCRIPTIVE STATEMENT. FROM THE NORMAL AND ABNORMAL BEHAVIOR OF ADOLESCENCE SERIES.
PROD-SIGINF   DIST-SIGINF

MANAGEMENT OF THE DEPENDENT ADOLESCENT   M 60 MIN
     3 3/4 IPS 2 TRACK AUDIO TAPE
SEE SERIES TITLE FOR DESCRIPTIVE STATEMENT. FROM THE PSYCHOTHERAPY OF ADOLESCENTS SERIES.
PROD-SIGINF   DIST-SIGINF

MANAGEMENT OF THE SUICIDAL PERSON   M 60 MIN
     3 3/4 IPS 2 TRACK AUDIO TAPE
SEE SERIES TITLE FOR DESCRIPTIVE STATEMENT. FROM THE SUICIDE AND SUICIDE PREVENTION SERIES.
PROD-SIGINF   DIST-SIGINF

MATCHING NOUNS AND VERBS - NOUN-VERB AGREEMENT   S
     1 7/8 IPS AUDIO TAPE CASSETTE   P
SEE SERIES TITLE FOR DESCRIPTIVE STATEMENT. FROM THE WORDS ARE FUN SERIES.
PROD-CORF   DIST-CORF

MENDING VERB ENDINGS - IRREGULAR VERBS   S
     1 7/8 IPS AUDIO TAPE CASSETTE   P
SEE SERIES TITLE FOR DESCRIPTIVE STATEMENT. FROM THE WORDS ARE FUN SERIES.
PROD-CORF   DIST-CORF

MENTAL AND PHYSICAL, THE   M 60 MIN
     3 3/4 IPS 2 TRACK AUDIO TAPE
DISCUSSES DISSOCIATIVE AND CONVERSION STATES AND 'PSYCHOSOMATIC' DISORDERS. FROM THE SPECIAL CLINICAL PROBLEMS IN INTENSIVE PSYCHOTHERAPY SERIES.
PROD-SIGINF   DIST-SIGINF

MESSAGE FROM OUR SPONSOR, A   S
     1 7/8 IPS AUDIO TAPE CASSETTE   I-J
EMPHASIZES LISTENING FOR ADVERTISING TECHNIQUES. FROM THE LISTENING WITH A PURPOSE SERIES.
PROD-CORF   DIST-CORF

MILITARY-INDUSTRIAL PERSONALITY - COMPASSION VS COMPULSION   M 60 MIN
     3 3/4 IPS 2 TRACK AUDIO TAPE
SEE SERIES TITLE FOR DESCRIPTIVE STATEMENT. FROM THE COMPASSION - TOWARD A SCIENCE OF VALUE SERIES.
PROD-SIGINF   DIST-SIGINF

MISCELLANEOUS TECHNIQUES   M 60 MIN
     3 3/4 IPS 2 TRACK AUDIO TAPE
SEE SERIES TITLE FOR DESCRIPTIVE STATEMENT. FROM THE BEHAVIOR MODIFICATION STRATEGIES FOR CHILD PSYCHOTHERAPISTS SERIES.
PROD-SIGINF   DIST-SIGINF

MORE THAN ONE - NOUN PLURALS   S
     1 7/8 IPS AUDIO TAPE CASSETTE   P
SEE SERIES TITLE FOR DESCRIPTIVE STATEMENT. FROM THE WORDS ARE FUN SERIES.
PROD-CORF   DIST-CORF

MOVIES   M
     3 3/4 IPS 2 TRACK AUDIO TAPE
SEE SERIES TITLE FOR DESCRIPTIVE STATEMENT. FROM THE WHAT'S YOUR PROBLEM SERIES.
PROD-BASCH   DIST-BASCH

MOVING - NEW HOME, NEW NEIGHBORHOOD   M
     3 3/4 IPS 2 TRACK AUDIO TAPE
SEE SERIES TITLE FOR DESCRIPTIVE STATEMENT. FROM THE WHAT'S YOUR PROBLEM SERIES.
PROD-BASCH   DIST-BASCH

MOVING - NEW SCHOOL, NEW PLAYMATES   M
     3 3/4 IPS 2 TRACK AUDIO TAPE
SEE SERIES TITLE FOR DESCRIPTIVE STATEMENT. FROM THE WHAT'S YOUR PROBLEM SERIES.

PROD-BASCH   DIST-BASCH

N

NAME GAMES - PROPER NOUNS
S
1 7/8 IPS AUDIO TAPE CASSETTE   P
SEE SERIES TITLE FOR DESCRIPTIVE STATEMENT. FROM THE WORDS ARE FUN SERIES.
PROD-CORF   DIST-CORF

NEUROSIS, CHARACTER AND BIOLOGY
M 60 MIN
3 3/4 IPS 2 TRACK AUDIO TAPE
DISCUSSES NEUROSIS AND CHARACTER AND THE PSYCHOLOGY OF WOMEN. FROM THE SPECIAL CLINICAL PROBLEMS IN INTENSIVE PSYCHOTHERAPY SERIES.
PROD-SIGINF   DIST-SIGINF

NEW APPROACH TO HUMAN EVOLUTION - INTRODUCTION
M 60 MIN
3 3/4 IPS 2 TRACK AUDIO TAPE
SEE SERIES TITLE FOR DESCRIPTIVE STATEMENT. FROM THE NEW APPROACH TO HUMAN EVOLUTION SERIES.
PROD-SIGINF   DIST-SIGINF

NEW APPROACH TO HUMAN EVOLUTION - SUMMATION AND CONCLUSIONS
M 60 MIN
3 3/4 IPS 2 TRACK AUDIO TAPE
SEE SERIES TITLE FOR DESCRIPTIVE STATEMENT. FROM THE NEW APPROACH TO HUMAN EVOLUTION SERIES.
PROD-SIGINF   DIST-SIGINF

NEW APPROACH TO HUMAN EVOLUTION--A SERIES
CARRIES EVOLUTIONARY CONCEPTS INTO AREAS OF INDIVIDUAL INTELLIGENCE AND SOCIAL INTERACTION. DRAWS ON THE SCIENCES OF COMMUNICATION, GENETICS AND HISTORICAL PERSPECTIVE. EXPLAINS A CHALLENGING NEW HYPOTHESIS UPON HUMAN INSTINCT, COMPETITION AND COOPERATION.
PROD-SIGINF   DIST-SIGINF

BIOLOGICAL EVOLUTION OF INTELLIGENCE, THE   60 MIN
BIOLOGY, MORALITY AND SOCIAL COHESION   60 MIN
EVOLUTION OF COMMUNICATION, THE   60 MIN
EVOLUTION OF WITHIN-GROUP COOPERATION, THE   60 MIN
GENES AND HUMAN EVOLUTION   60 MIN
GENES AND INTELLIGENCE   60 MIN
HISTORY AND HUMAN EVOLUTION   60 MIN
INSTINCT PROBLEM, THE   60 MIN
INTERGROUP COMPETITION AND PRIMATE EVOLUTION   60 MIN
NEW APPROACH TO HUMAN EVOLUTION - INTRODUCTION   60 MIN
NEW APPROACH TO HUMAN EVOLUTION - SUMMATION --   60 MIN
RECENT ATTITUDES TOWARD HUMAN EVOLUTION   60 MIN

NORMAL AND ABNORMAL BEHAVIOR OF ADOLESCENCE-- A SERIES
DEALS WITH ISSUES URGENTLY PERPLEXING EVERY THERAPIST INVOLVED WITH TODAY'S YOUTH AND ANALYZES PSYCHOLOGICAL DEVELOPMENT DURING ADOLESCENCE. PROVIDES INSIGHTS INTO THE DEVELOPMENTAL CRISES OF BLACK ADOLESCENTS AND INVESTIGATES PATTERNS OF DRUG ABUSE AMONG MIDDLE-CLASS ADOLESCENTS.
PROD-SIGINF   DIST-SIGINF

ADOLESCENT WITH A COMMUNICATION DISORDER, THE   60 MIN
ADOLESCENTS AND ADULTS   60 MIN
DEVELOPMENTAL CRISES IN BLACK ADOLESCENTS   60 MIN
HOSPITAL MANAGEMENT OF DISTURBED ADOLESCENTS,--   60 MIN
HOSPITAL MANAGEMENT OF DISTURBED ADOLESCENTS,1   60 MIN
INNOVATIVE SERVICES FOR YOUTH   60 MIN
MANAGEMENT OF DRUG ABUSE IN THE OUTPATIENT --   60 MIN
PATTERNS OF DRUG ABUSE AMONG MIDDLE-CLASS --   60 MIN
PSYCHOLOGICAL DEVELOPMENT DURING ADOLESCENCE   60 MIN
PSYCHOLOGICAL FUNCTIONS OF THE COUNTER CULTURE   60 MIN
SEVERELY NEUROTIC AND THE PSYCHOTIC --   60 MIN

SOCIOLOGIC PERSPECTIVES OF THE MARIJUANA   60 MIN

NOUN MARKERS - ARTICLES
S
1 7/8 IPS AUDIO TAPE CASSETTE   P
SEE SERIES TITLE FOR DESCRIPTIVE STATEMENT. FROM THE WORDS ARE FUN SERIES.
PROD-CORF   DIST-CORF

O

OBSERVATIONAL LEARNING
M 60 MIN
3 3/4 IPS 2 TRACK AUDIO TAPE
SEE SERIES TITLE FOR DESCRIPTIVE STATEMENT. FROM THE BEHAVIOR MODIFICATION STRATEGIES FOR CHILD PSYCHOTHERAPISTS SERIES.
PROD-SIGINF   DIST-SIGINF

OBSESSING AND LEARNING
M 60 MIN
3 3/4 IPS 2 TRACK AUDIO TAPE
DISCUSSES OBSESSING AND LEARNING. FROM THE SPECIAL CLINICAL PROBLEMS IN INTENSIVE PSYCHOTHERAPY SERIES.
PROD-SIGINF   DIST-SIGINF

OBSESSIONS AND PHOBIAS
M 60 MIN
3 3/4 IPS 2 TRACK AUDIO TAPE
SEE SERIES TITLE FOR DESCRIPTIVE STATEMENT. FROM THE CLINICAL PSYCHOPATHOLOGY SERIES.
PROD-SIGINF   DIST-SIGINF

OEDIPUS COMPLEX AND SEXISM, THE
M 60 MIN
3 3/4 IPS 2 TRACK AUDIO TAPE
SEE SERIES TITLE FOR DESCRIPTIVE STATEMENT. FROM THE IDENTITIES AND AFFINITIES - THE PROBLEM OF JUSTICE IN MARRIAGE AND OTHER UNIONS SERIES.
PROD-SIGINF   DIST-SIGINF

ON BECOMING IN-LAWS
M
3 3/4 IPS 2 TRACK AUDIO TAPE
SEE SERIES TITLE FOR DESCRIPTIVE STATEMENT. FROM THE WHAT'S YOUR PROBLEM SERIES.
PROD-BASCH   DIST-BASCH

ON BEING WIDOWED
M
3 3/4 IPS 2 TRACK AUDIO TAPE
SEE SERIES TITLE FOR DESCRIPTIVE STATEMENT. FROM THE WHAT'S YOUR PROBLEM SERIES.
PROD-BASCH   DIST-BASCH

OUR EMOTIONS
M
3 3/4 IPS 2 TRACK AUDIO TAPE
SEE SERIES TITLE FOR DESCRIPTIVE STATEMENT. FROM THE WHAT'S YOUR PROBLEM SERIES.
PROD-BASCH   DIST-BASCH

P

PARENTS AS THERAPEUTIC AGENTS
M 60 MIN
3 3/4 IPS 2 TRACK AUDIO TAPE
SEE SERIES TITLE FOR DESCRIPTIVE STATEMENT. FROM THE BEHAVIOR MODIFICATION STRATEGIES FOR CHILD PSYCHOTHERAPISTS SERIES.
PROD-SIGINF   DIST-SIGINF

PATIENTS WHO BEHAVE BADLY
M 60 MIN
3 3/4 IPS 2 TRACK AUDIO TAPE
DISCUSSES BASICALLY UNSOCIALIZED PATIENTS AND ADDICTED AND PERIODICALLY HYPERINJESTING PATIENTS. FROM THE SPECIAL CLINICAL PROBLEMS IN INTENSIVE PSYCHOTHERAPY SERIES.
PROD-SIGINF   DIST-SIGINF

PATTERNS OF DRUG ABUSE AMONG MIDDLE-CLASS ADOLESCENTS
M 60 MIN
3 3/4 IPS 2 TRACK AUDIO TAPE
SEE SERIES TITLE FOR DESCRIPTIVE STATEMENT. FROM THE NORMAL AND ABNORMAL BEHAVIOR OF ADOLESCENCE SERIES.
PROD-SIGINF   DIST-SIGINF

PEOPLE WATCHING
S
1 7/8 IPS AUDIO TAPE CASSETTE   I-J
EMPHASIZES LISTENING FOR ATTITUDES. FROM THE LISTENING WITH A PURPOSE SERIES.
PROD-CORF   DIST-CORF

PHILOSOPHIES OF MAN AND VALUE - SCIENTIFIC METHODS
M 60 MIN
3 3/4 IPS 2 TRACK AUDIO TAPE
SEE SERIES TITLE FOR DESCRIPTIVE STATEMENT. FROM THE COMPASSION - TOWARD A SCIENCE OF VALUE SERIES.
PROD-SIGINF   DIST-SIGINF

PHOBIC AND ANXIETY STATES
M 60 MIN
3 3/4 IPS 2 TRACK AUDIO TAPE
DISCUSSES THERAPEUTIC UNDERSTANDING AND PSYCHOTHERAPY AND DESENSITIZATION. FROM THE SPECIAL CLINICAL PROBLEMS IN INTENSIVE PSYCHOTHERAPY SERIES.
PROD-SIGINF   DIST-SIGINF

PREPARATION FOR CERTIFICATION BY THE AMERICAN BOARD OF PSYCHIATRY AND NEUROLOGY--A SERIES
PRESENTS INFORMATION AND CONCEPTS BASIC TO THE INFORMED PRACTICE OF PSYCHIATRY.
PROD-SIGINF   DIST-SIGINF

BIBLIOGRAPHY - HOW TO STUDY FOR BOARDS -   60 MIN
DRUG ABUSE - SOMATIC THERAPIES - PSYCHIATRIC --   60 MIN
EPIDEMIOLOGY - ETIOLOGY - PSYCHOLOGICAL --   60 MIN
FAMILY THERAPY - GROUP THERAPY - COMMUNITY --   60 MIN
INFORMATION FOR CANDIDATES - THE FORMAT OF --   60 MIN
PSYCHIATRIC DISORDERS OF CHILDHOOD - CHILD --   60 MIN
PSYCHIATRY AND THE LAW - ALCOHOLISM - DRUG --   60 MIN
SAMPLE EXAMINATIONS - THE CONCEPT OF --   60 MIN
SCHIZOPHRENIA - THE CONCEPT OF NEUROSIS AND --   60 MIN
SCHOOLS OF PSYCHODYNAMIC THEORY - THE HISTORY--   60 MIN
SPECIFIC NEUROSES - SPECIFIC PSYCHOSES - THE --   60 MIN
SUICIDE - HOMICIDE - THE CONCEPT OF --   60 MIN

PRESCHOOL ENRICHMENT AND LEARNING
M 60 MIN
3 3/4 IPS 2 TRACK AUDIO TAPE
SEE SERIES TITLE FOR DESCRIPTIVE STATEMENT. FROM THE BEHAVIOR DISORDERS OF CHILDREN SERIES.
PROD-SIGINF   DIST-SIGINF

PREVENTIVE MENTAL HEALTH WORK WITH PRESCHOOL TEACHERS
M 60 MIN
3 3/4 IPS 2 TRACK AUDIO TAPE
SEE SERIES TITLE FOR DESCRIPTIVE STATEMENT. FROM THE BEHAVIOR DISORDERS OF CHILDREN SERIES.
PROD-SIGINF   DIST-SIGINF

PROBLEMS RESULTING FROM THE DEPRIVATION OF PARENTAL AFFECTION, PT 1
M 60 MIN
3 3/4 IPS 2 TRACK AUDIO TAPE
SEE SERIES TITLE FOR DESCRIPTIVE STATEMENT. FROM THE THERAPY OF COMMON CHILDHOOD DISORDERS SERIES.
PROD-SIGINF   DIST-SIGINF

PROBLEMS RESULTING FROM THE DEPRIVATION OF PARENTAL AFFECTION, PT 2
M 60 MIN
3 3/4 IPS 2 TRACK AUDIO TAPE
SEE SERIES TITLE FOR DESCRIPTIVE STATEMENT. FROM THE THERAPY OF COMMON CHILDHOOD DISORDERS SERIES.
PROD-SIGINF   DIST-SIGINF

PROFESSOR STRUDEL'S SECRET FORMULA
S
1 7/8 IPS AUDIO TAPE CASSETTE   I-J
EMPHASIZES LISTENING TO ANNOUNCEMENTS AND INSTRUCTIONS. FROM THE LISTENING WITH A PURPOSE SERIES.
PROD-CORF   DIST-CORF

PSYCHIATRIC DISORDERS OF CHILDHOOD - CHILD PSYCHOTHERAPY - MARITAL MALADJUSTMENT AND...
M 60 MIN
3 3/4 IPS 2 TRACK AUDIO TAPE
SEE SERIES TITLE FOR DESCRIPTIVE STATEMENT. FROM THE PREPARATION FOR CERTIFICATION BY THE AMERICAN BOARD OF PSYCHIATRY AND NEUROLOGY SERIES.
PROD-SIGINF   DIST-SIGINF

P

**PSYCHIATRY AND THE LAW -
ALCOHOLISM - DRUG ABUSE** M 60 MIN
3 3/4 IPS 2 TRACK AUDIO TAPE
SEE SERIES TITLE FOR DESCRIPTIVE STATEMENT.
FROM THE PREPARATION FOR CERTIFICATION BY
THE AMERICAN BOARD OF PSYCHIATRY AND NEU-
ROLOGY SERIES.
PROD-SIGINF   DIST-SIGINF

**PSYCHOGENIC LEARNING
DISORDERS, PT 1** M 60 MIN
3 3/4 IPS 2 TRACK AUDIO TAPE
SEE SERIES TITLE FOR DESCRIPTIVE STATEMENT.
FROM THE THERAPY OF COMMON CHILDHOOD
DISORDERS SERIES.
PROD-SIGINF   DIST-SIGINF

**PSYCHOGENIC LEARNING
DISORDERS, PT 2** M 60 MIN
3 3/4 IPS 2 TRACK AUDIO TAPE
SEE SERIES TITLE FOR DESCRIPTIVE STATEMENT.
FROM THE THERAPY OF COMMON CHILDHOOD
DISORDERS SERIES.
PROD-SIGINF   DIST-SIGINF

**PSYCHOGENIC LEARNING
DISORDERS, PT 3** M 60 MIN
3 3/4 IPS 2 TRACK AUDIO TAPE
SEE SERIES TITLE FOR DESCRIPTIVE STATEMENT.
FROM THE THERAPY OF COMMON CHILDHOOD
DISORDERS SERIES.
PROD-SIGINF   DIST-SIGINF

**PSYCHOLOGICAL DEVELOPMENT
DURING ADOLESCENCE** M 60 MIN
3 3/4 IPS 2 TRACK AUDIO TAPE
SEE SERIES TITLE FOR DESCRIPTIVE STATEMENT.
FROM THE NORMAL AND ABNORMAL BEHAVIOR
OF ADOLESCENCE SERIES.
PROD-SIGINF   DIST-SIGINF

**PSYCHOLOGICAL FUNCTIONS OF
THE COUNTER CULTURE** M 60 MIN
3 3/4 IPS 2 TRACK AUDIO TAPE
SEE SERIES TITLE FOR DESCRIPTIVE STATEMENT.
FROM THE NORMAL AND ABNORMAL BEHAVIOR
OF ADOLESCENCE SERIES.
PROD-SIGINF   DIST-SIGINF

**PSYCHOLOGICAL REACTIONS TO
DIVORCE, PT 1** M 60 MIN
3 3/4 IPS 2 TRACK AUDIO TAPE
SEE SERIES TITLE FOR DESCRIPTIVE STATEMENT.
FROM THE THERAPY OF COMMON CHILDHOOD
DISORDERS SERIES.
PROD-SIGINF   DIST-SIGINF

**PSYCHOLOGICAL REACTIONS TO
DIVORCE, PT 2** M 60 MIN
3 3/4 IPS 2 TRACK AUDIO TAPE
SEE SERIES TITLE FOR DESCRIPTIVE STATEMENT.
FROM THE THERAPY OF COMMON CHILDHOOD
DISORDERS SERIES.
PROD-SIGINF   DIST-SIGINF

**PSYCHOLOGICAL REACTIONS TO
DIVORCE, PT 3** M 60 MIN
3 3/4 IPS 2 TRACK AUDIO TAPE
SEE SERIES TITLE FOR DESCRIPTIVE STATEMENT.
FROM THE THERAPY OF COMMON CHILDHOOD
DISORDERS SERIES.
PROD-SIGINF   DIST-SIGINF

**PSYCHOTHERAPEUTIC
INTERACTION, THE** M 60 MIN
3 3/4 IPS 2 TRACK AUDIO TAPE
DISCUSSES CLOSENESS AND ENCOUNTER AND
THE FLIGHT FROM PATIENTS. FROM THE SPECIAL
CLINICAL PROBLEMS IN INTENSIVE PSYCHOTHER-
APY SERIES.
PROD-SIGINF   DIST-SIGINF

PSYCHOTHERAPIST, THE M 60 MIN
3 3/4 IPS 2 TRACK AUDIO TAPE
DISCUSSES THE QUALIFICATIONS OF THE PSYCHO-
THERAPIST AND THE METHODS USED BY THE
PSYCHOTHERAPIST. FROM THE SPECIAL CLINICAL
PROBLEMS IN INTENSIVE PSYCHOTHERAPY SE-
RIES.
PROD-SIGINF   DIST-SIGINF

**PSYCHOTHERAPY OF
ADOLESCENTS--A SERIES**
PRESENTS A GUIDE TO TECHNICAL PROBLEMS
UNIQUE IN THE TREATMENT OF ADOLESCENTS.
DEALS WITH TRANSFERENCE DIFFICULTIES, RE-
BELLION, THE DILEMMA OF CONFIDENTIALITY VS
RESPONSIBILITY AND CONFLICTING LOYALTIES
WITHIN THE THERAPIST HIMSELF.
PROD-SIGINF   DIST-SIGINF

ADOLESCENT AND HIS PARENTS, THE 60 MIN
DELINQUENT AND PROMISCUOUS
HOMOSEXUAL -- 60 MIN
DEPRESSION AND SUICIDE 60 MIN
DIAGNOSTIC PROCESS AND THE
PLANNING OF -- 60 MIN
INITIAL EVALUATION, THE 60 MIN
LEARNING DISABILITIES -
PSYCHOTHERAPY AND -- 60 MIN
MANAGEMENT OF THE DEPENDENT
ADOLESCENT 60 MIN
REGRESSION AND ITS PREVENTION 60 MIN
TERMINATION OF THE TREATMENT OF
ADOLESCENTS 60 MIN
THERAPEUTIC ALLIANCE AND THE
EARLY STAGES OF -- 60 MIN
TRANSFERENCE AND
COUNTERTRANSFERENCE 60 MIN
TRANSFERENCE MANIFESTATIONS AND
THEIR -- 60 MIN

R

**RAPUNZEL AND THE GOLDEN
BIRD** M 15 MIN
7 1/2 IPS 1 TRACK AUDIO TAPE   I
TELLS THE STORIES OF 'RAPUNZEL' AND 'THE
GOLDEN BIRD.'
PROD-UTEX   DIST-UTEX

**RE-GRIEF WORK FOR THE
PATHOLOGICAL MOURNER** M 60 MIN
3 3/4 IPS 2 TRACK AUDIO TAPE
SEE SERIES TITLE FOR DESCRIPTIVE STATEMENT.
FROM THE CLINICAL PSYCHOPATHOLOGY SERIES.
PROD-SIGINF   DIST-SIGINF

**RECENT ATTITUDES TOWARD
HUMAN EVOLUTION** M 60 MIN
3 3/4 IPS 2 TRACK AUDIO TAPE
SEE SERIES TITLE FOR DESCRIPTIVE STATEMENT.
FROM THE NEW APPROACH TO HUMAN EVOLU-
TION SERIES.
PROD-SIGINF   DIST-SIGINF

**RECENT CONTRIBUTIONS
TOWARD A THEORY OF PAIN
BEHAVIOR** M 60 MIN
3 3/4 IPS 2 TRACK AUDIO TAPE
SEE SERIES TITLE FOR DESCRIPTIVE STATEMENT.
FROM THE CLINICAL PSYCHOPATHOLOGY SERIES.
PROD-SIGINF   DIST-SIGINF

**REGRESSION AND ITS
PREVENTION** M 60 MIN
3 3/4 IPS 2 TRACK AUDIO TAPE
SEE SERIES TITLE FOR DESCRIPTIVE STATEMENT.
FROM THE PSYCHOTHERAPY OF ADOLESCENTS SE-
RIES.
PROD-SIGINF   DIST-SIGINF

**REGRESSION AND SEMANTIC
SPEECH IN HYSTERIA AND
SCHIZOPHRENIA** M 60 MIN
3 3/4 IPS 2 TRACK AUDIO TAPE
SEE SERIES TITLE FOR DESCRIPTIVE STATEMENT.
FROM THE CLINICAL PSYCHOPATHOLOGY SERIES.
PROD-SIGINF   DIST-SIGINF

RIGHT TO FREEDOM, THE M 15 MIN
7 1/2 IPS 1 TRACK AUDIO TAPE   H A
PRESENTS DR ALICE SOWERS AND HUGH MIX DIS-
CUSSING THE RIGHTS OF PARENTS AS WELL AS
THOSE OF CHILDREN.
PROD-WNAD   DIST-WNAD

S

**SAMPLE EXAMINATIONS - THE
CONCEPT OF SCHIZOPHRENIA** M 60 MIN
3 3/4 IPS 2 TRACK AUDIO TAPE
SEE SERIES TITLE FOR DESCRIPTIVE STATEMENT.
FROM THE PREPARATION FOR CERTIFICATION BY
THE AMERICAN BOARD OF PSYCHIATRY AND NEU-
ROLOGY SERIES.
PROD-SIGINF   DIST-SIGINF

SCHERZO, SYMPHONY NO. 1 M 12 MIN
7 1/2 IPS 1 TRACK AUDIO TAPE   I-C A
FEATURES THE UNIVERSITY OF ILLINOIS BAND
PLAYING 'SCHERZO, SYMPHONY NO. 1,' 'NEWS-
REEL SUITE' AND 'THE POLKA AND FUGUE' FROM
SCHWANDA.
PROD-UILL   DIST-UILL

**SCHIZOPHRENIA - THE
CONCEPT OF NEUROSIS AND
PSYCHOSIS - SPECIFIC
NEUROSES** M 60 MIN
3 3/4 IPS 2 TRACK AUDIO TAPE
FROM THE PREPARATION FOR CERTIFICATION
BY THE AMERICAN BOARD OF PSYCHIATRY AND
NEUROLOGY SERIES.
PROD-SIGINF   DIST-SIGINF

SCHIZOPHRENIC PATIENT, THE M 60 MIN
3 3/4 IPS 2 TRACK AUDIO TAPE
DISCUSSES THERAPEUTIC UNDERSTANDING AND
THERAPEUTIC INTERVENTION. FROM THE SPECIAL
CLINICAL PROBLEMS IN INTENSIVE PSYCHOTHER-
APY SERIES.
PROD-SIGINF   DIST-SIGINF

SCHOOL DROP OUT M
SEE SERIES TITLE FOR DESCRIPTIVE STATEMENT.
FROM THE WHAT'S YOUR PROBLEM SERIES.
PROD-BASCH   DIST-BASCH

**SCHOOLS OF PSYCHODYNAMIC
THEORY - THE HISTORY OF
PSYCHIATRY** M 60 MIN
3 3/4 IPS 2 TRACK AUDIO TAPE
SEE SERIES TITLE FOR DESCRIPTIVE STATEMENT.
FROM THE PREPARATION FOR CERTIFICATION BY
THE AMERICAN BOARD OF PSYCHIATRY AND NEU-
ROLOGY SERIES.
PROD-SIGINF   DIST-SIGINF

SECRET MISSION, THE S
1 7/8 IPS AUDIO TAPE CASSETTE   I-J
EMPHASIZES LISTENING FOR DESCRIPTIONS.
FROM THE LISTENING WITH A PURPOSE SERIES.
PROD-CORF   DIST-CORF

**SELF-ADMINISTERED BEHAVIOR
THERAPY FOR CHILDREN** M 60 MIN
3 3/4 IPS 2 TRACK AUDIO TAPE
SEE SERIES TITLE FOR DESCRIPTIVE STATEMENT.
FROM THE BEHAVIOR MODIFICATION STRATEGIES
FOR CHILD PSYCHOTHERAPISTS SERIES.
PROD-SIGINF   DIST-SIGINF

SELF-ESTEEM PROBLEMS, PT 1 M 60 MIN
3 3/4 IPS 2 TRACK AUDIO TAPE
SEE SERIES TITLE FOR DESCRIPTIVE STATEMENT.
FROM THE THERAPY OF COMMON CHILDHOOD
DISORDERS SERIES.
PROD-SIGINF   DIST-SIGINF

SELF-ESTEEM PROBLEMS, PT 2 M 60 MIN
3 3/4 IPS 2 TRACK AUDIO TAPE
SEE SERIES TITLE FOR DESCRIPTIVE STATEMENT.
FROM THE THERAPY OF COMMON CHILDHOOD
DISORDERS SERIES.
PROD-SIGINF   DIST-SIGINF

**SERVICES OF UNIVERSITY
AUDIO-VISUAL CENTERS** M 15 MIN
7 1/2 IPS 1 TRACK AUDIO TAPE   A
INTRODUCES PROBLEMS OF ADMINISTRATION OF
AUDIO-VISUAL PROGRAMS AT SECONDARY COL-
LEGE LEVELS.
PROD-KENTSU   DIST-KENTSU

**SEVENTEENTH CENTURY
BEGINNING** M 15 MIN
7 1/2 IPS 1 TRACK AUDIO TAPE   J-C
DISCUSSES TODAY'S NEWSPAPER, HOW IT GOT TO
BE WHAT IT IS TODAY AND HOW NEWSPAPERS
DIFFER FROM ONE ANOTHER.
PROD-IU   DIST-IU

**SEVERELY NEUROTIC AND THE
PSYCHOTIC ADOLESCENT, THE** M 60 MIN
3 3/4 IPS 2 TRACK AUDIO TAPE
SEE SERIES TITLE FOR DESCRIPTIVE STATEMENT.
FROM THE NORMAL AND ABNORMAL BEHAVIOR
OF ADOLESCENCE SERIES.
PROD-SIGINF   DIST-SIGINF

**SISSIES AND TOMBOYS - CROSS
GENDER BEHAVIOR IN
CHILDREN** M 60 MIN
3 3/4 IPS 2 TRACK AUDIO TAPE
SEE SERIES TITLE FOR DESCRIPTIVE STATEMENT.
FROM THE BEHAVIOR DISORDERS OF CHILDREN
SERIES.
PROD-SIGINF   DIST-SIGINF

SLEEP AND PSYCHOPATHOLOGY
M 60 MIN
3 3/4 IPS 2 TRACK AUDIO TAPE
SEE SERIES TITLE FOR DESCRIPTIVE STATEMENT.
FROM THE CLINICAL PSYCHOPATHOLOGY SERIES.
PROD-SIGINF   DIST-SIGINF

SLIDE AND FILM EXCHANGE
M 14 MIN
7 1/2 IPS 1 TRACK AUDIO TAPE   H-C
PRESENTS AN INTERVIEW WITH THE LATE B S
AUGHINBAUGH, PIONEER AV LEADER AND FOR
MANY YEARS HEAD OF THE OHIO EDUCATIONAL
EXCHANGE.
PROD-DAVI   DIST-DAVI

SMALL OBSERVATORIES
M 15 MIN
7 1/2 IPS 1 TRACK AUDIO TAPE   H A
FEATURES MR BALFOUR S WHITNEY TALKING ON
HIS INTERPRETATION OF THE SMALL OBSERVA-
TORY AND ITS OPERATION.
PROD-UOKLA   DIST-UOKLA

**SOCIOLOGIC PERSPECTIVES OF
THE MARIJUANA CONTROVERSY**
M 60 MIN
3 3/4 IPS 2 TRACK AUDIO TAPE
SEE SERIES TITLE FOR DESCRIPTIVE STATEMENT.
FROM THE NORMAL AND ABNORMAL BEHAVIOR
OF ADOLESCENCE SERIES.
PROD-SIGINF   DIST-SIGINF

SOUND OF A CITY, THE
M
7 1/2 IPS 1 TRACK AUDIO TAPE   I
PRESENTS A TOUR OF A CITY, STRESSING THE
SOUNDS THAT CAN BE HEARD SUCH AS THAT OF
THE BUYERS IN FARMERS MARKET, THE BUSES
AND A RAINSTORM.
PROD-INSKY   DIST-IU

**SOUND OF THE WAY YOU
LOOK, THE**
M 15 MIN
7 1/2 IPS 1 TRACK AUDIO TAPE   I-J
SHOWS HOW DISCORD IN APPEARANCE CAN GIVE
A BAD IMPRESSION TO OTHERS. POINTS OUT
THAT GOOD GROOMING IS A KEY TO FRIENDS.
PROD-UTEX   DIST-MINNOE

**SPECIAL CLINICAL PROBLEMS
IN INTENSIVE PSYCHOTHERAPY-
-A SERIES**
BRINGS DR RICHARD D CHESSICK'S CONCEPTUAL
AND CLINICAL EXPERTISE TO BEAR ON MANY OF
THE UNIQUE AND CHALLENGING PROBLEMS ARIS-
ING IN THE COURSE OF INTENSIVE PSYCHOTHER-
APY. COVERS SPECIFIC AND EFFECTIVE THERA-
PEUTIC TECHNIQUES.
PROD-SIGINF   DIST-SIGINF

ADOLESCENT PATIENT AND THE
FAMILY, THE   60 MIN
BORDERLINE PATIENT, THE   60 MIN
LIMITATIONS OF PSYCHOTHERAPY, THE 60 MIN
MENTAL AND PHYSICAL, THE   60 MIN
NEUROSIS, CHARACTER AND BIOLOGY 60 MIN
OBSESSING AND LEARNING   60 MIN
PATIENTS WHO BEHAVE BADLY   60 MIN
PHOBIC AND ANXIETY STATES   60 MIN
PSYCHOTHERAPEUTIC INTERACTION,
THE   60 MIN
PSYCHOTHERAPIST, THE   60 MIN
SCHIZOPHRENIC PATIENT, THE   60 MIN
SUICIDE AND DEPRESSION   60 MIN

**SPECIFIC NEUROSES - SPECIFIC
PSYCHOSES - THE CONCEPT OF
DEPRESSION**
M 60 MIN
3 3/4 IPS 2 TRACK AUDIO TAPE
SEE SERIES TITLE FOR DESCRIPTIVE STATEMENT.
FROM THE PREPARATION FOR CERTIFICATION BY
THE AMERICAN BOARD OF PSYCHIATRY AND NEU-
ROLOGY SERIES.
PROD-SIGINF   DIST-SIGINF

SPOTS BEFORE YOUR EYES
M 15 MIN
7 1/2 IPS 1 TRACK AUDIO TAPE   J-C
PRESENTS A VISIT TO A TV STATION TO REVEAL
WHY TV VIEWERS HAVE SPOTS BEFORE THEIR
EYES.
PROD-IU   DIST-IU

**STAMP COLLECTING AND
MATHEMATICIANS**
M 15 MIN
7 1/2 IPS 1 TRACK AUDIO TAPE   H A
SHOWS GREAT MATHEMATICIANS HONORED
THROUGHOUT THE WORLD BY HAVING STAMPS IS-
SUED IN THEIR NAME.
PROD-UOKLA   DIST-UOKLA

**STATE OF THE UNION,
PRESENT AND FUTURE, THE**
M 60 MIN
3 3/4 IPS 2 TRACK AUDIO TAPE
SEE SERIES TITLE FOR DESCRIPTIVE STATEMENT.
FROM THE IDENTITIES AND AFFINITIES - THE
PROBLEM OF JUSTICE IN MARRIAGE AND OTHER
UNIONS SERIES.
PROD-SIGINF   DIST-SIGINF

**STILL-UNACCEPTABLE
AFFINITIES - OLDER WOMEN
YOUNGER MEN LIAISONS**
M 60 MIN
3 3/4 IPS 2 TRACK AUDIO TAPE
SEE SERIES TITLE FOR DESCRIPTIVE STATEMENT.
FROM THE IDENTITIES AND AFFINITIES - THE
PROBLEM OF JUSTICE IN MARRIAGE AND OTHER
UNIONS SERIES.
PROD-SIGINF   DIST-SIGINF

**STRATEGIC IMPORTANCE OF
CIVIL DEFENSE, THE**
M
7 1/2 IPS 1 TRACK AUDIO TAPE   J A
QUESTIONS WHETHER THERE ARE DEFENSE BEN-
EFITS BESIDES INDIVIDUAL.
PROD-NAEB   DIST-NAEB

**STRATEGIES OF CHILD
PSYCHOTHERAPY**
M 60 MIN
3 3/4 IPS 2 TRACK AUDIO TAPE
SEE SERIES TITLE FOR DESCRIPTIVE STATEMENT.
FROM THE BEHAVIOR DISORDERS OF CHILDREN
SERIES.
PROD-SIGINF   DIST-SIGINF

**STRUCTURE OF THE
COMMUNIST PARTY, PT 1**
M 75 MIN
7 1/2 IPS 1 TRACK AUDIO TAPE   A
FEATURES DR FRED C SCHWARZ GIVING A SUM-
MARY OF THE GOALS, METHODS AND STRUC-
TURES OF THE COMMUNIST PARTY.
PROD-PHLSAC   DIST-PHLSAC

**STRUCTURE OF THE
COMMUNIST PARTY, PT 2**
M 75 MIN
7 1/2 IPS 1 TRACK AUDIO TAPE   A
FEATURES DR FRED C SCHWARZ GIVING A SUM-
MARY OF THE GOALS, METHODS AND STRUC-
TURES OF THE COMMUNIST PARTY.
PROD-PHLSAC   DIST-PHLSAC

**SUBSTITUTE GAMES -
PRONOUNS**
S
1 7/8 IPS AUDIO TAPE CASSETTE   P
SEE SERIES TITLE FOR DESCRIPTIVE STATEMENT.
FROM THE WORDS ARE FUN SERIES.
PROD-CORF   DIST-CORF

SUICIDE - AN OVERVIEW
M 60 MIN
3 3/4 IPS 2 TRACK AUDIO TAPE
SEE SERIES TITLE FOR DESCRIPTIVE STATEMENT.
FROM THE SUICIDE AND SUICIDE PREVENTION
SERIES.
PROD-SIGINF   DIST-SIGINF

**SUICIDE - HOMICIDE - THE
CONCEPT OF
PSYCHOPHYSIOLOGIC
DISORDERS**
M 60 MIN
3 3/4 IPS 2 TRACK AUDIO TAPE
SEE SERIES TITLE FOR DESCRIPTIVE STATEMENT.
FROM THE PREPARATION FOR CERTIFICATION BY
THE AMERICAN BOARD OF PSYCHIATRY AND NEU-
ROLOGY SERIES.
PROD-SIGINF   DIST-SIGINF

SUICIDE AND DEPRESSION
M 60 MIN
3 3/4 IPS 2 TRACK AUDIO TAPE
DISCUSSES THE PROBLEM OF SUICIDE AND THER-
APEUTIC UNDERSTANDING OF SUICIDE AND DE-
PRESSION. FROM THE SPECIAL CLINICAL PROB-
LEMS IN INTENSIVE PSYCHOTHERAPY SERIES.
PROD-SIGINF   DIST-SIGINF

**SUICIDE AND SUICIDE
PREVENTION--A SERIES**
REVIEWS THE CURRENT KNOWLEDGE OF SUICIDE
AND SUICIDE PREVENTION. PRESENTS A SURVEY
OF THE ORGANIZATION, PHILOSOPHY AND DAY-
TO-DAY OPERATION OF A SUICIDE PREVENTION
CENTER.
PROD-SIGINF   DIST-SIGINF

ASSESSMENT OF SUICIDAL RISK   60 MIN
CURRENT ISSUES AND PROBLEMS IN
SUICIDE --   60 MIN
EXAMPLES AND DISCUSSION OF
SUICIDE CALLS, PT 1   60 MIN
EXAMPLES AND DISCUSSION OF
SUICIDE CALLS, PT 2   60 MIN
FAMILY SURVIVORS OF SUICIDE   60 MIN

HOW TO ESTABLISH A SUICIDE
PREVENTION PROGRAM   60 MIN
MANAGEMENT OF THE SUICIDAL
PERSON   60 MIN
SUICIDE - AN OVERVIEW   60 MIN
SUICIDE AND THE TERMINALLY ILL 60 MIN
SUICIDE AND VIOLENCE   60 MIN
SUICIDE IN PRISON   60 MIN
SUICIDE, SUICIDE ATTEMPTS AND SELF-
MUTILATION   60 MIN

**SUICIDE AND THE TERMINALLY
ILL**
M 60 MIN
3 3/4 IPS 2 TRACK AUDIO TAPE
SEE SERIES TITLE FOR DESCRIPTIVE STATEMENT.
FROM THE SUICIDE AND SUICIDE PREVENTION
SERIES.
PROD-SIGINF   DIST-SIGINF

SUICIDE AND VIOLENCE
M 60 MIN
3 3/4 IPS 2 TRACK AUDIO TAPE
SEE SERIES TITLE FOR DESCRIPTIVE STATEMENT.
FROM THE SUICIDE AND SUICIDE PREVENTION
SERIES.
PROD-SIGINF   DIST-SIGINF

SUICIDE IN PRISON
M 60 MIN
3 3/4 IPS 2 TRACK AUDIO TAPE
SEE SERIES TITLE FOR DESCRIPTIVE STATEMENT.
FROM THE SUICIDE AND SUICIDE PREVENTION
SERIES.
PROD-SIGINF   DIST-SIGINF

**SUICIDE, SUICIDE ATTEMPTS
AND SELF-MUTILATION**
M 60 MIN
3 3/4 IPS 2 TRACK AUDIO TAPE
SEE SERIES TITLE FOR DESCRIPTIVE STATEMENT.
FROM THE SUICIDE AND SUICIDE PREVENTION
SERIES.
PROD-SIGINF   DIST-SIGINF

**SUITE OF OLD AMERICAN
DANCES**
M 32 MIN
7 1/2 IPS 1 TRACK AUDIO TAPE   I-C A
FEATURES THE UNIVERSITY OF ILLINOIS BAND
PLAYING 'SUITE OF OLD AMERICAN DANCES,'
'CONCERT IN THE PARK' AND 'PORTRAIT OF A
FRONTIER TOWN.'
PROD-UILL   DIST-UILL

SUMMARY AND CONCLUSIONS
M 30 MIN
7 1/2 IPS 1 TRACK AUDIO TAPE   J A
PRESENTS COMMENTS AND CONCLUSIONS CON-
CERNING CIVIL DEFENSE. DISCUSSES ITS MERITS
AND DISADVANTAGES.
PROD-NAEB   DIST-NAEB

SUN SHINES BRIGHT, THE
M 30 MIN
7 1/2 IPS 1 TRACK AUDIO TAPE   H A
TELLS THE DRAMATIC STORY OF CIVIL AWAKEN-
ING ACROSS KENTUCKY TYPIFIED BY A DOCTOR'S
WIFE'S STRUGGLE FOR BETTER RURAL SCHOOLS
AND A VETERAN-STUDENT'S CAMPAIGN FOR LEG-
ISLATIVE REFORMS.
PROD-TCF   DIST-USOE

SWORD AND SICKLE
M 15 MIN
7 1/2 IPS 1 TRACK AUDIO TAPE   I-J
TELLS THE STORY OF THE FEUDAL SYSTEM AND
SERFDOM.
PROD-INSKY   DIST-INSKY

SYLVANIA STORY, THE
M 30 MIN
7 1/2 IPS 1 TRACK AUDIO TAPE   H A
TELLS HOW 51 FARMERS, ACTING TOGETHER TO
SAVE THE GUTTED SOIL INHERITED FROM THEIR
FOREBEARERS, FORM A CONSERVATION DISTRICT
AND DISCOVER A NEW SOLIDARITY.
PROD-TCF   DIST-USOE

SYMPHONY IN B FLAT
M 20 MIN
7 1/2 IPS 1 TRACK AUDIO TAPE   I-C A
FEATURES THE UNIVERSITY OF ILLINOIS BAND
PLAYING FAUCHET'S 'SYMPHONY IN B FLAT.'
PROD-UILL   DIST-UILL

T

TALK OF COLUMBUS, THE
S
1 7/8 IPS AUDIO TAPE CASSETTE   I-J
EMPHASIZES LISTENING TO CONVERSATIONS AND
DISCUSSIONS. FROM THE LISTENING WITH A PUR-
POSE SERIES.
PROD-CORF   DIST-CORF

**TALKING BOOKS FOR THE
BLIND**   M 14 MIN
        7 1/2 IPS 1 TRACK AUDIO TAPE   J A
FEATURES LEON PEARSON DISCUSSING THE TALK-
ING BOOKS FOR THE BLIND WITH ROBERT BAR-
NETT OF THE AMERICAN FOUNDATION FOR THE
BLIND.
PROD-AFB   DIST-AFB

**TEACHERS AS THERAPEUTIC
AGENTS**   M 60 MIN
        3 3/4 IPS 2 TRACK AUDIO TAPE
SEE SERIES TITLE FOR DESCRIPTIVE STATEMENT.
FROM THE BEHAVIOR MODIFICATION STRATEGIES
FOR CHILD PSYCHOTHERAPISTS SERIES.
PROD-SIGINF   DIST-SIGINF

TEACHING FILM   M 30 MIN
        7 1/2 IPS 1 TRACK AUDIO TAPE   H-C
PRESENTS AN INTERVIEW WITH CARL E MILLIKEN,
FORMER HEAD OF TEACHING FILM CUSTODIANS,
INC, CONCERNING THE DEVELOPMENT OF THE
USE OF FILMS FOR TEACHING.
PROD-DAVI   DIST-DAVI

TELEVISION   M
        3 3/4 IPS 2 TRACK AUDIO TAPE
SEE SERIES TITLE FOR DESCRIPTIVE STATEMENT.
FROM THE WHAT'S YOUR PROBLEM SERIES.
PROD-BASCH   DIST-BASCH

**TERMINATION OF THE
TREATMENT OF ADOLESCENTS**   M 60 MIN
        3 3/4 IPS 2 TRACK AUDIO TAPE
SEE SERIES TITLE FOR DESCRIPTIVE STATEMENT.
FROM THE PSYCHOTHERAPY OF ADOLESCENTS SE-
RIES.
PROD-SIGINF   DIST-SIGINF

TERMITES IN THE HOUSE   M 27 MIN
        7 1/2 IPS 1 TRACK AUDIO TAPE   H A
PRESENTS A DOCUMENTARY ON HOUSING DIS-
CRIMINATION IN THE UNITED STATES TODAY.
PROD-AJC   DIST-AJC

THAT YOU MAY KNOW - AGAIN   M 13 MIN
        7 1/2 IPS 1 TRACK AUDIO TAPE   J-C
PRESENTS A SUMMARY OF THE MASS MEDIA OF
COMMUNICATIONS.
PROD-IU   DIST-IU

**THERAPEUTIC ALLIANCE AND
THE EARLY STAGES OF
TREATMENT, THE**   M 60 MIN
        3 3/4 IPS 2 TRACK AUDIO TAPE
SEE SERIES TITLE FOR DESCRIPTIVE STATEMENT.
FROM THE PSYCHOTHERAPY OF ADOLESCENTS SE-
RIES.
PROD-SIGINF   DIST-SIGINF

THERAPEUTIC COMMUNITY, THE
                                      M 60 MIN
        3 3/4 IPS 2 TRACK AUDIO TAPE
SEE SERIES TITLE FOR DESCRIPTIVE STATEMENT.
FROM THE TOPICS IN CLINICAL PSYCHIATRY SE-
RIES.
PROD-SIGINF   DIST-SIGINF

**THERAPY OF COMMON
CHILDHOOD DISORDERS--A
SERIES**
        DETAILS THE APPLICATION OF PSYCHOTHERAPEU-
TIC TECHNIQUES WITH CHILDREN PRESENTING A
WIDE RANGE OF DIFFICULTIES.
PROD-SIGINF   DIST-SIGINF

ANGER INHIBITION PROBLEMS, PT 1   60 MIN
ANGER INHIBITION PROBLEMS, PT 2   60 MIN
PROBLEMS RESULTING FROM THE
DEPRIVATION OF --   60 MIN
PROBLEMS RESULTING FROM THE
DEPRIVATION OF 1-   60 MIN
PSYCHOGENIC LEARNING DISORDERS,
PT 1   60 MIN
PSYCHOGENIC LEARNING DISORDERS,
PT 2   60 MIN
PSYCHOGENIC LEARNING DISORDERS,
PT 3   60 MIN
PSYCHOLOGICAL REACTIONS TO
DIVORCE, PT 1   60 MIN
PSYCHOLOGICAL REACTIONS TO
DIVORCE, PT 2   60 MIN
PSYCHOLOGICAL REACTIONS TO
DIVORCE, PT 3   60 MIN
SELF-ESTEEM PROBLEMS, PT 1   60 MIN
SELF-ESTEEM PROBLEMS, PT 2   60 MIN

THEY CAN'T WAIT   M 26 MIN
        7 1/2 IPS 1 TRACK AUDIO TAPE   H A
DISCUSSES HOW TO GET THE BEST EDUCATION
FOR OUR CHILDREN AND THE PROBLEMS WHICH
FACE PUBLIC EDUCATION.

PROD-AJC   DIST-AJC

**THIRTY YEARS BEHIND A
CAMERA**   M 44 MIN
        7 1/2 IPS 1 TRACK AUDIO TAPE   H-C
PRESENTS A SPEECH ON '30 YEARS BEHIND A
CAMERA' GIVEN BY W F KRUSE, DAVI ARCHIVIST,
BEFORE THE CHICAGO FILM COUNCIL IN FEBRU-
ARY, 1957.
PROD-DAVI   DIST-DAVI

TIME TEASING VERBS - TENSE   S
        1 7/8 IPS AUDIO TAPE CASSETTE   P
SEE SERIES TITLE FOR DESCRIPTIVE STATEMENT.
FROM THE WORDS ARE FUN SERIES.
PROD-CORF   DIST-CORF

TO DIE THAT OTHERS MAY LIVE   M 15 MIN
        7 1/2 IPS 1 TRACK AUDIO TAPE   I
TELLS HOW JESSE LAZEAR CONDUCTED EXPERI-
MENTS ON HIMSELF TO DISCOVER THE CARRIER
OF MALARIA.
PROD-MINSA   DIST-MINSA

TOO YOUNG TO MARRY   M
        3 3/4 IPS 2 TRACK AUDIO TAPE
SEE SERIES TITLE FOR DESCRIPTIVE STATEMENT.
FROM THE WHAT'S YOUR PROBLEM SERIES.
PROD-BASCH   DIST-BASCH

**TOPICS IN CLINICAL
PSYCHIATRY--A SERIES**
        EMPHASIZES THE INTERACTION OF ENVIRONMEN-
TAL AND ORGANISMIC FACTORS IN CLINICAL PSY-
CHIATRY. COVERS THE INTEGRATION OF PSYCHO-
THERAPEUTIC   AND   PSYCHOPHARMACOLOGIC
TECHNIQUES.
PROD-SIGINF   DIST-SIGINF

ACUTE SCHIZOPHRENIA, PT 1   60 MIN
ACUTE SCHIZOPHRENIA, PT 2   60 MIN
CEREBRAL DYSFUNCTION   60 MIN
CEREBRAL DYSFUNCTION - SEIZURE
DISORDERS   60 MIN
CEREBRAL DYSFUNCTION - 14 AND SIX
CYCLES --   60 MIN
DEPRESSION - CLINICAL PICTURES AND
TREATMENT   60 MIN
DEPRESSION - DIFFERENTIAL
DIAGNOSIS AND --   60 MIN
GENERAL SYSTEMS - DIAGNOSTIC
CONCEPTS   60 MIN
GERIATRIC PSYCHIATRY   60 MIN
THERAPEUTIC COMMUNITY, THE   60 MIN
VIOLENCE IN CLINICAL STATES -
SYNDROMES   60 MIN
VIOLENCE IN CLINICAL STATES -
TREATMENT   60 MIN

**TRANSFERENCE AND
COUNTERTRANSFERENCE**   M 60 MIN
        3 3/4 IPS 2 TRACK AUDIO TAPE
SEE SERIES TITLE FOR DESCRIPTIVE STATEMENT.
FROM THE PSYCHOTHERAPY OF ADOLESCENTS SE-
RIES.
PROD-SIGINF   DIST-SIGINF

**TRANSFERENCE
MANIFESTATIONS AND THEIR
MANAGEMENT**   M 60 MIN
        3 3/4 IPS 2 TRACK AUDIO TAPE
SEE SERIES TITLE FOR DESCRIPTIVE STATEMENT.
FROM THE PSYCHOTHERAPY OF ADOLESCENTS SE-
RIES.
PROD-SIGINF   DIST-SIGINF

**TRAUMA OF EVENTLESSNESS,
THE**   M 60 MIN
        3 3/4 IPS 2 TRACK AUDIO TAPE
SEE SERIES TITLE FOR DESCRIPTIVE STATEMENT.
FROM THE IDENTITIES AND AFFINITIES - THE
PROBLEM OF JUSTICE IN MARRIAGE AND OTHER
UNIONS SERIES.
PROD-SIGINF   DIST-SIGINF

U

**UPROOTING AND ROLE-
TRANSFERENCE - ISSUES OF
IDENTITY CRISES IN WIVES**   M 60 MIN
        3 3/4 IPS 2 TRACK AUDIO TAPE
SEE SERIES TITLE FOR DESCRIPTIVE STATEMENT.
FROM THE IDENTITIES AND AFFINITIES - THE
PROBLEM OF JUSTICE IN MARRIAGE AND OTHER
UNIONS SERIES.
PROD-SIGINF   DIST-SIGINF

USE OF BANKS   M 15 MIN
        7 1/2 IPS 1 TRACK AUDIO TAPE   H-C
DISCUSSES THE VARIOUS KINDS OF BANKS, WHAT
SERVICES BANKS PROVIDE AND THE FUNCTIONS
OF BANKS IN OUR ECONOMY.
PROD-INSKY   DIST-INSKY

**USE OF LANTERN SLIDES IN
TEACHING**   M 40 MIN
        7 1/2 IPS 1 TRACK AUDIO TAPE   H-C
PRESENTS AN INTERVIEW WITH RITA HOCHEI-
MER, FORMER HEAD OF THE NEW YORK CITY
SCHOOLS AUDIO-VISUAL PROGRAM AND PIONEER
AV LEADER.
PROD-DAVI   DIST-DAVI

**USE OF SOMATIC TREATMENTS
IN SCHIZOPHRENIA**   M 60 MIN
        3 3/4 IPS 2 TRACK AUDIO TAPE
SEE SERIES TITLE FOR DESCRIPTIVE STATEMENT.
FROM THE CLINICAL PSYCHOPATHOLOGY SERIES.
PROD-SIGINF   DIST-SIGINF

V

**VALUE-ANALYSES OF POLITICAL
IDEOLOGIES**   M 60 MIN
        3 3/4 IPS 2 TRACK AUDIO TAPE
SEE SERIES TITLE FOR DESCRIPTIVE STATEMENT.
FROM THE COMPASSION - TOWARD A SCIENCE OF
VALUE SERIES.
PROD-SIGINF   DIST-SIGINF

**VALUES OF MATHEMATICS IN
SCHOOL CURRICULA**   M 15 MIN
        7 1/2 IPS 1 TRACK AUDIO TAPE   H A
POINTS OUT THAT UTILITY IS NOT THE ONLY PUR-
POSE FOR TAKING SUBJECTS IN SCHOOL, FOR
THESE SUBJECTS INFLUENCE OUR LIVES IN WAYS
NOT OFTEN DIRECTLY NOTICEABLE.
PROD-UOKLA   DIST-UOKLA

**VERB MAZES - ACTION AND
STATE-OF BEING VERBS**   S
        1 7/8 IPS AUDIO TAPE CASSETTE   P
SEE SERIES TITLE FOR DESCRIPTIVE STATEMENT.
FROM THE WORDS ARE FUN SERIES.
PROD-CORF   DIST-CORF

**VIOLENCE IN CLINICAL STATES
- SYNDROMES**   M 60 MIN
        3 3/4 IPS 2 TRACK AUDIO TAPE
SEE SERIES TITLE FOR DESCRIPTIVE STATEMENT.
FROM THE TOPICS IN CLINICAL PSYCHIATRY SE-
RIES.
PROD-SIGINF   DIST-SIGINF

**VIOLENCE IN CLINICAL STATES
- TREATMENT**   M 60 MIN
        3 3/4 IPS 2 TRACK AUDIO TAPE
SEE SERIES TITLE FOR DESCRIPTIVE STATEMENT.
FROM THE TOPICS IN CLINICAL PSYCHIATRY SE-
RIES.
PROD-SIGINF   DIST-SIGINF

W

WAR OR PEACE   M 65 MIN
        7 1/2 IPS 1 TRACK AUDIO TAPE   A
FEATURES WILLIAM P STRUBE SPEAKING ON THE
CHANCES OF COMMUNISM TAKING THE ENTIRE
WORLD WITHOUT WAR AND THE PATH OF RESIS-
TANCE NECESSARY.
PROD-PHLSAC   DIST-PHLSAC

WESTMINISTER BRIDGE   M 30 MIN
        7 1/2 IPS 1 TRACK AUDIO TAPE   C A
PRESENTS A DISCUSSION OF WILLIAM WORDS-
WORTH'S 'WESTMINISTER BRIDGE' WITH HAROLD
WHITEHALL, GEORGE JOHNSON AND SAUL MALICE
OF THE INDIANA UNIVERSITY STAFF.
PROD-IU   DIST-IU

**WHAT ARE AUDIO-VISUAL
MATERIALS**   M 14 MIN
        7 1/2 IPS 1 TRACK AUDIO TAPE   A
PRESENTS A DISCUSSION BY DR EDGAR DALE,
OHIO STATE UNIVERSITY, TO POINT OUT THE
GREAT VARIETY OF AUDIO-VISUAL MATERIALS
AVAILABLE TO TEACHERS.
PROD-OHIOSU   DIST-DAVI

WHAT DOES A POEM MEAN   M 30 MIN
      7 1/2 IPS 1 TRACK AUDIO TAPE   C A
FEATURES REED DRAGONET, POET AND SECRE-
TARY, DISCUSSING WITH FLORENCE BECKER LEN-
NON 'WHAT DOES A POEM MEAN.'
PROD-WEUD   DIST-WEUD

WHAT IS A BOOK   M 12 MIN
      7 1/2 IPS 1 TRACK AUDIO TAPE   I-J
DISCUSSES WHAT GOES INTO THE MAKING OF A
BOOK FROM THE TIME IT IS ONLY AN IDEA IN ONE
MAN'S MIND UNTIL THE MOMENT IT IS READY TO
BE PUT ON A BOOK SHELF.
PROD-INSKY   DIST-INSKY

**WHAT MAKES A HAPPY
MARRIAGE**   M
      3 3/4 IPS 2 TRACK AUDIO TAPE
SEE SERIES TITLE FOR DESCRIPTIVE STATEMENT.
FROM THE WHAT'S YOUR PROBLEM SERIES.
PROD-BASCH   DIST-BASCH

**WHAT MUSIC MEANS TO THE
BLIND**   M 14 MIN
      7 1/2 IPS 1 TRACK AUDIO TAPE   J A
FEATURES MARGARET TRUMAN DISCUSSING
WHAT MUSIC MEANS TO THE BLIND WITH MR
BARNETT AND ALBERT ASENJO OF THE AMERI-
CAN FOUNDATION FOR THE BLIND.
PROD-AFB   DIST-AFB

WHAT NOISES SAY   S
      1 7/8 IPS AUDIO TAPE CASSETTE   I-J
EMPHASIZES LISTENING FOR SOUNDS. ASKS THE
STUDENT TO PLAY THE RADIO GAME WHICH IN-
TRODUCES THE FUNCTIONS OF SOUND EFFECTS
IN 'OLD TIME' RADIO SHOWS. FROM THE LISTEN-
ING WITH A PURPOSE SERIES.
PROD-CORF   DIST-CORF

WHAT SHALL WE LISTEN TO   M 14 MIN
      7 1/2 IPS 1 TRACK AUDIO TAPE   J-C
EXPLAINS HOW TO BE SELECTIVE WHEN CHOOS-
ING PROGRAMS AND HOW TO REALLY LISTEN TO A
PROGRAM.
PROD-IU   DIST-IU

WHAT'S IN THE NEWS   S
      1 7/8 IPS AUDIO TAPE CASSETTE   I-J
EMPHASIZES LISTENING TO REPORTS AND
SPEECHES. FROM THE LISTENING WITH A PUR-
POSE SERIES.
PROD-CORF   DIST-CORF

WHAT'S NEWS   M 14 MIN
      7 1/2 IPS 1 TRACK AUDIO TAPE   J-C
GIVES A DEFINITION OF NEWS AND HOW IT AP-
PLIES TO OUR NEWSPAPERS AND THEIR READ-
ERS.
PROD-IU   DIST-INSKY

**WHAT'S YOUR PROBLEM--A
SERIES**
COVERS SUBJECTS OF LOVE AND LIFE WITH DR
OLGA LITTLE AND DR ROLAND SMITH.
PROD-BASCH   DIST-BASCH

ADOLESCENCE
ALCOHOLISM
BECOMING A PARENT
CAREER WIFE
COLLEGE OR JOB
DISCONTENTED HOUSEWIFE
INFIDELITY
INSECURITY

MOVIES
MOVING - NEW HOME, NEW
NEIGHBORHOOD
MOVING - NEW SCHOOL, NEW
PLAYMATES
ON BECOMING IN-LAWS
ON BEING WIDOWED
SCHOOL DROP OUT
TELEVISION
TOO YOUNG TO MARRY
WHAT MAKES A HAPPY MARRIAGE

WHO CAN BE HYPNOTIZED   M 60 MIN
      3 3/4 IPS 2 TRACK AUDIO TAPE
SEE SERIES TITLE FOR DESCRIPTIVE STATEMENT.
FROM THE CLINICAL PSYCHOPATHOLOGY SERIES.
PROD-SIGINF   DIST-SIGINF

WHO IS THE CENSOR WHAT   M 30 MIN
      7 1/2 IPS 1 TRACK AUDIO TAPE   A
FEATURES DOCTORS VAN DUSEN, BENNET, HYS-
LOP, WAGNER AND DWORKIN DISCUSSING OB-
SCENE LITERATURE AND CENSORSHIP.
PROD-UTS   DIST-UTS

WHO NEEDS CIVIL DEFENSE   M
      7 1/2 IPS 1 TRACK AUDIO TAPE   J A
QUESTIONS WHETHER CIVIL DEFENSE MEASURES
WILL BE AN AID TO EVERYONE OR TO JUST A
SMALL SEGMENT OF THE POPULATION.
PROD-NAEB   DIST-NAEB

WHO PAYS FOR THE NEWS   M 14 MIN
      7 1/2 IPS 1 TRACK AUDIO TAPE   J-C
TELLS WHAT MAKES IT POSSIBLE TO PURCHASE A
NEWSPAPER FOR THE LITTLE WE PAY. SHOWS
HOW ADVERTISING AND SUBSCRIPTION PLAY AN
IMPORTANT PART IN THE NEWSPAPER BUSINESS
AND DESCRIBES THEIR IMPORTANCE TO THE BUS-
INESSMAN.
PROD-IU   DIST-IU

**WHY AN OCEAN - THE OCEAN'S
HISTORY**   M 15 MIN
      7 1/2 IPS 1 TRACK AUDIO TAPE   J-H
FEATURES MATHEW WARREN TELLING ABOUT
THE OCEAN'S HISTORY.
PROD-VOA   DIST-VOA

WOMEN DID IT, THE   M 30 MIN
      7 1/2 IPS 1 TRACK AUDIO TAPE   H A
TELLS HOW WOMEN WORKING AS A GROUP LEAD
A WHOLE COMMUNITY TO CLEAN UP A SLUM
AREA, TO IMPROVE THE CITY GOVERNMENT AND
TO ORGANIZE AN EXPANDED SOCIAL SERVICE.
PROD-TCF   DIST-USOE

**WONDERS OF THE ANCIENT
WORLD**   M 11 MIN
      7 1/2 IPS 1 TRACK AUDIO TAPE   H-C
DESCRIBES THE SEVEN WONDERS OF THE AN-
CIENT WORLD, INCLUDING THE DATE, STYLE AND
MATERIAL USED.
PROD-NGART   DIST-NGART

WORD FROM THE WISE, A   S
      1 7/8 IPS AUDIO TAPE CASSETTE   I-J
EMPHASIZES LISTENING FOR LOGICAL CONCLU-
SIONS. FROM THE LISTENING WITH A PURPOSE
SERIES.
PROD-CORF   DIST-CORF

WORDS ARE FUN--A SERIES   P
REINFORCES STUDENTS' BASIC LANGUAGE SKILLS
BY MAKING IT FUN TO PRACTICE WORD USAGE.
PROD-CORF   DIST-CORF

ADJECTIVE PICTURE PUZZLES -
ADJECTIVES
ADVERB ABILITY - ADVERBS
LAST WORK, THE - REVIEW
LITTLE NOUN RIDDLES - COMMON
NOUNS
MATCHING NOUNS AND VERBS - NOUN-
VERB AGREEMENT
MENDING VERB ENDINGS - IRREGULAR
VERBS
MORE THAN ONE - NOUN PLURALS
NAME GAMES - PROPER NOUNS
NOUN MARKERS - ARTICLES
SUBSTITUTE GAMES - PRONOUNS
TIME TEASING VERBS - TENSE
VERB MAZES - ACTION AND STATE-OF
BEING VERBS

Y

**YANKEE DOODLEBUG AND THE
AW-THAT'S NOTHIN'**   M 15 MIN
      7 1/2 IPS 1 TRACK AUDIO TAPE   P-I
PRESENTS A STORY DEDICATED TO THE PROPOSI-
TION THAT BELITTLING THE POSSESSIONS AND
ACCOMPLISHMENTS OF OTHERS IS NO WAY TO
MAKE FRIENDS WHEN YOU MOVE TO A NEW COM-
MUNITY.
PROD-UTEX   DIST-UTEX.

YOU ARE THE TARGET   M 15 MIN
      7 1/2 IPS 1 TRACK AUDIO TAPE   J-C
DISCUSSES THE USE OF PROPAGANDA ON PUBLIC
OPINION.
PROD-IU   DIST-INSKY

YOU BE THE JUDGE   S
      1 7/8 IPS AUDIO TAPE CASSETTE   I-J
EMPHASIZES LISTENING FOR THE FACTS. FROM
THE LISTENING WITH A PURPOSE SERIES.
PROD-CORF   DIST-CORF

YOU HOLD THE KEY   M 27 MIN
      7 1/2 IPS 1 TRACK AUDIO TAPE   H A
PRESENTS AN APPROACH TO WHAT THE INTERNA-
TIONAL DECLARATION OF HUMAN RIGHTS MEANS
TO AMERICANS.
PROD-AJC   DIST-AJC

**YOUR HANDWRITING IS YOU--A
SERIES**
PRESENTS HANDWRITING ANALYSIS WITH DORO-
THY SARA.
PROD-BASCH   DIST-BASCH

Z

ZANONI   M 27 MIN
      7 1/2 IPS 1 TRACK AUDIO TAPE   I-C A
FEATURES THE UNIVERSITY OF ILLINOIS BAND
PLAYING 'ZANONI,' TWO SONGS FROM PORGY
AND BESS, 'AVE MARIA' AND 'SEA PIECES.'
PROD-UILL   DIST-UILL

ALPHABETICAL GUIDE TO OVERHEAD TRANSPARENCIES

A

A PHILIP RANDOLPH   C
8X10 PREPARED TRANSPARENCY   J-H
FROM THE BIOGRAPHIES OF OUTSTANDING
NEGRO AMERICANS SERIES.
PROD-LEART   DIST-LEART

**ACCUMULATING CAPITAL FOR
INVESTMENTS**   C
8X10 PREPARED TRANSPARENCY   J-H
FROM THE ECONOMICS - ECONOMICS IN
ACTION SERIES.
PROD-LEART   DIST-LEART

ADAM CLAYTON POWELL   C
8X10 PREPARED TRANSPARENCY   J-H
FROM THE BIOGRAPHIES OF OUTSTANDING
NEGRO AMERICANS SERIES.
PROD-LEART   DIST-LEART

**ADDITION AND MULTIPLICATION
OF RADICALS**   C
8X10 PREPARED TRANSPARENCY
FROM THE ALGEBRA, FIRST YEAR - REAL
NUMBERS SERIES.
PROD-LEART   DIST-LEART

**ADDITION OF COMPLEX
NUMBERS**   C
8X10 PREPARED TRANSPARENCY
FROM THE ALGEBRA, SECOND YEAR - COMPLEX
NUMBERS SERIES.
PROD-LEART   DIST-LEART

ADDITION OF FRACTIONS   C
8X10 PREPARED TRANSPARENCY   P-I
FROM THE ELEMENTARY-JUNIOR HIGH
MATHEMATICS SERIES.
PROD-LEART   DIST-LEART

ADDITION TABLE   C
8X10 PREPARED TRANSPARENCY   P-I
FROM THE ELEMENTARY-JUNIOR HIGH
MATHEMATICS SERIES.
PROD-LEART   DIST-LEART

**ADDRESSING ENVELOPES FOR
BUSINESS LETTERS**   I
8X10 PREPARED TRANSPARENCY
SEE SERIES TITLE FOR DESCRIPTIVE STATEMENT.
FROM THE LETTER WRITING SERIES.
PROD-BOW   DIST-BOW

**ADDRESSING ENVELOPES FOR
FRIENDLY LETTERS**   I
8X10 PREPARED TRANSPARENCY
SEE SERIES TITLE FOR DESCRIPTIVE STATEMENT.
FROM THE LETTER WRITING SERIES.
PROD-BOW   DIST-BOW

**ADJECTIVES - POSITIVE,
COMPARATIVE SUPERLATIVE**   C
8X10 PREPARED TRANSPARENCY   I-J
SEE SERIES TITLE FOR DESCRIPTIVE STATEMENT.
FROM THE WORD FORMS AND FUNCTIONS SE-
RIES.
PROD-BOW   DIST-BOW

ADOLESCENT CHANGE   C
8X10 PREPARED TRANSPARENCY   H
SEE SERIES TITLE FOR DESCRIPTIVE STATEMENT.
FROM THE GENERAL TOPICS SERIES.
PROD-BOW   DIST-BOW

**ADVENTURES IN PHONICS--A
SERIES**   P-J
PRESENTS CONSONANT GRAPHEMES. SHOWS
HOW TO INCREASE VOCABULARY AND LISTENING
SKILLS AND IMPROVE ENUNCIATION.
PROD-BOW   DIST-BOW

**ADVERBS - POSITIVE,
COMPARATIVE SUPERLATIVE**   C
8X10 PREPARED TRANSPARENCY   I-J
SEE SERIES TITLE FOR DESCRIPTIVE STATEMENT.
FROM THE WORD FORMS AND FUNCTIONS SE-
RIES.

PROD-BOW   DIST-BOW

**AFTER THE 'TAKE-OFF' - A
DRIVE TO MATURITY**   C
8X10 PREPARED TRANSPARENCY   J-H
FROM THE ECONOMICS - ECONOMIC HISTORY
SERIES.
PROD-LEART   DIST-LEART

AIRPLANE   C
8X10 PREPARED TRANSPARENCY   H
SEE SERIES TITLE FOR DESCRIPTIVE STATEMENT.
FROM THE APPLIED SCIENCE SERIES.
PROD-BOW   DIST-BOW

ALEXANDER DUMAS   C
8X10 PREPARED TRANSPARENCY   J-H
FROM THE BIOGRAPHIES OF OUTSTANDING
NEGRO AMERICANS SERIES.
PROD-LEART   DIST-LEART

**ALGEBRA, FIRST YEAR -
FUNCTIONS--A SERIES**

PROD-LEART   DIST-LEART

DIRECT VARIATION
FUNCTIONS
INVERSE VARIATION
RATIO AND PROPORTION
RELATIONS

**ALGEBRA, FIRST YEAR -
QUADRATIC SENTENCES--A
SERIES**

PROD-LEART   DIST-LEART

NATURE OF ROOTS OF QUADRATIC
EQUATIONS
PROPERTIES OF ROOTS OF QUADRATIC
EQUATIONS
QUADRATIC FORMULA
SOLVING OF QUADRATIC INEQUALITIES
SOLVING QUADRATIC EQUATIONS BY
FACTORING

**ALGEBRA, FIRST YEAR - REAL
NUMBERS--A SERIES**

PROD-LEART   DIST-LEART

ADDITION AND MULTIPLICATION OF
RADICALS
EXTENDING THE NUMBER LINE TO
INCLUDE --
IRRATIONAL NUMBERS
NTH ROOTS
PROPERTIES OF SQUARE ROOTS
RATIONALIZING THE DENOMINATOR
REAL NUMBERS
REPEATING DECIMALS
SIMPLIFYING RADICALS
SQUARE ROOTS

**ALGEBRA, FIRST YEAR - SYSTEM
OF LINEAR EQUATIONS--A
SERIES**

PROD-LEART   DIST-LEART

ALGEBRAIC SOLUTION OF SYSTEMS OF
LINEAR --
GRAPH OF A LINEAR EQUATION IN TWO
VARIABLES
GRAPHICAL SOLUTION OF INEQUALITIES
IN TWO --
GRAPHS OF OPEN SENTENCES IN TWO
VARIABLES
RECTANGULAR COORDINATE SYSTEM
SLOPE INTERCEPT FORM
SLOPE OF THE GRAPH OF AN
EQUATION
SOLUTION SET OF AN OPEN SENTENCE
IN TWO --

**ALGEBRA, FIRST YEAR - WORD
PROBLEMS--A SERIES**

PROD-LEART   DIST-LEART

MIXTURE PROBLEMS
MOTION PROBELMS
WORK PROBLEMS

**ALGEBRA, SECOND YEAR -
ALGEBRAIC EXPRESSIONS --A
SERIES**

PROD-LEART   DIST-LEART

COMBINING ALGEBRAIC FRACTIONS
COMPLEX FRACTIONS
EQUATIONS WITH RATIONAL ALGEBRAIC
EXPRESSIONS
MULTIPLYING AND DIVIDING RATIONAL
ALGEBRAIC --

**ALGEBRA, SECOND YEAR -
COMPLEX NUMBERS--A SERIES**

PROD-LEART   DIST-LEART

ADDITION OF COMPLEX NUMBERS
COMPLEX NUMBERS
CONJUGATE COMPLEX NUMBERS
DISCRIMINANT
MULTIPLICATION OF COMPLEX
NUMBERS
QUADRATIC FORMULA
QUOTIENTS OF COMPLEX NUMBERS
RADICAL EQUATIONS
SUM AND PRODUCT OF ROOTS

**ALGEBRA, SECOND YEAR -
CONICS--A SERIES**

PROD-LEART   DIST-LEART

ALGEBRAIC SOLUTION OF SYSTEM WITH
ONE --
ALGEBRAIC SOLUTION OF SYSTEM WITH
TWO --
CIRCLE
ELLIPSE - DEFINITION
EQUATION AND GRAPHING OF ELLIPSE
GRAPH OF SYSTEM WITH ONE
QUADRATIC AND ONE --
GRAPH OF SYSTEM WITH TWO
QUADRATIC EQUATIONS
HYPERBOLA - DEFINITION
HYPERBOLA - GRAPHING AND
EQUATION
HYPERBOLA OF FORM XY EQUALS K
PARABOLA - DEFINITION AND
EQUATION
PARABOLA - SKETCHING

**ALGEBRA, SECOND YEAR -
DETERMINANTS--A SERIES**

PROD-LEART   DIST-LEART

CRAMER'S RULE
DETERMINANT PROPERTIES FIVE AND
SIX
DETERMINANT PROPERTIES ONE AND
TWO
DETERMINANT PROPERTIES THREE AND
FOUR
DETERMINANT PROPERTY SEVEN
DETERMINANTS - DEFINITION AND
MINORS
EVALUATING DETERMINANTS
EXPANDING A DETERMINANT
USING DETERMINANTS

**ALGEBRA, SECOND YEAR -
FACTORING--A SERIES**

PROD-LEART   DIST-LEART

DIFFERENCE OF TWO SQUARES
FACTORING BY GROUPING
FACTORING BY USING EQUIVALENT
EXPRESSIONS
SUM OR DIFFERENCE OF TWO CUBES

**ALGEBRA, SECOND YEAR -
LINES AND PLANES--A SERIES**

PROD-LEART   DIST-LEART

ALGEBRAIC SOLUTION OF SYSTEM OF
THREE EQUATIONS
GRAPHING A FIRST-DEGREE EQUATION
IN THREE --
GRAPHING SOLUTION OF A SYSTEM OF
THREE --
PARALLEL LINES
PERPENDICULAR LINES
POSSIBLE RELATIONS OF THREE PLANES
IN SPACE
SLOPE OF A STRAIGHT LINE
THREE-DIMENSIONAL COORDINATE
SYSTEM
TWO-POINT AND POINT-SLOPE

WRITING EQUATIONS
WRITING EQUATIONS - EXAMPLES

**ALGEBRA, SECOND YEAR -
LOGARITHMS--A SERIES**

PROD-LEART   DIST-LEART

ANTILOGARITHMS
CALCULATING WITH LOGARITHMS
CHANGING BASES IN LOGARITHMS
COMMON LOGARITHM - TABLES
DEFINITION OF LOGARITHM
EQUATIONS WITH LOGARITHMS AND
EXPONENTS
GRAPH OF Y EQUALS B TO THE X
POWER
INTERPOLATING FOR ANTILOGARITHMS
INTERPOLATION IN TABLES
LINEAR INTERPOLATION
LOGARITHM OF A PRODUCT
LOGARITHM OF A QUOTIENT AND A
POWER

**ALGEBRA, SECOND YEAR -
RADICALS--A SERIES**

PROD-LEART   DIST-LEART

COMBINING RADICAL EXPRESSIONS
IRRATIONAL NUMBERS
PRODUCTS OF ROOTS
RATIONAL EXPONENTS
RATIONAL NUMBERS
ROOTS OF NUMBERS

**ALGEBRA, SECOND YEAR -
SOLUTION PROBLEMS**   C
          8X10 PREPARED TRANSPARENCY
    FROM THE ALGEBRA, SECOND YEAR - WORK
    PROBLEMS SERIES.
PROD-LEART   DIST-LEART

**ALGEBRA, SECOND YEAR -
STRUCTURE OF ALGEBRA-- A
SERIES**

PROD-LEART   DIST-LEART

INVERSE OF SUM AND OF PRODUCT
INVERSES OF EQUALS
MULTIPLICATION PROPERTY OF ZERO
POSTULATES FOR A FIELD
PRODUCTS OF ADDITIVE INVERSES
PROPERTIES OF EQUALITY
PROPERTIES OF EQUATIONS
RIGHT DISTRIBUTIVE PROPERTY
SUBTRACTION AND DIVISION
THEOREMS ON INVERSES, PT 1
THEOREMS ON INVERSES, PT 2
ZERO PRODUCTS

**ALGEBRA, SECOND YEAR -
WORK PROBLEMS**   C
          8X10 PREPARED TRANSPARENCY
    FROM THE ALGEBRA, SECOND YEAR - WORK
    PROBLEMS SERIES.
PROD-LEART   DIST-LEART

**ALGEBRA, SECOND YEAR -
WORK PROBLEMS--A SERIES**

PROD-LEART   DIST-LEART

ALGEBRA, SECOND YEAR - SOLUTION
PROBLEMS
ALGEBRA, SECOND YEAR - WORK
PROBLEMS
BASE TEN DIGIT PROBLEMS
MENSURATION PROBLEMS
MIXTURE, INVESTMENT AND RATIO
PROBLEMS
MOTION PROBLEMS
TWO VELOCITY MOTION PROBLEMS

**ALGEBRAIC SOLUTION OF
SYSTEM OF THREE EQUATIONS**   C
          8X10 PREPARED TRANSPARENCY
    FROM THE ALGEBRA, SECOND YEAR - LINES
    AND PLANES SERIES.
PROD-LEART   DIST-LEART

**ALGEBRAIC SOLUTION OF
SYSTEM WITH ONE QUADRATIC
AND ONE LINEAR**   C
          8X10 PREPARED TRANSPARENCY
    FROM THE ALGEBRA, SECOND YEAR - CONICS
    SERIES.
PROD-LEART   DIST-LEART

**ALGEBRAIC SOLUTION OF
SYSTEM WITH TWO QUADRATIC
EQUATIONS**   C
          8X10 PREPARED TRANSPARENCY
    FROM THE ALGEBRA, SECOND YEAR - CONICS
    SERIES.

PROD-LEART   DIST-LEART

**ALGEBRAIC SOLUTION OF
SYSTEMS OF LINEAR
EQUATIONS**   C
          8X10 PREPARED TRANSPARENCY
    FROM THE ALGEBRA, FIRST YEAR - SYSTEM OF
    LINEAR EQUATIONS SERIES.
PROD-LEART   DIST-LEART

ALTHEA GIBSON   C
          8X10 PREPARED TRANSPARENCY   J-H
    FROM THE BIOGRAPHIES OF OUTSTANDING
    NEGRO AMERICANS SERIES.
PROD-LEART   DIST-LEART

AMOEBA, THE   C
          8X10 PREPARED TRANSPARENCY   I-H
    SEE SERIES TITLE FOR DESCRIPTIVE STATEMENT.
    FROM THE MICROSCOPIC LIFE SERIES.
PROD-BOW   DIST-BOW

ANIMAL CELL TYPES   C
          8X10 PREPARED TRANSPARENCY   I-H
    SEE SERIES TITLE FOR DESCRIPTIVE STATEMENT.
    FROM THE MICROSCOPIC LIFE SERIES.
PROD-BOW   DIST-BOW

ANIMALS OF THE DEEP   C
          8X10 PREPARED TRANSPARENCY   I-H
    SEE SERIES TITLE FOR DESCRIPTIVE STATEMENT.
    FROM THE OCEANOGRAPHY SERIES.
PROD-BOW   DIST-BOW

ANIMALS OF THE OPEN OCEAN   C
          8X10 PREPARED TRANSPARENCY   I-H
    SEE SERIES TITLE FOR DESCRIPTIVE STATEMENT.
    FROM THE OCEANOGRAPHY SERIES.
PROD-BOW   DIST-BOW

ANTILOGARITHMS   C
          8X10 PREPARED TRANSPARENCY
    FROM THE ALGEBRA, SECOND YEAR -
    LOGARITHMS SERIES.
PROD-LEART   DIST-LEART

**APPAREL AND POSTURE AFFECT
YOUR ATTITUDE**   C
          8X10 PREPARED TRANSPARENCY
    SEE SERIES TITLE FOR DESCRIPTIVE STATEMENT.
    FROM THE GOOD GROOMING SERIES.
PROD-COF   DIST-COF

APPLICATION LETTER   C
          8X10 PREPARED TRANSPARENCY
    SEE SERIES TITLE FOR DESCRIPTIVE STATEMENT.
    FROM THE JOB APPLICATION AND JOB INTER-
    VIEW SERIES.
PROD-COF   DIST-COF

APPLIED SCIENCE--A SERIES
                                     H
    PRESENTS VARIOUS SCIENTIFIC PRINCIPLES.
PROD-BOW   DIST-BOW

AIRPLANE
BUOYANCY
COMPUTER
ELECTRICAL SWITCHES
FLIGHT PRINCIPLES
HEATING A HOME
LIFT PUMP
OIL WELL
PHOTOGRAPHY
REFRIGERATION
SYNTHETIC FIBERS
WATER FILTRATION PLANT

AREAS AS COVERING   C
          8X10 PREPARED TRANSPARENCY   P-I
    FROM THE ELEMENTARY GEOMETRY - AREA AS
    A MEASURE OF COVERING SERIES.
PROD-LEART   DIST-LEART

AROUSING INTEREST   C
          8X10 PREPARED TRANSPARENCY
    SEE SERIES TITLE FOR DESCRIPTIVE STATEMENT.
    FROM THE BASIC SALESMANSHIP SERIES.
PROD-COF   DIST-COF

ASSOCIATIVE LAW - GROUPING   C
          8X10 PREPARED TRANSPARENCY   P-I
    FROM THE ELEMENTARY-JUNIOR HIGH
    MATHEMATICS SERIES.
PROD-LEART   DIST-LEART

ASTRONOMY--A SERIES
                                     H
    DISCUSSES VARIOUS PHENOMENONS IN ASTRON-
    OMY.
PROD-BOW   DIST-BOW

DAY AND NIGHT
ECLIPSES
MOON
SEASONS
SOLAR SYSTEMS
STAR CHART

AT THE BEACH   C
          8X10 PREPARED TRANSPARENCY   K-P
    FROM THE LIFE SCIENCE - LIVING SOMEWHERE
    SERIES.
PROD-LEART   DIST-LEART

ATMOSPHERE   C
          8X10 PREPARED TRANSPARENCY   H
    SEE SERIES TITLE FOR DESCRIPTIVE STATEMENT.
    FROM THE WEATHER SERIES.
PROD-BOW   DIST-BOW

ATOMIC ENERGY--A SERIES
                                     H
    PRESENTS A DETAILED EXPLANATION OF ATOMIC
    ENERGY.
PROD-BOW   DIST-BOW

ATOMIC FISSION
ATOMIC FUSION
ATOMIC STRUCTURE
CHEMICAL CHANGE
ENGINES
NUCLEAR REACTOR
PERIODIC CHART

ATOMIC FISSION   C
          8X10 PREPARED TRANSPARENCY   H
    SEE SERIES TITLE FOR DESCRIPTIVE STATEMENT.
    FROM THE ATOMIC ENERGY SERIES.
PROD-BOW   DIST-BOW

ATOMIC FUSION   C
          8X10 PREPARED TRANSPARENCY   H
    SEE SERIES TITLE FOR DESCRIPTIVE STATEMENT.
    FROM THE ATOMIC ENERGY SERIES.
PROD-BOW   DIST-BOW

ATOMIC STRUCTURE   C
          8X10 PREPARED TRANSPARENCY   H
    SEE SERIES TITLE FOR DESCRIPTIVE STATEMENT. ,
    FROM THE ATOMIC ENERGY SERIES.
PROD-BOW   DIST-BOW

ATTITUDES   C
          8X10 PREPARED TRANSPARENCY   H
    FROM THE EMOTIONS AND SOCIAL ATTITUDES -
    ATTITUDES, VALUES SERIES.
PROD-LEART   DIST-LEART

AVOIDING DOUBLE NEGATIVES   C
          8X10 PREPARED TRANSPARENCY   I-J
    SEE SERIES TITLE FOR DESCRIPTIVE STATEMENT.
    FROM THE WORD USAGE SERIES.
PROD-BOW   DIST-BOW

B

BABY AND ME   C
          8X10 PREPARED TRANSPARENCY   K-P
    FROM THE LIFE SCIENCE - GROWING UP
    SERIES.
PROD-LEART   DIST-LEART

BABY ANIMALS   C
          8X10 PREPARED TRANSPARENCY   K-P
    FROM THE LIFE SCIENCE - COMING TO LIFE
    SERIES.
PROD-LEART   DIST-LEART

BABY AT ONE MONTH   C
          8X10 PREPARED TRANSPARENCY
    FROM THE SEX EDUCATION - THE BABY - ITS
    CONCEPTION, GROWTH AND BIRTH SERIES.
PROD-LEART   DIST-LEART

BABY FOR A YEAR   C
          8X10 PREPARED TRANSPARENCY   K-P
    FROM THE LIFE SCIENCE - GROWING UP
    SERIES.
PROD-LEART   DIST-LEART

BACTERIAL CELL TYPES   C
8X10 PREPARED TRANSPARENCY   I-H
SEE SERIES TITLE FOR DESCRIPTIVE STATEMENT.
FROM THE MICROSCOPIC LIFE SERIES.
PROD-BOW   DIST-BOW

BALANCE BEAM SCALE   C
8X10 PREPARED TRANSPARENCY   H
SEE SERIES TITLE FOR DESCRIPTIVE STATEMENT.
FROM THE INSTRUMENTS AND TECHNIQUES OF
SCIENCE SERIES.
PROD-BOW   DIST-BOW

**BANKS ACCUMULATE AND
DISTRIBUTE CAPITAL**   C
8X10 PREPARED TRANSPARENCY   J-H
FROM THE ECONOMICS - ECONOMICS IN
ACTION SERIES.
PROD-LEART   DIST-LEART

BAR GRAPH   C
8X10 PREPARED TRANSPARENCY   P-I
FROM THE ELEMENTARY-JUNIOR HIGH
MATHEMATICS SERIES.
PROD-LEART   DIST-LEART

BASE FOUR   C
8X10 PREPARED TRANSPARENCY   P-I
FROM THE ELEMENTARY-JUNIOR HIGH
MATHEMATICS SERIES.
PROD-LEART   DIST-LEART

**BASE FOUR - ADDING AND
SUBTRACTING**   C
8X10 PREPARED TRANSPARENCY   P-I
FROM THE ELEMENTARY-JUNIOR HIGH
MATHEMATICS SERIES.
PROD-LEART   DIST-LEART

BASE FOUR ADDITION TABLE   C
8X10 PREPARED TRANSPARENCY   P-I
FROM THE ELEMENTARY-JUNIOR HIGH
MATHEMATICS SERIES.
PROD-LEART   DIST-LEART

**BASE FOUR MULTIPLICATION
TABLE**   C
8X10 PREPARED TRANSPARENCY   P-I
FROM THE ELEMENTARY-JUNIOR HIGH
MATHEMATICS SERIES.
PROD-LEART   DIST-LEART

BASE TEN DIGIT PROBLEMS   C
8X10 PREPARED TRANSPARENCY
FROM THE ALGEBRA, SECOND YEAR - WORK
PROBLEMS SERIES.
PROD-LEART   DIST-LEART

BASIC PRINCIPLES   C
8X10 PREPARED TRANSPARENCY   P-I
FROM THE ELEMENTARY-JUNIOR HIGH
MATHEMATICS SERIES.
PROD-LEART   DIST-LEART

BASIC SALESMANSHIP--A SERIES

DEFINES SELLING AND POINTS OUT THE BASIC
CHANNELS OF DISTRIBUTION AND REASONS PEO-
PLE BUY. EXPLORES THE MAJOR STEPS IN A SALE.
PROD-COF   DIST-COF

AROUSING INTEREST
BE CONVINCING
BEFORE YOU MEET THE CUSTOMER
CREATING DESIRE
CUSTOMER ANALYSIS
DO
DON'T
DON'T SAY MAY I HELP YOU
FIVE MAJOR STEPS IN A SALE, THE
FUNCTIONS OF INDIVIDUALS
GAINING ATTENTION
GETTING ACTION
KEEPING UP WITH THE JONESES
OPENING THE SALE
OVERCOMING OBJECTIONS
PRODUCT KNOWLEDGE
SALES DEMONSTRATION CONTEST
SALES FLOW, THE
TURN OBJECTIONS INTO SELLING
POINTS
WHAT IS SELLING
WHEN YOU'RE NOT SELLING

**BASIC SOCIAL STUDIES
CONCEPTS - ECONOMICS--A
SERIES**   J-H

PROD-LEART   DIST-LEART

BUSINESS ORGANIZATION AND
OWNERSHIP
CONSUMPTION AND ECONOMICS
DEFINITION OF ECONOMIC ROLE
ECONOMIC INTERDEPENDENCE OF
PEOPLE
FACTORS OF PRODUCTION
HOW BANKS WORK
HOW DO CHECKS REPLACE MONEY
HOW PRICE IS DETERMINED
LABOR AND ECONOMICS
MONEY - HISTORY, TYPES AND
PURPOSES
NATURAL RESOURCES AND ECONOMICS
TAXES AND THE INDIVIDUAL
TYPES OF MARKET AND EXCHANGES
TYPES OF PRODUCTION
VALUES IN ECONOMIC DECISION
WHAT IS CAPITAL
WHAT IS ECONOMIC GROWTH
WHAT IS ECONOMICS

**BASIC SOCIAL STUDIES
CONCEPTS - POLITICS, SOCIAL-
ECONOMIC INTERDEPENDENCE-
-A SERIES**   J-H

PROD-LEART   DIST-LEART

CULTURE VS CIVILIZATION
INTERACTION OF POLITICAL, SOCIAL
AND ECONOMIC--
MAN'S COMMUNITY EXPANDS
THROUGH THE AGES
SOCIAL INSTITUTIONS AND ECONOMICS
SOCIETIES FORM GOVERNMENTS
WHAT IS SOCIAL STUDIES - AN
INTERDISCIPLINARY--

**BASIC SOCIAL STUDIES
CONCEPTS - SOCIETY--A SERIES**   J-H

PROD-LEART   DIST-LEART

GROUP PRESSURES
HOW CUSTOMS CHANGE
HOW DOES SOCIETY TEACH ITS VALUES
RELIGION AND SOCIETY
SOCIAL INSTITUTIONS MATCH THE LIFE
CYCLE
TYPES OF FAMILIES
WHAT ARE SOCIAL CLASSES
WHAT ARE SOCIAL VALUES AND NORMS
WHAT IS A SOCIAL INSTITUTION
WHAT IS A SOCIETY
WHAT IS AN OPEN SOCIETY
WHY A SOCIETY NEEDS TO STUDY IT'S
PAST

BASIS OF ROMANTIC IDEAL   C
8X10 PREPARED TRANSPARENCY   J
FROM THE DATING RELATIONS - ROMANCE AND
PEOPLE SERIES.
PROD-LEART   DIST-LEART

BATTERIES   C
8X10 PREPARED TRANSPARENCY   H
SEE SERIES TITLE FOR DESCRIPTIVE STATEMENT.
FROM THE MAGNETISM AND ELECTRICITY SERIES.
PROD-BOW   DIST-BOW

BE CONVINCING   C
8X10 PREPARED TRANSPARENCY
SEE SERIES TITLE FOR DESCRIPTIVE STATEMENT.
FROM THE BASIC SALESMANSHIP SERIES.
PROD-COF   DIST-COF

BEANS - BLOOM AND SEED   C
8X10 PREPARED TRANSPARENCY   K-P
FROM THE LIFE SCIENCE - COMING TO LIFE
SERIES.
PROD-LEART   DIST-LEART

**BEFORE YOU MEET THE
CUSTOMER**   C
8X10 PREPARED TRANSPARENCY
SEE SERIES TITLE FOR DESCRIPTIVE STATEMENT.
FROM THE BASIC SALESMANSHIP SERIES.
PROD-COF   DIST-COF

**BEGINNING OF THE CIVIL WAR
- 1860-1861**   C
8X10 PREPARED TRANSPARENCY   I-H
SEE SERIES TITLE FOR DESCRIPTIVE STATEMENT.
FROM THE CIVIL WAR SERIES.
PROD-BOW   DIST-BOW

BEGINNING SKILLS--A SERIES   K-P
PRESENTS ELEMENTARY CONCEPTS IN MATH AND
ENGLISH TO BEGINNING STUDENTS. INCLUDES
STORIES AND RHYMES.
PROD-BOW   DIST-BOW

LEARNING THE ALPHABET
LET'S HAVE A NURSERY RHYME PARTY
ON MY WAY TO SCHOOL I SAW
TELL THE STORY - CHANGE THE
ENDING
TELL THE STORY - MAKE IT RHYME
THREE-DIMENSIONAL LETTER SHAPES
THREE-DIMENSIONAL NUMERALS AND
COUNTING --
THREE-DIMENSIONAL TEN FRAME
THREE-DIMENSIONAL VISUAL
DISCRIMINATION KIT

BEING YOURSELF   C
8X10 PREPARED TRANSPARENCY   J
FROM THE DATING RELATIONS - POPULARITY
SERIES.
PROD-LEART   DIST-LEART

BENJAMIN BENNEKER   C
8X10 PREPARED TRANSPARENCY   J-H
FROM THE BIOGRAPHIES OF OUTSTANDING
NEGRO AMERICANS SERIES.
PROD-LEART   DIST-LEART

BENJAMIN L DAVIS   C
8X10 PREPARED TRANSPARENCY   J-H
FROM THE BIOGRAPHIES OF OUTSTANDING
NEGRO AMERICANS SERIES.
PROD-LEART   DIST-LEART

BILL COSBY   C
8X10 PREPARED TRANSPARENCY   J-H
FROM THE BIOGRAPHIES OF OUTSTANDING
NEGRO AMERICANS SERIES.
PROD-LEART   DIST-LEART

**BIOGRAPHIES OF OUTSTANDING
NEGRO AMERICANS--A SERIES**   J-H

PROD-LEART   DIST-LEART

A PHILIP RANDOLPH
ADAM CLAYTON POWELL
ALEXANDER DUMAS
ALTHEA GIBSON
BENJAMIN BENNEKER
BENJAMIN L DAVIS
BILL COSBY
BLANCHE K BRUCE
BOB GIBSON
BOOKER T WASHINGTON
CARTER G WOODSON
CHARLES DREW
COUNTEE CULLEN
CRISPUS ATTUCKS
DENMARK VESEY
DUKE ELLINGTON
FREDERICK A DOUGLASS
GEORGE WASHINGTON CARVER
GRANVILLE WOODS
GWENDOLYN BROOKS
HARRIET TUBMAN
HARRY BELAFONTE
HENRY O TANNER
JACK JOHNSON
JACKIE ROBINSON
JAMES BROWN
JAMES WELDON JOHNSON
JAN MATZELIGER
JOE LOUIS
LANGSTON HUGHES
LEONTYNE PRICE
LOUIS 'SATCHMO' ARMSTRONG
MAHALIA JACKSON
MALCOLM X
MARCUS GARVEY
MARIAN ANDERSON
MARTIN LUTHER KING
MARY MC LEOD BETHUNE
MATTHEW HENSON
NAT TURNER
PAUL LAURENCE DUNBAR
PHYLLIS WHEATLEY
RALPH J BUNCHE
RICHARD WRIGHT
ROBERT SMALLS
SAMMY DAVIS JR
SIDNEY POITIER
STOKELY CARMICHAEL
THURGOOD MARSHALL
W C HANDY
WILLIAM E B DU BOIS
WILLIE MAYS
WILTON N CHAMBERLAIN

BIRD ADAPTATION   C
   8X10 PREPARED TRANSPARENCY   H
SEE SERIES TITLE FOR DESCRIPTIVE STATEMENT.
FROM THE WARM-BLOODED VERTEBRATES SE-
RIES.
PROD-BOW   DIST-BOW

BIRD EMBRYOLOGY   C
   8X10 PREPARED TRANSPARENCY   H
SEE SERIES TITLE FOR DESCRIPTIVE STATEMENT.
FROM THE WARM-BLOODED VERTEBRATES SE-
RIES.
PROD-BOW   DIST-BOW

BIRD IDENTIFICATION   C
   8X10 PREPARED TRANSPARENCY   H
SEE SERIES TITLE FOR DESCRIPTIVE STATEMENT.
FROM THE WARM-BLOODED VERTEBRATES SE-
RIES.
PROD-BOW   DIST-BOW

BIRD MIGRATION   C
   8X10 PREPARED TRANSPARENCY   H
SEE SERIES TITLE FOR DESCRIPTIVE STATEMENT.
FROM THE WARM-BLOODED VERTEBRATES SE-
RIES.
PROD-BOW   DIST-BOW

BIRD NESTS   C
   8X10 PREPARED TRANSPARENCY   H
SEE SERIES TITLE FOR DESCRIPTIVE STATEMENT.
FROM THE WARM-BLOODED VERTEBRATES SE-
RIES.
PROD-BOW   DIST-BOW

BIRD STRUCTURE   C
   8X10 PREPARED TRANSPARENCY   H
SEE SERIES TITLE FOR DESCRIPTIVE STATEMENT.
FROM THE WARM-BLOODED VERTEBRATES SE-
RIES.
PROD-BOW   DIST-BOW

BIRTH OF THE BABY   C
   8X10 PREPARED TRANSPARENCY
FROM THE SEX EDUCATION - THE BABY - ITS
CONCEPTION, GROWTH AND BIRTH SERIES.
PROD-LEART   DIST-LEART

BLANCHE K BRUCE   C
   8X10 PREPARED TRANSPARENCY   J-H
FROM THE BIOGRAPHIES OF OUTSTANDING
NEGRO AMERICANS SERIES.
PROD-LEART   DIST-LEART

**BLENDS AND DIGRAPHS--A
SERIES**
HELPS THE STUDENT RELATE THE SOUNDS OF
CONSONANT BLENDS AND DIGRAPHS.
PROD-BOW   DIST-BOW

BLOOM TO FRUIT   C
   8X10 PREPARED TRANSPARENCY   K-P
FROM THE LIFE SCIENCE - COMING TO LIFE
SERIES.
PROD-LEART   DIST-LEART

BOB GIBSON   C
   8X10 PREPARED TRANSPARENCY   J-H
FROM THE BIOGRAPHIES OF OUTSTANDING
NEGRO AMERICANS SERIES.
PROD-LEART   DIST-LEART

BONE JOINTS   C
   8X10 PREPARED TRANSPARENCY   H
SEE SERIES TITLE FOR DESCRIPTIVE STATEMENT.
FROM THE HUMAN BODY SERIES.
PROD-BOW   DIST-BOW

BOOKER T WASHINGTON   C
   8X10 PREPARED TRANSPARENCY   J-H
FROM THE BIOGRAPHIES OF OUTSTANDING
NEGRO AMERICANS SERIES.
PROD-LEART   DIST-LEART

BREAKING OFF   C
   8X10 PREPARED TRANSPARENCY   J
FROM THE DATING RELATIONS - DATING
PROBLEMS SERIES.
PROD-LEART   DIST-LEART

**BREAST DEVELOPMENT AND
PURPOSE**   C
   8X10 PREPARED TRANSPARENCY
SEX EDUCATION - DEVELOPMENTAL PATTERNS
OF PUBESCENT GIRLS SERIES.
PROD-LEART   DIST-LEART

**BROAD GOALS OF DISTRIBUTIVE
EDUCATION**   C
   8X10 PREPARED TRANSPARENCY
SEE SERIES TITLE FOR DESCRIPTIVE STATEMENT.
FROM THE ORIENTATION TO DISTRIBUTIVE EDU-
CATION SERIES.
PROD-COF   DIST-COF

BUOYANCY   C
   8X10 PREPARED TRANSPARENCY   H
SEE SERIES TITLE FOR DESCRIPTIVE STATEMENT.
FROM THE APPLIED SCIENCE SERIES.
PROD-BOW   DIST-BOW

**BUSINESS - WHAT COMES
BEFORE PROFIT**   C
   8X10 PREPARED TRANSPARENCY   J-H
FROM THE ECONOMICS - ECONOMICS IN
ACTION SERIES.
PROD-LEART   DIST-LEART

**BUSINESS ORGANIZATION AND
OWNERSHIP**   C
   8X10 PREPARED TRANSPARENCY   J-H
FROM THE BASIC SOCIAL STUDIES CONCEPTS -
ECONOMICS SERIES.
PROD-LEART   DIST-LEART

C

**CALCULATING WITH
LOGARITHMS**   C
   8X10 PREPARED TRANSPARENCY
FROM THE ALGEBRA, SECOND YEAR -
LOGARITHMS SERIES.
PROD-LEART   DIST-LEART

CALENDAR   C
   8X10 PREPARED TRANSPARENCY   P-I
FROM THE ELEMENTARY-JUNIOR HIGH
MATHEMATICS SERIES.
PROD-LEART   DIST-LEART

CAPITALIZATION   C
   8X10 PREPARED TRANSPARENCY   P-I
SEE SERIES TITLE FOR DESCRIPTIVE STATEMENT.
FROM THE PUNCTUATION AND CAPITALIZATION
SERIES.
PROD-BOW   DIST-BOW

**CARD OF INTRODUCTION
(SAMPLE)**   C
   8X10 PREPARED TRANSPARENCY
SEE SERIES TITLE FOR DESCRIPTIVE STATEMENT.
FROM THE JOB APPLICATION AND JOB INTER-
VIEW SERIES.
PROD-COF   DIST-COF

**CARE OF MALE REPRODUCTIVE
ORGANS**   C
   8X10 PREPARED TRANSPARENCY
FROM THE SEX EDUCATION - DEVELOPMENTAL
PATTERNS OF PUBESCENT BOYS SERIES.
PROD-LEART   DIST-LEART

**CARE OF THE BODY DURING
MENSTRUATION**   C
   8X10 PREPARED TRANSPARENCY
SEX EDUCATION - DEVELOPMENTAL PATTERNS
OF PUBESCENT GIRLS SERIES.
PROD-LEART   DIST-LEART

CARS AND DATES   C
   8X10 PREPARED TRANSPARENCY   J
FROM THE DATING RELATIONS - DATING
PROBLEMS SERIES.
PROD-LEART   DIST-LEART

CARTER G WOODSON   C
   8X10 PREPARED TRANSPARENCY   J-H
FROM THE BIOGRAPHIES OF OUTSTANDING
NEGRO AMERICANS SERIES.
PROD-LEART   DIST-LEART

CASUAL-STEADY DATING   C
   8X10 PREPARED TRANSPARENCY   J
FROM THE DATING RELATIONS - DATING
CATEGORIES SERIES.
PROD-LEART   DIST-LEART

**CATEGORIES OF DATING
BEHAVIOR**   C
   8X10 PREPARED TRANSPARENCY   J
FROM THE DATING RELATIONS - DATING
CATEGORIES SERIES.
PROD-LEART   DIST-LEART

**CHANGING BASES IN
LOGARITHMS**   C
   8X10 PREPARED TRANSPARENCY
FROM THE ALGEBRA, SECOND YEAR -
LOGARITHMS SERIES.
PROD-LEART   DIST-LEART

CHAPTER ACTIVITIES   C
   8X10 PREPARED TRANSPARENCY
SEE SERIES TITLE FOR DESCRIPTIVE STATEMENT.
FROM THE DISTRIBUTIVE EDUCATION CLUBS OF
AMERICA SERIES.
PROD-COF   •   DIST-COF

**CHARACTERISTIC OF
DECIDUOUS TREES**   C
   8X10 PREPARED TRANSPARENCY   H
SEE SERIES TITLE FOR DESCRIPTIVE STATEMENT.
FROM THE PLANTS SERIES.
PROD-BOW   DIST-BOW

CHARLES DREW   C
   8X10 PREPARED TRANSPARENCY   J-H
FROM THE BIOGRAPHIES OF OUTSTANDING
NEGRO AMERICANS SERIES.
PROD-LEART   DIST-LEART

CHEMICAL CHANGE   C
   8X10 PREPARED TRANSPARENCY   H
SEE SERIES TITLE FOR DESCRIPTIVE STATEMENT.
FROM THE ATOMIC ENERGY SERIES.
PROD-BOW   DIST-BOW

CIRCLE   C
   8X10 PREPARED TRANSPARENCY   P-I
FROM THE ELEMENTARY-JUNIOR HIGH
MATHEMATICS SERIES.
PROD-LEART   DIST-LEART

CIRCUITS   C
   8X10 PREPARED TRANSPARENCY   H
SEE SERIES TITLE FOR DESCRIPTIVE STATEMENT.
FROM THE MAGNETISM AND ELECTRICITY SERIES.
PROD-BOW   DIST-BOW

CIRCULAR REGION   C
   8X10 PREPARED TRANSPARENCY   P-I
FROM THE ELEMENTARY GEOMETRY - AREA AS
A MEASURE OF COVERING SERIES.
PROD-LEART   DIST-LEART

CIRCULATORY SYSTEM   C
   8X10 PREPARED TRANSPARENCY   H
SEE SERIES TITLE FOR DESCRIPTIVE STATEMENT.
FROM THE HUMAN BODY SERIES.
PROD-BOW   DIST-BOW

CIVIL WAR IN 1862   C
   8X10 PREPARED TRANSPARENCY   I-H
SEE SERIES TITLE FOR DESCRIPTIVE STATEMENT.
FROM THE CIVIL WAR SERIES.
PROD-BOW   DIST-BOW

CIVIL WAR IN 1863   C
   8X10 PREPARED TRANSPARENCY   I-H
SEE SERIES TITLE FOR DESCRIPTIVE STATEMENT.
FROM THE CIVIL WAR SERIES.
PROD-BOW   DIST-BOW

CIVIL WAR IN 1864   C
   8X10 PREPARED TRANSPARENCY   I-H
SEE SERIES TITLE FOR DESCRIPTIVE STATEMENT.
FROM THE CIVIL WAR SERIES.
PROD-BOW   DIST-BOW

CIVIL WAR IN 1865   C
   8X10 PREPARED TRANSPARENCY   I-H
SEE SERIES TITLE FOR DESCRIPTIVE STATEMENT.
FROM THE CIVIL WAR SERIES.
PROD-BOW   DIST-BOW

CIVIL WAR--A SERIES   I-H

PRESENTS THE CIVIL WAR.
PROD-BOW   DIST-BOW

BEGINNING OF THE CIVIL WAR - 1860-
1861
CIVIL WAR IN 1862
CIVIL WAR IN 1863

CIVIL WAR IN 1864
CIVIL WAR IN 1865

CLASSIFICATION   C
   8X10 PREPARED TRANSPARENCY   H
   SEE SERIES TITLE FOR DESCRIPTIVE STATEMENT.
   FROM THE PLANTS SERIES.
PROD-BOW   DIST-BOW

**CLASSIFICATION-OPPOSITES-
SEQUENCES--A SERIES**   C 5 OVL
   8X10 PREPARED TRANSPARENCY
   PRESENTS SEQUENCE STORIES AND THINGS THAT
   GO TOGETHER.
PROD-BOW   DIST-BOW

**CLASSROOM-LABORATORY
ACTIVITIES**   C
   8X10 PREPARED TRANSPARENCY
   SEE SERIES TITLE FOR DESCRIPTIVE STATEMENT.
   FROM THE ORIENTATION TO DISTRIBUTIVE EDU-
   CATION SERIES.
PROD-COF   DIST-COF

**CLEANLINESS INFLUENCES
HEALTH**   C
   8X10 PREPARED TRANSPARENCY
   FROM THE SEX EDUCATION - PHYSICAL CARE
   AND SELF RESPECT SERIES.
PROD-LEART   DIST-LEART

CLIMATE   C
   8X10 PREPARED TRANSPARENCY   H
   SEE SERIES TITLE FOR DESCRIPTIVE STATEMENT.
   FROM THE WEATHER SERIES.
PROD-BOW   DIST-BOW

CLOCK   C
   8X10 PREPARED TRANSPARENCY   P-I
   FROM THE ELEMENTARY-JUNIOR HIGH
   MATHEMATICS SERIES.
PROD-LEART   DIST-LEART

CLOUDS   C
   8X10 PREPARED TRANSPARENCY   H
   SEE SERIES TITLE FOR DESCRIPTIVE STATEMENT.
   FROM THE WEATHER SERIES.
PROD-BOW   DIST-BOW

CLUB ACTIVITIES   C
   8X10 PREPARED TRANSPARENCY
   SEE SERIES TITLE FOR DESCRIPTIVE STATEMENT.
   FROM THE ORIENTATION TO DISTRIBUTIVE EDU-
   CATION SERIES.
PROD-COF   DIST-COF

COLONIES TO INDEPENDENCE   C
   8X10 PREPARED TRANSPARENCY   J-H
   FROM THE POLITICAL GEOGRAPHY AND
   NATIONALISM OF AFRICA SERIES.
PROD-LEART   DIST-LEART

COLOR WHEEL   C
   8X10 PREPARED TRANSPARENCY   I-H
   SEE SERIES TITLE FOR DESCRIPTIVE STATEMENT.
   FROM THE LIGHT AND COLOR SERIES.
PROD-BOW   DIST-BOW

**COMBINING ALGEBRAIC
FRACTIONS**   C
   8X10 PREPARED TRANSPARENCY
   FROM THE ALGEBRA, SECOND YEAR -
   ALGEBRAIC EXPRESSIONS SERIES.
PROD-LEART   DIST-LEART

COMBINING COLORS   C
   8X10 PREPARED TRANSPARENCY   I-H
   SEE SERIES TITLE FOR DESCRIPTIVE STATEMENT.
   FROM THE LIGHT AND COLOR SERIES.
PROD-BOW   DIST-BOW

**COMBINING RADICAL
EXPRESSIONS**   C
   8X10 PREPARED TRANSPARENCY
   FROM THE ALGEBRA, SECOND YEAR - RADICALS
   SERIES.
PROD-LEART   DIST-LEART

**COMMAS IN SERIES AND IN
DIRECT ADDRESS**   C
   8X10 PREPARED TRANSPARENCY   P-I
   SEE SERIES TITLE FOR DESCRIPTIVE STATEMENT.
   FROM THE PUNCTUATION AND CAPITALIZATION
   SERIES.
PROD-BOW   DIST-BOW

COMMON LOGARITHM - TABLES   C
   8X10 PREPARED TRANSPARENCY
   FROM THE ALGEBRA, SECOND YEAR -
   LOGARITHMS SERIES.
PROD-LEART   DIST-LEART

COMMUNICATION CONFUSION   C
   8X10 PREPARED TRANSPARENCY   J
   FROM THE DATING RELATIONS - EVALUATING
   DATING BEHAVIOR SERIES.
PROD-LEART   DIST-LEART

COMMUTATIVE LAW   C
   8X10 PREPARED TRANSPARENCY   P-I
   FROM THE ELEMENTARY-JUNIOR HIGH
   MATHEMATICS SERIES.
PROD-LEART   DIST-LEART

**COMPARATIVE SIZES - BOYS
AND GIRLS 11 YEARS**   C
   8X10 PREPARED TRANSPARENCY
   FROM THE SEX EDUCATION - GROWTH AND
   THE ENDOCRINE GLANDS SERIES.
PROD-LEART   DIST-LEART

**COMPARATIVE SIZES - BOYS
AND GIRLS 12 YEARS**   C
   8X10 PREPARED TRANSPARENCY
   FROM THE SEX EDUCATION - GROWTH AND
   THE ENDOCRINE GLANDS SERIES.
PROD-LEART   DIST-LEART

**COMPARATIVE SIZES - BOYS
AND GIRLS 13 YEARS**   C
   8X10 PREPARED TRANSPARENCY
   FROM THE SEX EDUCATION - GROWTH AND
   THE ENDOCRINE GLANDS SERIES.
PROD-LEART   DIST-LEART

**COMPARATIVE SIZES - BOYS
AND GIRLS 14 YEARS**   C
   8X10 PREPARED TRANSPARENCY
   FROM THE SEX EDUCATION - GROWTH AND
   THE ENDOCRINE GLANDS SERIES.
PROD-LEART   DIST-LEART

COMPARE VIEWPOINTS   C
   8X10 PREPARED TRANSPARENCY
   SEE SERIES TITLE FOR DESCRIPTIVE STATEMENT.
   FROM THE JOB APPLICATION AND JOB INTER-
   VIEW SERIES.
PROD-COF   DIST-COF

**COMPARING SIMPLE AND
COMPOUND VERBS**   C
   8X10 PREPARED TRANSPARENCY   I-J
   SEE SERIES TITLE FOR DESCRIPTIVE STATEMENT.
   FROM THE WORD FORMS AND FUNCTIONS SE-
   RIES.
PROD-BOW   DIST-BOW

COMPASS   C
   8X10 PREPARED TRANSPARENCY   H
   SEE SERIES TITLE FOR DESCRIPTIVE STATEMENT.
   FROM THE MAGNETISM AND ELECTRICITY SERIES.
PROD-BOW   DIST-BOW

COMPLEX FRACTIONS   C
   8X10 PREPARED TRANSPARENCY
   FROM THE ALGEBRA, SECOND YEAR -
   ALGEBRAIC EXPRESSIONS SERIES.
PROD-LEART   DIST-LEART

COMPLEX NUMBERS   C
   8X10 PREPARED TRANSPARENCY
   FROM THE ALGEBRA, SECOND YEAR - COMPLEX
   NUMBERS SERIES.
PROD-LEART   DIST-LEART

COMPLEXITY OF LOVE   C
   8X10 PREPARED TRANSPARENCY   J
   FROM THE DATING RELATIONS - MATURE LOVE
   SERIES.
PROD-LEART   DIST-LEART

**COMPROMISE RESULTING IN
THE TWO-HOUSE LEGISLATURE**   C
   8X10 PREPARED TRANSPARENCY   J-H
   FROM THE UNITED STATES GOVERNMENT AND
   HOW IT WORKS SERIES.
PROD-LEART   DIST-LEART

COMPUTER   C
   8X10 PREPARED TRANSPARENCY   H
   SEE SERIES TITLE FOR DESCRIPTIVE STATEMENT.
   FROM THE APPLIED SCIENCE SERIES.
PROD-BOW   DIST-BOW

**CONJUGATE COMPLEX
NUMBERS**   C
   8X10 PREPARED TRANSPARENCY
   FROM THE ALGEBRA, SECOND YEAR - COMPLEX
   NUMBERS SERIES.
PROD-LEART   DIST-LEART

CONSERVATION--A SERIES
                                                          H
   DISCUSSES THE VARIOUS ASPECTS OF CONSERVA-
   TION.
PROD-BOW   DIST-BOW

EROSION
FLOODING
FOREST FIRE
NATURAL RESOURCES
POLLUTION
SOIL DEPLETION

**CONSONANTS WITH TWO
SOUNDS--A SERIES**
   INTRODUCES A READING PROGRAM WHICH UTI-
   LIZES LISTENING, SPEAKING, READING AND WRIT-
   ING ACTIVITIES.
PROD-COF   DIST-COF

CONSTITUTION--A SERIES
   PRESENTS THE U S CONSTITUTION. INCLUDES
   HOW IT WAS CREATED, WHAT IT STANDS FOR
   AND HOW IT HAS BEEN IMPROVED BY THE
   AMENDMENTS.
PROD-BETECL   DIST-BETECL

**CONSUMPTION AND
ECONOMICS**   C
   8X10 PREPARED TRANSPARENCY   J-H
   FROM THE BASIC SOCIAL STUDIES CONCEPTS -
   ECONOMICS SERIES.
PROD-LEART   DIST-LEART

**CONTESTS AND AWARDS
PROGRAM**   C
   8X10 PREPARED TRANSPARENCY
   SEE SERIES TITLE FOR DESCRIPTIVE STATEMENT.
   FROM THE DISTRIBUTIVE EDUCATION CLUBS OF
   AMERICA SERIES.
PROD-COF   DIST-COF

CONVERSION CHART   C
   8X10 PREPARED TRANSPARENCY   P-I
   FROM THE ELEMENTARY-JUNIOR HIGH
   MATHEMATICS SERIES.
PROD-LEART   DIST-LEART

CORN   C
   8X10 PREPARED TRANSPARENCY   K-P
   FROM THE LIFE SCIENCE - COMING TO LIFE
   SERIES.
PROD-LEART   DIST-LEART

CORNER OF THE FIELD   C
   8X10 PREPARED TRANSPARENCY   K-P
   FROM THE LIFE SCIENCE - LIVING SOMEWHERE
   SERIES.
PROD-LEART   DIST-LEART

COUNTEE CULLEN   C
   8X10 PREPARED TRANSPARENCY   J-H
   FROM THE BIOGRAPHIES OF OUTSTANDING
   NEGRO AMERICANS SERIES.
PROD-LEART   DIST-LEART

COUNTRY OF NIGERIA, THE   C
   8X10 PREPARED TRANSPARENCY   J-H
   FROM THE POLITICAL GEOGRAPHY AND
   NATIONALISM OF AFRICA SERIES.
PROD-LEART   DIST-LEART

CRAMER'S RULE   C
   8X10 PREPARED TRANSPARENCY
   FROM THE ALGEBRA, SECOND YEAR -
   DETERMINANTS SERIES.
PROD-LEART   DIST-LEART

CREATING DESIRE   C
   8X10 PREPARED TRANSPARENCY
   SEE SERIES TITLE FOR DESCRIPTIVE STATEMENT.
   FROM THE BASIC SALESMANSHIP SERIES.
PROD-COF   DIST-COF

CREATIVE MARKETING PROJECT   C
    8X10 PREPARED TRANSPARENCY
SEE SERIES TITLE FOR DESCRIPTIVE STATEMENT.
FROM THE DISTRIBUTIVE EDUCATION CLUBS OF
AMERICA SERIES.
PROD-COF   DIST-COF

CRISPUS ATTUCKS   C
    8X10 PREPARED TRANSPARENCY   J-H
FROM THE BIOGRAPHIES OF OUTSTANDING
NEGRO AMERICANS SERIES.
PROD-LEART   DIST-LEART

CROSS-SECTION OF PENIS   C
    8X10 PREPARED TRANSPARENCY
FROM THE SEX EDUCATION - DEVELOPMENTAL
PATTERNS OF PUBESCENT BOYS SERIES.
PROD-LEART   DIST-LEART

CULTURE VS CIVILIZATION   C
    8X10 PREPARED TRANSPARENCY   J-H
FROM THE BASIC SOCIAL STUDIES CONCEPTS -
POLITICS, SOCIAL-ECONOMIC INTERDEPENDENCE
SERIES.
PROD-LEART   DIST-LEART

CUSTOMER ANALYSIS   C
    8X10 PREPARED TRANSPARENCY
SEE SERIES TITLE FOR DESCRIPTIVE STATEMENT.
FROM THE BASIC SALESMANSHIP SERIES.
PROD-COF   DIST-COF

D

DAD AND ME   C
    8X10 PREPARED TRANSPARENCY   K-P
FROM THE LIFE SCIENCE - GROWING UP
SERIES.
PROD-LEART   DIST-LEART

**DAILY SCHEDULE FOR GOOD
GROOMING, A**   C
    8X10 PREPARED TRANSPARENCY
SEE SERIES TITLE FOR DESCRIPTIVE STATEMENT.
FROM THE GOOD GROOMING SERIES.
PROD-COF   DIST-COF

DATA SHEET   C
    8X10 PREPARED TRANSPARENCY
SEE SERIES TITLE FOR DESCRIPTIVE STATEMENT.
FROM THE JOB APPLICATION AND JOB INTER-
VIEW SERIES.
PROD-COF   DIST-COF

DATING AND PARTYING   C
    8X10 PREPARED TRANSPARENCY
FROM THE SEX EDUCATION - DEVELOPMENT OF
CONCEPTS AND ATTITUDES SERIES.
PROD-LEART   DIST-LEART

DATING BEHAVIOR   C
    8X10 PREPARED TRANSPARENCY   J
FROM THE DATING RELATIONS - EVALUATING
DATING BEHAVIOR SERIES.
PROD-LEART   DIST-LEART

**DATING BEHAVIORS AND
EXPECTATIONS**   C
    8X10 PREPARED TRANSPARENCY   J
FROM THE DATING RELATIONS - EVALUATING
DATING BEHAVIOR SERIES.
PROD-LEART   DIST-LEART

**DATING RELATIONS - DATING
CATEGORIES--A SERIES**   J

PROD-LEART   DIST-LEART

CASUAL-STEADY DATING
CATEGORIES OF DATING BEHAVIOR
PLAYING THE FIELD
SERIOUS-STEADY DATING
SUMMARY OF DATING CATEGORIES

**DATING RELATIONS - DATING
PROBLEMS--A SERIES**   J

PROD-LEART   DIST-LEART

BREAKING OFF
CARS AND DATES
DRINKING AND DATING
LEARNING HOW TO SAY NO

LEARNING HOW TO VARY THE TEMPO
SETTING STANDARDS ON DATES
SEX AND DATING - CONSEQUENCES
SEX AND DATING - GUILT AND SHAME
SEX AND DATING - REPUTATION
STEADY DATES
SUMMARY OF DATING PROBLEMS

**DATING RELATIONS -
DIMENSIONS OF DATING--A
SERIES**   J

PROD-LEART   DIST-LEART

DIMENSIONS OF SEXUAL ATTRACTION -
FEMALE
DIMENSIONS OF SEXUAL ATTRACTION -
MALE
IDEAL FEMALE
IDEAL MALE
PSYCHOLOGICAL DIMENSIONS AND
DATING BEHAVIOR
SELF IMAGE

**DATING RELATIONS -
EVALUATING DATING BEHAVIOR
--A SERIES**   J

PROD-LEART   DIST-LEART

COMMUNICATION CONFUSION
DATING BEHAVIOR
DATING BEHAVIORS AND
EXPECTATIONS

**DATING RELATIONS - MATURE
LOVE--A SERIES**   J

PROD-LEART   DIST-LEART

COMPLEXITY OF LOVE
INDIVIDUAL DIFFERENCES IN CAPACITY
INTRODUCTION TO LOVE
LASTING LOVE
LOVE IS BOTH STURDY AND
PERISHABLE

**DATING RELATIONS - MIXED
DATING--A SERIES**   J

PROD-LEART   DIST-LEART

MIXED DATING AMONG CLASSES
MIXED DATING AMONG RACES
MIXED DATING AMONG RELIGIONS

**DATING RELATIONS -
POPULARITY--A SERIES**   J

PROD-LEART   DIST-LEART

BEING YOURSELF
DOING THINGS
FRIENDLINESS
INTERACTION WITH PEOPLE
SURFACE APPEAL
TRAITS OF POPULARITY

**DATING RELATIONS - ROMANCE
AND PEOPLE--A SERIES**   J

PROD-LEART   DIST-LEART

BASIS OF ROMANTIC IDEAL
IDEAL AND YOUR PARENTS
IDEALIZATION AND FANTASY
INFATUATION
INTRODUCTION OF ROMANCE
SUMMARY OF ROMANTIC LOVE
WHAT IS ROMANTIC LOVE

**DATING RELATIONS - THE FIRST
DATE--A SERIES**   J

PROD-LEART   DIST-LEART

FIRST DATE, THE - COSTS
FIRST DATE, THE - GROUP ACTIVITIES
FIRST DATE, THE - HOW
FIRST DATE, THE - WHAT TO DO
FIRST DATE, THE - WHO

DAY AND NIGHT   C
    8X10 PREPARED TRANSPARENCY   H
SEE SERIES TITLE FOR DESCRIPTIVE STATEMENT.
FROM THE ASTRONOMY SERIES.
PROD-BOW   DIST-BOW

DECA CREED, THE   C
    8X10 PREPARED TRANSPARENCY
SEE SERIES TITLE FOR DESCRIPTIVE STATEMENT.
FROM THE DISTRIBUTIVE EDUCATION CLUBS OF
AMERICA SERIES.
PROD-COF   DIST-COF

**DECA GROWTH AND WHY JOIN
DECA**   C
    8X10 PREPARED TRANSPARENCY
SEE SERIES TITLE FOR DESCRIPTIVE STATEMENT.
FROM THE DISTRIBUTIVE EDUCATION CLUBS OF
AMERICA SERIES.
PROD-COF   DIST-COF

**DECA OFFICERS, TERMINOLOGY,
EXCITEMENT**   C
    8X10 PREPARED TRANSPARENCY
SEE SERIES TITLE FOR DESCRIPTIVE STATEMENT.
FROM THE DISTRIBUTIVE EDUCATION CLUBS OF
AMERICA SERIES.
PROD-COF   DIST-COF

**DECIMAL NUMBER LINE -
ADDITION AND SUBTRACTION**   C
    8X10 PREPARED TRANSPARENCY   P-I
FROM THE ELEMENTARY-JUNIOR HIGH
MATHEMATICS SERIES.
PROD-LEART   DIST-LEART

**DECIMAL NUMBER LINE -
MULTIPLICATION AND DIVISION**   C
    8X10 PREPARED TRANSPARENCY   P-I
FROM THE ELEMENTARY-JUNIOR HIGH
MATHEMATICS SERIES.
PROD-LEART   DIST-LEART

**DEFINITION OF DISTRIBUTIVE
EDUCATION**   C
    8X10 PREPARED TRANSPARENCY
SEE SERIES TITLE FOR DESCRIPTIVE STATEMENT.
FROM THE ORIENTATION TO DISTRIBUTIVE EDU-
CATION SERIES.
PROD-COF   DIST-COF

DEFINITION OF ECONOMIC ROLE   C
    8X10 PREPARED TRANSPARENCY   J-H
FROM THE BASIC SOCIAL STUDIES CONCEPTS -
ECONOMICS SERIES.
PROD-LEART   DIST-LEART

DEFINITION OF LOGARITHM   C
    8X10 PREPARED TRANSPARENCY
FROM THE ALGEBRA, SECOND YEAR -
LOGARITHMS SERIES.
PROD-LEART   DIST-LEART

**DEGREE MEASUREMENT -
CIRCLE**   C
    8X10 PREPARED TRANSPARENCY   P-I
FROM THE ELEMENTARY-JUNIOR HIGH
MATHEMATICS SERIES.
PROD-LEART   DIST-LEART

DENMARK VESEY   C
    8X10 PREPARED TRANSPARENCY   J-H
FROM THE BIOGRAPHIES OF OUTSTANDING
NEGRO AMERICANS SERIES.
PROD-LEART   DIST-LEART

DEPRESSANTS   C
    8X10 PREPARED TRANSPARENCY   H
SEE SERIES TITLE FOR DESCRIPTIVE STATEMENT.
FROM THE DRUG ABUSE SERIES.
PROD-BOW   DIST-BOW

DESCENT OF THE TESTICLES   C
    8X10 PREPARED TRANSPARENCY
FROM THE SEX EDUCATION - DEVELOPMENTAL
PATTERNS OF PUBESCENT BOYS SERIES.
PROD-LEART   DIST-LEART

**DETERMINANT PROPERTIES
FIVE AND SIX**   C
    8X10 PREPARED TRANSPARENCY
FROM THE ALGEBRA, SECOND YEAR -
DETERMINANTS SERIES.
PROD-LEART   DIST-LEART

**DETERMINANT PROPERTIES
ONE AND TWO**   C
    8X10 PREPARED TRANSPARENCY
FROM THE ALGEBRA, SECOND YEAR -
DETERMINANTS SERIES.
PROD-LEART   DIST-LEART

**DETERMINANT PROPERTIES
THREE AND FOUR**   C
                8X10 PREPARED TRANSPARENCY
FROM THE ALGEBRA, SECOND YEAR -
DETERMINANTS SERIES.
PROD-LEART   DIST-LEART

**DETERMINANT PROPERTY
SEVEN**   C
                8X10 PREPARED TRANSPARENCY
FROM THE ALGEBRA, SECOND YEAR -
DETERMINANTS SERIES.
PROD-LEART   DIST-LEART

**DETERMINANTS - DEFINITION
AND MINORS**   C
                8X10 PREPARED TRANSPARENCY
FROM THE ALGEBRA, SECOND YEAR -
DETERMINANTS SERIES.
PROD-LEART   DIST-LEART

DICTIONARY SKILLS--A SERIES
SHOWS HOW TO BEST USE THE DICTIONARY.
PROD-BOW   DIST-BOW

DIESEL ENGINE   C
                8X10 PREPARED TRANSPARENCY   H
SEE SERIES TITLE FOR DESCRIPTIVE STATEMENT.
FROM THE ENGINES SERIES.
PROD-BOW   DIST-BOW

DIFFERENCE OF TWO SQUARES   C
                8X10 PREPARED TRANSPARENCY
FROM THE ALGEBRA, SECOND YEAR -
FACTORING SERIES.
PROD-LEART   DIST-LEART

**DIFFERENT MEDIUMS OF
EXCHANGE ARE USED IN
DIFFERENT TYPES OF MARKETS**
                                                 C
                8X10 PREPARED TRANSPARENCY   J-H
FROM THE ECONOMICS - ECONOMICS IN
ACTION SERIES.
PROD-LEART   DIST-LEART

**DIFFICULT CONSONANTS--A
SERIES**
INTRODUCES A READING PROGRAM WHICH UTI-
LIZES LISTENING, SPEAKING, READING AND WRIT-
ING ACTIVITIES.
PROD-COF   DIST-COF

DIGESTIVE SYSTEM   C
                8X10 PREPARED TRANSPARENCY   H
SEE SERIES TITLE FOR DESCRIPTIVE STATEMENT.
FROM THE HUMAN BODY SERIES.
PROD-BOW   DIST-BOW

**DIMENSIONS OF SEXUAL
ATTRACTION - FEMALE**   C
                8X10 PREPARED TRANSPARENCY   J
FROM THE DATING RELATIONS - DIMENSIONS
OF DATING SERIES.
PROD-LEART   DIST-LEART

**DIMENSIONS OF SEXUAL
ATTRACTION - MALE**   C
                8X10 PREPARED TRANSPARENCY   J
FROM THE DATING RELATIONS - DIMENSIONS
OF DATING SERIES.
PROD-LEART   DIST-LEART

DIRECT VARIATION   C
                8X10 PREPARED TRANSPARENCY
FROM THE ALGEBRA, FIRST YEAR - FUNCTIONS
SERIES.
PROD-LEART   DIST-LEART

DISCRIMINANT   C
                8X10 PREPARED TRANSPARENCY
FROM THE ALGEBRA, SECOND YEAR - COMPLEX
NUMBERS SERIES.
PROD-LEART   DIST-LEART

**DISTINGUISHING PROPER AND
COMMON NOUNS**   C
                8X10 PREPARED TRANSPARENCY   I-J
SEE SERIES TITLE FOR DESCRIPTIVE STATEMENT.
FROM THE WORD FORMS AND FUNCTIONS SE-
RIES.
PROD-BOW   DIST-BOW

**DISTRIBUTIVE EDUCATION
CLUBS OF AMERICA--A SERIES**
OUTLINES THE ACTIVITIES, BENEFITS AND PRO-
GRAM OF DECA, WHICH IS THE NATIONAL ORGA-
NIZATION DESIGNED FOR STUDENTS ENROLLED
IN DISTRIBUTIVE EDUCATION. COVERS THE PRO-
GRAM AT NATIONAL, STATE AND LOCAL LEVELS.
PROD-COF   DIST-COF

CHAPTER ACTIVITIES
CONTESTS AND AWARDS PROGRAM
CREATIVE MARKETING PROJECT
DECA CREED, THE
DECA GROWTH AND WHY JOIN DECA
DECA OFFICERS, TERMINOLOGY,
EXCITEMENT
NATIONAL DECA WEEK
NATIONAL GOALS OF DECA
OFFICIAL ITEMS
POST SECONDARY DIVISION
WHAT DECA SYMBOLIZES

**DISTRIBUTIVE EDUCATION IN
ACTION**   C
                8X10 PREPARED TRANSPARENCY
SEE SERIES TITLE FOR DESCRIPTIVE STATEMENT.
FROM THE ORIENTATION TO DISTRIBUTIVE EDU-
CATION SERIES.
PROD-COF   DIST-COF

**DISTRIBUTIVE EDUCATION
TRIANGLE, THE**   C
                8X10 PREPARED TRANSPARENCY
SEE SERIES TITLE FOR DESCRIPTIVE STATEMENT.
FROM THE ORIENTATION TO DISTRIBUTIVE EDU-
CATION SERIES.
PROD-COF   DIST-COF

**DIVERGENCE OF ATTITUDES OF
ADULTS LIVING ON YOUR
BLOCK**   C
                8X10 PREPARED TRANSPARENCY   H
FROM THE EMOTIONS AND SOCIAL ATTITUDES -
ATTITUDES, VALUES SERIES.
PROD-LEART   DIST-LEART

DIVISIONS OF THE OCEAN   C
                8X10 PREPARED TRANSPARENCY   I-H
SEE SERIES TITLE FOR DESCRIPTIVE STATEMENT.
FROM THE OCEANOGRAPHY SERIES.
PROD-BOW   DIST-BOW

DO   C
                8X10 PREPARED TRANSPARENCY
SEE SERIES TITLE FOR DESCRIPTIVE STATEMENT.
FROM THE BASIC SALESMANSHIP SERIES.
PROD-COF   DIST-COF

**DOES FOREIGN AID MEAN
FOREIGN CONTROL**   C
                8X10 PREPARED TRANSPARENCY   J-H
FROM THE ECONOMICS - POLITICAL ECONOMY
AND PHILOSOPHY SERIES.
PROD-LEART   DIST-LEART

**DOES GOOD GROOMING PAY
OFF**   C
                8X10 PREPARED TRANSPARENCY
SEE SERIES TITLE FOR DESCRIPTIVE STATEMENT.
FROM THE GOOD GROOMING SERIES.
PROD-COF   DIST-COF

DOING THINGS   C
                8X10 PREPARED TRANSPARENCY   J
FROM THE DATING RELATIONS - POPULARITY
SERIES.
PROD-LEART   DIST-LEART

DOMESTIC SYSTEM VS FACTORY
                                                 C
                8X10 PREPARED TRANSPARENCY   J-H
FROM THE ECONOMICS - ECONOMIC HISTORY
SERIES.
PROD-LEART   DIST-LEART

DON'T   C
                8X10 PREPARED TRANSPARENCY
SEE SERIES TITLE FOR DESCRIPTIVE STATEMENT.
FROM THE BASIC SALESMANSHIP SERIES.
PROD-COF   DIST-COF

DON'T SAY MAY I HELP YOU   C
                8X10 PREPARED TRANSPARENCY
SEE SERIES TITLE FOR DESCRIPTIVE STATEMENT.
FROM THE BASIC SALESMANSHIP SERIES.
PROD-COF   DIST-COF

DRESS FOR THE WEATHER   C
                8X10 PREPARED TRANSPARENCY
FROM THE SEX EDUCATION - PHYSICAL CARE
AND SELF RESPECT SERIES.
PROD-LEART   DIST-LEART

DRINKING AND DATING   C
                8X10 PREPARED TRANSPARENCY   J
FROM THE DATING RELATIONS - DATING
PROBLEMS SERIES.
PROD-LEART   DIST-LEART

DRUG ABUSE--A SERIES
                                                 H
COVERS THE SUBJECT OF DRUGS AND LAWS RE-
LATING TO DRUGS.
PROD-BOW   DIST-BOW

DEPRESSANTS
DRUGS AND THE LAW
GLUE SNIFFING
HALLUCINOGENIC DRUGS
MARIJUANA
NARCOTICS
STIMULANTS
USES AND ABUSES

DRUGS AND THE LAW   C
                8X10 PREPARED TRANSPARENCY   H
SEE SERIES TITLE FOR DESCRIPTIVE STATEMENT.
FROM THE DRUG ABUSE SERIES.
PROD-BOW   DIST-BOW

DUKE ELLINGTON   C
                8X10 PREPARED TRANSPARENCY   J-H
FROM THE BIOGRAPHIES OF OUTSTANDING
NEGRO AMERICANS SERIES.
PROD-LEART   DIST-LEART

DURING THE INTERVIEW   C
                8X10 PREPARED TRANSPARENCY
SEE SERIES TITLE FOR DESCRIPTIVE STATEMENT.
FROM THE JOB APPLICATION AND JOB INTER-
VIEW SERIES.
PROD-COF   DIST-COF

E

EAR   C
                8X10 PREPARED TRANSPARENCY   H
SEE SERIES TITLE FOR DESCRIPTIVE STATEMENT.
FROM THE HUMAN BODY SERIES.
PROD-BOW   DIST-BOW

EARTH AND SKY--A SERIES
                                                 K-P
DISCUSSES THE ROTATION OF THE EARTH, EM-
PHASIZING THE POSITION OF THE SUN AND
MOON.
PROD-BOW   DIST-BOW

HOW THE EARTH REVOLVES
HOW THE EARTH ROTATES
HOW THE MOON SENDS LIGHT
LEARNING ABOUT LIGHT AND SHADOWS
WHAT IS DAY, WHAT IS NIGHT

EARTH'S MAGNETIC FIELD   C
                8X10 PREPARED TRANSPARENCY   H
SEE SERIES TITLE FOR DESCRIPTIVE STATEMENT.
FROM THE MAGNETISM AND ELECTRICITY SERIES.
PROD-BOW   DIST-BOW

EASY CONSONANTS--A SERIES
INTRODUCES A READING PROGRAM WHICH UTI-
LIZES LISTENING, SPEAKING, READING AND WRIT-
ING ACTIVITIES.
PROD-COF   DIST-COF

ECLIPSES   C
                8X10 PREPARED TRANSPARENCY   H
SEE SERIES TITLE FOR DESCRIPTIVE STATEMENT.
FROM THE ASTRONOMY SERIES.
PROD-BOW   DIST-BOW

**ECONOMIC INTERDEPENDENCE
OF PEOPLE**   C
                8X10 PREPARED TRANSPARENCY   J-H
FROM THE BASIC SOCIAL STUDIES CONCEPTS -
ECONOMICS SERIES.
PROD-LEART   DIST-LEART

**ECONOMIC PHILOSOPHY IN
TRADITIONAL SOCIETY**   C
                8X10 PREPARED TRANSPARENCY   J-H
FROM THE ECONOMICS - POLITICAL ECONOMY
AND PHILOSOPHY SERIES.

PROD-LEART   DIST-LEART

**ECONOMICS - ECONOMIC
HISTORY--A SERIES**
                                    J-H

PROD-LEART   DIST-LEART

AFTER THE 'TAKE-OFF' - A DRIVE TO
MATURITY
DOMESTIC SYSTEM VS FACTORY
ECONOMICS IN A TRADITIONAL SOCIETY
FACTORS IN ECONOMIC GROWTH
GROWTH OF INTERNATIONAL TRADE
AND COMMERCE
HISTORY OF RECORD KEEPING
INDUSTRIAL REVOLUTION IS A 'TAKE-
OFF'
INDUSTRIAL REVOLUTION TODAY
MATURITY - HIGH MASS CONSUMPTION
REQUIREMENTS OF A 'TAKE-OFF'
STAGES OF ECONOMIC GROWTH
TOWN AND ECONOMICS

**ECONOMICS - ECONOMICS IN
ACTION--A SERIES**
                                    J-H

PROD-LEART   DIST-LEART

ACCUMULATING CAPITAL FOR
INVESTMENTS
BANKS ACCUMULATE AND DISTRIBUTE
CAPITAL
BUSINESS - WHAT COMES BEFORE
PROFIT
DIFFERENT MEDIUMS OF EXCHANGE
ARE USED IN --
ECONOMICS IN A DEVELOPING NATION
ECONOMICS TERMS
HOW TO EXPAND PRODUCTION
HOW WE MEASURE ECONOMIC GROWTH
INTERNATIONAL COMMERCIAL POLICY
INTERNATIONAL TRADE AND FINANCE
PATTERNS OF CONSUMPTION -
MARKETING
PER CAPITA INCOME AND
CONSUMPTION
PRICES AND THE ROLE OF
GOVERNMENT
PRODUCTION DEPENDS ON DEMAND
SAVINGS AND INVESTMENTS
SECTORS OF A MODERN ECONOMY
WHAT IS ECONOMIC PLANNING

**ECONOMICS - POLITICAL
ECONOMY AND PHILOSOPHY --A
SERIES**
                                    J-H

PROD-LEART   DIST-LEART

DOES FOREIGN AID MEAN FOREIGN
CONTROL
ECONOMIC PHILOSOPHY IN
TRADITIONAL SOCIETY
EDUCATION AND ECONOMICS
FEDERAL BUDGET - INCOME AND
EXPENDITURES
GUILD VS LABOR UNION
ROLE OF U S GOVERNMENT IN
ECONOMICS VS ROLE --
TODAY'S ISMS

**ECONOMICS IN A DEVELOPING
NATION**   C
        8X10 PREPARED TRANSPARENCY J-H
    FROM THE ECONOMICS - ECONOMICS IN
    ACTION SERIES.
PROD-LEART   DIST-LEART

**ECONOMICS IN A TRADITIONAL
SOCIETY**   C
        8X10 PREPARED TRANSPARENCY J-H
    FROM THE ECONOMICS - ECONOMIC HISTORY
    SERIES.
PROD-LEART   DIST-LEART

ECONOMICS TERMS   C
        8X10 PREPARED TRANSPARENCY J-H
    FROM THE ECONOMICS - ECONOMICS IN
    ACTION SERIES.
PROD-LEART   DIST-LEART

EDGE OF THE POND   C
        8X10 PREPARED TRANSPARENCY K-P
    FROM THE LIFE SCIENCE - LIVING SOMEWHERE
    SERIES.
PROD-LEART   DIST-LEART

EDGE OF THE WOODS   C
        8X10 PREPARED TRANSPARENCY K-P
    FROM THE LIFE SCIENCE - LIVING SOMEWHERE
    SERIES.
PROD-LEART   DIST-LEART

EDUCATION AND ECONOMICS   C
        8X10 PREPARED TRANSPARENCY J-H
    FROM THE ECONOMICS - POLITICAL ECONOMY
    AND PHILOSOPHY SERIES.
PROD-LEART   DIST-LEART

EFFECTS OF GONORRHEA   C
        8X10 PREPARED TRANSPARENCY
    FROM THE SEX EDUCATION - UNDERSTANDING
    VENEREAL DISEASE SERIES.
PROD-LEART   DIST-LEART

EFFECTS OF SYPHILIS   C
        8X10 PREPARED TRANSPARENCY
    FROM THE SEX EDUCATION - UNDERSTANDING
    VENEREAL DISEASE SERIES.
PROD-LEART   DIST-LEART

ELECTRIC BELL   C
        8X10 PREPARED TRANSPARENCY H
    SEE SERIES TITLE FOR DESCRIPTIVE STATEMENT.
    FROM THE MAGNETISM AND ELECTRICITY SERIES.
PROD-BOW   DIST-BOW

ELECTRIC MOTOR   C
        8X10 PREPARED TRANSPARENCY H
    SEE SERIES TITLE FOR DESCRIPTIVE STATEMENT.
    FROM THE MAGNETISM AND ELECTRICITY SERIES.
PROD-BOW   DIST-BOW

ELECTRICAL SWITCHES   C
        8X10 PREPARED TRANSPARENCY H
    SEE SERIES TITLE FOR DESCRIPTIVE STATEMENT.
    FROM THE APPLIED SCIENCE SERIES.
PROD-BOW   DIST-BOW

ELECTROSCOPE   C
        8X10 PREPARED TRANSPARENCY H
    SEE SERIES TITLE FOR DESCRIPTIVE STATEMENT.
    FROM THE MAGNETISM AND ELECTRICITY SERIES.
PROD-BOW   DIST-BOW

**ELEMENTARY GEOMETRY - AREA
AS A MEASURE OF COVERING--A
SERIES**
                                    P-I

PROD-LEART   DIST-LEART

AREAS AS COVERING
CIRCULAR REGION
PARALLELOGRAM REGION
RECTANGULAR REGION
TRIANGULAR REGION

**ELEMENTARY-JUNIOR HIGH
MATHEMATICS--A SERIES**
                                    P-I

PROD-LEART   DIST-LEART

ADDITION OF FRACTIONS
ADDITION TABLE
ASSOCIATIVE LAW - GROUPING
BAR GRAPH
BASE FOUR
BASE FOUR - ADDING AND
SUBTRACTING
BASE FOUR ADDITION TABLE
BASE FOUR MULTIPLICATION TABLE
BASIC PRINCIPLES
CALENDAR
CIRCLE
CLOCK
COMMUTATIVE LAW
CONVERSION CHART
DECIMAL NUMBER LINE - ADDITION
AND SUBTRACTION
DECIMAL NUMBER LINE -
MULTIPLICATION AND --
DEGREE MEASUREMENT - CIRCLE
EMPTY SET
EQUIVALENT SETS
EQUIVALENT SETS (MULTIPLICATION
SERIES)
FRACTIONAL NUMBER LINE
FREQUENCY DISTRIBUTION TABLE AND
LINE GRAPH
GRAPHING
LIQUID MEASURE
MAP PROBLEMS
MATHEMATICAL SYMBOLS
METRIC SYSTEM
MODERN BASE TEN ABACUS
MULTIPLICATION OF FRACTIONS
MULTIPLICATION PRINCIPLES
MULTIPLICATION TABLE
NAMES FOR NUMBERS
NATURAL ORDER OF NUMBERS, NO. 1
NATURAL ORDER OF NUMBERS, NO. 2
NON-EQUIVALENT SETS
NUMBER FACTS, PT 1
NUMBER FACTS, PT 2

NUMBER FACTS, PT 3
NUMBER FACTS, PT 4
NUMBER FACTS, PT 5
NUMBER FACTS, PT 6
NUMBER FACTS, PT 7
NUMBER FACTS, PT 8
NUMBER FACTS, PT 9
NUMBER LINE
NUMBER LINE - SIGNED NUMBERS
NUMBER LINE (MULT SERIES)
PASCAL'S TRIANGLE
PATTERN FORMATIONS
PLANE FIGURES
PROPERTIES OF SETS
PYTHAGOREAN THEOREM
REGULAR SOLIDS
SET, A
SETS AND SUBSETS
SIEVE OF ERATOSTHENES
SIMPLE GEOMETRIC FIGURES
SKIP COUNTING
SOLID FIGURES
SQUARE
SUBTRACTION - TAKE AWAY
SUBTRACTION OF FRACTIONS
SYSTEMS OF WRITING NUMERALS
TABLE OF MEASURE
TEMPERATURE
TIME ZONES
UNION OF SETS
UNITS OF TIME - YEAR, MONTH, DAY
VENN DIAGRAMS - INTERSECTION OF
SETS
VENN DIAGRAMS - SETS AND SUBSETS,
IDENTICAL --
VISUALIZING CROSS SECTIONS -
INTERSECTION OF --
VISUALIZING CROSS SECTIONS -
INTERSECTION OF 1-
VISUALIZING CROSS SECTIONS -
INTERSECTION OF 2
VISUALIZING CROSS SECTIONS -
INTERSECTION OF 3-
VOCABULARY

ELLIPSE - DEFINITION   C
        8X10 PREPARED TRANSPARENCY
    FROM THE ALGEBRA, SECOND YEAR - CONICS
    SERIES.
PROD-LEART   DIST-LEART

EMBRYO TO BABY   C
        8X10 PREPARED TRANSPARENCY
    FROM THE SEX EDUCATION - THE BABY - ITS
    CONCEPTION, GROWTH AND BIRTH SERIES.
PROD-LEART   DIST-LEART

**EMOTION AND BODY
FUNCTIONS**   C
        8X10 PREPARED TRANSPARENCY
    FROM THE SEX EDUCATION - PHYSICAL CARE
    AND SELF RESPECT SERIES.
PROD-LEART   DIST-LEART

**EMOTIONS AND SOCIAL
ATTITUDES - ATTITUDES,
VALUES--A SERIES**
                                    H

PROD-LEART   DIST-LEART

ATTITUDES
DIVERGENCE OF ATTITUDES OF ADULTS
LIVING ON --
NARROW VS BROAD EXPERIMENTATION
IN ATTITUDES
SOURCE OF ATTITUDES OF THE HIGH
SCHOOL PERSON
TASTES
VALUES IN THE ADULT
YOUR ATTITUDE IN FIVE YEARS

**EMPLOYEE'S WITHHOLDING
EXEMPTION CERTIFICATE**   C
        8X10 PREPARED TRANSPARENCY
    SEE SERIES TITLE FOR DESCRIPTIVE STATEMENT.
    FROM THE JOB APPLICATION AND JOB INTER-
    VIEW SERIES.
PROD-COF   DIST-COF

EMPTY SET   C
        8X10 PREPARED TRANSPARENCY P-I
    FROM THE ELEMENTARY-JUNIOR HIGH
    MATHEMATICS SERIES.
PROD-LEART   DIST-LEART

ENDOCRINE GLANDS   C
        8X10 PREPARED TRANSPARENCY
    FROM THE SEX EDUCATION - GROWTH AND
    THE ENDOCRINE GLANDS SERIES.
PROD-LEART   DIST-LEART

ENGINES   C
8X10 PREPARED TRANSPARENCY   H
SEE SERIES TITLE FOR DESCRIPTIVE STATEMENT.
FROM THE ATOMIC ENERGY SERIES.
PROD-BOW   DIST-BOW

ENGINES--A SERIES   H
PRESENTS VARIOUS KINDS OF ENGINES.
PROD-BOW   DIST-BOW

DIESEL ENGINE
FOUR-CYCLE ENGINE
INTERNAL COMBUSTION ENGINE
JET ENGINE
ROCKET ENGINE
STEAM ENGINE

**EQUATION AND GRAPHING OF
ELLIPSE**   C
8X10 PREPARED TRANSPARENCY
FROM THE ALGEBRA, SECOND YEAR - CONICS
SERIES.
PROD-LEART   DIST-LEART

**EQUATIONS WITH LOGARITHMS
AND EXPONENTS**   C
8X10 PREPARED TRANSPARENCY
FROM THE ALGEBRA, SECOND YEAR -
LOGARITHMS SERIES.
PROD-LEART   DIST-LEART

**EQUATIONS WITH RATIONAL
ALGEBRAIC EXPRESSIONS**   C
8X10 PREPARED TRANSPARENCY
FROM THE ALGEBRA, SECOND YEAR -
ALGEBRAIC EXPRESSIONS SERIES.
PROD-LEART   DIST-LEART

EQUIVALENT SETS   C   P-I
8X10 PREPARED TRANSPARENCY
FROM THE ELEMENTARY-JUNIOR HIGH
MATHEMATICS SERIES.
PROD-LEART   DIST-LEART

**EQUIVALENT SETS
(MULTIPLICATION SERIES)**   C   P-I
8X10 PREPARED TRANSPARENCY
FROM THE ELEMENTARY-JUNIOR HIGH
MATHEMATICS SERIES.
PROD-LEART   DIST-LEART

EROSION   C
8X10 PREPARED TRANSPARENCY   H
SEE SERIES TITLE FOR DESCRIPTIVE STATEMENT.
FROM THE CONSERVATION SERIES.
PROD-BOW   DIST-BOW *

EUGLENA, THE   C
8X10 PREPARED TRANSPARENCY   I-H
SEE SERIES TITLE FOR DESCRIPTIVE STATEMENT.
FROM THE MICROSCOPIC LIFE SERIES.
PROD-BOW   DIST-BOW

**EUROPEAN PARTITION
AGREEMENTS 1884-1885**   C
8X10 PREPARED TRANSPARENCY   J-H
FROM THE POLITICAL GEOGRAPHY AND
NATIONALISM OF AFRICA SERIES.
PROD-LEART   DIST-LEART

EVALUATING DETERMINANTS   C
8X10 PREPARED TRANSPARENCY
FROM THE ALGEBRA, SECOND YEAR -
DETERMINANTS SERIES.
PROD-LEART   DIST-LEART

EVERGREEN IDENTIFICATION   C
8X10 PREPARED TRANSPARENCY   H
SEE SERIES TITLE FOR DESCRIPTIVE STATEMENT.
FROM THE PLANTS SERIES.
PROD-BOW   DIST-BOW

EVOLUTION OF THE HORSE   C
8X10 PREPARED TRANSPARENCY   H
SEE SERIES TITLE FOR DESCRIPTIVE STATEMENT.
FROM THE WARM-BLOODED VERTEBRATES SE-
RIES.
PROD-BOW   DIST-BOW

**EXAMPLES OF DISTRIBUTIVE
BUSINESSES**   C
8X10 PREPARED TRANSPARENCY
SEE SERIES TITLE FOR DESCRIPTIVE STATEMENT.
FROM THE ORIENTATION TO DISTRIBUTIVE EDU-
CATION SERIES.
PROD-COF   DIST-COF

**EXAMPLES OF DISTRIBUTIVE
OCCUPATIONS**   C
8X10 PREPARED TRANSPARENCY
SEE SERIES TITLE FOR DESCRIPTIVE STATEMENT.
FROM THE ORIENTATION TO DISTRIBUTIVE EDU-
CATION SERIES.
PROD-COF   DIST-COF

EXERCISE AND ACTIVITIES   C
8X10 PREPARED TRANSPARENCY
FROM THE SEX EDUCATION - PHYSICAL CARE
AND SELF RESPECT SERIES.
PROD-LEART   DIST-LEART

EXPANDING A DETERMINANT   C
8X10 PREPARED TRANSPARENCY
FROM THE ALGEBRA, SECOND YEAR -
DETERMINANTS SERIES.
PROD-LEART   DIST-LEART

**EXPERIMENTING WITH LIGHT
AND OBJECTS**   C   I-H
8X10 PREPARED TRANSPARENCY
SEE SERIES TITLE FOR DESCRIPTIVE STATEMENT.
FROM THE LIGHT AND COLOR SERIES.
PROD-BOW   DIST-BOW

**EXPERIMENTS WITH COLORED
LIGHT**   C   I-H
8X10 PREPARED TRANSPARENCY
SEE SERIES TITLE FOR DESCRIPTIVE STATEMENT.
FROM THE LIGHT AND COLOR SERIES.
PROD-BOW   DIST-BOW

**EXPERIMENTS WITH COLORED
OBJECTS**   C   I-H
8X10 PREPARED TRANSPARENCY
SEE SERIES TITLE FOR DESCRIPTIVE STATEMENT.
FROM THE LIGHT AND COLOR SERIES.
PROD-BOW   DIST-BOW

**EXTENDING THE NUMBER LINE
TO INCLUDE IRRATIONAL
NUMBERS**   C
8X10 PREPARED TRANSPARENCY
FROM THE ALGEBRA, FIRST YEAR - REAL
NUMBERS SERIES.
PROD-LEART   DIST-LEART

EYE   C
8X10 PREPARED TRANSPARENCY   H
SEE SERIES TITLE FOR DESCRIPTIVE STATEMENT.
FROM THE HUMAN BODY SERIES.
PROD-BOW   DIST-BOW

F

FACTORING BY GROUPING   C
8X10 PREPARED TRANSPARENCY
FROM THE ALGEBRA, SECOND YEAR -
FACTORING SERIES.
PROD-LEART   DIST-LEART

**FACTORING BY USING
EQUIVALENT EXPRESSIONS**   C
8X10 PREPARED TRANSPARENCY
FROM THE ALGEBRA, SECOND YEAR -
FACTORING SERIES.
PROD-LEART   DIST-LEART

**FACTORS IN ECONOMIC
GROWTH**   C   J-H
8X10 PREPARED TRANSPARENCY
FROM THE ECONOMICS - ECONOMIC HISTORY
SERIES.
PROD-LEART   DIST-LEART

FACTORS OF PRODUCTION   C   J-H
8X10 PREPARED TRANSPARENCY
FROM THE BASIC SOCIAL STUDIES CONCEPTS -
ECONOMICS SERIES.
PROD-LEART   DIST-LEART

FAMILY OF CHILDREN   C   K-P
8X10 PREPARED TRANSPARENCY
FROM THE LIFE SCIENCE - GROWING UP
SERIES.
PROD-LEART   DIST-LEART

FAULT MOUNTAINS   C
8X10 PREPARED TRANSPARENCY   H
SEE SERIES TITLE FOR DESCRIPTIVE STATEMENT.
FROM THE GEOLOGY SERIES.
PROD-BOW   DIST-BOW

FAVORITE THINGS   C   K-P
8X10 PREPARED TRANSPARENCY
FROM THE LIFE SCIENCE - GROWING UP
SERIES.
PROD-LEART   DIST-LEART

**FEDERAL BUDGET - INCOME
AND EXPENDITURES**   C   J-H
8X10 PREPARED TRANSPARENCY
FROM THE ECONOMICS - POLITICAL ECONOMY
AND PHILOSOPHY SERIES.
PROD-LEART   DIST-LEART

FEEDER CONSTRUCTION   C
8X10 PREPARED TRANSPARENCY   H
SEE SERIES TITLE FOR DESCRIPTIVE STATEMENT.
FROM THE WARM-BLOODED VERTEBRATES SE-
RIES.
PROD-BOW   DIST-BOW

**FEMALE ORGANS OF EXCRETION
AND REPRODUCTION**   C
8X10 PREPARED TRANSPARENCY
SEX EDUCATION - DEVELOPMENTAL PATTERNS
OF PUBESCENT GIRLS SERIES.
PROD-LEART   DIST-LEART

**FEMALE REPRODUCTIVE
ORGANS - FRONT VIEW**   C
8X10 PREPARED TRANSPARENCY
SEX EDUCATION - DEVELOPMENTAL PATTERNS
OF PUBESCENT GIRLS SERIES.
PROD-LEART   DIST-LEART

FERTILIZATION   C
8X10 PREPARED TRANSPARENCY   H
SEE SERIES TITLE FOR DESCRIPTIVE STATEMENT.
FROM THE PLANTS SERIES.
PROD-BOW   DIST-BOW

FERTILIZATION   C
8X10 PREPARED TRANSPARENCY
FROM THE SEX EDUCATION - THE BABY - ITS
CONCEPTION, GROWTH AND BIRTH SERIES.
PROD-LEART   DIST-LEART

FIRST CLASS LEVER   C
8X10 PREPARED TRANSPARENCY   H
SEE SERIES TITLE FOR DESCRIPTIVE STATEMENT.
FROM THE MACHINES SERIES.
PROD-BOW   DIST-BOW

FIRST DATE, THE - COSTS   C   J
8X10 PREPARED TRANSPARENCY
FROM THE DATING RELATIONS - THE FIRST
DATE SERIES.
PROD-LEART   DIST-LEART

**FIRST DATE, THE - GROUP
ACTIVITIES**   C   J
8X10 PREPARED TRANSPARENCY
FROM THE DATING RELATIONS - THE FIRST
DATE SERIES.
PROD-LEART   DIST-LEART

FIRST DATE, THE - HOW   C   J
8X10 PREPARED TRANSPARENCY
FROM THE DATING RELATIONS - THE FIRST
DATE SERIES.
PROD-LEART   DIST-LEART

**FIRST DATE, THE - WHAT TO
DO**   C   J
8X10 PREPARED TRANSPARENCY
FROM THE DATING RELATIONS - THE FIRST
DATE SERIES.
PROD-LEART   DIST-LEART

FIRST DATE, THE - WHO   C   J
8X10 PREPARED TRANSPARENCY
FROM THE DATING RELATIONS - THE FIRST
DATE SERIES.
PROD-LEART   DIST-LEART

**FIVE MAJOR STEPS IN A SALE,
THE**   C
8X10 PREPARED TRANSPARENCY
SEE SERIES TITLE FOR DESCRIPTIVE STATEMENT.
FROM THE BASIC SALESMANSHIP SERIES.
PROD-COF   DIST-COF

FLIGHT PRINCIPLES   C
8X10 PREPARED TRANSPARENCY   H
SEE SERIES TITLE FOR DESCRIPTIVE STATEMENT.
FROM THE APPLIED SCIENCE SERIES.
PROD-BOW   DIST-BOW

FLOODING   C
       8X10 PREPARED TRANSPARENCY   H
SEE SERIES TITLE FOR DESCRIPTIVE STATEMENT.
FROM THE CONSERVATION SERIES.
PROD-BOW   DIST-BOW

FOLDED MOUNTAINS   C
       8X10 PREPARED TRANSPARENCY   H
SEE SERIES TITLE FOR DESCRIPTIVE STATEMENT.
FROM THE GEOLOGY SERIES.
PROD-BOW   DIST-BOW

FOOD AFFECTS GROWTH   C
       8X10 PREPARED TRANSPARENCY
FROM THE SEX EDUCATION - PHYSICAL CARE
AND SELF RESPECT SERIES.
PROD-LEART   DIST-LEART

FOOD WEB   C
       8X10 PREPARED TRANSPARENCY   I-H
SEE SERIES TITLE FOR DESCRIPTIVE STATEMENT.
FROM THE OCEANOGRAPHY SERIES.
PROD-BOW   DIST-BOW

FOOD, FUN, REST   C
       8X10 PREPARED TRANSPARENCY   K-P
FROM THE LIFE SCIENCE - GROWING UP
SERIES.
PROD-LEART   DIST-LEART

FOREST FIRE   C
       8X10 PREPARED TRANSPARENCY   H
SEE SERIES TITLE FOR DESCRIPTIVE STATEMENT.
FROM THE CONSERVATION SERIES.
PROD-BOW   DIST-BOW

FOSSIL PROTOZOANS   C
       8X10 PREPARED TRANSPARENCY   I-H
SEE SERIES TITLE FOR DESCRIPTIVE STATEMENT.
FROM THE MICROSCOPIC LIFE SERIES.
PROD-BOW   DIST-BOW

FOUR-CYCLE ENGINE   C
       8X10 PREPARED TRANSPARENCY   H
SEE SERIES TITLE FOR DESCRIPTIVE STATEMENT.
FROM THE ENGINES SERIES.
PROD-BOW   DIST-BOW

FRACTIONAL NUMBER LINE   C
       8X10 PREPARED TRANSPARENCY   P-I
FROM THE ELEMENTARY-JUNIOR HIGH
MATHEMATICS SERIES.
PROD-LEART   DIST-LEART

FREDERICK A DOUGLASS   C
       8X10 PREPARED TRANSPARENCY   J-H
FROM THE BIOGRAPHIES OF OUTSTANDING
NEGRO AMERICANS SERIES.
PROD-LEART   DIST-LEART

**FREQUENCY DISTRIBUTION
TABLE AND LINE GRAPH**   C
       8X10 PREPARED TRANSPARENCY   P-I
FROM THE ELEMENTARY-JUNIOR HIGH
MATHEMATICS SERIES.
PROD-LEART   DIST-LEART

FRESHWATER ALGAE   C
       8X10 PREPARED TRANSPARENCY   I-H
FROM THE MICROSCOPIC LIFE SERIES.
PROD-BOW   DIST-BOW

FRESHWATER PROTOZOANS   C
       8X10 PREPARED TRANSPARENCY   I-H
SEE SERIES TITLE FOR DESCRIPTIVE STATEMENT.
FROM THE MICROSCOPIC LIFE SERIES.
PROD-BOW   DIST-BOW

FRIENDLINESS   C
       8X10 PREPARED TRANSPARENCY   J
FROM THE DATING RELATIONS - POPULARITY
SERIES.
PROD-LEART   DIST-LEART

FROG - LIFE CYCLE   C
       8X10 PREPARED TRANSPARENCY   K-P
FROM THE LIFE SCIENCE - COMING TO LIFE
SERIES.
PROD-LEART   DIST-LEART

FUNCTIONS   C
       8X10 PREPARED TRANSPARENCY
FROM THE ALGEBRA, FIRST YEAR - FUNCTIONS
SERIES.
PROD-LEART   DIST-LEART

FUNCTIONS OF INDIVIDUALS   C
       8X10 PREPARED TRANSPARENCY
SEE SERIES TITLE FOR DESCRIPTIVE STATEMENT.
FROM THE BASIC SALESMANSHIP SERIES.
PROD-COF   DIST-COF

G

GAINING ATTENTION   C
       8X10 PREPARED TRANSPARENCY
SEE SERIES TITLE FOR DESCRIPTIVE STATEMENT.
FROM THE BASIC SALESMANSHIP SERIES.
PROD-COF   DIST-COF

GAME - OUR MAIN STREET   C
       8X10 PREPARED TRANSPARENCY
SEE SERIES TITLE FOR DESCRIPTIVE STATEMENT.
FROM THE ORIENTATION TO DISTRIBUTIVE EDU-
CATION SERIES.
PROD-COF   DIST-COF

GEARS   C
       8X10 PREPARED TRANSPARENCY   H
SEE SERIES TITLE FOR DESCRIPTIVE STATEMENT.
FROM THE MACHINES SERIES.
PROD-BOW   DIST-BOW

GENERAL TOPICS--A SERIES   H
PRESENTS VARIOUS TOPICS IN FAMILY LIVING
AND SEX EDUCATION.
PROD-BOW   DIST-BOW

ADOLESCENT CHANGE
HEREDITY (BASIC)
OVUM AND SPERM PHOTO
SINGLE FULL-TERM FETUS (X-RAY)
TWIN X-RAY
TWINS

GENERATING STATION   C
       8X10 PREPARED TRANSPARENCY   H
SEE SERIES TITLE FOR DESCRIPTIVE STATEMENT.
FROM THE MAGNETISM AND ELECTRICITY SERIES.
PROD-BOW   DIST-BOW

GEOLOGIC TIME   C
       8X10 PREPARED TRANSPARENCY   H
SEE SERIES TITLE FOR DESCRIPTIVE STATEMENT.
FROM THE GEOLOGY SERIES.
PROD-BOW   DIST-BOW

GEOLOGY--A SERIES   H
DISCUSSES VARIOUS PHENOMENA IN GEOLOGY.
PROD-BOW   DIST-BOW

FAULT MOUNTAINS
FOLDED MOUNTAINS
GEOLOGIC TIME
GLACIATION
ROCK CYCLE
VOLCANO

GEORGE WASHINGTON CARVER   C
       8X10 PREPARED TRANSPARENCY   J-H
FROM THE BIOGRAPHIES OF OUTSTANDING
NEGRO AMERICANS SERIES.
PROD-LEART   DIST-LEART

GERMINATION   C
       8X10 PREPARED TRANSPARENCY   H
SEE SERIES TITLE FOR DESCRIPTIVE STATEMENT.
FROM THE PLANTS SERIES.
PROD-BOW   DIST-BOW

**GET ACQUAINTED WITH
YOURSELF**   C
       8X10 PREPARED TRANSPARENCY
SEE SERIES TITLE FOR DESCRIPTIVE STATEMENT.
FROM THE JOB APPLICATION AND JOB INTER-
VIEW SERIES.
PROD-COF   DIST-COF

GETTING ACTION   C
       8X10 PREPARED TRANSPARENCY
SEE SERIES TITLE FOR DESCRIPTIVE STATEMENT.
FROM THE BASIC SALESMANSHIP SERIES.
PROD-COF   DIST-COF

GLACIATION   C
       8X10 PREPARED TRANSPARENCY   H
SEE SERIES TITLE FOR DESCRIPTIVE STATEMENT.
FROM THE GEOLOGY SERIES.
PROD-BOW   DIST-BOW

GLUE SNIFFING   C
       8X10 PREPARED TRANSPARENCY   H
SEE SERIES TITLE FOR DESCRIPTIVE STATEMENT.
FROM THE DRUG ABUSE SERIES.
PROD-BOW   DIST-BOW

GONORRHEA   C
       8X10 PREPARED TRANSPARENCY
FROM THE SEX EDUCATION - UNDERSTANDING
VENEREAL DISEASE SERIES.
PROD-LEART   DIST-LEART

GOOD GROOMING GAME A   C
       8X10 PREPARED TRANSPARENCY
SEE SERIES TITLE FOR DESCRIPTIVE STATEMENT.
FROM THE GOOD GROOMING SERIES.
PROD-COF   DIST-COF

GOOD GROOMING GAME B   C
       8X10 PREPARED TRANSPARENCY
SEE SERIES TITLE FOR DESCRIPTIVE STATEMENT.
FROM THE GOOD GROOMING SERIES.
PROD-COF   DIST-COF

GOOD GROOMING RULES   C
       8X10 PREPARED TRANSPARENCY
SEE SERIES TITLE FOR DESCRIPTIVE STATEMENT.
FROM THE GOOD GROOMING SERIES.
PROD-COF   DIST-COF

GOOD GROOMING--A SERIES
MAKES STUDENTS CONSCIOUS OF THE ROLE
GOOD GROOMING PLAYS IN DAILY LIFE AND PRE-
SENTS BASIC GOOD GROOMING RULES THAT AP-
PLY TO THE WORKING WORLD.
PROD-COF   DIST-COF

APPAREL AND POSTURE AFFECT YOUR
ATTITUDE
DAILY SCHEDULE FOR GOOD
GROOMING, A
DOES GOOD GROOMING PAY OFF
GOOD GROOMING GAME A
GOOD GROOMING GAME B
GOOD GROOMING RULES
HOW DO YOU MEASURE UP, NO. 1
HOW DO YOU MEASURE UP, NO. 2
IMPORTANCE OF A PLEASANT FACE
AND VOICE
ITEMS FOR THE WORKING GIRL'S
HANDBAG
ITEMS TO BE CARRIED BY THE
WORKING MAN
JOB REQUIREMENTS IN DRESS
SELECTING A HAIR STYLE
SELECTING CLOTHING FOR YOUR
BUDGET
SUMMARY OF GOOD GROOMING
FACTORS, PT 1
SUMMARY OF GOOD GROOMING
FACTORS, PT 2
WEEKLY SCHEDULE FOR GOOD
GROOMING, A
WELL-DRESSED YOUNG WORKING MAN,
THE
WELL-DRESSED YOUNG WORKING
WOMAN, THE

GRAFTING   C
       8X10 PREPARED TRANSPARENCY   H
SEE SERIES TITLE FOR DESCRIPTIVE STATEMENT.
FROM THE PLANTS SERIES.
PROD-BOW   DIST-BOW

GRAMMAR--A SERIES
REVIEWS THE RULES OF GRAMMAR FOR STU-
DENTS.
PROD-BETECL   DIST-BETECL

GRANVILLE WOODS   C
       8X10 PREPARED TRANSPARENCY   J-H
FROM THE BIOGRAPHIES OF OUTSTANDING
NEGRO AMERICANS SERIES.
PROD-LEART   DIST-LEART

**GRAPH OF A LINEAR EQUATION
IN TWO VARIABLES**   C
       8X10 PREPARED TRANSPARENCY
FROM THE ALGEBRA, FIRST YEAR - SYSTEM OF
LINEAR EQUATIONS SERIES.
PROD-LEART   DIST-LEART

**GRAPH OF SYSTEM WITH ONE
QUADRATIC AND ONE LINEAR
EQUATION**   C
       8X10 PREPARED TRANSPARENCY
FROM THE ALGEBRA, SECOND YEAR - CONICS
SERIES.
PROD-LEART   DIST-LEART

GRAPH OF SYSTEM WITH TWO QUADRATIC EQUATIONS C
8X10 PREPARED TRANSPARENCY
FROM THE ALGEBRA, SECOND YEAR - CONICS SERIES.
PROD-LEART   DIST-LEART

GRAPH OF Y EQUALS B TO THE X POWER C
8X10 PREPARED TRANSPARENCY
FROM THE ALGEBRA, SECOND YEAR - LOGARITHMS SERIES.
PROD-LEART   DIST-LEART

GRAPHICAL SOLUTION OF INEQUALITIES IN TWO VARIABLES C
8X10 PREPARED TRANSPARENCY
FROM THE ALGEBRA, FIRST YEAR - SYSTEM OF LINEAR EQUATIONS SERIES.
PROD-LEART   DIST-LEART

GRAPHING C
8X10 PREPARED TRANSPARENCY   P-I
FROM THE ELEMENTARY-JUNIOR HIGH MATHEMATICS SERIES.
PROD-LEART   DIST-LEART

GRAPHING A FIRST-DEGREE EQUATION IN THREE VARIABLES
C
8X10 PREPARED TRANSPARENCY
FROM THE ALGEBRA, SECOND YEAR - LINES AND PLANES SERIES.
PROD-LEART   DIST-LEART

GRAPHING SOLUTION OF A SYSTEM OF THREE EQUATIONS C
8X10 PREPARED TRANSPARENCY
FROM THE ALGEBRA, SECOND YEAR - LINES AND PLANES SERIES.
PROD-LEART   DIST-LEART

GRAPHS OF OPEN SENTENCES IN TWO VARIABLES C
8X10 PREPARED TRANSPARENCY
FROM THE ALGEBRA, FIRST YEAR - SYSTEM OF LINEAR EQUATIONS SERIES.
PROD-LEART   DIST-LEART

GROUP PRESSURES C
8X10 PREPARED TRANSPARENCY   J-H
FROM THE BASIC SOCIAL STUDIES CONCEPTS - SOCIETY SERIES.
PROD-LEART   DIST-LEART

GROWTH OF BODY HAIR C
8X10 PREPARED TRANSPARENCY
FROM THE SEX EDUCATION - DEVELOPMENTAL PATTERNS OF PUBESCENT BOYS SERIES.
PROD-LEART   DIST-LEART

GROWTH OF INTERNATIONAL TRADE AND COMMERCE C
8X10 PREPARED TRANSPARENCY   J-H
FROM THE ECONOMICS - ECONOMIC HISTORY SERIES.
PROD-LEART   DIST-LEART

GROWTH OF THE BABY, PT 1 C
8X10 PREPARED TRANSPARENCY
FROM THE SEX EDUCATION - THE BABY - ITS CONCEPTION, GROWTH AND BIRTH SERIES.
PROD-LEART   DIST-LEART

GROWTH OF THE BABY, PT 2 C
8X10 PREPARED TRANSPARENCY
FROM THE SEX EDUCATION - THE BABY - ITS CONCEPTION, GROWTH AND BIRTH SERIES.
PROD-LEART   DIST-LEART

GUILD VS LABOR UNION C
8X10 PREPARED TRANSPARENCY
FROM THE ECONOMICS - POLITICAL ECONOMY AND PHILOSOPHY SERIES.
PROD-LEART   DIST-LEART

GWENDOLYN BROOKS C
8X10 PREPARED TRANSPARENCY   J-H
FROM THE BIOGRAPHIES OF OUTSTANDING NEGRO AMERICANS SERIES.
PROD-LEART   DIST-LEART

H

HALLUCINOGENIC DRUGS C
8X10 PREPARED TRANSPARENCY   H
SEE SERIES TITLE FOR DESCRIPTIVE STATEMENT.
FROM THE DRUG ABUSE SERIES.
PROD-BOW   DIST-BOW

HARRIET TUBMAN C
8X10 PREPARED TRANSPARENCY   J-H
FROM THE BIOGRAPHIES OF OUTSTANDING NEGRO AMERICANS SERIES.
PROD-LEART   DIST-LEART

HARRY BELAFONTE C
8X10 PREPARED TRANSPARENCY   J-H
FROM THE BIOGRAPHIES OF OUTSTANDING NEGRO AMERICANS SERIES.
PROD-LEART   DIST-LEART

HEART C
8X10 PREPARED TRANSPARENCY   H
SEE SERIES TITLE FOR DESCRIPTIVE STATEMENT.
FROM THE HUMAN BODY SERIES.
PROD-BOW   DIST-BOW

HEATING A HOME C
8X10 PREPARED TRANSPARENCY   H
SEE SERIES TITLE FOR DESCRIPTIVE STATEMENT.
FROM THE APPLIED SCIENCE SERIES.
PROD-BOW   DIST-BOW

HEN AND CHICKS C
8X10 PREPARED TRANSPARENCY   K-P
FROM THE LIFE SCIENCE - COMING TO LIFE SERIES.
PROD-LEART   DIST-LEART

HENRY O TANNER C
8X10 PREPARED TRANSPARENCY   J-H
FROM THE BIOGRAPHIES OF OUTSTANDING NEGRO AMERICANS SERIES.
PROD-LEART   DIST-LEART

HEREDITY C
8X10 PREPARED TRANSPARENCY   H
SEE SERIES TITLE FOR DESCRIPTIVE STATEMENT.
FROM THE PLANTS SERIES.
PROD-BOW   DIST-BOW

HEREDITY (BASIC) C
8X10 PREPARED TRANSPARENCY   H
SEE SERIES TITLE FOR DESCRIPTIVE STATEMENT.
FROM THE GENERAL TOPICS SERIES.
PROD-BOW   DIST-BOW

HISTORY OF RECORD KEEPING C
8X10 PREPARED TRANSPARENCY   J-H
FROM THE ECONOMICS - ECONOMIC HISTORY SERIES.
PROD-LEART   DIST-LEART

HORMONES AND EMOTIONAL EFFECTS, PT 1 C
8X10 PREPARED TRANSPARENCY
FROM THE SEX EDUCATION - GROWTH AND THE ENDOCRINE GLANDS SERIES.
PROD-LEART   DIST-LEART

HORMONES AND EMOTIONAL EFFECTS, PT 2 C
8X10 PREPARED TRANSPARENCY
FROM THE SEX EDUCATION - GROWTH AND THE ENDOCRINE GLANDS SERIES.
PROD-LEART   DIST-LEART

HOW A BILL BECOMES A LAW C
8X10 PREPARED TRANSPARENCY   J-H
FROM THE UNITED STATES GOVERNMENT AND HOW IT WORKS SERIES.
PROD-LEART   DIST-LEART

HOW BANKS WORK C
8X10 PREPARED TRANSPARENCY   J-H
FROM THE BASIC SOCIAL STUDIES CONCEPTS - ECONOMICS SERIES.
PROD-LEART   DIST-LEART

HOW COLOR PICTURES ARE MADE C
8X10 PREPARED TRANSPARENCY   I-H
SEE SERIES TITLE FOR DESCRIPTIVE STATEMENT.
FROM THE LIGHT AND COLOR SERIES.
PROD-BOW   DIST-BOW

HOW CUSTOMS CHANGE C
8X10 PREPARED TRANSPARENCY   J-H
FROM THE BASIC SOCIAL STUDIES CONCEPTS - SOCIETY SERIES.
PROD-LEART   DIST-LEART

HOW DO CHECKS REPLACE MONEY C
8X10 PREPARED TRANSPARENCY   J-H
FROM THE BASIC SOCIAL STUDIES CONCEPTS - ECONOMICS SERIES.
PROD-LEART   DIST-LEART

HOW DO YOU MEASURE UP, NO. 1 C
8X10 PREPARED TRANSPARENCY
SEE SERIES TITLE FOR DESCRIPTIVE STATEMENT.
FROM THE GOOD GROOMING SERIES.
PROD-COF   DIST-COF

HOW DO YOU MEASURE UP, NO. 2 C
8X10 PREPARED TRANSPARENCY
SEE SERIES TITLE FOR DESCRIPTIVE STATEMENT.
FROM THE GOOD GROOMING SERIES.
PROD-COF   DIST-COF

HOW DOES SOCIETY TEACH ITS VALUES C
8X10 PREPARED TRANSPARENCY   J-H
FROM THE BASIC SOCIAL STUDIES CONCEPTS - SOCIETY SERIES.
PROD-LEART   DIST-LEART

HOW EMOTIONS ARE EXPRESSED C
8X10 PREPARED TRANSPARENCY
FROM THE SEX EDUCATION - DEVELOPMENT OF CONCEPTS AND ATTITUDES SERIES.
PROD-LEART   DIST-LEART

HOW HEAVY C
8X10 PREPARED TRANSPARENCY   K-P
FROM THE LIFE SCIENCE - GROWING UP SERIES.
PROD-LEART   DIST-LEART

HOW LENSES WORK C
8X10 PREPARED TRANSPARENCY   I-H
SEE SERIES TITLE FOR DESCRIPTIVE STATEMENT.
FROM THE LIGHT AND COLOR SERIES.
PROD-BOW   DIST-BOW

HOW PRICE IS DETERMINED C
8X10 PREPARED TRANSPARENCY   J-H
FROM THE BASIC SOCIAL STUDIES CONCEPTS - ECONOMICS SERIES.
PROD-LEART   DIST-LEART

HOW TALL C
8X10 PREPARED TRANSPARENCY   K-P
FROM THE LIFE SCIENCE - GROWING UP SERIES.
PROD-LEART   DIST-LEART

HOW TEMPERATURE AFFECTS US C
8X10 PREPARED TRANSPARENCY   K-P
SEE SERIES TITLE FOR DESCRIPTIVE STATEMENT.
FROM THE TEMPERATURE SERIES.
PROD-BOW   DIST-BOW

HOW THE EARTH REVOLVES C
8X10 PREPARED TRANSPARENCY   K-P
SEE SERIES TITLE FOR DESCRIPTIVE STATEMENT.
FROM THE EARTH AND SKY SERIES.
PROD-BOW   DIST-BOW

HOW THE EARTH ROTATES C
8X10 PREPARED TRANSPARENCY   K-P
SEE SERIES TITLE FOR DESCRIPTIVE STATEMENT.
FROM THE EARTH AND SKY SERIES.
PROD-BOW   DIST-BOW

HOW THE MOON SENDS LIGHT C
8X10 PREPARED TRANSPARENCY   K-P
SEE SERIES TITLE FOR DESCRIPTIVE STATEMENT.
FROM THE EARTH AND SKY SERIES.
PROD-BOW   DIST-BOW

I

HOW TO EXPAND PRODUCTION C
    8X10 PREPARED TRANSPARENCY   J-H
FROM THE ECONOMICS - ECONOMICS IN
ACTION SERIES.
PROD-LEART   DIST-LEART

HOW TO STUDY--A SERIES
PRESENTS THE KEYS TO LEARNING, INCLUDING
STUDY SETTING, PLANNING, NOTE-TAKING, ATTI-
TUDE, FITNESS AND OTHERS.
PROD-BETECL   DIST-BETECL

HOW TO USE THE
THERMOMETER C
    8X10 PREPARED TRANSPARENCY   K-P
SEE SERIES TITLE FOR DESCRIPTIVE STATEMENT.
FROM THE TEMPERATURE SERIES.
PROD-BOW   DIST-BOW

HOW WE MEASURE ECONOMIC
GROWTH C
    8X10 PREPARED TRANSPARENCY   J-H
FROM THE ECONOMICS - ECONOMICS IN
ACTION SERIES.
PROD-LEART.   DIST-LEART

HUMAN BODY--A SERIES H
ILLUSTRATES VARIOUS PARTS OF THE HUMAN
BODY.
PROD-BOW   DIST-BOW

BONE JOINTS
CIRCULATORY SYSTEM
DIGESTIVE SYSTEM
EAR
EYE
HEART
NERVOUS SYSTEM
RESPIRATORY SYSTEM
SKELETAL SYSTEM
SKIN
TOOTH STRUCTURE
VISION DEFECTS

HYPERBOLA - DEFINITION C
    8X10 PREPARED TRANSPARENCY
FROM THE ALGEBRA, SECOND YEAR - CONICS
SERIES.
PROD-LEART   DIST-LEART

HYPERBOLA - GRAPHING AND
EQUATION C
    8X10 PREPARED TRANSPARENCY
FROM THE ALGEBRA, SECOND YEAR - CONICS
SERIES.
PROD-LEART   DIST-LEART

HYPERBOLA OF FORM XY
EQUALS K C
    8X10 PREPARED TRANSPARENCY
FROM THE ALGEBRA, SECOND YEAR - CONICS
SERIES.
PROD-LEART   DIST-LEART

I

IDEAL AND YOUR PARENTS C
    8X10 PREPARED TRANSPARENCY   J
FROM THE DATING RELATIONS - ROMANCE AND
PEOPLE SERIES.
PROD-LEART   DIST-LEART

IDEAL FEMALE C
    8X10 PREPARED TRANSPARENCY   J
FROM THE DATING RELATIONS - DIMENSIONS
OF DATING SERIES.
PROD-LEART   DIST-LEART

IDEAL MALE C
    8X10 PREPARED TRANSPARENCY   J
FROM THE DATING RELATIONS - DIMENSIONS
OF DATING SERIES.
PROD-LEART   DIST-LEART

IDEALIZATION AND FANTASY C
    8X10 PREPARED TRANSPARENCY   J
FROM THE DATING RELATIONS - ROMANCE AND
PEOPLE SERIES.
PROD-LEART   DIST-LEART

IDENTIFYING ACTION VERBS C
    8X10 PREPARED TRANSPARENCY   I-J
SEE SERIES TITLE FOR DESCRIPTIVE STATEMENT.
FROM THE WORD FORMS AND FUNCTIONS SE-
RIES.

PROD-BOW   DIST-BOW

IDENTIFYING ADVERBIALS C
    8X10 PREPARED TRANSPARENCY   I-J
SEE SERIES TITLE FOR DESCRIPTIVE STATEMENT.
FROM THE WORD FORMS AND FUNCTIONS SE-
RIES.
PROD-BOW   DIST-BOW

IDENTIFYING APPOSITIVES C
    8X10 PREPARED TRANSPARENCY   P-I
SEE SERIES TITLE FOR DESCRIPTIVE STATEMENT.
FROM THE PUNCTUATION AND CAPITALIZATION
SERIES.
PROD-BOW   DIST-BOW

IDENTIFYING STATE-OF-BEING
VERBS C
    8X10 PREPARED TRANSPARENCY   I-J
SEE SERIES TITLE FOR DESCRIPTIVE STATEMENT.
FROM THE WORD FORMS AND FUNCTIONS SE-
RIES.
PROD-BOW   DIST-BOW

IMPLANTATION C
    8X10 PREPARED TRANSPARENCY
FROM THE SEX EDUCATION - THE BABY - ITS
CONCEPTION, GROWTH AND BIRTH SERIES.
PROD-LEART   DIST-LEART

IMPORTANCE OF A PLEASANT
FACE AND VOICE C
    8X10 PREPARED TRANSPARENCY
SEE SERIES TITLE FOR DESCRIPTIVE STATEMENT.
FROM THE GOOD GROOMING SERIES.
PROD-COF   DIST-COF

IN DISTRIBUTIVE EDUCATION
WE WILL STUDY C
    8X10 PREPARED TRANSPARENCY
SEE SERIES TITLE FOR DESCRIPTIVE STATEMENT.
FROM THE ORIENTATION TO DISTRIBUTIVE EDU-
CATION SERIES.
PROD-COF   DIST-COF

IN THE GROUND C
    8X10 PREPARED TRANSPARENCY   K-P
FROM THE LIFE SCIENCE - LIVING SOMEWHERE
SERIES.
PROD-LEART   DIST-LEART

INCLINED PLANE C
    8X10 PREPARED TRANSPARENCY   H
SEE SERIES TITLE FOR DESCRIPTIVE STATEMENT.
FROM THE MACHINES SERIES.
PROD-BOW   DIST-BOW

INDIVIDUAL DIFFERENCES IN
CAPACITY C
    8X10 PREPARED TRANSPARENCY   J
FROM THE DATING RELATIONS - MATURE LOVE
SERIES.
PROD-LEART   DIST-LEART

INDUSTRIAL REVOLUTION IS A
'TAKE-OFF' C
    8X10 PREPARED TRANSPARENCY   J-H
FROM THE ECONOMICS - ECONOMIC HISTORY
SERIES.
PROD-LEART   DIST-LEART

INDUSTRIAL REVOLUTION
TODAY C
    8X10 PREPARED TRANSPARENCY   J-H
FROM THE ECONOMICS - ECONOMIC HISTORY
SERIES.
PROD-LEART   DIST-LEART

INFATUATION C
    8X10 PREPARED TRANSPARENCY   J
FROM THE DATING RELATIONS - ROMANCE AND
PEOPLE SERIES.
PROD-LEART   DIST-LEART

INGUINAL AND SPERMATIC
CORD C
    8X10 PREPARED TRANSPARENCY
FROM THE SEX EDUCATION - DEVELOPMENTAL
PATTERNS OF PUBESCENT BOYS SERIES.
PROD-LEART   DIST-LEART

INITIAL AND FINAL
CONSONANTS--A SERIES
TEACHES INITIAL AND FINAL CONSONANT
SOUNDS AND THEIR RELATIONS TO THEIR SYM-
BOLS.
PROD-BOW   DIST-BOW

PROD-BOW   DIST-BOW

INSECT LIFE CYCLE C
    8X10 PREPARED TRANSPARENCY   K-P
FROM THE LIFE SCIENCE - COMING TO LIFE
SERIES.
PROD-LEART   DIST-LEART

INSTRUMENTS AND
TECHNIQUES OF SCIENCE--A
SERIES H
PRESENTS SOME SCIENTIFIC INSTRUMENTS AND
TECHNIQUES.
PROD-BOW   DIST-BOW

BALANCE BEAM SCALE
PREPARING SLIDES
PSYCHROMETER
TELESCOPE
TESTING FOR MINERALS
THERMOMETER

INTERACTION OF POLITICAL,
SOCIAL AND ECONOMIC
CAUSES AND EFFECTS C
    8X10 PREPARED TRANSPARENCY   J-H
FROM THE BASIC SOCIAL STUDIES CONCEPTS -
POLITICS, SOCIAL-ECONOMIC INTERDEPENDENCE
SERIES.
PROD-LEART   DIST-LEART

INTERACTION WITH PEOPLE C
    8X10 PREPARED TRANSPARENCY   J
FROM THE DATING RELATIONS - POPULARITY
SERIES.
PROD-LEART   DIST-LEART

INTERNAL COMBUSTION
ENGINE C
    8X10 PREPARED TRANSPARENCY   H
SEE SERIES TITLE FOR DESCRIPTIVE STATEMENT.
FROM THE ENGINES SERIES.
PROD-BOW   DIST-BOW

INTERNATIONAL COMMERCIAL
POLICY C
    8X10 PREPARED TRANSPARENCY   J-H
FROM THE ECONOMICS - ECONOMICS IN
ACTION SERIES.
PROD-LEART   DIST-LEART

INTERNATIONAL TRADE AND
FINANCE C
    8X10 PREPARED TRANSPARENCY   J-H
FROM THE ECONOMICS - ECONOMICS IN
ACTION SERIES.
PROD-LEART   DIST-LEART

INTERPOLATING FOR
ANTILOGARITHMS C
    8X10 PREPARED TRANSPARENCY
FROM THE ALGEBRA, SECOND YEAR -
LOGARITHMS SERIES.
PROD-LEART   DIST-LEART

INTERPOLATION IN TABLES C
    8X10 PREPARED TRANSPARENCY
FROM THE ALGEBRA, SECOND YEAR -
LOGARITHMS SERIES.
PROD-LEART   DIST-LEART

INTERVIEW RATING SHEET C
    8X10 PREPARED TRANSPARENCY
SEE SERIES TITLE FOR DESCRIPTIVE STATEMENT.
FROM THE JOB APPLICATION AND JOB INTER-
VIEW SERIES.
PROD-COF   DIST-COF

INTRODUCING ADVERBS C
    8X10 PREPARED TRANSPARENCY   I-J
SEE SERIES TITLE FOR DESCRIPTIVE STATEMENT.
FROM THE WORD FORMS AND FUNCTIONS SE-
RIES.
PROD-BOW   DIST-BOW

INTRODUCING QUOTATION
MARKS C
    8X10 PREPARED TRANSPARENCY   P-I
SEE SERIES TITLE FOR DESCRIPTIVE STATEMENT.
FROM THE PUNCTUATION AND CAPITALIZATION
SERIES.
PROD-BOW   DIST-BOW

INTRODUCTION OF ROMANCE C
    8X10 PREPARED TRANSPARENCY   J
FROM THE DATING RELATIONS - ROMANCE AND
PEOPLE SERIES.
PROD-LEART   DIST-LEART

INTRODUCTION TO LOVE   C
    8X10 PREPARED TRANSPARENCY   J
FROM THE DATING RELATIONS - MATURE LOVE
SERIES.
PROD-LEART   DIST-LEART

INTRODUCTIONS ALL AROUND   C
    8X10 PREPARED TRANSPARENCY
SEE SERIES TITLE FOR DESCRIPTIVE STATEMENT.
FROM THE ORIENTATION TO DISTRIBUTIVE EDU-
CATION SERIES.
PROD-COF   DIST-COF

**INVERSE OF SUM AND OF
PRODUCT**   C
    8X10 PREPARED TRANSPARENCY
FROM THE ALGEBRA, SECOND YEAR -
STRUCTURE OF ALGEBRA SERIES.
PROD-LEART   DIST-LEART

INVERSE VARIATION   C
    8X10 PREPARED TRANSPARENCY
FROM THE ALGEBRA, FIRST YEAR - FUNCTIONS
SERIES.
PROD-LEART   DIST-LEART

INVERSES OF EQUALS   C
    8X10 PREPARED TRANSPARENCY
FROM THE ALGEBRA, SECOND YEAR -
STRUCTURE OF ALGEBRA SERIES.
PROD-LEART   DIST-LEART

IRRATIONAL NUMBERS   C
    8X10 PREPARED TRANSPARENCY
FROM THE ALGEBRA, FIRST YEAR - REAL
NUMBERS SERIES.
PROD-LEART   DIST-LEART

**ISLAND AND CORAL REEF
FORMATION**   C
    8X10 PREPARED TRANSPARENCY   I-H
SEE SERIES TITLE FOR DESCRIPTIVE STATEMENT.
FROM THE OCEANOGRAPHY SERIES.
PROD-BOW   DIST-BOW

**ITEMS FOR THE WORKING
GIRL'S HANDBAG**   C
    8X10 PREPARED TRANSPARENCY
SEE SERIES TITLE FOR DESCRIPTIVE STATEMENT.
FROM THE GOOD GROOMING SERIES.
PROD-COF   DIST-COF

**ITEMS TO BE CARRIED BY THE
WORKING MAN**   C
    8X10 PREPARED TRANSPARENCY
SEE SERIES TITLE FOR DESCRIPTIVE STATEMENT.
FROM THE GOOD GROOMING SERIES.
PROD-COF   DIST-COF

J

JACK JOHNSON   C
    8X10 PREPARED TRANSPARENCY   J-H
FROM THE BIOGRAPHIES OF OUTSTANDING
NEGRO AMERICANS SERIES.
PROD-LEART   DIST-LEART

JACKIE ROBINSON   C
    8X10 PREPARED TRANSPARENCY   J-H
FROM THE BIOGRAPHIES OF OUTSTANDING
NEGRO AMERICANS SERIES.
PROD-LEART   DIST-LEART

JAMES BROWN   C
    8X10 PREPARED TRANSPARENCY   J-H
FROM THE BIOGRAPHIES OF OUTSTANDING
NEGRO AMERICANS SERIES.
PROD-LEART   DIST-LEART

JAMES WELDON JOHNSON   C
    8X10 PREPARED TRANSPARENCY   J-H
FROM THE BIOGRAPHIES OF OUTSTANDING
NEGRO AMERICANS SERIES.
PROD-LEART   DIST-LEART

JAN MATZELIGER   C
    8X10 PREPARED TRANSPARENCY   J-H
FROM THE BIOGRAPHIES OF OUTSTANDING
NEGRO AMERICANS SERIES.
PROD-LEART   DIST-LEART

JET ENGINE   C
    8X10 PREPARED TRANSPARENCY   H
SEE SERIES TITLE FOR DESCRIPTIVE STATEMENT.
FROM THE ENGINES SERIES.
PROD-BOW   DIST-BOW

**JOB APPLICATION AND JOB
INTERVIEW--A SERIES**
EXPLORES THE VARIOUS PHASES IN APPLYING
FOR A JOB AND PARTICIPATING IN A JOB INTER-
VIEW. ILLUSTRATES THE FORMS THAT MUST BE
FILLED OUT BEFORE SEEKING EMPLOYMENT.
PROD-COF   DIST-COF

APPLICATION LETTER
CARD OF INTRODUCTION (SAMPLE)
COMPARE VIEWPOINTS
DATA SHEET
DURING THE INTERVIEW
EMPLOYEE'S WITHHOLDING EXEMPTION
CERTIFICATE
GET ACQUAINTED WITH YOURSELF
INTERVIEW RATING SHEET
JOB APPLICATION FORM
OVERVIEW OF JOB APPLICATION AND
JOB INTERVIEW
PREPARATION
RELATED ITEMS FOR CLASSROOM
DISCUSSION
SOCIAL SECURITY AND TAX ACCOUNT
NUMBER
TIPS FOR THE INTERVIEW

JOB APPLICATION FORM   C
    8X10 PREPARED TRANSPARENCY
SEE SERIES TITLE FOR DESCRIPTIVE STATEMENT.
FROM THE JOB APPLICATION AND JOB INTER-
VIEW SERIES.
PROD-COF   DIST-COF

JOB REQUIREMENTS IN DRESS   C
    8X10 PREPARED TRANSPARENCY
SEE SERIES TITLE FOR DESCRIPTIVE STATEMENT.
FROM THE GOOD GROOMING SERIES.
PROD-COF   DIST-COF

JOE LOUIS   C
    8X10 PREPARED TRANSPARENCY   J-H
FROM THE BIOGRAPHIES OF OUTSTANDING
NEGRO AMERICANS SERIES.
PROD-LEART   DIST-LEART

**JURISDICTION OF THE SUPREME
COURT, THE**   C
    8X10 PREPARED TRANSPARENCY   J-H
FROM THE UNITED STATES GOVERNMENT AND
HOW IT WORKS SERIES.
PROD-LEART   DIST-LEART

K

**KEEPING UP WITH THE
JONESES**   C
    8X10 PREPARED TRANSPARENCY
SEE SERIES TITLE FOR DESCRIPTIVE STATEMENT.
FROM THE BASIC SALESMANSHIP SERIES.
PROD-COF   DIST-COF

L

LABOR AND ECONOMICS   C
    8X10 PREPARED TRANSPARENCY   J-H
FROM THE BASIC SOCIAL STUDIES CONCEPTS -
ECONOMICS SERIES.
PROD-LEART   DIST-LEART

LANGSTON HUGHES   C
    8X10 PREPARED TRANSPARENCY   J-H
FROM THE BIOGRAPHIES OF OUTSTANDING
NEGRO AMERICANS SERIES.
PROD-LEART   DIST-LEART

LASTING LOVE   C
    8X10 PREPARED TRANSPARENCY   J
FROM THE DATING RELATIONS - MATURE LOVE
SERIES.
PROD-LEART   DIST-LEART

LAW OF REFLECTION   C
    8X10 PREPARED TRANSPARENCY   I-H
SEE SERIES TITLE FOR DESCRIPTIVE STATEMENT.
FROM THE LIGHT AND COLOR SERIES.
PROD-BOW   DIST-BOW

LAWS OF MAGNETISM   C
    8X10 PREPARED TRANSPARENCY   H
SEE SERIES TITLE FOR DESCRIPTIVE STATEMENT.
FROM THE MAGNETISM AND ELECTRICITY SERIES.
PROD-BOW   DIST-BOW

LEAF IDENTIFICATION   C
    8X10 PREPARED TRANSPARENCY   H
SEE SERIES TITLE FOR DESCRIPTIVE STATEMENT.
FROM THE PLANTS SERIES.
PROD-BOW   DIST-BOW

LEAF STRUCTURE   C
    8X10 PREPARED TRANSPARENCY   H
SEE SERIES TITLE FOR DESCRIPTIVE STATEMENT.
FROM THE PLANTS SERIES.
PROD-BOW   DIST-BOW

**LEARNING ABOUT LIGHT AND
SHADOWS**   C
    8X10 PREPARED TRANSPARENCY   K-P
SEE SERIES TITLE FOR DESCRIPTIVE STATEMENT.
FROM THE EARTH AND SKY SERIES.
PROD-BOW   DIST-BOW

LEARNING HOW TO SAY NO   C
    8X10 PREPARED TRANSPARENCY   J
FROM THE DATING RELATIONS - DATING
PROBLEMS SERIES.
PROD-LEART   DIST-LEART

**LEARNING HOW TO VARY THE
TEMPO**   C
    8X10 PREPARED TRANSPARENCY   J
FROM THE DATING RELATIONS - DATING
PROBLEMS SERIES.
PROD-LEART   DIST-LEART

LEARNING THE ALPHABET   C
    8X10 PREPARED TRANSPARENCY   K-P
SEE SERIES TITLE FOR DESCRIPTIVE STATEMENT.
FROM THE BEGINNING SKILLS SERIES.
PROD-BOW   DIST-BOW

**LEARNING TO READ THE
THERMOMETER**   C
    8X10 PREPARED TRANSPARENCY   K-P
SEE SERIES TITLE FOR DESCRIPTIVE STATEMENT.
FROM THE TEMPERATURE SERIES.
PROD-BOW   DIST-BOW

LEONTYNE PRICE   C
    8X10 PREPARED TRANSPARENCY   J-H
FROM THE BIOGRAPHIES OF OUTSTANDING
NEGRO AMERICANS SERIES.
PROD-LEART   DIST-LEART

**LET'S HAVE A NURSERY RHYME
PARTY**   C
    8X10 PREPARED TRANSPARENCY   K-P
SEE SERIES TITLE FOR DESCRIPTIVE STATEMENT.
FROM THE BEGINNING SKILLS SERIES.
PROD-BOW   DIST-BOW

LETTER WRITING--A SERIES   I
PRESENTS THE PROPER METHODS OF WRITING A
LETTER.
PROD-BOW   DIST-BOW

ADDRESSING ENVELOPES FOR BUSINESS
LETTERS
ADDRESSING ENVELOPES FOR FRIENDLY
LETTERS
WRITING BUSINESS LETTERS
WRITING FRIENDLY LETTERS

LIBRARY SKILLS--A SERIES
DISCUSSES WHAT A LIBRARY CONTAINS, THE OR-
GANIZATION OF A LIBRARY, HOW TO FIND WHAT
YOU NEED AND THE RESPONSIBILITIES OF A PER-
SON AS A CITIZEN.
PROD-BOW   DIST-BOW

**LIFE SCIENCE - COMING TO
LIFE--A SERIES**   K-P
PROD-LEART   DIST-LEART

BABY ANIMALS
BEANS - BLOOM AND SEED
BLOOM TO FRUIT
CORN
FROG - LIFE CYCLE
HEN AND CHICKS
INSECT LIFE CYCLE
SEEDS IN FRUIT, VEGETABLES

LIFE SCIENCE - GROWING UP--A SERIES
K-P

PROD-LEART   DIST-LEART

BABY AND ME
BABY FOR A YEAR
DAD AND ME
FAMILY OF CHILDREN
FAVORITE THINGS
FOOD, FUN, REST
HOW HEAVY
HOW TALL
MANY COLORS
MANY FEET
MANY HANDS
MOM AND ME
TEETH COME AND GO

LIFE SCIENCE - LIVING SOMEWHERE--A SERIES
K-P

PROD-LEART   DIST-LEART

AT THE BEACH
CORNER OF THE FIELD
EDGE OF THE POND
EDGE OF THE WOODS
IN THE GROUND
LIVING THINGS NEAR HOME
LIVING THINGS NEAR SCHOOL
PLACES WHERE THINGS LIVE

LIFT PUMP   C
         8X10 PREPARED TRANSPARENCY   H
   SEE SERIES TITLE FOR DESCRIPTIVE STATEMENT.
   FROM THE APPLIED SCIENCE SERIES.
PROD-BOW   DIST-BOW

LIGHT AND COLOR--A SERIES
I-H
   DESCRIBES VARIOUS ASPECTS OF LIGHT AND
   COLOR.
PROD-BOW   DIST-BOW

COLOR WHEEL
COMBINING COLORS
EXPERIMENTING WITH LIGHT AND
OBJECTS
EXPERIMENTS WITH COLORED LIGHT
EXPERIMENTS WITH COLORED OBJECTS
HOW COLOR PICTURES ARE MADE
HOW LENSES WORK
LAW OF REFLECTION
LIGHT AND DARKNESS
PRISM AND SPECTRUM
REFRACTION OF LIGHT
TWO WAYS TO PRODUCE COLOR

LIGHT AND DARKNESS   C
         8X10 PREPARED TRANSPARENCY   I-H
   SEE SERIES TITLE FOR DESCRIPTIVE STATEMENT.
   FROM THE LIGHT AND COLOR SERIES.
PROD-BOW   DIST-BOW

LIGHT--A SERIES
I-C
   EXPLAINS THE VARIOUS ASPECTS OF LIGHT.
PROD-BOW   DIST-BOW

MATERIALS AND LIGHT
MICROSCOPE
PRIMARY COLORS OF LIGHT
REFLECTION OF LIGHT
REFRACTION AND LENSES
SPECTRUM

LINEAR INTERPOLATION   C
         8X10 PREPARED TRANSPARENCY
   FROM THE ALGEBRA, SECOND YEAR -
   LOGARITHMS SERIES.
PROD-LEART   DIST-LEART

LIQUID MEASURE   C
         8X10 PREPARED TRANSPARENCY   P-I
   FROM THE ELEMENTARY-JUNIOR HIGH
   MATHEMATICS SERIES.
PROD-LEART   DIST-LEART

LIVING THINGS NEAR HOME   C
         8X10 PREPARED TRANSPARENCY   K-P
   FROM THE LIFE SCIENCE - LIVING SOMEWHERE
   SERIES.
PROD-LEART   DIST-LEART

LIVING THINGS NEAR SCHOOL   C
         8X10 PREPARED TRANSPARENCY   K-P
   FROM THE LIFE SCIENCE - LIVING SOMEWHERE
   SERIES.
PROD-LEART   DIST-LEART

LOGARITHM OF A PRODUCT   C
         8X10 PREPARED TRANSPARENCY
   FROM THE ALGEBRA, SECOND YEAR -
   LOGARITHMS SERIES.
PROD-LEART   DIST-LEART

LOGARITHM OF A QUOTIENT AND A POWER   C
         8X10 PREPARED TRANSPARENCY
   FROM THE ALGEBRA, SECOND YEAR -
   LOGARITHMS SERIES.
PROD-LEART   DIST-LEART

LOUIS 'SATCHMO' ARMSTRONG   C
         8X10 PREPARED TRANSPARENCY   J-H
   FROM THE BIOGRAPHIES OF OUTSTANDING
   NEGRO AMERICANS SERIES.
PROD-LEART   DIST-LEART

LOVE IS BOTH STURDY AND PERISHABLE   C
         8X10 PREPARED TRANSPARENCY   J
   FROM THE DATING RELATIONS - MATURE LOVE
   SERIES.
PROD-LEART   DIST-LEART

M

MACHINES--A SERIES
H
   PRESENTS VARIOUS TYPES OF MACHINES.
PROD-BOW   DIST-BOW

FIRST CLASS LEVER
GEARS
INCLINED PLANE
PULLEY
SECOND CLASS LEVER
THIRD CLASS LEVER

MAGNETISM AND ELECTRICITY--A SERIES
H
   EXPLAINS THE PHENOMENON OF MAGNETISM
   AND ELECTRICITY, INCLUDING INVENTIONS
   WHICH HAVE EVOLVED FROM THEM.
PROD-BOW   DIST-BOW

BATTERIES
CIRCUITS
COMPASS
EARTH'S MAGNETIC FIELD
ELECTRIC BELL
ELECTRIC MOTOR
ELECTROSCOPE
GENERATING STATION
LAWS OF MAGNETISM
TELEGRAPH
TELEPHONE
TELEVISION

MAHALIA JACKSON   C
         8X10 PREPARED TRANSPARENCY   J-H
   FROM THE BIOGRAPHIES OF OUTSTANDING
   NEGRO AMERICANS SERIES.
PROD-LEART   DIST-LEART

MALCOLM X   C
         8X10 PREPARED TRANSPARENCY   J-H
   FROM THE BIOGRAPHIES OF OUTSTANDING
   NEGRO AMERICANS SERIES.
PROD-LEART   DIST-LEART

MALE ORGANS OF EXCRETION AND REPRODUCTION   C
         8X10 PREPARED TRANSPARENCY
   FROM THE SEX EDUCATION - DEVELOPMENTAL
   PATTERNS OF PUBESCENT BOYS SERIES.
PROD-LEART   DIST-LEART

MAMMALS' HOMES   C
         8X10 PREPARED TRANSPARENCY   H
   SEE SERIES TITLE FOR DESCRIPTIVE STATEMENT.
   FROM THE WARM-BLOODED VERTEBRATES SE-
   RIES.
PROD-BOW   DIST-BOW

MAN IN THE OCEAN   C
         8X10 PREPARED TRANSPARENCY   I-H
   SEE SERIES TITLE FOR DESCRIPTIVE STATEMENT.
   FROM THE OCEANOGRAPHY SERIES.
PROD-BOW   DIST-BOW

MAN'S COMMUNITY EXPANDS THROUGH THE AGES   C
         8X10 PREPARED TRANSPARENCY   J-H
   FROM THE BASIC SOCIAL STUDIES CONCEPTS -
   POLITICS, SOCIAL-ECONOMIC INTERDEPENDENCE
   SERIES.
PROD-LEART   DIST-LEART

MANY COLORS   C
         8X10 PREPARED TRANSPARENCY   K-P
   FROM THE LIFE SCIENCE - GROWING UP
   SERIES.
PROD-LEART   DIST-LEART

MANY FEET   C
         8X10 PREPARED TRANSPARENCY   K-P
   FROM THE LIFE SCIENCE - GROWING UP
   SERIES.
PROD-LEART   DIST-LEART

MANY HANDS   C
         8X10 PREPARED TRANSPARENCY   K-P
   FROM THE LIFE SCIENCE - GROWING UP
   SERIES.
PROD-LEART   DIST-LEART

MAP PROBLEMS   C
         8X10 PREPARED TRANSPARENCY   P-I
   FROM THE ELEMENTARY-JUNIOR HIGH
   MATHEMATICS SERIES.
PROD-LEART   DIST-LEART

MARCUS GARVEY   C
         8X10 PREPARED TRANSPARENCY   J-H
   FROM THE BIOGRAPHIES OF OUTSTANDING
   NEGRO AMERICANS SERIES.
PROD-LEART   DIST-LEART

MARIAN ANDERSON   C
         8X10 PREPARED TRANSPARENCY   J-H
   FROM THE BIOGRAPHIES OF OUTSTANDING
   NEGRO AMERICANS SERIES.
PROD-LEART   DIST-LEART

MARIJUANA   C
         8X10 PREPARED TRANSPARENCY   H
   SEE SERIES TITLE FOR DESCRIPTIVE STATEMENT.
   FROM THE DRUG ABUSE SERIES.
PROD-BOW   DIST-BOW

MARTIN LUTHER KING   C
         8X10 PREPARED TRANSPARENCY   J-H
   FROM THE BIOGRAPHIES OF OUTSTANDING
   NEGRO AMERICANS SERIES.
PROD-LEART   DIST-LEART

MARY MC LEOD BETHUNE   C
         8X10 PREPARED TRANSPARENCY   J-H
   FROM THE BIOGRAPHIES OF OUTSTANDING
   NEGRO AMERICANS SERIES.
PROD-LEART   DIST-LEART

MATERIALS AND LIGHT   C
         8X10 PREPARED TRANSPARENCY   I-C
   SEE SERIES TITLE FOR DESCRIPTIVE STATEMENT.
   FROM THE LIGHT SERIES.
PROD-BOW   DIST-BOW

MATHEMATICAL SYMBOLS   C
         8X10 PREPARED TRANSPARENCY   P-I
   FROM THE ELEMENTARY-JUNIOR HIGH
   MATHEMATICS SERIES.
PROD-LEART   DIST-LEART

MATTHEW HENSON   C
         8X10 PREPARED TRANSPARENCY   J-H
   FROM THE BIOGRAPHIES OF OUTSTANDING
   NEGRO AMERICANS SERIES.
PROD-LEART   DIST-LEART

MATURITY - HIGH MASS CONSUMPTION   C
         8X10 PREPARED TRANSPARENCY   J-H
   FROM THE ECONOMICS - ECONOMIC HISTORY
   SERIES.
PROD-LEART   DIST-LEART

MEANING OF DISTRIBUTION, THE   C
         8X10 PREPARED TRANSPARENCY
   SEE SERIES TITLE FOR DESCRIPTIVE STATEMENT.
   FROM THE ORIENTATION TO DISTRIBUTIVE EDU-
   CATION SERIES.
PROD-COF   DIST-COF

**MEASUREMENT IN ASTRONOMY-
-A SERIES**
I-J
DESCRIBES SYSTEMS OF MEASURING LIGHT AND DISTANCES BETWEEN THE PLANETS IN OUR SO-LAR SYSTEM.
PROD-BOW   DIST-BOW

MEASURING INDIRECTLY
MEASURING THE EARTH
MEASURING THE MOON
MEASURING THE SPEED OF LIGHT
MEASURING TO MARS
MEASURING TO THE STARS
MEASURING TO THE SUN
MODELS OF SOLAR SYSTEM

MEASUREMENT--A SERIES
PRESENTS THE EXPLANATION OF MEASUREMENT, HOW AND WHY IT IS NECESSARY, THE VARIOUS SYSTEMS AND THE CURRENT TREND TOWARD THE METRIC SYSTEM. DISCUSSES THE NEED FOR PRECISE LEARNING VALUES FROM THE SIMPLEST UNIT TO AN UNDERSTANDING OF EINSTEIN'S THEORY OF RELATIVITY.
PROD-BETECL   DIST-BETECL

MEASURING INDIRECTLY   C
8X10 PREPARED TRANSPARENCY   I-J
SEE SERIES TITLE FOR DESCRIPTIVE STATEMENT. FROM THE MEASUREMENT IN ASTRONOMY SE-RIES.
PROD-BOW   DIST-BOW

MEASURING THE EARTH   C
8X10 PREPARED TRANSPARENCY   I-J
SEE SERIES TITLE FOR DESCRIPTIVE STATEMENT. FROM THE MEASUREMENT IN ASTRONOMY SE-RIES.
PROD-BOW   DIST-BOW

MEASURING THE MOON   C
8X10 PREPARED TRANSPARENCY   I-J
SEE SERIES TITLE FOR DESCRIPTIVE STATEMENT. FROM THE MEASUREMENT IN ASTRONOMY SE-RIES.
PROD-BOW   DIST-BOW

**MEASURING THE SPEED OF
LIGHT**   C
8X10 PREPARED TRANSPARENCY   I-J
SEE SERIES TITLE FOR DESCRIPTIVE STATEMENT. FROM THE MEASUREMENT IN ASTRONOMY SE-RIES.
PROD-BOW   DIST-BOW

MEASURING TO MARS   C
8X10 PREPARED TRANSPARENCY   I-J
SEE SERIES TITLE FOR DESCRIPTIVE STATEMENT. FROM THE MEASUREMENT IN ASTRONOMY SE-RIES.
PROD-BOW   DIST-BOW

MEASURING TO THE STARS   C
8X10 PREPARED TRANSPARENCY   I-J
SEE SERIES TITLE FOR DESCRIPTIVE STATEMENT. FROM THE MEASUREMENT IN ASTRONOMY SE-RIES.
PROD-BOW   DIST-BOW

MEASURING TO THE SUN   C
8X10 PREPARED TRANSPARENCY   I-J
SEE SERIES TITLE FOR DESCRIPTIVE STATEMENT. FROM THE MEASUREMENT IN ASTRONOMY SE-RIES.
PROD-BOW   DIST-BOW

MENSTRUATION   C
8X10 PREPARED TRANSPARENCY
SEX EDUCATION - DEVELOPMENTAL PATTERNS OF PUBESCENT GIRLS SERIES.
PROD-LEART   DIST-LEART

MENSURATION PROBLEMS   C
8X10 PREPARED TRANSPARENCY
FROM THE ALGEBRA, SECOND YEAR - WORK PROBLEMS SERIES.
PROD-LEART   DIST-LEART

**METHODS OF AMENDING THE
CONSTITUTION**   C
8X10 PREPARED TRANSPARENCY   J-H
FROM THE UNITED STATES GOVERNMENT AND HOW IT WORKS SERIES.
PROD-LEART   DIST-LEART

METRIC SYSTEM   C
8X10 PREPARED TRANSPARENCY   P-I
FROM THE ELEMENTARY-JUNIOR HIGH MATHEMATICS SERIES.
PROD-LEART   DIST-LEART

MICROSCOPE   C
8X10 PREPARED TRANSPARENCY   I-C
SEE SERIES TITLE FOR DESCRIPTIVE STATEMENT. FROM THE LIGHT SERIES.
PROD-BOW   DIST-BOW

MICROSCOPIC LIFE--A SERIES
I-H
COMPARES THE MANY TYPES OF MICROSCOPIC LIFE.
PROD-BOW   DIST-BOW

AMOEBA, THE
ANIMAL CELL TYPES
BACTERIAL CELL TYPES
EUGLENA, THE
FOSSIL PROTOZOANS
FRESHWATER ALGAE
FRESHWATER PROTOZOANS
PARAMECIUM, THE
PLANT AND ANIMAL CELLS COMPARED
PLANT CELL TYPES
SMALL POND LIFE

**MIXED DATING AMONG
CLASSES**   C
8X10 PREPARED TRANSPARENCY   J
FROM THE DATING RELATIONS - MIXED DATING SERIES.
PROD-LEART   DIST-LEART

MIXED DATING AMONG RACES   C
8X10 PREPARED TRANSPARENCY   J
FROM THE DATING RELATIONS - MIXED DATING SERIES.
PROD-LEART   DIST-LEART

**MIXED DATING AMONG
RELIGIONS**   C
8X10 PREPARED TRANSPARENCY   J
FROM THE DATING RELATIONS - MIXED DATING SERIES.
PROD-LEART   DIST-LEART

MIXTURE PROBLEMS   C
8X10 PREPARED TRANSPARENCY
FROM THE ALGEBRA, FIRST YEAR - WORD PROBLEMS SERIES.
PROD-LEART   DIST-LEART

**MIXTURE, INVESTMENT AND
RATIO PROBLEMS**   C
8X10 PREPARED TRANSPARENCY
FROM THE ALGEBRA, SECOND YEAR - WORK PROBLEMS SERIES.
PROD-LEART   DIST-LEART

MODELS OF SOLAR SYSTEM   C
8X10 PREPARED TRANSPARENCY   I-J
SEE SERIES TITLE FOR DESCRIPTIVE STATEMENT. FROM THE MEASUREMENT IN ASTRONOMY SE-RIES.
PROD-BOW   DIST-BOW

MODERN BASE TEN ABACUS   C
8X10 PREPARED TRANSPARENCY   P-I
FROM THE ELEMENTARY-JUNIOR HIGH MATHEMATICS SERIES.
PROD-LEART   DIST-LEART

MOLD   C
8X10 PREPARED TRANSPARENCY   H
SEE SERIES TITLE FOR DESCRIPTIVE STATEMENT. FROM THE PLANTS SERIES.
PROD-BOW   DIST-BOW

MOM AND ME   C
8X10 PREPARED TRANSPARENCY   K-P
FROM THE LIFE SCIENCE - GROWING UP SERIES.
PROD-LEART   DIST-LEART

**MONEY - HISTORY, TYPES AND
PURPOSES**   C
8X10 PREPARED TRANSPARENCY   J-H
FROM THE BASIC SOCIAL STUDIES CONCEPTS - ECONOMICS SERIES.
PROD-LEART   DIST-LEART

MOON   C
8X10 PREPARED TRANSPARENCY   H
SEE SERIES TITLE FOR DESCRIPTIVE STATEMENT. FROM THE ASTRONOMY SERIES.
PROD-BOW   DIST-BOW

MOTION PROBLEMS   C
8X10 PREPARED TRANSPARENCY
FROM THE ALGEBRA, FIRST YEAR - WORD PROBLEMS SERIES.
PROD-LEART   DIST-LEART

**MULTIPLE OVULATION AND
FERTILIZATION**   C
8X10 PREPARED TRANSPARENCY
FROM THE SEX EDUCATION - THE BABY - ITS CONCEPTION, GROWTH AND BIRTH SERIES.
PROD-LEART   DIST-LEART

**MULTIPLICATION OF COMPLEX
NUMBERS**   C
8X10 PREPARED TRANSPARENCY
FROM THE ALGEBRA, SECOND YEAR - COMPLEX NUMBERS SERIES.
PROD-LEART   DIST-LEART

MULTIPLICATION OF FRACTIONS   C
8X10 PREPARED TRANSPARENCY   P-I
FROM THE ELEMENTARY-JUNIOR HIGH MATHEMATICS SERIES.
PROD-LEART   DIST-LEART

MULTIPLICATION PRINCIPLES   C
8X10 PREPARED TRANSPARENCY   P-I
FROM THE ELEMENTARY-JUNIOR HIGH MATHEMATICS SERIES.
PROD-LEART   DIST-LEART

**MULTIPLICATION PROPERTY OF
ZERO**   C
8X10 PREPARED TRANSPARENCY
FROM THE ALGEBRA, SECOND YEAR - STRUCTURE OF ALGEBRA SERIES.
PROD-LEART   DIST-LEART

MULTIPLICATION TABLE   C
8X10 PREPARED TRANSPARENCY   P-I
FROM THE ELEMENTARY-JUNIOR HIGH MATHEMATICS SERIES.
PROD-LEART   DIST-LEART

**MULTIPLYING AND DIVIDING
RATIONAL ALGEBRAIC
FRACTIONS**   C
8X10 PREPARED TRANSPARENCY
FROM THE ALGEBRA, SECOND YEAR - ALGEBRAIC EXPRESSIONS SERIES.
PROD-LEART   DIST-LEART

MUSHROOM   C
8X10 PREPARED TRANSPARENCY   H
SEE SERIES TITLE FOR DESCRIPTIVE STATEMENT. FROM THE PLANTS SERIES.
PROD-BOW   DIST-BOW

N

NAMES FOR NUMBERS   C
8X10 PREPARED TRANSPARENCY   P-I
FROM THE ELEMENTARY-JUNIOR HIGH MATHEMATICS SERIES.
PROD-LEART   DIST-LEART

NARCOTICS   C
8X10 PREPARED TRANSPARENCY   H
SEE SERIES TITLE FOR DESCRIPTIVE STATEMENT. FROM THE DRUG ABUSE SERIES.
PROD-BOW   DIST-BOW

**NARROW VS BROAD
EXPERIMENTATION IN
ATTITUDES**   C
8X10 PREPARED TRANSPARENCY   H
FROM THE EMOTIONS AND SOCIAL ATTITUDES - ATTITUDES, VALUES SERIES.
PROD-LEART   DIST-LEART

NAT TURNER   C
8X10 PREPARED TRANSPARENCY   J-H
FROM THE BIOGRAPHIES OF OUTSTANDING NEGRO AMERICANS SERIES.
PROD-LEART   DIST-LEART

NATIONAL DECA WEEK   C
8X10 PREPARED TRANSPARENCY
SEE SERIES TITLE FOR DESCRIPTIVE STATEMENT.
FROM THE DISTRIBUTIVE EDUCATION CLUBS OF
AMERICA SERIES.
PROD-COF   DIST-COF

NATIONAL GOALS OF DECA   C
8X10 PREPARED TRANSPARENCY
SEE SERIES TITLE FOR DESCRIPTIVE STATEMENT.
FROM THE DISTRIBUTIVE EDUCATION CLUBS OF
AMERICA SERIES.
PROD-COF   DIST-COF

**NATIONALIST LEADERS OF
BLACK AFRICA**   C
8X10 PREPARED TRANSPARENCY   J-H
FROM THE POLITICAL GEOGRAPHY AND
NATIONALISM OF AFRICA SERIES.
PROD-LEART   DIST-LEART

**NATIONALIST LEADERS OF
NORTH AFRICA**   C
8X10 PREPARED TRANSPARENCY   J-H
FROM THE POLITICAL GEOGRAPHY AND
NATIONALISM OF AFRICA SERIES.
PROD-LEART   DIST-LEART

**NATURAL ORDER OF NUMBERS,
NO. 1**   C
8X10 PREPARED TRANSPARENCY   P-I
FROM THE ELEMENTARY-JUNIOR HIGH
MATHEMATICS SERIES.
PROD-LEART   DIST-LEART

**NATURAL ORDER OF NUMBERS,
NO. 2**   C
8X10 PREPARED TRANSPARENCY   P-I
FROM THE ELEMENTARY-JUNIOR HIGH
MATHEMATICS SERIES.
PROD-LEART   DIST-LEART

NATURAL RESOURCES   C
8X10 PREPARED TRANSPARENCY   H
SEE SERIES TITLE FOR DESCRIPTIVE STATEMENT.
FROM THE CONSERVATION SERIES.
PROD-BOW   DIST-BOW

**NATURAL RESOURCES AND
ECONOMICS**   C
8X10 PREPARED TRANSPARENCY   J-H
FROM THE BASIC SOCIAL STUDIES CONCEPTS -
ECONOMICS SERIES.
PROD-LEART   DIST-LEART

**NATURE OF ROOTS OF
QUADRATIC EQUATIONS**   C
8X10 PREPARED TRANSPARENCY
FROM THE ALGEBRA, FIRST YEAR - QUADRATIC
SENTENCES SERIES.
PROD-LEART   DIST-LEART

NERVOUS SYSTEM   C
8X10 PREPARED TRANSPARENCY   H
SEE SERIES TITLE FOR DESCRIPTIVE STATEMENT.
FROM THE HUMAN BODY SERIES.
PROD-BOW   DIST-BOW

NON-EQUIVALENT SETS   C
8X10 PREPARED TRANSPARENCY   P-I
FROM THE ELEMENTARY-JUNIOR HIGH
MATHEMATICS SERIES.
PROD-LEART   DIST-LEART

**NORMAL ATTRACTION OF THE
SEXES, PT 1**   C
8X10 PREPARED TRANSPARENCY
FROM THE SEX EDUCATION - DEVELOPMENT OF
CONCEPTS AND ATTITUDES SERIES.
PROD-LEART   DIST-LEART

**NORMAL ATTRACTION OF THE
SEXES, PT 2**   C
8X10 PREPARED TRANSPARENCY
FROM THE SEX EDUCATION - DEVELOPMENT OF
CONCEPTS AND ATTITUDES SERIES.
PROD-LEART   DIST-LEART

NTH ROOTS   C
8X10 PREPARED TRANSPARENCY
FROM THE ALGEBRA, FIRST YEAR - REAL
NUMBERS SERIES.
PROD-LEART   DIST-LEART

NUCLEAR REACTOR   C
8X10 PREPARED TRANSPARENCY   H
SEE SERIES TITLE FOR DESCRIPTIVE STATEMENT.
FROM THE ATOMIC ENERGY SERIES.
PROD-BOW   DIST-BOW

NUMBER FACTS, PT 1   C
8X10 PREPARED TRANSPARENCY   P-I
FROM THE ELEMENTARY-JUNIOR HIGH
MATHEMATICS SERIES.
PROD-LEART   DIST-LEART

NUMBER FACTS, PT 2   C
8X10 PREPARED TRANSPARENCY   P-I
FROM THE ELEMENTARY-JUNIOR HIGH
MATHEMATICS SERIES.
PROD-LEART   DIST-LEART

NUMBER FACTS, PT 3   C
8X10 PREPARED TRANSPARENCY   P-I
FROM THE ELEMENTARY-JUNIOR HIGH
MATHEMATICS SERIES.
PROD-LEART   DIST-LEART

NUMBER FACTS, PT 4   C
8X10 PREPARED TRANSPARENCY   P-I
FROM THE ELEMENTARY-JUNIOR HIGH
MATHEMATICS SERIES.
PROD-LEART   DIST-LEART

NUMBER FACTS, PT 5   C
8X10 PREPARED TRANSPARENCY   P-I
FROM THE ELEMENTARY-JUNIOR HIGH
MATHEMATICS SERIES.
PROD-LEART   DIST-LEART

NUMBER FACTS, PT 6   C
8X10 PREPARED TRANSPARENCY   P-I
FROM THE ELEMENTARY-JUNIOR HIGH
MATHEMATICS SERIES.
PROD-LEART   DIST-LEART

NUMBER FACTS, PT 7   C
8X10 PREPARED TRANSPARENCY   P-I
FROM THE ELEMENTARY-JUNIOR HIGH
MATHEMATICS SERIES.
PROD-LEART   DIST-LEART

NUMBER FACTS, PT 8   C
8X10 PREPARED TRANSPARENCY   P-I
FROM THE ELEMENTARY-JUNIOR HIGH
MATHEMATICS SERIES.
PROD-LEART   DIST-LEART

NUMBER FACTS, PT 9   C
8X10 PREPARED TRANSPARENCY   P-I
FROM THE ELEMENTARY-JUNIOR HIGH
MATHEMATICS SERIES.
PROD-LEART   DIST-LEART

NUMBER LINE   C
8X10 PREPARED TRANSPARENCY   P-I
FROM THE ELEMENTARY-JUNIOR HIGH
MATHEMATICS SERIES.
PROD-LEART   DIST-LEART

**NUMBER LINE - SIGNED
NUMBERS**   C
8X10 PREPARED TRANSPARENCY   P-I
FROM THE ELEMENTARY-JUNIOR HIGH
MATHEMATICS SERIES.
PROD-LEART   DIST-LEART

NUMBER LINE (MULT SERIES)   C
8X10 PREPARED TRANSPARENCY   P-I
FROM THE ELEMENTARY-JUNIOR HIGH
MATHEMATICS SERIES.
PROD-LEART   DIST-LEART

**NUMERATION SYSTEMS--A
SERIES**
SHOWS SUBTRACTION PRINCIPLE, STANDARD
FORM, CONCEPT OF PLACE VALUE AND HOW THE
NUMBER SYSTEM STARTED.
PROD-BETECL   DIST-BETECL

OCEAN CURRENTS   C
8X10 PREPARED TRANSPARENCY   I-H
SEE SERIES TITLE FOR DESCRIPTIVE STATEMENT.
FROM THE OCEANOGRAPHY SERIES.
PROD-BOW   DIST-BOW

OCEANOGRAPHY--A SERIES   I-H
SHOWS AND EXPLAINS THE MANY FACETS OF LIFE
WITHIN THE SEA.
PROD-BOW   DIST-BOW

ANIMALS OF THE DEEP
ANIMALS OF THE OPEN OCEAN
DIVISIONS OF THE OCEAN
FOOD WEB
ISLAND AND CORAL REEF FORMATION
MAN IN THE OCEAN
OCEAN CURRENTS
PLANKTON
SEASHORE LIFE - COLD ROCKY SHORES
SEASHORE LIFE - TEMPERATE MARSHY
SHORES
SEASHORE LIFE - WARM SANDY SHORES
SUBMARINE GEOLOGY
TOOLS OF THE OCEANOGRAPHER

OFFICIAL ITEMS   C
8X10 PREPARED TRANSPARENCY
SEE SERIES TITLE FOR DESCRIPTIVE STATEMENT.
FROM THE DISTRIBUTIVE EDUCATION CLUBS OF
AMERICA SERIES.
PROD-COF   DIST-COF

OIL WELL   C
8X10 PREPARED TRANSPARENCY   H
SEE SERIES TITLE FOR DESCRIPTIVE STATEMENT.
FROM THE APPLIED SCIENCE SERIES.
PROD-BOW   DIST-BOW

ON MY WAY TO SCHOOL I SAW   C
8X10 PREPARED TRANSPARENCY   K-P
SEE SERIES TITLE FOR DESCRIPTIVE STATEMENT.
FROM THE BEGINNING SKILLS SERIES.
PROD BOW   DIST-BOW

OPENING THE SALE   C
8X10 PREPARED TRANSPARENCY
SEE SERIES TITLE FOR DESCRIPTIVE STATEMENT.
FROM THE BASIC SALESMANSHIP SERIES.
PROD-COF   DIST-COF

**OPPORTUNITIES THROUGH
DISTRIBUTIVE EDUCATION**   C
8X10 PREPARED TRANSPARENCY
SEE SERIES TITLE FOR DESCRIPTIVE STATEMENT.
FROM THE ORIENTATION TO DISTRIBUTIVE EDU-
CATION SERIES.
PROD-COF   DIST-COF

**ORIENTATION TO DISTRIBUTIVE
EDUCATION--A SERIES**
OUTLINES THE BASIC DISTRIBUTIVE EDUCATION
PROGRAM AND INCLUDES ITS MAJOR POINTS OF
INTEREST.
PROD-COF   DIST-COF

BROAD GOALS OF DISTRIBUTIVE
EDUCATION
CLASSROOM-LABORATORY ACTIVITIES
CLUB ACTIVITIES
DEFINITION OF DISTRIBUTIVE
EDUCATION
DISTRIBUTIVE EDUCATION IN ACTION
DISTRIBUTIVE EDUCATION TRIANGLE,
THE
EXAMPLES OF DISTRIBUTIVE
BUSINESSES
EXAMPLES OF DISTRIBUTIVE
OCCUPATIONS
GAME - OUR MAIN STREET
IN DISTRIBUTIVE EDUCATION WE WILL
STUDY
INTRODUCTIONS ALL AROUND
MEANING OF DISTRIBUTION, THE
OPPORTUNITIES THROUGH
DISTRIBUTIVE EDUCATION
PURPOSES OF DECA
STUDENT'S WEEKLY PRODUCTION
REPORT
TRAINING PLAN FOR DISTRIBUTIVE
EDUCATION --
VARIOUS PROGRAMS, THE

OVERCOMING OBJECTIONS   C
8X10 PREPARED TRANSPARENCY
SEE SERIES TITLE FOR DESCRIPTIVE STATEMENT.
FROM THE BASIC SALESMANSHIP SERIES.
PROD-COF   DIST-COF

**OVERVIEW OF JOB APPLICATION
AND JOB INTERVIEW**   C
8X10 PREPARED TRANSPARENCY
SEE SERIES TITLE FOR DESCRIPTIVE STATEMENT.
FROM THE JOB APPLICATION AND JOB INTER-
VIEW SERIES.
PROD-COF   DIST-COF

OVULATION   C
       8X10 PREPARED TRANSPARENCY
SEX EDUCATION - DEVELOPMENTAL PATTERNS
OF PUBESCENT GIRLS SERIES.
PROD-LEART   DIST-LEART

OVUM AND SPERM PHOTO   C
       8X10 PREPARED TRANSPARENCY   H
SEE SERIES TITLE FOR DESCRIPTIVE STATEMENT.
FROM THE GENERAL TOPICS SERIES.
PROD-BOW   DIST-BOW

P

**PARABOLA - DEFINITION AND
EQUATION**   C
       8X10 PREPARED TRANSPARENCY
FROM THE ALGEBRA, SECOND YEAR - CONICS
SERIES.
PROD-LEART   DIST-LEART

PARABOLA - SKETCHING   C
       8X10 PREPARED TRANSPARENCY
FROM THE ALGEBRA, SECOND YEAR - CONICS
SERIES.
PROD-LEART   DIST-LEART

PARALLEL LINES   C
       8X10 PREPARED TRANSPARENCY
FROM THE ALGEBRA, SECOND YEAR - LINES
AND PLANES SERIES.
PROD-LEART   DIST-LEART

PARALLELOGRAM REGION   C
       8X10 PREPARED TRANSPARENCY   P-I
FROM THE ELEMENTARY GEOMETRY - AREA AS
A MEASURE OF COVERING SERIES.
PROD-LEART   DIST-LEART

PARAMECIUM, THE   C
       8X10 PREPARED TRANSPARENCY   I-H
SEE SERIES TITLE FOR DESCRIPTIVE STATEMENT.
FROM THE MICROSCOPIC LIFE SERIES.
PROD-BOW   DIST-BOW

PASCAL'S TRIANGLE   C
       8X10 PREPARED TRANSPARENCY   P-I
FROM THE ELEMENTARY-JUNIOR HIGH
MATHEMATICS SERIES.
PROD-LEART   DIST-LEART

PASSAGE OF PLACENTA   C
       8X10 PREPARED TRANSPARENCY
FROM THE SEX EDUCATION - THE BABY - ITS
CONCEPTION, GROWTH AND BIRTH SERIES.
PROD-LEART   DIST-LEART

PATTERN FORMATIONS   C
       8X10 PREPARED TRANSPARENCY   P-I
FROM THE ELEMENTARY-JUNIOR HIGH
MATHEMATICS SERIES.
PROD-LEART   DIST-LEART

**PATTERNS OF CONSUMPTION -
MARKETING**   C
       8X10 PREPARED TRANSPARENCY   J-H
FROM THE ECONOMICS - ECONOMICS IN
ACTION SERIES.
PROD-LEART   DIST-LEART

PAUL LAURENCE DUNBAR   C
       8X10 PREPARED TRANSPARENCY   J-H
FROM THE BIOGRAPHIES OF OUTSTANDING
NEGRO AMERICANS SERIES.
PROD-LEART   DIST-LEART

**PER CAPITA INCOME AND
CONSUMPTION**   C
       8X10 PREPARED TRANSPARENCY   J-H
FROM THE ECONOMICS - ECONOMICS IN
ACTION SERIES.
PROD-LEART   DIST-LEART

PERIODIC CHART   C
       8X10 PREPARED TRANSPARENCY   H
SEE SERIES TITLE FOR DESCRIPTIVE STATEMENT.
FROM THE ATOMIC ENERGY SERIES.
PROD-BOW   DIST-BOW

PERPENDICULAR LINES   C
       8X10 PREPARED TRANSPARENCY
FROM THE ALGEBRA, SECOND YEAR - LINES
AND PLANES SERIES.
PROD-LEART   DIST-LEART

PHONIC-ANALYSIS--A SERIES
DESCRIBES MANY VOWEL, DIPTHONG AND LET-
TER COMBINATION RULES.
PROD-BOW   DIST-BOW

PHOTOGRAPHY   C
       8X10 PREPARED TRANSPARENCY   H
SEE SERIES TITLE FOR DESCRIPTIVE STATEMENT.
FROM THE APPLIED SCIENCE SERIES.
PROD-BOW   DIST-BOW

PHOTOSYNTHESIS   C
       8X10 PREPARED TRANSPARENCY   H
SEE SERIES TITLE FOR DESCRIPTIVE STATEMENT.
FROM THE PLANTS SERIES.
PROD-BOW   DIST-BOW

PHYLLIS WHEATLEY   C
       8X10 PREPARED TRANSPARENCY   J-H
FROM THE BIOGRAPHIES OF OUTSTANDING
NEGRO AMERICANS SERIES.
PROD-LEART   DIST-LEART

PHYSICAL CHANGES - BOYS   C
       8X10 PREPARED TRANSPARENCY
FROM THE SEX EDUCATION - DEVELOPMENTAL
PATTERNS OF PUBESCENT BOYS SERIES.
PROD-LEART   DIST-LEART

PHYSICAL CHANGES - GIRLS   C
       8X10 PREPARED TRANSPARENCY
SEX EDUCATION - DEVELOPMENTAL PATTERNS
OF PUBESCENT GIRLS SERIES.
PROD-LEART   DIST-LEART

PITUITARY GLAND   C
       8X10 PREPARED TRANSPARENCY
FROM THE SEX EDUCATION - GROWTH AND
THE ENDOCRINE GLANDS SERIES.
PROD-LEART   DIST-LEART

PLACES WHERE THINGS LIVE   C
       8X10 PREPARED TRANSPARENCY   K-P
FROM THE LIFE SCIENCE - LIVING SOMEWHERE
SERIES.
PROD-LEART   DIST-LEART

PLANE FIGURES   C
       8X10 PREPARED TRANSPARENCY   P-I
FROM THE ELEMENTARY-JUNIOR HIGH
MATHEMATICS SERIES.
PROD-LEART   DIST-LEART

PLANKTON   C
       8X10 PREPARED TRANSPARENCY   I-H
SEE SERIES TITLE FOR DESCRIPTIVE STATEMENT.
FROM THE OCEANOGRAPHY SERIES.
PROD-BOW   DIST-BOW

**PLANT AND ANIMAL CELLS
COMPARED**   C
       8X10 PREPARED TRANSPARENCY   I-H
SEE SERIES TITLE FOR DESCRIPTIVE STATEMENT.
FROM THE MICROSCOPIC LIFE SERIES.
PROD-LEART   DIST-LEART

PLANT CELL   C
       8X10 PREPARED TRANSPARENCY   H
SEE SERIES TITLE FOR DESCRIPTIVE STATEMENT.
FROM THE PLANTS SERIES.
PROD-BOW   DIST-BOW

PLANT CELL TYPES   C
       8X10 PREPARED TRANSPARENCY   I-H
SEE SERIES TITLE FOR DESCRIPTIVE STATEMENT.
FROM THE MICROSCOPIC LIFE SERIES.
PROD-BOW   DIST-BOW

PLANT TRANSPIRATION   C
       8X10 PREPARED TRANSPARENCY   H
SEE SERIES TITLE FOR DESCRIPTIVE STATEMENT.
FROM THE PLANTS SERIES.
PROD-BOW   DIST-BOW

PLANTING BULBS AND TUBERS   C
       8X10 PREPARED TRANSPARENCY   H
SEE SERIES TITLE FOR DESCRIPTIVE STATEMENT.
FROM THE PLANTS SERIES.
PROD-BOW   DIST-BOW

PLANTS--A SERIES   H
DISCUSSES DIFFERENT TYPES OF PLANTS AND
PROCESSES.
PROD-BOW   DIST-BOW

CHARACTERISTIC OF DECIDUOUS TREES
CLASSIFICATION
EVERGREEN IDENTIFICATION
FERTILIZATION
GERMINATION
GRAFTING
HEREDITY
LEAF IDENTIFICATION
LEAF STRUCTURE
MOLD
MUSHROOM
PHOTOSYNTHESIS
PLANT CELL
PLANT TRANSPIRATION
PLANTING BULBS AND TUBERS
TERRARIUM CONSTRUCTION
TREE BUDS
TREE TRUNK STRUCTURE

PLAYING THE FIELD   C
       8X10 PREPARED TRANSPARENCY   J
FROM THE DATING RELATIONS - DATING
CATEGORIES SERIES.
PROD-LEART   DIST-LEART

PLURAL NOUNS ENDING IN 'ES'   C
       8X10 PREPARED TRANSPARENCY   I-J
SEE SERIES TITLE FOR DESCRIPTIVE STATEMENT.
FROM THE WORD FORMS AND FUNCTIONS SE-
RIES.
PROD-BOW   DIST-BOW

**PLURAL NOUNS ENDING IN
'IES'**   C
       8X10 PREPARED TRANSPARENCY   I-J
SEE SERIES TITLE FOR DESCRIPTIVE STATEMENT.
FROM THE WORD FORMS AND FUNCTIONS SE-
RIES.
PROD-BOW   DIST-BOW

PLURAL NOUNS ENDING IN 'S'   C
       8X10 PREPARED TRANSPARENCY   I-J
SEE SERIES TITLE FOR DESCRIPTIVE STATEMENT.
FROM THE WORD FORMS AND FUNCTIONS SE-
RIES.
PROD-BOW   DIST-BOW

POCKET VETO, THE   C
       8X10 PREPARED TRANSPARENCY   J-H
FROM THE UNITED STATES GOVERNMENT AND
HOW IT WORKS SERIES.
PROD-LEART   DIST-LEART

**POLITICAL DIVISIONS AS OF
1968 - AFRICA**   C
       8X10 PREPARED TRANSPARENCY   J-H
FROM THE POLITICAL GEOGRAPHY AND
NATIONALISM OF AFRICA SERIES.
PROD-LEART   DIST-LEART

**POLITICAL GEOGRAPHY AND
NATIONALISM OF AFRICA --A
SERIES**   J-H
PROD-LEART   DIST-LEART

COLONIES TO INDEPENDENCE
COUNTRY OF NIGERIA, THE
EUROPEAN PARTITION AGREEMENTS
1884-1885
NATIONALIST LEADERS OF BLACK
AFRICA
NATIONALIST LEADERS OF NORTH
AFRICA
POLITICAL DIVISIONS AS OF 1968 -
AFRICA
POLITICALLY SOVEREIGN STATES OF
AFRICA
PURPOSES AND AIMS OF THE OAU
REGIONAL ORGANIZATIONS IN AFRICA
REPUBLIC OF SOUTH AFRICA
STRUCTURE OF THE OAU
UHURU
UNITED NATIONS ROLE IN THE
INDEPENDENCE OF --

**POLITICALLY SOVEREIGN
STATES OF AFRICA**   C
       8X10 PREPARED TRANSPARENCY   J-H
FROM THE POLITICAL GEOGRAPHY AND
NATIONALISM OF AFRICA SERIES.
PROD-LEART   DIST-LEART

POLLUTION C
8X10 PREPARED TRANSPARENCY H
SEE SERIES TITLE FOR DESCRIPTIVE STATEMENT.
FROM THE CONSERVATION SERIES.
PROD-BOW   DIST-BOW

**POSSIBLE RELATIONS OF THREE
PLANES IN SPACE** C
8X10 PREPARED TRANSPARENCY
FROM THE ALGEBRA, SECOND YEAR - LINES
AND PLANES SERIES.
PROD-LEART   DIST-LEART

POST SECONDARY DIVISION C
8X10 PREPARED TRANSPARENCY
SEE SERIES TITLE FOR DESCRIPTIVE STATEMENT.
FROM THE DISTRIBUTIVE EDUCATION CLUBS OF
AMERICA SERIES.
PROD-COF   DIST-COF

POSTULATES FOR A FIELD C
8X10 PREPARED TRANSPARENCY
FROM THE ALGEBRA, SECOND YEAR -
STRUCTURE OF ALGEBRA SERIES.
PROD-LEART   DIST-LEART

**POWERS OF THE PRESIDENT,
THE** C
8X10 PREPARED TRANSPARENCY J-H
FROM THE UNITED STATES GOVERNMENT AND
HOW IT WORKS SERIES.
PROD-LEART   DIST-LEART

PREPARATION C
8X10 PREPARED TRANSPARENCY
SEE SERIES TITLE FOR DESCRIPTIVE STATEMENT.
FROM THE JOB APPLICATION AND JOB INTER-
VIEW SERIES.
PROD-COF   DIST-COF

PREPARING SLIDES C
8X10 PREPARED TRANSPARENCY H
SEE SERIES TITLE FOR DESCRIPTIVE STATEMENT.
FROM THE INSTRUMENTS AND TECHNIQUES OF
SCIENCE SERIES.
PROD-BOW   DIST-BOW

**PRICES AND THE ROLE OF
GOVERNMENT** C
8X10 PREPARED TRANSPARENCY J-H
FROM THE ECONOMICS - ECONOMICS IN
ACTION SERIES.
PROD-LEART   DIST-LEART

PRIMARY COLORS OF LIGHT C
8X10 PREPARED TRANSPARENCY I-C
SEE SERIES TITLE FOR DESCRIPTIVE STATEMENT.
FROM THE LIGHT SERIES.
PROD-BOW   DIST-BOW

PRISM AND SPECTRUM C
8X10 PREPARED TRANSPARENCY I-H
SEE SERIES TITLE FOR DESCRIPTIVE STATEMENT.
FROM THE LIGHT AND COLOR SERIES.
PROD-BOW   DIST-BOW

PRODUCT KNOWLEDGE C
8X10 PREPARED TRANSPARENCY
SEE SERIES TITLE FOR DESCRIPTIVE STATEMENT.
FROM THE BASIC SALESMANSHIP SERIES.
PROD-COF   DIST-COF

**PRODUCTION DEPENDS ON
DEMAND** C
8X10 PREPARED TRANSPARENCY J-H
FROM THE ECONOMICS - ECONOMICS IN
ACTION SERIES.
PROD-LEART   DIST-LEART

**PRODUCTS OF ADDITIVE
INVERSES** C
8X10 PREPARED TRANSPARENCY
FROM THE ALGEBRA, SECOND YEAR -
STRUCTURE OF ALGEBRA SERIES.
PROD-LEART   DIST-LEART

PRODUCTS OF ROOTS C
8X10 PREPARED TRANSPARENCY
FROM THE ALGEBRA, SECOND YEAR - RADICALS
SERIES.
PROD-LEART   DIST-LEART

**PROPER SLEEP IS IMPORTANT
TO HEALTH** C
8X10 PREPARED TRANSPARENCY
FROM THE SEX EDUCATION - PHYSICAL CARE
AND SELF RESPECT SERIES.

PROD-LEART   DIST-LEART

PROPERTIES OF EQUALITY C
8X10 PREPARED TRANSPARENCY
FROM THE ALGEBRA, SECOND YEAR -
STRUCTURE OF ALGEBRA SERIES.
PROD-LEART   DIST-LEART

PROPERTIES OF EQUATIONS C
8X10 PREPARED TRANSPARENCY
FROM THE ALGEBRA, SECOND YEAR -
STRUCTURE OF ALGEBRA SERIES.
PROD-LEART   DIST-LEART

**PROPERTIES OF ROOTS OF
QUADRATIC EQUATIONS** C
8X10 PREPARED TRANSPARENCY
FROM THE ALGEBRA, FIRST YEAR - QUADRATIC
SENTENCES SERIES.
PROD-LEART   DIST-LEART

PROPERTIES OF SETS C
8X10 PREPARED TRANSPARENCY P-I
FROM THE ELEMENTARY-JUNIOR HIGH
MATHEMATICS SERIES.
PROD-LEART   DIST-LEART

PROPERTIES OF SQUARE ROOTS C
8X10 PREPARED TRANSPARENCY
FROM THE ALGEBRA, FIRST YEAR - REAL
NUMBERS SERIES.
PROD-LEART   DIST-LEART

**PSYCHOLOGICAL DIMENSIONS
AND DATING BEHAVIOR** C
8X10 PREPARED TRANSPARENCY J
FROM THE DATING RELATIONS - DIMENSIONS
OF DATING SERIES.
PROD-LEART   DIST-LEART

PSYCHROMETER C
8X10 PREPARED TRANSPARENCY H
SEE SERIES TITLE FOR DESCRIPTIVE STATEMENT.
FROM THE INSTRUMENTS AND TECHNIQUES OF
SCIENCE SERIES.
PROD-BOW   DIST-BOW

**PUBESCENCE - THE AGE OF
PUBERTY** C
8X10 PREPARED TRANSPARENCY
FROM THE SEX EDUCATION - GROWTH AND
THE ENDOCRINE GLANDS SERIES.
PROD-LEART   DIST-LEART

PULLEY C
8X10 PREPARED TRANSPARENCY H
SEE SERIES TITLE FOR DESCRIPTIVE STATEMENT.
FROM THE MACHINES SERIES.
PROD-BOW   DIST-BOW

**PUNCTUATING KINDS OF
SENTENCES** C
8X10 PREPARED TRANSPARENCY P-I
SEE SERIES TITLE FOR DESCRIPTIVE STATEMENT.
FROM THE PUNCTUATION AND CAPITALIZATION
SERIES.
PROD-BOW   DIST-BOW

**PUNCTUATION - INTRODUCING
KINDS OF SENTENCES** C
8X10 PREPARED TRANSPARENCY P-I
SEE SERIES TITLE FOR DESCRIPTIVE STATEMENT.
FROM THE PUNCTUATION AND CAPITALIZATION
SERIES.
PROD-BOW   DIST-BOW

**PUNCTUATION AND
CAPITALIZATION--A SERIES** P-I
INTRODUCES CONCEPTS IN PUNCTUATION AND
CAPITALIZATION.
PROD-BOW   DIST-BOW

CAPITALIZATION
COMMAS IN SERIES AND IN DIRECT
ADDRESS
IDENTIFYING APPOSITIVES
INTRODUCING QUOTATION MARKS
PUNCTUATING KINDS OF SENTENCES
PUNCTUATION - INTRODUCING KINDS
OF SENTENCES
UNDERSTANDING ABBREVIATIONS
UNDERSTANDING CONTRACTIONS
USING QUOTATION MARKS
USING THE PERIOD
USING THE QUESTION MARK

**PURPOSES AND AIMS OF THE
OAU** C
8X10 PREPARED TRANSPARENCY J-H
FROM THE POLITICAL GEOGRAPHY AND
NATIONALISM OF AFRICA SERIES.
PROD-LEART   DIST-LEART

PURPOSES OF DECA C
8X10 PREPARED TRANSPARENCY
SEE SERIES TITLE FOR DESCRIPTIVE STATEMENT.
FROM THE ORIENTATION TO DISTRIBUTIVE EDU-
CATION SERIES.
PROD-COF   DIST-COF

PYTHAGOREAN THEOREM C
8X10 PREPARED TRANSPARENCY P-I
FROM THE ELEMENTARY-JUNIOR HIGH
MATHEMATICS SERIES.
PROD-LEART   DIST-LEART

Q

QUADRATIC FORMULA C
8X10 PREPARED TRANSPARENCY
FROM THE ALGEBRA, FIRST YEAR - QUADRATIC
SENTENCES SERIES.
PROD-LEART   DIST-LEART

**QUALIFICATIONS FOR HOLDING
NATIONAL OFFICE, THE** C
8X10 PREPARED TRANSPARENCY J-H
FROM THE UNITED STATES GOVERNMENT AND
HOW IT WORKS SERIES.
PROD-LEART   DIST-LEART

**QUOTIENTS OF COMPLEX
NUMBERS** C
8X10 PREPARED TRANSPARENCY
FROM THE ALGEBRA, SECOND YEAR - COMPLEX
NUMBERS SERIES.
PROD-LEART   DIST-LEART

R

RADICAL EQUATIONS C
8X10 PREPARED TRANSPARENCY
FROM THE ALGEBRA, SECOND YEAR - COMPLEX
NUMBERS SERIES.
PROD-LEART   DIST-LEART

RALPH J BUNCHE C
8X10 PREPARED TRANSPARENCY J-H
FROM THE BIOGRAPHIES OF OUTSTANDING
NEGRO AMERICANS SERIES.
PROD-LEART   DIST-LEART

RATIO AND PROPORTION C
8X10 PREPARED TRANSPARENCY
FROM THE ALGEBRA, FIRST YEAR - FUNCTIONS
SERIES.
PROD-LEART   DIST-LEART

RATIONAL EXPONENTS C
8X10 PREPARED TRANSPARENCY
FROM THE ALGEBRA, SECOND YEAR - RADICALS
SERIES.
PROD-LEART   DIST-LEART

RATIONAL NUMBERS C
8X10 PREPARED TRANSPARENCY
FROM THE ALGEBRA, SECOND YEAR - RADICALS
SERIES.
PROD-LEART   DIST-LEART

**RATIONALIZING THE
DENOMINATOR** C
8X10 PREPARED TRANSPARENCY
FROM THE ALGEBRA, FIRST YEAR - REAL
NUMBERS SERIES.
PROD-LEART   DIST-LEART

**READING WRITING READINESS-
-A SERIES**
DEFINES RHYMING WORDS AND DISCUSSES HOW
TO DEVELOP THEM. PRESENTS PICTURES SHOW-
ING SHAPES, REQUIRING THE STUDENT TO DIS-
COVER WHAT ITEMS ARE MISSING AND ILLUS-
TRATES THE CONCEPTS OF THINGS THAT ARE
ALIKE AND THINGS THAT ARE DIFFERENT.
PROD-BOW   DIST-BOW

REAL NUMBERS   C
8X10 PREPARED TRANSPARENCY
FROM THE ALGEBRA, FIRST YEAR - REAL
NUMBERS SERIES.
PROD-LEART   DIST-LEART

REASONS FOR ERECTION   C
8X10 PREPARED TRANSPARENCY
FROM THE SEX EDUCATION - DEVELOPMENTAL
PATTERNS OF PUBESCENT BOYS SERIES.
PROD-LEART   DIST-LEART

RECOGNIZING NOUNS   C
8X10 PREPARED TRANSPARENCY   I-J
SEE SERIES TITLE FOR DESCRIPTIVE STATEMENT.
FROM THE WORD FORMS AND FUNCTIONS SE-
RIES.
PROD-BOW   DIST-BOW

RECOGNIZING ROOT WORDS,
PREFIXES AND SUFFIXES   C
8X10 PREPARED TRANSPARENCY   I-J
SEE SERIES TITLE FOR DESCRIPTIVE STATEMENT.
FROM THE WORD FORMS AND FUNCTIONS SE-
RIES.
PROD-BOW   DIST-BOW

RECTANGULAR COORDINATE
SYSTEM   C
8X10 PREPARED TRANSPARENCY
FROM THE ALGEBRA, FIRST YEAR - SYSTEM OF
LINEAR EQUATIONS SERIES.
PROD-LEART   DIST-LEART

RECTANGULAR REGION   C
8X10 PREPARED TRANSPARENCY   P-I
FROM THE ELEMENTARY GEOMETRY - AREA AS
A MEASURE OF COVERING SERIES.
PROD-LEART   DIST-LEART

REFLECTION OF LIGHT   C
8X10 PREPARED TRANSPARENCY   I-C
SEE SERIES TITLE FOR DESCRIPTIVE STATEMENT.
FROM THE LIGHT SERIES.
PROD-BOW   DIST-BOW

REFLECTION OF SOUND   C
8X10 PREPARED TRANSPARENCY   I-C
SEE SERIES TITLE FOR DESCRIPTIVE STATEMENT.
FROM THE SOUND SERIES.
PROD-BOW   DIST-BOW

REFRACTION AND LENSES   C
8X10 PREPARED TRANSPARENCY   I-C
SEE SERIES TITLE FOR DESCRIPTIVE STATEMENT.
FROM THE LIGHT SERIES.
PROD-BOW   DIST-BOW

REFRACTION OF LIGHT   C
8X10 PREPARED TRANSPARENCY   I-H
SEE SERIES TITLE FOR DESCRIPTIVE STATEMENT.
FROM THE LIGHT AND COLOR SERIES.
PROD-BOW   DIST-BOW

REFRIGERATION   C
8X10 PREPARED TRANSPARENCY   H
SEE SERIES TITLE FOR DESCRIPTIVE STATEMENT.
FROM THE APPLIED SCIENCE SERIES.
PROD-BOW   DIST-BOW

REGIONAL ORGANIZATIONS IN
AFRICA   C
8X10 PREPARED TRANSPARENCY   J-H
FROM THE POLITICAL GEOGRAPHY AND
NATIONALISM OF AFRICA SERIES.
PROD-LEART   DIST-LEART

REGULAR SOLIDS   C
8X10 PREPARED TRANSPARENCY   P-I
FROM THE ELEMENTARY-JUNIOR HIGH
MATHEMATICS SERIES.
PROD-LEART   DIST-LEART

RELATED ITEMS FOR
CLASSROOM DISCUSSION   C
8X10 PREPARED TRANSPARENCY
SEE SERIES TITLE FOR DESCRIPTIVE STATEMENT.
FROM THE JOB APPLICATION AND JOB INTER-
VIEW SERIES.
PROD-COF   DIST-COF

RELATIONS   C
8X10 PREPARED TRANSPARENCY
FROM THE ALGEBRA, FIRST YEAR - FUNCTIONS
SERIES.
PROD-LEART   DIST-LEART

RELIGION AND SOCIETY   C
8X10 PREPARED TRANSPARENCY   J-H
FROM THE BASIC SOCIAL STUDIES CONCEPTS -
SOCIETY SERIES.
PROD-LEART   DIST-LEART

REPEATING DECIMALS   C
8X10 PREPARED TRANSPARENCY
FROM THE ALGEBRA, FIRST YEAR - REAL
NUMBERS SERIES.
PROD-LEART   DIST-LEART

REPRODUCTIVE CELL DIVISION -
GROWTH   C
8X10 PREPARED TRANSPARENCY
FROM THE SEX EDUCATION - THE BABY - ITS
CONCEPTION, GROWTH AND BIRTH SERIES.
PROD-LEART   DIST-LEART

REPUBLIC OF SOUTH AFRICA   C
8X10 PREPARED TRANSPARENCY   J-H
FROM THE POLITICAL GEOGRAPHY AND
NATIONALISM OF AFRICA SERIES.
PROD-LEART   DIST-LEART

REQUIREMENTS OF A 'TAKE-
OFF'   C
8X10 PREPARED TRANSPARENCY   J-H
FROM THE ECONOMICS - ECONOMIC HISTORY
SERIES.
PROD-LEART   DIST-LEART

RESERVED POWERS AND
DELEGATED POWERS   C
8X10 PREPARED TRANSPARENCY   J-H
FROM THE UNITED STATES GOVERNMENT AND
HOW IT WORKS SERIES.
PROD-LEART   DIST-LEART

RESPIRATORY SYSTEM   C
8X10 PREPARED TRANSPARENCY   H
SEE SERIES TITLE FOR DESCRIPTIVE STATEMENT.
FROM THE HUMAN BODY SERIES.
PROD-BOW   DIST-BOW

RICHARD WRIGHT   C
8X10 PREPARED TRANSPARENCY   J-H
FROM THE BIOGRAPHIES OF OUTSTANDING
NEGRO AMERICANS SERIES.
PROD-LEART   DIST-LEART

RIGHT DISTRIBUTIVE PROPERTY
    C
8X10 PREPARED TRANSPARENCY
FROM THE ALGEBRA, SECOND YEAR -
STRUCTURE OF ALGEBRA SERIES.
PROD-LEART   DIST-LEART

ROBERT SMALLS   C
8X10 PREPARED TRANSPARENCY   J-H
FROM THE BIOGRAPHIES OF OUTSTANDING
NEGRO AMERICANS SERIES.
PROD-LEART   DIST-LEART

ROCK CYCLE   C
8X10 PREPARED TRANSPARENCY   H
SEE SERIES TITLE FOR DESCRIPTIVE STATEMENT.
FROM THE GEOLOGY SERIES.
PROD-BOW   DIST-BOW

ROCKET ENGINE   C
8X10 PREPARED TRANSPARENCY   H
SEE SERIES TITLE FOR DESCRIPTIVE STATEMENT.
FROM THE ENGINES SERIES.
PROD-BOW   DIST-BOW

ROLE OF U S GOVERNMENT IN
ECONOMICS VS ROLE OF
SOVIET GOVERNMENT   C
8X10 PREPARED TRANSPARENCY   J-H
FROM THE ECONOMICS - POLITICAL ECONOMY
AND PHILOSOPHY SERIES.
PROD-LEART   DIST-LEART

ROOTS OF NUMBERS   C
8X10 PREPARED TRANSPARENCY
FROM THE ALGEBRA, SECOND YEAR - RADICALS
SERIES.
PROD-LEART   DIST-LEART

S

SALES DEMONSTRATION
CONTEST   C
8X10 PREPARED TRANSPARENCY
SEE SERIES TITLE FOR DESCRIPTIVE STATEMENT.
FROM THE BASIC SALESMANSHIP SERIES.
PROD-COF   DIST-COF

SALES FLOW, THE   C
8X10 PREPARED TRANSPARENCY
SEE SERIES TITLE FOR DESCRIPTIVE STATEMENT.
FROM THE BASIC SALESMANSHIP SERIES.
PROD-COF   DIST-COF

SAMMY DAVIS JR   C
8X10 PREPARED TRANSPARENCY   J-H
FROM THE BIOGRAPHIES OF OUTSTANDING
NEGRO AMERICANS SERIES.
PROD-LEART   DIST-LEART

SAVINGS AND INVESTMENTS   C
8X10 PREPARED TRANSPARENCY   J-H
FROM THE ECONOMICS - ECONOMICS IN
ACTION SERIES.
PROD-LEART   DIST-LEART

SEASHORE LIFE - COLD ROCKY
SHORES   C
8X10 PREPARED TRANSPARENCY   I-H
SEE SERIES TITLE FOR DESCRIPTIVE STATEMENT.
FROM THE OCEANOGRAPHY SERIES.
PROD-BOW   DIST-BOW

SEASHORE LIFE - TEMPERATE
MARSHY SHORES   C
8X10 PREPARED TRANSPARENCY   I-H
SEE SERIES TITLE FOR DESCRIPTIVE STATEMENT.
FROM THE OCEANOGRAPHY SERIES.
PROD-BOW   DIST-BOW

SEASHORE LIFE - WARM SANDY
SHORES   C
8X10 PREPARED TRANSPARENCY   I-H
SEE SERIES TITLE FOR DESCRIPTIVE STATEMENT.
FROM THE OCEANOGRAPHY SERIES.
PROD-BOW   DIST-BOW

SEASONS   C
8X10 PREPARED TRANSPARENCY   H
SEE SERIES TITLE FOR DESCRIPTIVE STATEMENT.
FROM THE ASTRONOMY SERIES.
PROD-BOW   DIST-BOW

SECOND CLASS LEVER   C
8X10 PREPARED TRANSPARENCY   H
SEE SERIES TITLE FOR DESCRIPTIVE STATEMENT.
FROM THE MACHINES SERIES.
PROD-BOW   DIST-BOW

SECTORS OF A MODERN
ECONOMY   C
8X10 PREPARED TRANSPARENCY   J-H
FROM THE ECONOMICS - ECONOMICS IN
ACTION SERIES.
PROD-LEART   DIST-LEART

SEEDS IN FRUIT, VEGETABLES   C
8X10 PREPARED TRANSPARENCY   K-P
FROM THE LIFE SCIENCE - COMING TO LIFE
SERIES.
PROD-LEART   DIST-LEART

SELECTING A HAIR STYLE   C
8X10 PREPARED TRANSPARENCY
SEE SERIES TITLE FOR DESCRIPTIVE STATEMENT.
FROM THE GOOD GROOMING SERIES.
PROD-COF   DIST-COF

SELECTING CLOTHING FOR
YOUR BUDGET   C
8X10 PREPARED TRANSPARENCY
SEE SERIES TITLE FOR DESCRIPTIVE STATEMENT.
FROM THE GOOD GROOMING SERIES.
PROD-COF   DIST-COF

SELF DISCIPLINE   C
8X10 PREPARED TRANSPARENCY
FROM THE SEX EDUCATION - GROWTH AND
THE ENDOCRINE GLANDS SERIES.
PROD-LEART   DIST-LEART

SELF IMAGE   C
8X10 PREPARED TRANSPARENCY   J
FROM THE DATING RELATIONS - DIMENSIONS
OF DATING SERIES.
PROD-LEART   DIST-LEART

SEMINAL EMISSIONS   C
8X10 PREPARED TRANSPARENCY
FROM THE SEX EDUCATION - DEVELOPMENTAL
PATTERNS OF PUBESCENT BOYS SERIES.
PROD-LEART   DIST-LEART

**SEPARATION OF MOTHER AND
BABY**   C
8X10 PREPARED TRANSPARENCY
FROM THE SEX EDUCATION - THE BABY - ITS
CONCEPTION, GROWTH AND BIRTH SERIES.
PROD-LEART   DIST-LEART

SERIOUS-STEADY DATING   C
8X10 PREPARED TRANSPARENCY   J
FROM THE DATING RELATIONS - DATING
CATEGORIES SERIES.
PROD-LEART   DIST-LEART

SET, A   C
8X10 PREPARED TRANSPARENCY   P-I
FROM THE ELEMENTARY-JUNIOR HIGH
MATHEMATICS SERIES.
PROD-LEART   DIST-LEART

SETS AND SUBSETS   C
8X10 PREPARED TRANSPARENCY   P-I
FROM THE ELEMENTARY-JUNIOR HIGH
MATHEMATICS SERIES.
PROD-LEART   DIST-LEART

**SETTING STANDARDS ON
DATES**   C
8X10 PREPARED TRANSPARENCY   J
FROM THE DATING RELATIONS - DATING
PROBLEMS SERIES.
PROD-LEART   DIST-LEART

**SEX AND DATING -
CONSEQUENCES**   C
8X10 PREPARED TRANSPARENCY   J
FROM THE DATING RELATIONS - DATING
PROBLEMS SERIES.
PROD-LEART   DIST-LEART

**SEX AND DATING - GUILT AND
SHAME**   C
8X10 PREPARED TRANSPARENCY   J
FROM THE DATING RELATIONS - DATING
PROBLEMS SERIES.
PROD-LEART   DIST-LEART

**SEX AND DATING -
REPUTATION**   C
8X10 PREPARED TRANSPARENCY   J
FROM THE DATING RELATIONS - DATING
PROBLEMS SERIES.
PROD-LEART   DIST-LEART

**SEX EDUCATION -
DEVELOPMENT OF CONCEPTS
AND ATTITUDES--A SERIES**

PROD-LEART   DIST-LEART

DATING AND PARTYING
HOW EMOTIONS ARE EXPRESSED
NORMAL ATTRACTION OF THE SEXES,
PT 1
NORMAL ATTRACTION OF THE SEXES,
PT 2
UNDERSTANDING MALENESS AND
FEMALENESS
UNDERSTANDING SEXUALITY
WHAT MAKES PERSONALITIES
DIFFERENT

**SEX EDUCATION -
DEVELOPMENTAL PATTERNS OF
PUBESCENT BOYS--A SERIES**

PROD-LEART   DIST-LEART

CARE OF MALE REPRODUCTIVE ORGANS
CROSS-SECTION OF PENIS
DESCENT OF THE TESTICLES
GROWTH OF BODY HAIR
INGUINAL AND SPERMATIC CORD

MALE ORGANS OF EXCRETION AND
REPRODUCTION
PHYSICAL CHANGES - BOYS
REASONS FOR ERECTION
SEMINAL EMISSIONS
SPERM
WAYS OF CONTROL

**SEX EDUCATION - GROWTH
AND THE ENDOCRINE GLANDS-
-A SERIES**

PROD-LEART   DIST-LEART

COMPARATIVE SIZES - BOYS AND GIRLS
11 YEARS
COMPARATIVE SIZES - BOYS AND GIRLS
12 YEARS
COMPARATIVE SIZES - BOYS AND GIRLS
13 YEARS
COMPARATIVE SIZES - BOYS AND GIRLS
14 YEARS
ENDOCRINE GLANDS
HORMONES AND EMOTIONAL EFFECTS,
PT 1
HORMONES AND EMOTIONAL EFFECTS,
PT 2
PITUITARY GLAND
PUBESCENCE - THE AGE OF PUBERTY
SELF DISCIPLINE

**SEX EDUCATION - PHYSICAL
CARE AND SELF RESPECT--A
SERIES**

PROD-LEART   DIST-LEART

CLEANLINESS INFLUENCES HEALTH
DRESS FOR THE WEATHER
EMOTION AND BODY FUNCTIONS
EXERCISE AND ACTIVITIES
FOOD AFFECTS GROWTH
PROPER SLEEP IS IMPORTANT TO
HEALTH

**SEX EDUCATION - THE BABY -
ITS CONCEPTION, GROWTH
AND BIRTH--A SERIES**

PROD-LEART   DIST-LEART

BABY AT ONE MONTH
BIRTH OF THE BABY
EMBRYO TO BABY
FERTILIZATION
GROWTH OF THE BABY, PT 1
GROWTH OF THE BABY, PT 2
IMPLANTATION
MULTIPLE OVULATION AND
FERTILIZATION
PASSAGE OF PLACENTA
REPRODUCTIVE CELL DIVISION -
GROWTH
SEPARATION OF MOTHER AND BABY
TWINNING

**SEX EDUCATION -
UNDERSTANDING VENEREAL
DISEASE--A SERIES**

PROD-LEART   DIST-LEART

EFFECTS OF GONORRHEA
EFFECTS OF SYPHILIS
GONORRHEA
SYPHILIS
VENEREAL DISEASE

SHAKESPEARE--A SERIES
COVERS THE KEY FACTS ABOUT SHAKESPEARE,
HIS PLAYS AND THE ELIZABETHAN THEATRE.
PROD-BETECL   DIST-BETECL

SIDNEY POITIER   C
8X10 PREPARED TRANSPARENCY   J-H
FROM THE BIOGRAPHIES OF OUTSTANDING
NEGRO AMERICANS SERIES.
PROD-LEART   DIST-LEART

SIEVE OF ERATOSTHENES   C
8X10 PREPARED TRANSPARENCY   P-I
FROM THE ELEMENTARY-JUNIOR HIGH
MATHEMATICS SERIES.
PROD-LEART   DIST-LEART

SIMPLE GEOMETRIC FIGURES   C
8X10 PREPARED TRANSPARENCY   P-I
FROM THE ELEMENTARY-JUNIOR HIGH
MATHEMATICS SERIES.
PROD-LEART   DIST-LEART

SIMPLIFYING RADICALS   C
8X10 PREPARED TRANSPARENCY
FROM THE ALGEBRA, FIRST YEAR - REAL
NUMBERS SERIES.
PROD-LEART   DIST-LEART

**SINGLE FULL-TERM FETUS (X-
RAY)**   C
8X10 PREPARED TRANSPARENCY   H
SEE SERIES TITLE FOR DESCRIPTIVE STATEMENT.
FROM THE GENERAL TOPICS SERIES.
PROD-BOW   DIST-BOW

SKELETAL SYSTEM   C
8X10 PREPARED TRANSPARENCY   H
SEE SERIES TITLE FOR DESCRIPTIVE STATEMENT.
FROM THE HUMAN BODY SERIES.
PROD-BOW   DIST-BOW

SKIN   C
8X10 PREPARED TRANSPARENCY   H
SEE SERIES TITLE FOR DESCRIPTIVE STATEMENT.
FROM THE HUMAN BODY SERIES.
PROD-BOW   DIST-BOW

SKIP COUNTING   C
8X10 PREPARED TRANSPARENCY   P-I
FROM THE ELEMENTARY-JUNIOR HIGH
MATHEMATICS SERIES.
PROD-LEART   DIST-LEART

SLOPE INTERCEPT FORM   C
8X10 PREPARED TRANSPARENCY
FROM THE ALGEBRA, FIRST YEAR - SYSTEM OF
LINEAR EQUATIONS SERIES.
PROD-LEART   DIST-LEART

SLOPE OF A STRAIGHT LINE   C
8X10 PREPARED TRANSPARENCY
FROM THE ALGEBRA, SECOND YEAR - LINES
AND PLANES SERIES.
PROD-LEART   DIST-LEART

**SLOPE OF THE GRAPH OF AN
EQUATION**   C
8X10 PREPARED TRANSPARENCY
FROM THE ALGEBRA, FIRST YEAR - SYSTEM OF
LINEAR EQUATIONS SERIES.
PROD-LEART   DIST-LEART

SMALL POND LIFE   C
8X10 PREPARED TRANSPARENCY   I-H
SEE SERIES TITLE FOR DESCRIPTIVE STATEMENT.
FROM THE MICROSCOPIC LIFE SERIES.
PROD-BOW   DIST-BOW

**SOCIAL INSTITUTIONS AND
ECONOMICS**   C
8X10 PREPARED TRANSPARENCY   J-H
FROM THE BASIC SOCIAL STUDIES CONCEPTS -
POLITICS, SOCIAL-ECONOMIC INTERDEPENDENCE
SERIES.
PROD-LEART   DIST-LEART

**SOCIAL INSTITUTIONS MATCH
THE LIFE CYCLE**   C
8X10 PREPARED TRANSPARENCY   J-H
FROM THE BASIC SOCIAL STUDIES CONCEPTS -
SOCIETY SERIES.
PROD-LEART   DIST-LEART

**SOCIAL SECURITY AND TAX
ACCOUNT NUMBER**   C
8X10 PREPARED TRANSPARENCY
SEE SERIES TITLE FOR DESCRIPTIVE STATEMENT.
FROM THE JOB APPLICATION AND JOB INTER-
VIEW SERIES.
PROD-COF   DIST-COF

**SOCIETIES FORM
GOVERNMENTS**   C
8X10 PREPARED TRANSPARENCY   J-H
FROM THE BASIC SOCIAL STUDIES CONCEPTS -
POLITICS, SOCIAL-ECONOMIC INTERDEPENDENCE
SERIES.
PROD-LEART   DIST-LEART

SOIL DEPLETION   C
8X10 PREPARED TRANSPARENCY   H
SEE SERIES TITLE FOR DESCRIPTIVE STATEMENT.
FROM THE CONSERVATION SERIES.
PROD-BOW   DIST-BOW

SOLAR SYSTEMS   C
8X10 PREPARED TRANSPARENCY   H
SEE SERIES TITLE FOR DESCRIPTIVE STATEMENT.
FROM THE ASTRONOMY SERIES.
PROD-BOW   DIST-BOW

SOLID FIGURES C
8X10 PREPARED TRANSPARENCY P-I
FROM THE ELEMENTARY-JUNIOR HIGH
MATHEMATICS SERIES.
PROD-LEART   DIST-LEART

**SOLUTION SET OF AN OPEN
SENTENCE IN TWO VARIABLES** C
8X10 PREPARED TRANSPARENCY
FROM THE ALGEBRA, FIRST YEAR - SYSTEM OF
LINEAR EQUATIONS SERIES.
PROD-LEART   DIST-LEART

**SOLVING OF QUADRATIC
INEQUALITIES** C
8X10 PREPARED TRANSPARENCY
FROM THE ALGEBRA, FIRST YEAR - QUADRATIC
SENTENCES SERIES.
PROD-LEART   DIST-LEART

**SOLVING QUADRATIC
EQUATIONS BY FACTORING** C
8X10 PREPARED TRANSPARENCY
FROM THE ALGEBRA, FIRST YEAR - QUADRATIC
SENTENCES SERIES.
PROD-LEART   DIST-LEART

SONAR C
8X10 PREPARED TRANSPARENCY I-C
SEE SERIES TITLE FOR DESCRIPTIVE STATEMENT.
FROM THE SOUND SERIES.
PROD-BOW   DIST-BOW

OUND REPRODUCTION C
8X10 PREPARED TRANSPARENCY I-C
SEE SERIES TITLE FOR DESCRIPTIVE STATEMENT.
FROM THE SOUND SERIES.
D-BOW   DIST-BOW

ND WAVES C
8X10 PREPARED TRANSPARENCY I-C
E SERIES TITLE FOR DESCRIPTIVE STATEMENT.
OM THE SOUND SERIES.
BOW   DIST-BOW

SOUND--A SERIES
I-C
DISCUSSES THE PHENOMENON OF SOUND.
PROD-BOW   DIST-BOW

REFLECTION OF SOUND
SONAR
SOUND REPRODUCTION
SOUND WAVES
SPEECH
VIBRATION AND TRAVEL

**SOURCE OF ATTITUDES OF THE
HIGH SCHOOL PERSON** C
8X10 PREPARED TRANSPARENCY H
FROM THE EMOTIONS AND SOCIAL ATTITUDES -
ATTITUDES, VALUES SERIES.
PROD-LEART   DIST-LEART

SPECIFIC AMENDMENTS C
8X10 PREPARED TRANSPARENCY J-H
FROM THE UNITED STATES GOVERNMENT AND
HOW IT WORKS SERIES.
PROD-LEART   DIST-LEART

SPECTRUM C
8X10 PREPARED TRANSPARENCY I-C
SEE SERIES TITLE FOR DESCRIPTIVE STATEMENT.
FROM THE LIGHT SERIES.
PROD-BOW   DIST-BOW

SPEECH C
8X10 PREPARED TRANSPARENCY I-C
SEE SERIES TITLE FOR DESCRIPTIVE STATEMENT.
FROM THE SOUND SERIES.
PROD-BOW   DIST-BOW

**SPELLING GENERALIZATION--A
SERIES**
GIVES CLUES FOR SPELLING, VOWEL SOUNDS,
CONTRACTIONS, PLURALS AND PREFIXES.
PROD-BOW   DIST-BOW

SPERM C
8X10 PREPARED TRANSPARENCY
FROM THE SEX EDUCATION - DEVELOPMENTAL
PATTERNS OF PUBESCENT BOYS SERIES.
PROD-LEART   DIST-LEART

SQUARE C
8X10 PREPARED TRANSPARENCY P-I
FROM THE ELEMENTARY-JUNIOR HIGH
MATHEMATICS SERIES.
PROD-LEART   DIST-LEART

SQUARE ROOTS C
8X10 PREPARED TRANSPARENCY
FROM THE ALGEBRA, FIRST YEAR - REAL
NUMBERS SERIES.
PROD-LEART   DIST-LEART

STAGES OF ECONOMIC GROWTH
C
8X10 PREPARED TRANSPARENCY J-H
FROM THE ECONOMICS - ECONOMIC HISTORY
SERIES.
PROD-LEART   DIST-LEART

STAR CHART C
8X10 PREPARED TRANSPARENCY H
SEE SERIES TITLE FOR DESCRIPTIVE STATEMENT.
FROM THE ASTRONOMY SERIES.
PROD-BOW   DIST-BOW

STEADY DATES C
8X10 PREPARED TRANSPARENCY J
FROM THE DATING RELATIONS - DATING
PROBLEMS SERIES.
PROD-LEART   DIST-LEART

STEAM ENGINE C
8X10 PREPARED TRANSPARENCY H
SEE SERIES TITLE FOR DESCRIPTIVE STATEMENT.
FROM THE ENGINES SERIES.
PROD-BOW   DIST-BOW

STIMULANTS C
8X10 PREPARED TRANSPARENCY H
SEE SERIES TITLE FOR DESCRIPTIVE STATEMENT.
FROM THE DRUG ABUSE SERIES.
PROD-BOW   DIST-BOW

STOKELY CARMICHAEL C
8X10 PREPARED TRANSPARENCY J-H
FROM THE BIOGRAPHIES OF OUTSTANDING
NEGRO AMERICANS SERIES.
PROD-LEART   DIST-LEART

STRUCTURE OF MAMMALS C
8X10 PREPARED TRANSPARENCY H
SEE SERIES TITLE FOR DESCRIPTIVE STATEMENT.
FROM THE WARM-BLOODED VERTEBRATES SE-
RIES.
PROD-BOW   DIST-BOW

STRUCTURE OF THE OAU C
8X10 PREPARED TRANSPARENCY J-H
FROM THE POLITICAL GEOGRAPHY AND
NATIONALISM OF AFRICA SERIES.
PROD-LEART   DIST-LEART

**STUDENT'S WEEKLY
PRODUCTION REPORT** C
8X10 PREPARED TRANSPARENCY
SEE SERIES TITLE FOR DESCRIPTIVE STATEMENT.
FROM THE ORIENTATION TO DISTRIBUTIVE EDU-
CATION SERIES.
PROD-COF   DIST-COF

SUBMARINE GEOLOGY C
8X10 PREPARED TRANSPARENCY I-H
SEE SERIES TITLE FOR DESCRIPTIVE STATEMENT.
FROM THE OCEANOGRAPHY SERIES.
PROD-BOW   DIST-BOW

SUBTRACTION - TAKE AWAY C
8X10 PREPARED TRANSPARENCY P-I
FROM THE ELEMENTARY-JUNIOR HIGH
MATHEMATICS SERIES.
PROD-LEART   DIST-LEART

SUBTRACTION AND DIVISION C
8X10 PREPARED TRANSPARENCY
FROM THE ALGEBRA, SECOND YEAR -
STRUCTURE OF ALGEBRA SERIES.
PROD-LEART   DIST-LEART

SUBTRACTION OF FRACTIONS C
8X10 PREPARED TRANSPARENCY P-I
FROM THE ELEMENTARY-JUNIOR HIGH
MATHEMATICS SERIES.
PROD-LEART   DIST-LEART

SUM AND PRODUCT OF ROOTS C
8X10 PREPARED TRANSPARENCY
FROM THE ALGEBRA, SECOND YEAR - COMPLEX
NUMBERS SERIES.
PROD-LEART   DIST-LEART

**SUM OR DIFFERENCE OF TWO
CUBES** C
8X10 PREPARED TRANSPARENCY
FROM THE ALGEBRA, SECOND YEAR -
FACTORING SERIES.
PROD-LEART   DIST-LEART

**SUMMARY OF DATING
CATEGORIES** C
8X10 PREPARED TRANSPARENCY J
FROM THE DATING RELATIONS - DATING
CATEGORIES SERIES.
PROD-LEART   DIST-LEART

**SUMMARY OF DATING
PROBLEMS** C
8X10 PREPARED TRANSPARENCY J
FROM THE DATING RELATIONS - DATING
PROBLEMS SERIES.
PROD-LEART   DIST-LEART

**SUMMARY OF GOOD GROOMING
FACTORS, PT 1** C
8X10 PREPARED TRANSPARENCY
SEE SERIES TITLE FOR DESCRIPTIVE STATEMENT.
FROM THE GOOD GROOMING SERIES.
PROD-COF   DIST-COF

**SUMMARY OF GOOD GROOMING
FACTORS, PT 2** C
8X10 PREPARED TRANSPARENCY
SEE SERIES TITLE FOR DESCRIPTIVE STATEMENT.
FROM THE GOOD GROOMING SERIES.
PROD-COF   DIST-COF

SUMMARY OF ROMANTIC LOVE C
8X10 PREPARED TRANSPARENCY J
FROM THE DATING RELATIONS - ROMANCE AND
PEOPLE SERIES.
PROD-LEART   DIST-LEART

SURFACE APPEAL C
8X10 PREPARED TRANSPARENCY J
FROM THE DATING RELATIONS - POPULARITY
SERIES.
PROD-LEART   DIST-LEART

**SYLLABLE AND ACCENT CLUE--A
SERIES**
DESCRIBES PHONIC AND STRUCTURAL ANALYSIS
SKILLS. HELPS STUDENTS GAIN INDEPENDENCE
IN ATTACKING NEW WORDS.
PROD-BOW   DIST-BOW

SYNTHETIC FIBERS C
8X10 PREPARED TRANSPARENCY H
SEE SERIES TITLE FOR DESCRIPTIVE STATEMENT.
FROM THE APPLIED SCIENCE SERIES.
PROD-BOW   DIST-BOW

SYPHILIS C
8X10 PREPARED TRANSPARENCY
FROM THE SEX EDUCATION - UNDERSTANDING
VENEREAL DISEASE SERIES.
PROD-LEART   DIST-LEART

**SYSTEM OF CHECKS AND
BALANCES, THE** C
8X10 PREPARED TRANSPARENCY J-H
FROM THE UNITED STATES GOVERNMENT AND
HOW IT WORKS SERIES.
PROD-LEART   DIST-LEART

**SYSTEMS OF WRITING
NUMERALS** C
8X10 PREPARED TRANSPARENCY P-I
FROM THE ELEMENTARY-JUNIOR HIGH
MATHEMATICS SERIES.
PROD-LEART   DIST-LEART

T

TABLE OF MEASURE C
8X10 PREPARED TRANSPARENCY P-I
FROM THE ELEMENTARY-JUNIOR HIGH
MATHEMATICS SERIES.
PROD-LEART   DIST-LEART

TASTES   C
     8X10 PREPARED TRANSPARENCY   H
FROM THE EMOTIONS AND SOCIAL ATTITUDES -
ATTITUDES, VALUES SERIES.
PROD-LEART   DIST-LEART

TAXES AND THE INDIVIDUAL   C
     8X10 PREPARED TRANSPARENCY   J-H
FROM THE BASIC SOCIAL STUDIES CONCEPTS -
ECONOMICS SERIES.
PROD-LEART   DIST-LEART

TEETH COME AND GO   C
     8X10 PREPARED TRANSPARENCY   K-P
FROM THE LIFE SCIENCE - GROWING UP
SERIES.
PROD-LEART   DIST-LEART

TELEGRAPH   C
     8X10 PREPARED TRANSPARENCY   H
SEE SERIES TITLE FOR DESCRIPTIVE STATEMENT.
FROM THE MAGNETISM AND ELECTRICITY SERIES.
PROD-BOW   DIST-BOW

TELEPHONE   C
     8X10 PREPARED TRANSPARENCY   H
SEE SERIES TITLE FOR DESCRIPTIVE STATEMENT.
FROM THE MAGNETISM AND ELECTRICITY SERIES.
PROD-BOW   DIST-BOW

TELESCOPE   C
     8X10 PREPARED TRANSPARENCY   H
SEE SERIES TITLE FOR DESCRIPTIVE STATEMENT.
FROM THE INSTRUMENTS AND TECHNIQUES OF
SCIENCE SERIES.
PROD-BOW   DIST-BOW

TELEVISION   C
     8X10 PREPARED TRANSPARENCY   H
SEE SERIES TITLE FOR DESCRIPTIVE STATEMENT.
FROM THE MAGNETISM AND ELECTRICITY SERIES.
PROD-BOW   DIST-BOW

**TELL THE STORY - CHANGE THE
ENDING**   C
     8X10 PREPARED TRANSPARENCY   K-P
SEE SERIES TITLE FOR DESCRIPTIVE STATEMENT.
FROM THE BEGINNING SKILLS SERIES.
PROD-BOW   DIST-BOW

**TELL THE STORY - MAKE IT
RHYME**   C
     8X10 PREPARED TRANSPARENCY   K-P
SEE SERIES TITLE FOR DESCRIPTIVE STATEMENT.
FROM THE BEGINNING SKILLS SERIES.
PROD-BOW   DIST-BOW

TEMPERATURE   C
     8X10 PREPARED TRANSPARENCY   P-I
FROM THE ELEMENTARY-JUNIOR HIGH
MATHEMATICS SERIES.
PROD-LEART   DIST-LEART

TEMPERATURE--A SERIES   K-P

EXPLAINS DIFFERENT ASPECTS OF TEMPERATURE
AND HOW IT AFFECTS PEOPLE.
PROD-BOW   DIST-BOW

HOW TEMPERATURE AFFECTS US
HOW TO USE THE THERMOMETER
LEARNING TO READ THE
THERMOMETER

TERRARIUM CONSTRUCTION   C
     8X10 PREPARED TRANSPARENCY   H
SEE SERIES TITLE FOR DESCRIPTIVE STATEMENT.
FROM THE PLANTS SERIES.
PROD-BOW   DIST-BOW

TESTING FOR MINERALS   C
     8X10 PREPARED TRANSPARENCY   H
SEE SERIES TITLE FOR DESCRIPTIVE STATEMENT.
FROM THE INSTRUMENTS AND TECHNIQUES OF
SCIENCE SERIES.
PROD-BOW   DIST-BOW

THEOREMS ON INVERSES, PT 1   C
     8X10 PREPARED TRANSPARENCY
FROM THE ALGEBRA, SECOND YEAR
STRUCTURE OF ALGEBRA SERIES.
PROD-LEART   DIST-LEART

THEOREMS ON INVERSES, PT 2   C
     8X10 PREPARED TRANSPARENCY
FROM THE ALGEBRA, SECOND YEAR -
STRUCTURE OF ALGEBRA SERIES.
PROD-LEART   DIST-LEART

THERMOMETER   C
     8X10 PREPARED TRANSPARENCY   H
SEE SERIES TITLE FOR DESCRIPTIVE STATEMENT.
FROM THE INSTRUMENTS AND TECHNIQUES OF
SCIENCE SERIES.
PROD-BOW   DIST-BOW

THIRD CLASS LEVER   C
     8X10 PREPARED TRANSPARENCY   H
SEE SERIES TITLE FOR DESCRIPTIVE STATEMENT.
FROM THE MACHINES SERIES.
PROD-BOW   DIST-BOW

**THREE-DIMENSIONAL
COORDINATE SYSTEM**   C
     8X10 PREPARED TRANSPARENCY
FROM THE ALGEBRA, SECOND YEAR - LINES
AND PLANES SERIES.
PROD-LEART   DIST-LEART

**THREE-DIMENSIONAL LETTER
SHAPES**   C
     8X10 PREPARED TRANSPARENCY   K-P
SEE SERIES TITLE FOR DESCRIPTIVE STATEMENT.
FROM THE BEGINNING SKILLS SERIES.
PROD-BOW   DIST-BOW

**THREE-DIMENSIONAL NUMERALS
AND COUNTING DISC**   C
     8X10 PREPARED TRANSPARENCY   K-P
SEE SERIES TITLE FOR DESCRIPTIVE STATEMENT.
FROM THE BEGINNING SKILLS SERIES.
PROD-BOW   DIST-BOW

**THREE-DIMENSIONAL TEN
FRAME**   C
     8X10 PREPARED TRANSPARENCY   K-P
SEE SERIES TITLE FOR DESCRIPTIVE STATEMENT.
FROM THE BEGINNING SKILLS SERIES.
PROD-BOW   DIST-BOW

**THREE-DIMENSIONAL VISUAL
DISCRIMINATION KIT**   C
     8X10 PREPARED TRANSPARENCY   K-P
SEE SERIES TITLE FOR DESCRIPTIVE STATEMENT.
FROM THE BEGINNING SKILLS SERIES.
PROD-BOW   DIST-BOW

THURGOOD MARSHALL   C
     8X10 PREPARED TRANSPARENCY   J-H
FROM THE BIOGRAPHIES OF OUTSTANDING
NEGRO AMERICANS SERIES.
PROD-LEART   DIST-LEART

TIME ZONES   C
     8X10 PREPARED TRANSPARENCY   P-I
FROM THE ELEMENTARY-JUNIOR HIGH
MATHEMATICS SERIES.
PROD-LEART   DIST-LEART

TIPS FOR THE INTERVIEW   C
     8X10 PREPARED TRANSPARENCY
SEE SERIES TITLE FOR DESCRIPTIVE STATEMENT.
FROM THE JOB APPLICATION AND JOB INTER-
VIEW SERIES.
PROD-COF   DIST-COF

TODAY'S ISMS   C
     8X10 PREPARED TRANSPARENCY   J-H
FROM THE ECONOMICS - POLITICAL ECONOMY
AND PHILOSOPHY SERIES.
PROD-LEART   DIST-LEART

**TOOLS OF THE
OCEANOGRAPHER**   C
     8X10 PREPARED TRANSPARENCY   I-H
SEE SERIES TITLE FOR DESCRIPTIVE STATEMENT.
FROM THE OCEANOGRAPHY SERIES.
PROD-BOW   DIST-BOW

TOOTH STRUCTURE   C
     8X10 PREPARED TRANSPARENCY   H
SEE SERIES TITLE FOR DESCRIPTIVE STATEMENT.
FROM THE HUMAN BODY SERIES.
PROD-BOW   DIST-BOW

TOWN AND ECONOMICS   C
     8X10 PREPARED TRANSPARENCY   J-H
FROM THE ECONOMICS - ECONOMIC HISTORY
SERIES.
PROD-LEART   DIST-LEART

**TRAINING PLAN FOR
DISTRIBUTIVE EDUCATION
STUDENTS**   C
     8X10 PREPARED TRANSPARENCY
SEE SERIES TITLE FOR DESCRIPTIVE STATEMENT.
FROM THE ORIENTATION TO DISTRIBUTIVE EDU-
CATION SERIES.
PROD-COF   DIST-COF

TRAITS OF POPULARITY   C
     8X10 PREPARED TRANSPARENCY   J
FROM THE DATING RELATIONS - POPULARITY
SERIES.
PROD-LEART   DIST-LEART

TREE BUDS   C
     8X10 PREPARED TRANSPARENCY   H
SEE SERIES TITLE FOR DESCRIPTIVE STATEMENT.
FROM THE PLANTS SERIES.
PROD-BOW   DIST-BOW

TREE TRUNK STRUCTURE   C
     8X10 PREPARED TRANSPARENCY   H
SEE SERIES TITLE FOR DESCRIPTIVE STATEMENT.
FROM THE PLANTS SERIES.
PROD-BOW   DIST-BOW

TRIANGULAR REGION   C
     8X10 PREPARED TRANSPARENCY
FROM THE ELEMENTARY GEOMETRY - AREA A
A MEASURE OF COVERING SERIES.
PROD-LEART   DIST-I FART

**TURN OBJECTIONS INTO
SELLING POINTS**
     8X10 PREPARED TRANSPARENC
SEE SERIES TITLE FOR DESCRIPTIVE STATEM
FROM THE BASIC SALESMANSHIP SERIES.
PROD-COF   DIST-COF

TWIN X-RAY   C
     8X10 PREPARED TRANSPARENCY   H
SEE SERIES TITLE FOR DESCRIPTIVE STATEMENT.
FROM THE GENERAL TOPICS SERIES.
PROD-BOW   DIST-BOW

TWINNING   C
     8X10 PREPARED TRANSPARENCY
FROM THE SEX EDUCATION - THE BABY - ITS
CONCEPTION, GROWTH AND BIRTH SERIES.
PROD-LEART   DIST-LEART

TWINS   C
     8X10 PREPARED TRANSPARENCY   H
SEE SERIES TITLE FOR DESCRIPTIVE STATEMENT.
FROM THE GENERAL TOPICS SERIES.
PROD-BOW   DIST-BOW

**TWO VELOCITY MOTION
PROBLEMS**   C
     8X10 PREPARED TRANSPARENCY
FROM THE ALGEBRA, SECOND YEAR - WORK
PROBLEMS SERIES.
PROD-LEART   DIST-LEART

**TWO WAYS TO PRODUCE
COLOR**   C
     8X10 PREPARED TRANSPARENCY   I-H
SEE SERIES TITLE FOR DESCRIPTIVE STATEMENT.
FROM THE LIGHT AND COLOR SERIES.
PROD-BOW   DIST-BOW

TWO-POINT AND POINT-SLOPE   C
     8X10 PREPARED TRANSPARENCY
FROM THE ALGEBRA, SECOND YEAR - LINES
AND PLANES SERIES.
PROD-LEART   DIST-LEART

TYPES OF FAMILIES   C
     8X10 PREPARED TRANSPARENCY   J-H
FROM THE BASIC SOCIAL STUDIES CONCEPTS -
SOCIETY SERIES.
PROD-LEART   DIST-LEART

**TYPES OF MARKET AND
EXCHANGES**   C
     8X10 PREPARED TRANSPARENCY   J-H
FROM THE BASIC SOCIAL STUDIES CONCEPTS -
ECONOMICS SERIES.
PROD-LEART   DIST-LEART

TYPES OF PRODUCTION   C
     8X10 PREPARED TRANSPARENCY   J-H
FROM THE BASIC SOCIAL STUDIES CONCEPTS -
ECONOMICS SERIES.
PROD-LEART   DIST-LEART

TYPES OF PROTECTION   C
     8X10 PREPARED TRANSPARENCY
SEX EDUCATION - DEVELOPMENTAL PATTERNS
OF PUBESCENT GIRLS SERIES.
PROD-LEART   DIST-LEART

U

UHURU   C
     8X10 PREPARED TRANSPARENCY   J-H
FROM THE POLITICAL GEOGRAPHY AND
NATIONALISM OF AFRICA SERIES.
PROD-LEART   DIST-LEART

**UNDERSTANDING
ABBREVIATIONS**   C
     8X10 PREPARED TRANSPARENCY   P-I
SEE SERIES TITLE FOR DESCRIPTIVE STATEMENT.
FROM THE PUNCTUATION AND CAPITALIZATION
SERIES.
PROD-BOW   DIST-BOW

**UNDERSTANDING AND USING
ANTONYMS**   C
     8X10 PREPARED TRANSPARENCY   I-J
SEE SERIES TITLE FOR DESCRIPTIVE STATEMENT.
FROM THE WORD USAGE SERIES.
PROD-BOW   DIST-BOW

**UNDERSTANDING AND USING
HOMONYMS**   C
     8X10 PREPARED TRANSPARENCY   I-J
SEE SERIES TITLE FOR DESCRIPTIVE STATEMENT.
FROM THE WORD USAGE SERIES.
PROD-BOW   DIST-BOW

**UNDERSTANDING AND USING
SYNONYMS**   C
     8X10 PREPARED TRANSPARENCY   I-J
SEE SERIES TITLE FOR DESCRIPTIVE STATEMENT.
FROM THE WORD USAGE SERIES.
PROD-BOW   DIST-BOW

**UNDERSTANDING
CONJUNCTIONS**   C
     8X10 PREPARED TRANSPARENCY   I-J
SEE SERIES TITLE FOR DESCRIPTIVE STATEMENT.
FROM THE WORD FORMS AND FUNCTIONS SE-
RIES.
PROD-BOW   DIST-BOW

**UNDERSTANDING
CONTRACTIONS**   C
     8X10 PREPARED TRANSPARENCY   P-I
SEE SERIES TITLE FOR DESCRIPTIVE STATEMENT.
FROM THE PUNCTUATION AND CAPITALIZATION
SERIES.
PROD-BOW   DIST-BOW

**UNDERSTANDING MALENESS
AND FEMALENESS**   C
     8X10 PREPARED TRANSPARENCY
FROM THE SEX EDUCATION - DEVELOPMENT OF
CONCEPTS AND ATTITUDES SERIES.
PROD-LEART   DIST-LEART

**UNDERSTANDING MATH
CONCEPTS--A SERIES**
     I-J
PRESENTS PROBLEMS IN NEW MATH.
PROD-BOW   DIST-BOW

**UNDERSTANDING
PREPOSITIONS**   C
     8X10 PREPARED TRANSPARENCY   I-J
SEE SERIES TITLE FOR DESCRIPTIVE STATEMENT.
FROM THE WORD FORMS AND FUNCTIONS SE-
RIES.
PROD-BOW   DIST-BOW

UNDERSTANDING SEXUALITY   C
     8X10 PREPARED TRANSPARENCY
FROM THE SEX EDUCATION - DEVELOPMENT OF
CONCEPTS AND ATTITUDES SERIES.
PROD-LEART   DIST-LEART

UNION OF SETS   C
     8X10 PREPARED TRANSPARENCY   P-I
FROM THE ELEMENTARY-JUNIOR HIGH
MATHEMATICS SERIES.
PROD-LEART   DIST-LEART

**UNITED NATIONS ROLE IN THE
INDEPENDENCE OF AFRICAN
COUNTRIES**   C
     8X10 PREPARED TRANSPARENCY   J-H
FROM THE POLITICAL GEOGRAPHY AND
NATIONALISM OF AFRICA SERIES.
PROD-LEART   DIST-LEART

**UNITED STATES GOVERNMENT
AND HOW IT WORKS--A SERIES**
     J-H
PROD-LEART   DIST-LEART

COMPROMISE RESULTING IN THE TWO-
HOUSE --
HOW A BILL BECOMES A LAW
JURISDICTION OF THE SUPREME
COURT, THE
METHODS OF AMENDING THE
CONSTITUTION
POCKET VETO, THE
POWERS OF THE PRESIDENT, THE
QUALIFICATIONS FOR HOLDING
NATIONAL OFFICE, THE
RESERVED POWERS AND DELEGATED
POWERS
SPECIFIC AMENDMENTS
SYSTEM OF CHECKS AND BALANCES,
THE
WORK OF THE CONSTITUTIONAL
CONVENTION

**UNITS OF TIME - YEAR,
MONTH, DAY**   C
     8X10 PREPARED TRANSPARENCY   P-I
FROM THE ELEMENTARY-JUNIOR HIGH
MATHEMATICS SERIES.
PROD-LEART   DIST-LEART

UNUSUAL MAMMALS   C
     8X10 PREPARED TRANSPARENCY   H
SEE SERIES TITLE FOR DESCRIPTIVE STATEMENT.
FROM THE WARM-BLOODED VERTEBRATES SE-
RIES.
PROD-BOW   DIST-BOW

USES AND ABUSES   C
     8X10 PREPARED TRANSPARENCY   H
SEE SERIES TITLE FOR DESCRIPTIVE STATEMENT.
FROM THE DRUG ABUSE SERIES.
PROD-BOW   DIST-BOW

USING ADJECTIVES   C
     8X10 PREPARED TRANSPARENCY   I-J
SEE SERIES TITLE FOR DESCRIPTIVE STATEMENT.
FROM THE WORD FORMS AND FUNCTIONS SE-
RIES.
PROD-BOW   DIST-BOW

USING BETWEEN AND AMONG   C
     8X10 PREPARED TRANSPARENCY   I-J
SEE SERIES TITLE FOR DESCRIPTIVE STATEMENT.
FROM THE WORD USAGE SERIES.
PROD-BOW   DIST-BOW

USING DETERMINANTS   C
     8X10 PREPARED TRANSPARENCY
FROM THE ALGEBRA, SECOND YEAR -
DETERMINANTS SERIES.
PROD-LEART   DIST-LEART

USING DID AND DONE   C
     8X10 PREPARED TRANSPARENCY   I-J
SEE SERIES TITLE FOR DESCRIPTIVE STATEMENT.
FROM THE WORD USAGE SERIES.
PROD-BOW   DIST-BOW

USING I AND ME   C
     8X10 PREPARED TRANSPARENCY   I-J
SEE SERIES TITLE FOR DESCRIPTIVE STATEMENT.
FROM THE WORD USAGE SERIES.
PROD-BOW   DIST-BOW

**USING OBJECT FORM
PRONOUNS**   C
     8X10 PREPARED TRANSPARENCY   I-J
SEE SERIES TITLE FOR DESCRIPTIVE STATEMENT.
FROM THE WORD FORMS AND FUNCTIONS SE-
RIES.
PROD-BOW   DIST-BOW

USING POSSESSIVE NOUNS   C
     8X10 PREPARED TRANSPARENCY   I-J
SEE SERIES TITLE FOR DESCRIPTIVE STATEMENT.
FROM THE WORD FORMS AND FUNCTIONS SE-
RIES.
PROD-BOW   DIST-BOW

USING POSSESSIVE PRONOUNS   C
     8X10 PREPARED TRANSPARENCY   I-J
SEE SERIES TITLE FOR DESCRIPTIVE STATEMENT.
FROM THE WORD FORMS AND FUNCTIONS SE-
RIES.
PROD-BOW   DIST-BOW

USING PREDICATE ADJECTIVES   C
     8X10 PREPARED TRANSPARENCY   I-J
SEE SERIES TITLE FOR DESCRIPTIVE STATEMENT.
FROM THE WORD FORMS AND FUNCTIONS SE-
RIES.
PROD-BOW   DIST-BOW

USING PRONOUNS   C
     8X10 PREPARED TRANSPARENCY   I-J
SEE SERIES TITLE FOR DESCRIPTIVE STATEMENT.
FROM THE WORD FORMS AND FUNCTIONS SE-
RIES.
PROD-BOW   DIST-BOW

USING QUOTATION MARKS   C
     8X10 PREPARED TRANSPARENCY   P-I
SEE SERIES TITLE FOR DESCRIPTIVE STATEMENT.
FROM THE PUNCTUATION AND CAPITALIZATION
SERIES.
PROD-BOW   DIST-BOW

USING SAW AND SEEN   C
     8X10 PREPARED TRANSPARENCY   I-J
SEE SERIES TITLE FOR DESCRIPTIVE STATEMENT.
FROM THE WORD USAGE SERIES.
PROD-BOW   DIST-BOW

USING THE PERIOD   C
     8X10 PREPARED TRANSPARENCY   P-I
SEE SERIES TITLE FOR DESCRIPTIVE STATEMENT.
FROM THE PUNCTUATION AND CAPITALIZATION
SERIES.
PROD-BOW   DIST-BOW

USING THE QUESTION MARK   C
     8X10 PREPARED TRANSPARENCY   P-I
SEE SERIES TITLE FOR DESCRIPTIVE STATEMENT.
FROM THE PUNCTUATION AND CAPITALIZATION
SERIES.
PROD-BOW   DIST-BOW

**USING THERE, THEIR AND
THEY'RE**   C
     8X10 PREPARED TRANSPARENCY   I-J
SEE SERIES TITLE FOR DESCRIPTIVE STATEMENT.
FROM THE WORD USAGE SERIES.
PROD-BOW   DIST-BOW

USING TO, TOO AND TWO   C
     8X10 PREPARED TRANSPARENCY   I-J
SEE SERIES TITLE FOR DESCRIPTIVE STATEMENT.
FROM THE WORD USAGE SERIES.
PROD-BOW   DIST-BOW

V

**VALUES IN ECONOMIC
DECISION**   C
     8X10 PREPARED TRANSPARENCY   J-H
FROM THE BASIC SOCIAL STUDIES CONCEPTS -
ECONOMICS SERIES.
PROD-LEART   DIST-LEART

VALUES IN THE ADULT   C
     8X10 PREPARED TRANSPARENCY   H
FROM THE EMOTIONS AND SOCIAL ATTITUDES -
ATTITUDES, VALUES SERIES.
PROD-LEART   DIST-LEART

VARIOUS PROGRAMS, THE   C
     8X10 PREPARED TRANSPARENCY
SEE SERIES TITLE FOR DESCRIPTIVE STATEMENT.
FROM THE ORIENTATION TO DISTRIBUTIVE EDU-
CATION SERIES.
PROD-COF   DIST-COF

VENEREAL DISEASE   C
    8X10 PREPARED TRANSPARENCY
FROM THE SEX EDUCATION - UNDERSTANDING
VENEREAL DISEASE SERIES.
PROD-LEART   DIST-LEART

VENN DIAGRAMS -
INTERSECTION OF SETS   C
    8X10 PREPARED TRANSPARENCY   P-I
FROM THE ELEMENTARY-JUNIOR HIGH
MATHEMATICS SERIES.
PROD-LEART   DIST-LEART

VENN DIAGRAMS - SETS AND
SUBSETS, IDENTICAL SETS,
INTERSECTING SETS, DISJOINT
SETS   C
    8X10 PREPARED TRANSPARENCY   P-I
FROM THE ELEMENTARY-JUNIOR HIGH
MATHEMATICS SERIES.
PROD-LEART   DIST-LEART

VERTEBRATE ANIMALS   C
    8X10 PREPARED TRANSPARENCY   H
SEE SERIES TITLE FOR DESCRIPTIVE STATEMENT.
FROM THE WARM-BLOODED VERTEBRATES SE-
RIES.
PROD-BOW   DIST-BOW

VIBRATION AND TRAVEL   C
    8X10 PREPARED TRANSPARENCY   I-C
SEE SERIES TITLE FOR DESCRIPTIVE STATEMENT.
FROM THE SOUND SERIES.
PROD-DOW   DIST-BOW

VISION DEFECTS   C
    8X10 PREPARED TRANSPARENCY   H
SEE SERIES TITLE FOR DESCRIPTIVE STATEMENT.
FROM THE HUMAN BODY SERIES.
PROD-BOW   DIST-BOW

VISUALIZING CROSS SECTIONS -
INTERSECTION OF PLANE AND
CUBE   C
    8X10 PREPARED TRANSPARENCY   P-I
FROM THE ELEMENTARY-JUNIOR HIGH
MATHEMATICS SERIES.
PROD-LEART   DIST-LEART

VISUALIZING CROSS SECTIONS -
INTERSECTION OF PLANE AND
SPHERE   C
    8X10 PREPARED TRANSPARENCY   P-I
FROM THE ELEMENTARY-JUNIOR HIGH
MATHEMATICS SERIES.
PROD-LEART   DIST-LEART

VISUALIZING CROSS SECTIONS -
INTERSECTION OF PLANE AND
CYLINDER   C
    8X10 PREPARED TRANSPARENCY   P-I
FROM THE ELEMENTARY-JUNIOR HIGH
MATHEMATICS SERIES.
PROD-LEART   DIST-LEART

VISUALIZING CROSS SECTIONS -
INTERSECTION OF PLANE AND
CONE   C
    8X10 PREPARED TRANSPARENCY   P-I
FROM THE ELEMENTARY-JUNIOR HIGH
MATHEMATICS SERIES.
PROD-LEART   DIST-LEART

VOCABULARY   C
    8X10 PREPARED TRANSPARENCY   P-I
FROM THE ELEMENTARY-JUNIOR HIGH
MATHEMATICS SERIES.
PROD-LEART   DIST-LEART

VOLCANO   C
    8X10 PREPARED TRANSPARENCY   H
SEE SERIES TITLE FOR DESCRIPTIVE STATEMENT.
FROM THE GEOLOGY SERIES.
PROD-BOW   DIST-BOW

VOWEL CHARTS--A SERIES
SHOWS LONG AND SHORT SOUNDS, TWO LIKE
AND TWO DIFFERENT VOWELS TOGETHER, 'E'
ENDINGS, VOWEL PICTURES, SYMBOLS AND
RULES.
PROD-BOW   DIST-BOW

W

W C HANDY   C
    8X10 PREPARED TRANSPARENCY   J-H
FROM THE BIOGRAPHIES OF OUTSTANDING
NEGRO AMERICANS SERIES.
PROD-LEART   DIST-LEART

WARM AND COLD FRONTS   C
    8X10 PREPARED TRANSPARENCY   H
SEE SERIES TITLE FOR DESCRIPTIVE STATEMENT.
FROM THE WEATHER SERIES.
PROD-BOW   DIST-BOW

WARM-BLOODED VERTEBRATES-
-A SERIES   H
DISCUSSES VERTEBRATE ANIMALS, INCLUDING
THE EVOLUTION OF THE HORSE, BIRDS AND THE
STRUCTURE OF MAMMALS.
PROD-BOW   DIST-BOW

BIRD ADAPTATION
BIRD EMBRYOLOGY
BIRD IDENTIFICATION
BIRD MIGRATION
BIRD NESTS
BIRD STRUCTURE
EVOLUTION OF THE HORSE
FEEDER CONSTRUCTION
MAMMALS' HOMES
STRUCTURE OF MAMMALS
UNUSUAL MAMMALS
VERTEBRATE ANIMALS

WATER CYCLE   C
    8X10 PREPARED TRANSPARENCY   H
SEE SERIES TITLE FOR DESCRIPTIVE STATEMENT.
FROM THE WEATHER SERIES.
PROD-BOW   DIST-BOW

WATER FILTRATION PLANT   C
    8X10 PREPARED TRANSPARENCY   H
SEE SERIES TITLE FOR DESCRIPTIVE STATEMENT.
FROM THE APPLIED SCIENCE SERIES.
PROD-BOW   DIST-BOW

WAYS OF CONTROL   C
    8X10 PREPARED TRANSPARENCY
FROM THE SEX EDUCATION - DEVELOPMENTAL
PATTERNS OF PUBESCENT BOYS SERIES.
PROD-LEART   DIST-LEART

WEATHER--A SERIES   H
DISCUSSES VARIOUS PHENOMENA INVOLVING
WEATHER.
PROD-BOW   DIST-BOW

ATMOSPHERE
CLIMATE
CLOUDS
WARM AND COLD FRONTS
WATER CYCLE
WIND CIRCULATION

WEEKLY SCHEDULE FOR GOOD
GROOMING, A   C
    8X10 PREPARED TRANSPARENCY
SEE SERIES TITLE FOR DESCRIPTIVE STATEMENT.
FROM THE GOOD GROOMING SERIES.
PROD-COF   DIST-COF

WELL-DRESSED YOUNG
WORKING MAN, THE   C
    8X10 PREPARED TRANSPARENCY
SEE SERIES TITLE FOR DESCRIPTIVE STATEMENT.
FROM THE GOOD GROOMING SERIES.
PROD-COF   DIST-COF

WELL-DRESSED YOUNG
WORKING WOMAN, THE   C
    8X10 PREPARED TRANSPARENCY
SEE SERIES TITLE FOR DESCRIPTIVE STATEMENT.
FROM THE GOOD GROOMING SERIES.
PROD-COF   DIST-COF

WHAT ARE SOCIAL CLASSES   C
    8X10 PREPARED TRANSPARENCY   J-H
FROM THE BASIC SOCIAL STUDIES CONCEPTS -
SOCIETY SERIES.
PROD-LEART   DIST-LEART

WHAT ARE SOCIAL VALUES AND
NORMS   C
    8X10 PREPARED TRANSPARENCY   J-H
FROM THE BASIC SOCIAL STUDIES CONCEPTS -
SOCIETY SERIES.
PROD-LEART   DIST-LEART

WHAT DECA SYMBOLIZES   C
    8X10 PREPARED TRANSPARENCY
SEE SERIES TITLE FOR DESCRIPTIVE STATEMENT.
FROM THE DISTRIBUTIVE EDUCATION CLUBS OF
AMERICA SERIES.
PROD-COF   DIST-COF

WHAT IS A SOCIAL
INSTITUTION   C
    8X10 PREPARED TRANSPARENCY   J-H
FROM THE BASIC SOCIAL STUDIES CONCEPTS -
SOCIETY SERIES.
PROD-LEART   DIST-LEART

WHAT IS A SOCIETY   C
    8X10 PREPARED TRANSPARENCY   J-H
FROM THE BASIC SOCIAL STUDIES CONCEPTS -
SOCIETY SERIES.
PROD-LEART   DIST-LEART

WHAT IS AN OPEN SOCIETY   C
    8X10 PREPARED TRANSPARENCY   J-H
FROM THE BASIC SOCIAL STUDIES CONCEPTS -
SOCIETY SERIES.
PROD-LEART   DIST-LEART

WHAT IS CAPITAL   C
    8X10 PREPARED TRANSPARENCY   J-H
FROM THE BASIC SOCIAL STUDIES CONCEPTS -
ECONOMICS SERIES.
PROD-LEART   DIST-LEART

WHAT IS DAY, WHAT IS NIGHT   C
    8X10 PREPARED TRANSPARENCY   K-P
SEE SERIES TITLE FOR DESCRIPTIVE STATEMENT.
FROM THE EARTH AND SKY SERIES.
PROD-BOW   DIST-BOW

WHAT IS ECONOMIC GROWTH   C
    8X10 PREPARED TRANSPARENCY   J-H
FROM THE BASIC SOCIAL STUDIES CONCEPTS -
ECONOMICS SERIES.
PROD-LEART   DIST-LEART

WHAT IS ECONOMIC PLANNING   C
    8X10 PREPARED TRANSPARENCY   J-H
FROM THE ECONOMICS - ECONOMICS IN
ACTION SERIES.
PROD-LEART   DIST-LEART

WHAT IS ECONOMICS   C
    8X10 PREPARED TRANSPARENCY   J-H
FROM THE BASIC SOCIAL STUDIES CONCEPTS -
ECONOMICS SERIES.
PROD-LEART   DIST-LEART

WHAT IS ROMANTIC LOVE   C
    8X10 PREPARED TRANSPARENCY   J
FROM THE DATING RELATIONS - ROMANCE AND
PEOPLE SERIES.
PROD-LEART   DIST-LEART

WHAT IS SELLING   C
    8X10 PREPARED TRANSPARENCY
SEE SERIES TITLE FOR DESCRIPTIVE STATEMENT.
FROM THE BASIC SALESMANSHIP SERIES.
PROD-COF   DIST-COF

WHAT IS SOCIAL STUDIES - AN
INTERDISCIPLINARY APPROACH   C
    8X10 PREPARED TRANSPARENCY   J-H
FROM THE BASIC SOCIAL STUDIES CONCEPTS -
POLITICS, SOCIAL-ECONOMIC INTERDEPENDENCE
SERIES.
PROD-LEART   DIST-LEART

WHAT MAKES PERSONALITIES
DIFFERENT   C
    8X10 PREPARED TRANSPARENCY
FROM THE SEX EDUCATION - DEVELOPMENT OF
CONCEPTS AND ATTITUDES SERIES.
PROD-LEART   DIST-LEART

WHEN YOU'RE NOT SELLING C
8X10 PREPARED TRANSPARENCY
SEE SERIES TITLE FOR DESCRIPTIVE STATEMENT.
FROM THE BASIC SALESMANSHIP SERIES.
PROD-COF   DIST-COF

**WHY A SOCIETY NEEDS TO
STUDY IT'S PAST** C
8X10 PREPARED TRANSPARENCY   J-H
FROM THE BASIC SOCIAL STUDIES CONCEPTS -
SOCIETY SERIES.
PROD-LEART   DIST-LEART

WILLIAM E B DU BOIS C
8X10 PREPARED TRANSPARENCY   J-H
FROM THE BIOGRAPHIES OF OUTSTANDING
NEGRO AMERICANS SERIES.
PROD-LEART   DIST-LEART

WILLIE MAYS C
8X10 PREPARED TRANSPARENCY   J-H
FROM THE BIOGRAPHIES OF OUTSTANDING
NEGRO AMERICANS SERIES.
PROD-LEART   DIST-LEART

WILTON N CHAMBERLAIN C
8X10 PREPARED TRANSPARENCY   J-H
FROM THE BIOGRAPHIES OF OUTSTANDING
NEGRO AMERICANS SERIES.
PROD-LEART   DIST-LEART

WIND CIRCULATION C
8X10 PREPARED TRANSPARENCY   H
SEE SERIES TITLE FOR DESCRIPTIVE STATEMENT.
FROM THE WEATHER SERIES.
PROD-BOW   DIST-BOW

WORD BUILDING--A SERIES
SHOWS MANY CHANGES OF A ROOT WORD BY US-
ING SUFFIXES, PREFIXES AND OTHER ADDITIONS
AND DEVELOPING COMPOUND WORDS.
PROD-BOW   DIST-BOW

**WORD FORMS AND FUNCTIONS-
-A SERIES**
I-J
EXPLAINS HOW TO FORM DIFFERENT PARTS OF
SPEECH AND HOW TO CHANGE WORD FORMS.
PROD-BOW   DIST-BOW

ADJECTIVES - POSITIVE, COMPARATIVE

ADVERBS - POSITIVE, COMPARATIVE --
COMPARING SIMPLE AND COMPOUND
VERBS

DISTINGUISHING PROPER AND
COMMON NOUNS
IDENTIFYING ACTION VERBS
IDENTIFYING ADVERBIALS
IDENTIFYING STATE-OF-BEING VERBS
INTRODUCING ADVERBS
PLURAL NOUNS ENDING IN 'ES'
PLURAL NOUNS ENDING IN 'IES'
PLURAL NOUNS ENDING IN 'S'
RECOGNIZING NOUNS
RECOGNIZING ROOT WORDS, PREFIXES
AND --
UNDERSTANDING CONJUNCTIONS
UNDERSTANDING PREPOSITIONS
USING ADJECTIVES
USING OBJECT FORM PRONOUNS
USING POSSESSIVE NOUNS
USING POSSESSIVE PRONOUNS
USING PREDICATE ADJECTIVES
USING PRONOUNS

**WORD FUNCTION AND
SENTENCE PATTERNS--A SERIES**

DESCRIBES THE FUNCTION OF WORDS AND THE
PATTERNS OF SENTENCES.
PROD-BOW   DIST-BOW

WORD USAGE--A SERIES
I-J
EXPLAINS GRAMMATICAL USAGE OF DIFFERENT
TYPES OF WORDS.
PROD-BOW   DIST-BOW

AVOIDING DOUBLE NEGATIVES
UNDERSTANDING AND USING
ANTONYMS
UNDERSTANDING AND USING
HOMONYMS
UNDERSTANDING AND USING
SYNONYMS
USING BETWEEN AND AMONG
USING DID AND DONE
USING I AND ME
USING SAW AND SEEN
USING THERE, THEIR AND THEY'RE
USING TO, TOO AND TWO

**WORK OF THE
CONSTITUTIONAL CONVENTION** C
8X10 PREPARED TRANSPARENCY   J-H
FROM THE UNITED STATES GOVERNMENT AND
HOW IT WORKS SERIES.
PROD-LEART   DIST-LEART

WORK PROBLEMS C
8X10 PREPARED TRANSPARENCY
FROM THE ALGEBRA, FIRST YEAR - WORD
PROBLEMS SERIES.
PROD-LEART   DIST-LEART

WRITING BUSINESS LETTERS C
8X10 PREPARED TRANSPARENCY   I
SEE SERIES TITLE FOR DESCRIPTIVE STATEMENT.
FROM THE LETTER WRITING SERIES.
PROD-BOW   DIST-BOW

WRITING EQUATIONS C
8X10 PREPARED TRANSPARENCY
FROM THE ALGEBRA, SECOND YEAR - LINES
AND PLANES SERIES.
PROD-LEART   DIST-LEART

**WRITING EQUATIONS -
EXAMPLES** C
8X10 PREPARED TRANSPARENCY
FROM THE ALGEBRA, SECOND YEAR - LINES
AND PLANES SERIES.
PROD-LEART   DIST-LEART

WRITING FRIENDLY LETTERS C
8X10 PREPARED TRANSPARENCY   I
SEE SERIES TITLE FOR DESCRIPTIVE STATEMENT.
FROM THE LETTER WRITING SERIES.
PROD-BOW   DIST-BOW

Y

YOUR ATTITUDE IN FIVE YEARS C
8X10 PREPARED TRANSPARENCY   H
FROM THE EMOTIONS AND SOCIAL ATTITUDES -
ATTITUDES, VALUES SERIES.
PROD-LEART   DIST-LEART

Z

ZERO PRODUCTS C
8X10 PREPARED TRANSPARENCY
FROM THE ALGEBRA, SECOND YEAR -
STRUCTURE OF ALGEBRA SERIES.
PROD-LEART   DIST-LEART

ABCNEW ABC NEWS

ACI ACI PRODUCTIONS
ELEVENTH FLOOR
35 WEST 45TH ST
NEW YORK, NY 10036

AFB AMER FOUNDATION FOR
THE BLIND
15 W SIXTEENTH ST
NEW YORK, NY 10011

AFI ASSOCIATED FILMAKERS
INTERNATIONAL

AIMS AIMS INSTRUCTIONAL MEDIA
SERVICES, INC
P O BOX 1010
HOLLYWOOD, CA 90028

AJC AMER JEWISH COMMITTEE
590 N VERMONT AVE
LOS ANGELES, CA 90004

ALBM ALBERT (MARVIN) FILMS

ALDEN ALDEN FILMS
5113 SIXTEENTH AVE
BROOKLYN, NY 11204

ALEP AUDIOLINGUAL EDUCATIONAL PRESS
45 W PARK AVE BOX 390
LONG BEACH, NY 11561

ALTSUL GILBERT ALTSCHUL PRODUCTIONS
909 W DIVERSEY PARKWAY
CHICAGO, IL 60614

AMDA AMER DENTAL ASSN
BUREAU OF AUDIO VISUAL SERV
211 E CHICAGO AVE
CHICAGO, IL 60611

AMEDA AMER MEDICAL ASSN
535 N DEARBORN
CHICAGO, IL 60610

AMEDFL AMER EDUCATIONAL FILMS
9879 SANTA MONICA BLVD
BEVERLY HILLS, CA 90212

AMERFI AMER FILM INSTITUTE
1815 H ST NW
WASHINGTON, DC 20006

AMP ADMASTER PRINTS, INC
425 PARK AVE, S
NEW YORK, NY 10016

ARGSC ARGUS COMMUNICATIONS
3505 N ASHLAND AVE
CHICAGO, IL 60657

ARIC ATLANTIC RICHFIELD CO

ARIZSU ARIZ STATE UNIV
TEMPE, AZ 85281

ASPRSS ASSOCIATED PRESS

ATHI ATHLETIC INSTITUTE
ROOM 805 MERCHANDISE MART
CHICAGO, IL 60654

ATLAP ATLANTIS PRODUCTIONS, INC
1252 LA GRANADA DR
THOUSAND OAKS, CA 91360

AVDEV AIDS AUDIOVISUAL INSTRUCTIONAL
DEVICES, INC
24-20 LITTLE NECK BLVD
BAYSIDE, NY 11360

AVED AV-ED FILMS
7934 SANTA MONICA BLVD
HOLLYWOOD, CA 90046

AVEXP A-V EXPLORATIONS, INC
505 DELAWARE AVE
BUFFALO, NY 14202

AVIS AVIS FILMS
2408 W OLIVE AVE
BURBANK, CA 91506

AVNA AUDIO VISUAL NARRATIVE ARTS

BASCH BASCH RADIO AND TELEVISION
PRODUCTIONS
25 W 45TH ST
NEW YORK, NY 10036

BASCHE BASSETT-CHESNUT

BASSS SAUL BASS & ASSOCIATES
7039 SUNSET BLVD
LOS ANGELES, CA 90028

BBCTV BRITISH BROADCASTING CO-TV
630 FIFTH AVE
NEW YORK, NY 10020

BBF BILLY BUDD FILMS
235 E 57TH ST
NEW YORK, NY 10022

BEF BUSINESS EDUCATION FILMS
DIV OF ALDEN FILMS
5113 SIXTEENTH AVE
BROOKLYN, NY 11204

BELSON BELSON (JORDAN)
SAN FRANCISCO, CA

BETECL CHANNING L BETE CO, INC
45 FEDERAL ST
GREENFIELD, MA 01301

BFA BFA EDUCATIONAL MEDIA
2211 MICHIGAN AVE
SANTA MONICA, CA 90404

BNA BNA FILMS
A DIV OF THE BUREAU OF NATL
AFFAIRS, INC
5615 FISHERS LANE
ROCKVILLE, MD 20852

BOSUST STEPHEN BOSUSTOW PRODUCTIONS
20548 PACIFIC COAST HWY
MALIBU, CA 90265

BOUCH BOUCHE PRODUCTIONS
1050 PECAS TRAIL
SANTA FE, NM 87501

BOW STANLEY BOWMAR CO
4 BROADWAY
VALHALLA, NY 10595

BRNDNL BRANDON (LIANE)
19 LANGLEY RD
BRIGHTON, MA 02135

BSF BASIC SKILL FILMS
1355 INVERNESS DR
PASADENA, CA 91103

CAED CAEDMAN RECORDS, INC
DIV HOUGHTON MIFFLIN CO
110 TREMONT ST
BOSTON, MA 02107

CAHILL CHARLES CAHILL AND ASSOC, INC
P O BOX 1010
HOLLYWOOD, CA 90028

CARMAN CARMAN EDUCATIONAL ASSOC, INC
BOX 205
YOUNGSTOWN, NY 14174

CAROUF CAROUSEL FILMS, INC
1501 BROADWAY
NEW YORK, NY 10036

CBSTV COLUMBIA BROADCASTING SYSTEM
383 MADISON AVE
NEW YORK, NY 10017

CCMFI CCM FILMS, INC
866 THIRD AVE
NEW YORK, NY 10022

CENTEF CENTRON EDUCATIONAL FILMS
SUITE 652, 1255 POST ST
SAN FRANCISCO, CA 94109

CER COMMUNITY EDUCATIONAL RESOURCES
DEPT OF EDUCATION
SAN DIEGO COUNTY
6401 LINDA VISTA RD
SAN DIEGO, CA 92111

CEURED CENTER FOR URBAN EDUCATION

CF CHURCHILL FILMS
662 N ROBERTSON BLVD
LOS ANGELES, CA 90069

CFS CREATIVE FILM SOCIETY
14558 VALERIO ST
VAN NUYS, CA 91405

CHM CLEVELAND HEALTH MUSEUM
8911 EUCLID AVE
8711 EUCLID AVE
CLEVELAND, OH 44106

CLOPSD CLOVER PARK SCHOOL DISTRICT 400
LAKEWOOD CENTER, WA

CLSMAT CLASSROOM MATERIALS, INC
93 MYRTLE DR
GREAT NECK, NY 11021

CMC CENTER FOR MASS COMMUNICATION
OF COLUMBIA UNIV PRESS
440 W 110TH ST
NEW YORK, NY 10025

COF COLONIAL FILMS
752 SPRING ST NW
ATLANTA, GA 30308

COMG COMMON GROUND, LTD
44 FULHAM RD
LONDON, S W 3, ENGLAND

COMICO COMMUNICO
1335 N HIGHWAY DR
FENTON, MO 63206

CONMED CONCEPT MEDIA
P O 1893
COSTA MESA, CA 92626

CONNF CONN FILMS, INC
6 COBBLE HILL RD
WESTPORT, CT 06880

CONSFI CONSOLIDATED FILM INDUSTRIES
959 SEWARD ST
HOLLYWOOD, CA 90028

COPI COMPRENETICS, INC
9021 MELROSE AVE
LOS ANGELES, CA 90069

CORF CORONET INSTRUCTIONAL FILMS
65 E SOUTH WATER ST
CHICAGO, IL 60601

CREATV CREATIVE VISUALS, INC
P O BOX 1911
BIG SPRING, TX 79720

CRMP CRM PRODUCTIONS
9263 THIRD ST
BEVERLY HILLS, CA 90210

CUNIV CORNELL UNIV
FILM CENTER
ITHACA, NY 14850

DARTNL DARTNELL CORP
4660 RAVENSWOOD
CHICAGO, IL 60640

DATA DATA FILMS
2625 TEMPLE ST
LOS ANGELES, CA 90026

DAVFMS DAVIDSON FILMS
3701 BUCHANAN ST
SAN FRANCISCO, CA 94123

DAVI NATL EDUCATION ASSN OF THE U S
DIV OF AV INSTRUCTION
1201 SIXTEENTH ST
WASHINGTON, DC 20036

DIMFIV DIMENSION 5

DISNEY WALT DISNEY PRODUCTIONS
EDUCATIONAL FILM DIVISION
500 S BUENA VISTA AVE
BURBANK, CA 91503

DOUBLE DOUBLEDAY MULTIMEDIA
1370 REYNOLDS AVE
SANTA ANA, CA 92705

DWYLIE WYLLIE (DIANA) LTD
3 PARK RD
BAKER ST
LONDON NWI, ENGLAND

EAGLE ARNOLD EAGLE PRODUCTIONS
41 WEST 47TH ST
NEW YORK, NY 10036

EAV EDUCATIONAL AUDIO-VISUAL
29 MARBLE AVE
PLEASANTVILLE, NY 10570

EBEC ENCYCLOPEDIA BRITANNICA
EDUCATIONAL CORP
425 N MICHIGAN AVE
CHICAGO, IL 60611

ECCCW ECCENTRIC CIRCLE CINEMA WORKSHOP
347 FLORENCE AVE
EVANSTON, IL 60202

EDC EDUCATION DEVELOPMENT CENTER
55 CHAPEL ST
NEWTON, MA 02160

EDCOM EDCOM PRODUCTIONS
285 W SIXTH ST
MARSFIELD, OH 44902

EDDIM EDUCATIONAL DIMENSIONS CORP
BOX 146
GREAT NECK, NY 11023

EDLACT EDUCATIONAL ACTIVITIES, INC
ACTIVITY RECORDS
P O BOX 392
FREEPORT, NY 11520

EDPRC EDUCATIONAL PROJECTION CORP
527 S COMMERCE
JACKSON, MS 39205

EDREC EDUCATIONAL DIRECTION, INC
181 W STATE ST
WESTPORT, CT 06880

EGH EYE GATE HOUSE, INC
146-01 ARCHER AVE
JAMAICA, NY 11435

EMP EXCEL MOVIE PRODUCTS

EPRI E P RESEARCH, INC
SUITE N VILLAGE CORNER
LOS ALTOS, CA 94022

EVNSR RUTH EVANS

FI FILMS, INC
1144 WILMETTE
WILMETTE, IL 60091

FIELEP FIELD EDUCATIONAL PUBLICATIONS

FILIM FILM IMAGES
DIST NOW BY RADIM FILMS

FILMSW FILMS/WEST, INC
1522 N VAN NESS
518 N LA CIENIGA BLVD
HOLLYWOOD, CA 90028

FLMFR FILMFAIR, INC
10820 VENTURA BLVD
STUDIO CITY, CA 91604

FMCMP FORD MOTOR CO
MOTION PICTURE DEPT
3000 SCHAEFER ROAD
DEARBORN, MI 48122

FORD HENRY FORD MUSEUM AND
GREENFIELD VILLAGE
AUDIO-VISUAL SERVICES
DEARBORN, MI 48124

FOTH FILMS FOR THE HUMANITIES AND
SCIENCES
PO BOX 378
PRINCETON, NJ 08540

FPC FOLLETT PUBLISHING CO
1010 W WASHINGTON BLVD
CHICAGO, IL 60607

FSH   FILMSTRIP HOUSE
432 PARK AVE S
NEW YORK, NY 10016

GA   GUIDANCE ASSOC
HARCOURT, BRACE AND WORLD
23 WASHINGTON AVE
PLEASANTVILLE, NY 10570

GEIGY   GEIGY CHEMICAL CORP
SAW MILL RIVER RD
ARDSLEY, NY 10502

GLDWER   GOLDBERG-WERRENROTH PRODUCTIONS

2096 PARK LANE
HIGHLAND PARK, IL 60035

GMS   GOLDSMITH'S MUSIC SHOP, INC
LANGUAGE DEPT
401 W 42ND ST
NEW YORK, NY 10036

GPITVL   GREAT PLAINS INSTRUCTIONAL TV
LIBRARY
UNIV OF NEBRASKA
P O BOX 80669
LINCOLN, NB 68501

GRANDY   ROY GRANDY PRODUCTIONS
1881 ROLLINS RD, BLDG C
BURLINGAME, CA 94010

GREAVW   GREAVES (WILLIAM) PRODUCTIONS

HAR   HARPER AND ROW PUBLISHERS
49 EAST 33RD ST
NEW YORK, NY 10016

HEARST   HEARST METROTONE NEWS
450 W 56TH ST
NEW YORK, NY 10019

HESTER   HESTER AND ASSOC
P O BOX 20812
11422 HARRY HINES BLVD
SUITE 212
DALLAS, TX 75220

HRAW   HOLT, RINEHART AND WINSTON
383 MADISON AVE
NEW YORK, NY 10017

HUBDSC   HUBBARD SCIENTIFIC CO
P O BOX 105
NORTHBROOK, IL 60062

HUNGFM   HUNGAROFILM
BUDAPEST, HUNGARY

IDEA   INSTITUTE FOR DEVELOPMENT OF
EDUCATIONAL ACTIVITIES
P O BOX 446
MELBOURNE, FL 32901

ILBELL   ILL BELL TELEPHONE CO
225 W RANDOLPH ST
CHICAGO, IL 60606

INTXC   INSTITUTE OF TEXAN CULTURES

IOWA   IOWA STATE UNIV
FILM PRODUCTION UNIT
ALICE NORTON HOUSE
AMES, IA 50010

IU   IND UNIV
AUDIO-VISUAL CENTER
BLOOMINGTON, IN 47401

IWANMI   IWANMI PRODUCTIONS, INC
TOKYO, JAPAN

JOU   JOURNAL FILMS
909 W DIVERSEY PKWY
CHICAGO, IL 60614

KCET   KCET/LOS ANGELES
C/O ETS PROGRAM SERVICE
317 E SECOND ST
BLOOMINGTON, IN 47401

KEGPL   KEG PRODUCTIONS, LTD
556 CHURCH ST
TORONTO, ONTARIO, CANADA

KELLRP   PAUL F KELLER & ASSOCIATES
6412 INDIAN HILLS RD
MINNEAPOLIS, MN 55435

KENTSU   KENT STATE UNIVERSITY
AV SERVICES
KENT, OH 44240

KINGSP   KING SCREEN PRODUCTIONS
A DIV OF KING BROADCASTING CO
320 AURORA AVE N
SEATTLE, WA 98109

KRI   KENNY REHABILITATION INSTITUTE
1800 CHICAGO AVE
MINNEAPOLIS, MN 55404

LACFD   L A CITY FIRE DEPT
217 S HILL
LOS ANGELES, CA 90015

LCOA   LEARNING CORPORATION OF AMERICA
711 FIFTH AVE
NEW YORK, NY 10022

LEART   LEARNING ARTS
P O BOX 917
WICHITA, KS 67201

LESAM   LES FILMS ARMORIAL
6 RUE LAMMENAIS
PARIS 8, FRANCE

LIBFSC   LIBRARY FILMSTRIP CENTER
3033 ALOMA
WICHITA, KS 67211

LIEB   JACK LIEB PRODUCTIONS
1230 W WASHINGTON ST
CHICAGO, IL 60607

LIFE   LIFE FILMSTRIPS
TIME AND LIFE BUILDING
9 ROCKEFELLER PLAZA
NEW YORK, NY 10020

LILC   LONG ISLAND LIGHTING CO
250 OLD COUNTRY ROAD
MINEOLA, NY 11501

LONWTV   LONDON WEEKEND TV
LONDON, ENGLAND

LYCEUM   LYCEUM PRODUCTIONS
2605 W LAKE AVE
ALTADENA, CA 91001

MANTLH   HAROLD MANTELL, INC
PO BOX 378
PRINCETON, NJ 08540

MENKNS   SHEPHERD MENKEN

METROM   METROMEDIA PRODUCERS CORP
485 LEXINGTON AVE
NEW YORK, NY 10017

MFLMC   MONUMENT FILM CORP
267 W 25TH ST
NEW YORK, NY 10001

MGHT   MC GRAW-HILL TEXTFILMS
330 W 42ND ST
NEW YORK, NY 10036

MSCF   MEDIA SERVICES AND CAPTIONED
FILMS
7TH AND D STREETS, SW
WASHINGTON, DC 20202

MTP   MODERN TALKING PICTURE SERV
1212 AVENUE OF THE AMERICAS
NEW YORK, NY 10036

MTSJC   MT SAN JACINTO COLLEGE

NAEB   NATL ASSN OF EDUCATIONAL
BROADCASTERS
317 SECOND ST
UNIVERISTY OF ILLINOIS
BLOOMINGTON, IN 47403

NASA   NATL AERONAUTICS AND
SPACE ADMIN
CODE FAD
WASHINGTON, DC 20546

NAVA   NATL AUDIO VISUAL ASSN, INC
3150 SPRING ST
FAIRFAX, VA 22030

NBCTV   NATL BROADCASTING CO, TV
30 ROCKEFELLER PLAZA RM 914
NEW YORK, NY 10020

NET   NATL EDUCATIONAL TV, INC
INDIANA UNIVERSITY
BLOOMINGTON, IN 47401

NFBC   NATL FILM BOARD OF CANADA
680 FIFTH AVE, SUITE 819
NEW YORK, NY 10019

NHTSA   NATL HIGHWAY TRAFFIC SAFETY
ADMIN

NITC   NATL INSTRUCTIONAL TV CENTER
BOX A
BLOOMINGTON, IN 47401

NLC   NEW LINE CINEMA
121 UNIVERSITY PLACE
NEW YORK, NY 10003

NOWAKA   AMRAM NOWAK ASSOCIATES
254 W 54TH ST
NEW YORK, NY 10019

NRMA   NATL RETAIL MERCHANTS ASSN
DOWNTOWN DEVELOPMENT COMMITTEE
100 W 31ST ST
NEW YORK, NY 10001

NSF   NATL SCIENCE FOUNDATION
1951 CONSTITUTION AVE, NW
WASHINGTON, DC 20550

NULSEN   NULSEN (DAVID) ENTERPRISES
3211 PICO BLVD
SANTA MONICA, CA 90405

NVFP   NEUBACHER-VETTER FILM PRODUCTION
1750 WESTWOOD BLVD
LOS ANGELES, CA 90024

NWFLMP   NORTHWEST FILM PRODUCTIONS
P O BOX 1030
SPOKANE, WA 99210

OF   OXFORD FILMS, INC
1136 N LAS PALMAS AVE
HOLLYWOOD, CA 90038

OHIOSU   OHIO STATE UNIVERSITY
190 W 17TH AVE
COLUMBUS, OH 44223

PART   PARTHENON PICTURES
2625 TEMPLE ST
HOLLYWOOD, CA 90026

PATED   PATHESCOPE EDUCATIONAL FILMS INC
71 WEYMAN AVE
NEW ROCHELLE, NY 10802

PAULST   PAULIST PRODUCTIONS
17575 PACIFIC COAST HIGHWAY
PACIFIC PALISADES, CA 90272

PERSPF   PERSPECTIVE FILMS
65 E SOUTH WATER ST
CHICAGO, IL 60601

PFP   PYRAMID FILM PRODUCTIONS
P O BOX 1048
317 GEORGINA AVE
SANTA MONICA, CA 90406

PHENIX   PHOENIX FILMS

PHLSAC   PHILADELPHIA SCHOOL FOR
ANTI-COMMUNISTS

PHOTO   PHOTO LAB, INC
3825 GEORGIA AVE, N W
WASHINGTON, DC 20011

PIC   PICTURA FILMS CORP
43 W 16TH ST
NEW YORK, NY 10011

PILOT   PILOT PRODUCTIONS, INC
1819 RIDGE AVE
EVANSTON, IL 60201

POPHAM   POPHAM (W JAMES)
5640 WISH AVE
ENCINO, CA 91316

PPFA   PLANNED PARENTHOOD FEDERATION
OF AMERICA, INC

PUI   PRODUCTIONS UNLIMITED, INC
1564 BROADWAY
NEW YORK, NY 10036

RADIM   RADIM FILMS, INC
220 WEST 42ND ST
NEW YORK, NY 10036

RARIG   RARIG'S INC
5510 UNIVERSITY WAY
SEATTLE, WA 98105

RAYM   MARIAN RAY
36 VILLIERS AVE
SURBITON, SURREY
ELMBRIDGE 5020, ENGLAND

REPRO   REDISCOVERY PRODUCTIONS
2 HALFMILE COMMON
WESTPORT, CT 06880

RMI   RMI FILM PRODUCTIONS
4916 MAIN ST
KANSAS CITY, MO 64112

ROAS   ROAS'S FILMS
1696 N ASTOR ST
MILWAUKEE, WI 53202

ROBINP   ROBINSON (PETER) ASSOC
176 W 87TH ST
NEW YORK, NY 10024

SAFECO   SAFECO INSURANCE CO
SEATTLE, WA

SAIF   SANDLER INSTITUTIONAL FILMS,
INC
1001 N POINSETTIA PLACE
HOLLYWOOD, CA 90046

SALVA   SALVATION ARMY

SAUNDW   W B SAUNDERS CO
WEST WASHINGTON SQUARE
PHILADELPHIA, PA 19105

SCCOE   SANTA CLARA COUNTY OFFICE
OF EDUCATION
1000 MARKET
SANTA CLARA, CA 95050

SCHLAT   WARREN SCHLOAT PRODUCTIONS, INC
115 TOMPKINS AVE
PLEASANTVILLE, NY 10570

SCHNDL   MORTON SCHINDEL
WESTON, CT 06880

SCORER   R S SCORER

SCREEI   SCREEN EDUCATION ENTERPRISES,
INC
2800 SMITH TOWER
SEATTLE, WA 98104

SDCDE   SAN DIEGO COUNTY DEPT EDUCATION

SED   SCOTT EDUCATION DIV
104 LOWER WESTFIELD RD
HOLYOKE, MA 01040

SFI   SPORTLITE FILMS
20 N WACKER DR
CHICAGO, IL 60606

SKF   SMITH, KLINE AND FRENCH
MEDICAL FILM CENTER
1530 SPRING GARDEN ST
PHILADELPHIA, PA 19101

SNBRST   SUNBURST FILMS, INC
7466 BEVERLY BLVD
LOS ANGELES, CA 90036

SPA   SPOKEN ARTS
59 LOCUST AVE
NEW ROCHELLE, NY 10801

SSR   SPECIAL SERVICE RECORDS

STDYSC   STUDYSCOPES PRODUCTIONS
P O BOX 25943
LOS ANGELES, CA 90025

STNHM   H M STONE PRODUCTIONS
6 E 45TH ST
NEW YORK, NY 10017

SVE   SOCIETY FOR VISUAL EDUCATION,
INC
DIV THE SINGER CO
1345 DIVERSEY PARKWAY
CHICAGO, IL 60614

SWANK   SWANK MOTION PICTURES, INC
201 S JEFFERSON
ST LOUIS, MO 63166

TCF   TWENTIETH CENTURY FUND
41 EAST 70TH ST
NEW YORK, NY 10021

TECVIS   TECNIFAX/VISUCOM
20 FIRST AVE
CHICOPEE, MA 01020

TERF   TEACHING RESOURCES FILMS

TEXFLM	TEXTURE FILMS, INC 1600 BROADWAY NEW YORK, NY 10019
TF	TRAINING FILMS, INC LAUREL PARK BUTLER, NJ 07405
TIMLIF	TIME-LIFE FILMS, INC 16 MM DEPT 43 W 16TH ST NEW YORK, NY 10011
TRNAID	TRAIN-AIDE EDUCATIONAL SYSTEMS
TROLA	TROLL ASSOCIATES 320 ROUTE 17 MAHWAH, NJ 07430
UEUWIS	UNIV EXTENSION, UNIV OF WISC 432 N LAKE ST MADISON, WI 53706
UEVA	UNIVERSAL EDUCATION AND VISUAL ARTS 221 PARK AVE, S NEW YORK, NY 10003
UILL	UNIV OF ILL 501 SOUTH WRIGHT ST CHAMPLAIGN, IL 61820
UILVAS	UNIV OF ILL VOCATIONAL AGRICULTURE SERVICE 434 MUMFORD HALL URBANA, IL 61801
UMITV	UNIV OF MICH TV CENTER 310 MAYNARD ST ANN ARBOR, MI 48104
UMM	URBAN MEDIA MATERIALS 212 MINEOLA AVE ROSLYN HEIGHTS, NY 11577
UNIPUB	UNIPUB
UNISYS	UNIV SYSTEMS, INC 268 WHEATLEY RD OLD WESTBURY, NY 11741
UOKLA	UNIV OF OKLA, AUDIO-VISUAL SERVICES 650 PARRINTON OVAL 109 NORMAN, OK 73069
USA	U S ARMY THE PENTAGON WASHINGTON, DC 20310
USAEC	U S ATOMIC ENERGY COMMISSION DIVISION OF PUBLIC INFORMATION AUDIO-VISUAL BRANCH WASHINGTON, DC 20545

USDA	U S DEPT OF AGRICULTURE MOTION PICTURES SERV ROOM 1850 SOUTH BLDG WASHINTON, DC 20250
USDD	U S DEPT OF DEFENSE THE PENTAGON WASHINGTON, DC 20301
USDL	U S DEPT OF LABOR 14TH ST AND CONSTITUTION AVE, WASHINGTON, DC 20210
USN	U S NAVY DEPT OFFICE OF INFORMATION PENTAGON BLDG WASHINGTON, DC 20350
USNAC	U S NATL AUDIOVISUAL CENTER NATL ARCHIVES AND RECORDS SERV WASHINGTON, DC 20408
USOE	U S OFFICE OF EDUCATION 400 MARYLAND AVE, SW WASHINGTON, DC 20202
USOPA	U S OFFICE OF PRICE ADMIN THIS OFFICE DEFUNCT SEND INQUIRIES TO USNA
UTEX	UNIV OF TEX VISUAL INSTRUCTION BUREAU AUSTIN, TX 78712
UTS	UNION THEOLOGICAL SEMINARY
UWASHP	UNIV OF WASH PRESS 1416 NE 41ST ST SEATTLE, WA 98105
UWF	UNITED WORLD FILMS, INC 221 PARK AVE S NEW YORK, NY 10003
UWFKD	UNITED WORLD FILMS, KINETIC DIV 2001 S VERMONT AVE LOS ANGELES, CA 90007
UWISC	UNIV OF WISC, BUREAU OF AUDIO VISUAL INSTRUCTION AV CENTER LA CROSSE, WI 54601
UWLA	UNITED WAY, INC (LOS ANGELES) 729 S FIGUEROA LOS ANGELES, CA 90017
VIEWLX	VIEW LEX, INC BROADWAY AVE HOLBROOK, NY 11741
VIMCET	VIMCET ASSOC P O BOX 24714 LOS ANGELES, CA 90024

VIP	VIKING PRESS 625 MADISON AVE NEW YORK, NY 10022
VISED	VISUAL EDUCATION, INC 4546 VIA MARIA SANTA BARBARA, CA 93105
VISIN	VISUAL INSTRUCTION PRODUCTIONS 295 W 4TH ST NEW YORK, NY 10014
VISPUB	VISUAL PUBLICATIONS, LTD LONDON, ENGLAND
VISTAP	VISTAPRO
VOA	VOICE OF AMERICA, WASHINGTON
VOFI	VOCATIONAL FILMS 111 EUCLID AVE PARK RIDGE, IL 60068
WASHBF	WASHBURN FILMS NEW YORK, NY
WB	WARNER BROTHERS 4000 WARNER BURBANK, CA 91505
WGBH	WGBH EDUCATIONAL FOUNDATION 125 WESTERN AVE BOSTON, MA 02134
WILCOX	ROY WILCOX PRODUCTIONS ALLEN HILL MERIDEN, CT 06450
WILETS	BERNARD WILETS 11559 SANTA MONICA BLVD LOS ANGELES, CA 90025
WNAD	WNAD RADIO STATION, UNIV OF OKLA
WWS	WESTON WOODS STUDIOS WESTON WOODS ST WESTON, CT 06880
XEROX	XEROX CORP ADVERTISING DIVISION P O BOX 1540 ROCHESTER, NY 14600
YAF	YOUNG AMERICA FILMS DIST NOW BY MC GRAW HILL
ZAGREB	ZAGREB FILMS ZAGREB 1, YUGOSLAVIA

CODE SECTION - BY NAME

A-V EXPLORATIONS, INC — AVEXP

ABC NEWS — ABCNEW
ACI PRODUCTIONS — ACI
ACTIVITY RECORDS — EDLACT
  EDUCATIONAL ACTIVITIES, INC
ADMASTER PRINTS, INC — AMP
AIDS AUDIOVISUAL INSTRUCTIONAL — AVDEV
  DEVICES, INC
AIMS INSTRUCTIONAL MEDIA — AIMS
  SERVICES, INC
ALBERT (MARVIN) FILMS — ALBM
ALDEN FILMS — ALDEN
ALDEN FILMS — BEF
  BUSINESS EDUCATION FILMS
ALTSCHUL (GILBERT) PRODUCTIONS — ALTSUL
AMER DENTAL ASSN — AMDA
AMER EDUCATIONAL FILMS — AMEDFL
AMER FILM INSTITUTE — AMERFI
AMER FOUNDATION FOR — AFB
  THE BLIND
AMER JEWISH COMMITTEE — AJC
AMER MEDICAL ASSN — AMEDA
AMRAM NOWAK ASSOCIATES — NOWAKA
ARGUS COMMUNICATIONS — ARGSC
ARIZ STATE UNIV — ARIZSU
ARNOLD EAGLE PRODUCTIONS — EAGLE
ASSOCIATED FILMAKERS — AFI
  INTERNATIONAL
ASSOCIATED PRESS — ASPRSS
ATHLETIC INSTITUTE — ATHI
ATLANTIC RICHFIELD CO — ARIC
ATLANTIS PRODUCTIONS, INC — ATLAP
AUDIO VISUAL NARRATIVE ARTS — AVNA
AUDIOLINGUAL EDUCATIONAL PRESS — ALEP
AV-ED FILMS — AVED
AVIS FILMS — AVIS

BAILEY FILM ASSOC — BFA
BASCH RADIO AND TELEVISION — BASCH
  PRODUCTIONS
BASIC SKILL FILMS — BSF
BASS (SAUL) & ASSOCIATES — BASSS
BASSETT-CHESNUT — BASCHE
BELSON (JORDAN) — BELSON
BERNARD WILETS — WILETS
BETE (CHANNING L) CO, INC — BETECL
BFA EDUCATIONAL MEDIA — BFA
BILLY BUDD FILMS — BBF
BNA FILMS — BNA
BOSUSTOW (STEPHEN) PRODUCTIONS — BOSUST
BOUCHE PRODUCTIONS — BOUCH
BOWMAR (STANLEY) CO — BOW
BRANDON (LIANE) — BRNDNL
BRITISH BROADCASTING CO-TV — BBCTV
BUDD (BILLY) FILMS — BBF
BUREAU OF NATL AFFAIRS, INC — BNA
BUSINESS EDUCATION FILMS — BEF
  DIV OF ALDEN FILMS

CAEDMAN RECORDS, INC — CAED
  DIV HOUGHTON MIFFLIN CO
CAHILL (CHARLES) AND ASSOC, INC — CAHILL
CARMAN EDUCATIONAL ASSOC, INC — CARMAN
CAROUSEL FILMS, INC — CAROUF
CBS TELEVISION — CBSTV
CCM FILMS, INC — CCMFI
CENTER FOR MASS COMMUNICATION — CMC
  OF COLUMBIA UNIV PRESS
CENTER FOR URBAN EDUCATION — CEURED
CENTRON EDUCATIONAL FILMS — CENTEF
CHANNING L BETE CO, INC — BETECL
CHARLES CAHILL AND ASSOC, INC — CAHILL
CHURCHILL FILMS — CF
CLASSROOM MATERIALS, INC — CLSMAT
CLEVELAND HEALTH MUSEUM — CHM
CLOVER PARK SCHOOL DISTRICT 400 — CLOPSD
COLONIAL FILMS — COF
COLUMBIA BROADCASTING SYSTEM — CBSTV
COLUMBIA UNIV PRESS (SEE CENTER — CMC
  FOR MASS COMMUNICATION)
COMMON GROUND, LTD — COMG
COMMUNICATIONS RESEARCH — CRMP
  MACHINES
COMMUNICO — COMICO
COMMUNITY EDUCATIONAL RESOURCES — CER
COMPRENETICS, INC — COPI
CONCEPT MEDIA — CONMED
CONN FILMS, INC — CONNF
CONSOLIDATED FILM INDUSTRIES — CONSFI
CORNELL UNIV — CUNIV
CORONET INSTRUCTIONAL FILMS — CORF
CREATIVE FILM SOCIETY — CFS
CREATIVE VISUALS, INC — CREATV
CRM PRODUCTIONS — CRMP

DARTNELL CORP — DARTNL
DATA FILMS — DATA
DAVI — DAVI

DAVIDSON FILMS — DAVFMS
DIMENSION 5 — DIMFIV
DISNEY (WALT) PRODUCTIONS — DISNEY
DOUBLEDAY MULTIMEDIA — DOUBLE

E P RESEARCH, INC — EPRI
EAGLE (ARNOLD) PRODUCTIONS — EAGLE
ECCENTRIC CIRCLE CINEMA WORKSHOP — ECCCW
EDCOM PRODUCTIONS — EDCOM
EDUCATION DEVELOPMENT CENTER — EDC
EDUCATIONAL ACTIVITIES, INC — EDLACT
  ACTIVITY RECORDS
EDUCATIONAL AUDIO-VISUAL — EAV
EDUCATIONAL DIMENSIONS CORP — EDDIM
EDUCATIONAL DIRECTION, INC — EDREC
EDUCATIONAL PROJECTION CORP — EDPRC
ENCYCLOPEDIA BRITANNICA — EBEC
  EDUCATIONAL CORP
EVANS (RUTH) — EVNSR
EXCEL MOVIE PRODUCTS — EMP
EYE GATE HOUSE, INC — EGH

FIELD EDUCATIONAL PUBLICATIONS — FIELEP
FILM IMAGES — FILIM
FILMFAIR, INC — FLMFR
FILMS FOR THE HUMANITIES AND — FOTH
  SCIENCES
FILMS/WEST, INC — FILMSW
FILMS, INC — FI
FILMSTRIP HOUSE — FSH
FOLLETT PUBLISHING CO — FPC
FORD (HENRY) MUSEUM AND — FORD
  GREENFIELD VILLAGE
FORD MOTOR CO — FMCMP

GEIGY CHEMICAL CORP — GEIGY
GENERAL PRECISION EQUIPMENT CORP — SVE
  SOCIETY FOR VISUAL ED DIV
GILBERT ALTSCHUL PRODUCTIONS — ALTSUL
GOLDBERG-WERRENROTH PRODUCTIONS — GLDWER
GOLDSMITH'S MUSIC SHOP, INC — GMS
GRANDY (ROY) PRODUCTIONS — GRANDY
GREAT PLAINS INSTRUCTIONAL TV — GPITVL
  LIBRARY
GREAVES (WILLIAM) PRODUCTIONS — GREAVW
GUIDANCE ASSOC — GA
  HARCOURT, BRACE AND WORLD

H M STONE PRODUCTIONS — STNHM
HARCOURT, BRACE AND WORLD — GA
  GUIDANCE ASSOC DIV
HAROLD MANTELL, INC — MANTLH
HARPER AND ROW PUBLISHERS — HAR
HEARST METROTONE NEWS — HEARST
HENRY FORD MUSEUM AND — FORD
  GREENFIELD VILLAGE
HESTER AND ASSOC — HESTER
HOLT, RINEHART AND WINSTON — HRAW
HOUGHTON MIFFLIN CO — CAED
  CAEDMON RECORDS DIV
HUBBARD SCIENTIFIC CO — HUBDSC
HUNGAROFILM — HUNGFM

ILL (UNIV OF) — UILL
ILL BELL TELEPHONE CO — ILBELL
IND UNIV — IU
INSTITUTE FOR DEVELOPMENT OF — IDEA
  EDUCATIONAL ACTIVITIES
INSTITUTE OF TEXAN CULTURES — INTXC
IOWA STATE UNIV — IOWA
IWANMI PRODUCTIONS, INC — IWANMI

JACK LIEB PRODUCTIONS — LIEB
JOURNAL FILMS — JOU

KCET/LOS ANGELES — KCET
KEG PRODUCTIONS, LTD — KEGPL
KELLER (PAUL F) & ASSOCIATES — KELLRP
KENNY REHABILITATION INSTITUTE — KRI
KENT STATE UNIVERSITY — KENTSU
KING BROADCASTING — KINGSP
  KING SCREEN PRODUCTIONS DIV
KING SCREEN PRODUCTIONS — KINGSP
  A DIV OF KING BROADCASTING CO

L A CITY FIRE DEPT — LACFD
LEARNING ARTS — LEART
LEARNING CORPORATION OF AMERICA — LCOA
LES FILMS ARMORIAL — LESAM
LIBRARY FILMSTRIP CENTER — LIBFSC
LIEB (JACK) PRODUCTIONS — LIEB
LIFE FILMSTRIPS — LIFE
LONDON WEEKEND TV — LONWTV
LONG ISLAND LIGHTING CO — LILC
LYCEUM PRODUCTIONS — LYCEUM

MANTELL (HAROLD,) INC — MANTLH
MARIAN RAY — RAYM
MC GRAW-HILL TEXTFILMS — MGHT

MEDIA SERVICES AND CAPTIONED — MSCF
  FILMS
MENKEN (SHEPHERD) — MENKNS
METROMEDIA PRODUCERS CORP — METROM
MODERN TALKING PICTURE SERV — MTP
MONUMENT FILM CORP — MFLMC
MORTON SCHINDEL — SCHNDL
MT SAN JACINTO COLLEGE — MTSJC

NATL AERONAUTICS AND — NASA
  SPACE ADMIN
NATL ASSN OF EDUCATIONAL — NAEB
  BROADCASTERS
NATL AUDIO VISUAL ASSN, INC — NAVA
NATL BROADCASTING CO, TV — NBCTV
NATL EDUCATION ASSN OF THE U S — DAVI
  DIV OF AV INSTRUCTION
NATL EDUCATIONAL TV, INC — NET
NATL FILM BOARD OF CANADA — NFBC
NATL HIGHWAY TRAFFIC SAFETY — NHTSA
  ADMIN
NATL INSTRUCTIONAL TV CENTER — NITC
NATL RETAIL MERCHANTS ASSN — NRMA
NATL SCIENCE FOUNDATION — NSF
NEUBACHER-VETTER FILM PRODUCTION — NVFP
NEW LINE CINEMA — NLC
NORTHWEST FILM PRODUCTIONS — NWFLMP
NOWAK (AMRAM) ASSOCIATES — NOWAKA
NULSEN (DAVID) ENTERPRISES — NULSEN

OHIO STATE UNIVERSITY — OHIOSU
OKLA, UNIV OF — UOKLA
OXFORD FILMS, INC — OF

PARTHENON PICTURES — PART
PATHESCOPE EDUCATIONAL FILMS INC — PATED
PAUL F KELLER & ASSOCIATES — KELLRP
PAULIST PRODUCTIONS — PAULST
PERSPECTIVE FILMS — PERSPF
PHILADELPHIA SCHOOL FOR — PHLSAC
  ANTI-COMMUNISTS
PHOENIX FILMS — PHENIX
PHOTO LAB, INC — PHOTO
PICTURA FILMS CORP — PIC
PILOT PRODUCTIONS, INC — PILOT
PLANNED PARENTHOOD FEDERATION — PPFA
  OF AMERICA, INC
POPHAM (W JAMES) — POPHAM
PRODUCTIONS UNLIMITED, INC — PUI
PYRAMID FILM PRODUCTIONS — PFP

R S SCORER — SCORER
RADIANT FILMS, SEE RADIM FILMS — RADIM
RADIM FILMS, INC — RADIM
RARIG'S INC — RARIG
RAY (MARIAN) — RAYM
REDISCOVERY PRODUCTIONS — REPRO
RMI FILM PRODUCTIONS — RMI
ROAS'S FILMS — ROAS
ROBINSON (PETER) ASSOC — ROBINP
ROY GRANDY PRODUCTIONS — GRANDY
ROY WILCOX PRODUCTIONS — WILCOX
RUTH EVANS — EVNSR

SAFECO INSURANCE CO — SAFECO
SALVATION ARMY — SALVA
SAN DIEGO COMMUNITY — CER
  EDUCATIONAL RESOURCES
SAN DIEGO COUNTY DEPT EDUCATION — SDCDE
SANDLER INSTITUTIONAL FILMS, — SAIF
  INC
SANTA CLARA COUNTY OFFICE — SCCOE
  OF EDUCATION
SAUL BASS & ASSOCIATES — BASSS
SAUNDERS (W B) CO — SAUNDW
SCHINDEL (MORTON) — SCHNDL
SCHLOAT (WARREN) PRODUCTIONS INC — SCHLAT
SCORER (R S) — SCORER
SCOTT EDUCATION DIV — SED
SCREEN EDUCATION ENTERPRISES, — SCREEI
  INC
SCREEN NEWS DIGEST (SAME AS — HEARST
  HEARST METROTONE NEWS)
SHEPHERD MENKEN — MENKNS
SMITH, KLINE AND FRENCH — SKF
SOCIETY FOR VISUAL EDUCATION, — SVE
  INC
SPECIAL SERVICE RECORDS — SSR
SPOKEN ARTS — SPA
SPORTLITE FILMS — SFI
STANLEY BOWMAR CO — BOW
STEPHEN BOSUSTOW PRODUCTIONS — BOSUST
STONE (H M) PRODUCTIONS — STNHM
STUDYSCOPES PRODUCTIONS — STDYSC
SUNBURST FILMS, INC — SNBRST
SWANK MOTION PICTURES, INC — SWANK

TEACHING RESOURCES FILMS — TERF
TECNIFAX/VISUCOM — TECVIS

TEX, UNIV OF	UTEX
TEXTURE FILMS, INC	TEXFLM
TIME-LIFE FILMS, INC	TIMLIF
TRAIN-AIDE EDUCATIONAL SYSTEMS	TRNAID
TRAINING FILMS, INC	TF
TROLL ASSOCIATES	TROLA
TWENTIETH CENTURY FUND	TCF
U S ARMY	USA
U S ATOMIC ENERGY COMMISSION	USAEC
U S DEPT OF AGRICULTURE	USDA
U S DEPT OF DEFENSE	USDD
U S DEPT OF LABOR	USDL
U S NATL AUDIOVISUAL CENTER	USNAC
U S NAVY DEPT	USN
U S OFFICE OF EDUCATION	USOE
U S OFFICE OF PRICE ADMIN	USOPA
UNION THEOLOGICAL SEMINARY	UTS
UNIPUB	UNIPUB
UNITED WAY, INC (LOS ANGELES)	UWLA
UNITED WORLD FILMS, INC	UWF
UNITED WORLD FILMS, KINETIC DIV	UWFKD
UNIV EXTENSION, UNIV OF WISC	UEUWIS
UNIV OF ILL	UILL
UNIV OF ILL VOCATIONAL	UILVAS

AGRICULTURE SERVICE	
UNIV OF MICH TV CENTER	UMITV
UNIV OF OKLA, AUDIO-VISUAL SERVICES	UOKLA
UNIV OF TEX	UTEX
UNIV OF WASH PRESS	UWASHP
UNIV OF WISC, BUREAU OF AUDIO VISUAL INSTRUCTION	UWISC
UNIV OF WISC, UNIV EXTENSION	UEUWIS
UNIV SYSTEMS, INC	UNISYS
UNIVERSAL EDUCATION AND VISUAL ARTS	UEVA
URBAN MEDIA MATERIALS	UMM
VIEW LEX, INC	VIEWLX
VIKING PRESS	VIP
VIMCET ASSOC	VIMCET
VISTAPRO	VISTAP
VISUAL EDUCATION, INC	VISED
VISUAL INSTRUCTION PRODUCTIONS	VISIN
VISUAL PUBLICATIONS, LTD	VISPUB
VOCATIONAL FILMS	VOFI
VOICE OF AMERICA, WASHINGTON	VOA
W B SAUNDERS CO	SAUNDW

WALT DISNEY PRODUCTIONS	DISNEY
WARNER BROTHERS	WB
WARREN SCHLOAT PRODUCTIONS, INC	SCHLAT
WASHBURN FILMS	WASHBF
WESTON WOODS STUDIOS	WWS
WGBH EDUCATIONAL FOUNDATION	WGBH
WILCOX (ROY) PRODUCTIONS	WILCOX
WILETS (BERNARD)	WILETS
WISC, UNIV OF	UWISC
WNAD RADIO STATION, UNIV OF OKLA	WNAD
WYLLIE (DIANA) LTD	DWYLIE
XEROX CORP	XEROX
YOUNG AMERICA FILMS	YAF
ZAGREB FILMS	ZAGREB
WISC, UNIV OF	UWISC
WNAD RADIO STATION, UNIV OF OKLA	WNAD
WYLLIE (DIANA) LTD	DWYLIE
XEROX CORP	XEROX
YOUNG AMERICA FILMS	YAF

22-102